KU-306-461

THE TIMES HISTORY OF THE WORLD

NEW EDITION

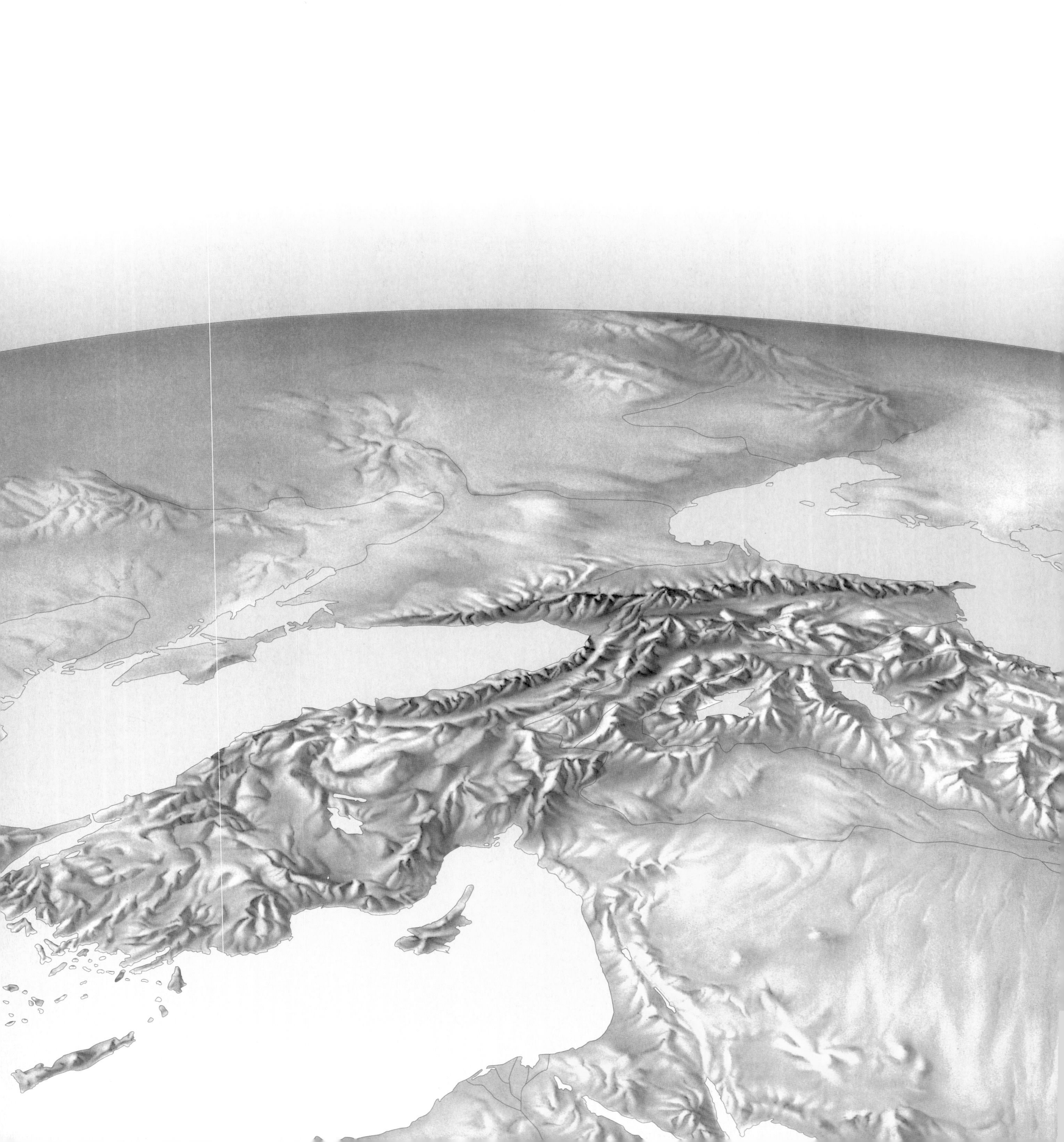

Edited by GEOFFREY BARRACLOUGH

NEW EDITION

Edited by RICHARD OVERY

TED SMART

This edition produced for
The Book People Ltd,
Hall Wood Avenue, Haydock,
St. Helens, WA11 9UL

New Edition
First published in 1999 by
TIMES BOOKS
HarperCollins*Publishers*
77-85 Fulham Palace Road
London W6 8JB

Reprinted 1999, 2000

The HarperCollins website address is
www.**fireandwater**.com

First edition published 1978
Reprinted with revisions 1979
Reprinted 1979, 1980, 1981, 1983
Second edition published 1984
Reprinted 1985
Reprinted with revisions 1986
Reprinted 1988
Third edition published 1989
Reprinted 1992
Fourth edition published 1993
Reprinted 1994, 1996, 1997

British Library Cataloguing in Publication Data
A catalogue record for this book is available from the British Library

ISBN 0-00-761900-6

Editorial direction
Philip Parker
Thomas Cussans
Matthew Parker

Design
Mabel Chan
Kathryn Gammon

Cartographic direction
Martin Brown

Cartographers
Stephen Brooks, Ruth Coombs, Martin Curran, Loraine Eddy, Mark Eldridge, Alan Grimwade, John Howes, Richard Jones, Kevin Klein, David Maltby, Isobel Morison, Laura Morris, Ian Spizick, Marcella Warner at **Cosmographics**, Watford, England.

Karen Marland, Vaila McAllister, David F. White, Tom Dougan, Ewen Ross, Mark Steward at **Bartholomew Mapping Services**, Glasgow, Scotland.

Graphs and charts
Stephen John Scanlan
Laurence Kryzanek

Picture research
Anne-Marie Ehrlich

Place-name consultant and place-name index
Pat Geelan

Subject index
Sue Hibbert

Original conception
Barry Winkleman
Malcolm Swanston

The publishers would also like to thank the following:
Andras Bereznay; Natalie Cade; Tim Dobson; Ben Edwards, *The Economist*; Jacob Nell; Barbara Nash; Tania Monckton; Dr Niru Ratnam; Jonathan Shepherd; Janet Smy; Dennis Taylor, *The Times*, London; Emma Tolkien; Geoff Wilson

Colour origination
Saxon Photo Litho Ltd, England

Printed and bound in Spain
by Graficas Estella

CONTRIBUTORS

Editor:
Geoffrey Barraclough
Late President, Historical Association
Chichele Professor of Modern History
University of Oxford

Editor, New Edition:
Richard Overy
Professor of Modern History
King's College
University of London

Editor, Third Edition:
Norman Stone
Professor of History
Bilkent University, Ankara

Editor, Fourth Edition:
Geoffrey Parker FBA
Andreas Dorpalen Distinguished Professor of History
The Ohio State University

David Abulafia
Reader in Mediterranean History
University of Cambridge

Daud Ali
Lecturer in South Asian History
School of Oriental and African Studies
University of London

Amira K. Bennison
Lecturer in Middle Eastern and Islamic Studies
Faculty of Oriental Studies
University of Cambridge

Hugh Bowden
Lecturer in Ancient History
King's College
University of London

John Breen
Senior Lecturer in Japanese Studies
School of Oriental and African Studies
University of London

Carl Bridge
Head of the Sir Robert Menzies Centre for Australian Studies
Institute of Commonwealth Studies
University of London

Kent Deng
Lecturer in Economic History
London School of Economics
University of London

Robert I. Frost
Lecturer in Early Modern History
King's College
University of London

Clive Gamble
Professor of Archaeology
University of Southampton

Ian Glover
Emeritus Reader in Southeast Asian Archaeology
Institute of Archaeology
University College
University of London

Graham Gould
Lecturer in Early Church History
King's College
University of London

David R. Harris
Professor of Human Environment
Institute of Archaeology
University College
University of London

Nicholas James

David Killingray
Professor of Modern History
Goldsmiths' College
University of London

Rosamond McKitterick
Professor of History
University of Cambridge

Thomas Nelson
Okinaga Junior Research Fellow in Japanese Studies
Wadham College
University of Oxford

Joan Oates
Fellow of the MacDonald Institute for Archaeological Research
University of Cambridge

David W. Phillipson
Director and Curator
Museum of Archaeology and Anthropology
University of Cambridge

Andrew Porter
Rhodes Professor of Imperial History
King's College
University of London

Francis Robinson
Professor of the History of South Asia
Royal Holloway College
University of London

Stephen Shennan
Professor of Theoretical Archaeology
Institute of Archaeology
University College
University of London

Peter Sluglett
Professor of History and Director
Middle East Center
University of Utah

Sarah Stockwell
Lecturer in History
King's College
University of London

Melvyn Stokes
University College
University of London

Julian Swann
Lecturer in European History
Birbeck College
University of London

CONTRIBUTORS TO PREVIOUS EDITIONS

F R Allchin
R W Van Alstyne
David Arnold
Anthony Atmore
John Barber
James R Barrett
Iris Barry
Peter Bauer
Christopher Bayly
W G Beasley
Ralph Bennett
A D H Bivar
Brian Bond
Hugh Borton
David Brading
Warwick Bray
Michael G Broers
F R Bridge
Roy C Bridges
Hugh Brogan
Tom Brooking
Ian Brown
Anthony Bryer
Muriel E Chamberlain
David G Chandler
John Channon
Eric Christiansen
Peter Coates
Irene Collins
Michael Crawford
James Cronin
Douglas Dakin
John Darwin
Ralph Davis
I E S Edwards
Robert Evans
John Ferguson
Felipe Fernández-Armesto
Stefan Fisch
David H Fischer
John R Fisher
Kate Fleet
Michael Flinn
Timothy Fox
Alan Frost
W J Gardner
Carol Geldart
John Gillingham
Martin Goodman
D G E Hall
Norman Hammond
John D Hargreaves
Jonathan Haslam
Ragnhild Hatton
M Havinden
Harry Hearder
W O Henderson
Colin J Heywood
Sinclair Hood
Albert Hourani
Henry Hurst
Jonathan Israel
Edward James
Richard H Jones

CONTRIBUTORS CONTINUED

Ulrich Kemper
Mark H Leff
Colin Lewis
Karl Leyser
Wolfgang Liebeschuetz
D Anthony Low
David Luscombe
John Lynch
James M McPherson
Isabel de Madriaga
J P Mallory
P J Marshall
A R Michell
Christopher D Morris
A E Musson
F S Northedge
David Ormrod
J H Parry
Thomas M Perry
Sidney Pollard
Avril Powell
T G E Powell
John Poynter
Benjamin Ravid
Tapan Raychaudhuri
B H Reid
Michael Roaf
A N Ryan
Gören Rystad
H W F Saggs
S B Saul
Peter Sawyer
Chris Scarre
Roger Schofield
D J Schove
H M Scott
H H Scullard
Andrew Sharf
Andrew Sherratt
R B Smith
Frank C Spooner
Jocelyn Statler
L S Stavrianos
Zara Steiner
W C Sturtevant
Alan Sykes
E A Thompson
Hugh Tinker
Malcolm Todd
R C Trebilcock
Hugh R Trevor-Roper
Denis C Twitchett
Frans von der Dunk
F R von der Mehden
Ernst Wangermann
Geoffrey Warner
D Cameron Watt
Bodo Wiethoff
D S M Williams
Glyn Williams
H P Willmott
David M Wilson
George D Winius

In addition to the contributors listed above and on page 5, the publishers would also like to thank the following for their generous advice and help:

Correlli Barnett; Professor C D Cowan; J Morland Craig; Dr Elizabeth Dunstan; Professor John Erickson; Professor D W Harding; Professor David Hawkins; Thomas M Jordan; Morton Keller; Jonathan King; Dr Michael Leifer; George Maddocks; Professor Roland Oliver; Professor P J Parish; Professor M C Rickleffs; Dr R L Sims; Denis Mack Smith; Professor Jan van Houtte; Patricia A Wenzel; Dr Joachim Whaley; Dr L R Wright.

CONTENTS

SECTION ONE

SECTION TWO

The first civilizations 50

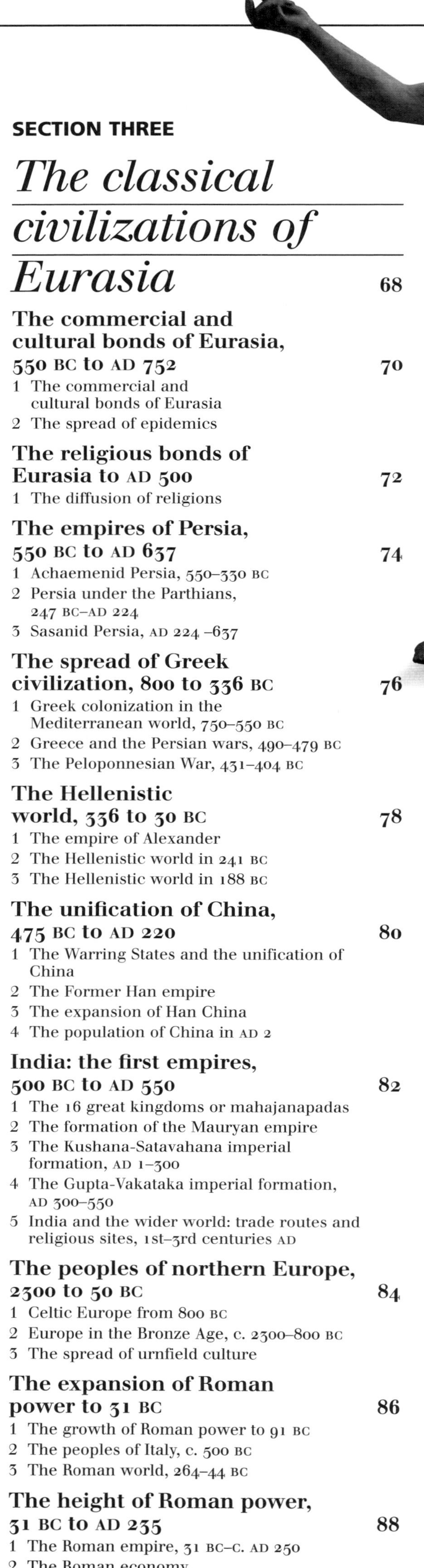

SECTION THREE

The classical civilizations of Eurasia 68

SECTION FOUR

The world of divided regions 94

SECTION FIVE

The world of the emerging West

SECTION SIX

The age of European dominance

SECTION SEVEN

The age of global civilization 252

INTRODUCTION

Over the past 21 years, *The Times Atlas of World History*, now in this new edition *The Times History of the World*, has established itself as the undisputed leader in its field. Its reputation owes a great deal to the conception of its founding editor, Geoffrey Barraclough, who set out in the early 1970s to create a work that would provide an authoritative history of the world in maps, pictures and text. His priorities were to avoid too Eurocentric a treatment and too great an emphasis on the modern age. The result was a history that did indeed cover the whole globe, and devoted more space to the pre-modern age than was general in world histories. Barraclough was also determined that the atlas should reflect history as a process, not simply as a series of unconnected stories. Many of the maps from the original edition show change over time, often a long period of time, and try to demonstrate the forces that shaped such changes.

One significant innovation has been introduced. The original maps were hand-drawn. This was repeated with the changes undertaken in the second edition of 1984, edited again by Barraclough, and in the third and fourth editions, edited respectively by Norman Stone and Geoffrey Parker following Barraclough's death in 1984. For this new edition, the old method has been discarded in favour of digitized map-making. For the first time, all the maps in this edition have been generated by computer. The opportunity afforded by this technological leap has been taken to revise the atlas in its entirety. The old format has been replaced with an entirely new design, incorporating a chronology, a quotation significant for the text, more pictures and the redrawing and re-colouring of all of the maps. A box at the top of each page provides an easy cross-referencing system. The redesigned spreads have new or revised texts as well, updated to take account of the swelling volume of historical research from the past decade.

The new edition has also made possible other changes. There are four new spreads at the end of the book to reflect developments in the quarter century since the book was first conceived: for example, the rise of religious fundamentalism, the growth of multinational organizations and the proliferation of nuclear weapons. Other spreads have been added to strengthen the commitment of the editors to a balanced chronological treatment and adequate balance between the world's different regions and civilizations. Additions to the history of Asia and the Middle East have strengthened the coverage of the non-European world and, I hope, removed any lingering suspicion of Eurocentrism. Finally, the opportunity has been taken to incorporate 20th-century genocide more fully, a change that reflects the widespread contemporary interest in the whole subject and the quite exceptional character of this particular historical experience.

The new edition coincides with the end of the millennium. It is no part of the task of a work of world history to gaze into the future, but in this case it is difficult to avoid the temptation to suggest some of the themes with which the next century will have to come to terms. Population growth has always featured on the last spread of the book. When Barraclough was writing, the population explosion was in full flood and there were the darkest predictions of demographic catastrophe. The majority of all humans in history are alive today thanks to that population boom. But the latest projections show a sharp slow-down in growth by the middle of the next century. There will still be a demographic crisis but it may well be more manageable than the doom-laden scenarios popular two decades ago.

A more serious problem is posed by environmental damage produced by economic modernization. A new spread has been introduced to show the extent of that damage and to demonstrate some of the unexpected consequences of global warming. Of course, issues of environment feature throughout world history. Yet most were the result of circumstances dictated by nature: now man is dictating to the natural world. In the next century, ecological issues may well come to replace the issues of national and racial rivalry which have bedevilled world politics for more than a century.

A third change was barely evident when the first edition was completed. In the 1970s, western liberals confidently assumed that religion was a force on the wane in world history. A glance at the book might have suggested that this belief was premature, for conflicts between and within faiths play a very large part throughout its pages. Since the 1970s, religion has revived as a social, even political phenomenon. Religious fundamentalism, a return to ancient religious principles, can be found across the globe, but particularly in the Islamic and Hindu worlds. Even in the bloc of communist states that were once officially atheistic, change has come. The former Soviet states have seen a remarkable religious flowering, and religion has revived even in China. Armed conflict with a strong religious core has punctuated the past decade, and it is more than probable that religious faith, rather than communism or fascism, will be the chief ideological torch handed on from this millennium to the next.

All of these perspectives on the future can be found in the later spreads of the book. As in the earlier editions, there has been no attempt simply to chase headlines. There is also a positive aspect to the new millennium which is more difficult to reflect in map terms. Much of the world is more prosperous than was thought possible a quarter of a century ago. Citizens in the most developed states are richer than man has ever been. They are also healthier and more secure. 'Progress' is no longer a fashionable term, for it is always shadowed by poverty, conflict and discrimination, yet improvements have been tangible for hundreds of millions of people. The development of world history has been anything but a straight upward line, as the pages of this book make abundantly clear, but on the eve of the new millennium more people are able to influence the course of their own lives through the ballot-box or in the market-place than was remotely possible 100 years ago let alone 1,000 years ago. That process of emancipation, so often distorted, interrupted, paradoxical, has not ended. Its development is the chief challenge for the next millennium, just as it played a central theme throughout the last.

This new edition has been made possible through the exceptional efforts of the team at Times Books – Thomas Cussans, Philip Parker, Matthew Parker, Martin Brown, Mabel Chan and Kathryn Gammon – and through the work of some 25 new contributors who have added to the work assembled by Barraclough's team of more than 100 consultants. Thanks are also due to Anne-Marie Ehrlich for searching out the magnificent new photographs. The new edition now provides an authoritative and accessible volume, building on the strengths inherited from almost a quarter of a century of the book in its many editions worldwide. It is a work designed for a global audience, capturing global history in ways that continue to be visually arresting and intellectually stimulating.

Richard Overy
October 1998

CHRONOLOGY OF WORLD HISTORY

9000 BC

ASIA EXCLUDING THE NEAR EAST

c. 7000 Evidence of rice cultivation in China

c. 3000 First agricultural settlements in southeast Asia

c. 2500 Beginnings of Harappan culture in the Indus valley

c. 1750 Abandonment of major Indus valley cities

c. 1650 Indo-Aryans begin to arrive in China

c. 1600 Start of Bronze Age in China
c. 1550 Aryans destroy Indus valley civilization and settle in N India
c. 1520 Beginnings of Shang dynasty in China
c. 1500 Bronze Age in northeast Thailand and north Vietnam

c. 1030 Shang dynasty in China overthrown by Chou; Aryans in India expand eastwards down Ganges valley
c. 1000 Indo-Aryan settlements established in the Upper Ganges plains

c. 800 Aryans expand southwards in India

771 Collapse of Chou feudal order in China

EUROPE

c. 7000 First farming in Greece and Aegean; reaches Iberia and Low Countries c. 5000; Britain and southern Scandinavia c. 4000

3200–2000 Early Cycladic civilization

c. 3000 Spread of copper-working. Beginning of Greek Early Bronze Age

c. 2000 Indo-European speakers (early Greeks) invade and settle Peloponnese; beginnings of 'Minoan' civilization in Crete

1628 Massive volcanic eruption on Aegean island of Thera
c. 1600 Beginnings of Mycenaean civilization in Greece

c. 1300 Start of Urnfield culture

c. 1100 Earliest fortified hilltop sites in western Europe

c. 1000 Etruscans arrive in Italy

753 Traditional date for foundation of Rome
c. 750 Greek city-states begin to found settlements throughout Mediterranean
c. 750–450 Hallstatt culture in central and western Europe: mixed farming, iron tools

c. 700 Scythians spread from central Asia to eastern Europe

NEAR EAST AND NORTH AFRICA

9000–8000 Evidence of domesticated cereals and pulses in the Levant – the 'Neolithic revolution' – in the Near East; first permanent settlements
8350–7350 Jericho founded: first walled town in the world (ten acres)
c. 7000 Early experiments with copper ores in Anatolia
6250–5400 Çatal Höyük (Anatolia) flourishes: largest city of its day (32 acres)

c. 6000 Earliest cereal cultivation in north Africa
c. 5000 Colonization of Mesopotamian alluvial plain by groups practising irrigation. Agricultural settlements in Egypt
c. 4000–3000 Desiccation of Sahara begins; north African populations expand south and east
c. 4000 Bronze casting begins in Near East; first use of plough

c. 3500 Eanna in Uruk and other ceremonial complexes built as centres of the earliest cities in Mespotamia

c. 3100 Traditional date of unification of Egypt under Menes
c. 3000 Development of major cities in Sumer
c. 2686 The 'Old Kingdom' (pyramid age) of Egypt begins (to 2181 BC)

2296 Sargon I of Agade founds first empire in world history
c. 2000 Hittites invade Anatolia and found empire (1650)
c. 1990 Egyptian conquests of Nubia begin
c. 1749 Shamshi-Adad founds Assyrian state
c. 1728 Hammurabi founds Babylonian empire

c. 1648 Hyksos control Egypt

c. 1540 Kamose and Amose expel Hyksos invaders and inaugurate Egyptian 'New Kingdom' (to 1069 BC)

c. 1420 Tudhaliya I begins expansion of Hittite power

1275 Battle of Kadesh between Ramses II of Egypt and Hittites
c. 1200 Collapse of Hittite empire. Jewish exodus from Egypt and settlement in Palestine
1152 Death of Ramses III, last great pharaoh of Egypt
c. 1100 Spread of Phoenicians in Mediterranean region (to 700 BC)
c. 1025 Emergence of Israelite kingdom

c. 900 Kingdom of Meroe established
c. 840 Rise of Urartu
814 Traditional date for foundation of Phoenician colony at Carthage

721–705 Assyria at height of military power

OTHER REGIONS

c. 9000 Southern tip of South America colonized

c. 3000 Maize first cultivated in Mesoamerica. First pottery in Americas (Ecuador and Colombia)

c. 2000 First metal-working in Peru. Settlement of Melanesia by immigrants from Indonesia begins
c. 1750 Northernmost Greenland settled

c. 1300 Settlers of Melanesia reach Fiji, later spreading to Western Polynesia

c. 1150 Beginning of Olmec civilization in Mexico

CULTURE AND TECHNOLOGY

c. 6000 First known pottery and woolen textiles (Çatal Höyük)

c. 3500 Construction of Megalithic tombs and circles in Brittany, Iberian peninsula and British Isles (Stonehenge c. 2000). Invention of wheel and plough (Mesopotamia) and sail (Egypt)
c. 3200 Earliest readable documents from Mesopotamia
c. 3100 Pictographic writing invented in Sumer

c. 2590 Cheops builds great pyramid at Giza
c. 2500 Domestication of horse (central Asia)

c. 2000 Use of sail on sea-going vessels (Aegean)

c. 1500 Ideographic script in use in China; 'Linear B' script in Crete and Greece; Hittite cuneiform in Anatolia
c. 1450 Development of Brahma worship; composition of *Vedas* (earliest Indian literature) begins
c. 1360 Akhenaten enforces monotheistic sun worship in Egypt; builds new capital, Akhetaten
c. 1200 Beginning of Jewish religion (worship of Yahweh). Teachings of Zoroaster

c. 1100 Phoenicians develop alphabetic script (basis of all modern European script)

800–400 Composition of *Upanishads*, Sanskrit religious treatises
776 Traditional date for first Olympic Games, in Greece

c. 750 Amos, first great prophet in Israel. Homer's *Iliad* and Hesiod's poetry first written down

146 BC

ASIA EXCLUDING THE NEAR EAST

c. 660 Jimmu, legendary first emperor of Japan
c. 650 Introduction of iron technology in China

c. 600 Kausambi and Ujjayini develop as earliest post-Harappan cities

c. 500 Sinhalese, an Aryan people, reach Ceylon. Iron introduced to southeast Asia; development of political elites

475–221 'Warring States' period in China

322 Chandragupta founds Mauryan empire at Magadha, India

265 Ashoka, Mauryan emperor, converted to Buddhism

221 Shih Huang-ti, of Ch'in dynasty, unites China (to 207)

202 Former Han dynasty (to AD 9) reunites China; capital at Chang-an

185 Demetrius and Menander, kings of Bactria, conquer northwest India

EUROPE

c. 650 Rise of 'Tyrants' in Corinth and other Greek cities

511 Expulsion of Tarquinius Superbus, last of Rome's kings
c. 505 Cleisthenes establishes democracy in Athens

490 Battle of Marathon: Persian attack on Athens defeated

480 Battles of Salamis and Plataea (479): Persian invasion of Greece defeated

478 Foundation of Confederacy of Delos, later transformed into Athenian empire
c. 450 Celtic (La Tène) culture emerges in central and western Europe
431–404 Peloponnesian War between Sparta and Athens
390 Sack of Rome by Gauls
356 Philip II, king of Macedon (to 336)
338 Battle of Chaeronea gives Macedon control of Greece

290 Rome completes conquest of central Italy

241 First Punic War (264–241) with Carthage gives Rome control of Sicily

218 Second Punic War (218–201): Hannibal of Carthage invades Italy

206 Rome gains control of Spain

168 Rome defeats and partitions Macedonia

146 Rome sacks Carthage and Corinth; Greece under Roman domination

NEAR EAST AND NORTH AFRICA

671 Assyrian conquest of Egypt; introduction of iron-working

612 Sack of Nineveh by Medes and Scythians; collapse of Assyrian power
586 Babylonian captivity of the Jews

539 Cyrus the Great of Persia captures Babylon

521 Persia under Darius I (the Great) rules from the Nile to the Indus
c. 520 Darius I completes canal connecting Nile with Red Sea

494 Persians suppress Ionian revolt

334 Alexander the Great (of Macedon) invades Asia Minor; conquers Egypt (332), Persia (330) reaches India (327)
323 Death of Alexander: empire divided between Macedon, Egypt, Syria and Pergamum
304 Ptolemy I, Macedonian governor of Egypt, founds independent dynasty (to 30 BC)

238 Arsaces I seizes Parthia from the Seleucids

149 Third Punic War (149–146): Rome destroys Carthage and founds province of Africa

OTHER REGIONS

c. 550 Iron use begins in sub-Saharan Africa; Bantu speakers expand southwards

c. 500 Foundation of Zapotec capital, Monte Albán, in Mexico. Iron-making techniques spead to sub-Saharan Africa
c. 500–AD 200 Period of Nok culture in northern Nigeria

c. 300 Rise of Hopewell chiefdoms in North America

c. 150 Settlement of Marquesas Islands

CULTURE AND TECHNOLOGY

c. 650 First coins: Lydia (Asia Minor) and Greece (c. 600). Rise of Greek lyric poetry (Sappho born c. 612)

585 Thales of Miletus predicts an eclipse: beginnings of Greek rationalist philosophy

c. 551 Birth of Confucius
550 Zoroastrianism becomes official religion of Persia
c. 550 Chinese silks known in Athens
540 Deutero-Isaiah, Hebrew prophet, at work during exile in Babylon
c. 530 Pythagoras, mathematician and mystic, active
528 Traditional date for death of Mahavira, founder of Jain sect

520 Death of Lao-tzu (born 605), traditional founder of Daoism

c. 500 Achaemenid Persians transmit food plants (rice, peach, apricot, etc.) to western Asia. Caste system established in India. First hieroglyphic writing in Mexico (Monte Albán)

c. 486 Birth of Buddha

479–338 Period of Greek classical culture: poetry, Pindar (518–438); drama, Aeschylus (525–456), Sophocles (496–406), Euripides (480–406), Aristophanes (c. 440–385); history, Herodotus (c. 486–429), Thucydides (c. 460–400); medicine, Hippocrates (c. 470–406); philosophy, Socrates (469–399), Plato (c. 437–347), Aristotle (384–322); sculpture, Phidias (c. 490–417), Praxiteles (c. 364); architecture, Parthenon (447–431)
479 Death of Confucius

447 Parthenon begun in Athens

350–200 Great period of Chinese thought: formation of Daoist, Legalist and Confucian schools; early scientific discoveries

312/311 Start of Seleucid era; first continuous historical dating-system

c. 290 Foundation of Alexandrian library

277 Death of Ch'ü Yüan (b. 343), earliest major Chinese poet

142 BC

ASIA EXCLUDING THE NEAR EAST

141 Wu-ti, Chinese emperor, expands Han power in eastern Asia
c. 138 Chang Chien explores central Asia
130 Yüeh-chih tribe (Tocharians) establish kingdom in Transoxania

c. 112 Opening of 'Silk Road' across central Asia linking China to West

88 BC Bactria and Indus valley overrun by the Shakas

AD 9–23 Hsin dynasty in China
25 Later Han dynasty (to AD 220); capital at Lo-yang

c. 60 Rise of Kushana empire

78–102 Kanishka, Kushana emperor, controls north India
91 Chinese defeat Hsiungnu in Mongolia

166 Roman merchants at the Chinese imperial court
184 'Yellow Turbans' rebellions disrupt Han China

220 Last Han emperor Hsien-ti abdicates

245 Chinese envoys visit Funan (modern Cambodia), first major southeast Asian state

280 China unified under Western Chin

304 Hsiungnu invade China; China fragmented to 589

320 Chandragupta I founds Gupta empire in northern India

c. 350 Hunnish invasions of Persia and India

420 Overthrow of Eastern Chin dynasty

EUROPE

133–122 Failure of reform movement in Rome, led by Tiberius and Gaius Gracchus

89 All Italy receives Roman citizenship

58–51 Julius Caesar conquers Gaul

49 Julius Caesar crosses Rubicon; begins march on Rome
47–45 Civil war in Rome; Julius Caesar becomes sole ruler (45)

31 Battle of Actium: Octavian (later Emperor Augustus) establishes domination over Rome
27 BC Collapse of Roman republic and beginning of empire

AD 43 Roman invasion of Britain

117 Roman empire at its greatest extent

165 Smallpox epidemic ravages Roman empire

212 Roman citizenship conferred on all free inhabitants of empire

238 Gothic incursions into Roman empire begin

293 Emperor Diocletian reorganizes Roman empire

312 Conversion of Constantine
313 Edict of Milan: toleration proclaimed for all religions in the Roman empire
330 Capital of Roman empire transferred to Constantinople

361–3 Emperor Julian attempts to restore pagan religion
370 First appearance of Huns in Europe
378 Visigoths defeat and kill Roman emperor at Adrianople
395 Division between east and west Roman empire permanent

406 Vandals invade and ravage Gaul and Spain (409)
410 Visigoths invade Italy, sack Rome and overrun Spain

NEAR EAST AND NORTH AFRICA

64 Pompey the Great conquers Syria; end of Seleucid empire
53 Battle of Carrhae; Parthia defeats Roman invasion

30 BC Death of Antony and Cleopatra: Egypt a Roman province

AD 44 Mauretania (Morocco) annexed by Rome

70 Romans destroy the Jewish Temple in Jerusalem

97 Chinese ambassador Kan Ying visits Persia

116 Roman Emperor Trajan completes conquest of Mesopotamia

132 Jewish rebellion against Rome leads to 'diaspora' (dispersal of Jews)

224 Foundation of Sasanid dynasty in Persia

429 Vandal kingdom in North Africa

OTHER REGIONS

100 BC Camel introduced into Saharan Africa

c. AD 50 Expansion of kingdom of Aksum (Ethiopia) begins

c. 100 Rise of Teotihuacán in Mesoamerica

c. 150 Berber and Mandingo tribes begin domination of the Sudan

c. 250 Kingdom of Aksum gains control of Red Sea trade

c. 300 Rise of Maya civilization in Mesoamerica; large civilized states in Mexico (Teotihuacán, Monte Albán, El Tajín). Settlement of eastern Polynesia

c. 400 Aksum destroys kingdom of Meroe (Kush). Settlement of Hawaiian islands

CULTURE AND TECHNOLOGY

142 Completion of first stone bridge over river Tiber

79 Death of Ssu-ma Ch'ien, Chinese historian

46 Julius Caesar reforms calendar; Julian calendar in use until AD 1582 (England 1752, Russia 1917)
31 BC–AD 14 The Augustan Age at Rome: Virgil (70–19 BC), Horace (65–27 BC), Ovid (43 BC–AD 17), Livy (59 BC–AD 17)
c. 5 BC Birth of Jesus Christ

c. AD 33 Jesus of Nazareth, founder of Christianity, crucified in Jerusalem

46–57 Missionary journeys of St Paul

65 First Buddhist missionaries arrive in China

c. 90–120 Great Silver period of Latin: Tacitus (c. 55–120), Juvenal (c. 55–c. 140), Martial (c. 38–102)

105 First use of paper in China

c. 125 Third Buddhist conference: widespread acceptance of the sculptural Buddha image
150 Earliest surviving Sanskrit inscription (India). Buddhism reaches China

c. 200 Completion of *Mishnah* (codification of Jewish Law). Indian epic poems *Mahabharata*, *Ramayana* and *Bhagavad Gita*. Earliest Sanskrit writing in southeast Asia
c. 200–250 Development of Christian theology: Tertullian (c. 160–220), Clement (c. 150–c. 215), Origen (185–254)

271 Magnetic compass in use (China)
274 Unconquered Sun proclaimed god of Roman empire
276 Crucifixion of Mani (b. 215), founder of Manichaean sect
285 Confucianism introduced into Japan
c. 300 Foot-stirrup invented in Asia

350 Buddhist cave temples, painting, sculpture (to 800)

404 Latin version of Bible completed

413 Kumaragupta; great literary era in India
426 Augustine of Hippo completes *City of God*

ASIA EXCLUDING THE NEAR EAST

480 Gupta empire overthrown

511 Huns rule northern India

534 Northern Wei dynasty fragments

589 China reunified by Sui dynasty

607 Unification of Tibet

617 China in state of anarchy
618 China united under T'ang dynasty (to 907)

c. 640 Empire of Sri Harsha in northern India
645 Fujiwara's 'Taika reform' remodels Japan on Chinese lines
658 Maximum extension of Chinese power in central Asia ; protectorates in Afghanistan, Kashmir, Sogdiana and Oxus valley
665 Tibetan expansion into Turkestan, Tsinghai
676 Korea unified under Silla

712 Arabs conquer Sind and Samarkand

745 Beginning of Uighur empire in Mongolia
751 Battle of Talas River establishes boundary between China and Abbasid caliphate
755 An Lu-shan's rebellion in China

793 Japanese capital moved to Kyoto from Nara
c. 802 Jayaxarman II establishes Angkorean kingdom (Cambodia)
836 Struggle for control of Indian Deccan
840 Collapse of Uighur empire
842 Tibetan empire disintegrates

EUROPE

449 Angles, Saxons and Jutes begin conquest of Britain

476 Deposition of last Roman emperor in west
481 Clovis becomes king of the Franks
493 Ostrogoths take power in Italy

533 Justinian restores Roman power in north Africa and Italy (552)

c. 542 Bubonic plague ravages Europe

568 Lombard conquest of north Italy

590 Gregory the Great extends papal power

610 Accession of East Roman Emperor Heraclius; beginning of Hellenization of (East) Roman empire, henceforth known as Byzantine empire

680 Bulgars invade Balkans
687 Battle of Tertry: Carolingians dominate Frankish state

711 Muslim invasion of Spain

733/4 Battle of Tours halts Arab expansion in western Europe

751 Lombards overrun Ravenna, last Byzantine foothold in northern Italy

774 Charlemagne conquers northern Italy

793 Viking raids begin
800 Charlemagne crowned emperor in Rome; beginning of new Western (later Holy Roman) empire

843 Treaty of Verdun: partition of Carolingian empire

NEAR EAST AND NORTH AFRICA

540 Chosroes I sacks Antioch

611 Persian armies capture Antioch and Jerusalem and overrun Asia Minor (to 626)

622 *Hegira* of Mohammed; beginning of Islamic calendar

628 Heraclius defeats Persians at Nineveh
632 Death of Mohammed: Arab expansion begins
636 Arabs overrun Syria
637 Arabs overrun Iraq

641 Arabs conquer Egypt and begin conquest of north Africa

717 Arab siege of Constantinople repulsed

750 Abbasid caliphate established

809 Death of caliph Harun al-Rashid

OTHER REGIONS

c. 600 Apogee of Maya civilization

c. 700 Rise of empire of Ghana. Decline of kingdom of Aksum. Teotihuacán destroyed

c. 850 Collapse of Classic Maya culture in Mesoamerica

CULTURE AND TECHNOLOGY

497 Franks converted to Christianity

c. 520 Rise of mathematics in India: Aryabhata and Varamihara invent decimal system
529 Rule of St Benedict regulates Western monasticism
534 Justinian promulgates Legal Code
538 Hagia Sophia, Constantinople, consecrated
c. 540 Silkworms brought into Byzantine empire from China
c. 550 Buddhism introduced into Japan from Korea
563 St Colomba founds monastery of Iona: beginning of Irish mission to Anglo-Saxons

597 Mission of Augustine to England
607 Chinese cultural influence in Japan begins

625 Mohammed begins his prophetic mission

c. 645 Buddhism reaches Tibet (first temple 651)

c. 690 Arabic replaces Greek and Persian as language of Umayyad administration
692 Completion of Dome of Rock in Jerusalem; first great monument of Islamic architecture
c. 700 Buddhist temples built at Nara, Japan. Golden age of Chinese poetry: Li Po (701–62), Tu Fu (712–70), Po Chü-i (772–846)
722 St Boniface's mission to Germany
725 Bede (673–735) introduces dating by Christian era
c. 730 Printing in China

751 Paper-making spreads from China to Muslim world and Europe (1150)

760 Arabs adopt Indian numerals and develop algebra and trigonometry
c. 780–850 Temple at Borobudur (Java) constructed by Shailendra kings
782 Alcuin of York (735–804) organizes education in Carolingian empire: 'Carolingian renaissance'
788 Great mosque in Córdoba

802 Foundation of Angkor, Cambodia

849 Pagan (Burma) founded

853 First printed book in China

862

ASIA EXCLUDING THE NEAR EAST

907 Last T'ang emperor deposed

916 Khitan kingdom in Mongolia founded
918 State of Koryo founded in Korea

939 Vietnam independent of China
947 Khitans overrun northern China, establish Liao dynasty with capital at Peking

967 Fujiwara domination of Japan begins

979 Sung dynasty reunites China

1018 Turkic armies sack Kanauj, ending the reign of the Pratiharas. Rajendra Chola conquers Ceylon

c. 1022 Cholas invade Bengal
1025 Mahmud of Ghazni destroys Shiva temple at Somnath
1038 Tangut tribes form Hsi-hsia state in northwest China
1044 Establishment of first Burmese national state at Pagan

1126 Chin overrun northern China; Sung rule restricted to south

1170 Apogee of Sri Vijaya kingdom in Java under Shailendra dynasty
1175 Muhammad Ghuri invades India and begins the establishment of a Muslim empire
c. 1180 Angkor empire (Cambodia) at greatest extent
1185 Battle of Dannoura (Japan): first shogunate founded

EUROPE

862 Novgorod founded by Rurik the Viking

871 Alfred, king of Wessex, halts Danish advance in England
882 Capital of Russia moved to Kiev

906 Destruction of Moravia by Magyars

911 Vikings granted duchy of Normandy

929 Abd ar-Rahman III establishes caliphate at Córdoba

955 Otto I defeats Magyars at Lechfeld
959 Unification of England under Edgar
960 Mieszko I founds Polish state
962 Otto I of Germany crowned emperor in Rome

972 Beginning of Hungarian state under Duke Geisa

983 Great Slav rebellion against German eastward expansion
987 Accession of Capetians in France

1001 Stephen recognized as first king of Hungary

1014 Battle of Clontarf breaks Viking domination of Ireland
1018 Byzantines annex Bulgaria (to 1185)
1019 Cnut the Great rules England, Denmark and Norway (to 1035). Kievan Rus at height of its political influence (to 1054)
1031 Collapse of caliphate of Córdoba

1054 Schism between Greek and Latin Christian churches begins

1066 Norman conquest of England
1071 Fall of Bari completes Norman conquest of Byzantine Italy
1073 Gregory VII elected Pope: beginning of conflict of Empire and Papacy

1125 Renewal of German eastwards expansion

1154 Accession of Henry II: Angevin empire in England and France

1198 Innocent III elected Pope

NEAR EAST AND NORTH AFRICA

936 Caliphs of Baghdad lose effective power

969 Fatimids conquer Egypt and found Cairo

1055 Seljuk Turks take Baghdad
1056 Almoravids conquer north Africa and southern Spain
1071 Battle of Manzikert: defeat of Byzantium by Seljuk Turks

1096 First Crusade: Franks invade Anatolia and Syria, and found crusader states

1135 Almohads dominant in north-west Africa and Muslim Spain

1171 Saladin defeats Fatimids and conquers Egypt

1187 Saladin destroys Frankish crusader kingdoms

OTHER REGIONS

c. 990 Expansion of Inca empire (Peru)

c. 1000 Vikings colonize Greenland and discover America (Vinland). First Iron Age settlement at Zimbabwe

1076 Almoravids destroy kingdom of Ghana

c. 1100 Toltecs build their capital at Tula (Mexico). Height of Pueblo culture (North America)

c. 1150 Beginnings of Yoruba city states (Nigeria)

c. 1175 Tula abandoned by Toltecs; political fragmentation in Mesoamerica

c. 1200 Rise of empire of Mali in west Africa

CULTURE AND TECHNOLOGY

863 Creation of Cyrillic alphabet in eastern Europe
864 Mission of Cyril and Methodius to Moravia
865 Bulgars and Serbs accept Christianity

c. 890 Japanese cultural renaissance: novels, landscape painting and poetry

910 Abbey of Cluny founded

935 Text of *Koran* finalized

988 Foundation of Russian church

c. 1000 Great age of Chinese painting and ceramics

1020 Completion of *Tale of Genji* by Lady Murasaki. Death of Avicenna, Persian philosopher

c. 1045 Moveable type printing invented in China

1094 Composition of old Javanese *Ramayana* by Yogisvara
c. 1100 First universities in Europe: Salerno (medicine), Bologna (law), Paris (theology and philosophy). Omar Khayyam composes *Rubaiyyat*
1111 Death of al-Ghazali, Muslim theologian

c. 1150 Hindu temple of Angkor Wat (Cambodia) built
1154 Chartres Cathedral begun; Gothic architecture spreads through western Europe

c.1160 Development of European vernacular verse: *Chanson de Roland* (c.1100), *El Cid* (c.1150), *Parzifal*, *Tristan* (c.1200)

1193 Zen Buddhist order founded in Japan
1198 Death of Averroës, Arab scientist and philosopher

ASIA EXCLUDING THE NEAR EAST

1206 Mongols under Genghis Khan begin conquest of Asia. Sultanate of Delhi founded

c. 1220 Emergence of first Thai kingdom

1234 Mongols destroy Chin empire

1264 Kublai Khan founds Yüan dynasty in China

1274 Mongol attack on Japan defeated (and in 1281)

1279 Mongols conquer southern China
1289 Mongol attacks on Pagan defeated

1333 End of Minamoto shogunate: civil war in Japan
1335 Sultan Muhammad ibn Tughluq rules most of India

c. 1342 'Black Death' starts in Asia

1349 First Chinese settlement at Singapore; beginning of Chinese expansion in southeast Asia
1350 Golden age of Majapahit empire in Java

1368 Ming dynasty founded in China
1370 Hindu state of Vijayanagar dominant in south India

1380 Tamerlane (Timur) begins conquests

1392 Korea reduced to vassal status
1394 Thais invade Cambodia; Khmer capital moved to Phnom Penh
1398 Tamerlane invades India and sacks Delhi
c. 1400 Establishment of Malacca as a major commercial port of SE Asia
1405 Chinese voyages in Indian Ocean begin

1427 Chinese expelled from Vietnam

1467–77 Onin Wars: Japan plunged into civil war
1471 Vietnamese southward expansion: Champa annexed

EUROPE

1204 Fourth Crusade: Franks conquer Constantinople and found Latin empire
1212 Battle of Las Navas de Tolosa
1215 Magna Carta: King John makes concessions to English barons

1237 Mongols invade and conquer Russia (1238)
1241 Mongols invade Poland, Hungary, Bohemia
1242 Alexander Nevsky defeats Teutonic Order
1250 d. of Emperor Frederick II: collapse of imperial power in Germany and Italy
1260 Expulsion of Jews from England
1261 Greek empire restored in Constantinople

1291 Beginnings of Swiss Confederation

1305 Papacy moves from Rome to Avignon (to 1376)
1314 Battle of Bannockburn: Scotland defeats England
1315–17 Great Famine in northern Europe
1325 Ivan I begins recovery of Moscow

1337 Hundred Years' War between France and England begins (to 1453)

1347 Black Death from Asia ravages Europe (to 1351)

1354 Ottoman Turks capture Gallipoli, gain first foothold in Europe
1360 Peace of Brétigny ends first phase of Hundred Years' War
1361 Ottomans capture Adrianople

1378 Great Schism in West (to 1417)

1386 Union of Poland and Lithuania

1389 Battle of Kosovo: Ottomans gain control of Balkans
1394 Expulsion of Jews from France

1397 Union of Kalmar (Scandinavia)

1410 Battle of Tannenberg: Poles defeat Teutonic Knights
1415 Battle of Agincourt: Henry V of England resumes attack on France
1428 Joan of Arc: beginning of French revival

1453 England loses Continental possessions (except Calais). Ottoman Turks capture Constantinople: end of Byzantine empire

1475 Burgundy at height of power (Charles the Bold, d.1477)
1478 Ivan III, first Russian tsar, subdues Novgorod and throws off Mongol yoke (1480)

NEAR EAST AND NORTH AFRICA

1228 Hafsid dynasty established at Tunis

1258 Mongols sack Baghdad; end of Abbasid caliphate

1299 Ottoman Turks begin expansion in Anatolia

1402 Battle of Ankara: Tamerlane defeats Ottomans in Anatolia

1415 Portuguese capture Ceuta: beginning of Portugal's African empire

OTHER REGIONS

c. 1200 Emergence of Hausa city states (Nigeria). Aztecs occupy valley of Mexico
1200–1400 Buildings of Great Zimbabwe

c. 1250 Mayapan becomes dominant Maya city of Yucatán

c. 1300 Kanuri empire moves capital from Kanem to Bornu. Emergence of empire of Benin (Nigeria)

1325 Rise of Aztecs in Mexico: Tenochtitlán founded

1375 Chimú conquest of central Andes begins

c. 1400 Songhay breaks away from Mali

1434 Portuguese explore south of Cape Bojador
c. 1450 Apogee of Songhay empire; university at Timbuktu. Mwenemutapa empire founded

1470 Incas conquer Chimú kingdom

1487 Bartolomeu Dias rounds Cape of Good Hope

CULTURE AND TECHNOLOGY

c. 1215 Islamic architecture spreads to India
1216 Foundation of Dominican and Franciscan orders
1226 Death of St Francis of Assisi

1272 Death of St Thomas Aquinas: his *Summa Theologica* defines Christian dogma
1275 Marco Polo (1254–1324) arrives in China

1290 Spectacles invented (Italy)

c. 1320 Cultural revival in Italy: Dante (1265–1321), Giotto (1276–1337), Petrarch (1304–71)

1339 Building of Kremlin (Moscow)

c. 1350 Japanese cultural revival

1377 Death of Ibn Battuta (b. 1309), Arab geographer and traveller

1387 Lithuania converted to Christianity
1392 Death of Hafiz, Persian lyric poet

1400 Death of Chaucer, first great poet in English

1406 Death of Ibn Khaldun, Muslim historian

1455 Johannes Gutenberg (1397–1468) prints first book in Europe using moveable type

1492

ASIA

1498 Vasco da Gama: first European sea-voyage to India and back
1500 Shah Ismail founds Safavid dynasty in Persia

1511 Portuguese take Malacca

1516–7 Ottomans overrun Syria, Egypt and Arabia (1517)

1526 Battle of Panipat: Babur conquers Delhi sultanate and founds Mughal dynasty

1543 Portuguese traders arrive in Japan

1550 Mongol Altan-khan invades northern China; Japanese 'pirate' raids in China

1557 Portuguese enclave established at Macao (China)

1565 Akbar extends Mughal power to Deccan

1581 Yermak begins Russian conquest of Siberia
1584 Phra Narai creates independent Siam
1587 Accession of Shah Abbas: apogee of Safavid state

1603 Beginning of Tokugawa shogunate in Japan

1619 Foundation of Batavia (Jakarta) by Dutch: start of Dutch colonial empire in East Indies

EUROPE

1492 Fall of Granada: end of Muslim rule in Spain; Jews expelled from Spain

1494 Italian wars: beginning of Franco-Habsburg struggle for hegemony in Europe

1499–1552 Jews expelled from many German states

1519 Charles V, ruler of Spain and Netherlands, elected Holy Roman Emperor
1521 Martin Luther outlawed: beginning of Protestant Reformation. Suleiman the Magnificent, Ottoman sultan, conquers Belgrade
1523 Collapse of Union of Kalmar; Sweden independent
1526 Battle of Mohács: Ottoman Turks overrun Hungary

1529 First Ottoman siege of Vienna

1534 Henry VIII of England breaks with Rome

1541 John Calvin founds reformed church at Geneva

1545 Council of Trent: beginning of Catholic Reformation

1555 Charles V abdicates; divides inheritance
1556 Ivan IV of Russia conquers Volga basin

1562 Wars of religion in France (to 1598)
1563–70 Nordic Seven Years' War

1569 Union of Lublin unites Poland and Lithuania

1571 Battle of Lepanto: end of Turkish sea power in central Mediterranean
1572 Dutch Revolt against Spain

1588 Spanish Armada defeated by English

1598 'Time of Troubles' in Russia
1600 Foundation of English and Dutch (1602) East India Companies
1603 Union of Crowns between England and Scotland

1609 Dutch Republic becomes independent

1618 Outbreak of Thirty Years' War

AFRICA

1492 Spaniards begin conquest of north Africa coast
1493 Askia the Great ruler of Songhay

1505 Portuguese establish trading posts in east Africa

1546 Mali empire destroyed by Songhay

1571 Portuguese colony established in Angola

1578 Battle of Al-Kasr al-Kebir: Moroccans destroy Portuguese power in northwest Africa

1591 Battle of Tondibi: Moroccans destroy Songhay kingdom

c. 1600 Oyo empire at height of its power

1628 Portuguese destroy Mwenemutapa empire

NEW WORLD

1492 Columbus reaches America: discovery of New World
1493 First Spanish settlement in New World (Hispaniola). Treaty of Tordesillas divides New World between Portugal and Spain

1497 Cabot reaches Newfoundland
1498 Columbus discovers South America

c. 1510 First African slaves to America

1519 Cortés begins conquest of Aztec empire (to 1520)
1520–1 Magellan crosses Pacific

1531 Pizarro begins conquest of Inca empire for Spain (to 1533)

1545 Discovery of silver mines at Potosí (Peru) and Zacatecas (Mexico)

c. 1560 Portuguese begin sugar cultivation in Brazil

1571 Spanish conquer Philippines

1607 First permanent English settlement in America (Jamestown, Virginia)
1608 French colonists found Quebec

1620 Puritans land in New England (*Mayflower*)

1625 Dutch settle New Amsterdam

CULTURE AND TECHNOLOGY

c. 1500 Italian Renaissance: Leonardo da Vinci (1452–1519), Michelangelo (1475–1564), Raphael (1483–1520), Botticelli (1444–1510), Machiavelli (1469–1527), Ficino (1433–99)

1509 Watch invented by Peter Henle (Nuremberg)

1539 Death of Kabir Nanak, founder of Sikh religion

1543 Copernicus publishes *Of the Revolution of Celestial Bodies*

1559 Tobacco first introduced into Europe

c. 1565 Introduction of potato from South America to Europe

1598 Shah Abbas I creates imperial capital at Isfahan

1607 Monteverdi's *La Favola d'Orfeo* establishes opera as art form

1609 Telescope invented (Holland)
c. 1610 Scientific revolution in Europe begins: Kepler (1571–1610), Bacon (1561–1626), Galileo (1564–1642), Descartes (1596–1650)

1616 Death of Shakespeare (b. 1564) and Cervantes (b. 1547)

1620 First weekly newspapers in Europe (Amsterdam)

1775

ASIA

1638 Russians reach Pacific

1641 Dutch caputure Malacca from Portuguese
1644 Ming dynasty toppled; Manchus found new dynasty (Ch'ing)

1674 Sivaji creates Hindu Maratha kingdom

1689 Treaty of Nerchinsk between Russia and China
1690 Foundation of Calcutta by English
1697 Chinese occupy Outer Mongolia

1707 Death of Aurangzeb: decline of Mughal power in India

1722 Last Safavid shah overthrown by Afghan rebels

1739 Nadir Shah invades India and sacks Delhi

1747 Ahmad Khan Abdali founds kingdom of Afghanistan
1751 China overruns Tibet, Dzungaria and Tarim Basin (1756–9). French gain control of Deccan and Carnatic
1755 Alaungpaya founds Rangoon and reunites Burma (to 1824)
1757 Battle of Plassey: British defeat French

1761 Capture of Pondicherry; British destroy French power in India

1765 British granted the revenues of Bengal by Mughal emperor

EUROPE

1630 Gustavus Adolphus of Sweden intervenes in Thirty Years' War

1642 English Civil War begins

1648 Peace of Westphalia ends Thirty Years' War
1649 First Anglo-Dutch War: beginning of Dutch decline

1654 Ukraine passes from Polish to Russian rule
1655–60 Second Northern War; zenith of Swedish power

1667 Beginning of French expansion under Louis XIV

1683 Turkish siege of Vienna

1688 'Glorious Revolution'; constitutional monarchy in England
1689 'Grand Alliance' against Louis XIV

1699 Treaty of Carlowitz: Habsburgs recover Hungary from Turks
1700 Great Northern War (to 1721)
1702 War of the Spanish Succession (to 1713)
1703 Foundation of St Petersburg, capital of Russian empire (1712)
1707 Union of England and Scotland
1709 Battle of Poltava: Peter the Great of Russia defeats Swedes

1713 Treaty of Utrecht ends War of the Spanish Succession

1740 War of the Austrian Succession (to 1748): Prussia annexes Silesia

1756 Seven Years' War begins

1772 First Partition of Poland (Second and Third Partitions 1793, 1795)
1774 Treaty of Kuchuk Kainarji: beginning of Ottoman decline

AFRICA

1652 Foundation of Cape Colony by Dutch

1659 French found trading station on Senegal coast

1662 Battle of Ambuila: destruction of Kongo kingdom by Portuguese

c. 1700 Rise of Ashanti power (Gold Coast)

c. 1730 Revival of ancient empire of Bornu (central Sudan)

NEW WORLD

1645 Tasman circumnavigates Australia and discovers New Zealand

1664 New Amsterdam taken by English from Dutch (later renamed New York)

1684 La Salle explores Mississippi and claims Louisiana for France

1693 Gold discovered in Brazil

1718 New Orleans founded by France

1728 Bering begins Russian reconnaissance of Alaska

1754 Renewed war between Britain and France for control of North America

1760 New France conquered by British: Quebec (1759) and Montreal (1760)

1763 Treaty of Paris transfers most French North American possessions to Britain

1768 Cook begins exploration of Pacific

1775 American revolution begins

CULTURE AND TECHNOLOGY

c. 1630 Apogee of Netherlands art: Hals (1580–1666), Rembrandt (1606–69), Vermeer (1632–75), Rubens (1577–1640)

1636 Foundation of Harvard College, first university in north America

1653 Taj Mahal, Agra, India, completed

1656 St Peter's Rome, completed (Bernini)

c. 1660 Classical period of French culture: drama, Molière (1622–73), Racine (1639–99), Corneille (1606–84); painting, Poussin (1594–1665), Claude (1600–82); music, Lully (1632–87), Couperin (1668–1733)
1662 Royal Society founded in London and (1666) Académie Française in Paris

1687 Isaac Newton's *Principia*

1690 John Locke's *Essay concerning Human Understanding*

c. 1700 Great age of German baroque music: Buxtehude (1637–1707), Handel (1685–1759), Bach (1685–1750)

1709 Abraham Darby discovers coke-smelting technique for producing pig iron (England)

1730 Wesley brothers create Methodism
c. 1735 Wahabite movement to purify Islam begins in Arabia

c. 1760 European enlightenment: Voltaire (1694–1778), Diderot (1713–84), Hume (1711–76)

1762 J. J. Rousseau's *Social Contract*

c. 1770 Advance of science and technology in Europe: J Priestley (1733–1804), A. Lavoisier (1743–94), A. Volta (1745–1827), Harrison's chronometer (1762), Watt's steam engine (1765), Arkwright's water-powered spinning-frame (1769)

1776

ASIA

1793 British embassy under Macartney to the Chinese court

1796 British conquer Ceylon

1813 British defeat the Marathas and become the effective rulers of India

1819 British found Singapore as free trade port

1824 Treaty of London formalizes British control of Malaya and Dutch control of East Indies. British begin conquest of Burma and Assam
1825–30 Java war: revolt of Indonesians against Dutch

1830 Russia begins conquest of Kazakhstan (to 1854)

1833 Death of Rammohan Roy (b. 1772), father of modern Indian nationalism

1839–42 First Opium War: Britain annexes Hong Kong

1843 British conquer Sind
1845–9 British conquest of Punjab and Kashmir

1850 T'ai-p'ing rebellion in China (to 1846), with immense loss of life

1853 First railway and telegraph lines in India. Perry arrives in Japan; proposes commercial arrangements between Japan and US

1856–60 Second Opium War

EUROPE

1783 Russia annexes Crimea

1789 French revolution begins; abolition of feudal system and proclamation of Rights of Man
1791 Russia gains Black Sea steppes from Turks
1792 French republic proclaimed; beginning of revolutionary wars
1793 Attempts to reform Ottoman empire by Selim III

1799 Napoleon becomes First Consul and (1804) emperor of France

1805 Battle of Trafalgar: Britain defeats French and Spanish fleets
1806 Abdication of Emperor Francis I; end of the Holy Roman Empire
1807 Abolition of serfdom in Prussia

1812 Napoleon invades Russia; suffers catastrophic defeat. Last major outbreak of bubonic plague in Europe (to 1815)
1815 Napoleon defeated at Waterloo, exiled to St Helena. Congress of Vienna

1821 Greek declaration of independence

1825 'Decembrist' uprising in Russia suppressed

1830 Revolutionary movements in France, Germany, Poland and Italy; Belgium wins independence. Greece independent
1833 Slavery abolished in British empire.
1834 Formation of German customs union, *Zollverein*

1845 Irish famine (to 1849) stimulates hostility to Britain and emigration to US
1846 Britain repeals Corn Laws and moves towards complete free trade
1846–7 Last major famine in Europe
1848 Revolutionary movements in Europe; proclamation of Second Republic in France

1852 Fall of French republic; Louis Napoleon (Napoleon III, 1803–73) becomes French emperor

1853 Crimean War (to 1855)

AFRICA

1798 Napoleon attacks Egypt

1804 Usuman dan Fodio begins to establish Fulani empire

1806 Cape Colony recaptured by Britain
1807 Slave trade abolished within British empire
1811 Mohammed Ali takes control in Egypt

1818 Shaka forms Zulu kingdom in SE Africa

1822 Liberia founded as colony for freed slaves
1824 British merchants establish post in Natal; first Anglo-Ashanti war

1830 French begin conquest of Algeria

1836 'Great Trek' of Boer colonists from Cape, leading to foundation of Republic of Natal (1839), Orange Free State (1848) and Transvaal (1849)

1852 South African Republic (Transvaal) established by agreement between Britain and Boers
1853 Livingstone's explorations begin

AMERICAS AND AUSTRALASIA

1776 American Declaration of Independence
1778 France enters American War of Independence

1783 Treaty of Paris: Britain recognizes American independence
1788 British colony of Australia founded
1789 George Washington becomes first president of United States of America

1803 Louisiana Purchase nearly doubles size of US

1808 Independence movements in Spanish and Portuguese America: 13 new states created by 1828

1819 US purchases Florida from Spain
1820 Missouri Compromise bans slavery north of 36 degrees 30 minutes

1823 Monroe Doctrine asserts that Europe should not interfere in affairs of the Americas

1840 Britain annexes New Zealand

1845 Texas annexed by US

1846 Mexican War begins: US conquers New Mexico and California (1848). Oregon Treaty delimits US-Canada boundary

1850 Australian colonies and (1856) New Zealand granted responsible government

CULTURE AND TECHNOLOGY

1776 Publication of *The Wealth of Nations* by Adam Smith (1723–90) and *Common Sense* by Tom Paine (1737–1809)
1781 Immanuel Kant's *Critique of Pure Reason*

c. 1790 Great age of European orchestral music: Mozart (1756–91), Haydn (1732–1809), Beethoven (1770–1827)
1792 Cartwright invents steam-powered weaving loom
1793 Decimal system introduced (France). Eli Whitney's 'cotton gin' (US)
1796 Jenner discovers smallpox vaccine (UK)

1798 Malthus publishes *Essay on the Principle of Population*

1812 Cylinder printing press invented, adopted by *The Times* (London)

1817 Foundation of Hindu college, Calcutta, first major centre of Western influence in India

c. 1820 Romanticism in European literature and art: Byron (1788–1824), Chateaubriand (1768–1848), Heine (1797–1856), Turner (1775–1851), Delacroix (1798–1863)
1821 Electric motor and generator invented by M. Faraday (Britain)
1822 First photographic image produced, by J-N. Niepce (France)

1825 First passenger steam railway: Stockton and Darlington (England)
1828 Foundation of Brahmo-samaj, Hindu revivalist movement

1832 Death of Goethe (born 1749)
1833 First regulation of industrial working conditions (Britain)
1834 First mechanical reaper patented (US)
1836 Needle-gun invented (Prussia), making breech-loading possible
1837 Pitman's shorthand invented
1838 First electric telegraph (Britain)

1840 First postage stamp (Britain)

1848 *Communist Manifesto* issued by Marx (1818–83) and Engels (1820–95)
1849 Death of Chopin (b. 1810); apogee of Romantic music with Berlioz (1803–69), Liszt (1811–86), Wagner (1813–83), Brahms (1833–97), Verdi (1813–1901)
1851 Great Exhibition in London

1853 Haussmann begins rebuilding of Paris

1855 Bessemer process permits mass-production of steel

1905

ASIA

1857 Indian Mutiny
1858 Treaty of Tientsin: further Treaty Ports opened to foreign trade in China

1860 Treaty of Peking: China cedes Maritime Province to Russia

1863 France establishes protectorate over Cambodia, Cochin China (1865), Annam (1874), Tonkin (1885) and Laos (1893)

1868 End of Tokugawa shogunate; Meiji restoration in Japan

1877 Start of Tanzimat reform era in Ottoman empire. Queen Victoria proclaimed empress of India

1879 Second Afghan War gives Britain control of Afghanistan

1885 Foundation of Indian National Congress
1886 British annex Upper Burma

1887 French establish Indo-Chinese Union

1894–5 Russo-Japanese War: Japan occupies Formosa

1898 Abortive 'Hundred Days' reform in China

1900 Boxer uprising in China

1904 Partition of Bengal: nationalist agitation in India
1904–5 Russo-Japanese War; Japanese success stimulates Asian nationalism

EUROPE

1859 Sardinian-French war against Austria; Piedmont acquires Lombardy (1860); unification of Italy begins

1861 Emancipation of Russian serfs

1864 Prussia defeats Denmark: annexes Schleswig-Holstein (1866). Russia suppresses Polish revolt

1866 Establishment of North German confederation and of dual monarchy in Austria-Hungary

1870 Franco-Prussian war
1871 Proclamation of German empire, beginning of Third French Republic: suppression of Paris commune

1875 Growth of labour/socialist parties: Germany (1875), Holland (1877), Belgium (1885), Britain (1893), Russia (1898)

1878 Congress of Berlin held; leads to the Treaty of Berlin: Romania, Montenegro and Serbia become independent and Bulgaria autonomous.
1879 Dual alliance between Germany and Austria-Hungary

1890 Dismissal of Bismarck; Wilhelm II begins new policy

1894 Franco-Russian alliance

1898 Germany embarks on naval building programme: beginning of German 'world policy'

1904 Anglo-French entente

1905 Revolution in Russia, followed by tsarist concessions. Norway independent of Sweden

AFRICA

1860 French expansion in west Africa from Senegal

1869 Suez canal opens

1875 Disraeli buys Suez Canal Company shares to ensure British control of sea route to India

1881 French establish protectorate over Tunisia
1882 Revolt in Egypt leading to British occupation
1884 Berlin Conference on the partition of Africa. Germany acquires SW Africa, Togoland, Cameroons
1885 King of Belgium acquires Congo
1886 Germany and Britain partition east Africa

1889 British South Africa Company formed by Cecil Rhodes; begins colonization of Rhodesia (1890)

1896 Battle of Adowa: Italians defeated by Ethiopians

1898 Fashoda crisis between Britain and France

1899 The South African ('Boer War') begins (to 1902): Britain conquers Boer republics, Transvaal and Orange Free State
1900 Copper mining begins in Katanga

1905 First Moroccan crisis

AMERICAS AND AUSTRALASIA

1860 Abraham Lincoln US president; South secedes

1861 Outbreak of American Civil War

1863 Slavery abolished in US

1864 War of Paraguay against Argentina, Brazil and Uruguay (to 1870)
1865 End of American Civil War

1867 Russia sells Alaska to US. Dominion of Canada established

1869 Prince Rupert's Land, Manitoba (1870) and British Columbia (1871) join Canada

1876 Porfirio Diaz (1830–1915) gains control of Mexico (to 1911)
1877 Reconstruction formally ended in Southern states of US

1879 War of the Pacific (Chile, Bolivia, Peru)

1885 Completion of Canadian Pacific railway

1888 Brazil becomes last Latin American country to abolish slavery

1890 US Bureau of Census declares the western frontier closed

1898 Spanish-American war: US annexes Guam, Puerto Rico and Philippines

1901 Commonwealth of Australia created
1903 Panama Canal Zone ceded to US

CULTURE AND TECHNOLOGY

1859 Darwin publishes *The Origin of Species*. First oil well drilled (Pennsylvania, USA)

c. 1860 Great age of European novel: Dickens (1812–70), Dumas (1802–70), Flaubert (1821–80), Turgenev (1818–83), Dostoyevsky (1821–81), Tolstoy (1828–1910)

1861 Pasteur evolves germ theory of disease. Women first given vote (Australia)
1863 First underground railway (London)

1864 Foundation of Red Cross (Switzerland)

1866 First trans-Atlantic telegraph cable laid

1867 Marx publishes *Das Kapital* (vol. 1)

1869 First trans-continental railroad completed (US)
1870 Declaration of Papal infallibility

1874 First electric tram (New York); telephone patented by Bell (US 1876); first electric steetlighting (London 1878). Emergence of Impressionist school of painting: Monet (1840–1926), Renoir (1841–1919), Degas (1834–1917)
1878 First oil tanker built (Russia)

1879 F. W. Woolworth opens first '5 and 10 cent store'
1880 First consignment of frozen Australian beef arrives in London

1882 First hydro-electric plant (Wisconsin, US)
1884 Maxim gun perfected

c. 1885 Daimler and Benz pioneer the automobile (Germany)

1888 Dunlop invents pneumatic tyre

c. 1890 Beginnings of modern literature in Japan on western models. Europe – realistic drama: Ibsen (1828–1906), Strindberg (1849–1912), Chekhov (1860–1904), Shaw (1856–1950)
1891–1905 Trans-Siberian railway built

1895 Röntgen discovers X-rays (Germany); first public showing of motion picture (France)
1896 Marconi builds first radio transmitter. Herzl publishes *The Jewish State* calling for Jewish National Home
1898 Pierre and Marie Curie observe radioactivity and isolate radium (France)
1899 Howard's *Garden Cities of Tomorrow* initiates modern city planning

1900 Planck evolves quantum theory (Germany). Freud's *Interpretation of Dreams*, beginning of psychoanalysis (Austria)
1901 First wireless message sent across Atlantic
1903 First successful flight of petrol-powered aircraft (Wright Brothers, US)

1905 Einstein's Theory of Relativity (Germany)

1907

ASIA

1908 Young Turk revolution: Ottoman sultan deposed
1910 Japan annexes Korea

1911 Chinese revolution; Sun Yat-sen provisional president of new republic; rise to power of Warlords (to 1926)
1914 German concessions in China and colonies in Pacific taken over by Japan, Australia and New Zealand
1915–16 Armenian massacres in Turkey
1917 Balfour Declaration promises Jews a National Home in Palestine
1917–18 Arab revolt: Ottoman territories in Middle East lost

1919 Amritsar incident; upsurge of Indian nationalism

1920 Mustafa Kemal (Atatürk) leads resistance to partition of Turkey; Turkey Nationalist Movement
1920–2 Gandhi leads Indian non-cooperation movement
1921–2 Washington Conference on situation in east Asia
1922 Greek army expelled from Turkey; last Ottoman sultan deposed; republic proclaimed (1923)

1926 Chiang Kai-shek begins reunification of China

1930–1 Civil disobedience campaign in India (and in 1932–4)
1931 Japan invades Manchuria
1932 Iraq independent. Kingdom of Saudi Arabia formed by Ibn Saud
1934 'Long March' of Chinese communists begins
1935 Government of India Act: Indians gain provincial autonomy
1936 Japan signs anti-Comintern pact with Germany. Arab revolt in Palestine against Jewish immigration
1937 Beginning of full-scale war between Japan and China

1939 Russian forces defeat Japan at Khalkin Gol (Manchuria); Russo-Japanese neutrality pact (1941)

1941 Japan attacks US at Pearl Harbor; US declares war
1942 Japan overruns SE Asia. Battle of Midway: US halts Japanese expansion. Gandhi and Indian Congress leaders arrested

1945 US drops atom bombs on Japan forcing surrender
1946 Civil war in China (to 1949). Creation of Philippine Republic. Beginning of Vietnamese struggle against France (to 1954)
1947 India and Pakistan partitioned and granted independence

1948 Burma and Ceylon independent. Establishment of State of Israel; first Arab-Israeli war (to 1949)
1949 Communist victory in China; Chiang Kai-shek retreats to Formosa (Taiwan). Indonesia independent
1950 China invades Tibet. Korean War begins (to 1953)
1951 US ends occupation of Japan

1953 Military coup in Iran

EUROPE

1907 Anglo-Russian entente
1908 Bulgaria becomes independent; Austria annexes Bosnia and Herzegovina

1912–13 Balkan wars: Turkey loses bulk of remaining European territory
1914 Outbreak of First World War

1915 Italy enters war on the side of the Allies
1917 Revolution in Russia: tsar abdicates (February), Bolsheviks take over (October); first socialist state established
1918 Treaty of Brest-Litovsk; Russia withdraws from First World War. Germany and Austria-Hungary sue for armistice (November): end of First World War. Civil war and foreign intervention in Russia
1919 Paris treaties redraw map of Europe

1920 League of Nations established (headquarters Geneva)

1921 Lenin introduces New Economic Policy
1922 Mussolini takes power in Italy

1924 Death of Lenin; Stalin eventually emerges as Soviet leader (1929)
1925 Locarno treaties stabilize frontiers in west

1928 First Five-Year Plan and (1929) collectivization of agriculture in USSR
1931 Collapse of central European banks begins major recession

1933 Hitler made Chancellor in Germany; beginning of Nazi revolution

1936 German reoccupation of Rhineland. Spanish Civil War begins (to 1939). 'Great Terror' launched by Stalin in Russia

1938 Germany occupies Austria. Munich conference: Czechoslovakia dismembered
1939 Germany occupies Czechoslovakia; Germany-Soviet non-aggression pact; Germany invades Poland; Britain and France declare war on Germany
1940 Germany overruns Norway, Denmark, Belgium, Netherlands, France; Italy invades Greece but is repulsed; Battle of Britain
1941 Germany invades Russia; declares war on US. 'Final solution' initiated by Nazis
1943 German VI army surrenders at Stalingrad; Italian capitulation
1944 Anglo-American landing in Normany; Russian advance in E Europe
1945 Yalta Conference; defeat of Germany and suicide of Hitler

1947 Development of Cold War; Truman Doctrine enunciated. Marshall Plan for economic reconstruction in Europe
1948 Communist takeover in Czechoslovakia and Hungary; Berlin airlift (to 1949). Split between Yugoslavia under Tito and USSR
1949 USSR tests its first atomic bomb. Formation of NATO alliance and of COMECON

1952 European Coal and Steel Community founded

1953 Death of Stalin; East Berlin revolt crushed

AFRICA

1908 Belgian state takes over Congo from King Leopold
1910 Formation of Union of South Africa

1911 Italy conquers Libya

1914–15 French and British conquer German colonies except German East Africa

1919 Former German colonies distributed as League of Nations mandates. Nationalist revolt in Egypt against British protectorate

1921 Battle of Anual: Spanish army routed by Moroccans
1922 Egypt independent

1926 Revolt of Abd-el Krim crushed in Morocco

1934 Italians suppress Senussi resistance in Libya
1935–6 Italy conquerors Abyssinia

1936 Anglo-Egyptian alliance; British garrison Suez Canal Zone

1940–1 Italians expelled from Somalia, Eritrea and Ethiopia

1941 Germans conquer Cyrenaica and advance into Egypt (1942)
1942 Battle of El-Alamein; German defeat and retreat. Anglo-American landings in Morocco and Algeria. Apartheid programme inaugurated in S Africa

1952 Beginning of Mau Mau rebellion in Kenya. Military revolt in Egypt; proclamation of republic (1953)

AMERICAS AND AUSTRALASIA

1907 Peak year for immigration into USA. New Zealand acquires dominion status
1910 Mexican revolution begins

1914 Panama canal opens

1917 US declares war on Central Powers

1918 President Wilson announces 'Fourteen Points'

1920 US refuses to ratify Paris treaties and withdraws into isolation

1921 US restricts immigration

1923 General Motors established: world's largest manufacturing company

1929 Wall Street crash precipitates Great Depression
1930 Military revolution in Brazil; Vargas becomes president

1933 US President Franklin D. Roosevelt introduces New Deal
1935 Cárdenas president of Mexico: land redistribution and (1938) nationalization of oil
1936 Pan-American congress; US proclaims 'good neighbour' policy

1941 US enters war against Germany and Japan

1945 Death of Roosevelt; Harry Truman US president. United Nations established (headquarters New York)
1946 Perón comes to power in Argentina

1948 Organization of American States established

1951 Australia, New Zealand and US sign ANZUS Pact

CULTURE AND TECHNOLOGY

1907 Exhibition of Cubist paintings in Paris: Picasso (1881–1973), Braque (1882–1963)
1910 Development of abstract painting: Kandinsky (1866–1944), Mondrian (1872–1944). Development of plastics

1913 Henry Ford develops conveyor belt assembly for production of Model T automobile (Detroit, US)

1917 First use of massed tanks (Battle of Cambrai)

1919 Rutherford (1871–1973) splits atom (UK). Bauhaus school of design at Weimar (Germany). First crossing of Atlantic by air (Alcock and Brown)
1920 First general radio broadcasts (US and UK). Emergence of jazz in US: Louis Armstrong (1900–71), Duke Ellington (1899–1974), Count Basie (1904–84)

1923 Development of tuberculosis vaccine (France)
1924 Thomas Mann (1875–1955) publishes *The Magic Mountain*
1925 Franz Kafka (1883–1924), *The Trial*; Adolf Hitler, *Mein Kampf*

1927 Emergence of talking pictures. Rise of great film makers: D.W. Griffith (1874–1948), Chaplin (1889–1977), John Ford (1895–1973), Eisenstein (1896–1948), Clair (1898–1981), Hitchcock (1899–1980), Disney (1901–66)

1936 First regular public television transmissions (UK)

1937 Jet engine first tested (UK); invention of nylon (USA)

1939 Development of penicillin (UK). Development of DDT (Switzerland)

1942 Fermi builds first nuclear reactor (US)

1945 Atom bomb first exploded (US)

1946 First electronic computer built (US)

1947 First supersonic flight (US)

1948 Transistor invented (US)

1951 First nuclear power stations
1952 Hydrogen bomb first exploded (US). Contraceptive pill developed (US)
1953 Crick and Watson explain structure of DNA (UK)

ASIA	EUROPE	AFRICA	AMERICAS AND AUSTRALASIA	CULTURE AND TECHNOLOGY
1954 Geneva conference: Laos, Cambodia and Vietnam become independent states **1956** Second Arab-Israeli war	**1955** Four-power occupation of Austria ended. Warsaw Pact signed **1956** Soviet leader Khrushchev denounces Stalin at Party Congress. Polish revolt, Gomulka in power. Hungarian revolt crushed by Russians **1957** Treaty of Rome: Formation of European Economic Community and (1959) of European Free Trade Association **1958** Fifth Republic in France: de Gaulle first president	**1954** Beginnings of nationalist revolt in Algeria (to 1962) **1956** Suez crisis: Anglo-French invasion of Canal Zone **1957** Beginning of decolonization in sub-Saharan Africa: Gold Coast (Ghana) becomes independent	**1955** Overthrow of Perón regime in Argentina **1956** Civil rights protests in Alabama	**1956** Beginning of rock and roll music (US): Elvis Presley (1935–77) **1957** First space satellite launched (USSR)
1958 'Great Leap Forward' in China (to 1961) **1959** War between North and South Vietnam (to 1975) **1960** Sino-Soviet dispute begins		**1960** 'Africa's year'; many states become independent; outbreak of civil war in former Belgian Congo. Sharpeville massacre in South Africa	**1959** Fidel Castro takes power after Cuban insurgency **1960** John F. Kennedy elected US president	
1961 Increasing US involvement in Vietnam **1962** Sino-Indian war	**1961** East Germans build Berlin Wall	**1961** South Africa becomes independent republic **1962** Algeria becomes independent **1963** Nationalist uprising against Portuguese rule in Angola	**1962** Cuban missile crisis **1963** Kennedy assassinated; Lyndon Johnson succeeds (to 1968)	**1961** First man in space: Gagarin (USSR) **1962** Second Vatican Council reforms Catholic liturgy and dogma
1964 China tests first atomic bomb **1965** Sukarno overthrown in Indonesia. Indo-Pakistan war **1966** Cultural Revolution in China (to 1976) **1967** Third Arab-Israeli war (Six-Day War) **1968** Viet Cong launch Tet Offensive in Vietnam	**1964** Khrushchev ousted as Soviet leader; succeeded by Leonid Brezhnev **1968** Liberalization in Czechoslovakia halted by Russian invasion **1969** Outbreak of violence in N Ireland	**1965** Rhodesia declares independence – UDI **1966** South African prime minister, Hendrik Verwoerd, assassinated **1967** Civil war in Nigeria with secessionist Biafra (to 1970)	**1964** US Civil Rights Act inaugurates President Johnson's 'Great Society' programme **1966** Eruption of Black American discontent; growth of Black Power **1968** Assassinations of Martin Luther King and Robert Kennedy; R.M. Nixon elected US president **1970** Allende elected president of Chile (killed 1973)	**1964** Publication of *Thoughts of Chairman Mao* **1968** World-wide student protest movement **1969** First man lands on moon: Armstrong (US)
1971 Indo-Pakistan war leads to breakaway of East Pakistan (Bangladesh) **1973** US forces withdraw from South Vietnam. Fourth Arab-Israeli war; OPEC countries triple oil price	**1973** Oil crisis ends post-war economic boom. Britain, Ireland and Denmark join EEC **1974** Death of Salazar; end of dictatorship in Portugal. Turkish invasion of Cyprus **1975** Death of Franco; end of dictatorship in Spain		**1971** US initiates policy of detente with China and USSR. USA abandons Gold Standard and depreciates dollar **1972** President Nixon visits China **1973** Overthrow of Allende regime in Chile. Major recession in US triggered by oil crisis **1974** President Nixon resigns after Watergate scandal; Gerald Ford succeeds	
1975 Civil war in Lebanon: Syria invades (1976). Communists take over Vietnam, Laos and Cambodia **1976** Death of Mao Zedong; paves way for economic re-orientation and modernization under Deng Xiaoping **1977** Egypt/Israeli peace talks (Camp David Peace Treaty, 1978). Military coup ends democratic rule in Pakistan **1978** Vietnam invades Cambodia **1979** Fall of shah of Iran, establishment of Islamic Republic under Ayatollah Khomeini (d.1989). Afghanistan invaded by USSR (to 1989). Sino-Vietnamese War. Vietnam expels Khmer Rouge government from Cambodia		**1974** Emperor Haile Selassie of Ethiopia deposed by Marxist junta **1975** Portugal grants independence to Mozambique and Angola **1976** Morocco and Mauritania partition Spanish Sahara. Unrest in Soweto, South Africa, suppressed **1979** Tanzanian forces invade Uganda and expel President Amin	**1976** Jimmy Carter elected US president **1979** Civil war in Nicaragua (to 1990). Civil war in El Salvador (to 1992)	**1976** First supersonic trans-Atlantic passenger service begins with Concorde
1980 Outbreak of Iran/Iraq War (to 1988) **1982** Israel invades Lebanon, expulsion of PLO from Beirut. Israel withdraws from Sinai peninsula **1984** Indira Gandhi assassinated **1985** Israel withdraws from Lebanon **1986** Fall of Marcos in the Phillipines; Cory Aquino succeeds	**1980** Death of Marshal Tito. Creation of independent Polish trade union Solidarity; martial law (1981) **1981** Greece joins EEC **1982** Death of USSR president, Brezhnev, succession of Yuri Andropov (d.1984), then Konstantin Chernenko (d.1985) **1985** Mikhail Gorbachev leader of USSR (to 1991) **1986** Spain and Portugal join EEC	**1980** Black majority rule established in Zimbabwe (Rhodesia) **1981** President Sadat of Egypt assassinated **1984** Famine in Sahel and Ethiopia; continuing war against secession **1986** US bomb Libya in retaliation for terrorist activities	**1980** Ronald Reagan elected US president **1981** US hostages released after 444 days in US embassy in Iran **1982** Argentina occupies South Georgia and Falkland Islands; surrenders to UK forces **1983** Democracy restored in Argentina. US invades Grenada **1985** Democracy restored in Brazil, Bolivia and Uruguay	**1980s** Computer revolution: spread of computers in offices and homes in Western world **1981** First re-usable shuttle space flight (USA)
1988 Benazir Bhutto restores civilian rule in Pakistan. Palestine uprising (*intifada*) against Israeli occupied territories. PLO recognizes State of Israel **1989** Death of Ayatollah Khomeini. Student pro-democracy demonstration crushed in Beijing	**1988** Gorbachev introduces *glasnost* and *perestroika* in USSR **1989** Communist bloc in E Europe disintegrates; Berlin Wall demolished		**1987** INF treaty between USSR and USA: phased elimination of intermediate-range nuclear weapons. US stock market crash **1988** George Bush elected US president (to 1993) **1989** Democracy restored in Chile **1989–90** US military intervention in Panama; arrest and extradition of Manuel Noriega	**1986** Launch of world's first permanently manned space station (USSR). Major nuclear disaster at Chernobyl power reactor (Ukraine). US space shuttle *Challenger* explodes **1987** World population reaches 5 billion **1988** Global recognition that ozone layer is being depleted; global ban on CFCs (chlorofluorocarbons) (1990)
1990 Iraq invades Kuwait **1991** Gulf War: UN Coalition forces led by US attack Iraq and liberate Kuwait. Rajiv Gandhi assassinated	**1990** Reunification of Germany **1991** Boris Yeltsin elected president of Russian Federation; USSR disintegrates. Disintegration of Yugoslavia; Slovenia and Croatia declare independence **1992** Civil War in Bosnia-Herzegovina. Czech Republic and Slovakia emerge as separate states	**1990** Namibia independent. S African government moves towards accommodation with ANC, frees Nelson Mandela, and (1991) announces intention to dismantle apartheid **1992** US forces intervene to end Somalia's famine and civil war. Prolonged terrorism in Algeria after elections are cancelled	**1990** Democratic elections in Nicaragua end Sandinista rule **1992** Bill Clinton elected US president	**1990** *Voyager* space probe mission completed; last planetary encounter (Neptune)
1993 Israel and PLO sign Palestinian autonomy agreement for limited Palestinian self-rule **1997** Hong Kong returned to China. Death of Deng Xiaoping; Jiang Zemin emerges as Chinese leader **1998** India and Pakistan carry out nuclear tests. President Suharto resigns after Indonesian unrest	**1993** Russian parliament building shelled after its occupation by hardline opponents of Yeltsin **1995** Dayton Agreement temporarily halts war in former Yugoslavia **1998** Fighting in Albanian-majority province of Kosovo (Serbia). **1999** European single currency (euro) launched	**1994** Nelson Mandela elected as South Africa's first black president. Up to one million Tutsis and moderate Hutus massacred by Hutu extremists in Rwanda **1997** President Mobutu Sese Soko overthrown by Laurent Kabila as ruler of Congo	**1994** US military intervention in Haiti **1995** Oklahoma City terrorist bombing **1996** President Clinton re-elected **1997** Pope visits Cuba **1998** US bombs Afghanistan and Sudan after terrorist attacks on US embassies in Kenya and Tanzania	**1994** Cross-Channel rail link between Britain and France inaugurated **mid-1990s** Growth of the world-wide web

1

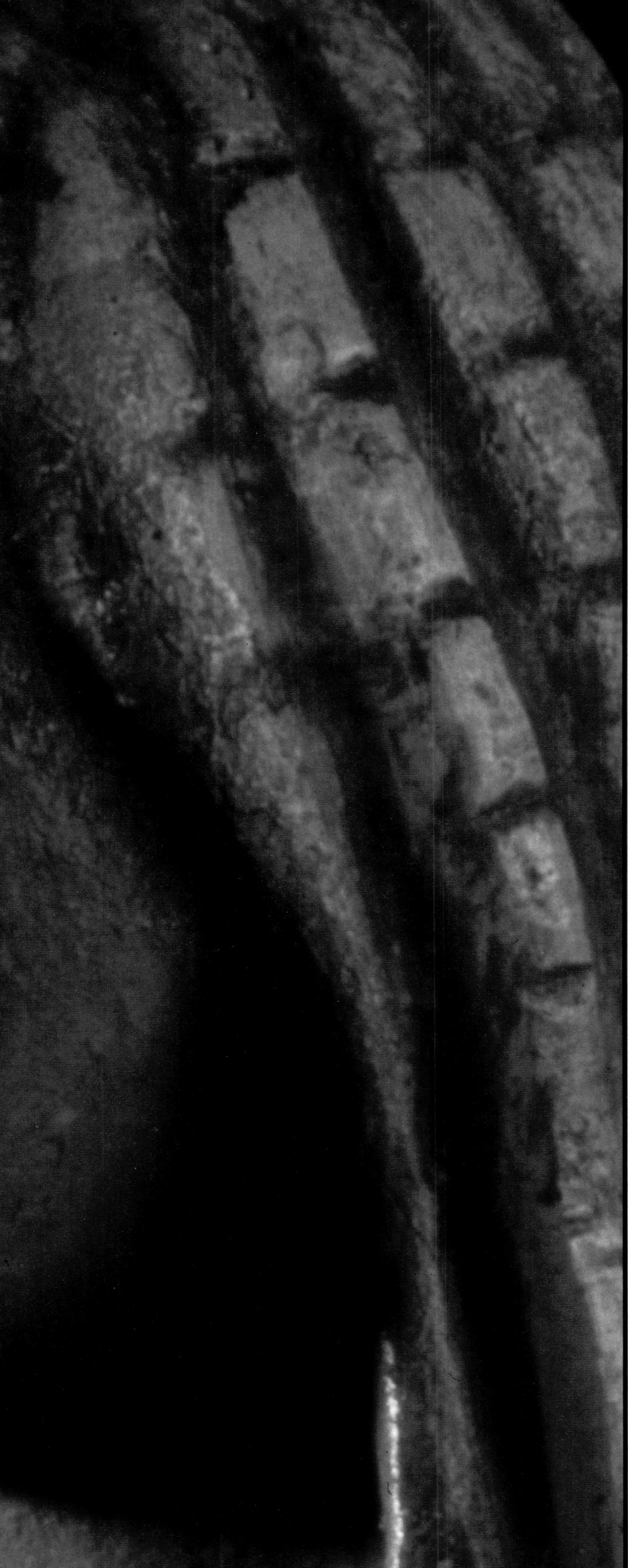

Human origins and early cultures

RECORDED HISTORY is only the tip of an iceberg reaching back to the first appearance on earth of the human species. Anthropologists, prehistorians and archaeologists have extended our vista of the past by hundreds of thousands of years: we cannot understand human history without taking account of their findings. The transformation of humankind (or, more accurately, of certain groups of humans in certain areas) from hunters and fishers to agriculturists, and from a migratory to a sedentary life, constitutes the most decisive revolution in the whole of human history. The climatic and ecological changes which made it possible have left their mark on the historical record down to the present day.

Agriculture made possible not merely a phenomenal growth of human population, which is thought to have increased some 16-fold between 8000 and 4000 BC, but also gave rise to the familiar landscape of village communities which still characterized Europe as late as the middle of the 19th century and which even today prevails in many parts of the world. Nowhere are the continuities of history more visible. The enduring structures of human society, which transcend and outlive political change, carry us back to the end of the Ice Age, to the changes which began when the shrinking ice-cap left a new world to be explored and tamed.

Carved head from Brassempouy, southwest France, c. 20,000 BC

From c. 5 million years ago

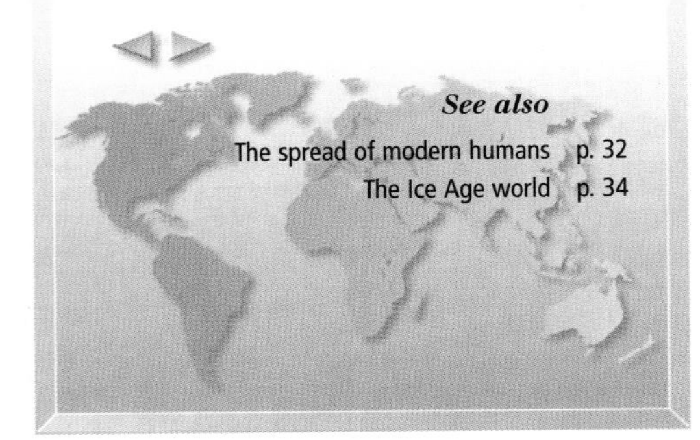
See also
The spread of modern humans p. 32
The Ice Age world p. 34

Human origins

Global cooling between five and six million years ago saw savannahs replace the tropical forests of sub-Saharan Africa. The appearance of this new environment was in turn matched by an evolutionary pulse that gave rise to new carnivores and omnivores. Among them were the hominines, the ancestors of modern man.

THE EARLIEST HOMININE FOSSILS, discovered in the Afar region of Ethiopia, are the fragmentary 4.5-million year-old remains of *Ardipithecus ramidus*. Better evidence is available of the later and more widespread Australopithecenes, or 'southern apes'. Skeletal and fossilized footprints of *Australopithecus afarensis*, dated to between three and four million years ago, indicate a serviceable if not fully bipedal gait, hands still partly adapted for specialized tree climbing and a brain approximately one-third the size of ours. This species is the probable ancestor both of the robustly built Australopithecines *boisei*, *aethiopicus* and *robustus*, all with large teeth and herbivorous diets, and of our genus, *Homo*, meaning 'man'. A major discovery thrown up by fieldwork since the 1950s has revealed that these closely related but nonetheless distinctive species not only lived at the same time but side by side in the same habitats. Finds of more species are expected.

From between two and three million years ago, there is evidence of important evolutionary trends in *Homo*: brains became much bigger, a process known as encephalization; and full bipedalism was attained. As larger brains need better diets to sustain them, the increase in brain size could only have occurred as a result of significant evolutionary pressures. The problem was compounded because hominines stayed the same size, with the result that their bigger brains could be achieved only by reducing the size of another organ, the stomach, a trade-off which in turn reduced the efficiency of the digestive tract, which in turn demanded a still better diet.

Early technologies

The most convincing explanation of this development – the expensive tissue hypothesis – holds that a move towards an energy-rich diet, particularly animal proteins, was responsible. And indeed the earliest-known stone tools, found in Gona, Ethiopia, suggest that 2.5 million years ago meat was a central part of hominines' diet, with the sharpened stones used to cut flesh and pound marrow-rich bones from carcasses either scavenged or brought down and then defended against

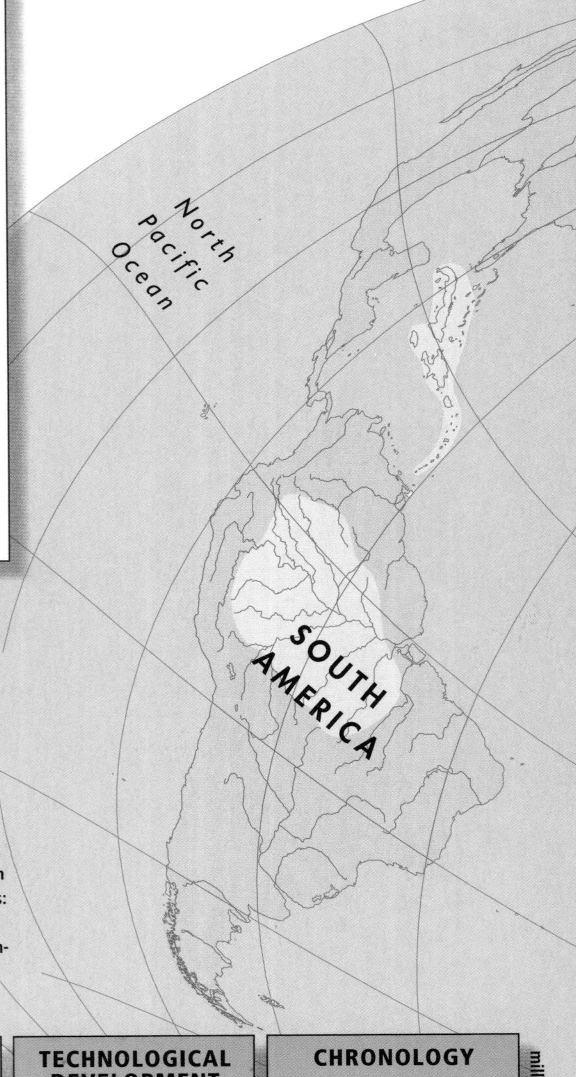

1 Important fossils of human ancestors have been found at sites in Africa, Asia and Australia *(map right)*. East Africa's Great Rift Valley is a crucial area since fossils found here in the stratified deposits can be reliably dated. The location of the remains suggest that these early humans lived away from the more densely populated forests and inhabited the grasslands where a different range of resources could be exploited with less competition. Even here, life was not without its dangers: some Australopithecine skulls found in southern Africa have leopard teeth-marks on them.

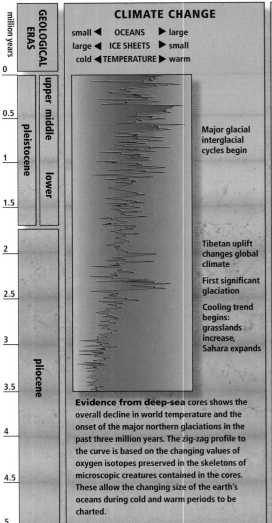

2 Hominine development

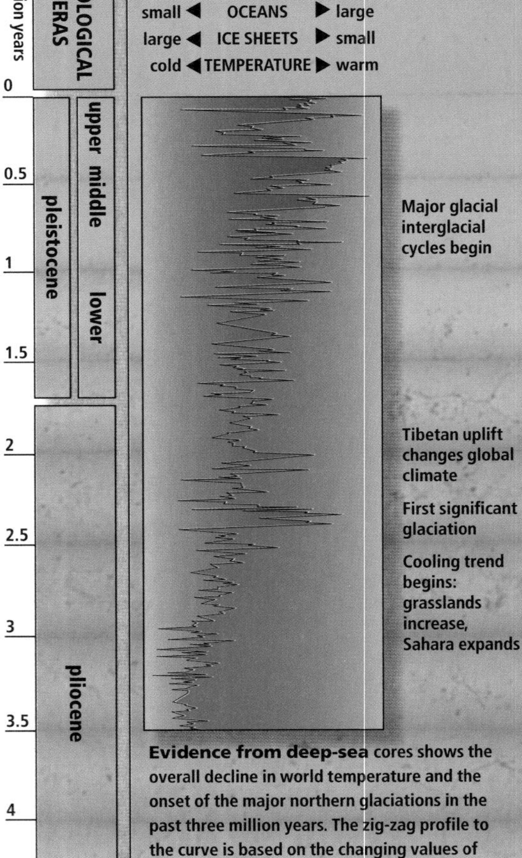

Evidence from deep-sea cores shows the overall decline in world temperature and the onset of the major northern glaciations in the past three million years. The zig-zag profile to the curve is based on the changing values of oxygen isotopes preserved in the skeletons of microscopic creatures contained in the cores. These allow the changing size of the earth's oceans during cold and warm periods to be charted.

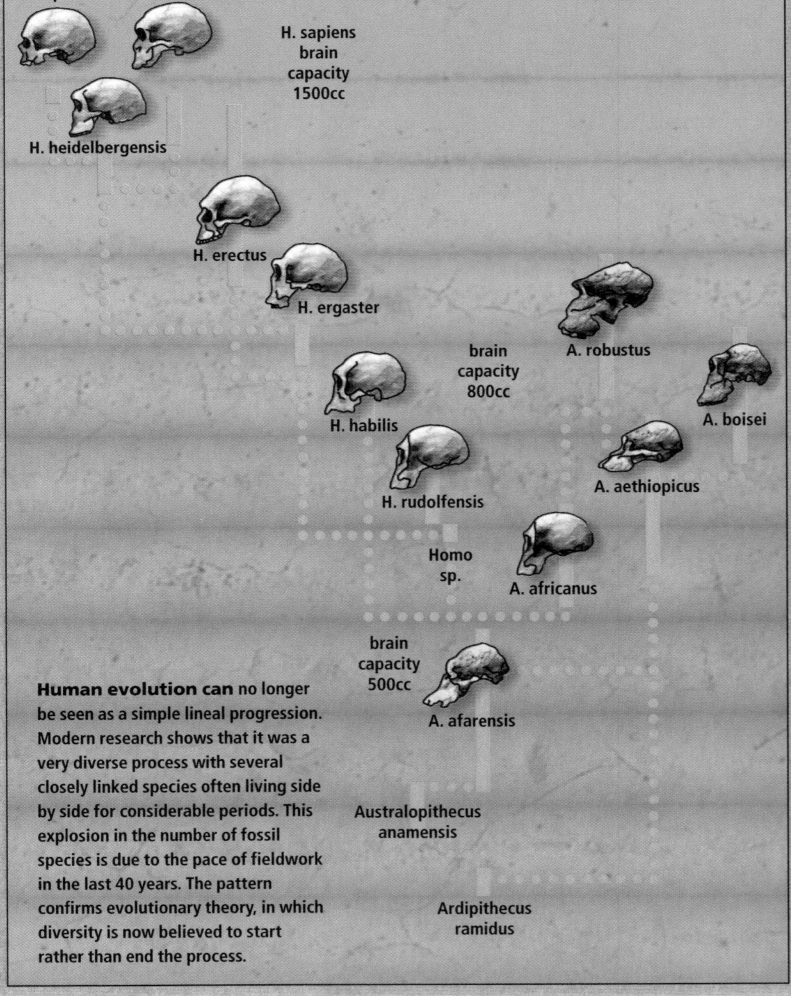

Human evolution can no longer be seen as a simple lineal progression. Modern research shows that it was a very diverse process with several closely linked species often living side by side for considerable periods. This explosion in the number of fossil species is due to the pace of fieldwork in the last 40 years. The pattern confirms evolutionary theory, in which diversity is now believed to start rather than end the process.

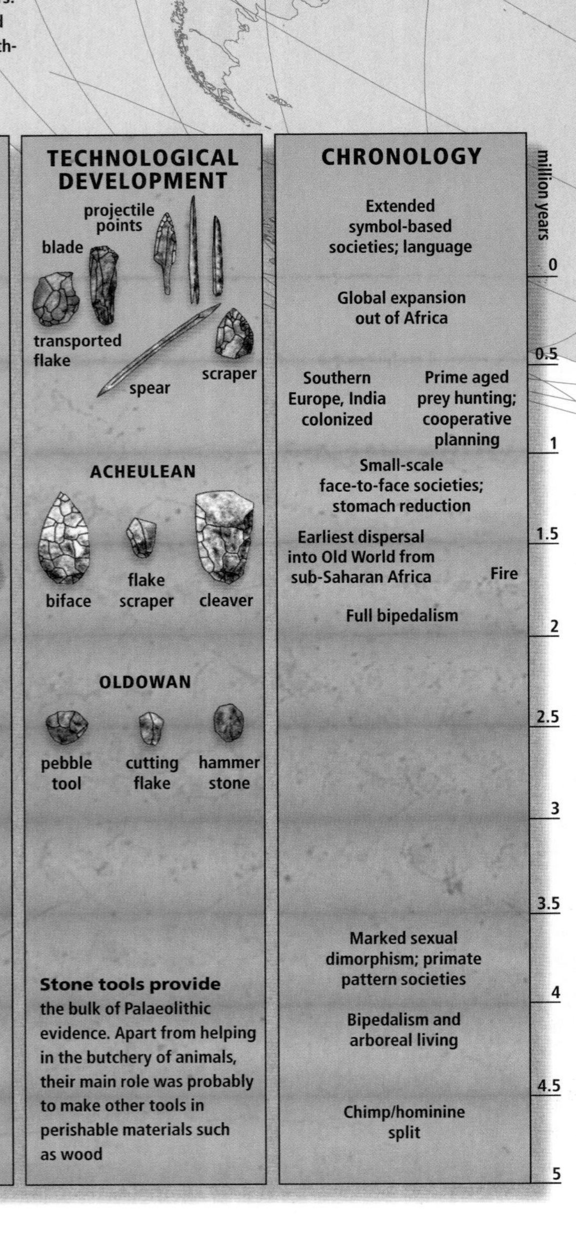

Stone tools provide the bulk of Palaeolithic evidence. Apart from helping in the butchery of animals, their main role was probably to make other tools in perishable materials such as wood

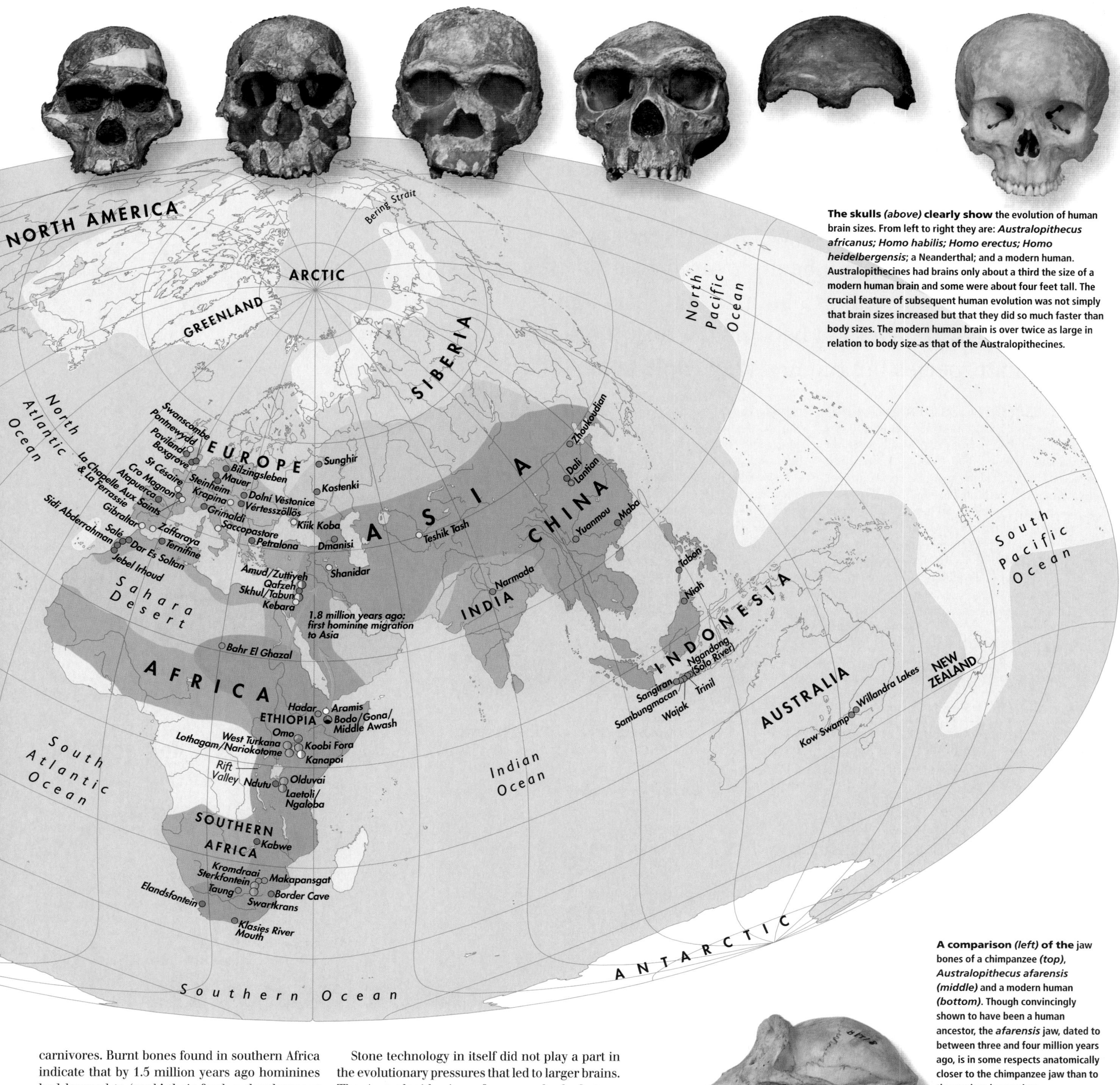

The skulls *(above)* **clearly show** the evolution of human brain sizes. From left to right they are: *Australopithecus africanus; Homo habilis; Homo erectus; Homo heidelbergensis*; a Neanderthal; and a modern human. Australopithecines had brains only about a third the size of a modern human brain and some were about four feet tall. The crucial feature of subsequent human evolution was not simply that brain sizes increased but that they did so much faster than body sizes. The modern human brain is over twice as large in relation to body size as that of the Australopithecines.

A comparison *(left)* **of the** jaw bones of a chimpanzee *(top)*, *Australopithecus afarensis* *(middle)* and a modern human *(bottom)*. Though convincingly shown to have been a human ancestor, the *afarensis* jaw, dated to between three and four million years ago, is in some respects anatomically closer to the chimpanzee jaw than to the modern human jaw.

carnivores. Burnt bones found in southern Africa indicate that by 1.5 million years ago hominines had learned to 'cook' their food, a development which again would have compensated for smaller stomachs by breaking down animal proteins before digestion took place.

Out of Africa

This pattern of development was the basis for the first colonization, by *Homo erectus*, 1.8 million years ago of areas outside sub-Saharan Africa. Then, a million years ago *Homo heidelbergensis* migrated into north Africa and the Near East, reaching northern Europe about 500,000 years ago. Both *Homo erectus* and *heidelbergensis* probably shared a common ancestor, *Homo ergaster*, best known from the skeleton found at Nariokotome in Kenya's Rift Valley. By perhaps 1.5 million years ago, all three had brains of about 1,000 cubic centimetres and an adaptable stone technology: the weight and careful shaping of the edges of their distinctive handaxes, whether pointed or oval, made them effective butchery tools.

Stone technology in itself did not play a part in the evolutionary pressures that led to larger brains. The Australopithecines, for example, had stone tools but their brains did not grow as a result, nor did they migrate from Africa. Instead, the importance of *Homo*'s larger brain had less to do with the food quest, more to do with allowing hominines to remember, to manipulate, to support and to organize others in more complex ways. Perhaps paradoxically, as hominines developed these more sophisticated social structures, so they simultaneously became less reliant on one another and better adapted to living in smaller groups. This in turn allowed them to colonize harsher barrier habitats such as the Sahara at the margins of their homelands from where they could colonize new, more temperate areas beyond.

Modern humans

From about 500,000 years ago, this early burst of colonization came to a halt. Instead, though there were undoubtedly many dispersals of populations and much intermingling of genes, regional groups of separate populations living side by side such as the Neanderthals developed. But from 100,000 years ago, a second major dispersal began when anatomically modern people – *Homo sapiens sapiens* – emigrated from sub-Saharan Africa. By 50,000 years ago, Australia had been reached, by boat; 33,000 years ago, the western Pacific islands were colonized; 15,000 years ago, the Americas were reached. Major expansion into the Arctic began about 4500 years as the continental ice sheets retreated. Finally, 2000 years ago, humans began to settle the deep Pacific islands from where they reached New Zealand around 1200 years ago, 1000 years before the island's discovery by Captain Cook.

From c. 200,000 years ago

The spread of modern humans

See also
Human origins p. 30
The Ice Age world p. 34
From hunting to farming: the origins of agriculture p. 36

DNA studies have revealed that the first anatomically modern humans – *Homo sapiens sapiens* – arose in Africa between 200,000 and 140,000 years ago. Though much has still to be discovered about their origins and dispersal, by about 15,000 years ago *Homo sapiens sapiens* had become not only the sole human species but the first truly global one.

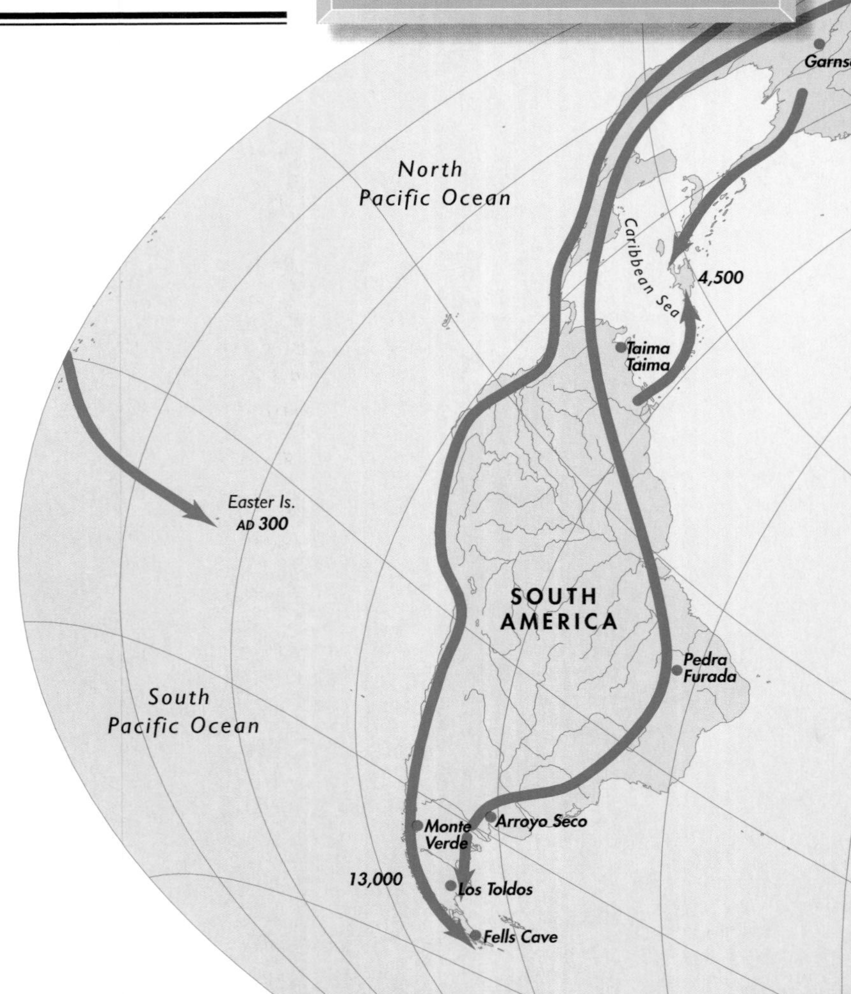

THE EARLIEST MODERN-LOOKING human skulls yet found are about 130,000 years old and come from the Omo basin in Ethiopia and Klasies River Mouth in southern Africa, the latter one of the best-researched sites of early human habitation. Perhaps 100,000 years ago, these early populations began to disperse, migrating northwards out of Africa. These migrations were followed by a process known as 'bottlenecking' in which population levels among the dispersed peoples remained small for thousands of years. It's possible that a contributory factor to bottlenecking was the eruption of Toba in northwest Sumatra 71,000 years ago, an environmental catastrophe on an extraordinary scale: parts of India were covered with ash up to 10 feet deep, global temperatures were lowered for a millennium. At the same time, the restricted populations generated by bottlenecking had the side effect of encouraging rapid changes in genetic structures thereby increasing the pace of evolutionary change.

Archaeological and genetic evidence then point to a further rapid expansion of modern human populations and settlements about 50,000 years ago. The archaeological evidence in particular highlights growing sophistication and the mastery of a wide and increasing range of skills. In some regions, lighter, multi-component weapons have been found, including spears made from skilfully produced stone blades fixed to wooden shafts and handles. There is evidence, too, of textiles and baskets and of more orderly layouts of camp-sites, including cold-weather dwellings and underground food stores. Trading networks are also

2 The evolution of modern humans

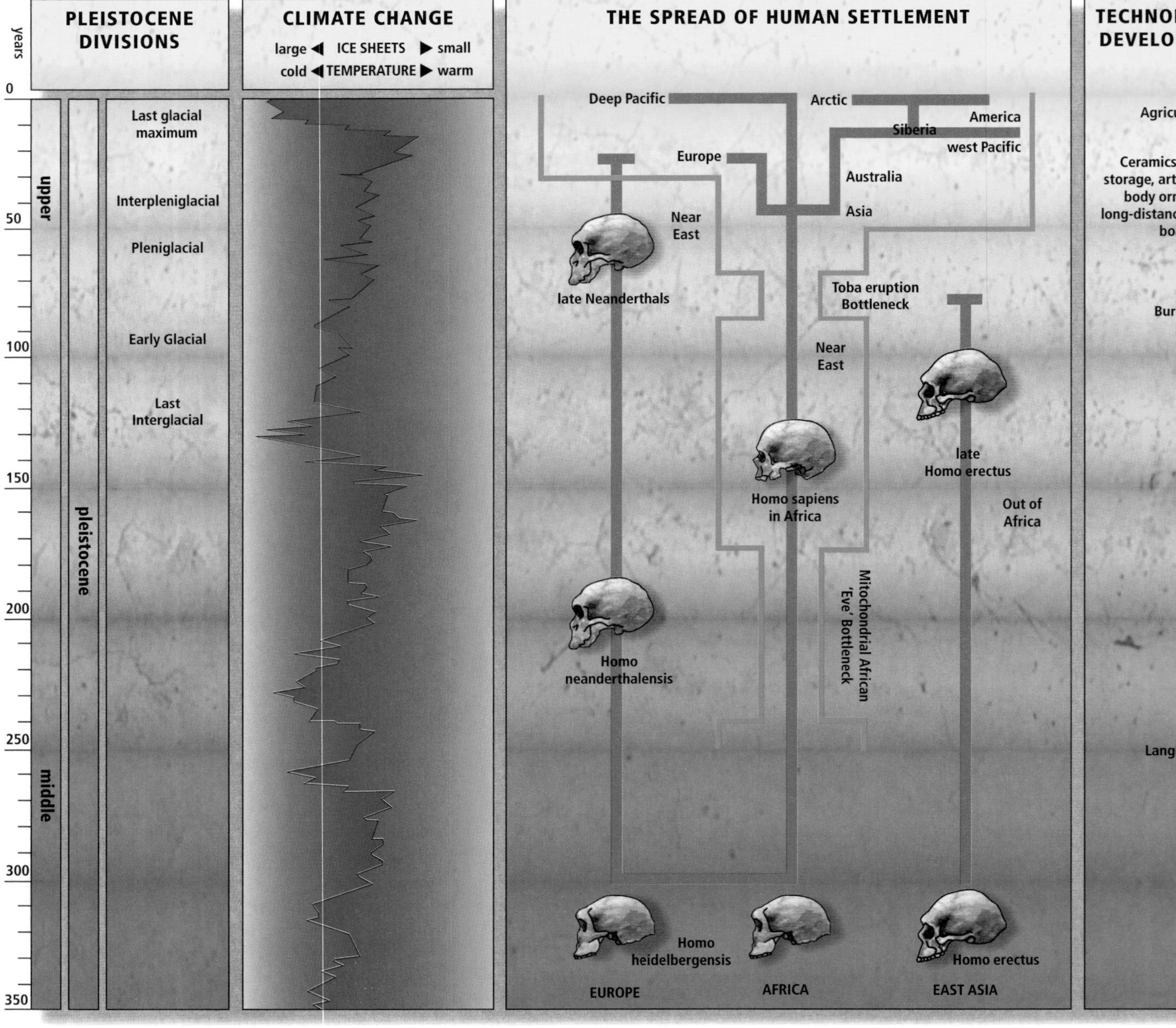

1 & 2 The appearance of anatomically modern humans – *Homo sapiens sapiens* – in Africa between 150,000 and 200,000 years ago was followed by the relatively rapid dispersal of these new populations. However, between 100,000 and 50,000 years ago, population movements stopped. About 50,000 years ago, modern human populations began to grow again and migrations to many new areas of the world took place *(map above and chart left)*. There was nothing inevitable about the ultimate success of *Homo sapiens sapiens* in becoming not only the sole hominine species but the only global one as well. For many thousands of years, *Homo sapiens sapiens* shared the world with *Homo erectus* in Asia and the Neanderthals in Europe and the Near East, both groups in many ways as sophisticated and successful in their mastery of their environments as *Homo sapiens sapiens*. The similarities between these contemporary hominine species – all with small populations and simple technologies and all vulnerable to climate change or environmental catastrophes such as the Toba eruption 70,000 years – are in most respects more striking than the differences. Nonetheless, it was the greater social sophistication of *Homo sapiens sapiens* which was decisive in allowing these early peoples to colonize a much wider range of habitats than any previous hominine.

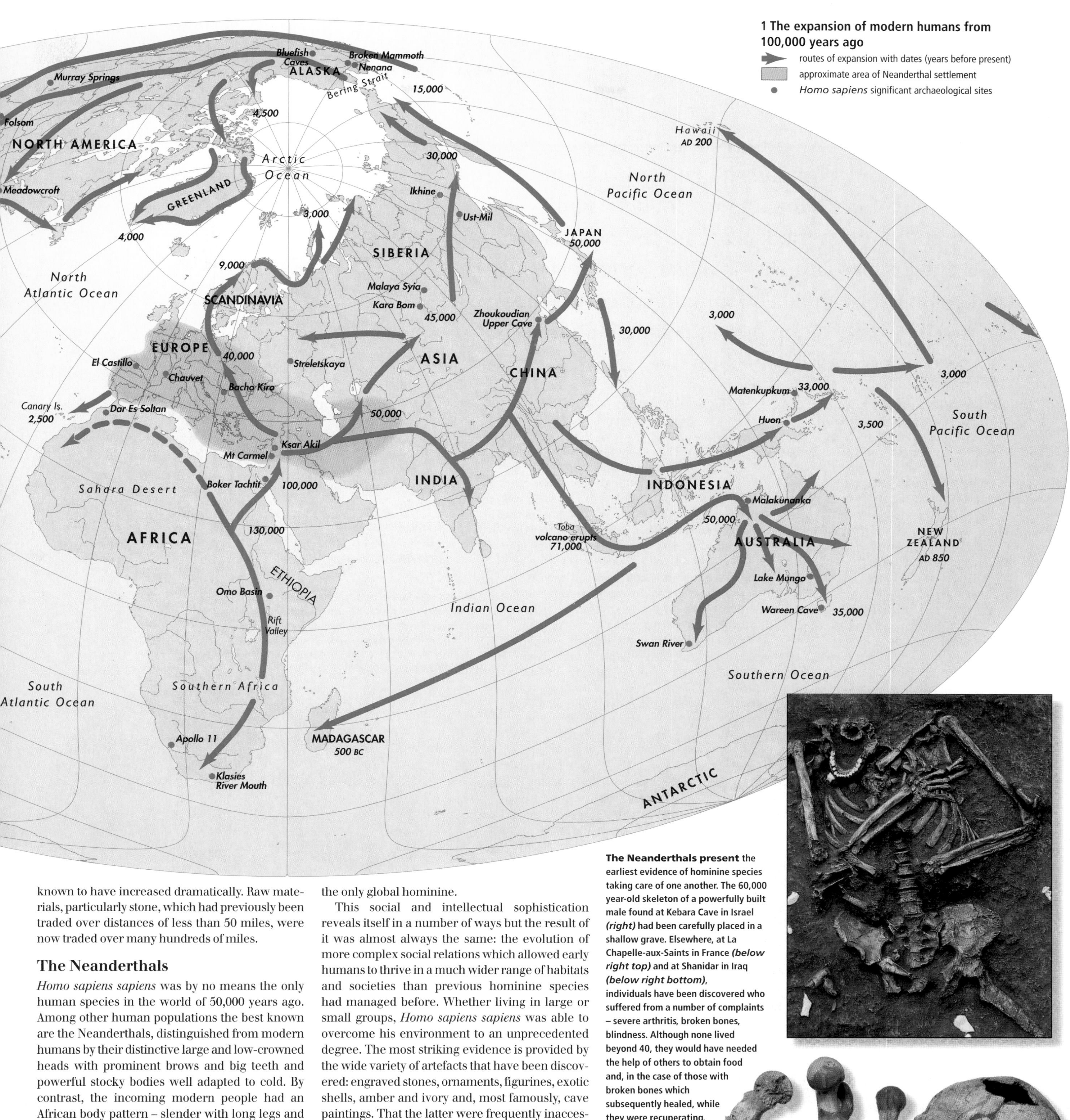

1 The expansion of modern humans from 100,000 years ago

known to have increased dramatically. Raw materials, particularly stone, which had previously been traded over distances of less than 50 miles, were now traded over many hundreds of miles.

The Neanderthals

Homo sapiens sapiens was by no means the only human species in the world of 50,000 years ago. Among other human populations the best known are the Neanderthals, distinguished from modern humans by their distinctive large and low-crowned heads with prominent brows and big teeth and powerful stocky bodies well adapted to cold. By contrast, the incoming modern people had an African body pattern – slender with long legs and small torsos – that copes better with heat stress. The Neanderthals had brains as large as modern humans and were in many ways highly successful. They adapted well to a wide range of habitats and climates ranging from the relatively arid Middle East to the cold of central Europe; their use of tools was sophisticated; and they were effective hunters of animals in prime condition such as bison, horse and reindeer. Their burial of their dead, often with some elaboration, also indicates signs of a recognizably modern humanity. They almost certainly had language, too. But what the Neanderthals seem not to have possessed is the degree of social flexibility and cultural tradition that more than any other characteristic singles out *Homo sapiens sapiens* and explains our ultimate success in becoming the only global hominine.

This social and intellectual sophistication reveals itself in a number of ways but the result of it was almost always the same: the evolution of more complex social relations which allowed early humans to thrive in a much wider range of habitats and societies than previous hominine species had managed before. Whether living in large or small groups, *Homo sapiens sapiens* was able to overcome his environment to an unprecedented degree. The most striking evidence is provided by the wide variety of artefacts that have been discovered: engraved stones, ornaments, figurines, exotic shells, amber and ivory and, most famously, cave paintings. That the latter were frequently inaccessible and could have been seen only with ladders and artificial light suggests that a variety of factors motivated its creators. Whatever the explanation, these early works of art are an evocative monument to the humanity of these early hunters.

It is significant that the Neanderthals had almost no cultural traditions of this kind. A few incised bones have been found; similarly, the very occasional exotic piece of raw material occurs. By about 27,000 years ago, the Neanderthals, having co-existed with modern man for perhaps 8,000 years, had disappeared. Their extinction is unlikely to have been the violent event sometimes portrayed so much as a slow contraction in their numbers. With their disappearance, *Homo sapiens sapiens* became the first global species in hominine evolution.

The Neanderthals present the earliest evidence of hominine species taking care of one another. The 60,000 year-old skeleton of a powerfully built male found at Kebara Cave in Israel ***(right)*** had been carefully placed in a shallow grave. Elsewhere, at La Chapelle-aux-Saints in France ***(below right top)*** and at Shanidar in Iraq ***(below right bottom)***, individuals have been discovered who suffered from a number of complaints – severe arthritis, broken bones, blindness. Although none lived beyond 40, they would have needed the help of others to obtain food and, in the case of those with broken bones which subsequently healed, while they were recuperating. At death, they, too, were buried.

See also
Human origins p. 30
The spread of modern humans p. 32
From hunting to farming: the origins of agriculture p. 36

20,000 to 10,000 BC

The Ice Age world

By 10,000 years ago, humans had colonized almost the whole of the habitable world. It was an achievement made in the face of the last of a series of Ice Ages, when vast sheets of ice periodically advanced and retreated. The human species today is the product of this long process of adaptation to the varied conditions of the Ice Ages.

THERE HAVE BEEN EIGHT Ice Ages in the last 800,000 years, each interspersed with warmer periods of about 10,000 years known as interglacials, brief and extreme parts of this cycle. The Ice Ages were periods of exceptional cold away from the equator. Ice sheets advanced across the frozen wastes of the northern hemisphere as temperatures fell by up to 15 degrees centigrade. With so much of the earth's water locked into the ice sheets, sea levels fell, by up to 500 feet. As they did so, land bridges appeared, linking most major land areas and present-day islands into a single continental land mass.

Equatorial regions were also affected: as rainfall diminished, half the land area between the tropics became desert. With each advance of the ice, the plants and animals of the northern hemisphere withdrew to warmer latitudes. As the ice retreated, so they moved northwards again. Humans, too, must have migrated with these changing climates. Yet despite the extremes of cold, the human species continued to develop, spreading from its original African homeland to east and southeast Asia and to Europe. Mastery of fire and the invention of clothing were crucial to this achievement, as were new social and communication skills.

Ice Age man

The height of the last Ice Age or LGM (last glacial maximum) was reached about 20,000 years ago. As the ice expanded, so human populations contracted into a small number of more favourable habitats. Across practically the whole of the Eurasian landmass between the ice to the north and the deserts to the south, from the glacial cul-de-sac of Alaska to southern France, productive grasslands and steppes were created. Rich in seasonal grasses, they were capable of sustaining large herds of mammoth, bison, horse and reindeer, all of them important food sources for Palaeolithic hunters.

Much the same sort of habitat seems to have developed in North America. By the time modern humans migrated there about 15,000 years ago, the rolling grasslands were teeming with animal life: giant bison with a six-foot horn spread; towering beaver-like creatures called casteroides; camels; ground sloths; stag moose; two types of musk-oxen; several varieties of large, often lion-sized cats; mastodons; and three types of mammoth. So effectively did the new human population hunt them that by about 10,000 years ago almost all of them were extinct, including the horse, re-introduced to the New World only by Europeans following in the wake of Columbus.

South of the Eurasian mammoth steppe lay an extensive zone of drier conditions, indeed parts of the Sahara, the Near East and India became almost entirely arid, forcing their populations along permanent watercourses such as the Nile. Similar patterns of settlement are found in Australia, where cemeteries discovered along the Murray river bear marked resemblances to those along the Nile.

Modern man was a late arrival in western Europe, replacing Neanderthal populations only from about 35,000 years ago. Yet the new communities developed remarkable levels of cultural expression. In southwest France, the Pyrenees and northern Spain, hundreds of caves decorated with paintings of symbols and animals have been discovered, evidence of a rich cultural tradition.

By 12,000 years ago, the last Ice Age was declining. As temperatures rose, vegetation spread and animals re-colonized the cold northern wastes. With them went hunters and gatherers. By 10,000 BC in Central America and the Near East, people had begun to move beyond their existing resources and to investigate new ways of producing food and manipulating plants and animals in the first experiments in farming.

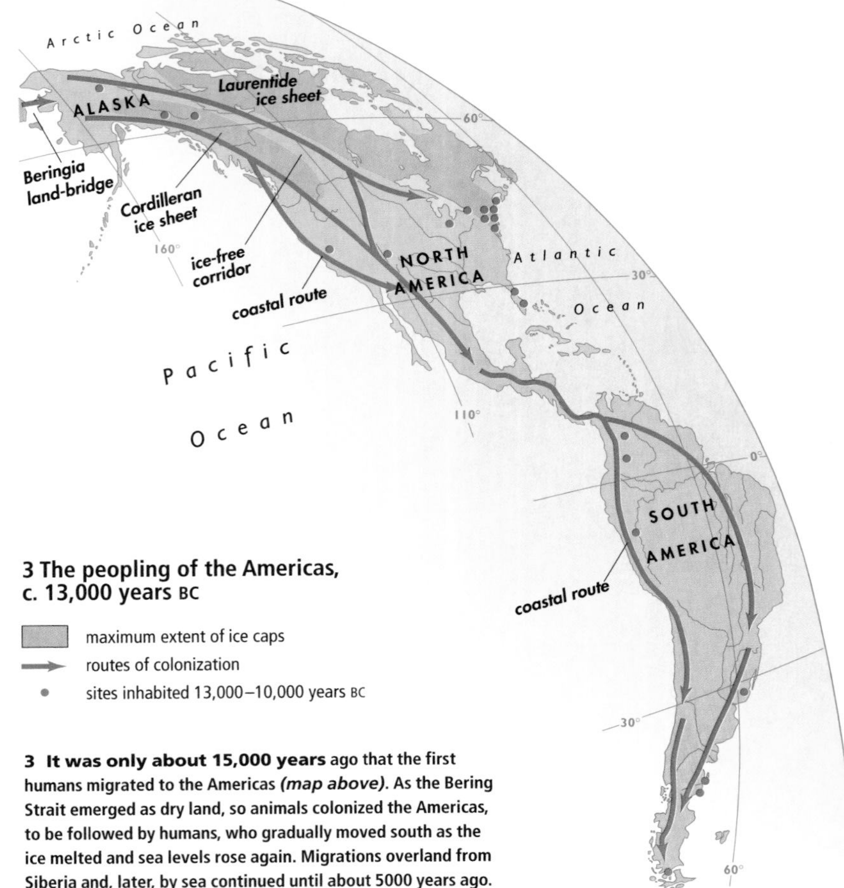

3 The peopling of the Americas, c. 13,000 years BC

maximum extent of ice caps
routes of colonization
sites inhabited 13,000–10,000 years BC

3 It was only about 15,000 years ago that the first humans migrated to the Americas *(map above)*. As the Bering Strait emerged as dry land, so animals colonized the Americas, to be followed by humans, who gradually moved south as the ice melted and sea levels rose again. Migrations overland from Siberia and, later, by sea continued until about 5000 years ago.

2 Small or 'portable' works of art have been found throughout the area inhabited by European hunters between about 30,000 and 10,000 years ago. These include sculptures and engravings of animals on bone and antler and thousands of engravings on small stone plaques. Very occasionally the engravings take the form of abstract patterns of lines and dots, or sequences of notches or grooves, which might conceivably have been hunting tallies or even calendars for plotting the movements of the Moon. Decorated ornaments were also made, such as fine carved amber swan pendants from Russia or cut beads of ivory and antler from the same region. Venus figurines are particularly striking. These pieces are carved in the round and are representations of a highly striking female form with exaggerated breasts and buttocks. An analogous style is found in wall art where bas-relief engravings of Venuses, perhaps representations of the mother goddess, have been discovered. Portable works of art have been discovered across Europe but the bulk of cave art from the period is in the valleys of the Vézère and the Dordogne in southwest France, the Pyrenees and the Cantabrian Mountains of northern Spain, though paintings and engravings have also been found in sites far beyond these areas *(map left)*.

The sophistication of Ice Age artists is amply attested by this delicately carved and elegant female head, found at Brassempouy in southwest France *(above)*. No more than 3.5 cm high, it dates from about 20,000 years ago.

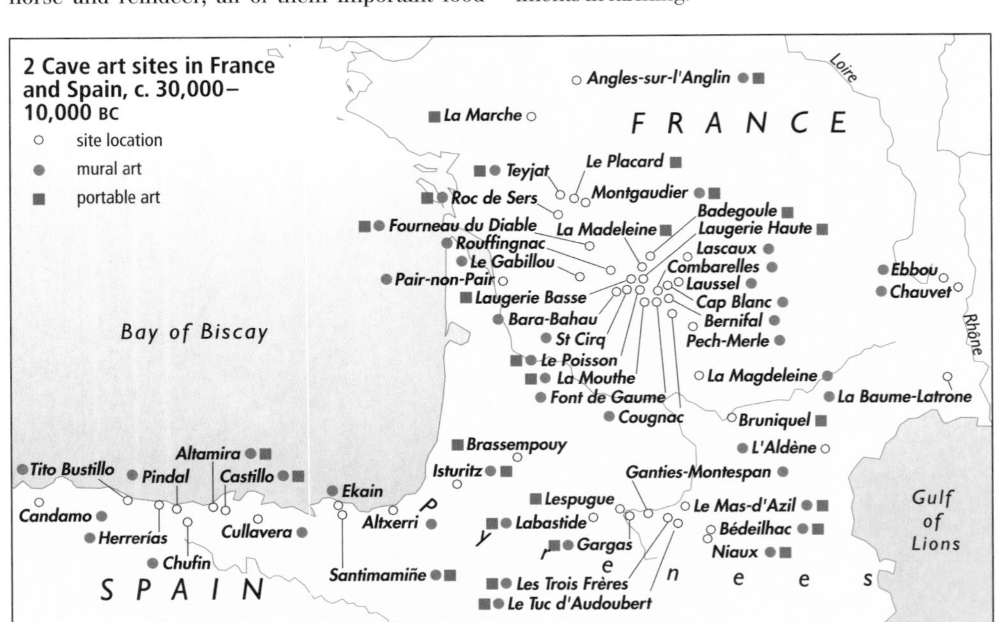

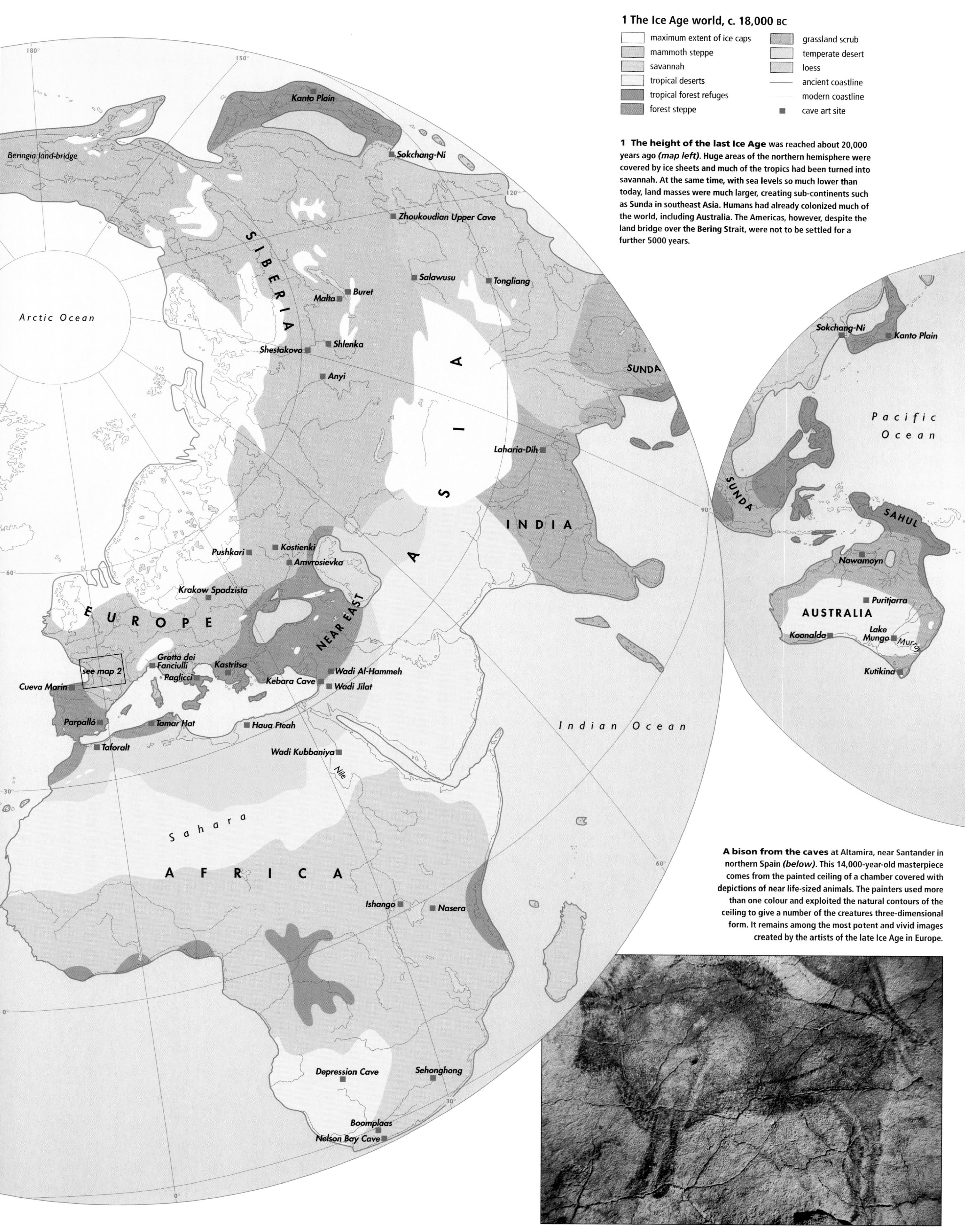

1 The height of the last Ice Age was reached about 20,000 years ago *(map left)*. Huge areas of the northern hemisphere were covered by ice sheets and much of the tropics had been turned into savannah. At the same time, with sea levels so much lower than today, land masses were much larger, creating sub-continents such as Sunda in southeast Asia. Humans had already colonized much of the world, including Australia. The Americas, however, despite the land bridge over the Bering Strait, were not to be settled for a further 5000 years.

A bison from the caves at Altamira, near Santander in northern Spain *(below)*. This 14,000-year-old masterpiece comes from the painted ceiling of a chamber covered with depictions of near life-sized animals. The painters used more than one colour and exploited the natural contours of the ceiling to give a number of the creatures three-dimensional form. It remains among the most potent and vivid images created by the artists of the late Ice Age in Europe.

From hunting to farming: the origins of agriculture

See also
The spread of modern humans p. 32
The Ice Age world p. 34
Before the first cities: the Near East, 10,000–4000 BC p. 38
Early Europe: the colonization of a continent, 7000–2000 BC p. 40

The transition from hunting and gathering to agriculture irreversibly changed human society, but it involved the domestication of relatively few plants and animals and occurred independently in a very few areas. The earliest evidence of agriculture comes from the Levant 10,000 years ago, from where it spread to Europe, northern Africa and central Asia.

TEN THOUSAND YEARS AGO, at the end of the last Ice Age, the human population numbered only a few millions and all their food came from wild plants and animals. Then people began to domesticate some of those species, so that today almost the entire world population depends for food on a relatively small range of crops and domestic animals. During the 150,000 years that preceded the "agricultural revolution", anatomically modern humans had colonized most of the the globe (*see* p. 32) and had learned to survive as foragers, subsisting on a great diversity of plant and animal foods. Foragers moved seasonally in small groups to obtain their food supplies and population densities remained low for many millennia.

Foraging to farming

By 8000 BC, some groups of foragers had settled down and occupied favourable sites year-round. Their populations increased, as restraints on fertility imposed by the seasonally mobile way of life were relaxed, and they ranged less far for their food. This profound change in human behaviour led to the beginnings of agriculture, enabling more people to be supported on a given area of land – although at the cost of the greater effort needed to cultivate crops and raise domestic animals. The effects of settling down, population increase, and growing dependence on agriculture led to increases in the number and size of settlements, to the development of more complex, less egalitarian societies, and, eventually, to urban life and civilization.

The earliest evidence of agriculture consists of the remains of wild species which have been altered in their morphology or behaviour by human intervention. Foremost among the crops are the cereals and pulses (peas, beans and other herbaceous legumes), the seeds of which provide carbohydrate and some protein and are easily stored. They sustained early civilizations and have become staples of world agriculture. They were domesticated from wild grasses in subtropical regions, for example wheat, barley, lentil, pea and chickpea in southwestern Asia; rice, soya and mung bean in southern and eastern Asia; sorghum, other millets and cowpea in tropical Africa; and maize and the common bean in Mexico. Root crops have also become staples in many areas, for example the potato which was domesticated in the Andes and is now a major crop of temperate latitudes, and manioc (cassava), yams, taro and sweet potato, all of which were native to the tropics

Domestication of animals

Whereas cereals and root crops were brought into cultivation and domesticated in all the habitable continents except Australia (where agriculture was introduced by European settlers in the 18th century AD), animals were domesticated in relatively few areas, principally in western Asia, where there is evidence for the early domestication of sheep, goats, pigs and cattle, followed later by asses, horses and camels. Some forms of cattle and pigs, as well as chickens, were domesticated in southern and eastern Asia, and cattle and pigs may also have been domesticated independently in Europe. Very few animals were domesticated in the Americas – turkey in North America and llama, alpaca and guinea pig in South America – and none in tropical Africa or Australia.

The spread of farming

Archaeological evidence indicates that the earliest transition to agriculture took place in the 'Fertile Crescent' of southwestern Asia during the Neolithic period starting about 8000 BC. Sites in the Levant have yielded charred seeds and chaff of barley, wheat and various pulses, as well as the bones of domestic goats and sheep. Radiocarbon dating shows that grain cultivation began here about 1000 years before goat and sheep pastoralism. Dependence on agriculture increased very gradually, paralleled by the spread of village settlement, the development of techniques of irrigation and terracing, and the cultivation of fruits such as dates, figs, grapes and olives. By the end of the Neolithic in southwestern Asia, about 6000 years ago, agriculture had spread west and east into Europe, northern Africa and central and southern Asia, where new domesticates were added to the growing repertoire of crops.

Agriculture began independently in China between 7000 and 6000 BC, in the Americas by about 3000 BC and in tropical Africa by about 2000 BC. By the time of the European expansion in the 16th century AD agricultural and pastoral economies occupied most of Eurasia, Africa and Central and South America.

c. 8000 BC *Foragers using sites year-round*

c. 8000 BC *Evidence of domesticated cereals and pulses in the Levant*

c. 7000 BC *Evidence of rice cultivation in China*

c. 4000 BC *Agriculture established across Europe*

c. 3000 BC *Evidence of maize cultivation in Mesoamerica*

c. 3000 BC *Evidence of tree crop cultivation in tropical Africa*

NORTHERN SOUTH AMERICA

Pulses	Root Crops
Common bean	Manioc
Lima bean	Potato
	Sweet Potato
	Yam

Fruits	Other Crops
Guava	Cashew
Pineapple	Chili pepper
Soursop	Cocoa
Sweetsop	Peanut
	Quinoa
	Squashes

MESOAMERICA

Cereals	Pulses
Maize	Common bean
Teosinte	Runner bean
	Tepary bean

Fruits	Other Crops
Avocado	Chilli pepper
Tomato	Squashes

NORTH AMERICA
Turkey
MESOAMERICA
ANDES
LOWLANDS
Guinea pig
Llama
Alpaca

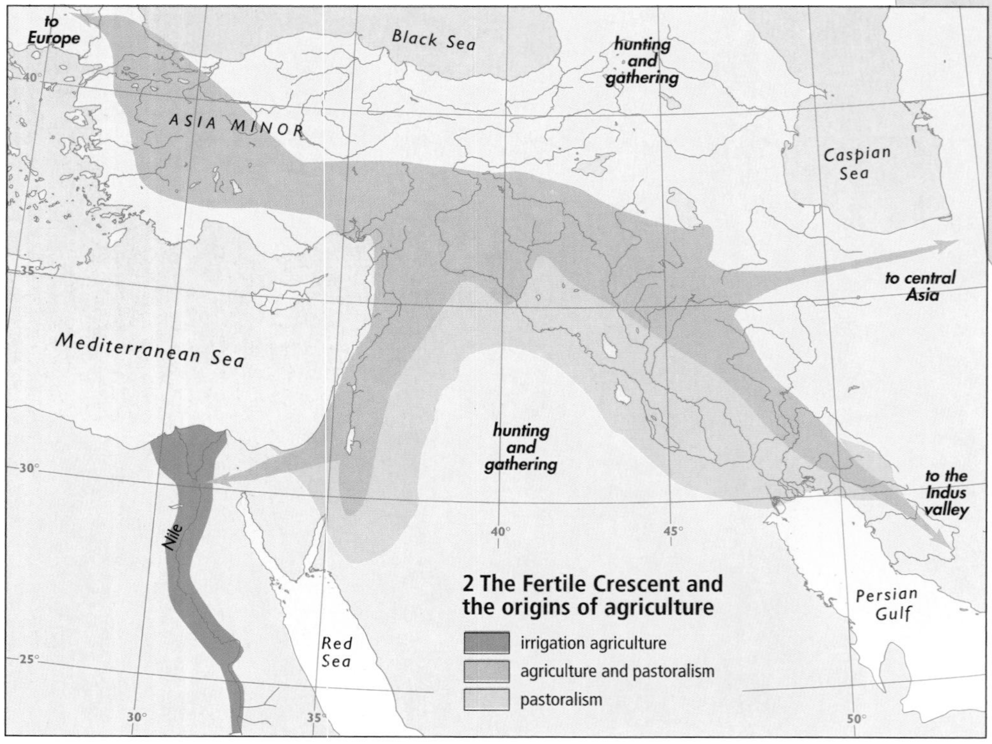

to Europe
Black Sea
hunting and gathering
ASIA MINOR
Caspian Sea
to central Asia
Mediterranean Sea
hunting and gathering
Nile
to the Indus valley
Red Sea
Persian Gulf

2 The Fertile Crescent and the origins of agriculture

- irrigation agriculture
- agriculture and pastoralism
- pastoralism

2 The Fertile Crescent, where the transition from foraging to farming first occurred. The map *(left)* shows an early stage in the development of agricultural and pastoral economies around 6000 BC when the new way of life had begun to spread northwest across Asia Minor into Europe, southwest to the Nile valley and east towards central Asia and the Indus valley.

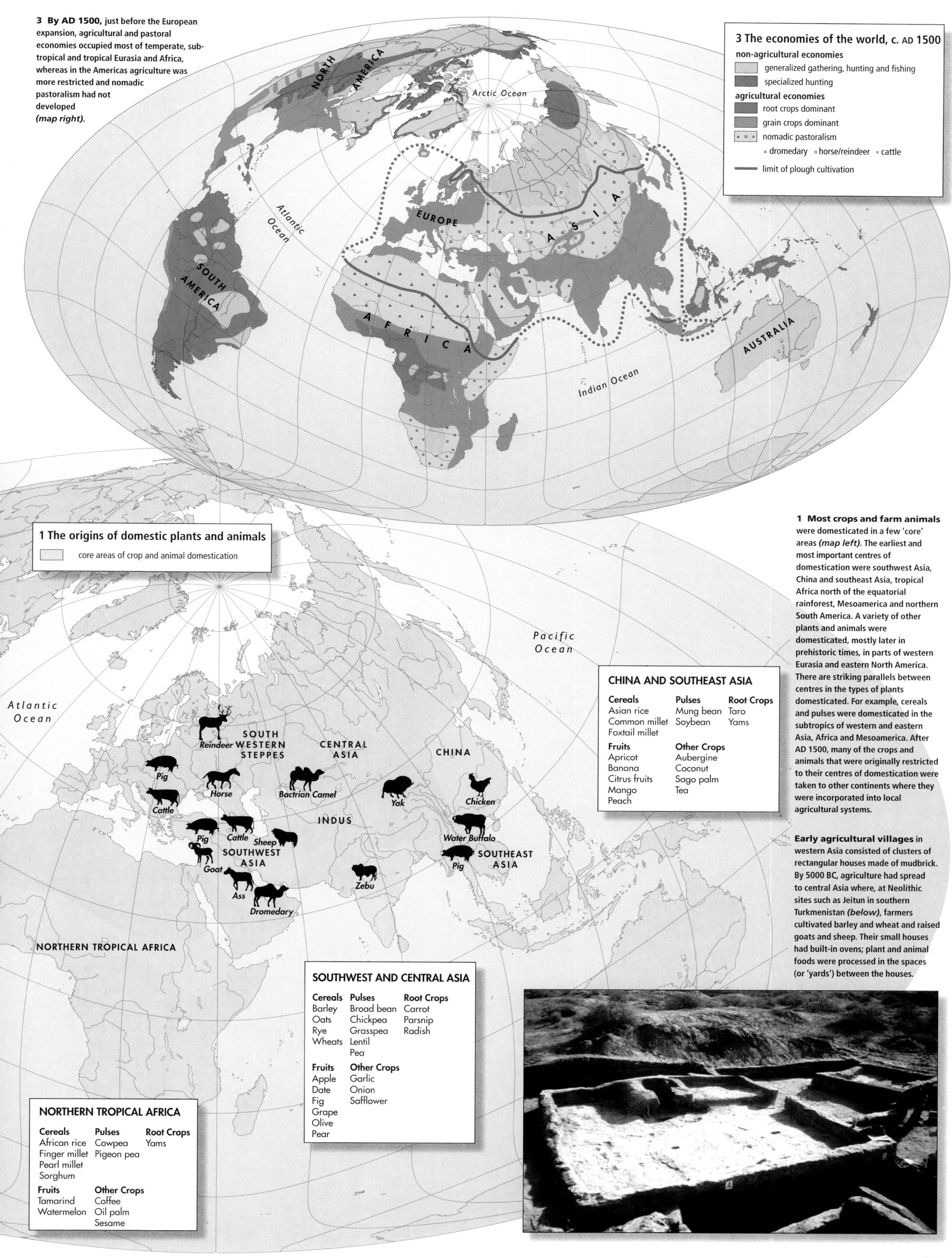

3 By AD 1500, just before the European expansion, agricultural and pastoral economies occupied most of temperate, sub-tropical and tropical Eurasia and Africa, whereas in the Americas agriculture was more restricted and nomadic pastoralism had not developed *(map right)*.

1 Most crops and farm animals were domesticated in a few 'core' areas *(map left)*. The earliest and most important centres of domestication were southwest Asia, China and southeast Asia, tropical Africa north of the equatorial rainforest, Mesoamerica and northern South America. A variety of other plants and animals were domesticated, mostly later in prehistoric times, in parts of western Eurasia and eastern North America. There are striking parallels between centres in the types of plants domesticated. For example, cereals and pulses were domesticated in the subtropics of western and eastern Asia, Africa and Mesoamerica. After AD 1500, many of the crops and animals that were originally restricted to their centres of domestication were taken to other continents where they were incorporated into local agricultural systems.

Early agricultural villages in western Asia consisted of clusters of rectangular houses made of mudbrick. By 5000 BC, agriculture had spread to central Asia where, at Neolithic sites such as Jeitun in southern Turkmenistan *(below)*, farmers cultivated barley and wheat and raised goats and sheep. Their small houses had built-in ovens; plant and animal foods were processed in the spaces (or 'yards') between the houses.

10,000 to 4000 BC

Before the first cities: the Near East

See also
From hunting to farming: the origins of agriculture p. 36
Early Europe: the colonization of a continent, 7000–2000 BC p. 40
The beginning of civilization in the Eurasian world, 3500–1500 BC p. 52
The early empires of Mesopotamia, c. 3500–1600 BC p. 54

12,000–9000 BC *Epipalaeolithic: earliest semi-permanent villages*

9000–6500 BC *Pre-pottery Neolithic: beginnings of food production; extensive ritual evidence*

6500–5500 BC *Pottery Neolithic (Hassuna, Samarra): craft specialization*

5500–4200 BC *Chalcolithic ('Ubaid period): regional centres; administration*

4200–3100 BC *Chalcolithic (Uruk period): growth of cities; earliest writing*

The period 10,000 to 4000 BC witnessed three critical developments: the origins of settled life; the first farming; and the first cities. The origin of agriculture is often referred to as the 'Neolithic revolution', but archaeology reveals only gradual changes in techniques of food acquisition over thousands of years, which by 7000 BC led to villages dependent on food production.

THE EARLIEST CHANGES visible in the archaeological record relate not to food production but to social relations, indicated not only in the tendency to reside in one location over longer periods and in the investment of labour in more substantial and more permanent structures, but also in the growth of ritual, an important factor in social cohesion. Indeed it is possible that this 'symbolic revolution' was of greater immediate significance than the economic changes we associate with the origins of agriculture.

Lakeshore and riverine sites were important for their rich and varied resources, while the utilitarian date palm flourished in marsh areas in southern Mesopotamia, rich also in fish and water fowl. The earliest permanent settlements tend to be found at the junctions of discrete environmental zones, with greater access to a variety of resources (for example Abu Hureyra on the boundary of the dry steppe and the Euphrates flood plain, and Ain Mallaha in the Jordan valley). The importance of ritual house fittings and skull cults, perhaps suggestive of the increasing importance of the family and property, is attested at some of the earliest sites (Qermez Dere), while 9th-millennium villages in Anatolia, with early evidence for the cultivation of cereals, contain impressive ritual buildings (Çayönü, Nevali Çori). The carving of stone (Hallan Çemi, Jerf al Ahmar, Nemrik) and the working of copper (Çayönü) are found well before the appearance of true farming villages. The early use of clay for containers is attested at Mureybet on the Euphrates (9000 BC) and at Ganj Dareh in the Zagros; white lime plaster vessels are characteristic of the latest pre-pottery Neolithic phases, especially at sites in the Levant and Anatolia.

The development of villages

Among the best-known pre-pottery Neolithic sites is Jericho, in the 9th millennium BC already a settlement of some four acres with, uniquely, a massive rock-cut ditch and stone wall with a huge circular tower ascended by means of an internal circular stair. A millennium later Basta and Ain Ghazal in Jordan are farming settlements of over 24 acres. Human skulls on which faces had been realistically modelled were kept by the inhabitants of these sites, while at Ain Ghazal deposits of cultic statues have been recovered.

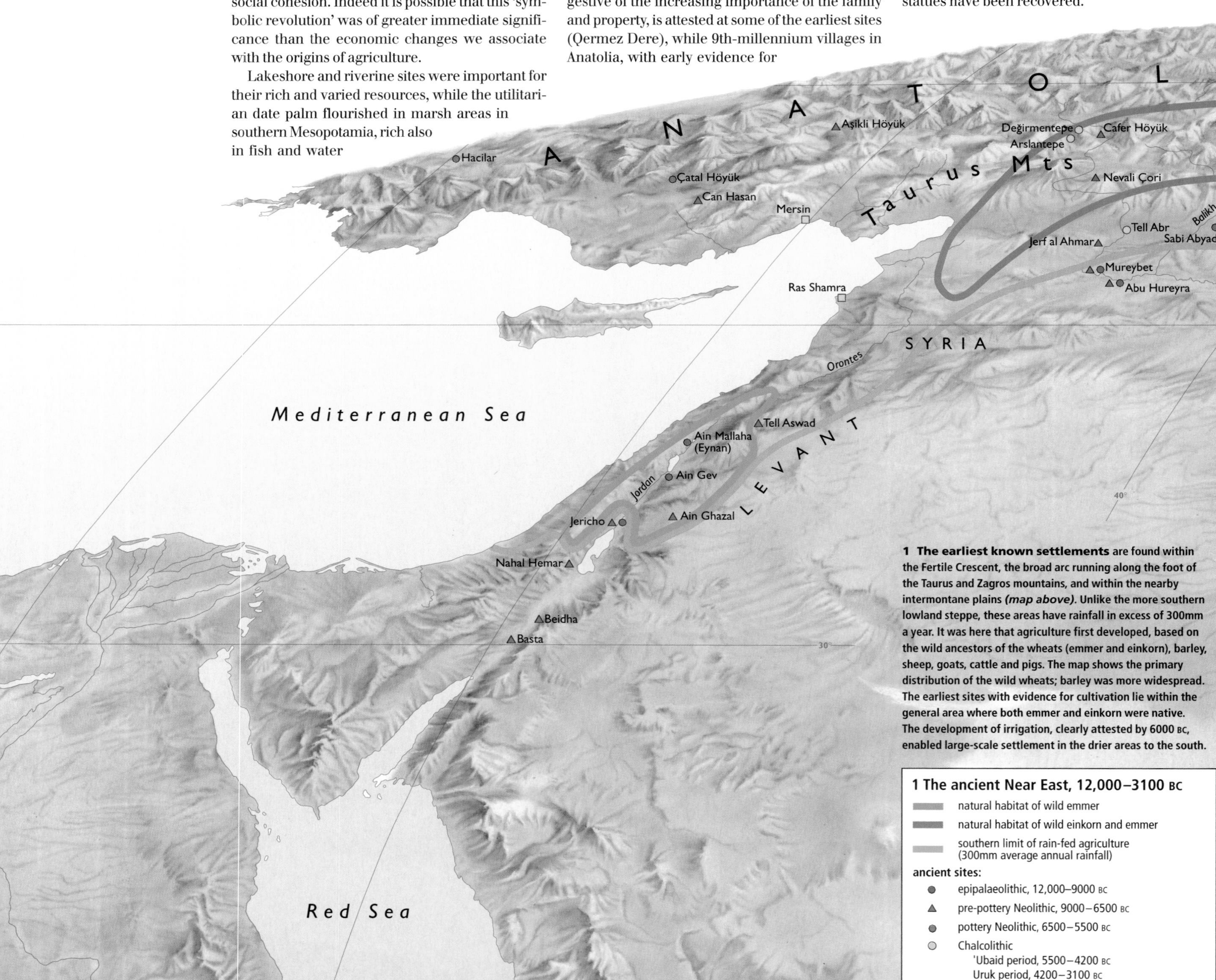

1 The earliest known settlements are found within the Fertile Crescent, the broad arc running along the foot of the Taurus and Zagros mountains, and within the nearby intermontane plains ***(map above)***. Unlike the more southern lowland steppe, these areas have rainfall in excess of 300mm a year. It was here that agriculture first developed, based on the wild ancestors of the wheats (emmer and einkorn), barley, sheep, goats, cattle and pigs. The map shows the primary distribution of the wild wheats; barley was more widespread. The earliest sites with evidence for cultivation lie within the general area where both emmer and einkorn were native. The development of irrigation, clearly attested by 6000 BC, enabled large-scale settlement in the drier areas to the south.

In the 7th and 6th millennia BC developed Neolithic villages appear over much of the landscape. They are characterized by economies dependent on domesticated plants and animals, and on sophisticated technological developments (for example an 'industrial' area of two-stage pottery kilns, and the presence of lead and copper at Yarim Tepe around 6000 BC). Well-fired painted pottery characterizes these villages, which are often classified by their ceramic styles. One of the most spectacular early pottery sites is Çatal Höyük, 32 acres in area, with extensive evidence for wealth in the form of valuable commodities such as obsidian and semi-precious stones. The house fittings bear elaborate ornaments including wall paintings and the plastered skulls of wild cattle.

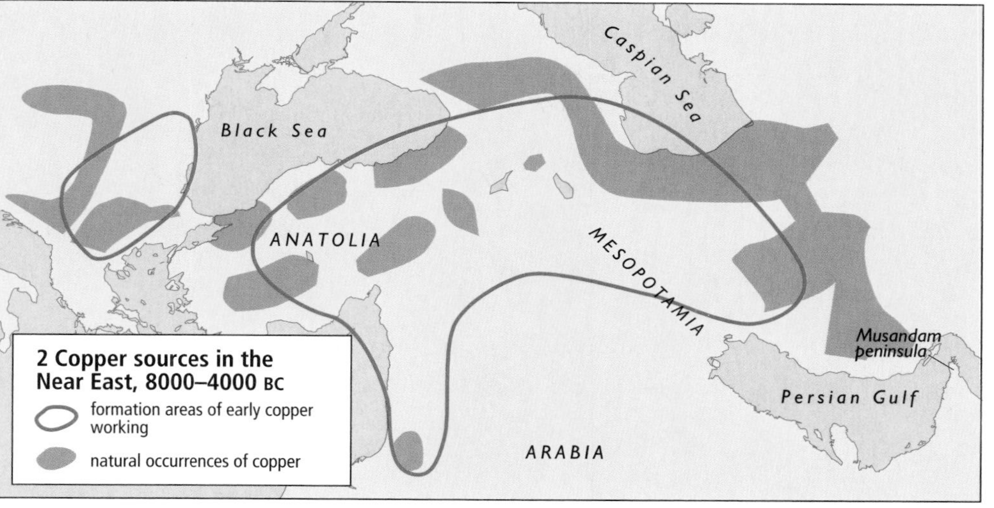

2 Copper sources were abundant in the highland areas of the Near East *(map left)*, and the attractive colours of both the native metal and the weathered ores led to their widespread use as ornaments. Small hammered objects of native copper have been found at 9th-millennium Çayönü while by the 6th millennium there is evidence for both smelting and casting. The presence of both furnaces and workshops at 'Ubaid Değirmentepe emphasizes the early importance of Anatolian metal for the Mesopotamian world.

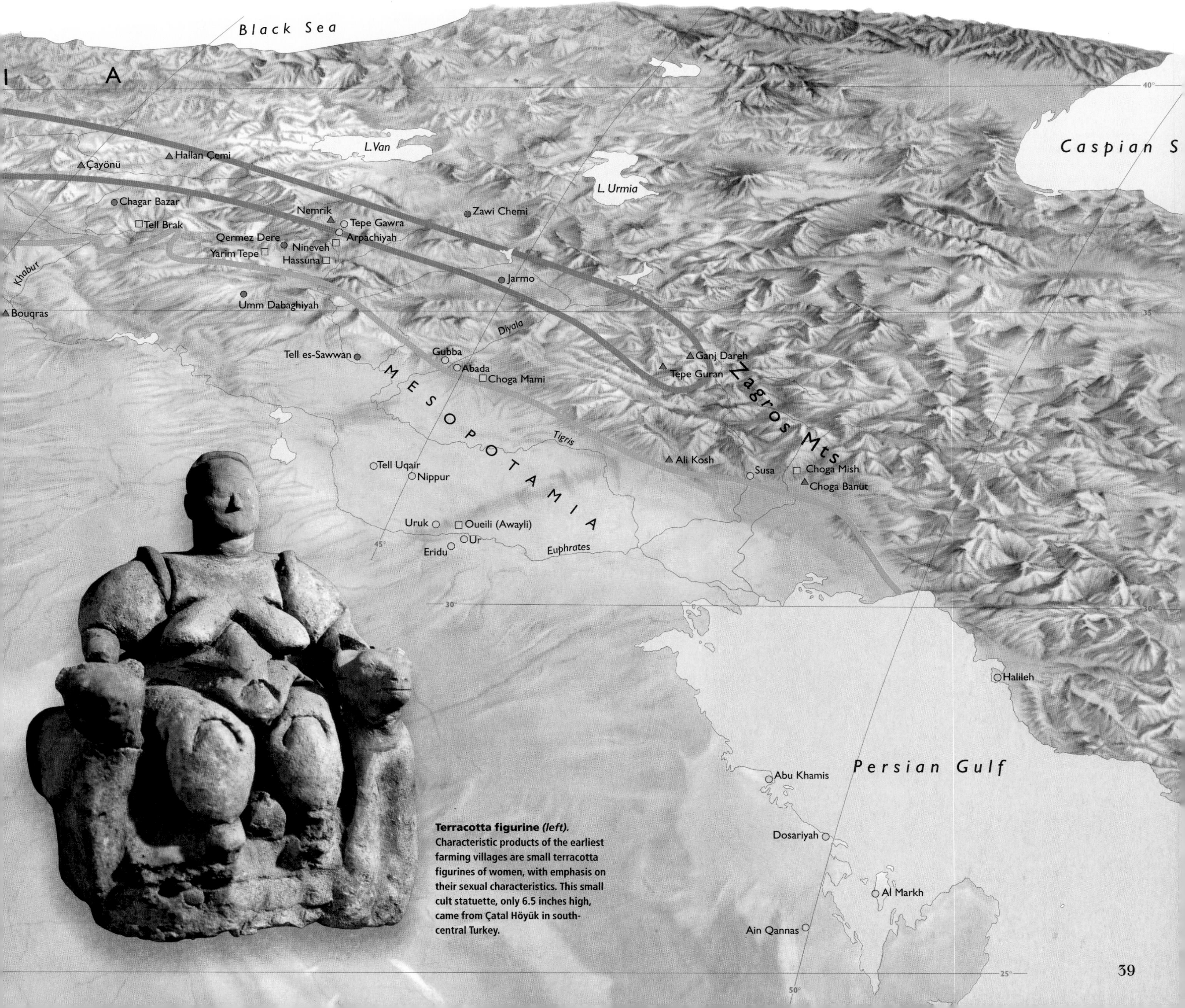

Trade and temples

An important development attested in the Neolithic villages of north Mesopotamia and Syria constitutes the earliest record-keeping, effected by the use of combinations of small clay tokens and the stamping of distinctive clay or stone seals onto clay lids and other fastenings (most importantly at Sabi Abyad in the Samarran period and slightly later at Arpachiyah). Such simple methods of validating social contracts and other transactions formed the basis of later literate urban recording systems.

Mesopotamia had no metals or semi-precious stones, and by the 5th millennium BC demand for such luxury goods led to the establishment of small colonies in Anatolia, even as far as the Malatya plain (Değirmentepe) and the sea-borne exploitation of the resources of the Persian Gulf (Dosariyah, Abu Khamis), even as far as the Musandam peninsula. The first temples were built at this time in southern Mesopotamia, precursors of the institutions around which the earliest urban states were organized. There was a temple on the same site at Eridu for 3500 years, striking evidence of the continuity of tradition which was one remarkable feature of the world's earliest city-states.

Despite their precocious development, sites like Jericho and Çatal did not form the focus of more complex polities. By 4000 BC the foundations of literate, urban civilization had been laid in Mesopotamia, where it was the organizational and economic potential of the highly productive irrigation economy in the south and the powerful, strategic positions of sites like Nineveh in the north, controlling access to areas rich in raw materials, that saw the growth of the world's first complex states.

Terracotta figurine ***(left).*** Characteristic products of the earliest farming villages are small terracotta figurines of women, with emphasis on their sexual characteristics. This small cult statuette, only 6.5 inches high, came from Çatal Höyük in south-central Turkey.

7000 to 2000 BC

Early Europe: the colonization of a continent

See also
From hunting to farming: the origins of agriculture p. 36
Before the first cities: the Near East, 10,000–4500 BC p. 38
The beginnings of civilization in the Eurasian world p. 52
The peoples of northern Europe, 2300–50 BC p. 84

7000 BC *First agricultural settlement of Europe*

5000 BC *Agriculture reaches Iberian Peninsula and the Low Countries*

4500 BC *Beginning of significant copper production in the Balkans*

4000 BC *Agricultural economy in Britain and southern Scandinavia*

3500 BC *Spread of cart and plough across Europe*

3000 BC *Megalithic tombs in western Europe*

2000 BC *Beginning of large-scale tin-bronze production in central Europe*

Farming first spread from the Near East to southeast Europe c.7000 BC and then along the Mediterranean coast and across central Europe, reaching the Low Countries by 5000 BC. After a brief pause it spread to Britain and northern continental Europe by 4000 BC. It was only c. 2000 BC that farming reached the more northerly parts of European Russia and the Baltic.

2 Megalithic monuments *(map below)* The farmers of the loess lands built their houses and cult-centres of wood. Further west, while houses continued to be built mostly of wood, public monuments were constructed from large undressed boulders or slabs of stone. Such monuments, built to serve many generations, were mainly concerned with mortuary rituals and ancestor-worship. Three or four main areas began independently to build simple structures, but as the monuments grew more elaborate, ideas and techniques were exchanged.

THE EARLIEST FARMING VILLAGES in Europe, dating to immediately after 7000 BC, were on the western side of the Aegean (eg Argissa) and on Crete (eg Knossos), but by 5500 BC such villages were distributed widely across the Balkans. They consisted of clusters of mudbrick buildings, each with an identical layout of hearth and cooking and sleeping areas. Their economy was based on keeping sheep and cultivating wheat and legumes. Such villages were situated in areas of good soil with a plentiful water supply and were often occupied for hundreds of years.

Agricultural villages

Villages of this kind spread inland as far as Hungary but from here northwards a new pattern developed. The mudbrick dwellings were replaced by wooden longhouses whose remains did not build up into settlement mounds. Agricultural settlement spread in a broad band from northeast France to southwest Russia on soils produced by the weathering of loess – a highly fertile windblown dust laid down during the Ice Age. Over this area the characteristic pottery was decorated with incised lines in spiral or meandering bands, a uniformity which reflects the rapid spread of settlement between 5500 and 5000 BC. Cattle were more important than sheep in the forested interior of Europe but wheat continued as the main cereal crop. The settlers did not clear wide areas of land but practised intensive horticulture in the valleys around their settlements.

At the same time as it was spreading into continental Europe, aspects of an agricultural way of life were also spreading westwards along the northern shore of the Mediterranean, reaching Spain by around 5000 BC; in this zone environmental conditions were much closer to those where agriculture started and fewer adjustments had to be made.

Alongside the early agricultural communities, small groups of foragers pursued their way of life in areas untouched by the new economy. Hunting populations were rather sparse in the areas first selected by agriculturists, and the rapidity with which farming spread across the loess lands may in part reflect a lack of local competition, but elsewhere foragers were more numerous. They were especially well-established in the lake-strewn landscapes left by the retreating ice sheets around the Alps and on the northern edge of the North European Plain.

There has been much debate about whether the spread of agriculture was due to the expansion of colonizing populations from the southeast or to the adoption of the new way of life by existing foragers. Current evidence from archaeology and the analysis of the DNA of modern populations suggests that there was a colonizing element, probably associated with the expansion through the Balkans and the loess lands of central Europe, but that in most of Europe the dominant process was the adoption of agriculture and its material attributes by existing populations, perhaps in part because of the prestige of the new way of life.

Megalithic Europe

In much of western Europe farming was first adopted around 4000 BC and the clearance of land in rocky terrain provided the opportunity to build large stone (megalithic) monuments as burial places and mortuary shrines for the scattered hamlets of early farmers. Some of the earliest megalithic tombs were built in Brittany and Portugal around 4500 BC, but particularly elaborate forms were being made in Ireland and Spain up to 2000 years later. Alongside the tombs, other kinds of megalithic monuments came to be constructed in some regions, such as the stone circles of the British Isles.

From 4500 to 2500 BC, important developments occurred which were to change the established pattern of life. Early metallurgy of copper and gold developed in the Balkans from 4500 BC, although whether this was an independent invention or came from the Near East is still in dispute. Fine examples of the products come from the rich Copper Age cemetery of Varna on the Black Sea coast.

From around 3500 BC there is evidence of contact between eastern Europe and the steppe zone north of the Black Sea; this has been linked by some to the spread of Indo-European languages into Europe. The period around 3500 BC also saw the rapid spread across Europe of wheeled vehicles and the plough, both associated with the first large-scale use of draught animals. These gradually changed the nature of agricultural production. Widespread clearance of forests took place and flint mines produced the stone required for large quantities of axes. It was only after 2000 BC that stone axes were superseded by metal ones.

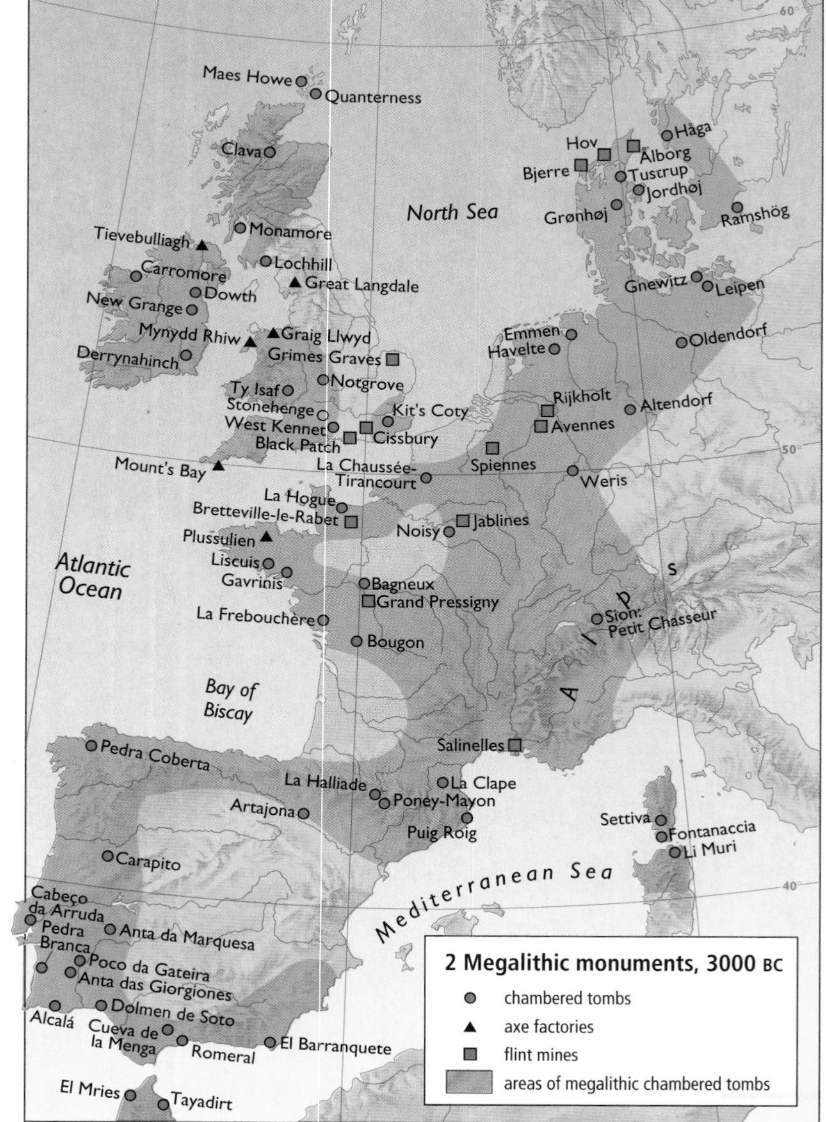

PORTUGAL
SPAIN
Verdelpino
Grotte d'Escoural
impressed
Coveta de l'Or
hunters and pastoralists

1 The spread of agricultural settlement

main routes of agrarian expansion

dates of agricultural settlement (based on tree-ring corrected radiocarbon dating)
by 7000 BC
7000–6000 BC
6000–5000 BC
5000–3000 BC
3000–2000 BC
bowl cultures early farming groups
Hembury site of excavated farming village
SPAIN modern state names

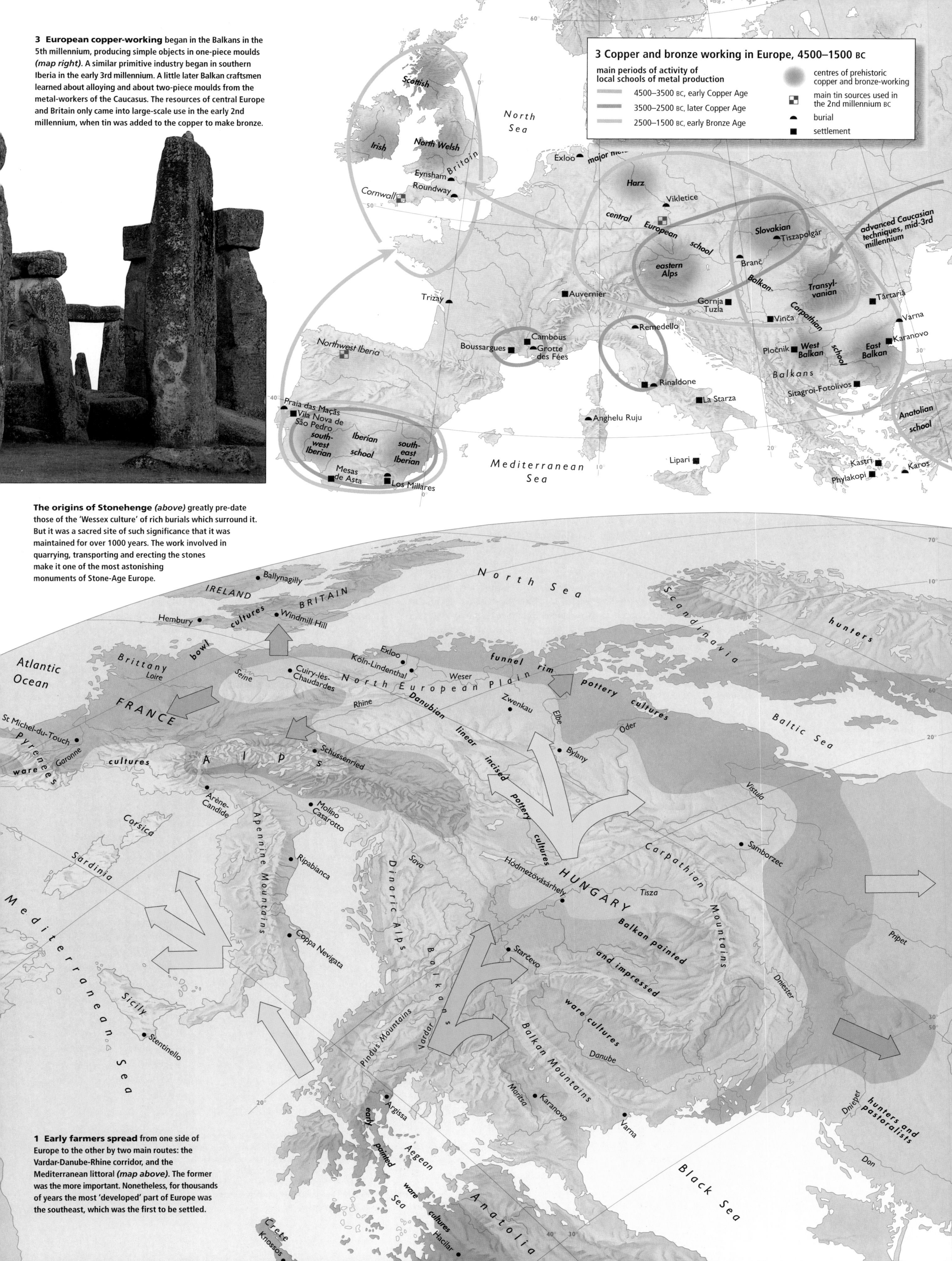

3 European copper-working began in the Balkans in the 5th millennium, producing simple objects in one-piece moulds *(map right)*. A similar primitive industry began in southern Iberia in the early 3rd millennium. A little later Balkan craftsmen learned about alloying and about two-piece moulds from the metal-workers of the Caucasus. The resources of central Europe and Britain only came into large-scale use in the early 2nd millennium, when tin was added to the copper to make bronze.

The origins of Stonehenge *(above)* greatly pre-date those of the 'Wessex culture' of rich burials which surround it. But it was a sacred site of such significance that it was maintained for over 1000 years. The work involved in quarrying, transporting and erecting the stones make it one of the most astonishing monuments of Stone-Age Europe.

1 Early farmers spread from one side of Europe to the other by two main routes: the Vardar-Danube-Rhine corridor, and the Mediterranean littoral *(map above)*. The former was the more important. Nonetheless, for thousands of years the most 'developed' part of Europe was the southeast, which was the first to be settled.

African peoples and cultures

See also
The spread of modern humans p. 32
The Ice Age world p. 34
From hunting to farming: the origins of agriculture p. 36
Ancient Egypt: civilization and empire p. 56
The Muslim world: the Middle East and north Africa, 800–1350 p. 136
The emergence of states in Africa, 1000–1500 p. 140

7th millennium BC *Earliest cereal cultivation*

4th millennium BC *Copper worked in Egypt; first tropical crops*

4th –3rd millennia BC *Desiccation of the Sahara begins; populations expand south and east*

3rd–2nd millennia BC *Peak of civilization in Egypt*

c. 900 BC *Kingdom of Meroe established*

c. 550 BC *Iron use begins in sub-Saharan Africa; Bantu speakers expand southwards*

c. AD 400 *Eclipse of Meroe*

c. AD 700 *Decline of Aksum*

Africa south of the equator, probably the birthplace of humankind, is slowly revealing its later prehistory to archaeological researchers. New evidence dispels the belief that this was a technological and intellectual backwater, showing instead the richness and adaptability of African cultural traditions.

FROM THE 10TH MILLENNIUM BC, much of what is now the Sahara Desert enjoyed wetter conditions than today, supporting Africa's first (and one of the world's oldest) settled human populations, fishermen who lived beside the waters, which provided year-round food supplies. These settlements, characterized by barbed bone harpoon heads, extended from the northern Rift Valley and the Sudanese Nile Valley to Ghana between the 10th and 2nd millennia BC.

Around the 7th millennium BC, there is evidence for cattle-herding in western Egypt and near the Hoggar Massif in the Sahara. At broadly the same time, beside the Nile delta, cultivation of wheat and barley introduced from western Asia began. In the Sudanic lowlands, by contrast, it was indigenous cereals that were brought under cultivation, notably sorghum and varieties of millet. In the Ethiopian Highlands a range of local plants was domesticated, including the cereal teff, the banana-like ensete and the oil-yielding noog. On the northern fringes of the equatorial forest, the cultivation of yams may have begun around this time. However, these definitely African developments cannot yet be dated with any precision.

Climatic change

With the desiccation of the Sahara during the 4th and 3rd millennia BC, some farming peoples penetrated the Nile valley, while others expanded southwards. Over the next two millennia human populations increased markedly in the Sudanic belt, supported by cattle-herding and the development of tropical crops. The southernmost African farmers by 500 BC were probably those in the area of Narosura. By the last centuries BC urban centres are attested not only in the Sudanese Nile valley and Ethiopian highlands, but also around the inland Niger delta where indigenous African Guinea rice was cultivated.

The spread of iron

To the north, Egyptian civilization arose in virtual isolation from these southerly developments (*see* p. 56). Use of copper began in Egypt during the 4th millennium BC, and in the 3rd millennium was superseded by bronze. Copper and bronze objects found along the North African coast may indicate contacts with the early metal-using societies of southern Europe. Rare unsmelted iron has been found in Egyptian tombs, including that of Tutankhamun (c. 1350 BC), but it was not until the 1st millennium that it was commonly used. At about the same period, iron use also began in the Phoenician colonies of North Africa.

Egypt's fortunes declined in the 1st millennium BC, when it was conquered by a series of foreign powers. But the Kushite state prospered in the Sudanese Nile Valley, centred first at Napata and then at Meroe. In the 4th century AD Meroe declined, perhaps overthrown by Aksum, a major state in northern Ethiopia. By the early centuries AD it dominated the Red Sea both commercially and militarily; but in the 7th century Aksum came into conflict with the rising power of Islam, and declined into comparative obscurity.

Iron came into use in parts of sub-Saharan Africa during the second quarter of the last millennium BC. Controversy surrounds the extent to which this was a local development or one inspired from more northerly regions. The earliest Iron Age sites south of the Equator mark a change far more dramatic than that in the north, for here the introduction of iron not only represented an important breakthrough in itself, but was also associated with the earliest cereal agriculture, cattle-keeping and pottery. Almost all of sub-equatorial Africa is occupied today by the descendants of these early food producers, speaking the closely related Bantu languages which may have been disseminated by early agriculturists.

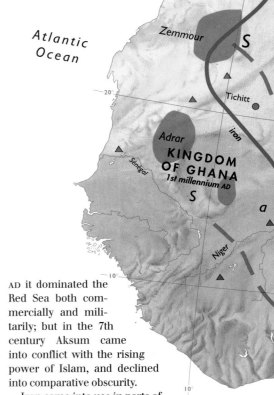

2 African cultures were crucially determined by the continent's physical constraints and its changing vegetation *(map below)*. Over large areas the existence of desert and equatorial forest restricted cultivation and herding respectively. Indigenous African crops were all initially cultivated in the zone south of the Sahara and north of the equatorial forest.

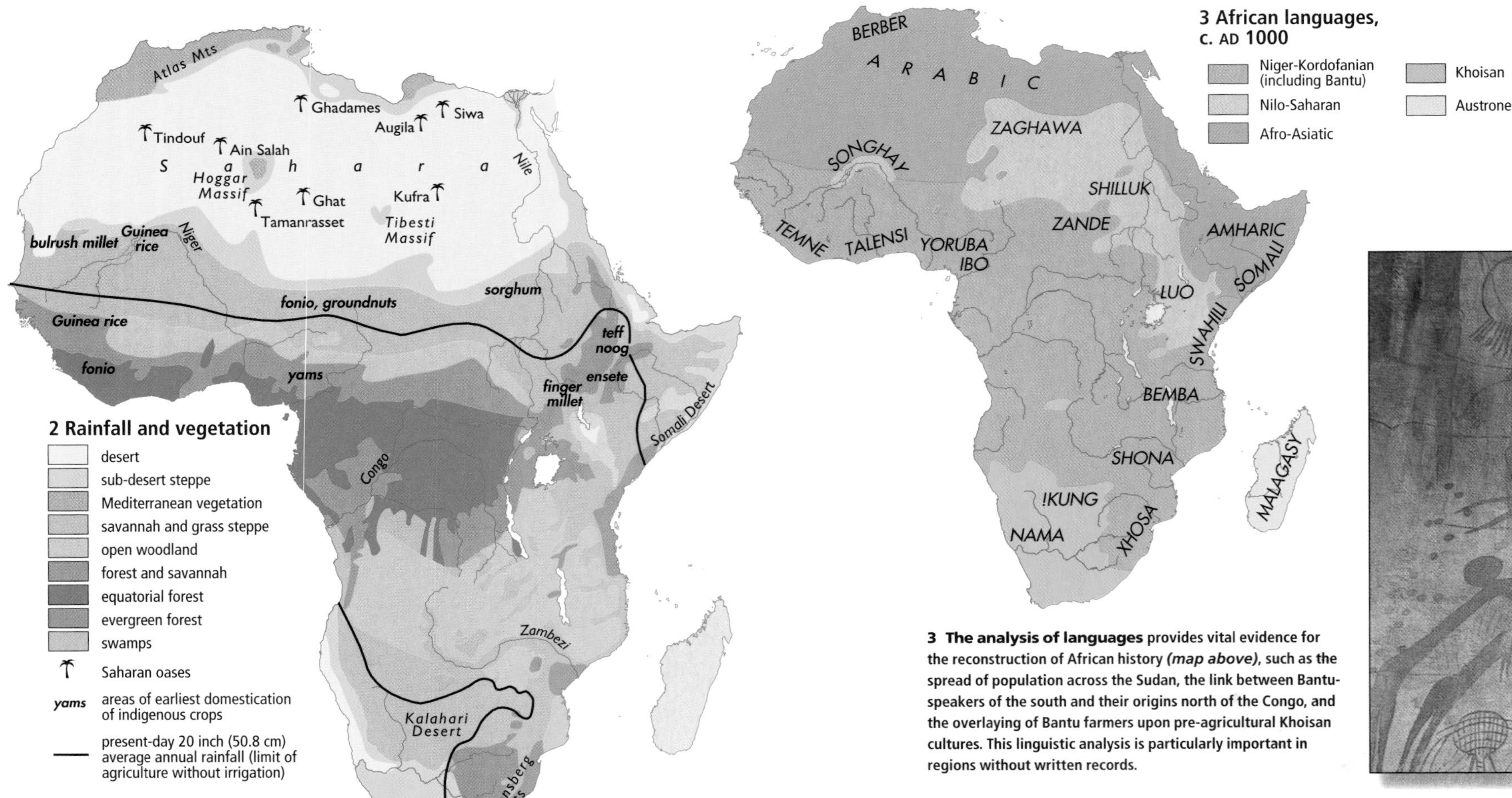

3 The analysis of languages provides vital evidence for the reconstruction of African history *(map above)*, such as the spread of population across the Sudan, the link between Bantu-speakers of the south and their origins north of the Congo, and the overlaying of Bantu farmers upon pre-agricultural Khoisan cultures. This linguistic analysis is particularly important in regions without written records.

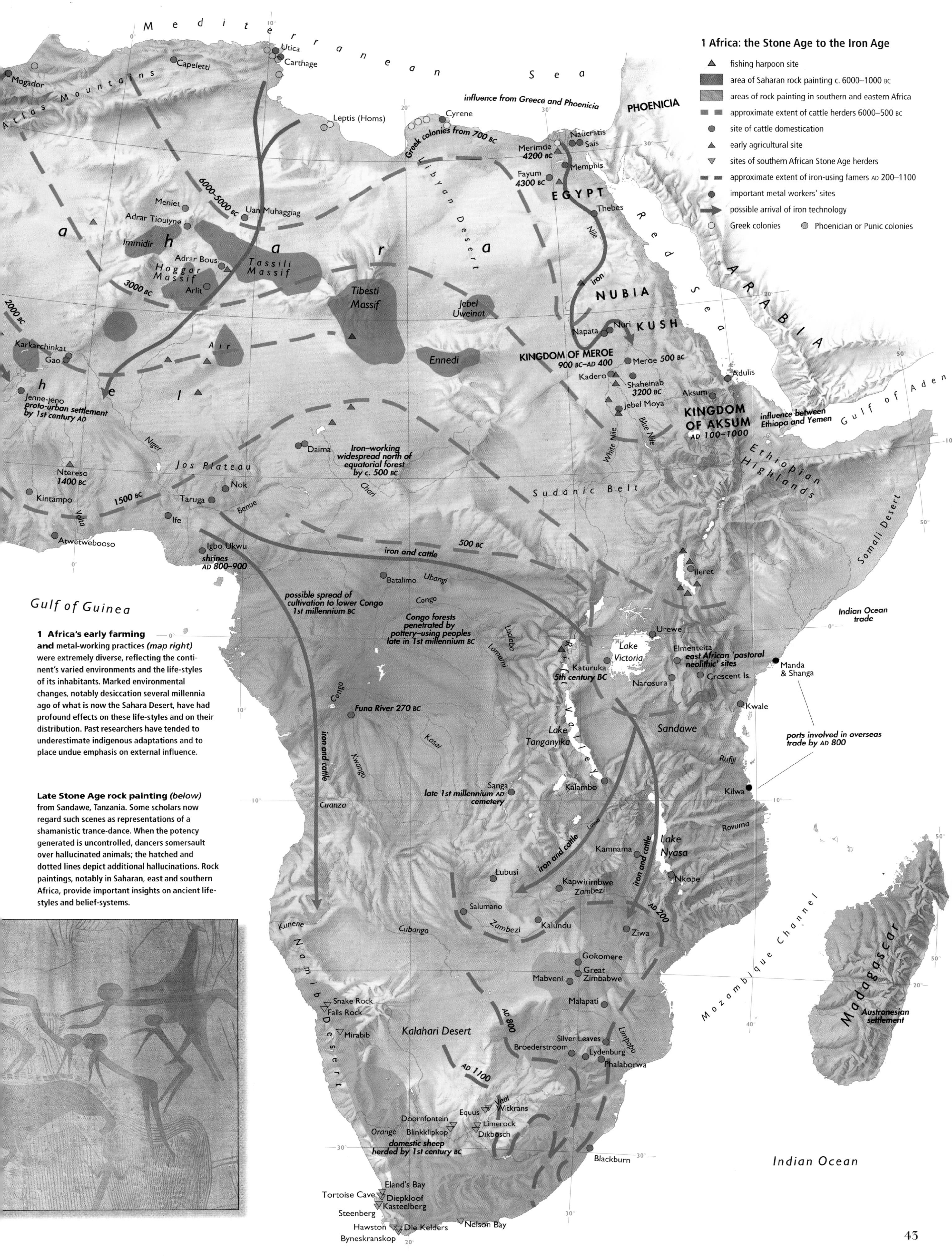

1 Africa's early farming and metal-working practices *(map right)* were extremely diverse, reflecting the continent's varied environments and the life-styles of its inhabitants. Marked environmental changes, notably desiccation several millennia ago of what is now the Sahara Desert, have had profound effects on these life-styles and on their distribution. Past researchers have tended to underestimate indigenous adaptations and to place undue emphasis on external influence.

Late Stone Age rock painting ***(below)*** from Sandawe, Tanzania. Some scholars now regard such scenes as representations of a shamanistic trance-dance. When the potency generated is uncontrolled, dancers somersault over hallucinated animals; the hatched and dotted lines depict additional hallucinations. Rock paintings, notably in Saharan, east and southern Africa, provide important insights on ancient life-styles and belief-systems.

Peoples of the Americas

See also
The spread of modern humans p. 32
The Ice Age world p. 34
From hunting to farming: the origins of agriculture p. 36
Peoples of the Americas, 300 BC–c. AD 1300 p. 60
The Americas on the eve of European conquest p. 148

The staple foods were the ingredients for ... the human design, and the water was for the blood ... our first mother-fathers ... talked and they made words ... looked and listened. They walked, they worked.

From the Popol Vuh, *the sacred book of the Quiché Maya*

First colonized by Siberians during the Ice Age, the Americas then developed in complete isolation from the rest of the world. Nonetheless, ways of life and forms of social organization evolved in much the same ways as in the Old World, though languages and customs were distinct as was much of the technology that was developed.

c. 13,000 BC *First human settlement*

c. 11,000 BC *Mammoth kill near Clovis (North America)*

c. 9000 BC *Southern tip of South America colonized*

c. 3600 BC *Mesoamerica: evidence maize cultivated*

c. 3000 BC *First pottery in America (northern South America)*

c. 2000 BC *First metal-working in the Central Andes*

c. 1750 BC *Northernmost Greenland settled*

c. 1150 BC *Beginnings of Olmec civilization in Mexico*

c. 500 BC *Foundation of Zapotec capital, Monte Albán, in Mexico*

When were the Americas first peopled and by whom? Long controversy is now deepening with the results of new research on genetics. But the general view remains that humans first entered the Americas from Siberia around 15,000 years ago. A second Asiatic immigration in about 8000 BC brought the first speakers of the Na-Dene languages of northern and western North America, and then came the ancestors of the Aleuts and Inuit. From this point on, the Americas remained almost entirely isolated from further human contact until the European discovery of the continent 500 years ago.

Linguistic diversity today shows that these early colonists soon spread. Archaeology confirms that the southernmost tip of South America was inhabited by 9000 BC and northernmost Greenland by 1750 BC (by 'Independence' cultures). The way of life – travelling in small bands, gathering, fishing and hunting – encouraged such wide dispersal. Yet in some areas large groups assembled regularly. Buffalo hunts on the Great Plains of North America called for extensive cooperation. Gatherings on this scale would have been annual highlights for the people involved. They continued in remoter areas into the early 1900s, allowing anthropologists to discover something of the organization, knowledge and skills of this largely unchanged way of life.

The first settlements

With the end of the Ice Age, peoples in the temperate and tropical zones of the region came to rely increasingly on both non-migratory prey and migratory wildfowl, on shellfish beds and on seasonal farming, all of which encouraged settled ways of life and population growth. Along the west coast of North America and the southeast coast of South America, fishing was to remain a mainstay but elsewhere – in Mesoamerica, the Central Andes and Amazonia – gathering and hunting gradually declined in favour of farming. Both cause and effect, villages were flourishing in many areas by 1500 BC.

The most widely grown crop was maize, though manioc (cassava) became important in lowland South America and potatoes and cotton in the Andes. Other early crops included gourds, squashes, beans, tomatoes, avocados, chillies and aloes. Turkeys and dogs were kept for food in Mesoamerica, guinea pigs in the Andes. Herding was restricted to the Andes, where llamas were important as pack animals, and both llamas and alpacas were raised for wool.

Settled village life did not preclude long-distance trade. Sea shells and metal tools and ornaments were circulated widely in eastern North America. Pottery provides evidence that sailors ranged along much of the west coast of South America as well as north to Central America. It is not known whether it is diffusion of this kind or a common and older Siberian heritage that explains the cultural similarities widespread among native Americans even today.

Early civilizations

Settled life permitted rising populations. Similarly, the need for farm labour may have encouraged the trend. But how were larger groups to live together? Across the continent, political leaders emerged. They used religious institutions to reflect and mould new forms of organization. Across the eastern half of North America, families gathered around ceremonial earthworks for festivals. Their tombs suggest that funerals were political occasions, too. There is evidence from these burial places of distinctions between rich and poor, governors and governed.

In the Central Andes, temples stood guard over warehouses built to store seasonal surpluses and precious imports. Community assets were the objects not only of local rivalry but of outsiders' jealousy as well. Gruesome sculptures at Cerro Sechín may depict warfare. Later, around 700–400 BC, the Chavín cult transcended local rivalries. Associated with ideas about supernatural spirits, its rites, architecture, sculpture, goldwork and fine textiles were used in many districts, probably partly to justify the privileges of chieftains. These ideas were to last long (*see* p. 60).

In Mesoamerica during the same period religion was almost certainly used to the same ends by the Olmecs, whose cult was also widespread and also part of a tradition that lived on. Chiefs seem to have claimed pivotal roles in the organization of the cosmos. Earthworks, rock art, sculpture and decorated pottery served the cult and illustrated it. Again probably for the same reasons, the Maya adorned their pyramids with similar religious and political symbols.

All the while, chiefs were supposed not to order their people but to depend on them. The break came in Mexico, in about 500 BC, with the foundation of Monte Albán as a new capital for the Zapotecs. Whether or not this move was prompted by a need for local cooperation in managing water resources or by common interests in defence, it was soon evident – from the site's architecture, its symbolism, and the rulers' effects on the surrounding villages and their conquests further afield – that a more powerful and centralized form of rule had arisen: the state. From the same period at Monte Albán is the earliest evidence for hieroglyphic writing: dated records of conquest.

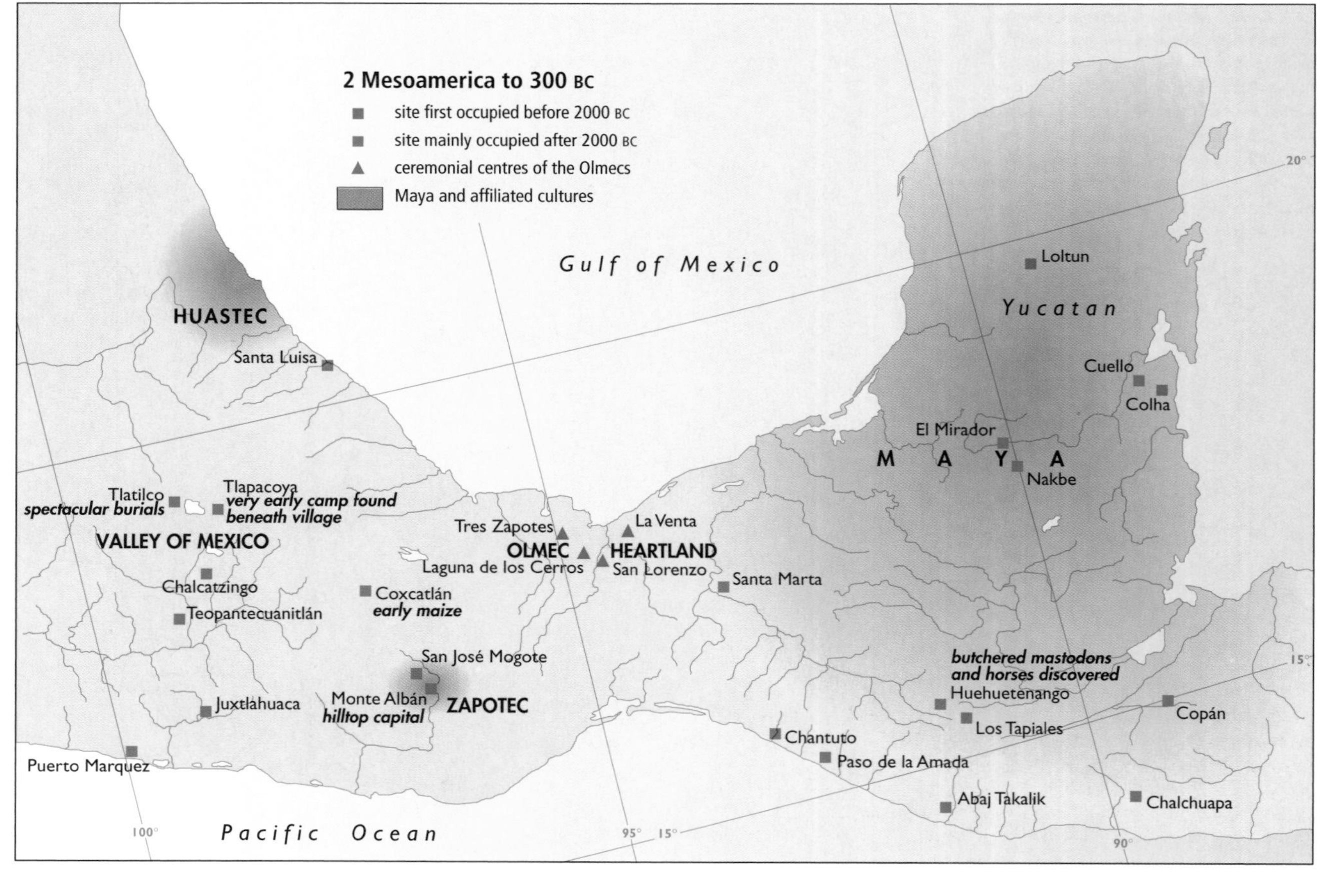

2 The first millennium BC saw the emergence of a series of increasingly developed societies in Mesoamerica *(map right)*. The Gulf of Mexico was the main area of settlement of the Olmecs, though there were major Olmec highland sites, too. The Huastecs to the north seem to have been closely affiliated to the Maya on the Yucatan peninsula. But by 500 BC the Maya had emerged as a distinct group. At the same time, the Zapotecs were also emerging as a distinct culture.

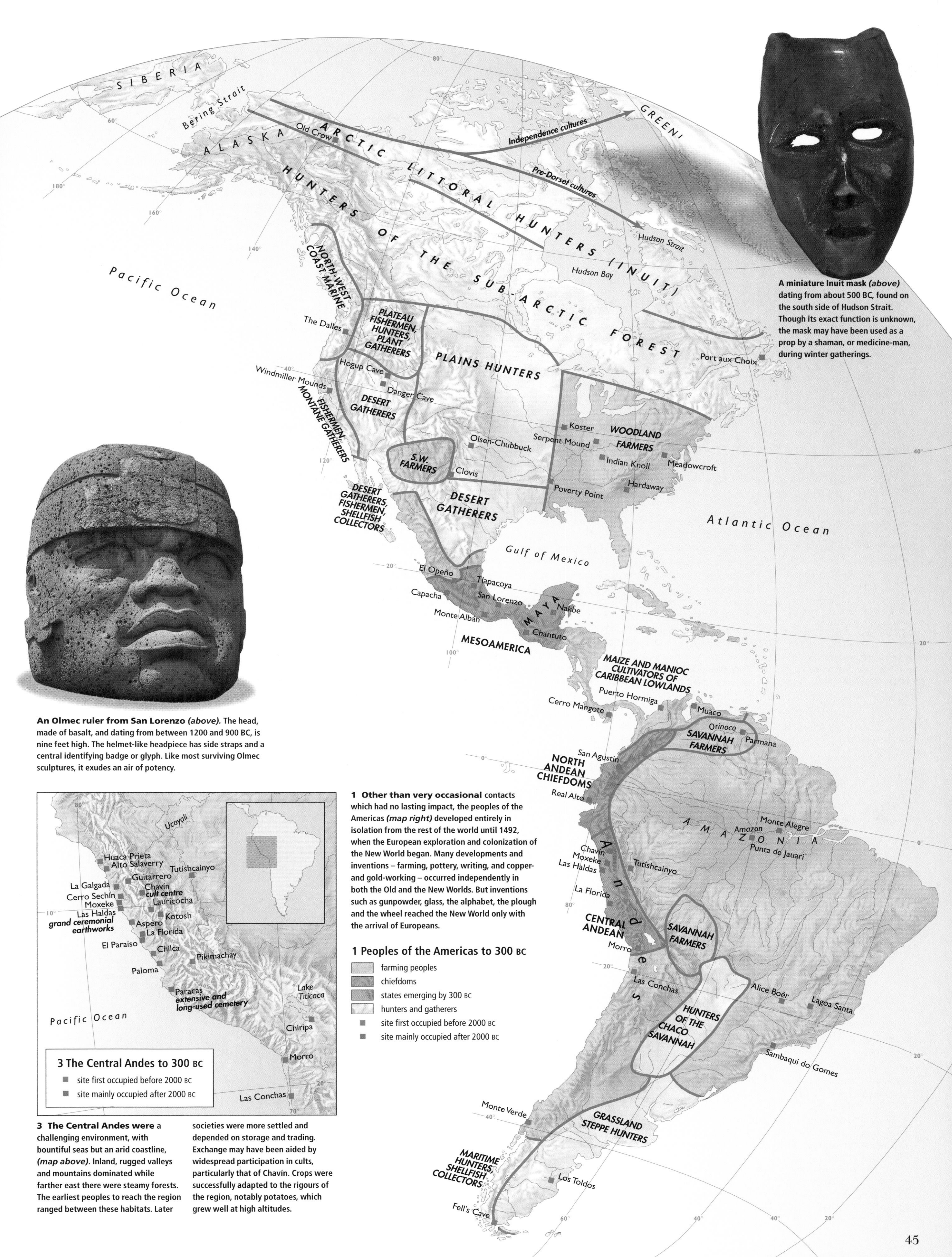

A miniature Inuit mask *(above)* dating from about 500 BC, found on the south side of Hudson Strait. Though its exact function is unknown, the mask may have been used as a prop by a shaman, or medicine-man, during winter gatherings.

An Olmec ruler from San Lorenzo *(above)*. The head, made of basalt, and dating from between 1200 and 900 BC, is nine feet high. The helmet-like headpiece has side straps and a central identifying badge or glyph. Like most surviving Olmec sculptures, it exudes an air of potency.

1 Other than very occasional contacts which had no lasting impact, the peoples of the Americas ***(map right)*** developed entirely in isolation from the rest of the world until 1492, when the European exploration and colonization of the New World began. Many developments and inventions – farming, pottery, writing, and copper- and gold-working – occurred independently in both the Old and the New Worlds. But inventions such as gunpowder, glass, the alphabet, the plough and the wheel reached the New World only with the arrival of Europeans.

3 The Central Andes were a challenging environment, with bountiful seas but an arid coastline, ***(map above)***. Inland, rugged valleys and mountains dominated while farther east there were steamy forests. The earliest peoples to reach the region ranged between these habitats. Later societies were more settled and depended on storage and trading. Exchange may have been aided by widespread participation in cults, particularly that of Chavín. Crops were successfully adapted to the rigours of the region, notably potatoes, which grew well at high altitudes.

Southeast Asia before civilization

See also
The spread of modern humans p. 32
The Ice Age world p. 34
From hunting to farming: the origins of agriculture p. 36
The early civilizations of southeast Asia to AD 1511 p. 134

Before 1,000,000 BC Homo erectus *enters Asia*

c. 60,000 BC Homo sapiens *spreads through southeast Asia*

c. 40,000–10,000 BC *Late Pleistocene flake-and-blade-tool tradition*

c. 10,000–4000 BC *Hoabinhian hunter-gathering traditions on the mainland*

c. 7000–4000 BC *Rice agriculture expands through central and south China*

c. 3000 BC *First agricultural settlements in southeast Asia*

c. 1500–500 BC *Bronze Age in northeast Thailand and north Vietnam*

c. 500 BC *Introduction of iron, trade with India and development of political elites*

With its long coastlines, mountain ranges and great river valleys fed by heavy seasonal rains, both the mainland and islands of southeast Asia provided a wealth of resources for early humankind. The diversity of flora and the abundance of metal ores allowed the growth of agricultural communities from at least the 4th millennium BC.

THERE SEEMS LITTLE DOUBT that *Homo erectus*, the ancestor of all modern humans, was established in southeast Asia west of the 'Wallace Line' more than one million years ago. But only Java, with its favourable geological conditions, has provided the skeletal evidence; elsewhere only discoveries of stone tools along river terraces and in some limestone fissure deposits reveal his passing.

Archaeological evidence

Abundant archaeological evidence for modern human hunter-gatherers comes only in the Late Pleistocene, and mainly from sites in the limestone mountains: among the best known are Tham Khuong and Nguom in northern Vietnam, Lang Rongrien in Thailand, Leang Burung in Celebes, and Tabon Cave in the island of Palawan in the Philippines. From about 40,000 years ago a varied range of flake stone tools have been found in these caves, left by people who exploited a wide range of plants, small and large animals and molluscs. This way of life persisted until about the 6th millennium BC, with changes in the tool kit from flake tools to pebble choppers – the Hoabinhian tradition, called after the region in north Vietnam where it was first described.

From at least 6000 BC village settlements with evidence for rice growing and pottery making have been found in southern China, but perhaps because there has been relatively little research on early village sites in southeast Asia no settlements of rice farmers older than 3000 BC have been found in northern Vietnam and inland areas of Thailand, although Phung Nguyen in the Red River valley of Vietnam and Ban Chiang and Non Nok Tha in northern Thailand have all been well investigated. But the best evidence for late Neolithic occupation of southeast Asia comes from Khok Phanom Di, a seven-metre deep village mound occupying about five hectares near the coast southeast of modern-day Bangkok. Here over 150 burials and rich occupation layers dated to between 2000 and 1400 BC provide evidence of intensive exploitation of the sea and adjacent mangrove forests, and the beginnings of social differentiation.

Metal technologies

From early in the 2nd millennium BC bronze tools were added to the existing stone, bone and antler tool kits in central and northeast Thailand and northern Vietnam, where we can refer to a true Bronze Age from about 1500 to 500 BC. The best known Bronze-Age locations in Thailand are Ban Chiang and Ban Na Di in the northeast and Nil Kham Haeng near Lopburi in the Chao Phraya valley. In Vietnam more sites of this phase are known including Dong Dau, Viet Khe, Cau Chan, Trang Khen, Lang Vac and Dong Son on the Ma river where a rich burial ground has been excavated since the 1920s and given its name to the late Bronze Age culture of the region, best known for its great bronze drums. These are widely distributed from Yunnan in Southwest China to Thailand, Malaya and many parts of Indonesia where they seem to have been traded in antiquity as objects of great prestige and magical power.

Influence from India

In western and peninsular Thailand, Malaysia, Burma, Indonesia and the Philippines bronze metallurgy seems to have arrived only with iron after about 500 BC and to have been introduced from India as maritime trade routes were extended across the Bay of Bengal. In graves of this period are found glass and semi-precious stone jewellery of great aesthetic and technical sophistication together with iron tools and weapons, while in

2 The great river systems of southeast Asia together with its extended coastlines encouraged the use of boats which carried natural products and manufactured goods such as iron, glass and ceramics throughout the region *(map below)* linking the islands and the mainland in a complex network of trade routes which extended north to China and Japan and westwards to India and the Mediterranean world.

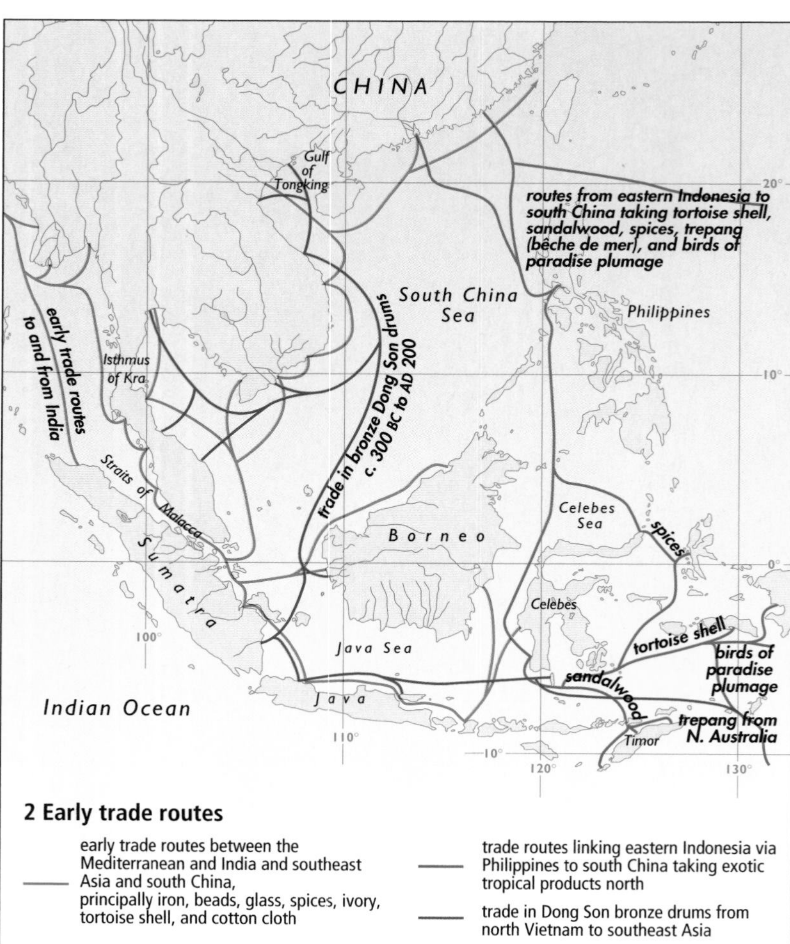

3 Mainland southeast Asia is linguistically highly complex *(map right)* with at least eight major language families represented, but most of the languages of the Philippines and Indonesia belong to the Austronesian family which is thought to have expanded from a homeland in south China 6000 years ago. But this pattern hides considerable diversity and in Timor alone over 43 distinct languages are spoken.

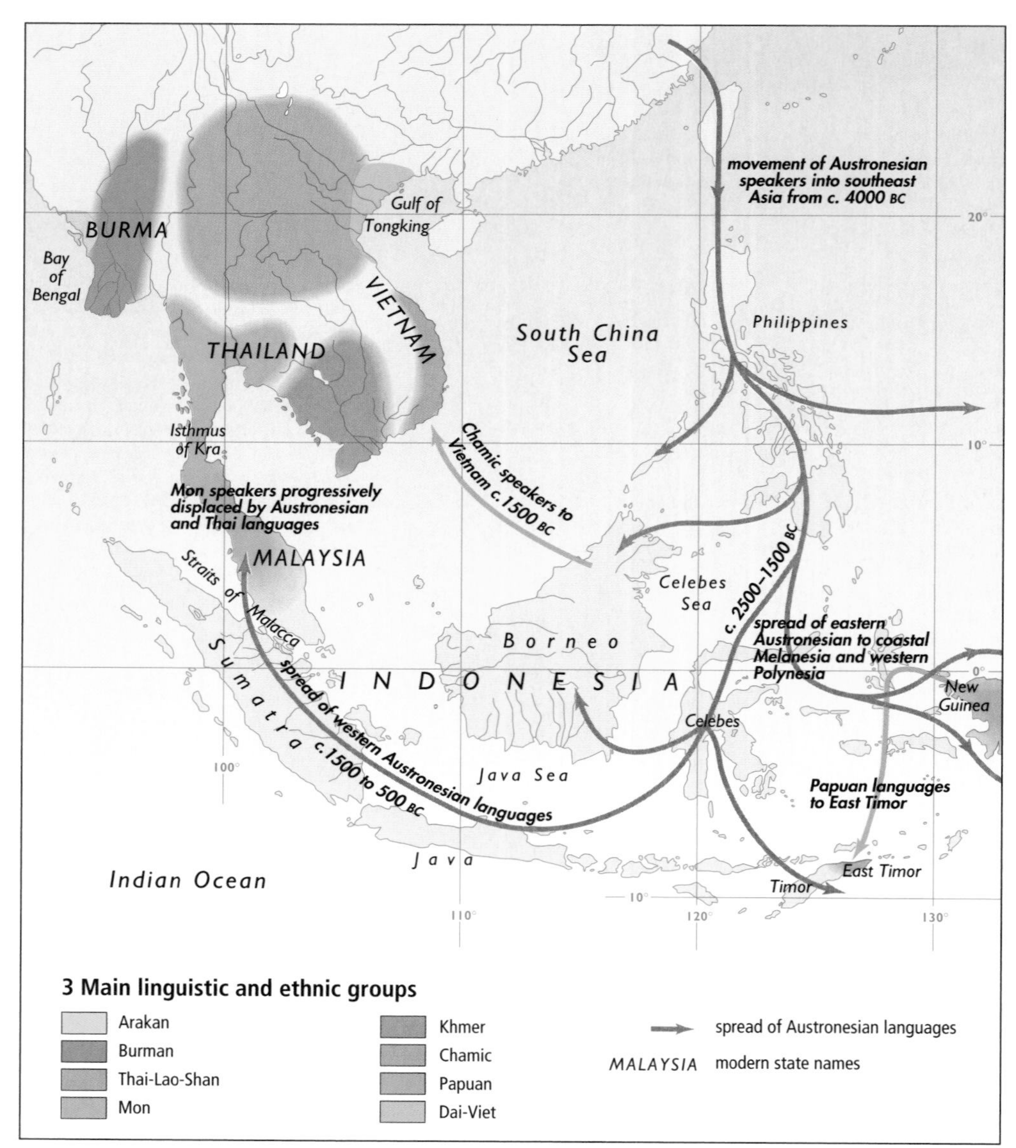

inland areas large moated-mound settlements and well-laid out cemeteries mark the emergence of powerful chiefdoms whose rulers, attracted by the rituals and prestige of Indian culture, soon adapted these to enhance their own status and power. Sites such as Ban Don Ta Phet, Khao Jamook, Khuan Lukpad, Ban Prasat, Non U-Loke, Ban Lum Khao and Ban Chieng Hian in Thailand, Giong Ca Vo, Giong Phet, Doc Chua, Long Giao, Hang Gon and Hau Xa in southern and central Vietnam have all produced rich examples from this last stage of prehistoric culture on the mainland of southeast Asia, as have Plawangan and Lamongan in Java and Gilimanuk and Sembiran in Bali, where glass beads imported from south India and a potsherd with a Brahmi inscription serve to mark the end of prehistory.

Magnificent cast bronze drums *(right)* were made in southwest China and northern Vietnam from at least 500 BC and served in ceremonies to initiate agricultural work and to summon villagers in times of war. Many were traded south to Indonesia and along the riverine routes into Laos and Thailand.

1 The past 30 years has seen much new archaeological research including, very recently, in the south of Vietnam, and this is reflected in the distribution of marked sites *(map above)*, of which only the more important or better investigated are shown. Many sites are multi-period and most village settlements include some burials. Symbols are chosen to indicate the most significant aspect of each archaeological site. The 'Wallace Line' marks a major biogeographical boundary between the Asian fauna to the west and Australasian fauna to the east. The islands to the west were connected to the Asian mainland as recently as 12,000 years ago, while the islands to the east are separated by deep submarine trenches.

Australia and Oceania before European contact

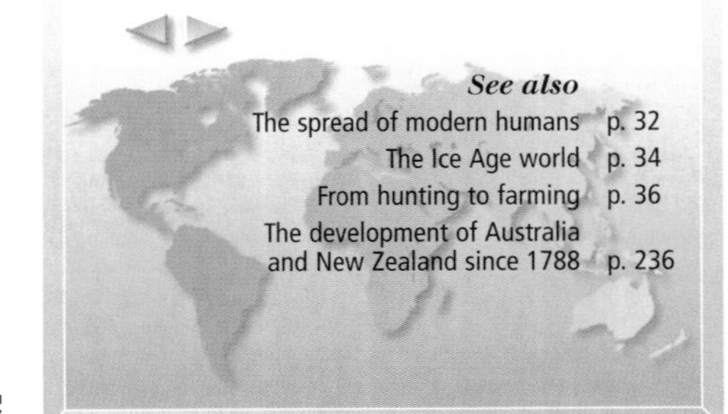

The Australian continent was first settled from 50,000 years ago when lower land levels permitted the sea-crossing from southeast Asia. Around 5,000 years ago sea-levels rose and thereafter Australia, New Guinea, New Zealand, Melanesia and Polynesia developed in isolation from the rest of the world, developing rich and uniquely adapted cultures.

c. 50,000 BC *Settlement of Australia from southeast Asia*

c. 40,000 BC *Settlement of New Guinea*

c. 2000 BC *Settlement of Melanesia by immigrants from Indonesia begins*

c. 1300 BC *Settlers of Melanesia reach Fiji*

c.150 BC *Settlement of Marquesas Islands*

c. AD 400 *Settlement of Hawaiian islands*

c. 750 *Settlers reach New Zealand*

1642–3 *Tasman circumnavigates Australia and discovers New Zealand*

1768 *Cook begins exploration of the Pacific*

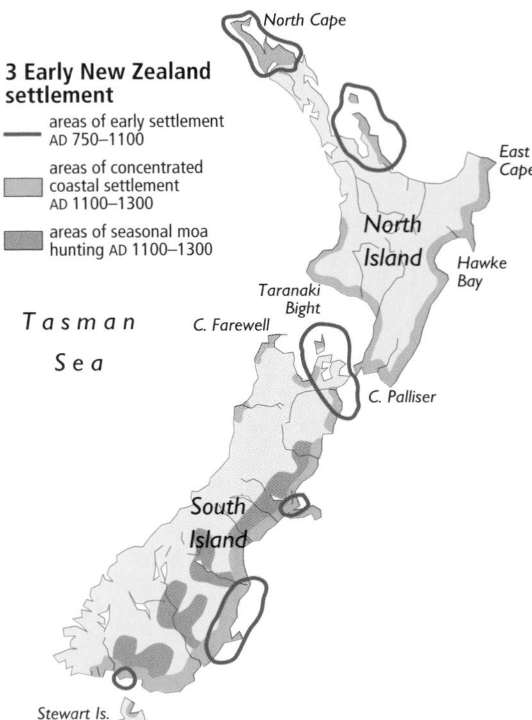

ABOUT 50,000 YEARS AGO, when lower sea levels linked Tasmania, Australia and New Guinea, man first ventured onto the Greater Australian Continent. That journey, from a southeast Asian homeland, was a pioneering one, as it involved at least one major sea crossing. The original Australians were therefore among the world's earliest mariners. A strange new world greeted these newcomers: of enormous size, and ranging from tropical north to temperate south. Some of the edible plants found in more northerly latitudes were related to those of Asia and were therefore familiar, but this was not so of the animals. In addition to the mammals which have survived, there was a bewildering assortment of giant forms: ten-foot tall kangaroos, various enormous ox-like beasts, a large native lion, and rangy ostrich-like birds.

Pleistocene Australia

Despite this terrestrial abundance, it was the plentiful supply of fish and shellfish available along the coasts and in the rivers that drew most attention, and it was in these areas of Australasia that the first human settlements were concentrated. Most of the sites are lost to us, for between 50,000 and 5000 years ago the sea was lower than the present level and they now lie offshore, on the continental shelf.

The Pleistocene inhabitants of Australasia used red ochre to create elaborate rock paintings, thus laying the foundations of a rich and long-lived Aboriginal custom. Their stone core implements and crude scrapers belong to what is known as the Australian Core Tool Tradition. This tradition, which underwent remarkably little change in more than 40,000 years, is pan-Australian, but there are a number of regional elements that have links with New Guinea and southeast Asia. One of these is the edge-ground axe, which has been dated to 22,000 years in Arnhem Land. Similar ground-stone tools found in Japan are up to 30,000 years old. Ground-stone tools were ultimately developed in most other parts of the world also, but only at a much later period.

Rock art ***(above)*** **became common in Australia 5000 years ago. This much more recent painting shows the two 'Lightning Brothers', ancestral spirits of the Wardaman Aboriginal people from northwestern Australia.**

Aboriginal society

Around 5000 years ago the sea rose to its present level, and while Aboriginal settlements were still concentrated along the coasts there was a rapid increase in the exploitation of inland resources. At about this time a range of small, finely finished flake implements especially developed for hafting, and known as the Australian Small Tool Tradition, appeared across the continent; the dingo was also introduced.

Political, economic and religious development continued and by the time the first European settlers arrived in the 18th century, there were at least 750,000 Aborigines living in around 500 tribal territories. Although the Aborigines' way of life was still based on hunting and gathering (they never became full-scale agriculturists), they had developed some very intricate relationships with their environment. In desert areas, small nomadic groups ranged over thousands of square miles, while in richer parts of the continent there were settled, permanent villages. Fish traps were constructed, grasses and tubers replanted to assist nature, and fire was used to burn old vegetation and encourage the growth of rich new plant cover.

New Guinea

New Guinea was first occupied at the same time as Australia. A settlement in northern New Guinea has been dated to at least 40,000 years ago, when it was covered by a deposit of volcanic ash, and New Ireland to the north is known to have been occupied some 33,000 years ago.

Other sites in the highlands of the northwest evidence the widespread distribution of man in New Guinea by 8000 BC. Major changes took place about 6000 years ago with the introduction of domesticated Asian plants and animals, and the creation of drained fields at places such as Kuk Swamp. The hunting and gathering tradition of earlier times persisted into recent times, however, alongside agriculture.

Most of island Melanesia (to the east, northeast and southeast of the New Guinea mainland) saw its first occupants during the 2nd and 1st millennia BC, as maritime trading groups bearing domesticated plants and animals spread through the area. These Austronesian people, with their distinctive pottery, belonging to the Lapita tradition (which can be traced back to the Moluccas area of Indonesia), reached Fiji, the eastern boundary of present-day Melanesia, by 1300 BC, and soon after made their way into western Polynesia via Tonga and Samoa. And it was in these two island groups, but particularly in the latter, that a typically

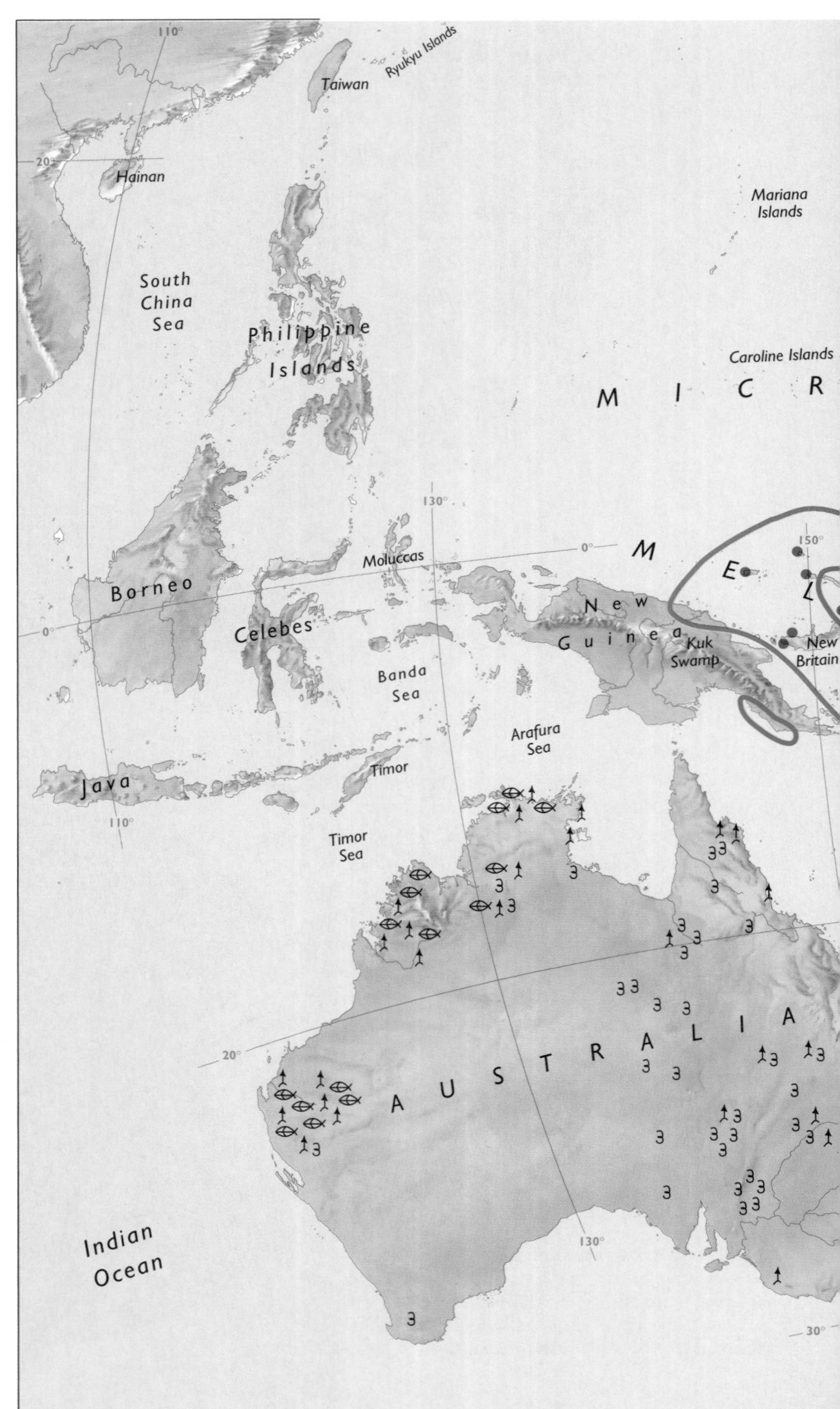

3 New Zealand's early settlers were basically coastal hunter-gatherers, though South Island inland resources were seasonally exploited *(map below left)*. Cultivated plants were only grown in sheltered North Island localities.

4 At the time of European contact in 1769 most Maoris were settled in North Island, along the coast and rivers *(map below)*. Food obtained by hunting and gathering was in some areas supplemented by horticultural products.

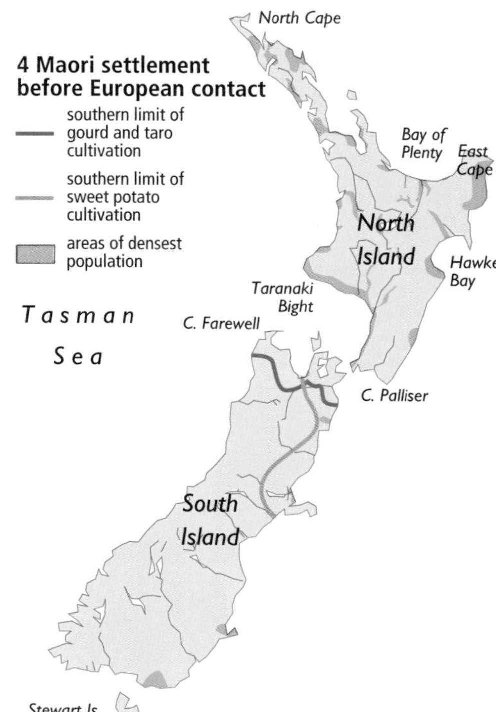

Melanesian material culture gradually evolved into a Polynesian-style one, during more than 1000 years of geographical isolation. Around 150 BC, a time when Lapita pottery was disappearing throughout island Melanesia and western Polynesia, prehistoric Samoans ventured eastward in their canoes and settled the distant Marquesas Islands. After a brief pause, settlers spread to the Hawaiian Islands around AD 400, while at about the same time the first Polynesians reached Easter Island, there to give birth to an extraordinary and impressive culture. All the other major island groups of Polynesia, including New Zealand, were first settled, mainly from Samoa-Tonga or Society Islands-Marquesas, between AD 750 and 1300, and a multitude of largely independent cultures evolved on these little 'island universes', only to be shattered by the shock of European contact during the 17th, 18th and 19th centuries.

Because of its climatic range, comparative size, and unfamiliar plants and animals, New Zealand presented its initial Polynesian settlers with special adaptive problems. Most of the domesticated plants and animals characteristic of the ancestral homeland were lost en route to New Zealand or else failed to withstand the more rigorous climatic conditions; the only important survivors were the dog and native rat, and the taro, yam and sweet potato (albeit these last three were basically restricted to coastal North Island localities). Nevertheless, the New Zealand environment offered these early settlers unexpected dietary compensation in the form of a whole suite of giant flightless birds, the best known of which are the moas. The original New Zealanders of North Island and northern South Island (the Maoris) thus became hunter-farmers, and a pattern of seasonal movement was developed to take advantage of local conditions. Settlements were predominantly coastal and were restricted to several clearly defined regions. Meanwhile, new forms of tools were developed in response to the new environment. During the ensuing centuries the growing population expanded around the coasts of both islands, and inland resources were intensively exploited on South Island.

As hunting and man-made bushfires continued there was a gradual change in the environment, culminating in the 13th and 14th centuries with widespread deforestation, and virtual extinction of large birds. It was probably at about this time that many of the implements derived from ancestral Polynesian types were abandoned, and that distinctly New Zealand artifacts began to emerge. So too did warfare, and with it the appearance of specially developed fortified settlements termed *pa*. By the time of European contact, Cook and other explorers found New Zealand occupied by up to 150,000 Maoris. A hunting-farming lifestyle was still in evidence, except in the southern half of South Island, which was beyond the limits of horticulture. European contact and settlement soon led to violent confrontation which resulted in the rapid breakdown of traditional Maori society and culture.

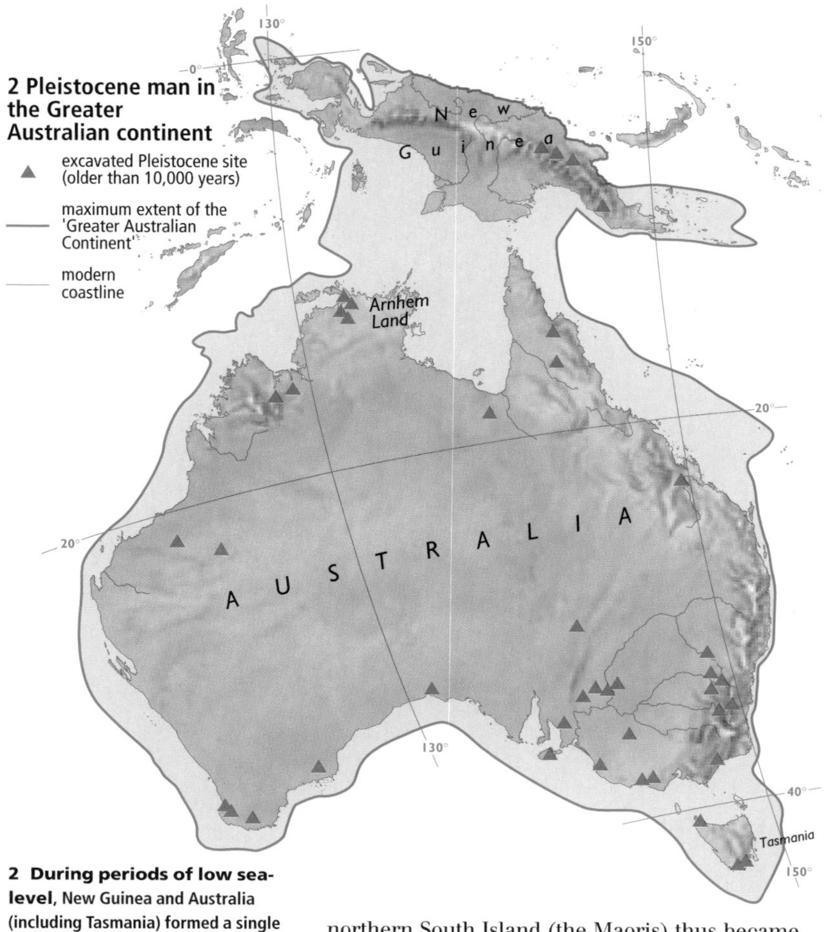

2 Pleistocene man in the Greater Australian continent

- ▲ excavated Pleistocene site (older than 10,000 years)
- maximum extent of the 'Greater Australian Continent'
- modern coastline

2 During periods of low sea-level, New Guinea and Australia (including Tasmania) formed a single large landmass *(map above)*. Settlement was concentrated along the major river systems and the coast, but Pleistocene coastal sites now lie submerged offshore. In this map, the comparative abundance of sites in southeast Australia is simply a result of the greater attention devoted to this region by archaeologists.

1 Most of the main groups of island Melanesia and western Polynesia were first settled over the last two millennia by maritime colonists bearing Lapita-style pottery *(map below)*. After 1000 years of geographical isolation, a distinctly Polynesian material culture evolved in Tonga and Samoa, and this was introduced to eastern Polynesia in about AD 400. Between AD 400 and 1000, Polynesian settlers travelling with crops and livestock in small double canoes and outrigger canoes reached virtually every island in the Polynesian triangle.

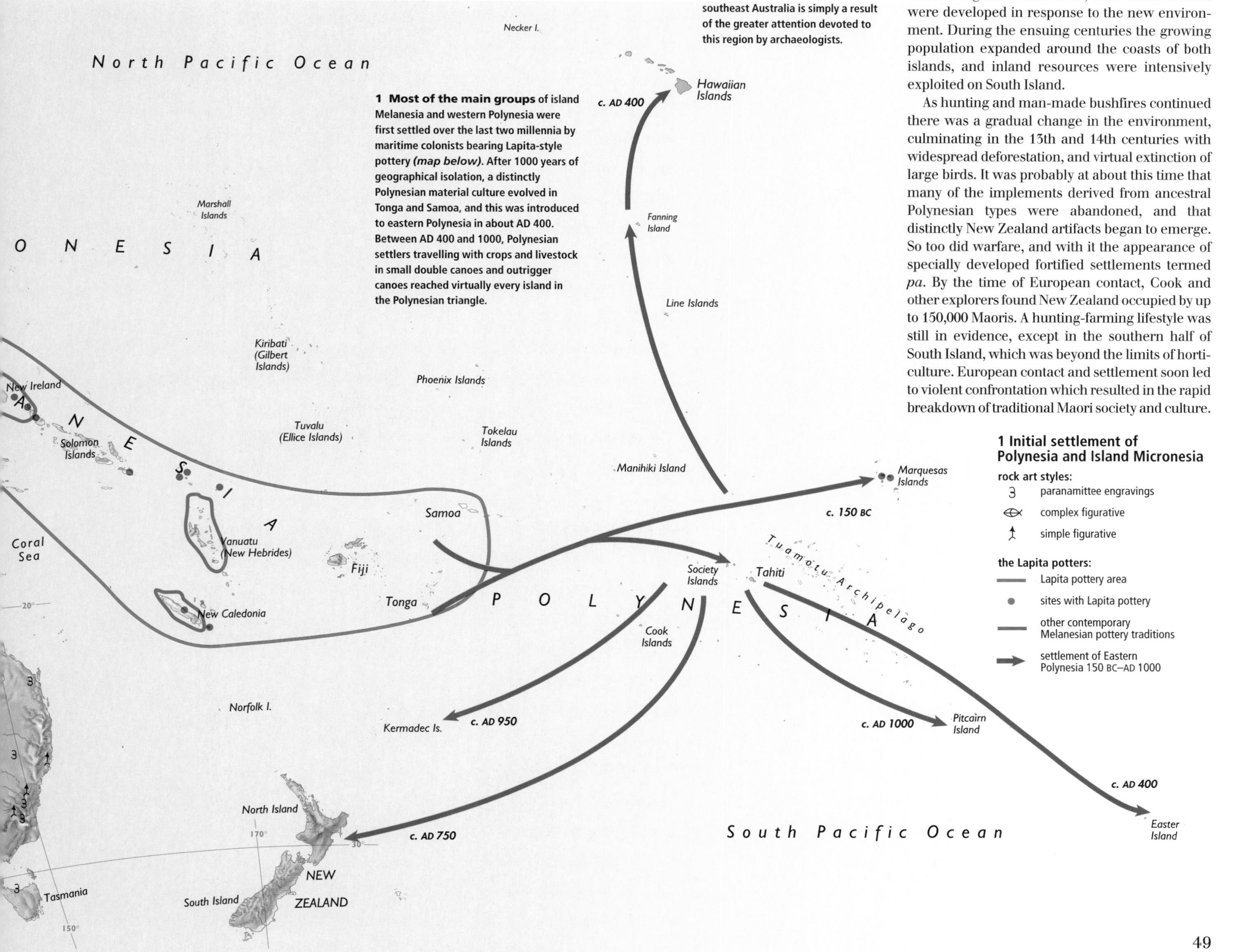

1 Initial settlement of Polynesia and Island Micronesia

rock art styles:
- paranamittee engravings
- complex figurative
- simple figurative

the Lapita potters:
- Lapita pottery area
- sites with Lapita pottery
- other contemporary Melanesian pottery traditions
- settlement of Eastern Polynesia 150 BC–AD 1000

2

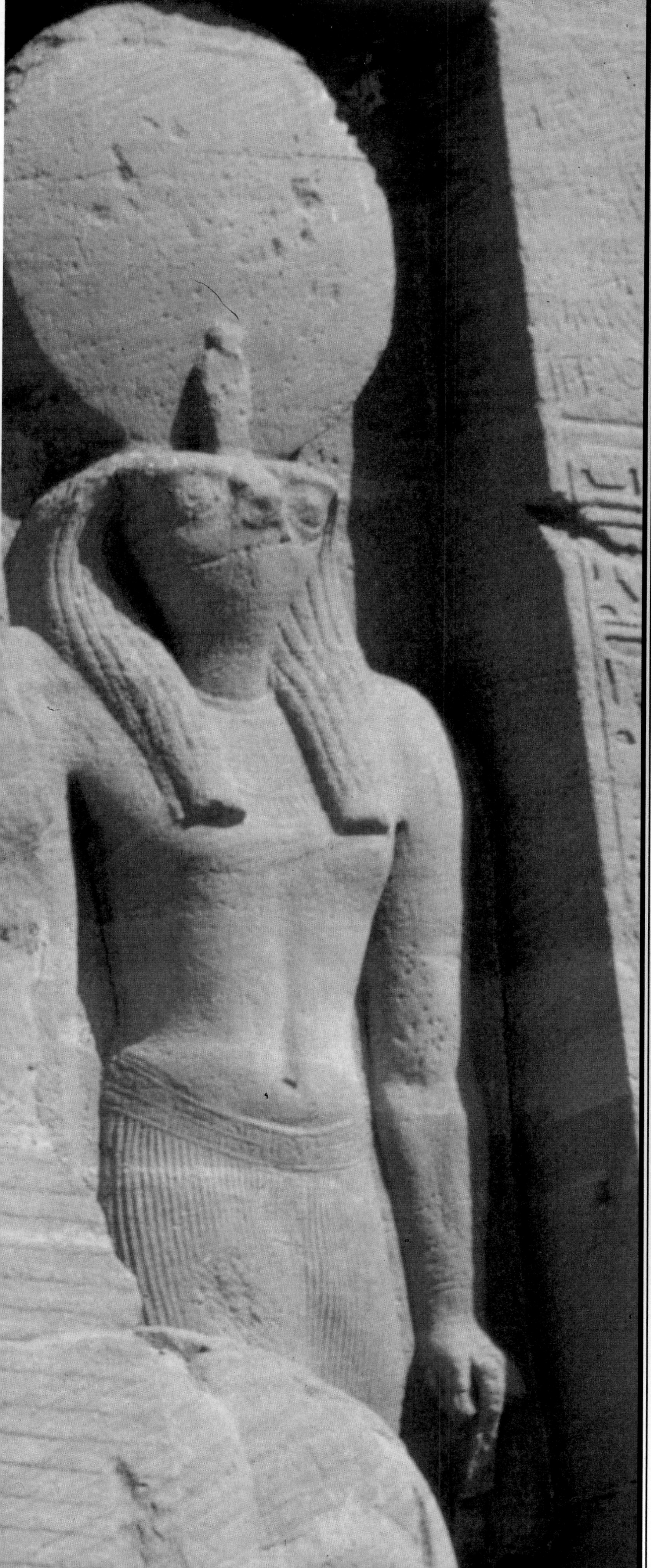

The first civilizations

ABOUT 6000 YEARS AGO, in a few areas of particularly intensive agriculture, the dispersed villages of Neolithic peoples gave way to more complex societies. These were the first civilizations, and their emergence marks the start of a new phase of world history. They arose, apparently independently, in four widely dispersed areas (the early civilizations of America emerged considerably later): the lower Tigris and Euphrates valleys; the valley of the Nile; the Indus valley around Harappa and Mohenjo-Daro; and the Yellow River around An-yang. The characteristic feature of them all was the city, which now became an increasingly dominant social form, gradually encroaching on the surrounding countryside, until today urban civilization has become the criterion of social progress. But the city possessed other important connotations: a complex division of labour; literacy and a literate class (usually the priesthood); monumental public buildings; political and religious hierarchies; a kingship descended from the gods; and ultimately empire, or the claim to universal rule. A dichotomy already existed between the civilized world and the barbarian world outside. The onslaught of nomadic peoples eager to enjoy the fruits of civilization became a recurrent theme of world history until the advent of effective firearms in the 15th century AD tilted the balance in favour of the civilized peoples.

Statue of Ramses II,
Great Temple of Abu Simbel, c. 1257 BC

The beginnings of civilization in the Eurasian world

See also

Before the first cities: the Near East, 8000–3500 BC p. 38
Early Europe : the colonization of a continent p. 40
The early empires of Mesopotamia p. 54
Ancient Egypt: civilization and empire p. 56
The beginnings of Chinese civilization to 475 BC p. 62
The beginnings of Indian civilization to 500 BC p. 64
The peoples of northern Europe, 2300–50 BC p. 84

c. 3500 BC *Eanna in Uruk and other ceremonial complexes built as the centres of the earliest cities in Mesopotamia*

c. 3200 BC *Earliest readable documents from Mesopotamia*

c. 3100 BC *Palatial complexes at Abydus established under First Dynasty of Egypt*

c. 2500 BC *Growth of urbanism in the Indus valley*

c. 2350 BC *First ceremonial centre built at Troy in western Anatolia*

c. 1800 BC *Beginning of Shang dynasty in China*

Urban civilizations developed independently in four different areas of Eurasia, as the exploitation of fertile river valleys allowed complex forms of social organization. The sudden growth of cities was a dramatic development in human history, and was accompanied by the beginnings of literacy. From this period it becomes possible to write true history.

'DRAW NEAR TO EANNA, THE DWELLING OF ISHTAR, WHICH NO FUTURE KING, NO MAN, CAN EQUAL. GO UP AND WALK ON THE WALLS OF URUK, INSPECT THE BASE TERRACE, EXAMINE THE BRICKWORK: IS NOT ITS BRICKWORK OF BURNT BRICK? DID NOT THE SEVEN SAGES LAY ITS FOUNDATION'

The Epic of Gilgamesh

THE DEVELOPMENT OF URBAN societies seems to have been triggered by a sudden concentration of population in certain river valleys, which in some cases may have been a result of climate change which made the surrounding areas outside the valleys less attractive for habitation. The need to exploit the fertile land of these valleys and their alluvial plains to feed a growing population then led to the development of irrigation and flood-control mechanisms. In Mesopotamia and China this involved the construction of canals to carry water away to the land around the Tigris-Euphrates and the Yellow River, while in Egypt and India the annual flooding of the Nile and Indus provided fertile silt in which crops were grown.

The first cities

The concentrated populations were able to produce surplus crops which could be exported to areas beyond the rivers in return for raw materials and precious items not locally available, above all bronze. The food surplus also made possible social groups not directly involved in agriculture, whether specialized craftsmen or rulers and military leaders. It was when ambitious individuals and families succeeded in diverting resources into the construction of monumental ceremonial centres that provided a focus for the populations living near them that the first true cities appeared. This took place in Mesopotamia in c. 3500 BC and in Egypt in c. 3100 BC, while the Indus valley cities appeared in c. 2500 BC, and in China urbanism began in c. 1800 BC.

The political development of these different regions was not uniform: in Egypt a single unified kingdom emerged almost immediately, extending from the Nile delta as far south as the first cataract; in China the earliest civilization is associated with the Shang dynasty,

1 Between c. 3500 and c. 1500 BC, complex societies characterized by urbanism, literacy and specialization of labour grew up independently in the valleys of the Tigris-Euphrates, Nile, Indus and Yellow rivers *(map right)*. In the 2nd millennium BC urban societies developed in Anatolia and the Aegean, and these further influenced the communities of the Balkans, south of the Carpathian mountains. Although amber from the Baltic found its way as far south as Mycenae, changes in the Near East had little impact on north and west Europe, where the 3rd and 2nd millennia saw the emergence of a common culture, the Bell-Beaker groups, while villages remained the normal form of community. At the same time the steppes of central Asia saw the domestication of the horse and the rise of nomad pastoralists who were to be a continuing influence on the urban civilizations of west and east.

1 The spread of civilization

- Bell-Beaker exchange routes, c. 2800–1800 BC
- amber routes after c. 1800 BC
- trade routes between urbanized areas
- area of Carpathian and Balkan Bronze Age groups
- area of Shang Chinese bronze working
- areas of irrigated agriculture
- early urban centres

Temple at Eridu in Mesopotamia, built c. 3000 BC. The large platform on which it stands is a forerunner of later Mesopotamian ziggurats. The 'Sumerian king list' names Eridu as the earliest seat of power in Mesopotamia. All early cities were important as ceremonial centres with large temple-complexes constructed early in their development: works which required both large-scale labour and considerable organization.

although the Shang rulers may have been leaders of a loose confederacy rather than absolute rulers. In Mesopotamia, by contrast, no one city was able to establish control for any length of time, and competition for dominance between the leading cities came to characterize the history of the area for nearly three millennia. The situation in the Indus valley is less clear, but the major cities of Harappa and Mohenjo-Daro appear to have coexisted until the decline of the Indus cities in c. 1750 BC. It appears that in all these civilizations religious, political and military power was concentrated in the hands of a small number of ruling families.

Trade and exchange were important in the expansion of the first civilizations. The possession of prestige goods and the desire to acquire more resources were instrumental in the emergence of the first empires in Mesopotamia. During the 3rd millennium BC goods were being traded between the Indus and the Mediterranean. In the 2nd millennium BC urbanization spread to Anatolia and the Aegean, and the cultural influence of the Near East can be seen in the bronze-working of the Balkan communities. However, in many parts of Eurasia, including the fertile river deltas of the Ganges and Mekong, the nature of the landscape did not favour concentrations of population, and village communities remained the normal form of social organization until the 1st millennium BC.

The development of writing occurred almost at the start of each of the four civilizations. The earliest known use of writing in China was for divination: the Shang rulers used prepared turtle shells and ox scapulae heated in a fire to establish the will of the gods, and the result of the enquiry was scratched onto the shell or bone. In Mesopotamia, Egypt and the Indus valley writing was used mainly for administrative activities, with inventories and accounts being inscribed on clay, a substance easy both to obtain and to re-use when necessary. Early examples of writing have often survived because clay tablets were accidentally baked, fixing the messages permanently. Clay inscriptions spread to Crete and Greece by around 1500 BC. In Egypt and Mesopotamia the use of writing developed rapidly, as large public inscriptions, including law-codes, were erected by the rulers as monuments to their wisdom, justice and power. It is from monuments such as these, celebrating their victories or their public works, that the earliest true history can be reconstructed.

THE EARLIEST FORMS OF WRITING

Methods of writing can use signs in two distinct ways: logographically and phonographically. Logograms are semantic symbols, signs that stand for words and ideas. Some logograms, known as pictograms, are actually pictures of the objects or actions they represent.

Other logograms work indirectly: ancient Egyptian used a picture of a shepherd's crook as the symbol for 'ruler'. Phonograms represent sounds, often syllables, and can also develop from pictograms. Where known, meanings (in bold) and sounds are shown below.

Mesopotamian pictograms and cuneiform, c. 3000 BC & 2400 BC

The earliest script developed gradually over a wide area of Mesopotamia: it was pictographic, inscribed on damp clay with a stick or reed. Used for record-keeping in economic transactions, the characteristic use of a stylus to make wedge-shaped marks ('cuneus' is Latin for 'wedge') led to stylized signs. It developed into a syllabic system for writing Sumerian, and later other Mesopotamian languages.

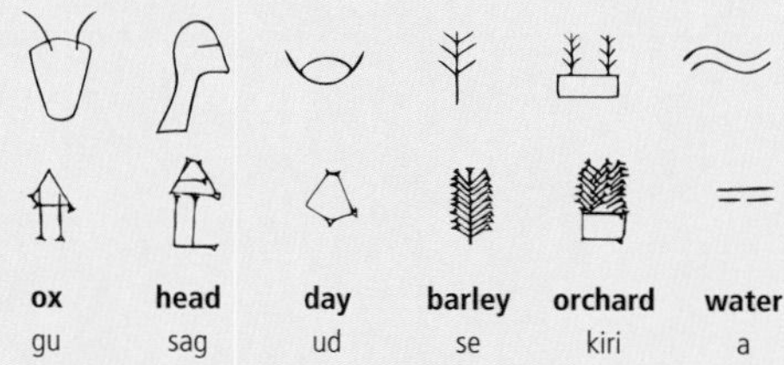

Egyptian hieroglyphics, c. 3100 BC

The earliest examples are found as labels on small objects. They use a combination of logographic and phonographic signs. Over 6000 are known, but fewer than 1000 are thought to have been in use at any one time, and only a small proportion used frequently. Fully developed from its earliest appearance, it continued in use until the 4th century AD. The ancient Egyptian language was the ancestor of Coptic.

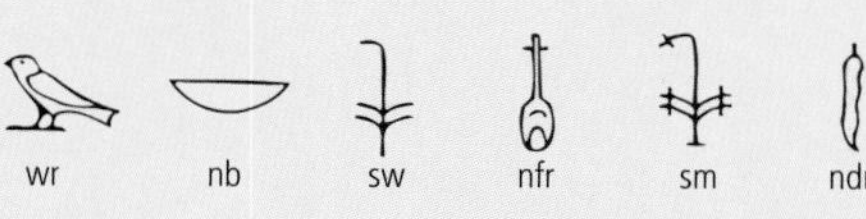

Indus valley script, c. 2500 BC

These signs are found mainly on seal stones, pottery, copper tablets, bone and ivory. About 400 separate signs have been distinguished in about 3500 short inscriptions. The script is not yet deciphered, but this language may be related to the Dravidian group which includes modern Tamil and Malayalam

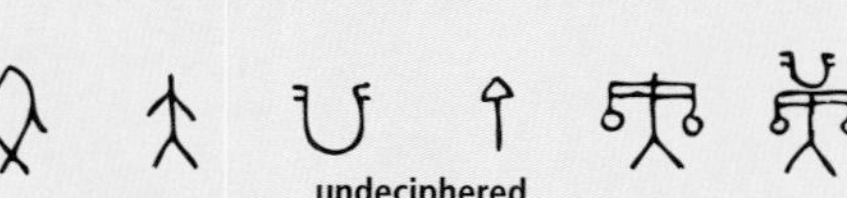

Linear A & B, c. 1800 BC & c. 1500 BC

Both have been found on clay tablets used for record-keeping: Linear A only in Crete, Linear B in later contexts in Crete and on mainland Greece. About 90 signs have been found and they suggest that these were syllabic systems, with some logographic elements. Linear A is as yet undeciphered; Linear B was adapted from it by Mycenaeans to write Greek, and a version was used in Cyprus down to the 5th century BC.

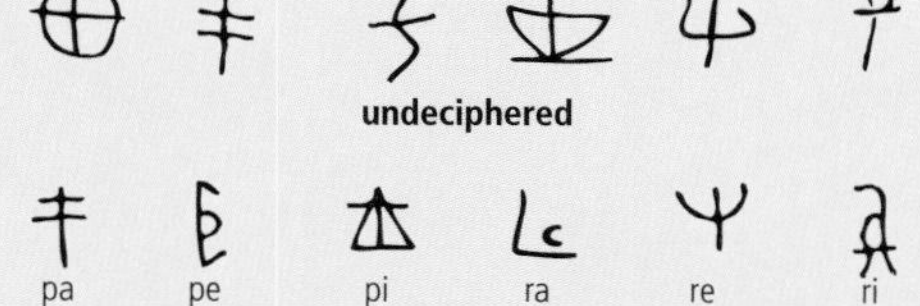

Shang 'Oracle Bone' script, c. 1400 BC

The earliest examples are found on 'oracle bones', pieces of bone and turtle shell used for divination by later rulers of Shang dynasty (c. 1500-1000 BC). About 4500 signs have been distinguished, of which about 1000 have been identified. Some signs are pictographic, but not all. It is a direct ancestor of modern Chinese scripts.

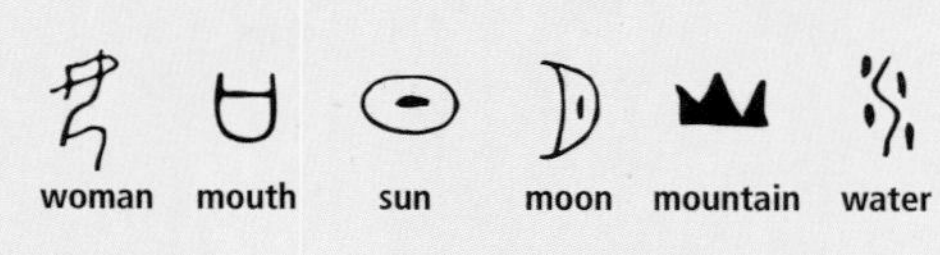

c. 3500 to 1600 BC

The early empires of Mesopotamia

See also
Before the first cities: the Near East, 10,000–4000 BC p. 38
The beginnings of civilization in the Eurasian world, 3500–1500 BC p. 52
Ancient Egypt: civilization and empire p. 56
The Near East, 1600–539 BC p. 58
The beginnings of Indian civilization to 500 BC p. 64

c. 3500–3200 BC *Earliest written records from Mesopotamia*

c. 2900 BC *Beginning of Early Dynastic period*

c. 2296 BC *Beginning of the reign of Sargon, first ruler of the empire of Agade*

c. 2029 BC *Beginning of the reign of Shulgi of Ur*

c. 1749 BC *Amorite Shamshi-Adad I conquers Ashur and takes the Assyrian throne*

c. 1728 BC *Beginning of the reign of Hammurabi of Babylon*

c. 1686 BC *Hammurabi publishes his law code shortly before his death*

c. 1595 BC *Hittite Mursili I sacks Babylon*

The broad plain through which the Tigris and Euphrates rivers flow gave birth to the world's first cities. Irrigation systems made it possible to support substantial populations and complex administrative structures. With urbanization came more developed economies and trade, while competition between cities led to warfare and the first empires.

May a citizen who has been wronged and is involved in a lawsuit come before my statue named 'King of Justice', may he read my law code, may my law code make clear the law for him, may he see his judgement, may he let his heart breathe easily and say 'Hammurabi, the lord, who exists for the people like a true father, has cared at the command of his lord, Marduk, pleased the heart of his lord Marduk and determined the well-being of his people for ever, and helped the land obtain justice.'

Hammurabi (1728–1686 BC)
Law Code

The earliest cities appeared in Mesopotamia in the second half of the 4th millennium BC: at Uruk, Ur, Tell 'Uqair and Susa vast and elaborately decorated ceremonial complexes were built as the centres of urban settlements, probably under the leadership of families eager to display their power and their respect for the gods. The fertile plains and valleys watered by the Tigris and the Euphrates produced food surpluses sufficient to support these elaborate new centres and their complex social structures.

The cities were the basic political units of Mesopotamia. Religion was fundamental to their social organization: the rulers of cities presented themselves as favoured servants of the gods, while lower down the social scale agricultural workers had a necessary role in producing the materials for sacrifices and offerings to the gods. The cities established diplomatic and trade relationships with each other, although little is known of the mechanisms for this. Finds of goods from Uruk, the predominant city in Mespotamia from around 3500 BC have come from as far afield as Susa and Syria. The effect of trade and gift-exchange between cities encouraged the development of a common culture from the edges of the Persian Gulf to Mari in the northwest and Ashur in the north. Although other languages were spoken, the early use of Sumerian as a written language has led to the use of the term 'Sumerian' to describe the culture

1 Mesopotamia occupies a key position *(map below)* on the lines of communication between the central Asia and Europe and between the Persian Gulf and the Mediterranean. Southern Mesopotamia had no sources of metals, and the need to ensure the supply of bronze and other goods including timber was an important stimulus for military campaigns and imperialism. Although the rulers of Agade and Ur gained control over large territories, they did not establish new imperial identities to replace loyalty to individual cities.

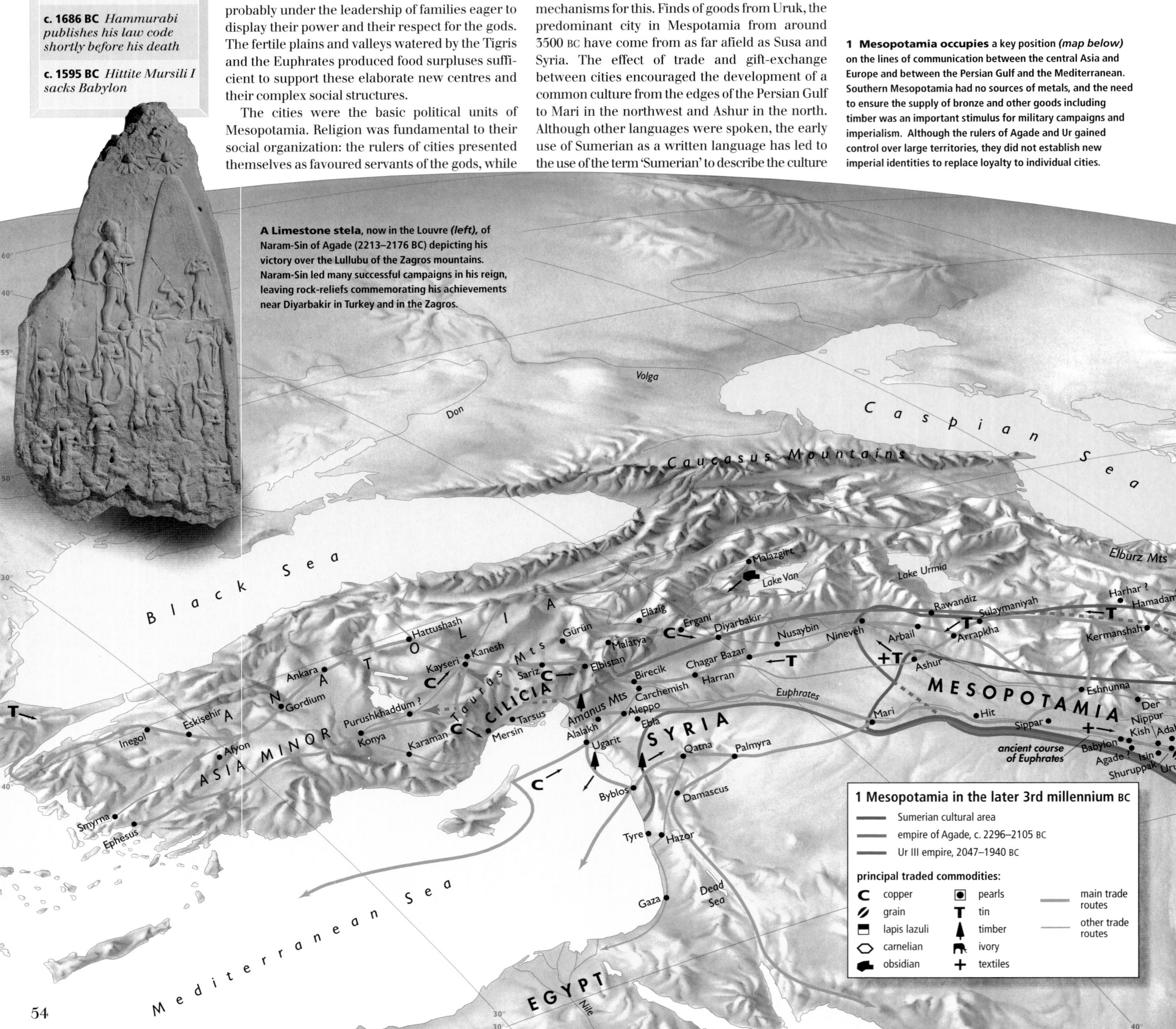

A Limestone stela, now in the Louvre *(left)*, of Naram-Sin of Agade (2213–2176 BC) depicting his victory over the Lullubu of the Zagros mountains. Naram-Sin led many successful campaigns in his reign, leaving rock-reliefs commemorating his achievements near Diyarbakir in Turkey and in the Zagros.

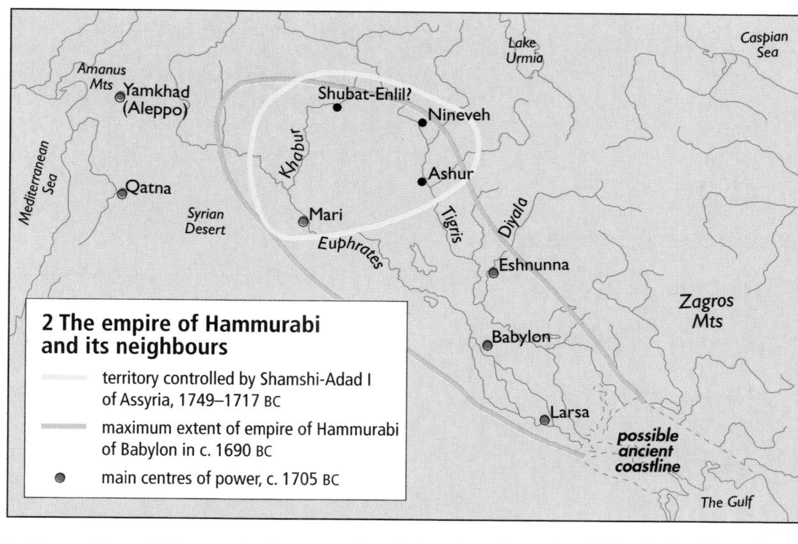

2 The politics of Mesopotamia in the 18th century BC was characterized by shifting alliances between the rulers of the major cities *(map above)*. Shamshi-Adad I seized control of Ashur and carved out an empire in northern Mesopotamia, while establishing good relations with cities to the south. His former ally Hammurabi of Babylon later absorbed Assyria into his own empire.

and society of early and middle 3rd millennium.

The empire of Agade

Towards the end of the 3rd millennium powerful leaders attempted to expand their influence over a wider area. The first was Sargon (c. 2296–2240 BC), who created a new political centre at Agade, also known as Akkad, before conquering the cities of southern Mesopotamia and claiming authority over areas as far west as Byblos. The empire of Agade was enlarged by Sargon's grandson Naram-Sin (2213–2176 BC), but within a generation of his death it had disappeared, as its subject cities reasserted their independence. The rise of Agade had long-lasting effects on the region, with Akkadian (whose variants included Babylonian and Assyrian) replacing Sumerian as the main language of Mesopotamia.

A century later the rulers of the Third Dynasty of Ur (Ur III: 2047–1940 BC), beginning with Ur-Nammu, built an empire in southern Mesopotamia, but in common with the other early Mesopotamian empires it was not long-lasting and its decline left a number of important cities competing for power. The centre of activity moved to northern Mesopotamia, and a new elite emerged – the Amorites – who had previously been excluded from power. The most successful Amorite leader was Shamshi-Adad I, who established a short-lived empire in Assyria in the years after 1750 BC. After his death the region returned to a period of competing rulers, as reflected by the assessment of an advisor to Zimri-Lim of Mari (c. 1714–1700 BC): 'There is no king who is strong by himself: 10 or 15 kings follow Hammurabi of Babylon, as many follow Rim-Sin of Larsa, Ibalpiel of Eshnunna and Amutpiel of Qatna, while 20 kings follow Yarim-Lim of Yamkhad.' Soon after this Hammurabi was able to establish an empire of his own, and Babylon became a leading power in the region for the first time.

The law code of Hammurabi

Hammurabi is most famous for his law code, inscribed on a large stone with a carving of the king in the presence of Shamash, the Babylonian sun-god. Although it is presented as a practical collection of laws including the principle of punishment with 'an eye for an eye', the primary function of the document was probably to advertize the achievements of Hammurabi's reign. After his death, his successors in the First Dynasty of Babylon ruled for about 90 years before the city was raided by the Hittites, and a new phase in the history of Mesopotamia began (*see* p. 58).

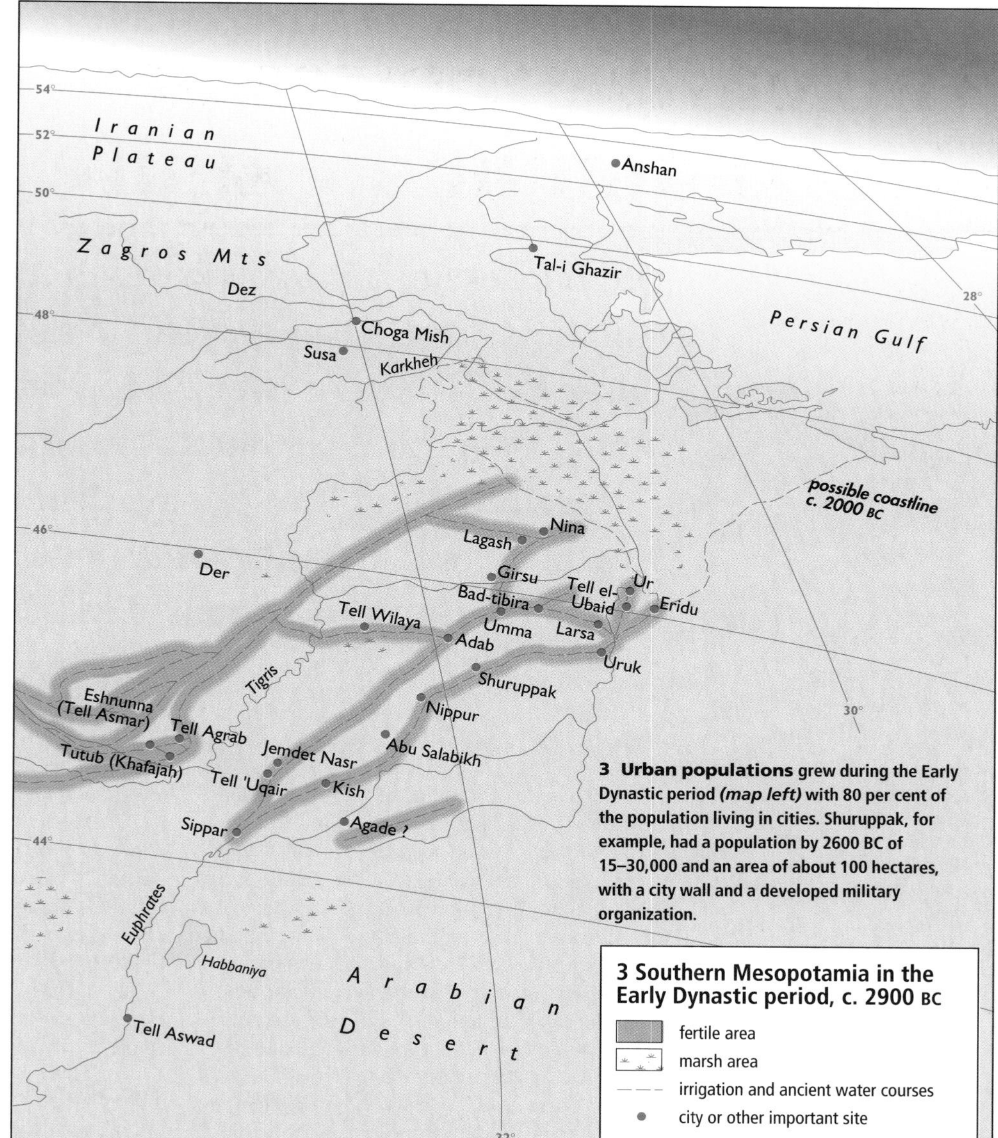

3 Urban populations grew during the Early Dynastic period *(map left)* with 80 per cent of the population living in cities. Shuruppak, for example, had a population by 2600 BC of 15–30,000 and an area of about 100 hectares, with a city wall and a developed military organization.

3100 to 30 BC
Ancient Egypt: civilization and empire

See also
African peoples and cultures to AD 1000 p. 42
The beginnings of civilization in the Eurasian world, 3500–1500 BC p. 52
The Near East, 1600–539 BC p. 58
The empires of Persia, 550 BC–AD 637 p. 74
The Hellenistic world, 336–30 BC p. 78

c. 3100 BC *Traditional date of unification of Egypt under Menes*

c. 2590 BC *Cheops builds great pyramid at Giza*

c. 1990 BC *Egyptian conquests of Nubia begin*

c. 1648–1540 BC *Hyksos control Egypt*

c. 1550 BC *Egyptian conquests of Palestine and Syria begin*

c. 1360 BC *Akhenaten builds new capital, Akhetaten*

1152 BC *Death of Ramses III, last great pharaoh of Egypt*

525 BC *Persians under Cambyses invade Egypt*

332 BC *Alexander the Great conquers Egypt*

The harnessing of the Nile's annual floods to irrigate the fields on its banks made possible a civilization that was to last for over 25 centuries. Though the history of the Egyptian state is one of successive periods of unification and disintegration, the language, religion and culture of Egypt demonstrate a continuity unequalled in the Near East.

EGYPT'S HISTORY is usually divided into 32 dynasties, a scheme deriving from the 3rd century BC Egyptian historian Manetho. He followed a New Kingdom tradition that Egypt was created when the first pharaoh, Menes, united the lands of Upper and Lower Egypt. However, archaeological evidence suggests that Egypt emerged gradually as a single state in the Early Dynastic period, possibly as a result of growing desertification and the concentration of the population along the Nile valley. The increasing requirement for irrigation works led to the emergence of local rulers, and ultimately the merging of their territories into a state with a single ruler.

The first period of Egyptian unity, the Old Kingdom, lasted for 500 years. It was at this time that writing in hieroglyphic script was invented. Memphis was the centre of administration, and around it the pharaohs of the 3rd and 4th Dynasties built their massive pyramid tombs. The great pyramids of Cheops and his successors were not emulated by the following dynasties, who put their resources into building vast temples to the sun-god Re, and introduced the practice of including the term 'son of Re' in their names. At the end of the 6th Dynasty, for reasons which are unclear, rule from Memphis broke down. There followed a period of disorder and civil war with rival rulers based at Herakleopolis (9th to 10th Dynasties) and Thebes (11th Dynasty), which was ended when Mentuhotep II (2060–2010 BC) reunited the entire country.

The Middle and New Kingdoms

In the following period, the Middle Kingdom, Thebes emerged as a major centre, its local god, Amun, now identified with Re. The state was administered from El-Lisht, near Memphis, where its rulers were buried. Under the 12th Dynasty military advances were made in the south (*see* map 3) and diplomatic and trading relations established with the Levant in the north. It was now that classical styles of Egyptian literature were developed, while the forms of hieroglyphic writing became the model for later periods.

During the 13th Dynasty, centralized rule of Egypt broke down once more. The delta appears to have been divided into small areas ruled by princelets (14th Dynasty) before the whole of Egypt as far south as Koptos was taken over by foreign rulers, called by the Egyptians 'Hyksos' (15th Dynasty). The Hyksos governed from Avaris in the eastern Delta with their vassal kings (16th Dynasty) while a small independent southern kingdom was ruled from Thebes (17th Dynasty). New Kingdom propaganda is hostile to the Hyksos, portraying them as oppressive. But there is no reason to suppose that their rule was harmful to Egypt's development, and they may have been responsible for introducing two-wheeled chariots and bronze-working into the country.

Hyksos rule was brought to an end by Kamose, last king of the 17th Dynasty, and his brother Amose, first king of the 18th Dynasty, who expanded their control northwards from Thebes, eventually taking over the whole delta. Their achievements were built upon by Amose's successors, who conquered territory to the north and south of Egypt (*see* maps 2 and 3). Queen Hatshepsut (1490–1469 BC), regent for Tuthmosis III, also sent an expedition by sea to Eritrea.

This period of imperial expansion was matched by construction works in Egypt. Under Tuthmosis I Memphis was re-established as the centre of administration and Thebes was largely rebuilt, with a vast temple complex created for Amun-Re at Karnak where the Valley of the Kings became the burial place for New Kingdom pharaohs. The cult of the sun-god, in the form of the solar disc, called the Aten, reached a peak under Amenophis IV, who renamed himself Akhenaten ('he who is beneficial to the Aten'), and built a new city, Akhetaten, at el-Amarna. The emphasis on the Aten led to a decline in the worship of the other Egyptian gods, though this was reversed after Akhenaten's death, possibly in response to an outbreak of plague which killed several members of the royal family and which was taken as a sign of the displeasure of the old gods.

Disunity and conquest

Although Egypt reached a height of wealth and influence under Ramses II (1290–1224 BC) it did not escape the upheaval that affected the whole of the Near East at the end of the Bronze Age. The end of the New Kingdom in 1069 BC was followed by four centuries of disunity, with external rule from Libya, Nubia and Assyria, before Psammetichus I (664–610 BC) was able to reunite the country.

In the following century Egypt was conquered by the Persians and although it regained independence between 404 and 341 BC, it was only under the Ptolemies (323–30 BC), a dynasty originated by one of Alexander the Great's conquering generals (*see* p. 78), that it again became a significant power.

HOW MANY ARE YOUR DEEDS
THOUGH UNKNOWN TO US,
O SOLE GOD WHO HAS NO EQUAL!
YOU MADE THE WORLD IN YOUR FASHION,
YOU ALONE,
ALL MEN, HERDS AND WILD BEASTS
ALL THAT IS ON EARTH AND WALKS ON LEGS,
ALL THAT IS IN THE AIR AND FLIES
WITH WINGS OUTSTRETCHED,
ALL THE FOREIGN LANDS,
FROM SYRIA TO THE SUDAN,
AND THE LAND OF EGYPT.

Akhenaten (1364–1347 BC)
The Great Hymn to the Sun

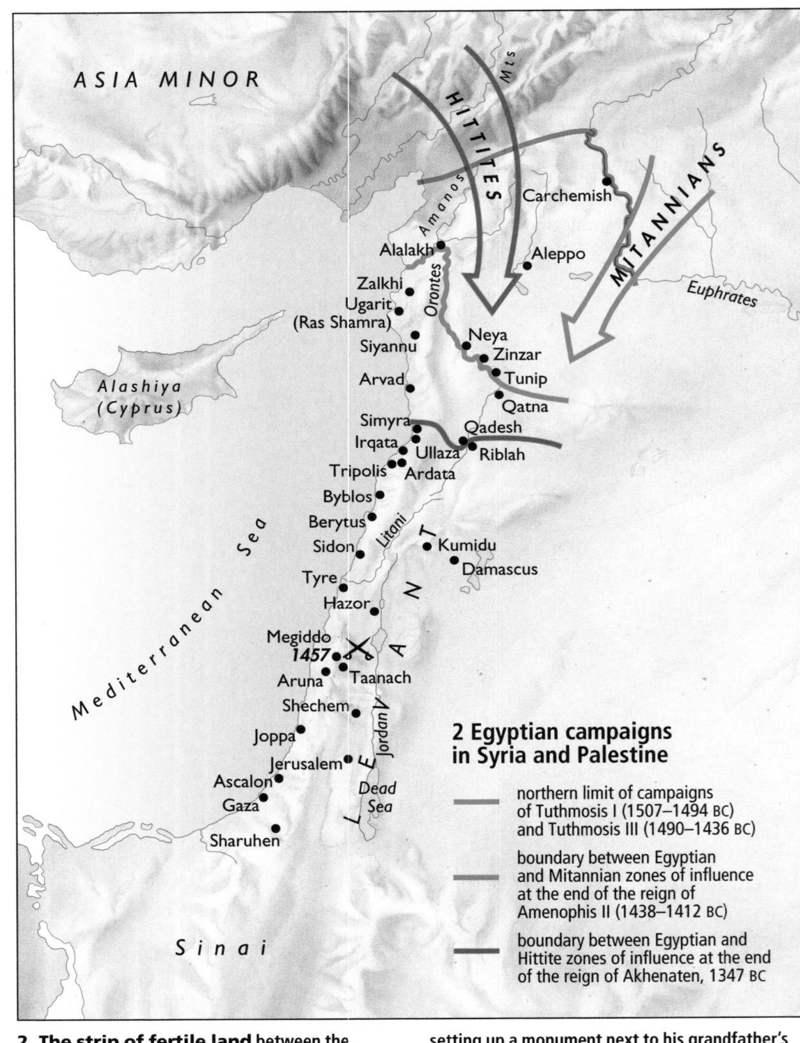

2 The strip of fertile land between the Mediterranean and the Syrian desert was a target for Egyptian imperialism ***(map above)***, beginning with the campaigns of the early pharaohs of the 18th Dynasty. By the reign of Tuthmosis I, Egypt's power reached north from the Third Cataract in Nubia to the Euphrates. His grandson, Tuthmosis III, fought 17 campaigns in Palestine and Syria, setting up a monument next to his grandfather's on the Euphrates in the region of Carchemish. Boundaries were established by treaties first with the land of Mitanni, later with the Hittites. After much of this empire had crumbled away in the next 130 years, Seti I and Ramses II recovered some of the region. But all these territories were lost after the reign of Ramses VI (1142–1134).

THE DYNASTIES OF ANCIENT EGYPT

Early Dynastic, 3100–2686 BC
1st Dynasty, 3100–2890 BC
2nd Dynasty, 2890–2686 BC

Old Kingdom, 2686–2181 BC
3rd Dynasty, 2686–2613 BC
4th Dynasty, 2613–2494 BC
Cheops (Khufu)
5th Dynasty, 2494–2345 BC
6th Dynasty, 2345–2181 BC

First Intermediate Period, 2180–2040 BC
7th Dynasty, 2181–2173 BC
8th Dynasty, 2173–2160 BC
9th and 10th Dynasties, 2160–2040 BC

Middle Kingdom, 2040–1730 BC
11th Dynasty, 2040–1991 BC
12th Dynasty, 1991–1783 BC
Sesostris I (1971–1926 BC)
Sesostris III (1878–1841 BC)
13th Dynasty, 1783–1730

Second Intermediate Period, 1730–1552 BC
13th Dynasty, 1730–1648 BC
14th Dynasty, 1720–1648 BC
15th Dynasty, 1648–1540 BC
16th Dynasty, 1648–1540 BC
17th Dynasty, 1648–1552 BC

New Kingdom, 1552–1069 BC
18th Dynasty, 1552–1306 BC
Amenophis I (1527–1507 BC)
Tuthmosis I (1507–1494 BC)
Tuthmosis III (1490–1436 BC)
Amenophis II (1436–1412 BC)
Akhenaten (1364–1347 BC)
Tutankhamun (1345–1335 BC)
19th Dynasty, 1306–1187 BC
Ramses II (1290–1224 BC)
20th Dynasty, 1186–1069
Ramses III (1184–1152)

Third Intermediate Period, 1069–664 BC
21st Dynasty, 1069–945 BC
22nd Dynasty, 945–712 BC
23rd Dynasty, 828–712 BC
24th Dynasty, 724–712 BC
25th Dynasty, 770–664 BC

Late Period, 664–30 BC
26th Dynasty, 664–525 BC
27th Dynasty, 525–404 BC
28th Dynasty, 404–399 BC
29th Dynasty, 399–379 BC
30th Dynasty, 379–341 BC
31st Dynasty, 341–332 BC
32nd Dynasty, 332–30 BC

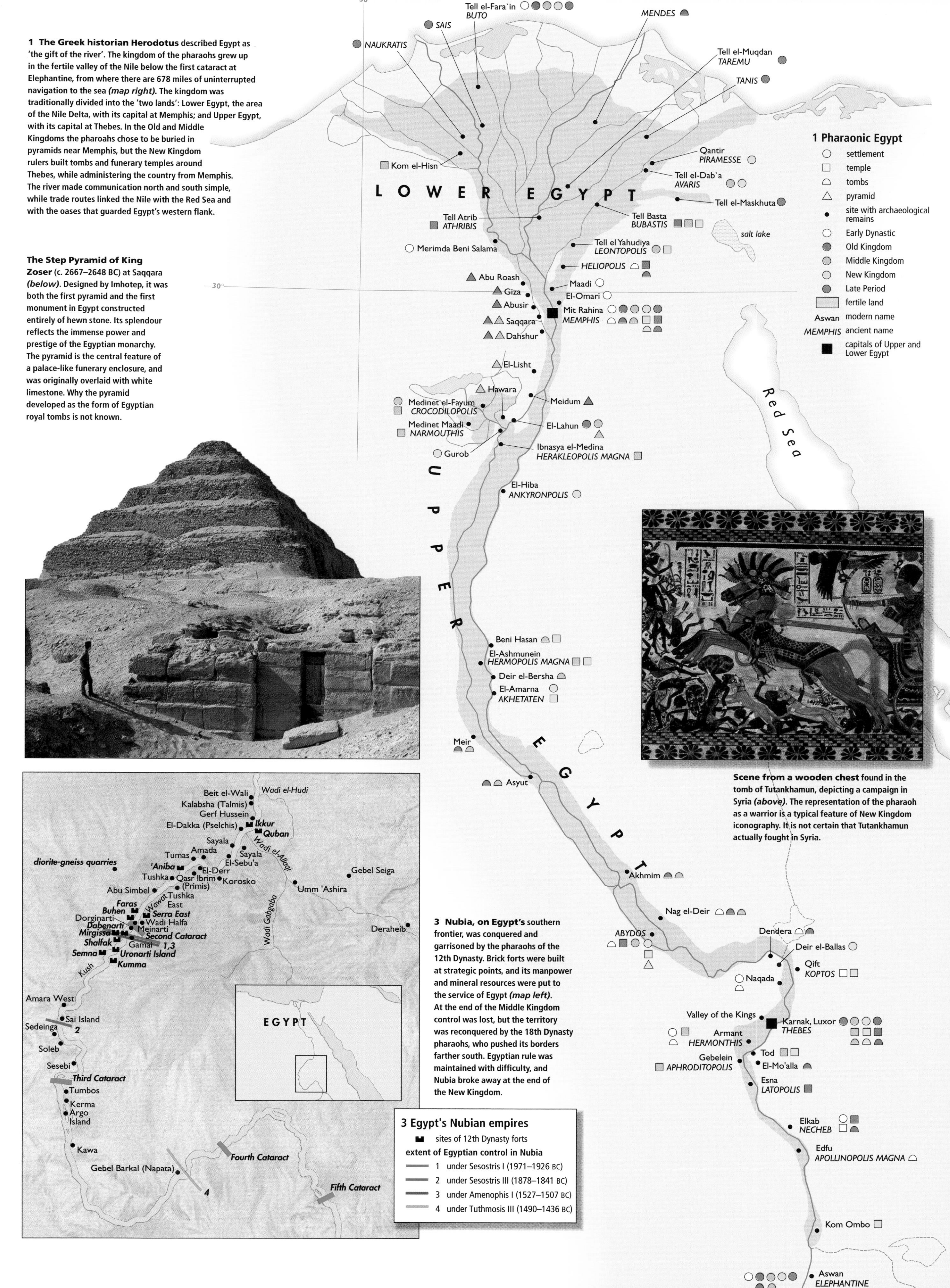

1 The Greek historian Herodotus described Egypt as 'the gift of the river'. The kingdom of the pharaohs grew up in the fertile valley of the Nile below the first cataract at Elephantine, from where there are 678 miles of uninterrupted navigation to the sea *(map right)*. The kingdom was traditionally divided into the 'two lands': Lower Egypt, the area of the Nile Delta, with its capital at Memphis; and Upper Egypt, with its capital at Thebes. In the Old and Middle Kingdoms the pharoahs chose to be buried in pyramids near Memphis, but the New Kingdom rulers built tombs and funerary temples around Thebes, while administering the country from Memphis. The river made communication north and south simple, while trade routes linked the Nile with the Red Sea and with the oases that guarded Egypt's western flank.

The Step Pyramid of King Zoser (c. 2667–2648 BC) at Saqqara *(below)*. Designed by Imhotep, it was both the first pyramid and the first monument in Egypt constructed entirely of hewn stone. Its splendour reflects the immense power and prestige of the Egyptian monarchy. The pyramid is the central feature of a palace-like funerary enclosure, and was originally overlaid with white limestone. Why the pyramid developed as the form of Egyptian royal tombs is not known.

Scene from a wooden chest found in the tomb of Tutankhamun, depicting a campaign in Syria *(above)*. The representation of the pharaoh as a warrior is a typical feature of New Kingdom iconography. It is not certain that Tutankhamun actually fought in Syria.

3 Nubia, on Egypt's southern frontier, was conquered and garrisoned by the pharaohs of the 12th Dynasty. Brick forts were built at strategic points, and its manpower and mineral resources were put to the service of Egypt *(map left)*. At the end of the Middle Kingdom control was lost, but the territory was reconquered by the 18th Dynasty pharaohs, who pushed its borders farther south. Egyptian rule was maintained with difficulty, and Nubia broke away at the end of the New Kingdom.

1600 to 539 BC

The Near East

See also

The early empires of Mesopotamia c. 3500–1600 BC p. 54

Ancient Egypt: civilization and empire p. 56

Minoan and Mycenaean civilizations c. 3000–950 BC p. 66

The empires of Persia, 550 BC–AD 637 p. 74

c. 1420 BC *Tudhaliya I begins expansion of Hittite power*

c. 1390 BC *Amenophis III of Egypt marries the daughter of Kassite King Kurigalzu I of Babylon*

1275 BC *Battle of Kadesh between Ramses II of Egypt and the Hittites*

c. 1025 BC *Emergence of Israelite kingdom*

934 BC *Ashur-dan II begins Assyrian recovery*

671–656 BC *Assyrians gain temporary control of Egypt*

612 BC *Nabopolassar of Babylon sacks Nineveh*

539 BC *Cyrus the Great of Persia captures Babylon*

The period after 1600 BC saw the fertile lands of Mesopotamia and the Levant become the battleground between rival empires: Egyptians, Hittites, Mitannians, Assyrians, Babylonians and Elamites. Following the collapse of these powers in the 12th century, Assyria re-emerged as the region's greatest power until it was overthrown by Babylon, soon to be conquered in its turn by the Persians.

I BROUGHT BACK THE EXHAUSTED PEOPLE OF ASSYRIA WHO HAD ABANDONED THEIR CITIES AND HOUSES IN THE FACE OF WANT, HUNGER AND FAMINE, AND HAD GONE UP TO OTHER LANDS. I SETTLED THEM IN CITIES AND HOUSES WHICH WERE SUITABLE AND THEY DWELT IN PEACE. I CONSTRUCTED PALACES IN THE DISTRICTS OF MY LAND. I HITCHED UP PLOUGHS IN THE DISTRICTS OF MY LAND AND PILED UP MORE GRAIN THAN EVER BEFORE. I HITCHED UP MANY TEAMS OF HORSES FOR THE FORCES OF ASSYRIA.

Ashur-dan II (934–912 BC)

AFTER THE FALL of the first dynasty of Babylon in c.1595 BC (*see* p. 54), the city came under the control of the Kassites, who probably originally inhabited the Zagros mountains. They held it for nearly 400 years and established diplomatic relations with Egypt, but were increasingly threatened by the growing power of their neighbours, Elam and Assyria.

In Anatolia the Hittites had been expanding their power from their centre at Hattushash since the reign of Hattusili I (c. 1650–c. 1620 BC). Mursili I (c. 1620–c. 1590 BC) led an expedition that destroyed Aleppo and Babylon, but it was Tudhaliya I (c. 1420–1400 BC) and Suppiluliuma I (1344–1322 BC) who made the Hittites an imperial power, bringing them into conflict with Mitanni on the upper Euphrates, and then with the 18th Dynasty pharaohs of Egypt (*see* p. 56). The kingdom of Mitanni became the Hittites' main opponent to the east, and for about 140 years it dominated Syria and the surrounding area until internal disorder and Hittite pressure led to its collapse in c. 1340 BC.

The remnants of Mitanni then became a buffer for the Hittites against the growing power of the Assyrians, until its conquest by the Assyrian ruler Adad-nirari I (1295–1264 BC). Assyrian expansion had started under Ashur-uballit I (1353–1318 BC), and continued under Tikulti-ninurta I (1233–1197 BC) who marched on Babylon and installed a series of puppet rulers, actions that led to a damaging counter-invasion from Elam .

Collapse of the Bronze Age empires

No universally accepted explanation has been found for the crises in the 12th and 11th centuries that affected the powers of the region from Greece (*see* p. 66) to Elam. Raids by the 'sea peoples' are reported in Egyptian texts, but it is more likely that political collapse was the result of other factors, perhaps a break in the supply of the copper and tin needed for making bronze. The peoples living in the territories previously under imperial control took advantage of the situation to develop their own states: Aramaeans and Chaldaeans in the fertile Levant-Mesopotamia crescent (*see* map 2), Phrygians in Anatolia and Persians east of Elam.

One of the new Aramaean states was the Israelite kingdom, a confederation of smaller groups united under David (c. 1000–c. 960 BC) and Solomon (c. 960–c. 922 BC). After Solomon's death the kingdom was divided, and in 722 BC the northern part was destroyed by the Assyrians, while Nebuchadnezzar II of Babylon sacked the capital of the southern kingdom, Jerusalem, in 587 BC. Meanwhile, from the 9th to the 7th centuries the kingdom of Urartu in the mountainous area around Lake Van, north of Assyria, rapidly expanded, came into conflict with the Assyrians, then just as rapidly disappeared.

The revival of Assyria

Babylon and Assyria weathered the storms of the 12th and 11th centuries, with greatly reduced territories, and the 10th century saw the beginning of Assyrian recovery (*see* map 3). In the following century Ashurnasirpal II (883–859 BC) sent his armies north and west and used the wealth they gained to build a spectacular new palace at Nimrud. Even greater gains were made by Tiglath-pileser III (744–727 BC) and Sargon II (721–705 BC) who annexed Babylonia and conquered the

1 The second half of the 2nd millennium saw the growth of a number of competing powers in the Near East. The map *(below)* indicates the territorial position in c. 1330 BC. To the west, New Kingdom Egypt fought for control of Syria-Palestine first with Mitanni and then with the Hittites, while to the east the Kassite kings of Babylon were increasingly threatened by the emergent powers of Assyria to the north and Elam to the east.

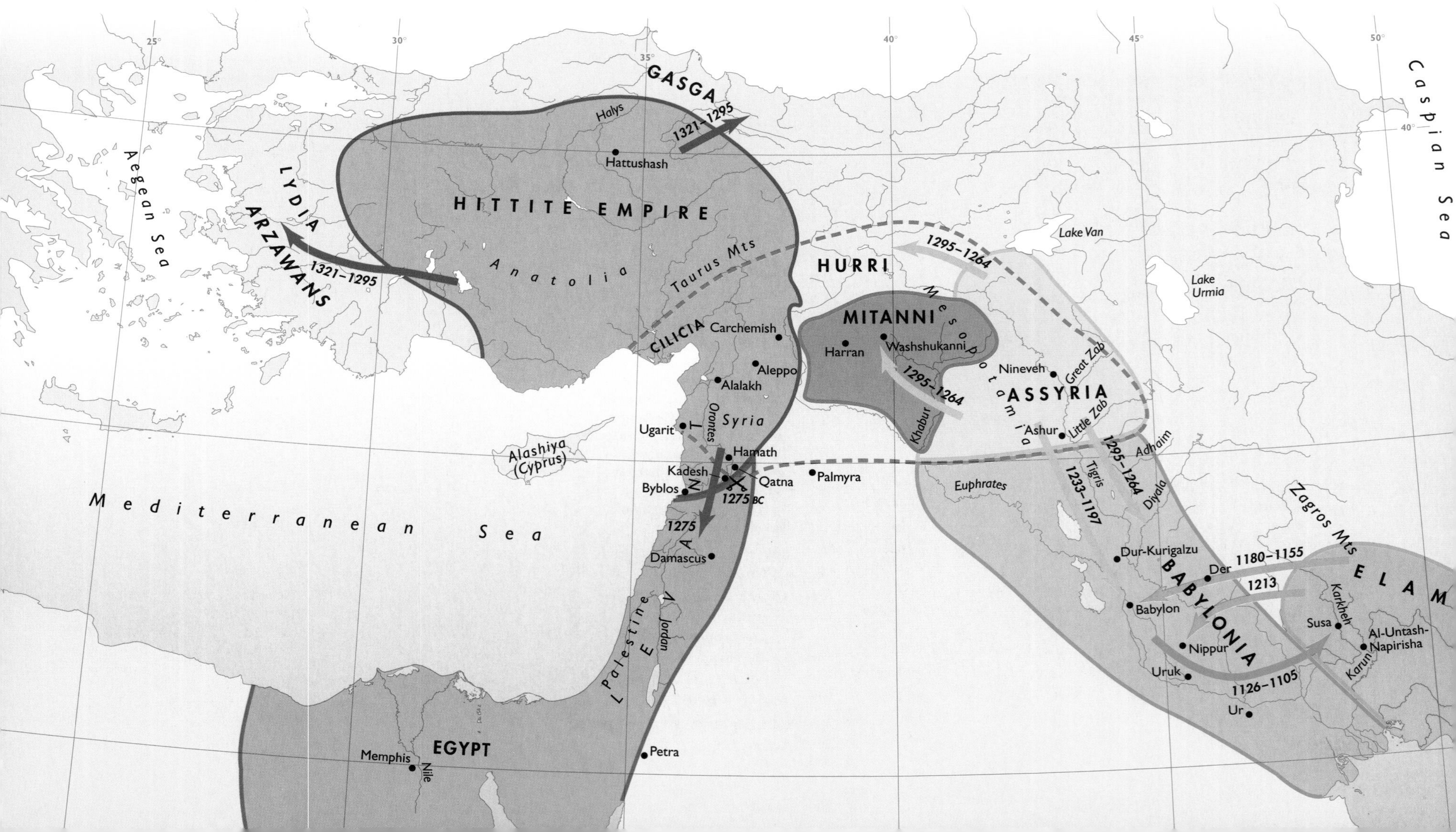

3 The Near East that emerged from the upheavals of the late Bronze Age *(map right)* was characterized by new forms of political organization. Along the Mediterranean coast city-states developed, sometimes united by powerful rulers into temporary kingdoms while to the north the new power of Urartu appeared. Meanwhile Assyria recovered to become the main power of the region, until its overthrow by the Babylonians and Medes.

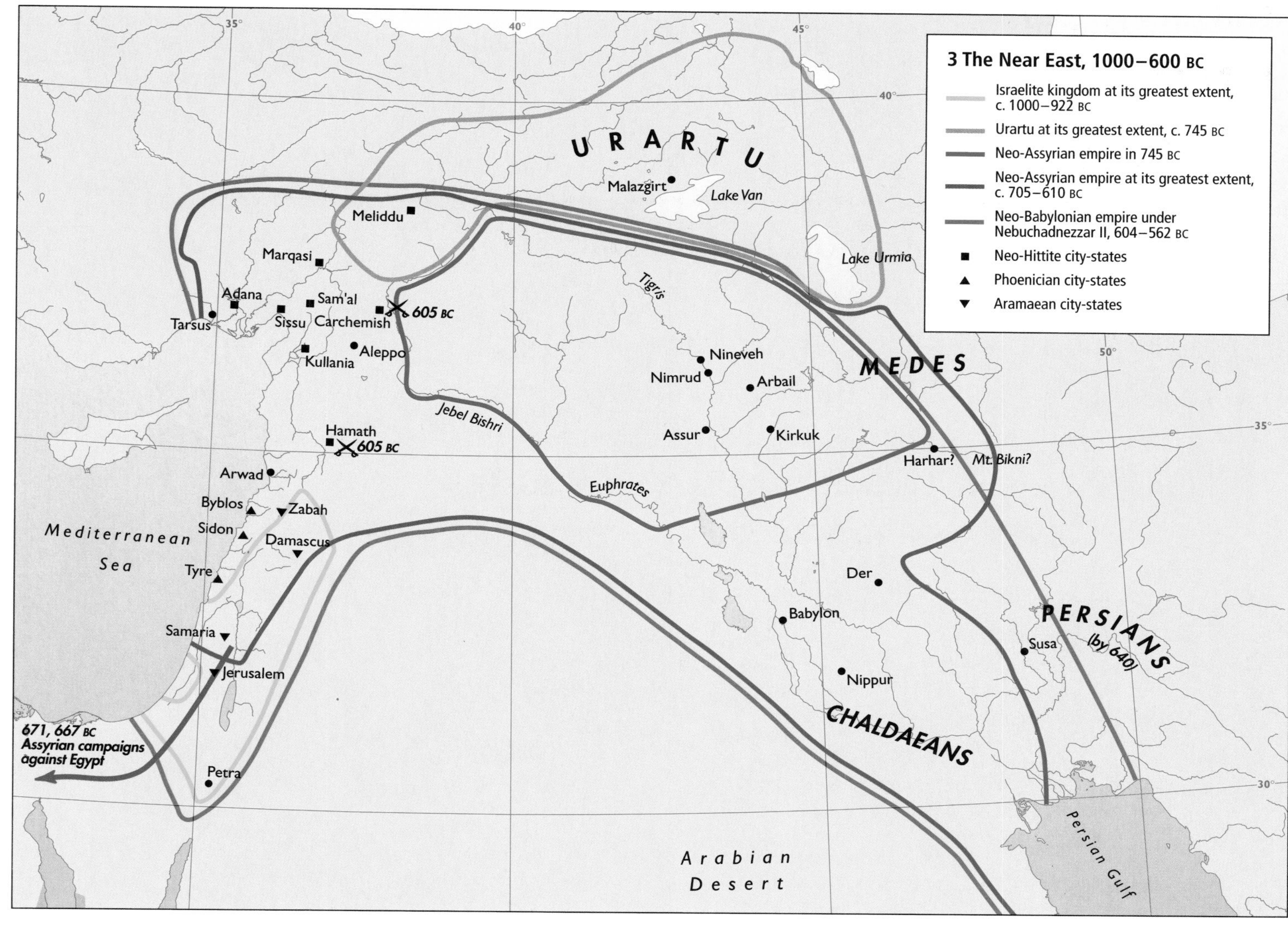

2 Between c. 1200 and c. 1050 BC a political shockwave ran through the eastern Mediterranean and Near East *(map right)*. It affected different areas in different ways, but may have resulted from a disruption of the supply of bronze weakening the hold of the ruling powers and allowing subordinate populations such as the Aramaeans, Philistines, Chaldaeans, Phrygians and Persians to establish their own governments in the ruins of the former empires.

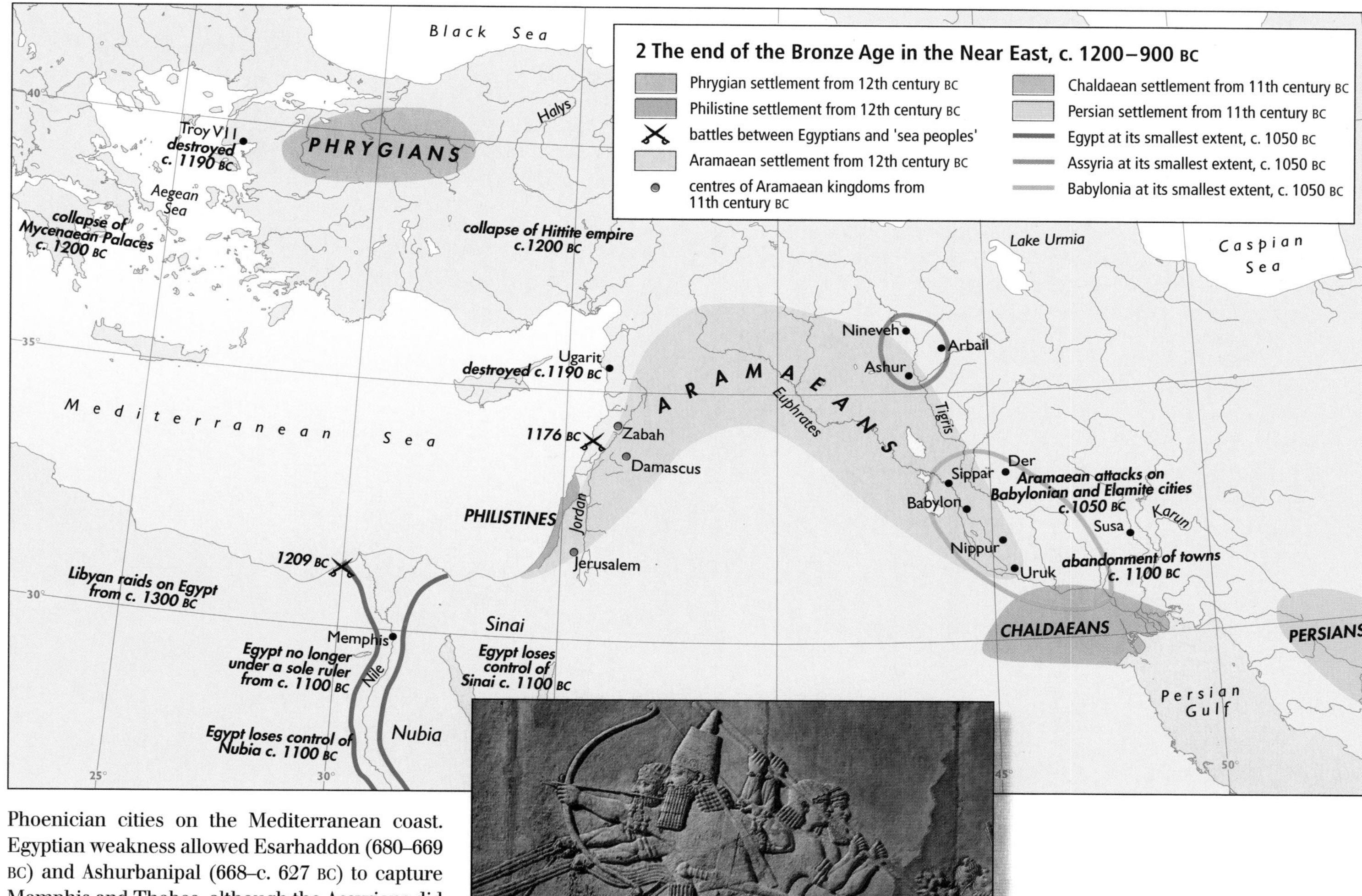

1 Kingdoms and empires, c. 1500–1100 BC

- Hittite empire established by Suppiluliuma I, 1344–1322 BC
- Mitanni territory at its greatest extent, c. 1480–1340 BC
- Mitanni after c. 1340 BC (under Hittite and Assyrian control)
- Assyrian territory gained by Ashur-uballit I, 1353–1318 BC
- Babylonia under Burnaburiash II, 1347–1321 BC
- Elam under Tepti-ahar, c. 1353–1318 BC
- Egypt under Amenophis IV and Tutankhamun, 1352–1335 BC

Anshan

Phoenician cities on the Mediterranean coast. Egyptian weakness allowed Esarhaddon (680–669 BC) and Ashurbanipal (668–c. 627 BC) to capture Memphis and Thebes, although the Assyrians did not attempt to formalize their control of Egypt.

Assyrian control of Babylonia was never secure: the Babylonian king, Nabopolassar (626–605 BC), rebelled and, aided by the Medes, sacked the major Assyrian cities including Ashur and Nineveh. The Babylonians inherited the Assyrian empire, but had to fight to keep it. In 605 BC the Egyptians attempted to annex Syria, but were defeated at Carchemish and Hamath. Nebuchadnezzar (604–562 BC) consolidated Babylonian rule, but his successors were unable to maintain the position, and Babylon fell to the Persians in 539 BC (*see* p.74).

Relief from the palace of Ashurbanipal (668–c. 627 BC) at Nineveh showing a royal lion-hunt *(left)*. The king is using his bow while attendants armed with spears ward off a wounded animal. Depictions of the king hunting were a common subject for royal propaganda throughout the Near East, and similar scenes can be found from Egypt in the Middle and New Kingdom periods.

Peoples of the Americas

See also
Peoples of the Americas to 300 BC p. 44
The Americas on the eve of the European conquest p. 148
European voyages of discovery, 1487–1780 p. 156
The Americas, 1500–1810 p. 162

Many societies in the Americas changed little in the 2,000 years before 1300. In Mesoamerica and the Central Andes, however, complex societies were developing by the end of the first millennium BC. They then underwent cycles of growth and decline that included periods of outstanding intellectual and artistic achievement.

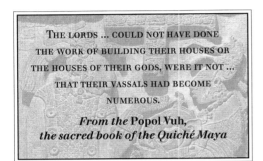

> THE LORDS ... COULD NOT HAVE DONE THE WORK OF BUILDING THEIR HOUSES OR THE HOUSES OF THEIR GODS, WERE IT NOT ... THAT THEIR VASSALS HAD BECOME NUMEROUS.
>
> *From the* Popol Vuh, *the sacred book of the Quiché Maya*

BY 300 BC, ALMOST EVERY way of life had developed in the Americas that the Europeans were later to encounter. While some societies – in western and northern North America and in southern South America – remained relatively simple, others – in Mesoamerica and in the Andes – were highly developed.

North America

In Ohio and Illinois (*see* map 3) between 250 BC and AD 400, Hopewell chiefdoms buried their dead in elaborate cemeteries with goods imported from as far as Florida and the Rockies. The addition of beans to farmers' repertoires made farming more efficient and permitted urbanization (Mississippian culture). By AD 1000, Cahokia was the biggest town, with 30,000 inhabitants. It was linked with others in southeastern North America in a ceremonial cult, the Southern Cult. By this time, too, the Pueblo villages were flourishing in the southwest, partly perhaps on the strength of trade with Mesoamerica. Climate change upset their economy but the same process encouraged new farms in the Mid West and, from Alaska to Greenland, the spread of the whale hunters of the 'Thule' culture.

Mesoamerica

Earlier developments in Mesoamerica were eclipsed in about AD 100 by the sudden rise of Teotihuacán. Its population grew eventually to some 200,000. There are doubts about the nature of the city's economy but the centre, with two mighty pyramids, was planned for rites which included extensive human sacrifice. Whether or not in association with trade, the Teotihuacános' influence spread widely. They colonized some neighbouring districts and possibly sponsored new towns further afield.

At the same time the small but brilliant kingdoms of the Maya flourished. Their capitals were pyramid-studded ceremonial centres with extensive suburbs. Voluminous inscriptions reveal a sophisticated but typically Mesoamerican concern with astrology. However, whether on account of the chronic wars that are recorded too, or of popular discontent, or of environmental degradation by excessive population – or of all of these factors – most of the towns were abandoned between 790 and the mid-9th century. Many districts revived later in what is known as the 'Post-Classic' period, but the Maya never regained their grandeur.

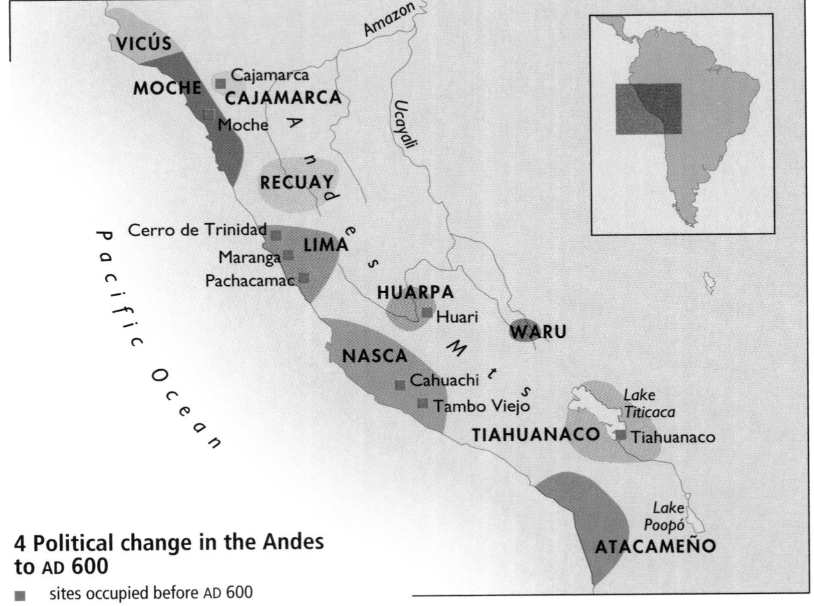

4 Political change in the Andes to AD 600
■ sites occupied before AD 600

4 & 5 By the 6th century AD each of the major regions of the Andes had its own local art style. This diversity probably reflects a lack of political unity and the existence of many independent and fragmentary states *(maps above and below)*. With soldiers, battle scenes and severed heads a frequent theme in pottery decoration, relations between these states may have been warlike. In artistic terms, the people of Moche and Nasca were supreme. After AD 600, the balance of power began to shift from the coast to the highlands, where the cities of Tiahuanaco and Huari between them came to dominate the central Andes. Except in the north, regional styles of architecture and pottery decoration fell under the influence of a single new art style whose subject matter was taken from Tiahuanaco-Huari mythology.

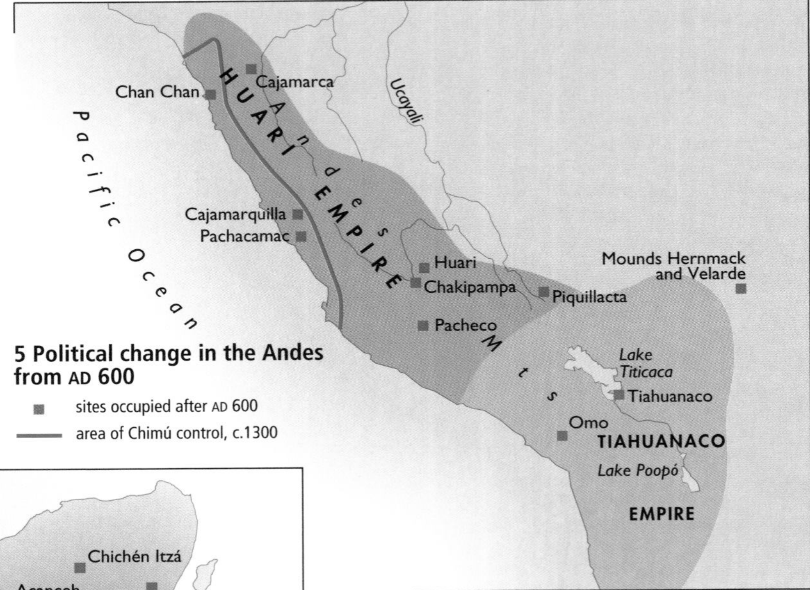

5 Political change in the Andes from AD 600
■ sites occupied after AD 600
— area of Chimú control, c.1300

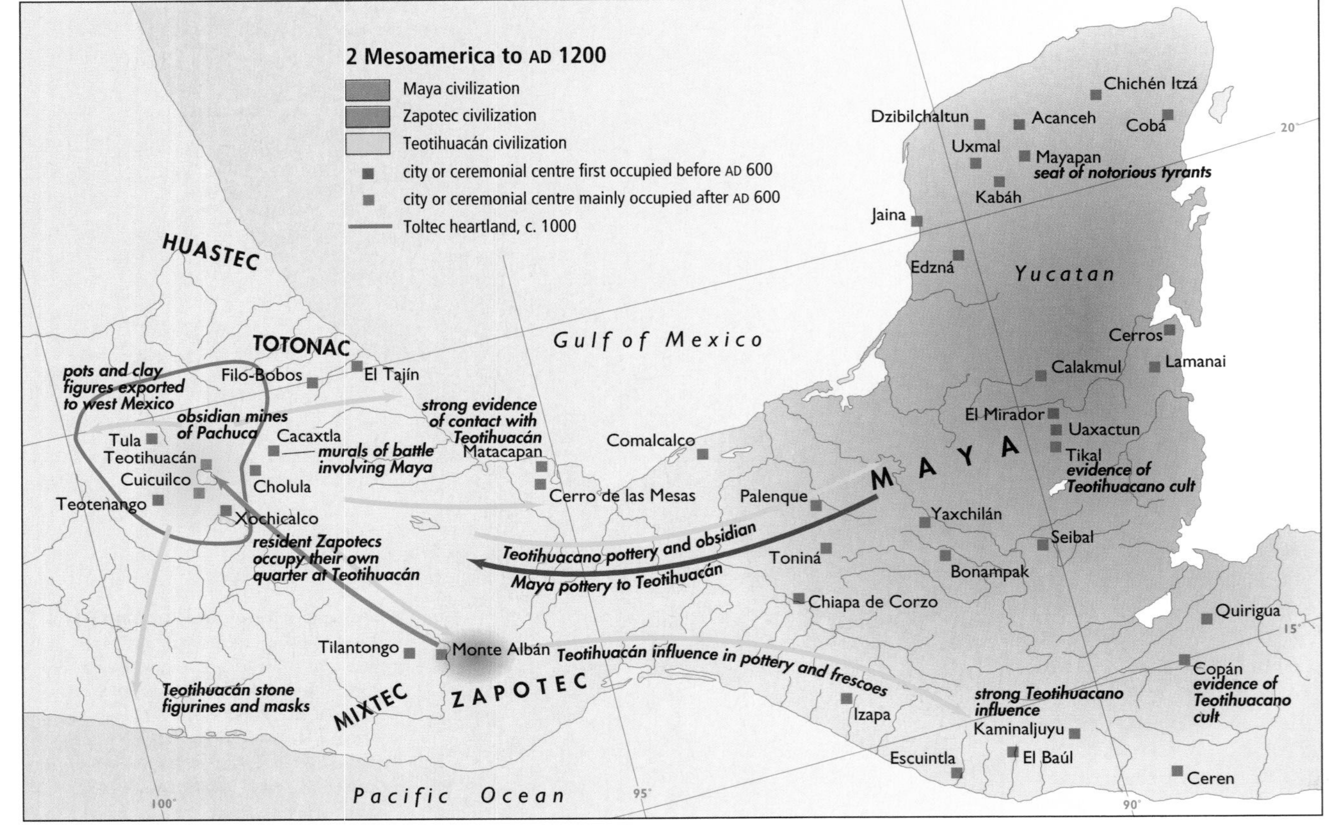

The Maya 'collapse' followed the dissolution of Teotihuacán in about 700. But between these poles of power a new generation of thriving towns had emerged, including some of Teotihuacán's protégés, that established their independence from the traditional order. They appear to have been eclipsed in turn by the Toltecs, soldiers and probably traders, whose influence subsequently extended throughout Mesoamerica and beyond. In about 1175 their reign, too, ended, possibly on account of refugees from the north escaping climatic change.

South America

In the northern Andes and southern Central America, along the Amazon and in the plains southwest of the Amazon there were other large populations. Much of the most telling evidence for them is extensive field systems. In northwestern South America and the southernmost parts of

2 By AD 250, Mesoamerica was dominated by Teotihuacán, the Maya and the Zapotecs *(map left)*. Three centuries later, new civilizations – the Totonacs, the Mixtecs and others – were emerging. From about AD 1000 another cycle began: the age of the Toltecs.

c. 300 BC *Rise of Hopewell chiefdoms in North America*

c. AD 100 *Rise of Teotihuacán*

c. AD 600 *Apogee of Maya civilization; Huari and Tiahuanaco expansion begins*

c. AD 700 *Teotihuacán destroyed*

c. AD 850 *Collapse of Maya civilization*

c. AD 1100 *Height of Pueblo culture (North America)*

c. AD 1175 *Tula abandoned by Toltecs; political fragmentation in Mesoamerica*

c. AD 1275 *Chimú conquests begin*

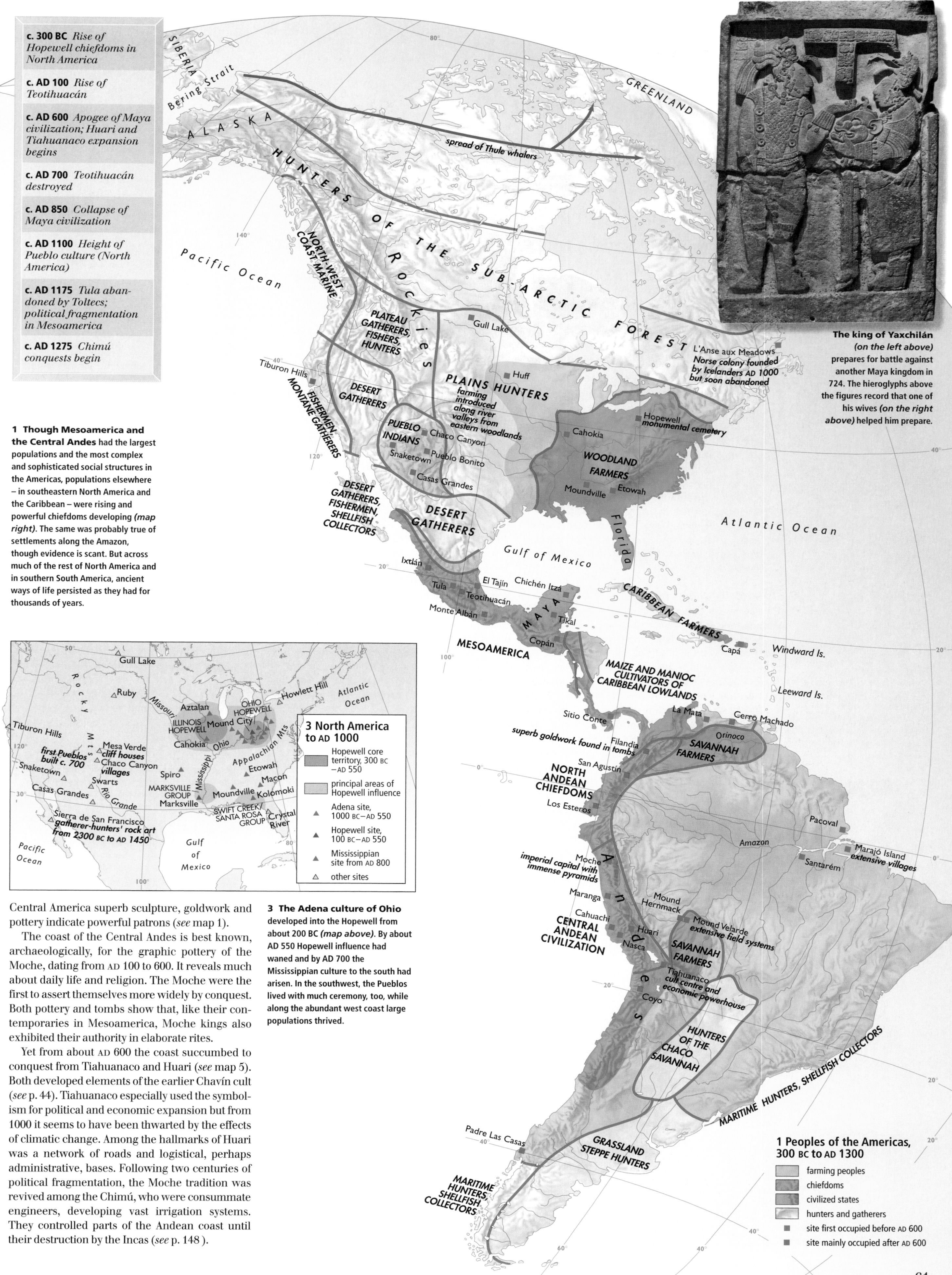

The king of Yaxchilán ***(on the left above)*** **prepares for battle against another Maya kingdom in 724. The hieroglyphs above the figures record that one of his wives** ***(on the right above)*** **helped him prepare.**

1 Though Mesoamerica and the Central Andes had the largest populations and the most complex and sophisticated social structures in the Americas, populations elsewhere – in southeastern North America and the Caribbean – were rising and powerful chiefdoms developing *(map right)*. The same was probably true of settlements along the Amazon, though evidence is scant. But across much of the rest of North America and in southern South America, ancient ways of life persisted as they had for thousands of years.

3 The Adena culture of Ohio developed into the Hopewell from about 200 BC *(map above)*. By about AD 550 Hopewell influence had waned and by AD 700 the Mississippian culture to the south had arisen. In the southwest, the Pueblos lived with much ceremony, too, while along the abundant west coast large populations thrived.

Central America superb sculpture, goldwork and pottery indicate powerful patrons (*see* map 1).

The coast of the Central Andes is best known, archaeologically, for the graphic pottery of the Moche, dating from AD 100 to 600. It reveals much about daily life and religion. The Moche were the first to assert themselves more widely by conquest. Both pottery and tombs show that, like their contemporaries in Mesoamerica, Moche kings also exhibited their authority in elaborate rites.

Yet from about AD 600 the coast succumbed to conquest from Tiahuanaco and Huari (*see* map 5). Both developed elements of the earlier Chavín cult (*see* p. 44). Tiahuanaco especially used the symbolism for political and economic expansion but from 1000 it seems to have been thwarted by the effects of climatic change. Among the hallmarks of Huari was a network of roads and logistical, perhaps administrative, bases. Following two centuries of political fragmentation, the Moche tradition was revived among the Chimú, who were consummate engineers, developing vast irrigation systems. They controlled parts of the Andean coast until their destruction by the Incas (*see* p. 148).

To 475 BC

The beginnings of Chinese civilization

See also
Human origins p. 30
The spread of modern humans p. 32
The beginnings of civilization in the Eurasian world, 3500–1500 BC p. 52
The unification of China, 475 BC–AD 220 p. 80

c. 2,000,000 BC *Earliest archaeologically proven hominine activity in China*

c. 500,000 BC *Emergence of 'Peking Man'*

c. 30,000 BC *Emergence of* Homo sapiens *in China*

c. 30,000–7500 BC *Palaeolithic period*

c. 7500–3500 BC *Neolithic period*

c. 2500–1800 BC *Longshan period*

c. 1600 BC *Start of the Bronze Age in China*

c. 1520–1030 BC *Shang dynasty*

c. 1030–771 BC *Chou dynasty*

770–476 BC *Spring and Autumn period*

Geographically and climatically China has a range of favourable conditions for human settlement, which took place 500,000 years ago. A turning point was reached at about 1600 BC when China entered the Bronze Age. It was then that Chinese culture took shape, as written languages, philosophies and stable socio-political and economic structures gradually emerged.

A COUNTRY OF A THOUSAND WAR-CHARIOTS CANNOT BE ADMINISTERED UNLESS THE RULER ATTENDS STRICTLY TO BUSINESS, PUNCTUALLY OBSERVES HIS PROMISES, IS ECONOMICAL IN EXPENDITURE, SHOWS AFFECTION TOWARDS HIS SUBJECTS IN GENERAL, AND USES THE LABOUR OF THE PEASANTRY ONLY AT THE PROPER TIMES OF THE YEAR.

Confucius, 551–479 BC
Analects

CHINA HAS BEEN INHABITED continuously by humans since very early times. Remains of early hominines, which are similar to those from Java, have been found across large areas of southeast China. In about 500,000 BC Peking Man – *Homo erectus* – was living around Po Hai and in the southeast and possibly in central and southern China as well. *Homo sapiens* first appeared in Palaeolithic cultures in the Ordos region, in the north and in the southwest in about 30,000 BC (*see* p. 30). Later Mesolithic cultures flourished in the north, south and southwest and in Taiwan (*see* p. 32).

Early agriculturalists

Neolithic agricultural communities, the immediate ancestors of Chinese civilization, arose around 7500 BC in what is now southern China and in the loess-covered lands of the north and northeast, where the well-drained soil of the river terraces was ideal for primitive agriculture (*see* map 1). One of the best early sites is Pan-p'o, with round and rectangular houses, pottery kilns and a cemetery area. In the valley of the Yellow River, early agriculture depended heavily on millet, but in the Yangtze delta area evidence of rice-paddies dates from the 5th millennium BC. By 3000 BC, more sophisticated skills developed, including the carving of jade, and small townships rather than villages began to emerge.

Around 1600 BC China entered the Bronze Age with its first archaeologically proven dynasty, the Shang (c. 1520–1030 BC). Chasing copper mines, the Shang moved their capital at least six times, and three, at Cheng-chou, Erh-li-t'ou and An-yang, have been excavated. Many smaller Shang sites have been found and some are now known from the Yangtze valley in central China indicating the Shang expansion southward. In addition, the Shang had trade relations with most of the northern and central east Asian mainland.

The Chou dynasty

In the 11th century BC the Shang territory was conquered by the Chou, of different ethnic origin, who inhabited the northwest border of the Shang domain. The Chou gradually extended their sovereignty beyond the Shang boundaries, including the entire middle and lower reaches of the Yellow River and parts of the middle basin of the Yangtze. At first their capital lay near Hsi-an. The Chou territory was divided into numerous domains among the king and the elites – a system of delegated authority similar to the later European feudal system.

Until the 8th century BC the Chou constantly extended the area under their control. About 770 BC, however, internal disorders broke the kingdom into numerous units and forced the Chou king to abandon his homeland in the Wei valley and move to the eastern capital at Lo-yang, where his power diminished. Over the next two and a half centuries wars caused more than 100 petty units to be swallowed up by some 20 of the more powerful ones, among whom there emerged a clear pecking order.

The Shang and early Chou periods were differentiated from their predecessors not only by their political organization and their bronze technology, but also by the use of writing, and their culture was already recognizably 'Chinese'. Their cities maintained a hierarchy of nobles, royal officers and court servants. They drew support from communities of craftsmen working in bronze, jade, wood, stone, ceramics and textiles. Peasants working the various domains that belonged to the landed classes produced revenues and foodstuffs. Market activities were common and mint currencies were in use.

Bronze was used for ritual objects and a wide range of weapons and tools, with the exception of farming equipment. Farmers working in the fields continued to use stone implements, growing rice, millet, barley and hemp and raising pigs, poultry and silkworms, and the practice of fallow became the norm.

Towards the end of the period, the old social order began to collapse. The more powerful units employed bureaucrats rather than the hereditary nobility of older times. A new group of administrators (*shih*) emerged. A leading figure among this group, Confucius, formulated a new ethos, which was to have currency far into the future and far beyond China's territory.

Shang ritual food vessel ***(below)*** in Ho or Yu style, in the form of a tiger protecting a man. The vessel is covered with animal motifs related to a fertility cult.

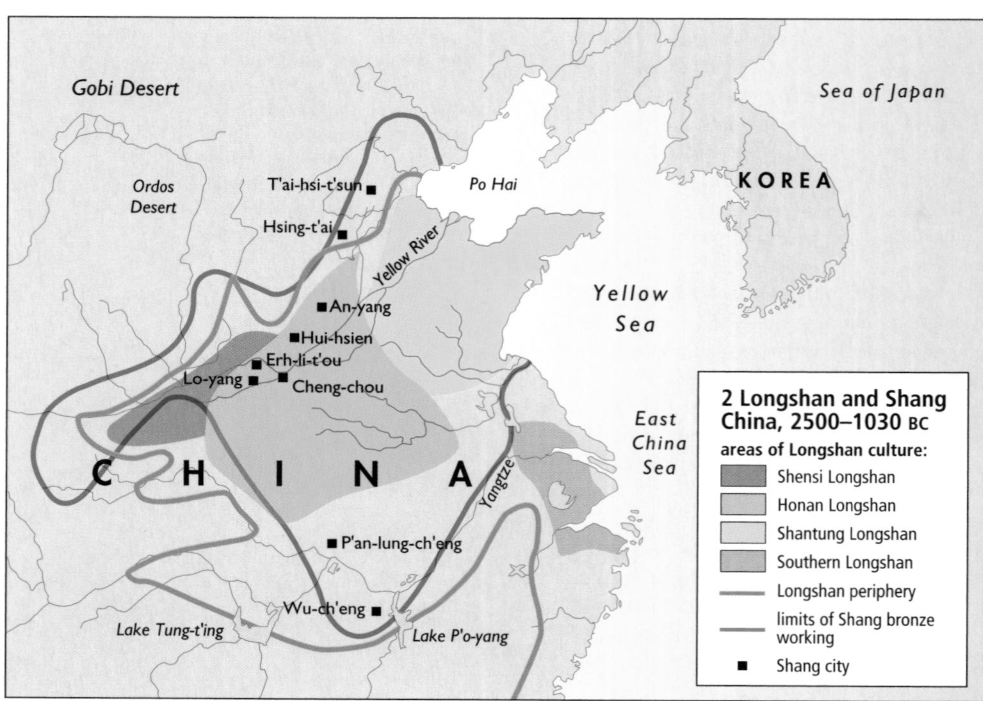

2 The Longshan period, named after its characteristic black pottery, saw the first signs of cultural homogenization spreading from the east coast Shantung Longshan ***(map below)***. Increasing social and cultural complexity emerged, as well as walled settlements and more sophisticated technology, including the potter's wheel. These developments formed the prelude to the rise of the first Chinese civilization, named after the Shang dynasty. Extensive walled cities, rich tombs, sophisticated craftsmanship and the earliest Chinese writing all demonstrate the wealth and originality of Shang civilization.

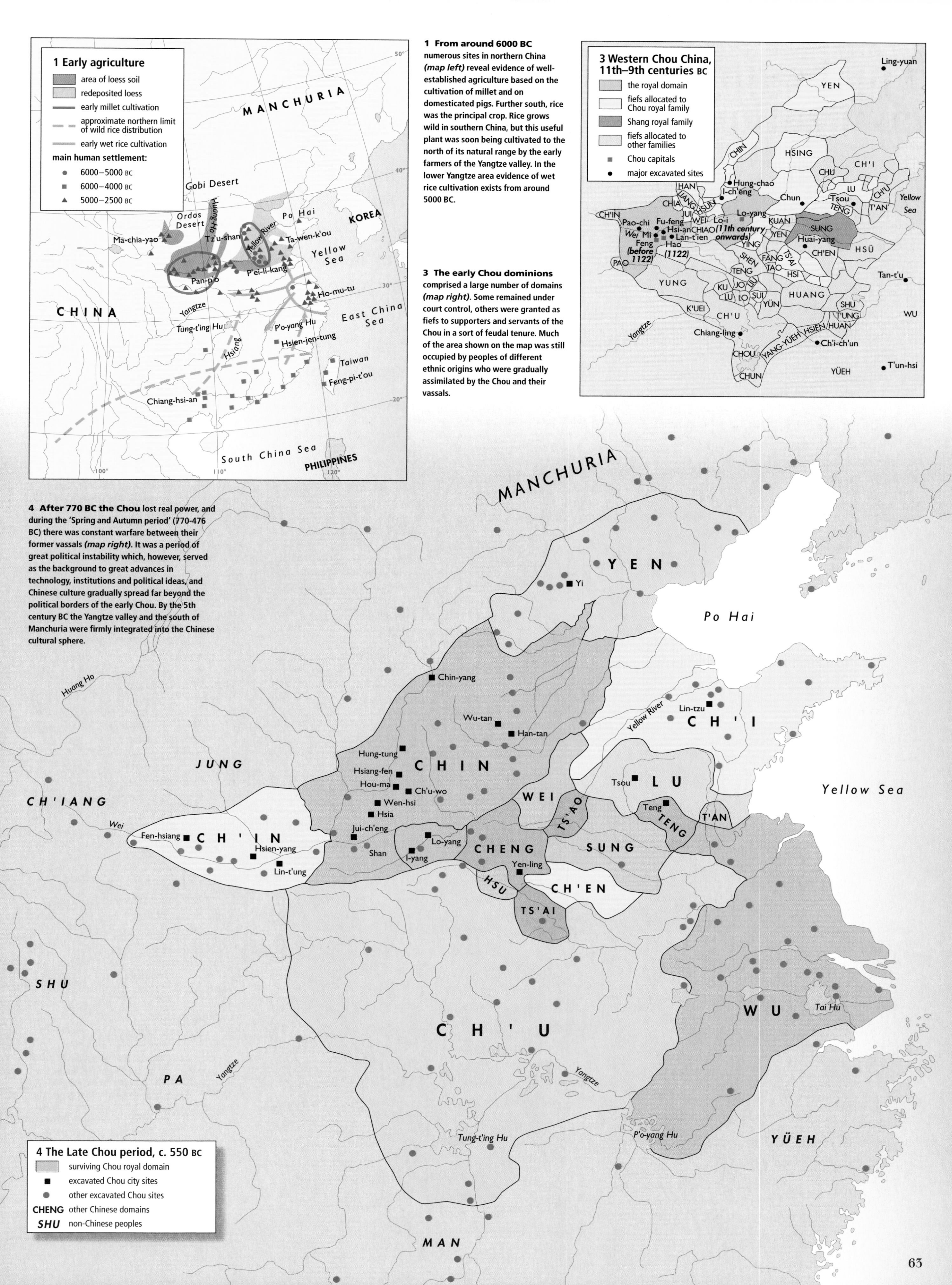

1 From around 6000 BC numerous sites in northern China ***(map left)*** reveal evidence of well-established agriculture based on the cultivation of millet and on domesticated pigs. Further south, rice was the principal crop. Rice grows wild in southern China, but this useful plant was soon being cultivated to the north of its natural range by the early farmers of the Yangtze valley. In the lower Yangtze area evidence of wet rice cultivation exists from around 5000 BC.

3 The early Chou dominions comprised a large number of domains ***(map right)***. Some remained under court control, others were granted as fiefs to supporters and servants of the Chou in a sort of feudal tenure. Much of the area shown on the map was still occupied by peoples of different ethnic origins who were gradually assimilated by the Chou and their vassals.

4 After 770 BC the Chou lost real power, and during the 'Spring and Autumn period' (770-476 BC) there was constant warfare between their former vassals ***(map right)***. It was a period of great political instability which, however, served as the background to great advances in technology, institutions and political ideas, and Chinese culture gradually spread far beyond the political borders of the early Chou. By the 5th century BC the Yangtze valley and the south of Manchuria were firmly integrated into the Chinese cultural sphere.

The beginnings of Indian civilization

See also
The beginnings of civilization in the Eurasian world, 3500–1500 BC p. 52
India: the first empires, 500 BC–AD 550 p. 82

With the bow let us win cows, with the bow let us win the contest and violent battles with the bow. The bow ruins the enemy's pleasure; with the bow let us conquer all the corners of the world. Neighing violently, the horses with their showering hoofs outstrip everyone with their chariots. Trampling down the foes with the tips of their hoofs, they destroy their enemies without veering away.

Hymn to Arms, Rig Veda
(c. 1200–900 BC)

India was the home of one of the oldest civilizations of history, which grew up along the banks of the Indus river. The Indus Valley culture and the Vedic culture, which succeeded and was influenced by it, were the basis for the development of later Indian society, in particular for the major religious systems of Hinduism, Buddhism and Jainism.

c. 3500 BC *Beginning of Early Indus period*

c. 2500 BC *Beginning of Harappan culture in the Indus valley*

c. 1750 BC *Abandonment of major Indus valley cities*

c. 1650 BC *Indo-Aryans begin to arrive in India*

c. 1000 BC *Indo-Aryan settlements established in the Upper Ganges plains*

c. 600 BC *Kausambi and Ujjayini develop as earliest post-Harappan cities*

Terracotta figurine ***(right)*** **from Mohenjo-Daro, probably representing a mother goddess. A large number of such figurines have been found in the Indus valley. The worship of goddesses was common in this period, and became a feature of Hindu worship. The figurine may, however, be more closely connected with Sumerian deities.**

The early history of India is very difficult to recover. Archaeology can reveal something about the way of life of its earliest inhabitants, but little can be learned from written evidence. The earliest works of Indian literature, the *Vedas*, were composed in the centuries after 1200 BC, but they were not written down until probably the 5th century.

Harappa and Mohenjo-Daro

Although the subcontinent had substantial human occupation from the Stone Age onwards (*see* map 1), the first great Indian civilization was the Harappan culture which emerged in the Indus valley in the 3rd millennium BC. Like the slightly older civilizations of Mesopotamia and Egypt it was based on flood-plain agriculture, as the cultivation of the fertile land on either side of the Indus was able to provide enough of a surplus to support a complex urban society. Several substantial cities were built (*see* map 2), of which the best explored are Harappa and Mohenjo-Daro.

The Indus civilization also developed writing, and about 2000 seals with short pictographic inscriptions on them have been discovered. Although it has not yet been convincingly deciphered, the language was almost certainly an early form of Dravidian related to languages still spoken in southern India and the hills of Pakistan and distinct from the Indo-European languages, such as Sanskrit, that became prominent in the following millennium.

The cities of the Indus valley engaged in some kind of trade with Mesopotamia, as goods marked with Indus seals have been found in Mesopotamia, and Mesopotamian cylinder seals have been found in Mohenjo-Daro. However, in the first half of the 2nd millennium the major Indus valley cities declined, probably as a result of climatic change, although smaller settlements remained inhabited.

Vedic culture

From around 1500 BC a new culture becomes apparent in India. This is now known as Vedic civilization, and was characterized by a new language and rituals, and the use of horses and two-wheeled chariots. The traditional way to explain the changes was to talk of an 'Aryan invasion', with mounted bands of warriors riding in from the northwest and conquering the indigenous Indus population before moving eastwards to the Ganges. Support for this picture was claimed from one of the *Vedas*, the *Rig Veda*, where the Aryans are presented as conquering the cities of the darker skinned indigenous Dasas. It is more likely that the process was gradual and that small groups of nomads entered the subcontinent from the northwest in the early 2nd millennium and settled alongside the existing populations. They absorbed elements of Harappan culture, but were able to establish themselves as the dominant elite ('arya' is the Sanskrit word for 'nobility'). Over the next centuries their Aryan language was adopted by more of the population, and at the same time their influence spread eastwards to the upper Ganges.

The south

Southern India was left largely untouched by the civilizations of the north. There were probably trading links between the Indus valley and the southern tip of the peninsula, but there was no urbanism in the south, where villages were the normal form of social organization. However, some limited form of common culture in the south

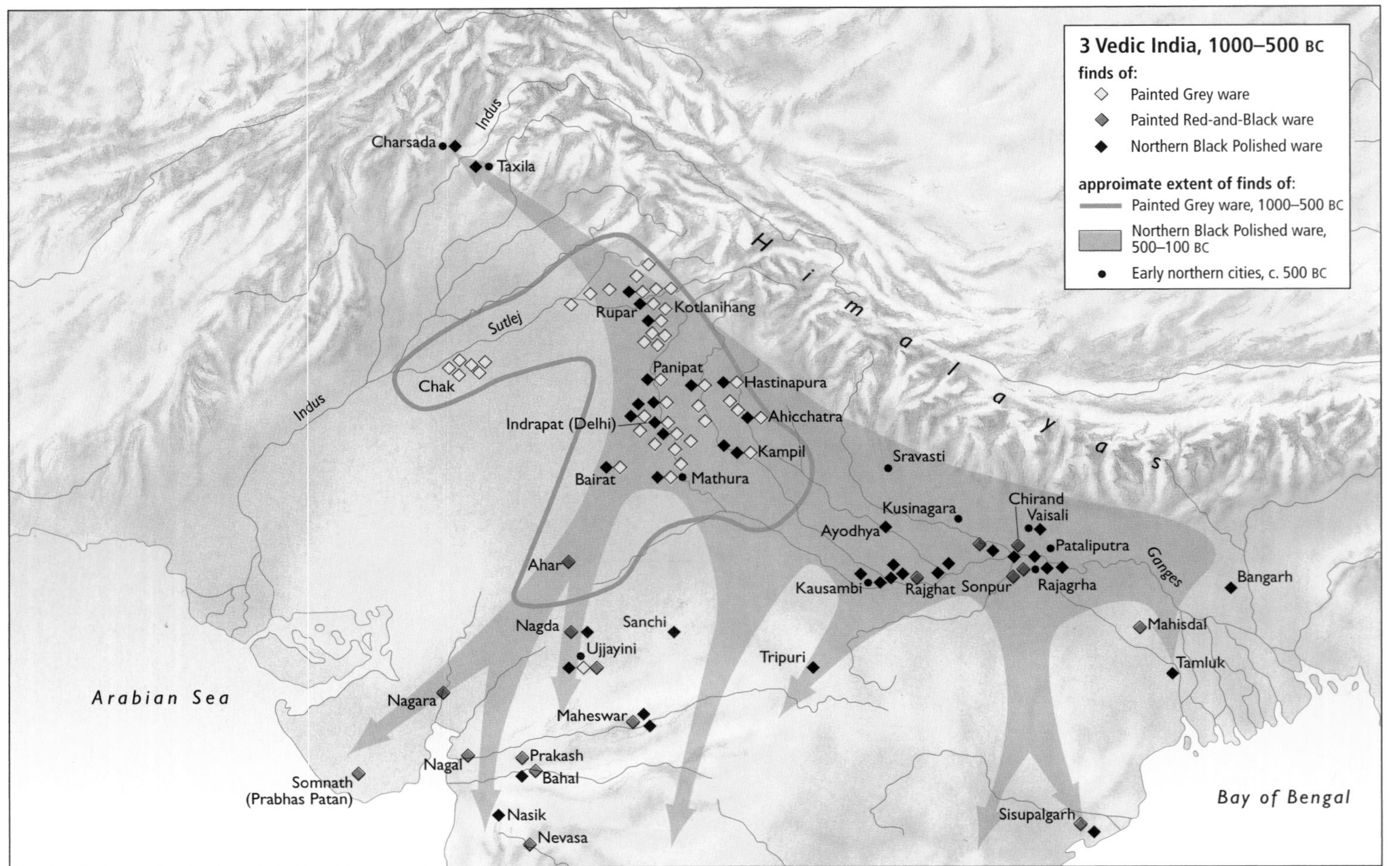

3 The spread of Vedic civilization in the 1st millennium BC can be followed using the evidence of pottery ***(map left)***. Painted Grey ware, found in central north India, is associated with the earlier Aryan settlement in the upper and middle Ganges, while the later Red-and-Black ware is found further east and south. The spread of Northern Black Polished ware, which dates from the time of the foundation of the first cities on the Ganges, indicates the growing influence of Vedic culture throughout northern and central India.

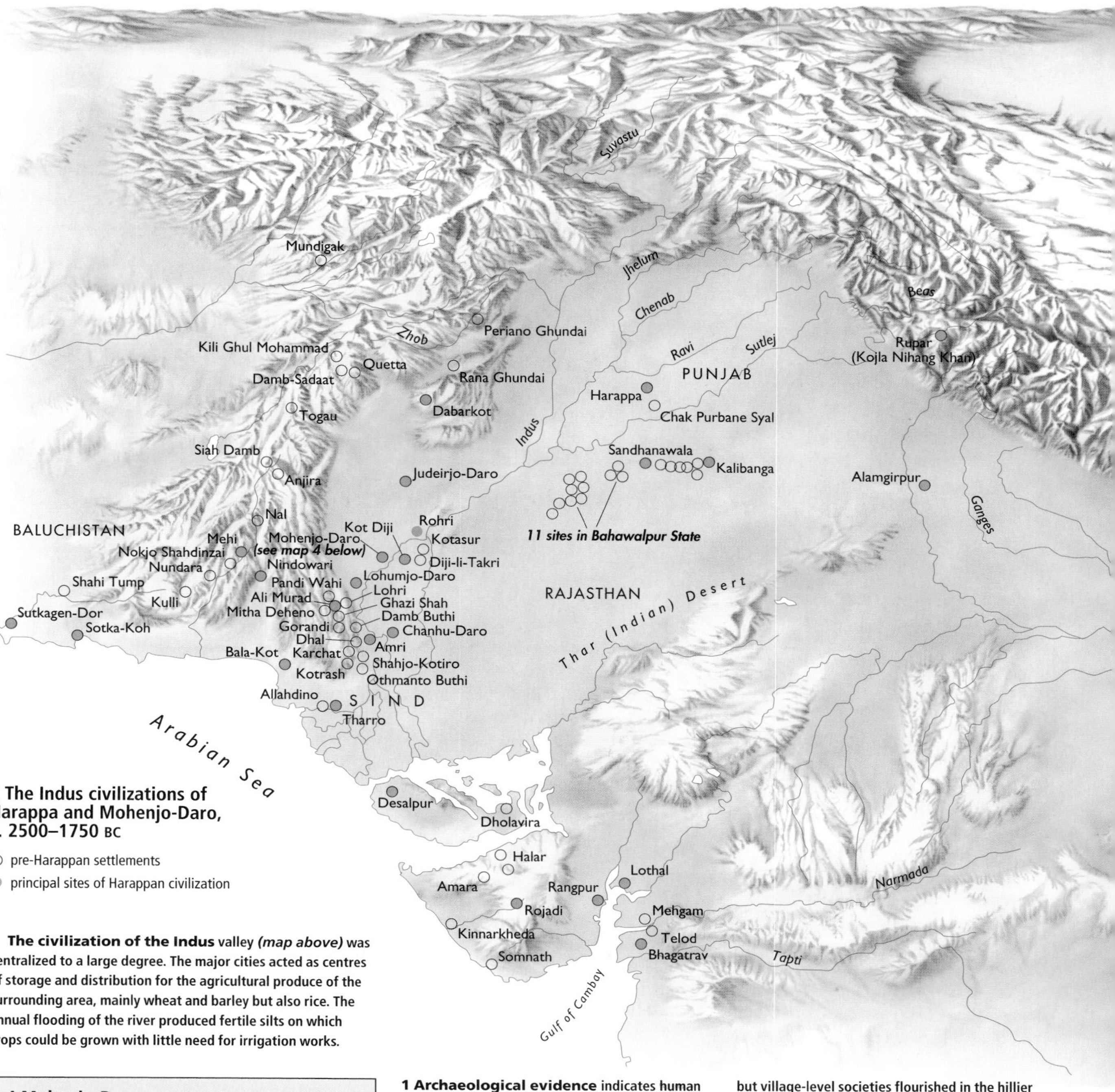

is suggested by the distinctive megalithic tombs found over most of the area.

In the north, where, unlike the hilly, fragmented geography of the south, great plains lent themselves to large-scale agriculture and the growth of substantial kingdoms, cultural coherence became more widespread as, in the centuries that followed the emergence of the Vedic culture, the new civilization spread gradually east from the Indus to the Ganges. Evidence from finds of pottery characteristic of particular periods suggests that there was also movement southwards (*see* map 3). The early Aryans had been pastoralists, but over time they adopted agricultural practices, and as they became increasingly settled they established larger communities. Once again cities began to be built, although they were not on the scale of Harappa and Mohenjo-Daro, being constructed largely from mud-bricks. No known public buildings survive from this period. Yet by the 5th century BC there were political entities that might be called states or polities, most significantly Magadha, with its substantial fortified capital at Pataliputra (*see* p. 82).

Vedic religion

The religious practices of Vedic society were influenced in part by the earlier Indus Valley culture, and animal sacrifice had a central role in it. Vedic religion was polytheistic, and the *Rig Veda* includes hymns to a number of deities, including the warrior god Indra, the fire god Agni, and Soma, identified with a mind-altering drug of some kind, possibly derived from mushrooms. Vedic religion is the forerunner of Hinduism, and the urban societies that developed along the Ganges were the communities among whom appeared in the 5th century Mahavira, the founder of Jainism, and the Buddha himself.

4 Mohenjo-Daro ***(right)*** **was one of the major cities of the Indus valley, covering an area of 60 hectares and with a population of about 40,000. It was laid out in a regular grid pattern and the major buildings were constructed with baked bricks. The 'lower town' was the main residential area, and the citadel acted as the administrative and ceremonial centre of the city. The 'college' may have been the residence of a priestly elite.**

2 The Indus civilizations of Harappa and Mohenjo-Daro, c. 2500–1750 BC

○ pre-Harappan settlements
● principal sites of Harappan civilization

2 The civilization of the Indus valley ***(map above)*** **was centralized to a large degree. The major cities acted as centres of storage and distribution for the agricultural produce of the surrounding area, mainly wheat and barley but also rice. The annual flooding of the river produced fertile silts on which crops could be grown with little need for irrigation works.**

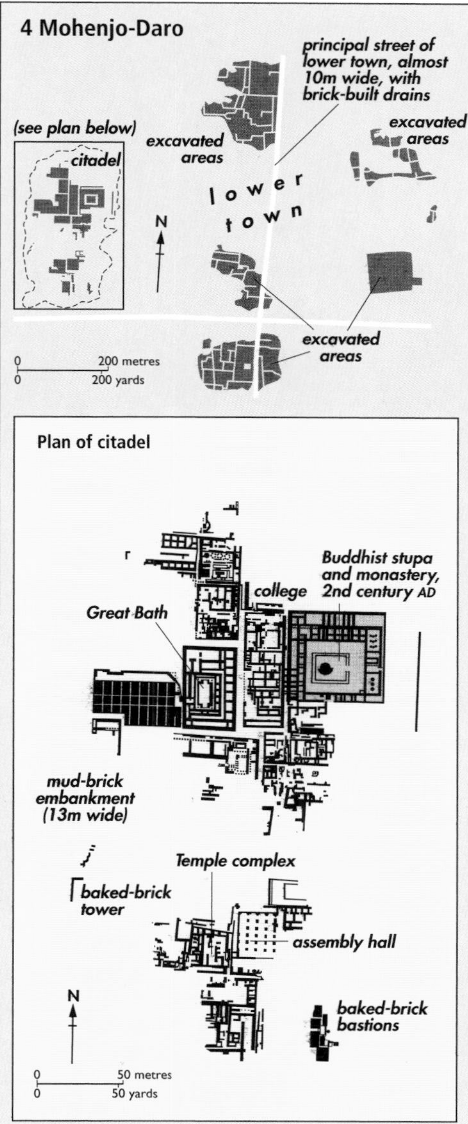

1 Archaeological evidence indicates human occupation throughout the whole Indian peninsula from the Stone Age onwards ***(map below)*****. Intensive agriculture made possible the growth of cities in the Indus valley and, later, on the Ganges, but village-level societies flourished in the hillier land to the south. The spread of metal-working from the north and the diffusion of Iron Age megalithic burials in the south indicates regular contact between the scattered communities.**

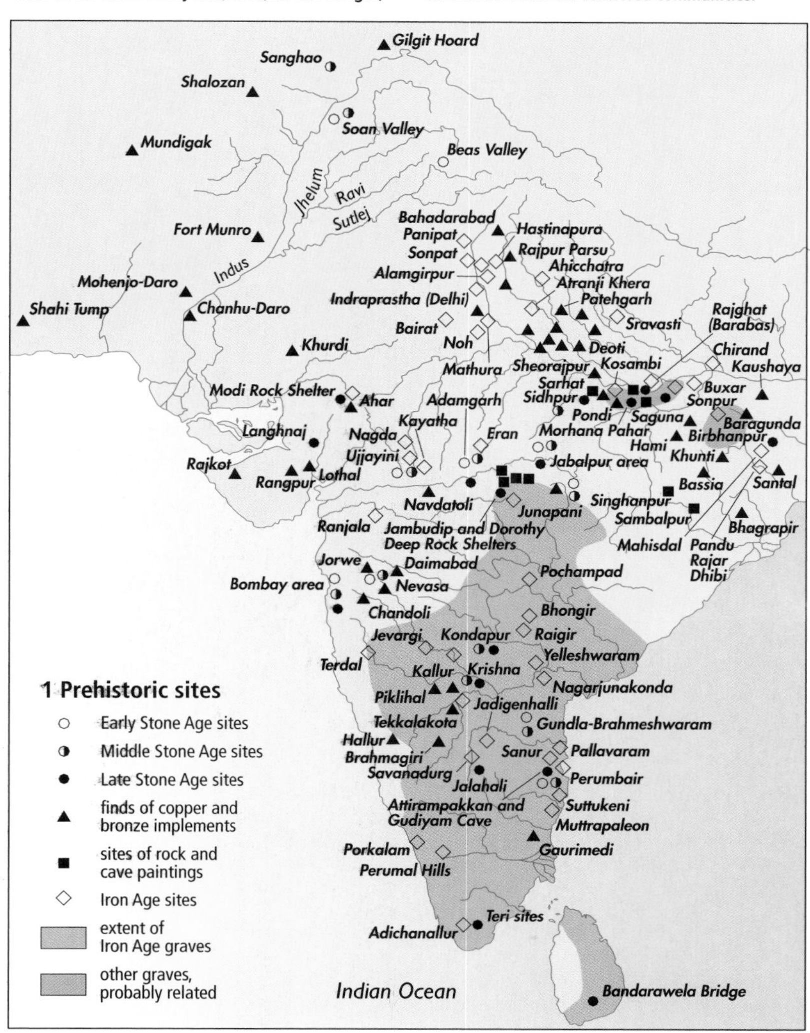

Minoan and Mycenaean civilizations

See also
Ancient Egypt: civilization and empire p. 56
The Near East, c. 1600–539 BC p. 58
The spread of Greek civilization p. 76

> THERE IS A LAND CALLED CRETE, IN THE MIDDLE OF THE WINE-DARK SEA, FAIR AND FERTILE AND SEAGIRT; IT HAS COUNTLESS NUMBERS OF MEN, AND NINETY CITIES, AND LANGUAGES MIX THERE ONE WITH ANOTHER … AND THERE IS KNOSSOS, THE GREAT CITY, WHERE MINOS RULES, NINE YEARS BY NINE YEARS, WHO HAS THE EAR OF MIGHTY ZEUS.
>
> **Homer, *Odyssey***
>
> FATHER ZEUS, LET THE LOT FALL TO AJAX, OR TO THE SON OF TYDEUS, OR TO HIM WHO IS KING OF GOLDEN MYCENAE.
>
> **Homer, *Iliad***

In the late 19th century, Heinrich Schliemann and Sir Arthur Evans unearthed the remains of previously unknown civilizations. Although the names of Troy, Mycenae and Knossos were familiar from the poems of Homer, the Bronze Age societies of the Aegean revealed by these excavations had much more in common with contemporary Near Eastern societies than they had with later Greece.

SUBSTANTIAL SETTLEMENTS appeared in mainland Greece and Crete by the end of the 3rd millennium BC. These were subsistence farmers, with households producing goods for their own consumption. The subsequent appearance in Crete of large stone-built complexes marked the emergence of a new form of social organisation. There are some parallels between these 'Old Palaces' and Near Eastern buildings, and they are accompanied by other signs of such influence, including the appearance of a form of hieroglyphic writing in Crete. However, it is likely that local needs as much as outside influence determined the island's overall development.

There is no agreed explanation for the later destruction of the 'Old Palaces', but in their place the large complexes of the 'New Palace Period' emerged. These were not fortified, but they were the focus of the economic and religious life of the Minoan communities.

By 1600 BC Knossos had achieved a dominant position within Crete, and the palace there reveals much information about Minoan society. Surviving frescoes depict scenes of communal activity including processions, bull-leaping, dining and dancing. It is clear from Knossos and other palaces that Cretan society depended upon intensive agriculture – the palaces incorporate large storage areas where crops could be gathered for later redistribution to the population. Outside the towns, especially in eastern Crete, large 'villas' (*see* map 2) had a similar role, and acted as processing centres for grape and olive crops.

The three and a half centuries of the New Palace Period witnessed considerable destruction and rebuilding at a number of sites. The eruption of Thera in 1628 BC left its mark on sites in eastern Crete but otherwise appears to have had little long-term impact. More significantly, a little over a century later many Cretan settlements underwent widespread devastation, possibly as a result of invasion from the Greek mainland.

Mycenaean Greece

Mainland Greece did not share in the prosperity of Crete and the Aegean islands until c. 1700 BC, when rich burials, especially in the 'shaft-graves' at Mycenae and in *tholos* tombs, point to the emergence of a powerful warlike elite. After 1500 BC mainlanders, called Mycenaeans by archaeologists, appear to have been in control of Knossos, where the palace continued to function for another century. It was only after that that palaces started to appear on the mainland. While they owed something to Minoan models, and, like them, acted as centres for agricultural storage and redistribution,

c. 3000 BC *Beginning of Greek Early Bronze Age*

c. 1900 BC *Beginning of Old Palace Period on Crete*

c. 1750 BC *Destruction of Old Palaces. Beginning of New Palace Period*

1628 BC *Massive volcanic eruption on the Aegean island of Thera*

c. 1500 BC *Mycenaean invasion of Crete*

c. 1400 BC *Appearance of Palaces on the mainland*

c. 1190 BC *Abandonment of Mycenaean Palaces*

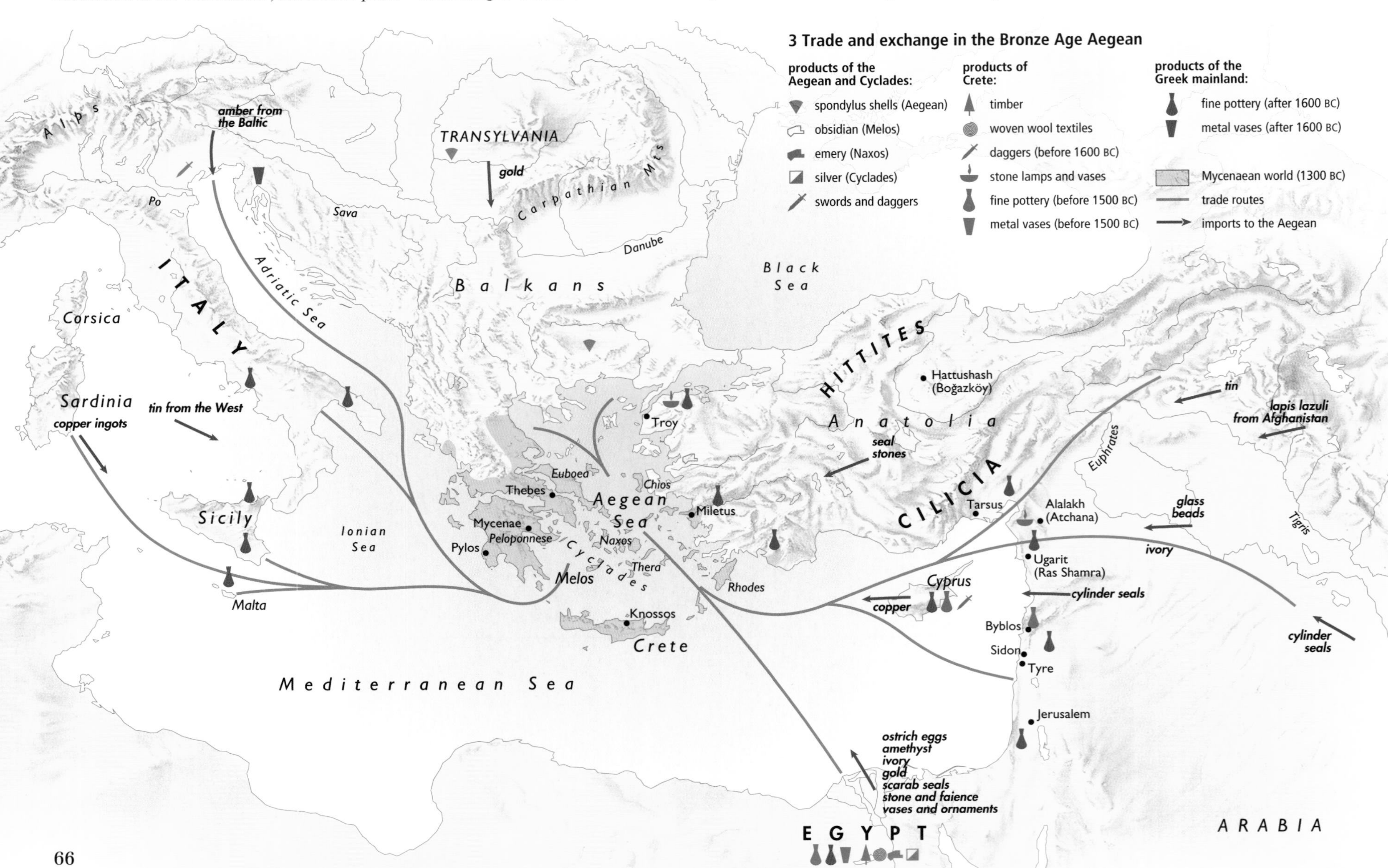

3 Bronze Age Greece and Crete were part of the wider eastern Mediterranean and Near East *(map below)*. The rulers of these developing civilizations needed raw materials such as copper and tin to make bronze, as well as luxury goods. In return, the Aegean supplied rare materials such as obsidian and fine works of craftsmanship. These goods often circulated as gifts or dowries rather than as items of trade.

they were fortified and less luxurious (*see* map 1). The Mycenaeans spoke a form of Greek, and wrote in a syllabic script, Linear B, adapted from the still-undeciphered script already in use in Crete, Linear A. Documents inscribed on clay tablets have survived to reveal a strongly hierarchical society, with the ruler (*wanax*) at the top, lesser lords below and the mass of the people at the bottom.

Soon after 1200 BC, more or less simultaneously, the palaces on the mainland were destroyed. In the centuries following there is no trace of Linear B writing, nor of the figurative decoration that characterises Mycenaean art. When written Greek appears again in the 8th century, it uses a version of the Phoenician alphabet.

The absence of firm evidence – mirrored by the lack of firm dates for this period – has led historians to examine myths in the search for historical facts. On this basis it has been suggested that the Mycenaeans fell victim to Dorian invaders from the north, or that a long war against Troy caused revolution in the Greek homeland. Neither finds support from archaeology, and an agreed explanation for the complete social breakdown of Mycenaean society is yet to emerge. One contributing factor may have been major political upheavals further east, cutting off access to the tin (*see* map 3) needed to make the bronze on which the Mycenaean rulers based their power. Certainly the society which emerged from the 'dark age' that followed the collapse was reliant on the more widely available iron.

The massive ruins of the Mycenaean palaces remained visible to the Greeks of later times, and these, together with a tradition of oral poetry that developed over the following centuries, led to the invention of a heroic world, most famously celebrated in the epic poems of Homer, that was very different from Bronze Age reality.

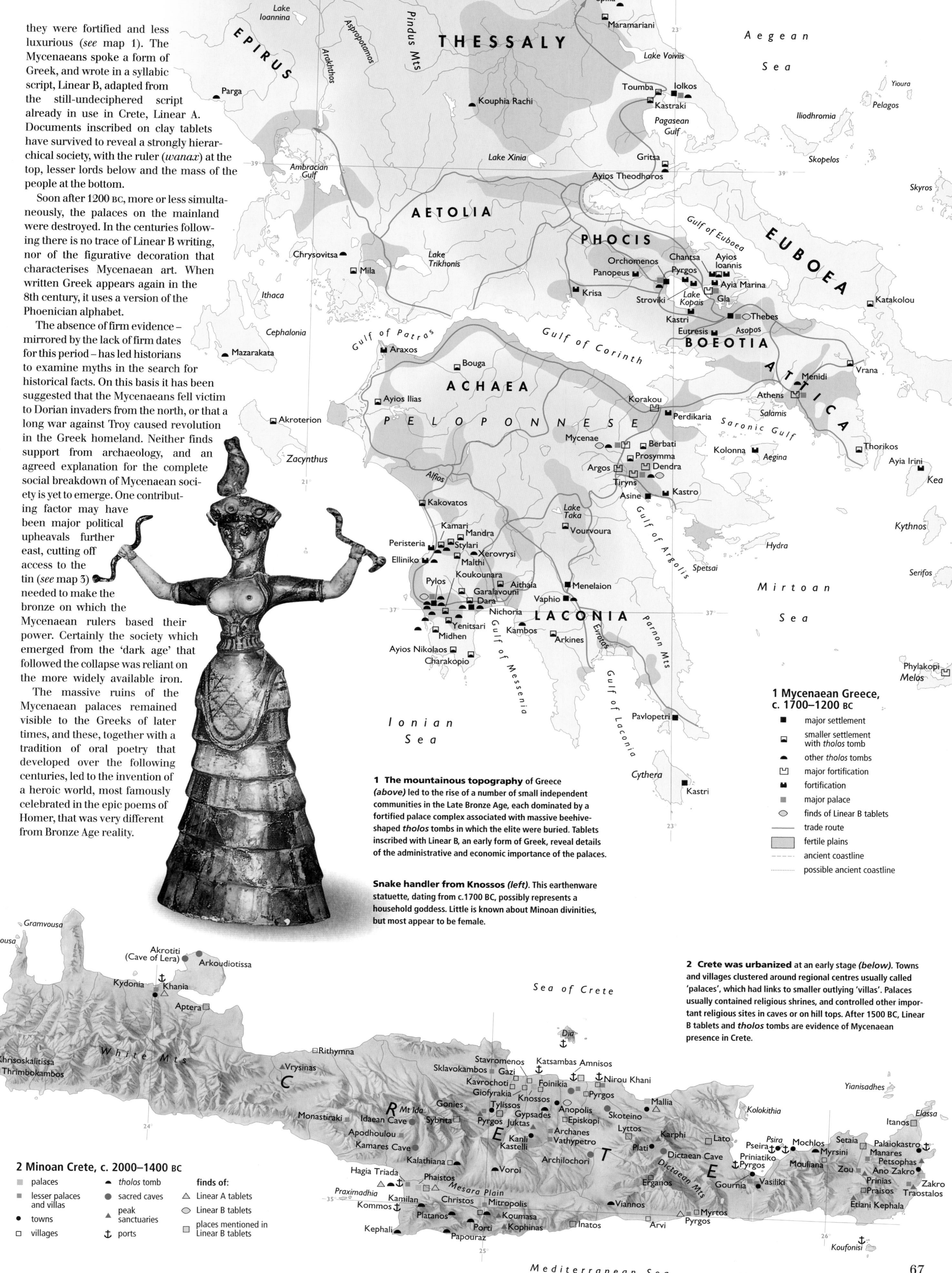

1 The mountainous topography of Greece *(above)* led to the rise of a number of small independent communities in the Late Bronze Age, each dominated by a fortified palace complex associated with massive beehive-shaped *tholos* tombs in which the elite were buried. Tablets inscribed with Linear B, an early form of Greek, reveal details of the administrative and economic importance of the palaces.

Snake handler from Knossos *(left)*. This earthenware statuette, dating from c.1700 BC, possibly represents a household goddess. Little is known about Minoan divinities, but most appear to be female.

2 Crete was urbanized at an early stage *(below)*. Towns and villages clustered around regional centres usually called 'palaces', which had links to smaller outlying 'villas'. Palaces usually contained religious shrines, and controlled other important religious sites in caves or on hill tops. After 1500 BC, Linear B tablets and *tholos* tombs are evidence of Mycenaean presence in Crete.

3

The classical civilizations of Eurasia

THE EARLIEST civilizations arose at a few scattered points in the vast and sparsely inhabited Eurasian landmass. Between 1000 BC and AD 500 the pattern began to change. Although America, Australasia and Africa south of the Sahara still stood outside the mainstream of world history, and were to stay so for a further thousand years, the civilizations of Europe and Asia now formed a continuous belt. By AD 100, when the classical era was at its height, a chain of empires extended from Rome via Parthia and the Kushana empire to China, constituting an unbroken zone of civilized life from the Atlantic to the Pacific.

This was a new and important fact in the history of the Eurasian world. The area of civilization remained narrow and exposed to unrelenting barbarian pressures, and developments in the different regions remained largely autonomous. But with the expansion of the major civilizations and the elimination of the geographical gaps between them, the way lay open for inter-regional contacts and cultural exchanges which left a lasting imprint. In the west, the expansion of Hellenism created a single cultural area which extended from the frontiers of India to Britain; in the east, the expansion of the Chinese and Indian civilizations resulted in a kind of cultural symbiosis in Indo-China. These wider cultural areas provided a vehicle not only for trade but for the transmission of ideas, technology and institutions, and above all for the diffusion of the great world religions. Beginning with Buddhism, and continuing with Judaism, Zoroastrianism, Christianity and Islam, religion became a powerful unifying bond in the Eurasian world.

Detail from the Altar of Zeus, Pergamum, c. 180 BC

See also
The beginnings of civilization in the Eurasian world p. 52
The religious bonds of Eurasia to AD 500 p. 72

550 BC to AD 752
The commercial and cultural bonds of Eurasia

c. 550 BC *Chinese silks known in Athens*

c. 116 BC *Eudoxus of Cyzicus sails from Arabia to India using the monsoons*

102 BC *Chinese emperor leads an expedition to Ferghana to seize horses*

AD 97 *Chinese ambassador Kan Ying visits Persia*

AD 166 *Roman merchants at the Chinese imperial court*

c. AD 540 *Silkworms brought into the Byzantine empire*

The rulers of the empires of the ancient world had no commercial policies, and were seldom interested in trade. Yet the activities of traders, operating at the margins of society, and rarely mentioned in ancient literature, had a profound effect on the development of the world, transmitting not only goods, but also cultural ideas – and occasionally deadly organisms.

AFTER THIS, HEADING EAST WITH THE OCEAN ON THE RIGHT, YOU REACH THE GANGES REGION AND NEAR IT THE EASTERNMOST POINT OF THE MAINLAND, CHRYSE. THERE IS A RIVER NEAR IT THAT IS ITSELF CALLED THE GANGES, THE GREATEST OF ALL RIVERS IN INDIA, WHICH RISES AND FALLS LIKE THE NILE. ON IT IS A TRADING POST WITH THE SAME NAME AS THE RIVER, GANGES, WHICH EXPORTS MALABATHRON, GANGETIC NARD, PEARLS AND COTTON GARMENTS OF THE VERY FINEST QUALITY, WHICH IS CALLED 'GANGETIC'.

Anonymous (1st century AD)
A Voyage around the Red Sea

THE QUANTITY OF GOODS passing across the Eurasian landmass varied enormously depending on the political conditions of the time. Between 200 BC and AD 200 stable regimes in the Roman Mediterranean, the Persian Parthian empire, the Kushana empire and China under the Han dynasty, helped to stabilize the routes between Europe, Persia and China. Such favourable conditions for the movement of goods and people did not recur until the 8th century AD when T'ang China and Abbasid Persia once more linked east with west. These earlier empires were not, however, directly interested in facilitating trade. Chinese campaigns in the area of the Silk Road in Sinkiang, north of Tibet, such as that of Pan Ch'ao against the Kushanas in c. AD 90 confronted a military rather than a commercial threat. The Han emperors certainly wanted valuable commodities like horses from Ferghana, but they expected to receive them either as diplomatic gifts, as tribute or as booty from war.

Since the time of Assyrian merchants in Anatolia in the 2nd millennium BC there are examples of communities of traders who settled in foreign territories to import goods from their homelands. In the 8th century BC Greek and Phoenician trading posts were established across the Mediterranean for the same purpose. These 'trade diasporas' made possible effective communication between different cultural groups. The people who made up the diaspora communities were not wealthy merchants, but of much lower status. The 'Roman' traders who sailed across the Indian Ocean or visited the Chinese court would not have been Italians, but inhabitants of the eastern provinces, who were probably not even Roman citizens.

Trade was not the only way in which goods travelled across this route. The Han rulers of China maintained peace on their northwest frontier by regular gifts of large quantities of silk and lacquerware to the Hsiungnu tribes outside the Great Wall. Some of these items would have been passed on in dowries or as gifts, and gradually made their way to the Mediterranean where silken clothing was sought by Roman senators, much to the distaste of more austere emperors.

While silk was the major import from China to the Mediterranean, a variety of goods found their way westwards. The Roman writer Pliny (AD 23–79) complains that the desire for eastern goods was draining the empire of its gold and silver, but this is not supported by the archaeological evidence. Glass was certainly sought after, but slaves were probably also a significant item of trade, and there are references in Chinese sources to 'Syrian jugglers' reaching the Chinese court.

Maritime trade

Maritime trade developed at the same time as the overland routes, as increasing use was made of the monsoons for trade between southern Arabia and south India. Vital information about the goods traded between the Roman empire and the east comes from *A Voyage around the Red Sea*, an anonymous handbook for traders written in the 1st century AD, which describes the coastal routes from the Egyptian Red Sea ports of Myos Hormus and Berenice to east Africa and the Ganges delta. The author knows of China as a vast city, but east of India his geographical knowledge is hazy.

The exchange of goods might have profound cultural effects. Begram in Gandhara was the location of the summer palace of the Kushana emperors. A rich hoard from there dating from around AD 100 included lacquer from China and ivory from India, as well as bronzes, glassware and pottery from the Mediterranean. The Kushana interest in Mediterranean artefacts illustrated by the Begram hoard had a profound effect on local practices, acting as a catalyst for the development of Gandharan art which emerged in the 2nd century AD, in part modelled on Greco-Roman styles.

A wall painting ***(below)*** **from Tun-huang shows a Chinese official mounted on a horse from Ferghana. The Han Chinese emperors needed to equip their cavalry to fight against the nomads north of the Great Wall, and the horses of Ferghana were highly prized. Chinese tradition claimed that they were descended from winged heavenly horses. In 102 BC the emperor Wu-ti attempted to purchase a supply from Ferghana, and when he was refused sent two military expeditions into Ferghana to attempt to seize them.**

1 The carrying of goods along the Silk Road to the Mediterranean began in the 6th century BC ***(map right)*****, and trade along this route flourished between c. 200 BC and AD 200 when stable empires controlled the territories through which the traders passed. The usual starting point, on the edge of China proper, was Tun-huang, from which the route continued west over the Pamirs, to Samarkand and Merv. At the same time traders began to take advantage of the monsoons for seaborne trade with India and beyond. Archaeology has done much to reveal the extent of trade over the Eurasian landmass. Chinese silks have been found in Britain, and a Roman coin in Vietnam. The Shoso-in, the treasure-house of the Todaiji temple at Nara in Japan, built by 752, contains glass from the Byzantine empire as well as goods from Sasanid Persia and China.**

1 The commercial and cultural bonds of Eurasia

- trading centre
- trade route
- Silk Road

distribution of:
- Han mirrors
- Chinese silks
- treasures of the Shoso-in
- Graeco-Roman objects found in southeast Asia AD 1–300
- sites known to the author of *A Voyage around the Red Sea*

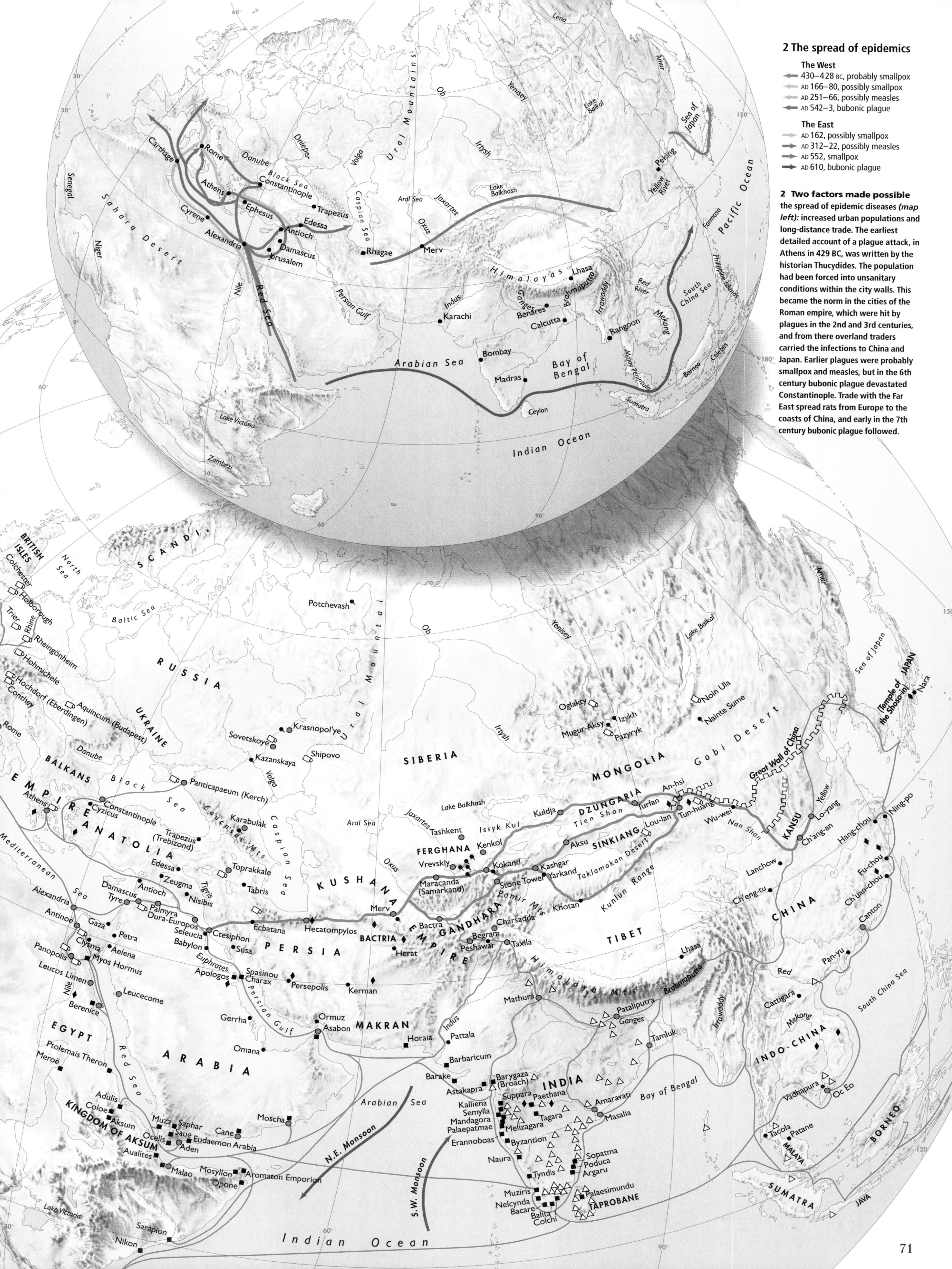

2 Two factors made possible the spread of epidemic diseases *(map left)*: increased urban populations and long-distance trade. The earliest detailed account of a plague attack, in Athens in 429 BC, was written by the historian Thucydides. The population had been forced into unsanitary conditions within the city walls. This became the norm in the cities of the Roman empire, which were hit by plagues in the 2nd and 3rd centuries, and from there overland traders carried the infections to China and Japan. Earlier plagues were probably smallpox and measles, but in the 6th century bubonic plague devastated Constantinople. Trade with the Far East spread rats from Europe to the coasts of China, and early in the 7th century bubonic plague followed.

The religious bonds of Eurasia

See also

The commercial and cultural bonds of Eurasia, 550 BC–AD 752 p. 70

The rise of Christianity to AD 600 p. 92

The spread of Islam from AD 622 p. 98

The Jewish diaspora, AD 70—1800 p. 102

c. 1200 BC *Teachings of Zoroaster*

c. 551 BC *Birth of Confucius*

c. 520 BC *Building of Temple in Jerusalem begins*

c. 486 BC *Birth of Gautama Buddha*

c. 265 BC *Conversion of Ashoka to Buddhism*

c. 5 BC *Birth of Jesus Christ*

AD 313 *Edict of Milan: toleration proclaimed for all religions in the Roman empire*

Before the 1st millennium BC, polytheism was the dominant form of religious activity throughout Eurasia, with individual communities worshipping their own gods. As the empires of the ancient world were established, a number of major religions, each characterized by single doctrine and claims to universality, largely replaced these myriad cults.

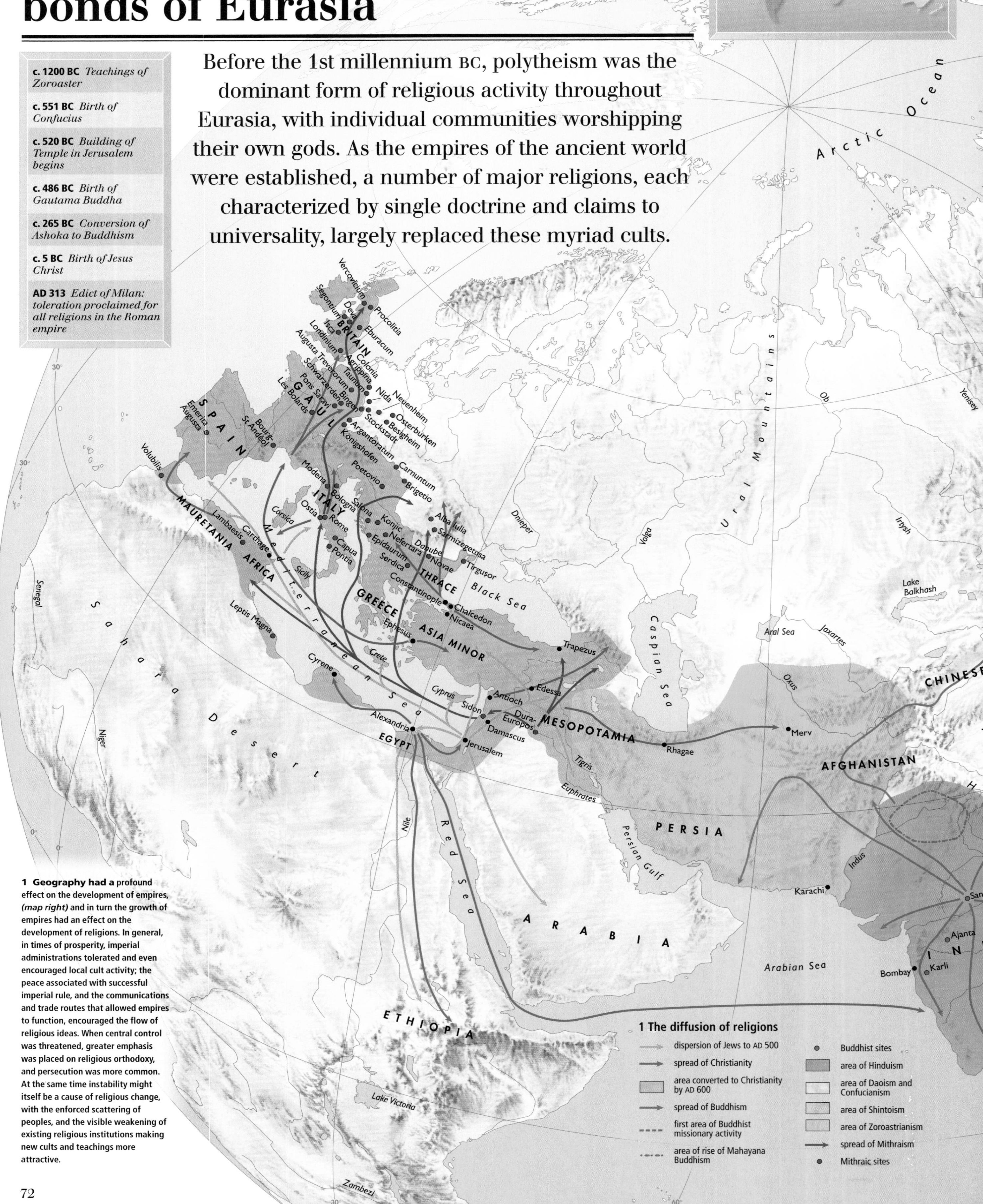

1 Geography had a profound effect on the development of empires, *(map right)* and in turn the growth of empires had an effect on the development of religions. In general, in times of prosperity, imperial administrations tolerated and even encouraged local cult activity; the peace associated with successful imperial rule, and the communications and trade routes that allowed empires to function, encouraged the flow of religious ideas. When central control was threatened, greater emphasis was placed on religious orthodoxy, and persecution was more common. At the same time instability might itself be a cause of religious change, with the enforced scattering of peoples, and the visible weakening of existing religious institutions making new cults and teachings more attractive.

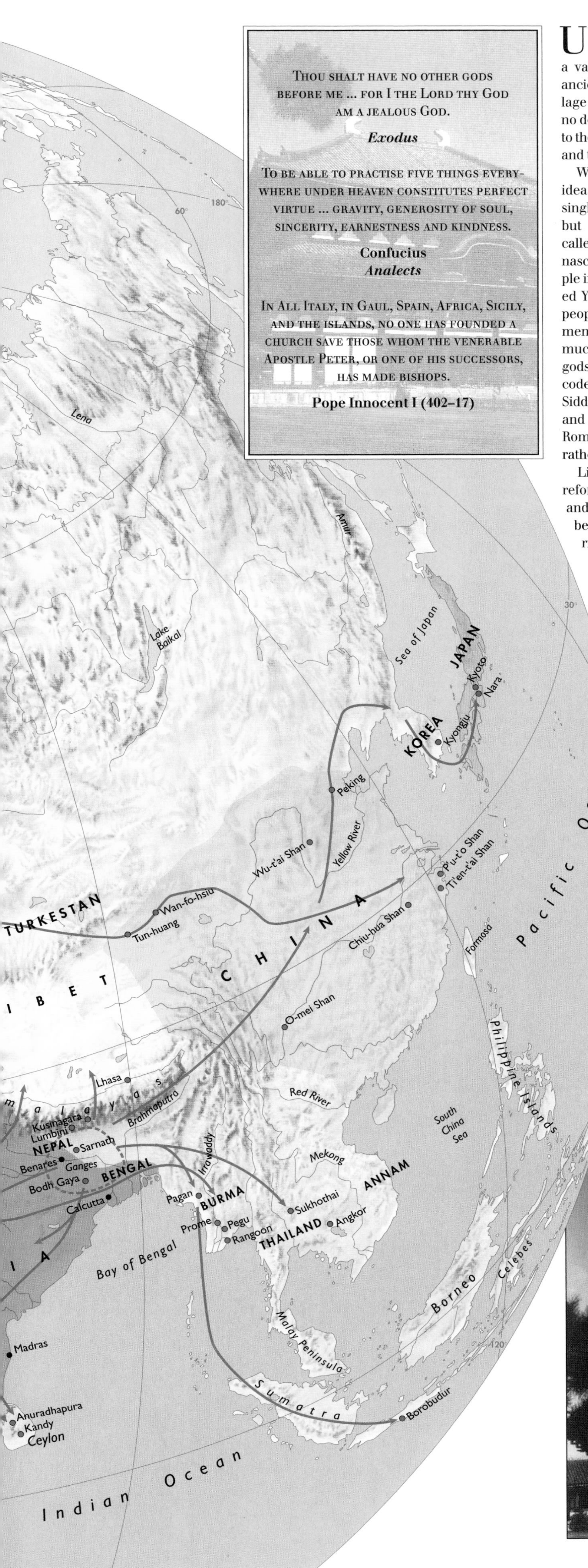

Thou shalt have no other gods before me ... for I the Lord thy God am a jealous God.

Exodus

To be able to practise five things everywhere under heaven constitutes perfect virtue ... gravity, generosity of soul, sincerity, earnestness and kindness.

Confucius
Analects

In all Italy, in Gaul, Spain, Africa, Sicily, and the islands, no one has founded a church save those whom the venerable Apostle Peter, or one of his successors, has made bishops.

Pope Innocent I (402–17)

Until the emergence of Christianity in the 1st century AD and of Islam 600 years later, a variety of religious beliefs proliferated in the ancient world. In some places, every town and village had its own gods and cults. These faiths had no defined dogma but were more often a response to the circumstances of the lives of the worshippers and their varying social structures.

Within this polytheistic world, new religious ideas were born which advocated reliance on a single god, denying not the existence of other gods but their worthiness. Zoroaster, for example, called for respect for Ahura Mazda alone, while the nascent Jewish community which rebuilt the temple in Jerusalem after the fall of Babylon, demanded Yahweh be acknowledged the sole god of his people. Among rich élites elsewhere, other movements developed which were concerned not so much with religion or with the nature of a god or gods as with establishing a philosophical or ethical code. The teaching of Confucius, of Gautama Siddhartha, of Laozi (a principal figure in Daoism) and of Stoicism or Epicurianism in the Greco-Roman world dealt with how life should be lived rather than which gods should be worshipped.

Little is known of the men who established or reformulated Buddhism, Judaism, Confucianism and Daoism in this period. But all seem to have been reacting to the tensions of the age: to the rise of warring states and empires which, as they reduced the power and independence of cities and smaller communities, lessened the appeal and impact of local cults. The development of larger, more centralized states and empires and the rise of these new religions and codes thus went hand in hand, the new religions either becoming associated with or adopted by the great empires of the ancient world: Zoroastrianism with the Persian empire of Cyrus and Darius the Great; Buddhism with Ashoka's Indian empire; Confucianism and Daoism with China under the Chou.

Christianity, based on the teachings of Jesus, began as another call for a new way of living, though one attractive to the poor. In the first centuries AD, the administration of the Roman empire remained in the hands of cities, each responsible for its own religious practices. As their power waned and that of the emperor grew, city cults began to lose their appeal while cults such as Christianity and Mithraism gained in popularity. Rome's emperors encouraged worship of themselves and the gods who protected them, and when the emperor Constantine identifed his protecting god with the god of the Christians Christianity became the central cult of the later Roman empire.

RELIGIONS OF THE ANCIENT WORLD

Hinduism: Polytheistic religion of India. Hinduism spread through India in the Vedic period (c. 1500–500 BC) but was probably linked to earlier cult practice. It was further developed in the Epic period (c. 500 BC–AD 500) when major works, including the *Mahabharata*, were composed.

Buddhism: Ascetic movement pointing towards enlightenment through the extinguishing of desire. The importance of Buddhism grew after it was adopted by Mauryan emperor Ashoka, who spread it through India. Missionary activity then brought Buddhist ideas to many places in east Asia, where it developed under the influence of different local religious traditions.

Confucianism: Developed by Confucius (b. 551 BC), a member of the Chinese intellectual and administrative élite, whose disciples recorded his precepts about correct conduct. Temples were built to Confucius throughout China from the 2nd century BC and his teachings subsequently became part of Chinese ideology.

Daoism: Ethical system developed in China in the 6th century BC, associated with Laozi. Emphasized importance of living in accordance with 'the Way' or Dao. With Confucianism it developed as an important strand in Chinese religious ideology.

Shinto: Traditional Japanese polytheistic religion. Did not develop any literature or specific ethical teachings of its own until the 8th century AD.

Judaism: Monotheistic cult focussed on temple of Yahweh in Jerusalem; developed during exile of Israelite elite in Babylon (c. 587-539 BC). Religious outlook saw both adversity and prosperity as controlled by Yahweh and faithfulness to him alone as the way of salvation. Repeated exiles spread Diaspora Jewish communities across the Mediterranean.

Christianity: Jesus of Nazareth (c. 5 BC–AD 30) advocated ethical reforms within Judaism. After his execution by the Romans, disciples proclaimed his divinity and missionary activity spread the cult across the Roman empire. Christianity developed a network of communities headed by bishops, who were members of the elite, and was well placed to benefit from the patronage of emperors from the 4th century onwards.

Zoroastrianism: Teachings of Zoroaster, concerned with purity and the conflict between light and dark, were adopted in the 6th century BC by the Achaemenid Persians to create a religious system emphasizing the role of the king as agent of the god Ahura Mazda.

Mithraism: Roman cult using Persian imagery. Open only to male initiates and particularly popular in the Roman army.

Despite the parallel rise of great empires and world religions, the periods of greatest missionary activity of the new religions almost always coincided with upheaval within the state structures which nourished them. Even so, as the empires of the ancient world fell, their religions were left intact or even prospered.

The 'Great Buddha Hall' of the Todaiji Temple at Nara ***(below)***. **Buddhism was introduced into Japan, via China and Korea, in the mid-6th century AD. The 'Buddha Hall', built around 745, is the world's largest wooden building.**

550 BC to AD 637

The empires of Persia

539 BC *Cyrus the Great captures Babylon*

525 BC *Cambyses conquers Egypt*

330 BC *Darius III, last Achaemenid King, assassinated*

238 BC *Arsaces I seizes Parthia from the Seleucids*

53 BC *Parthians defeat Roman legions under Marcus Crassus at Carrhae*

AD 259 *Sasanid Shapur I captures the Roman emperor Valerian at Edessa*

AD 540 *Chosroes I sacks Antioch*

AD 637 *Arabs capture Sasanid capital Ctesiphon*

The Iranian plateau was the heartland of three great empires whose territory stretched from the ancient centres of civilization in Mesopotamia to India. For more than a millennium, the Persian empire was governed successively by the Achaemenid, Arsacid and Sasanid ruling families, and offered a constant challenge to the Mediterranean lands to the west.

THE DOWNFALL OF THE Assyrian empire around 612 BC (*see* p. 58) was brought about by the Babylonians and the Medes, a loose confederacy of tribes in western Iran. It was the Persians, however, who proved to be the main beneficiaries. The Persian state emerged in the 7th century BC on the edge of the area dominated by Assyria, and in 550 BC its ruler, Cyrus (559–530 BC), defeated an invading Median army at Pasargadae. The next 11 years saw attempts to stop the growth of Persian power by both Croesus of Lydia and Nabonidus of Babylon. Both were defeated, leaving Cyrus in possession of Anatolia, the Levant and Mesopotamia.

The absorption of Lydian territory into Cyrus's empire brought Persia into contact with the Greeks. He then turned his attention eastwards, gaining control of much of Afghanistan and south central Asia. Though Cyrus's successor, Cambyses, (530–522 BC) added Egypt to the empire in 525 BC, his death was followed by the first of several upheavals within the empire as uncertainty over the succession encouraged widespread revolts.

These were quickly suppressed by Darius (522–486 BC), who also incorporated northwest India into the empire. The northwestern boundary of the empire remained a problem, but after the failure of expeditions into Europe (*see* p. 76) by Darius and Xerxes (486–465 BC), the Persians protected their interests by a series of peace treaties with the Greek states.

Achaemenid rule was brought to an end by the invasion of Alexander the Great in 334 BC (*see* p. 78). Dynastic struggles in the 330s may have had an effect, but no entirely satisfactory explanation has been given for the rapidity with which the Achaemenid empire fell.

> DARIUS THE KING SAYS: THESE ARE THE LANDS WHICH CAME TO ME. I BECAME THEIR KING BY THE WILL OF AHURA MAZDA: PERSIA, ELAM, BABYLONIA, ASSYRIA, ARABIA, EGYPT, THOSE BY THE SEA, SARDIS, IONIA, MEDIA, ARMENIA, CAPPADOCIA, PARTHIA, DRANGIANA, ARIA, KHWARAZM, BACTRIA, SOGDIANA, GANDHARA, SHAKALAND, SATTAGYDIA, ARACHOSIA, MAKA, A TOTAL OF TWENTY-THREE LANDS.
>
> **Inscription of Darius (522–486 BC) at Behistun**

The Parthian empire

After Alexander's death, Iran and its neighbouring territories became part of the Seleucid kingdom (*see* p. 78). In the 3rd century BC internal disputes and conflict with other Hellenistic kingdoms weakened Seleucid control of their eastern territories. Bactria broke away to become an independent kingdom, and the provinces of Parthia and Hyrcania were taken over by Arsaces, leader of the Parni in 238.

The early history of the new kingdom of Parthia

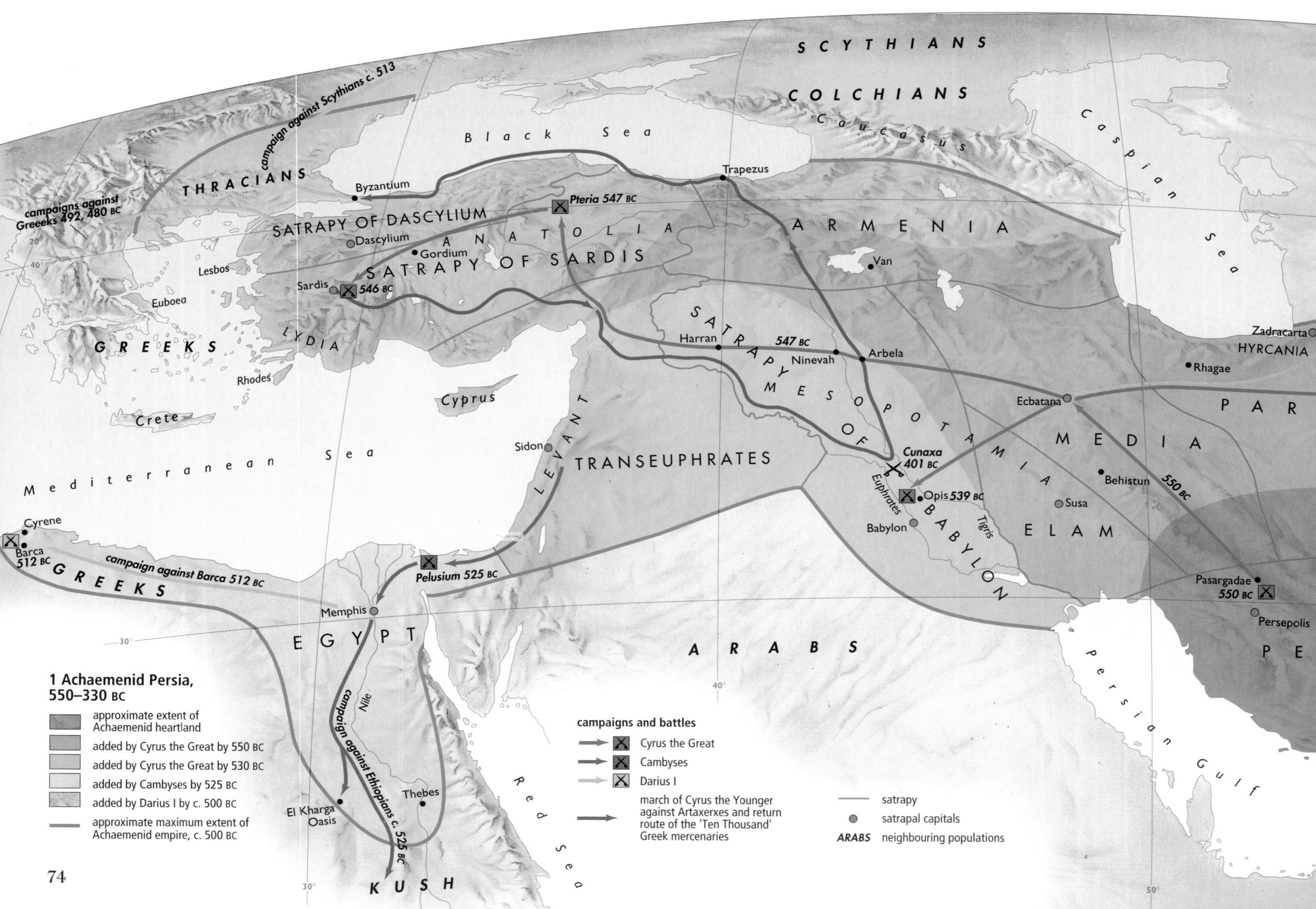

2 The Parthians overran much of the territory of the Seleucid kingdom *(map right)*. Their advance westwards brought them into contact with the expanding power of Rome and in 53 BC their mounted archers surrounded and destroyed the legions of the Roman general Crassus. In the following centuries several Roman campaigns against the Parthians were mounted, including one under Trajan (AD 98–117), who briefly annexed Armenia and Mespotamia, but the Euphrates came to be acknowledged as the uncertain frontier. In the east, the Parthians had to endure raids by a number of nomadic peoples until the rise of the Kushana empire provided some stability.

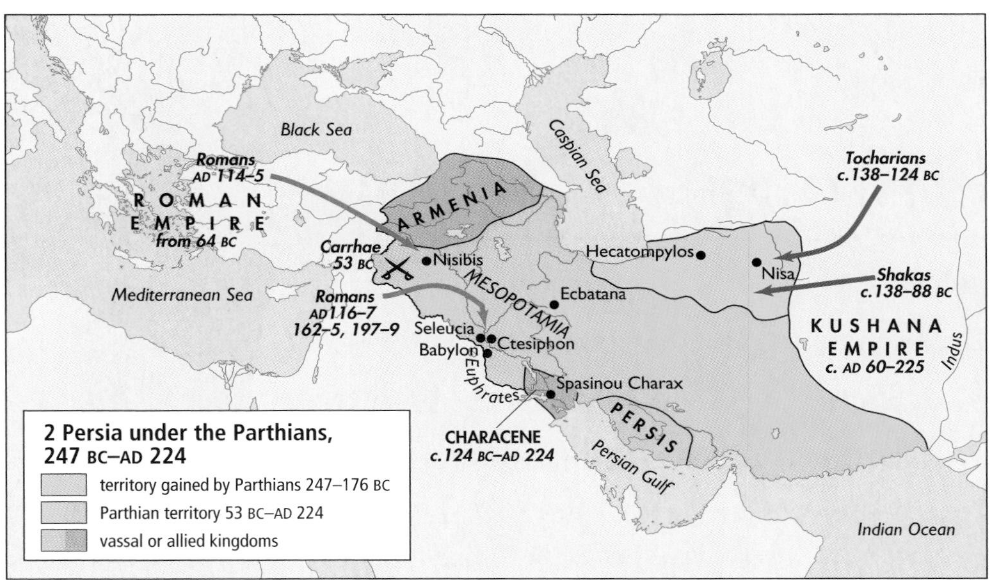

3 The new rulers of Persia rapidly annexed the western parts of the Kushana empire and installed their own governors under the title 'king of the Kushans' *(map right)*. Control of this part of their territory was threatened by further nomadic invasions of Hephthalite and Chionite Huns from the 4th century. On the western frontier, the Sasanids were able to withstand further attacks from Roman armies, capturing the Emperor Valerian at Edessa in 259. Their greatest successes came under Shapur II (310–79) and Chosroes I (531–79), under whose rule Arab territory was annexed as far south as Yemen. But conflict to the west continued, draining Sasanid resources and leaving the empire vulnerable to the Arab invasion of the 7th century.

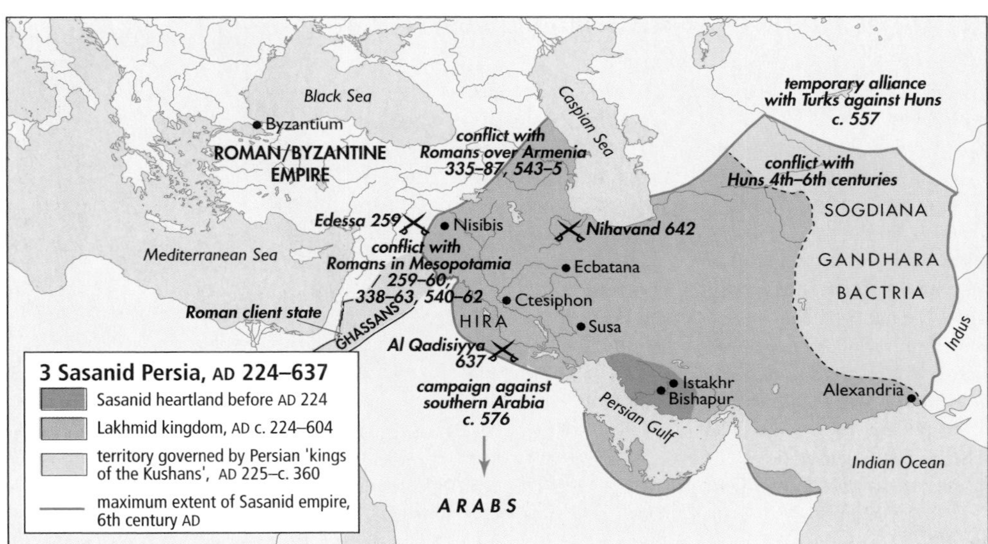

is uncertain, but under Mithradates I (171–138 BC) its territory was extended into Mesopotamia and as far east as the mouth of the Indus, its success, like that of Sasanid Persia later, largely the result of the use of mounted archers and armoured cavalry. In the years after Mithradates's death the empire was threatened by the Tocharians and the Shakas in the east, but order was restored by Mithradates II (123–87 BC). From the 1st century BC onwards, in spite of further severe Shaka incursions from the east, the main threat to Parthian security was Rome. But although there were a number of wars between the two empires, they were well matched militarily and Arsacid, or Parthian, rule remained secure until it was challenged from within.

Sasanid Persia

Considerable autonomy was left in the hands of local ruling families, and it was from one of these in Persis that the new rulers of Persia arose. The first Sasanid ruler, Ardashir, defeated his Arsacid overlord Ardavan in AD 224 and rapidly took control over the whole of Parthia's empire and the areas beyond. Roman and Byzantine rule in Mesopotamia, Syria and eastern Anatolia was constantly challenged over the next centuries. The last century of Parthian rule had seen the rise of the Kushana empire in the east (*see* p. 82). This came to an end in 225 and Gandhara, Bactria and Sogdiana were brought under Sasanid control. From the 4th century this territory was threatened by Hephthalite and Chionite Huns and in the 6th century by the Turks.

The Arabs were a constant presence to the southwest of Persia's empires. The Achaemenids had established some control over northern Arabia, but in the Parthian period an independent state of Characene emerged at the head of the Persian Gulf, whose rulers styled themselves 'kings of the Arabs'. The Sasanids ended the independence of Characene, but maintained friendly relations with the Lakhmid Arab kingdom of Hira in western Mesopotamia which supported them against the Romans. Southern Arabia was never brought under Persian control, and in c. 604, after the Sasanid Chosroes II had ended Lakhmid independence, the Persians were defeated in battle by a confederacy of Arabs from the south. Success created confidence and increased Arab unity to such an extent that with further victories at Al Qadisiyya (637) and Nihavand (642) they brought Sasanid power to an end.

1 The Achaemenid empire was the creation of the first three Persian kings – Cyrus, Cambyses and Darius – who in less than 50 years united the very disparate inhabitants of the area from the Mediterranean to the Indus under a single administration *(map left)*. According to the Greek historian Herodotus, there was a Persian saying that 'Cyrus was a father, Cambyses a tyrant and Darius a tradesman', and indeed it was under Darius that the empire was organized into satrapies, tribute-paying provinces usually ruled by Persian governors which nonetheless retained a variety of local forms of administration. The sheer size of the empire meant that its kings were sometimes slow to react to problems. The Greek mercenary and historian Xenophon described his involvement in an abortive attempt in 401 BC by the crown prince Cyrus to overthrow his brother Artaxerxes: Cyrus and his 'Ten Thousand' Greek mercenaries were able to march nearly half-way across the empire before they were stopped and Cyrus killed. Nonetheless, the empire was strong enough to withstand such shocks and remained a potent and united force until it was invaded by Alexander the Great in 334 BC.

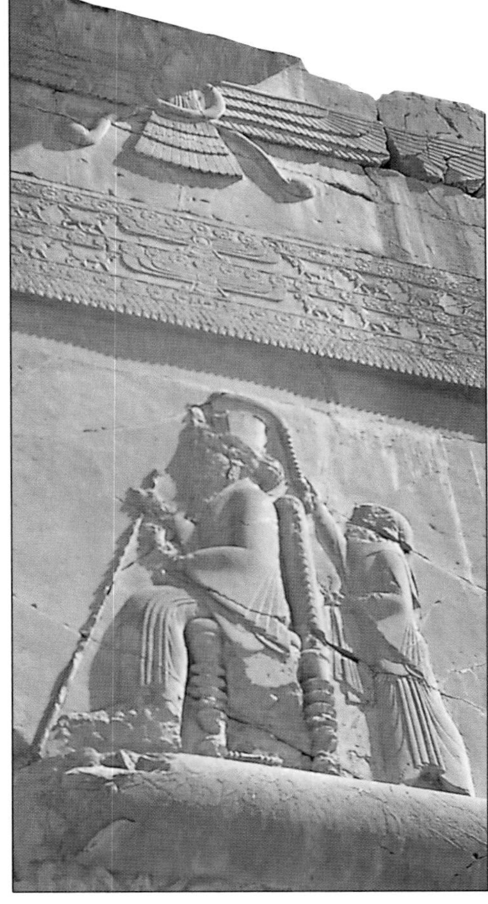

Relief from the royal palace at Persepolis *(right)*. King Darius is shown on his throne, and above him is the flying disk of Ahura Mazda, the chief god of Zoroastrianism, a religion whose origins lie in the second millennium BC. All three Persian regimes adopted versions of Zoroastrianism and the kings claimed a special relationship with Ahura Mazda.

800 to 336 BC
The spread of Greek civilization

See also
Minoan and Mycenaean civilizations p. 66
The commercial and cultural bonds of Eurasia p. 70
The empires of Persia, 550 BC–AD 637 p. 74
The Hellenistic world, 336–30 BC p. 78

776 BC *Traditional date for first Olympic Games*

c. 750 BC *First Greek colonizing expeditions*

7th–6th centuries BC *Emergence of tyrants in many Greek states*

508 BC *Reforms of Cleisthenes establish Athenian democracy*

478-404 BC *Athens dominates Aegean through Delian League*

447 BC *Parthenon begun in Athens*

399 BC *Socrates tried and executed at Athens*

371 BC *Thebans defeat Spartans at Leuctra: end of Spartan influence in Greek affairs*

338 BC *Battle of Chaeronea: Philip II of Macedon gains control of Greece*

The Greek heartland is an area of islands and plains divided by mountains. After the collapse of the Mycenaean palace system, a new form of political and religious community emerged here, the *polis*, or city-state, which became the Mediterranean world's dominant form of political organization.

THE EIGHTH CENTURY BC was a period of great transformation in Greece. It saw the appearance of the first monumental public buildings, and with them other indications of the emergence of new communities, including changes in burial practices and artistic styles. At the same time literacy was reintroduced into Greece, with a new alphabet. Though contact with the wider world had not been totally broken in previous centuries, it now increased dramatically, above all on the island of Euboea. Although it is impossible to be certain what produced this transformation, one important factor was the activities of the Phoenicians, who at this time began to explore and settle throughout the Mediterranean.

The age of expansion

From the middle of the century, following in the wake of the Phoenicians, groups of Greeks began to create settlements around the Mediterranean (*see* map 1). The earliest were in Italy and Sicily, but by the middle of the 6th century there were numerous Greek communities in north Africa and, to the east, along the Black Sea coast. These colonies were set up for a variety of reasons. Some of the earliest were trading posts, which over time developed into permanent settlements. Others were formally dispatched as a response to land shortage in the mother city. Others may have been founded by bands of discontented young men looking for a new and better life away from old Greece. It is probable that the experience of the colonists had an effect on the political development of their mother cities.

From its earliest existence, decision-making in the Greek *polis* lay with an assembly of adult male citizens. Leadership, however, would have been in the hands of the wealthy elite. Increasing wealth and overseas contact in the 7th and 6th centuries led to the emergence in many city-states of powerful individuals, known as tyrants, who were able to impose their will on the community, usually with popular support. The 'age of the tyrants' was a period of urban development, with new buildings, in particular enormous temples such as those of Hera on Samos, Artemis at Ephesus and Olympian Zeus at Athens. City-states published law-codes on large stone tablets, advertizing to the world that they were communities governed by the rule of law. Poetry flourished, with the *Iliad* and *Odyssey* of Homer and the poems of Hesiod appearing in the early 7th century, followed by the great lyric poets, among them Archilochus, Anacreon and Sappho. Certain religious sanctuaries, above all Olympia and Delphi, gained 'pan-Hellenic' status, and became meeting places for the leading members of the different Greek communities.

The Athenian empire

The experience of the Persian invasion of Greece under Xerxes (*see* map 2) encouraged the Greeks in the Aegean and Asia Minor to band together to

3 The whole Greek world became involved in the prolonged war between Athens and Sparta *(map below)*. Sparta was stronger on land, but Athens kept firm control of the sea. After ten years an uneasy peace was made (421 BC), but when Athens lost almost its entire fleet in Sicily, the Spartans pressed home their advantage. Even so, it was only with considerable naval and financial support from the Persians that they were able to overcome the Athenian navy.

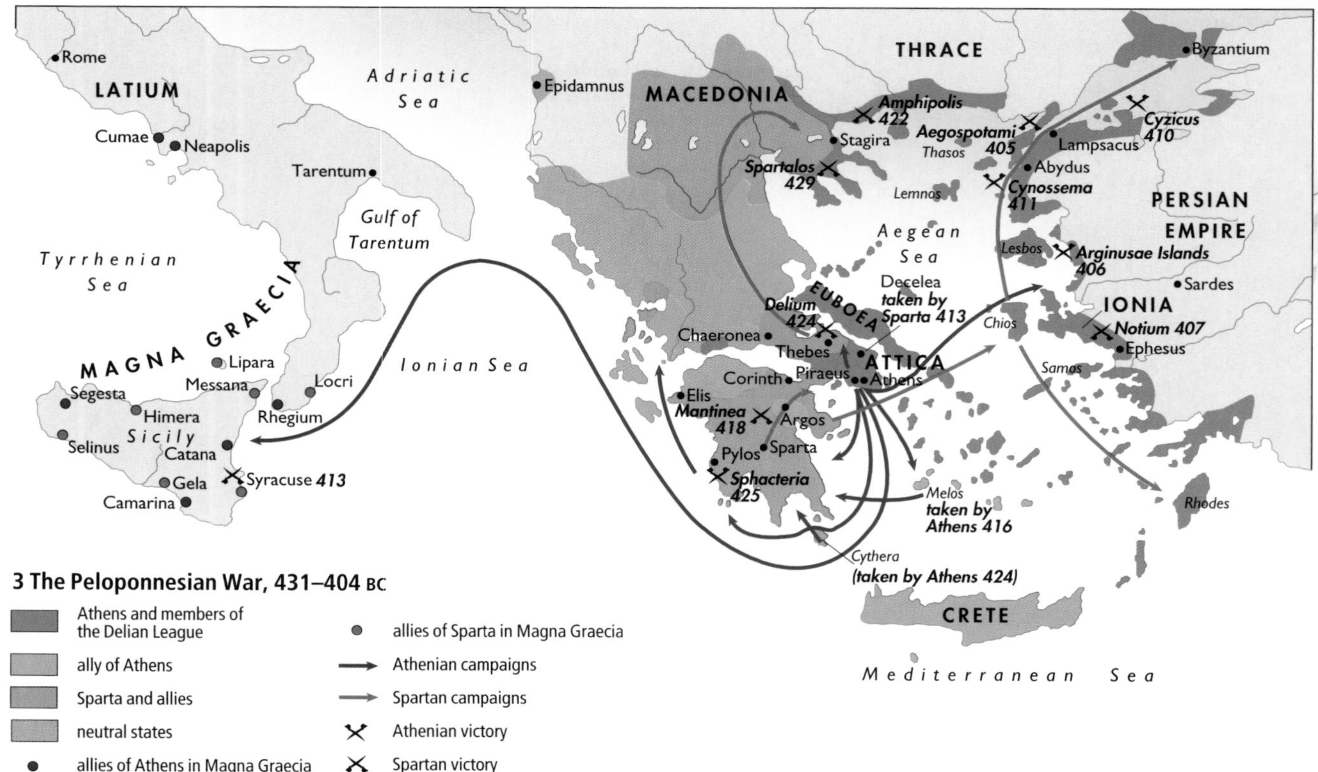

3 The Peloponnesian War, 431–404 BC

PEOPLE NOW AND IN TIME TO COME WILL MARVEL AT US, AND WE HAVE NO NEED OF A HOMER TO PRAISE US, OR OF ANYONE ELSE WHO MAY DELIGHT US FOR THE MOMENT BY THEIR WORDS, BUT WHOSE ESTIMATION OF OUR ACHIEVEMENTS WILL FALL SHORT OF THE TRUTH. FOR WE HAVE MADE EVERY SEA AND EVERY LAND ACCESSIBLE TO OUR DARING SPIRIT; AND EVERYWHERE WE HAVE ESTABLISHED EVERLASTING MEMORIALS OF GOOD TO OUR FRIENDS AND HARM TO OUR ENEMIES.

Thucydides (c. 460–400 BC)
Pericles' Funeral Oration

Bronze statue of Zeus ***(left)*** **of around 460 BC. The work, more than life-size, was retrieved from a wreck off Cape Artemisium. Few large bronze sculptures have survived from the period, and this is a superb example of early classical statuary.**

defend themselves from future threats from the still-powerful Persian empire. Athens, which had by far the largest fleet, inevitably took command, turning this alliance of city-states into an Athenian empire. Member states were required to pay tribute to finance the Athenian fleet, which guaranteed security. The existence of the Athenian empire had considerable effects on life in Athens. The fleet gave employment and status to the poorer citizens, who served as oarsmen and were able to participate in political activity to an extent unequalled elsewhere in the Greek world. A proportion of the tribute, along with some of the booty from successful naval campaigns, was given to the gods, funding great building programmes in Athens. The last three decades of the 5th century were also the period of Athens' most enduring literary achievements. Following the work of Aeschylus earlier in the century, Sophocles and Euripides wrote tragedies, and Aristophanes his comedies, for performance at the great dramatic festivals, the City Dionysia and the Lenaea. Herodotus, the first historian, lived in Athens for some time, while sophists, philosophers and rhetoricians flocked there to make their names and their fortunes. Athens also produced its own great historian, Thucydides.

At the same time, Athens' growing power was seen as a threat by the states of the Peloponnese, above all Sparta. After some inconclusive conflicts in the mid-century, in 431 BC Sparta declared war on Athens. This, the Peloponnesian War, developed into a conflict which ended 27 years later in the defeat of Athens and the disbanding of its empire (*see* map 3).

The rise of Macedon

The economies of all Greek city-states were dominated by agriculture, and, except perhaps in Sparta, which relied on the labour of its conquered Messenian subjects (the 'helots'), most of the population was made up of small-scale farmers, who were available for military service in the periods of less intense agricultural activity. One effect of this was that even prolonged periods of warfare had little long-term impact on the economies of the city-states involved. Thus within a decade of surrendering to the Peloponnesians, Athens was again at war with Sparta, this time supported by several of her former opponents.

The Spartans had originally defeated the Athenians with help from Persia. In 387 BC the Persian king attempted to impose a peace settlement on Greece, and the next 30 years saw Athens, Sparta and Thebes vying for dominance in Greece, looking always for backing from Persia. In 359 BC Philip II became king of Macedon. He united the country and took advantage of conflicts elsewhere in Greece to gain control of Thrace to the east and Thessaly to the south. This gave him a firm base for involvement in Greek affairs, and, after Philip had brought to an end the 'Sacred War' of 356–46, Macedon was left as the major power in Greece. In 338 BC Philip defeated the Athenians and Thebans at Chaeronea, and imposed a settlement on the whole of Greece, the 'League of Corinth'. His death two years later left his son Alexander the legacy of a more or less united Greece, from which he was able to launch his invasion of the Persian empire.

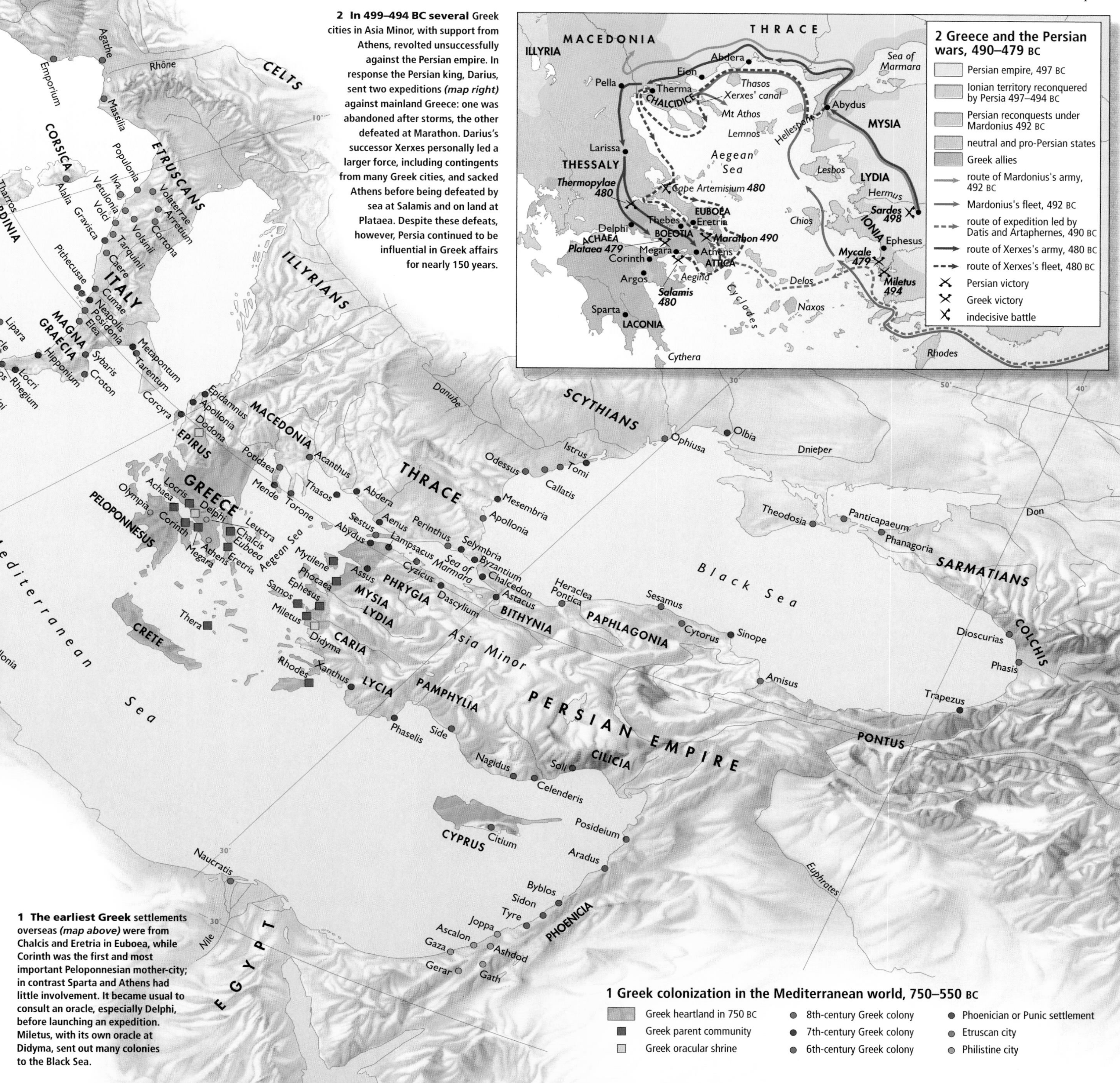

2 In 499–494 BC several Greek cities in Asia Minor, with support from Athens, revolted unsuccessfully against the Persian empire. In response the Persian king, Darius, sent two expeditions *(map right)* against mainland Greece: one was abandoned after storms, the other defeated at Marathon. Darius's successor Xerxes personally led a larger force, including contingents from many Greek cities, and sacked Athens before being defeated by sea at Salamis and on land at Plataea. Despite these defeats, however, Persia continued to be influential in Greek affairs for nearly 150 years.

1 The earliest Greek settlements overseas *(map above)* were from Chalcis and Eretria in Euboea, while Corinth was the first and most important Peloponnesian mother-city; in contrast Sparta and Athens had little involvement. It became usual to consult an oracle, especially Delphi, before launching an expedition. Miletus, with its own oracle at Didyma, sent out many colonies to the Black Sea.

336 to 30 BC
The Hellenistic world

See also
The empires of Persia, 550 BC–AD 637 p. 74
The spread of Greek civilization p. 76
India: the first empires, 500 BC–AD 550 p. 82
The expansion of Roman power to 31 BC p. 86

WHEN ALEXANDER WAS DYING AT BABYLON, HE WAS ASKED BY HIS FRIENDS TO WHOM HE WAS LEAVING HIS KINGDOM. WITH HIS LAST BREATH HE REPLIED, 'TO THE STRONGEST: FOR I FORESEE THAT A GREAT COMBAT BETWEEN MY FRIENDS WILL BE MY FUNERAL GAMES.'

Diodorus Siculus
Library of History, c. 50 BC

EVERYTHING IN THE WORLD THAT EXISTS OR IS MADE IS NOW IN EGYPT: WEALTH, WRESTLING SCHOOLS, POWER, PEACE, FAME, SPECTACLES, PHILOSOPHERS, GOLD, YOUTHS, THE SANCTUARY OF THE BROTHER-SISTER GODS, THE NOBLE KING, THE MUSEUM, WINE, EVERY GOOD THING ONE COULD NEED.

Herodas
The Procuress, c. 250 BC

Alexander the Great's conquest of the Persian empire transformed the eastern Mediterranean and Middle Eastern world. The spread of Greek culture and political organisation which followed in his wake shaped the region for a millennium. Greek became the common language, and the city-state the common form of social organisation.

336 *Philip of Macedon assassinated*

334 *Alexander invades the Persian empire*

323 *Death of Alexander*

301 *Battle of Ipsus; final break-up of Alexander's empire*

146 *Following rebellions, Macedonia becomes a Roman province*

133 *Attalus III of Pergamum dies, leaving his kingdom to Rome*

64 *Romans annex Syria, ending Seleucid rule*

30 *Death of Cleopatra; Romans annex Egypt*

ALONG WITH THE KINGDOM of Macedon, in 336 BC Alexander inherited from his father the leadership of a league of Greek states that he had intended to use to campaign against the Persian empire. Through his ambition and brilliant generalship, by the time of his death less than 13 years later at the age of 32, he was recognized as legitimate ruler of an empire stretching from Egypt to India (*see* map 1). From the moment he died there was competition between his closest companions and generals. Until the assassination of Alexander's young son in 307 BC, the contenders, for all that each had ambitions to take over the whole empire, could at least claim to be acting as regents. Thereafter, they were fighting for themselves, rapidly styling themselves as kings, and attempting to carve out areas of personal influence. By 276 BC, a division of the empire into three main kingdoms – Antigonid Macedon, Seleucid Asia and Ptolemaic Egypt – had been established.

Cultural life in the successor states

The basic political units of these new kingdoms was the city-state, some nominally independent, but most owing allegiance to one of the successor kings. The cities of old Greece, such as Athens, retained their prestige, but they were eclipsed by the newly created or reorganized cities of the east, named inevitably after their founders or rulers: Alexandria, Seleucia, Antioch. The new cities had all the elements of their older counterparts, with gymnasia, theatres and temples to the gods, and regular festivals, some including athletics, which might be attended by Greeks from far afield. Citizenship was restricted almost entirely to the Greek and Macedonian minority, and the land was in the hands of citizens or of the kings and their friends. The local populations might farm the land as tenants or as labourers, but they were excluded from administrative positions. The network of cities helped the spread of a common Greek culture and language throughout the region: Clearchus, a pupil of Aristotle, brought a collection of maxims from Delphi in central Greece to the city of Ai Khanoum in eastern Afghanistan. In a number of cities, but above all in Alexandria, with its access to papyrus, and Pergamum, from where parchment got its name, the kings established great libraries, and these became centres for literary work.

Even before Alexander's conquest, some communities within the Persian empire had adopted aspects of Greek culture. This 'Hellenization' continued, at least among the elites: conflict between 'Hellenizers' and 'traditionalists' in the 2nd century led to violence in Jerusalem. However, especially in Seleucid territories, elements of older cultures, including cuneiform writing, remained important, and in those areas which were to become the Parthian empire (*see* p. 74), Greek culture was never firmly established.

There were advances in geometry and mathematics, especially with Euclid of Alexandria and Archimedes. The great Alexandrian librarian, Eratosthenes of Cyrene, attempted with some success to calculate the circumference of the earth.

However, this was not a period of great technological change. The basis of the Hellenistic economy was agriculture, and this changed little. Merchants continued to trade, and writers of the time praise the range of goods available in the great cities, but there is evidence too of an increasing gulf between rich and poor. Only in warfare were there major developments, with the creation of ever more advanced artillery and siege engines, and the introduction by the Seleucids and the Ptolemies of elephants onto the battlefield.

From the late 3rd century, a new player entered the game. Threats to Roman

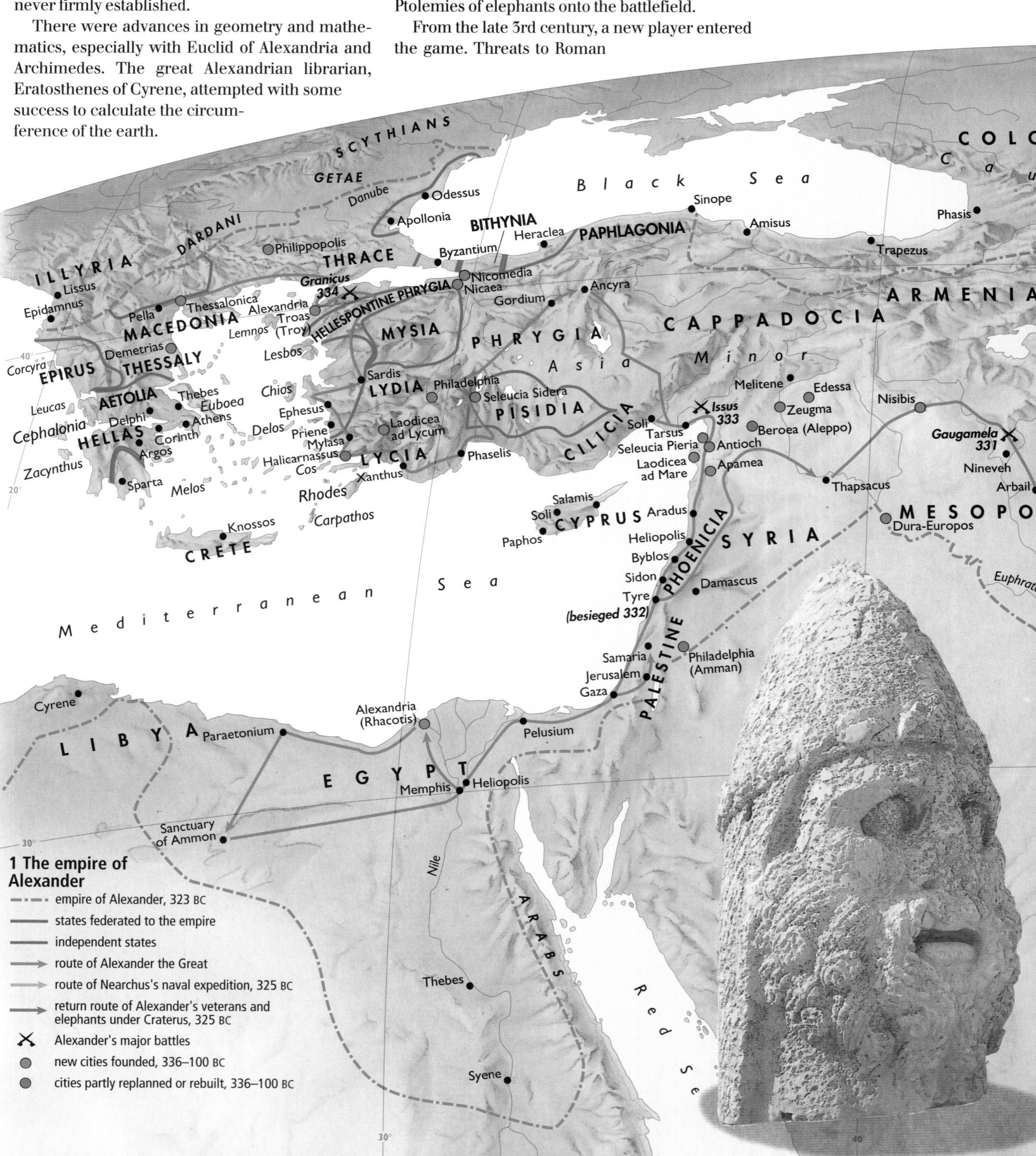

operations in the Adriatic, and Macedonian support for the Carthaginian Hannibal, led to a Roman invasion of Greece and Asia Minor. The Macedonian phalanx proved inferior to the Roman legions.

The growth of Roman power

Wars gave Roman commanders an opportunity for booty and glory, and initially they withdrew their forces after each campaign; but as Rome acquired more allies in the east, the reasons for maintaining their presence grew. After the battle of Pydna (168) the kingdom of Macedon was divided into four independent republics. 18 years later it was made a Roman province. The involvement of Cleopatra VII in the civil war between Mark Antony and the future emperor Augustus led after the battle of Actium (*see* p. 87) to the Roman annexation of Egypt, the last major successor kingdom. A few small client kingdoms, tolerated by the Romans for a while, were all that remained of Alexander's territorial inheritance.

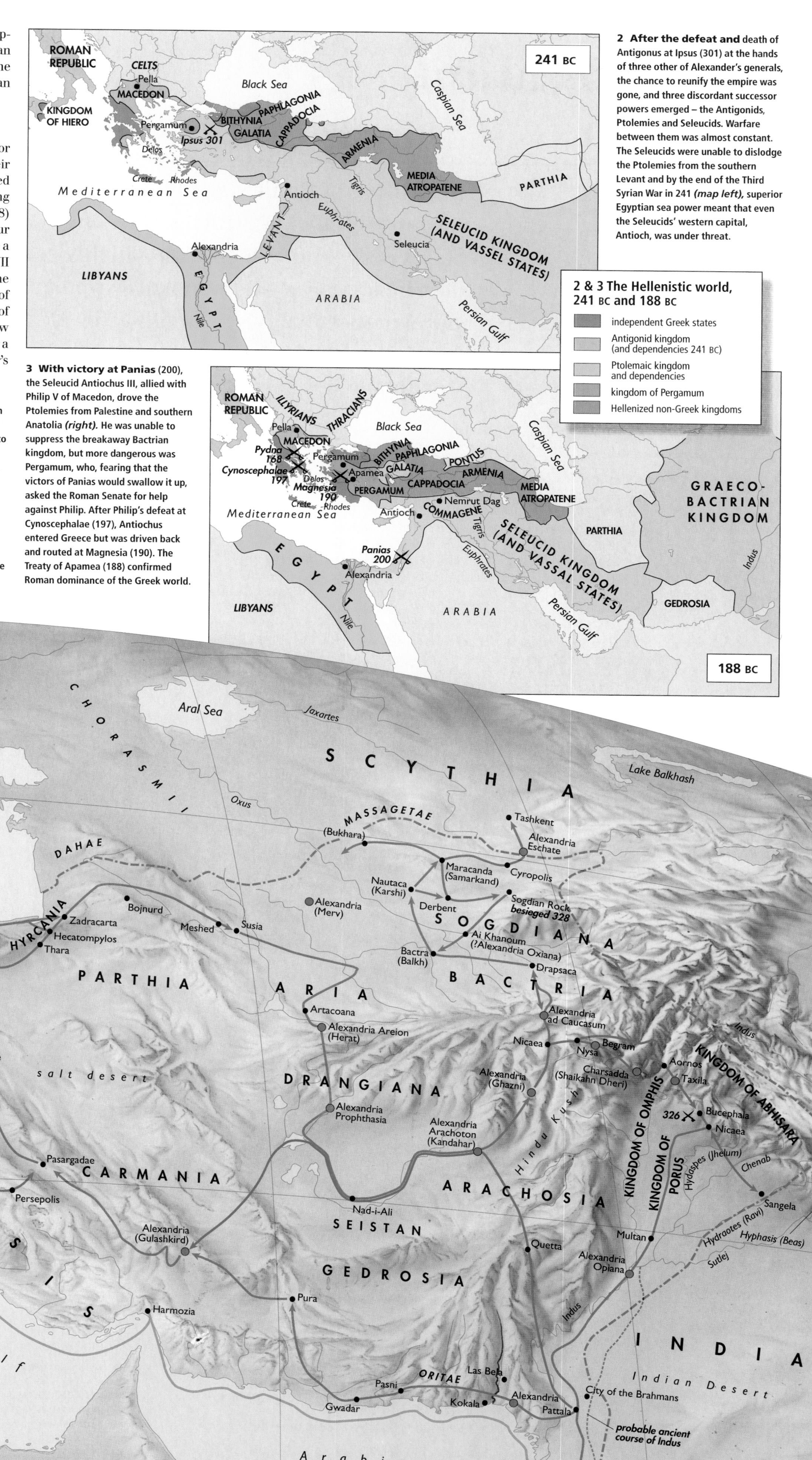

2 After the defeat and death of Antigonus at Ipsus (301) at the hands of three other of Alexander's generals, the chance to reunify the empire was gone, and three discordant successor powers emerged – the Antigonids, Ptolemies and Seleucids. Warfare between them was almost constant. The Seleucids were unable to dislodge the Ptolemies from the southern Levant and by the end of the Third Syrian War in 241 ***(map left)***, superior Egyptian sea power meant that even the Seleucids' western capital, Antioch, was under threat.

3 With victory at Panias (200), the Seleucid Antiochus III, allied with Philip V of Macedon, drove the Ptolemies from Palestine and southern Anatolia ***(right)***. He was unable to suppress the breakaway Bactrian kingdom, but more dangerous was Pergamum, who, fearing that the victors of Panias would swallow it up, asked the Roman Senate for help against Philip. After Philip's defeat at Cynoscephalae (197), Antiochus entered Greece but was driven back and routed at Magnesia (190). The Treaty of Apamea (188) confirmed Roman dominance of the Greek world.

1 Alexander spent almost his whole reign on campaign in the Persian empire ***(below)***. Victories over the Persians at Granicus (334), Issus (333) and Gaugamela (331) allowed him to take over the title of Great King. He continued eastwards to end resistance to his rule, and reached the mouth of the Indus. Having sent his older veterans back to Macedonia under the general Craterus, and while his fleet under Nearchus explored the Persian Gulf, he led his army on a gruelling march through the Gedrosian desert back to Babylon, where he died. The legacy of his campaigns was a series of colonies, made up of veteran soldiers, each named Alexandria. His successors continued the founding of new Hellenistic cities throughout the area of his former empire.

Antiochus I of Commagene (c. 69–36 BC) ***(left)***. Commagene on the upper Euphrates broke away from the Seleucid empire c. 162 BC, and remained autonomous until AD 72. Antiochus claimed descent from the Achaemenid Persian kings and from Alexander, emphasizing this joint heritage in his vast mausoleum-temple at Nemrut Dag, from where this portrait-head comes.

475 BC to AD 220
The unification of China

See also
The beginnings of Chinese civilization to 475 BC p. 62
The commercial and cultural bonds of Eurasia p. 70
The religious bonds of Eurasia to AD 500 p. 72
China and east Asia, AD 220–618 p. 124
Early civilizations of southeast Asia to AD 1511 p. 134

> They recall the age of disordered confusion when the land was divided and separate states established, so opening wide the fissures of strife, when assaults and battles every day arose, and blood flowed on the plains, as it has since earliest antiquity ... Until now, when this our emperor has made the world one family, and weapons of warfare are lifted up no longer.
>
> **Imperial edict**
> *Found on Mount Yi, from c. 215 BC*

The process of China's nation- and empire-building began with the political anarchy of the Warring States period but ended with a highly centralized state headed by a single monarch and an efficient bureaucracy that reached village level. The new system attained its full glory under the Han, whose wealth and territory matched the Roman empire.

475–221 BC *Warring States period*

221–207 BC *Ch'in dynasty*

221 BC *Shih Huang-ti crowned the first emperor of China*

210 BC *Death of Shih Huang-ti; decline of the Ch'in*

202 BC–AD 9 *Former Han dynasty*

87 BC *Death of emperor Han Wu-ti; decline of Former Han*

AD 9–23 *Hsin dynasty*

AD 25–220 *Later Han dynasty*

AD 220 *Last Han emperor Hsien-ti abdicates*

THROUGHOUT THE WARRING States period (475–221 BC) seven major rivals contended for supremacy. At first, following the decline of the power of the Chou king (*see* p. 62), the principal contenders were the old-established dukedoms of Ch'i, Ch'u, Han and Wei. But from the beginning of the 3rd century BC the border state of Ch'in established firm control over the northwest and west, adopting the title 'king' in 325 BC, and during the latter half of the 3rd century BC it began gradually destroying its rivals (*see* map 1).

Throughout China, it was period of constant warfare, waged on a massive scale by powerful and well-organized political units. But at the same time, this period of 'Warring States' coincided with major economic and social changes. The introduction of iron tools from about 500 BC and the use of animal power for cultivation greatly increased agricultural productivity, and farming zones expanded. Population multiplied, commerce and industry flourished and large cities emerged. It was also a period of innovation in technology and science and of philosophical ferment, in which the main schools of thought – Confucianism, Daoism and Legalism – took shape.

That the Ch'in emerged from this period to unify China under their leadership was at least in part due to the success of the 'Legalist' system adopted by them in the 4th century, whereby a universal code of rewards and punishments was established that induced a high level of popular obedience and military discipline. In the place of the old feudal aristocracy a centralized bureaucracy took measures to improve the production and distribution of grain, and organized the population to provide manpower for construction works and for the army, enforcing the system through a ruthless penal code.

The first emperor

When the Ch'in king, Shih Huang-ti, was crowned the first emperor of China in 221, these 'Legalist' institutions were extended throughout the country. But although the emperor tried to eliminate all hostile factions, under the burdens imposed on the

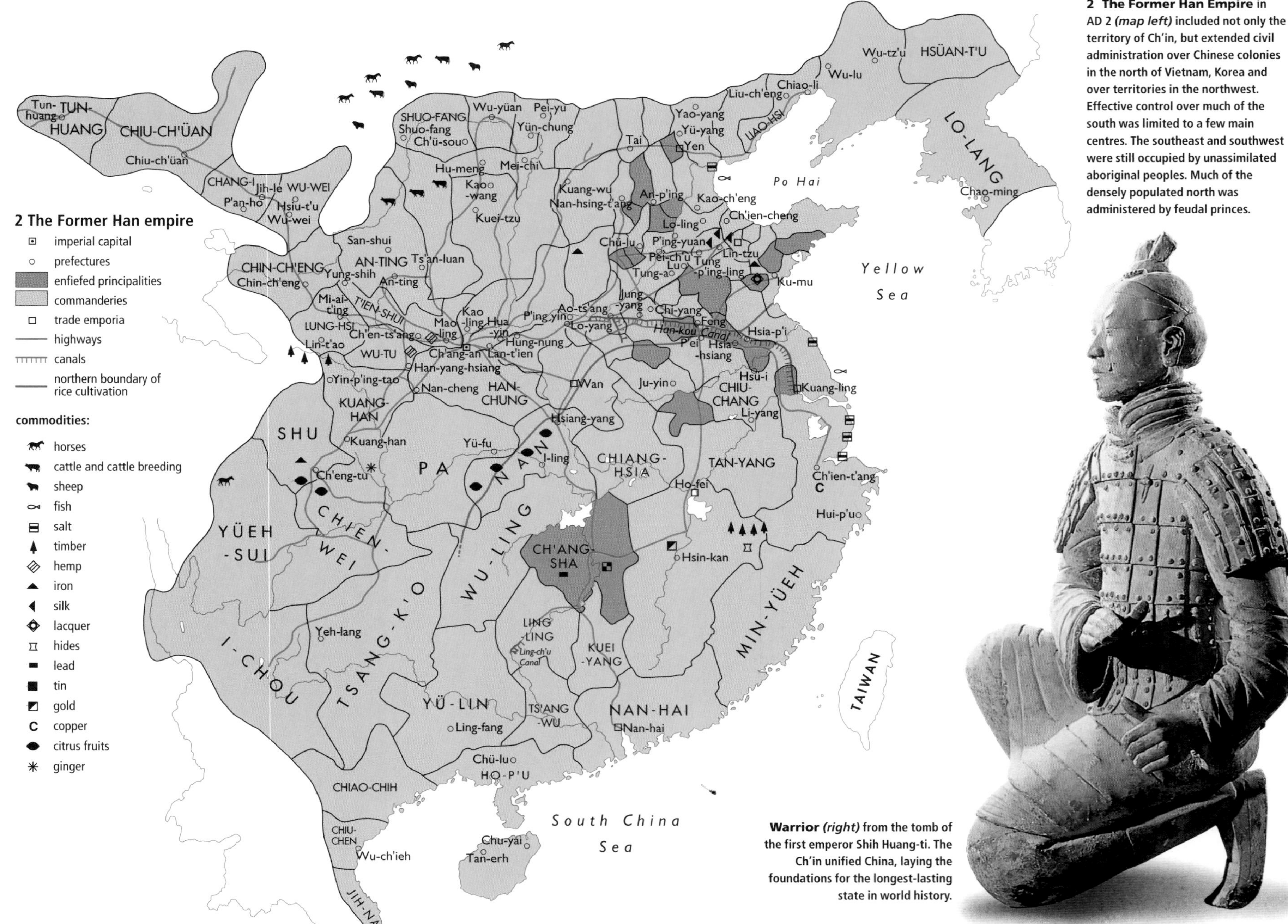

2 The Former Han Empire in AD 2 *(map left)* included not only the territory of Ch'in, but extended civil administration over Chinese colonies in the north of Vietnam, Korea and over territories in the northwest. Effective control over much of the south was limited to a few main centres. The southeast and southwest were still occupied by unassimilated aboriginal peoples. Much of the densely populated north was administered by feudal princes.

Warrior *(right)* from the tomb of the first emperor Shih Huang-ti. The Ch'in unified China, laying the foundations for the longest-lasting state in world history.

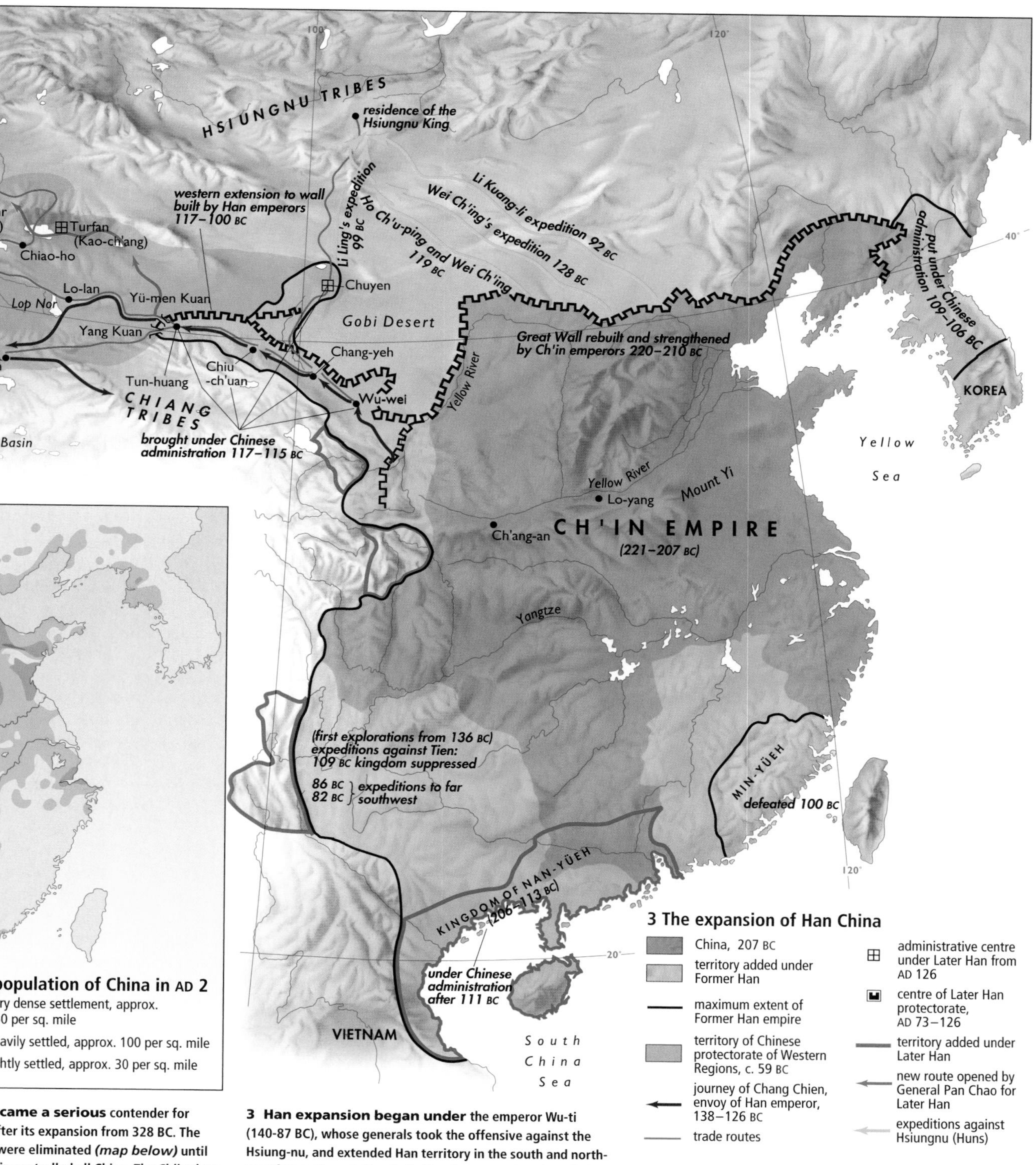

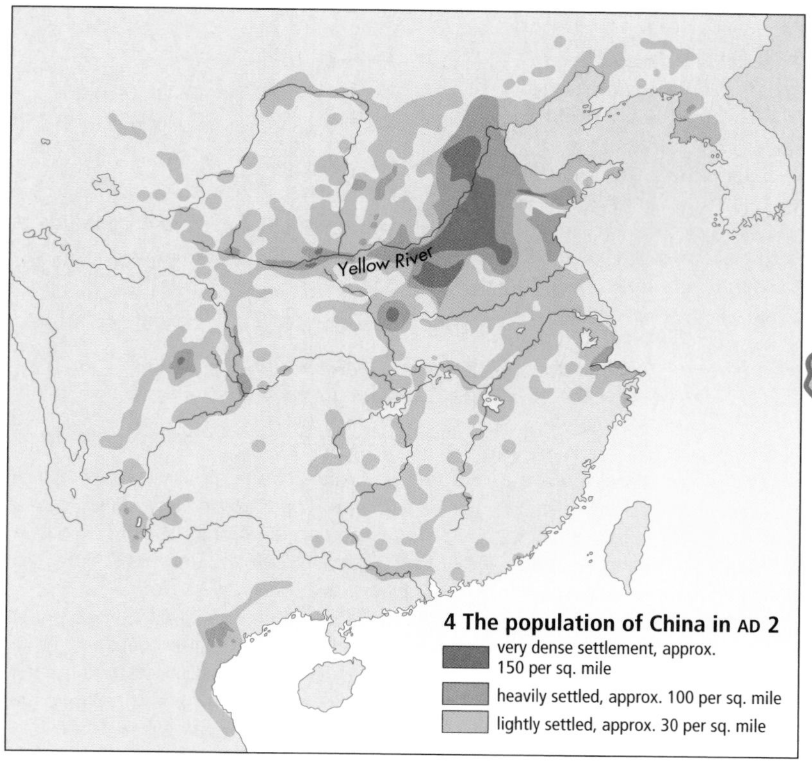

4 The population of China in AD 2

very dense settlement, approx. 150 per sq. mile

heavily settled, approx. 100 per sq. mile

lightly settled, approx. 30 per sq. mile

4 The earliest surviving Chinese census is from AD 2, and shows a population of 57 million, concentrated in the lower Yellow River plain *(map above)*. Before 500 BC, population growth had been limited by the lack of the technology needed to clear new land for cultivation, but after the introduction of iron, and with the emergence of large-scale new states in the 5th century BC, massive drainage and irrigation projects were undertaken. Population growth was further boosted by the wealth and stability of Han China.

1 Ch'in became a serious contender for supremacy after its expansion from 328 BC. The other states were eliminated *(map below)* until in 221 BC Ch'in controlled all China. The Ch'in then expanded its territories to the south and northeast. Earlier, several of the 'warring' kingdoms had erected earthworks as a defence against their neighbours or potential invasions from the non-Chinese peoples to the north. Faced with a threat from the Hsiung-nu, the first Ch'in emperor unified these into a single coordinated system.

3 Han expansion began under the emperor Wu-ti (140-87 BC), whose generals took the offensive against the Hsiung-nu, and extended Han territory in the south and northeast *(map above)*. Thanks to the pioneer exploration of Chang Chien, diplomatic initiatives were started to expand trade and forge alliances with some of the peoples of the northwest, and under his promptings the 'Silk Road' was established carrying Chinese trade to central Asia and beyond. To protect these routes, annexations and extensions to the Great Wall in the northwest followed. Chinese power was again briefly extended to the west under the Later Han after AD 94.

3 The expansion of Han China

China, 207 BC

territory added under Former Han

maximum extent of Former Han empire

territory of Chinese protectorate of Western Regions, c. 59 BC

journey of Chang Chien, envoy of Han emperor, 138–126 BC

trade routes

administrative centre under Later Han from AD 126

centre of Later Han protectorate, AD 73–126

territory added under Later Han

new route opened by General Pan Chao for Later Han

expeditions against Hsiungnu (Huns)

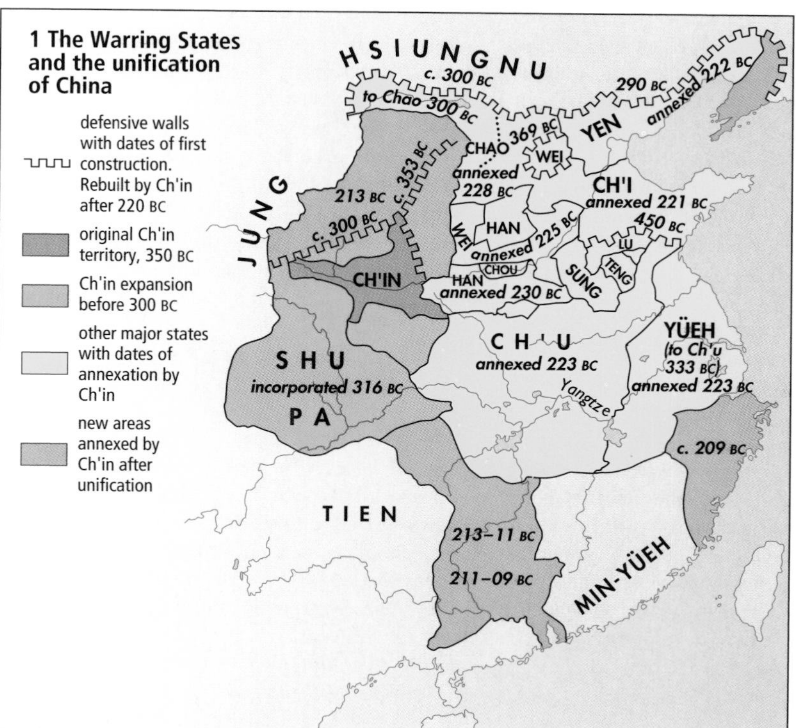

people by his military campaigns and vast construction works, his dynasty collapsed in a nationwide mass rebellion in 206 BC, shortly after his death

After a period of civil war a new dynasty, the Han, was established by Liu Pang (256–195 BC). Copying the general outlines of the Ch'in system, but softening its harshness and in part restoring a system of feudal principalities, the Han gradually evolved an effective central government and system of local administration. The 'Legalist' approach was replaced by Confucianism which emphasized benevolent rule and good statesmanship.

Han expansion

The Ch'in had taken strong defensive measures against the nomad Hsiung-nu (Huns) in the north. Under the emperor Wu-ti (140–87 BC), though probably driven by his generals in the north, Han China again took the offensive against the Hsiung-nu, and opened up the route to central Asia known as the Silk Road. A large export trade, mainly in silk, reached as far as the Roman empire. The Han also reaffirmed the Ch'in conquests in the southern region, eliminated the Yüeh kingdoms of the southeast coast, and occupied northern Vietnam. Chinese armies also drove deep into the southwest, seeking to establish Han control. In addition, Wu-ti's armies placed parts of northern Korea under Chinese administration.

The Han empire grew extremely prosperous and China's population reached some 57 million. Many large cities grew up and the largest, the capital Ch'ang-an, housed a population of a quarter of a million and was the centre of a brilliant culture. At the beginning of the Christian era the Han empire rivalled that of Rome in size and wealth.

But under a series of weak emperors during the latter half of the 1st century BC, the authority of the throne was challenged by powerful court families. In AD 9 Wang Mang usurped the throne. His reign (the Hsin dynasty, AD 9–23) ended in a widespread rebellion that restored the Han (Later Han, AD 25–220), and the capital was moved to Lo-yang.

The collapse of the Han empire

After some decades of consolidation, in the late 1st century the Chinese resumed active hostilities to drive the Hsiung-nu westward to central Asia. But trouble with the Chiang tribes of the northwest and virulent factionalism at court had seriously weakened the Han state by AD 160. A wave of agrarian distress culminated in 184 in a massive uprising led by the 'Yellow Turbans', a religious movement based on popular cults. Although the Han survived in name until 220, power in fact now lay with regional commanders. In 220 the empire was divided into three independent kingdoms, ushering in a long period of territorial fragmentation.

500 BC to AD 550
India: the first empires

See also

The beginnings of Indian civilization p. 64
The commercial and cultural bonds of Eurasia p. 70
The religious bonds of Eurasia to AD 500 p. 72
The empires of Persia, 550 BC–AD 637 p. 74
The Hellenistic world, 336–30 BC p. 78
From Rome to Byzantium, AD 235–565 p. 90
India: the emergence of temple kingdoms p. 130
The early civilizations of southeast Asia p. 134

From 500 BC to AD 550 south Asia witnessed a succession of metropolitan empires centred in north India – the Mauryas, the Kushanas and the Guptas. Although centralized political control was often weak, for the first time the entire subcontinent was integrated within a single but diverse cultural field.

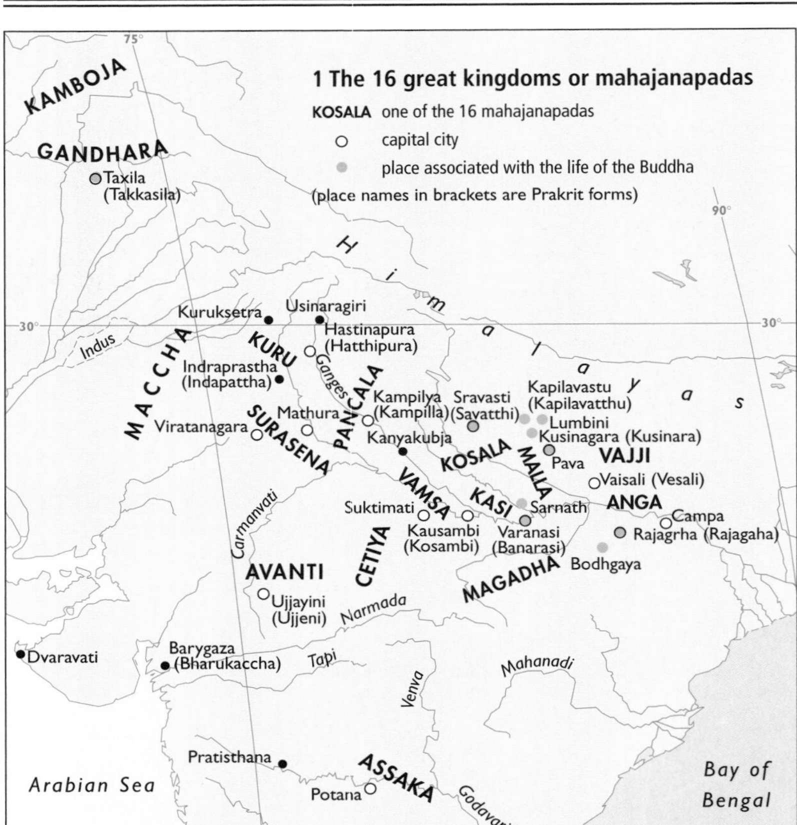

1 In 500 BC, north India ***(map above)*** **was dominated by small polities, one of which, the eastern kingdom of Magadha contained the seeds of empire. Eastern India was also the home of Gautama Buddha who, born in around 486 BC in Lumbini near Kapilavastu, renounced the pleasures of royal life and attained spiritual enlightenment at Bodhgaya. He gave his first sermon at Sarnath and died at Kusinagara, from where his remains were carried away by kings and enshrined in burial mounds known as stupas.**

3 In the 1st century BC migrations by the Shaka clans had destabilized the northwest. They were followed by new invaders, the Kushanas, who reduced the Shakas settled in western India to provincial governors (Satrapas) and subjugated much of north India, although they failed to dislodge the powerful Satavahanas of central west India ***(map below)*****. By the 3rd century AD, the Kushana empire had ended: its western reaches were tributary to the Persian Sasanids and its eastern provinces fragmented into small polities.**

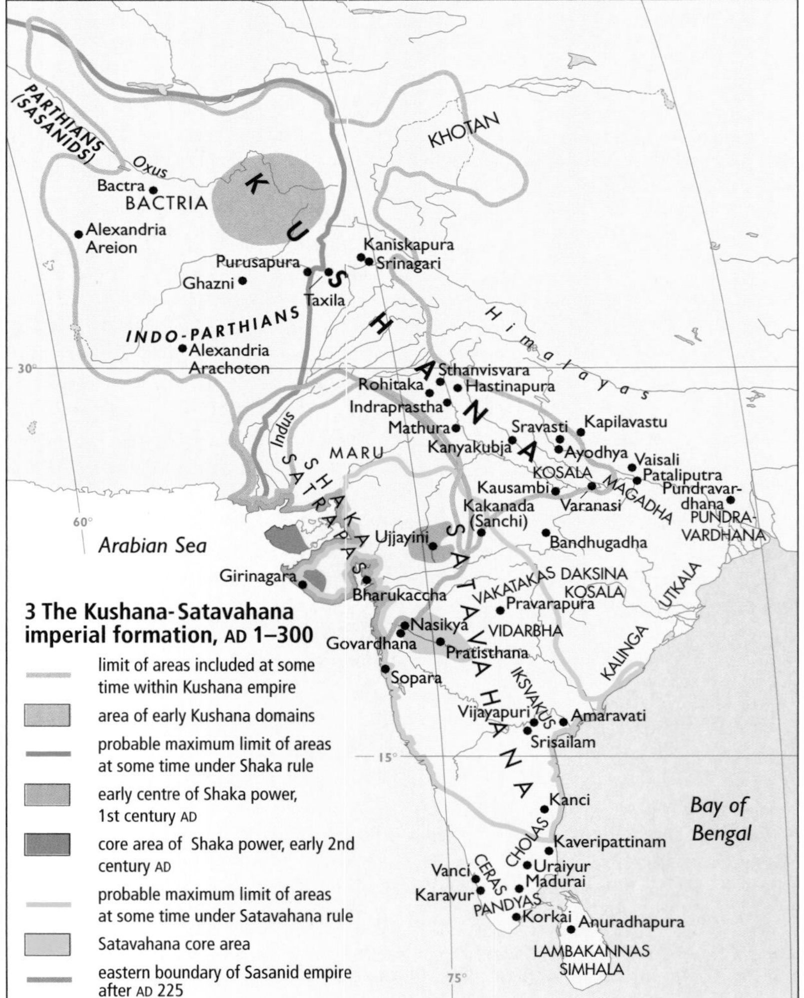

BY ABOUT 500 BC NORTH India sustained 16 well-articulated polities, or 'mahajanapadas', some still essentially tribal republics and others already monarchies (*see* map 1). This region witnessed tremendous change, as the consolidation of settled agriculture led to the emergence of cities and more complex political systems. Such changes made the older sacrificial cult of the Vedas, which had its origins in the pastoral communities of the Aryan tribes, increasingly obsolete. In its place, at the end of the 5th century BC in the heart of the Gangetic plains, the founders of Buddhism and Jainism formulated their radical new teachings.

> I HAVE GIVEN THE GIFT OF INSIGHT IN VARIOUS FORMS. I HAVE CONFERRED MANY BENEFITS ON MAN, ANIMALS, BIRDS, AND FISH, EVEN TO SAVING THEIR LIVES, AND I HAVE DONE MANY OTHER COMMENDABLE DEEDS. I HAVE HAD THIS INSCRIPTION OF DHAMMA ENGRAVED THAT MEN MAY CONFORM TO IT AND THAT IT MAY ENDURE.
>
> ***Second Pillar Edict, Lauriya Nandangarh***

The first empire

During the 5th century BC the number of mahajanapadas gradually diminished to four – Vajji, Kosala, Kasi and Magadha. After a century of wars, the single kingdom of Magadha dominated, with its splendid new capital of Pataliputra. This was to be the nucleus of the first Indian empire. Shortly after Alexander's incursion into India in 327 BC, the Mauryan prince Chandragupta seized the Magadhan throne. Chandragupta then conquered the land east of the Indus, swung south to occupy much of central India, and in 305 BC decisively defeated Alexander's successor in the northwest, Seleucus Nicator. The Mauryan empire that Chandragupta founded reached its zenith under his grandson, Ashoka, who established his rule over most of the subcontinent (*see* map 2). Ashoka's empire was composed of a centralized administrative system spread over a number of thriving cities and their hinterlands. After his conquest of Kalinga in 260 BC, Ashoka publicly converted to Buddhism and adopted a policy of 'conquest through righteousness', or *dhammavijaya*. In a number of public orders inscribed on pillars and rockfaces throughout the subcontinent, Ashoka called for peace, propagated moral teachings (*dhamma*), and prohibited Vedic animal sacrifices. These edicts, written in Prakrit, are the first specimens of royal decrees in south Asia, a type of public communication which would remain important in subsequent times.

The Kushana empire

Mauryan rule did not long survive Ashoka's death in 232 BC. In the 2nd century BC, the northwest was repeatedly invaded, both by Greeks from Bactria and Parthia, and then by new nomad groups themselves displaced from central Asia. First among these were Scythian tribes called the Shakas who overran Bactria and the Indus valley in the 1st century BC. Then the Kushana branch of the Yüeh-chih horde, who had settled in the Oxus valley after 165 BC, gradually extended their rule inland, subduing the Shakas in western India and reaching Varanasi in the 1st century AD. As well as the Oxus and Indus valleys, large parts of Khotan were included in their cosmopolitan empire, centred in Purusapura. Kushana India was a melting pot of cultures – Indian, Chinese, central Asian and Helleno-Roman. The empire reached its height of power and influence under Kanishka, who patronized Buddhism and became extensively involved in political conflicts in central Asia.

Both the Shakas and the Kushanas took Indian names and were the first kings to adopt Sanskrit at their courts – the first courtly poems and inscriptions in Sanskrit date from this period – though the native kingdom of the Satavahanas of the Deccan continued to use Prakrit. In the northwest Mahayana Buddhism emerged at this time from the more conservative teachings known as Theravada, and developed a more eclectic outlook, emphasizing compassion and worship in an enlarged Buddhist pantheon.

In the same period, India's ancient trading links with the west were revitalized and greatly extended as the Roman empire rose to power (*see* map 5). Ports such as Barbaricum, on the Indus delta, and the entrepot of Barygaza exported turquoise, diamonds, indigo and tortoise-shell, receiving in return a flow of pearls, copper, gold and slaves from the Arab and Mediterranean worlds. Much of the Chinese silk traffic found its way to the city of Taxila, before caravans took it further west. Trade led to other exchanges, as Buddhism spread to central Asia and China.

By the middle of the 2nd century AD the south had also witnessed economic development. The Satavahanas of the Deccan developed a powerful empire and established overland and coastal trading networks and the weaker Tamil-speaking kingdoms of the south established ports on both coasts of the peninsula.

The Guptas

In the 4th century, the native dynasty of the Guptas, imposed a new rule, based again in Pataliputra. Following the campaigns of Samudragupta and his son Chandragupta II, their suzerainty was acknowledged over an area almost as great as that of the Mauryan empire. Until repeated Hun incursions ended Gupta power in the 6th century (*see* map 4), the Gupta period saw the blossoming of earlier cultural trends, and has become known as the 'classical' or 'epic' age of Indian history.

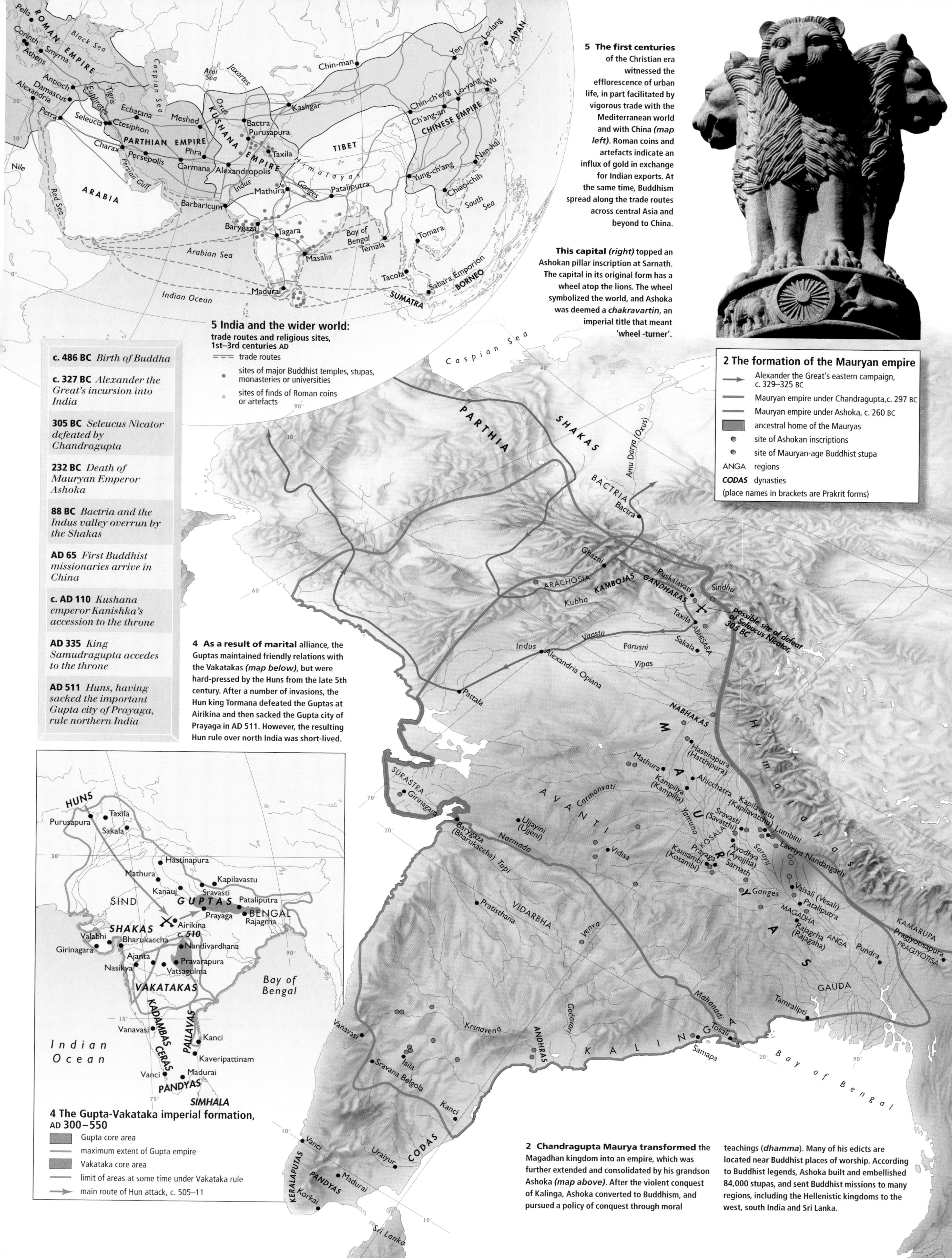

c. 486 BC *Birth of Buddha*

c. 327 BC *Alexander the Great's incursion into India*

305 BC *Seleucus Nicator defeated by Chandragupta*

232 BC *Death of Mauryan Emperor Ashoka*

88 BC *Bactria and the Indus valley overrun by the Shakas*

AD 65 *First Buddhist missionaries arrive in China*

c. AD 110 *Kushana emperor Kanishka's accession to the throne*

AD 335 *King Samudragupta accedes to the throne*

AD 511 *Huns, having sacked the important Gupta city of Prayaga, rule northern India*

5 The first centuries of the Christian era witnessed the efflorescence of urban life, in part facilitated by vigorous trade with the Mediterranean world and with China *(map left)*. Roman coins and artefacts indicate an influx of gold in exchange for Indian exports. At the same time, Buddhism spread along the trade routes across central Asia and beyond to China.

This capital *(right)* topped an Ashokan pillar inscription at Sarnath. The capital in its original form has a wheel atop the lions. The wheel symbolized the world, and Ashoka was deemed a *chakravartin*, an imperial title that meant 'wheel -turner'.

4 As a result of marital alliance, the Guptas maintained friendly relations with the Vakatakas *(map below)*, but were hard-pressed by the Huns from the late 5th century. After a number of invasions, the Hun king Tormana defeated the Guptas at Airikina and then sacked the Gupta city of Prayaga in AD 511. However, the resulting Hun rule over north India was short-lived.

2 Chandragupta Maurya transformed the Magadhan kingdom into an empire, which was further extended and consolidated by his grandson Ashoka *(map above)*. After the violent conquest of Kalinga, Ashoka converted to Buddhism, and pursued a policy of conquest through moral teachings (*dhamma*). Many of his edicts are located near Buddhist places of worship. According to Buddhist legends, Ashoka built and embellished 84,000 stupas, and sent Buddhist missions to many regions, including the Hellenistic kingdoms to the west, south India and Sri Lanka.

The peoples of northern Europe

See also
Early Europe: the colonization of a continent p. 40
The beginnings of civilization in the Eurasian world, 3500–1500 BC p. 52
The spread of Greek civilization, 800–336 BC p. 76
The expansion of Roman power to 31 BC p. 86
The height of Roman power, 31 BC–AD 235 p. 88

c. 2000 BC *High-point of 'Únětice' metal-working in north-central Europe*

c. 1300 BC *Start of Urnfield culture*

c. 1100 BC *Earliest fortified hilltop sites in western Europe*

c. 750 BC *Start of 'Hallstatt' Iron Age*

c. 600 BC *Foundation of Greek colony at Massilia (Marseilles)*

c. 450 BC *Collapse of West Hallstatt system leads to spread of Celtic (La Tène) culture*

c. 390 BC *Celts sack Rome*

279 BC *Celts under Brennus attack Delphi*

58–51 BC *Julius Caesar conquers Gaul*

Northern Europe did not see the development of the large territorial empires that characterized the ancient Near East. Until the Roman conquests it remained an area of small autonomous communities. Nonetheless in the late Bronze Age common European cultures emerged, culminating in the appearance of the Celts, whose warrior bands briefly threatened the Mediterranean world.

THE WHOLE CELTIC RACE IS OBSESSED WITH WAR, HIGH-SPIRITED AND QUICK TO BATTLE, BUT OTHERWISE STRAIGHTFORWARD AND NOT UNCOUTH. THEY ARE ALSO BOASTFUL AND FOND OF DECORATING THEMSELVES. NOT ONLY DO THEY WEAR GOLDEN ORNAMENTS – CHAINS ROUND THEIR NECKS AND BRACELETS ROUND THEIR ARMS AND WRISTS – BUT THEIR CHIEFTAINS WEAR CLOTHES WHICH HAVE BEEN DYED AND SPRINKLED WITH GOLD.

Strabo (c. 64 BC–AD 21)
Geography

BRONZE WORKING APPEARED in Europe around 2300 BC. North of the sub-Carpathian plain autonomous villages were the usual form of settlement rather than larger units. In some of these 'Únětice' communities powerful individuals emerged, gaining status by controlling access to sources of metals and the technology for working them. They were buried under large mounds at sites such as Leubingen, Helmsdorf and Łęki Małe, often with metal-working tools as part of their grave goods.

In the sub-Carpathian plain and to the south earlier Bronze Age society developed differently. The area had links with the communities of the steppe to the east and with the Aegean area to the south, probably by way of the Danube and the Black Sea. Here, as evidenced by the weapon hoards found at Hajdusámson and Apa, the development of bronze-working skills in the early centuries of the 2nd millennium are revealed. The geography of the sub-Carpathian plain, coupled with the wealth generated by exporting worked bronze, also allowed the development of larger communities, often fortified, such as Spišsky Štvrtok, Nitriansky Hrádok and Barca in modern Slovakia.

The Urnfield period

The centuries after 1300 BC saw great upheavals in the Near East, including the Aegean, possibly the result of interruptions to the supply of the tin needed to make bronze. Though there was no shortage of bronze in northern Europe, the turmoil in the Near East may nonetheless have had an indirect effect on social development there. This is the start of the 'Urnfield' period, named after the cemeteries which begin to appear in eastern and central Europe and, later, farther west. The dead were now more usually cremated in large cemeteries, rather than buried, and with few or no grave-goods. The spread of urnfields also indicates an increasing cultural conformity over a large part of northern Europe. It represents a change of focus from powerful individuals to communities, and with it the need for fortifications and new kinds of weapons. The Urnfield period prepared the way for the emergence of a warrior elite in the following centuries.

The Celtic world

The 8th century BC saw the re-establishment of contact with the centres of civilization in the eastern Mediterranean and beyond as well as with the new Greek and Phoenician colonies in the western Mediterranean and the emerging Etruscans in Italy. At the same time the techniques of iron-working were widely adopted. This development had little impact on the Atlantic coasts of Europe, which were still characterized by small-scale trade between communities with little interest in Mediterranean luxury goods. But to the east the Rhône valley provided a trade-route from the Mediterranean, especially after the foundation of the Greek colony of Massilia (Marseilles). It was this that lead to the development of a 'prestige goods economy' in Burgundy, seen in the rich finds from Mont Lassois and Vix, which acted as staging posts between the Mediterranean and central Europe, as well as farther east at the hill fort at the Heuneburg on the upper Danube. Contact with the steppe communities on the eastern flank of the Celtic world also continued, and by this route goods from the Far East could reach central Europe. This is well illustrated by the discovery in a burial mound beside the Heuneburg site of textiles embroidered with Chinese silk.

Among the chief exports to the Mediterranean from this period onwards was slaves, which raised the status of warriors who were able to trade prisoners of war for prestige goods from Etruria and Greece. This 'West Hallstatt system' collapsed when the Etruscans started to make direct contact

1 Early Iron Age ('Hallstatt') society emerged in the area between eastern France and the Danube *(map below)*. It was dominated by an aristocratic elite occupying hillforts, whose wealth was displayed in rich burials. In the later 'La Tène' period from the 5th century BC to the 1st century AD, the characteristic curvilinear style of Celtic art appeared throughout Europe, spread by conquest and by exchange. The

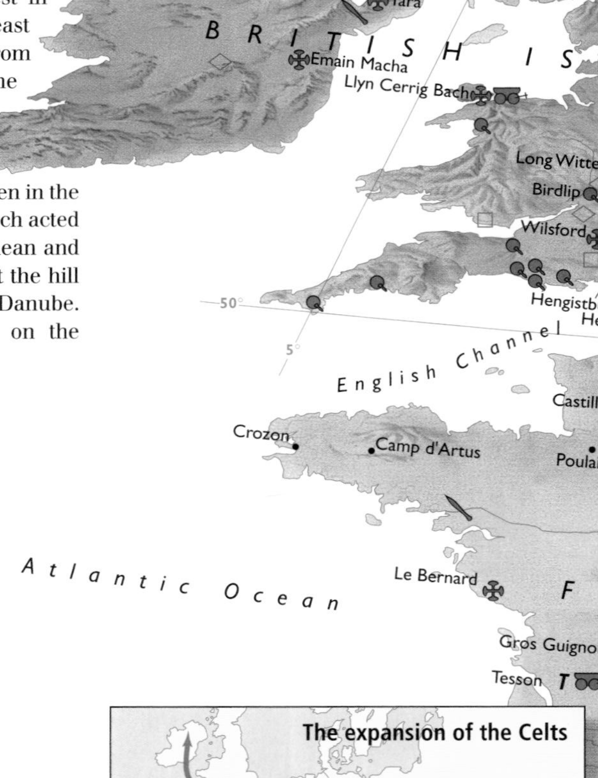

Maiden Castle in Dorset, southern England *(left)* was the site of an Iron Age settlement established in c. 300 BC. Defensive earthworks and walls were built up in the 1st century BC. It was besieged by the Romans in AD 44.

with the area around the Marne and Moselle. The same period also saw the emergence of a distinctive decorative aristocratic style known as 'Celtic' art. Spectacular finds have been made at sites such as Somme-Bionne and Basse-Yutz.

The following centuries saw Celtic war-bands spreading out from central Europe into Italy and Greece – Rome was attacked in 390 BC, Delphi in 279 BC – and settling as far south as Galatia in Anatolia and Galicia in Spain. Other areas, such as western France and Britain, were absorbed into the Celtic world by peaceful means, with the native aristocracies adopting the new continental fashions of art and warfare. From the 3rd century BC fortified urban settlements known as 'oppida' became more common, and unified Celtic states began to appear.

Celtic social organization was increasingly influenced by the growing power of Rome, and the Celts were the first peoples of northern Europe to be incorporated within the Roman empire. Already by the end of the 2nd century BC the Mediterranean part of Gaul was a Roman province. Julius Caesar's conquests in Gaul then brought the western Celtic world under Roman control as far as the English Channel by 50 BC. Thus the most economically advanced areas of the barbarian world were rapidly integrated within the Roman world.

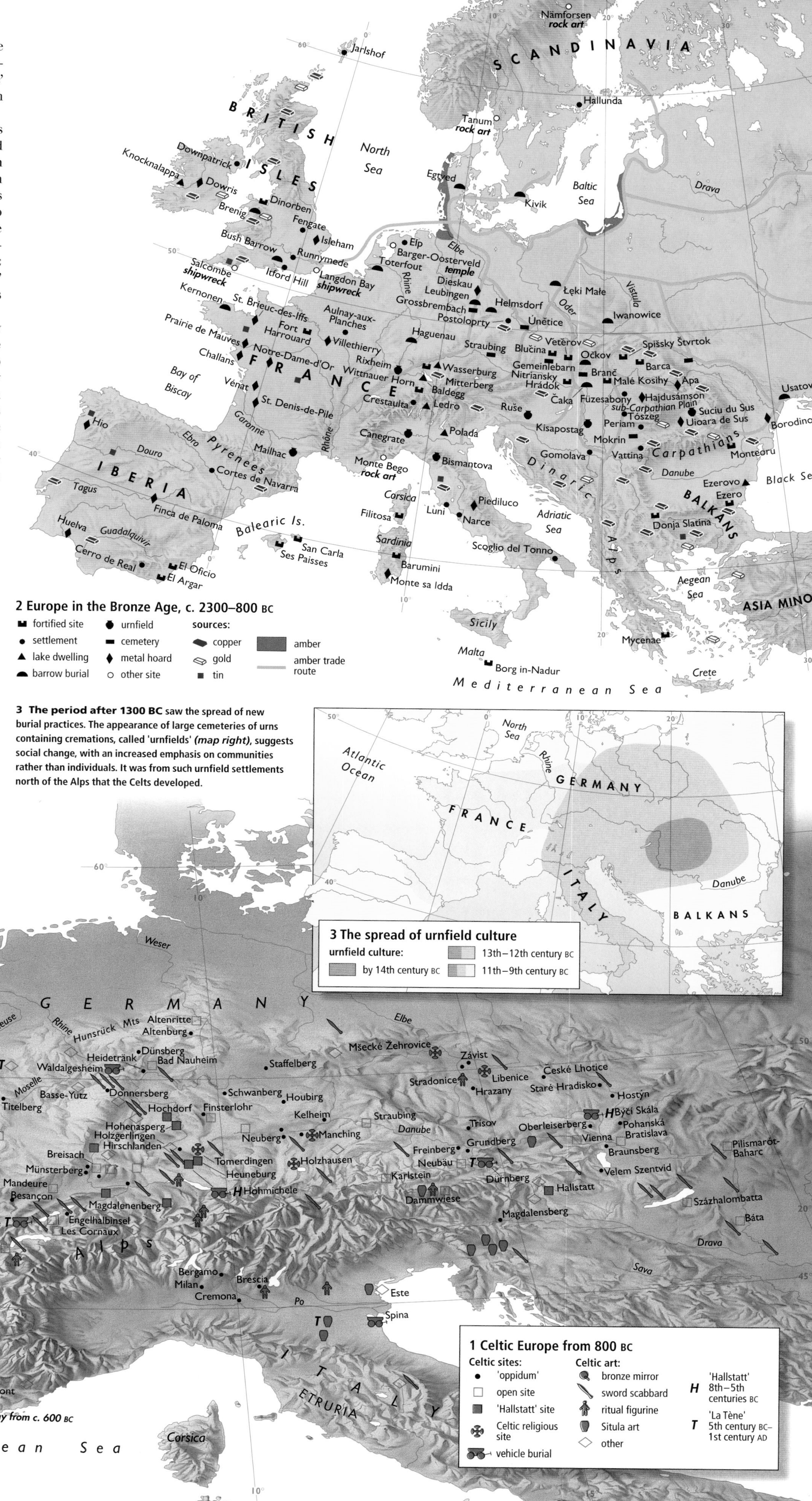

2 Long-distance trade in metals was a crucial factor in the development of Bronze Age Europe *(map right)*. Copper was widespread but tin was restricted to parts of western Britain and France, northwest Spain and northern Italy, from where it was carried to central and eastern Europe in exchange for a range of goods such as amber. Maritime routes were clearly important: two Bronze Age shipwrecks have been found in the English Channel. Increased contact contributed to cultural uniformity: by the end of the Bronze Age similar types of weapons and tools were being produced all along the Atlantic coasts of Iberia, France and the British Isles.

rapid movement of Celtic warrior bands in the 4th and 3rd centuries BC was followed by increasing settlement in fortified 'oppida'. Some, such as Manching in Bavaria, were both large and extremely sophisticated. By the 1st century AD, the Celtic world had been almost entirely absorbed within the Roman empire: only Ireland and northern Scotland remained outside Roman control to carry Celtic culture into the Middle Ages.

3 The period after 1300 BC saw the spread of new burial practices. The appearance of large cemeteries of urns containing cremations, called 'urnfields' *(map right)*, suggests social change, with an increased emphasis on communities rather than individuals. It was from such urnfield settlements north of the Alps that the Celts developed.

To 31 BC

The expansion of Roman power

See also
The empires of Persia, 550 BC–AD 637 p. 74
The Hellenistic world, 336–30 BC p. 78
The peoples of northern Europe p. 84
The height of Roman power, 31 BC–AD 235 p. 88

Rome, a city-state governed by aristocratic families leading an army of peasant soldiers, came to control an empire that stretched from the Atlantic to the Euphrates and from the English Channel to the Sahara. But military success brought social disorder; rivalries between warlords led to civil war; and republican institutions became an autocracy.

THE CITY OF ROME grew up on the banks of the Tiber at the lowest point the river could be bridged. Although there were settlements on several of Rome's hills from around 1000 BC, the earliest signs of urbanization date from the 7th century. According to tradition, Rome was ruled by a line of seven kings, and the expulsion of the last of these in 511 BC resulted in the creation of a republic ruled by two annually elected consuls or magistrates. It is probable, however, that the government of the emerging city-state was less formalized than this tradition suggests and that republican systems reached their developed form only in the 4th century.

> WHO IS SO WORTHLESS OR INDOLENT THAT THEY DO NOT WISH TO KNOW BY WHAT MEANS AND UNDER WHAT POLITICAL SYSTEM THE ROMANS, IN LESS THAN 53 YEARS, HAVE SUCCEEDED IN BRINGING NEARLY THE WHOLE INHABITED WORLD UNDER A SINGLE GOVERNMENT, SOMETHING NEVER BEFORE ACHIEVED?
>
> **Polybius (c. 200–c. 118 BC)**
> ***Histories***

Consuls held office for no more than a single year and ruled with the support of the Senate, a council of former magistrates and priests. Legislation proposed by them had also to be ratified by a popular assembly. However, their main task was to protect the city, which in effect meant to lead military campaigns. Success in war brought material gains to the people of Rome and prestige to the commanders making imperialism an inevitable feature of Roman policy.

The Punic Wars

By 264 BC Rome controlled the whole of the Italian peninsula and had emerged as a powerful confederacy and the principal rival to the other major power in the western Mediterranean, Carthage. The Romans were forced to develop naval skills to defeat Carthage in the First Punic War (264–241 BC), in which Rome drove the Carthaginians out of Sicily; soon after Corsica and Sardinia were seized as well. In the Second Punic War (218–201 BC), Rome was invaded from the north, when Hannibal brought his army and elephants from Spain over the Alps into Italy. Though Rome suffered devastating defeats at Lake Trasimene (217 BC) and Cannae (216 BC) it was able to draw on great reserves of Italian manpower to drive Hannibal out of Italy and defeat him at Zama in north

2 Italy in 500 BC was inhabited by a mixture of peoples *(map above)*. In the south and in Sicily the coastal plains had been settled in the 8th and 7th centuries by colonists from Greece while the city-states of Etruria had long had cultural and economic links with the eastern Mediterranean. As Rome's power spread through Italy, its culture was transformed by its contacts with these older civilizations.

3 The acquisition of overseas provinces by Rome *(map below)* was seldom by design. Although Roman commanders needed little encouragement to undertake military campaigns, they preferred to make treaties with defeated enemies rather than turn their territories into provinces. However, the wars against Carthage in the 3rd century and against the Hellenistic kingdoms of the eastern Mediterranean in the 2nd and 1st centuries left the Romans with possessions which could yield substantial tribute.

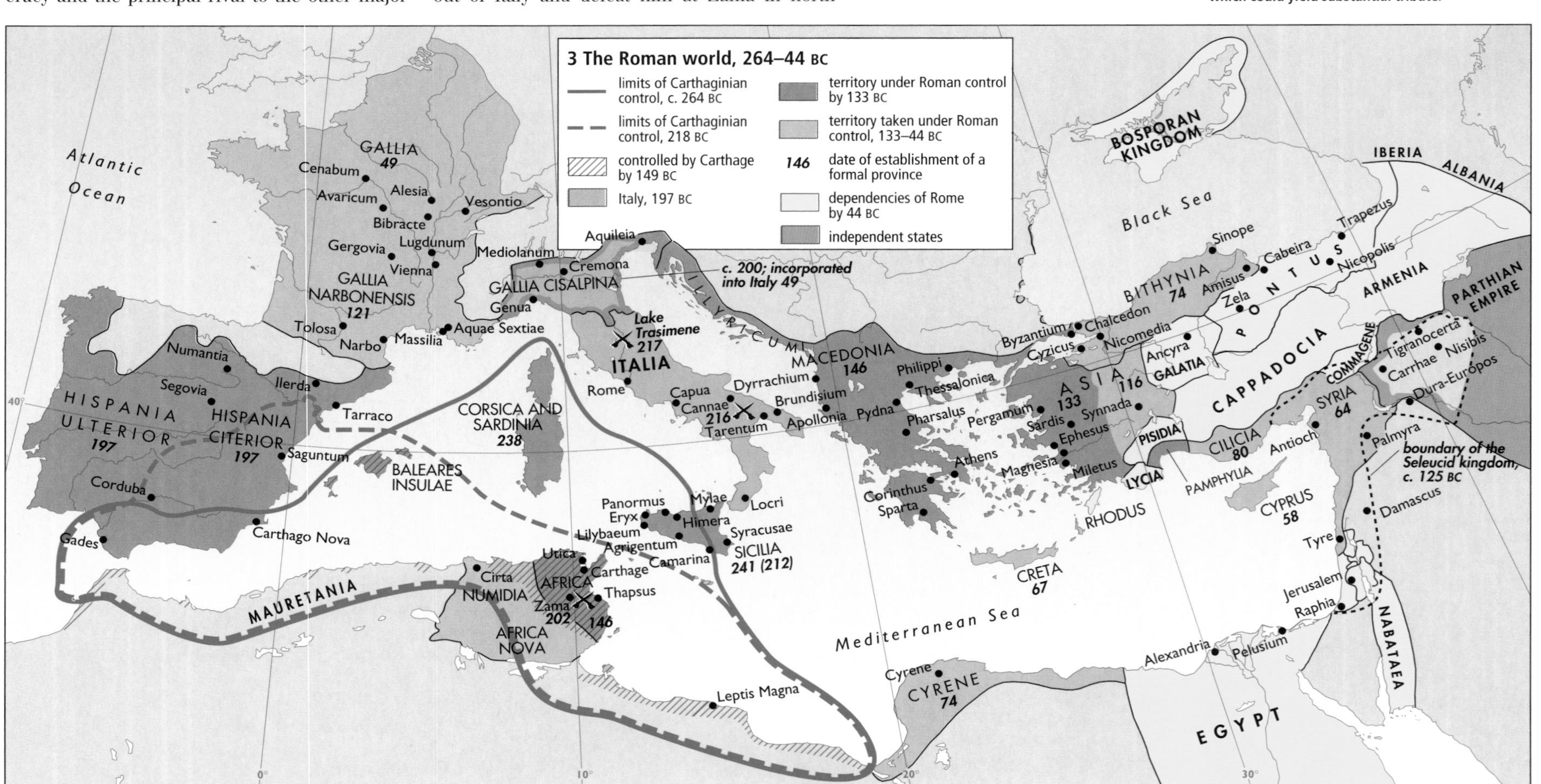

c. 640 BC *Roman Forum laid out*

511 BC *Expulsion of Tarquinius Superbus, last of Rome's kings*

496 BC *Battle of Lake Regillus; Rome defeats the Latins*

390 BC *Sack of Rome by the Gauls*

218–201 BC *Second Punic War: Hannibal defeated, Spain a Roman province*

146 BC *Romans sack Carthage and Corinth*

91–89 BC *Social War: Roman citizenship extended to all Italians*

49 BC *Julius Caesar crosses the Rubicon and marches on Rome*

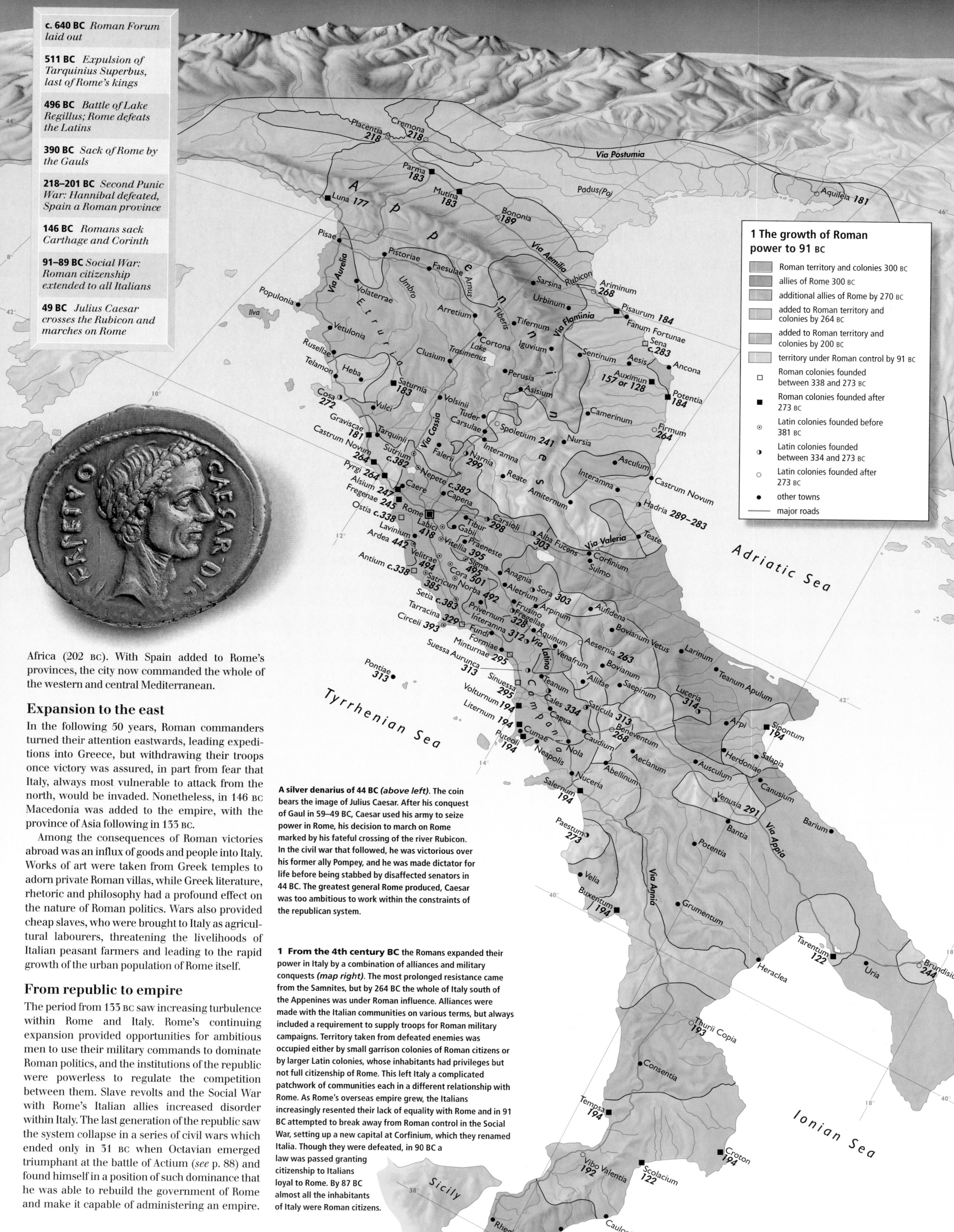

A silver denarius of 44 BC *(above left)*. The coin bears the image of Julius Caesar. After his conquest of Gaul in 59–49 BC, Caesar used his army to seize power in Rome, his decision to march on Rome marked by his fateful crossing of the river Rubicon. In the civil war that followed, he was victorious over his former ally Pompey, and he was made dictator for life before being stabbed by disaffected senators in 44 BC. The greatest general Rome produced, Caesar was too ambitious to work within the constraints of the republican system.

1 From the 4th century BC the Romans expanded their power in Italy by a combination of alliances and military conquests *(map right)*. The most prolonged resistance came from the Samnites, but by 264 BC the whole of Italy south of the Appenines was under Roman influence. Alliances were made with the Italian communities on various terms, but always included a requirement to supply troops for Roman military campaigns. Territory taken from defeated enemies was occupied either by small garrison colonies of Roman citizens or by larger Latin colonies, whose inhabitants had privileges but not full citizenship of Rome. This left Italy a complicated patchwork of communities each in a different relationship with Rome. As Rome's overseas empire grew, the Italians increasingly resented their lack of equality with Rome and in 91 BC attempted to break away from Roman control in the Social War, setting up a new capital at Corfinium, which they renamed Italia. Though they were defeated, in 90 BC a law was passed granting citizenship to Italians loyal to Rome. By 87 BC almost all the inhabitants of Italy were Roman citizens.

Africa (202 BC). With Spain added to Rome's provinces, the city now commanded the whole of the western and central Mediterranean.

Expansion to the east

In the following 50 years, Roman commanders turned their attention eastwards, leading expeditions into Greece, but withdrawing their troops once victory was assured, in part from fear that Italy, always most vulnerable to attack from the north, would be invaded. Nonetheless, in 146 BC Macedonia was added to the empire, with the province of Asia following in 133 BC.

Among the consequences of Roman victories abroad was an influx of goods and people into Italy. Works of art were taken from Greek temples to adorn private Roman villas, while Greek literature, rhetoric and philosophy had a profound effect on the nature of Roman politics. Wars also provided cheap slaves, who were brought to Italy as agricultural labourers, threatening the livelihoods of Italian peasant farmers and leading to the rapid growth of the urban population of Rome itself.

From republic to empire

The period from 133 BC saw increasing turbulence within Rome and Italy. Rome's continuing expansion provided opportunities for ambitious men to use their military commands to dominate Roman politics, and the institutions of the republic were powerless to regulate the competition between them. Slave revolts and the Social War with Rome's Italian allies increased disorder within Italy. The last generation of the republic saw the system collapse in a series of civil wars which ended only in 31 BC when Octavian emerged triumphant at the battle of Actium (*see* p. 88) and found himself in a position of such dominance that he was able to rebuild the government of Rome and make it capable of administering an empire.

31 BC to AD 235

The height of Roman power

See also
The empires of Persia, 550 BC–AD 637 p. 74
The expansion of Roman power to 31 BC p. 86
From Rome to Byzantium, AD 235–565 p. 90
The rise of Christianity p. 92
Germanic settlement in western Europe p. 96

27 BC *Augustus becomes Roman emperor*

AD 14 *Tiberius becomes emperor*

AD 43 *Claudius invades Britain*

AD 69 *Year of the Four Emperors: civil wars between Galba, Otho, Vitellius and Vespasian*

AD 101–106 *Trajan's Dacian Wars*

AD 131 *Hadrian establishes Panhellenion at Athens*

AD 180 *Death of Marcus Aurelius*

AD 212 *Caracalla extends citizenship to all free inhabitants of the empire*

Augustus, the first emperor, transformed the government of the Roman empire. He brought an end to internal conflicts and created a standing army to guard the empire's frontiers and extend its power. As Roman culture and organization spread throughout the empire, it laid the foundations for the development of the Mediterranean world.

IN 31 BC OCTAVIAN, the future emperor Augustus, was undisputed master of Rome. His popularity as adopted son of Julius Caesar and victor over Cleopatra and Mark Antony at the battle of Actium allowed him to rebuild the shattered Roman republic into a system of government capable of controlling a vast empire, reforms which were to bring Rome a new and intense surge of life and two and a half centuries of almost uninterrupted peace and prosperity

Augustus's reforms were far-reaching. He restored the prestige of the Senate, though not, in practice, its influence. He reorganized the army and, in 27 BC, took command of those parts of the empire where legions were stationed. From then on responsibility for the defence of the empire lay with the emperor alone. At the same time he took the religiously significant name Augustus, and stressed his relationship to the now deified Julius Caesar. Among his many priesthoods was that of Pontifex Maximus, chief priest, and from the time of Augustus onward the emperor became the focus of all Roman religious ritual.

In 19 BC Augustus was given the power to rule by decree, and although he continued to pay due respect to the Senate, whose members he needed to command the legions and to administer the provinces, his authority was now absolute. The vast wealth he had inherited and won (his defeat of Antony and Cleopatra left Egypt as his personal domain) was further increased by bequests from the rich throughout the empire. At his death his property was worth thousands of times as much as that of even the richest senator. That his heir should also inherit his position as head of the empire was inevitable.

In the event, Augustus had great difficulty in finding an heir, eventually settling on his stepson Tiberius (AD 14–37), who had been a successful military commander but took on the role of emperor with reluctance. Neither he nor his successors were able to maintain good relations with the Senate, and the failure of Nero (54–68) to prevent revolt in the provinces led to his enforced suicide and the end of the Julio-Claudian dynasty. After a year of civil war, Vespasian (69–79) restored order. He was succeeded by his sons, Titus (79–81) and Domitian (81–96). Though the latter was generally regarded as a cruel and probably insane tyrant, many of his imperial policies were adopted by his successors, especially Trajan (98–117), who began the practice of appearing before the Senate not in a toga but in the purple cloak and armour of a triumphant general. This was to become the uniform of the emperor for the next thousand years.

Stability and strife

Domitian's assassination was followed by nearly a century of stability as emperors without sons of their own chose their successors from the Senate. Civil war returned in 193, from which Septimius Severus (193–211) emerged victorious. He ruled with his sons Caracalla (198–217) and Geta (209–12), setting a pattern that was to be followed in the following centuries. Caracalla was murdered, and after him came a series of short-lived emperors, of whom Severus Alexander (222–35) was the last who could claim a dynastic link to his predecessors.

The nature of Rome

The figure of the emperor was central to the empire: everywhere statues and coins were constant reminders of his presence. In the former Hellenistic kingdoms the kings had been the objects of religious worship, a practice which continued with the cult of the emperors. In the western provinces, temples and altars dedicated to the emperor became focuses of Romanization.

The early 2nd century saw important cultural developments: it was a time when Greek and Latin literature flourished; the distinction between Italy and the provinces dissolved as rich men from all over the empire were admitted to the Senate, with some, such as Trajan and Hadrian (117–138), even becoming emperor. For the poor, there were fewer benefits, and differences in the rights and privileges of rich and poor grew. By the time Caracalla extended Roman citizenship throughout the empire in AD 212, it gave little advantage to the newly enfranchised citizens. Later in the 2nd century, pressures grew on the frontiers. Marcus Aurelius (161–180) spent much of his reign at war with barbarian invaders, and his successors faced threats both from the north, and, after 224, from the rejuvenated Persian empire under the Sasanids.

REMEMBER, ROMAN, WHERE YOUR SKILLS LIE: IT IS YOUR TASK TO RULE THE PEOPLES BY YOUR POWER, TO ADD CIVILIZATION TO PEACE, TO SPARE THE DEFEATED AND TO BEAT DOWN THE PROUD IN WAR.

Virgil (70–19 BC)
Aeneid

THE AFFAIRS OF THE ROMANS OF THAT TIME [AD 180] DESCENDED FROM A KINGDOM OF GOLD, TO ONE OF IRON AND RUST – AND SO TOO DOES OUR HISTORY.

Cassius Dio (c. AD 164–230)
Roman History

Although campaigns in the 1st century AD in Germany had only limited success, the eastern Balkans, north Africa, Arabia and Britain were all added to Rome while in the following century Trajan added Dacia, Armenia, Assyria and Mesopotamia. Trajan's rule marked Rome's greatest territorial extent. Hadrian, his successor, abandoned Trajan's conquests other than Arabia and Dacia to consolidate more defensible frontiers.

1 From 27 BC, the emperor himself was responsible for the administration of the imperial provinces (those in which legions were stationed). The others were governed by proconsuls appointed by the Senate. At the start of the imperial period some parts of the empire were ruled by friendly client kings; as they died their lands became Roman provinces. Emperors could gain great glory by extending the empire.

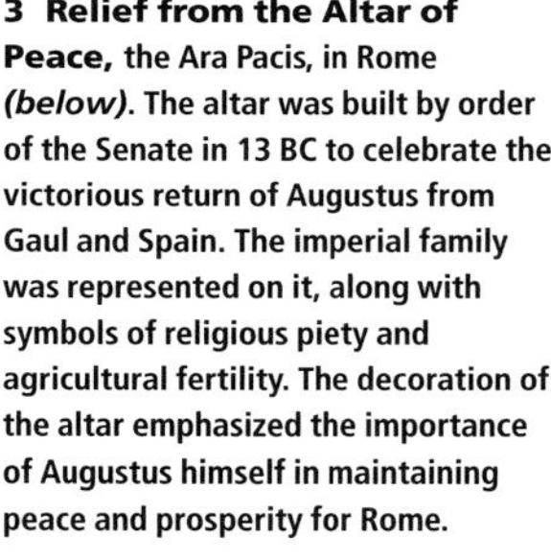

3 Relief from the Altar of Peace, the Ara Pacis, in Rome ***(below)***. The altar was built by order of the Senate in 13 BC to celebrate the victorious return of Augustus from Gaul and Spain. The imperial family was represented on it, along with symbols of religious piety and agricultural fertility. The decoration of the altar emphasized the importance of Augustus himself in maintaining peace and prosperity for Rome.

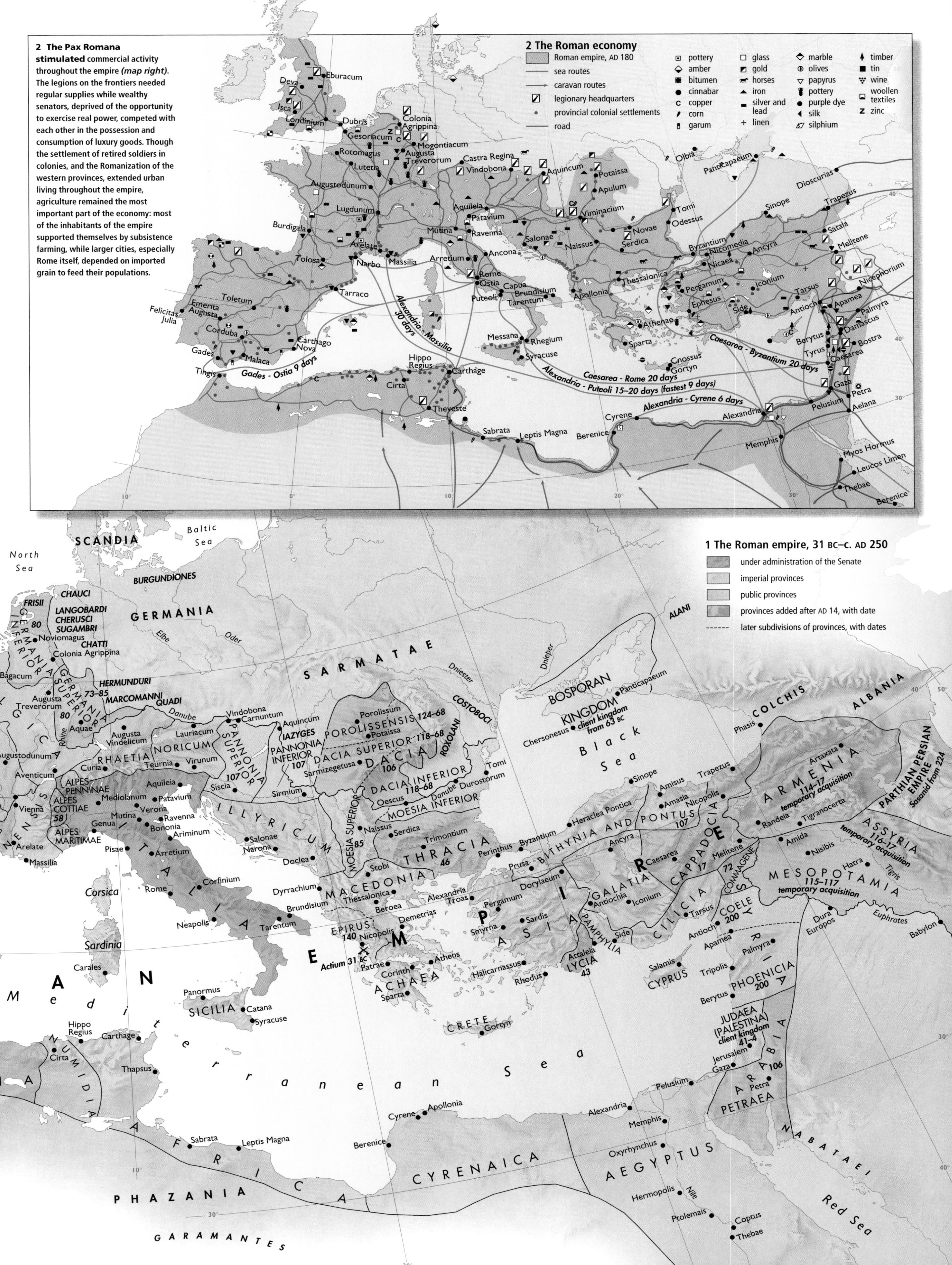

2 The Pax Romana stimulated commercial activity throughout the empire *(map right)*. The legions on the frontiers needed regular supplies while wealthy senators, deprived of the opportunity to exercise real power, competed with each other in the possession and consumption of luxury goods. Though the settlement of retired soldiers in colonies, and the Romanization of the western provinces, extended urban living throughout the empire, agriculture remained the most important part of the economy: most of the inhabitants of the empire supported themselves by subsistence farming, while larger cities, especially Rome itself, depended on imported grain to feed their populations.

From Rome to Byzantium

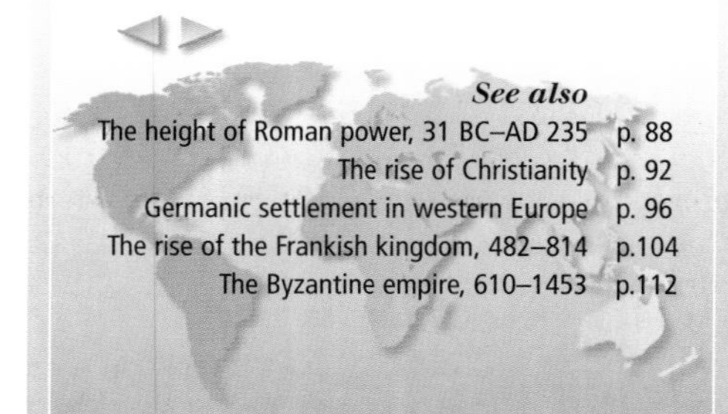
See also
The height of Roman power, 31 BC–AD 235 p. 88
The rise of Christianity p. 92
Germanic settlement in western Europe p. 96
The rise of the Frankish kingdom, 482–814 p.104
The Byzantine empire, 610–1453 p.112

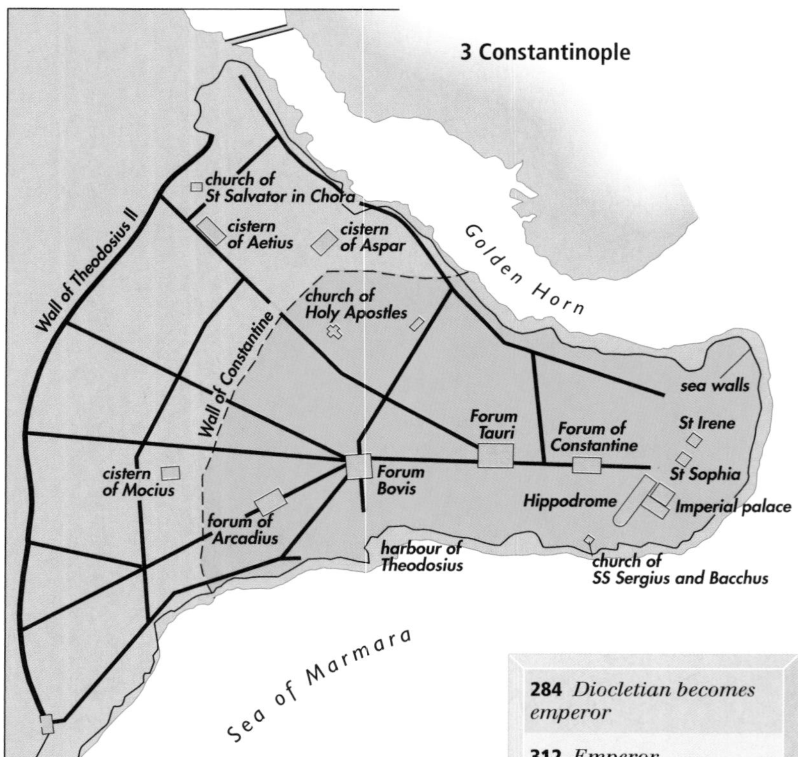

3 Constantinople was founded by Constantine in 330, on the site of the Greek city of Byzantium *(map above)* as the base from which to govern the eastern part of his empire. It had its own Senate, and rapidly became the largest city in the eastern empire, with a population reaching 500,000. Although the masses had no formal power, emperors could not afford to antagonize them. The Hippodrome, where chariot-racing took place, was linked to the imperial palace and became the main point of communication between ruler and subjects.

2 Between 235 and 284 the frontiers of the empire were threatened by Germans, Goths and Sasanid Persians *(map below)*. The Roman legions struggled to meet the challenge, and there were more than 20 emperors in 50 years, each replaced after failure to stem the barbarian incursions. Under Gallienus (253–68) large parts of the empire broke away. Aurelian (270–5) was able to reunite the empire, and military reorganization enabled him and his successors to repel the invaders. Only Dacia and the Agri Decumates were lost.

284 *Diocletian becomes emperor*

312 *Emperor Constantine declares toleration for all religions in the empire*

361–3 *Emperor Julian attempts to restore pagan religion*

395 *Death of Theodosius I: division between east and west becomes permanent*

410 *Alaric and Visigoths sack Rome*

476 *Romulus Augustulus, last western emperor, deposed*

527 *Justinian becomes emperor in the east*

The 4th century AD saw Roman emperors still ruling an empire that stretched from Spain to Syria. In the 5th century the two halves of the empire experienced different fortunes. Roman administration in the west dissolved in the face of increasing barbarian settlement, but in the east Byzantine civilization, combining Greek and Roman practices and culture, grew and flourished.

THE EMPIRE EMERGED from the storms of the 3rd century (*see* map 2) intact but not unchanged. Diocletian and his successors owed their position to the army, not the Senate, and the military now provided most of the provincial governors. Rome itself ceased to be the centre of empire, as the emperors based themselves in cities nearer the frontiers: Mediolanum (Milan) in Italy; and, after AD 330, Constantinople in the east. The emperors were surrounded by large courts, increasingly turning to eunuchs as their closest advisors. To maintain the army, the taxation system was reformed and military service became a hereditary obligation. But as the senators in Italy and other rich landowners were increasingly excluded from power, so they became less inclined to support the emperor, a development which was to have a profound effect on the western half of the empire.

The rise of Christianity

But the greatest change to the empire was religious. In 312 Constantine defeated his rival Maxentius outside Rome, and he came to attribute his victory to the support of the Christian god. In his reign and that of his son Constantius II the churches received many favours from the emperor, and Christianity began to establish itself as the dominant religion of the empire. The last pagan emperor, Julian, died in AD 363 on campaign against the Persians before he had the opportunity to reverse the trend. Bishops such as St Ambrose in Milan (374–97) became increasingly powerful figures in the empire.

Barbarian incursions continued to erode central control of the empire. The arrival of the Huns in eastern Europe in 376 drove many Goths across the Danube, forcing them into Roman territory. Having in 378 defeated the Romans at Adrianople, in 405 they invaded Italy. In the winter of 406 German tribes then crossed the frozen river Rhine in unstoppable masses. The situation deteriorated throughout the century. The Vandals marched through Gaul and Spain before crossing to Africa where they captured Carthage, the chief city, in 439 and set up their own kingdom.

Where in the 4th century the Roman army had made use of barbarian officers, now the western emperors had little choice but to make grants of land for the invaders to settle on and to employ them in the army. With landowners unwilling to allow their tenants to fight, what had been a

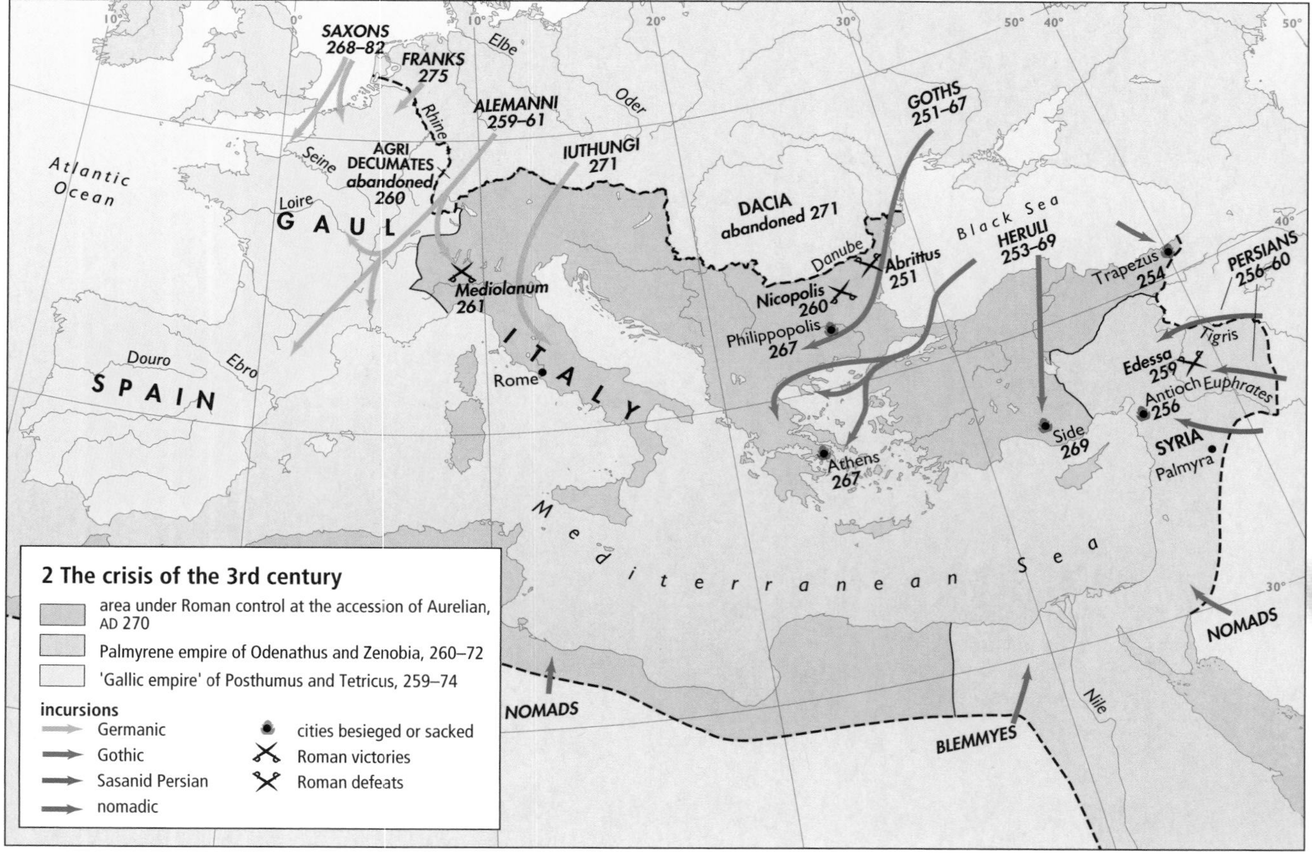

Porphyry relief of Constantine and his sons *(above)*. In his imperial propaganda Constantine emphasized the fact that he had three adult sons, a sign of divine favour. After their father's death, his sons – Constantine II (337–40), Constans (337–50) and Constantius II (337–61) – shared control of the empire until Constantius eliminated his brothers and assumed sole power.

Roman citizen army became a barbarian mercenary one. Since the frontiers were no longer preventing barbarians from entering the western empire, and since the army was itself largely barbarian, the role of the emperor in the west was effectively redundant.

In 476 the *magister militum* (the chief military officer of the western empire) Odoacer, a German, deposed the emperor Romulus Augustulus, and did not replace him. With the eastern emperor making no attempt to resist this, the western empire ceased to exist (*see* map 4). In 490 the Ostrogoths took control of Italy, and by 507 the Franks had established an extensive kingdom in Gaul (*see* p. 104). Yet Roman institutions survived: the Roman Senate continued to sit, and Latin remained the language of government.

The reconquests of Justinian

The eastern part of the empire possessed greater resources than the west, and eastern emperors could use their wealth to persuade would-be invaders to move away westwards. Although Roman culture continued to flourish in the eastern part of the empire (*see* p. 112), there were growing cultural differences between east and west: when Justinian launched his attempt to reconquer the former western empire, he was trying to impose a Greek-speaking administration on Latin-speaking territories.

Justinian's reign was a mixture of triumph and disaster. In Constantinople it saw the building of the great church of St Sophia (532–63) as well as a devastating plague in 542. His general Belisarius took Africa from the Vandals in 533–4 while in 554, after a campaign lasting 20 years, Ostrogothic rule in Italy was ended. But Justinian's successes in Italy were short-lived: the Lombard invasion of 568 left only Ravenna in Byzantine hands. Meanwhile in the east there was war with Persia (540–62): Antioch was sacked in 540 and peace was eventually bought only at great financial cost. Justinian's wars left Byzantium seriously weakened. The dream of a reunited empire died with him.

THUS THE ALMIGHTY SOVEREIGN HIMSELF ACCORDS AN INCREASE BOTH OF YEARS AND OF CHILDREN TO OUR MOST PIOUS EMPEROR, AND RENDERS HIS SWAY OVER THE NATIONS OF THE WORLD STILL FRESH AND FLOURISHING, AS THOUGH IT WERE EVEN NOW SPRINGING UP IN ITS EARLIEST VIGOUR. EVERY ENEMY, WHETHER VISIBLE OR UNSEEN, HAS BEEN UTTERLY REMOVED: AND HENCEFORWARD PEACE, THE HAPPY NURSE OF YOUTH, EXTENDS HER REIGN THROUGHOUT THE WORLD.

Eusebius of Caesarea
Speech in praise of Constantine, AD 336

4 Southwest Europe at the overthrow of the last western emperor, 476

1 Diocletian (284–305) and Constantine (306–37) oversaw the reorganization of the empire ***(map below)***. Military and civil commands were separated and the existing provinces split into smaller units, which were grouped together into 12 dioceses, each headed by a 'Vicarius'. They in turn were subordinate to up to four 'Praetorian Prefects'. In the 4th century imperial power was several times divided between two or three senior emperors (called 'Augusti'), usually supported by a junior ('Caesar'), a division which became permanent after 395. Milan (Mediolanum), Trier (Treveri), Nicaea, Nicomedia and later Constantinople replaced Rome as centres of imperial administration.

4 By the deposition of Romulus Augustulus by Odoacer in 476, the western empire had already suffered a series of calamitous losses ***(map above)***. Spain, Portugal and southwest France were under the control of the Sueves and the Visigoths while the largest Roman-controlled area in France, governed by Syagrius, did not acknowledge the authority of the emperor. Odoacer, until his murder in 493, in fact maintained peace and stability in Italy, which he ruled from Ravenna, retaining Roman administrative structures and rewarding Roman senators for their support. He made some attempts to expand his territory, conquering Dalmatia in 480 after the murder of the imperial claimant, Julius Nepos.

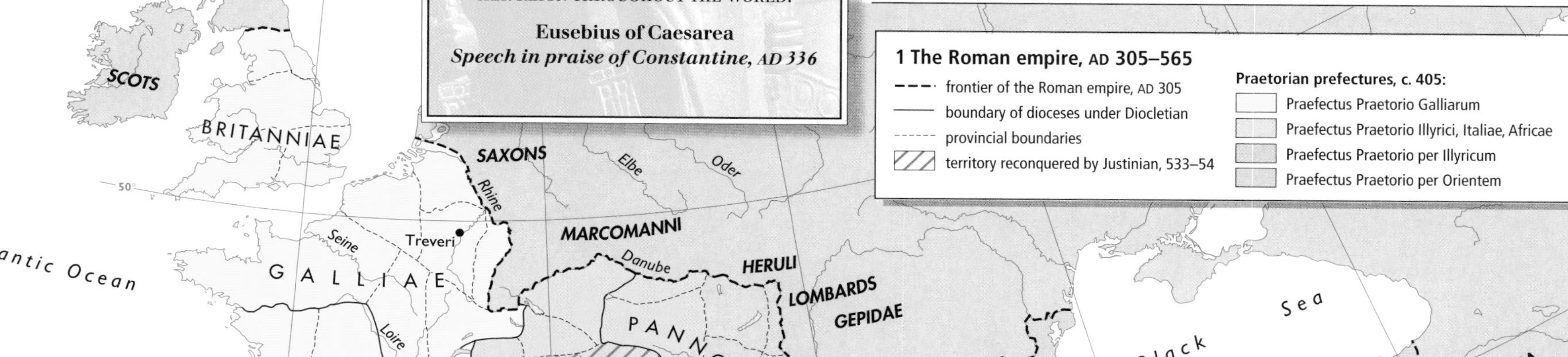

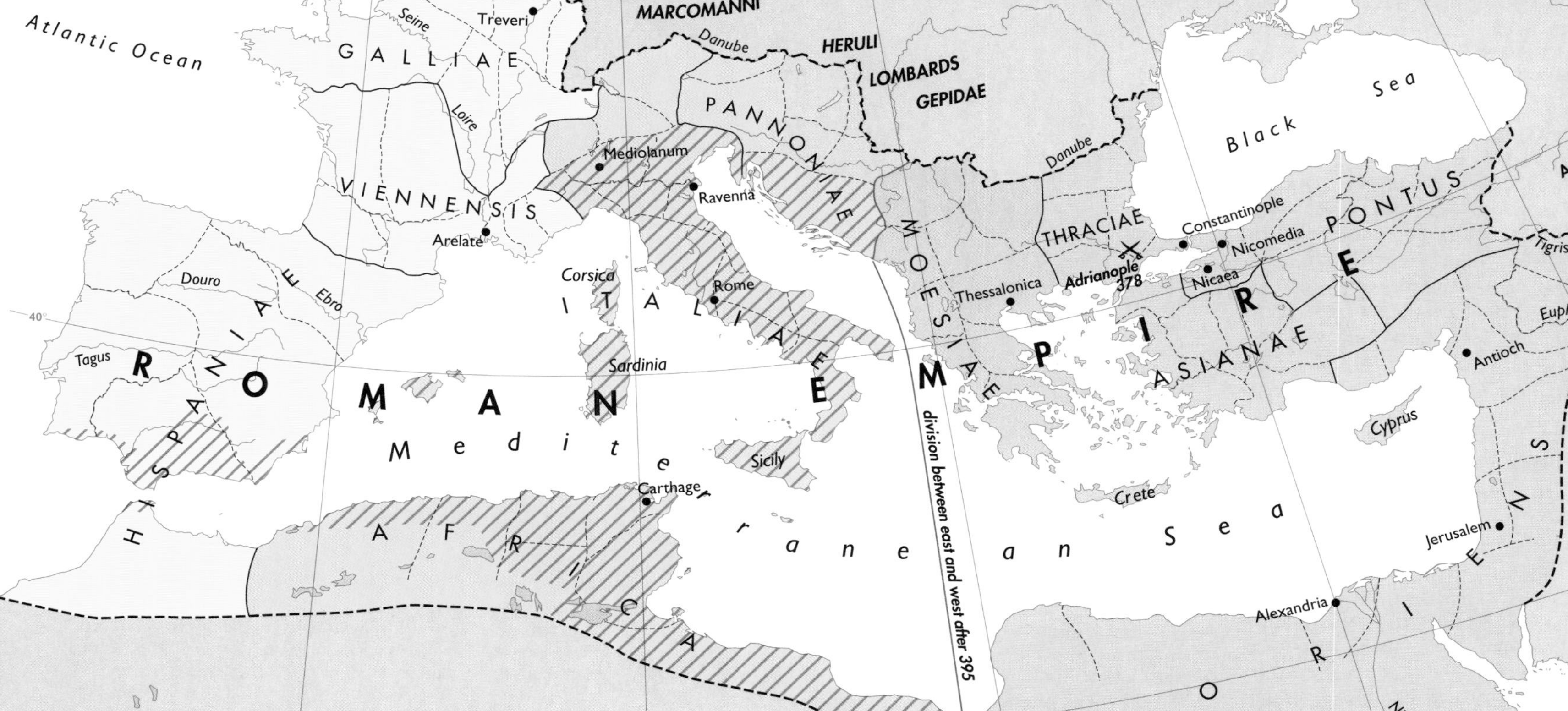

To AD 600

The rise of Christianity

See also

The religious bonds of Eurasia to AD 500 p. 72
From Rome to Byzantium, AD 235 – 565 p. 90
The expansion of Christianity AD 600–1500 p. 100
Reformation and Catholic Reformation p. 182

AN IMMENSE MULTITUDE WAS CONVICTED, NOT SO MUCH OF THE CRIME OF ARSON, AS OF HATRED OF THE HUMAN RACE

Tacitus
on Nero's persecution of the Christians in AD 64

YOU ARE BISHOPS WHOSE JURISDICTION IS WITHIN THE CHURCH: I ALSO AM A BISHOP, ORDAINED BY GOD TO OVERLOOK THOSE OUTSIDE THE CHURCH

Constantine
c. AD 274–337

Christianity began as a small sect within Judaism, but gradually established itself as a significant religious and intellectual force throughout the Roman empire. It offered both a promise of eternal salvation to individuals and, from the 4th century onwards, a powerful new vision of an empire united under a Christian ruler which was to be of enormous significance for the future of Europe.

c. AD 33 *Crucifixion of Jesus*

46–57 *Missionary journeys of St Paul*

64 *Nero persecutes Christians in Rome*

303–12 *The 'Great Persecution' of Christians in the Roman empire*

312 *Conversion of Constantine*

325 *Council of Nicaea*

391 *Legislation to ban pagan rites in the Roman empire*

451 *Council of Chalcedon*

590 *Gregory the Great extends papal power*

THE EARLIEST CHRISTIANS did not see themselves as founders of a new religion but as witnesses to the fulfilment of God's promise to provide his people, the Jews, with a Messiah or redeemer. By raising him from the dead, they believed that God had shown that Jesus of Nazareth was this Messiah and that the risen Jesus had commissioned his disciples to preach the good news of God's kingdom.

Though the earliest Christians were Jews, they did not interpret the message of Jesus in political or national terms. Christianity was attractive to people besides Jews for its promise of eternal life and for the spiritual benefits of membership of a close-knit, supportive community. So the conversion of gentiles soon began in the cities of the eastern Roman empire and was enthusiastically advocated by Paul, a converted Pharisee and former opponent of Christianity. With the rejection of Christianity's claims by the majority of Jews, Christianity had become a distinct religion by the end of the 1st century. Christian expansion was much slower in the west: while there was a Christian community in Rome by AD 50, the earliest evidence for Christianity in France and north Africa is to be found from the late 2nd century.

Christianity added to the Jewish belief in one true God a commitment to the divinity of Jesus and the Holy Spirit. This implicit rejection of the polytheism of the Roman world led to accusations that the Christians were atheists and to periodic Roman persecutions. Tacitus provides evidence that the emperor Nero was able to exploit the unpopularity of the Christians to blame them for the great fire of Rome of AD 64. But it was not until the 3rd century that a systematic attempt was made to eliminate Christianity throughout the empire, first by Decius in 250, and then by Diocletian and Galerius in the 'Great Persecution' of 303–12.

By this time the Church had grown from a network of small communities, meeting in the homes of richer members, into a well-organized body owning buildings and burial grounds and led by a ministry of bishops, presbyters and deacons. During the Great Persecution church property was confiscated and the leaders of the churches arrested. Christianity survived, however, to emerge into a new era of growth and change during the 4th century.

Constantine

The conversion of the emperor Constantine to Christianity in 312 was probably the most significant event in the early history of the church. The exact motives for his conversion are unclear (later Christians believed it has been the result of a supernatural vision), but he rapidly became aware that Christianity could act as a unifying force in the Roman empire, and to see himself as a Christian ruler endowed with divine authority, a self-imposed role accepted by many Christians, who relished a new era of favour from the state. But Constantine did not make Christianity into the state religion of the empire overnight. This was a gradual process, interrupted by the reign of the pagan emperor Julian (361–3), which was to reach its conclusion – the banning of the pagan rites which Christians found so offensive – only in the reign of Theodosius (379–95).

In the 5th century there were still many pagans, even at court, but the empire was gradually Christianized through a programme of church building and the demolition of pagan shrines. Monks took a leading role in evangelization from the 4th century onwards. Meanwhile, Christianity had also spread east to Persia and west among the

1 Except in Palestine, 1st-century Christianity was confined mainly to Greek-speaking cities *(map above)*. By the early 4th century, Christians may have numbered 10 per cent of the population of the Roman empire, but were still found mainly in the east, in heavily urbanized areas and along trade routes. Following the conversion of Constantine, the expansion of Christianity was helped by imperial support. By 400 it was probably the majority religion of the Roman empire, and by 600 the whole of the empire (including its former territories in the west) was predominantly Christian. Christianity owed much to the writings of its leading bishops and theologians, most of whom lived in the larger cities and were able to express their beliefs in terms drawn from the sophisticated literary and intellectual culture of the Greco-Roman world.

barbarian tribes which were eventually to invade and destroy the western Roman empire.

Doctrinal development

From its roots in Jewish monotheism, early Christianity underwent a good deal of doctrinal development. Many theologians from the 2nd century onwards attempted to combine the teachings of Christianity with the intellectual assumptions of Greek philosophy. In the 4th and 5th centuries the church embodied its beliefs about God and Jesus in a succession of doctrinal statements intended to prohibit heretical views (*see panel right*). The statements of faith in the Trinity and the Incarnation produced by the church councils of Nicaea (325) and Chalcedon (451) were especially important. In them, the early church bequeathed to later Christianity a set of doctrinal assumptions that were not to be seriously challenged until the Reformation in the 16th century and which remain the basis of their faith for many Christians even today.

EARLY CHRISTIAN HERESIES AND SCHISMS

In contrast to its later reputation for fostering doctrinal conformity, early Christianity allowed room for intellectual speculation. Not all speculation led to heresy, but some Christians developed ideas which were eventually judged unacceptable by the church as a whole.

In the 2nd century, various forms of **Gnosticism** were the main heresies. Gnostics, such as Valentinus and Basilides, were dualists who taught that matter was evil and distinguished between the creator of the world and the true God – views which most Christians thought inconsistent with the Bible. **Montanism**, a movement of prophetic revival which arose in Asia Minor in the 160s, was also significant. Christians who continued to obey the Jewish law (often called **Ebionites**, from a Hebrew word meaning 'poor') also became separated from the mainstream during the 2nd century.

In the 3rd century came the first controversies over the doctrines of the Trinity and the church and sacraments. **Monarchianism**, popular in Rome, taught the unity of God rather than the distinction of the three persons of the Trinity. **Adoptionism**, whose leading representative was Paul of Samosata, stressed the humanity rather than the divinity of Christ. In Rome, **Novatianism** (named after the presbyter Novatian) was a puritan movement which withheld forgiveness from those who had denied the faith in times of persecution or committed other serious sins.

The 4th century was dominated by the **Arian** controversy, which led to the first agreed definition of the relationship between the persons of the Trinity. The Alexandrian presbyter Arius taught that the Son of God was created, and therefore different in nature from the Father. His views were rejected at the Council of Nicaea, which issued a creed stating that the Son is 'of one substance with the Father'. After further controversy over the interpretation of the creed, this teaching was reaffirmed by the Council of Constantinople in 381.

In the 5th century there were controversies over the doctrine of the Incarnation, or the relationship between the divine and human elements in Jesus. **Nestorianism**, named after Bishop Nestorius of Constantinople, regarded the divine and human elements as distinct in principle, so that the human Jesus could be spoken of as different from the divine Son of God who dwelt in him. Nestorius was accused by his opponents of teaching that Christ was 'two Sons'. At the Council of Chalcedon Nestorianism was rejected, but the opposite extreme, **Eutychianism**, which denied any distinction between Jesus's divine and human natures, was also avoided. In the west the doctrine of grace and the relationship between faith and works were controversial. **Pelagianism**, which emphasized free will and the capacity of human beings for righteousness, was rejected by Augustine of Hippo, who was more pessimistic about fallen human nature.

By the 5th century many groups of Christians existed whose views had been condemned and who were out of communion with the wider church. Their freedom of worship and action were often restricted by the authorities of the Christian Roman empire. In more recent times it has been generally recognized that the divisions which occurred were often the result of misunderstandings or of different (but equally valid) interpretations of the Bible and Christian tradition, and not just a product of the malice of heretics, as orthodox theologians of the period usually claimed.

A stone slab of the Apostles Peter and Paul from the sepulchre of the child Amellus dating from after 313 *(above)*. Following the conversion of Constantine, Christian art became more public and explicit representations of Christ and the saints are common from this period. Portraits of Peter and Paul from Rome proudly allude to the connection of the two leading apostles with the city and its powerful bishops. In this example, they are depicted as Roman gentlemen of high social status, as the purple stripe of their togas attests.

2 Almost from the very beginning of organized Christianity, there were Christians who adopted a life of celibacy and renunciation, though they did not at first live in monastic communities separated from society at large. Monasticism originated in Egypt and Syria early in the 4th century, and monasteries were soon found both in desert areas and in villages and towns *(map right)*. By 340 Egyptian monks had visited Rome. Later in the 4th century monasticism spread to Asia Minor, north Africa and France, and in the 5th century to Britain, Ireland and Spain. Women as well as men founded monasteries, though the surviving documentation is biased towards male communities, both anchoritic (groups of hermits) and cenobitic (monks living together under a common rule). Monks and nuns were widely admired and exercised a powerful influence on Christian life and thought.

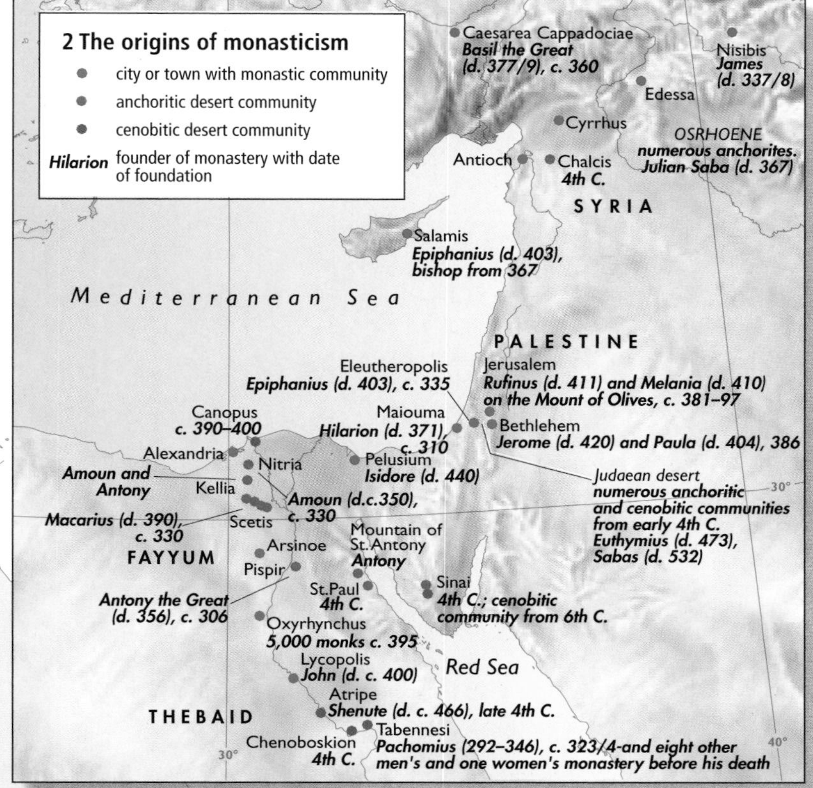

Sarcophagus of Livia Primitiva, from the early 3rd century, found in Rome *(below)*. The inscription and decoration on this early Christian gravestone are typical of the period. The former reads: 'Livia Nicarus set this up for her sister Livia Primitiva, who lived 24 years 9 months'. The incised carvings show Christ as the good shepherd (carrying a sheep on his shoulders) and a fish and anchor, which were popular early Christian symbols. Christ is dressed in Roman style, in a short tunic.

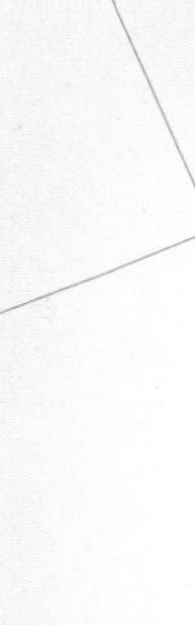

4

The world of divided regions

THE PERIOD around AD 500 saw upheaval throughout the Eurasian world, when nomads from the steppes of Asia descended upon all the existing centres of civilization. Although the gains of the classical period never entirely disappeared, contacts dwindled between China and the West, between north Africa and Italy and between Byzantium and western Europe. For the next few centuries each region was thrown back on its own resources and forced to fend for itself.

In western Europe this period is traditionally known as 'the Middle Ages'. The description may be appropriate for European history but it makes little sense in the wider perspective of world history. Here, two outstanding events dominated: the rise and expansion of Islam after 632; and the emergence of the Mongol empire in the 13th century. At the same time, important developments transformed hitherto isolated regions. The appearance of the Maya, Aztec and Inca civilizations in America, the creation of the empires of Sri Vijaya and Majapahit in southeast Asia, and the rise of the empires of Ghana, Mali and Songhay in Africa all attested to a new vitality and to the expansion of the area of civilized life.

Europe, by comparison, remained backward. Even here, however, it was a formative age, when primitive societies were welded into feudal monarchies. But the process of consolidation was slow, interrupted by barbarian incursions and by economic setbacks. Not until the second half of the 15th century did Europe begin to draw level with the other world civilizations, laying the foundations for overseas expansion with a series of path-breaking voyages of exploration. Even then, however, it remained overshadowed by the expanding power of the Ottoman Turks for another century.

Stone Buddha from Wat Mahathat in Lop Buri, Thailand, 13th–14th century

341 to 597

Germanic settlement in western Europe

See also

The peoples of northern Europe, 2300–50 BC p. 84
From Rome to Byzantium, 235–565 p. 90
The expansion of Christianity, 600–1500 p. 100
The rise of the Frankish kingdom, 482–814 p. 104
Magyars, Saracens and Vikings in 9th and 10th century Europe p. 106

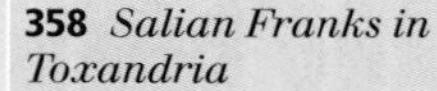

358 *Salian Franks in Toxandria*

378 *Battle of Adrianople*

410 *Alaric the Visigoth in Rome*

418 *Visigothic kingdom of Toulouse founded*

429 *Vandal kingdom founded in north Africa*

451 *Attila the Hun defeated at Catalaunian Fields*

476 *Deposition of Romulus Augustulus, last Roman emperor in the west*

481 *Clovis becomes king of the Franks (to 511)*

493 *Theodoric the Ostrogoth defeats Odoacer (rules Italy to 526)*

506 *Visigoths promulgate Breviary of Alaric (lawcode)*

536-61 *Ostrogothic wars in Italy*

568 *Lombards enter Italy*

With the foundation of barbarian kingdoms within the western Roman empire, Europe began to take on the configurations of the medieval period. The Germanic kingdoms were in a real sense the heirs of Rome, and local populations accommodated the barbarian groups, many of whom originally settled among them as Roman allies or 'federates'.

> YOU WHO HAVE BEEN RESTORED TO IT AFTER MANY YEARS SHOULD GLADLY OBEY THE ROMAN CUSTOM, FOR IT IS GRATIFYING TO RETURN TO THAT STATE FROM WHICH YOUR ANCESTORS ASSUREDLY TOOK THEIR RISE. AND THEREFORE AS MEN OF GOD'S FAVOUR RESTORED TO ANCIENT LIBERTY, CLOTHE YOURSELVES IN THE MORAL OF THE TOGA, CAST OFF BARBARIAN WAYS, THROW ASIDE SAVAGERY OF MIND, FOR IT IS WRONG OF YOU IN MY JUST TIMES, TO LIVE BY ALIEN WAYS.
>
> **King Theodoric of Italy to all the provincials of the Gauls, c. 510**

THE SETTLEMENT OF GERMANIC and, later, Slav peoples within the former Roman empire was part of a general political and cultural shift within the Mediterranean world in relation to the rest of Europe. Trading and diplomatic relations – both secular and ecclesiastical – between eastern and western Mediterranean and between the Mediterranean and northern Europe were not interrupted.

The origins of the various Germanic tribes are obscured by their own and Roman ethnographers' legends about them, but long before the Christian era West and East Germanic groups (distinguished from each other on linguistic grounds) probably migrated from the far north of Europe and east central Europe respectively. Between 370 and 470, the build-up of the Asiatic Huns on the eastern fringes of the Roman empire, despite their pastoral economy and lack of political integration, presented

1 In the frontier regions of the Roman empire, there was much interchange with, as well as raids by, neighbouring peoples *(map above)*. On occasion entire peoples were settled as 'federates' associated with the army for defence purposes. Other 'barbarians' served in the ranks and in the top military posts of the imperial armies. The Huns created a major disruption and pushed groups such as the Goths and Vandals from the frontier regions of the empire. By the early 6th century, especially in the west, a number of successor states of mixed population had emerged on its former territory.

a powerful concentration of force and their attack on the Ostrogoths forced the latter to settle, with Roman permission, south of the Danube in Thrace.

The Huns' advances appear to have forced other groups into Roman territory, some of whom were recruited to defend the Romans and given the notional status of 'federates' or allied peoples. The relationship with the Romans on occasion could turn sour: the Goths, for example, inflicted a major defeat on the Emperor Valens at the battle of Adrianople (378), but it was Romans and Germanic tribes who together defeated Attila and his Huns on the Catalaunian Fields near Troyes in Gaul in 451.

Franks and Visigoths

With the cooperation of the Romans among whom they lived in Spain, Gaul and Italy, the military role of the federate groups became a governing role as well. In northern Gaul Clovis, the Frankish leader, ruled over Gallo-Romans and Franks (settled in Toxandria probably since the 4th century) from 486. The Visigoths, military allies of the empire who had briefly set up their own emperor in Rome itself, founded the kingdom of Toulouse in Gaul in 418. They subsequently expanded their territory in Gaul, but were pushed south into Spain by the Franks at the beginning of the 6th century. The Burgundians founded a kingdom around the city of Worms, but were settled in Savoy in 443. The Sueves founded a kingdom in Galicia, though this was in due course absorbed into the Visigothic kingdom. The Vandals and Alans crossed from Spain into Africa in 429, and in 442 the imperial government recognized their king, Gaiseric, as an independent ruler of the former Roman province.

Ostrogothic Italy

In 476 the last Roman emperor in the west, Romulus Augustulus, was deposed by Odoacer, the commander-in-chief of the Roman army. Odoacer then ruled Italy peacefully until the Ostrogothic leader Theodoric, sent from Constantinople under an arrangement with the Eastern emperor, defeated him and established an Ostrogothic kingdom in Italy in 493. This was effectively destroyed in the middle of the 6th century by the Byzantine emperor Justinian's wars of reconquest, led by the great general Belisarius. He briefly secured the Vandal kingdom of north Africa and the Ostrogothic kingdom until the Byzantines were ousted by the Arabs and Lombards respectively.

The European periphery

Meanwhile in Britain, during the 5th and 6th centuries, Angles and Saxons occupied the eastern and southern coastal areas, from which the Roman garrisons had been withdrawn. The early history of the peoples of southeast Europe is more obscure; but by the end of the 8th century independent Croatian, Serbian and Bulgarian kingdoms were taking shape. In all of these centres of settlement and assimilation, a fusion of Greco-Roman institutions, Germanic traditions and the Judaeo-Christian legacy together transformed the Roman world and heralded the emergence of early medieval Europe.

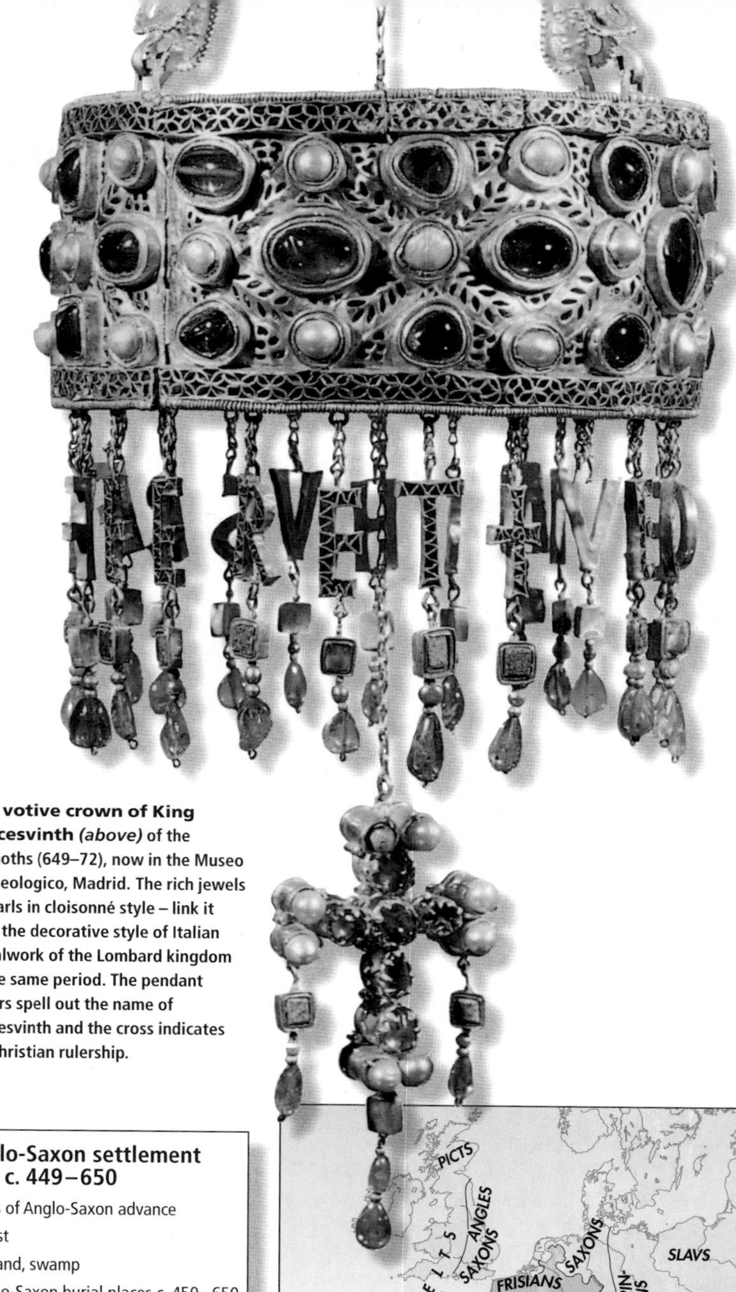

The votive crown of King Reccesvinth *(above)* of the Visigoths (649–72), now in the Museo Arqueologico, Madrid. The rich jewels – pearls in cloisonné style – link it with the decorative style of Italian metalwork of the Lombard kingdom in the same period. The pendant letters spell out the name of Reccesvinth and the cross indicates his Christian rulership.

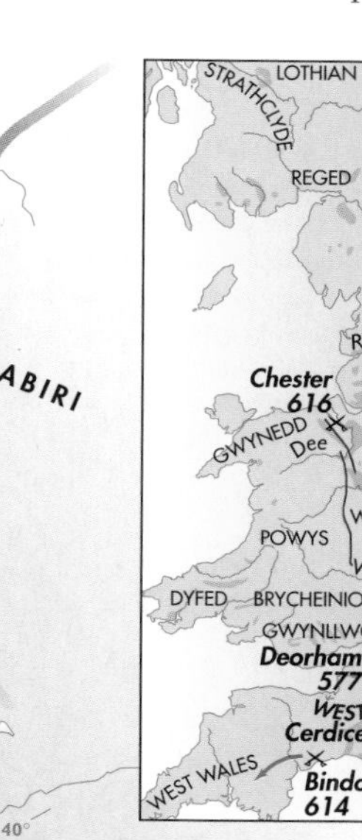

4 The Anglo-Saxon settlement in Britain, c. 449–650
lines of Anglo-Saxon advance
forest
fenland, swamp
Anglo-Saxon burial places c. 450–650
British fortifications

4 The first Germanic settlers in Britain were probably mercenaries in Roman service. In the early 5th century the last Roman legions left Britain and the numbers of barbarian incomers increased *(map above)*. According to the Anglo-Saxon Chronicle, the Anglo-Saxons set up their own kingdoms from about the middle of the 5th century, establishing control of most of modern England by about 650.

2 The Visigoths settled in Aquitaine as a Roman allied army from 418 *(map below)*. Gradually their rule extended over a defined area, the kingdom of Toulouse. They invaded Spain in 454, driving out the Sueves. The Visigothic conquest of Spain was consolidated under Euric (466–84), but following their defeat by the Franks at Vouillé, they lost most of Gaul. The Vandals crossed from Spain into North Africa in 429 and in 439 took Carthage. Their kingdom survived until 534.

3 In 493 Theodoric the Ostrogoth overthrew Odoacer to become ruler of Italy. By this time the former territory of the western Roman empire was occupied by Germanic successor kingdoms *(map above)*. These kingdoms were the heirs of Rome in every sense. Much that was Roman – in government, law, social organization, religion and intellectual culture – was maintained and even promoted under Germanic rule.

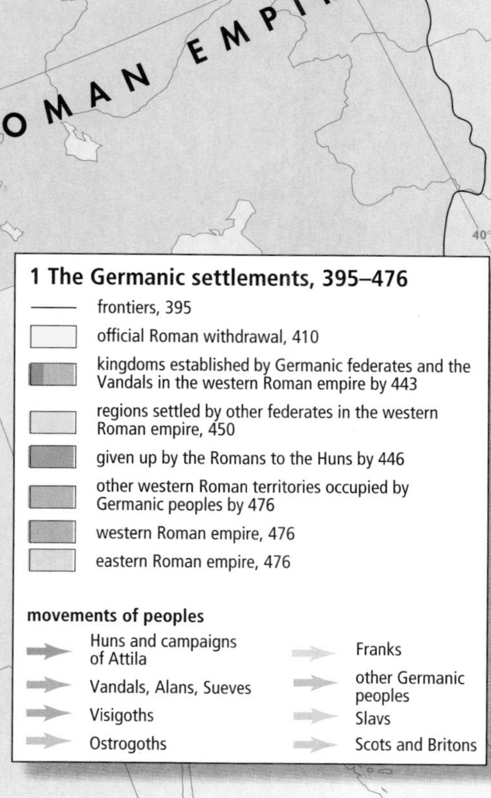

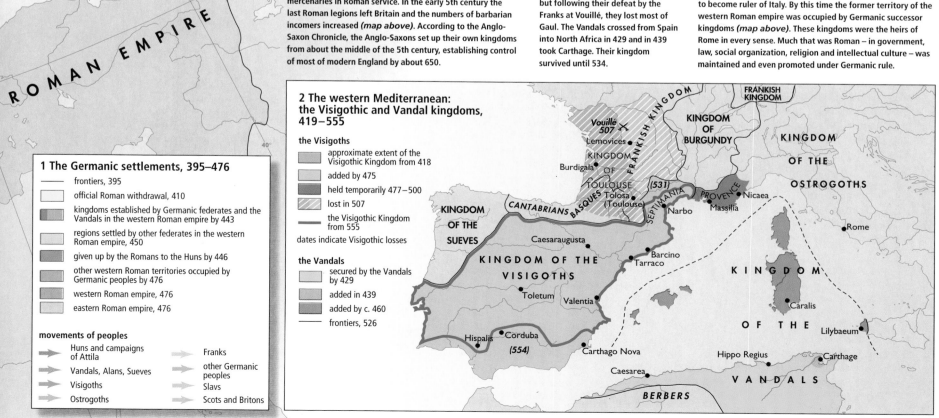

From AD 632
The spread of Islam

See also
The religious bonds of Eurasia to AD 500 p. 72
The expansion of Christianity, 600–1500 p. 100
Crusading in Europe, 11th to the 15th century p. 110
The Byzantine empire, 610–1453 p. 112
The Muslim world: the Middle East and north Africa, 800–1350 p. 136
The emergence of states in Africa, 1000–1500 p. 140
The rise of the Otoman empire, 1281–1522 p. 142

In the century after the death of Mohammed, Islam was spread by Arab armies through much of the Middle East and north Africa. It also spread to the Far East. This Muslim world retained a considerable degree of cultural unity. In the Middle Ages it conserved much ancient Greek learning, crucially enabling its later transmission to medieval European civilization.

ISLAM MEANS 'submission to the will of God'. Muslims believe that God's message to mankind has been expressed through a series of prophets, culminating in Mohammed, the Apostle and Prophet of God; that God has spoken through Mohammed; and that the Koran (meaning 'recitation') is the Word of God. Mohammed is the final Prophet, and no others will come after him.

Mohammed was born in Mecca in about AD 570. The city was the principal commercial centre in western Arabia, and was also an important pilgrimage centre because of its shrine, the Ka'ba. Mohammed received his first revelations in 610 and his followers soon grew in number. However, the hostility of the merchant aristocracy in Mecca developed into persecution, and Mohammed and his followers withdrew to Medina, some 280 miles northeast of Mecca. This 'migration', *hijra* in Arabic, on 16 July 622 marks the beginning of the Islamic era and thus of the Muslim calendar.

The Muslim conquests

In Medina, Mohammed organized the Muslims into a community, and consolidated his base with the assistance of his Medinan hosts. He returned to Mecca in triumph in 630 and cast out the idols from the Ka'ba, transforming it into the focal point of the new religion of Islam. At Mohammed's death in 632, his authority extended over the Hejaz and most of central and southern Arabia.

The first of Mohammed's successors, the caliph Abu Bakr (632–4), completed the conquest of Arabia and entered southern Palestine. Caliph Omar (634–44) advanced to Damascus, and followed victory over the Byzantines at the Yarmuk river in 636 with thrusts east into Mesopotamia and northwest into Asia Minor. By 643 Persia had been overrun, and the last Persian emperor, Yazdigird, was killed in 651 after a final stand at Merv. The conquest of Herat and Balkh and the fall of Kabul opened the way to India; Sind, in northeast India, fell to the Muslims in 712.

Simultaneously, Arab forces pushed west into Egypt, occupying Alexandria in 643, and advancing across north Africa into Cyrenaica and the Maghreb. Independent Arab forces under the leadership of Tariq ibn Ziyad and Musa crossed the Straits of Gibraltar in 711 and conquered the southern part of Spain (al-Andalus). Raids into southern France, however, were successfully deflected by the Franks. In the east, the Byzantines succeeded in preventing the Arabs from capturing Constantinople and retained control of much of Asia Minor until the 11th century.

Initially, Islam did not particularly encourage, far less insist upon, conversion. The Koran enjoins Muslims to respect the 'people of the book', that is, members of the other monotheistic religions with written scriptures. The peaceful co-existence of substantial Christian (and, until comparatively recently, Jewish) communities throughout the Muslim world is ample evidence that this injunction was heeded. Under the Abbasid dynasty (750–1258), however, large-scale conversion to Islam became common.

Politics and culture

The Muslim world split in the mid-7th century between the minority, who supported the claims of the Prophet's cousin Ali and his descendants to the caliphate (the Shi'a), and the mainstream (Sunni). In the long-run the two traditions developed religious as well as political differences. The Muslim world lost any real political unity when the Abbasid caliphate began to disintegrate and rival caliphates were established in Cairo and Córdoba in the mid-10th century. It did retain a considerable degree of cultural unity, however, largely through the Arabic language. As well as their own fine intellectual and cultural contributions, the Arabs helped to preserve much of the ancient learning of the Greeks in mathematics, astronomy and medicine. Transmitted through Arabic Spain and Sicily, this learning was a crucial contribution to medieval European civilization. Islam itself continued to expand as a religious force (*see* maps 2 and 3). This expansion was due to both conquest and, notably in southeast Asia and west Africa, missionary activity by traders and preachers.

3 Indonesia and the Malay peninsula were converted to Islam by a gradual process of proselytization ***(map above)***, probably beginning with Muslim traders from Gujerat who acquired a permanent foothold at Perlak on the northern tip of Sumatra by 1290. From there they spread to the Malay peninsula (c. 1400), Java and the Moluccas (c. 1430–90). By the 16th century most of the archipelago had accepted Islam, as had the southern Philippines.

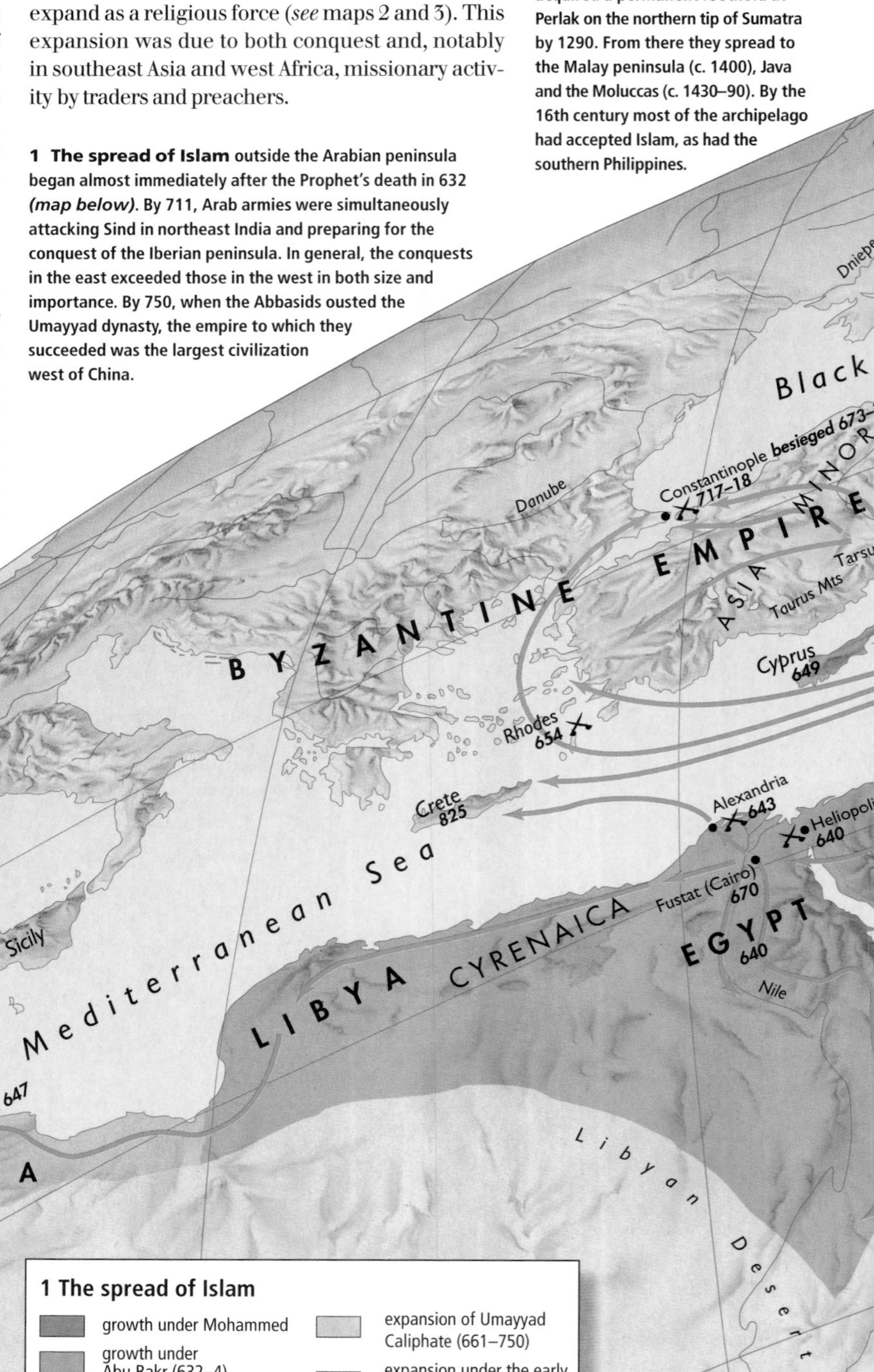

1 The spread of Islam outside the Arabian peninsula began almost immediately after the Prophet's death in 632 ***(map below)***. By 711, Arab armies were simultaneously attacking Sind in northeast India and preparing for the conquest of the Iberian peninsula. In general, the conquests in the east exceeded those in the west in both size and importance. By 750, when the Abbasids ousted the Umayyad dynasty, the empire to which they succeeded was the largest civilization west of China.

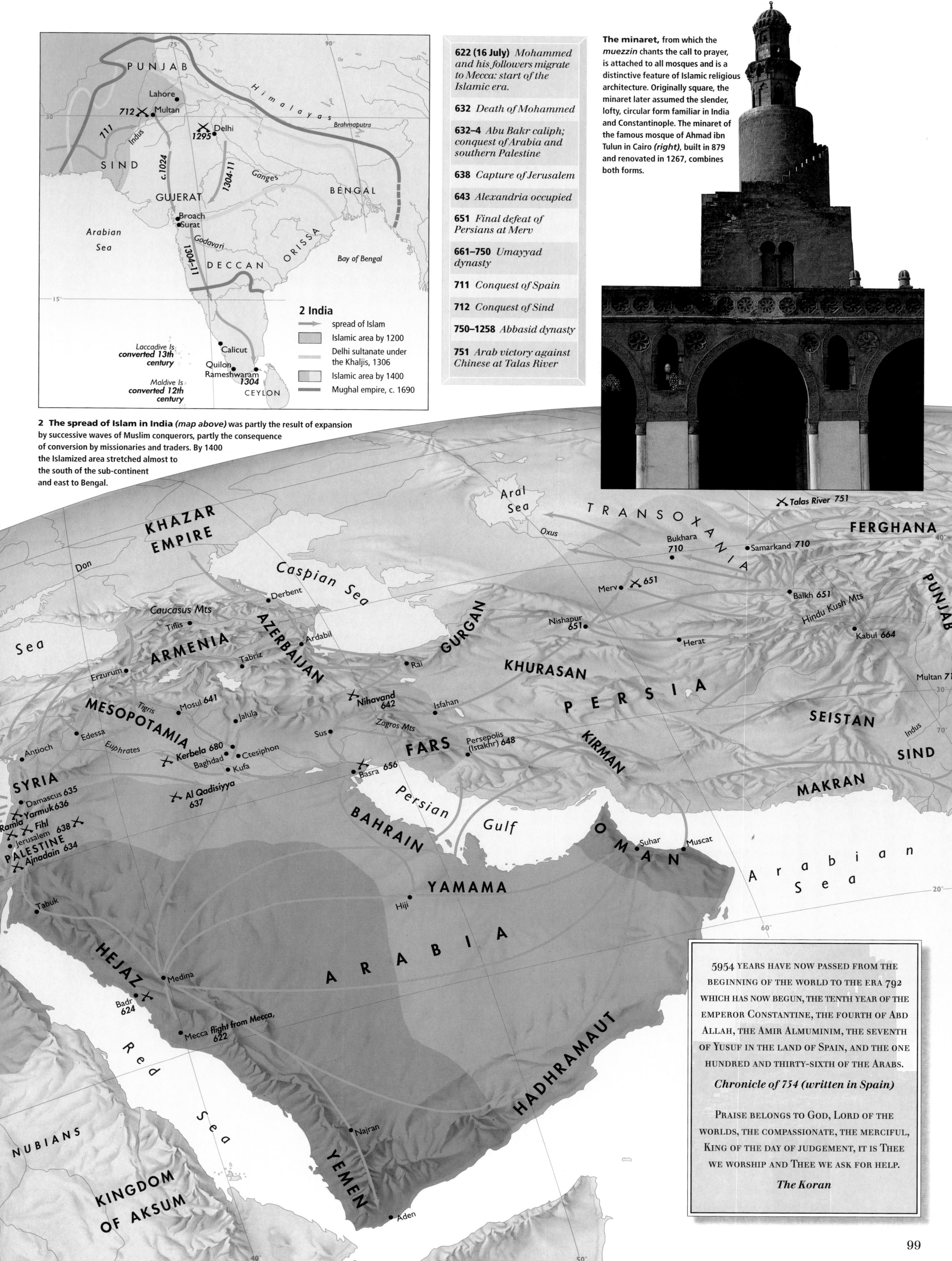

2 The spread of Islam in India *(map above)* was partly the result of expansion by successive waves of Muslim conquerors, partly the consequence of conversion by missionaries and traders. By 1400 the Islamized area stretched almost to the south of the sub-continent and east to Bengal.

622 (16 July) *Mohammed and his followers migrate to Mecca: start of the Islamic era.*

632 *Death of Mohammed*

632–4 *Abu Bakr caliph; conquest of Arabia and southern Palestine*

638 *Capture of Jerusalem*

643 *Alexandria occupied*

651 *Final defeat of Persians at Merv*

661–750 *Umayyad dynasty*

711 *Conquest of Spain*

712 *Conquest of Sind*

750–1258 *Abbasid dynasty*

751 *Arab victory against Chinese at Talas River*

The minaret, from which the *muezzin* chants the call to prayer, is attached to all mosques and is a distinctive feature of Islamic religious architecture. Originally square, the minaret later assumed the slender, lofty, circular form familiar in India and Constantinople. The minaret of the famous mosque of Ahmad ibn Tulun in Cairo *(right)*, built in 879 and renovated in 1267, combines both forms.

5954 years have now passed from the beginning of the world to the era 792 which has now begun, the tenth year of the emperor Constantine, the fourth of Abd Allah, the Amir Almuminim, the seventh of Yusuf in the land of Spain, and the one hundred and thirty-sixth of the Arabs.

Chronicle of 754 (written in Spain)

Praise belongs to God, Lord of the worlds, the compassionate, the merciful, King of the day of judgement, it is Thee we worship and Thee we ask for help.

The Koran

600 to 1500

The expansion of Christianity

See also

The rise of Christianity p. 92
The spread of Islam from AD 632 p. 98
The Jewish diaspora, AD 70–1800 p. 102
The rise of the Frankish kingdom, 482–814 p. 104
Northern and eastern Europe, 900–1050 p. 108
Crusading in Europe, 11th–15th century p. 110
The Byzantine empire, 610–1453 p. 112
Reformation and Catholic Reformation p. 182

597 *Mission of Augustine of Canterbury to England*

864 *Mission of Cyril and Methodius to Moravia*

988 *Foundation of Russian church*

1054 *Schism between Roman (Catholic) and Byzantine (Orthodox) churches*

1096–9 *First Crusade and capture of Jerusalem*

1216 *Foundation of Dominican and Franciscan orders*

1378 *Beginning of Papal schism*

1492 *Destruction of Moorish kingdom of Granada*

Having begun as a Middle Eastern religion, Christianity became a predominantly European one during the Middle Ages. Christianity gave ideological unity to medieval Europe, especially in the west. But by 1500, divisions within the Church and criticism of its teaching and institutions had paved the way for the religious turmoil of the Reformation.

IN THE FIRST FIVE CENTURIES OF ITS history, Christianity was largely confined to the Roman empire. As Rome declined and parts of the empire were settled by non-Christian invaders, the Church had to redefine itself outside the framework of imperial protection. Nonetheless by AD 600 Christianity had become the dominant religion of the Mediterranean world. However, from the 7th century the Islamic conquests deprived the Christian Byzantine empire of its lands in the Middle East and north Africa: after several centuries of Islamic rule only small Christian minorities remained in these areas. Despite the tolerance extended by Islam to Christians, the rise of Islam isolated the churches of Europe from the Monophysite and Nestorian Christians of the east, who carried out their own missions in Asia in later centuries (*see* map 1).

In Europe, meanwhile, Pope Gregory the Great (590–604) inaugurated a new era of missionary expansion, sending Augustine (later known as Augustine of Canterbury) to England. Differences between Irish missionaries already active in England and Roman missionaries over issues such as the date of Easter were the result of over a century of independent development in the Irish church (since c. 450). Nonetheless these disputes were resolved in the 7th century.

Rome and Constantinople

The same was not true of the differences between the Roman and Byzantine churches, which grew steadily greater during the early Middle Ages. Though theology played a part, many of the disputes were over liturgical practices (for example, the use in the west of unleavened bread in the Eucharist) or questions of church government and spheres of influence, especially after the conversion of the Slavs of central Europe had been inaugurated by Cyril and Methodius at the end of the 9th century.

The Byzantines were used to a regime in which the patriarch of Constantinople governed the church under the protection of a Christian emperor, and distrusted the growing power of the Popes in the west. Although the schism between Rome and Constantinople which occurred in 1054 was not technically a permanent breach, it was an important symbol of the gradual separation of the two churches. The Orthodox church in Byzantium was eventually to come under the authority of an Islamic ruler when Constantinople fell to the Turks in 1453. From then on, Russia, converted to Christianity from 988, was the most important Orthodox Christian power in Europe.

The power of the Papacy

From the 11th century the Papacy assumed a position of leadership in western Europe, which included presiding over the organization of the crusades (*see* p. 110). Gregory VII (1073–85) campaigned to end simony (the purchase of ecclesiastical office) and to enforce clerical celibacy. Innocent III (1198–1216) continued his work and was probably the most powerful Pope of the Middle Ages. Papal pretensions to superiority over secular rulers often led to political conflicts. In 1302 Boniface VIII propounded the theory of the 'two swords', which held that both temporal and spiritual leadership in Christendom should be under the control of the papacy.

> WE LEARN FROM THE WORDS OF THE GOSPEL THAT IN THIS CHURCH AND IN HER POWER ARE TWO SWORDS, THE SPIRITUAL AND THE TEMPORAL.
>
> **Pope Boniface VIII, 1302**

> LET US SEE HOW SUCH PRELATES ARE INFECTED BY THE SPLENDOUR OF THE WORLD AND BY AVARICE ... SO THAT THEY BECOME RICH MEN IN THE WORLD'S EYE.
>
> **John Wyclif, (1330–84)**

The wealth and political pretensions of the church in the west also led to opposition at a popular level. From the 11th century, heretical movements existed in western Europe. The Cathars of southern France revived the ancient gnostic and Manichaean belief that the flesh was evil, but attracted popular support because of their holiness of life and rejection of the power of the Church. Though the Cathars, like other heretics, were brutally suppressed, some churchmen realized that reform of the church, rather than the violence of the Inquisition, was the answer to heresy. The foundation of orders of friars by Dominic (1172–1221) and Francis of Assisi (1181–1226) was a response to the need of the Church for anti-heretical preachers. The friars played an important role in preaching the gospel in later medieval Europe, as well as leading what few attempts were made to convert

A section from the 8th-century Ruthwell Cross in Scotland *(above)*, one of the most important surviving Anglo-Saxon sculptures and a fascinating example of early medieval Christian art. The figures represent different aspects of the divine power of Christ. The runic characters on the borders contain an excerpt from *The Dream of the Rood*, an Old English Christian poem.

1 The medieval expansion of Christianity into central and east Asia *(map below)* was largely the work of Nestorian and Monophysite Christians, who had been separated from the rest of the church since the 5th century. Their work along the trade routes of central Asia and the Persian Gulf was tolerated by non-Christian rulers until the 14th century. China was also the scene of missionary work by the Manichees, whose dualist religion (founded in the 3rd century) had been banned and persecuted in the Christian west. Nestorianism and Manichaeism in China eventually died out, but Nestorianism survives in modern Iraq and Monophysitism remains the indigenous form of Christianity in Egypt (the Coptic church), Ethiopia and India (the Syrian Orthodox or St Thomas Christians), where distinctive traditions of worship and theology are preserved.

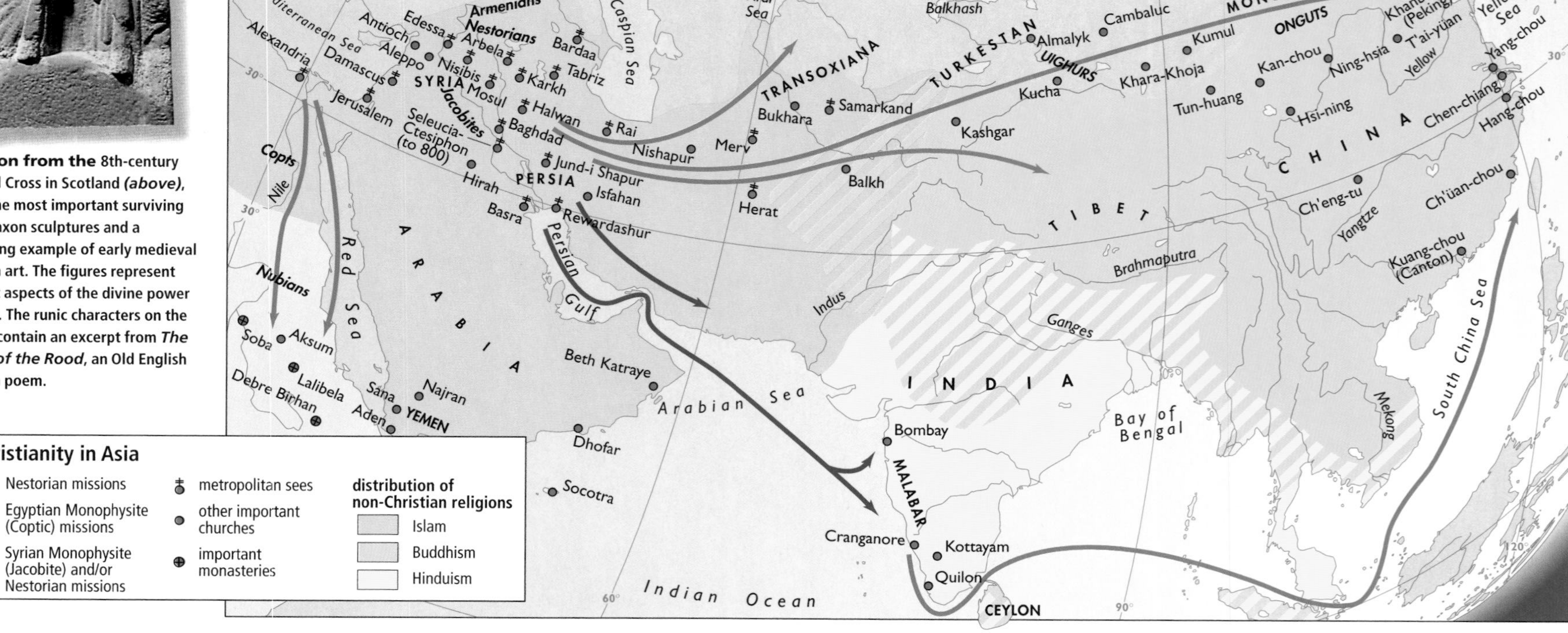

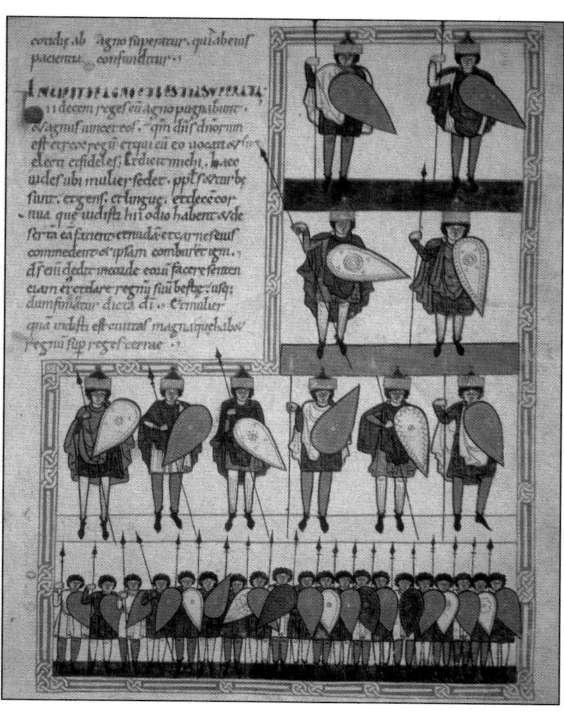

The ten kings and their troops from the 11th-century *Beatus of Liébana Apocalypse (left)*. The important 8th-century commentary on the Book of Revelation (or the Apocalypse) by Beatus of Liébana was usually copied with a series of illustrations, some of which originally alluded to political events such as the Muslim conquest of Spain. The 'ten kings' (probably, in the New Testament, representing enemies of the Roman empire) are mentioned in Revelation 17.12–14

3 Irish missionaries such as Columba (c. 521–97) and Aidan (d. 651) were instrumental in converting Scotland and northern England to Christianity; Columbanus (d. 615) founded monasteries in the Frankish kingdom *(map right)*. The Anglo-Saxon kingdoms also sent missionaries (with Roman and Frankish support) to western Germany. The most important were Willibrord (658–739) and Boniface (c. 675–754), bishops of Utrecht and Mainz.

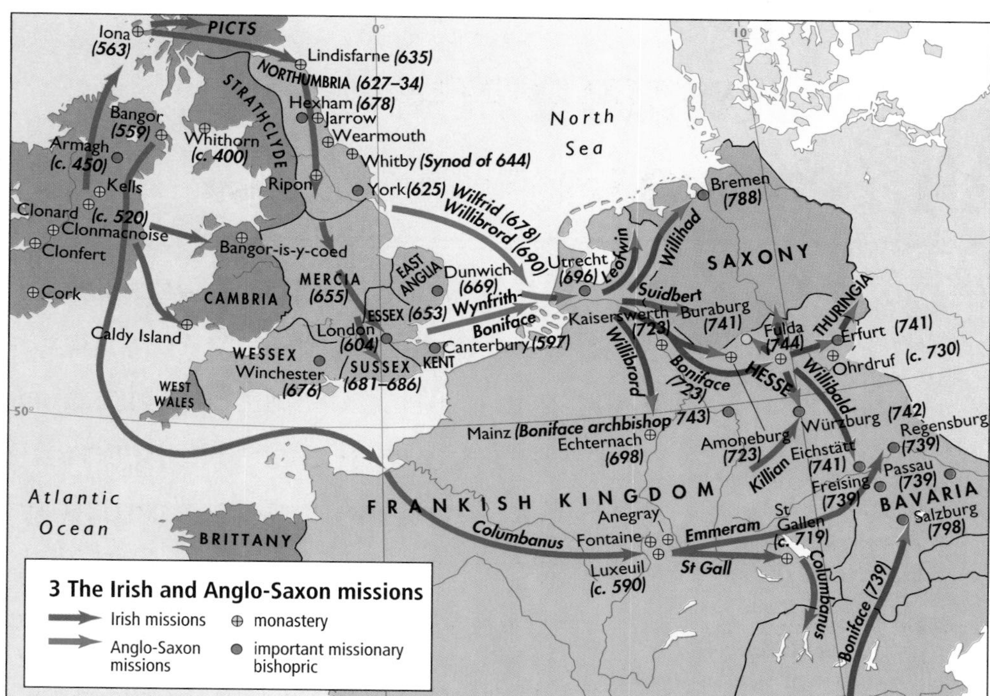

Muslims to Christianity.

In the 14th century there were further challenges to the church in western Europe. The English scholar John Wyclif (1330–84) led a movement of protest against both its wealth and some of its teachings, and there were similar protests elsewhere. The papal schism of 1378 to 1415, when two rival claimants to the papacy were supported by different secular rulers, did much to encourage calls for reform. Though such proposals came to nothing during the Middle Ages, hostility to the papacy played a large part in the Reformation of the 16th century (*see* p. 182). Nonetheless, by 1500 Europe was a wholly Christian civilization. Despite protests against the papacy, there is little to suggest that the Catholic church did not continue to provide adequately for the spiritual needs of most west Europeans.

2 From about 700, Christianity began to expand into Germany and, from the 9th century, into central Europe, where the Roman and Byzantine churches competed for the allegiance of newly converted rulers *(map right)*. The conversion of Scandinavia began in the mid-10th century, that of Russia in 988. Most of Spain was overrun by Islam in 711 but slowly reconquered by Christian rulers during the rest of the Middle Ages. From 1096, crusader armies from western Europe campaigned to recover the Holy Land from Islam: Christian rule was established in Jerusalem and Antioch, but these territories were lost by 1291. With the conversion of Prussia and Lithuania in the 14th century most of Europe had become at least nominally Christian, though the Church had been permanently divided between Catholic west and Byzantine east.

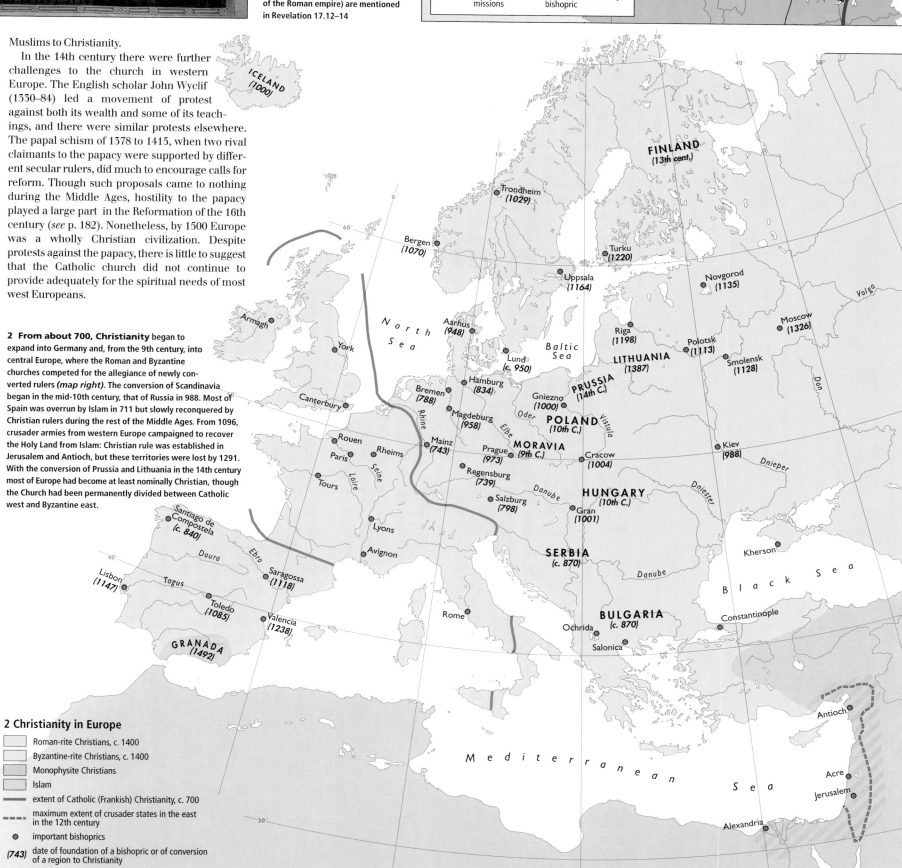

2 Christianity in Europe

- Roman-rite Christians, c. 1400
- Byzantine-rite Christians, c. 1400
- Monophysite Christians
- Islam
- extent of Catholic (Frankish) Christianity, c. 700
- maximum extent of crusader states in the east in the 12th century
- important bishoprics
- *(743)* date of foundation of a bishopric or of conversion of a region to Christianity

AD 70 to 1800
The Jewish diaspora

See also
The religious bonds of Eurasia to AD 500 p. 72
The height of Roman power, 31 BC–AD 235 p. 88
The rise of Christianity p. 92
The spread of Islam from AD 632 p. 98

> THESE JEWISH MERCHANTS SPEAK ARABIC, PERSIAN, THE LANGUAGES OF THE ROMAN EMPIRE, OF THE FRANKS, THE SPANISH AND THE SLAVS. THEY GO FROM WEST TO EAST BY LAND AND SEA. FROM THE WEST THEY CARRY EUNUCHS, FEMALE AND MALE SLAVES, SILKEN CLOTH, VARIOUS KINDS OF FURS, AND SWORDS. THEY SHIP OUT FROM FRANKISH TERRITORY ON THE MEDITERRANEAN SEA AND HEAD FOR FARAM IN THE NILE DELTA.
>
> **Ibn Kurradadhbah**
> ***Treatise on the Routes and the Kingdoms, 9th century***

After their persecution in Palestine by the Romans in the 1st century AD, Jews settled across much of north Africa and then Europe, contributing decisively to the cultural, intellectual and economic development of their new countries. Further expulsions in the Middle Ages led to a new round of enforced Jewish migrations, above all to Poland and Lithuania.

FOR OVER 2000 YEARS the history of the Jews has combined external dispersal with internal cohesion. The decisive dispersal of the Jewish people took place under Rome. Although the Jewish revolts of AD 66–73 and 132–5 and their vigorous suppression by the Romans, as well as Hadrian's measures to de-Judaize Jerusalem, caused rapid deterioration in the position of the Jews in Judaea, elsewhere in the Roman world their legal and economic status and the viability of their communities remained unaffected. This stimulated a constant flow of migration from Palestine, Mesopotamia and Alexandria to the western and northern shores of the Mediterranean. Consequently, widely scattered but internally cohesive Jewish communities developed all over the west and north of the Roman empire: in Italy, in Spain and as far north as Cologne. The Cairo community was a major element in Mediterranean commerce and has left its detailed records (the Cairo 'Genizah') of life there during the Middle Ages.

Medieval Jewry and the expulsions

The resilience of Judaism can be chiefly ascribed to the evolution of the Jewish religion following the destruction of the First Temple in Jerusalem in 586 BC, and the gradual emergence of a faith based on synagogue and communal prayer. New local leaders of Jewish life, the men of learning, or rabbis, emerged. Jewish religious and civil law was gradually codified in the *Mishnah* (AD 200) and the commentary and discussions systematized as the *Talmud* (AD 500).

During the High Middle Ages Jews from the Near East and north Africa settled in southern Italy, Spain, France, and southern Germany. They flourished in Spain under the first Umayyad caliph of Córdoba, 'Abd ar-Rahman III (912–61), and continued to play a major role in society, learning and commerce until 1391. Despite the massacres which attended the First Crusade in the 1090s, the 11th and 12th centuries constituted the golden age of medieval German Jewry.

A series of expulsions from western Europe, beginning in England in 1290, led to a steady eastwards migration of German Jews (*Ashkenazim*) to Prague (from the 11th century) and Vienna. Jewish communities arose in Cracow, Kalisz, and other towns in western and southern Poland in the 13th

63 BC *Judaea becomes Roman protectorate*

AD 66–73 *First Jewish revolt*

AD 70 *Destruction of the Temple in Jerusalem*

AD 132–5 *Second Jewish revolt under Bar Kokhba*

1290 *Expulsion of Jews from England*

1394 *Expulsion from France*

1492 *Expulsion from Spain*

1497 *Expulsion from Portugal*

1499–1552 *Expulsion from many German states*

The seven-branched candlestick *(right)* from the Temple in Jerusalem was taken to Rome by Titus when the Romans destroyed the Temple in AD 70 during the suppression of the Jewish revolt. A second revolt in AD 132–5 was similarly crushed.

1 & 2 The Jews in medieval Europe were tolerated by the authorities for economic reasons, but were subjected to restrictions and frequent persecution. They formed two major sub-groups *(map right)*: *Sephardim* from the Hebrew word *Sepharad* (for Spain) who lived in Spain until 1492; and *Ashkenazim* (from the Hebrew word *Ashkenaz*, for the Germanic lands) who originally lived in the Rhineland until, as a result of migration and expulsion *(map far right)*, by the late 15th century they flourished primarily in Poland and Lithuania. By 1500 much of Europe, including England, France, Spain and Portugal was closed to Jews.

century and, further east, at Lvov, Brest-Litovsk, and Grodno in the 14th. The period of heaviest immigration from the west into Poland-Lithuania came in the late 15th and 16th. Most of the expelled Spanish and Portuguese Jews (*Sephardim*) settled in the Ottoman empire and north Africa, though in the late 16th century a trickle migrated to Rome and northern Italy.

The revival of Jewish life

After the disruption of the Thirty Years' War (1618–48), Jews from central and eastern Europe, as well as the Near East, were once again able to settle, usually in ghettos, with the permission of both trading cities and princely governments, in northern Italy, Germany, Holland and, from the 1650s, in England and the English colonies in the New World (first those in the Caribbean and later in North America). Small groups also migrated from Germany to Denmark and Sweden. In the central European cities of Vienna, Berlin, Hamburg and Budapest, Jewish communities grew considerably during the 18th and 19th centuries and made major contributions to the development of their countries, in particular engaging in financial enterprises forbidden to Christians. During the 17th and 18th centuries, some of the largest and wealthiest, as well as culturally most sophisticated, communities in the Jewish world lived in Amsterdam, Hamburg, Frankfurt, Livorno, Venice, Rome, Berlin and London. Amsterdam's Jews were especially important in the areas of commerce, finance, printing and book production.

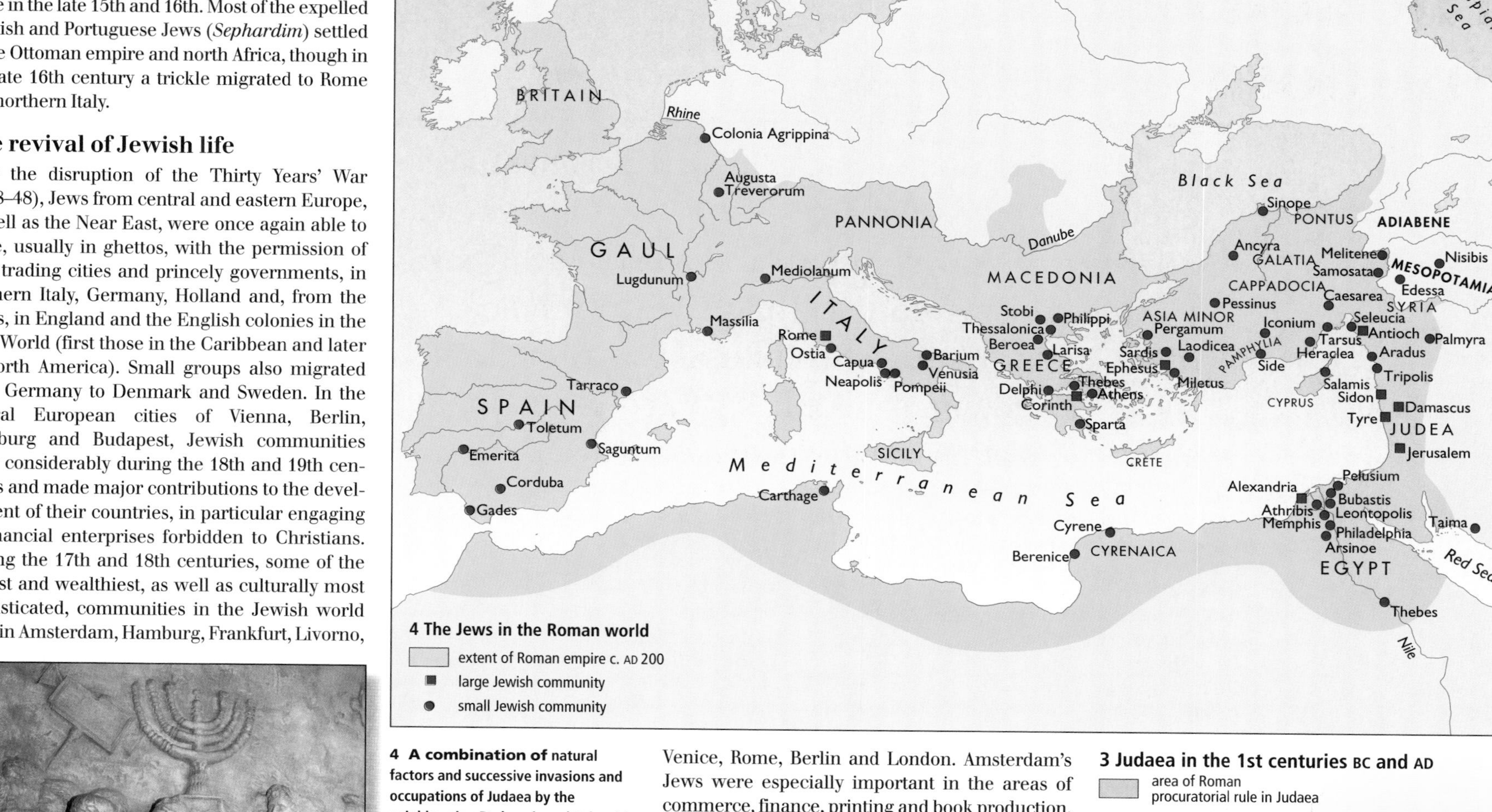

4 A combination of natural factors and successive invasions and occupations of Judaea by the neighbouring Ptolemaic and Seleucid rulers (c. 312–165 BC) encouraged sustained emigration of Jews all over the Mediterranean world ***(map above)***. Not subject to any restrictions, and with their favoured status confirmed by the Roman emperors, most fared well until the Christianization of the Roman empire from the 4th century AD onwards.

Eastern Europe

Nevertheless until the 1940s by far the greater proportion of world Jewry continued to live in eastern Europe. The small Jewish populations in Hungary and Romania in 1700 increased in the 18th and 19th centuries through immigration from Poland and the Czech lands. Under the tsars, the bulk of the Jewish population in the Russian empire was confined by law to western areas (the 'Pale of Settlement'). The demographic preponderance of eastern Europe in world Jewry ended with the Nazis: Jewish life in Poland, Czechoslovakia and the old Pale of Settlement was largely destroyed though significant Jewish populations survived in the USSR, Romania, Bulgaria and Hungary.

3 In 140 BC an independent Jewish state emerged under Simon the Hasmonean. It became a Roman protectorate in 63 BC. Herod I (37–4 BC) divided it in his will among his three sons. Judaea was governed by Roman procurators from AD 6 to 66 ***(map right)***, with an interlude when the whole of Herod's kingdom was reunited under his grandson Agrippa I (AD 41–4). After Agrippa's death, the rule of the procurators provoked an unsuccessful revolt by Jewish nationalists in AD 66–73, who made a last stand at the fortress of Masada.

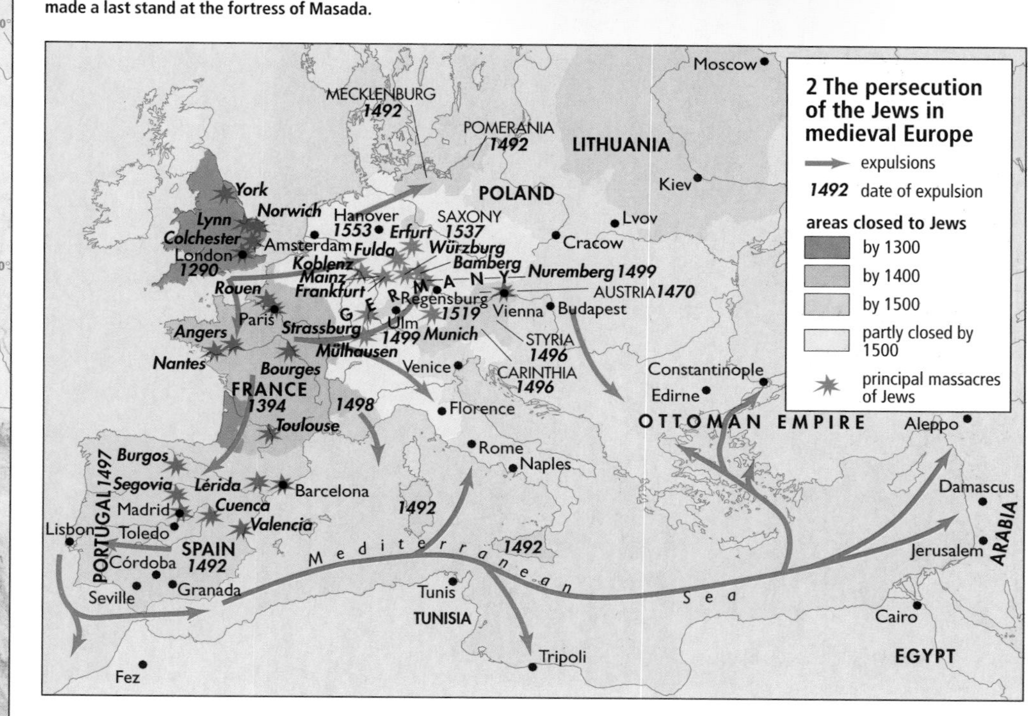

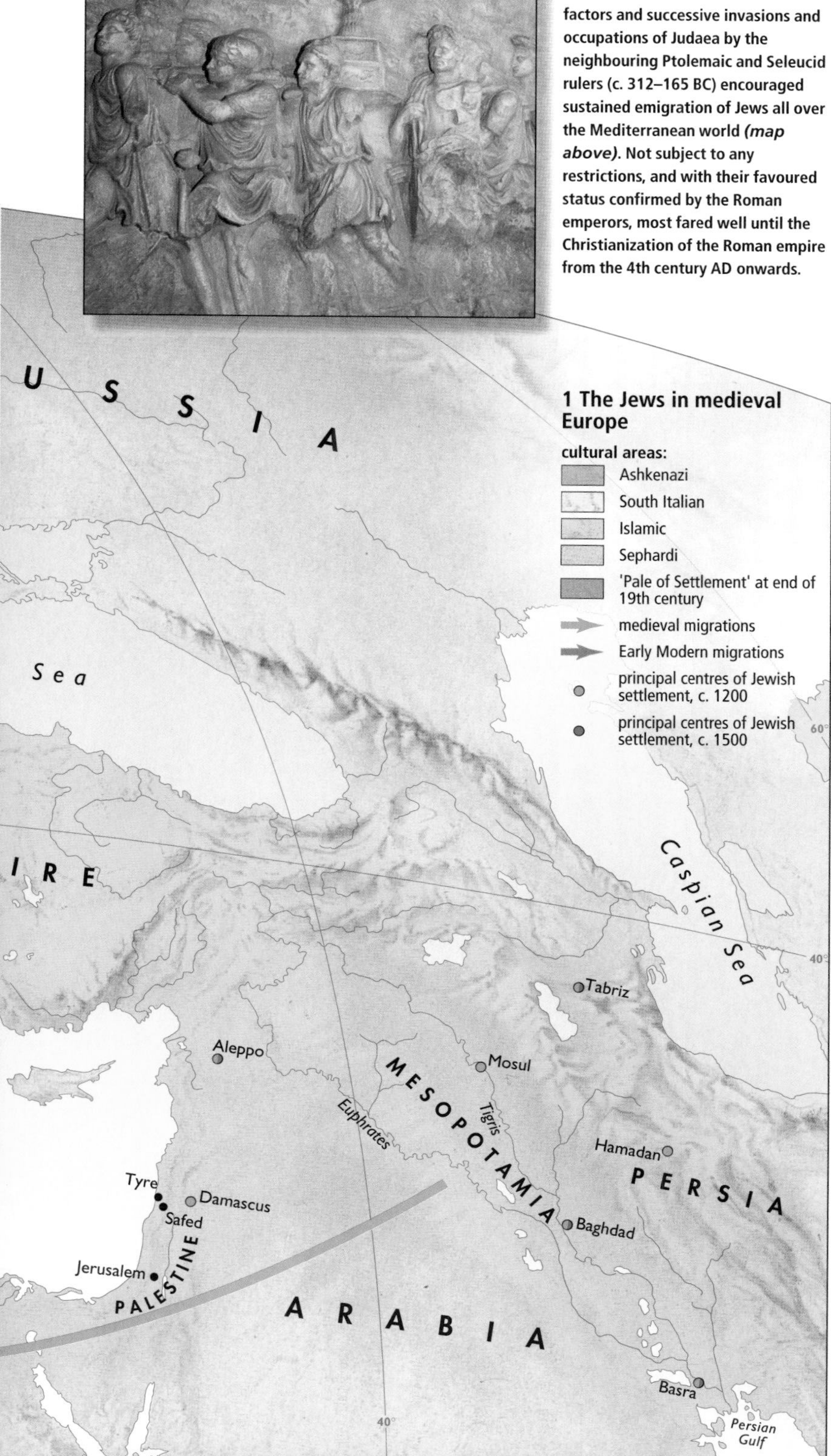

482 to 814
The rise of the Frankish kingdom

See also
Germanic settlement in western Europe p. 96
The expansion of Christianity, 600–1500 p. 100
Magyars, Saracens and Vikings in 9th and 10th century Europe p. 106
The German empire and the Papacy, 962–1250 p. 116
Economic growth in Europe, 950–1150 p. 120

496–508 *Conversion to Catholicism and baptism of Clovis*

507 *Battle of Vouillé; Frankish conquest of Visigothic Aquitania*

687 *Battle of Tertry*

714–18 *Charles Martel effective ruler in Francia*

733/4 *Battle of Tours; Charles Martel defeats Arabs*

751 *Pippin III usurps Merovingian throne*

774 *Lombard kingdom conquered by Charlemagne*

788 *Charlemagne annexes Bavaria*

794 *Synod of Frankfurt; reform of coinage, weights and measures*

800 *Coronation of Charlemagne as emperor in Rome*

814 *Death of Charlemagne; Louis the Pious becomes emperor*

The kingdom of the Franks in Gaul was the most enduring of the barbarian successor states to the Roman empire. Under the Carolingians the Franks dominated western Europe. They combined remarkable political and cultural coherence with crucial developments in kingship and government, culture, education, religion and social organization.

A STRONG REPORT HAS COME TO US THAT YOU HAVE TAKEN OVER THE ADMINISTRATION OF THE SECOND BELGIC PROVINCE. THERE IS NOTHING NEW IN THAT YOU BEGIN TO BE WHAT YOUR PARENTS ALWAYS WERE. YOU SHOULD DEFER TO YOUR BISHOPS AND ALWAYS HAVE RECOURSE TO THEIR ADVICE. IF YOU ARE ON GOOD TERMS WITH THEM YOUR PROVINCE WILL BE BETTER ABLE TO STAND FIRM.

Bishop Remigius of Rheims
Letter to King Clovis of the Franks, 481

THE MEROVINGIAN KINGDOM of the Franks in Gaul (so called because the kings claimed Meroveus, a sea monster, as their legendary ancestor) proved to be the most enduring of the barbarian successor states to the Roman empire. The conquests of Clovis and his sons and grandsons created a powerful basis for Frankish hegemony and one which was built on by their Carolingian successors who later dominated western Europe. Frankish rule in western Europe was a time of remarkable political and cultural coherence, combined with crucial, diverse and formative developments in almost every sphere of life.

The Merovingians

The splendid grave of Clovis's father, Childeric (d. 481), discovered at Tournai in 1653, shows that, although a pagan, he had ruled as Roman military governor in the north of Gaul. Clovis's conversion to Catholicism was a major factor in winning over the Gallo-Roman population to acceptance of his rule. Gallo-Romans and Franks merged; by the 7th century it is not possible to determine who among the counts and bishops who were so prominent in Merovingian administration and politics was descended from Gallo-Romans and who from Franks. It is symptomatic of the assimilation of peoples in Gaul that the French language has developed from Latin, though it was not until the 9th century that the first small adjustments to the orthography of the written language began to be made. For the whole of the period of Frankish dominance in Europe, Latin was the language of law, religion and education. West of the Rhine it was the vernacular as well.

Under Clovis's descendants, Frankish power was largely concentrated north of the Loire and especially in the areas known as Neustria and Austrasia. From 613 the kings increasingly relied on officials known as the 'mayors of the palace' and other aristocrats who governed the far flung regions of the realm. It was from Austrasia's most powerful family, the Arnulfings, later known as the Carolingians, that the most concerted challenge to Merovingian rule emerged. It was led by Pippin II, mayor of the palace, for whom the Battle of Tertry

An image of Charlemagne from his tomb at Aachen *(below)*. The tomb was endowed by Frederick Barbarossa in the 12th century. The masterpiece of gold enamels and gems shows that, for the later emperor, Charlemagne was a saint and a personal patron, able to confer political legitimacy.

2 The Frankish empire reached its greatest extent by the time of Charlemagne's coronation as emperor in Rome *(map below)*. The Lombard kingdom of Italy had been seized in 774; large parts of Germany were added, in the face of prolonged and determined resistance, after 772; and a march, or boundary province, was created across the Pyrenees between 795 and 812.

2 The empire of Charlemagne
- Frankish realm 714
- added to Frankish empire by 814
- Frankish dependencies (with date of formation)
- Frankish royal residences
- archbishoprics
- important monasteries
- GASCONY 769 province with date of acquisition

in 687 was a crucial if short-term victory. It was Pippin II's son Charles Martel, however, who rebuilt the family's and Frankish fortunes in the face of opposition from the Neustrian mayors of the palace, the Frisians, Aquitainians and Saracens. By the time of his death in 741 Charles, although still nominally only the mayor of the palace, handed on to his sons Pippin and Carloman a greatly enlarged and strengthened realm.

It was Pippin III who in 751, on the advice and with the consent of the Frankish magnates, made himself king and so established the new Carolingian dynasty. Pippin's position was further strengthened in 754 when the Pope crossed the Alps and anointed him and his sons as the rightful rulers of the Franks. The realm was again expanded under Pippin III to include Alemannia and Aquitania.

Charlemagne

Pippin's son Charlemagne conquered the Lombard kingdom and annexed Bavaria. In a series of bloody campaigns he then beat the Saxons into submission and obliged them to accept Christianity. Despite the setback at Roncesvalles (778) immortalized in the *Chanson de Roland*, Charlemagne established control of the Spanish march. He also achieved a celebrated victory against the Avars (796). Charlemagne's rule over many peoples was recognized in his coronation as emperor on Christmas Day 800, though this event was largely symbolic and did not materially affect Charlemagne's status or power: it had more to do with the role of the Frankish king in relation to Italy and his protection of Rome. Later generations, however, were to capitalize on its implications. The arrangements for the succession, devised in 806 but never put into effect, did not in fact preserve the imperial title. However, with the death by 813 of all his sons save one, Louis, Charlemagne crowned him as his successor. The triumphalist narratives of the 9th century created a strong image of Carolingian continuity and success which inspired later rulers in Europe.

Carolingian government

The Carolingian conquests were accompanied by the consolidation of the Christian church. The support as well as the protection of the Papacy, the close relationship with the church, the clerics' key role in all aspects of government alongside lay magnates and the status of the Carolingian ruler as Christian king, responsible for the faith and welfare of the Christians under his dominion, are hall marks of the Carolingian regime. Scholars, poets and artists from all over Europe were gathered at the court, centred on Aachen from the end of the 8th century, and at other cultural centres throughout the realm. Many innovations were made in government, not least the reform of the coinage and of weights and measures, and a restructuring of the administration, relying heavily on written communications, to rule the vast territories effectively. Laws were compiled and officials charged to ensure justice in society. Christian learning and education, church and monastic life were all regulated and supported systematically. Copies of specified liturgical books for use in the churches, as well as of a corrected Bible text and canon law (ecclesiastical law) were prepared by Carolingian scholars under court auspices for dissemination throughout the kingdom. Although many may have come reluctantly under the Frankish yoke, the Carolingian realm knit together a great diversity of peoples in a remarkable way and laid the foundations of modern western Europe.

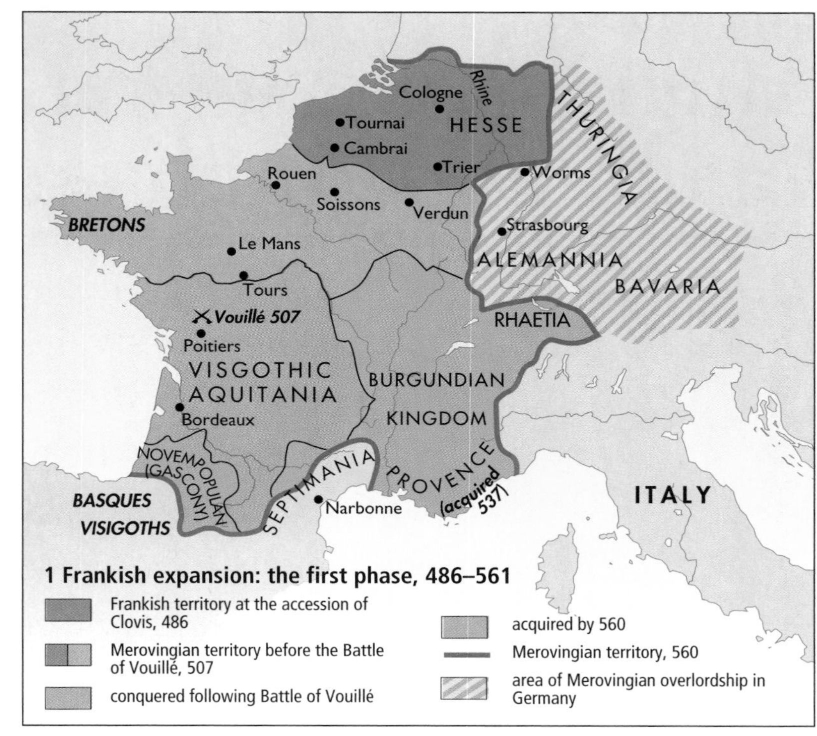

1 The Franks under Clovis and his sons extended their kingdom from their homeland near the Rhine at remarkable speed *(map above)*. Most of this came at the expense of Roman ambitions and barbarian rulers, notably Visigoths and Burgundians. By 560 the Franks were masters of the greater part of Gaul and had extensive tribute-paying regions in the east.

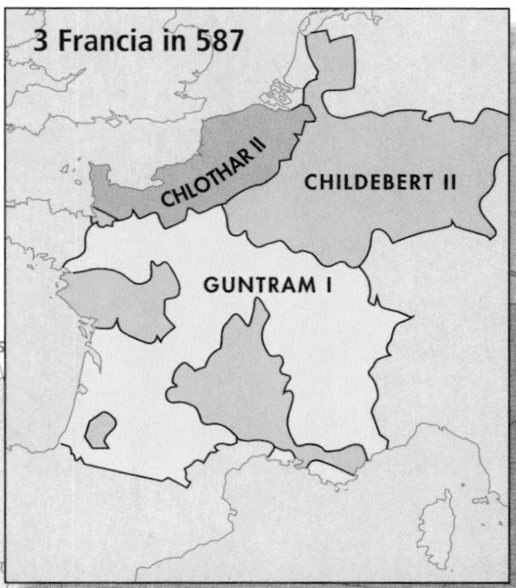

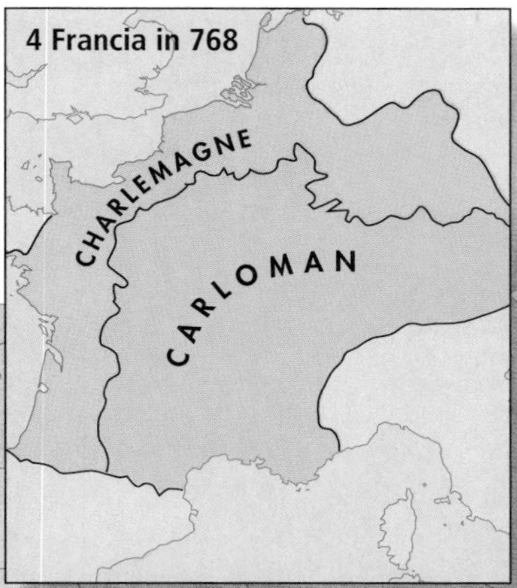

3 Francia in 587 *(map above)*. The treaty of 587 was one of many agreements which divided the Frankish kingdom between the descendants of Clovis. Childebert's portion was in effect ruled by his mother, the Visigoth Brunhild, who dominated Frankish politics until she was executed in 613.

4 Francia in 768 *(map above)*. The custom of partitioning the kingdom was continued by the Carolingians: on the death of Pippin III (768) his two sons divided their inheritance. The elder, Charlemagne, held most of the key area of Austrasia until Carloman died (771), when he inherited the whole.

Magyars, Saracens and Vikings in 9th and 10th century Europe

See also

The spread of Islam from AD 632 p. 98
The expansion of Christianity, 600–1500 p. 100
The rise of the Frankish kingdom, 482–814 p. 104
Northern and eastern Europe, 900–1050 p. 108
The first Russian state: Kievan Russia, 882–1242 p. 114
Economic growth in Europe, 950–1150 p. 120

793 *Sack of Lindisfarne*

826 *Baptism of Danish king Harold*

827 *First Muslim attack on Sicily*

841–71 *Muslims occupy Bari*

856–62 *The great Viking raids*

880 *Muslims driven from Taranto*

862 *Weland the Viking swears fealty to Charles the Bald*

885–6 *Viking siege of Paris*

896 *Magyars settle Hungarian Plain*

911 *Rouen ceded to Rollo by Charles the Simple*

955 *Battle of the Lechfeld*

Three main groups – Magyars, Saracens and Vikings – launched raids on Europe in the 9th and 10th centuries, as well as being involved in trade. It was the Vikings who proved the most adaptable colonists. Settlements established by them in the north Atlantic and North Sea, Russia and the Mediterranean developed into strong independent states.

THE RELATIVELY EFFECTIVE RULE of the Carolingians in western Europe (*see* p. 104) and of the various kings in Britain gave some assurance of security from attacks both to religious communities and merchants. By the 8th century abbeys and markets were not fortified and the masonry from Roman defences was often used for other building work. The wealth accumulated in such places offered tempting bait to external raiders. They came from countries whose rulers and people were often also partners in trade, the objects of missionary activity and political overtures or attempts at control, and who interacted with the politics of the countries their countrymen raided by entering into political agreements with them or acting as mercenaries. In the 9th and 10th centuries western Europe suffered attacks in particular from bands of Saracens, Magyars and Vikings.

After the Muslim occupation of Sicily, begun in 827 (though conquest was not complete until 902), Saracen pirates, possibly mainly from Crete and the eastern Mediterranean, established temporary bases such as Bari and Taranto on the coast of southern Italy, and later in southern Gaul, from which they were able to attack centres in the western Mediterranean until ousted by Byzantine armies in the late 9th century. Corsica and Sardinia were frequently attacked and many monasteries and towns in central and southern Italy (including Rome itself) were pillaged.

> INGIFAST HAD THIS STONE CUT IN MEMORY OF HIS FATHER SIGVID. HE FELL IN HOLMGARD [NOVGOROD], A SHIP'S CAPTAIN WITH HIS CREW.
>
> INGA PUT UP THIS STONE FOR OLAEIF HER HEIR. IN THE EAST HIS KEEP HE PLOUGHED. IN THE LOMBARD'S LAND HE BREATHED HIS LAST.
>
> ALTIK SIGVID'S SON PUT UP THIS STONE FOR HIS FATHER'S SPIRIT WHO HAD BEEN IN THE WESTERN WORLD, STORMED CITIES AND FOUGHT WITHIN THEM.
>
> ***Inscriptions from rune stones in Sweden***

The Magyars

The nomadic Magyars, who may have moved into the Hungarian Plain from the east in the last years of the 9th century, plundered the neighbouring areas: northern Italy, Germany and even France. Their skill as horsemen and their advantages of speed and surprise made opposition difficult. They also acted as mercenaries against the Moravians and the Bulgars. Major defeats were inflicted on east Frankish armies between 899 and 910, but thereafter the German rulers achieved important successes, culminating in the defeat of the Magyars at the Lechfeld in 955. In the east, the threat of Magyar raids was halted by a joint enterprise by the ruler of Kiev and the Byzantine emperor. A Magyar embassy to the German emperor Otto I in 973 marked the beginning of a more settled way of life for the Magyars. Missionary activities thereafter from Regensburg and Passau resulted in Stephen (977–1038), the first Christian king of Hungary, being given the right to set up the Hungarian church with its own bishoprics.

The Viking raids

Frankish expansion into Frisia and Saxony in the 8th century may have prompted defensive aggression on the part of the Danes. Franks and Danes were able to conclude various agreements in the first half of the 9th century, including the conversion to Christianity of a number of leading Danes and the settlement of Viking groups at strategic points to defend outlying regions of the Carolingian empire. However, raids on Lindisfarne in 793 and on the important trading emporium of Dorestad in 834 were the beginning of a grim record of attacks on both France and England until the end of the 9th century. Although the raids were no doubt described in exaggerated terms by survivors, they undoubtedly caused much misery and distress; for example the bishop of Nantes and all his clergy were murdered in 842. Increasingly effective defence (including buying time with tribute payments and the building of new fortifications) against the raids was mounted by the Frankish and English rulers. The practice of ceding the Vikings territory in order to act as a buffer culminated in the granting of the county of Rouen in 911 to Rollo, which with hindsight can be recognized as the

2 The first Viking colonists were Norwegians who settled in Ireland and Scotland, whence they raided the coast of Britain. Other Norwegians settled in Iceland, Greenland and the Scottish islands. The Danes, who had tended to raid the rich lowlands of England and France, settled in East Anglia, the Midlands and north of the Humber from 876 onwards, leaving a permanent linguistic mark on eastern and northern areas *(map right)*. In England control of the area of Viking settlement – the 'Danelaw' – was only finally secured by the kings of Wessex in the mid-10th century. In Scotland, the earldom of Orkney encompassed much of the highlands and islands by 1000 and it was only in the 15th century that Denmark finally ceded Orkney and Shetland to Scotland.

foundation of Normandy.

The Vikings were highly adaptable colonists as well as traders and raiders and their shipbuilding and seafaring prowess enabled them to journey far afield. The Danes settled in England as well as France. The Norse ventured to Ireland, Man, Scotland, the Orkneys, the Faroes, Iceland, Greenland and even as far as Newfoundland. The Swedes travelled down the great rivers of Russia and founded the kingdom of the Rus based at Kiev and Novgorod where they formed links with Byzantium.

1 No part of the Christian west was immune from either internal war or external attack in the 9th and 10th centuries *(map above)*. The Magyars traversed vast distances, but as they moved on quickly, the disruption they caused was short-lived. In contrast, Saracens and Vikings established bases in the west. The Saracens were expelled, but the Norwegians, Danes and Swedes were in time assimilated.

3 The settlement of Iceland by Norwegians began in about 870 and was completed in two generations *(map below)*. Later emigrants found limited opportunities there, but after the discovery of Greenland in the last years of the 10th century, some went on to create new settlements which survived for some five centuries. The Vikings later reached Newfoundland, but only temporary settlements have been found there and further south.

A carved wooden head *(above)* from the Oseberg cart (c. 800) depicts a fearsome Viking warrior. Viking success was in large part achieved not through superior organization or tactical skill, but depended on their greater mobility. They were able to launch lightning attacks on undefended coastal settlements and penetrate far inland in shallow boats or on horseback.

900 to 1050

Northern and eastern Europe

See also
Germanic settlement in western Europe p. 96
Magyars, Saracens and Vikings in 9th and 10th century Europe p. 106
The first Russian state: Kievan Russia, 882–1242 p. 114
The German empire and the Papacy, 962–1250 p. 116
Economic growth in Europe, 950–1150 p. 120

Stable political regimes in some northern and eastern European regions outside the former Roman empire emerged only in the period from 850 to 1050. Their conversion to Christianity created essential bonds with the rest of Latin Christendom, despite political tensions and enmities between them.

POLITICAL CONDITIONS WERE not as favourable to political consolidation in northern and eastern Europe as they were further south and west. In England the kings of Wessex were only gradually able to absorb the Scandinavian-controlled Danelaw and most settlers were apparently able to retain their land, giving a partly Scandinavian character to the customs and place-names of the region. The conquest of the Danelaw and an expanding economy paved the way for the unification of 'England' and for the religious reforms introduced by Eadgar (959–75). Nonetheless England remained subject to Danish attacks, and these culminated in the reign of the Danish king, Cnut, who ruled Norway and Denmark as well as England and introduced many Danish and 'Norman' connections into English politics. Emma of Normandy, descended from Vikings, married first Aethelred 'the Unready' and then Cnut. It was her son by Aethelred, Edward the Confessor, who succeeded to the English throne in 1042. Emma symbolizes the international sphere of politics at this time. In the wake of the Norman Conquest of England in 1066, links with France, Flanders and the Mediterranean were strengthened still further at the expense of those with the Scandinavian world.

Ireland, Scotland and Wales

Ireland at this time was characterized by political fragmentation. The Irish were rarely united and much of the period was punctuated by war between the various Irish and Viking dynasties, notably the northern and southern Uí Néill. Brian Boru became king of Munster in 976 and then made himself king of Ireland. But the Vikings of Ireland, Orkney, the Hebrides and Man together with the Leinstermen defeated Brian in 1014. His successors, concentrating on the possession of Dublin, still attempted to establish their rule over the whole country until defeated by the Norman invasion of the 12th century.

The Jelling stones *(above)* are both a symbol and a proof of the unity of Denmark and its official conversion to Christianity in the 10th century. The inscription reads 'King Harald had this monument made in memory of Gorm his father and in memory of Thyre his mother. That Harald who won for himself all Denmark and Norway and made the Danes Christian.' Harald died c. 986.

In Scotland, too, Scandinavian control hampered the consolidation of political power. Vikings settled in the western and southern parts of Scotland from the beginning of the 10th century, and different groups of Picts, Scots (originally from Ireland) and Norsemen formed many shifting alliances until a measure of stability and unity was achieved under the Scottish king Malcom II (1005–34). Relations with England fluctuated; there was frequent border warfare, and a firm boundary was fixed only in the 13th century. In Wales a similar process of consolidation took place: the dynasty of Rhodri Mawr established their rule over much of Gwynedd and Dyfed. Ultimately the instability of the conglomeration of Welsh kingdoms made them vulnerable to Norman attack.

Scandinavia

In Scandinavia itself, powerful kingdoms began to emerge out of the disarray of the Viking age. Most notable was the emergence of Denmark under three kings, Gorm, Harald and Sven. By the 10th century Denmark had become a powerful kingdom, and, under Cnut (1014–35), the centre of an Anglo-Scandinavian empire. Much of southern Norway was united under the rule of Harald Finehair after the battle of Hafrsfjord in the 890s, but after his death in the 930s Norway occasionally came under Danish lordship. Sweden, meanwhile, was united only at the end of the 11th century under the kings of Uppland. On the fringes of the Scandinavian world, Iceland by 930 was an independent commonwealth (without a king) while Greenland was colonized by Norwegians from about 985.

Eastern Europe

In eastern Europe, Moravia was attacked in 906 by Magyar invaders, but a new phase of political consolidation began shortly thereafter, probably in response to pressure from the Saxon kings Henry I and Otto I. Although the Slav peoples along the Elbe successfully resisted the Germans in the great Slav revolt of 983, they remained disunited and loosely organized. It

3 After the unification of the tribes of Great (northern) Poland under Mieszko I, his son Bolesław Chrobry ('the Brave') attempted to carve out a larger kingdom *(map left)*. Most of gains were temporary and involved long debilitating wars on all frontiers; but Little Poland, centred on Cracow, was permanently acquired, and became the royal residence under Casimir I (1038–58).

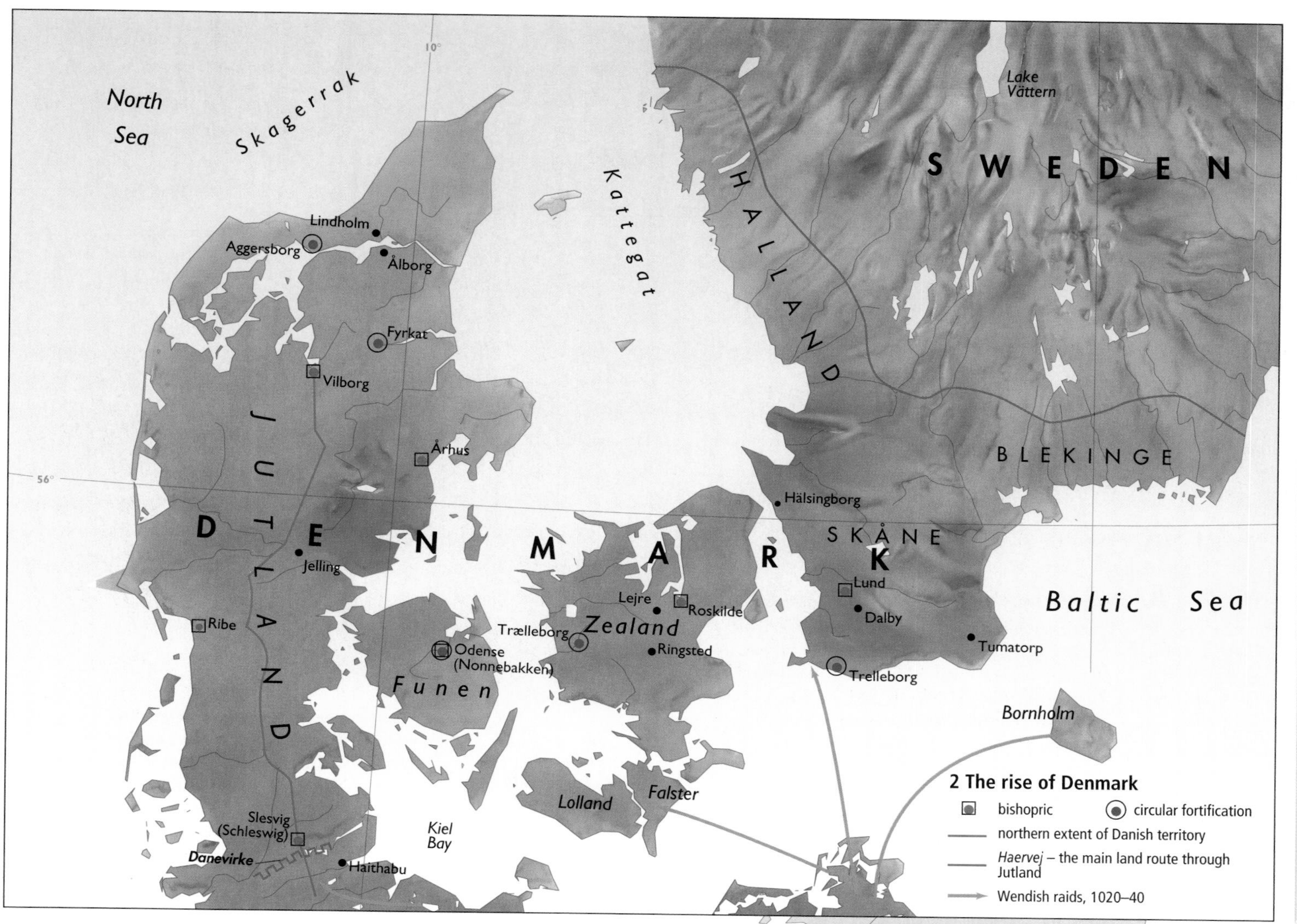

844–78 *Rule of Rhodri Mawr in Wales*

906 *Destruction of Moravia by the Magyars*

948 *Three bishops appointed to sees in Denmark*

954 *Erik Bloodaxe, last Scandinavian king of York, killed*

960–92 *Mieszko of Poland expands territory*

c. 986 *Harald Bluetooth, who restored Danish overlordship in Scandinavia, dies*

992–1025 *Bolesław I forms kingdom of Poland*

999 *Revolt of Sitric Silkenbeard Norse king of Dublin*

1013 *Sven Forkbeard, king of Denmark, attacks England and makes himself king*

1019–54 *Kievan Russia at height of its political influence under Jaroslav the Wise*

1047 *Harald Hardrada establishes control over Norway*

was in Poland that a major Slav state arose: Mieszko I (960–92) united the tribes of northern Poland, and his son, Bolesław Chrobry (992–1025), extended control to the south. Meanwhile the Magyars, led by Duke Geisa (972–97) and his more famous son, King Stephen (997–1038), the first Christian king of Hungary, established their kingdom. Bohemia, caught between Germany and Poland, had also emerged as a political unit by the time of the Přemyslid prince Bolesław I (929–67). The creation of Bohemia, Poland and Hungary – by the Přemyslid, Piast and Arpád dynasties respectively – was based on agricultural development, suppression of tribal differences and independent tribal aristocracies, and on the organizing and civilizing influence of the Church. All three dynasties made use of western institutions and connections to strengthen their position, though a notable feature in eastern Europe in the succeeding centuries was the power of the nobility as distinct from that of the monarchs. Nonetheless Bohemia, Poland and Hungary did not lose their identities, although it was only in the 14th century that a restoration of royal power took place there.

2 Denmark was the first Scandinavian kingdom to achieve full statehood in the Latin Christian tradition ***(map above)***. Four kings were responsible: Gorm the Old (c. 940–c. 58), Harald Bluetooth (c. 958–c. 86), Sven Forkbeard (c. 986–c. 1014) and Cnut the Great (c. 1014–35). Harald was instrumental in persuading the Danes to accept Christianity, while politically he countered a German threat and brought Norway under his sway. Sven concentrated largely on campaigns in England from which he drew large amounts of tribute ('Danegeld'), while his son Cnut ruled an empire which stretched from northern Norway to the English Channel. In the 10th and 11th centuries a number of towns developed in Denmark, some on the basis of the earlier 8th- and 9th-century emporia such as Ribe and Haithabu. Also a remarkable series of fortifications was constructed – including at least part of the Danevirke (the fortified southern frontier) and the fortresses at Trælleborg, Odense, Fyrkat and Aggersborg.

937: In this year King Aethelstan, lord of nobles, dispenser of treasure to men, and his brother also, Edmund Aetheling, won by the sword's edge undying glory in the battle around Brunanburh ... There lay many a man destroyed by the spears, many a Northern warrior shot over his shield and likewise many a Scot lay weary, sated with battle.
1030: In this year King Olaf was killed in Norway by his own people and was afterwards holy. And previously in this year the brave Earl Hakon died at sea.

from the Anglo-Saxon Chronicle,

1 By his death in 899, Alfred, who had styled himself king of the Anglo-Saxons, had successfully consolidated the kingdom of Wessex ***(map right)***; was in effect the overlord of Mercia; reached a *modus vivendi* with the Danes in the Danelaw; and in 886 occupied London. His sons and grandsons, Edward the Elder (899–924), Aethelstan (924–39), Edmund (939–46) and Eadred (946–55) extended and consolidated the English kingdom. Edward established his rule over the entire area south of the Humber, and east of the Welsh and secured Mercia. His successors pushed north: the last Viking ruler of York, Erik Bloodaxe, fell in battle in 954.

Crusading in Europe from the 11th to the 15th century

See also
The Byzantine empire, 610–1453 p. 112
The Muslim world: the Middle East and north Africa, 800–1350 p. 136
Islam and Christianity at the end of the 15th century p. 138
European states in the 14th century p. 146
The Mediterranean world, 1494–1797 p. 186

A Crusade was a Christian war concerned with the recovery and defence of lost lands. For those taking part it was means of salvation. Starting with the First Crusade in 1096–9, the crusaders altered the political balance in the eastern Mediterranean for many centuries. Christian holy war also remained a recurrent feature of northern European politics.

1095 *Pope Urban II preaches First Crusade at Council of Clermont*

1099 *Crusaders capture Jerusalem*

1119 *Templars founded*

1142 *Krak des Chevaliers built*

1144 *Edessa falls to Turks*

1146–8 *Second Crusade*

1187 *Saladin takes Jerusalem and Acre*

1189–91 *Third Crusade*

1199 *Livonian Crusade in Baltic*

1204 *Fourth Crusade; sack of Constantinople*

1212 *Muslims defeated at Las Navas de Tolosa*

1291 *Fall of Acre*

1312 *Templars suppressed*

1453 *Constantinople falls to Turks*

1492 *Granada captured by Christians*

BOHEMUND GAVE ORDERS SAYING 'CHARGE AT TOP SPEED, LIKE A BRAVE MAN AND FIGHT VALIANTLY FOR GOD AND THE HOLY SEPULCHRE, FOR YOU KNOW IN TRUTH THAT THIS IS NO WAR OF THE FLESH, BUT OF THE SPIRIT. SO BE VERY BRAVE, AS BECOMES A CHAMPION OF CHRIST.'

Anon. Gesta Francorum, VI

WE CONCEDE TO ALL FIGHTING IN THIS EXPEDITION [IN SPAIN] THE SAME REMISSION OF SINS WHICH WE HAVE GIVEN TO THE DEFENDERS OF THE EASTERN CHURCH.

Pope Calixtus II, 1123

CHRISTIANS HAD MADE pilgrimages to the Holy Land since the 2nd century AD. The combination of religious tourism and spiritual inspiration offered by pilgrimage had greatly increased the number of visitors after the conversion of Constantine and the discovery by his mother, Helena, of the supposed True Cross in Jerusalem. Many new churches and monasteries were built in the Holy Land, often on newly identified holy sites of both Old and New Testament events. Jerusalem in particular held pride of place in the imagination and hearts of Christians everywhere, which not even its conquest by Arab forces in the 7th century could overturn. Indeed, access thereafter was far from denied and throughout the 8th, 9th and 10th centuries there are reports from travellers from Britain, France and Italy who prayed at the holy sites. A constant stream of souvenirs and holy relics, furthermore, reached the west and were treated with great reverence in churches across Europe. Allied to the importance of pilgrimage to the Holy Land were the missionary endeavours to convert pagans conducted in western Europe. Between the 6th and 11th centuries this saw the conversion of the English, the Frisians, Saxons, Slavs, Scandinavians, Bulgars and Rus by Irish, Roman, English, Frankish, Saxon and Byzantine missionaries. Within the Christian church, moreover, there were intense bouts of eradication of heresy. Pilgrimage, the striving to achieve orthodoxy and the conversion of pagans, coupled with the religious piety and devotion of the laity, came together in the crusading movement of the central and later Middle Ages.

The movement was concerned not only with the recovery of the Holy Land from those who were regarded by the Christian church as 'infidels'. There were also crusades against the Albigensian heretics in southern France from 1208, the pagan Slavs in Livonia in the Baltic from the end of the 12th century and the Reconquista of Spain from the Arabs by the Catholic monarchs of northern Spain which became a national liberation movement. Even such European rulers as the Emperor Frederick II of Germany and King Beta of Aragon were the objects of crusades to defend the Catholic faith and liberty of the church against their rulers' alleged depredations.

The First Crusade

The crusading movement was precipitated by a plea from a Byzantine embassy to Pope Urban II in 1095 for help to defend the eastern church against the Turks who had overrun Asia Minor. In November of that year the Pope preached the first crusade at the Council of Clermont. The enthusiasm for the call to wage Christian holy war was remarkable. Nobles and knights made considerable sacrifices which affected both themselves and their families in order to go on crusade, for it was a genuinely popular devotional activity. Many sold their patrimonies to raise money for the expeditions, though only a minority actually 'took the Cross' and went to fight. Only a few noble families from France joined the First Crusade, though kings, notably Richard I (the Lionheart) of England and Louis IX of France, were involved in later expeditions to the east.

The crusaders

Crusaders made a public, formal vow to join a military expedition in response to an appeal by the Pope on Christ's behalf. It was a legal obligation and crusaders became subject to the jurisdiction of the ecclesiastical courts. In return special privileges were granted to a crusader including the protection of their families' interests and assets while they were absent, and major spiritual privileges in the form of Indulgences to reduce the time spent in purgatory atoning for sins on earth. Closely associated with the crusading movement were the military orders, such as the Templars and Hospitallers, whose members had made a permanent commitment to wage holy war. Both the Templars and Hospitallers had their headquarters in Jerusalem, but soon acquired extensive properties in the west. The rulers of the crusader states, frequently starved of manpower, entrusted great strongholds and large stretches of land to the military orders and by the 13th century they formed the backbone of the military strength of the crusading states.

The later Crusades

The First Crusade led to the foundation of the Latin kingdom of Jerusalem following the crusaders' capture of Jerusalem and Antioch in 1098 and 1099 The focus of subsequent expeditions was the defence, ultimately unsuccessful, of these gains against Muslim attack. The Second Crusade (1146–8) was inspired by the loss of the city of Edessa to al-Din Zengi, the Muslim ruler of Aleppo, while the Third Crusade (1189–91) was launched as a response to the conquest by Saladin of most of the crusader territories in the Levant, including the catastrophic loss of Jerusalem. Although the city was not recovered, the crusaders reoccupied most of the coastal ports, so ensuring the survival of the crusader states.

In Spain the Reconquista or recovery of land from the Muslims was given impetus by crusading ideals. In contrast to the Crusades to the east this was a local affair, with little help received from outside. Yet in Spain, too, military orders such as Calatrava (from 1158) and Santiago (from 1170)

3 Norman invasions and Crusader penetration encouraged western ambitions against Byzantium. Fostered by Venice, eager to destroy her main commercial rival, the Fourth Crusade ***(map below)*** sacked Constantinople, dismembered the Byzantine empire and established a short-lived Latin empire (1204–61).

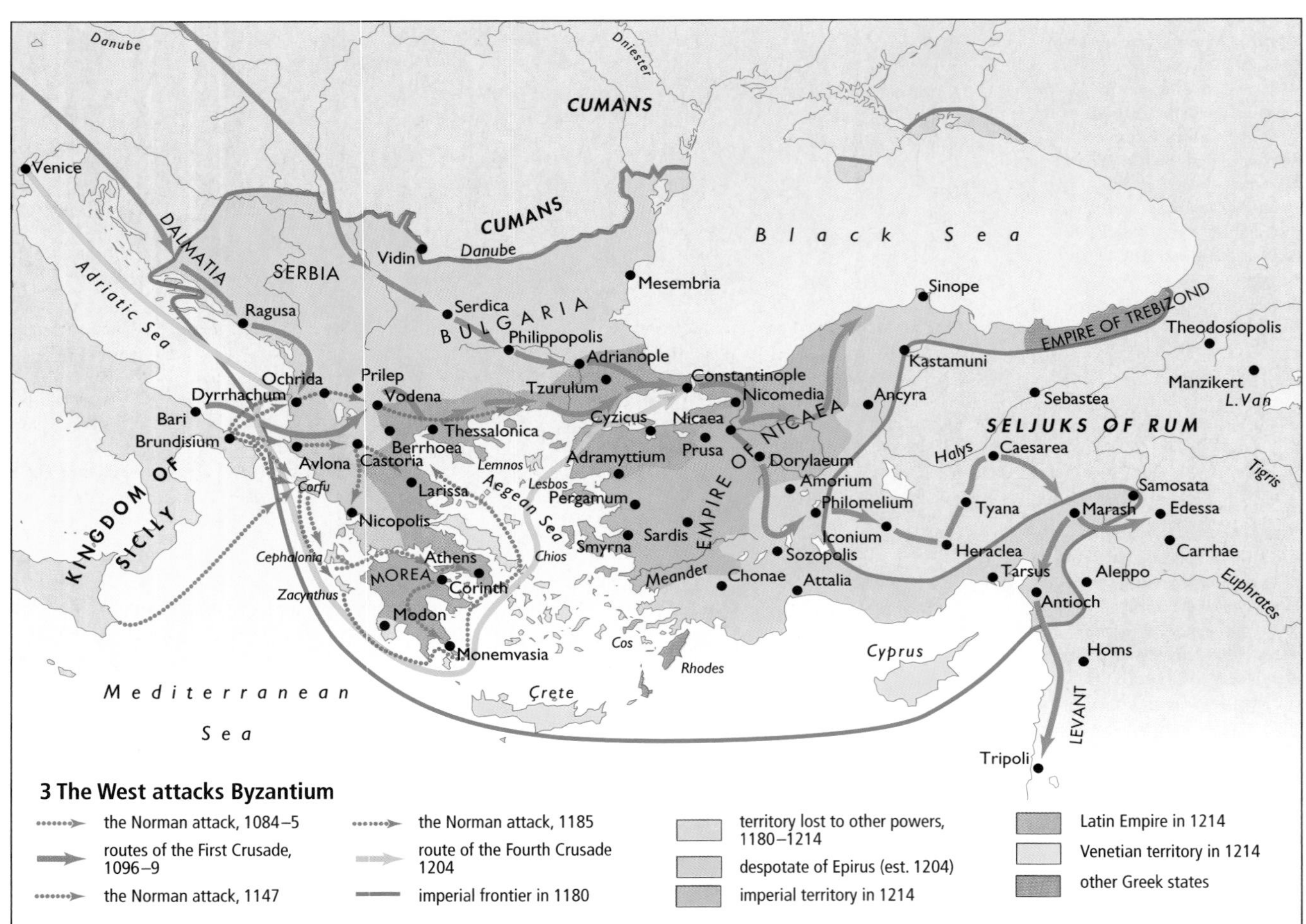

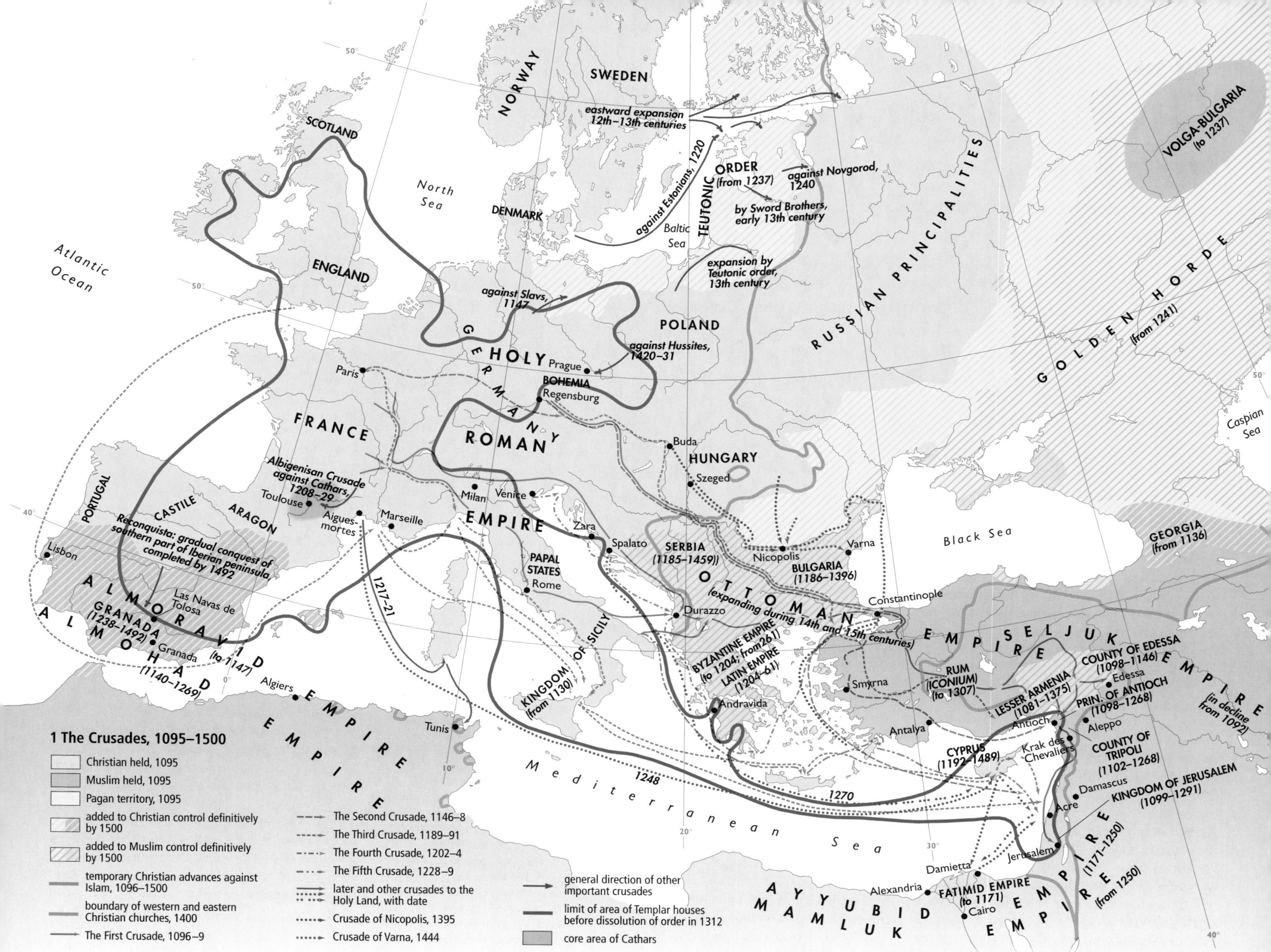

1 The Crusades, 1095–1500

- Christian held, 1095
- Muslim held, 1095
- Pagan territory, 1095
- added to Christian control definitively by 1500
- added to Muslim control definitively by 1500
- temporary Christian advances against Islam, 1096–1500
- boundary of western and eastern Christian churches, 1400
- The First Crusade, 1096–9
- The Second Crusade, 1146–8
- The Third Crusade, 1189–91
- The Fourth Crusade, 1202–4
- The Fifth Crusade, 1228–9
- later and other crusades to the Holy Land, with date
- Crusade of Nicopolis, 1395
- Crusade of Varna, 1444
- general direction of other important crusades
- limit of area of Templar houses before dissolution of order in 1312
- core area of Cathars

1 Beginning with the First Crusade, preached by Pope Urban II at the Council of Clermont (1095), the crusading movement inspired Christian Europe's struggle against the enemies of the faith – both internal and external – for four centuries *(map above)*. Even after the fall of the last stronghold in Palestine in 1291, Crusades were fought to defend the Balkans against the Ottoman Turks, to complete the Reconquista in Spain, and against pagans around the Baltic.

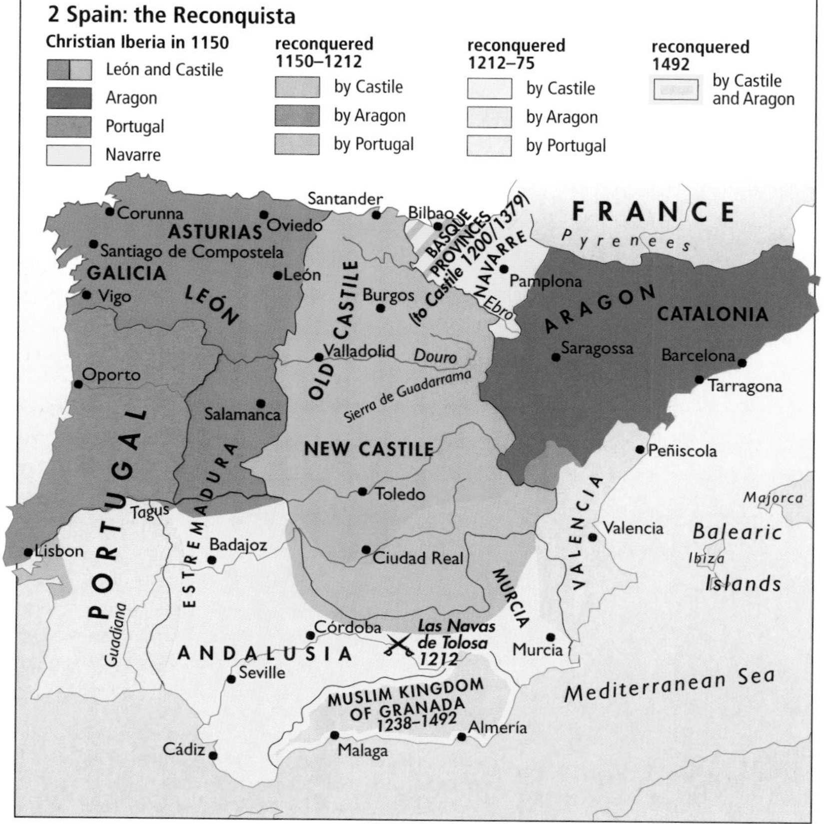

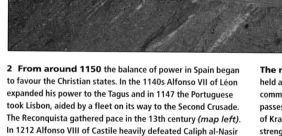

2 From around 1150 the balance of power in Spain began to favour the Christian states. In the 1140s Alfonso VII of Léon expanded his power to the Tagus and in 1147 the Portuguese took Lisbon, aided by a fleet on its way to the Second Crusade. The Reconquista gathered pace in the 13th century *(map left)*. In 1212 Alfonso VIII of Castile heavily defeated Caliph al-Nasir at Las Navas de Tolosa. The subsequent collapse of the Almohad empire helped the Christians overrun most of southern Spain by 1275, including Córdoba in 1235 and Seville in 1248.

The military orders (Hospitallers and Templars) held a series of important strongholds in the Holy Land, commanding strategic locations such as ports, valleys and passes. Perhaps the most impressive was the Hospitaller castle of Krak des Chevaliers *(above)*. Its imposing fortifications were strengthened at the beginning of the 13th century, but in the end, isolated by the Mamluks' occupation of the surrounding territories, the castle surrendered to them in 1271 after a siege of barely more than a month.

contributed vitally to the war against Islam. In 1212 the armies of Castile, Navarre and Aragon crushed the Muslim army at Las Navas de Tolosa, winning the most important victory of the whole Reconquista. In 1492 Christian armies took Granada, the last remaining Muslim stronghold in Spain.

The crusading movement was seriously compromised in 1204 by the bloodshed of the capture of Constantinople by an army of Latin Christians, who diverged from a planned campaign in Palestine. They dismembered the Byzantine empire and, together with the Genoese and Venetians, set up Latin states around the Aegean.

The crusading ideal, however, lived on. Further Crusades targeted Egypt and the Levant. The crusader states in the east survived until the late 13th century, with the loss of the last stronghold at Acre in 1291. Even then further Crusades were still mounted against the Muslims as late as 1444 (the Crusade of Varna), and the language of crusading was employed to describe the struggle against the Ottoman Turks and Spanish incursions into north Africa in the 16th century. Crusades were launched against heretics, such as the Hussites in Bohemia (1420–31) and by the Teutonic Knights in the Baltic against pagan Prussians from 1309 (*see* p. 146).

610 to 1453

The Byzantine empire

See also
From Rome to Byzantium, AD 235–565 p. 90
Crusading in Europe, from the 11th to the 15th century p. 110
The first Russian state: Kievan Russia, 882–1242 p. 114
The Muslim world: The Middle East and north Africa, 800–1350 p. 136
The rise of the Ottoman empire, 1281–1522 p. 142

The Roman empire in the east continued – as Byzantium – long after the political transformation of the west by the barbarian successor states. Its distinctive, Greek-speaking, Christian and culturally diverse civilization dominated the east Mediterranean, exerting a crucial cultural influence on western Europe despite the steady loss of territory to the Turks.

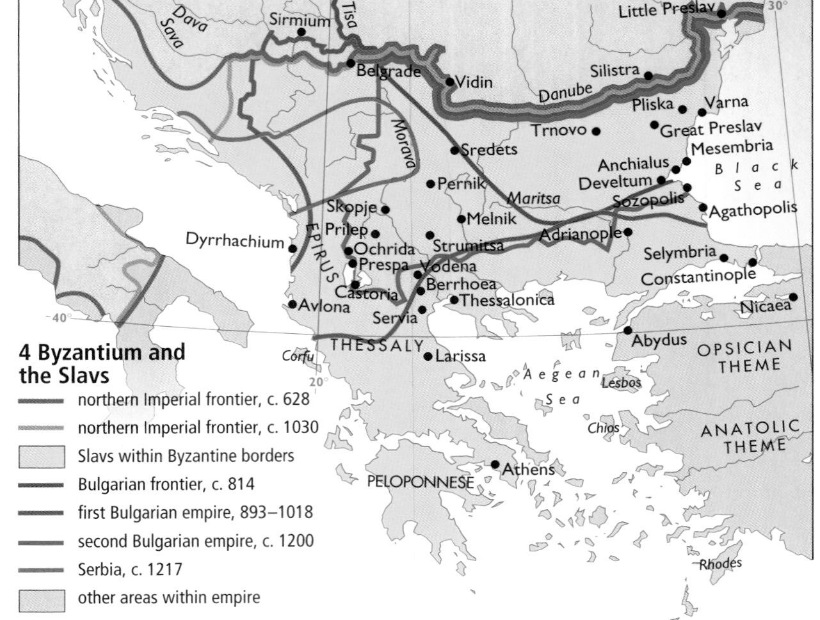

ALTHOUGH HERACLIUS (610–41) had ended the struggle with the Sasanid rulers of Persia, for so long Rome's most formidable rival, before his death the southern and eastern frontiers of the empire came under attack from the forces of Islam. Constantinople withstood two Arab sieges, in 674–8 and again in 717–8. At the same time the Bulgars settled in the Balkans with armed outposts less than 60 miles from Constantinople itself.

Renewal and retreat

Within Byzantium major disruption to society between 726 and 843 was caused by the controversy over the banning of Christian images, known as iconoclasm. Not long after images in churches were restored, a fresh and vigorous Macedonian dynasty of emperors embarked on a new era of expansion. Between 863, when a strong force of Arabs was annihilated at Poson, on the Halys river in Anatolia, and the death of the great warrior-emperor Basil II (976–1025), a series of dramatic victories pushed back the frontiers, often close to where they had been in the heyday of Rome. In the southeast the Arabs at one stage (976) retreated to the very gates of Jerusalem; the Rus were held and routed at Silistra on the Danube (971); and Bulgaria, after long bitter campaigning, became a group of Byzantine provinces. But the new frontiers, exhaustingly won, proved indefensible, especially as the previously invincible Byzantine armed forces now found themselves starved of funds by a civilian administration fearful of a military coup. In 1071, the Byzantine army was heavily defeated by Seljuk Turks at the battle of Manzikert (*see* p. 136). The Turks then established a permanent occupation of the Anatolian plateau. In the same year, the empire's last Italian possession fell to the Normans.

The Comeneni and the Crusades

Paradoxically, the 11th and 12th centuries proved to be among the most fertile in Byzantine history in artistic and theological terms. Yet for all their genius, the emperors Alexius I (1081–1118), John II (1118–43) and Manuel I (1143–80) ultimately proved unable to recover much of the vast territory that had been lost, though they succeeded by diplomatic means in maintaining a strong balance of the various interests between themselves and their neighbours. The First Crusade (1096–9) had certainly created serious difficulties for the Byzantine rulers while the ferocious assault of the Christian Latin Crusaders in 1204 inflicted great damage on both Constantinople and the empire.

Byzantium's strength, apart from its religious cohesion, was two-fold: the *themes* (*see* map 3) with their independent freeholding peasantry, ready both to farm and to defend its land; and an army and a navy often manned by native officers and troops. By the 11th and 12th centuries, mercenaries – themselves often Seljuk, Muslim or Norman – came to form the bulk of the armed forces, and the important civilian posts in the civilian bureaucracy fell more and more under the control of a few rich dynasties. These owed much of their new wealth and power to the *pronoia* system, under which key state functions, including

4 By 600, Slavic peoples had settled most of the Balkans. Though they were driven back, by the 10th century the first Bulgarian empire became a serious rival to Byzantium ***(map above)***. Symeon of Bulgaria (d. 927) brought effective rule to Bulgaria: in 904 Byzantium recognized his possession of Thrace and Macedonia. A Byzantine counter-offensive began in 1001. Basil II (976–1025) annexed Bulgaria in 1018 after bitter campaigning. In 1180 a revolt against Byzantine rule led to the rise of a new Bulgarian empire based at Trnovo. Serbia under Stefan Nemanja (1168–96) also carved out a large independent territory. The introduction of Orthodox Christianity helped pacify Slav peoples, and took strong root despite the conflicts.

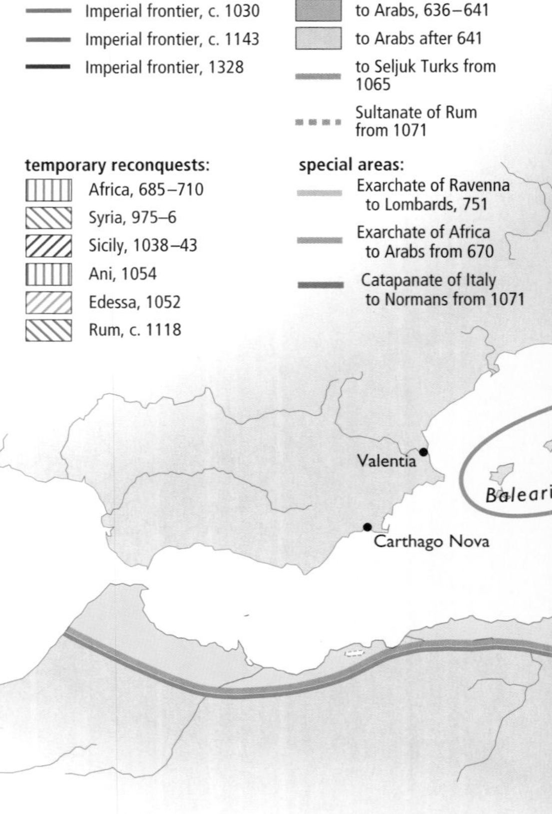

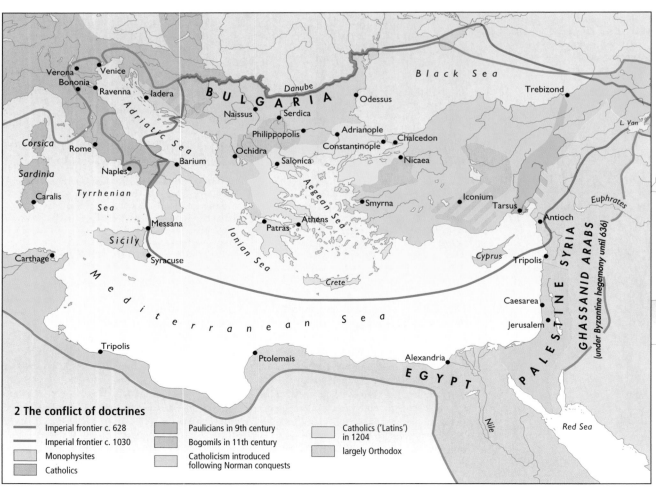

2 The conflict of doctrines
Imperial frontier c. 628
Imperial frontier c. 1030
Monophysites
Catholics
Paulicians in 9th century
Bogomils in 11th century
Catholicism introduced following Norman conquests
Catholics ('Latins') in 1204
largely Orthodox

2 Doctrinal disputes helped weaken central imperial control ***(map left)***. The areas where Monophysitism (a heterodox view of the nature of Christ) was strong were conquered by the Arabs in the 7th century. Paulicians and Bogomils (9th–10th centuries) preached varieties of the dualistic heresy of Manichaeism (holding there to be a good god and and evil one) and their adherents occupied key areas of Asia Minor and the Balkans. A large part of the empire came under Catholic 'Latin' control after 1204 but this was the faith of the new rulers, not of the people.

THE KING OF THE GREEKS HAS LONG HAIR AND WEARS A TUNIC WITH LONG SLEEVES AND A BONNET; HE IS LYING, CRAFTY, MERCILESS, FOXY, PROUD, FALSELY HUMBLE, MISERLY AND GREEDY; HE EATS GARLIC, ONIONS AND LEEKS, AND HE DRINKS BATH WATER.

Liutprand of Cremona
The Embassy to Constantinople in 968

628 *Heraclius defeats Persians at Nineveh*

726 *Leo III declares all images to be idols; images finally restored in 843*

976–1025 *Reign of Basil II, the Bulgar slayer*

1054 *Schism between Orthodox and Catholic churches*

1071 *Seljuk Turks defeat Byzantines at Manzikert*

1096–9 *First Crusade*

1204 *Constantinople sacked by Fourth Crusade; Latin empire established*

1261 *Greek empire re-established*

1438–9 *Council of Florence; attempt to unify eastern and western churches*

1453 *Fall of Constantinople*

tax collection, were handed over to large local landowners – originally for their lifetime, but increasingly on a hereditary basis. In religious matters, Rome and Constantinople moved even further apart. There had been tension, if not actual schism, between the Roman and Orthodox churches since 1054 (*see* p. 100).

The last centuries

Both Seljuks and Normans resumed full-scale frontier aggression in the 1170s and many Byzantine provinces were lost. The immediate beneficiary of the Fourth Crusade (1204) was the rising power of Venice, whose fleets had carried the Crusaders and who established colonies on the Aegean islands and Crete. A Latin empire was created with many principalities in Thessaly, Athens and Achaia and Greek enclaves at Nicaea and Epirus. The Greeks still constituted a majority within the truncated empire and in 1261, aided by Genoa, a rival of Venice, they drove out the westerners. But the Greek empire was only a shadow of the Byzantium of the past and was unable to prevent the steady advance of the Ottoman empire into Anatolia, Thrace, Macedonia and Bulgaria in the 14th century and the conquest of Constantinople itself by Mehmet the Conqueror in 1453.

3 The themes and Arab invasions

organization of *themes* in late 9th century

first five *themes* with date of foundation

Armeniac, 667
Anatolic, 669
Opsician, 680
Carabisiani, 680
Thracian, 680

Arab invasion routes

by land
by sea
invasion bases

Byzantine frontier, 867

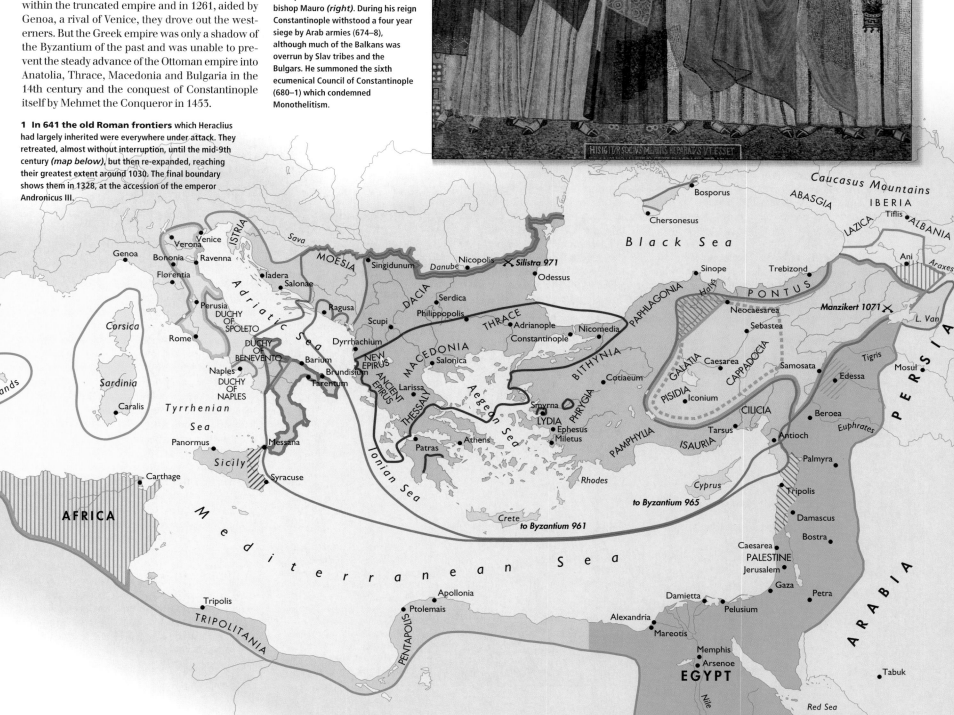

3 The *themes* were administrative districts in which peasants were granted farms in exchange for service in the local army ***(map above right)***. They prevented Arab settlement, although they could not stop raids.

The emperor Constantine IV Pogonatus and his brothers hand privileges to the Ravenna church of San Apollinare in Classe and to archbishop Mauro ***(right)***. During his reign Constantinople withstood a four year siege by Arab armies (674–8), although much of the Balkans was overrun by Slav tribes and the Bulgars. He summoned the sixth ecumenical Council of Constantinople (680–1) which condemned Monothelitism.

1 In 641 the old Roman frontiers which Heraclius had largely inherited were everywhere under attack. They retreated, almost without interruption, until the mid-9th century ***(map below)***, but then re-expanded, reaching their greatest extent around 1030. The final boundary shows them in 1328, at the accession of the emperor Andronicus III.

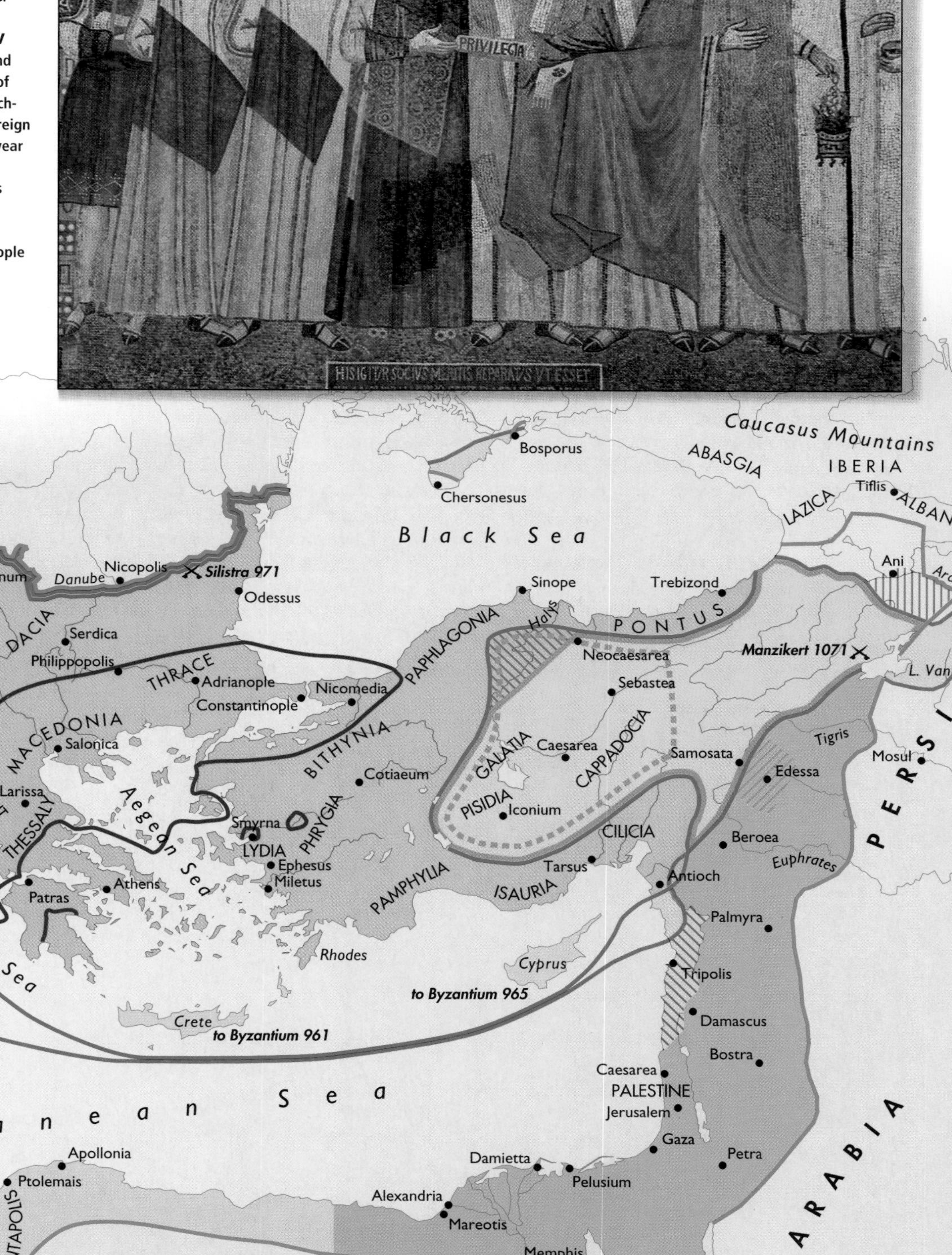

882 to 1242
The first Russian state: Kievan Russia

See also
Magyars, Saracens and Vikings in 9th and 10th century Europe p. 106
The Byzantine empire, 610–1453 p. 112
The Mongol empire, 1206–1405 p. 128
Russian expansion in Europe and Asia p. 160

Russia first emerged under the Vikings (or Rus) in the 9th century. Steppe, forests and rivers determined the course of the history of Kievan Rus. It received Christianity from Byzantium, was attacked by Mongols and split into various principalities. When the Kievan Rus lost their southern steppe territory to nomads they resumed eastward colonization.

THE RIVERS BETWEEN the Baltic and the Black Sea assumed great importance from the 9th century with the coming of the Vikings or Rus, who established, dominated and exploited trade routes along these rivers and adjoining lands. The polity the Rus established ran north and south across forests and steppes, and these barriers ultimately proved too strong for a river-based north-south alignment to survive. The main waterway route established by the Vikings ran from the Gulf of Finland up the river Neva, the river Volkhov and thence by portages to the Dnieper and on across the Black Sea to Byzantium. As Viking control spread south, Novgorod, Smolensk and Kiev (in 882) became their headquarters. Kiev grew rapidly from the early 10th century, and strong links developed with Byzantium, its chief trading partner. It was from Byzantium that Christianity was introduced to Kiev during the reign of Vladimir Svyatoslavich (980–1015).

> THE CHUDS, THE SLAVS, THE KRIVICHIANS AND THE VES THEN SAID TO THE PEOPLE OF THE RUS, 'OUR LAND IS GREAT AND RICH, BUT THERE IS NO ORDER IN IT. COME TO RULE AND REIGN OVER US.'
>
> **Russian Primary Chronicle, 1113**
>
> I HAVE NEVER SEEN MORE PERFECT PHYSICAL SPECIMENS, TALL AS DATE PALMS, BLOND AND RUDDY. EACH MAN HAS AN AXE, A SWORD AND A KNIFE, AND KEEPS THEM BY HIM AT ALL TIMES ... THEY ARE THE FILTHIEST OF GOD'S CREATURES.
>
> **Ibn Fadlan, of Rus traders at Itil, 922**

Expansion of Kievan Rus

At the time of the Viking incursions the Khazars and the Magyars held the steppes. The Rus succeeded in dominating the lands of the lower Prut, Dniester and Bug, and in controlling the upper Dnieper route to the Black Sea and thence to Byzantium. Grand Prince Svyatoslav (c. 962–72) determined to strengthen and expand Rus power by crushing the Khazars. But by destroying the relatively peaceful Khazars, he opened the way to the fierce Pechenegs (Turkic nomads) who dominated the south Russian steppes until displaced by the equally warlike Polovtsy in the 12th century. Vladimir I had some defensive success against the Pechenegs, constructing a steppe-frontier south of Kiev, and the Rus princes held the initiative over the nomads through most of the 11th and first half of the 12th centuries.

The southern Rus lands, relatively secure and prosperous, became the bone of contention between rival branches of Vladimir's offspring and from the mid-12th century disputes proliferated. But the resulting multiplication of princely seats opened up outlying areas to Christianity and commerce and in urban centres stone church building and functional literacy flourished. Uniquely, Novgorod's oligarchy was powerful enough to 'hire and fire' princes and to organize the collection of tribute in the form of furs from as far north as the Arctic Ocean. However, in the early 13th century, Novgorod increasingly came under the sway of the princes of Vladimir-Suzdal, who were emerging as the dominant Rus princes. On the eve of the Mongol attack of 1237, Vladimir-Suzdal was about to challenge the Volgar Bulgars whose stranglehold on the middle Volga obstructed further Russian expansion eastward. Nizhniy Novgorod was built as a first move in this campaign.

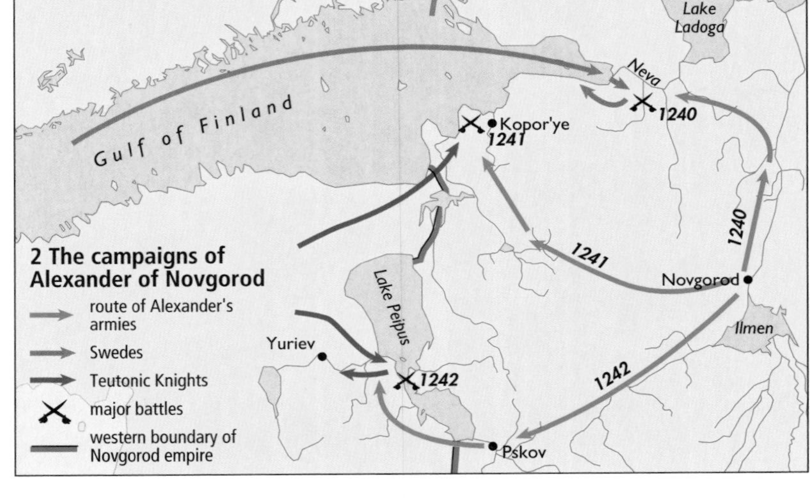

2 An attempt by the Swedes and Germans in 1240 to drive Russia from the Baltic was frustrated by Prince Alexander of Novgorod *(map above)*. His decisive victory on the Neva earned him the title 'Nevsky'. Two years later he defeated the Teutonic Knights at Lake Peipus, thus effectively stopping Swedish and German attempts at eastward expansion.

3 The first Russian state was established by the Vikings with the Dnieper as its axis *(map right)*. It lay athwart the northern forest and the southern steppe. Kiev was a natural capital.

3 Vegetation belts and early migrations

forest belt with marshes
wooded steppe
open steppe
Viking route
associated waterway trade route
movement of nomadic peoples
early movements of Russians and other East Slavs

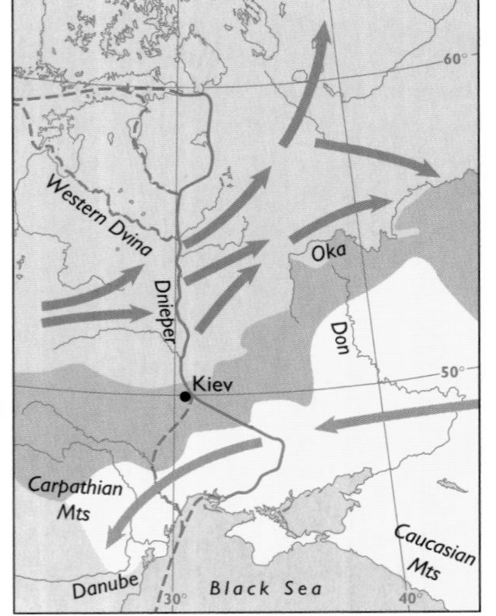

- **750** *Settlement at Staraya Ladoga*
- **862** *Vikings seize Kiev*
- **882** *Oleg unites Novgorod and Kiev*
- **922** *Ibn Fadlan's visit to the middle Volga*
- **941** *Rus attack on Constantinople*
- **after 987** *Vladimir of Kiev converts to Christianity*
- **1019–54** *Reign of Iaroslav the Wise*
- **1041** *Expedition of Ingvar the Widefarer*
- **1237–8** *Mongols attack Vladimir-Suzdal*
- **1240** *Mongols sack Kiev*
- **1240** *Alexander defeats Swedes at River Neva*

The Mongol invasions

The Mongols, led by Khan Batu, attacked the middle and upper Volga regions in 1237–8. They displaced the Polovtsy who fled to Hungary where they settled between the Tisza and the Danube rivers and came to be known as Kuns. That winter, when the protective rivers were frozen, the Mongols overcame the Volga Bulgars and set upon Vladimir-Suzdal, destroying its wealthy towns. Only the approach of spring saved Novgorod, as the invaders dared not be caught by the thaw among its surrounding marshes. In 1239 it was the turn of the southern principalities of the Rus. Kiev itself was sacked in 1240. Novgorod escaped the Mongol fury but was threatened by incessant attacks from Swedes and Germans in the Baltic region. Its prince, Alexander Nevsky, beat the Swedes decisively on the River Neva (1240) and the Teutonic Knights on the ice of Lake Peipus (1242).

The Mongols established the Kipchak Khanate or Golden Horde which came to control the lucrative trade routes between central Asia and the Black Sea. Much of western Rus, however, came under Lithuanian or Polish rule in the 14th century. At first based in Kiev, the metropolitan of the Orthodox church moved to Moscow in the early 14th century. This lent prestige to the princes of Moscow and contributed to Moscow's emergence as the predominant Rus polity in the northeast.

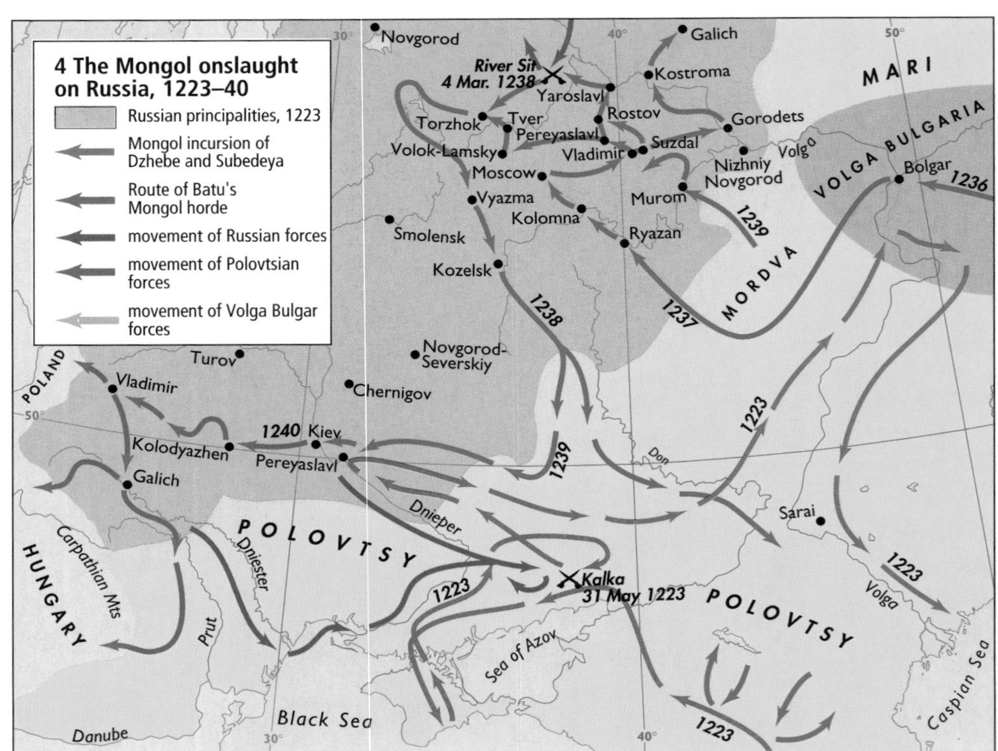

4 Until 1236, northern Russia was relatively immune from the steppe nomads' raids, and its cities prospered. But in the winter of 1237–8, the Mongols struck north into the forest and subjugated its princes *(map left)*. An exploratory raid in 1221, and a larger incursion which defeated a combined Russian and Polovtsy force at the Kalka river in 1223 was followed by the massive invasion of 1237.

A scene from Novgorod's victory over Suzdal in 1169 *(left)*. Novgorod was the capital of the Rus until Oleg moved his capital to Kiev in 882. In 1019 Iaroslav I granted Novgorod a charter of self-government, and thereafter the town elected its own prince. Grown rich on the trade in furs, Novgorod became pre-eminent in northern Russia. During the 12th century it came into conflict with the growing power of Vladimir-Suzdal to the south. However Novgorod defeated Vladimir-Suzdal in 1169 and 1216. It avoided the Mongol destruction and defeated the Germans and Swedes in 1240–2. A struggle for supremacy with Moscow in the 14th and 15th centuries saw the eclipse of Novgorod.

1 In 1054 there was still a unified Russian state, but by the early 13th century it had disintegrated ***(map below)***. Southern centres, such as Kiev, were weakened by nomadic attack, while northern towns, such as Novgorod, Vladimir and Moscow, exploited their positions on river trade routes in the security of the forest. Novgorod established a vast fur-trading empire stretching to the Arctic and the Urals.

The German empire and the Papacy

See also
The expansion of Christianity, 600–1500 p. 100
The rise of the Frankish kingdom, 482–814 p. 104
Northern and eastern Europe, 900–1050 p. 108
Monarchy in Britain and France, 1154–1314 p. 118
Economic growth in Europe, 950–1150 p. 120

The right to allocate the Imperial title, to consecrate kings and nominate new bishops or the Pope was vital in medieval Europe. Individual German emperors or popes attempted to assert either Imperial or Papal prerogatives. Popes ultimately sought to promote the authority of the bishops, while the Emperors' priority was to rule their vast territories.

911 *Death of Louis, last Carolingian king of east Frankish kingdom*

932 *Election of Otto I*

962 *Otto I crowned emperor in Rome*

1076 *Pope Gregory VII excommunicates Emperor Henry IV*

1095 *Pope Urban II preaches the First Crusade*

1122 *Concordat of Worms concludes Investiture controversy*

1197 *Death of Emperor Henry VI*

1215 *Lateran Council on doctrine and church reform*

1305 *Pope takes up residence in Avignon – the 'Babylonian captivity'*

HENRY, KING NOT BY USURPATION BUT BY THE PIOUS ORDINATION OF GOD, TO HILDEBRAND, NOT NOW POPE, BUT FALSE MONK. OUR LORD, JESUS CHRIST, HAS CALLED US TO THE KINGSHIP, BUT HAS NOT CALLED YOU TO THE PRIESTHOOD. FOR YOU HAVE RISEN BY THESE STEPS: NAMELY, BY CUNNING, WHICH THE MONASTIC PROFESSION ABHORS, TO MONEY; BY MONEY TO FAVOUR; BY FAVOUR TO THE SWORD. BY THE SWORD YOU HAVE COME TO THE THRONE OF PEACE AND FROM THE THRONE OF PEACE YOU HAVE DESTROYED THE PEACE.

Letter of Emperor Henry IV to Pope Gregory VII, 1076

FOR ALL THEIR DIFFERENCES, the separate Frankish kingdoms created between 840 and 843 were nonetheless bound together by many cultural, religious and kinship ties, as well as by the retention of the Imperial title in the Carolingian family. In 911, however, the Carolingians were replaced in the East Frankish (German) kingdom first by the Franconian noble Conrad and then by a member of the Saxon Liudolfing family, Henry I (911–36). Henry I's son, Otto I (936–73), consolidated his position, extended his influence over the German duchies and into Italy and defeated the Magyars. His Imperial coronation in 962 was the symbol of his aspirations and the southern and Italian orientation of his policies.

Imperial government

Government in the German empire was intensely personal with the king constantly on the move with his court. Only 13th-century Sicily possessed a centralized administrative system. The Ottonians stayed in their royal residences, supplied by the produce of their estates, as well as at royal convents, presided over by female members of the royal house. Bishops, notably those from the reformed monastic houses of Gorze in Lorraine, played a major role in government. The rulers themselves were devoted supporters of the church and were behind many of the missionary efforts and founding of new bishoprics, where Christianization and political expansion went hand in hand. It was the royal women, many of whom became abbesses, on the other hand, who appear, together with the bishops, to have done most to patronize culture and learning. The Salian and Staufen emperors continued these traditions.

The Papacy and the empire

The connection forged between Church reformers and the Papacy inaugurated a long dispute between the Emperors and the popes over who had the authority to appoint bishops or depose kings (the Investiture controversy). The conflict came to a head under Pope Gregory VII (1073–85). Gregory excommunicated and deposed the emperor Henry IV in 1076, forced him to perform public penance at Canossa, and allied with the Emperor's enemies – the Normans of southern Italy, the recalcitrant German nobility, and a chain of states around the periphery which feared German power.

Although Gregory failed in his immediate objectives, the launching of the First Crusade (*see* p. 110) by Pope Urban II (1088–99) testified to the success of the claims for papal authority. The Investiture dispute was settled in 1122 by the Concordat of Worms when the emperor granted canonical election and the free consecration of bishops.

The political involvement of the Papacy in the struggle for the control of Italy became clear when Pope Alexander III (1154–81) allied with the Lombard League to resist the attempts of Frederick I (1152–90) to restore German Imperial authority in Italy. The issue was settled by a compromise but the Papacy failed to prevent the Hohenstaufen from acquiring the Norman Kingdom of Sicily in 1194.

The apogee of papal power

Only the early death of Frederick's son, Henry VI (1190–7), and civil war in Germany enabled Pope Innocent III (1198–1216) to achieve the temporary supremacy of the Papacy. He successfully protected Rome and he claimed the right and authority of examining the person elected Emperor. At the same time Innocent compelled the French king to be reconciled with his wife and become his ally.

2 Otto I established a firm grip on the East Frankish lands *(map below left)*. After the ducal revolts of 938–9 he was able to exercize power even in the more prosperous south and west. Magyar raids were halted. The drive eastward against the Slavs was normally left to the margraves, while Otto himself ranged more widely.

3 Monastic reform movements *(map below)*, which aimed to promote the Rule of Benedict as the sole guide to the monastic life, built on the reforming zeal of the Carolingian period and gathered strength in the later 10th century, mainly in eastern France, Lorraine and Flanders. The principal centres were Cluny, Brogne and Gorze, whose influence extended into Germany, Spain and England.

The Pope also forced King John of England to submit to him. He also had some success in dealing with anti-clericalism. The heretics of southern France were viciously suppressed in the Albigensian Crusade (1208), but Innocent also encouraged the evangelism of the new orders of friars, the Franciscans and Dominicans, and sought to remove sources of discontent with the church by reforming clerical behaviour. However, like Alexander III before him, Pope Innocent IV (1243–54) allied with the Italian cities to resist the Emperor Frederick II. Nonetheless the Papacy only succeeded in undermining German influence in Italy when Pope Clement IV (1265–8) called in Charles of Anjou, the brother of Louis IX of France, to evict the Germans from Italy. Disputes thereafter with the increasingly centralized French monarchy over taxation of the clergy and royal sovereignty led to open conflict. Pope Boniface VIII (1294–1303) was kidnapped by his French and Italian enemies. In 1305 his successor took up residence in Avignon, under direct French supervision.

1 At the height of their power, the Emperors held sway over territories stretching from the Baltic to Sicily *(map above)*. Within these extended frontiers they faced the German princes, the growing wealth and independence of the north Italian towns of the Lombard League and the Papacy at its most aggressive.

A dedicatory miniature of the Emperor Otto III (996–1002) from his gospel book *(right)*. The emperor is enthroned between two lords spiritual and two lords temporal. Asked by the Roman nobility to nominate a new pope, he chose a cousin, Bruno of Carinthia, who as Pope Gregory V was the first German pope. Gregory crowned Otto emperor in 996.

1154 to 1314

Monarchy in Britain and France

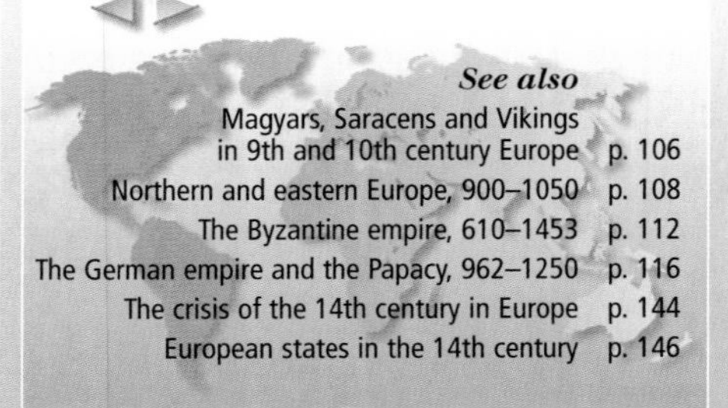

See also
Magyars, Saracens and Vikings in 9th and 10th century Europe p. 106
Northern and eastern Europe, 900–1050 p. 108
The Byzantine empire, 610–1453 p. 112
The German empire and the Papacy, 962–1250 p. 116
The crisis of the 14th century in Europe p. 144
European states in the 14th century p. 146

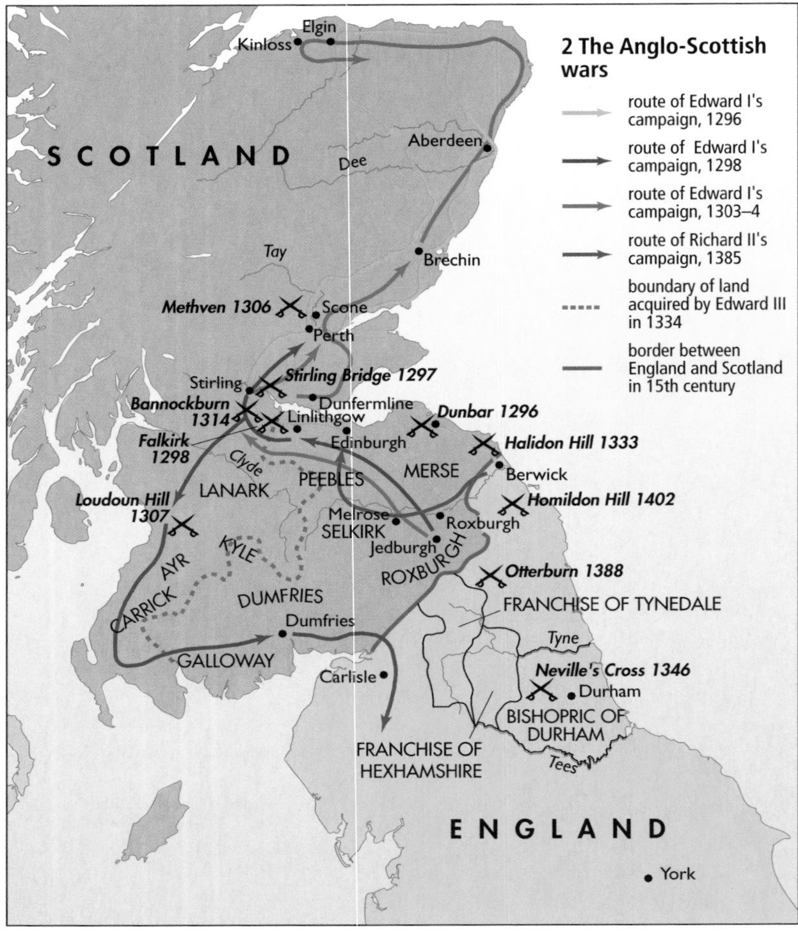

2 The efforts of Edward I of England (1272–1307) to subjugate Scotland culminated in Edward II's disastrous defeat by the Scots under Robert the Bruce (1282–1327) at Bannockburn *(map above)*. Throughout the century and beyond, the Scots, often fighting in alliance with France, were a significant threat to England's security.

3 Henry II of England (1154–89) created a powerful empire spanning the English Channel *(map below)*. His marriage to Eleanor of Aquitaine brought him control over most of western France. Combined with his Norman and Angevin inheritance this made him the most powerful ruler in France. In 1157 he acquired Cumbria and settled the Scottish border and in 1171 invaded Ireland.

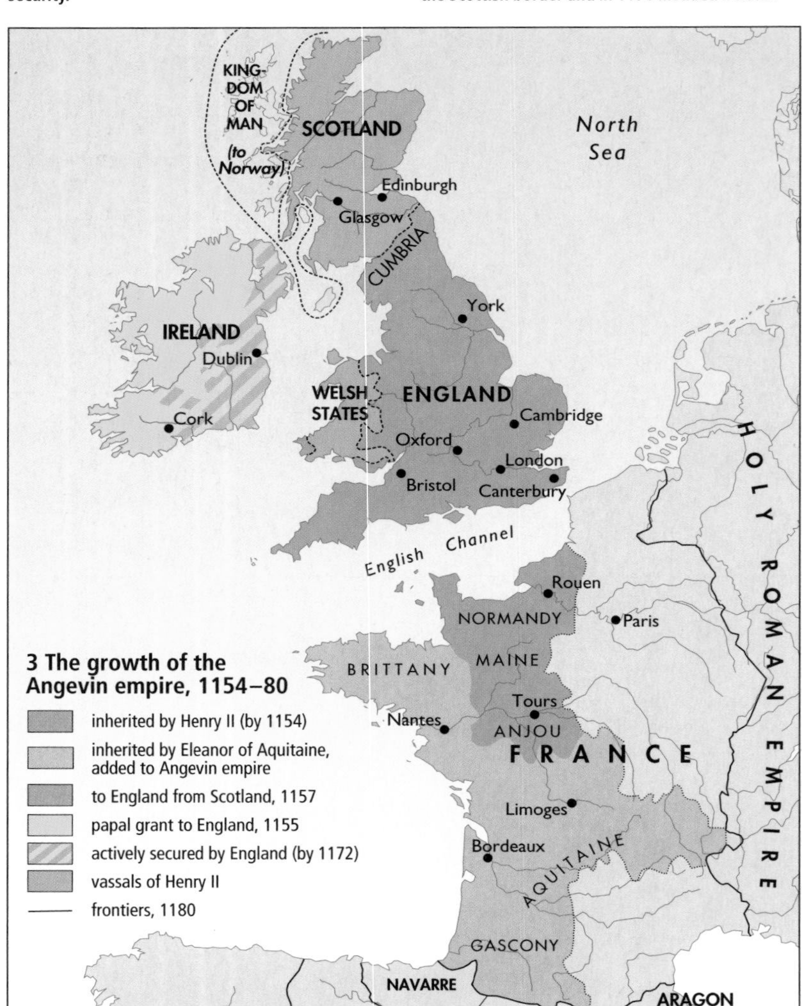

Within a distinctive blend of public office and landholding in medieval Britain and France, great stress was laid on authority, especially that of kings. Contemporaries did not think in terms of borders or national entities so much as of territorial and legal jurisdictions, where varied social bonds and political obligations and rights were interdependent.

DESPITE THE GROWTH of principalities in France and the strength of the earls in England in the 10th and 11th centuries, kingship survived. The king's position at the apex of the social hierarchy was hallowed by religious and legal sanctions which might bear little relationship to the realities of political power. In the 12th century kings used their position and fortuitous agglomerations of territory to assert their prerogatives. In the hands of the Emperor Frederick Barbarossa and later of the French Capetians, Roman law became a powerful instrument of royal authority. But the main weapons used by 12th- and 13th-century kings were the king's rights as 'liege lord'; the duty of tenants-in-chief to render service; the theory that all land was held of the king; and all rights of justice were delegations of royal authority, which therefore reverted, or 'escheated', to the crown in case of abuse or treason. Grave misdemeanours (felonies) were reserved to the king's courts or 'pleas of the crown'. Much of this process was piecemeal; but by the middle of the 13th century the great lawyers (Bracton in England, Beaumanoir in France) had created a systematic theory of royal government, which kings such as Edward I of England (1272–1307) and Philip IV of France (1285–1314) proceeded to implement.

The Normans and England

The process was most rapid in the Norman kingdoms of England and Sicily, both of which were acquired by conquest. In England this enabled William the Conqueror (1066-87) to retain and build up the fiscal and jurisdictional prerogatives inherited from his Anglo-Saxon predecessors. Henry II's coronation as king of England meant that Anjou, Normandy, the Touraine, Aquitaine and Gascony also came under his rule, creating an Angevin 'empire' which, at least initially, held together quite successfully.

The consolidation of France

In France, on the other hand, Louis VI (1108–37) spent his reign asserting authority over the petty barons of the Ile de France, and it was scarcely before the reign of Philip Augustus (1180–1223) that expansion of the royal demesne began in earnest. The turning point was the conquest of Normandy in 1204 which effectively meant the destruction of the Angevin empire. After 1214 English continental possessions were limited to Gascony while a third of France was now under royal control. Much of Languedoc was subdued in a campaign against the Albigensian heretics (1209–29) and royal authority was extended south of the Loire.

Kings exercised powers of taxation and legislation (often in consultation with parliaments or 'estates of the realm') and controlled the administration of justice. Nowhere was the network of overlapping rights and jursidictions more complex than in France. Indeed, the determination of the French kings to assert their lordship over these lands and over Flanders gave rise to a series of major wars.

> THE DUKE OF NORMANDY OR THE PRINCE IS THE ONE WHO HOLDS THE LORDSHIP OVER THE ENTIRE DUCHY. THIS DIGNITY THE LORD KING OF FRANCE HOLDS TOGETHER WITH THE OTHER HONOURS TO WHICH, WITH THE AID OF THE LORD, HE HAS BEEN RAISED. FROM THIS IT PERTAINS TO HIM TO PRESERVE THE PEACE OF THE LAND, TO CORRECT THE PEOPLE BY THE ROD OF JUSTICE, AND BY THE MEASURE OF EQUITY TO END PRIVATE DISPUTES. THEREFORE HE SHOULD THROUGH THE JUSTICIARS SUBJECT TO HIM SEE TO IT THAT THE PEOPLE UNDER HIS AUTHORITY REJOICE IN THE RULE OF JUSTICE AND THE TRANQUILLITY OF PEACE.
>
> *The Summa de legibus of Normandy, c. 1258*

The limits of royal power

Meanwhile the English kings were asserting similar claims in Scotland, Wales and Ireland. Henry II's attempt to conquer Ireland (1171) achieved only a precarious foothold, but in 1284 Edward I subdued Wales. He tried to repeat the process in Scotland in 1296, but met with resistance under Wallace and Bruce, and his son Edward II suffered a crushing defeat at Bannockburn in 1314 (*see* map 2).

Edward's failure in Scotland was matched by Philip IV's failure in Flanders. Defeated by the Flemings at Courtrai (1302), the French king, who had seized Gascony in 1294, was compelled to restore it to the English in 1303. In England Edward I was compelled in 1297 to confirm and extend the concessions wrested by the barons from his grandfather, King John, in 1215. In France the Estates-General met for the first time in 1302. Everywhere, nobles, many of them well versed in the law, were challenging royal jurisdictions and prerogatives.

Harlech Castle *(right)*. The castle was the symbol of the conquering monarchies of western Europe in the 13th century. During the reign of Henry III of England (1216–72) much of Wales had become autonomous under Llewelyn ap Gruffydd, but Edward I, infuriated by Llewelyn's refusal to perform homage, invaded in force in 1277. A subsequent Welsh rebellion ended in the death of Llewelyn and, by the Statute of Wales (1284), Edward completed the reorganization of the Principality on English lines. Harlech Castle is one of the best preserved and most impressive of the series of fortifications built by Edward to hold down the conquered country.

1 The institutional strength of monarchy, developing in the 12th century, expanded rapidly in the 13th century. In France the kings extended the extent of their control from a tiny 10th-century royal domain around Paris and Orléans *(map below)*. By 1300 western kings, like their early medieval predecessors, were acknowledged executors of effective public authority.

Economic growth in Europe

See also
The spread of Islam from AD 632 p. 98
Northern and eastern Europe, 900–1050 p. 108
Crusading in Europe from the 11th to the 15th century p. 110
The German empire and the Papacy, 962–1250 p. 116

7th century *Trading settlement at Dorestad founded*

688–726 *Hamwic founded*

755 *Frankish king Pippin takes control of coinage*

794 *Major coinage, weights and measures reforms of Charlemagne*

802 *Caliph of Baghdad sends an elephant to Charlemagne at Aachen*

830–40 *Viking raids on Dorestad*

c. 850 *Dorestad abandoned due to silting up of Rhine*

c. 860 *Flanders fairs begin*

893 *Frisian merchants recorded in Duisberg*

992 *Venetian merchants accorded special privileges in Constantinople*

1096 *First Crusade*

As new archaeological evidence reveals, the early Middle Ages was a vital period of economic activity, in which important new developments in the northwest, the opening up of new trade routes, wealth created by new agricultural land and the foundation of trading towns all built on the earlier economic patterns of the Roman empire.

From the 7th century onwards the northwest of Europe grew in importance as a trading area. In the North Sea and the Baltic region, the Scandinavians built on trading networks already established by the Frisians, Franks and English. The extension of Scandinavian activity overseas coincided with the growing demand for goods that could only be obtained from the north; walrus tusks were at that time the main source of ivory in Europe, and furs from the arctic regions of Scandinavia and Russia were greatly prized. There was a growing commerce in coastal markets called *wics*. The greatest was Dorestad at the mouth of the Rhine, but there were many others, including Quentovic (near Boulogne), Ipswich, London and Hamwic, later to develop into Southampton. Other small trading towns flourished, such as Starya Ladoga in Russia, Birka in Sweden, Wastergarn in Gotland, Kaupang in Norway and Ribe and Haithabu in Denmark.

The Scandinavian world

Scandinavians now sought even further afield for fresh supplies of skin, furs and tusks and a contemporary account by a 9th-century Norwegian, Ottar, narrates the voyage he made from his home in northern Norway into the White Sea in search of walrus. Dublin's fortunes fluctuated politically but her function as the chief of the Scandinavian towns in Ireland (founded in the 9th century) is emphasized by the striking of the first Irish coins there in the 990s. From the late 10th century her economic power and international connections grew apace, and the existence of continuous building and growth up to the 12th century bears witness to her prosperity. The town served as the chief market for the Isle of Man, the Western Isles of Scotland and the Atlantic islands all of which remained under Scandinavian control throughout the period.

The opening of new regions

By 1000 it is estimated that the population of western Europe may have reached a total of 30 million and 150 years later it may have increased by a further 40 per cent. Most of this was concentrated in France, Germany and England and was probably related to the opening up of new land by clearing forests. It took three main forms: steady encroachment by the peasants of the old villages on the woods which surrounded their fields; the migration of settlers, presumably driven by land-hunger to the uninhabited uplands and mountains, where they carved out scattered fields and enclosures from the forest and scrub; and planned development by lay lords and monasteries, wealthy promoters and speculators who founded villages and towns, at the foot of a castle or outside a monastery gate, with the aim of increasing their income. All three types of clearing are found juxtaposed in all countries, and their history is revealed by field patterns and by place-names – Newport, Neuville, Neustadt, Bourgneuf, Nieuwpoort. In a few regions – the Po valley of northern Italy, Flanders, the country around the Wash in England – marshes were drained and land reclaimed from the sea.

Markets and trade

The agricultural surplus further stimulated the foundation and growth of towns, markets and fairs (notably the fairs of Champagne) which initially served a local market but became internationally renowned after 1150. In the Mediterranean, the survival of silks, pottery and other goods indicated a continuation of connections across the Mediterranean and with northern Europe.

In Italy, Pisa, Genoa and Venice extended their overseas trade, assisted by the opportunities offered by the crusading movement in the eastern Mediterranean. North of the Alps, rivers such as the Rhine, Seine, Danube, Meuse and Rhône, conveyed bulk transport and connected the cloth towns of Flanders and the Rhineland with the south. The western Alpine passes (Mont Cenis, Great St Bernard) were in regular use. The central passes (St Gotthard, and Splügen) and the Brenner in the east were developed in the later 12th century. The Rhineland was a major focus of artistic and intellectual as well as of economic life. Cologne, in particular, was at the height of its prosperity, but the cathedral-building throughout the region – as at Mainz and Worms – is a testimony to the wealth which 'the great age of clearing' had made available.

Let all know that for the love of God we have granted the petition of Adaldag, the reverend archbishop of Hamburg, and have given him permission to establish a market in the place called Bremen. In connection with the market we grant him jurisdiction, tolls, a mint, and all other things connected therewith to which our royal treasury would have a right. We also take under our special protection all the merchants who live in that place.

Grant by the Emperor Otto I of Saxony to the archbishop of Hamburg, 965

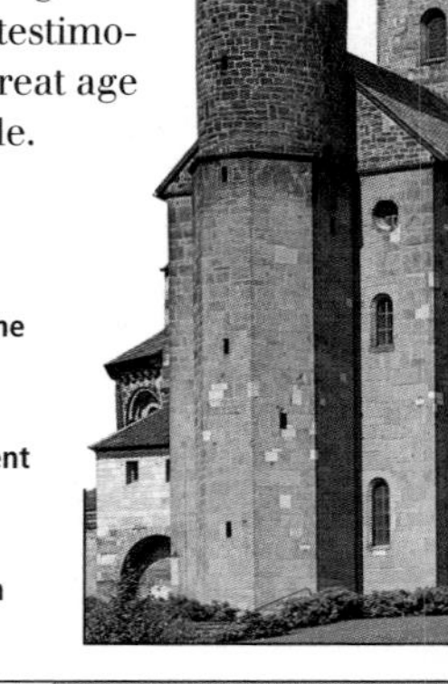

St Michael's church at Hildesheim ***(right)*** is a supreme example of Saxon architecture from the early 11th century (1010–30). It was overseen by the cultured Bishop Bernward. The interior is as magnificent as the exterior, complemented by the ornate bronze doors, nearly 5 metres high, carved in relief with scenes from the Old and New Testaments.

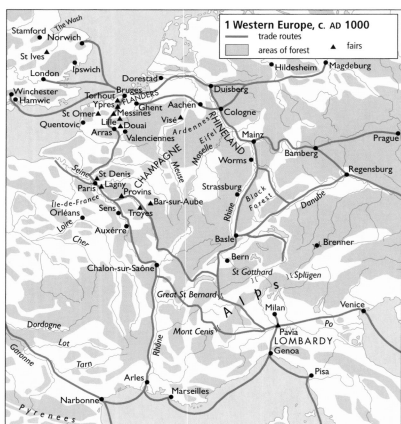

1 Before AD 1000 perhaps four-fifths of Europe north of the Alps and Pyrenees was covered by dense forest (*map below*). Over the next 200 years much of this was cleared to make land available for human settlement and agriculture. Even in the Rhineland the highlands bounding the river were still largely uninhabited (*see* map 3). Forests such as the Ardennes and the Eifel constituted an almost impenetrable barrier to communications. Certain areas – Flanders, Lombardy, and the Rhine valley – became centres of commerce from 1100. But it was only after 1150 that Italian merchants regularly attended the Champagne fairs (Troyes, Provins, Lagny), buying Flemish cloths in exchange for Oriental goods.

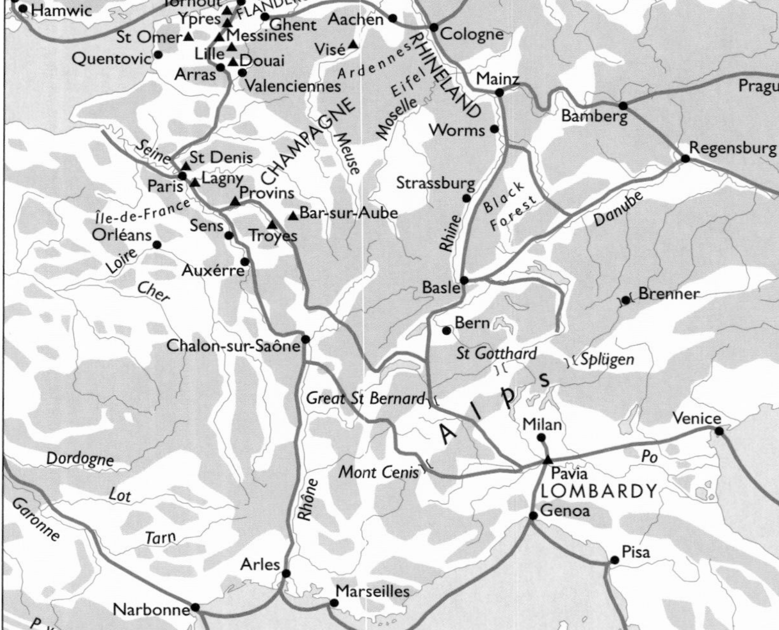

2 In 950 the Mediterranean was almost entirely a 'Muslim lake' *(map right)*. Such trade as there was between western Europe and the Orient was in the hands of the cities of Byzantine Italy, especially Amalfi. But their connections with northern Europe were at best indirect, and it was Venice that first engaged in trade with Europe north of the Alps. In the western Mediterranean trade was risky so long as the Saracens held the islands. The weakening of their hold from the 11th century enabled the fleets of Pisa and (later) of Genoa to wrest control of the Ligurian and Tyrrhenian seas. The First Crusade (1096–99) opened up trading stations in the Levant; but it was only after the Venetian naval victory off Ascalon in 1123 that the Italian cities came to dominate the Mediterranean from Spain to Syria.

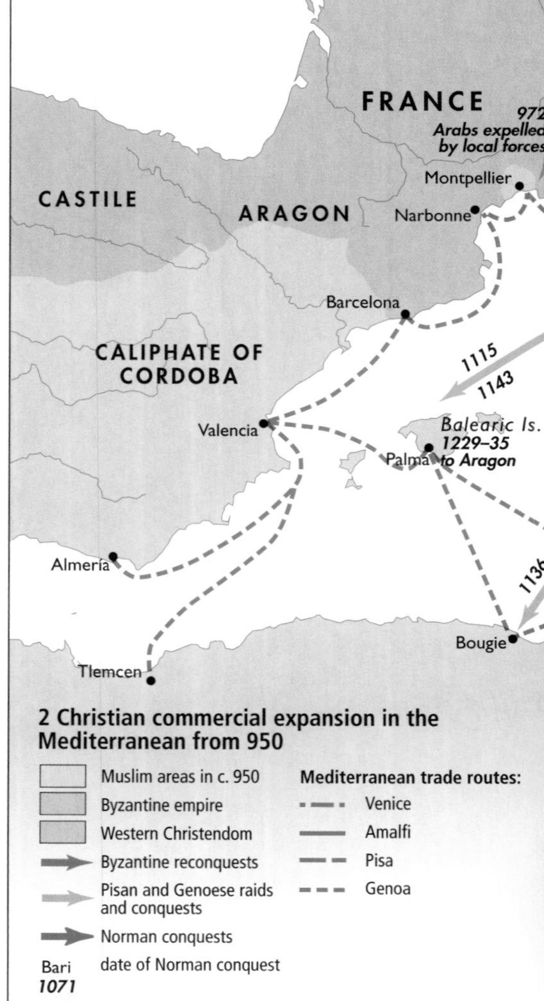

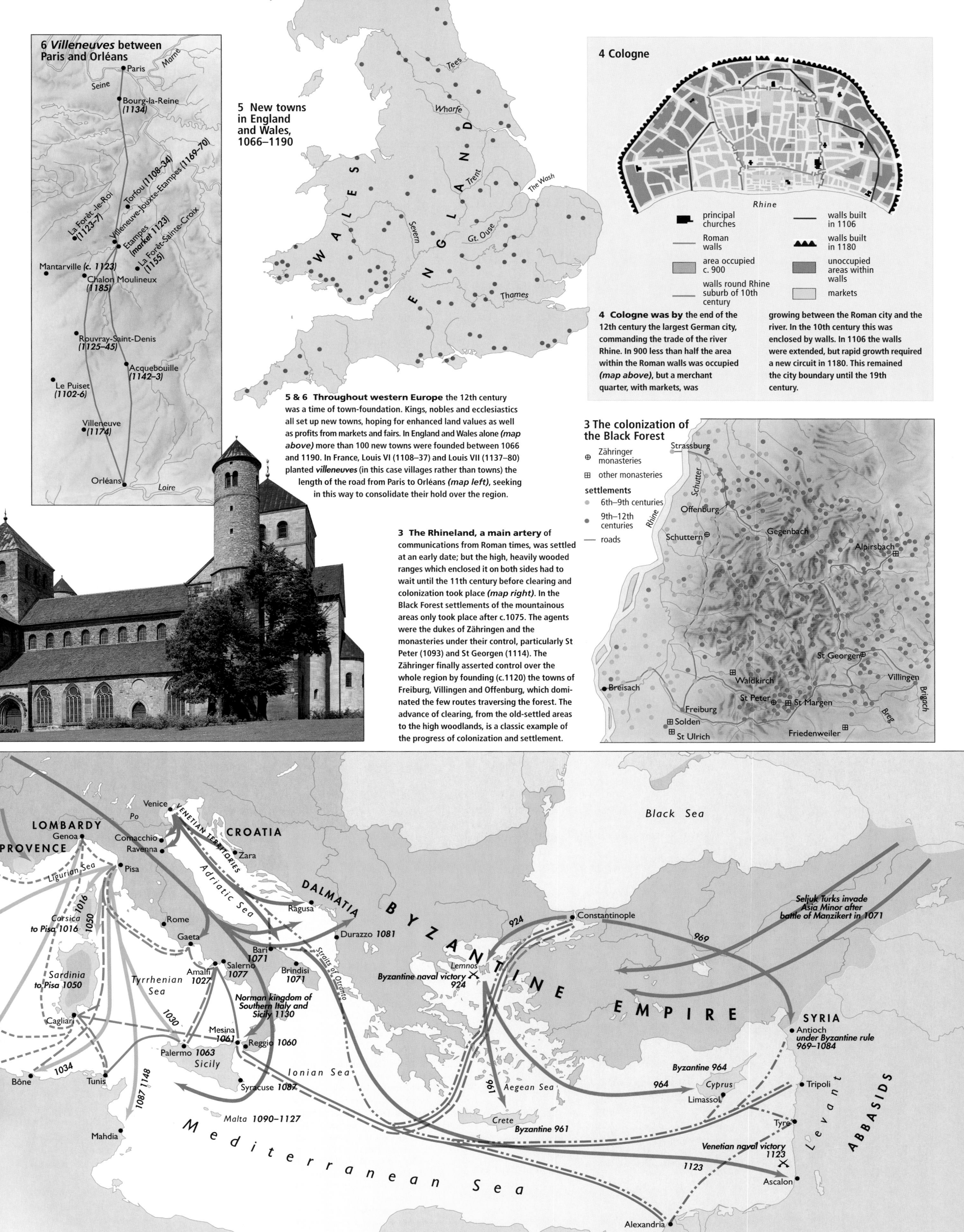

5 & 6 Throughout western Europe the 12th century was a time of town-foundation. Kings, nobles and ecclesiastics all set up new towns, hoping for enhanced land values as well as profits from markets and fairs. In England and Wales alone *(map above)* more than 100 new towns were founded between 1066 and 1190. In France, Louis VI (1108–37) and Louis VII (1137–80) planted ***villeneuves*** (in this case villages rather than towns) the length of the road from Paris to Orléans *(map left)*, seeking in this way to consolidate their hold over the region.

4 Cologne was by the end of the 12th century the largest German city, commanding the trade of the river Rhine. In 900 less than half the area within the Roman walls was occupied *(map above)*, but a merchant quarter, with markets, was growing between the Roman city and the river. In the 10th century this was enclosed by walls. In 1106 the walls were extended, but rapid growth required a new circuit in 1180. This remained the city boundary until the 19th century.

3 The Rhineland, a main artery of communications from Roman times, was settled at an early date; but the high, heavily wooded ranges which enclosed it on both sides had to wait until the 11th century before clearing and colonization took place *(map right)*. In the Black Forest settlements of the mountainous areas only took place after c.1075. The agents were the dukes of Zähringen and the monasteries under their control, particularly St Peter (1093) and St Georgen (1114). The Zähringer finally asserted control over the whole region by founding (c.1120) the towns of Freiburg, Villingen and Offenburg, which dominated the few routes traversing the forest. The advance of clearing, from the old-settled areas to the high woodlands, is a classic example of the progress of colonization and settlement.

To 1477

Imperial Japan and the early shogunates

See also
China and east Asia, 220–618 p. 124
Chinese civilization from the T'ang to the Sung, 618–1279 p. 126
The Mongol empire, 1206–1405 p. 128
China at the time of the Ming dynasty, 1368–1644 p. 166
Japan under the shogunate, 1477–1868 p. 174

The early Japanese state achieved stability in the 8th century when the great families clustered around the emperor swapped military power for rank in a Chinese-inspired bureauracy. This ruled for four centuries until, in 1185, its own warrior clients founded the first in a series of shogunates, which were to rule Japan until 1868.

JAPAN IS FIRST MENTIONED in Chinese records of the 3rd century AD. These state that the archipelago was divided into a series of small kingdoms, a number of them tributary to the Chinese emperor and most acknowledging the spiritual leadership of the Empress Himiko. Over the next three centuries, a line of emperors, possibly Himiko's descendants, unified most of what is today Japan either by absorbing or destroying other leading families.

The influence of China

Early Japan was consistently overshadowed by its much larger and more powerful neighbour, China – so much so that Japan consciously tried to model itself on China. Embassies were dispatched, imperial records drafted on the Chinese model and Buddhism introduced. The changes culminated in the Taika revolution of 645, when a new emperor, backed by the powerful Fujiwara family, first tried to mirror the role played by the Chinese emperors. Further impetus to reform came in 668 when T'ang Chinese and Sillan armies unified the Korean peninsula, in the process decisively defeating at Hakusukinoe a Japanese fleet sent to help the allied kingdom of Paekche in Korea. Fear of invasion proved a powerful spur to reform.

Early in the following century, Japan accordingly sought to model itself more closely still on the highly centralized Chinese state, continuing the 'Taika' process began in 645. A new Chinese-style capital was established at Nara in 710 and provincial governors and magistrates, all answerable to the emperor, were appointed. At the same time, all rice-growing land was declared the property of the emperor – was in effect nationalized – and then allotted to households on a per capita basis. Farmers paid the government a tax in the form of rice and were obliged to perform military service.

Soon, however, this structure proved unworkable. After smallpox epidemics had slashed the workforce and conscript armies had been mauled by the northern Emishi tribesmen, conscription was abandoned and the tax system simplified. Whereas earlier land had been allocated to farmers by the state only for life, now private individuals owned income-bearing land-rights (*shiki*), which they could pass on to their descendants. The type of *shiki* varied with the owner's status. At the bottom of the hierarchy, a farmer's *shiki* gave him some of the crop for tilling the soil. A *samurai*'s *shiki* conferred on him a portion of the harvest from the lands he managed. At the top of the scale, an aristocrat's *shiki* gave him income in return for defending the legality of the *shiki* belonging to those below him. Thus the castes were linked by chains of fealty, which were known as *kenmon*.

645 *'Taika' reforms*
794 *Kyoto established as imperial court*
1156–9 *Hogen and Heiji Disturbances pit rival Taira and Minamoto factions against each other*
1185 *Battle of Dannoura: first shogunate founded*
1221 *Emperor Go-Toba unsuccessfully attempts to restore imperial authority*
1274 & 1281 *Mongol invasions defeated*
1333–6 *Go-Daigo briefly re-establishes imperial rule before being expelled from Kyoto by the new Ashikaga shogunate*
1467–77 *Onin Wars: Japan plunged into civil war*

GREAT JAPAN IS THE DIVINE LAND. THE HEAVENLY PROGENITOR FOUNDED IT, AND THE SUN GODDESS BEQUEATHED IT TO HER DESCENDANTS TO RULE ETERNALLY. ONLY IN OUR COUNTRY IS THIS TRUE; THERE ARE NO SIMILAR EXAMPLES IN OTHER COUNTRIES. THIS IS WHY OUR COUNTRY IS CALLED THE DIVINE LAND.

***The Jinno Shotoki*, 1339**

These changes radically altered the power structure of the country. Previously the imperial family had been dominated by the Fujiwara family, who provided the emperors' consorts. Most emperors were children, very much under the influence of their maternal Fujiwara relatives and, moreover, after coming of age the emperor was required to 'retire'. However by the 11th century the imperial family had begun to reassert itself, and the retired emperors had organized themselves as a *kenmon*. With the other new *kenmon* emerging, the Fujiwara now faced real competition, and the scope for factionalism grew.

Now government became merely the arena where *kenmon* heads hammered out their differences. The *kenmon* were largely autonomous, but, when there was a need for military operations beyond the scope of any one *kenmon*, *kenmon* heads would meet and commission as general a Taira or Minamoto, clans who over the generations had acquired a reputation for producing able military commanders. But recurrent factional feuds, culminating in the Genpei Wars (1180–5), allowed one of these generals, Minamoto Yoritomo, to emerge as Japan's first military leader (*shogun*).

The first *shogun*

Yoritomo based his regime not in the existing capital of Kyoto, but far to the east in Kamakura. There, he gave justice and protection to any *samurai* who swore him allegiance. After Yoritomo's death, his two sons were eliminated by his Hojo in-laws, who then dominated the Kamakura shogunate. Initially, the shogunate deliberately limited its role to defending the interests of its warrior clients within the existing framework of *shiki* and *kenmon*, but in the wake of two major crises, its authority grew: in 1221 a bid by the Emperor Go-Toba to re-establish imperial primacy was crushed in the Jokyu War; and in 1274 and 1281 two Mongol invasions were thwarted.

But the Hojo family, with no genealogical rights, overreached themselves in their efforts to control ever-larger swathes of the country. The Hojo's fall came about in 1333 through an alliance between the Emperor Go-Daigo and Ashikaga Takauji, one of the surviving scions of the Minamoto. Within three years, however, the emperor and Takauji had fallen foul of one another. The emperor was forced to flee with his supporters to the mountain fastness of Yoshino, where he established what came to be known as the 'southern' court. In his absence, Takauji replaced him in Kyoto with a

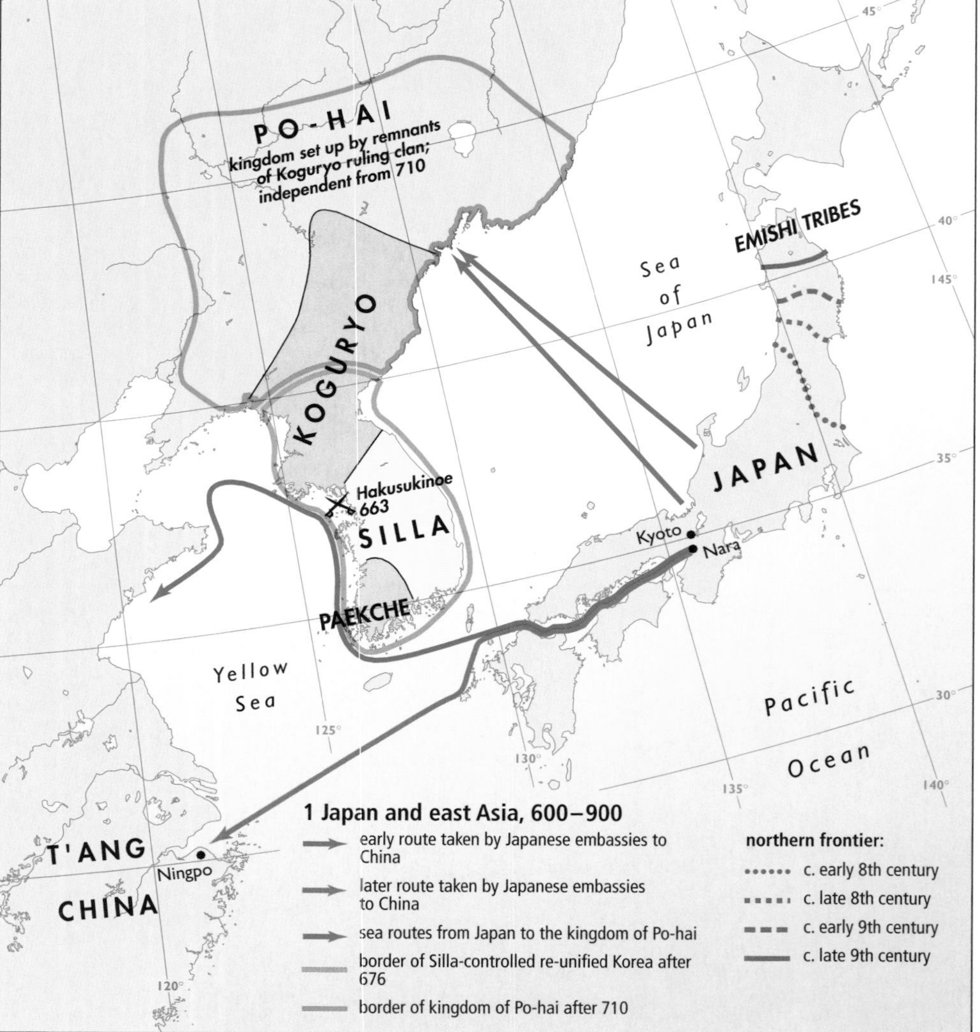

1 The resurgence of China under the T'ang and the unification of the Korean peninsula under the Silla in 668 faced Japan with a real threat of invasion. The imperial court sought to counter this by borrowing Chinese military and administrative practices, subduing the Emishi tribesmen in the north, and thereby pushing the border of Japanese-controlled territory progressively further north, and establishing itself as an acknowledged peer of the states of the region: China, Korea and Po-hai *(map left).*

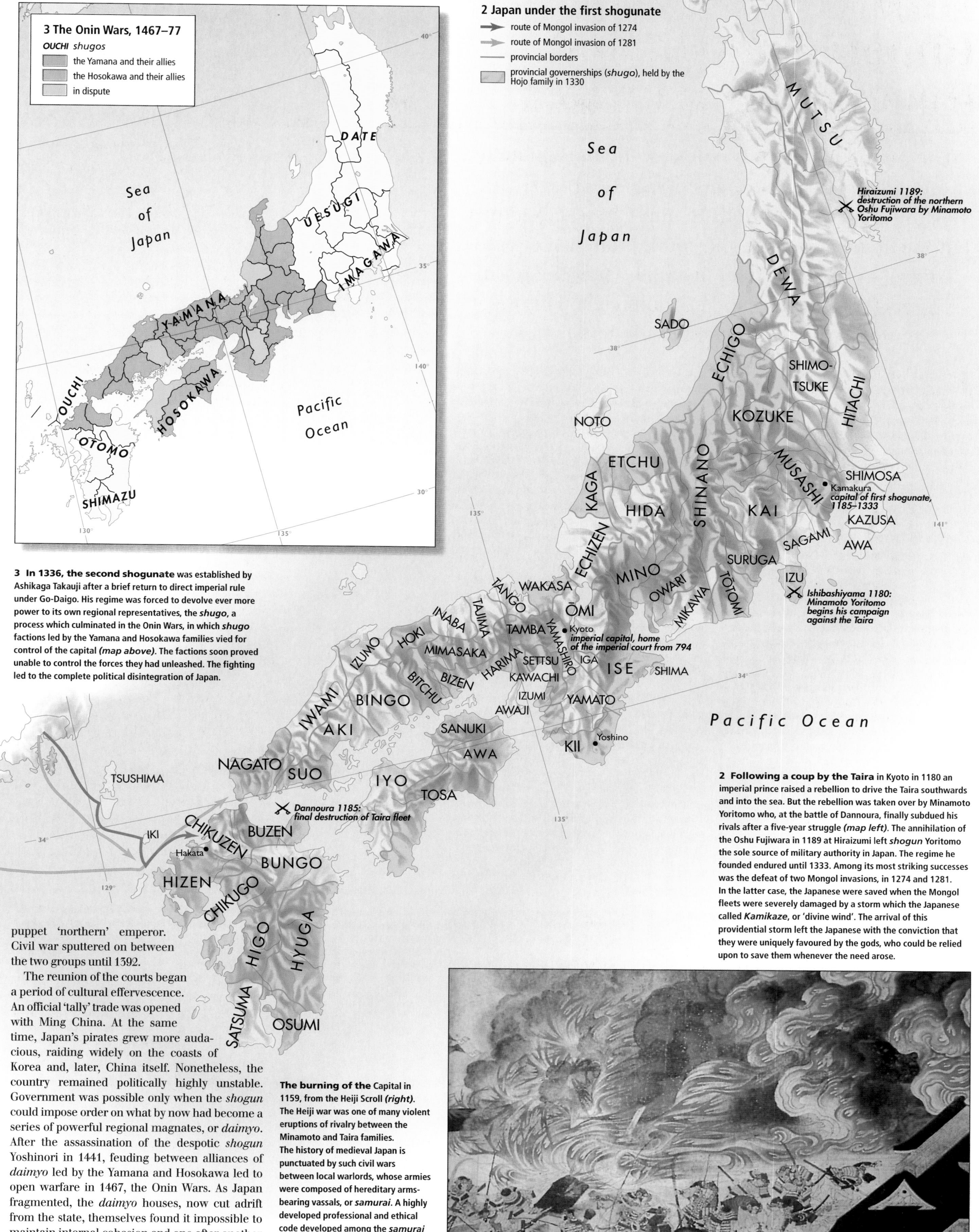

3 In 1336, the second shogunate was established by Ashikaga Takauji after a brief return to direct imperial rule under Go-Daigo. His regime was forced to devolve ever more power to its own regional representatives, the *shugo*, a process which culminated in the Onin Wars, in which *shugo* factions led by the Yamana and Hosokawa families vied for control of the capital *(map above)*. The factions soon proved unable to control the forces they had unleashed. The fighting led to the complete political disintegration of Japan.

2 Following a coup by the Taira in Kyoto in 1180 an imperial prince raised a rebellion to drive the Taira southwards and into the sea. But the rebellion was taken over by Minamoto Yoritomo who, at the battle of Dannoura, finally subdued his rivals after a five-year struggle *(map left)*. The annihilation of the Oshu Fujiwara in 1189 at Hiraizumi left *shogun* Yoritomo the sole source of military authority in Japan. The regime he founded endured until 1333. Among its most striking successes was the defeat of two Mongol invasions, in 1274 and 1281. In the latter case, the Japanese were saved when the Mongol fleets were severely damaged by a storm which the Japanese called *Kamikaze*, or 'divine wind'. The arrival of this providential storm left the Japanese with the conviction that they were uniquely favoured by the gods, who could be relied upon to save them whenever the need arose.

The burning of the Capital in 1159, from the Heiji Scroll *(right)*. The Heiji war was one of many violent eruptions of rivalry between the Minamoto and Taira families. The history of medieval Japan is punctuated by such civil wars between local warlords, whose armies were composed of hereditary arms-bearing vassals, or *samurai*. A highly developed professional and ethical code developed among the *samurai* at the time, similar to, but more complex than, the chivalric code among European feudal knights. Their exploits were meticulously recorded.

puppet 'northern' emperor. Civil war sputtered on between the two groups until 1392.

The reunion of the courts began a period of cultural effervescence. An official 'tally' trade was opened with Ming China. At the same time, Japan's pirates grew more audacious, raiding widely on the coasts of Korea and, later, China itself. Nonetheless, the country remained politically highly unstable. Government was possible only when the *shogun* could impose order on what by now had become a series of powerful regional magnates, or *daimyo*. After the assassination of the despotic *shogun* Yoshinori in 1441, feuding between alliances of *daimyo* led by the Yamana and Hosokawa led to open warfare in 1467, the Onin Wars. As Japan fragmented, the *daimyo* houses, now cut adrift from the state, themselves found it impossible to maintain internal cohesion and one after another they were brought down by their own retainers. It would be more than a century before Japan was unified again.

China and east Asia

See also
The unification of China, 475 BC–AD 220 p. 80
Imperial Japan and the early shogunates p. 122
Chinese civilization from the T'ang to the Sung, 618–1279 p. 126
The early civilizations of southeast Asia, 500 BC–AD 1511 p. 134

The period after 220 was one of the most chaotic and bloody in Chinese history. Not only was the north lost for long periods to non-Chinese regimes, but the governments in the south often lost effective control as well. Political instability was the norm across the country, and economic growth was minimal until the advent of the Sui dynasty.

205 *Ts'ao Ts'ao, founder of the Wei dynasty, in effective control of north China*

220 *Last Han emperor abdicates*

280 *China unified under Western Chin*

311 *Ch'ang-an first attacked by Ti armies*

316 *Lo-yang sacked by Hsiungnu*

420 *Overthrow of Eastern Chin dynasty*

534 *Northern Wei dynasty fragments*

611–14 *Sui launches unsuccessful and draining invasions of north Korea*

618 *Last Sui emperor, Yang-ti, assassinated*

K'UNG-MING OFFERED HIS PRAYER: 'BORN INTO AN AGE OF TROUBLES, I WOULD HAVE BEEN CONTENT TO LIVE OUT MY TIMES AMONG THE GROVES AND STREAMS, BUT FOR THE LATE KING, WHO COMMITTED ME TO TOIL IN THE SERVICE OF OUR CAUSE ...'

Lo Kuan-chung (c. 1330–c. 1400)
Three Kingdoms (Romance based on The Records of the Three Kingdoms by Ch'en Shou, AD 297)

THE HAN EMPIRE BROKE up into three kingdoms in 220: the Wei in the north; the Wu in the south; and the Shu in the west. The militarily strong Wei had conquered the Shu in the southwest by 263, but in 265 a military family, the Ssuuma, took over the Wei kingdom through a coup d'état. They then proceeded with a series of military campaigns to unify China under the name of the Western Chin dynasty. The target of unification was finally achieved in 280.

The Western Chin

The new authorities granted farmers land-holding rights to re-establish household farming in accordance with the Han model. 'Salary land' for officials was granted and cultivated by tenants. Overall, this helped the recovery of the agricultural economy. The adoption of a laissez-faire Daoism by the new rulers as the state philosophy was also precedented in the Han. At the same time Buddhism became increasingly widespread.

Politically, however, the ruling class were deeply divided. In the period from 291 to 306, there were numerous assassinations and violent struggles within the royal family, known as the 'Wars between Eight Princes'. The unitary empire existed only in name. The weakness of the Western Chin regime created opportunities for the non-Chinese peoples within and on the borders of the empire – the Hsienpei, Hsiungnu, Chieh, Ti and Ch'iang – to move in and establish their own kingdoms, as many as 16 at one time, known as the 'Five Barbarians' Disruption of China' which practically ended the Western Chin. The Chinese regime managed to survive under the Eastern Chin only in south China. Its territory was much smaller than the area controlled by those non-Chinese regimes in the north and its authority over the population severely weakened. Tax avoidance became endemic.

During the years of the Eastern Chin, north China saw near permanent conflict among the non-Chinese regimes. The unification of the north finally arrived in 382 under the Ch'ien Ch'in and after their failed invasion of the south in the following year an era of co-existence was ushered in between the non-Chinese regime in the north and the Chinese one in the south. Based on this ethnic division, the period is called the 'Northern and Southern Dynasties' (*see* chart 5).

In the south the Eastern Chin dynasty ended with its overthrow in 420 by one of its generals, who established the Sung dynasty. There followed another three short-lived dynasties, each in turn brought down by either a general or another member of the ruling family, although outside the court there was a measure of peace and prosperity.

The Northern Wei

In the north a dynasty of Hsienpei descent, the Northern Wei, managed to conquer all of north China in the early 5th century, but split into two lines in 534, to become, in 550 and 557 respectively, the Northern Ch'i and Northern Chou. Although the latter was smaller and poorer, it had a more efficient military organization, and overcame the Northern Ch'i in 577. Within a few years, however, its ruling family was overthrown by one of its partly-Chinese generals, Yang Chien, who went on to conquer the south and establish the Sui dynasty. Although it was itself short-lived, the Sui had at last reunified China.

1 After the collapse of the Han dynasty the strongest military forces were commanded by the Wei in the north *(map below)*, who further expanded their fighting strength through a huge programme of public farming projects to support the vast armies. Although the Shu and the Wu forged an alliance for their mutual protection, both were overrun by the Wei between 263 and 280.

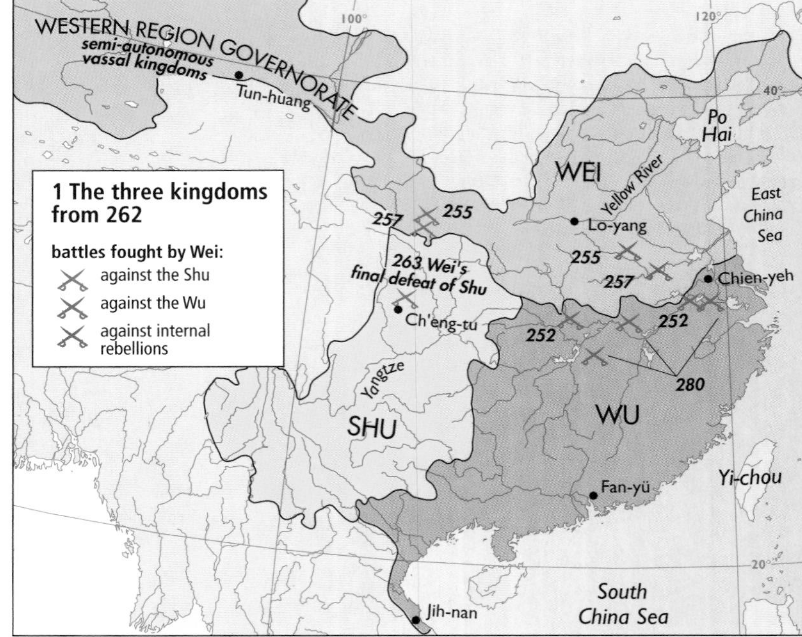

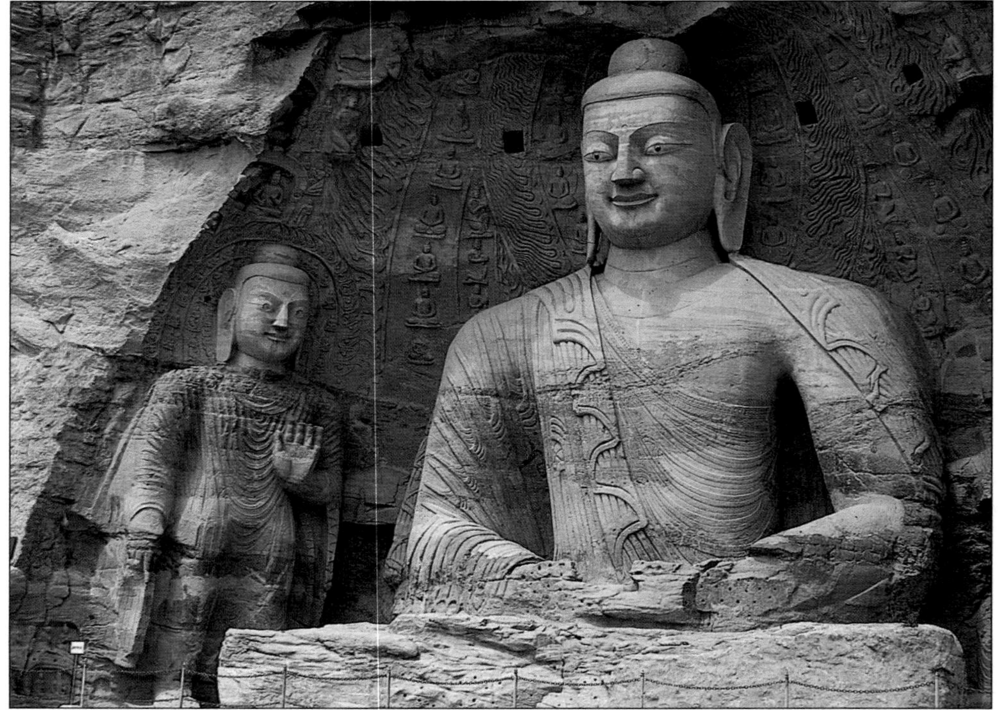

The lasting turmoil between 218 and 618 left few cultural relics of the period. However, a corridor of Buddhists sculptures *(left)*, 51,000 in all, in the 53 'Yun-gang Caves' built in AD 460–94, have survived to this day. These two clearly show the strong Indian influence of the time. Buddhism and Daoism were to undermine or even replace Confucianism during this period.

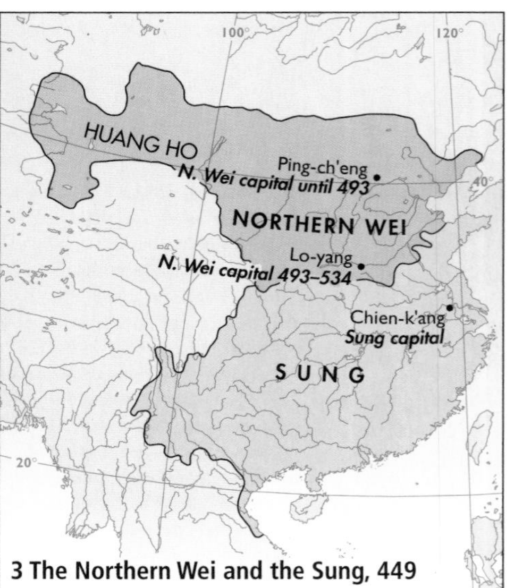

3 The Northern Wei and the Sung, 449

3 Having eliminated their rivals in north China, the Northern Wei *(map left)* proceeded to attempt to balance the claims of their own Hsienpei people and the ethnic Han Chinese. In fact the dynasty became thoroughly Sinicized to the extent that under the emperor Hsiao-wen-ti (471–99) many of the old Hsienpei ways and even the use of the Hsienpei language in court were outlawed. The same emperor undertook a programme of drastic reform, including a reorganization of the civil service and an overhaul of civil laws. He also moved the capital to the ruined site of Lo-yang, which within 20 or 30 years had a population of half a million people, with magnificent buildings. The forced pace of change, however, together with the greed and incompetence of the court, destabilized the ever-fractious border regions, and led to the sacking of the new capital and the end of the dynasty. In the south the Sung, established by the general Liu Yu,provided only 30 years of capable rule before falling into decline.

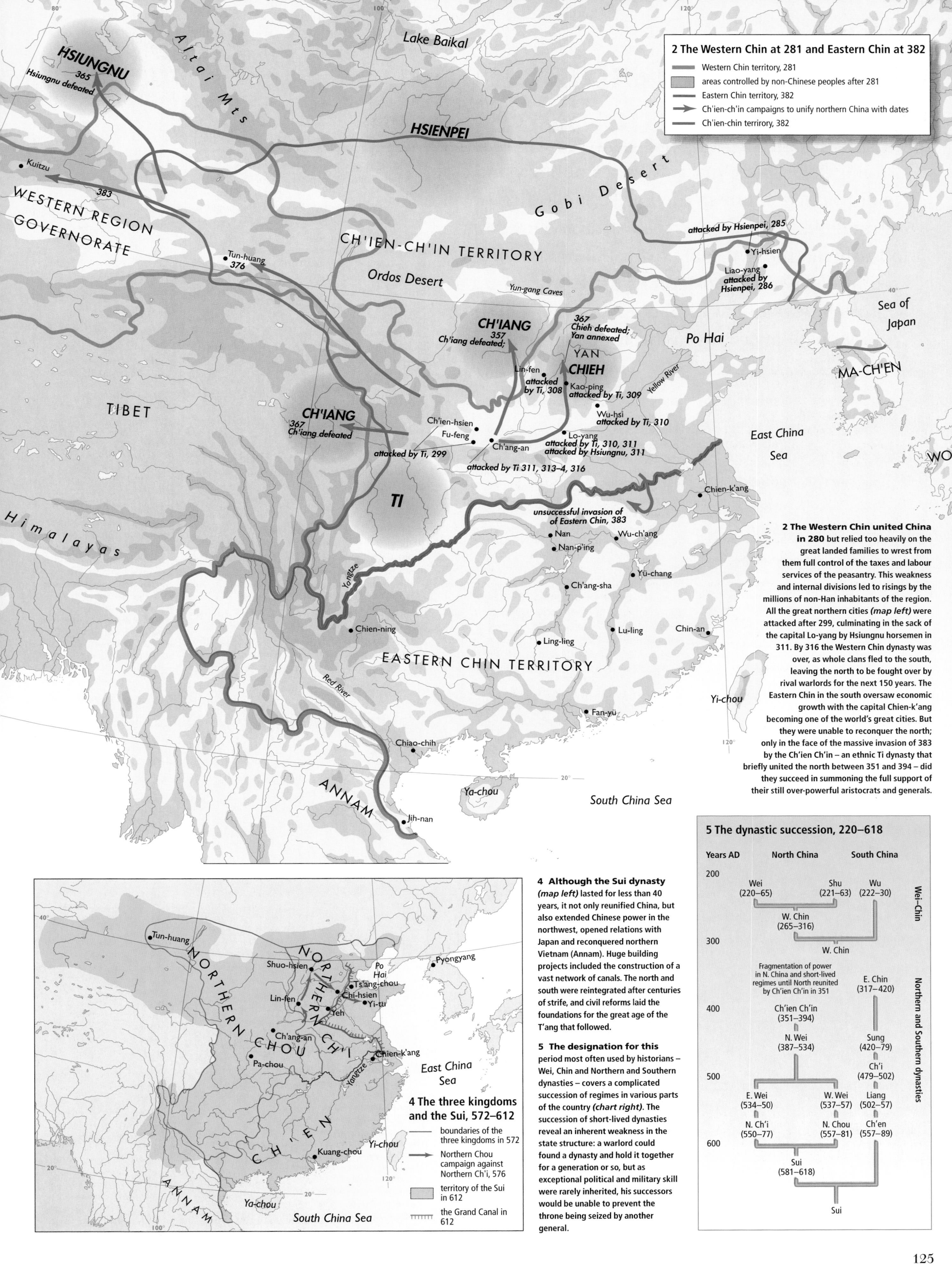

2 The Western Chin united China in 280 but relied too heavily on the great landed families to wrest from them full control of the taxes and labour services of the peasantry. This weakness and internal divisions led to risings by the millions of non-Han inhabitants of the region. All the great northern cities *(map left)* were attacked after 299, culminating in the sack of the capital Lo-yang by Hsiungnu horsemen in 311. By 316 the Western Chin dynasty was over, as whole clans fled to the south, leaving the north to be fought over by rival warlords for the next 150 years. The Eastern Chin in the south oversaw economic growth with the capital Chien-k'ang becoming one of the world's great cities. But they were unable to reconquer the north; only in the face of the massive invasion of 383 by the Ch'ien Ch'in – an ethnic Ti dynasty that briefly united the north between 351 and 394 – did they succeed in summoning the full support of their still over-powerful aristocrats and generals.

4 Although the Sui dynasty *(map left)* lasted for less than 40 years, it not only reunified China, but also extended Chinese power in the northwest, opened relations with Japan and reconquered northern Vietnam (Annam). Huge building projects included the construction of a vast network of canals. The north and south were reintegrated after centuries of strife, and civil reforms laid the foundations for the great age of the T'ang that followed.

5 The designation for this period most often used by historians – Wei, Chin and Northern and Southern dynasties – covers a complicated succession of regimes in various parts of the country *(chart right)*. The succession of short-lived dynasties reveal an inherent weakness in the state structure: a warlord could found a dynasty and hold it together for a generation or so, but as exceptional political and military skill were rarely inherited, his successors would be unable to prevent the throne being seized by another general.

618 to 1279

Chinese civilization from the T'ang to the Sung

See also

The spread of Islam from AD 632 p. 98

Imperial Japan and the early shogunates p. 122

China and east Asia, AD 220–618 p. 124

The Mongol empire, 1206–1405 p. 128

East Asia at the time of the Ming dynasty p. 166

Under the T'ang dynasty, China's military and cultural hegemony in the Far East was firmly entrenched. Its successor dynasty, the Sung, was a less dynamic external power but nonetheless reinforced China's position as the world's most sophisticated country until the disruptions of the Mongol invasions in the 13th century.

> THE BOAT IS LIKE THE MONARCH; AND WATER, THE CITIZENS. WATER IS CAPABLE OF SUPPORTING THE BOAT AS WELL AS CAPSIZING IT.
>
> **Emperor T'ang T'ai-tsung** (AD 627–49)

1 The whole of China, excepting the far southwest, was permanently organized with a centralized administration under the T'ang *(map below)*. The empire was linked by a network of post-roads, while transport of commodities between the rapidly developing regions of the Yangtze valley and the north was provided by an efficient system of canals and waterways. The road system centred on the capital, Ch'ang-an, which remained the political and strategic hub of the empire. However, the northern plain and the area around the Lower Yangtze were the principal economic centres.

AFTER CENTURIES OF DISUNION (*see* p. 124), China had been reunified in 589 by the Sui dynasty (581–618). This collapsed, partly from the burden imposed by public works like the Grand Canal, partly from expensive attempts to conquer Koguryo (northern Korea).

The T'ang rose from the widespread rebellions that followed to become a strong centralized empire with an effective administrative system. Underpinning T'ang rule was the Imperial Examination System, which was designed to recruit well-educated citizens to serve the empire. It was to endure until the early 20th century.

After some years of internal consolidation the T'ang began to expand abroad. By the 660s T'ang armies had intervened in India, had occupied the Tarim Basin and Dzungaria and had briefly set up protectorates in Tukharistan, Sogdiana, and Ferghana. In the same period Koguryo was finally conquered. By the 660s the Chinese empire reached its greatest extent until the 18th century. Chinese culture and administrative methods were spread alongside its military exploits, establishing a Chinese cultural hegemony in the Far East that would endure long after T'ang power had decayed.

In 755 An Lu-shan, a frontier general, mutinied, severely weakening the T'ang. In the years of turmoil which followed, China withdrew from central Asia and became more inward-looking, in part also as the result of the spread of Islam, which by the 8th century had reached Ferghana and later became dominant in Turkestan (*see* p. 98). Internally, imperial authority was much reduced. Power passed to the provinces, and many provincial capitals grew into large and wealthy metropolises. At the same time there was a massive movement of population to the Yangtze valley, where new methods of farming developed. Trade boomed, and a network of small market towns grew up.

The rise of the Sung

At the end of the 9th century, massive peasant uprisings reduced central authority to a cipher. China split into ten states with an imperial rump controlled by five successive short-lived dynasties (*see* map 3). Control was lost of the northeastern area to the Khitan (Liao) who set up an empire in Manchuria and Inner Mongolia. In the northwest another powerful kingdom, the Hsi-hsia, was founded by the Tanguts. These areas remained under foreign domination until 1368.

Following a coup d'état at the palace of the last of the 'Five Dynasties', the Later Chou, a new dynasty, the Sung, seized power, led by a skilled military and political operator, determined to reunify China and nullify the threat from the north. The new state that emerged was organized on less uniform lines than the T'ang, and was weaker

618–907 *T'ang dynasty*

Jan. 960 *Coup d'état of General Chao K'unag-yin, later Emperor Sung T'ai-tsu (960–76)*

963–79 *Sung's war to reunite China*

979–1004 *Sung-Liao border war*

982–1126 *Sung-Hsi-hsia border war*

1126–7 *Tatar (Chin) war to conquer north China*

1210–34 *Mongol war to conquer Chin-held north China*

1235–79 *Mongol war to conquer Sung-held south China*

2 During the 660s and 670s Chinese military power reached a peak, and briefly extended the power of the T'ang from Sogdiana to north Korea *(map right)*. The Tarim Basin and parts of northwest China fell to the Tibetans in 763–83 after T'ang garrisons were withdrawn. Chinese institutions and literary culture extended over parts of the Far East which although never ruled by China still came under Chinese cultural hegemony.

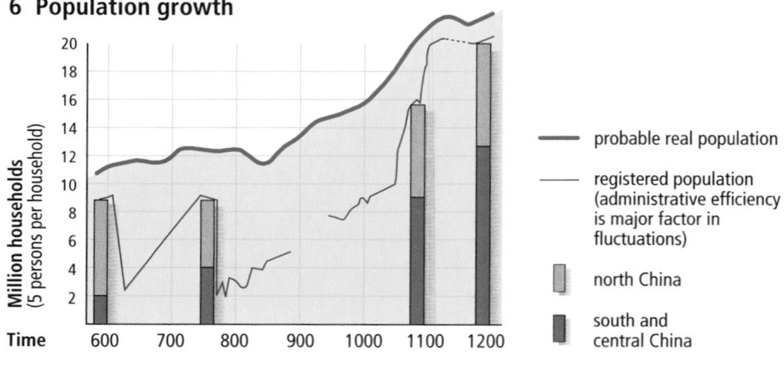

4 & 6 The period from 750 to 1250 saw a very rapid growth of the Chinese population, which probably doubled *(chart above and map right)*. At the same time the demographic distribution changed. In the 7th century, 73 per cent of the population lived in the northeast of China, and less than a quarter in south and central China. By the 13th century the situation was reversed and China's economic centre of gravity had shifted from the northern plain to the Yangtze valley.

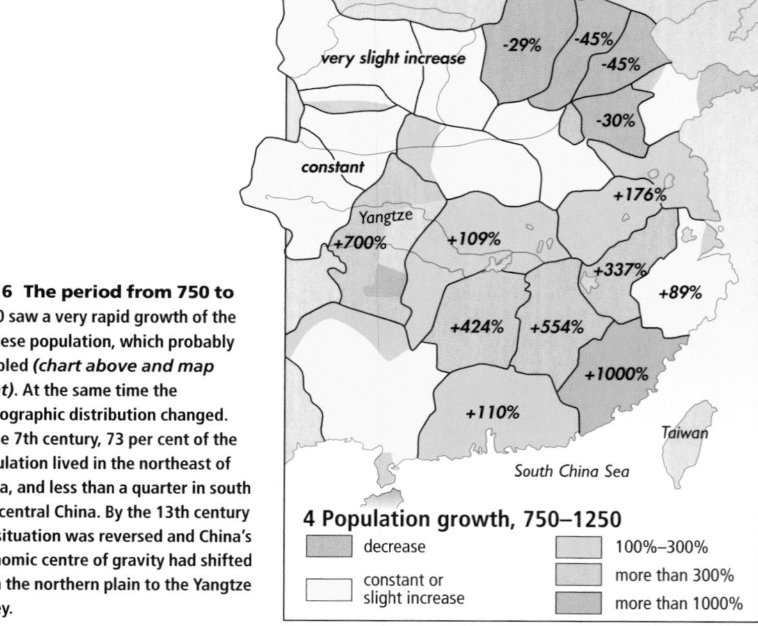

2 The Chinese world, 7th–8th centuries

under permanent T'ang civil administration
area of temporary occupation during 7th century
under T'ang military control
zone of Chinese cultural dominance
trade routes
canals
Tibetan expansion
advance of Islam

Turkish people, converted to Judaism. Their nomad empire destroyed by Russia at end of the 10th century

powerful unified Turkish kingdom in 6th century, split into Eastern and Western groups c.585. Eastern Turks conquered by T'ang 630, but re-emerge from 681 and 699–715 are re-united with Western Turks. In 715 Western Turks break away: Eastern Turks finally destroyed 744

Talas River 751 Arabs defeat T'ang armies

Uighurs replace Turks in the steppe 745–840; more stable, less anti-Chinese than Turks. Destroyed by Kirghiz

proto-Mongol people, raid T'ang border from 695, sometimes vassals of Turks. Set up own empire (Liao) in Manchuria in early 10th century

powerful kingdom on the T'ang model set up by remnants of Korean ruling clan of Koguryo. Independent from 710. Destroyed by Khitan 934

still occupied by Emishi aboriginal peoples

under T'ang control 645–763

to Tibet 763–843

T'ang occupation 668–676

Arabs invade Khurasan 667, settle from 670; settle Transoxiana 705–15. Final Arab dominance from 739 in central Asia as far as Ferghana

unified kingdom c.600. Expansion after 650; under Chinese cultural influence until c.750 then Indian influence. Central control collapsed c.840

Arabs invade Sind 711

independent politically; increasing Chinese cultural influence from 6th century. In 7th century a strong centralized kingdom developed, based on T'ang institutions

before 660 there were three states in Korea: Koguryo, Paekche and Silla. The T'ang destroyed Paekche in 660, Koguryo in 668 and occupied N. Korea. Strong resistance led to Chinese withdrawal in 676, leaving all Korea under Silla, a powerful, centralized state on T'ang lines

NAN-CHAO kingdom formed by federation of tribal groups organized on T'ang model

Indianized Buddist kingdom invaded by Nan-chao in 8th and 9th centuries

kingdom under strong Indian/Hindu influence

kingdom centred on Hue. Strong Indian influence

militarily as well. However, the imperial examinations for the recruiting of officials were further streamlined and a meritocracy of career bureaucrats became established. This, too, was a period of rapid economic growth. Between 750 and 1100 the population nearly doubled, trade reached new levels with the help of paper currency and a great concentration of industries arose around the early Sung capital, K'ai-feng. But the Sung paid a heavy price for its weak military defence along the northern border. In 1126–7 the Tatar Chin conquered north China. The Sung territory was soon reduced to central and southern China, and was only maintained by paying vast ransoms to the Tatars.

Nevertheless, economic growth continued in the south. The population continued to increase rapidly, trade and industry boomed and the new capital, Hang-chou, became indisputably the world's greatest city. This was also a period of great cultural achievement ranging from the visual arts to literature and philosophy. New heights were reached in science and technology also, most significantly in metallurgy, porcelain manufacture, ship-building and compass-guided navigation. Education became more widespread, aided by the dissemination of block printing. Merchants established complex commercial organizations with credit systems. In the countryside a free market in land emerged. Since the old overland routes to central Asia and the Middle East were no longer in Chinese hands, the Chinese became a major sea power, regularly trading with southeast Asia, south Asia and the Persian Gulf. A powerful navy was also built.

In the 13th century, the pace of change slowed markedly. This was mainly the result of the immense destruction and social disruption caused by the Mongol invasion and conquest of both Tatar and Sung territory (*see* p. 128). Nonetheless, 13th-century China remained far more populous and wealthy than contemporary Europe.

A foreign merchant *(right)*. Most of the trade along the Silk Road was handled by the Chinese and the nomadic peoples of central and western Asia. The T'ang generally regarded them with interested amusement, as is evident in this glazed pottery figure of a camel groom or trader with his exaggeratedly large nose.

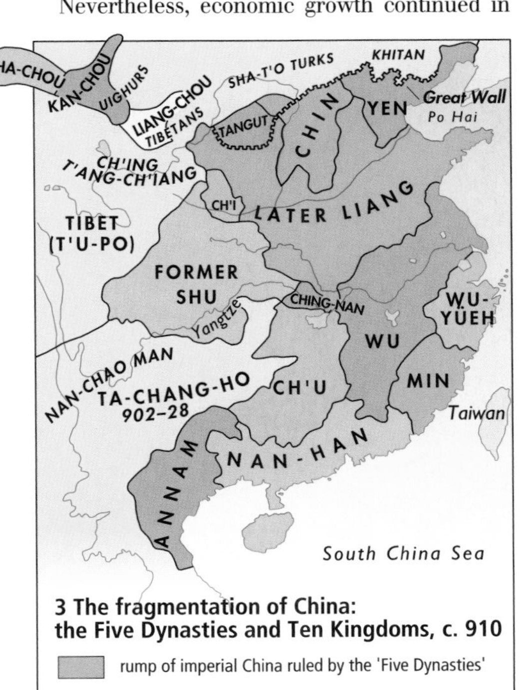

3 The fragmentation of China: the Five Dynasties and Ten Kingdoms, c. 910

rump of imperial China ruled by the 'Five Dynasties'

3 After the fall of the T'ang, a variety of independent local kingdoms developed on the basis of Late T'ang provincial divisions *(map left)*. A rump was left, ruled by five successive dynasties from 907 to 959. Although the area under imperial control expanded after the Later Liang, the last of the 'Five Dynasties' emperors still controlled China only north of the Yangtze.

5 The Sung never recovered all of the territory of T'ang China *(map right)*: Annam had broken away; the Khitan state of Liao still occupied the border areas to the northeast; and the Tangut state of Hsi-hsia the northwest. The centre of the Sung state was the great commercial city of K'ai-feng, hub of the canal system and road network, and seat of industries.

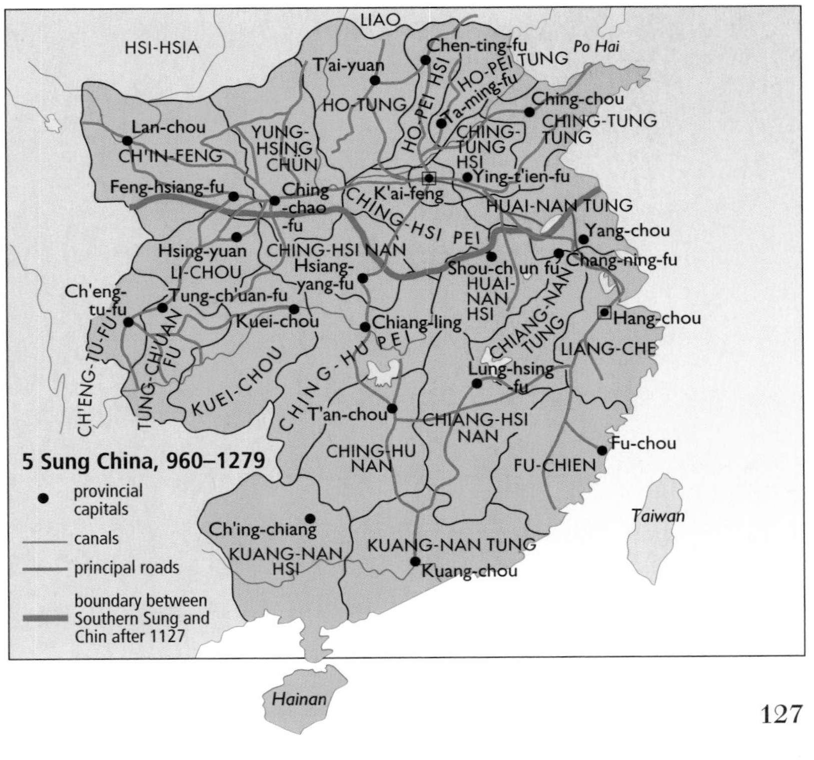

5 Sung China, 960–1279

provincial capitals
canals
principal roads
boundary between Southern Sung and Chin after 1127

The Mongol empire

See also
The first Russian state: Kievan Russia, 882–1242 p. 114
Imperial Japan and the early shogunates p. 122
Chinese civilization from the T'ang to the Sung p. 126
The Delhi sultanate, 1206–1526 p. 132
The rise of the Ottoman empire, 1281–1522 p. 142
Russian expansion in Europe and Asia p. 160
China at the time of the Ming dynasty p. 166

The Mongols, pastoral nomads from the depths of Asia, achieved conquests of unrivalled range, from the eastern frontiers of Germany to Korea and from the Arctic Ocean to Turkey and the Persian Gulf, though their invasions of Japan and Java failed. Whole peoples were uprooted and dispersed, permanently changing the ethnic character of many regions.

1206 *Temujin proclaimed Genghis Khan ('universal ruler') of Mongol tribes*

1219 *Genghis attacks Samarkand*

1211–34 *Mongol conquest of China*

1227 *Death of Genghis*

1237–8 *Moscow and Vladimir fall to Mongols*

1241 *Mongols invade Poland and Hungary*

1258 *Mongols destroy Baghdad*

1260 *Mongol defeat at Ain Jalut*

1274–81 *Mongol attempts to conquer Japan*

c. 1360–1405 *Campaigns of Tamerlane*

THE TITLE KHAN MEANS IN OUR LANGUAGE 'GREAT LORD OF LORDS'. AND CERTAINLY HE HAS A RIGHT TO THIS TITLE; FOR EVERYONE SHOULD KNOW THAT THIS GREAT KHAN IS THE MIGHTIEST MAN, WHETHER IN RESPECT OF SUBJECTS OR TERRITORY OR OF TREASURE, WHO IS IN THE WORLD TODAY OR WHO HAS EVER BEEN, FROM ADAM OUR FIRST PARENT DOWN TO THE PRESENT MOMENT ... HE IS INDEED THE GREATEST LORD THE WORLD HAS EVER KNOWN.

Marco Polo
The Travels of Marco Polo, c. 1298

MONGOL-SPEAKING TRIBES had lived for centuries in the general area of present-day Mongolia, but only an extraordinary leader could unite the Mongols and transform them into a world power. Genghis Khan was born in around 1162, the son of a tribal chief. After years of struggle he had united all the Mongol tribes by 1206. Originating in barren lands, the Mongols themselves were relatively few, but from the outset Genghis recruited into his armies Turkish tribes, and used traditional battle tactics, relying on light cavalry. In 1211 he invaded northern China, subduing the independent Chin empire, piercing the Great Wall and opening a struggle that was to end only in 1234, after Genghis's death. Genghis was drawn away to the west in campaigns against the Kara-khitai and Khwarizm, the first Muslim state to experience the full fury of the Mongol onslaught. In spite of bitter resistance, answered with horrific massacres, the Mongols slashed their way across Asia to the Caucasus. One effect of the Mongol conquests was that a trade route flourished briefly, linking east to west across the Asian land mass. The Venetian merchant Marco Polo came this way in 1271, and after 1300 Italian merchants settled as far away as Zaitun in China. However, conflict between the Mongols of Russia, Persia and China soon discouraged travellers from this heroic journey.

4 Tamerlane, the last great Mongol conqueror, actually destroyed what remained of the empire – the khanates of the Golden Horde and Chagatai. He established his control over Transoxiana by the 1360s and then campaigned ceaselessly for 30 years ***(map below)***. His defeat of the Ottoman sultan at Ankara in 1402 gave Byzantium a temporary respite. The empire he created stretched from Baghdad to Delhi, and although it fragmented after his death in 1405, his descendants ruled from Samarkand for a century, and one, Babur, became the first Mughal emperor.

Mongol conquests in Europe

Genghis died in 1227, but his conquests were continued and extended by his successors. Before he died, he divided his empire among his four sons. Batu, a grandson of Genghis, directed the invasion of Europe (*see* map 2). The northern Russian principalities were smashed in a lightning winter campaign in 1237–8; Kiev was razed in 1240; Poland and Hungary were attacked, and in 1241 a Christian army was annihilated at Legnica. Mongol troops even reached the coastline of Croatia near Trogir (Traù). The death of the Great Khan Ogedei in December 1241 saved Europe; Batu withdrew eastwards to immerse himself in internal Mongol affairs.

Mongols, Islam and Christianity

The Mongol conquerors came into contact with three main religions: Buddhism, Islam and Christianity (in its many forms). Themselves shamanists, they were attracted by the high culture associated with the great religions. Islam at first seemed to be the loser: Baghdad itself was captured in 1258 amid horrific massacres; the caliph was slain, and for a time the Mongols promoted Nestorian Christianity and Buddhism in Persia, though by the early 14th

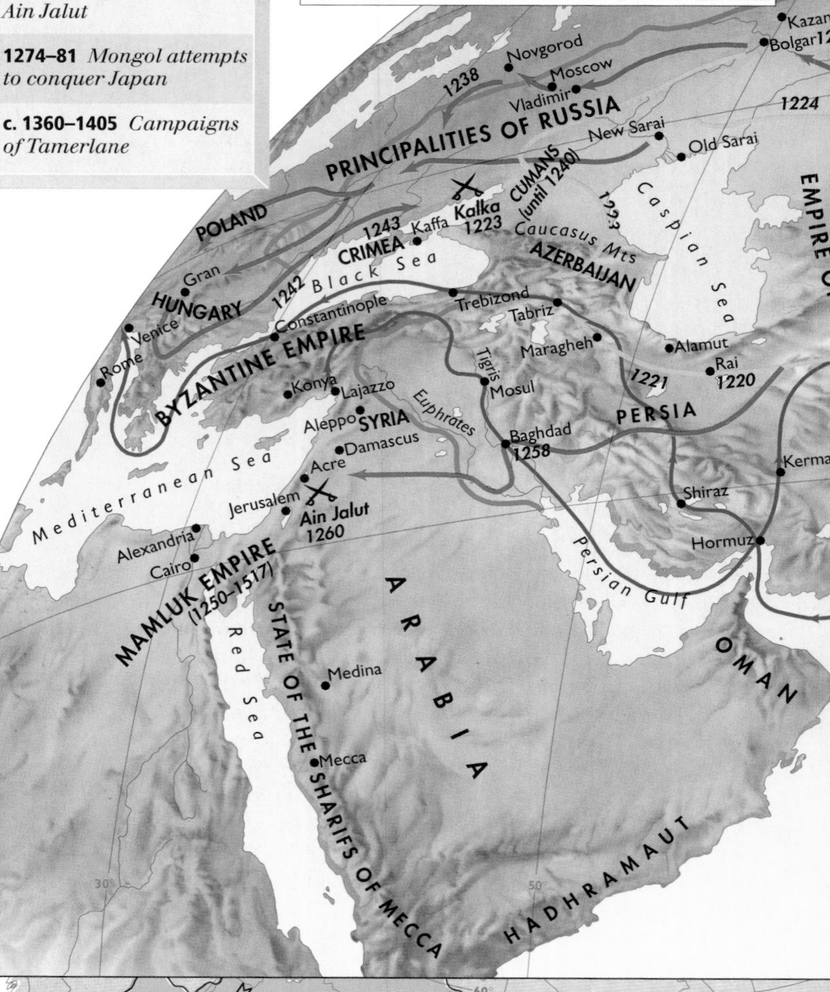

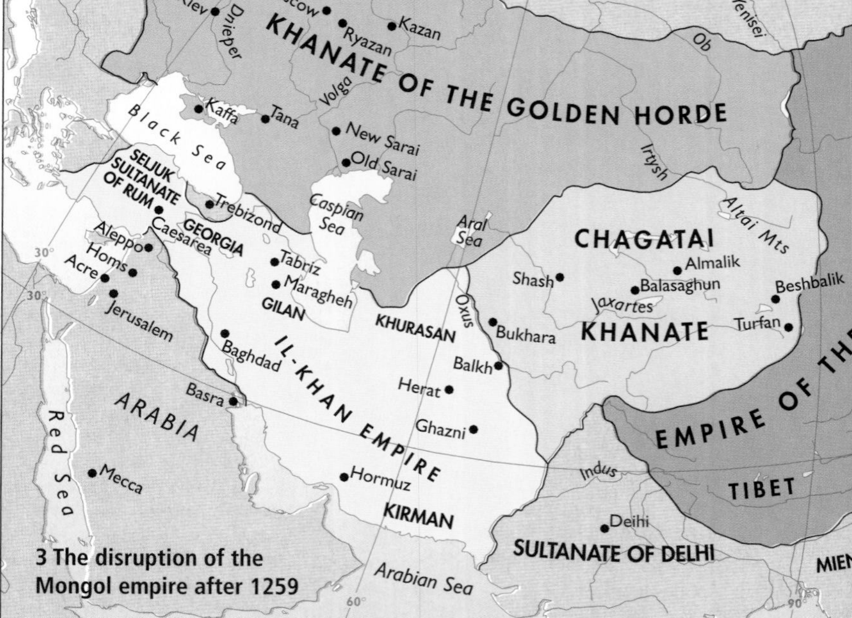

3 The disruption of the Mongol empire after 1259

4 The conquests of Tamerlane, c. 1360–1405

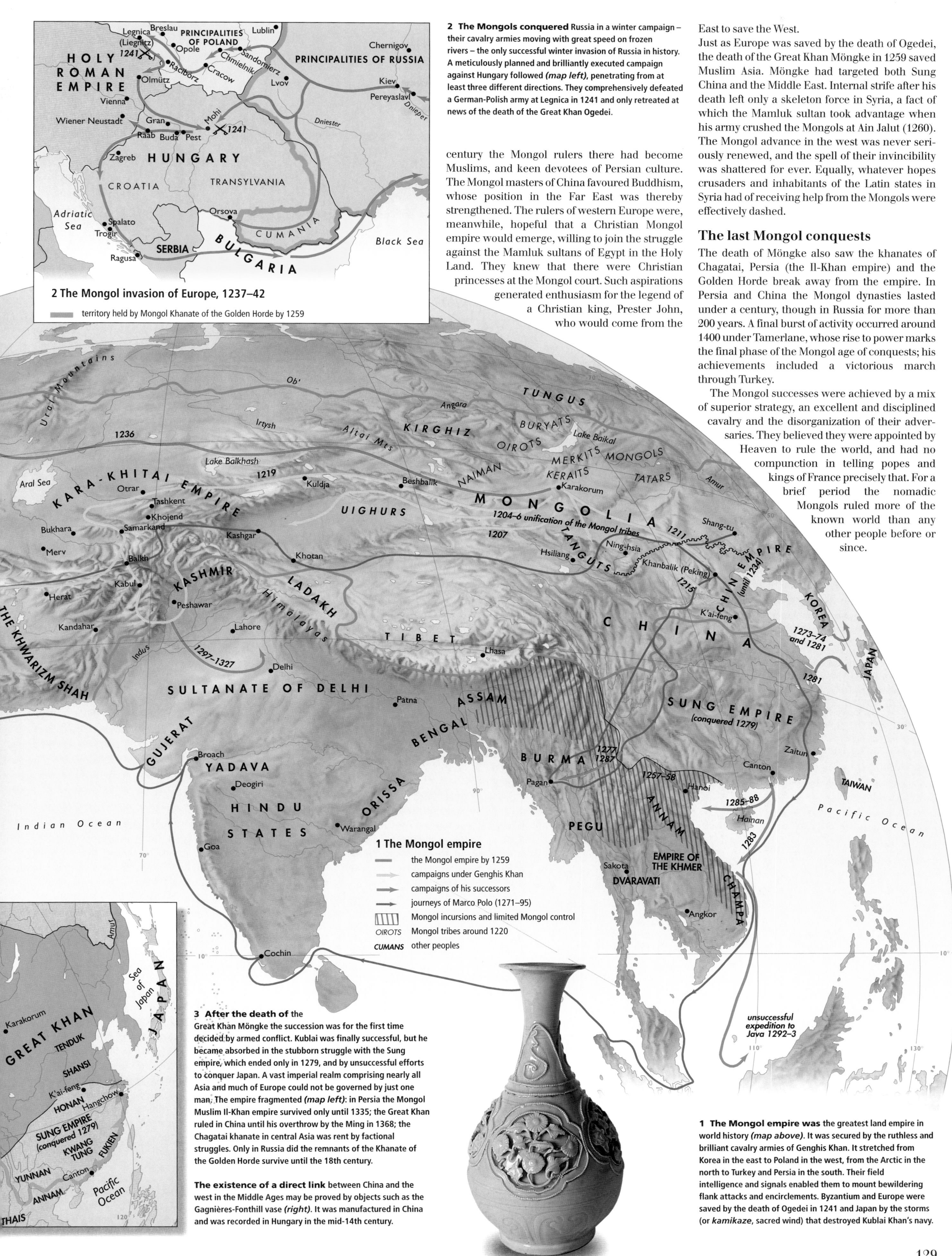

2 The Mongols conquered Russia in a winter campaign – their cavalry armies moving with great speed on frozen rivers – the only successful winter invasion of Russia in history. A meticulously planned and brilliantly executed campaign against Hungary followed *(map left)*, penetrating from at least three different directions. They comprehensively defeated a German-Polish army at Legnica in 1241 and only retreated at news of the death of the Great Khan Ogedei.

century the Mongol rulers there had become Muslims, and keen devotees of Persian culture. The Mongol masters of China favoured Buddhism, whose position in the Far East was thereby strengthened. The rulers of western Europe were, meanwhile, hopeful that a Christian Mongol empire would emerge, willing to join the struggle against the Mamluk sultans of Egypt in the Holy Land. They knew that there were Christian princesses at the Mongol court. Such aspirations generated enthusiasm for the legend of a Christian king, Prester John, who would come from the East to save the West.

Just as Europe was saved by the death of Ogedei, the death of the Great Khan Möngke in 1259 saved Muslim Asia. Möngke had targeted both Sung China and the Middle East. Internal strife after his death left only a skeleton force in Syria, a fact of which the Mamluk sultan took advantage when his army crushed the Mongols at Ain Jalut (1260). The Mongol advance in the west was never seriously renewed, and the spell of their invincibility was shattered for ever. Equally, whatever hopes crusaders and inhabitants of the Latin states in Syria had of receiving help from the Mongols were effectively dashed.

The last Mongol conquests

The death of Möngke also saw the khanates of Chagatai, Persia (the Il-Khan empire) and the Golden Horde break away from the empire. In Persia and China the Mongol dynasties lasted under a century, though in Russia for more than 200 years. A final burst of activity occurred around 1400 under Tamerlane, whose rise to power marks the final phase of the Mongol age of conquests; his achievements included a victorious march through Turkey.

The Mongol successes were achieved by a mix of superior strategy, an excellent and disciplined cavalry and the disorganization of their adversaries. They believed they were appointed by Heaven to rule the world, and had no compunction in telling popes and kings of France precisely that. For a brief period the nomadic Mongols ruled more of the known world than any other people before or since.

3 After the death of the Great Khan Möngke the succession was for the first time decided by armed conflict. Kublai was finally successful, but he became absorbed in the stubborn struggle with the Sung empire, which ended only in 1279, and by unsuccessful efforts to conquer Japan. A vast imperial realm comprising nearly all Asia and much of Europe could not be governed by just one man. The empire fragmented *(map left)*: in Persia the Mongol Muslim Il-Khan empire survived only until 1335; the Great Khan ruled in China until his overthrow by the Ming in 1368; the Chagatai khanate in central Asia was rent by factional struggles. Only in Russia did the remnants of the Khanate of the Golden Horde survive until the 18th century.

The existence of a direct link between China and the west in the Middle Ages may be proved by objects such as the Gagnières-Fonthill vase *(right)*. It was manufactured in China and was recorded in Hungary in the mid-14th century.

1 The Mongol empire was the greatest land empire in world history *(map above)*. It was secured by the ruthless and brilliant cavalry armies of Genghis Khan. It stretched from Korea in the east to Poland in the west, from the Arctic in the north to Turkey and Persia in the south. Their field intelligence and signals enabled them to mount bewildering flank attacks and encirclements. Byzantium and Europe were saved by the death of Ogedei in 1241 and Japan by the storms (or *kamikaze*, sacred wind) that destroyed Kublai Khan's navy.

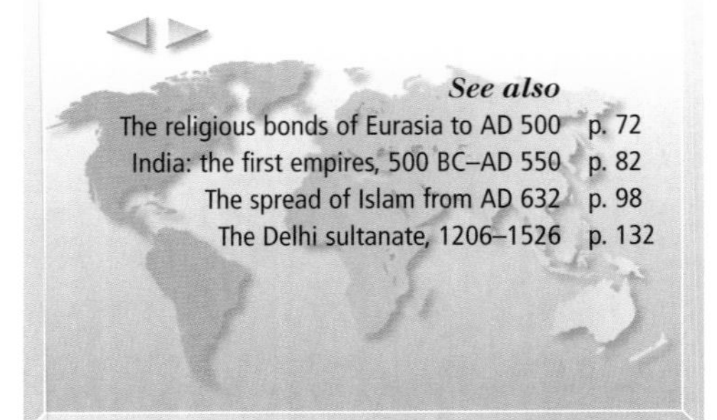

550 to 1206

India: the emergence of temple kingdoms

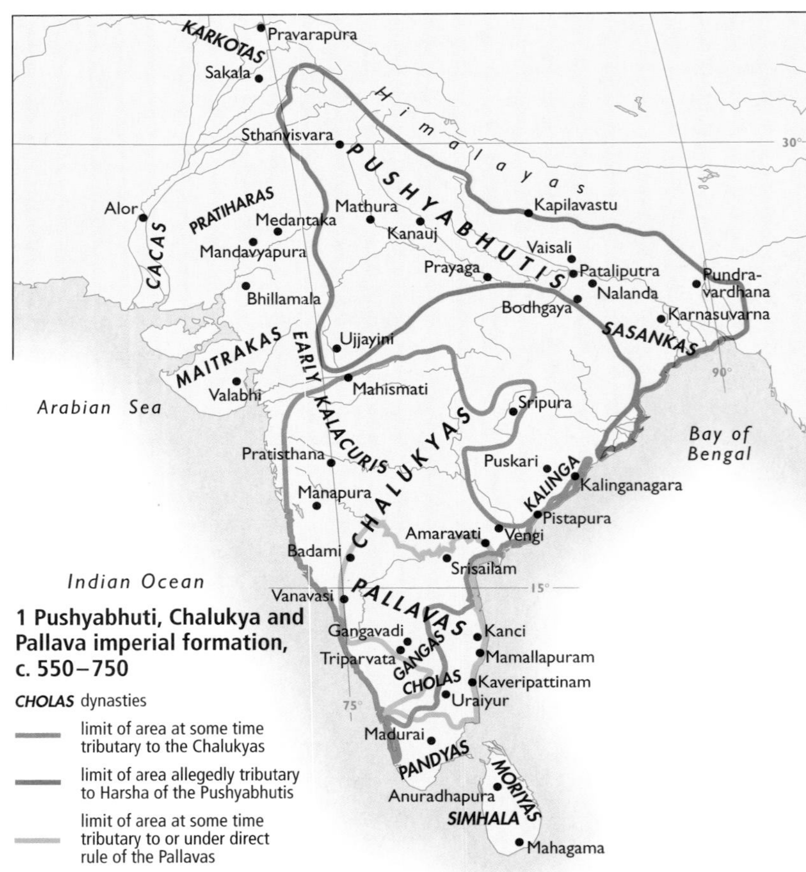

1 Pushyabhuti, Chalukya and Pallava imperial formation, c. 550–750

CHOLAS dynasties

limit of area at some time tributary to the Chalukyas

limit of area allegedly tributary to Harsha of the Pushyabhutis

limit of area at some time tributary to or under direct rule of the Pallavas

1 The famous Pushyabhuti king Harsha of Kanauj, whose court has been detailed by the Sanskrit poet Bana as well as the Chinese traveller Hsüan-tsang, was perhaps the last major king of northern India ***(map above)*** as the political centre of India shifted to the south until the establishment of the sultanate (*see* p. 132). The Chalukyas, who defeated Harsha, and the Pallavas, who developed links with southeast Asia, were powerful dynasties that vied for control of the south throughout this period.

2 Arab travellers in the 9th century reported that the Rashtrakuta king ruled all India, but in fact there were at least two other dynasties that claimed regional paramountcy ***(map below)***. The Rashtrakutas, who had arisen to prominence when their king Dantidurga had led a rebellion in the 750s against their Chalukya overlords, met fierce resistance from the Gurjara-Pratiharas, and were able to defeat them only intermittently. The weaker Buddhist empire of the Palas claimed dominance over eastern India.

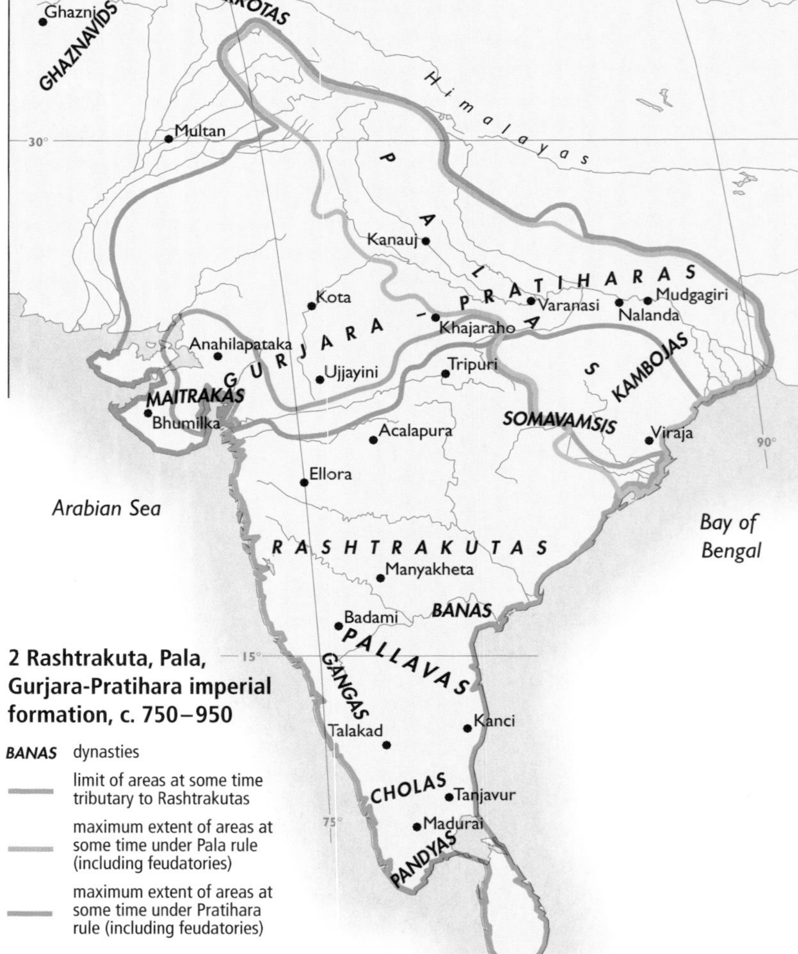

2 Rashtrakuta, Pala, Gurjara-Pratihara imperial formation, c. 750–950

BANAS dynasties

limit of areas at some time tributary to Rashtrakutas

maximum extent of areas at some time under Pala rule (including feudatories)

maximum extent of areas at some time under Pratihara rule (including feudatories)

The integration of early India led to agrarian expansion, the proliferation of rival states and the triumph of Hinduism over its rivals. The political centre of India gradually shifted southward to powerful agrarian empires such as the Rashtrakutas and Cholas. As north India fragmented, it became vulnerable to Turkic incursions from the northwest.

THE THOUSANDS OF inscriptions that have come down to us from medieval India reveal an intricate mosaic of kings, lords and priests superimposed on an agrarian populace. Overall, civilization and its revenue-extracting agents now penetrated into regions previously beyond the reach of the more urbanized polities of ancient India. The great metropolises of earlier times contracted as the countryside became filled with smaller settlements integrated into local trade networks. Temple Hinduism triumphed over Buddhism and provided the political theology of royal courts as well as the religious sentiments of the peasantry.

Dynastic struggles

Politically, this epoch was composed of successive 'imperial formations', hierarchies of dynastic empires in struggle and alliance, vying for paramountcy. After the the decline of the power of the Guptas (*see* p. 82), north India suffered political instability until the Huns were gradually pushed northward from India by local rulers. Not long afterwards, three major dynasties emerged as powerful contenders for imperial paramountcy – the Pushyabhutis of Kanauj, the Chalukyas of Badami and the Pallavas of Kanci. Harsha Pushyabhuti, who hosted the famous Chinese traveller Hsüan-tsang, was defeated in 630 by the Chalukya king Pulakesin II, although the location of this battle is not known. The Chalukyas, who claimed descent from the Satavahana dynasty that had held sway in the south 500 years earlier (*see* p. 82), gained initial victories against the southern Pallavas, but were later defeated by them and finally faced rebellion by one of their ablest underlords, the Rashtrakutas, who rose to become the chief power in south India for nearly 200 years (c. 750–950). The Rashtrakutas, builders of the famous Kalaisanatha temple at Ellora, were perceived by the Arab traveller Masudi as the most powerful dynasty of India. Their rivals were the Pratiharas to the north and the Palas of eastern India, followers of Mahayana Buddhism and patrons of the Buddhist university at Nalanda.

The rise of the Cholas

By the close of the 10th century these empires had weakened and contracted as the ancient Chola lineage of the south revitalized itself to become the dominant force in a new imperial formation that would last nearly 250 years (c. 950-1200). The Cholas made daring military expeditions to north India, Sri Lanka and southeast Asia, gaining tremendous wealth with which they constructed elaborate imperial temples and patronized Brahmin religious elites. In the Deccan, two families revived the Chalukya dynasty and further north the Pratihara empire fragmented into a number of smaller kingdoms warring amongst themselves, that eventually came to be known as the Rajputs. Perhaps the most powerful of these smaller dynasties were the Paramaras based in Dhar. The political instability of north India made it particularly vulnerable to the militarily superior Turkic armies, which under the leadership of Mahmud of Ghazni conducted looting raids in the 11th century.

From the time of the Pallavas the dynasties of eastern India – particularly the Palas and the Cholas – established trade links and cultural exchanges with the kingdoms of southeast Asia. Several Buddhist kings of southeast Asia patronized Buddhist institutions in eastern India and maintained trading enclaves at coastal cities. After the decline of Rome, trade links with southeast Asia were further strengthened, as peninsular India eventually became an important depot in a trans-regional trade circuit connecting China to the Arab Middle East. Despite these trading links, medieval Indian empires remained primarily agrarian in nature. Their royal families, courtly officials and ritual specialists enjoyed the revenue extracted from vast tracts of land cultivated by the lower orders, who in turn were divided into hierarchies of cultivators, tenants and labourers. The Cholas, for example, relied on the flourishing wet-cultivation of rice in the Kaveri river delta. Political authority was not directly administered but was sustained through relations of tribute and dependence among a hierarchy of lords, giving India an almost feudal complexion.

Temple Hinduism

Saivism and Vaisnavism, the two main orders of theistic Hinduism, which centred their philosophy and ritual around the exaltation of the gods Vishnu and Shiva respectively, facilitated this chain of medieval lordships. These religions, which had been growing since the time of the Guptas, gained the commitments of most royal courts by the 7th century. Two of the most important early texts of these theistic orders were the *Ramayana*, a tale of the mythical king Rama of Ayodhya (*see* map 4), and the voluminous *Mahabharata*, recounting the war between two royal families for paramount sovereignty of the earth. The latter contained the *Bhagavad-gita*, which developed the theology of devotion called 'bhakti'. Through theocentric histories called 'Puranas', ancient pedigrees and divine identities were provided for medieval rulers, and images of Hindu gods were housed in royal fashion in hundreds of temples which dotted the countryside, reinforcing the ideology of sovereignty and devotion integral to the authority of kings. Occasionally devotion to god ('bhakti') could be turned against the chain of secular lordships, but such subversions were limited. Temples became the beneficiaries of royal and lordly largesse, accumulating considerable wealth and emerging as significant landholders by the end of the medieval period. This no doubt explains their attraction for the raiding Turks who laid the foundation of Muslim rule in India (*see* p. 132).

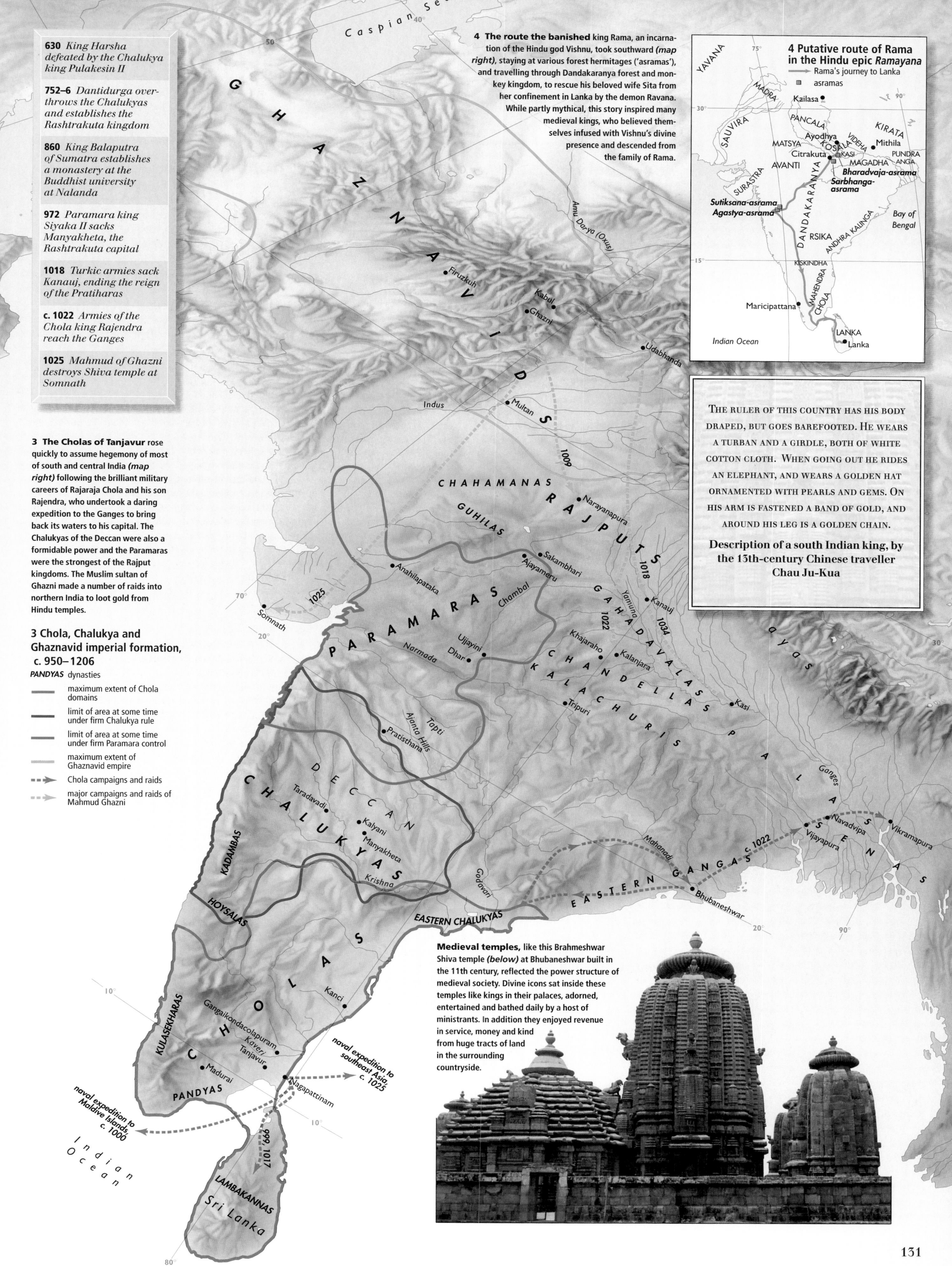

630 *King Harsha defeated by the Chalukya king Pulakesin II*

752–6 *Dantidurga overthrows the Chalukyas and establishes the Rashtrakuta kingdom*

860 *King Balaputra of Sumatra establishes a monastery at the Buddhist university at Nalanda*

972 *Paramara king Siyaka II sacks Manyakheta, the Rashtrakuta capital*

1018 *Turkic armies sack Kanauj, ending the reign of the Pratiharas*

c. 1022 *Armies of the Chola king Rajendra reach the Ganges*

1025 *Mahmud of Ghazni destroys Shiva temple at Somnath*

4 The route the banished king Rama, an incarnation of the Hindu god Vishnu, took southward *(map right)*, staying at various forest hermitages ('asramas'), and travelling through Dandakaranya forest and monkey kingdom, to rescue his beloved wife Sita from her confinement in Lanka by the demon Ravana. While partly mythical, this story inspired many medieval kings, who believed themselves infused with Vishnu's divine presence and descended from the family of Rama.

3 The Cholas of Tanjavur rose quickly to assume hegemony of most of south and central India *(map right)* following the brilliant military careers of Rajaraja Chola and his son Rajendra, who undertook a daring expedition to the Ganges to bring back its waters to his capital. The Chalukyas of the Deccan were also a formidable power and the Paramaras were the strongest of the Rajput kingdoms. The Muslim sultan of Ghazni made a number of raids into northern India to loot gold from Hindu temples.

3 Chola, Chalukya and Ghaznavid imperial formation, c. 950–1206

- *PANDYAS* dynasties
- maximum extent of Chola domains
- limit of area at some time under firm Chalukya rule
- limit of area at some time under firm Paramara control
- maximum extent of Ghaznavid empire
- Chola campaigns and raids
- major campaigns and raids of Mahmud Ghazni

THE RULER OF THIS COUNTRY HAS HIS BODY DRAPED, BUT GOES BAREFOOTED. HE WEARS A TURBAN AND A GIRDLE, BOTH OF WHITE COTTON CLOTH. WHEN GOING OUT HE RIDES AN ELEPHANT, AND WEARS A GOLDEN HAT ORNAMENTED WITH PEARLS AND GEMS. ON HIS ARM IS FASTENED A BAND OF GOLD, AND AROUND HIS LEG IS A GOLDEN CHAIN.

Description of a south Indian king, by the 13th-century Chinese traveller Chau Ju-Kua

Medieval temples, like this Brahmeshwar Shiva temple *(below)* at Bhubaneshwar built in the 11th century, reflected the power structure of medieval society. Divine icons sat inside these temples like kings in their palaces, adorned, entertained and bathed daily by a host of ministrants. In addition they enjoyed revenue in service, money and kind from huge tracts of land in the surrounding countryside.

1206 to 1526

India: the Delhi sultanate

I ENCOURAGED MY INFIDEL SUBJECTS TO EMBRACE THE RELIGION OF THE PROPHET, AND I PROCLAIMED THAT EVERY ONE WHO REPEATED THE CREED AND BECAME A MUSLIM SHOULD BE EXEMPT FROM THE POLL TAX. INFORMATION OF THIS CAME TO THE PEOPLE AT LARGE, AND LARGE NUMBERS OF HINDUS PRESENTED THEMSELVES, AND WERE ADMITTED TO THE HONOUR OF ISLAM.

Firoz Shah Tughluq

The Delhi sultanate spread Muslim rule throughout most of south Asia. It created the circumstances in which large numbers of Indians began to convert to Islam. In the mid-14th century the sultanate reached the peak of its power after which India began to divide into many smaller sultanates, making it an easy target for invaders from the northwest.

1175 *Muhammad Ghuri invades India and begins the establishment of a Muslim empire*

1206 *Delhi sultanate founded*

1335 *Sultan Muhammad ibn Tughluq rules most of India*

1341 *Bengal breaks away from the Delhi sultanate*

1370 *Hindu state of Vijayanagar dominant in south India*

1398 *Tamerlane invades India and sacks Delhi*

1526 *Battle of Panipat (see p. 170): Babur conquers Delhi sultanate and founds Mughal empire*

FROM THE BEGINNING of the 11th century the Turkish Muslim rulers of central Asia and Afghanistan had been expanding their power into north India (*see* p. 130). First Mahmud of Ghazni (927–1030) invaded India 17 times, bringing the Punjab under his sway. Then, from 1175, having overthrown Mahmud's successors, Muhammad Ghuri built his power in northwest India. In 1206, Qutbuddin Aibak, a Ghurid general who had risen from slave status, established in his own name the sultanate of Delhi.

Over the following 320 years northern India was ruled from Delhi by five dynasties of Turkish and Afghan extraction: the Slave Kings (1206–90); the Khaljis (1290–1320); the Tughluqs (1320–1414); the Sayyids (1414–51); and the Lodis (1451–1526). For the first century and a half they strove to spread their rule throughout India. In 1311 the army of Alauddin Khalji (1296–1316) reached the subcontinent's southern tip. Under Muhammad ibn Tughluq (1325–51) the sultanate reached its maximum extent, drawing taxes from more than 20 provinces (*see* map 1). Greater security was promised, moreover, by the decline of the Mongol threat from the northwest. But controversial decisions by Muhammad to levy higher taxes and to transfer the population of Delhi to a new capital in the Deccan led to the disintegration of the sultanate as it reached its peak. In 1341 Bengal broke away to form a separate sultanate; in 1347 so did the Bahmani rulers of the Deccan. Between 1382 and 1396 Khandesh, Malwa, Jaunpur and Gujerat followed suit. The invasion of Tamerlane in 1398, when Delhi was razed, rendered the sultanate's power nominal, and allowed the emergence of regional powers (*see* map 3). From the mid-15th century the Afghan Lodis managed to stretch Delhi's sway once more over northern India. Dissensions among them between 1517 and 1526, however, facilitated the final overthrow of the sultanate by Tamerlane's descendant, Babur.

The Hindu south

From the mid-14th to the mid-16th century the south was not disturbed by powers from the north. Here the Bahmani sultanate of the Deccan and its successors faced a strong Hindu polity in the Vijayanagar empire (*see* map 2), founded in 1336,

2 The mid-14th century *(map below)* saw the establishment of two major states in southern India, the Muslim Bahmani sultanate and the Hindu Vijayanagar (City of Victory) empire. The two states were involved in almost continuous and inconclusive warfare. In the 15th century the Gajapatis were able to press their rule southward down the east Indian coast. In the 1480s the Bahmani state split into five separate sultanates.

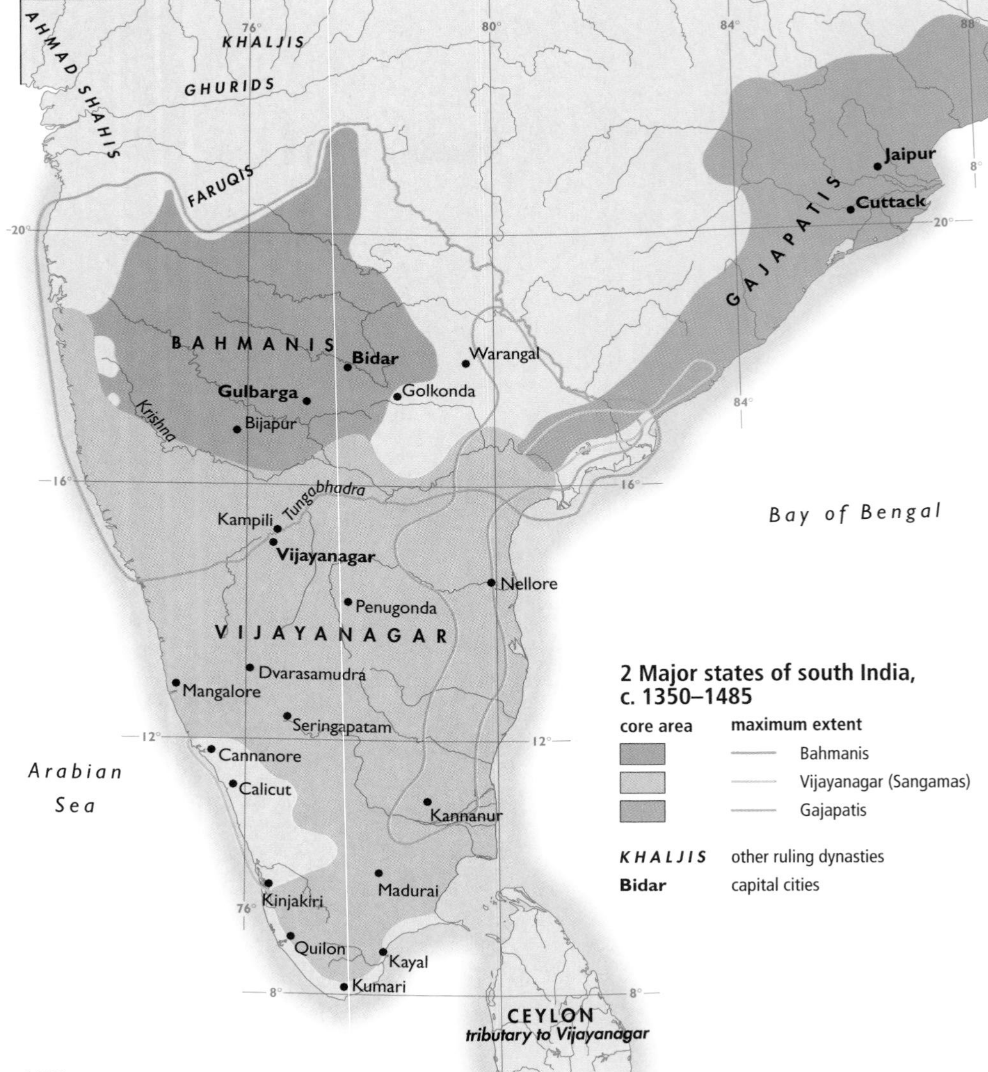

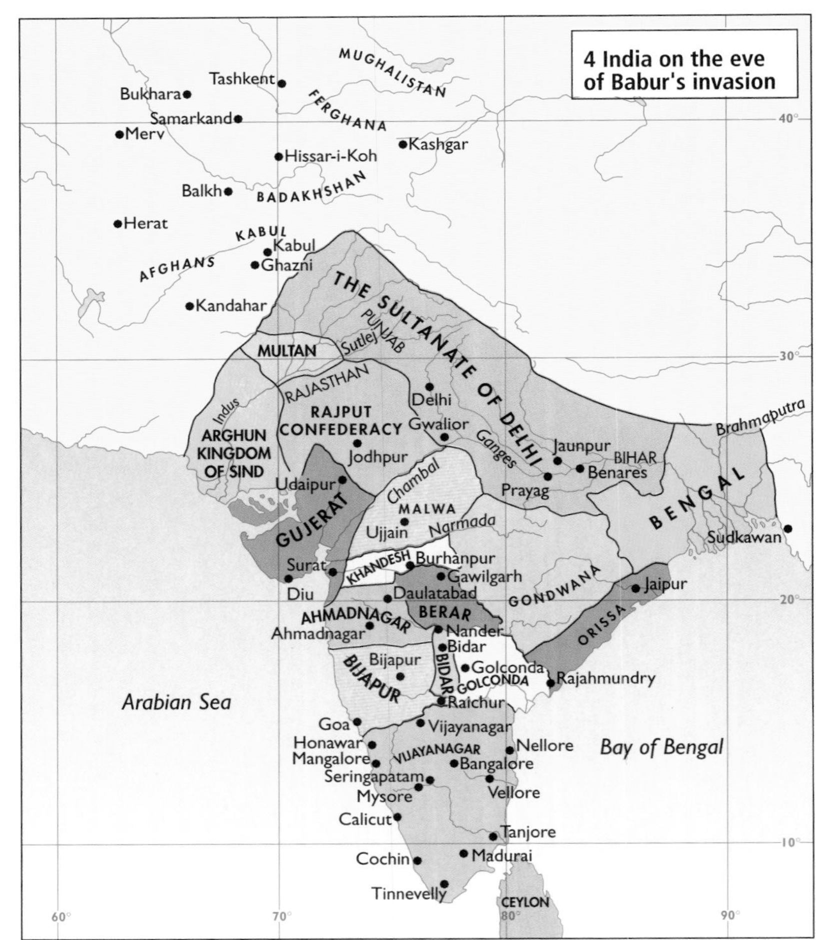

4 In 1526 one of the Lodi dynasty, which had gained power in Delhi in the second half of the 15th century, ruled the Punjab *(map above)* and another controlled the Gangetic plain as far east as Bihar. The Bahmani kingdom in the Deccan had broken up into five warring sultanates. Rajput dynasties controlled Rajasthan and threatened territories to the north.

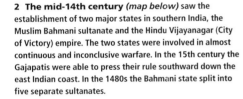

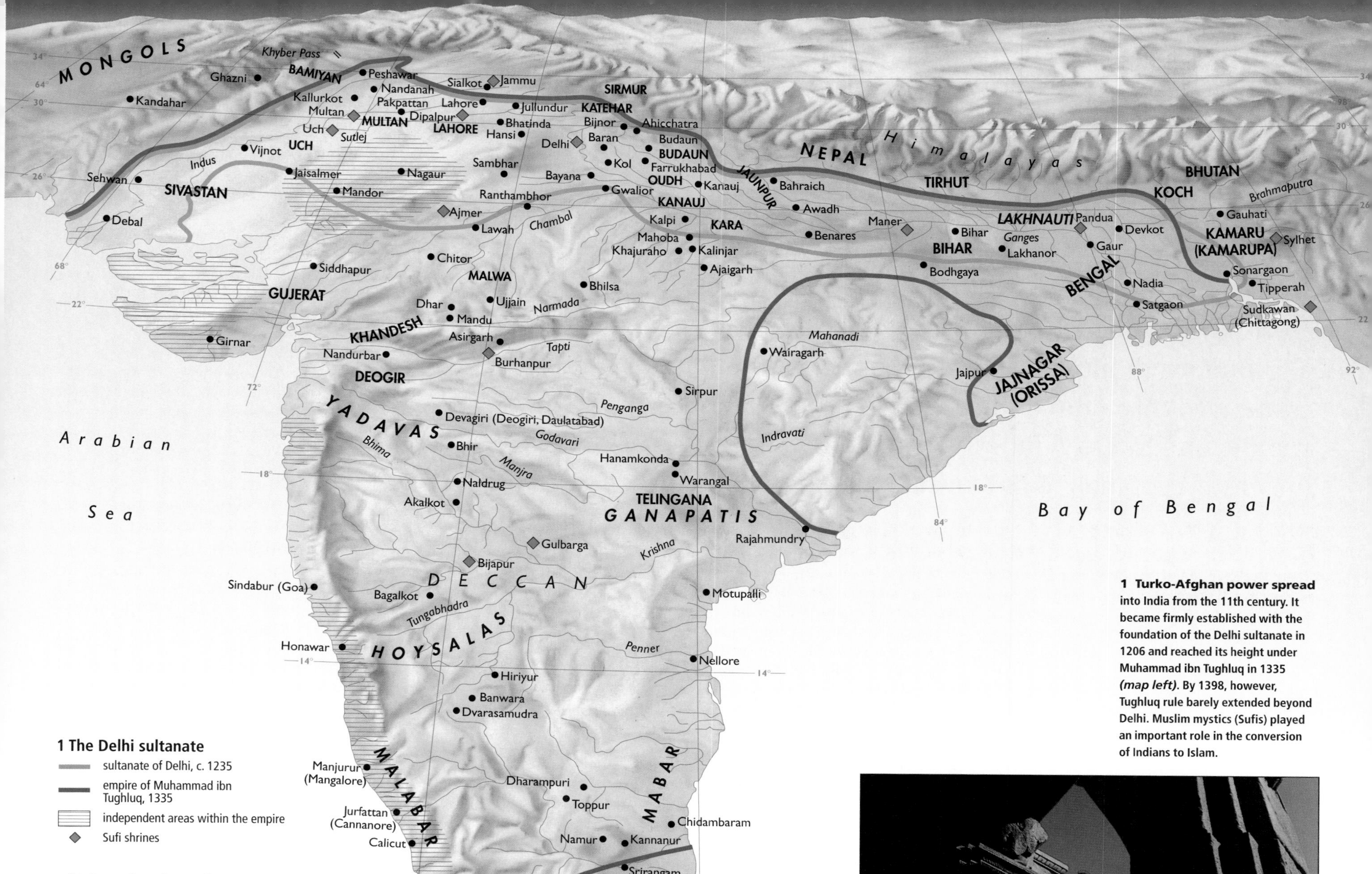

1 The Delhi sultanate

- sultanate of Delhi, c. 1235
- empire of Muhammad ibn Tughluq, 1335
- independent areas within the empire
- Sufi shrines

1 Turko-Afghan power spread into India from the 11th century. It became firmly established with the foundation of the Delhi sultanate in 1206 and reached its height under Muhammad ibn Tughluq in 1335 *(map left)*. By 1398, however, Tughluq rule barely extended beyond Delhi. Muslim mystics (Sufis) played an important role in the conversion of Indians to Islam.

which under three dynasties dominated south India until its fall in 1565. It is a mistake, however, to regard this competition as simply one of Muslim versus Hindu. Men of each faith fought on both sides.

India and Islam

One consequence of the Muslim conquest of much of India was that it came to be linked more closely to the worlds of central and western Asia. Large numbers of scholars, poets and craftsmen, often uprooted by the havoc wrought by the Mongols and their successors, came to seek their fortunes at Indian courts, providing a great stimulus to Indian arts. Persian became the leading language of literature and government. The dome and the arch became major features of Indian architecture.

Another consequence was the conversion of Indians from all levels of society, but particularly from the lower levels, to Islam. This was a largely peaceful development in which Sufi saints played an important role. One third of the world's Muslims now live in the region.

There was much interaction between Hinduism and Islam, particularly at the mystical level. Teachers emerged who drew from both traditions, for instance Kabir (1440–1518) and Nanak (1469–1539), who founded Sikhism. There was fruitful interaction, too, in literature and architecture, where distinctive traditions developed in the regional kingdoms. Nevertheless, orthodox Muslims continued to find much in Hinduism that offended their belief in the unity of God and His revelation through the Prophet Mohammed.

Hindu culture also saw important achievements. Bhakti devotionalism (love of God) spread from south India to Bengal, leading to a revival of the worship of Vishnu as the Universal God in eastern and northern India. Magnificent temples were built in the rich Hindu civilization of Vijayanagar in the south. Nevertheless, in this period Delhi was established as the political centre of India. It was to remain so until the 19th century.

3 The invasion of Tamerlane in 1398–9 had a great impact on the politics of northern India *(map below)*. The power of the Delhi sultanate was greatly reduced and numerous regional powers were able to assert themselves. It was not until the mid-15th century that significant power returned to Delhi under the Lodi sultans.

Quwwat al-Islam Mosque with Qutb Minar in the background *(above)*. The picture shows the arched screen of the Quwwat al-Islam (Might of Islam) mosque built by Qutbuddin Aibak inside a captured Hindu citadel, close to Delhi, on the platform of a demolished Hindu temple. He also built the Qutb Minar as a tower of victory to symbolize the supremacy of Islam in India.

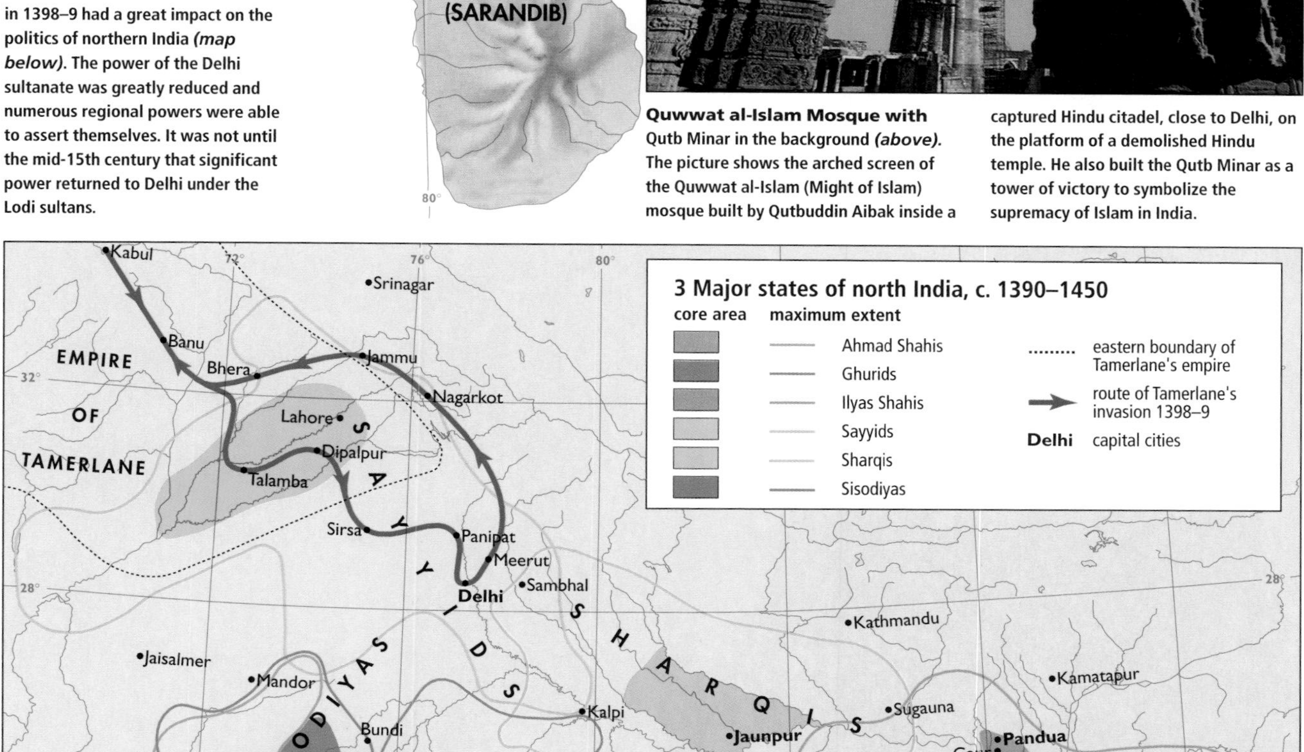

500 BC to AD 1511

The early civilizations of southeast Asia

See also

Southeast Asia before civilization p. 46
The unification of China, 475 BC–AD 220 p. 80
India: the first empires, 500 BC–AD 550 p. 82
The spread of Islam from AD 632 p. 98
China and east Asia, 220–618 p. 124
Chinese civilization from the T'ang to the Sung p. 126
China at the time of the Ming dynasty p. 166
Southeast Asia and the European powers p. 176

Maritime trade routes linked India with southeast Asia from the last few centuries of the pre-Christian era. By the middle of the first millennium AD the influence of Indian Hindu-Buddhist civilization extended throughout the region other than in the remote and forested interior of the mainland and in the eastern islands of Indonesia and the Philippines.

111 BC *Han invasion of northern Vietnam under emperor Wu-ti*

Early 3rd century AD *Earliest Sanskrit writing in southeast Asia in the 'Vo Canh' inscription of central Vietnam*

780–850 *Construction of Borobudur, Java*

802 *Foundation of Angkor in Cambodia*

849 *Pagan (Burma) founded*

1287 *Mongol attacks on Pagan and elsewhere defeated by Thai-Lao and Viet-Cham alliances*

1471 *Capture of Cham capital of Vijaya by Vietnamese*

1511 *Portuguese capture of Malacca*

FOLLOWING EARLIER TRENDS (*see* p. 46), from about the 3rd and 4th centuries AD there was an increasing adoption of Hindu and Buddhist cults among the local rulers of southeast Asia. They adopted Sanskrit titles and personal names, constructed numerous religious monuments and commissioned statuary modelled on Indian prototypes. In addition, Indian scripts and languages came to be used for political and religious texts. By the 6th century Buddhist images and votive inscriptions in Sanskrit had spread over continental southeast Asia, Sumatra and Java.

Early kingdoms

By the 6th century AD numerous kingdoms, whose locations are not always easy to identify, seem to have emerged. They were in frequent conflict with one another yet at the same time most maintained commercial and political relations with China, which welcomed tribute missions from the south.

An ancient port has been identified at Oc Eo (3rd–6th centuries AD), and from at least the 7th century Hindu temples were being built in lower Cambodia, notably at Angkor Borei, on the Dieng Plateau in central Java and in the valleys of central Vietnam. Buddhist shrines have been excavated at Beikthano and Sri Ksetra in central Burma and in Thailand (Siam) at U-Thong, Ku Bua and Nakhon Pathom. The best-studied temple complexes are those of Borobudur and Prambanan in central Java (8th–10th centuries); around Angkor in Cambodia (9th–13th centuries); at Pagan in Burma (11th–13th centuries); and the Cham Shivite temple towers of central Vietnam (7–13th centuries). All combined Hindu and Buddhist elements to varying degrees.

A centre of Buddhist culture developed from the 7th century at Sri Vijaya in southeast Sumatra, the capital of the maritime empire of Sri Vijaya, which for centuries controlled trade passing through the straits of Malacca and Sunda. However, by the 14th century Malacca, on the west coast of Malaya, had replaced Sri Vijaya as the dominant regional power.

Decline of the temple states

The Salendra kingdom, centred on the temple complexes at Prambanan, was devastated by volcanic ash falls in the early 10th century, and was replaced by a succession of smaller states and, eventually, the Majapahit empire. On the mainland, Pagan was sacked by Mongol invaders in the late 13th century. The Khmer rulers, under pressure from the Thai kingdom of Sukhothai from the 14th century, abandoned Angkor for the greater security of Phnom Penh.

Sukhothai was itself in decline by the late 14th century and the Thai political centre moved south to Ayutthaya while independent regional capitals were established at Chieng Mai in the northwest and Luang Prabang on the Mekong river. About the same time in Burma new political centres emerged at Ava on the upper Irrawaddy and at Toungoo on the Sittang, while Pegu became the capital of a new Mon kingdom in the south.

The rise of Vietnam

Northern Vietnam had been incorporated into the Chinese empire following the Han invasions of the 2nd century BC (*see* p. 80) but broke free at the end of the 10th century. Despite Chinese attempts at reconquest, a new Vietnamese kingdom emerged which gradually absorbed the Cham principalities to the south, annexing their last capital of Vijaya in 1471. However, with the advent of the Ming dynasty in China from the late 14th century Vietnam again fell within China's tributary system (*see* p. 166).

The political changes of the 14th and 15th centuries were accompanied by significant religious developments. While Theravada Buddhism spread through the mainland, Islam, which had a foothold at Atjeh in northern Sumatra before 1300, expanded through the archipelago as far as Mindanao in the Philippines. Rulers of the north Javanese trading ports and those of Ternate and Tidore converted to Islam, whose advance was only halted by the Portugese capture of Malacca in 1511 (*see* p. 176) and the Spanish setttlement in the Philippines from the 1560s.

2 Before the arrival of the Portuguese and Spanish the 15th century there were many conflicts between the major polities and religions of the region *(map below)*. Hindu cultures were yielding to Islam in Indonesia, the sinicized Dai-Viet rulers were absorbing the remaining Cham kingdoms while Ayutthaya, having driven the Khmer from Angkor, struggled for supremacy with the Burmese to the west.

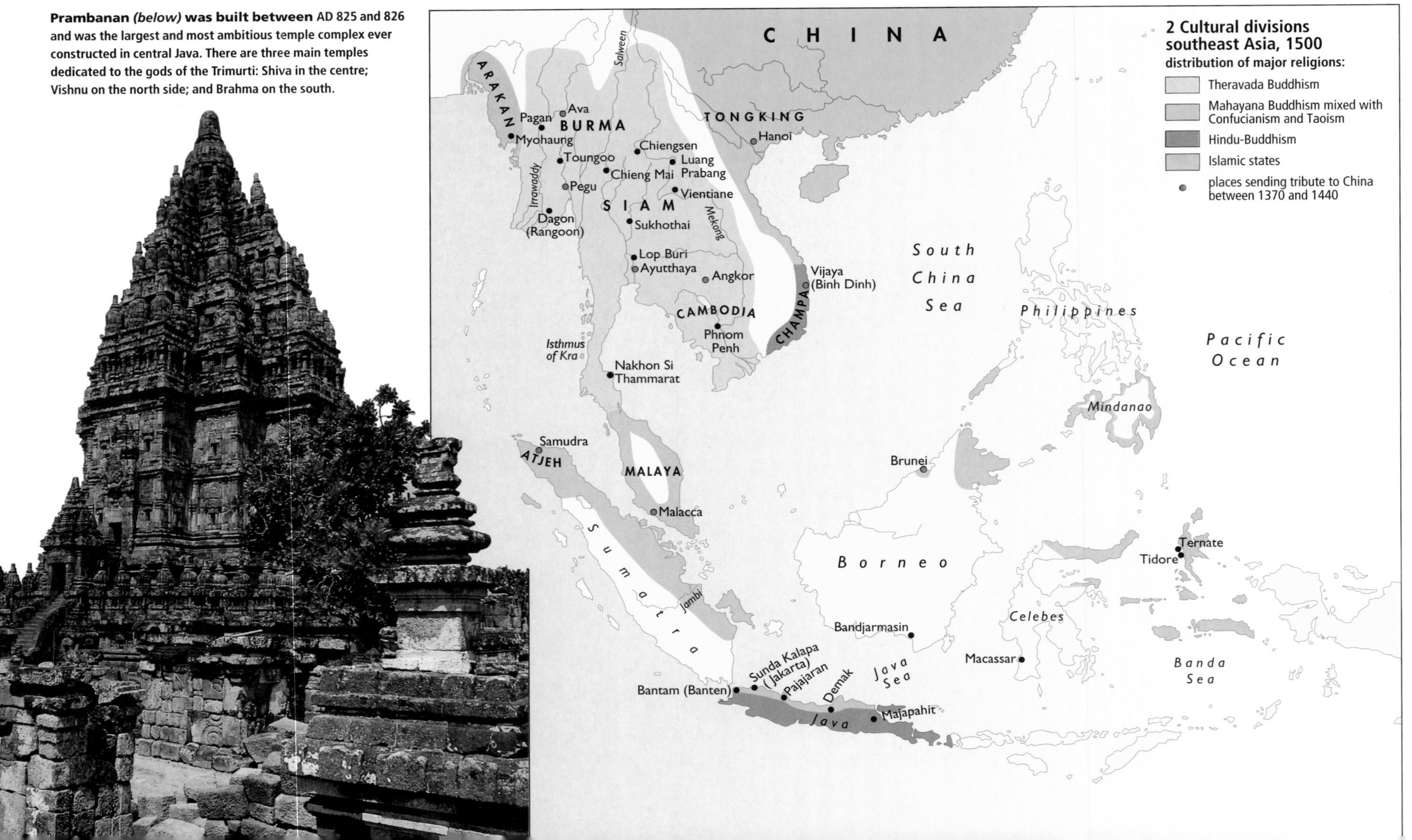

Prambanan *(below)* was built between AD 825 and 826 and was the largest and most ambitious temple complex ever constructed in central Java. There are three main temples dedicated to the gods of the Trimurti: Shiva in the centre; Vishnu on the north side; and Brahma on the south.

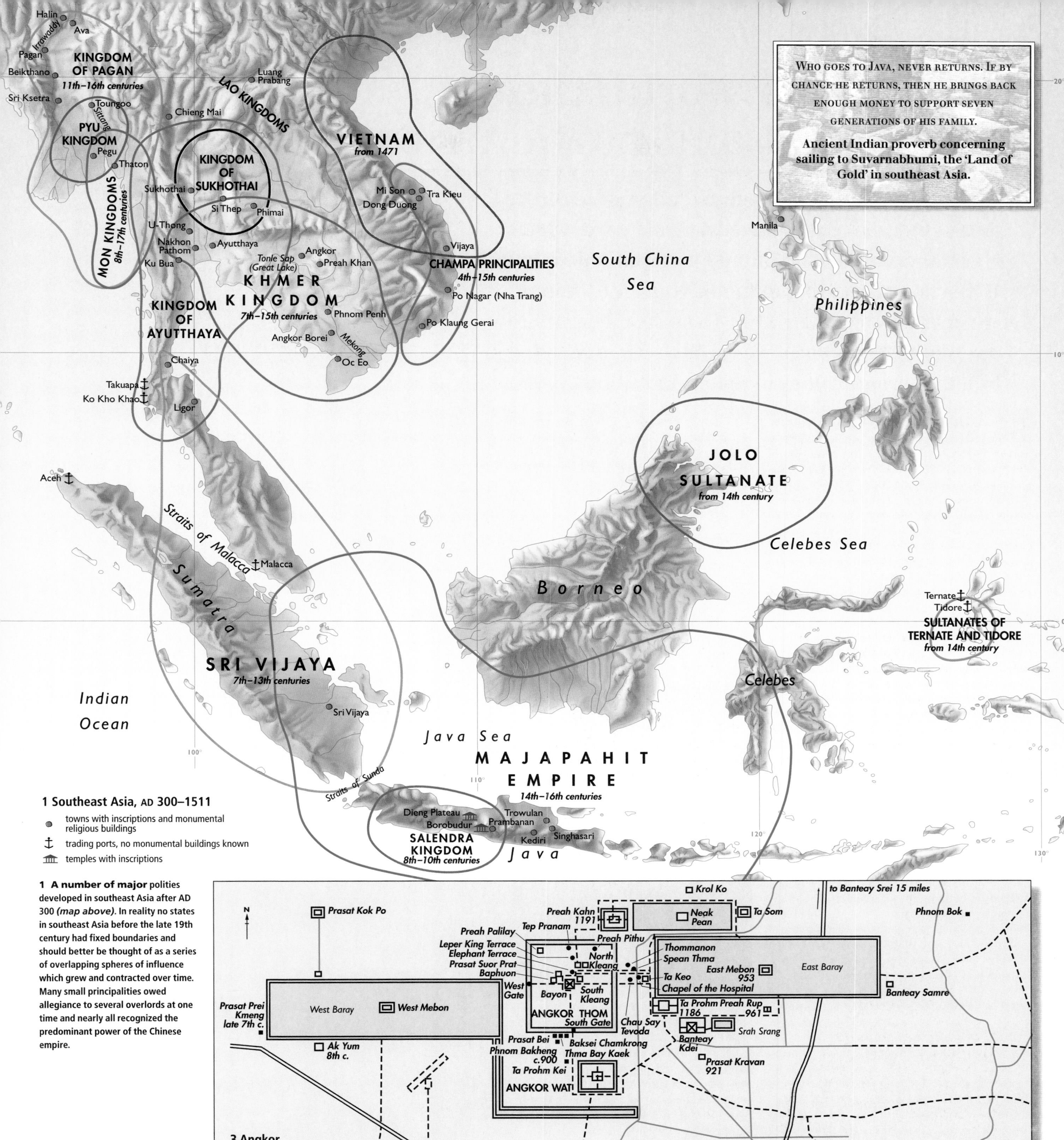

WHO GOES TO JAVA, NEVER RETURNS. IF BY CHANCE HE RETURNS, THEN HE BRINGS BACK ENOUGH MONEY TO SUPPORT SEVEN GENERATIONS OF HIS FAMILY.

Ancient Indian proverb concerning sailing to Suvarnabhumi, the 'Land of Gold' in southeast Asia.

1 A number of major polities developed in southeast Asia after AD 300 *(map above)*. In reality no states in southeast Asia before the late 19th century had fixed boundaries and should better be thought of as a series of overlapping spheres of influence which grew and contracted over time. Many small principalities owed allegiance to several overlords at one time and nearly all recognized the predominant power of the Chinese empire.

3 The region immediately north of the Great Lake of Cambodia witnessed the construction of the greatest complex of monumental religious buildings of the ancient world *(plan right)*. Angkor Wat is the best preserved but far from the largest of these temples. All were planned according to rigid geometric alignments and served by huge reservoirs whose function is still debated.

800 to 1350

The Muslim world: the Middle East and north Africa

See also
The spread of Islam from 632 p. 98
Crusading in Europe from the 11th to the 15th century p. 110
The Byzantine empire, 610–1453 p. 112
The Mongol empire, 1206–1405 p. 128
Islam and Christianity at the end of the 15th century p. 138
The emergence of states in Africa, 1000–1500 p. 140

The Muslim world disintegrated after 900, as rival states emerged and unified Arab rule gave way to Berbers and Turks, who founded substantial empires in north Africa and the Middle East. A Christian counter-attack began by 1100. Even so, the prosperity of the Islamic economies was reflected in magnificent building programmes in Spain, Egypt and Syria.

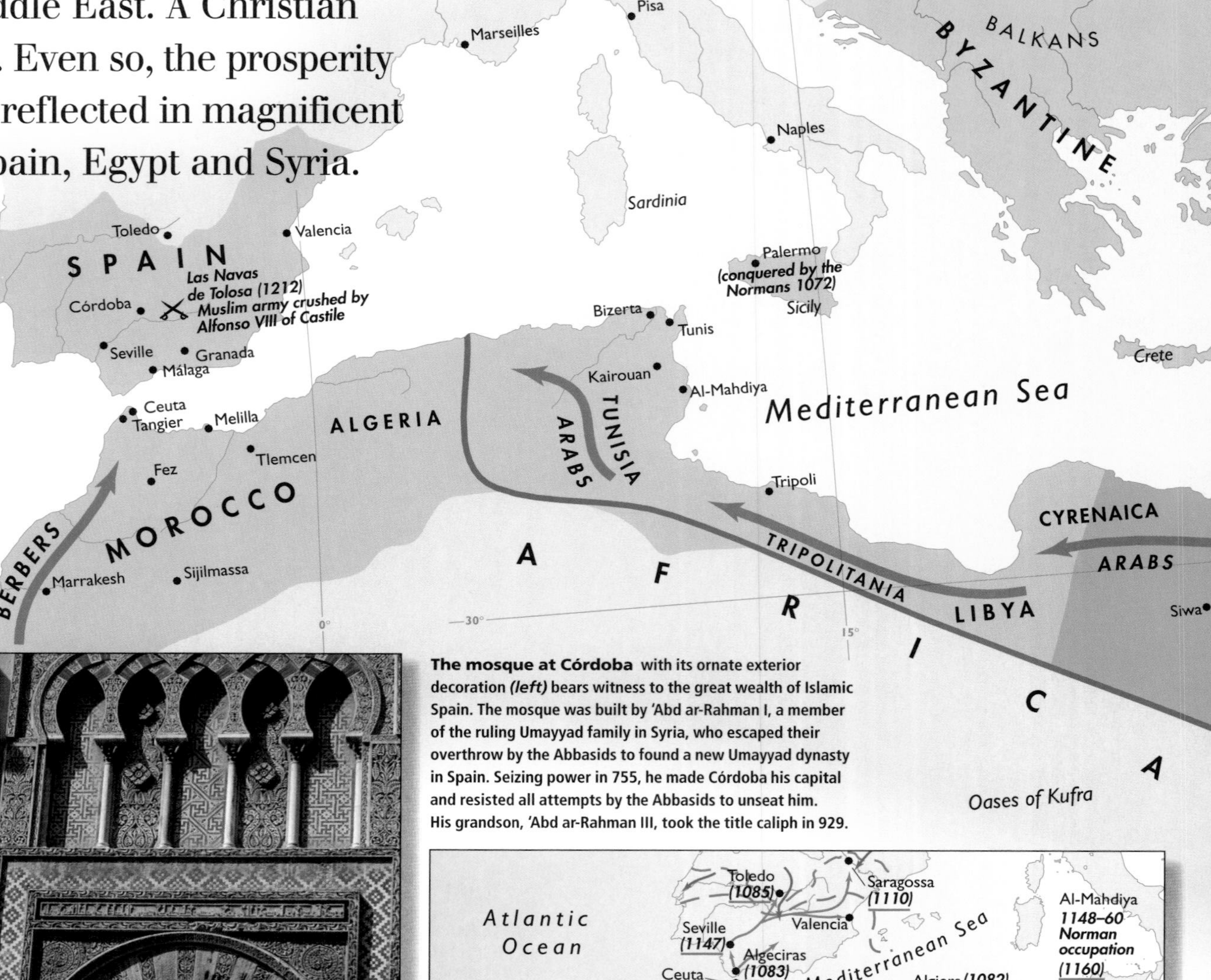

The mosque at Córdoba with its ornate exterior decoration *(left)* bears witness to the great wealth of Islamic Spain. The mosque was built by 'Abd ar-Rahman I, a member of the ruling Umayyad family in Syria, who escaped their overthrow by the Abbasids to found a new Umayyad dynasty in Spain. Seizing power in 755, he made Córdoba his capital and resisted all attempts by the Abbasids to unseat him. His grandson, 'Abd ar-Rahman III, took the title caliph in 929.

BY 900, THE MUSLIM WORLD had lost the fundamental unity of the original caliphate (*see* p. 98). The Abbasid caliphs were challenged in every corner, and ibn Tulun's creation of an independent regime in Egypt in the late 9th century foreshadowed the appearance of rival caliphates in Spain, north Africa and Iraq during the 10th century. Yet despite political fragmentation, this was a period of flourishing trade that generally ignored political boundaries and created a common market from the Atlantic to Persia.

The Shi'a posed a particularly serious threat to mainstream Islam. They challenged Sunni claims to caliphal authority, believing that Mohammed's authority passed to their imams through his son-in-law Ali. Shi'a Islam tended to adopt more radical views of Islamic law and appealed to disaffected groups, as reflected in the rise of the Fatimids. They set up a rival caliphate first in Tunisia and then in Cairo, which had fallen to the Fatimids in 969; their rule in Egypt lasted 200 years, and was marked by great artistic achievements. The Fatimid threat to the Mediterranean and to Morocco inspired the Umayyad rulers of Spain to reclaim in 929 the caliphal title their ancestors had held in the 7th century. A struggle for control of the Mediterranean began between Fatimids, Umayyads and Byzantines.

Islamic Spain and Morocco

Islamic Spain was a wealthy society in which Muslims were beginning to outnumber Christians by 950, and in which Islamic and Jewish culture flourished. Córdoba above all was a great centre of poetry and the fine arts. By the early 11th century, however, factional struggles led to the break up of the caliphate of Córdoba, whose last caliph abdicated in 1031. Spain was divided among dozens of *taifas* or 'petty kings'; among the most powerful were the rulers of Seville, Granada and Saragossa.

In Morocco, Islamization was much slower than it had been in Spain, and it was only in the 11th and 12th centuries that religious and political unity was achieved, promoted by two radical Berber religious reform movements: the Almoravids and the still more radical Almohads; they also conquered southern Spain and extinguished the last vestiges of Christianity in north Africa.

This was the age of non-Arab Muslim peoples. The Turks established themselves in the highlands of Anatolia, pressing on to Syria and Iraq and threatening Byzantine Asia Minor. Religious zealots enthusiastic for the struggle against the unbeliever were attracted to the Turkish frontier. Their expansion was also aided by the emergence of a well-organized military regime in eastern Anatolia, the Seljuk sultanate of Rum, which survived until the Mongol conquests of the 13th century.

The Christian counter-attack began in Spain, Sicily and Syria in the late 11th and early 12th centuries, for the first time leaving significant numbers of Muslims under Christian rule (in Valencia until 1525); of the Muslim states only the small kingdom of Granada retained an independent existence until 1492. Christian attempts to extend the reconquest of Spain to north Africa were less successful; in the 13th century the Marinids in Morocco and the Hafsids in Tunisia established long-lasting states which drew wealth from the trade of Catalan and Italian merchants. However, Ceuta fell to the Portuguese in 1415 and Melilla to Castile in 1497.

The rise of Egyptian power

Christian rule in Syria, established through the Crusades (*see* p. 110), was always more fragile than in Spain or Sicily, and collapsed in 1291 with the conquest of Acre by the Mamluk sultans of Egypt, soldiers of slave origin who had gained power in 1250 and whose independent rule lasted until the Ottoman conquest in 1517. Well before the sack of Baghdad by the Mongols (1258) the centre of gravity of the Islamic world, politically and economically, had shifted to Egypt; Alexandria was the transit point for vast quantities of spices transhipped from the Far East to western Europe, and the revenues from this trade enriched the Mamluk sultans. By 1200 Italian merchants in the Mediterranean and Muslim ones in the Red Sea dominated these exchanges. In the east, Persia became economically more important than Iraq.

The late 14th and 15th centuries saw a further shift as the Ottoman Turks became the leaders of Islamic expansion, eyeing not merely the former Byzantine empire and the Balkans but Syria and Egypt. Economic decline had already set in in the Arab lands of the Middle East, and the golden age of Islamic prosperity and culture drew to an end.

2 The Almoravids and Almohads, c. 1050–c. 1269

The Almoravids (1056–1147)
- Almoravid homeland
- route of Almoravid advance
- *(1055)* town captured by Almoravids (with date)
- limit of Almoravid territory in 1115

The Almohads (1140–1269)
- route of Almohad advance
- *(1146)* town captured by Almohads (with date)
- frontier of Almohad empire, c.1160–1200
- Christian attacks against Almohads
- area occupied by Normans (with date)

Atlantic Ocean; Mediterranean Sea; Toledo (1085); Saragossa (1110); Valencia; Seville (1147); Algeciras (1083); Ceuta (1083); Al-Mahdiya 1148–60 Norman occupation (1160); Algiers (1082); Bougie (1151); Rabat; Fez (1069) (1146); Oran (1151); Tinmallal (1130); Marrakesh (1146); Sfax (1148–60); Djerba (1135–60); Taroudant (1056); Sijilmassa (1055); Tripoli (1146–58); Walata (1076); Timbuktu (1100); Gao

2 The Berbers of North Africa submitted to Islam at the end of the 7th century; but its real penetration among them was slight. In the mid-11th century a radical renewal movement, the Almoravids, imposed strict Sunni Muslim observance on the nomadic tribes of the northwestern Sahara. From a newly founded capital at Marrakesh, the Almoravids seized much of Spain and large areas south of Morocco *(map above)*, until they were overthrown in turn in the 12th century by the even more radical Almohads.

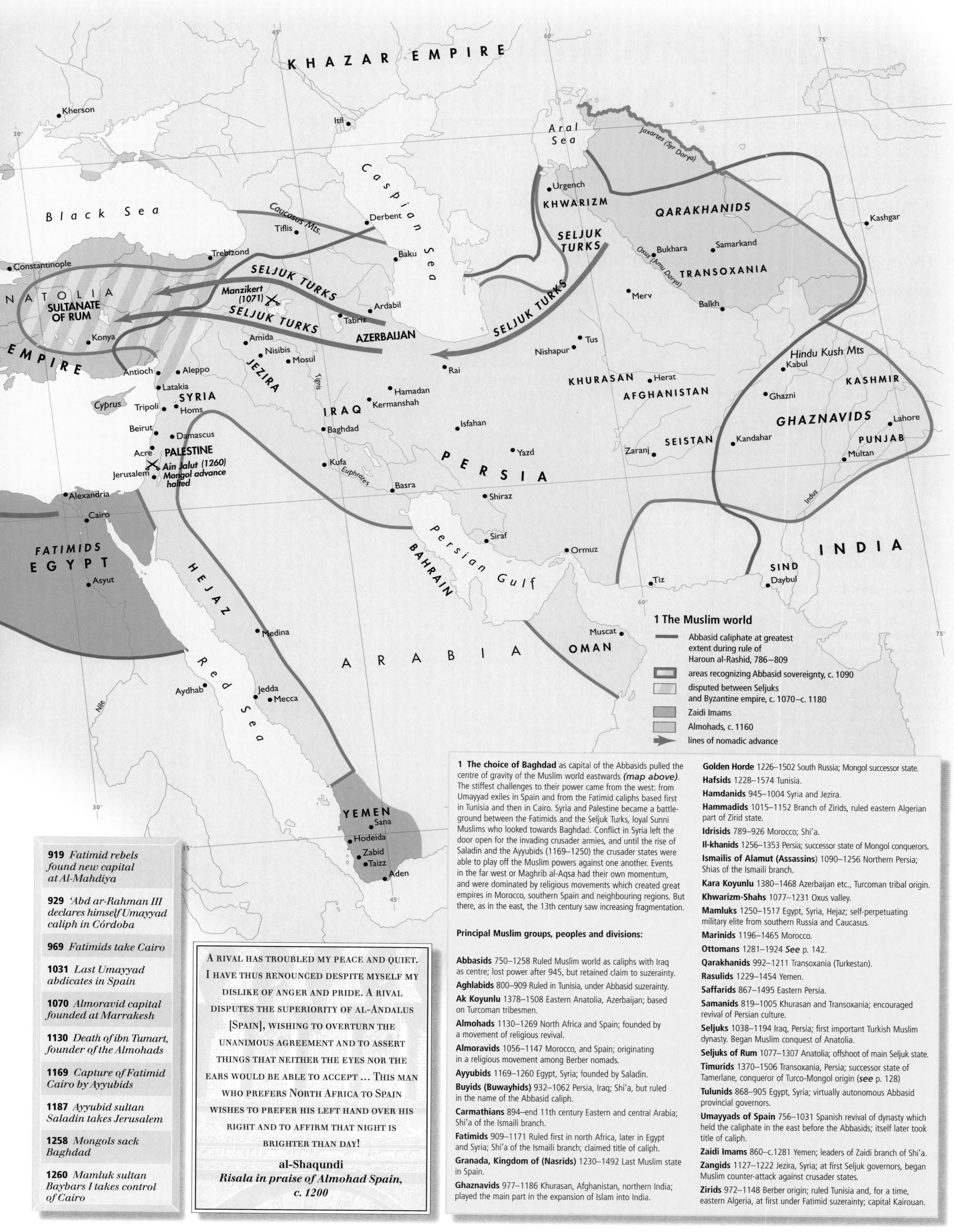

919 *Fatimid rebels found new capital at Al-Mahdiya*

929 *'Abd ar-Rahman III declares himself Umayyad caliph in Córdoba*

969 *Fatimids take Cairo*

1031 *Last Umayyad abdicates in Spain*

1070 *Almoravid capital founded at Marrakesh*

1130 *Death of ibn Tumart, founder of the Almohads*

1169 *Capture of Fatimid Cairo by Ayyubids*

1187 *Ayyubid sultan Saladin takes Jerusalem*

1258 *Mongols sack Baghdad*

1260 *Mamluk sultan Baybars I takes control of Cairo*

A RIVAL HAS TROUBLED MY PEACE AND QUIET. I HAVE THUS RENOUNCED DESPITE MYSELF MY DISLIKE OF ANGER AND PRIDE. A RIVAL DISPUTES THE SUPERIORITY OF AL-ANDALUS [SPAIN], WISHING TO OVERTURN THE UNANIMOUS AGREEMENT AND TO ASSERT THINGS THAT NEITHER THE EYES NOR THE EARS WOULD BE ABLE TO ACCEPT ... THIS MAN WHO PREFERS NORTH AFRICA TO SPAIN WISHES TO PREFER HIS LEFT HAND OVER HIS RIGHT AND TO AFFIRM THAT NIGHT IS BRIGHTER THAN DAY!

al-Shaqundi
Risala in praise of Almohad Spain, c. 1200

1 The choice of Baghdad as capital of the Abbasids pulled the centre of gravity of the Muslim world eastwards ***(map above)***. The stiffest challenges to their power came from the west: from Umayyad exiles in Spain and from the Fatimid caliphs based first in Tunisia and then in Cairo. Syria and Palestine became a battle-ground between the Fatimids and the Seljuk Turks, loyal Sunni Muslims who looked towards Baghdad. Conflict in Syria left the door open for the invading crusader armies, and until the rise of Saladin and the Ayyubids (1169–1250) the crusader states were able to play off the Muslim powers against one another. Events in the far west or Maghrib al-Aqsa had their own momentum, and were dominated by religious movements which created great empires in Morocco, southern Spain and neighbouring regions. But there, as in the east, the 13th century saw increasing fragmentation.

Principal Muslim groups, peoples and divisions:

Abbasids 750–1258 Ruled Muslim world as caliphs with Iraq as centre; lost power after 945, but retained claim to suzerainty.
Aghlabids 800–909 Ruled in Tunisia, under Abbasid suzerainty.
Ak Koyunlu 1378–1508 Eastern Anatolia, Azerbaijan; based on Turcoman tribesmen.
Almohads 1130–1269 North Africa and Spain; founded by a movement of religious revival.
Almoravids 1056–1147 Morocco, and Spain; originating in a religious movement among Berber nomads.
Ayyubids 1169–1260 Egypt, Syria; founded by Saladin.
Buyids (Buwayhids) 932–1062 Persia, Iraq; Shi'a, but ruled in the name of the Abbasid caliph.
Carmathians 894–end 11th century Eastern and central Arabia; Shi'a of the Ismaili branch.
Fatimids 909–1171 Ruled first in north Africa, later in Egypt and Syria; Shi'a of the Ismaili branch; claimed title of caliph.
Granada, Kingdom of (Nasrids) 1230–1492 Last Muslim state in Spain.
Ghaznavids 977–1186 Khurasan, Afghanistan, northern India; played the main part in the expansion of Islam into India.
Golden Horde 1226–1502 South Russia; Mongol successor state.
Hafsids 1228–1574 Tunisia.
Hamdanids 945–1004 Syria and Jezira.
Hammadids 1015–1152 Branch of Zirids, ruled eastern Algerian part of Zirid state.
Idrisids 789–926 Morocco; Shi'a.
Il-khanids 1256–1353 Persia; successor state of Mongol conquerors.
Ismailis of Alamut (Assassins) 1090–1256 Northern Persia; Shias of the Ismaili branch.
Kara Koyunlu 1380–1468 Azerbaijan etc., Turcoman tribal origin.
Khwarizm-Shahs 1077–1231 Oxus valley.
Mamluks 1250–1517 Egypt, Syria, Hejaz; self-perpetuating military elite from southern Russia and Caucasus.
Marinids 1196–1465 Morocco.
Ottomans 1281–1924 ***See*** p. 142.
Qarakhanids 992–1211 Transoxania (Turkestan).
Rasulids 1229–1454 Yemen.
Saffarids 867–1495 Eastern Persia.
Samanids 819–1005 Khurasan and Transoxania; encouraged revival of Persian culture.
Seljuks 1038–1194 Iraq, Persia; first important Turkish Muslim dynasty. Began Muslim conquest of Anatolia.
Seljuks of Rum 1077–1307 Anatolia; offshoot of main Seljuk state.
Timurids 1370–1506 Transoxania, Persia; successor state of Tamerlane, conqueror of Turco-Mongol origin (***see*** p. 128)
Tulunids 868–905 Egypt, Syria; virtually autonomous Abbasid provincial governors.
Umayyads of Spain 756–1031 Spanish revival of dynasty which held the caliphate in the east before the Abbasids; itself later took title of caliph.
Zaidi Imams 860–c.1281 Yemen; leaders of Zaidi branch of Shi'a.
Zangids 1127–1222 Jezira, Syria; at first Seljuk governors, began Muslim counter-attack against crusader states.
Zirids 972–1148 Berber origin; ruled Tunisia and, for a time, eastern Algeria, at first under Fatimid suzerainty; capital Kairouan.

Islam and Christianity at the end of the 15th century

See also
Crusading in Europe from the 11th to the 15th century p. 110
The Muslim world:
The Middle East and north Africa, 800–1350 p. 136
The emergence of states in Africa, 1000–1500 p. 140
The rise of the Ottoman empire, 1281–1522 p. 142
The Early Modern Muslim empires, 1520–1700 p. 168

The balance of power between the Islamic world and western Europe shifted decisively in the 15th century. While the Ottoman Turks became a major power in the Balkans, the Mediterranean Arab states found themselves politically and economically enfeebled. Europeans, meanwhile, sought to by-pass the Muslim world to gain access to the spices of the Far East.

1415 *Fall of Ceuta to Portuguese*

1424–6 *Mamluk expeditions against Cyprus*

1492 *Fall of Granada to Ferdinand and Isabella*

1496 *Alonso de Lugo gains control of Tenerife*

1497–8 *Vasco da Gama opens sea route around Africa to India*

1497 *Fall of Melilla to Ferdinand and Isabella*

1510 *Fall of Tripoli to Ferdinand the Catholic*

1516–17 *Ottoman conquest of Syria and Egypt*

1525 *Practice of Islam banned in Aragon*

1565 *Siege of Malta*

THE ENTHRONEMENT OF KANSUH AL-GHURI AS SULTAN COULD BE LEGALIZED BY THE CALIPH ONCE THE RELIGIOUS JUDGES HAD ARRIVED. THEY BROUGHT THE NEW SULTAN THE EMBLEMS OF SOVEREIGNTY, THE BLACK CLOAK AND TURBAN IN WHICH THEY NOW ARRAYED HIM ... THE WHOLE OF CAIRO WAS LIT UP LIKE A HALO ... THE NEW SULTAN WAS AT THIS TIME ABOUT SIXTY. HIS BEARD SHOWED NOT ONE WHITE HAIR. THIS WAS CONSIDERED AN AUSPICIOUS OMEN.

Enthronement of the 46th Mamluk sultan, 1501

BY THE END OF THE 15TH CENTURY the pressure of western invaders on the Muslims of Spain and the Maghreb was reaching its peak. The fall of Granada in 1492 meant the end of Islamic rule within Spain, and it foreshadowed the suppression of Muslim observance in the whole of Spain (Castile, 1502; Aragon, 1525). The war against Islam could now be carried over the Straits of Gibraltar, where the Portuguese had already taken Ceuta in 1415. Spanish navies captured Melilla in 1497 and pushed relentlessly eastwards, as far as Tripoli (1510). The need to establish Spanish *presidios* or garrisons on the African coast was enhanced by the emerging threat of the Barbary pirates to Catalan merchants trading towards north Africa.

Trade, exploration and empire

The dream of encircling Islam had economic dimensions. Shortages of gold in Europe stimulated attempts at penetration of the gold-rich empire of Songhay. The traditional camel caravans that navigated across the desert bound for the ports of the north African coast also kept the Islamic economies supplied with gold. The idea of diverting gold away from the heartlands of Islam towards western Europe had fascinated crusade theorists since Marino Sanudo of Venice (early 14th century). The Genoese merchant Malfante is said to have reached Tuat in 1477. More promising was a sea route that would carry Italian or Catalan ships down to the entrance of the supposed River of Gold, in search of which Jaume Ferrer of Majorca set out in 1346. Throughout the late 14th century, trading expeditions regularly penetrated as far as the Canary Islands, and schemes were hatched for a great pincer attack on the Muslims of north Africa via the Canaries and the western Mediterranean islands. In the event, the conquest of the Canaries was definitively achieved only at the end of the 15th century, when a Neolithic population ignorant of metals, weaving and – surprisingly – navigation was overwhelmed by ruthless *conquistadores* such as Alonso de Lugo acting in the name of Castile. The process of colonization that took place in the 1490s bears comparison with the Caribbean after 1492. Those navigating the African coasts also found their way, thanks to the winds, to the empty islands of Madeira and the Azores. The former became a major source of sugar cane after the 1420s, reducing dependence on Islamic sources.

Muslim north Africa

The Muslim states of north Africa underwent fatal weakening in the late 15th century. The Marinids

A Hispano-Moresque plate dating from the end of the 14th century *(left)* bears witness to the the rich material culture of Islamic Spain or al-Andalus. Yet by the mid-13th century the Islamic kingdom had dwindled to a small territory in south-east Spain. Riven by civil wars and unable to rely on the Berber principalities of north Africa, it was politically impotent. Between 1482 and 1492 Ferdinand of Aragon and Isabella of Castile conquered it. In 1492 they captured the capital of Granada itself, putting an end to nearly 800 years of Muslim rule in Spain.

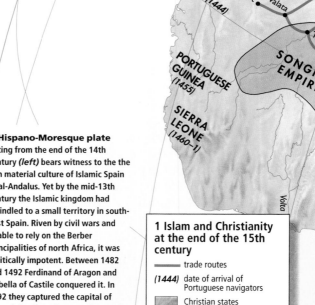

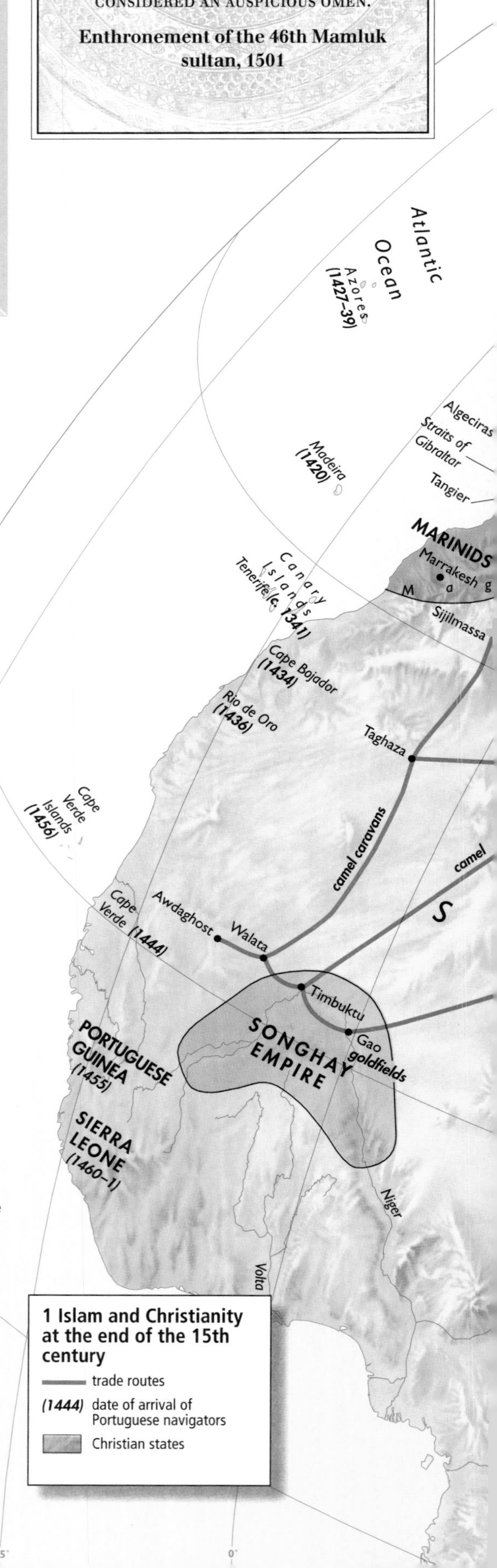

1 Islam and Christianity at the end of the 15th century

trade routes

(1444) date of arrival of Portuguese navigators

Christian states

in Morocco had reached their apogee with the occupation of Tunis in 1347. Until the fall of Algeciras in 1344 they were able to give support to the beleaguered kingdom of Granada. But dynastic and religious strife led to further fragmentation, and the loss by the 1480s of almost everything apart from Fez; meanwhile the Portuguese had occupied many of the coastal towns of Atlantic Morocco, culminating in Tangier in 1471. In western Algeria, too, a highpoint was passed with the dethronement of Abu Hammu in 1389, and thereafter Tlemcen was generally a tributary of Fez, Tunis or later on of Aragon, with which it continued to enjoy very close trading relations. The Hafsids of Tunis, originally heirs to the rigorous Almohad tradition (*see* p. 136), in fact practised a tolerant outlook in the 15th century, and they were able to impose renewed unity on much of the Maghreb; but the successes that culminated in the reign of Uthman (1434–88) were followed by a period of anarchy; nothing was done to take advantage of growing hostility between the Spaniards and the Ottomans in the Mediterranean.

Mamluk Egypt

Little better was in store for the inhabitants of Egypt and Syria, under the increasingly corrupt rule of the Mamluk soldiers who had been in power since 1250. A caliph technically reigned in Cairo, but effective power was transferred from one sultan to another with bewildering speed and the fact that the Mamluks were descended from Circassian and other foreign slaves meant that the Egyptian population saw them as alien in culture. Living off the profits of the Venetian spice trade through Alexandria, the Mamluks squandered their wealth; they did little to promote economic welfare in a time of growing difficulties. Meanwhile, attempts by Spain (Columbus, 1492) and Portugal (Vasco da Gama, 1497–8) to find new routes to the Spice Islands threatened the monopoly of Alexandria as the distribution point for pepper and ginger bound for Europe. The Ottoman conquest of Egypt in 1517 further revealed the Mamluk failure to modernize their armies in the way that other Muslim rulers, whether in Turkey or Morocco, were managing to do. The Mamluks succumbed with barely a whimper. The Ottomans, both in north Africa and the Balkans were to prove much more effective opponents for the Christian powers.

1 By the end of the 15th century the balance of power between Christian states and Islam had shifted decisively in the western Mediterranean ***(map below)***. All hope of Islamic political unity was now lost. In Spain only the Nasrid kingdom of Granada survived as an independent Islamic polity, but this was conquered in 1492 by Ferdinand and Isabella. There was growing pressure from the Christian powers on the Islamic states in Africa: the Portuguese captured Ceuta in 1415; while the Spanish took Melilla in 1497 and Tripoli in 1510. At the same time Portuguese explorers moved down the African coast hoping to discover new routes to the east and thus bypass the land routes still controlled by Islamic powers. Only in the east did the growing power of the Ottoman empire provide a counter-challenge to the Christian powers.

The emergence of states in Africa

See also
African peoples and cultures to AD 1000 p. 42
The spread of Islam from AD 632 p. 98
The Muslim World: the Middle East and north Africa, 800 to 1350 p. 136
Islam and Christianity at the end of the 15th century p. 138
The rise of the Ottoman empire, 1281–1522 p. 142
European voyages of discovery p. 156

The period from 1000 to 1500 saw the emergence of states over much of Africa, crucially assisted by the need to control and secure trading routes and by the wealth which flowed from them. The spread of trade often went hand in hand with the dissemination of Islam. By 1500, sub-Saharan African states had made their first contacts with European explorers.

THE PERIOD FROM 1000 to 1500 saw two principal developments in Africa: the spread of Islam and the emergence of organized states throughout the continent. In many places these were linked. By 1000 the Maghreb (northwest Africa) had been in Islamic hands for over three centuries). Between 1000 and 1500 Islam spread south: up the Nile into the Christian kingdoms of Nubia; along the northern and eastern coasts of the Horn; and across the Sahara into the states of the 'Sudanic belt', stretching from the Senegal to the Nile. Muslim merchants crossed the Sahara with caravans of camels which regularly made the hazardous journey from trading depots on either edge of the desert, such as Sijilmassa, south of the Atlas Mountains, and Walata in Mali. This dangerous trade carried luxury goods (and, in time, firearms) and salt to the black African lands of the south. In exchange, leather-work, slaves and gold went northwards: by 1250 the economies of both the Muslim Middle East and Christian Europe depended to a great extent upon African gold.

The states of western Africa

Although the beginnings of urbanism in the Sudanic belt can be traced as far back as the last centuries BC, expanding trans-Saharan trade gave an impetus to the growth of states. Two of the earliest of these were Ghana and Mali. Ghana, an essentially African polity, which flourished from the 8th to the 11th centuries, was established in the area north of the Senegal and Niger rivers, far from the modern state which has taken its name. Its successor, Mali, extended from the Atlantic across the great bend of the Niger. In 1324 the Mali king Mansa Musa went on pilgrimage to Mecca, and is said to have taken so much gold with his retinue that he caused inflation in Cairo. The empire of Mali gave way to that of Songhay, centred on the Niger cities of Gao and Timbuktu. East of Mali lay the city states of Hausaland, some of which – Zaria, Kano, Katsina – became extremely prosperous, although they never united to form a single state. Further east was Kanem, founded by desert people to the east of Lake Chad. Their ruling dynasty, the Kanuri kings, retained authority until their final overthrow in the 19th century.

By the late Middle Ages, at a time of crisis in western Europe (*see* p. 144), the black kingdoms of the western and central Sudan flourished. A number of African kings, among them Mansa Musa and Sunni Ali (of Songhay), enjoyed renown throughout Islam and Christendom for their wealth, brilliance and the artistic achievements of their subjects. Their capitals were large walled cities with many mosques and at least two, Timbuktu and Jenne, had universities that attracted scholars and poets from far and wide. Their power derived from a mixture of military force and diplomatic alliances with local leaders; their prosperity was based on control of rich local resources; their bureaucracies administered taxation and controlled trade, the life-blood of these empires.

To the south of the Sudanic states, Hausa and Malinke merchants traded among the peoples on the edge of the tropical forests, especially in the gold-producing regions. The prosperity this trade brought led, by 1500, to the foundation of many forest states, such as Benin. Around this time, also, the first contacts occurred with Portuguese sailors exploring the west African sea lanes.

The states of east and central Africa

In the east, after the decline of Aksum (*see* p. 42), the centre of political power in Christian Ethiopia shifted southwards, first under the Kushitic-speaking Zagwe dynasty in the 11th century and then, in the 13th century, under the Amharic-speaking Solomonids who later clashed with the Muslim coastal states of the Horn of Africa, notably Adal.

Along the east coast there arose a string of Muslim city states. Kilwa Kisiwani, with its handsome mosques and palaces, prospered as the entrepôt for the gold of Zimbabwe, brought via Sofala. The arrival of the Portuguese there in 1498 marked the beginning of European encroachment in this lucrative system of oceanic trade.

Meanwhile, in the interior of the southern half of the continent, many other African peoples coalesced to form states. These processes are best known in two regions: the upper Lualaba where wealth was accumulated in the form of metal, and south of the Zambezi where, from the 10th century, prosperous cattle-herders gave rise to the polity that was centred at Great Zimbabwe. Other states, many of them Bantu-speaking, emerged in the region south of the lower Congo river, and in the area between the great lakes of east Africa.

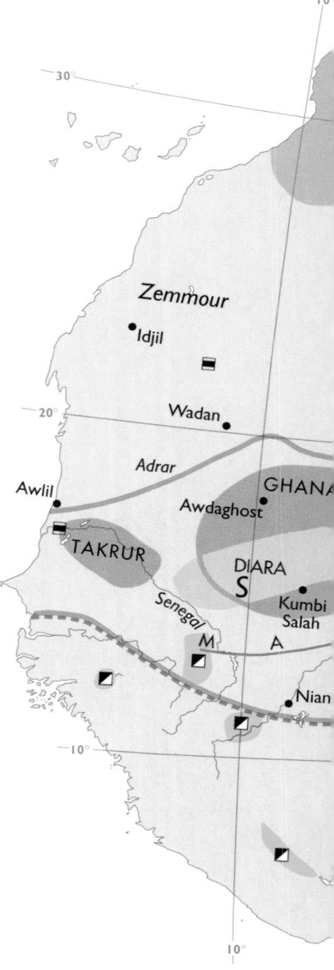

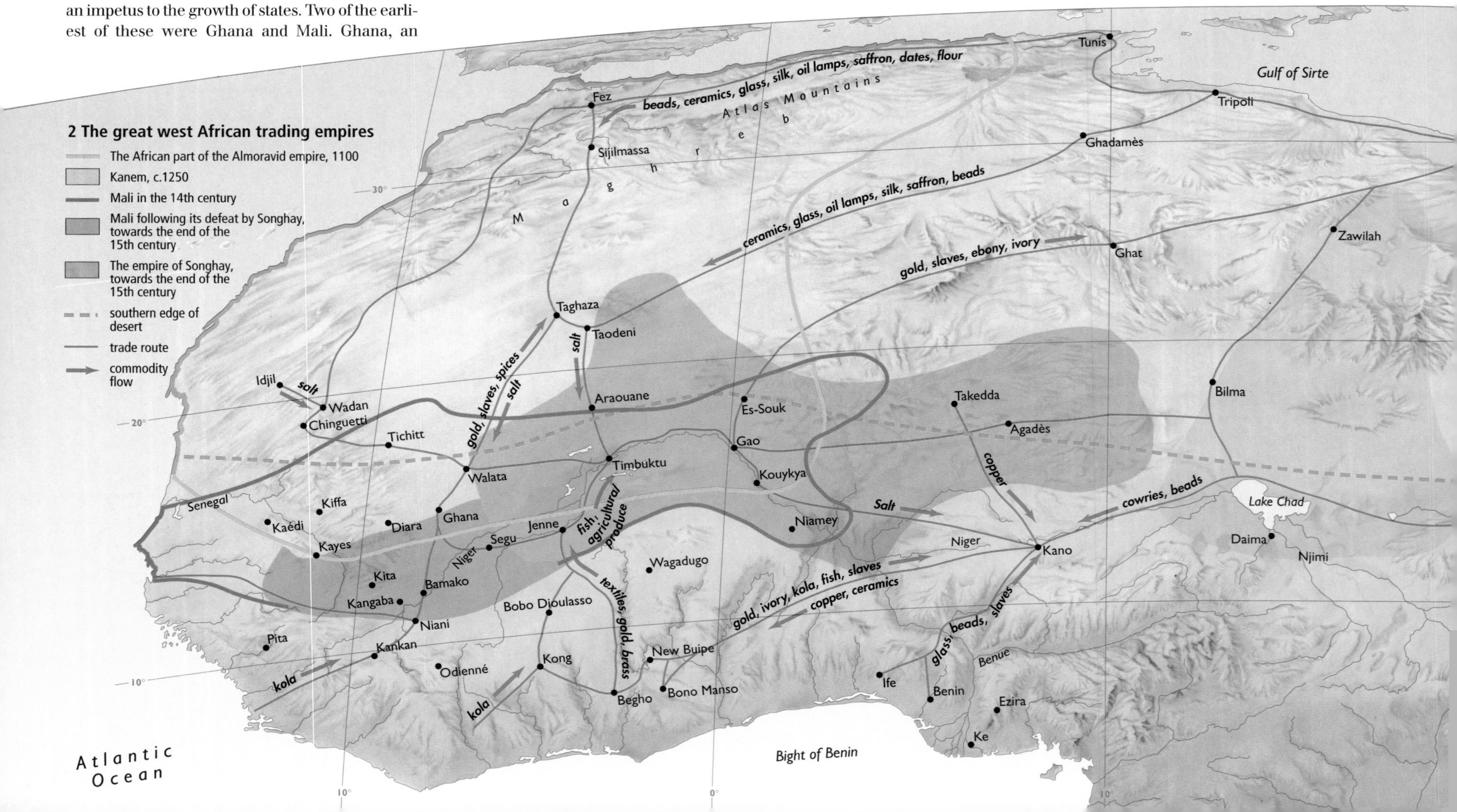

2 The great west African trading empires

- The African part of the Almoravid empire, 1100
- Kanem, c.1250
- Mali in the 14th century
- Mali following its defeat by Songhay, towards the end of the 15th century
- The empire of Songhay, towards the end of the 15th century
- southern edge of desert
- trade route
- commodity flow

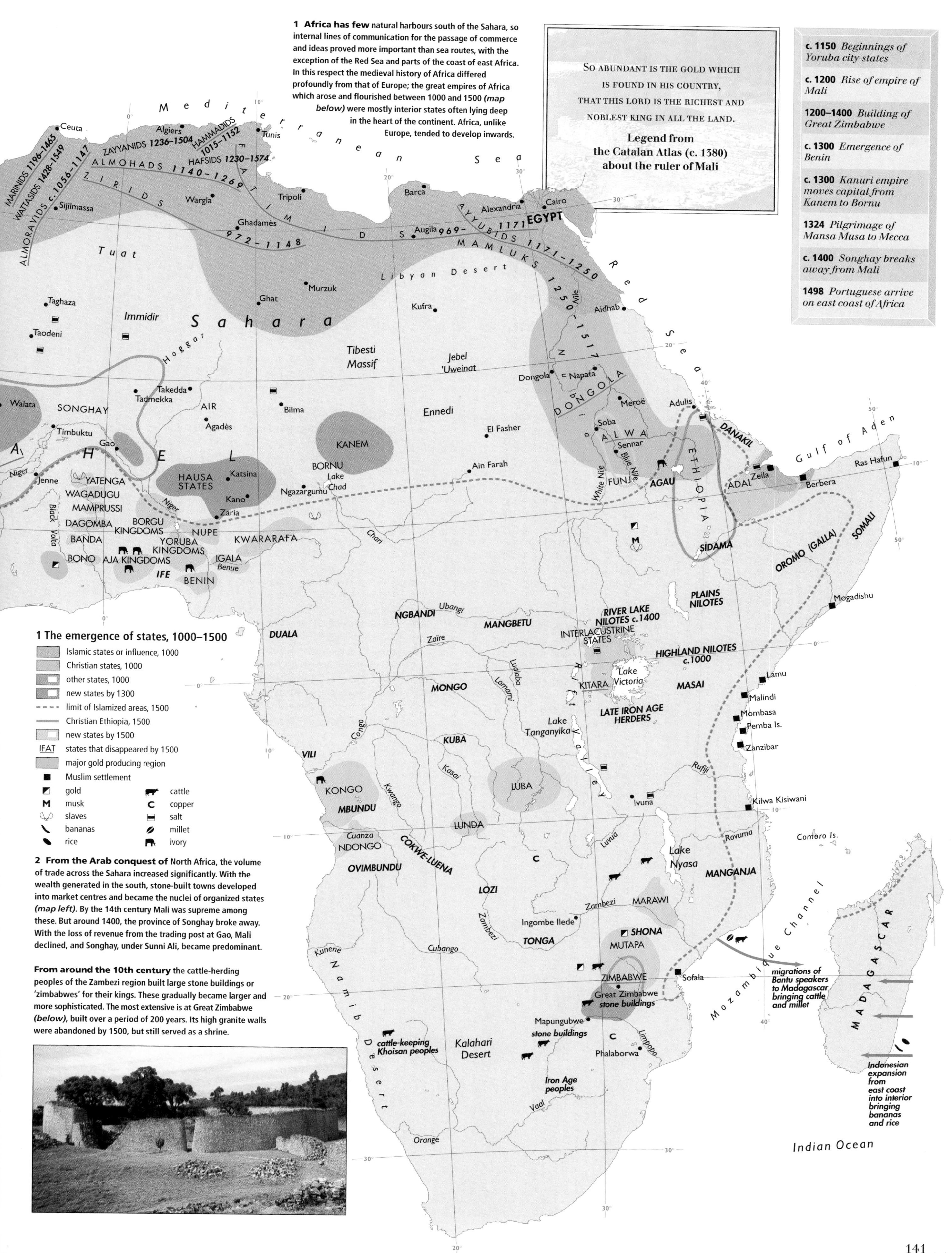

1 Africa has few natural harbours south of the Sahara, so internal lines of communication for the passage of commerce and ideas proved more important than sea routes, with the exception of the Red Sea and parts of the coast of east Africa. In this respect the medieval history of Africa differed profoundly from that of Europe; the great empires of Africa which arose and flourished between 1000 and 1500 *(map below)* were mostly interior states often lying deep in the heart of the continent. Africa, unlike Europe, tended to develop inwards.

2 From the Arab conquest of North Africa, the volume of trade across the Sahara increased significantly. With the wealth generated in the south, stone-built towns developed into market centres and became the nuclei of organized states *(map left)*. By the 14th century Mali was supreme among these. But around 1400, the province of Songhay broke away. With the loss of revenue from the trading post at Gao, Mali declined, and Songhay, under Sunni Ali, became predominant.

From around the 10th century the cattle-herding peoples of the Zambezi region built large stone buildings or 'zimbabwes' for their kings. These gradually became larger and more sophisticated. The most extensive is at Great Zimbabwe *(below)*, built over a period of 200 years. Its high granite walls were abandoned by 1500, but still served as a shrine.

1281 to 1522

The rise of the Ottoman empire

See also
The Mongol empire, 1206–1405 p. 128
The Muslim world: the Middle East and north Africa, 800–1350 p. 136
Islam and Christianity at the end of the 15th century p. 138
The Early Modern Muslim empires, 1520–1700 p. 168
The Mediterranean world, 1494–1797 p. 186

I AM GOD'S SLAVE AND SULTAN OF THIS WORLD. BY THE GRACE OF GOD I AM HEAD OF MOHAMMED'S COMMUNITY. GOD'S MIGHT AND MOHAMMED'S MIRACLES ARE MY COMPANIONS. I AM CALIPH IN MECCA AND MEDINA. IN BAGHDAD I AM THE SHAH, IN BYZANTINE REALMS THE CAESAR, AND IN EGYPT THE SULTAN; WHO SENDS HIS FLEETS TO THE SEAS OF EUROPE, NORTH AFRICA AND INDIA. I AM THE SULTAN WHO TOOK THE CROWN AND THRONE OF HUNGARY AND GRANTED THEM TO A HUMBLE SLAVE ...

Inscription celebrating Suleiman the Magnificent (1520–66)

Originally a petty principality in western Anatolia, from the late 13th century the Ottoman state was transformed into an astonishingly dynamic imperial and military power. By 1522, it had expanded to embrace the Balkans, the Black Sea and the Middle East and had become a major player in the international power politics of the day.

THE RETREAT OF THE Mongols from Anatolia into Iran in the 13th century created a vacuum in Anatolia which a series of rival Turcoman states fought to fill. Among them was a small polity based on Söğüt. With the accession in 1281 of Osman, after whom the Ottoman dynasty came to be called, it began a period of rapid expansion. By 1354 it had gained its first foothold in Europe with the acquisition of Gallipoli. By 1361 the Ottomans had taken Edirne (Adrianople), which they made their capital. The decisive defeat of the Serbians and Bosnians at Kosovo in 1389 then established Ottoman supremacy in the Balkans. By 1393, Bulgaria had been absorbed as had most of the remaining independent emirates of Anatolia. Ottoman rule stretched from the Danube to the Euphrates.

Defeat and reconstruction

Renewed Mongol incursions under Tamerlane saw the Ottomans' first serious setback. Though the Mongol advance ended with Tamerlane's death in 1405, their victory at Ankara in 1402 had provided the opportunity for the Balkan states and the Anatolian emirates to escape Ottoman hegemony. But reconstruction of the Ottoman state by Mehmed I (1413–21) and renewed campaigns by his son Murad II (1421–51) again brought most of eastern and central Anatolia and the southern and eastern Balkans under Ottoman control.

The emergence of the Ottoman state as a world power was the work of Mehmed II, Fatih, 'The Conqueror' (1451–81), whose conquest of Constantinople in 1453 made possible Ottoman expansion into northern Anatolia and their dominance of the Straits and southern Black Sea. The conquest of Serbia, Herzegovina and much of Bosnia now left Hungary as the major European power facing the Ottomans. Mehmed's failure to take Belgrade in 1456 established the Danube and lower Sava as the Ottoman boundary with Hungary for over 60 years.

With the final re-absorption of Karaman in 1468 the last of the independent Anatolian emirates disappeared. Farther north, Mehmed established a bridgehead in the Crimea by the capture of Kefe (Caffa) from the Genoese in 1475, bringing the Khanate of the Crimea under Ottoman control.

In Europe, the middle years of Mehmed's reign saw the ending of Byzantine and Frankish control over the Morea, and the erosion of Venetian and Genoese power in the Aegean and the Black Sea. Mehmed's death in 1481, which occurred soon after the Turks overwhelmed Otranto in southern Italy, put paid to his ambition to conquer Rome. The struggle for the succession between Bayezid II (1481–1512) and his brother, Jem, was then skilfully manipulated by the West, protecting it from further Ottoman incursions for many years. However, with the conquests of Akkerman and Kilia the land route from Constantinople to the Crimea was secured in 1484, while the Ottoman-Venetian war of 1499–1502 underlined the growing Ottoman naval power.

Expansion in the Middle East

The last years of Bayezid II's reign, and most of that of his successor Selim I (1512–20), were taken up with conquests in the Middle East. The rise of the Safavids in Iran after 1501 brought to power a state militarily strong and ideologically hostile to the Ottomans. Risings among the Turcoman tribes of eastern Anatolia in the last years of Bayezid II's reign were a prelude to the war which broke out in the reigns of Selim and Shah Isma'il (1501–24), culminating in the defeat of the Safavids at Çaldiran in 1514. Eastern Anatolia was secured and the threat of religious separatism removed.

Selim's annexation of the emirate of Dhu'l-Qadr in 1515 brought the Ottomans into direct contact with the Mamluk empire for the first time. Over the next two years Selim swept the Mamluks aside, conquering Aleppo and Damascus in 1516 and taking Cairo in 1517. As well as bringing Syria and Egypt under Ottoman control, his campaign added the holy places of Christendom and Islam to the empire. His successor, Suleiman the Magnificent was to continue Ottoman expansion (*see* p. 168).

2 On the eve of the Ottoman conquest, invasion and war between Latins, Byzantines, Muslims and Mongols had destroyed the last shred of the former Byzantine and Muslim empires in the Middle East *(map below)*. The Balkans and Anatolia, entirely fragmented by the early 14th century, were to become, under the Ottomans, the provinces of a single empire.

The siege of Rhodes in 1522 ***(below)*****,** depicting the elite of the Ottoman army storming the walls of the city, defended by knights of St John. The troops shown consisted of the janissaries, the infantry corps founded early in the Ottoman state's history, and the sipahis, the Muslim feudal cavalry. The janissaries were raised by the *Devshirme*, a compulsory levy of Christian boys begun late in the 14th century and which soon became a fundamental institution of the empire. Christian Europe saw them as the most formidable component of the Ottoman army.

1281 *Accession of Osman*

1354 *Ottomans capture Gallipoli and gain first foothold in Europe*

1361 *Edirne (Adrianople) taken; becomes new Ottoman capital*

1389 *Battle of Kosovo: Ottoman supremacy in the Balkans established*

1402 *Tamerlane destroys Ottoman army at Ankara*

1413–51 *Ottoman control of Balkans and Anatolia reinforced*

1453 *Constantinople falls to Mehmed II, Fatih*

1456 *Hungary defeats Ottoman army at Belgrade*

1516–7 *Ottomans overrun Syria, Egypt and Arabia*

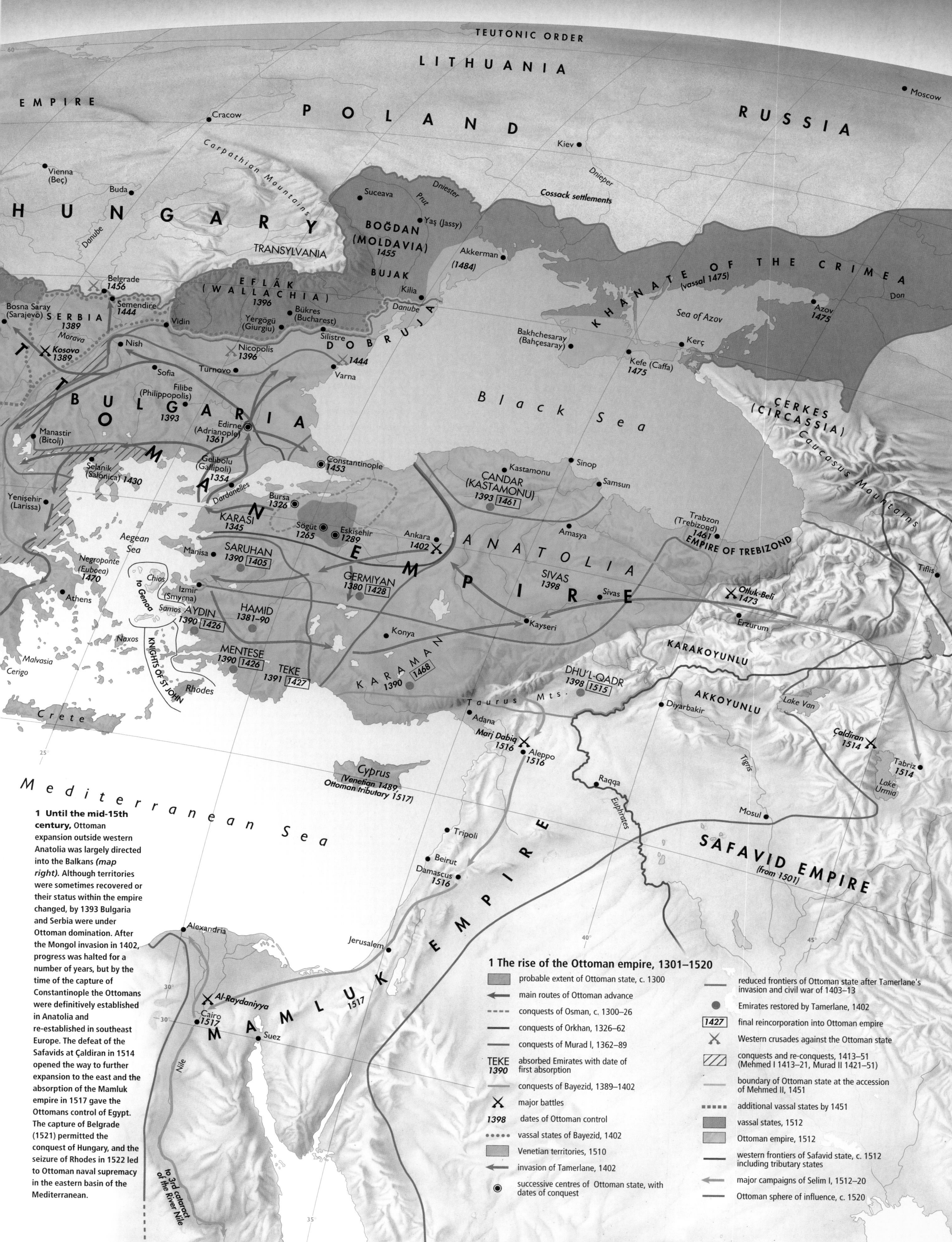

1 Until the mid-15th century, Ottoman expansion outside western Anatolia was largely directed into the Balkans *(map right)*. Although territories were sometimes recovered or their status within the empire changed, by 1393 Bulgaria and Serbia were under Ottoman domination. After the Mongol invasion in 1402, progress was halted for a number of years, but by the time of the capture of Constantinople the Ottomans were definitively established in Anatolia and re-established in southeast Europe. The defeat of the Safavids at Çaldiran in 1514 opened the way to further expansion to the east and the absorption of the Mamluk empire in 1517 gave the Ottomans control of Egypt. The capture of Belgrade (1521) permitted the conquest of Hungary, and the seizure of Rhodes in 1522 led to Ottoman naval supremacy in the eastern basin of the Mediterranean.

1252 to 1381

The crisis of the 14th century in Europe

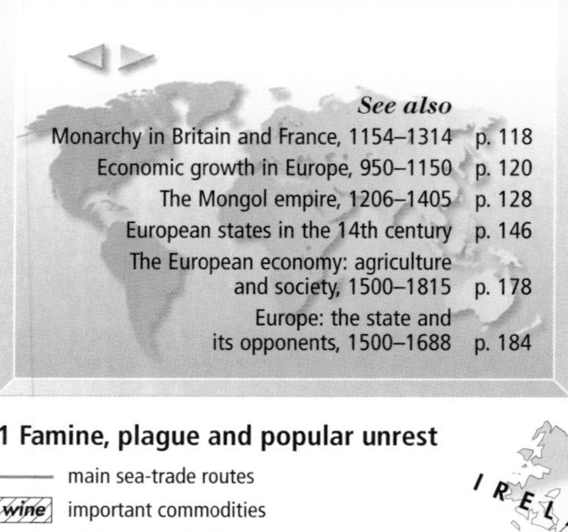

See also
Monarchy in Britain and France, 1154–1314 p. 118
Economic growth in Europe, 950–1150 p. 120
The Mongol empire, 1206–1405 p. 128
European states in the 14th century p. 146
The European economy: agriculture and society, 1500–1815 p. 178
Europe: the state and its opponents, 1500–1688 p. 184

1252 *First western European gold coins for 450 years minted in Genoa and Florence*

1277 *Opening of sea route from Italy to Flanders*

1277 *Sheep guild or Mesta organized in Castile*

1315–17 *Great Famine in northern Europe*

1346–51 *Black Death*

1347 *Bankruptcy of Peruzzi bankers, Florence*

1362–3 *Second plague pandemic in Europe*

1370 *Peace of Stralsund guarantees passage to Hansa merchants*

1378 *Rebellion of Florentine clothworkers (Ciompi)*

1381 *Peasants' Revolt, England*

2 The function of medieval universities was to train candidates for the upper clergy and parish priests. The first universities were founded in Italy (Bologna, 1088) and France (Paris, late 11th century). The early 14th century saw a new wave of foundations *(map below)* and by the early 15th almost every state in Christian Europe had its own university. In the period after the Black Death the universities played a valuable role in providing new recruits for the priesthood, but they also often became centres of religious dissent.

The 14th century saw dramatic change in Europe and Asia as the Black Death spread westward, reaching the Black Sea in 1346, Sicily in 1347 and most of Europe by 1350. In Europe and the Islamic world between a quarter and a half of the population died of plague. The economy and society of East and West underwent radical transformations as a result.

THE INTENSE PRESSURE on the land of a densely packed population combined with a succession of poor harvests to cause the Great Famine in northern Europe of 1315–17. Yet though Europe was to be afflicted with a series of further harvest failures, this was also a period of expanding markets, meeting the needs of increasingly active regional trade in wine, grain, dyestuffs and raw materials. Further new opportunities grew after the Black Death, when labour, previously in surplus, leading to low wages, suddenly became scarce.

Black Death and economic crisis

Signs of crisis were visible before the Black Death. Textile manufacture in Flemish and Italian cities was in decline on the eve of the plague. Banking failures, beginning with the Buonsignori of Siena (1298), culminated in the collapse of the great Florentine banking houses of Bardi and Peruzzi in the 1340s. The plague struck in 1346, and by 1350 had swept through most of Europe (*see* map 1). Population levels did not recover until the late 15th century because of the recurrence of plague, which became endemic in Europe, though outbreaks were increasingly localized.

Yet though the effects on the European economy were profound, there were many who benefited from the new economic climate, and this was not necessarily a period of severe depression. Thus English cloth exports expanded greatly, as did Castilian wool exports. Farmland was converted to pasture for sheep in England, Italy and Spain and for cattle in the Netherlands, Spain and northern Germany. New products such as saffron were cultivated in southern Germany, where Nuremberg and Augsburg were front-runners in a new wave of economic expansion, partly based on the mineral resources of the lands to the east.

On the other hand, monopolistic guild restrictions meant that some of the once prosperous cloth towns in northern Europe lost out to more agile competitors in the restructured economy of the late 14th century. Florence, too, lost its pre-eminence in woollen cloth, and attempted to become a major centre of silk production instead; but by now there were several lively competitors. Barcelona found a market for its upper-middle quality cloths, but financial crises and internal power struggles sapped the city's energy and Valencia took over as the powerhouse of western Mediterranean trade. In the north, the German Hansa became a powerful confederation of trading cities which dominated Baltic and North Sea trade in fish, grain, dairy goods and furs, operating through bases at London, Lynn, Bergen, Bruges and Novgorod; for long it was able to keep competitors such as the Dutch and the English at bay.

Peasant unrest and revolt

Economic change brought new wealth to some and undermined the wealth of others, such as landlords who lost their source of cheap labour. Villages were abandoned in areas as far apart as the English Midlands and Russia, as peasants moved – often without permission – to the lands of lords who made less demands on them or which had more fertile soil. Many moved to towns, especially when villages were abandoned to make

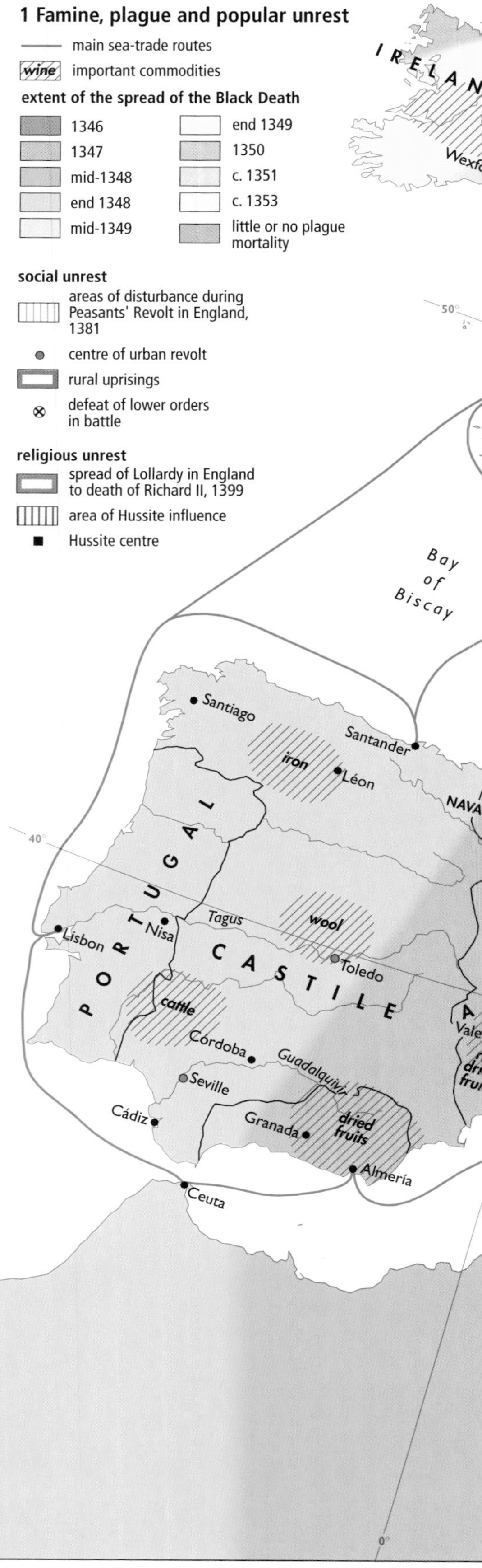

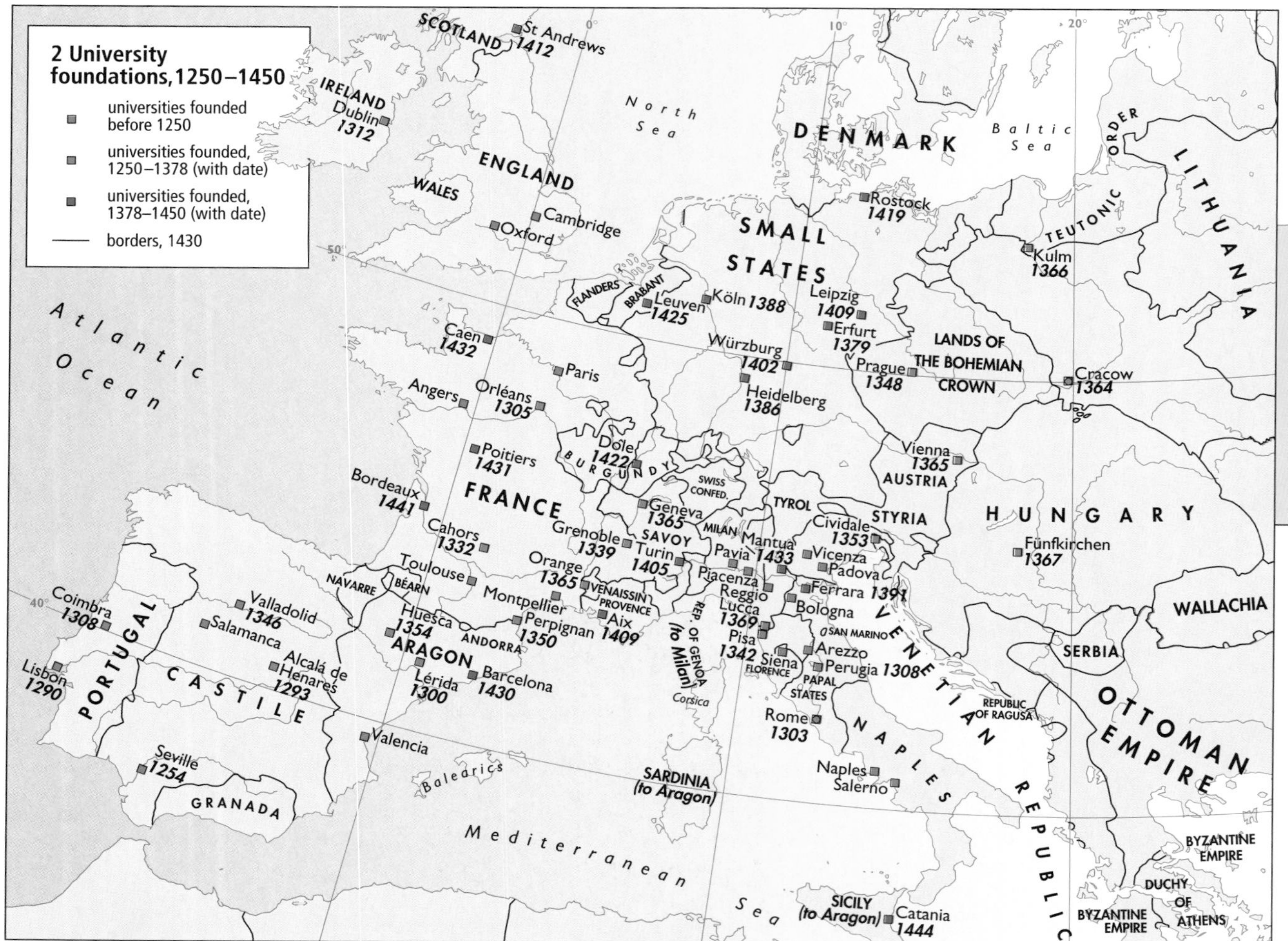

Unlike famine, the pestilence affected every social class, and the psychological impact was profound. Until the early 18th century, scarcely a decade passed without a recurrent outbreak. The disease, spread by infected fleas carried by rats, was particularly virulent, and few who caught it ever recovered. This illustration *(above)* from the Stiny Codex shows death strangling a plague victim.

1 Inadequately financed and weakened by war and internal dissension, western Europe underwent severe strains in the 14th century *(map above)*. Recession, compounded by famine and pestilence, led to conflicts in almost all countries between the autocracy and the urban oligarchies on the one hand and the peasants and urban workers on the other. The effect of the Black Death was particularly severe. After 1346 plague of Asiatic origin spread from the southeast across virtually all of Europe, wiping out between a quarter and a half of the population. As well as economic and social turmoil, Europe saw religious dissent, too, with the Lollard movement in England and the Hussites in Bohemia.

way for sheep. Yet some peasants were able to accumulate large amounts of land, as relatives died of the plague and left them their possessions. To many it seemed that the world was turned topsy-turvy. Social unrest became strident in town and country, exemplified by the Ciompi rebellion in Florence (1378) or the Peasants' Revolt in England (1381), particularly among those whose depressed social status did not match their rising economic status. Generally, however, serfdom was a thing of the past in much of western Europe by 1400; in eastern Europe it was, in contrast, reinforced, as landlords such as the Teutonic Knights sought to produce grain for their Hanseatic customers.

> Some say that it descended upon the human race through the influence of heavenly bodies, others that it was a punishment signifying God's anger at our iniquitous way of life. But whatever its cause, it had originated some years earlier in the East, where it had claimed countless lives before it unhappily spread westward, growing in strength as it swept relentlessly from one place to the next.
>
> **Boccaccio**
> ***The Decameron, 1358***

The 14th century saw severe readjustment, the restructuring of economies in the wake of massive depopulation. Yet by the end of the century the Hansa was enjoying its Golden Age, the maritime trade routes linking Italy and Catalonia to England and Flanders (opened around 1277) were flourishing, and Venice and Genoa had secured a strong hold on eastern markets: the Genoese mainly in the Black Sea, whence they brought grain and dried fruits; the Venetians in Egypt and Syria, whence they brought spices and cotton. The Black Death was a dramatic demographic earthquake, with severe aftershocks, yet the European economy was successfully rebuilt on its own shattered remains.

European states in the 14th century

The 14th century was a tumultuous period of state building in which rulers sought to define frontiers and develop centralized bureaucracies. They were challenged by parliaments of nobles, knights and townsmen, seeking concessions in return for taxation. Furthermore, the cost of frontier wars forced rulers back into the arms of their subjects.

1302 *War of Sicilian Vespers ends*

1305–76 *Papacy in residence at Avignon*

1323–4 *Aragonese invasion of Sardinia*

1337–1453 *Hundred Years' War between France and England*

1378–1417 *Great Schism*

1378 *Death of Emperor Charles IV*

1386 *Union of Poland and Lithuania*

1397 *Union of Kalmar brings together Scandinavian kingdoms*

1399 *Deposition of Richard II of England*

1400 *Deposition of enzel of Bohemia from imperial throne*

WAR ADDED TO THE TURMOIL caused to 14th-century Europe by famine and plague (see p. 144). Italy was particularly affected. The struggle for Sicily after 1282 between the French house of Anjou and Aragonese invaders (the War of the Sicilian Vespers) continued long after its formal ending in 1302 by the Treaty of Caltabellotta. Around 1300 northern Italy remained divided between competing cities, themselves often torn apart by Guelph and Ghibelline factions, the former able to count on the support of Naples or the Papacy. As regional despots gained power over the cities, conflict within their walls died, culminating in the conquest of large areas of Lombardy and Tuscany by Giangaleazzo Visconti, duke of Milan. Few Italian republics stood firm against the trend, though Florence made much capital out of its self-proclaimed dedication to the cause of republican liberty.

The pope himself decamped in 1305 to Avignon in southern France, a more peaceful city than Rome. Papal centralization was visible in the tighter control over Church appointments and taxation, successes that generated bitter criticism from reformers such as Wyclif in Oxford and Hus in Prague. The return of the Papacy to Rome in 1376 led to deep divisions among the cardinals and the outbreak of a schism that lasted nearly 40 years.

The conflict between France and England (*see* p. 118) for control of France, above all Gascony, erupted again in 1294 and then in 1337 (the Hundred Years' War). Initial English successes coupled with internal strife gravely weakened France and great princes such as the Valois dukes of Burgundy exploited this royal debility to create powerful statelets of their own.

Rulers and subjects

Against this disturbed background, rulers sought to create a sound financial base for themselves. Often this meant, as in Germany and Aragon, negotiating with parliaments that controlled their budget. Conflicts between rulers and their leading subjects led to the deposition of Edward II and Richard II in England (1327, 1399), and of Wenzel in Bohemia (1400). In Germany, the great princely houses vied for the crown, but were more concerned to strengthen their own patrimonies than to stabilize the German monarchy. A web of leagues emerged, of which the Swiss Confederation (from 1291) was the most successful.

In the Mediterranean, the Crown of Aragon consolidated its hold. Sardinia, promised by Pope Boniface VIII to the Aragonese in 1297, was invaded in 1323–4, though it took many decades before Aragonese rule became a reality; Majorca, an autonomous kingdom since 1276, was reconquered in 1343, giving access to prime trade routes; by the end of the century Sicily, too, was under Aragonese rule. Castile, on the other hand, was wracked in mid-century by civil war, and social tensions took a brutal toll on the Jewish

3 Italy after 1282

- Papal states
- ◑ Republican communes
- ⊙ cities under Signorial domination c. 1310

the Signori

1. Avvocati	5. Da Camino	9. Este	13. Malatesta
2. Bonacolsi	6. Da Correggio	10. Fissiraga	14. Robert of Anjou
3. Brusati	7. Da Polenta	11. Langosco	15. Scotti
4. Cavalcabo	8. Della Scala	12. Maggi	16. Visconti

2 Throughout the 14th century, Prussia was gradually conquered by the Teutonic knights *(map below)*. In 1231 Hermann Balke, provincial master of the Teutonic Order, crossed the river Vistula with a crusading army, swiftly founding new fortified cities such as Königsberg. Eastern expansion was checked by defeat at Lake Peipus and in the west at Tannenberg. Systematic subjection of the pagan Prussian tribes gave way, after 1309, to 100 years of prosperity.

3 Papal-imperial controversy and the wealth of the municipalities inhibited consolidation in Italy *(map above)*. After 1250, public power in independent city-states was exercised by republican oligarchies or by despots who often succeeded as alternatives to the factional violence of civic politics.

1 The 14th century saw the definitive emergence of many of the European states which were to survive into the modern age. The map *(right)* shows the situation in about 1380. The great German dynasties were consolidating their hold on lands in central Europe, while the Ottoman empire was gaining ever greater authority in the Balkans. France expanded its power in the Rhône valley.

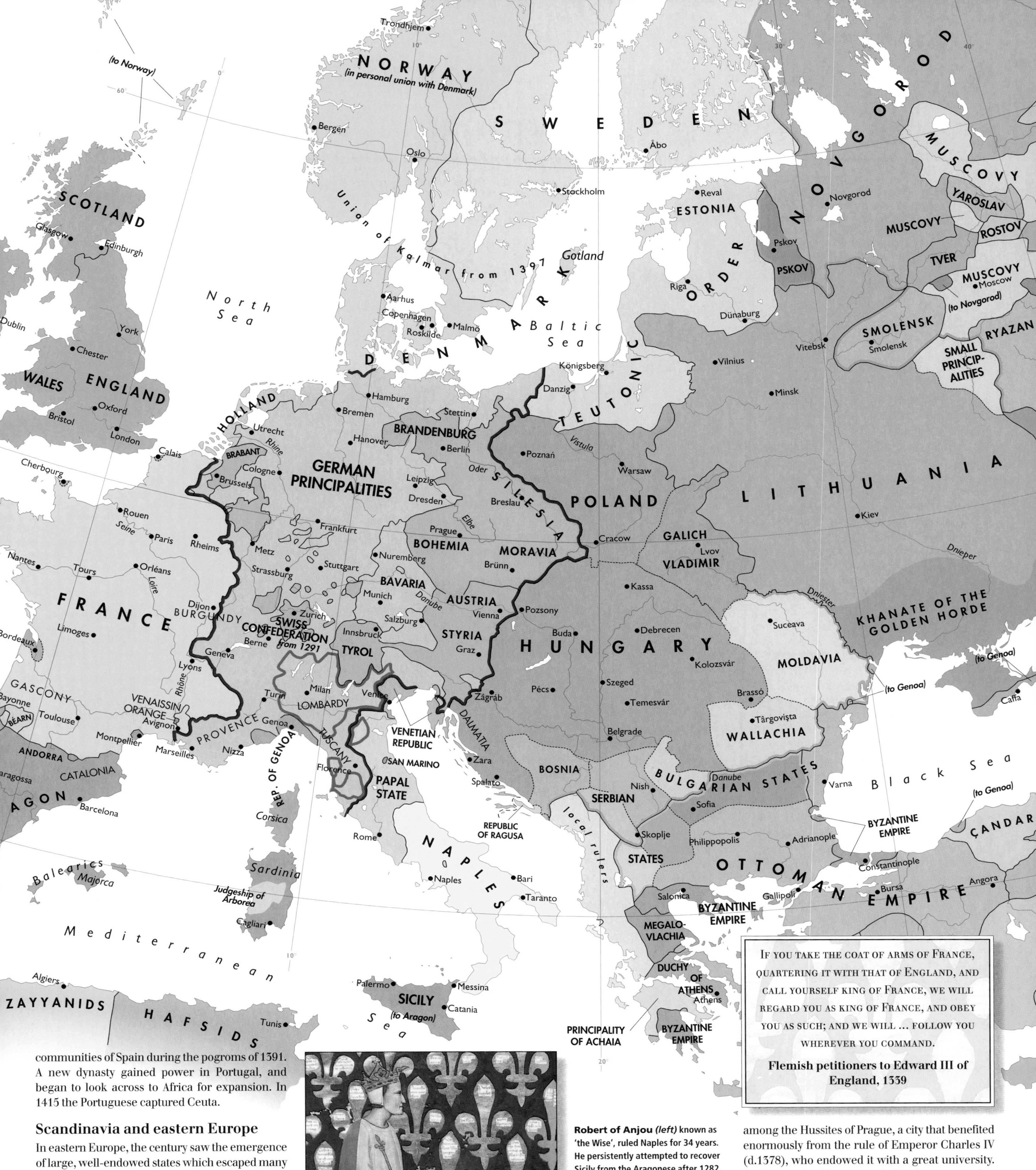

If you take the coat of arms of France, quartering it with that of England, and call yourself king of France, we will regard you as king of France, and obey you as such; and we will ... follow you wherever you command.

Flemish petitioners to Edward III of England, 1339

communities of Spain during the pogroms of 1391. A new dynasty gained power in Portugal, and began to look across to Africa for expansion. In 1415 the Portuguese captured Ceuta.

Scandinavia and eastern Europe

In eastern Europe, the century saw the emergence of large, well-endowed states which escaped many of the economic difficulties afflicting western Europe. Hungary at its peak dominated an area between the Adriatic (acquiring Dalmatia from Venice in 1352) and Poland, though an attempt to gain permanent control of the Polish crown failed. Lithuania had possessions from the Black Sea almost to the Baltic, and the marriage of its newly baptized duke, Jagiello, to the Polish heiress in 1386 extended its territories still further. In Bohemia, religious dissent flourished by 1400 among the Hussites of Prague, a city that benefited enormously from the rule of Emperor Charles IV (d.1378), who endowed it with a great university. In Denmark, Norway and Sweden, one ruler, Margaret of Norway, acquired loose control of all three kingdoms by the Union of Kalmar in 1397. Yet they were not permanently united and the supremacy of the aristocracy persisted.

Amid these rivalries, a sense of national identity, generally built more around language than race, was emerging in areas such as Catalonia, Bohemia and England. Frontiers between states were being drawn, some of which lasted into the 20th century.

Robert of Anjou *(left)* **known as 'the Wise', ruled Naples for 34 years. He persistently attempted to recover Sicily from the Aragonese after 1282. By the Treaty of Caltabellotta, Aragon agreed to restore the island on the death of the Aragonese ruler of Sicily, Frederick III. Robert fought from 1309 to 1319 on the side of the pro-papal Guelph party against the Visconti of Milan. He ultimately failed to regain Sicily on Frederick's death. However, he was an excellent administrator and patron of leading literary figures such as the poet Petrarch.**

c. 1300 to 1535
The Americas on the eve of European conquest

See also
Peoples of the Americas, 300 BC–c. AD 1300 p. 60
The world on the eve of European expansion p. 154
European voyages of discovery, 1487–1780 p. 156
The Americas, 1500–1810 p. 162

THE INDIANS WERE BURIED WITH AS MUCH WEALTH AS POSSIBLE, AND SO THEY STROVE WITH THE UTMOST DILIGENCE THROUGHOUT THEIR LIVES TO ACQUIRE AND AMASS ALL THE GOLD THEY COULD, WHICH THEY TOOK FROM THEIR OWN LAND AND WERE BURIED WITH IT, BELIEVING THAT THE MORE OF THE METAL THEY CARRIED AWAY WITH THEM THE MORE ESTEEMED THEY WOULD BE IN THE PLACES AND REGIONS TO WHICH THEY IMAGINED THEIR SOULS WOULD GO.

Pedro de Cieza de León, 1554

To see the pre-colonial inhabitants of the Americas, as many Europeans came to do after 1492, as much the same everywhere and collectively condemned to conquest because of technological backwardness was to ignore the profound diversity of 'Native Americans' and their resourcefulness in dealing with their natural environment.

c. 1250 *Mayapán becomes dominant city of Yucatán*

1325 *Rise of Aztecs in Mexico*

1375 *Chimú conquests of central Andes begin*

1470 *Incas conquer Chimú kingdom*

1492 *Columbus reaches Americas*

1493 *Treaty of Tordesillas divides New World between Spain and Portugal*

1519 *Cortés begins conquest of Aztec empire*

1532 *Pizarro begins conquest of Inca empire*

IN 1492, WHEN COLUMBUS SET SAIL on his historic voyage, the continent he would open to European conquest was already peopled from the Arctic Circle to the South Atlantic (*see* p. 60). These indigenous inhabitants were astonishingly diverse. It has been estimated that they spoke 2,200 different languages. They also varied greatly, from the sophistication of the Aztec and Inca polities which – in the course of the 15th century – expanded faster and more vigorously than any state in western Europe, to the small groups of hunters chasing bison on the Great Plains.

The Aztecs

The origins of the Aztec empire which dominated the Valley of Mexico at the time of European discovery are shrouded in myth. It probably began with nomads who settled among the agrarian states of the Lake Texcoco area near the beginning of the 14th century. Their lake-bound city of Tenochtitlán slowly achieved dominance, as a result of alliance or submission, over neighbouring communities until it became the principal beneficiary of a network of tributary relationships that stretched across the region as a whole.

In around 1500, Aztec armies extended the sway of their system of tribute-exaction as far as the Pánuco river in the north and Xoconusco province in the south. Borne by trade, their influence reached across the northern deserts into southwest North America, over the Caribbean to the Taino of Haiti (who adopted their ritual ball games with stone courts) and to the east past Xicalango (where the remotest Aztec garrison was stationed) into Yucatán.

The principal source of this empire's strength – and weakness – was tribute. The large, dense population of Tenochtitlán could not survive on local resources alone. Huge quantities of food, clothing, and ritual goods had to be levied and transported from far afield. A surviving tribute-roll (which may itself be incomplete) lists over 225,000 bushels of maize and 123,400 cotton mantles, with corresponding quantities of beans, herbs such as sage and purslane, as well as chillies, cacao, lime, salt, incense and other precious exotica due every year. Other Aztec cities had comparable rates of consumption. The market of Tlatelolco, Tenochtitlán's neighbour, was said to be regularly patronized by 50,000 people.

The Aztec empire was prodigious – and perhaps prodigal – in other fields. Its material culture featured monumental stone building, vital sculpture, sumptuous goldwork and extravagant featherwork, all requiring intensive labour and expensive raw materials. Its religion exacted a fearful toll in human sacrifices. According to the varying estimates of European colonial sources, between 10,000 and 80,000 were offered at the dedication of the main temple of Tenochtitlán in 1487, most of them acquired through capture in war or ritual exchange of victims with other communities.

The voracious appetites of the Aztec system, while forcing its beneficiaries to be skilled in war, also made it vulnerable to a concerted withdrawal of tribute by suppliers. This was despite campaigns in the last generation of Aztec history into evermore distant territories to levy the exotic products on which the metropolitan life of the Aztec elite increasingly depended. Isolated by the diplomacy of the Spanish invaders after 1519, the Aztec capital was starved into surrender.

The Incas

Because of its Andean location, the Inca empire was very different from that of the Aztecs. For this was a territorial state, organizing and enforcing collaboration between producers of complementary goods at different micro-climatic levels. The Incas were able, in the interests of maximizing production or increasing security, to re-locate large populations. In the early 16th century, the Inca ruler Huayna Capac was said to have re-settled in Cochabamba some 14,000 people from areas as far apart as Cuzco and what is now northern Chile. The most conspicuous demonstration of the unity of the empire lay in its road system, more than 12,500 miles in length.

However, though different in character, the Inca empire revealed some of the structural weaknesses of the Aztec. While the tally of human sacrifice was less extravagant, religion still strained resources as a result of the vast households maintained for the cults of dead rulers. The costs this involved may have contributed to divisions among the elite, which developed into the devastating civil war raging at the time of the Spanish conquest. Also, many subject peoples found the burden of Inca rule so oppressive that they were willing to collaborate with the invader.

North America

It has been estimated that in 1492 there were about one and a half million Native Americans spread across what is now the United States. Most supported themselves through agriculture, with maize (corn), beans and squash as the most prominent crops. Women were particularly active in

An Aztec or Miztec sacrificial knife *(above)*. The Aztecs believed that the continuation of human society required that the sun and earth be nourished with human blood and hearts. War was necessary to provide the sacrificial victims, whose hearts were removed with knives such as this. It is 12 inches long with an inlaid handle in the form of a warrior costumed as an eagle, or *quauhtli*, which was also a name for the sun.

2 The Aztec empire to 1519

Post-Classic Maya area
area of Aztec domination, 1519
Post-Classic trading routes

Pánuco
Tamuín
late Huastec centre
Aztec capital founded AD1325
late Post-Classic Tarascan site
Tzintzuntzán
Tula
Teayo
El Tajín
Azcapotzalco
L.Texcoco
Texcoco
Tenochtitlán
Tlatelolco
Tlacopán
Tlaxcala
Malinalco
Cacaxtla
Aztec period temple carved in rock
Xochicalco
Cholula
Cempoala
major centre of Aztec allies
Balsas
Teotitlán
Tehuacán Valley
Monte Albán
Valley
Oaxaca
Yagul
Mitla
tombs in old Zapotec ceremonial centre
Guiengola
XOCONUSCO
rich province supplying cacao to the Aztec capital
Xoconocho
Bay of Campeche
long-distance contacts from 9th century AD
trading exchanges between Aztec and Maya
Champotón
Xicalango
Chichén Itzá
Mayapán
site of the last centralized government of Yucatán destroyed in 1441
Yucatán Peninsula
Tulum
Cozumel island trading centre
late Post-Classic fortified town
Ichpaatun
late Post-Classic fortified town
Santa Rita
murals in Mixtec style
ACALAN
Lamanai
Tipu
Tayasal
Maya centres occupied continuously until mid-17th century
lakeside town; last centre of Maya resistance to Spain
highland Maya kingdoms under central Mexican influences
Gulf of Honduras
Zaculeu
Iximché
Wild Cane Cay
island trading centre

2 The Aztecs entered central Mexico from the north. In the course of the 15th century they built a large, tribute-based empire *(map left)* controlled from Tenochtitlán, their capital city, which was founded in the early 14th century. The gargantuan appetite of the Aztec empire for food, gold and sacrificial victims was the source alike of its strength and weakness, explaining both its tentacular reach and its unsustainable consumption. The descendants of the 'Classic Maya' civilization still controlled the Yucatán peninsula in 1535, although the 16 separate provinces were constantly at odds with each other over land rights.

The colour categories in this map show culture areas defined by modern anthropologists, classifying the multitude of Aboriginal societies (only a few are shown here). Within each area the economic basis of life was similar, as were the social and political systems.

1 By the time the European conquest began in the Americas, its native inhabitants were divided into more than 1,000 independent societies belonging to over 20 unrelated language families and possessing an immense variety of cultures *(map right)*. At one extreme were Stone Age hunters such as the Inuit of the far north and the Mataco of the southern Chaco; at the other were the highly developed and affluent civilizations of Mesoamerica and the Andes, where the Aztecs and the Incas respectively built on cultural traditions more than 1,500 years old.

A Navajo blanket showing two supernatural 'holy people' flanking the sacred maize plant, which was their gift to the mortals *(above)*. Maize was just one of the foods Europeans found Native Americans exploiting – foods that would later spread to Europe and the rest of the world. Among the others were potatoes, sweet potatoes, tomatoes, squash, beans, pumpkins, cacao, vanilla, pineapples, papayas, chillies, pecans, peanuts, sunflower seeds and avocados.

cultivating crops in most areas apart from the southwest. Despite the lack of wheels, ploughs and animals used for traction (or hunting – the horse was introduced by Europeans), Native Americans were skilled plant breeders and agriculturalists. They had no concept of buying and selling land, since they regarded themselves as trustees of it for future generations, although they recognized individual rights to cultivated land and group rights to uncultivated land. While the tribes differed greatly in language, religious observance and customs, they were themselves united by the interconnecting obligations of extended families or kinship groups. If there were no great civilizations such as those of the Aztecs and the Incas, early Europeans arriving on the southeast coast of North America reported fabulous surplus wealth, signs of long-range trade and high standards of craftsmanship. The Pueblo Indians of the southwest had learned to farm in arid lands using irrigation techniques, lived mostly in towns, had advanced arts and crafts and were believers in a form of supernaturalist ceremonialism that long resisted the spread of Christianity.

3 The Inca empire expanded rapidly in the 15th century *(map left)*. From Cuzco, the Inca emperor exerted rigid control over this extensive territory by means of a highly trained bureaucracy, a state religion, a powerful army and an advanced communications network. The final expansion under Huayna Capac put the Inca world under great strain, however, and by the arrival of the Spanish conqueror Pizarro, in 1533, civil war had split the empire in two.

1450 to c.1600

The Renaissance and Early Modern state in Europe

See also
The rise of the Ottoman empire, 1281–1522 p. 142
The crisis of the 14th century in Europe p. 144
European states in the 14th century p. 146
Russian expansion in Europe and Asia p. 160
Europe: the state and its opponents, 1500–1688 p. 184
The Mediterranean world, 1494–1797 p. 186

1455 *Gutenberg prints first book using moveable type*

1477 *Battle of Nancy: death of Charles the Bold of Burgundy*

1492 *Spanish reconquest of Granada*

1519 *Charles V elected Holy Roman Emperor*

1526 *Battle of Mohács: Ottomans conquer most of Hungary; Habsburgs gain kingdom of Bohemia*

1555–6 *Charles V abdicates; divides inheritance.*

1569 *Union of Lublin: union between Poland and Lithuania.*

1603 *Union of the Crowns between Scotland and England*

Increasing knowledge of the classical past and a desire to return to the Greek and Roman roots of European civilization stimulated the movement known as the Renaissance, which, beginning in Italy, spread rapidly around Europe after the invention of printing. This awakening of interest in its classical past was to affect Europe's politics profoundly.

SOVEREIGNTY IS THE ABSOLUTE AND PERPETUAL POWER OF A COMMONWEALTH, WHICH THE LATINS CALL MAIESTAS; THE GREEKS AKRA EXOUSIA, KURION ARCHE, AND KURION POLITEUMA; AND THE ITALIANS SEGNIORIA ...WHILE THE HEBREWS CALL IT TOMECH SHÉVET – THAT IS THE HIGHEST POWER OF COMMAND ...

Jean Bodin,
Six Livres de la République, 1576

THE RENAISSANCE SAW a flowering of literature and the arts across Europe. Writers and artists, seeking to emulate the cultures of Greece and Rome, developed new techniques and formulated new ideas in their attempts to apply the knowledge of the Ancients to the very different world of the 16th century. Important scientific and technological advances were made. At the same time, increased exploitation of the invention of printing promoted the emergence of literate secular elites and created a new political environment as secular rulers used artists to display their power visually and written propaganda to appeal directly to their most important subjects.

State consolidation

Such incipient secularization of political life enabled monarchs to challenge the power of the church: in concordats with the Holy Roman Emperor (1448), France (1516) and Spain (1523), the papacy was forced to concede far-reaching rights over the national churches, while in a number of Protestant countries the ruler openly assumed control of spiritual affairs.

These changes aided the internal consolidation of states across Europe after 1450, now recovering from the economic and demographic ravages of the 14th century (*see* p. 144), when so many apparently powerful states had proved ephemeral. The strengthening of the principle of male primogeniture, under which only the eldest son inherited his father's property, thus keeping estates intact, ensured that states could be consolidated more effectively as well as stimulating desires to recover lost territories. Such 'reunifications' brought conflict across Europe, since there were inevitably rival claims to be considered and rulers now enjoyed an enhanced capacity to wage war. This was in part the result of increasing economic prosperity and demographic recovery after 1450. By increasing the tax base of all European states, rulers gained greater access to credit, which enabled them to afford the new military technologies made possible by the development of gunpowder. Large artillery trains destroyed the castles of over-mighty subjects, most of whom were usually in no position to compete financially, while only states could afford the new large, infantry-based armies and elaborate fortifications.

The result was a series of large-scale dynastic and territorial wars. In the east, Muscovy, the Ottoman empire and Poland-Lithuania struggled for control; in the west, Burgundy, the rising star of the 15th century, was partitioned after Charles the Bold was killed in 1477 (*see* map 2), while in 1453 the English were expelled from France (except Calais). In Spain, Castile and Aragon were united in 1479 and in 1492 consolidated their rule of Spain when their combined forces completed the conquest of the Muslim kingdom of Granada. In England, though defeat by France in the Hundred Years' War had provoked civil war ('the Wars of the Roses'), after 1485 the new Tudor dynasty restored order and extended royal control in the turbulent north and west. In Germany, a series of dynastic alliances united the Habsburg lands with those of

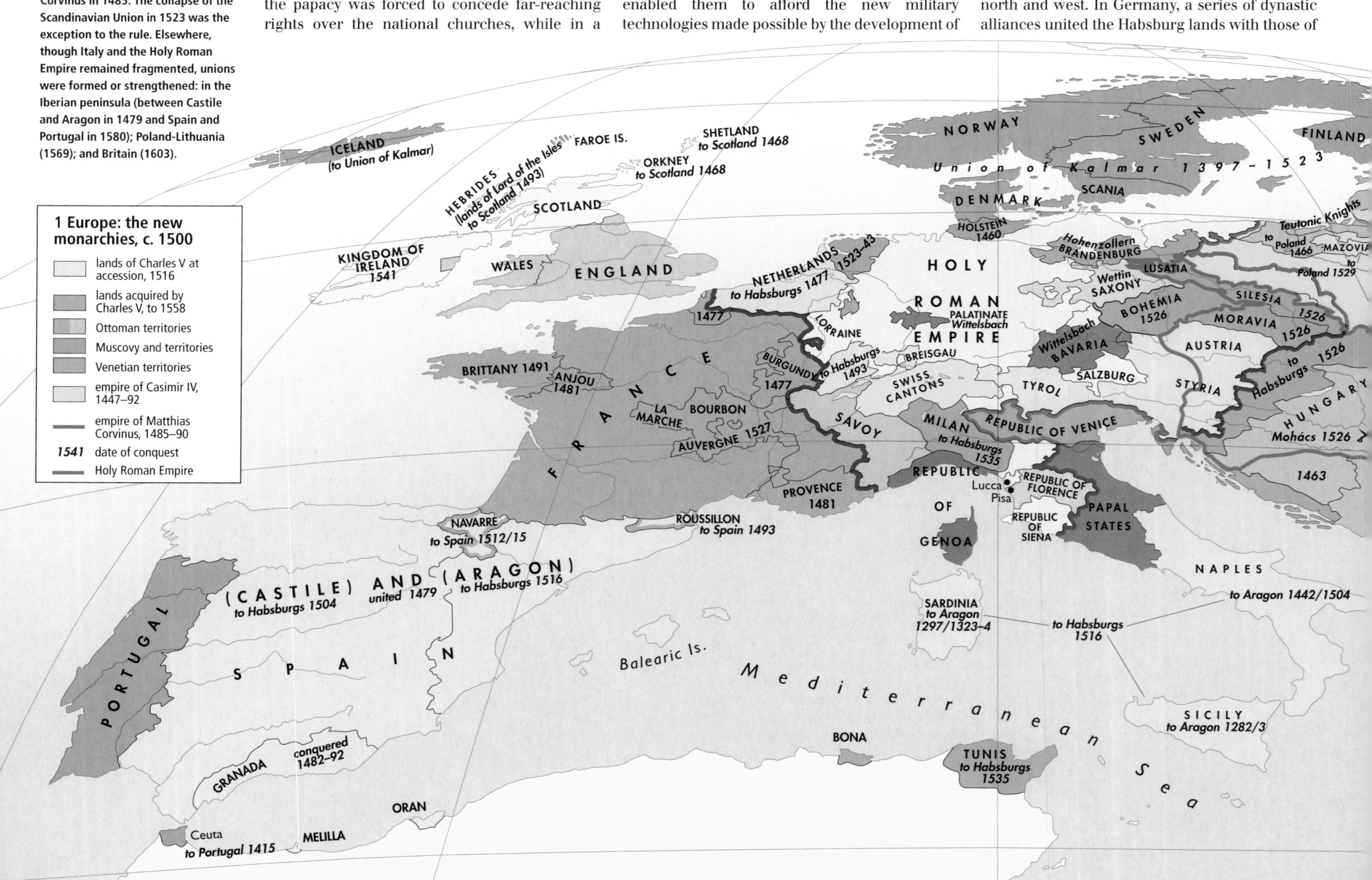

1 In the early 16th century, more consolidated state structures began to emerge *(map below)*. In the east, Muscovy challenged Poland-Lithuania for the inheritance of Kievan Rus, while in the 1520s the Ottomans destroyed the composite monarchy of Hungary and Bohemia which had reached its zenith under Matthias Corvinus in 1485. The collapse of the Scandinavian Union in 1523 was the exception to the rule. Elsewhere, though Italy and the Holy Roman Empire remained fragmented, unions were formed or strengthened: in the Iberian peninsula (between Castile and Aragon in 1479 and Spain and Portugal in 1580); Poland-Lithuania (1569); and Britain (1603).

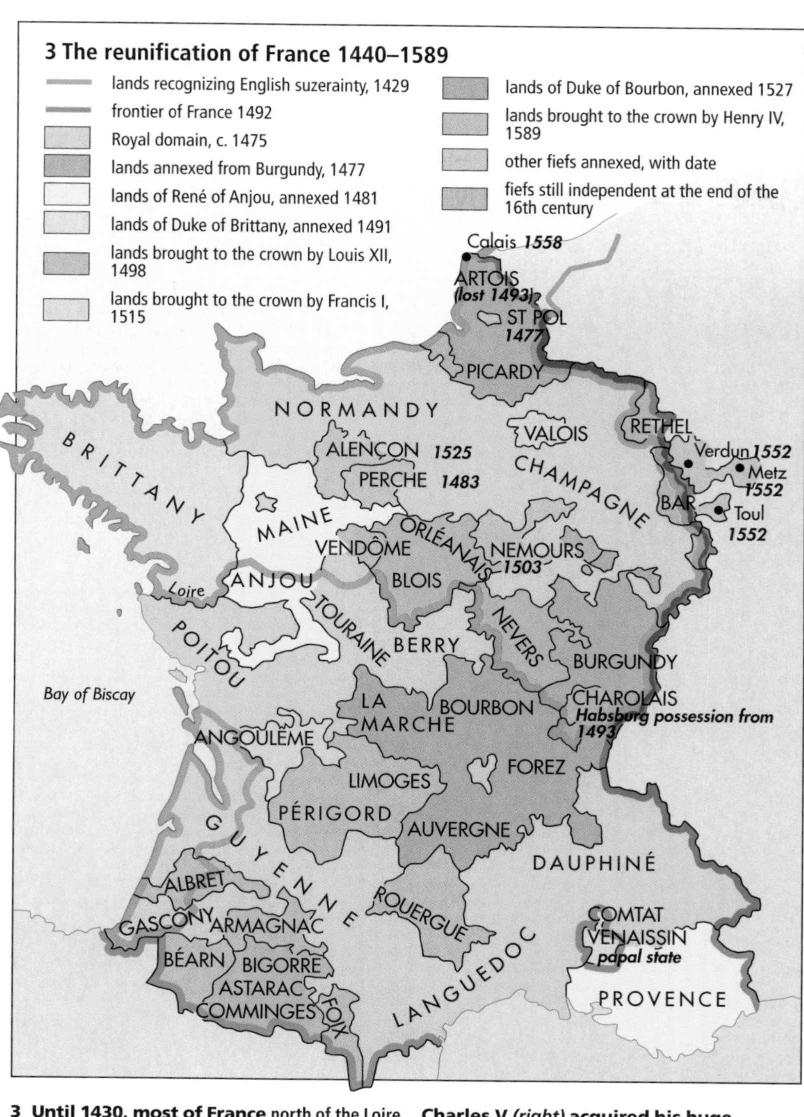

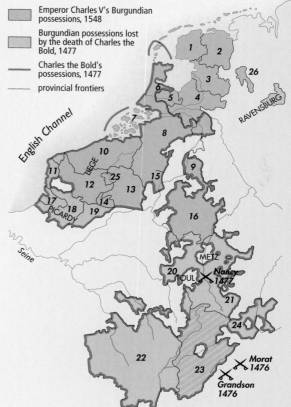

2 STATE-BUILDING IN THE LOW COUNTRIES

From the late 14th century, the Valois dukes of Burgundy built a powerful state along the northeastern borders of France, its lands among the most prosperous in Europe *(map and numbered list below)*. Charles the Bold (1467–77) overreached himself, however. Defeated at Morat and Grandson (1476), he was killed at Nancy (1477). His French fiefs (Picardy and Burgundy) were confiscated by Louis XI; the rest passed to Charles's son-in-law Maximilian Habsburg, and thence to Maximilian's grandson Charles V, who added further lands in the Netherlands. In 1548, Charles united his 17 territories in the Low Countries into a single federation. Barely 20 years later, rebellion tore the new state asunder.

1 Friesland: acquired by purchase 1523–4
2 Groningen: acquired by negotiation 1536
3 Overijssel: acquired by negotiation 1536
4 Gelderland: conquered 1473, lost 1477; conquered 1481, lost 1492; conquered again 1543
5 Utrecht: acquired by negotiation 1536
6 Holland: acquired by treaty 1433
7 Zeeland: acquired by treaty 1433
8 Brabant: inherited 1404
9 Limburg: acquired by gift 1396
10 Flanders: acquired by marriage 1384
11 Boulonnais: ceded by marriage treaty 1435, lost 1477
12 Artois: acquired by marriage 1384, lost 1477; regained 1493
13 Hainaut: acquired by treaty 1433
14 Cambrai: conquered 1543
15 Namur: acquired by purchase 1429
16 Luxembourg: inherited 1451
17 Ponthieu: ceded by treaty 1435, lost 1477
18 Amiens: ceded by treaty 1435, lost 1463; regained 1465, lost 1477
19 Vermandois: ceded by treaty 1435, lost 1463; regained 1465, lost 1477
20 Bar: conquered 1475, lost 1476
21 Lorraine: conquered 1475, lost 1476
22 Burgundy: inherited 1363, lost 1477
23 Franche-Comté: acquired by marriage 1384, lost 1477; regained 1493
24 Alsace: partially conquered 1469, lost 1477
25 Tournai: conquered 1521
26 Lingen: acquired 1543

Emperor Charles V's Burgundian possessions, 1548
Burgundian possessions lost by the death of Charles the Bold, 1477
Charles the Bold's possessions, 1477
provincial frontiers
English Channel
RAVENSBURG
LIEGE
PICARDY
Seine
METZ
TOUL
Nancy 1477
Morat 1476
Grandson 1476

3 Until 1430, most of France north of the Loire was in English or Burgundian hands *(map above)*; to the south, the royal domain constituted less than half the total territory. The reconquest in the 1440s of Normandy, Gascony and other lands held by the English doubled the French crown's territory. A series of confiscations and deaths then added the lands of the dukes of Burgundy (1477), Anjou (1481), Brittany (1491) and Bourbon (1527). This left only a handful of fiefs, many of which reverted to the crown when Henry of Navarre became Henry IV in 1589.

Charles V *(right)* acquired his huge inheritance largely by dynastic accident; after his election as Holy Roman Emperor in 1519, however, he projected himself as the temporal head of Christendom, the successor of Charlemagne and the Roman emperors, arguing that Christian unity was the vital precondition to defeat the Ottomans. Charles's claims were rejected by contemporary monarchs, in particular Francis I of France and Henry VIII of England. Although he remained emotionally attached to the imperial ideal, Charles acted largely as a practical dynastic politician, ruling his various lands as separate entities, conducting vigorous dynastic wars – in particular with Francis I in a vain attempt to reclaim the parts of his Burgundian inheritance lost in 1477 – and dividing his lands upon his abdication.

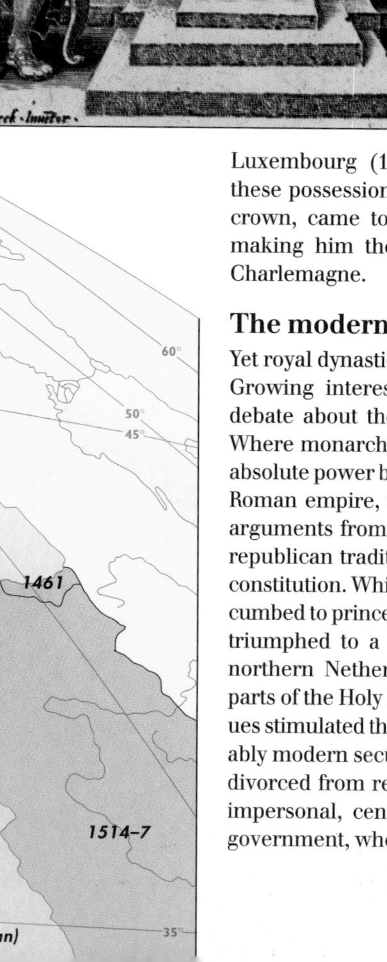

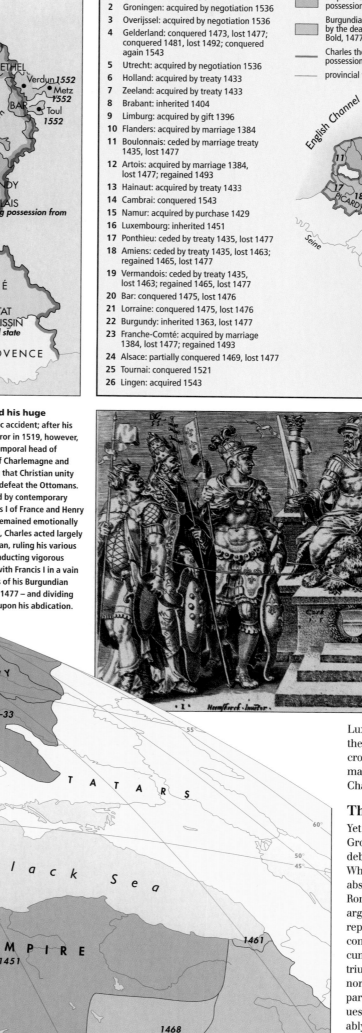

Luxembourg (1437) and Burgundy (1477). All these possessions, and later those of the Spanish crown, came to Emperor Charles V (1519–56), making him the greatest Christian ruler since Charlemagne.

The modern state

Yet royal dynasticism did not triumph unchecked. Growing interest in the classical past sparked debate about the nature of legitimate authority. Where monarchs sought to justify their claims to absolute power by reference to Roman law and the Roman empire, their opponents sought counter-arguments from the classical past, citing Rome's republican traditions and arguing for a balanced constitution. While most Italian city-republics succumbed to princely power, the republican tradition triumphed to a greater or lesser degree in the northern Netherlands, Poland-Lithuania and in parts of the Holy Roman Empire. This clash of values stimulated the gradual emergence of recognizably modern secular states, in which politics were divorced from religion and organized around an impersonal, centralized and unifying system of government, whether monarchical or republican.

5

The world of the emerging West

THE INDIAN HISTORIAN K. M. Panikkar described the period from 1498 to 1947, from Vasco da Gama's discovery of the sea route to India to Indian independence, as the European age in history. Others have pointed out the element of exaggeration in this definition: if, in 1750, the Europeans had abandoned their isolated settlements on the coasts of Asia and Africa, they would have left few traces. Nevertheless, around 1500 the balance, which hitherto had weighed on the side of Asia, began to change, and after 1750 that change was momentous.

Before 1500 civilization had been essentially land-centred, and contacts by sea relatively unimportant. If the year 1500 marks a new period in world history it is because thereafter direct sea contact linked the continents. This resulted not only in the integration in a global system of regions which hitherto had developed in isolation, but in a challenge to the age-old, land-centred balance between the Eurasian civilizations.

Nonetheless, the impact of European expansion should not be exaggerated. The 16th century saw a remarkable resurgence of Muslim power in the Ottoman empire, Safavid Persia and Mughal India. China, meanwhile, remained the world's most advanced state. Indeed to many in 18th-century Europe, Turkey and China were the exemplars of civilized living. The industrial revolution put Europe ahead; but the fruits of that process – some of them poisonous – were only garnered in the 19th century. Europe between 1500 and 1815, for all its thrusting novelty, was still an agricultural society of lords and peasants, closer to its agrarian past than to its industrial future.

Marble bust of Louis XIV by Bernini, 1665

c. 1500

The world on the eve of European expansion

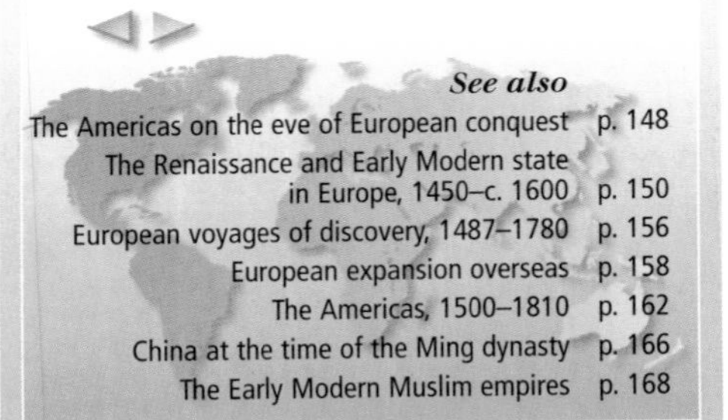

The central feature of world history between 1500 and 1815 was the expansion of Europe and the gradual spread of European civilization throughout the globe. Until 1500 the world had, on the whole, pressed in on Europe. After 1500, Europe increasingly pressed out on the world. By 1775 a new global balance was in existence.

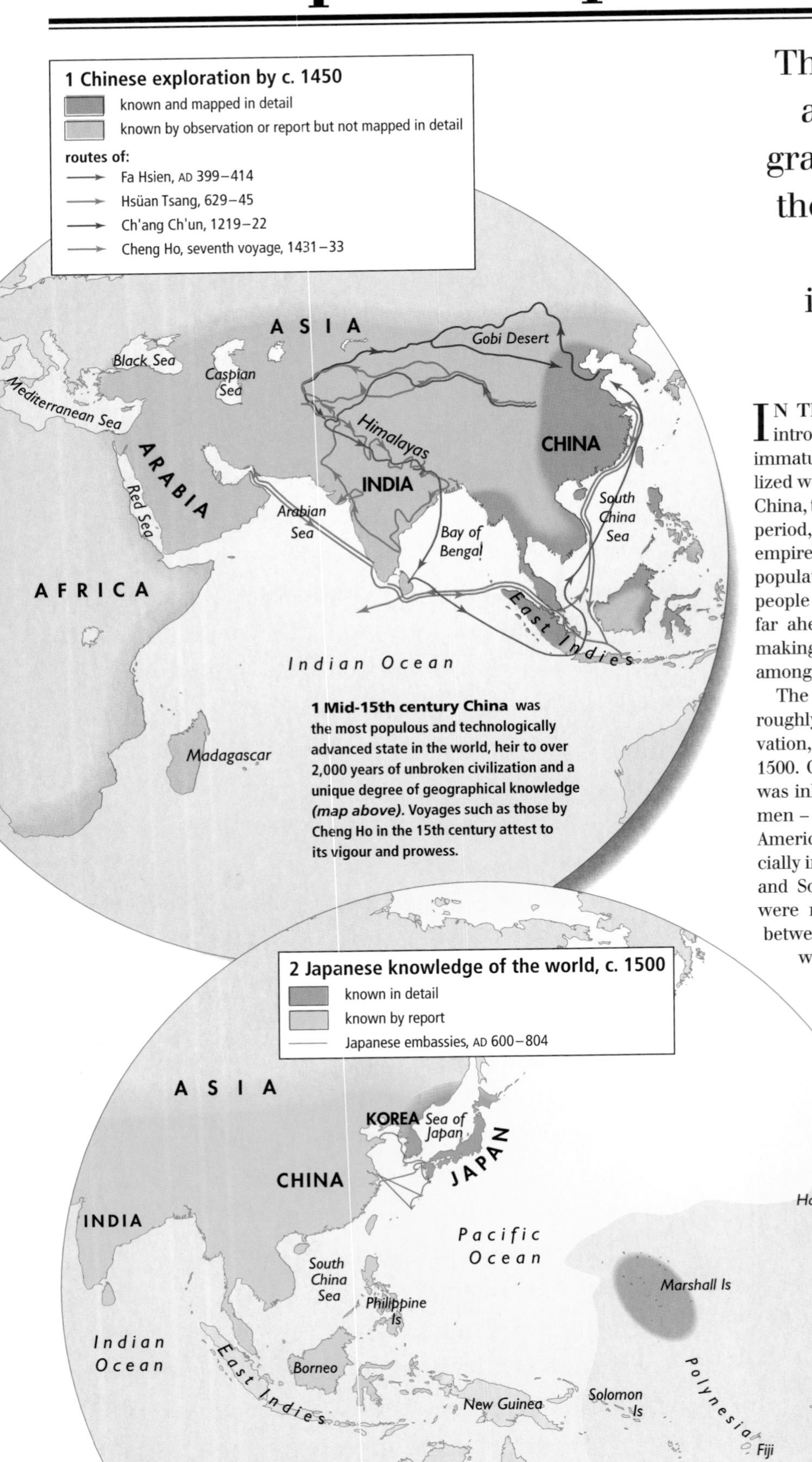

1 Mid-15th century China was the most populous and technologically advanced state in the world, heir to over 2,000 years of unbroken civilization and a unique degree of geographical knowledge *(map above)*. Voyages such as those by Cheng Ho in the 15th century attest to its vigour and prowess.

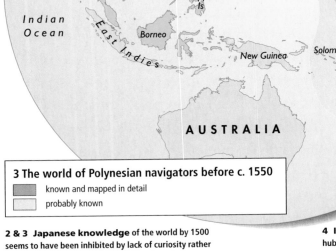

3 The world of Polynesian navigators before c. 1550
known and mapped in detail
probably known

2 & 3 Japanese knowledge of the world by 1500 seems to have been inhibited by lack of curiosity rather than of means *(map above)*. Until the first direct contacts with the West in 1543, first-hand Japanese knowledge of the wider world was largely restricted to China and Korea, though the existence of India was recognized. The Polynesians, meanwhile, surrounded by the immensity of the Pacific, seem to have attained the limits of the world accessible to them with the technology at their disposal.

IN THE EARLY 16TH CENTURY, Europe – introspective, uncertain and technologically immature – still stood on the periphery of the civilized world, overshadowed by the Ming empire in China, the most powerful and advanced state of the period, and by the rising Ottoman and Safavid empires of the Middle East. Both in wealth and population, China, with more than 100 million people (more than the whole of Europe), loomed far ahead. Islam, meanwhile, was still actively making converts in central and southeast Asia and among the peoples of sub-Saharan Africa.

The area occupied by the major civilizations, roughly equivalent to the area under plough cultivation, was nonetheless still relatively small in 1500. Over three-quarters of the world's surface was inhabited either by food gatherers or herdsmen – as in Australia and most of Siberia, North America and Africa – or by hand cultivators, especially in southeast Asia, parts of Africa and central and South America. But the plough cultivators were more productive and it is probable that between two-thirds and three-quarters of the world's population was concentrated in the relatively small area which was being farmed by the plough.

This concentration of people and wealth closely matches the location of the major Eurasian civilizations. The comparative fragility of the Aztec and Inca civilizations in the Americas and of the African kingdoms immediately south of the Sahara, all of them highly developed in many respects, may be partly explained first by their geographic isolation and lack of external stimulus and second by their dependence on hand cultivation. After 1500, when the expansion of Europe brought all continents into direct contact with each other for the first time, these non-Eurasian civilizations sometimes found themselves unable to put up more than feeble resistance to outside aggression.

The tempo of change

It is nevertheless important not to exaggerate the tempo of change. Although in America the Aztec and Inca empires were destroyed by 1521 and 1535 respectively, elsewhere the political impact of Europe was extremely limited before the the second half of the 18th century. China and Japan remained intact, and in India the Europeans were kept at arm's length for 250 years following the arrival of Vasco da Gama in 1498. There, as in west Africa and southeast Asia, the European presence was largely confined to isolated coastal trading stations. The cultural influence of Europe was even more negligible: Christianity, for example, made little headway except where it was imposed by force in the Philippines and the Americas until it

ASIA
Caspian Sea
ARABIA
Red Sea
CHINA
Arabian Sea
INDIA
Bay of Bengal
South China Sea
AFRICA
Maldives
Seychelles
Indian Ocean
East Indies
Madagascar
AUSTRALIA

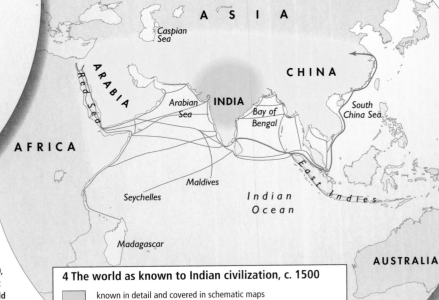

4 The world as known to Indian civilization, c. 1500
known in detail and covered in schematic maps
known by observation or report but not known to have been mapped
Indian Ocean trade routes
route of Bodhidharma, c. AD 525

4 Indian civilization, at the hub of long-established trade routes across the Indian Ocean *(map right)*, was remarkably well informed about much of the rest of the Eurasian world and benefitted, too, from great journeys, by sea and overland, such as that of the Buddhist missionary Bodhidharma.

> THE WORLD IS NOT EVENLY DIVIDED. OF ITS THREE PARTS, OUR ENEMIES HOLD ASIA AS THEIR HEREDITARY HOME ... BUT NOW THE CHRISTIANS OF THOSE PARTS, IF THERE ARE ANY LEFT, SQUEEZE A BARE SUBSISTENCE FROM THE SOIL AND PAY TRIBUTE TO THEIR ENEMIES ... AFRICA, TOO, HAS BEEN HELD BY OUR ENEMIES FOR 200 YEARS AND MORE ... THIRDLY, THERE IS EUROPE ... THIS LITTLE PORTION OF THE WORLD IS PRESSED UPON BY WARLIKE TURKS AND SARACENS: FOR 300 YEARS THEY HAVE HELD SPAIN AND THE BALEARIC ISLANDS, AND THEY LIVE IN HOPE OF DEVOURING THE REST.
>
> **William of Malmesbury**
> **c. 1090–1143**

c. 1450 *Population of Ming China reaches one million*

1492 *Columbus reaches Americas: European discovery of New World*

1493 *First Spanish settlement in New World*

1498 *Vasco da Gama reaches India by sea*

1500 *Shah Ismail founds Safavid dynasty in Persia*

1505 *Portuguese establish trading posts in east Africa*

c. 1510 *First African slaves shipped to Americas*

c. 1565 *Potato introduced to Europe from South America*

was backed by the resources of western industrial technology in the mid- to late 19th century.

The global impact

On the other hand, the European discoveries opened the way to a global redistribution of resources: migrations of peoples, diffusions of animals and plants, release of mineral wealth, expansion of cultivation and re-alignment of trade. The spread of food plants – almost all domesticated by prehistoric man in various parts of the world – had proceeded slowly until 1500. Thereafter, they became common to every continent. In addition, the American Indians pioneered two major cash crops: tobacco and cotton (derived largely in its commercial form from varieties they had domesticated, though other species were known and used in the Orient before 1500). Cane sugar, introduced by Europeans into Brazil and the West Indies from the late 16th century, also quickly became a staple of foreign trade.

This interchange of plants produced an enormous surge in food supplies, which made possible the unprecedented population growth after 1500. It also initiated a corresponding increase in intercontinental trade. Before 1500, this trade was limited to Eurasia and Africa and involved mostly luxury goods. After 1500, the combination of regional economic specialization and improved sea transport made possible the gradual transformation of the limited medieval luxury trade into the modern mass trade of new bulky necessities – hence the flourishing 'triangular trade' of rum, cloths, guns and other metal products from Europe to Africa, slaves from Africa to the New World and sugar, tobacco and bullion from the New World to Europe.

It was not until the 19th century, with the opening of the Suez and Panama canals and the construction of transcontinental railways in Canada, the United States, Siberia and Africa, that areas and lines of commerce which had previously been separate finally blended into a single economy on a world scale (*see* p. 254). But the first stages of global integration were completed in just over two centuries beginning in 1500.

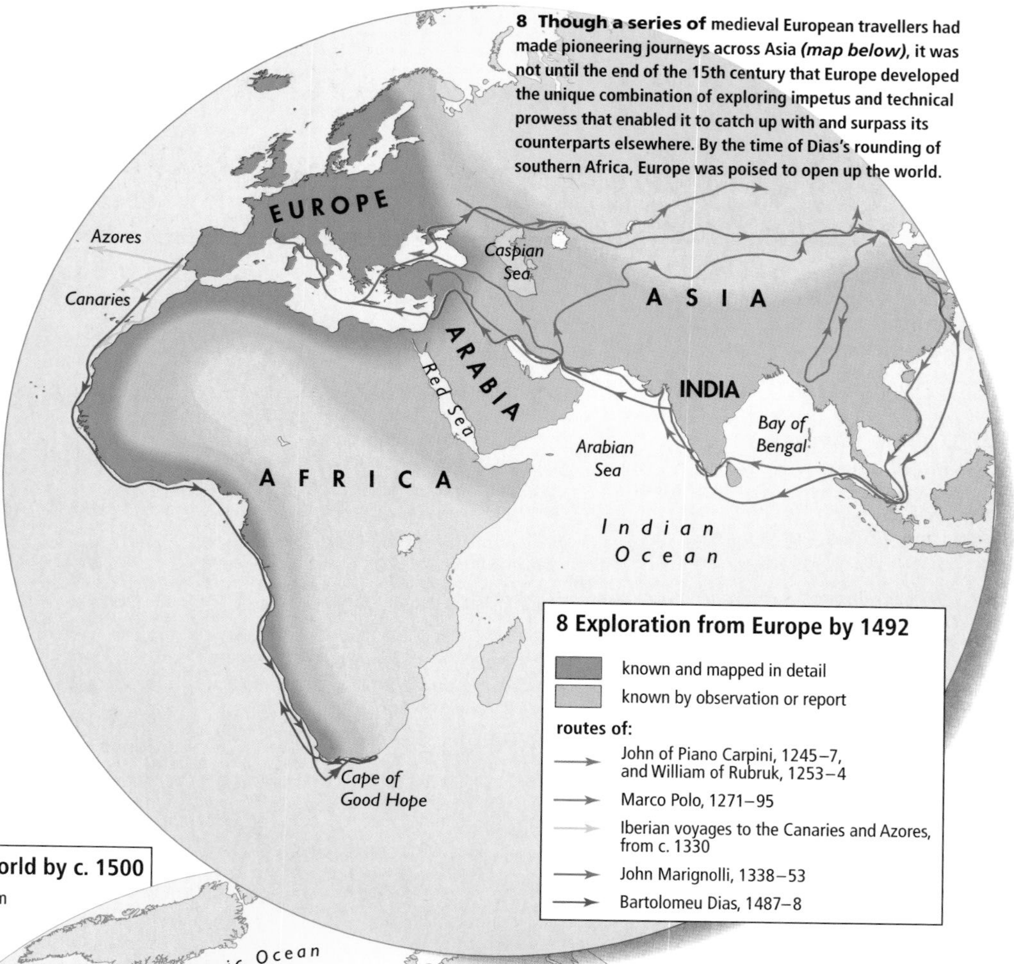

8 Though a series of medieval European travellers had made pioneering journeys across Asia *(map below)*, it was not until the end of the 15th century that Europe developed the unique combination of exploring impetus and technical prowess that enabled it to catch up with and surpass its counterparts elsewhere. By the time of Dias's rounding of southern Africa, Europe was poised to open up the world.

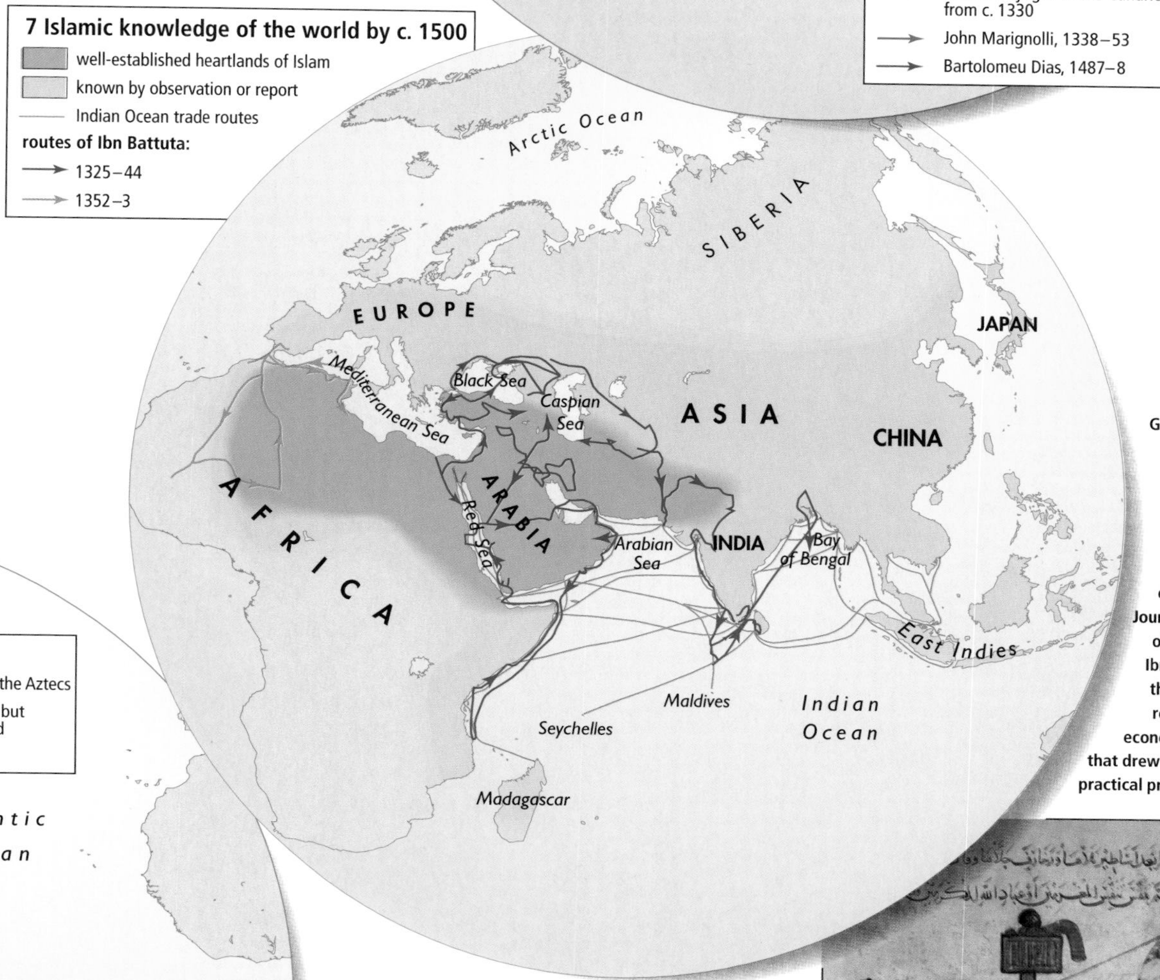

8 Exploration from Europe by 1492
- known and mapped in detail
- known by observation or report

routes of:
- John of Piano Carpini, 1245–7, and William of Rubruk, 1253–4
- Marco Polo, 1271–95
- Iberian voyages to the Canaries and Azores, from c. 1330
- John Marignolli, 1338–53
- Bartolomeu Dias, 1487–8

7 Islamic knowledge of the world by c. 1500
- well-established heartlands of Islam
- known by observation or report
- Indian Ocean trade routes

routes of Ibn Battuta:
- 1325–44
- 1352–3

7 Heir, with Europe, to the Greco-Roman legacy of geographical information and imbued with missionary zeal, Islam proved a dynamic exploring culture *(map left)*. Journeys such as those of the indefatigable Ibn Battuta testify to the unified political, religious, social and economic world-system that drew its theoretical and practical precepts from Islam.

5 Mesoamerica, c. 1500
- known and mapped in detail by the Aztecs
- known by observation or report, but not known to have been mapped
- trade routes

6 The Inca world, c. 1510
- known in detail and linked by paved roads
- probably known by observing or report, but not reached by the road system
- Inca roads

5 & 6 A combination of geography and technical deficiencies restricted both Aztec and Inca knowledge of the world *(map above)*. Deserts to their north and no more than basic maritime skills limited Aztec horizons to Mesoamerica. The Incas, meanwhile, hemmed in by the Andes and the Pacific, suffered from possessing no written means of transmitting information.

Descriptions of the volume and direction of maritime trade in the Indian Ocean prove beyond doubt that Arab shipowners and their captains were well able to navigate out of sight of land. This Indian ship from an Iraqi manuscript of 1238 *(above)* has a square sail ideal for monsoonal winds and ample space for passengers and cargo in its hold.

1487 to 1780

European voyages of discovery

See also
The emergence of states in Africa, 1000–1500 p. 140
The world on the eve of European expansion p. 154
European expansion overseas p. 158
The Americas, 1500–1800 p. 162
Southeast Asia and the European powers, 1511–1826 p. 176
The struggle for empire, 1713–1815 p. 194
The emerging global economy c. 1775 p. 198

VOYAGES INTENDED FOR SOUTH ASIA BY SOUTHEAST ROUTE:

1/Dias 1487–8 (outward) discovered open waters. of Cape Agulhas; entered Indian Ocean; reached Great Fish River.

2/Vasco da Gama 1497–8 (outward) made best use of Atlantic winds on way to Cape of Good Hope; reached India, guided by local pilot.

3/Cabral 1500 (outward) second Portuguese voyage to India; landed Brazil, probably accidentally.

4/First Portuguese voyage to Malacca, 1509.

5/Abreu 1512–3 visited Moluccas.

6/First Portuguese visits to Macao, 1516.

VOYAGES INTENDED FOR CHINA AND SOUTH ASIA BY WEST OR SOUTHWEST ROUTE:

7/Da Mota, Zeimoto and Peixoto 1542–3 Portuguese discovery of Japan.

8/Columbus 1492–3 (outward and homeward) discovered Bahama group, explored n. coasts of Cuba and Hispaniola; found best return route.

9/Columbus 1493–4 (outward) explored s. coast of Cuba; reported it as peninsula of mainland China.

10/Columbus 1498 (outward) discovered Trinidad and Venezuela; recognized coast as mainland.

11/Columbus 1502–4 explored coast of Honduras, Nicaragua and the Isthmus.

12/Ojeda and Vespucci 1499–1500 (outward) reached Guiana coast, failed to round Cape São Roque, followed coast w. to Cape de la Vela.

13/Coelho and Vespucci 1501 (outward) followed coast s. from Cape São Agostinho to 35°S.

14/Solís 1515 entered River Plate estuary and investigated n. bank.

15/Magellan and Elcano 1519-22 discovered Strait of Magellan, crossed Pacific, reached Moluccas via Philippines; first circumnavigation.

16/Saavedra 1527 discovered route from Mexico across Pacific to Moluccas.

17/Urdaneta 1565 found feasible return route Philippines to Mexico in 42°N. using w. winds.

18/Schouten and Le Maire 1616 discovered route into Pacific via Le Maire Strait and Cape Horn.

VOYAGES INTENDED FOR ASIA BY NORTHWEST AND NORTHEAST ROUTE:

19/Cabot 1497 (outward) re-discovered Newfoundland, first sighted by Norsemen 11th C.

20/Corte-Real 1500 re-discovered Greenland.

21/Verazzano 1524 traced e. coast of N. America from (probably) 34°N. to 47°N.; revealed continental character of N. America.

22/Cartier 1534 and 1535 explored Strait of Belle Isle and St Lawrence as far as Montreal.

23/Willoughby and Chancellor 1553 rounded North Cape and reached Archangel.

24/Frobisher 1576 reached Frobisher Bay in Baffin Island, which he took for a 'strait'.

25/Davis 1587 explored w. coast of Greenland to the edge of the ice in 72° N.

26/Barents 1596–7 discovered Bear Island and Spitsbergen; wintered in Novaya Zemlya.

27/Hudson 1610 sailed through Hudson Strait to the s. extremity of Hudson Bay.

28/Button 1612 explored w. coast of Hudson Bay, concluded Bay landlocked on the w.

29/Baffin and Bylot 1616 explored whole coast of Baffin Bay; concluded no navigable nw. passage existed in that area.

Between 1480 and 1780, European explorers discovered and mapped almost all of the world's seas and the outlines of almost all the continents. Impelled by a variety of motives – trade, personal enrichment, glory and, by the 18th century, scientific knowledge – their legacy is today's world map, a common resource of all mankind.

IN 1480 THE PRINCIPAL SEAFARING peoples of the world were separated not only by great expanses of uncharted sea but by continental landmasses whose extent and shape were unknown. Regular European shipping was still mainly confined to the north Atlantic, the Mediterranean and the Baltic. The west African coast had been explored cursorily and only very recently by Europeans, while the coast from Gaboon to Mozambique was unknown to any regular long-range shipping. In the Americas, limited raft and canoe-borne navigation took place on the Pacific coasts of Ecuador and Peru and in the Caribbean, but there was no communication with Europe nor – so far as is known – with other parts of the Pacific.

In the east, several seafaring peoples overlapped. Indian, Persian and Arab ships plied the northern Indian Ocean. Chinese shipping, which in the past had sailed intermittently to east Africa, by 1480 usually went no farther than Malacca, sharing the shallow seas of the Malay archipelago with local shipping, chiefly Javanese. To the east, it

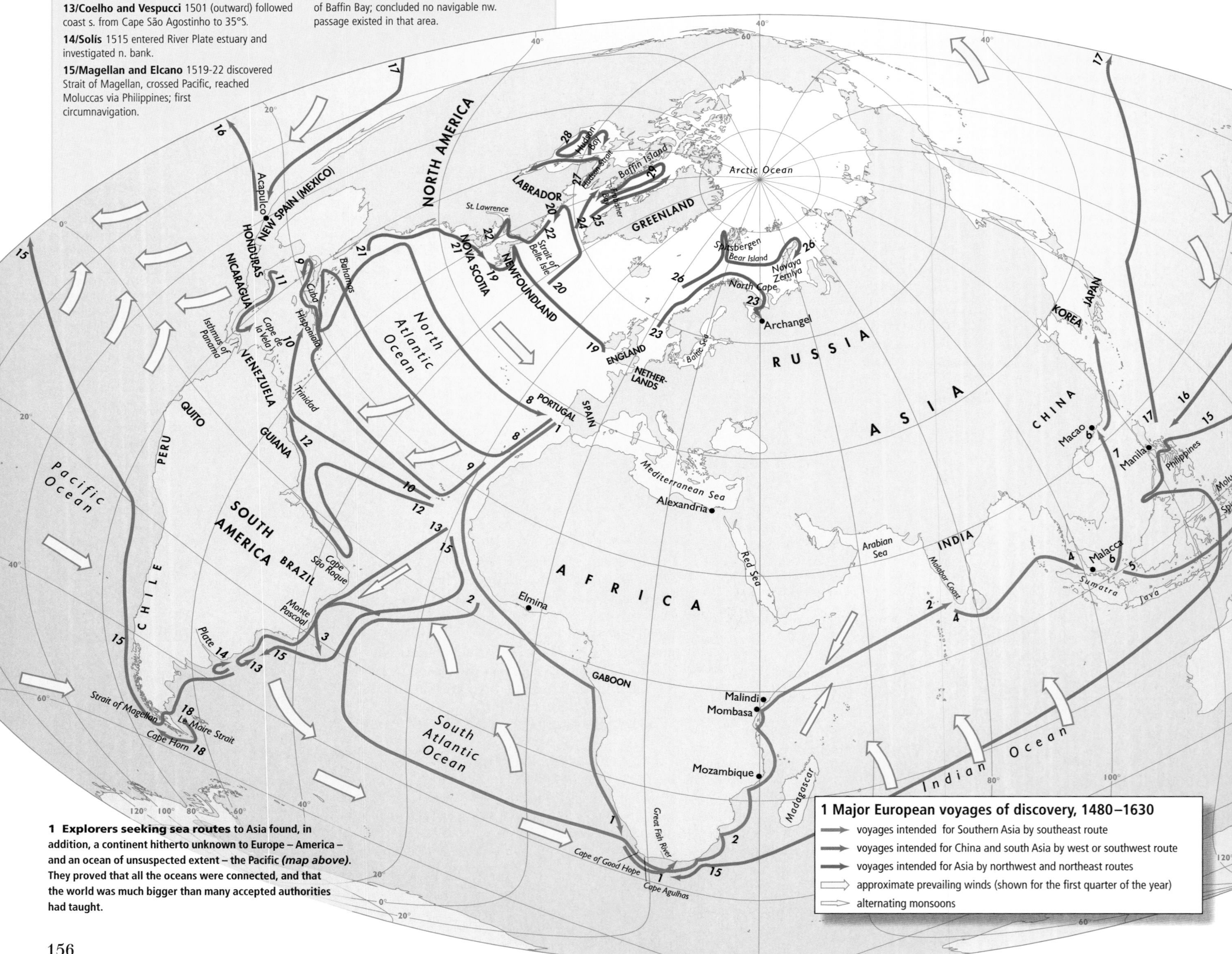

1 Explorers seeking sea routes to Asia found, in addition, a continent hitherto unknown to Europe – America – and an ocean of unsuspected extent – the Pacific *(map above)*. They proved that all the oceans were connected, and that the world was much bigger than many accepted authorities had taught.

went no farther than the Philippines. No shipping used the southern Indian Ocean: Javanese contacts with Madagascar had long ceased. The great expanses of the central Pacific were crossed only occasionally and perilously by Polynesian canoes. In the north Pacific, except in Japanese and Korean coastal waters, there was no shipping at all.

The Spanish and Portuguese

The European voyages of discovery began early in the 15th century when Portuguese navigators advanced southward, round the west coast of Africa, in search of gold, slaves and spices, until in 1487 Dias and de Covilha brought them into the Indian Ocean. Thenceforth voyages of exploration multiplied, particularly after the resurgence of Islam made the old route to the east via Alexandria and the Red Sea precarious.

While the Spanish sailed west, the Portuguese explored the eastern route to Asia. Once in the Indian Ocean they quickly reached their goal: Malabar (1498), Malacca (1509) and the Moluccas (1512). The Spanish search for a western route to the Spice Islands was less successful but its unintended and momentous result was Columbus's discovery of the New World in 1492 followed by the Spanish conquest of the Americas (see p. 162). But it was not until after 1524, when Verazzano traced the coastline of North America as far north as Nova Scotia, that the existence of the new continent was generally accepted.

Meanwhile the search for a western route to Asia continued, leading to extensive exploration of the Caribbean. Finally, in 1521 Magellan rounded South America, entered the Pacific and reached the Philippines, but his route would prove too long and too hazardous for commercial purposes. In 1557 the Portuguese occupied Macao and after 1571 Spanish galleons traded between Manila and Acapulco in Mexico. The combined effect of these Spanish and Portuguese voyages had been to show that all the oceans of the southern hemisphere were connected. At the same time, for about a century Spain and Portugal were able to prevent other Europeans from using these connecting sea passages, other than for occasional raids.

The French, British and Dutch

As a result, the exploration of the Pacific was delayed until the 18th century. In part at least it was inspired as much by scientific curiosity as by hope of commercial gain. It was the work of British, Dutch and Russians seeking a navigable passage via the Arctic between the Atlantic and the Pacific and hoping also to locate a hypothetical southern continent. Both proved illusory but the result was the charting of New Zealand and the eastern coast of Australia, both opened in a few years to European colonization.

Meanwhile, England and France, unwilling to recognize the monopoly claimed by Spain and Portugal in the Treaty of Tordesillas of 1494 (see p. 158), had embarked on a series of voyages intended to reach Asia by a northern route. All these proved abortive and were abandoned after 1632, but they resulted in the opening of North America to European settlement. The English, French and Dutch were also unwilling to abandon the profitable trade with south and southeast Asia to the Portuguese and Spaniards and the later years of the 16th and first half of the 17th centuries saw a determined and ultimately successful effort to breach their privileged position (see p. 176).

After 1500 direct sea contact was established between continents and regions which hitherto had developed in isolation. It was necessarily a slow process and for a long time the European footholds in Asia and Africa remained tenuous. But by the time of the death of the last great explorer, James Cook in 1779, few of the world's coastlines remained to be explored.

To discover what lay beyond the Canaries and Cape Bojador; to trade with any Christians who might dwell in the lands beyond; to discover the extent of the Mohammedan dominions; to find a Christian king who would help him to fight the infidel; to spread the Christian faith; to fulfil the predictions of his horoscope, which bound him to engage in great and noble conquests and attempt the discovery of things that were hidden from other men; to find Guinea.

Gomez Eannes de Azurara
15th-century chronicler of Henry the Navigator

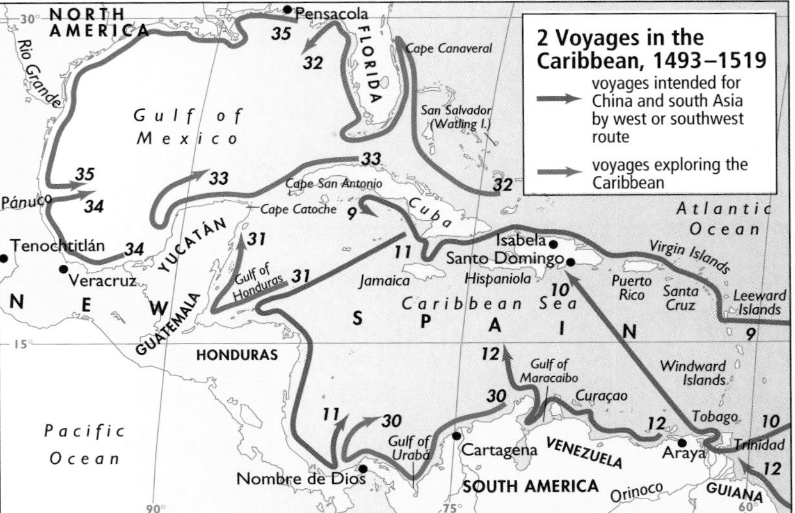

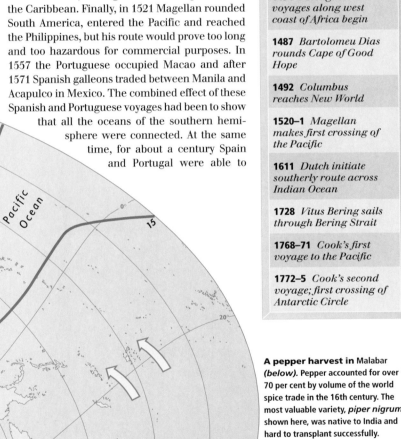

2 VOYAGES IN THE CARIBBEAN, 1492–1519

Spanish expeditions explored the Caribbean searching for a seaway to China, India and the Golden Chersonese. They found it landlocked on the west; took to slaving, pearling and plunder; encountered settled, city-building peoples; and founded a European empire

30/Bastidas and La Cosa 1501–2 explored coast from Gulf of Maracaibo to Gulf of Urabá.

31/Pinzón and Solís 1508 sent from Spain to find strait to Asia, perhaps followed e. coast of Yucatán.

32/Ponce de León 1512–3 sailed from Puerto Rico, explored Florida from n. of Cape Canaveral to (possibly) Pensacola; may have sighted Yucatán on return; first explorer to note force of Gulf Stream.

33/Hernández de Córdoba 1517 sailed from Cuba, explored n. and w. coasts of Yucatán; first report of Maya cities.

34/Grijalva 1518 followed s. and w. coasts of Gulf of Mexico as far as River Pánuco.

35/Pineda 1519 explored n. and w. coasts of Gulf of Mexico from Florida to River Pánuco; ended hope of strait to Pacific in that region.

- **1434** *Portuguese voyages along west coast of Africa begin*
- **1487** *Bartolomeu Dias rounds Cape of Good Hope*
- **1492** *Columbus reaches New World*
- **1520–1** *Magellan makes first crossing of the Pacific*
- **1611** *Dutch initiate southerly route across Indian Ocean*
- **1728** *Vitus Bering sails through Bering Strait*
- **1768–71** *Cook's first voyage to the Pacific*
- **1772–5** *Cook's second voyage; first crossing of Antarctic Circle*

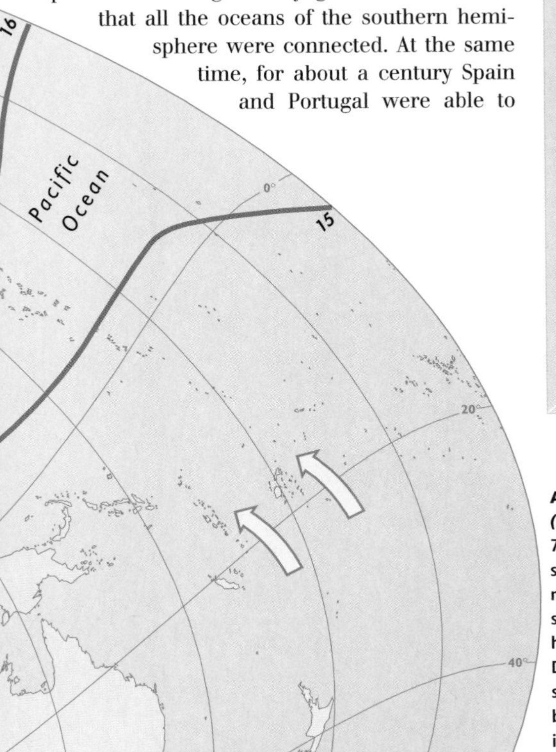

A pepper harvest in Malabar *(below)*. Pepper accounted for over 70 per cent by volume of the world spice trade in the 16th century. The most valuable variety, *piper nigrum*, shown here, was native to India and hard to transplant successfully. Demand from Europe and China spread it to selective parts of the East, but Portuguese efforts to introduce it in Africa and America in the 17th century met with little success.

3 European exploration in the Pacific, 1720–80

Cook's first voyage, 1768–71
Cook's second voyage, 1772–5
Cook's third voyage, 1776–80
other 18th-century voyages

3 18TH-CENTURY VOYAGES IN THE PACIFIC:

Most 18th-century voyages of discovery in the Pacific were searches for a habitable southern continent or for a usable northern strait between the Pacific and Atlantic. Both proved imaginary. The expeditions instead confirmed the immensity of the Pacific and revealed the islands of New Zealand, a habitable eastern Australia, numerous islands and a valuable whale fishery.

36/Roggeveen 1722 discovered Easter Island and some of the Samoan group; circumnavigated globe.

37/Bering 1728 sailed from Kamchatka, discovered strait separating ne. Asia and nw. America.

38/Wallis 1766–8 discovered Society Islands (Tahiti), encouraged hope of habitable southern continent; circumnavigated globe.

39/Cook 1768–71 charted coasts of New Zealand, explored e. coast of Australia, confirmed existence of Torres Strait; circumnavigated globe.

40/Cook 1772–5 made circuit of southern oceans in high latitude, charted New Hebrides, discovered many islands, ended hope of habitable southern continent; circumnavigated globe.

41/Cook and Clerke 1776–80 discovered Sandwich Islands (Hawaii), explored nw. coast of N. America from Vancouver Island to Unimak Pass, sailed through Bering Strait to edge of pack ice, ended hope of navigable passage through Arctic to Atlantic.

European expansion overseas

Portuguese 16th-century traders established Europe's trading links with Africa, India, the Malay archipelago, China and Japan and dominated the African trade in gold and slaves. But by the 17th century growing Dutch, British and French competition was challenging both Portugal's position and Spain's dominance in the West Indies.

1480 *Portuguese found and fortify Elmina*

1507 *Portuguese occupy Mozambique*

1510 *Portuguese capture Goa*

1511 *Portuguese capture and occupy Malacca*

1515 *Portuguese occupy Ormuz*

1557 *Portuguese established at Macao*

1600 *English East India Company incorporated*

1602 *Dutch East India Company incorporated*

1619 *Dutch East India Company established at Batavia*

1652 *Dutch settlement at Cape of Good Hope*

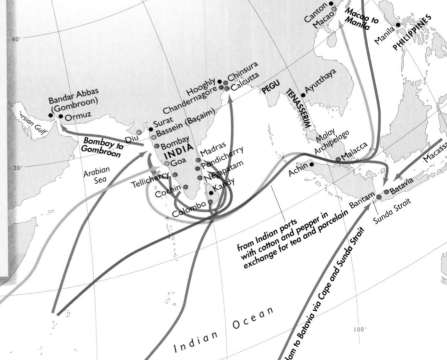

THE DISCOVERIES BY EUROPEAN explorers in the late 15th century were rapidly exploited. By 1500, Portuguese possessions outside Europe included several island groups in the Atlantic and the Gulf of Guinea, and a number of trading stations on the west coast of Africa – above all the fortress-factory of Elmina. A dozen or so ships made the voyage between Portugal and Guinea every year, bartering hard-ware and cloth for slaves and gold dust.

After the sea route to India was discovered (*see* p. 156), the Portuguese attempted to become the main suppliers of spices to Europe by capturing or leasing trading posts and fortified bases on the east coast of Africa, around the north shores of the Indian Ocean and in the Malay archipelago. By the mid-16th century, they had a tenuous string of more than 50 forts and factories. Strategically, the most important were Mozambique (1507), Goa (1510), Ormuz (1515) and Malacca (1511). East of Malacca, the Portuguese position was precarious and their activity completely commercial. In 1557, with the agreement of the Chinese, they established a base at Macao. From there, they traded to Nagasaki, where they were welcomed as carriers of Chinese goods, since the Chinese themselves were forbidden to trade with Japan. At Ternate, they maintained a warehouse until 1575, when they were expelled by a league of Muslim princes.

Portugal's trading empire

All these Far Eastern enterprises, together with the gold of the Zambezi basin, exported through Sofala, paid for the pepper and other spices shipped annually from Goa to Lisbon for distribution to western Europe. Though the Portuguese never achieved anything like a monopoly, their power was sufficient to channel much of the Indian Ocean trade through harbours under their control, and for 100 years they had no real European rivals. Only the Spanish, whose main interest lay in the Americas, showed a parallel interest in the Far East (*see* p. 162).

Once the Portuguese had started to settle Brazil in the 1530s, the Brazilian demand for slave labour breathed new life into the Portuguese trading stations in west Africa, where the gold trade had dwindled as the gold became exhausted and caused traders to extend their operations from Guinea south to Angola. The Portuguese slave depot of Luanda was founded in 1575 and slave ships shuttled directly between Angola and Brazil, with the slaves paid for by Brazilian tobacco.

Dutch expansion

From the opening years of the 17th century, the Portuguese in the East began to experience significant competition from other European countries. This usually organized itself in the form of joint

Bahamas English from 1670 (Treaty of Madrid)
Belize Acknowledged as Spanish but occupied c. 1660 by English logwood cutters
Curaçao Captured from Spain by Dutch 1634; formally ceded 1648 (Treaty of Münster)
Jamaica Captured from Spain by English 1655; formally ceded 1670 (Treaty of Madrid)
Leeward Islands Barbuda (1628), Nevis (1628), Antigua (1632), Anguilla (1650): continuously English. Montserrat: English (1632); taken by French, restored 1668. St Christopher: shared by English and French settlers (1625–1713), then wholly English. St Barthélemy, Guadeloupe and Marie Galante: French from first settlement (1648, 1635, 1648). St Eustatius (1648), Saba (1640), St Martin (1648): confirmed as Dutch 1648. Dominica: claimed by England and France; inhabited only by Caribs in 1713
Mosquito Coast English alliance with local Indians; a few English settlers; claimed by Spain
St-Domingue Evacuated by Spain c.1605; occupied by French buccaneers; formally ceded to France 1697 (Treaty of Rijswijk)
Tobago French from 1677
Virgin Islands Tortola: English from 1666. St Thomas: Danish from 1671
Windward Islands Martinique: continuously French since first settlement (1635). Grenada: claimed by France 1650; by 1713 a few French settlers. St Lucia and St Vincent: disputed between England and France; inhabited only by Caribs in 1713.

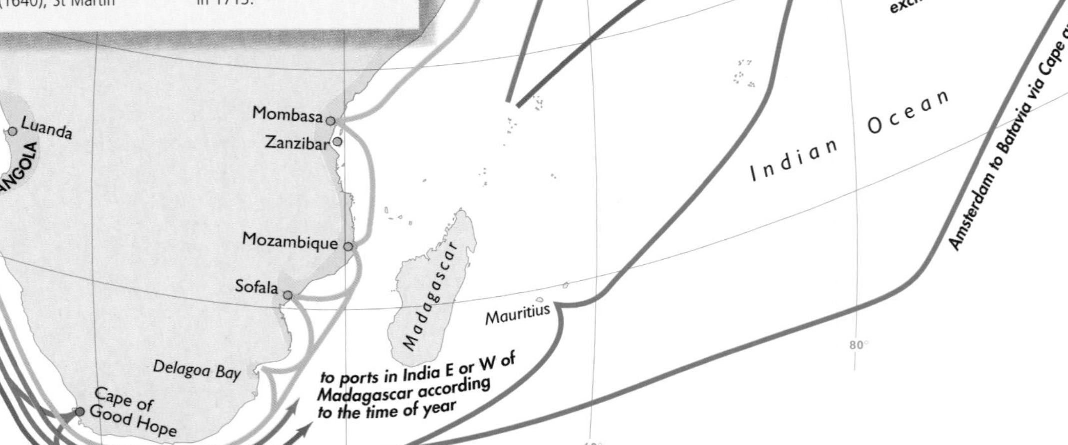

3 Columbus's first landfall in 1492 was in the West Indies *(map above right)*. On his second visit, in 1493, he encountered the Carib Indians who would subsequently give their name to this region of tropical islands. The Spanish settlement of Hispaniola began in the same year, with the settlers hoping to find gold and to use the island as a launch-pad for trade with China, which they erroneously thought nearby. Hispaniola became the Spanish base for the settlement of Central America, Cuba for that of Mexico. In the 17th century, the British, French and Dutch began to challenge the supremacy Spain had established over the Caribbean. Over the course of time, the West Indies would become famous for their sugar crop (sugar was the most profitable of all the exotic products imported into Europe in Early Modern times). From the middle of the 17th century until after the end of the 18th, sugar-producing islands in the West Indies were frequently regarded by the British, French and Dutch governments as the most valuable of all their colonial possessions. They were often subjects of dispute between the governments.

Captured by the Portuguese in 1510, Goa, on the west coast of India, became the capital of Portugal's empire in the East. This illustration *(left)* is by the Dutchman Jan van Linschoten, sent to the East at the end of the century on an intelligence-gathering mission which went far to helping the Dutch in their subsequent expansion. Despite the apparent prosperity of the town, its security was threatened by the Dutch expansion in the East. Unlike many of the Portuguese outposts in the East, which were easily taken by the Dutch early in the 17th century as their own commercial empire took shape, Goa remained Portuguese until 1961.

1 & 2 The Portuguese empire in the East consisted of fortified bases and trading posts, few of them bigger than a single city and its immediate hinterland *(maps above and far left)*. Some of them were mere warehouse compounds. Nonetheless, by 1600, there were more than 50 such establishments. In the next century, the Dutch, English and French established their own trading stations and gradually supplanted the Portuguese. But as their trading posts in the East were eliminated, so the Portuguese reinforced their position in South America. By 1600, coastal Brazil had become the foremost sugar-producing territory in the western hemisphere.

THE HOLLANDERS SAY WE GO ABOUTE TO REAPE THE FRUITS OF THEIR LABOURS. IT IS RATHER THE CONTRARYE FOR THAT THEY SEEM TO BARRE US OF OUR LIBERTIE TO TRADE IN A FREE COUNTRYE, HAVING MANIE TIMES TRADED IN THESE PLACES, AND NOWE THEY SEEKE TO DEFRAUD US OF THAT WE HAVE SO LONG SOUGHT FOR.

John Jourdain of the English East India Company on Anglo-Dutch rivalry for control of the spice trade, 1613

stock companies, empowered to trade, settle, conquer, administer and defend. The most formidable, at least to begin with, was the Dutch East India Company, formally incorporated in 1602. In 1619, this vast concern, the biggest trading corporation in Europe, established its eastern headquarters at Batavia, well to the south (and east) of Goa and Malacca, thus acquiring a permanent strategic advantage. Its ships pioneered a direct route to Batavia, provisioning (after 1652) at the new Dutch settlement at the Cape of Good Hope, then running east before the 'roaring forties' and entering the archipelago by the Sunda Strait. By acquiring bases in strategic locations, by bringing pressure on local rulers and by squeezing other Europeans out, it established a monopoly of the more valuable trades of the archipelago. Elsewhere in the East it traded in competition with native and European merchants on terms dictated by local rulers, though throughout the 17th century it held its own against all European rivals.

European rivalries

The English East India Company, incorporated in 1600, was a rather smaller concern and usually proved unable to resist Dutch pressure in the archipelago. It engaged principally in trade in cotton goods and pepper from India, first at the Mughal port of Surat, later at stations of its own at Madras, Bombay and Calcutta. In 1685 it began a modest trade with China, purchasing tea and porcelain at Amoy and later at Canton, where from 1698 its agents found themselves in direct competition with the French Compagnie de Chine.

As a result of the commercial competition and naval aggression of these corporations (which continued irrespective of whether there was formal war or peace in Europe), the Portuguese Estado de India shrank both in territorial extent and in commercial profit. The Red Sea and the Persian Gulf both became commercial backwaters as the joint-stock companies carried more and more of the trade between Europe and Asia in their own capacious and well-armed ships. Meanwhile, the Dutch West India Company – less well entrenched than its eastern counterpart, but formidable nonetheless – conquered the Brazilian coastal region of Pernambuco in 1630 and over the next few years seized the Portuguese slaving stations in west Africa, without which the Brazilian plantation system appeared unworkable. But in the 1640s, with the end of the long period of union (1580–1640) of the Spanish and Portuguese crowns, the Portuguese recovered the Angola slave-pens and in 1654 drove the Dutch from Brazil. The West India Company now turned its attention to the Caribbean.

1462 to 1815
Russian expansion in Europe and Asia

See also
The first Russian state: Kievan Rus, 882–1242 p. 114
The Mongol empire, 1206–1405 p. 128
The struggle for the Baltic, 1523–1721 p. 188
The age of partition: eastern Europe, 1648–1795 p. 196
The Russian empire: expansion and modernization, 1815–1917 p. 230

The Grand Duchy of Muscovy emerged in the late 15th century as a powerful state with claims to the legacy of Kievan Rus. Though it spread rapidly east and south, expansion in the west was blocked by Lithuania, which included many of the lands of Kievan Rus. Only after 1648 did Muscovy prevail, laying the foundations of the Russian empire.

Russian woodcut showing a procession of merchants carrying furs at the court of the Holy Roman Emperor c. 1570 ***(above)***. By the early 17th century the demand for luxury furs fuelled expansion eastwards into Siberia to tap its seemingly inexhaustible supply.

3 The Union of Lublin (1569) between Poland and Lithuania created a formidable barrier to Russian expansion to the west ***(map below)***. Poland-Lithuania expanded steadily at Muscovy's expense after 1569, until the tables turned following the 1648 Cossack revolt.

THE EBBING OF MONGOL POWER and the collapse of the Byzantine empire opened the way for the emergence of Muscovy as a European power. Proclaiming Muscovy's independence from the Mongols in 1480, Ivan III (1462–1505) laid claim to the heritage of Kievan Rus and, by marrying the daughter of the last Byzantine emperor and adopting the double-headed eagle as his emblem, to that of Byzantium. The last independent Orthodox state after 1453, Muscovy proclaimed itself the leader of the Orthodox world, with Moscow raised to a metropolitanate in 1448 and a patriarchate in 1589.

Muscovy's growing power was manifested in the ruthless annexations of Novgorod (1478) and Pskov (1510) and the seizure of Smolensk from Lithuania (1514). The conquest of the khanates of Kazan (1552) and Astrakhan (1556) conferred control of the Volga and opened the way to the east and the south. Expansion was not so easy to the west, where the tsars' claim to rule 'all the Russias' was challenged by the grand dukes of Lithuania, most of whose subjects were eastern Slavs with elites increasingly attracted by the participative political system of Poland. The 1569 Union of Lublin between Poland and Lithuania, which saw the direct incorporation of Lithuania's Ukrainian territories into the kingdom of Poland, led to the creation of a sophisticated noble democracy with a common diet (parliament) and an elective monarchy that was in stark contrast to the centralized Muscovite autocracy.

Between 1558 and 1634, Poland-Lithuania repulsed all Muscovite attempts to expand westwards. Ivan IV's attempts to take Livonia were beaten off, Sigismund III regained Smolensk and Chernigov at the Treaty of Deulino (1618/19), while during the 'Time of Troubles' (1605–13), Sigismund's son Władysław was elected tsar by a group of boyars, and a Polish garrison occupied the Kremlin (1610–12). A Muscovite attempt to retake Smolensk in 1632–4 was repulsed decisively.

Growth of empire

The turning-point came during the Thirteen Years' War (1654–67). At the 1654 Treaty of Pereyaslav, Tsar Alexis Mikhailovich (1645–76) extended Muscovy's protection to the Zaporozhian Cossacks, who had rebelled against Poland in 1648. Although Alexis failed to hold on to the large areas of Lithuania annexed in 1654–5, the 1667 Treaty of Andrusovo granted Muscovy those areas of the Ukraine on the left bank of the Dnieper and, albeit only for three years, Kiev, though in 1686 the Poles were forced to recognize its permanent loss. The capture of Kiev and left-bank Ukraine made good part of the tsars' claim to rule all the Russias; the Ukraine was dubbed 'Little Russia' in contrast to 'Great Russia', the empire's Muscovite heartland. Muscovy had become Russia.

As Poland-Lithuania weakened, Russian expansion continued. The military improvements under Alexis were completed by his son, Peter I (the Great), who captured Azov from the Ottomans before turning his attention northwards. In a long war, marked by his great victory at Poltava in 1709, Peter finally wrested Estonia and Livonia from Sweden at the Treaty of Nystad (1721), acquired the ancient port of Riga and founded the new one of St Petersburg.

His successors reverted to the policy of expansion in the south, which was carried to a successful conclusion by Catherine II (the Great) in her first (1768–74) and second (1787–92) Turkish wars. The Crimea was annexed, and Russia now controlled the northern shore of the Black Sea from the Dniester to the Caucasus. The period from 1772 to 1815 then saw the Russian land frontier advanced by 600 miles at the expense of Poland. By the partitions of 1772, 1793 and 1795 (*see* p. 196), Russia obtained much of the former Polish-Lithuanian Commonwealth, in the process acquiring a further 5.5 million inhabitants. Indeed throughout the period as a whole the population of Russia expanded dramatically from an estimated 10 million in 1600 to nearly 43 million in 1812.

1569 *Union of Lublin*

1618 *Treaty of Deulino: highpoint of Polish-Lithuanian eastward expansion*

1648 *Revolt of the Zaporozhian Cossacks against Poland-Lithuania*

1654 *Treaty of Pereyaslav: Tsar Alexis extends protection over Ukraine*

1667 *Treaty of Andrusovo: Russia acquires Kiev and the Ukraine lands on the left bank of the Dnieper*

1703 *Foundation of St Petersburg*

1772–95 *Partitions of Poland-Lithuania*

2 Though the Russian population of Siberia was only 200,000 by the mid-17th century, the speed of Russia's expansion was nonetheless prodigious ***(map left)***. Other than the Amur basin, annexed from China but returned by the 1689 Treaty of Nerchinsk, most of this vast area was acquired from indigenous peoples .

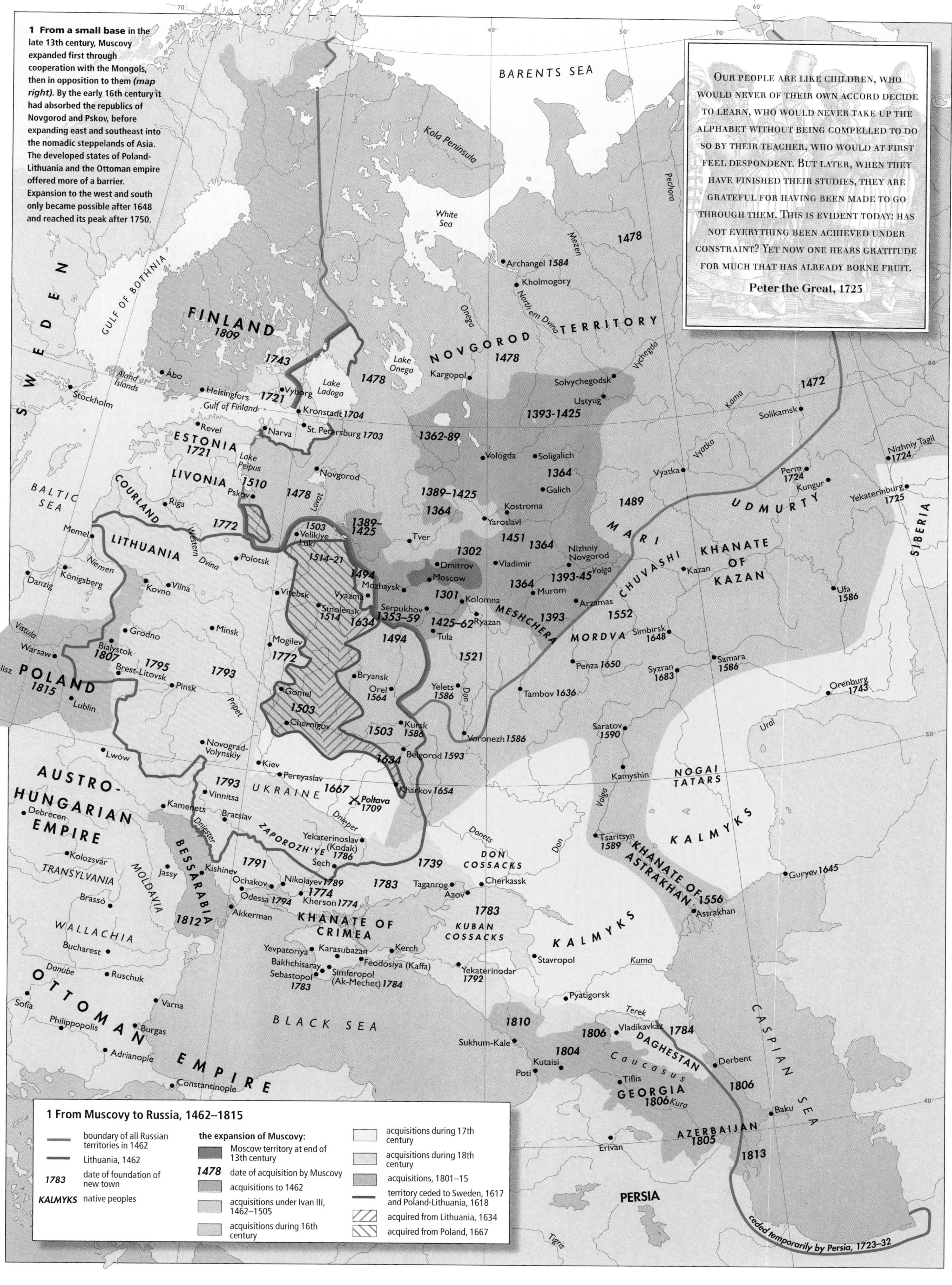

1 From a small base in the late 13th century, Muscovy expanded first through cooperation with the Mongols, then in opposition to them *(map right)*. By the early 16th century it had absorbed the republics of Novgorod and Pskov, before expanding east and southeast into the nomadic steppelands of Asia. The developed states of Poland-Lithuania and the Ottoman empire offered more of a barrier. Expansion to the west and south only became possible after 1648 and reached its peak after 1750.

OUR PEOPLE ARE LIKE CHILDREN, WHO WOULD NEVER OF THEIR OWN ACCORD DECIDE TO LEARN, WHO WOULD NEVER TAKE UP THE ALPHABET WITHOUT BEING COMPELLED TO DO SO BY THEIR TEACHER, WHO WOULD AT FIRST FEEL DESPONDENT. BUT LATER, WHEN THEY HAVE FINISHED THEIR STUDIES, THEY ARE GRATEFUL FOR HAVING BEEN MADE TO GO THROUGH THEM. THIS IS EVIDENT TODAY: HAS NOT EVERYTHING BEEN ACHIEVED UNDER CONSTRAINT? YET NOW ONE HEARS GRATITUDE FOR MUCH THAT HAS ALREADY BORNE FRUIT.
Peter the Great, 1723

1 From Muscovy to Russia, 1462–1815
boundary of all Russian territories in 1462
Lithuania, 1462
1783 date of foundation of new town
KALMYKS native peoples
the expansion of Muscovy:
Moscow territory at end of 13th century
1478 date of acquisition by Muscovy
acquisitions to 1462
acquisitions under Ivan III, 1462–1505
acquisitions during 16th century
acquisitions during 17th century
acquisitions during 18th century
acquisitions, 1801–15
territory ceded to Sweden, 1617 and Poland-Lithuania, 1618
acquired from Lithuania, 1634
acquired from Poland, 1667

BARENTS SEA
Kola Peninsula
White Sea
SWEDEN
GULF OF BOTHNIA
FINLAND 1809
Åland Islands
Åbo
Stockholm
Helsingfors
Gulf of Finland
Vyborg 1721
Lake Ladoga
Lake Onega
Kronstadt 1704
St. Petersburg 1703
Narva
Revel
ESTONIA 1721
Lake Peipus
LIVONIA
Pskov 1510
Novgorod
Riga
COURLAND
BALTIC SEA
Memel
LITHUANIA
Königsberg
Danzig
Kovno
Vilna
Polotsk
Vitebsk
Smolensk 1514
Minsk
Grodno
Bialystok 1807
Warsaw
Kalisz
POLAND 1815
Lublin
Brest-Litovsk
Pinsk
Mogilev 1772
Gomel
Chernigov
Novograd-Volynskiy
Lwów
Kiev
Pereyaslav
AUSTRO-HUNGARIAN EMPIRE
Debrecen
Kolozsvár
TRANSYLVANIA
MOLDAVIA
BESSARABIA 1812
Jassy
Kishinev
Kamenets
Vinnitsa
Bratslav
UKRAINE
Poltava 1709
ZAPOROZH'YE
Yekaterinoslav (Kodak) 1786
Sech
Ochakov
Nikolayev 1789
Odessa 1794
Kherson 1774
Akkerman
KHANATE OF CRIMEA
Yevpatoriya
Karasubazar
Kerch
Bakhchisaray
Feodosiya (Kaffa)
Sebastopol 1783
Simferopol (Ak-Mechet) 1784
Brassó
WALLACHIA
Bucharest
Danube
Ruschuk
OTTOMAN EMPIRE
Sofia
Varna
Philippopolis
Burgas
Adrianople
Constantinople
BLACK SEA
Archangel 1584
Kholmogory
Northern Dvina
NOVGOROD TERRITORY 1478
Kargopol
Onega
Mezen
Pechora
Vychegda
Solvychegodsk
Ustyug
Vologda
Soligalich
Galich
Kostroma
Yaroslavl
Tver
Velikiye Luki
Dmitrov
Moscow
Vladimir
Mozhaysk
Vyazma
Kolomna
Serpukhov
Ryazan
Tula
Murom
Nizhniy Novgorod
Arzamas
MESHCHERA
Bryansk
Orel 1564
Yelets 1586
Kursk 1586
Belgorod 1593
Kharkov 1654
Voronezh 1586
Tambov 1636
Penza 1650
MORDVA
Simbirsk 1648
Syzran 1683
Samara 1586
Kazan
KHANATE OF KAZAN
CHUVASHI
MARI
UDMURTY
Vyatka
Kama
Perm 1724
Kungur
Solikamsk
Nizhniy Tagil 1724
Yekaterinburg 1725
SIBERIA
Ufa 1586
Orenburg 1743
Ural
Saratov 1590
Kamyshin
NOGAI TATARS
KALMYKS
Volga
Don
Donets
Tsaritsyn 1589
KHANATE OF ASTRAKHAN
Astrakhan 1556
Guryev 1645
DON COSSACKS
Taganrog
Azov
Cherkassk
KUBAN COSSACKS
Yekaterinodar 1792
Stavropol
Kuma
Pyatigorsk
Terek
Vladikavkaz 1784
DAGHESTAN
Derbent
Caucasus
Sukhum-Kale
Kutaisi
Poti
Tiflis
GEORGIA 1806
Kura
Baku
AZERBAIJAN 1805
Erivan
CASPIAN SEA
PERSIA
Tigris
ceded temporarily by Persia, 1723–32

See also
The Americas on the eve of European conquest p. 148
The world on the eve of European expansion p. 154
European voyages of discovery, 1487–1780 p. 156
European expansion overseas p. 158
The struggle for empire, 1713–1815 p. 194
The age of revolt, 1773–1814 p. 202
Latin America: independence and national growth, 1810–1930 p. 226

The Americas

1519–20 *Cortés conquers the Aztec empire*

1531–33 *Spanish invasion of Peru*

1549 *Bahia founded in Portuguese Brazil*

1607 *English settlement founded at Jamestown, Virginia*

1620 *Arrival of the* Mayflower *pilgrims*

1664 *English seize New Amsterdam (later New York) from the Dutch*

1718 *New Orleans founded by France*

1763 *Treaty of Paris transfers most French North American possessions to Britain*

1776 *Declaration of American independence*

Within 40 years of Columbus's discovery of America, the Spanish had overturned two rich empires, the Aztecs and Incas. They and the Portuguese dominated the 'New World' for over a century more, but by 1700 the French and English held sway over much of North America. New colonial societies were emerging, however, which were to cast off European control.

By 1500, IN THE WAKE of Columbus's voyages, around 6,000 Spaniards had already emigrated to the New World. For over a century the Spanish were to dominate the settlement of the Americas. The pace of colonization accelerated enormously after the discovery and conquest of two fabulously rich empires: the Aztec in Mesoamerica and the Inca in the Andean region. Relatively small Spanish forces were able to exploit existing divisions within these societies to replace the old dominant groups without arousing much new opposition. News of the conquest of central Mexico attracted a rush of emigrants during the 1520s. A similar movement followed the conquest of Inca Peru in the early 1530s. The two areas became the main foci of Spanish settlement in the New World. Greatly productive silver mines were discovered, both in Mexico and Peru. By the 1560s, silver had become the chief export to Spain.

The Portuguese, French and English

In 1494 the Spanish and Portuguese had established a line of demarcation between them in the New World by the Treaty of Tordesillas, with the Portuguese allocated the territories east of the line. However, the Portuguese only settled Brazil in the 1530s. With its administrative capital at Bahia in 1549 and huge African slave-worked sugar plantations, Brazil attracted many land-hungry emigrants from Portugal and the Azores.

From the later 16th century the French, Dutch and English challenged the Iberian domination of the Americas, particularly in the Caribbean and in North America. The French extended their territories in a vast sweep from Acadia (later Nova Scotia) beyond the Great Lakes and down the Mississippi to the Gulf of Mexico and the settlement of New Orleans, founded in 1718. French trappers, soldiers and missionaries pushed far into the forests founding future cities (Quebec, 1608; Ville-Marie, later Montreal, 1642; Detroit, 1701). But political support for the venture was weak and the colonies were few and widely scattered. Conflict with other Europeans, such as the Dutch at New Amsterdam and the more numerous British colonists along the eastern seaboard, further hampered French efforts at expansion.

English settlement began with the founding of Jamestown, Virginia (1607) and the Mayflower landing in Massachusetts Bay (1620). Led by ambition or the wish to attain religious freedom, large numbers of English migrated to North America. By the end of the 17th century, they numbered around 250,000, supporting a thriving economy based on agriculture, fishing and commerce.

Political development and society

In the early 18th century Spain extended its authority into Texas, the Mississippi valley and California, where Spanish miners, soldiers and priests met Russians probing south from Alaska. But the major contest in North America was between the British and the French. In 1713 as a result of the Peace of Utrecht, Britain gained Nova Scotia, Newfoundland and a clear field for the Hudson Bay Company to exploit the region's rich hunting grounds. The French and Indian War against Britain (1754–60) finally ended France's American ambitions. With the Treaty of Paris (1763) Britain gained all Canada and the land east of the Mississippi, while Louisiana went to Spain.

The societies that emerged in the New World were very different from those in Europe, conditioned by varied environments, the mix of traditions brought by settlers and the indigenous peoples they encountered. Nearly everywhere, the 'pioneering spirit' of the colonists and the vast distances separating them from their homelands prevented effective metropolitan control. Attempts from the mid-18th century to increase the taxes they produced led to tension between colonies and the mother country that finally exploded into the American War of Independence in 1775–83.

4 The Spanish invasion of Peru, 1531–3 *(map right)* showing Tumbes, where Pizarro landed; Cajamarca, where the Inca ruler, Atahuallpa, was seized at his first meeting with Pizarro; Jauja, the site of the first serious battle; Vilcaconga, where Soto was ambushed; and Cuzco, the Inca highland capital. The small Spanish force took advantage of an opponent split by a civil war. Despite the apparent ease of their victory, active opposition to the Spanish continued until 1572.

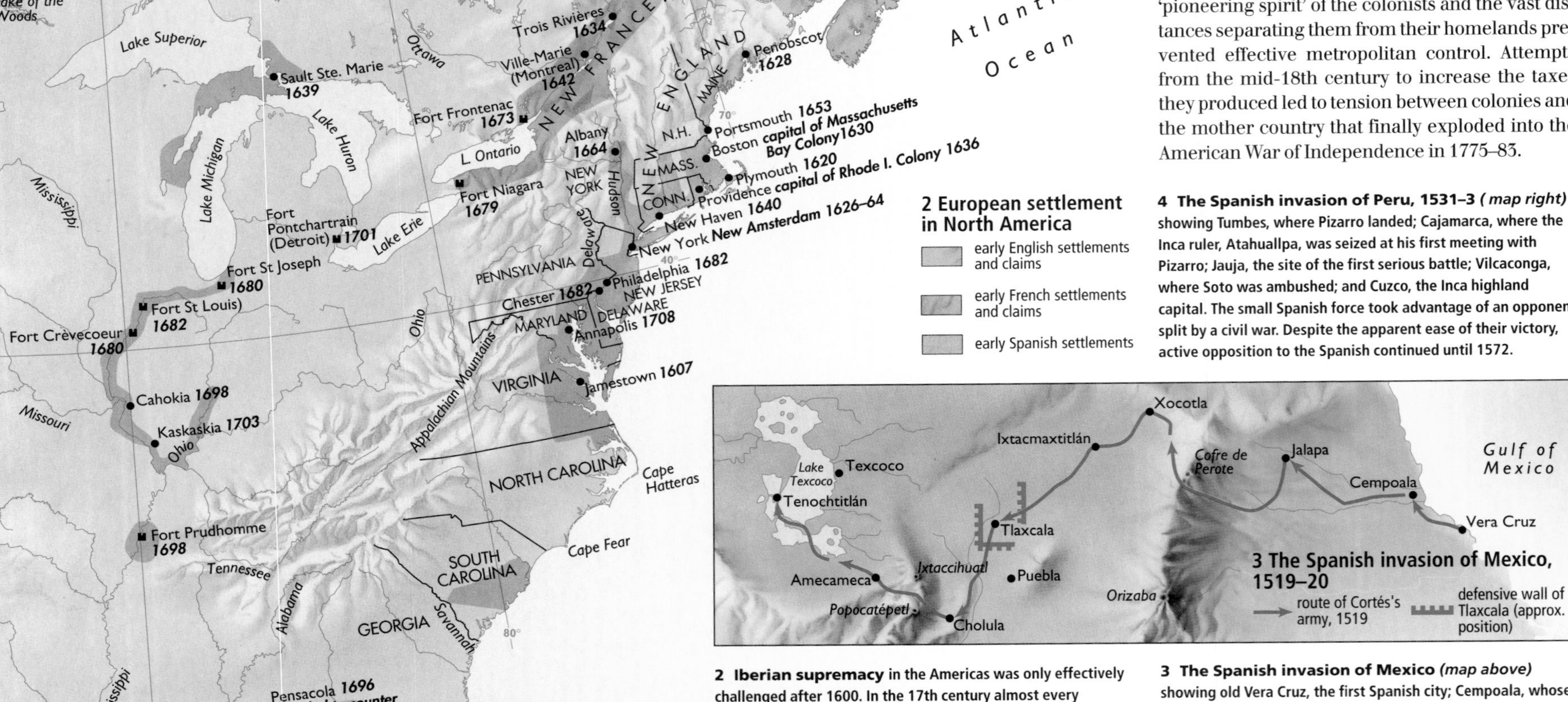

2 Iberian supremacy in the Americas was only effectively challenged after 1600. In the 17th century almost every European state which possessed an Atlantic seaboard established settlements in North America *(map left)*. The English settled in 12 colonies (Georgia became the 13th in 1733) along the eastern seaboard, while the French dominated the waterways of the St Lawrence and Mississippi.

3 The Spanish invasion of Mexico *(map above)* showing old Vera Cruz, the first Spanish city; Cempoala, whose ruler was encouraged by Cortés in revolt against the Aztecs; Tlaxcala, home of Cortés's principal allies; and Tenochtitlán, capital of the Aztecs, on its island in Lake Texcoco. The conquest was not easy: Cortés's small force only just escaped destruction in the first stages of the conflict.

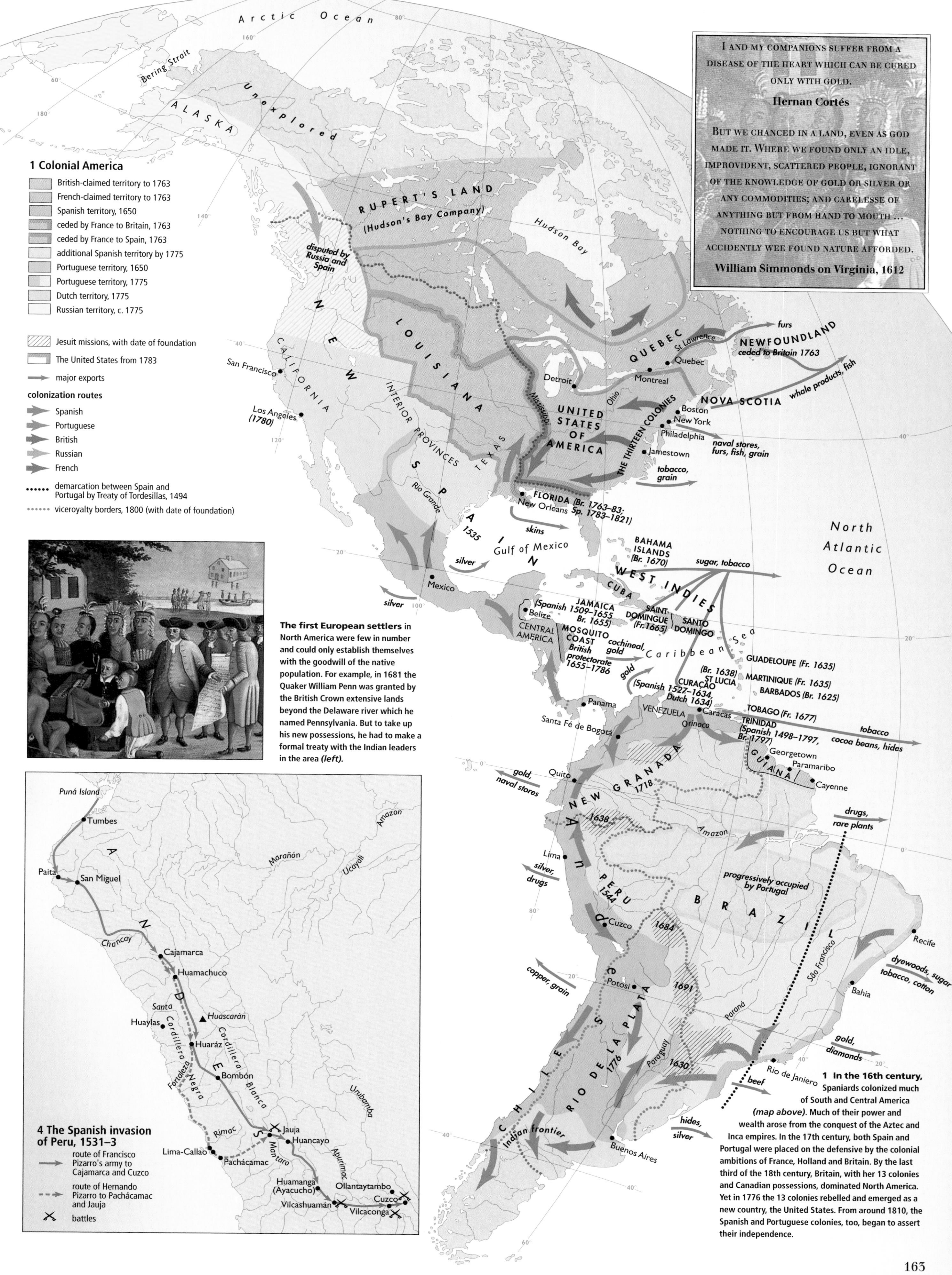

The first European settlers in North America were few in number and could only establish themselves with the goodwill of the native population. For example, in 1681 the Quaker William Penn was granted by the British Crown extensive lands beyond the Delaware river which he named Pennsylvania. But to take up his new possessions, he had to make a formal treaty with the Indian leaders in the area *(left)*.

1 In the 16th century, Spaniards colonized much of South and Central America *(map above)*. Much of their power and wealth arose from the conquest of the Aztec and Inca empires. In the 17th century, both Spain and Portugal were placed on the defensive by the colonial ambitions of France, Holland and Britain. By the last third of the 18th century, Britain, with her 13 colonies and Canadian possessions, dominated North America. Yet in 1776 the 13 colonies rebelled and emerged as a new country, the United States. From around 1810, the Spanish and Portuguese colonies, too, began to assert their independence.

Trade and empire in Africa

See also
The emergence of states in Africa, 1000–1500 p. 140
The rise of the Ottoman empire p. 142
The world on the eve of European expansion p. 154
European voyages of discovery p. 156
European expansion overseas p. 158
The emerging global economy, c. 1775 p. 198
Africa before the partition by the European powers, 1800–1880 p. 238

1493–1528 *Askia the Great ruler of Songhay*

1505 *Portuguese establish trading posts in east Africa*

1546 *Mali empire destroyed by Songhay*

1571 *Portuguese colony established in Angola*

1590 *Morocco invades Songhay*

c. 1600 *Oyo empire at height of its power*

1628 *Portuguese destroy Mwenemutapa empire*

1652 *Foundation of Cape Colony by Dutch*

c. 1700 *Rise of Ashanti power*

From 1500 to 1800 African history was dominated by three main processes: the expansion of large political units; the spread of Islam; and the increasing involvement of Europeans. By 1800 Africans had made great progress in evolving distinctive social and political forms, but their independence was already seriously compromised.

FROM THE LATE 15TH CENTURY, large political units multiplied in Africa. In 1464, Sunni Ali became ruler of the Songhay people around Gao in the eastern Niger bend. Under Askia the Great (1493–1528), Songhay became a great empire, incorporating a number of important commercial cities including Timbuktu and Jenne, which developed into centres of learning and Muslim piety. In the savannah and forest country to the south, trading communities gave rise to comparable polities. Well before 1500 Oyo and Benin had emerged in the woodlands to the west of the Niger delta, producing superb terracottas and bronzes.

Elsewhere, similar processes gave rise to centralized states of iron-working agriculturists and cattle-keepers. Increased populations, diversified economies and trade promoted stronger political control. When the Portuguese arrived south of the Congo mouth in 1484, they encountered the brilliant Kongo kingdom. Inland and to the south were other Bantu-speaking African states including those of the Luba and Lunda, while in the fertile lands between the east African lakes a series of states evolved, notably Rwanda and Buganda.

Equally prosperous was the Zimbabwe plateau with its kingdom based initially at Great Zimbabwe, later replaced by a number of successors including the Mwenemutapa empire centred northeast of modern Harare. At its peak Great Zimbabwe was the political and religious centre of a major state with trade links extending as far as China.

The spread of Islam

Between 1500 and 1800 Islam consolidated its position in the Sudanic lands, and spread southward along the east African coast. Bitter rivalry between Christian Ethiopia and Muslim coastal states in the Horn then developed: Sultan Ahmad Gran of Adal invaded the Christian highlands in the 1520s, and was only defeated by Portuguese intervention.

Meanwhile, in 1517, the Ottomans conquered the Mamluks in Egypt, and subsequently extended their control over Tripoli and Tunis; Algiers was ruled by corsair princes subject to the Ottomans. Only Morocco remained independent, governed for much of this period by Sharifian dynasties. In 1590, Morocco invaded the Songhay empire and set up a client state, disrupting economic life throughout the region. Later, in the 18th century, the politics and commerce of Muslim west Africa recovered again in a burst of Islamic proselytizing.

Europeans and the slave trade

Throughout the period, Europeans became more involved in Africa, seeking gold, ivory, wood and, above all, slaves to work the mines and plantations of the Americas. Although by 1800 the number of European territorial possessions was small, their domination of oceanic trade had considerable effects in many parts of Africa. In southernmost Africa, Dutch and French Huguenot settlers arrived after 1652 and subjected the Khoisan peoples, but by 1800 they encountered serious resistance from the southeastern Bantu-speakers.

The Dutch, French and British established 'factories' along the coast where slaves were bought. From 1450 to 1870, some 11,500,000 Africans were exported to the Americas, perhaps 75 per cent of whom survived the passage. Most came from west Africa, though by 1800 east Africa, which had long provided slaves to the Muslim world, was contributing to the Atlantic system. The precise effects of the slave trade are unclear. Overall, Europeans gained and Africa's development was inhibited.

2 Under the patronage of Prince Henry the Navigator Portuguese explorers sailed south in search of gold, spices and slaves *(map right)*. By Henry's death the lower reaches of the Gambia and Senegal had been reached. Fernão Gomes and Diogo Cão pushed the limit of exploration to the river Congo. In 1488 one Portuguese expedition reached the Cape of Good Hope, and another reconnoitred east Africa, preparing the way for Vasco da Gama's journey to India in 1497.

Within the rich artistic traditions of west Africa, the bronzes produced in Benin from the 15th century onwards are outstanding. In court art designed for the *oba* (king), naturalism gave way to stylized designs, emphasizing power. Here *(right)* the *oba*'s butchers sacrifice a cow, the most prestigious animal sacrifice. This form of sculpture may have drawn its inspiration from woodcuts in books shown to the artists by early Portuguese visitors. Benin, which became powerful under Ewuare the Great (1440–73), was first reached by a Portuguese envoy as early as 1486. By the 17th century, Portuguese and Dutch traders were regular visitors.

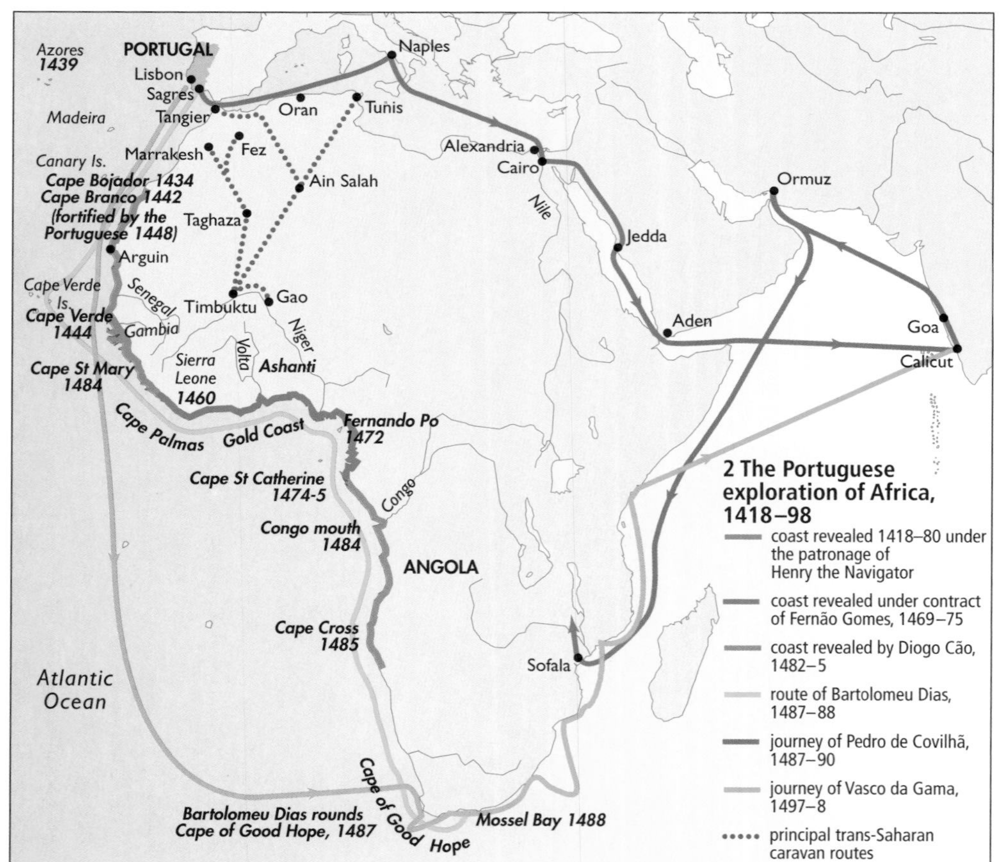

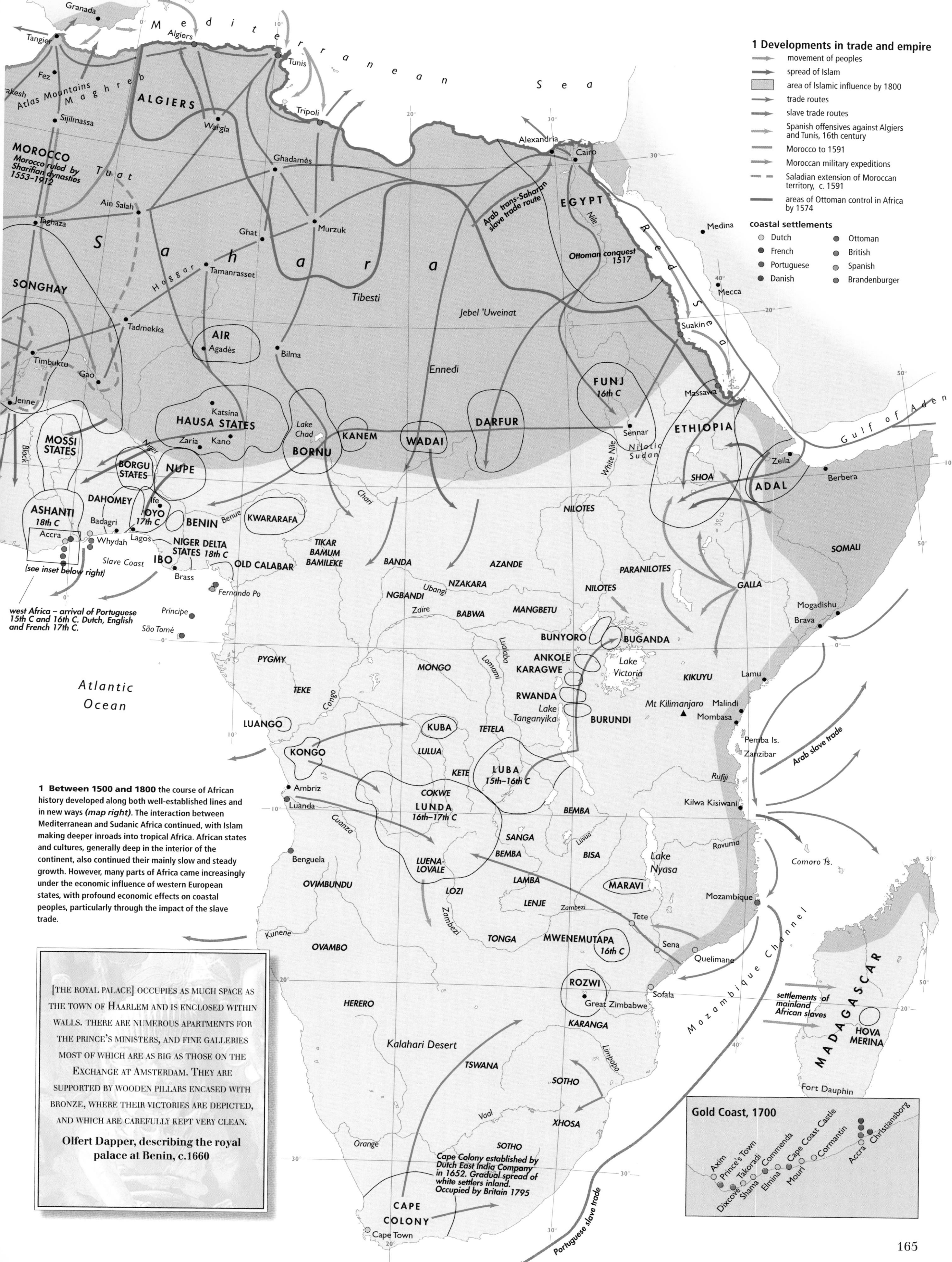

1 Between 1500 and 1800 the course of African history developed along both well-established lines and in new ways *(map right)*. The interaction between Mediterranean and Sudanic Africa continued, with Islam making deeper inroads into tropical Africa. African states and cultures, generally deep in the interior of the continent, also continued their mainly slow and steady growth. However, many parts of Africa came increasingly under the economic influence of western European states, with profound economic effects on coastal peoples, particularly through the impact of the slave trade.

[THE ROYAL PALACE] OCCUPIES AS MUCH SPACE AS THE TOWN OF HAARLEM AND IS ENCLOSED WITHIN WALLS. THERE ARE NUMEROUS APARTMENTS FOR THE PRINCE'S MINISTERS, AND FINE GALLERIES MOST OF WHICH ARE AS BIG AS THOSE ON THE EXCHANGE AT AMSTERDAM. THEY ARE SUPPORTED BY WOODEN PILLARS ENCASED WITH BRONZE, WHERE THEIR VICTORIES ARE DEPICTED, AND WHICH ARE CAREFULLY KEPT VERY CLEAN.

Olfert Dapper, describing the royal palace at Benin, c.1660

1368 to 1644

China at the time of the Ming dynasty

See also
Imperial Japan and the early shogunates p. 122
Chinese civilization from the T'ang to the Sung p. 126
The Mongol empire, 1206–1405 p. 128
The world on the eve of European expansion p. 154
China under the Ch'ing dynasty, 1644–1839 p. 172
Japan under the shogunate, 1477–1868 p. 174

ONLY SUCH AS HAVE EARNED A DOCTOR'S DEGREE OR THAT OF LICENTIATE ARE ADMITTED TO TAKE PART IN THE GOVERNMENT OF THE KINGDOM, AND DUE TO THE INTEREST OF THE MAGISTRATES AND OF THE KING HIMSELF THERE IS NO LACK OF SUCH CANDIDATES. EVERY PUBLIC OFFICE IS THEREFORE FORTIFIED WITH AND DEPENDENT UPON THE ATTESTED SCIENCE, PRUDENCE, AND DIPLOMACY OF THE PERSON ASSIGNED TO IT, WHETHER HE BE TAKING OFFICE FOR THE FIRST TIME OR IS ALREADY EXPERIENCED IN THE CONDUCT OF CIVIL LIFE.

Nicholas Trigault's description of the Chinese civil service in 1615

By the late 14th century a new Chinese dynasty, the Ming, had overthrown the Mongols. For 200 years it brought order and prosperity to much of China. The population more than doubled, new crops were introduced, industry flourished and trade greatly increased. By the early 17th century, corruption, external attack and crop failures conspired to weaken Ming rule and bring about its collapse.

1368 *Ming dynasty founded*

1392 *Korea reduced to vassal status*

1405 *China sends the first of seven huge fleets into the Indian Ocean*

1407 *China occupies Annam (Vietnam)*

1427 *China expelled from Annam*

1448 *Rebellions in Fukien and Chekiang lead to one million deaths*

1449 *Chinese invasion of Mongolia ends in the emperor's capture.*

1550 *Mongol threat re-emerges; Japanese pirate attacks increase*

1627 *Wave of rebel movements begins*

1644 *Ming dynasty toppled*

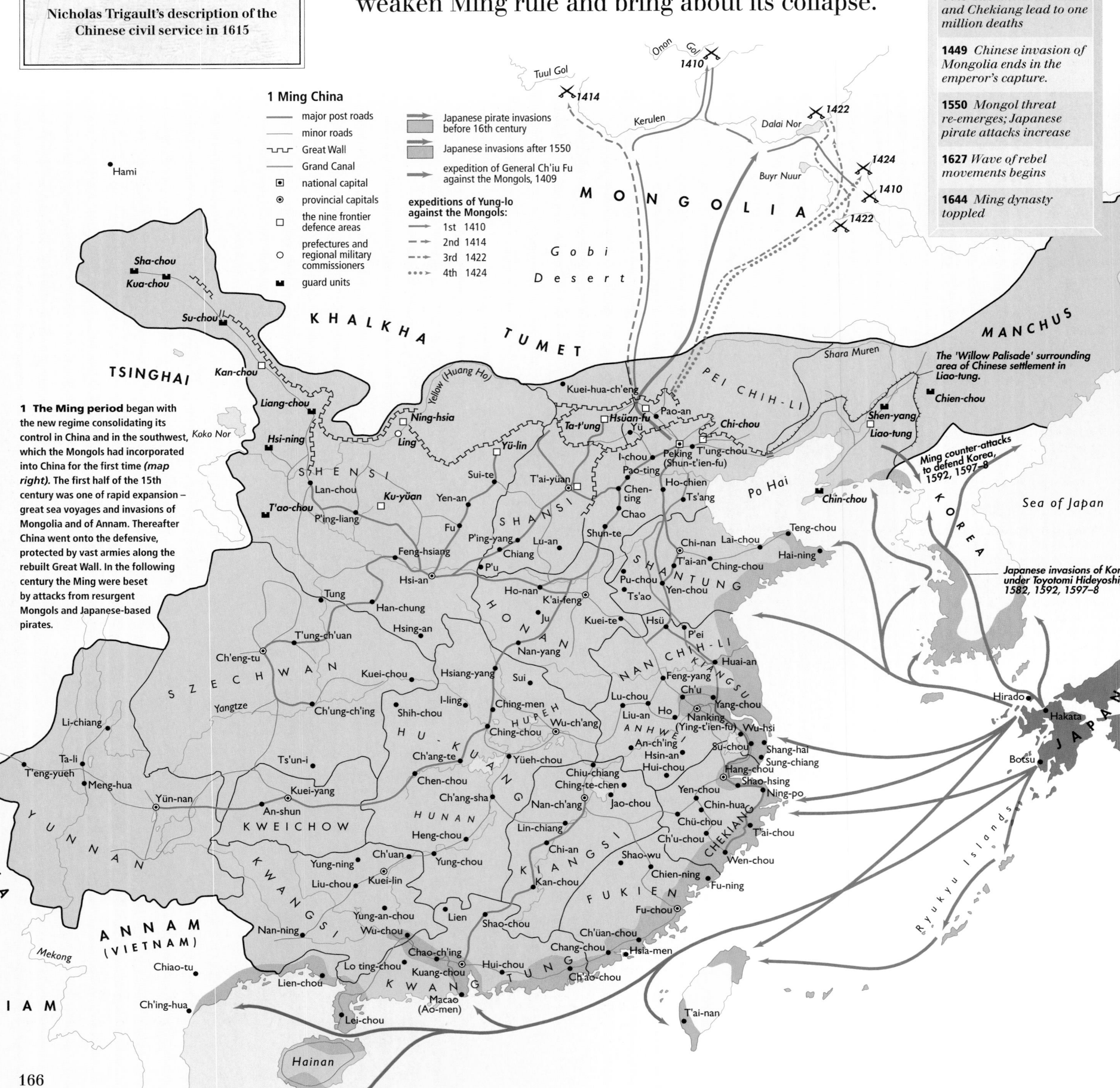

1 The Ming period began with the new regime consolidating its control in China and in the southwest, which the Mongols had incorporated into China for the first time *(map right)*. The first half of the 15th century was one of rapid expansion – great sea voyages and invasions of Mongolia and of Annam. Thereafter China went onto the defensive, protected by vast armies along the rebuilt Great Wall. In the following century the Ming were beset by attacks from resurgent Mongols and Japanese-based pirates.

BY THE LATE 13th century Mongol rule in China had brought a measure of stability even to the north of the country, which had endured the worst of the Mongol depredations 50 years earlier. But the death of the Mongol emperor Kublai Khan in 1294 sparked further instability as rival claimants fought for the imperial throne. By the 1340s and '50s, dynastic decline was accelerated by floods, droughts and disease. Together with increasing discontent with Mongol rule, these touched off a series of uprisings against the government. The most serious was in central and southeastern China where, in 1368, Chu Yüan-chang, the most powerful of the rebels, proclaimed a new dynasty, the Ming. By 1388, the Mongols were driven back to the steppe and the Ming controlled all China.

Consolidation

Under the Ming, stability was restored and numerous improvements to the country's agricultural base made. Throughout the period, new agricultural techniques enabled the country to feed its rapidly growing population (*see* chart 5) more efficiently. New crops were introduced – some, such as yams, maize, peanuts and potatoes, by the Portuguese and Spanish – and new areas opened up to cultivation. To facilitate the movements of products and people, the Grand Canal, which would eventually stretch 1,000 miles, from Hang-chou to Peking, was built. Upwards of 20,000 barges carrying 200,000 tons of grain a year used the canal. The administration of the burgeoning Chinese state was simple and practical. Though it discouraged innovation and, being highly centralized, was dangerously dependent on the emperor, it proved effective. Control over the vast population was effected largely through the 'gentry', or *shen-shih*, degree-holders who had been through the education system and shared the values of the bureaucracy without actually holding office.

Within the new stability provided by the Ming, industry boomed. The great cities of the Yangtze delta – Nanking, Su-chou, Wu-hsi, Sung-chiang and Hang-chou – developed as major industrial centres, particularly for textiles. The enormous volume of trade that flowed through them gave rise to a number of powerful groups of merchants, whose influence came to extend across the country. By the late 16th century, the economy was further stimulated by inflows of silver from the New World, which were used to pay for Chinese exports of tea, silk and ceramics.

Overseas expansion

Ming China, especially under the Yung-lo emperor, successor to Chu Yüan-chang, was exceptionally expansionist and aggressive. Campaigns against the Mongols in the far north, the restoration of Korea to vassal status in 1392, the occupation of Annam from 1407 to 1427 and a series of immense seaborne expeditions (*see* map 4) extended China's reach to new and unprecedented limits. But the return on these extravagant ventures was never enough to justify them. Following a further and abortive attack against the Mongols in 1449, which ended with the capture of the Ming emperor himself, China reverted to its traditional defensive posture. Renewed Mongol attacks coupled with a succession of political and economic demands placed the empire under increasing strain. It was made considerably worse by persistent attacks on the south coast by Japanese-based pirates and smugglers. By the 1550s, the seas around China were infested by heavily armed bands who terrorized coastal regions. Exacerbating China's difficulties, at the end of the century Japan launched two costly and destructive invasions of Korea, obliging China to send huge armies to aid their vassals.

These threats both coincided with and were partly responsible for a decline in Ming power, a process made worse by growing government corruption and a series of crop failures in the north. By 1636, much of the country was in rebellion, with the Manchus in the forefront. Though it was to be another rebel leader, Li Tzu-ch'eng, who in 1644 toppled the Ming, his regime was itself overthrown almost immediately by the new Ch'ing dynasty from Manchuria. It was to exercise its iron grip over China until 1911.

2 The Ming economy

agrarian productivity
relative production of grain (cattles per mou)*
49–62 | 89–115 | 160–210
northern limit of rice cultivation

merchant groups
major merchant groups under the Ming all operated on a national scale
merchant groups
trade routes

population in 1393
density per sq. mile
under 20 | 21–40 | 41–90 | 100–200 | over 200

* 1 cattle = ½ kilo or 1.1 lbs 7 mou = 1acre

2 China enjoyed an economic boom under the Ming *(map left)*. Silk, cotton textiles and ceramics were exchanged in the Philippines for Spanish silver from the New World. From the early 17th century tea was exported to Europe via Dutch traders. China imported silver, spices, sulphur, sandalwood and copper from Japan. The Grand Canal was crucial to China's economic growth: 160,000 guards were stationed on it to secure this lifeline of empire. At the same time, agricultural productivity was improved as new techniques and crops were introduced.

Chu Yüan-chang (1328–98), founder of the Ming dynasty *(right)*. In 1368 he proclaimed himself the founder of a new imperial dynasty, taking the title Hung-wu, meaning 'mightily martial'.

5 China's population rose steadily for most of the Ming period *(chart below)*, the result of political stability and rising productivity. By the mid-17th century renewed violence and two outbreaks of plague caused a further fall in population.

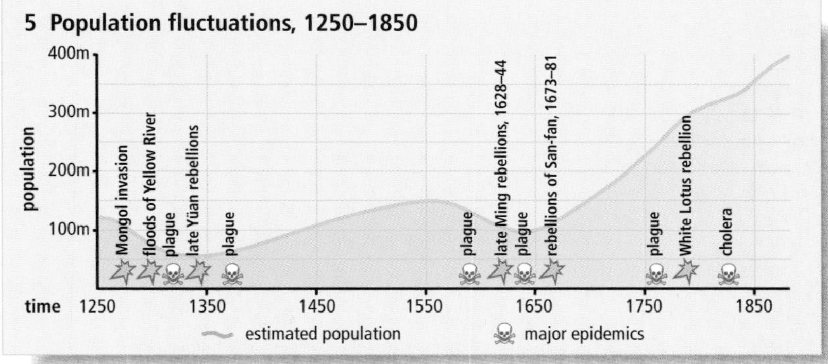

3 Rural distress produced a number of rebellions during the 15th century, mostly in central and southeastern China *(map left)*. In the early 17th century taxation and economic pressures produced urban risings in the great cities while from the 1620s peasant rebellions broke out in central and northern China . By the 1640s, two rival contenders, both struggling to found new dynasties, had emerged to fill the power vacuum: Li Tzu-ch'eng and Chang Hsien-ch'ung.

3 Rebellions under the Ming

local risings:
outbreaks, 1628–36
outbreaks, 1636–41
urban riots
15th, 16th century: early uprisings

major rebel regimes, 1641–7:
Chang Hsien-ch'ung
Li Tzu-ch'eng

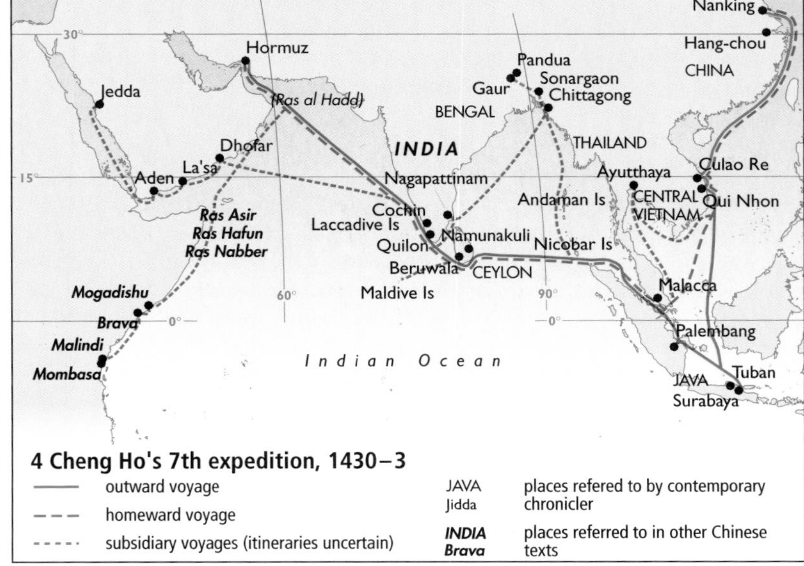

4 Between 1405 and 1433 China became a significant maritime country, sending seven great fleets under the command of Cheng Ho, a Muslim eunuch, as far as east Africa *(map above)*. In the 1420s these expeditions were attacked as expensive and serving no state interest. They were stopped and China restricted her maritime activity to the southwest coast.

1520 to c.1700

The Early Modern Muslim empires

The emergence of the mature Ottoman empire in the 16th century was accompanied by the rise of two other Muslim military empires: the Safavids in Persia and the Mughals in India. These three states dominated the politics and trade of an area stretching from central Europe to China, and presided over an era of Islamic cultural efflorescence.

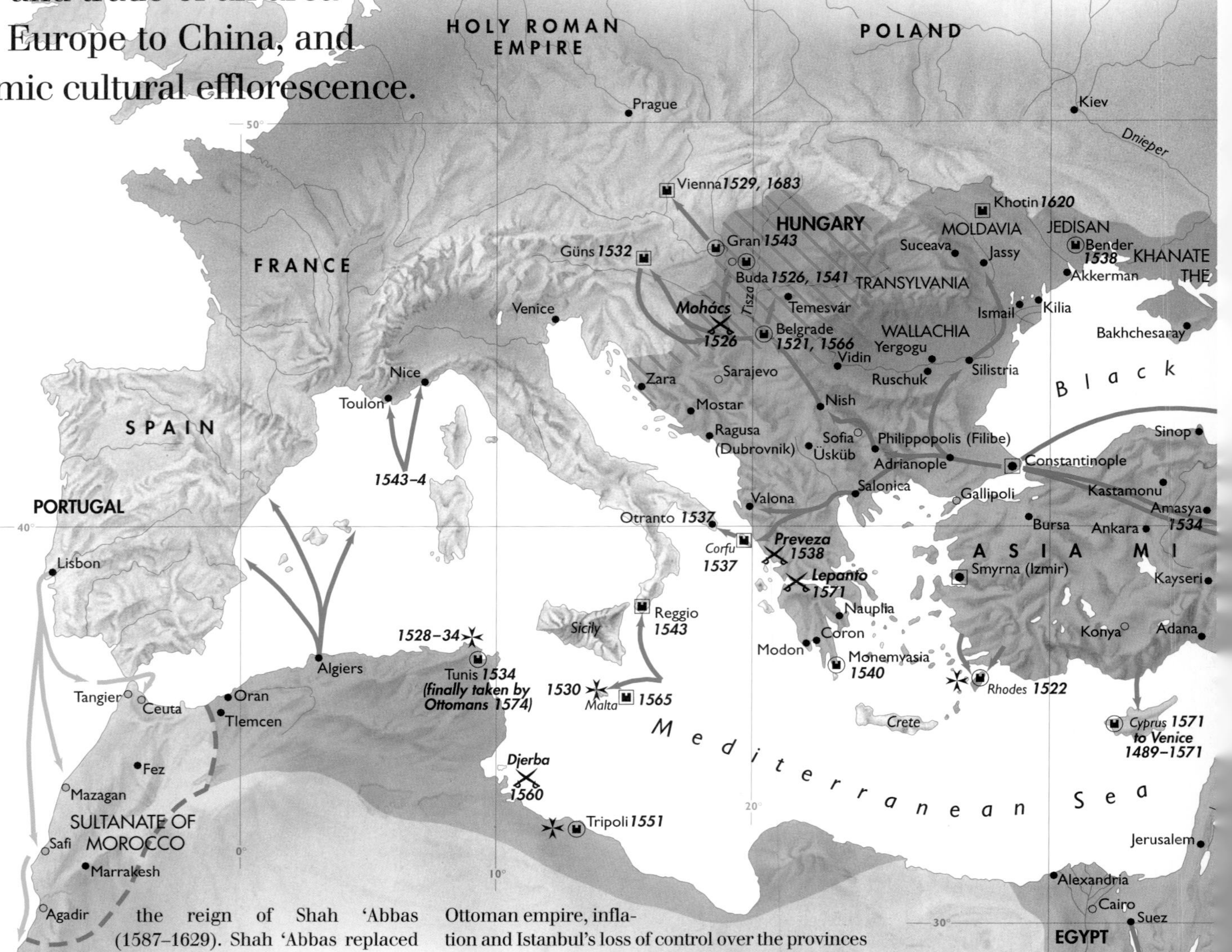

THE 16TH CENTURY WITNESSED the formation of three Muslim empires: the Ottoman empire in the Middle East and north Africa; the Safavid state in Iran; and the Mughal empire in India. In each, dynasties assisted by military elites of tribal or slave origin dominated large territories through their adoption of gunpowder weaponry. Smaller Muslim states, organized along similar lines, clustered around these giants. To the west of Ottoman north Africa lay the sultanate of Morocco, while to the east a series of Muslim khanates stretched from the Crimea to Turfan. The most important of these khanates was the Uzbek Shaybanid khanate of Bukhara which controlled much of central Asia. Most of these states professed Sunni Islam. The Safavids, however, adopted Shi'a Islam, a decision which gave clashes between the Safavids and their Ottoman and Uzbek neighbours an ideological edge. All three empires were characterized by their strong central bureaucracies and opulent court cultures, which fostered the development of imperial styles in art and architecture. They also encouraged the expansion of interregional Muslim trade by land from the Levant through Iraq and Persia to India and by sea from the Mediterranean to the Red Sea and Indian Ocean.

The Ottoman empire

The Ottomans made their state into an empire with the transformation of Constantinople into Istanbul, the cosmopolitan seat of the sultans. The empire expanded steadily during the reign of Suleiman the Magnificent (1520–66), whose armies occupied Hungary after the Battle of Mohács (1526) and advanced to Vienna in 1529. Vienna, however, proved to be beyond Ottoman reach and the Habsburg-Ottoman frontier stabilized. Expansion on land was matched by naval expansion in the Mediterranean where Ottomans and Habsburgs struggled for control until the Habsburg victory at the Battle of Lepanto (1571) and the fall of Tunis to the Ottomans (1574) confirmed Habsburg and Ottoman control of the northern and southern Mediterranean respectively, a situation verified by treaty in 1580. Further east, Ottoman navies prevented Portuguese intrusion into the Red Sea spice trade, but failed to prevent their participation in Indian Ocean commerce.

The Safavids

The neighbouring Safavid state was founded in the early 16th century by Shah Isma'il, a young Turcoman warrior, whose tribal followers were known as Qizilbash (Red Hats) after their distinctive red headgear. The Ottomans' military might prevented the Safavids from expanding westwards into Anatolia, and forced the new state to move its capital steadily eastwards from Tabriz to Qazvin, then to Isfahan on the Iranian plateau. This movement contributed to the steady Persianization of the Safavid state, which reached its zenith during the reign of Shah 'Abbas (1587–1629). Shah 'Abbas replaced the dynasty's tribal contingents with troops from the Caucasus, who were supplied with muskets by an English diplomat and merchant, Sir Robert Sherley. The wealth of the state reflected its participation in the overland trade in raw silk, Persia's main export, and enabled Shah 'Abbas to add a sumptuous imperial quarter to his capital of Isfahan.

The Mughal empire

East of Safavid Iran lay the third Muslim empire, the Mughal empire, founded in north India in the early 16th century by Babur, a descendant of Tamerlane, and extended by his successors to include most of the Indian sub-continent. The Mughal governing military elite was drawn from Afghan and Chagatai Turkish warrior lineages. Although political power lay in Muslim hands, Mughal culture was a unique synthesis between the Perso-Muslim and Hindu traditions. Its greatest achievements were in such architectural creations as the Taj Mahal and in painting and poetry. Like the Safavids, the Mughals were not a naval power: their lack of interest in controlling maritime trade allowed the Portuguese, Dutch and then British to establish the coastal footholds which later facilitated the colonization of India.

All three empires remained strong throughout the 17th century but internal weaknesses saw them begin to falter in the early 18th century. In the Ottoman empire, inflation and Istanbul's loss of control over the provinces weakened the state, whilst in Persia, state imposition of Shi'a Islam alienated Sunni Afghan tribesmen who rebelled in the early 18th century. The Mughal empire faced similar problems from the Hindu Rajputs and Marathas who resented the Islamization policies of Aurangzeb (1658–1707).

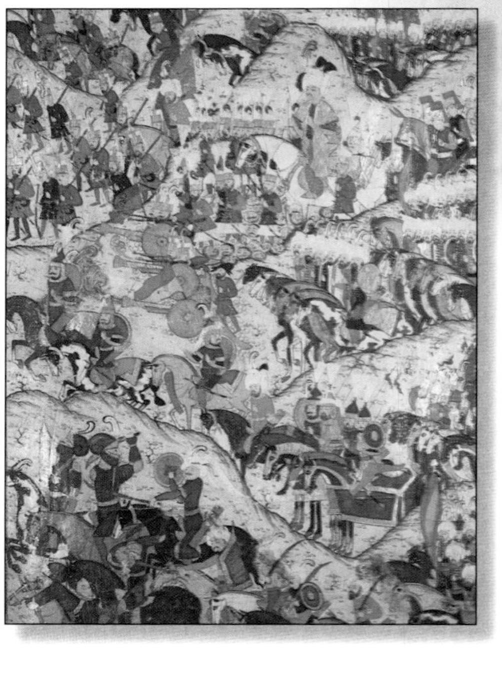

1 By the mid-16th century Muslim powers controlled a vast swathe of territory from Morocco to Bengal ***(map below)***. The dominant powers within this area were the Ottoman, Safavid and Mughal empires. The Ottoman empire reached its greatest extent in the reign of Suleiman I (1520–66). It only started to lose significant territories in Europe between 1682 and 1699. The Safavids ruled Persia from 1501–1722. In the Indian sub-continent Mughal expansion southwards continued until the 18th century when Hindu-Muslim conflict began to undermine the empire.

The military might, order and discipline of the Ottomans in the first half of the 16th century are vigorously depicted in this miniature of Suleiman I at the Battle of Mohács in 1526 ***(left)***. He is shown surrounded by his vezirs, sipahis and janissaries. At Mohács the Turks broke the power of Hungary and seriously threatened the Habsburgs in Austria; in 1529 Suleiman laid siege unsuccessfully to Vienna. Under Suleiman, the Ottomans also seized much of eastern Asia Minor from the Safavids, and in north Africa took Tripoli in 1551.

There can be no sultan without the military.
There can be no military without wealth.
The flock of subjects produce wealth.
Justice preserves the subjects' loyalty to the sultan.
Justice requires harmony in the state.
Islamic law maintains harmony in the state.
There is no support for Islamic law except the sultan.
The Ottoman Circle of Equity, 16th–17th century
1520 Suleiman the Magnificent becomes Ottoman sultan
1526 Babur establishes Mughal rule in India. Ottomans conquer Hungary
1529 First Ottoman siege of Vienna
1556 Accession of Akbar: apogee of Mughal empire
1577 Habsburg-Ottoman truce
1587 Accession of Shah 'Abbas: apogee of Safavid state
1683–99 Second Ottoman siege of Vienna; Ottoman-Habsburg war and Ottoman loss of Hungary
1707 Death of Aurangzeb
1722 Last Safavid shah overthrown by Afghan rebels
1 The Early Modern Muslim empires, 1520–c. 1700
Ottoman empire, 1520
Ottoman vassal states, 1520
expansion of Ottoman empire under Suleiman, 1520–66
expansion of Ottoman empire, 1566–1600
Ottoman territory lost to Habsburgs, 1682–99
Ottoman territory lost to Muscovites, 16th–17th centuries
major Ottoman campaigns, 1520–1629
Ottoman conquest, with date
Ottoman siege, with date
administrative centre of major regions (beglerbegliks)
Safavid empire, 16th century
areas of Safavid–Ottoman conflict
area of Safavid–Uzbek conflict
campaigns of 'Abbas I, 1588–1629
Mughal empire, 1530
expansion of Mughal empire under Akbar, 1556–1605
expansion of Mughal empire, 1605–1707
campaigns of Shah Jehan and Aurangzeb, 1628–1707
area of Safavid–Mughal conflict
area of Maratha power, c.1700
other Muslim areas
Portuguese expansion 15th–16th centuries
Portuguese enclaves until 1540s
main centres of Western trade
Knights of St John
Volga
1569
Don
Azov (Azak)
RIMEA
ffa (Kefe)
Astrakhan
Caspian Sea
Aral Sea
Syr Darya
Sea
Sukhum-Kale
DAGHESTAN
Makhachkala
Caucasus
Tiflis 1578
Derbend 1579
GEORGIA
amsun
Trebizond
Erzurum
Kars 1578
Arash 1578
SHIRWAN
Baku 1583
Ganja 1588
Erevan
Sivas
Erzincan
Nakhichevan 1557
QARABAGH
Tabriz 1534, 1548, 1585
Van
Bitlis
Malatya
Aleppo
skenderun
ntakya
Qazvin
1603–07
AZERBAIJAN
Teheran
Mosul
Euphrates
SYRIA
IRAQ
Hamadan 1587
Damascus
Baghdad 1534
1623–38
LEVANT
PERSIA
Qum
Isfahan
LURISTAN 1587
Basra 1546
Kerman
Shiraz
1622
Bandar Abbas 1551
Ormuz (Portuguese 1515–1622)
Bahrein 1554
Muscat 1551
Medina
Arabia
Jedda
Mecca
Red Sea
Sana
Zabid
YEMEN
Aden 1538
Socotra (Portuguese 1507)
to Malindi (1584)
Urgench
Khiva
UZBEK KHANATE
Bukhara
Amu Darya
Samarkand
Merv
Meshed
Nishapur 1588–9 Safavid conquests
Herat 1506, 1588–9
1598
1622
Kandahar
Balkh
Tashkent
Khokand
KHANATE OF KASHGAR
Kashgar
Yarkand
Khotan
Tarim Basin
KHANATE OF TURFAN
Turfan
Kabul
Mughal conquest 1504
Khyber Pass
Peshawar
Indus
Lahore
SIND 1590
RAJPUTANA
Panipat 1526
Delhi
Mughal conquest 1504
Agra
Jaipur
Lucknow
Allahabad
BENGAL
Ganges
INDIA
GUJERAT
Diu 1538 (Portuguese)
Surat 1554
Indian Ocean
Goa (Portuguese 1509)
Madras
Bangalore
Mysore

Mughal India and the growth of British power

See also
The Delhi sultanate, 1206–1526 p. 132
European expansion overseas p. 158
The Early Modern Muslim empires, 1520–1700 p. 168
The struggle for empire, 1713–1815 p. 194
India under British rule, 1805–1935 p. 234

1526 *Battle of Panipat: Babur conquers the Delhi sultanate and founds Mughal dynasty*

1674 *Sivaji creates Maratha kingdom*

1707 *Death of Aurangzeb; decline of Mughal power in India*

1739 *Nadir Shah invades India and sacks Delhi*

1761 *Capture of Pondicherry; British destroy French power in India*

1765 *British granted the revenues of Bengal by the Mughal emperor*

1803 *British defeat the Marathas at Delhi; the Mughal empire accepts British protection*

Founded in the early 16th century, the Mughal empire was at its height from the 1550s to the 1650s, presiding over a golden age of religious cooperation and cultural synthesis. But in the 18th century it rapidly disintegrated, with the British emerging as the victors over the French and the Maratha Hindus in the struggle for the succession.

IN THE 1520s BABUR, who counted both Genghis Khan and Tamerlane among his ancestors, invaded India from Afghanistan. After defeating the Lodi sultan at Panipat in 1526, he began the establishment of the Mughal empire, but died before the foundations were secure. His son, Humayun, was expelled by the Afghans of Bihar under Sher Shah and it took a full-scale invasion, brilliantly consolidated by Babur's grandson, Akbar (1556–1605), to restore Mughal rule. This now stretched from Bengal in the east and the Godavari river in the south, to Kashmir in the north and the Indus valley in the west (*see* map 1). Most of the Hindu Rajput princes became tributary allies, and the empire was administered by a new class of bureaucrats, the *mansabdars*, ranked in a military hierarchical system.

Akbar's reign is one of the golden ages of Indian history. A standardized tax system was introduced; there was agricultural prosperity and buoyant trade (*see* map 2). Policies of tolerance were adopted towards the non-Muslim majority and Akbar himself took wives from Rajput families. His patronage laid the foundations for a remarkable synthesis of Persian and Indian cultural forms. He presided over the development of Mughal miniature painting, which combined the traditions of the Safavid and Rajput schools. Under his son Jahangir (1605–27), Mughal painting reached its peak. Akbar's red sandstone capital at Fatehpur Sikri expressed a striking synthesis of Islamic and Hindu traditions of architecture. The new style reached its climax under his grandson Shahjahan (1628–57), the builder of the Taj Mahal.

Akbar's political inheritance included a ceaseless thrust towards territorial expansion, especially southwards. Under Aurangzeb (1658–1707) this brought confrontation with a new Hindu power, the Marathas, a kingdom founded by Sivaji in 1674. By 1700 the Marathas were ravaging the land from the Deccan to Bengal. There was also open internal disaffection from Rajputs, Sikhs and Jats. It used to be thought that these developments were the outcome of Aurangzeb's revision of Akbar's policies of toleration. It now seems clear that they arose from weaknesses in the economic and administrative structures of the empire.

Mughal decline

After Aurangzeb's death the empire quickly declined. The finishing stroke came from Persia when Nadir Shah's army sacked Delhi in 1739. The former Mughal provinces of Oudh, Bengal and Hyderabad now offered only nominal allegiance to Delhi. In the south the Muslim state of Mysore grew into a formidable power under Haidar Ali and his son, Tipu Sultan. Over the course of the century the Maratha chiefs spread their territories deep into north, west, central and eastern India (*see* map 4). The Mughal emperor became no more than a Maratha protégé.

The East India Company

Simultaneously, India was undergoing its first major invasion from the sea. By the 1760s the English East India Company, having both defeated the French and been granted control over the revenues of Bengal by the Mughal emperor, was firmly established on the Indian shore. With these resources the Company was now able to sustain an army of over 100,000 men. Through military victories over the Marathas and Mysore, it came to occupy a continuous band of territory from the Gangetic plain to India's southern coasts (*see* map 3). In addition, by a system of subsidiary alliances, its suzerainty was recognised by many Indian rulers beyond its actual borders. In 1803 the Mughal emperor himself accepted British protection. British supremacy was now widely acknowledged.

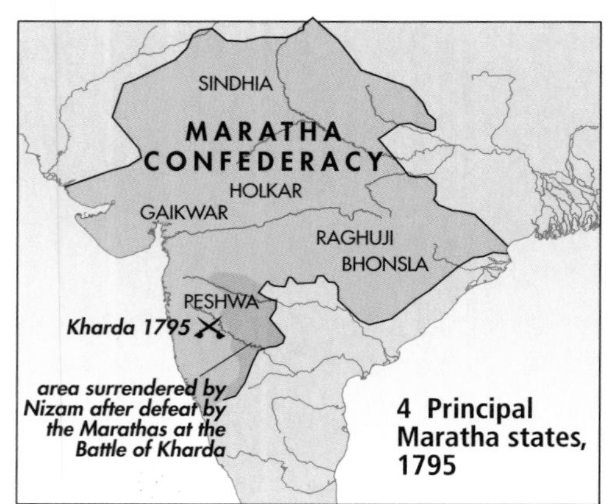

4 Principal Maratha states, 1795

2 The rich and populous Mughal empire *(below)* produced many craft goods and cash crops. Textiles from Bengal, Gujerat and Coromandel were the main export, along with sugar to Japan and Iran and pepper and saltpetre to Europe. The main imports were gold and silver.

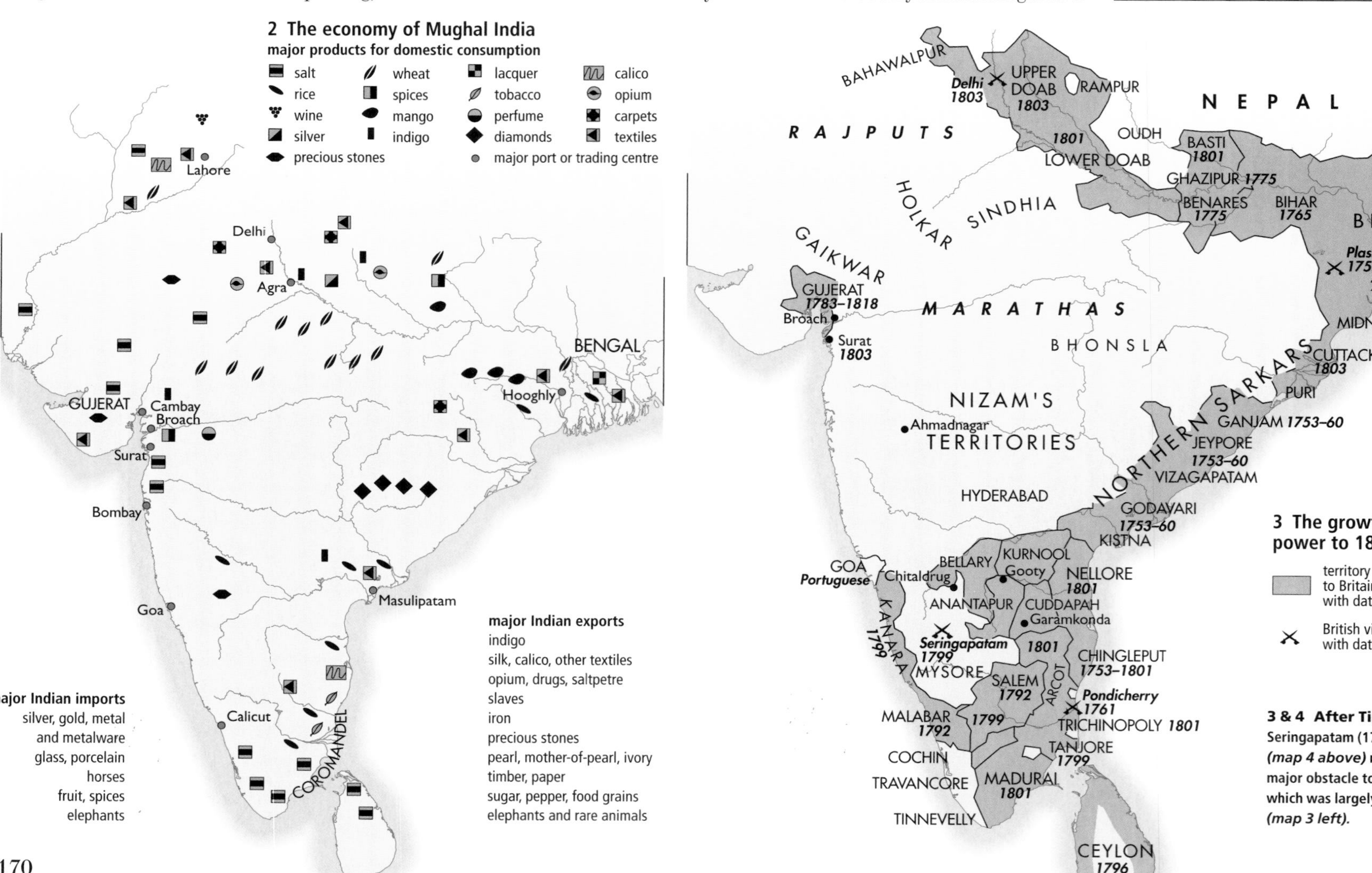

3 & 4 After Tipu's death at Seringapatam (1799), the Marathas *(map 4 above)* represented the only major obstacle to British supremacy, which was largely achieved by 1805 *(map 3 left)*.

A MONARCH SHOULD BE EVER INTENT ON CONQUEST, OTHERWISE HIS NEIGHBOURS RISE IN ARMS AGAINST HIM.

Saying of the Emperor Akbar

I ASSERT THAT IN THE MUGHAL KINGDOM THE NOBLES, AND ABOVE ALL THE KING, LIVE WITH SUCH OSTENTATION THAT THE MOST SUMPTUOUS OF EUROPEAN COURTS CANNOT COMPARE IN RICHNESS AND MAGNIFICENCE WITH THE LUSTRE BEHELD IN THE INDIAN COURT.

Niccolo Manucci, artilleryman and physician at the Mughal Court, c. 1656–86

Much of the early part of Akbar's reign was spent in the conquest of the Hindu Rajputs, who were to become important allies of the Mughals. In this typically sumptuous miniature *(above)* of 1569, Surjan Hara, ruler of the fort of Ranthanbhur, submits to Akbar, offering him the keys to the fort and many gifts.

1 The territory controlled by the Mughal administration grew with each emperor, until the death of Aurangzeb (1707) *(map above)*. But by the end of the 17th century Mughal rule was everywhere under attack, both from within and without. The most important opposition came from the Maratha Hindus, under Sivaji, fanning out from their homeland in the Western Ghats. At the same time, the European trading nations, who had taken serious interest in India's rich resources and markets, had by now established significant footholds along the coast.

1644 to 1839
China under the Ch'ing dynasty

See also
European expansions overseas p. 158
Russian expansion in Europe and Asia p.160
China at the time of the Ming dynasty, 1368–1644 p. 166
The collapse of the Chinese empire, 1839–1911 p. 232

1644 *Manchus found the Ch'ing dynasty*

1674 *Rebellion of the Three Feudatories begins*

1689 *Treaty of Nerchinsk between China and Russia*

1697 *China occupies Outer Mongolia*

1746 *Chin-ch'uan tribal rebellion begins*

1751 *China overruns Tibet, Dzungaria and Tarim Basin (1756–9)*

1793 *British embassy under Macartney to the Chinese Court*

Under the Ch'ing dynasty China doubled in size and experienced a century of peaceful prosperity. But by the late 18th century economic decline brought about by rapid population growth sparked repeated revolts. The developing crisis was exacerbated by growing government inefficiency and Western economic intervention. By the 1830s China's problems demanded urgent and radical change.

PEACEFUL RULE HAVING LASTED NOW FOR MORE THAN ONE HUNDRED YEARS, IT MAY BE CONSIDERED OF LONG DURATION. BUT IF WE CONSIDER THE POPULATION, WE CAN SEE THAT IT HAS INCREASED FIVE TIMES OVER WHAT IT WAS THIRTY YEARS AGO, TEN TIMES OVER WHAT IT WAS SIXTY YEARS AGO, AND AT LEAST TWENTY TIMES OVER WHAT IT WAS ONE HUNDRED AND SOME TENS OF YEARS AGO.

The scholar-official Hung Lian-chi (1746–1809) on China's population problem

THE CH'ING DYNASTY was founded by a non-Chinese people, the Manchus, who in the early 17th century had established a Chinese-style state in Manchuria with its capital at Mukden (*see* p. 166). When the Ming were toppled by the rebel Li Tzu-ch'eng in 1644, the Manchus invaded China and proclaimed a new dynasty. Though Ming resistance continued in the south and west for several decades, notably in the rebellion of the Three Feudatories of 1674–81, from 1652 Manchu rule was effectively established. The Ch'ing brought to China more than a century of internal peace and prosperity under three rulers of great ability, the emperors K'ang-hsi (1661–1722), Yung-cheng (1722–35) and Ch'ien-lung (1736–96), who also led the expansion of the Chinese empire into central Asia until it was almost double its earlier size.

The Manchus maintained their predominant place in government, and above all in the military, but also established good working relationships with their Chinese officials. Only towards the end of the 18th century, as they became more and more influenced by Chinese education and culture, did the distinctive Manchu identity begin to fade. Exploitation by Chinese and Manchu alike led to many rebellions of peoples on the periphery: in Yunnan in 1726–9, among the Chinese Muslim minority in Kansu in 1781–4, among the Yao people of Kwangsi in 1790, among the Miao people of Kweichow in 1795–7, and most notably the massive Chin-ch'uan tribal risings in western Szechwan in 1746–9 and again in 1771–6, when order was finally restored only after ruinously expensive military operations.

Population growth

From the end of the 18th century rebel movements began to take new forms. The background was a developing economic crisis. The area available for agriculture, which had been expanded by the introduction of maize, sweet potato, ground nuts and tobacco in the 16th and 17th centuries, was now fully used. The population, meanwhile, grew inexorably, from 100 million to 300 million between 1650 and 1800 and to 450 million by 1850. This constantly growing population had to be fed by ever-more intensive cultivation of a limited area. By the end of the 18th century, there was widespread hardship and impoverishment which in turn sparked rebellions, usually inspired by secret societies: the rebellions of the Heaven and Earth Society, 1787–8; the White Lotus, 1796–1805; and the Eight Trigrams of 1813, which was accompanied by an attempted coup in Peking. Further risings took place among border peoples.

The crisis of government

The developing economic crisis was exacerbated by the strains that external expansion placed on imperial financial administration and by a sharp decline in the quality of government. Corruption became endemic at every level of administration while the government itself failed to keep up with population growth, delegating more and more power to local gentry. A further factor was the import of opium by foreign powers into China to help pay for their extensive purchases of tea, silk, porcelain and handicrafts. By the 1830s opium imports were leading to a substantial drain of silver from China with concomitant damage to the economy and state finances.

By this time Manchu China was the world's largest and most populous empire, directly controlling vast territories in inner Asia and treating as tributary states still larger areas: Korea, Indo-China, Siam, Burma, Nepal. But within this huge empire, effective Ch'ing administrative and military control was gradually declining, while inexorable economic pressures increased which could be cured only by large-scale technological innovation and radical reorganization. Neither was imminent and in the meantime China faced new pressures from the expansionist Western powers.

3 By the 17th century China had developed considerable regional specialization and a nationwide marketing system *(map below)*. Some cities in the lower Yangtze sustained large and varied handicraft industries, their raw materials and food transported over great distances via the Grand Canal and the Yangtze.

3 The Ch'ing economy

main manufacturing and trading areas, 16th and 17th centuries
major trade routes, with principal traded commodities

iron · gold · silver · copper · lead · tin · mercury · salt · coal · silk textiles · cotton textiles · paper · tea · sugar · iron utensils · ceramics (porcelain)

furs, gold, ginseng · raw cotton, grain · copper · tea · tea, porcelain, silk, cotton · limited Dutch trade · overseas trade with West: tea, silk, fine cottons, porcelain, lacquer

KANSU · SHANSI · CHIHLI · SHANTUNG · HONAN · SHENSI · KIANGSU · ANHWEI · HUPEH AND HUNAN · SZECHWAN · KIANGSI · CHEKIANG · FUKIEN · KWEICHOW · YUNNAN · KWANGSI · KWANGTUNG · TAIWAN · Peking · Lin-ch'ing · Chi-ning · Grand Canal (Yun Ho) · Huai-an · Yang-chou · Nanking · Su-chou · Hang-chou · Sian · Ch'eng-tu · Yangtze · Nan-ch'ang · Ch'ang-sha · Amoy · Canton

The most important development of Ch'ien-lung's reign was the expansion of the Chinese empire into central Asia. The new acquisitions were known as 'Xingjiang' or the 'New Territories'. The outcome was that China now established a firm western border with Russia alongside the northern borders settled by the Treaty of Nerchinsk (1689). China also added extra populations of Muslims and Buddhists to its subjects. In this 18th-century scroll *(below)* Kirghiz tribesmen from the western frontier present horses, their most treasured possessions, to the emperor Ch'ien-lung.

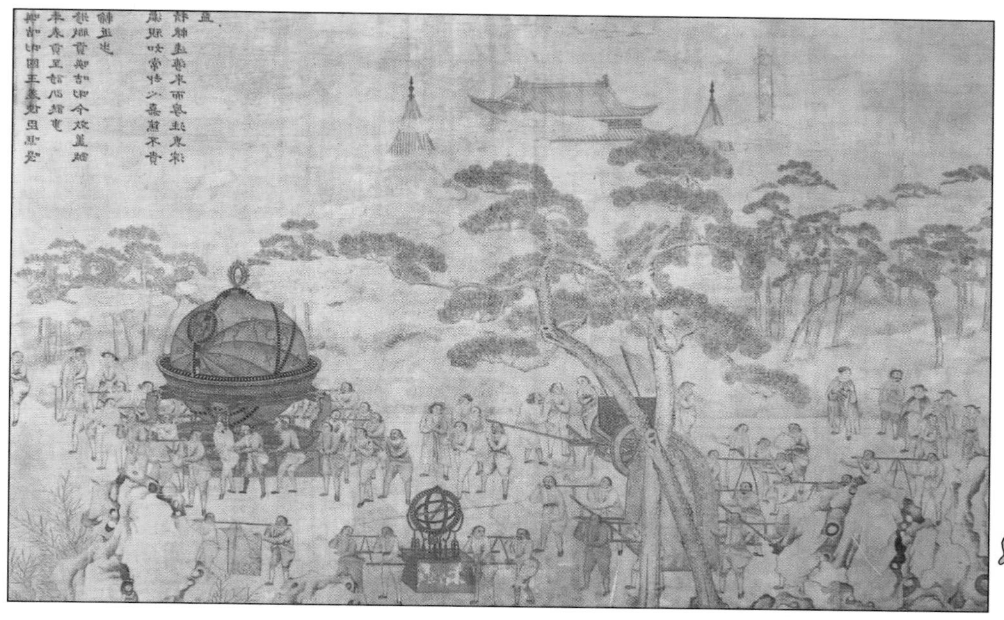

In June 1793, an embassy from Britain arrived off Canton. It lacked nothing which might emphasize its prestige. Among the gifts to the Chinese court were a letter from George III in a gold box and samples of early British industrialization including a globe that needed more than 12 men to carry it *(above)*. The emissary was dismissively received. Europe may have been catching up but the Chinese empire was still the world's largest and most powerful state.

4 Chinese exports of tea increased by over 50 per cent in the first third of the 19th century. Over the same period, silk exports quadrupled. But by the 1830s opium imports by western powers had outstripped Chinese exports and a drain of silver out of China began *(chart right)*. This had increasingly serious effects on the Chinese economy and further impoverished the state finances.

4 The Chinese economy in the 19th century

+5
+4
+3
+2
+1
NIL
-1
-2
-3
-4
-5
millions of ounces of silver
value of opium imports
net inflow of silver
date
1800 1804 1808 1812 1816 1820 1824 1828 1832 1836

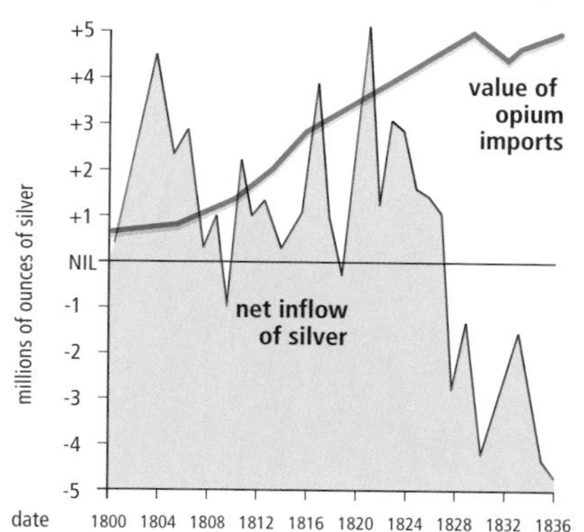

2 The rebellion of the Three Feudatories, 1674–81

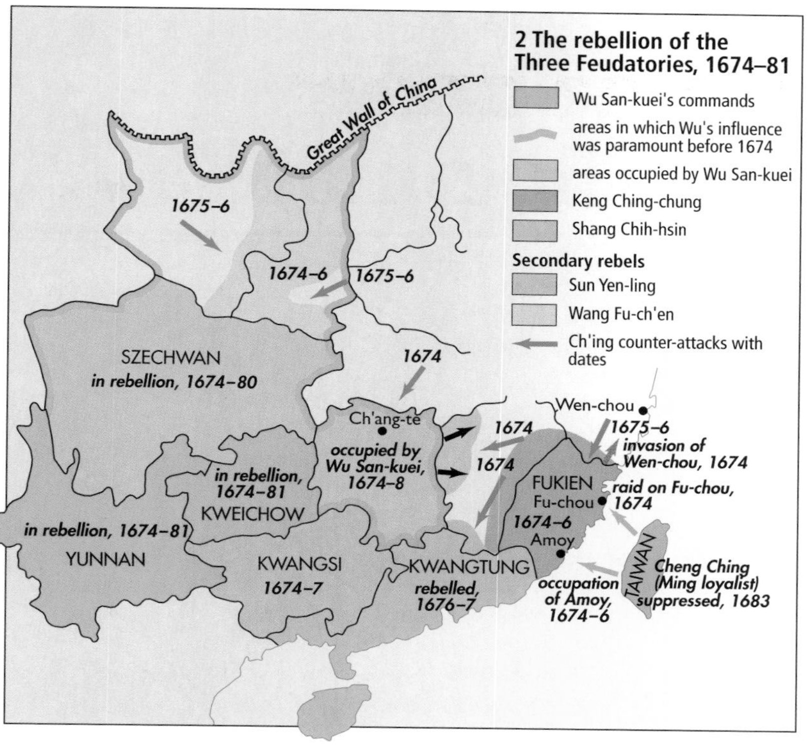

Wu San-kuei's commands
areas in which Wu's influence was paramount before 1674
areas occupied by Wu San-kuei
Keng Ching-chung
Shang Chih-hsin
Secondary rebels
Sun Yen-ling
Wang Fu-ch'en
Ch'ing counter-attacks with dates
Great Wall of China
1675–6
1674–6
1675–6
1674
SZECHWAN
in rebellion, 1674–80
Ch'ang-te
occupied by Wu San-kuei, 1674–8
in rebellion, 1674–81
KWEICHOW
in rebellion, 1674–81
YUNNAN
KWANGSI
1674–7
KWANGTUNG
rebelled, 1676–7
1674
1674
Wen-chou
1675–6
invasion of Wen-chou, 1674
FUKIEN
Fu-chou
raid on Fu-chou, 1674
1674–6
Amoy
occupation of Amoy, 1674–6
TAIWAN
Cheng Ching (Ming loyalist) suppressed, 1683

1 Throughout the late 17th and 18th centuries, the Manchus pursued an expansionist policy which left them in control of vast new regions *(map below)*. But these conquests, triggered in part by fear of Russian, French and British expansion, were enormously expensive. Undeterred, Chinese military expeditions went still further: four attacks on Burma in 1766–9, an expedition into Nepal in 1788–92 and a large-scale invasion of Tonking in 1788. All ended in failure. At the same time, a series of peasant revolts began as China struggled with growing economic crisis.

2 Resistance to Ch'ing rule continued for many years after the collapse of the Ming , above all in the southern provinces, which effectively became the personal domains of a series of rebel generals *(map above)*. In 1674, the Ch'ing attempted to reassert control over Kwangtung, provoking a rebellion that lasted until 1681. For a time most of southern and western China was in rebel hands, though by 1677 only the southwest remained. With the death in 1678 of the most prominent rebel, Wu San-kuei, the Ch'ing slowly regained control.

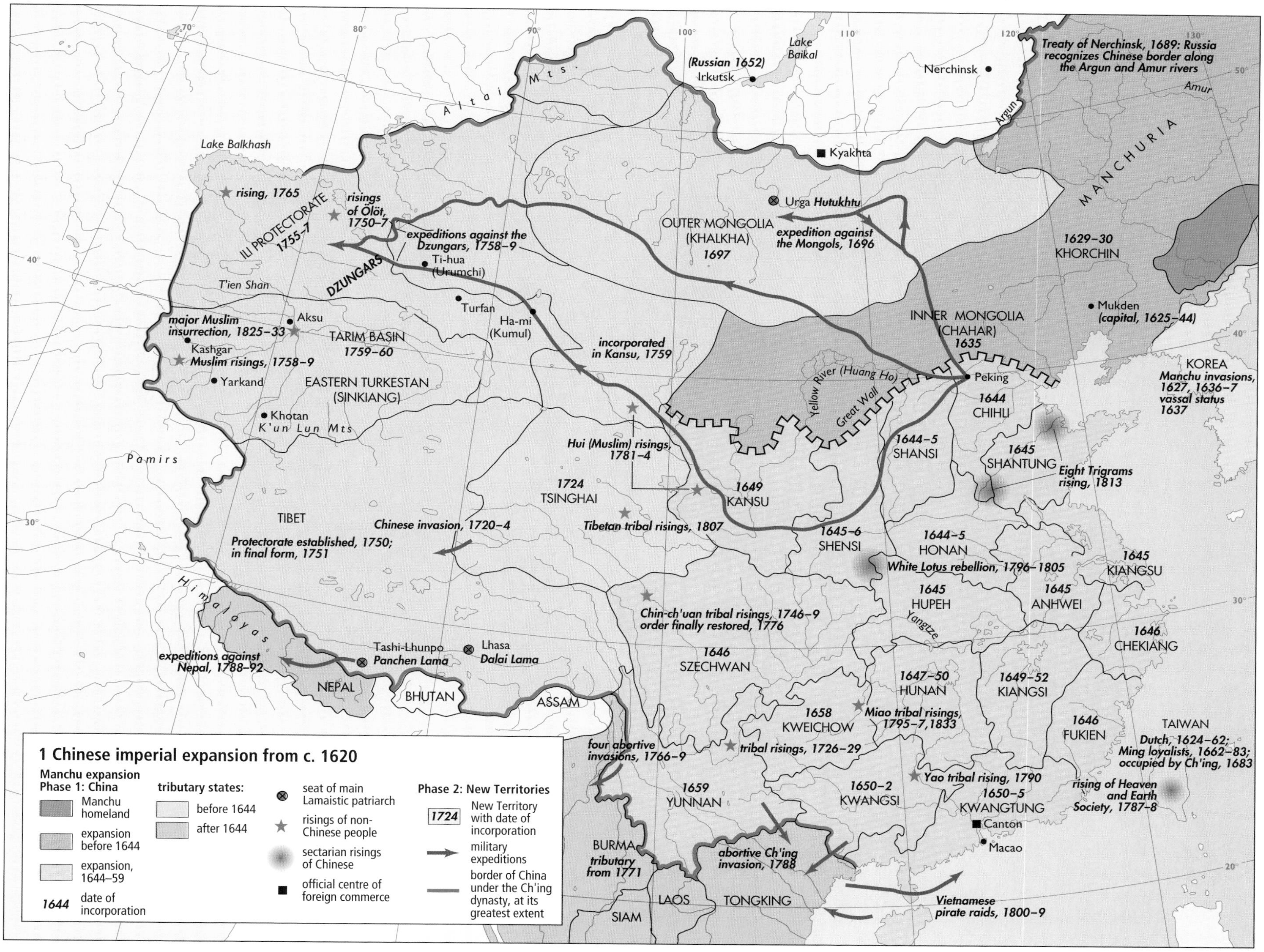

Lake Baikal
(Russian 1652)
Irkutsk
Nerchinsk
Treaty of Nerchinsk, 1689: Russia recognizes Chinese border along the Argun and Amur rivers
Amur
Argun
Altai Mts
Lake Balkhash
Kyakhta
MANCHURIA
rising, 1765
ILI PROTECTORATE 1755–7
risings of Ölöt, 1750–7
expeditions against the Dzungars, 1758–9
Urga Hutukhtu
OUTER MONGOLIA (KHALKHA) 1697
expedition against the Mongols, 1696
1629–30 KHORCHIN
Ti-hua (Urumchi)
DZUNGARS
T'ien Shan
Turfan
Ha-mi (Kumul)
Mukden (capital, 1625–44)
major Muslim insurrection, 1825–33
Aksu
Kashgar
TARIM BASIN 1759–60
incorporated in Kansu, 1759
INNER MONGOLIA (CHAHAR) 1635
Muslim risings, 1758–9
Yarkand
EASTERN TURKESTAN (SINKIANG)
Khotan
K'un Lun Mts
Yellow River (Huang Ho)
Great Wall
Peking
1644 CHIHLI
KOREA
Manchu invasions, 1627, 1636–7 vassal status 1637
Pamirs
Hui (Muslim) risings, 1781–4
1644–5 SHANSI
1645 SHANTUNG
Eight Trigrams rising, 1813
1724 TSINGHAI
1649 KANSU
TIBET
Chinese invasion, 1720–4
Tibetan tribal risings, 1807
Protectorate established, 1750; in final form, 1751
1645–6 SHENSI
1644–5 HONAN
White Lotus rebellion, 1796–1805
1645 KIANGSU
1645 HUPEH
1645 ANHWEI
Himalayas
Chin-ch'uan tribal risings, 1746–9 order finally restored, 1776
Yangtze
1646 CHEKIANG
expeditions against Nepal, 1788–92
Tashi-Lhunpo Panchen Lama
Lhasa Dalai Lama
1646 SZECHWAN
NEPAL
BHUTAN
ASSAM
1647–50 HUNAN
1649–52 KIANGSI
1658 KWEICHOW
Miao tribal risings, 1795–7, 1833
1646 FUKIEN
TAIWAN
Dutch, 1624–62; Ming loyalists, 1662–83; occupied by Ch'ing, 1683
four abortive invasions, 1766–9
tribal risings, 1726–29
1659 YUNNAN
1650–2 KWANGSI
Yao tribal rising, 1790
1650–5 KWANGTUNG
rising of Heaven and Earth Society, 1787–8
Canton
Macao
BURMA tributary from 1771
abortive Ch'ing invasion, 1788
LAOS
TONGKING
SIAM
Vietnamese pirate raids, 1800–9
1 Chinese imperial expansion from c. 1620
Manchu expansion
Phase 1: China
Manchu homeland
expansion before 1644
expansion, 1644–59
1644 date of incorporation
tributary states:
before 1644
after 1644
seat of main Lamaistic patriarch
risings of non-Chinese people
sectarian risings of Chinese
official centre of foreign commerce
Phase 2: New Territories
1724 New Territory with date of incorporation
military expeditions
border of China under the Ch'ing dynasty, at its greatest extent

Japan under the shogunate

See also
The commercial and cultural bonds
of Eurasia, 550 BC–AD 752 p. 70
The religious bonds of Eurasia to AD 500 p. 72
Imperial Japan and the early
shogunates to 1477 p. 122
China at the time of the Ming
dynasty, 1368–1644 p. 166
The expansion and modernization
of Japan, 1868–1922 p. 242

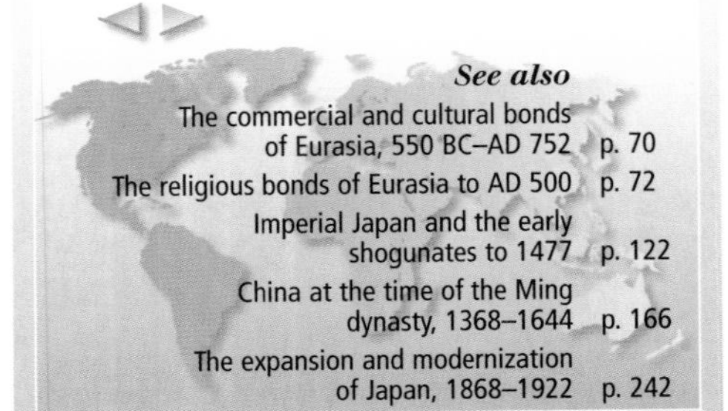

By 1600, the Tokugawa *shoguns* had pacified Japan. They tamed the feudal barons, controlled Buddhist institutions, disarmed the peasantry, harnessed imperial authority and monopolized diplomacy. Not until 1868 did the Tokugawa fall, powerless in the face of economic crisis, the return of Western powers and new enthusiasm for imperial rule.

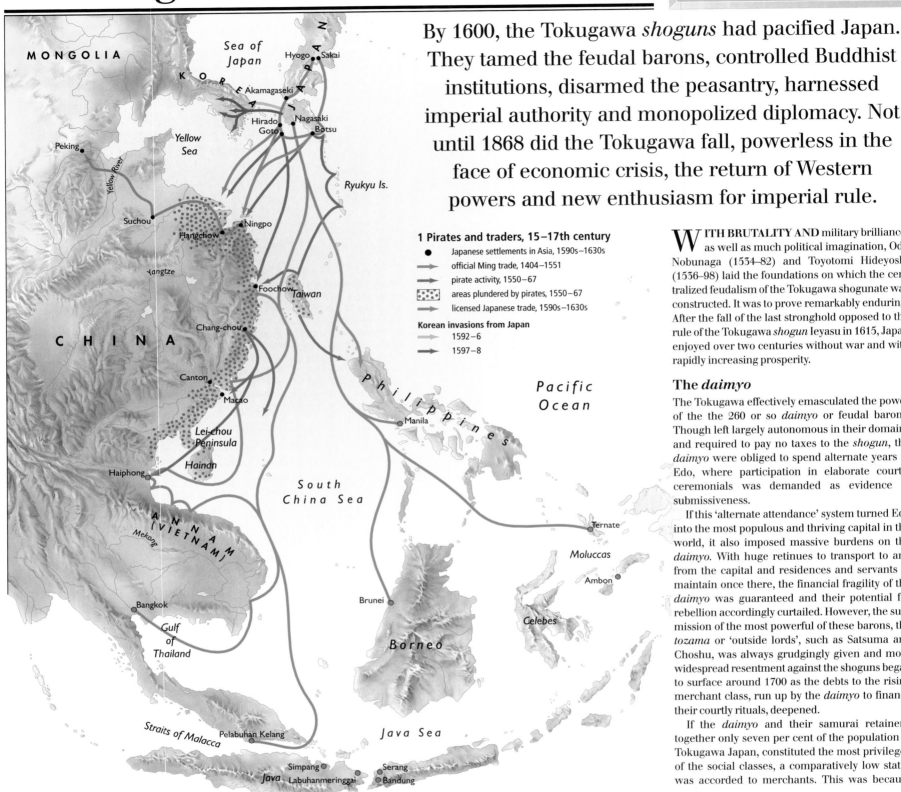

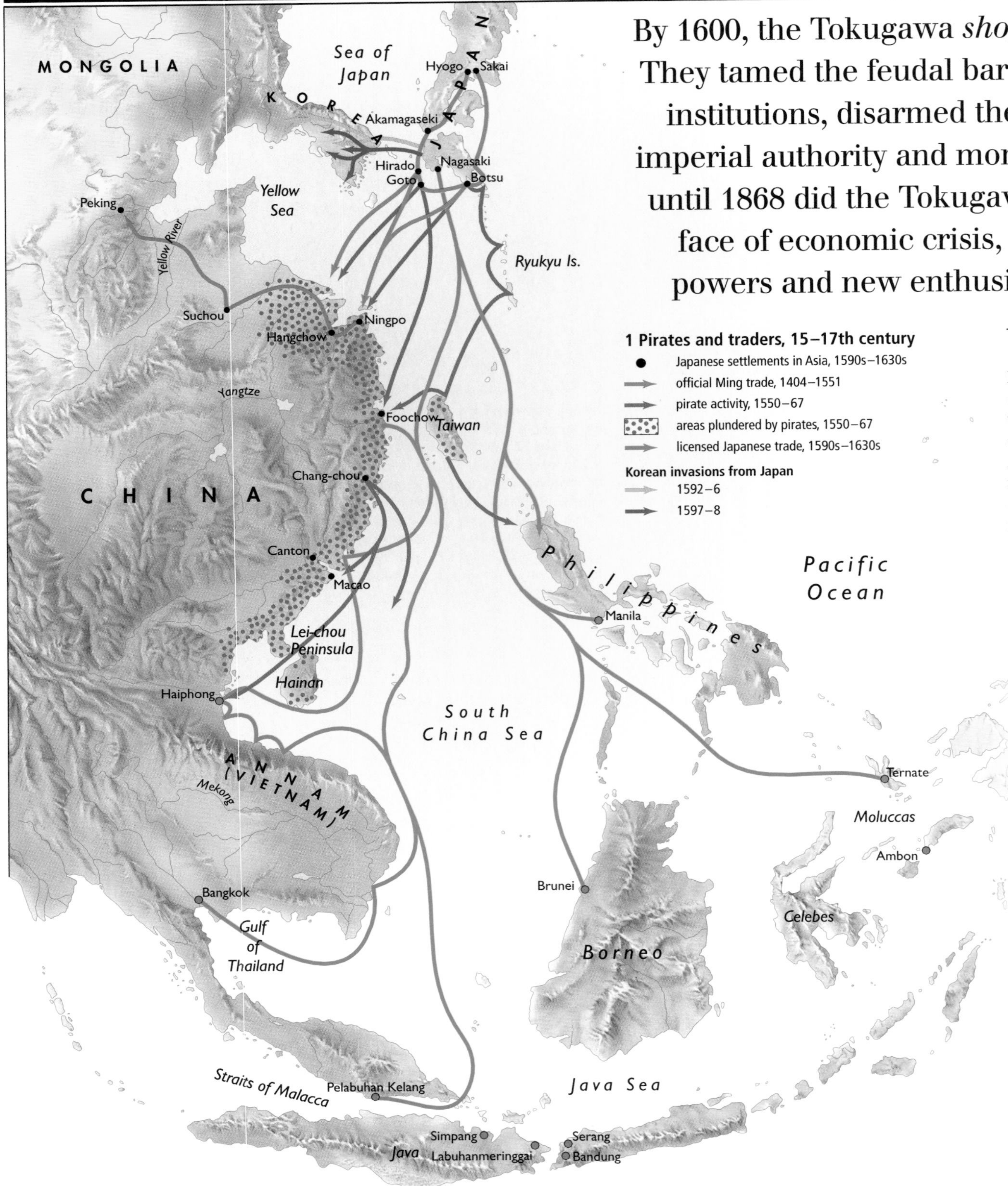

1 Pirates and traders, 15–17th century

- Japanese settlements in Asia, 1590s–1630s
- official Ming trade, 1404–1551
- pirate activity, 1550–67
- areas plundered by pirates, 1550–67
- licensed Japanese trade, 1590s–1630s

Korean invasions from Japan

- 1592–6
- 1597–8

WITH BRUTALITY AND military brilliance, as well as much political imagination, Oda Nobunaga (1534–82) and Toyotomi Hideyoshi (1536–98) laid the foundations on which the centralized feudalism of the Tokugawa shogunate was constructed. It was to prove remarkably enduring. After the fall of the last stronghold opposed to the rule of the Tokugawa *shogun* Ieyasu in 1615, Japan enjoyed over two centuries without war and with rapidly increasing prosperity.

The *daimyo*

The Tokugawa effectively emasculated the power of the the 260 or so *daimyo* or feudal barons. Though left largely autonomous in their domains and required to pay no taxes to the *shogun*, the *daimyo* were obliged to spend alternate years in Edo, where participation in elaborate courtly ceremonials was demanded as evidence of submissiveness.

If this 'alternate attendance' system turned Edo into the most populous and thriving capital in the world, it also imposed massive burdens on the *daimyo*. With huge retinues to transport to and from the capital and residences and servants to maintain once there, the financial fragility of the *daimyo* was guaranteed and their potential for rebellion accordingly curtailed. However, the submission of the most powerful of these barons, the *tozama* or 'outside lords', such as Satsuma and Choshu, was always grudgingly given and more widespread resentment against the shoguns began to surface around 1700 as the debts to the rising merchant class, run up by the *daimyo* to finance their courtly rituals, deepened.

If the *daimyo* and their samurai retainers, together only seven per cent of the population of Tokugawa Japan, constituted the most privileged of the social classes, a comparatively low status was accorded to merchants. This was because

> IT WAS THE WISH OF TOKUGAWA IEYASU, VENERATED NOW AS THE DEITY WHO SHINES OVER THE EAST, THAT RURAL PEASANTS BE TAXED NOT SO HEAVILY THAT THEY DIE, NOR YET SO LIGHTLY THAT THEY LIVE.
>
> **Takano Jodo, 1796**
>
> OUR DIVINE REALM IS THE HEAD AND SHOULDERS OF THE GLOBE AND CONTROLS ALL NATIONS. RECENTLY THE FOUL BARBARIANS FROM THE WEST, IGNORANT OF THEIR POSITION AT THE LOWER EXTREMITIES, HAVE BEEN TRAMPLING OTHER NATIONS UNDERFOOT. WHAT MANNER OF IMPUDENCE IS THIS?
>
> **Aizawa Seishisai, 1825**

1 Japanese pirates responded to Ming China's banning of trade in 1550 by plundering the Chinese coast *(map above)*. In 1567, the ban was lifted for all but the Japanese, allowing the Portuguese to take over as middlemen between China and Japan. Later, under Hideyoshi and Ieyasu, Japanese contacts with the region increased markedly. By 1600, 70,000 Japanese were engaged in trade in east Asia and 10,000 lived outside Japan.

3 The extent of Japan's isolation from the wider world under the Tokugawa is much exaggerated *(map right)*. While Japan shrank from contact with European powers from the 1640s, it sought to recreate itself as the centre of a new Asian order. Nonetheless, it was mid-19th century American demands that Japan open itself to trade with the West that brought down the Tokugawa.

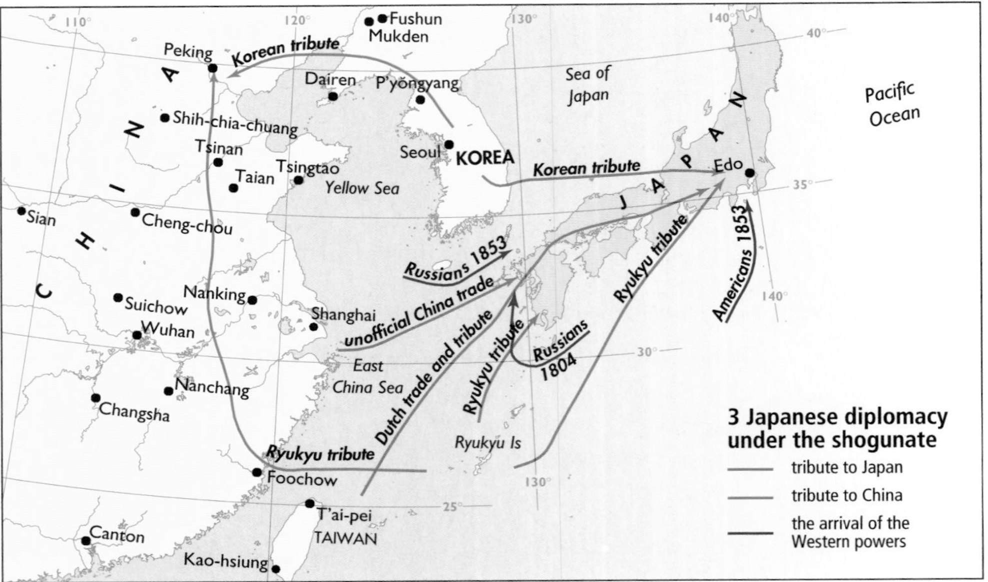

3 Japanese diplomacy under the shogunate

- tribute to Japan
- tribute to China
- the arrival of the Western powers

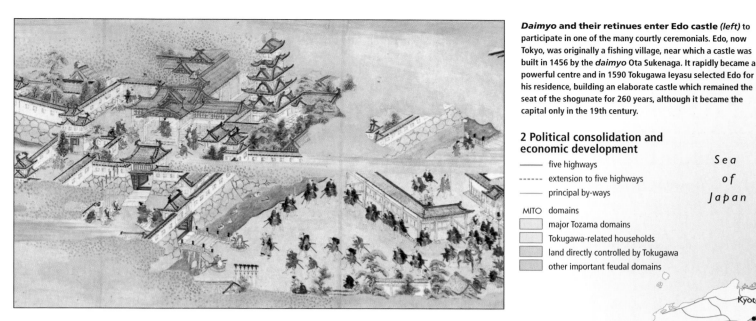

Daimyo* and their retinues enter Edo castle *(left) to participate in one of the many courtly ceremonials. Edo, now Tokyo, was originally a fishing village, near which a castle was built in 1456 by the *daimyo* Ota Sukenaga. It rapidly became a powerful centre and in 1590 Tokugawa Ieyasu selected Edo for his residence, building an elaborate castle which remained the seat of the shogunate for 260 years, although it became the capital only in the 19th century.

2 Political consolidation and economic development

five highways
extension to five highways
principal by-ways
MITO domains
major Tozama domains
Tokugawa-related households
land directly controlled by Tokugawa
other important feudal domains

MATSUMAE
MORIOKA
AKITA
SENDAI
Sea of Japan
Honshu
Oshu-kaido
Nikko
Nikko kaido
MITO
KAGA
Nakasendo
Koshu-kaido
Edo
Tokaido
Sekigahara
Kyoto
OWARI
Osaka
Sakai
KII
Pacific Ocean
CHOSHU
Shikoku
TOSA
HIZEN
Kyushu
Nagasaki
SATSUMA

2 Tokugawa Ieyasu and his successors reinforced their rule by using trusted *daimyo*, or barons, as buffers around the capital, Edo *(map above)*. All *daimyo* were subject to the 'alternate attendance' system, compulsory attendance at court every other year. To facilitate their movements to and from the court five major highways were built. The Tokugawa controlled economic centres, mines and ports; promoted a cult of Ieyasu, centred at Nikko; and effectively sidelined the emperor, confining him to his palace at Kyoto. However despotic, Tokugawa Japan thrived and enjoyed vigorous economic growth. By the 19th century, the country was far better prepared to meet the challenge of Western expansion than its larger neighbour, China.

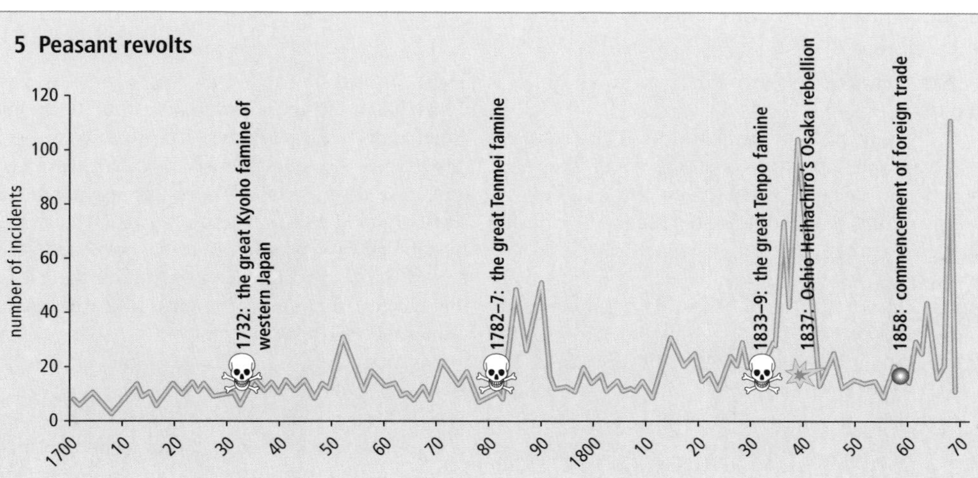

5 'Peasants are like sesame seeds: the more they are squeezed, the more they produce.' This comment, attributed to Tokugawa Ieyasu, sums up official attitudes to the rice-producing peasant class. The country's peasants, 80 per cent of the population of Tokugawa Japan, responded to their often desperate plight with frequent and destructive uprisings *(chart above)*.

Confucianism, used by the Tokugawa as an ideological buttress, despised money-making. Paradoxically, Japanese merchants, based in cities such as Osaka, Kyoto and Edo, were left alone to develop their trading contacts and a number, such as the Sumitomo family, acquired fabulous wealth. Though excluded from all forms of government, they left an increasingly important mark on the development of Japan. From around 1700, a brilliant and sophisticated alternative culture developed characterized by *kabuki* drama in Osaka in the 18th century and wood-block prints in Edo in the 18th and 19th centuries.

The bulk of the population, perhaps 80 per cent, consisted of the peasantry. The tax burden they owed their *daimyo* could be crippling, however, especially at times of poor harvests. Rural and urban uprisings in the 1730s, 1780s, 1830s and 1860s were directed at the *daimyo* and the merchant class alike and exposed the contradictions inherent in the Tokugawa system.

Tokugawa control

Aware of the emperor's potential as a rival focus of authority, the Tokugawa isolated and carefully controlled the imperial court. The emperor himself, silent and symbolic, served to bestow legitimacy on Tokugawa rule. It was not until the 1850s, when the arrival of Westerners demanding trade with Japan effectively paralyzed the Tokugawa, that the imperial court, backed by unrest at the inability of the Tokugawa to stand up to the West, reasserted itself.

But long before this undermining of their authority, the Tokugawa had established complete control over the country, monopolizing foreign trade and diplomacy and expelling most European merchants and missionaries. Yet however self-sufficient and hierarchical, Japan did not withdraw entirely from contact with the wider world. Diplomatic initiatives in east Asia were launched. Trade with the Chinese and the Dutch continued.

Nonetheless, by the end of the 18th century financial crisis and rural unrest prompted attempts at reform by the Tokugawa. All ended in failure. In 1854 and 1855, the Americans, British, Dutch and Russians extracted 'friendship' treaties from the Tokugawa. These aggressive foreign intrusions coupled with the weak Japanese response provoked crisis. For once unsure of itself, the Tokugawa solicited advice from the *daimyo* and authorization from the imperial court, thus drawing both groups on to the political stage. In 1858, the Tokugawa signed trade treaties, with the Americans, then with the British, but without first seeking imperial approval. A wave of radicalism swept Japan which led to the fall of the Tokugawa.

4 Togukawa legitimacy was fatally undermined by the intrusion of the Western powers in the 1850s *(map below)*. The diplomatic crisis prompted outbursts of anti-foreign, pro-imperial violence, which was soon turned on the Tokugawa. When foreign powers flexed their muscles, anti-foreign Tokugawa loyalists realized that the West could not be repulsed, only accommodated. The sense of social chaos was compounded by widespread millenarian activity in 1867.

1467 *Onin Wars: civil unrest throughout Japan*
1543 *Portuguese traders arrive*
1603 *Tokugawa Ieyasu first Tokugawa* shogun
1640s *Christian missionaries and European traders (except Dutch) expelled*
1700 *Osaka, Kyoto and Edo flourish as merchant centres*
1833–9 *Nationwide famine and unrest*
1853 *Commodore Perry arrives; proposes commercial arrangements between Japan and US*
1858 *Trade treaties signed with US and Britain*
1868 *Fall of Tokugawa; Meiji restoration*

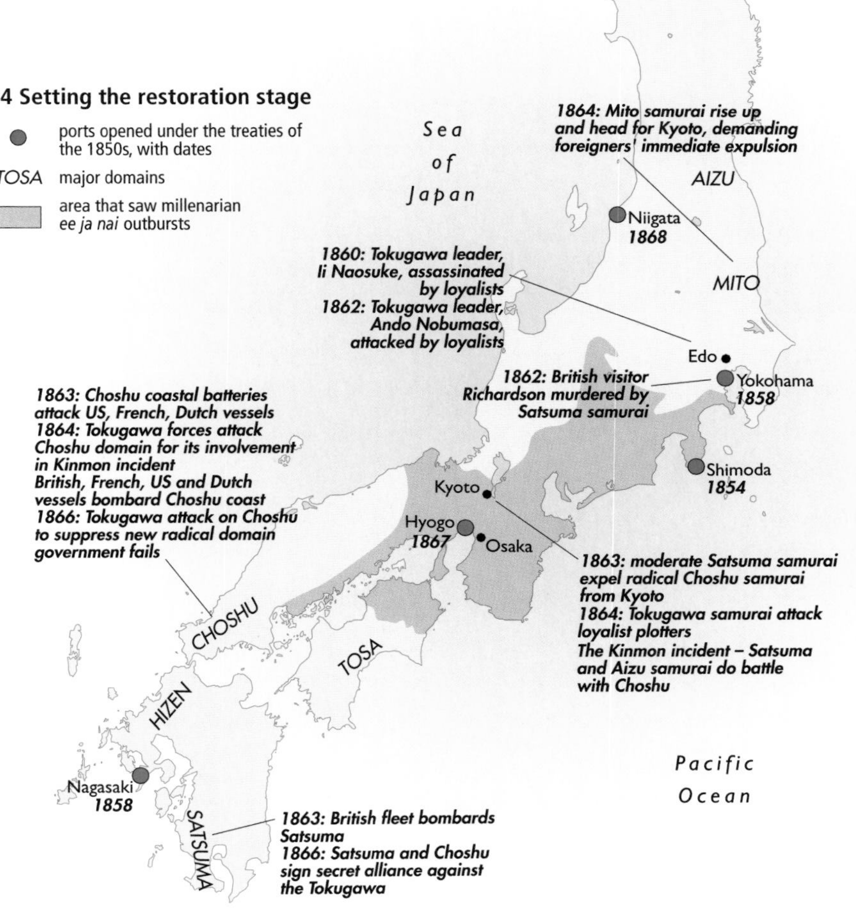

1511 to 1826

Southeast Asia and the European powers

See also

The early civilizations of southeast Asia p. 134
The world on the eve of European expansion p. 154
European expansion overseas p. 158
The struggle for empire, 1713–1815 p. 194
The emerging global economy p. 198
The collapse of the Chinese empire p. 232
India under British rule, 1805–1935 p. 234
European colonial empires, 1815–1914 p. 244

1511 *Portuguese take control of Malacca*

1557 *Portuguese become established in Macao (China)*

1619 *Batavia founded by Dutch; beginnings of Dutch colonial empire in the East Indies*

1641 *Dutch capture Malacca from the Portuguese*

1786 *Penang acquired by English East India Company*

1819 *Singapore founded by Britain as free trade port*

1824 *Treaty of London formalizes British control of Malaya and Dutch control of East Indies*

At the beginning of the 16th century the first Europeans, lured by the lucrative spice trade, arrived in southeast Asia. Though the Spanish and Portuguese established the first European settlements, in the longer run the Dutch and the British, exploiting divisions among the southeast Asians themselves, were the major beneficiaries.

YOUR HONOURS SHOULD KNOW BY EXPERIENCE THAT TRADE IN ASIA MUST BE DRIVEN AND MAINTAINED UNDER THE PROTECTION AND FAVOUR OF YOUR HONOURS' OWN WEAPONS, AND THAT THE WEAPONS MUST BE PAID FOR BY THE PROFITS FROM THE TRADE; SO THAT WE CANNOT CARRY ON TRADE WITHOUT WAR NOR WAR WITHOUT TRADE.

Jan Pietersz Coen, 1614, founder of Batavia

WHEN EUROPEAN TRADERS and adventurers broke through into the Indian Ocean at the close of the 15th century, the great prize drawing them forward was the spices of southeast Asia. Here was untold wealth to be tapped. But here also, at one of the world's main crossroads, where cultural influences from China and India intermingled, they found themselves in a region of great complexity – politically fragmented, unstable and divided between Buddhism, Hinduism and Islam.

On the mainland, rival peoples and dynasties competed for hegemony. In the Malayan archipelago, the empires of Sri Vijaya and Majapahit were little more than memories (*see* p. 134), having split into many small states with little cohesion between them. This was the situation when Europeans first arrived in the region in the person of Alfonso de Albuquerque who in 1511 conquered the great international emporium of Malacca for the king of Portugal.

The Portuguese presence changed little at first. Albuquerque and his successors were there to dominate the spice trade and to this end built a chain of fortified trading stations linked by naval power. Provided this was accepted, they had no wish to interfere with the native potentates. Far more important, after the arrival on the scene of the Dutch and the English, was the challenge to the Portuguese trading monopoly presented by their European rivals. For most of the 17th century, this rivalry was the dominant factor.

The Dutch and English conquests

The Dutch in particular began a systematic conquest of the Portuguese settlements, capturing Malacca in 1641, before turning against the British. But in doing so, they were inevitably drawn into local politics. After establishing a base at Batavia in 1619, they interfered in succession disputes among the neighbouring sultans, to ensure their own position, and in this way gradually extended control over Java, expelling the British from Bantam in 1682. They had already driven them out of the Spice Islands at the 'massacre of Amboina' (1623) and by the seizure of Macassar (1667), as a result forcing the English East India Company to turn instead to the China trade. With this in view, the British acquired Penang on the west coast of Malaya in 1786, the first step in a process which was ultimately to make them masters of the Malay peninsula.

But this was still exceptional. Though European activities encroached on the outlying islands they had little impact on the mainland monarchies, which had no direct interest in European trade and were mainly concerned with extending their power at the expense of that of their neighbours. At the same time (*see* map 1) all the main centres were under pressure from the hill peoples of the interior, always waiting to assert their independence. But the main lines of development include the advance of Annam (Vietnam) at the expense of Cambodia, the rise of a new Burmese empire under Alaungpaya (1735–60) and successful Siamese resistance to Burmese enchroachment, in spite of Burmese conquest in 1767.

These events occured for the most part without European involvement even if, during the struggle for empire between France and England in the 18th century (*see* p. 194), some states were implicated. Already under Louis XIV, France had intervened in Siam against the Dutch. But such was the popular hostility engendered by French meddling in Siam that the dynasty they supported was overthrown and the French themselves were expelled. During the Anglo-French war in India after 1746, France supported the Mon rebellion in Burma, provoking the English East India Company to seize in reply the island of Negrais at the mouth of the Bassein river. Later, when the Burmese, foiled in their attempt to capture Siam, switched their efforts to the north, the British, fearing for the security of Bengal, again intervened. The result was the first Anglo-Burmese war (1824–6) and the British annexation of Assam, Arakan and Tenasserim (*see* p. 234).

Anglo-Dutch agreement

In Malaya there was similar encroachment on the native states when the British, rulers of Penang since 1786, established Singapore in 1819 as a free trade port after its acquisition by Sir Stamford Raffles, the British Lieutenant-Governor of Benkulen in Sumatra. This led to a conflict of interest with Holland which was only settled by the Anglo-Dutch Treaty of London of 1824, under which the British withdrew from Sumatra in return for Dutch withdrawal from Malacca (*see* map 4).

But if by the early years of the 19th century the future Dutch and British colonial empires in southeast Asia were taking shape, the control directly exercised by the European powers was still loose, more concerned with trade than with imperial rule. The Portuguese and Dutch had dominated the spice and pepper trades, but they were largely content to receive surpluses produced by local peasants; it was not until 1830 that the Dutch introduced the 'Culture System' in which the Javanese were forced to devote one-fifth of their lands to export crops. Only with the impact of the industrial revolution in Europe, and the rapidly expanding market for raw materials and the increased exports of finished goods it created, were the lives and fortunes of the peoples of the region seriously affected by the European presence.

2 The spice routes
English routes — Portuguese routes — Spanish routes — Dutch routes

2 European penetration of the Spice Islands was driven by the desire to capture and control the lucrative trade in spices originating in the East Indies *(map left)*. The Portuguese were first on the scene, in 1511. To the east, an early and unsuccesful Spanish expedition to Tidore was followed by their capture of Manila in 1571. By the early 17th century, Dutch and British penetration sparked a continuing struggle between the European powers for control of the region.

3 Dutch territorial expansion in Java began through Sultan Agung of Mataram's attempts to capture Batavia *(map below)*. After his death in 1646 the Dutch East India Company, by intervening in succession disputes, gradually became the strongest political force in the island, with the ruling houses coming under its control and paying their debts by cessions of territory. The maintenance of its trade monopoly played a vital part in this expansion.

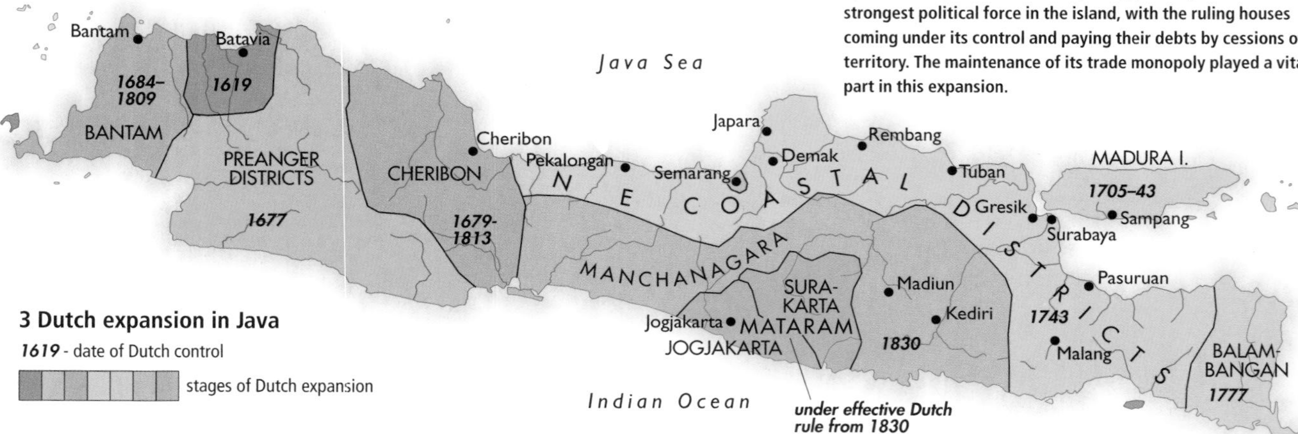

3 Dutch expansion in Java
1619 - date of Dutch control
stages of Dutch expansion

1 European contact with southeast Asia *(map above)*, though driven initially by demand in Europe for spices, paved the way for the foundation of substantial European empires across the region. The Spanish had ruled the Philippines since the 16th century and, though other European contacts had little impact on mainland societies, by the early 19th century the British had put in place the basis of their subsequent colonial rule in Malaya, while Dutch control of the East Indies was also firmly established.

4 Under the Treaty of London of 1824 the Dutch were to withdraw from the Malay peninsula *(map left)*. The British settlements there – Penang, Singapore and Malacca – were bound by the doctrine of non-intervention laid down in Pitt's India Act. The immediate danger to the independence of the Malay states in 1826 lay in Siamese expansionism; the Burney Treaty in that year halted Siam's pressure upon them, though only after two incidents in which the Penang government safeguarded Perak's independence.

Javanese culture provided a strong strand of continuity even under Dutch rule. Indeed the new rulers were incorporated into traditional art forms. This 19th-century batik *(right)* depicts a street scene in Jogjakarta – a marriage procession with musicians, street vendors and Dutchmen driven in carriages.

The European economy: agriculture and society

See also
The European economy: trade and industry, 1550–1775 p. 180
Europe: the state and its opponents, 1500–1688 p. 184
The industrial revolution begins: Great Britain, 1760–1860 p. 200
Population growth and movements, 1815–1914 p. 208

European agriculture as a whole improved only slowly between 1500 and 1800 and with marked regional contrasts. Southern and eastern Europe, the latter severely handicapped by feudalism, saw slow growth. But in northern Europe there were dramatic increases in agricultural productivity, above all in Britain and the Low Countries

FROM THE EARLY 16TH CENTURY Britain and the Low Countries enjoyed an agricultural revolution which by 1800 had produced a highly efficient, commercialized farming system. But elsewhere in Europe agricultural techniques and levels of productivity had hardly changed since Roman times and most peasants produced only about 20 per cent more a year than they needed to feed their families and their livestock and to provide the next year's seed. Consequently, in many countries about 80 per cent of the people worked on the land. In Britain and the Low Countries, however, the proportion fell rapidly during the later 18th century as improved agriculture met the food needs of the growing urban population.

The new crops

Except in Britain and the Netherlands, most improvements came from the introduction of new, more productive crops, mainly from America. Thus the potato became a basic staple in western Europe, starting in Spain and Italy. In Ireland it allowed such a massive increase in population (from 2.5 to 8 million) that disaster struck when the crop failed in 1846. American maize, like the potato, gave a far higher yield than the established cereals – barley, millet and sorghum – and was widely adopted in southern Europe. Buckwheat, useful on poor soils, entered northern Europe from Russia while in the Mediterranean sugar cane, rice and citrus fruits had arrived from Asia before 1500. Sugar production declined after 1550, however, in the face of competition from Madeira, the Canaries and, after 1600, the West Indies and Brazil.

These slow crop changes contrasted strongly with the rapidly developing northwest. The Dutch began the process by pouring capital into reclaiming land from the sea. Naturally wishing to avoid having to leave land fallow every third year (necessary under the traditional system), they discovered that fertility could be maintained by simple crop rotation involving the alternation of arable with artificial grasses and industrial crops such as rapeseed, flax and dyestuffs. Turnips, on which sheep could be grazed in winter to produce manure as well as mutton and wool, were especially important, as were peas, beans and clovers. English farmers copied and developed these innovations. Irrigation, drainage schemes and woodland clearance increased the productive acreage, while land enclosure and soil treatments encouraged improved husbandry. By the 1740s, grain exports accounted for 10 per cent of England's export earnings, and the old fear of starvation had been banished.

Such techniques gradually spread as the growth of towns encouraged more specialization in food production. Holland concentrated on dairy products and was exporting 90 per cent of her cheese by 1700. The Danes were sending 80,000 head of cattle a year to Germany, and the Dutch, German and Italian cloth industries were sustained by massive imports of Spanish wool. The exchange of northern Europe's cereals and timber for the fruits, wines and oils of the Mediterranean grew apace.

Peasants and feudalism

All improvements in productivity depended on breaking the old feudal relationships which oppressed the peasants, however, and here there was a sharp east-west cleavage. Before 1500 feudalism had been stronger in the older settled areas of western Europe than in the sparsely peopled lands of eastern Europe and Russia. After 1500 this changed completely: peasants in northwest Europe exchanged the traditional labour services on their lords' land for a money rent (especially in England and the Netherlands) or, in France and farther south, for share-cropping tenancies. They also gradually freed themselves from burdensome personal services and dues, though this required revolutionary action, inspired by France in 1789, before it was complete.

In total contrast, feudal power grew and spread in eastern Europe until it approached slavery. Feudal lords increased their power, halting

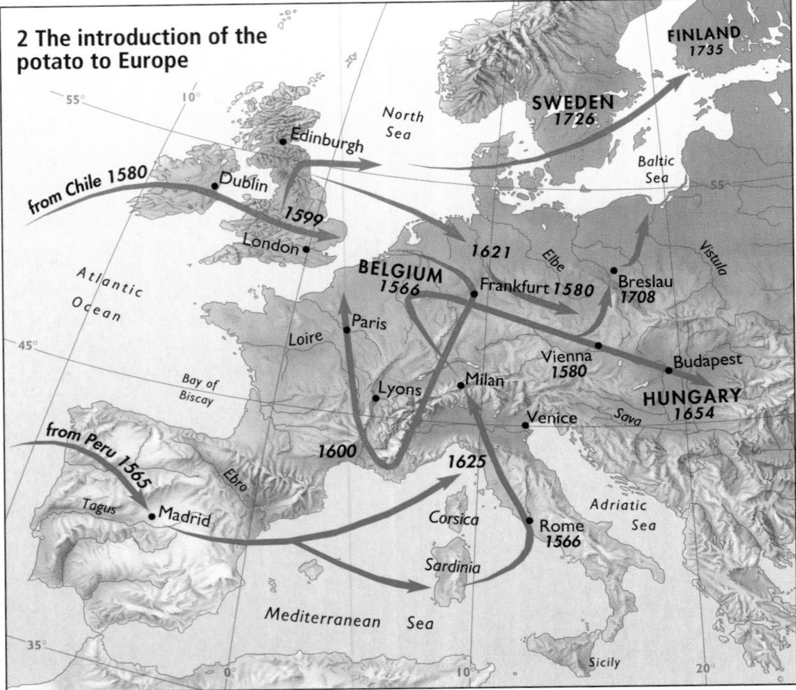

2 Yielding four times as much carbohydrate per acre as wheat, the potato, a South American import, spread rapidly after its arrival in 1565 – first in gardens, after 1700 as a key field crop *(map above)*.

1 By 1812, the peasants of Britain, Scandinavia and the Netherlands had long been free *(map below)*. Those of Denmark and Austria were encouraged in their efforts by the French revolution, which had revived emancipation movements in Poland and Germany, the latter scene of the most famous peasant revolt (1525). Only Russia, Spain, Portugal and Italy remained fully under the landlords' yoke.

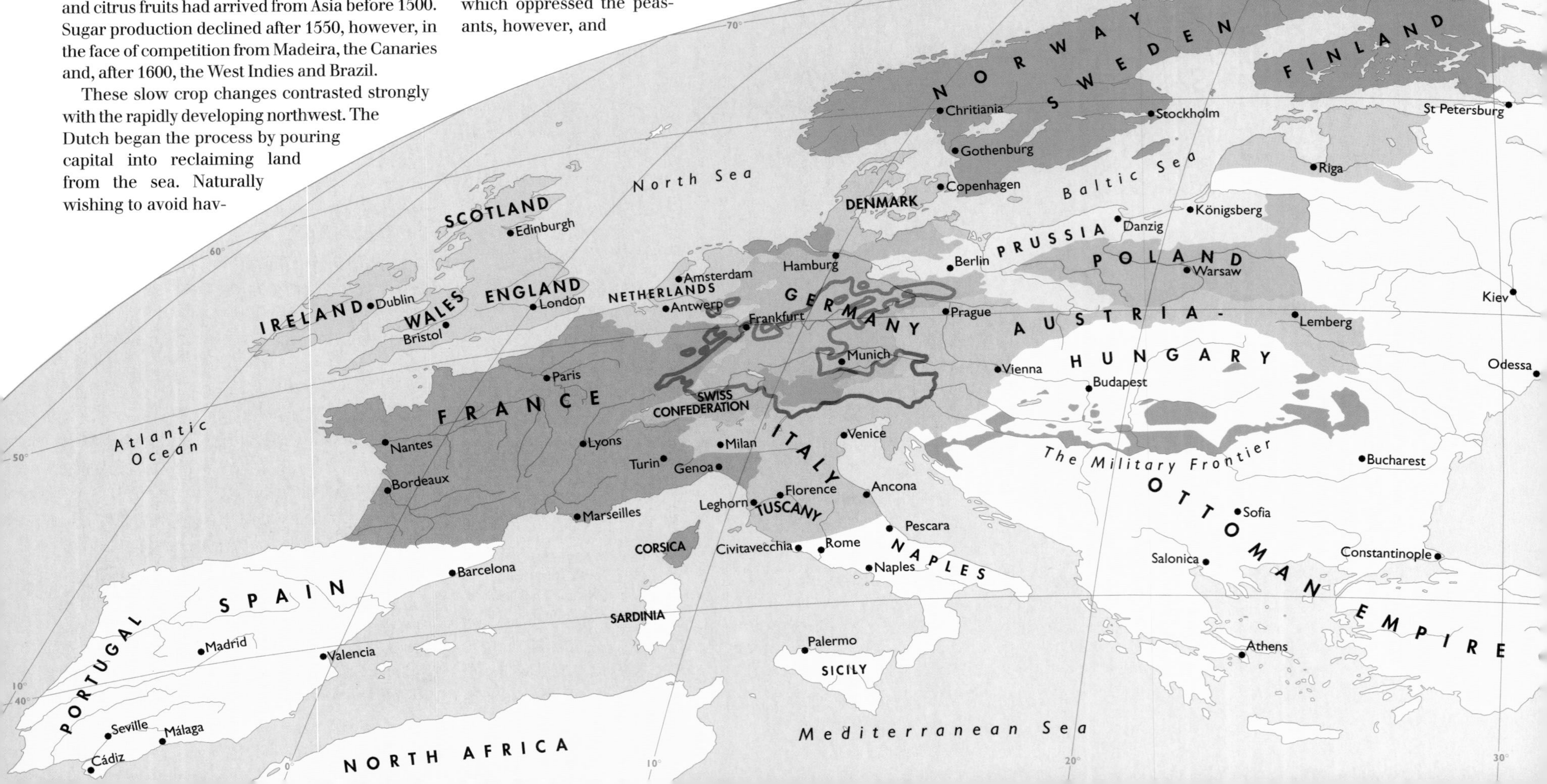

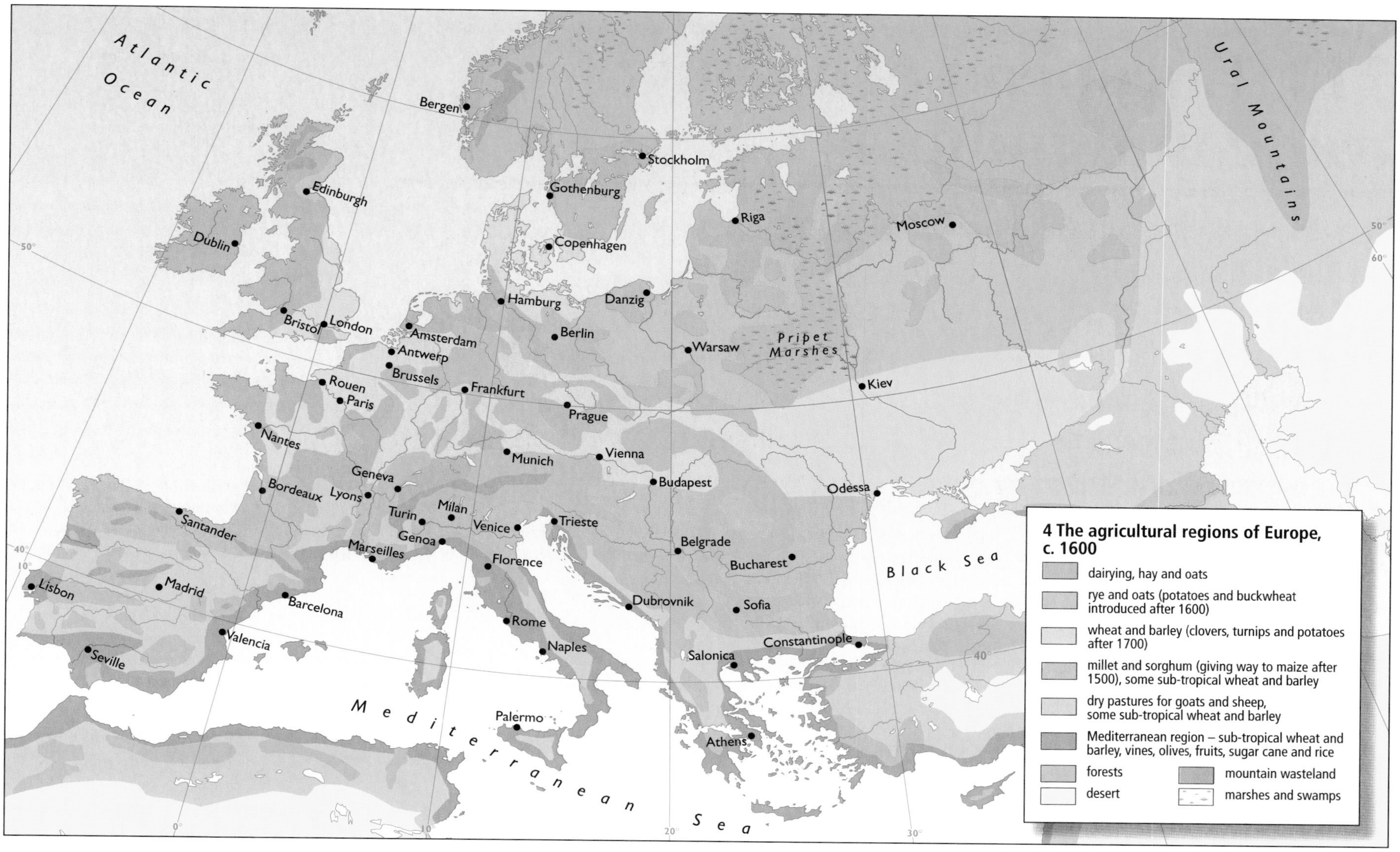

4 The agricultural regions of Europe, c. 1600

- dairying, hay and oats
- rye and oats (potatoes and buckwheat introduced after 1600)
- wheat and barley (clovers, turnips and potatoes after 1700)
- millet and sorghum (giving way to maize after 1500), some sub-tropical wheat and barley
- dry pastures for goats and sheep, some sub-tropical wheat and barley
- Mediterranean region – sub-tropical wheat and barley, vines, olives, fruits, sugar cane and rice
- forests
- mountain wasteland
- desert
- marshes and swamps

> We ride abroad a league or two into the country which they call Grave. [Talked] with a poore paisant's wife. Their ordinary food riebread and water. Flesh is a thing [which] seldome seasons their pots, and, as she said, they make no distinction between flesh and fast days; but when their money reaches to a more costly meale, they buy the inwards of some beast in the market and then they feast themselves. And yet they say in San Longe and severall other parts of France the paisants are much more miserable than these, for these they count the flourishing paisants which live in Grave.
>
> **John Locke**
> ***Travels in France, 1675–9***

1525 *German peasants revolt*

1565 *Potato introduced into Europe. Netherlands begins large-scale land reclamation*

1594–7 *Peasant wars in Austria and Hungary*

1649 *Serfdom legalized in Russia*

1730s *Jethro Tull's seed drill invented. Charles Townshend advocates crop rotation*

1778 *Sardinia frees serfs*

1789 *The French revolution abolishes feudal privileges in the countryside*

1807 *Prussia abolishes serfdom*

4 The main agricultural areas shown are as they were in 1600 *(map above)*. Boundaries are only approximate. Potatoes gradually took over from cereals in many parts of northern and central Europe, while in the south maize replaced millet and sorghum.

3 Between 1540 and 1715 the people of Friesland, Zeeland and Holland wrested 364,565 acres from the sea, and 84,638 acres from the edges of the inland lakes *(map right)*. Their capital-intensive methods, based on widespread use of windmills and pumps, were adapted with great success in England and, to a lesser extent, in France, Italy and north Germany.

migration to empty lands farther east (as in Russia) and increasing grain-export profits (as in eastern Germany and Poland-Lithuania). Free peasants only survived in newly conquered lands if they performed military service instead of paying rent. The peasants of western Germany occupied a middle position. They had tried to win their freedom in a great revolt in 1525, and briefly controlled most of southern Germany before the rebellion was savagely crushed. Yet the excesses of eastern Europe were averted, and the peasants gradually gained greater freedom by 1800. Their slow emancipation was, however, an important reason why the German industrial revolution came so late.

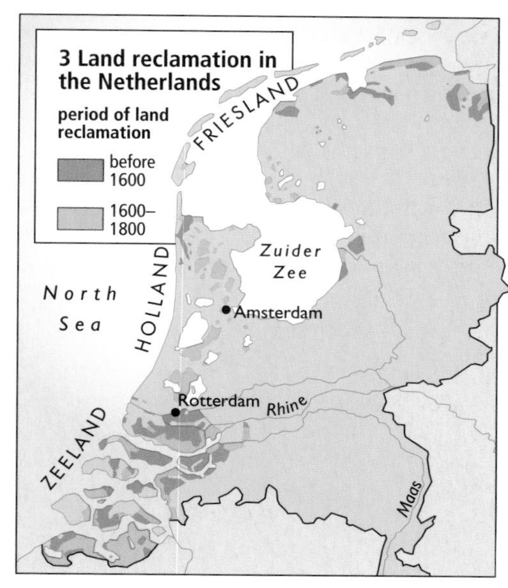

Improvements in animal husbandry in 18th-century England were remarkable. The average weight of bullocks grew from 370 lbs in 1700 to 840 lbs in 1786, that of sheep from 28 lbs to 100 lbs. ***Mr Healey's Sheep (below)*** **is a graphic illustration of the effects of selective breeding.**

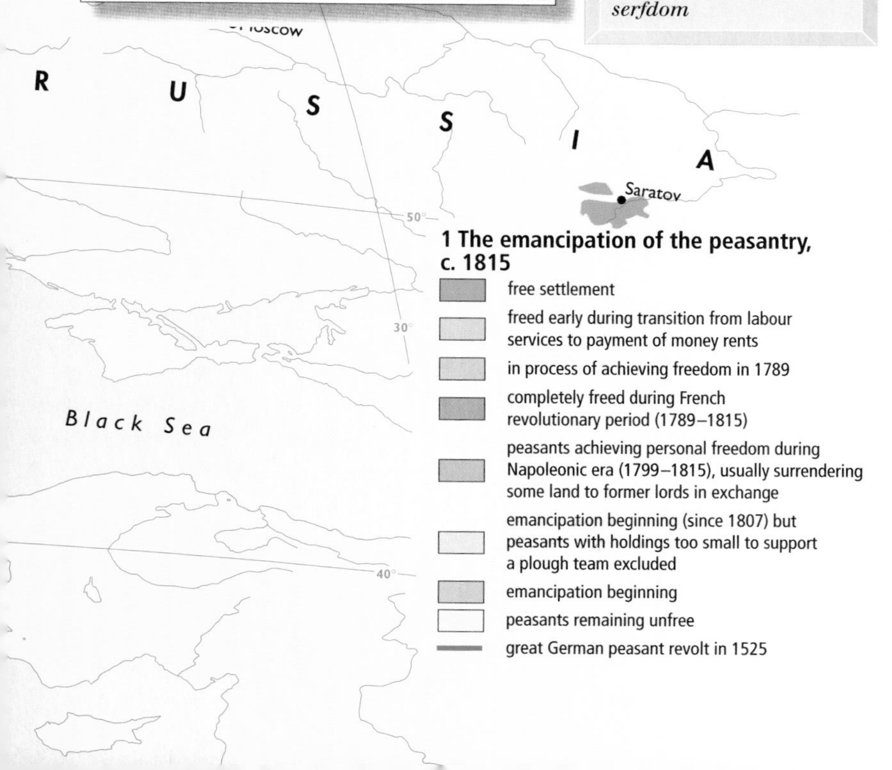

1 The emancipation of the peasantry, c. 1815

- free settlement
- freed early during transition from labour services to payment of money rents
- in process of achieving freedom in 1789
- completely freed during French revolutionary period (1789–1815)
- peasants achieving personal freedom during Napoleonic era (1799–1815), usually surrendering some land to former lords in exchange
- emancipation beginning (since 1807) but peasants with holdings too small to support a plough team excluded
- emancipation beginning
- peasants remaining unfree
- great German peasant revolt in 1525

The European economy: trade and industry

See also
The Renaissance and Early Modern state in Europe, 1450–c. 1600 p. 150
The European economy: agriculture and society, 1500–1815 p. 178
Europe: the state and its opponents, 1500–1688 p. 184
The emerging global economy, c. 1775 p. 198
The industrial revolution begins: Great Britain, 1760–1860 p. 200

Population growth, expanding industry, the impact of colonial trade and changes to the banking system transformed Europe's economic performance after 1500. At the same time, there was a decisive shift in the economic centre of gravity from southern to northern Europe. The Dutch Republic and, later, Britain emerged as the new economic powerhouses.

1545 *Discovery of silver mines at Potosí (Peru) and Zacatecas (Mexico)*

1559 *Tobacco first introduced into Europe*

c. 1560 *Portuguese begin sugar cultivation in Brazil*

1600 *English East India Company established*

1602 *Dutch East India Company founded*

1609 *Amsterdam Exchange Bank established*

1693 *Gold discovered in Brazil*

1694 *Bank of England established*

1776 *Publication of The Wealth of Nations, Adam Smith*

EUROPE'S POPULATION EXPANDED fast in the 16th century, was retarded by famine, plague and war in the 17th century, but grew rapidly again from the mid-18th century. In 1500 only three cities – Constantinople (by far the largest), Paris and Naples – had more than 200,000 inhabitants. By 1700 this number had doubled, and London, Paris and Constantinople had passed the half-million mark.

The increased complexity of government, an acceleration of trade and finance, a growing taste for conspicuous consumption, and a feeling that survival was better assured in the cities, all helped to hasten this trend. The resulting problems, particularly the need to guarantee reliable urban food supplies, also created new opportunities. Most notably, until the mid-17th century, they generated a massive demand for eastern Europe's wheat and rye, a trade which fed the burgeoning economic strength of Holland, now nearly monopolizing the Baltic carrying trade.

The Netherlands in fact formed the hinge for a gradual but decisive shift in commercial power. In 1500 industry was largely concentrated in the corridor running north–south from Antwerp and Bruges to Florence and Milan. By 1700 this axis had swung through almost 90 degrees. At one end stood Britain and the Dutch Republic, increasingly the most dynamic commercial centres in Europe; eastward the line extended through the metal and woollen districts of the Rhine to the great industrial concentrations of Saxony, Bohemia and Silesia.

Industry, trade and finance

At the same time, however, technology advanced only in patches and much industrial expansion was chiefly achieved by increasing the number of workers while still using the old methods. But even this helped improve industrial organization, by splitting up production processes, developing production in rural areas free of urban restriction, and drawing on the cheap part-time labour of peasant families. Much industry was controlled by traders who organized a scattered cottage labour force. By the 18th century this had become the typical form of all but local and luxury industry.

More impressive than the erratic spread of industry was the increase in international trade. The maritime powers, with their colonies and ports in Asia and the Americas, imported a fast-growing stream of new products: tea, coffee, sugar, chocolate, tobacco. They were purchased with European manufactures and with the shipping, insurance and merchandising services that built up the wealth of ports such as Bordeaux, London, Amsterdam and Marseilles.

Governments assisted those sectors of economic activity that they favoured. Holland and England waged wars to protect and expand their shipping and trading interests, but did not consistently aid industry. The governments of France and the central European states, by contrast, established new industries and subsidized old ones. Increasingly costly wars, however, had an even more powerful influence. They called for heavy taxation and large borrowings that undermined the precarious stability of Europe's gradually evolving monetary

Europe was permanently short of silver and gold before the discovery and exploitation by Spain in the 16th century of the New World's more plentiful silver mines. This German silver mine *(right)*, painted in 1521, highlights the small-scale and largely rural nature of much pre-industrial European economic activity.

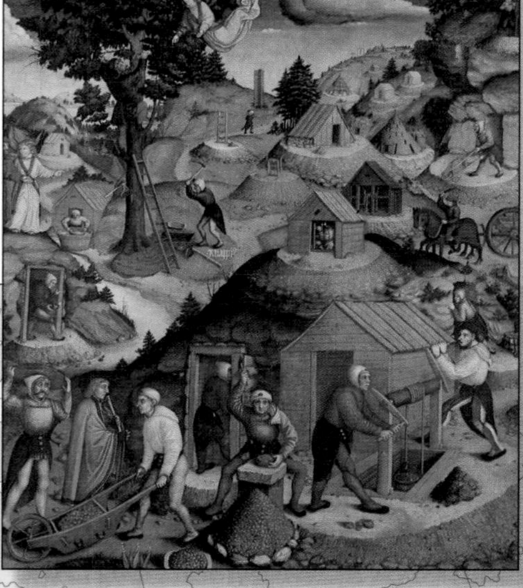

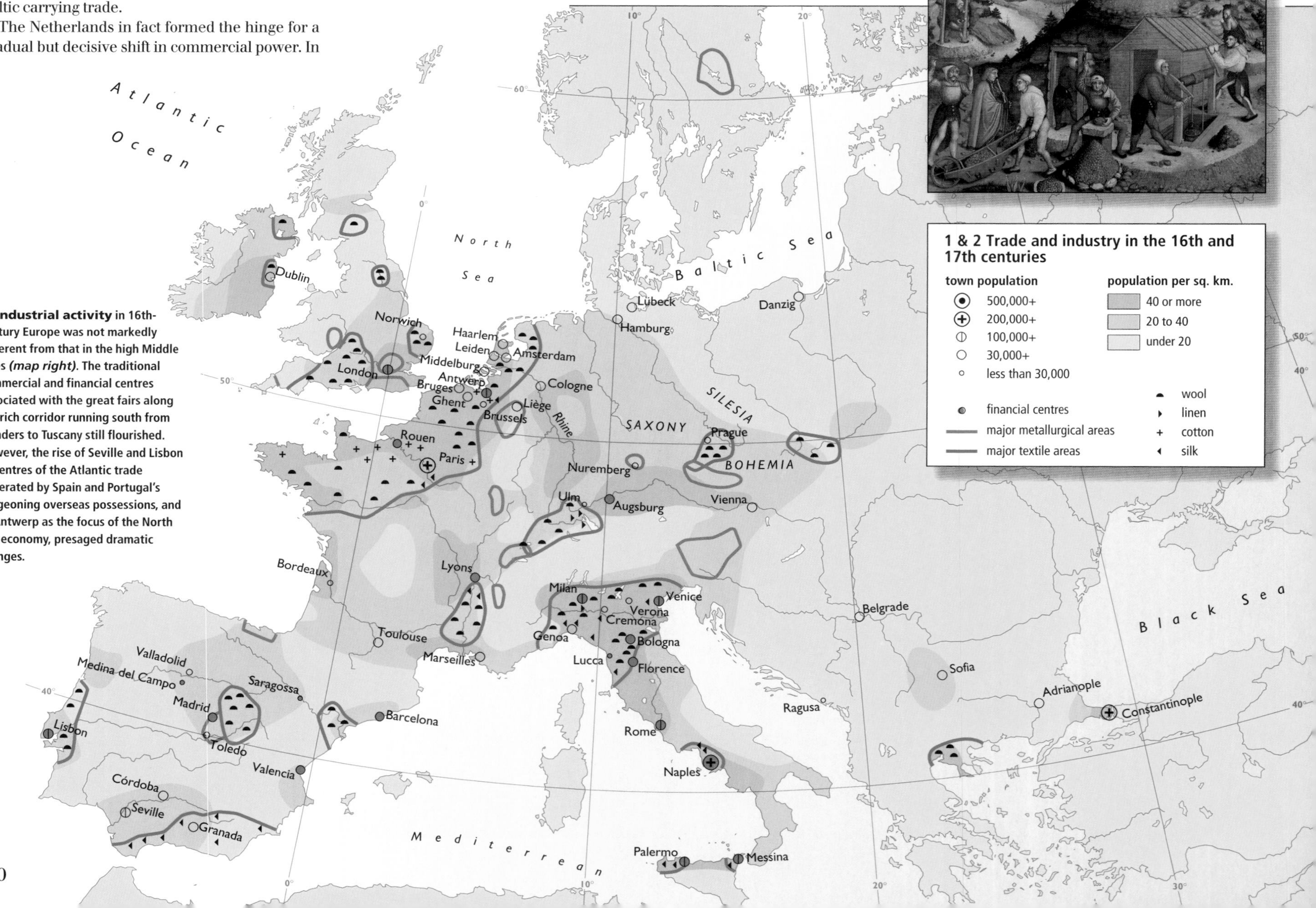

1 & 2 Trade and industry in the 16th and 17th centuries

town population: 500,000+; 200,000+; 100,000+; 30,000+; less than 30,000

population per sq. km.: 40 or more; 20 to 40; under 20

financial centres; major metallurgical areas; major textile areas

wool; linen; cotton; silk

1 Industrial activity in 16th-century Europe was not markedly different from that in the high Middle Ages *(map right)*. The traditional commercial and financial centres associated with the great fairs along the rich corridor running south from Flanders to Tuscany still flourished. However, the rise of Seville and Lisbon as centres of the Atlantic trade generated by Spain and Portugal's burgeoning overseas possessions, and of Antwerp as the focus of the North Sea economy, presaged dramatic changes.

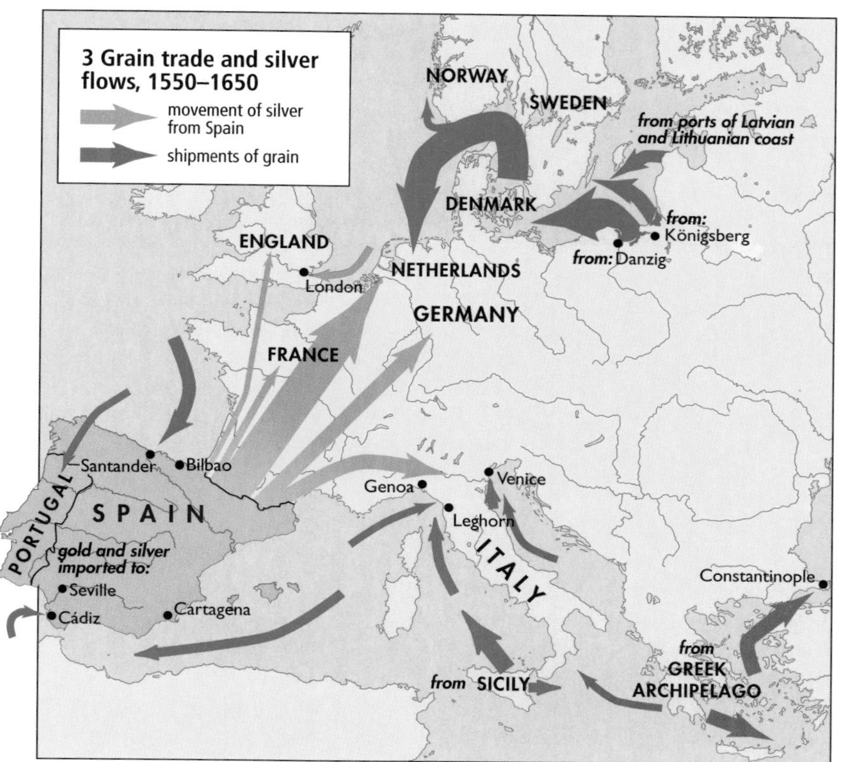

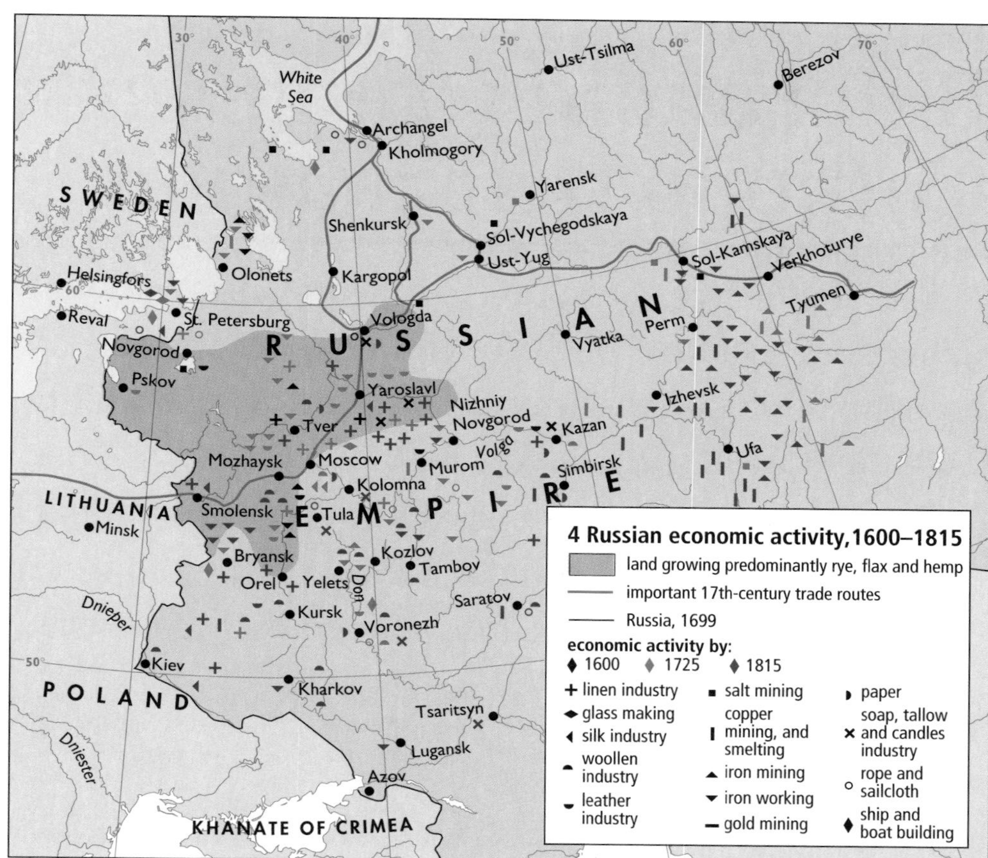

> It is upon these two classes of People, the Manufacturers and the Shopkeepers, that I build the Hypothesis which I have taken upon me to offer to the public, 'tis upon the gain they make either by their Labour, or their Industry in Trade, and upon their inconceivable Numbers, that the Home Consumption of our own Produce, and of the Produce of foreign Nations imported here is so exceeding great, that our Trade is raised up to such a Prodigy of Magnitude...
>
> **Daniel Defoe**
> ***Tour Through the Whole Island of Great Britain, 1724–6***

3 From the mid-16th century, the bullion-bearing galleons from the Indies brought a flood of liquid funds to Spain ***(map above)***. But it flowed out as fast as it arrived – to finance Habsburg imperialism and to pay for the Baltic grain for a Mediterranean largely unable to feed itself.

4 Russia was a late developer economically ***(map above right)***. By 1600 economic activity, concentrated around Moscow, consisted mainly of the processing of animal and vegetable products. By 1725, the extensive smelting of copper and iron was established in the Urals. By 1815, a third important industrial area, around St Petersburg, had developed.

systems. The wars were ruinous to Spain and damaging to France and many smaller states; only Britain and the Dutch Republic kept their military commitments within realistic financial bounds.

Trade and war also generated an unprecedented demand for money. Gold and silver were amply provided from Spanish Mexico and Peru after 1545, supported from the 1690s by Brazilian gold. This bullion was redistributed across Europe by merchants and by Spanish government transactions, much of it financing Europe's trade deficits with the East Indies and the Levant. The money supply was also supplemented by the growth of banking. In contrast to the established German and Italian banks, which were heavily engaged in government lending, Dutch and English banks served private interests with giro and foreign-exchange facilities and short-term credits. In the century after its opening in 1609, the Amsterdam Exchange Bank was the undisputed focus of continental trade; Britain could compete only after 1694, when the Bank of England provided a focus for older private banking firms. With low interest rates, free capital movement, secure international payments and an assured savings flow, the foundations of modern finance were firmly laid.

2 Dramatic changes in 18th-century European trade and industry occurred even before the industrial revolution ***(map right)***. Italy and Spain lost ground, while England (with major metal-working and mining interests), Holland (building ships for the whole of Europe), France (behind a high protective wall), and Sweden (exploiting her mineral resources), all forged ahead fast. At the same time, the increasing sophistication of her banking mechanisms gave Britain an important and growing advantage.

1517 to 1670
Reformation and Catholic Reformation

See also
The Renaissance and Early Modern state in Europe, 1450–c. 1600 p. 150
Europe: the state and its opponents, 1500–1688 p. 184
The Holy Roman Empire, 1493–1806 p. 190

The shattering of the unity of Latin Christendom altered the course of European history. The rise of assertive Protestant churches and the reaction of the Catholic church stimulated a battle for the consciences of ordinary Europeans which disrupted traditional loyalties and political arrangements. It was 150 years before an uneasy religious balance was restored.

IN 1500 THE CATHOLIC CHURCH seemed stronger than ever. Paganism was vanquished; the Iberian Reconquista had destroyed the last Islamic state in western Europe and the overthrow of the Byzantine empire in 1453 had weakened the Orthodox church. Lay piety was booming, as was popular interest in the church's promise of salvation. Yet this very success brought profound problems. The moral and spiritual quality of many clergy left much to be desired. There was widespread concern at the state of the church and of popular religious belief which, although often enthusiastic, was frequently characterized by ignorance or heterodoxy. Attempts at reform, however, were often undermined by the unresolved problem of authority within the Church, while the invention of the printing press, by dramatically quickening the pace of debate, facilitated the questioning of established truth by clergy and laity alike.

The Reformation

The Reformation began as a revolt of the clergy, as Martin Luther (1483–1546), Huldrych Zwingli (1484–1531), Martin Bucer (1491–1551) and many others rejected the authority of the Catholic church, attacking the Papacy and basing their challenge on the authority of scripture, increasingly available in vernacular translations. These ideas proved attractive to many princes, who embraced reform. With the emergence of a second wave of Protestant reform spearheaded by the followers of the French reformer John Calvin (1509–64), an increasing number turned Protestant. Protestantism was already the official religion in large parts of northern Germany, Sweden, Denmark, Scotland and England, and Calvinism, which developed sophisticated theories justifying resistance to political authority, was spreading rapidly in the Netherlands, Poland-Lithuania, Hungary and France, where there were perhaps 1200 Calvinist churches by 1570.

Challenges to Protestantism

Yet confessional divisions were by no means fixed, and Protestantism faced growing problems. The Catholic church began a vigorous recovery after the Council of Trent reaffirmed its doctrine in response to the Protestant challenge and launched an ambitious programme of reform. Protestantism, by rejecting Catholic mechanisms for sustaining orthodoxy, could not establish the universal church to which the early reformers had aspired while discipline was always a problem, with radical sects such as Anabaptists and Antitrinitarians surviving vigorous persecution.

The second half of the 16th century was a period of adjustment, as rulers switched from one brand of Protestantism to another, or even considered reunification with Rome, as in England under Mary Tudor (1552–8) or, more ambiguously, in Sweden under John III (1568–92). In eastern Europe, Catholicism outflanked Protestantism by negotiating the 1596 Union of Brest, in which most of the Orthodox hierarchy in Poland-Lithuania

1517 *Luther launches debate over church reform*

1520 *Luther burns papal bull of excommunication*

1541–64 *Calvin reforms Genevan Church*

1563 *End of the Council of Trent*

1589 *Independent Orthodox patriarchate established in Moscow*

1596 *Union of Brest establishes Greek Catholic (Uniate) church in Poland-Lithuania*

1598 *Edict of Nantes: religious peace in France (revoked 1685)*

1648 *Peace of Westphalia: religious peace in the Holy Roman Empire*

2 Religion in Europe, c. 1670

2 By 1670, the religious dividing lines were much firmer *(map right)*. Most striking was the recovery of Catholicism after the Council of Trent. Where Protestantism had failed to win support from state authorities, it had withered. In France in 1685, Louis XIV revoked the Edict of Nantes, forcing thousands of Huguenots into exile. In eastern Europe, Calvinism had all but been eradicated in Poland-Lithuania, although Lutheranism was still strong in Prussia. Meanwhile, the Uniate Church had begun to blossom in Poland-Lithuania.

1 & 2 Reformation and Catholic Reformation

Roman Catholic, Orthodox, Greek Catholic (Uniate), Islam, Lutheran, Calvinist, Anabaptist, Anglican, Hussite

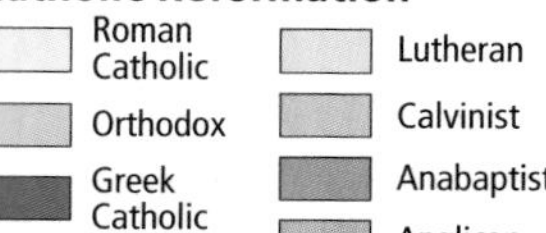

3 delegates sent to last session of Council of Trent
■ date of change from Catholicism to Lutheranism
▲ date of change to Calvinism, Zwinglianism or Anglicanism
— borders, 1572 (*map 1*) and 1683 (*map 2*)

Of the 250,000 or so works printed in Europe between 1447 and 1600, about 75 per cent concerned religion. The Reformation and the Catholic response would have been impossible without printing presses like this one *(right)*, from the cover of a book printed in Frankfurt in the early 17th century.

1 In 1570, Catholicism appeared to be in retreat on virtually every front *(map above)*. Yet Protestantism, despite its introduction as the official religion in England, Scotland, Denmark, Sweden and much of north Germany and its rapid spread in France, Poland and Hungary, was not yet firmly rooted anywhere. It took time for people to be educated in the new faith, especially where rulers had not turned Protestant and church land had not been secularized,

accepted papal authority in return for keeping the Orthodox rite. Orthodox resistance to this Uniate (Greek Catholic) church was powerful, and it was only after 1650 that it began to flourish; similar Unions were established with the Ruthenians of northeast Hungary (1646) and the Romanian Orthodox church (1697). In such unstable circumstances, it took time for new religious convictions to take root among the ordinary people and Protestant rulers found that old beliefs died hard even where people welcomed the destruction of the power of the Catholic clergy. Nevertheless, the religious differentiation of Europe proceeded apace and was accompanied by vicious civil wars and widespread persecution. It was only after 1660 that the religious map took on a more permanent shape, as the success of evangelization made it difficult for rulers to challenge the religious beliefs of their subjects. Only now were the religious divisions of the continent accepted, if not welcomed.

THE PEOPLE AS A WHOLE, OR THE OFFICERS OF THE KINGDOM WHOM THE PEOPLE HAVE ESTABLISHED ... VERY GRAVELY SIN AGAINST THE COVENANT WITH GOD IF THEY DO NOT USE FORCE AGAINST A KING WHO CORRUPTS GOD'S LAW OR PREVENTS ITS RESTORATION, IN ORDER TO CONFINE HIM TO HIS PROPER BOUNDS.

Philippe du Plessis-Mornay (1549–1623)
Vindiciæ contra Tyrannos (A Defence of Liberty against Tyrants), 1579

Europe: the state and its opponents

See also
Monarchy in Britain and France, 1154–1314 p. 118
European states in the 14th century p. 146
The Renaissance and Early Modern state in Europe, 1450–c. 1600 p. 150
The Reformation and Catholic Reformation p. 182
The ascendancy of France, 1648–1715 p. 192
The struggle for empire, 1713–1815 p. 194

1520 *Comuneros and Germaniá revolts in Spain*

1562 *Start of the French Wars of Religion (1562–98)*

1566–7 *Outbreak and suppression of the first Dutch revolt*

1572 *Dutch revolt renewed; continues until 1648*

1640 *Revolts of Portugal (1640–68) and of Catalonia (1640–52) against Spain*

1642 *Outbreak of the English Civil War (1642–9)*

1648 *Revolt of the Fronde (1648–53)*

1649 *Execution of Charles I*

1688 *The Glorious Revolution: James II overthrown*

Before 1688 European rulers struggled to impose their authority. Nobles, townspeople and peasants fought to protect privileges and to resist the fiscal demands of the state. The Dutch and Portuguese revolts led to independence while in France and Spain monarchs could only increase their power by working with the elites. In England cooperation with Parliament was essential, as Charles I discovered.

DESPITE THEIR APPARENT strength, the monarchies of Europe continued to govern through the personal ties of clientage which had characterized monarchy in the feudal period (*see* p. 118). The state still relied on the goodwill of its nobles for the enforcement of its policies, and failure to retain the support of the landed classes could provoke major revolts. The French aristocracy staged several rebellions against the crown, culminating in the Fronde (1648–53); a section of the English aristocracy rebelled against Elizabeth I in 1569–70 (the 'Northern Rising') and many English peers supported Parliament's stand against Charles I after 1640. Similarly, nobles in the Netherlands opposed their 'natural prince', Philip II of Spain, in 1566, 1572 and 1576 while those in Portugal rose against Philip IV in 1640.

These were only the most important rebellions of the period. Uprisings against the state were a continuing fact of life throughout the 16th and 17th centuries. Some revolts arose from attacks on the privileges of the 'estates'; others were caused by economic hardship – from taxes imposed at a time of high prices and widespread unemployment, as was the case in most French popular revolts, or from the enclosing of common land, which caused the revolts of 1549 and 1607 in England. Other uprisings – the Pilgrimage of Grace in England in 1536 and the Covenanting Movement in Scotland in 1638 – were triggered by unpopular religious policies. In all cases the revolts were a response to attempts at innovation. Governments everywhere were endeavouring to create what James I of England described as: 'one worship to God, one kingdom entirely governed, one uniformity of laws'. The problem, however, was one of means, not ends. Neither James nor any of his fellow sovereigns had the resources to enforce such ambitions. They simply lacked the revenues and the officials required.

The age of revolt

The barriers to centralization in Early Modern Europe were formidable. Many subjects did not speak the same language as their government (Breton and Provençal in France, Catalan and Basque in Spain, Cornish in England, Frisian in the Netherlands); certain 'corporations', notably the Church, possessed privileges which protected them against state interference; and many provinces possessed charters guaranteeing their traditional way of life.

Serious political upheavals occurred when the state tried to undermine these rights: the Dutch rebelled largely because they believed that the central government, controlled from Madrid, threatened their traditional liberties. They continued their armed opposition until 1609, when Spain, in effect, recognized the independence of the seven provinces still in rebellion. In England, Parliament began a civil war against Charles I in 1642 because it believed that he intended to destroy the established rights of 'free-born Englishmen'. They, too, maintained their armed resistance until the power of the king was shattered in battle, and Charles himself was tried and executed in 1649. Although Charles's son was restored in 1660 with full powers and even a small standing army, another revolt, in 1688, supported by the Dutch, drove James II into exile.

While opposition in France did not go to such lengths, the absolutist policies and fiscal exactions of Cardinal Mazarin, chief minister of the boy king Louis XIV, so alienated the crown's officials, the nobles and the people of Paris that in 1649 they drove Louis from his capital and forced him to make major concessions. Royal control was not fully restored until 1655. Philip IV of Spain pushed the Portuguese aristocracy to revolt in support of the House of Braganza and by 1668 Portugal was independent. The Spanish king was fortunate not to lose Catalonia in a similar fashion during the revolt of 1640 to 1652.

> LET HIM [PHILIP II] BE A KING IN CASTILE, IN ARAGON, AT NAPLES, AMONGST THE INDIANS, AND IN EVERY PLACE WHERE HE COMMANDS AT HIS PLEASURE; YEA LET HIM BE A KING, IF HE WILL, IN JERUSALEM, AND A PEACEABLE GOVERNOR IN ASIA AND AFRICA, YET FOR ALL THAT I WILL NOT ACKNOWLEDGE HIM IN THIS COUNTRY FOR ANY MORE THAN A DUKE AND A COUNT, WHOSE POWER IS LIMITED ACCORDING TO OUR PRIVILEGES, WHICH HE SWORE TO OBSERVE.
>
> **William of Orange**
> *'Apology' for the Dutch Revolt, 1584*

The structure of the state

Despite these upheavals, however, the structure of the state survived. None of the rebels seriously questioned the need for strong government, only the location of it. After 1660, and even more after 1688, power in England was shared between Parliament, representing merchants and landowners, and the crown. The last major effort to resist the rise of central power and defend local autonomy had failed. In France, the Fronde was a frightening lesson for Louis XIV whose re-establishment of royal authority was based upon a policy of compromise with aristocratic and office-owning elites (*see* p. 192). A more sensitive government, combined with a rapidly expanding standing army after 1661, ensured that France saw no repetition of the Fronde before 1789.

The Dutch Revolt, on the other hand, achieved its primary goal of protecting local independence against central encroachment. Despite the preponderance of Holland within the Republic, the other six provinces retained a large measure of autonomy within a decentralized political system reminiscent of the 15th century. It was to leave the Dutch at a permanent disadvantage in a world which permitted no profit without power and no security without war. The 18th century and its profits – particularly in the colonial world – would belong to their rivals, France and Britain.

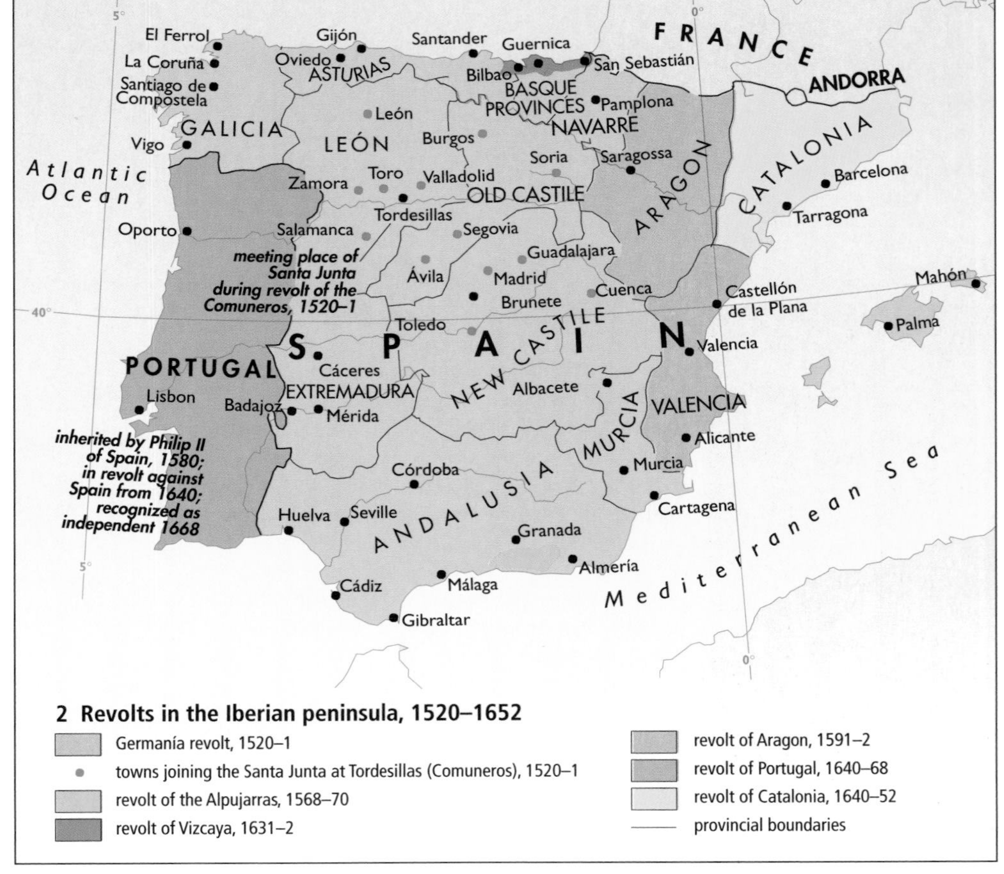

2 Philip II's inheritance of the Portuguese throne in 1580 united the Iberian peninsula *(map right)*. Yet the authority of the Spanish monarchs was fragile. Charles I had been threatened in 1520 by the revolt of the Castilian towns (the Comuneros) and that of the peasants of Valencia, the Germanía, the same year. Philip II's persecution of the Moriscos provoked the revolt of the Alpujarras of 1568–70. Fear of centralization from Madrid then sparked the revolts of Aragon (1591) and Catalonia (1640–52). The Portuguese revolt of 1640–68 marked the end of Iberia's brief union.

1 The states of northwest Europe were plagued by rebellion between 1500 and 1688 *(map left)*. More than a dozen major rebellions broke out in England. Spain faced a continuous revolt in the Netherlands from 1572 onwards as well as having to face revolts in Portugal and Catalonia in 1640. In France, over 500 popular uprisings culminated in the Fronde of 1648. After 1660, however, the rise of standing armies coupled with greater attention to the interests of landed elites meant that revolts were increasingly rare. But as internal tensions subsided, the three governments took to fighting each other, above all for control of the seas. England emerged the stronger from the Anglo-Dutch Wars, and, as the Dutch republic was drawn into war with France, the English established their naval prowess not just in Europe but in the wider world.

A propaganda piece justifying the Dutch revolt against the tyranny of the Spanish duke of Alba *(left)*. The devil crowns Alba and Cardinal Granvelle, who wields bellows in allusion to the fires of heresy. Alba holds allegorical figures of the Dutch provinces on a chain, while the execution of Counts Egmont and Horn, defenders of the rights and liberties of the Netherlands, can be seen through the arch. The execution itself took place in Brussels on 5 June 1568.

1494 to 1797

The Mediterranean world

See also
Crusading in Europe from the 11th to the 15th century p. 110
Islam and Christianity at the end of the 15th century p. 138
The rise of the Ottoman empire, 1281–1522 p. 142
The Renaissance and the Early Modern state in Europe p. 150
The Early Modern Muslim empires, 1520–1700 p. 168

The Ottoman conquest of the eastern Mediterranean and the French invasion of Italy in 1494 opened a new phase in Mediterranean history. Both the sea and the Italian peninsula became the focus for power-struggles between states whose interests were only partly Mediterranean. Meanwhile, Europe's economic centre of gravity shifted northwest.

AFTER 1500, EVEN AS the civilization of the Italian Renaissance was spreading round Europe, Italy and the Mediterranean were losing their dominant position within the cultural and economic worlds of Europe. The invasion of Italy by Charles VIII of France in 1494 (*see* map 2) initiated over 60 years of warfare between the Habsburgs and the French Valois for control of Italy which undermined the political primacy of the Italian cities, just as the Ottoman drive into the eastern Mediterranean threatened their economic dominance. The loss of Italian primacy was precipitated in part, too, by the creation of the Habsburg empire. Charles V, elected Holy Roman Emperor in 1519, ruled not only the Habsburg lands in Austria, south Germany and the Netherlands, but also the realms bequeathed by his maternal grandparents, Ferdinand and Isabella, in Spain, Italy and north Africa. His inheritance was soon expanded: in 1526 his brother and close ally Ferdinand succeeded to the crowns of Bohemia and Hungary, creating a huge Habsburg power block running from the Adriatic almost to the Baltic. In 1535 Charles himself acquired both Milan and Tunis.

By the peace of Câteau-Cambrésis (1559), France was excluded from Italy, which now came under the domination of the Habsburgs. Although Charles V divided his empire on his death, his son Philip II of Spain retained Milan and the kingdoms of Naples and Sicily. Henceforth, Spanish viceroys ruled in Naples, Sicily and Sardinia, with a Spanish governor in Lombardy.

The Ottoman threat

Even Italy's largest states lacked room for manoeuvre in the face of Spain's overwhelming dominance. 80 per cent of Genoese seaborne trade was conducted with Spain, and Venice, whose eastern Mediterranean empire was falling gradually into Ottoman hands, was surrounded by Habsburg territory. Papal attempts to oppose the Habsburgs ended in catastrophe: the sack of Rome itself in 1527 and a humiliating invasion in 1556–7. Yet the Spaniards at least provided effective defence against the Ottomans who, despite their successful advance along the north African coast with the capture of Algiers (1529), Tripoli (1551) and Bugia (1555), were unable to secure a foothold in Italy. The climactic moment came with the unsuccessful siege of Malta in 1565, although the Spanish victory at Lepanto (1571) could not prevent the fall of Cyprus the same year.

Italy and the Holy Roman Empire

The fading of the Turkish threat after the Ottoman-Spanish truce of 1577 ensured that the new status quo lasted until the 1790s. Southern Italy and Sardinia were ruled by Spain, the Papal States dominated central Italy, while the north, apart from Venice, was still part of the Holy Roman Empire, and was a complex network of imperial and papal fiefs and semi-independent territories:

1 Spanish-Ottoman rivalry dominated the Mediterranean until 1577 *(map right)*, as each state sought to expand along the north African coast. The climax came with the Ottoman failure to seize Malta, the gateway to the western Mediterranean (1565). Philip II and Murad III, both preoccupied with other imperial concerns, concluded an uneasy but lasting peace in 1577. Spain turned northwards, to the Netherlands and the Holy Roman Empire, while the Ottomans attacked Persia.

2 The Italian wars, 1494–1559

F - Fornovo 1495
A - Agnadello 1509
N - Novara 1513
M - Marignano 1515
B - Bicocca 1522
P - Pavia 1525
L - Landriano 1529

- frontiers in 1500
- boundary of areas brought under French control, 1494–1512
- under French control from 1515
- to France under agreement with Spain, 1500
- attempted French conquest
- added to France (with dates)
- French occupied, 1536–59
- Swiss Confederation, 1512
- to Swiss Confederation by 1536
- added to Florence (with dates)
- to Savoy, 1529
- Papal control re-established or established by 1513
- frontier of areas lost by Venice (with dates)
- frontier of temporary Venetian control (with dates)
- autonomy or independence from Papal States re-established (with dates)
- Habsburg possessions, 1520
- The Holy Roman Empire, 1550
- battles (with dates)

2 In the late 15th century increased rivalry between the major Italian states sucked in foreign powers *(map left)*. In 1494 Charles VIII of France intervened in the Milanese succession. By 1495 he had occupied the kingdom of Naples. The Habsburgs (in alliance with the Papacy, the Emperor and Venice) then acted to halt the French advance, driving the French from the south by 1504 and taking Naples for themselves. Habsburg influence continued to grow: at the Battle of Pavia (1525) Charles V drove out the French from Milan, and restored the native duke, but in 1535 he occupied the duchy himself. Florence and Venice kept or expanded their territories, but by 1559 the French were excluded from Italy and the Habsburgs were effective arbiters of the whole peninsula.

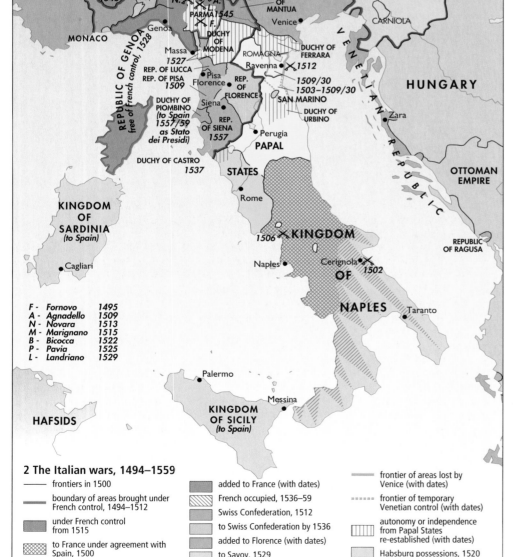

IN SUCH A STATE OF MIND AND IN SUCH A CONFUSION OF AFFAIRS … BEGAN THE YEAR 1494 – A MOST UNHAPPY YEAR FOR ITALY, AND IN TRUTH THE BEGINNING OF THOSE YEARS OF MISFORTUNE, BECAUSE IT OPENED THE DOOR TO INNUMBERABLE HORRIBLE CALAMITIES, IN WHICH … FOR VARIOUS REASONS, A GREAT PART OF THE WORLD WAS SUBSEQUENTLY INVOLVED.

Francesco Guicciardini
The History of Italy, 1540

1494 *Charles VIII of France invades Italy; temporary French capture of Naples*

1535 *Habsburgs take Milan*

1559 *Treaty of Câteau-Cambrésis ends Habsburg-Valois wars*

1565 *Failed Ottoman siege of Malta*

1571 *Battle of Lepanto*

1577 *Habsburg-Ottoman truce*

1629–31 *War of the Mantuan Succession*

1702–13 *War of the Spanish Succession*

1797 *Napoleon conquers Austrian Lombardy and Venice*

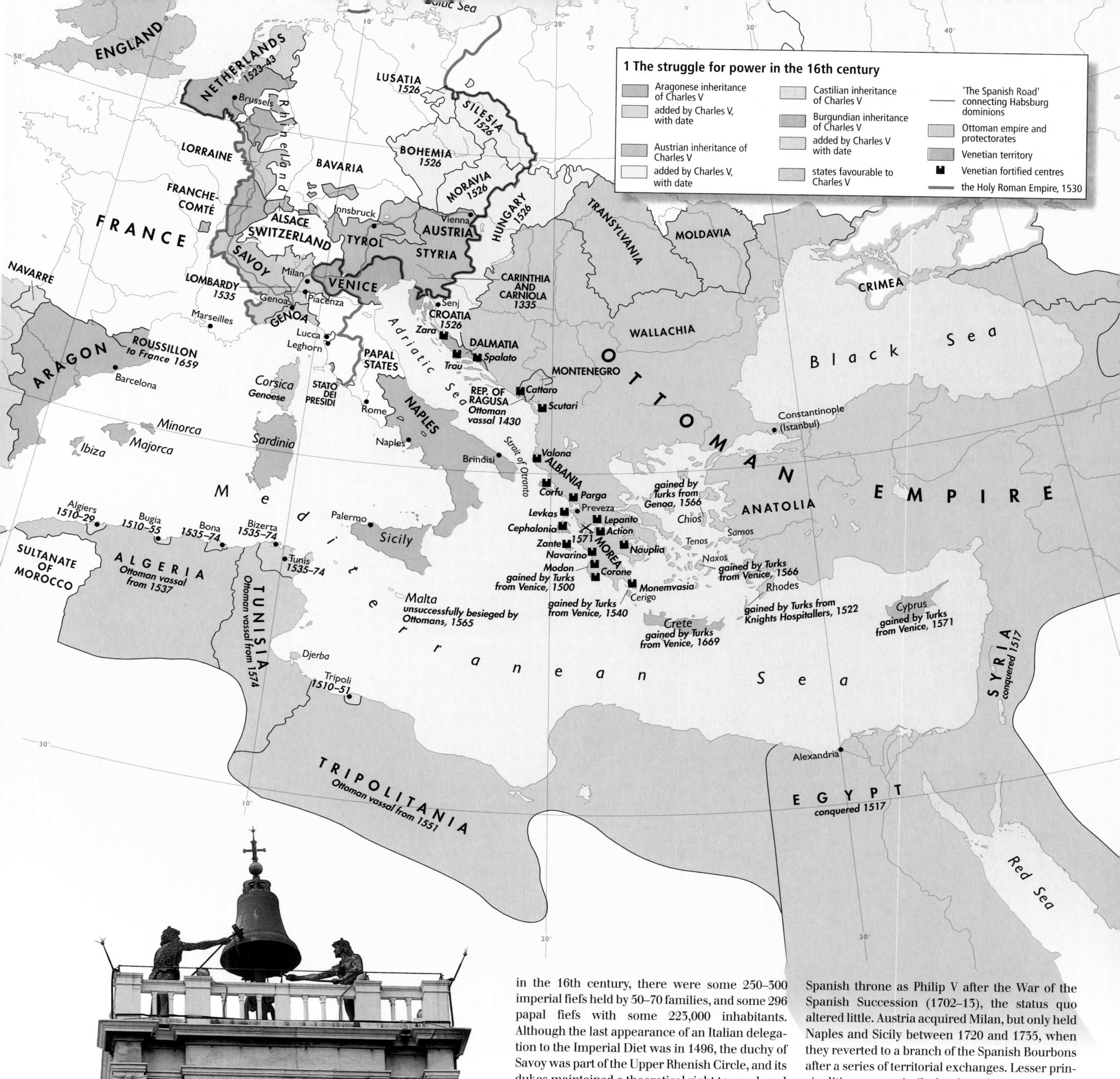

in the 16th century, there were some 250–300 imperial fiefs held by 50–70 families, and some 296 papal fiefs with some 223,000 inhabitants. Although the last appearance of an Italian delegation to the Imperial Diet was in 1496, the duchy of Savoy was part of the Upper Rhenish Circle, and its dukes maintained a theoretical right to speak and vote in the Diet until 1806. Many important north Italian families, such as the Doria or the Spinola, were imperial princes, and the Imperial Aulic Council heard 1500 cases involving Italians between 1555 and 1806 (400 in the 16th century; 490 in the 17th; and 540 in the 18th). Northern Italy was strategically vital to Spain during the Dutch Revolt and the Thirty Years' War: with the sea-route to the Netherlands through the English Channel dominated by the Dutch and the English, Milan was the mustering-ground for Spanish troops sent overland down the 'Spanish Road' through the Valtellina, Alsace and the Rhineland to the Netherlands. Thus Italy was vital to Spain's long war against the Dutch rebels; this led to a renewal of Franco-Spanish war in Italy during the War of the Mantuan Succession (1629–31), which saw the victory of the French-backed candidate, Charles Gonzaga, duke of Nevers.

Even when the Spanish Habsburgs died out in 1700, and the grandson of Louis XIV secured the Spanish throne as Philip V after the War of the Spanish Succession (1702–13), the status quo altered little. Austria acquired Milan, but only held Naples and Sicily between 1720 and 1735, when they reverted to a branch of the Spanish Bourbons after a series of territorial exchanges. Lesser principalities were similarly shared out. Only the republics of Venice, Genoa and Lucca remained relatively undisturbed.

Britain in the Mediterranean

The principal guardian of this stability was Great Britain, attracted to the Mediterranean by trading opportunities in the late 16th century, when the Levant Company established a base in Istanbul (1581). In the 1650s, British fleets entered to pursue royalist vessels and punish the Barbary pirates. From 1662 to 1683, Britain held Tangier, guarding the entrance to the Mediterranean; in 1704 it took Gibraltar on the other side of the straits. Sardinia was a British base between 1708 and 1714, as was Minorca from 1708 to 1783. On the whole, though, Britain preferred diplomacy to force; it was only when Napoleon's invasion of Italy and annexation of Egypt and Malta in the late 1790s destroyed the status quo and convulsed the eastern and western Mediterranean alike that British naval power came to dominate both.

The Venetian Republic controlled extensive territories in the eastern Mediterranean and its symbol, the Lion of St Mark *(above)*, stood guard on coastal fortresses in Greece, the Balkans, Crete and Cyprus. The Venetian empire was not purely maritime, however: there were extensive Venetian territories in Italy itself. Nonetheless its lifeline was the Adriatic and, despite territorial losses elsewhere in this period, chiefly to the Ottomans, and the decline throughout the 18th century of its once dominant trading position in the eastern Mediterranean, Venice was able to cling on to its fortresses guarding the entrance to the Adriatic – Cattaro, Corfu, Levkas, Cephalonia, Zante – until the extinction of the republic itself by Napoleon in 1797.

The struggle for the Baltic

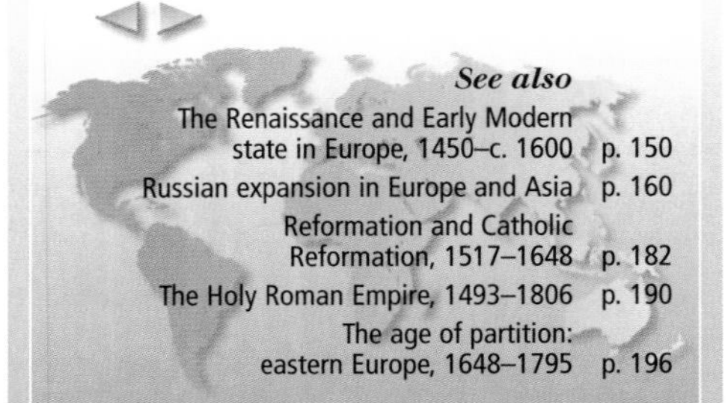
See also
The Renaissance and Early Modern state in Europe, 1450–c. 1600 p. 150
Russian expansion in Europe and Asia p. 160
Reformation and Catholic Reformation, 1517–1648 p. 182
The Holy Roman Empire, 1493–1806 p. 190
The age of partition: eastern Europe, 1648–1795 p. 196

The growing economic importance of the Baltic after 1500 coincided with the decay of the political status quo as the powers which had dominated the sea in the medieval period entered terminal decline or were seriously weakened. The resultant struggle for control of the Baltic Sea lasted two centuries before Russia emerged as the most significant Baltic power.

3 The Swedish empire, 1561–1721

Swedish empire

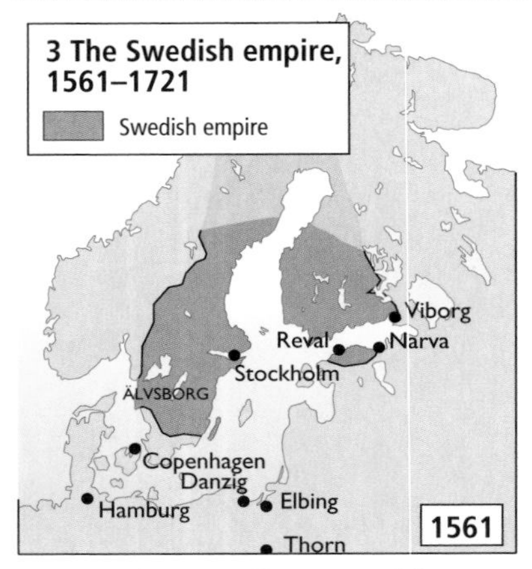

1561 Reval, threatened by Ivan IV and the commercial rivalry of Viborg and Narva, put itself under Swedish protection, rejecting Polish and Danish claims to overlordship and giving Sweden its first foothold across the Gulf of Finland.

1595 Peace of Teusina with Muscovy added Narva and effectively all Estonia, turned the Gulf of Finland into a Swedish waterway and pushed the northern border across the Arctic circle.

1617 Peace of Stolbovo with Muscovy confirmed possession of Estonia, added Ingria (Ingermanland), and Karelia cutting off Russia, including its great trading centre of Novgorod (occupied by Sweden, 1610–6) from the Baltic.

H. HÄRJEDALEN
HA. HALLAND

1645 De facto Swedish possession of Livonia by truces of Altmark (1629) and Stuhmsdorf (1635) with Poland-Lithuania. Peace of Brömsebro with Denmark-Norway (1645) transferred Ösel, Gotland, Jämtland, Härjedalen and (for 30 years) Halland.

1648 At the Peace of Westphalia, which ended the Thirty Years' War, Sweden gained West Pomerania, including the important ports of Stettin and Wismar, and the bishoprics of Bremen and Verden.

B. BOHUSLÄN
BL. BLEKINGE

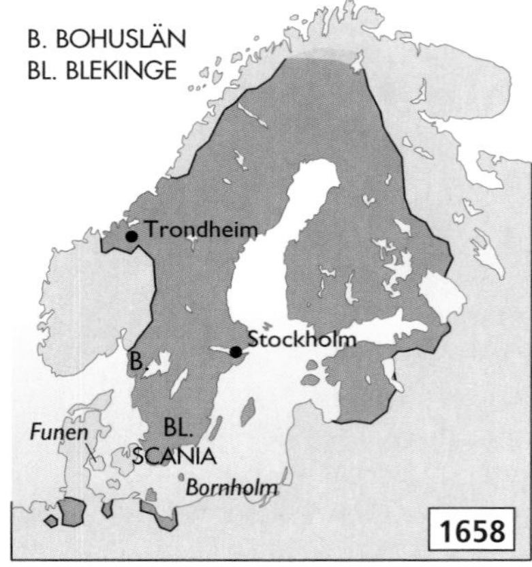

1658 Peace of Roskilde with Denmark. Sweden acquired Scania, Blekinge, Bohuslän, Trondheim and Bornholm; possession of Halland confirmed. Renewed Swedish attack in summer of 1658 led to Danish-Dutch alliance, rebellion in Scania and defeat on Funen in 1659.

1660 Fighting ceased after the death of Charles X. Treaty of Copenhagen returned Trondheim and island of Bornholm to Denmark and formally abandoned Swedish attempts to close the Baltic to foreign warships.

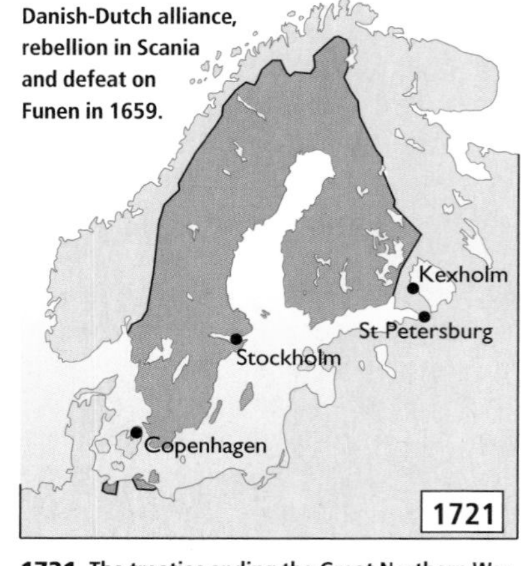

1721 The treaties ending the Great Northern War (1700–21) dismantled Sweden's Baltic empire. In the east, Karelia, Ingermanland, Estonia and Livonia were lost, as were Bremen & Verden and most of West Pomerania in the Holy Roman Empire.

FROM 1500 THE BALTIC provided most of the timber, tar, pitch, hemp and flax for the ships with which European powers built their world empires, as well as copper and huge supplies of cheap grain. This increasingly lucrative trade provoked serious rivalry, as neighbouring powers sought to control ports at the mouths of the great rivers which bore goods from the interior, while Denmark's control of both sides of The Sound, the narrow entrance to the Baltic, enabled it to impose the hotly contested Sound Tolls on most of the commerce passing through. After 1500, no power was strong enough to dominate the Baltic or its trade; the resultant conflicts constantly interlocked with wider European affairs.

In 1523 Sweden under Gustav Vasa broke away from the Scandinavian Union of Kalmar (*see* p. 150). Meanwhile, the Hanseatic League of Baltic trading towns began to unravel, while the Teutonic Order, which controlled the southern Baltic shore from Pomerania to Estonia, slowly decayed. A rebellion led by the burghers of Thorn, Danzig and Elbing in alliance with Poland had already seen the Order lose much of Prussia by the Peace of Thorn (1466); in 1525, Grand Master Albrecht of Hohenzollern then secularized the Order, creating the Duchy of Prussia as a Lutheran fief of the Polish crown. The decaying rump of the Order held on in Livonia, but ancient claims and a desire to profit from Baltic trade led Ivan IV of Muscovy to invade in 1558.

Sweden's Baltic empire

Ivan failed to establish Muscovite power on the Baltic. The early beneficiaries of the Order's collapse were Poland-Lithuania and Sweden. Poland accepted the overlordship of Livonia in 1561 and granted Courland to Gotthard Kettler, Grand Master of the Order, as a fief of the Polish crown. Sweden, meanwhile, seized Reval and Estonia and became involved in the Nordic Seven Years' War with Denmark (1563–70), in which Denmark struggled to re-establish the Union of Kalmar and Sweden sought to expand its foothold on the North Sea at Älvsborg, on the site of the future city of Gothenburg. The Muscovite armies could terrorize but not conquer; they were driven back by determined resistance from the Poles and the Swedes under John III (1568–92), who then married a Polish princess and had his son Sigismund elected king of Poland in 1587. Muscovy gradually subsided into anarchy after Ivan's death in 1584; by 1619, it was cut off from the Baltic, as Sweden secured Karelia, Ingria (Ingermanland) and Estonia, and Poland-Lithuania took Livonia and regained Smolensk. Denmark, despite seizing Älvsborg in the War of Kalmar (1611–3), was unable to secure a decisive advantage, and had to remain content with control of The Sound, returning Älvsborg for a large ransom.

But the Polish-Swedish alliance was short-lived. Sigismund, raised a Catholic, was driven off the Swedish throne in 1599; for 60 years, Poland-Lithuania and Sweden were locked in a dynastic struggle which gave Muscovy time to recover.

Under the brilliant Gustavus Adolphus (1611–32) Sweden seized Livonia in the 1620s, while the powerful military system which matured in his reign enabled Sweden to play a leading role in the Thirty Years' War (*see* p. 190) after his brilliant victory at Breitenfeld (Sep. 1631). By 1648, despite Gustavus Adolphus's death in the battle of Lützen (Nov. 1632), Sweden had gained substantial territories in northern Germany and, after a devastating war with Denmark (1643–5), had widened its bridgehead on the North Sea.

Under Charles X (1654–60) Swedish power reached its zenith. Charles invaded Poland-Lithuania in 1655 and pushed the Muscovites back from Riga. Denmark, keen for revenge, attacked Sweden in 1657, but was defeated and made peace at Roskilde (Feb. 1658). Charles's decision to attack Denmark again in the summer of 1658 proved rash, however: he lost the chance to secure concessions from Poland-Lithuania or Russia, while England, the United Provinces and France, fearing

1466 *Peace of Thorn: Poland acquires Royal Prussia*
1523 *Collapse of the Union of Kalmar; Sweden independent kingdom*
1525 *Secularization of the Duchy of Prussia*
1558 *Ivan IV invades Livonia; the Livonian War (1558–82)*
1563–70 *Nordic Seven Years' War*
1655–60 *Second Northern War; zenith of Swedish power*
1676–9 *Scanian War*
1700–21 *Great Northern War; Russia becomes a Great Power*

Swedish domination of the Baltic, supported Denmark. After the Peace of Copenhagen (1660), though Denmark's grip on the Sound was broken, Sweden had failed to find security.

The decline of Swedish power

Sweden's success brought it many enemies. Swedish support of the house of Holstein-Gottorp, a junior branch of the Danish royal family which shared control of the duchy of Holstein, ensured that relations with Denmark remained tense. Attacked by Brandenburg and Denmark in the Scanian War (1676–9), Sweden's precarious control of its scattered Baltic empire was revealed: it only preserved its southern Baltic holdings thanks to the intervention of Louis XIV of France.

Charles XI (1660–97) adopted a pacific policy after 1679 and revived the army, but when he was succeeded by his teenage son Charles XII (1697–1718), Denmark, Saxony-Poland and Russia formed an alliance which attacked Sweden in 1700, launching the Great Northern War (1700–21). Although Charles immediately knocked Denmark out of the war, smashed the Russian army at Narva (1700) and forced Saxony to make peace at Altranstädt (1706), he became bogged down in Poland. Peter I, given breathing-space after Narva, built a formidable army and fleet; by 1704, Ingermanland and much of Livonia was in his hands. After Charles's crushing defeat at Poltava (1709), Brandenburg-Prussia, Hanover and Denmark joined Russia in a struggle for Sweden's Baltic empire. By 1721, Sweden was once more a second-rank power, and Russia was the dominant force in the region.

HE CARRIED ALL THE HEROIC VIRTUES TO EXTREMES, AT WHICH TIME THEY BECAME AS DANGEROUS AS THE OPPOSING VICES ... HIS GREAT QUALITIES, ANY ONE OF WHICH WOULD HAVE IMMORTALIZED ANOTHER PRINCE, WERE THE RUIN OF HIS NATION.

Voltaire
Lion of the North: Charles XII of Sweden, 1731

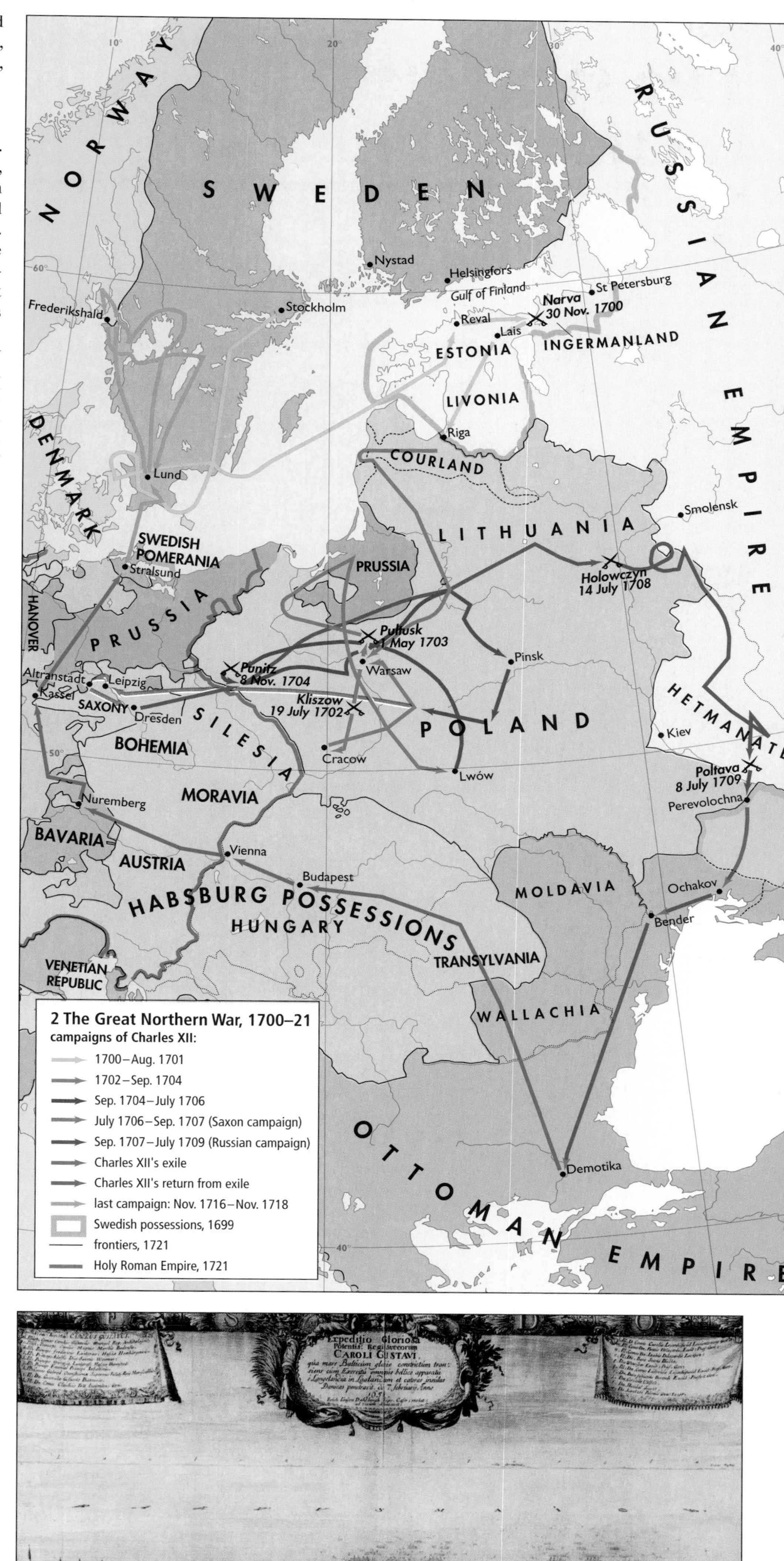

1 At the Peace of Brömsebro in 1645, Denmark was forced to cede Halland to Sweden, marking the beginning of Denmark's loss of control of the strategic Sound *(map below)*. Denmark's efforts in 1657 to recover Halland were unsuccessful, and further territorial concessions had to be made to Sweden in February 1658. But Sweden then overreached herself. An attempt to storm Copenhagen in February 1659 was repulsed, and when Swedish forces then occupied Funen in October, they were defeated the next month at Nyborg by a Danish-Dutch force and half the Swedish army was destroyed.

1 Denmark's Baltic empire, 1618–60
- Denmark-Norway, 1618
- lost to Sweden, 1645
- lost to Sweden, 1658
- Swedish lands in Germany, 1648
- Charles X's march over the ice, 1658

SWEDEN · GOTLAND · Kalmar · Brömsebro · SCANIA · Baltic Sea · Lund · Bornholm (to Sweden 1658–60) · RÜGEN · Peenemünde · Oliva · Danzig · EAST POMERANIA · POMERANIA · Stettin · POLAND · BRANDENBURG · Bärwalde

2 Sweden's aggressive empire-building made it many enemies. When Sweden was attacked by Russia, Denmark and Saxony-Poland in 1700, Charles XII launched a series of brilliant campaigns *(map right)* which saw him defeat Denmark, devastate Poland and invade Saxony before catastrophic defeat at Poltava ended his invasion of Russia. Charles spent five years in Turkish exile, before returning to die on campaign in Norway in 1718, thus opening the way to a peace settlement and the loss of Sweden's Baltic empire.

The march over the ice in February 1658 *(right)*. In 1657 Frederick III of Denmark took advantage of Sweden's involvement in Poland during the Second Northern War to attempt to recover Halland, lost in 1645. Charles X responded by moving rapidly through Germany into Jutland, then astonished the Danes by marching his army across the frozen Baltic Sea via the island of Funen to threaten unprotected Copenhagen *(see map left)*, thereby forcing Frederick to accept the humiliating Peace of Roskilde. Erik Dahlbergh, on whose drawing this engraving is based, was an eyewitness; he investigated the thickness of the ice before the army crossed.

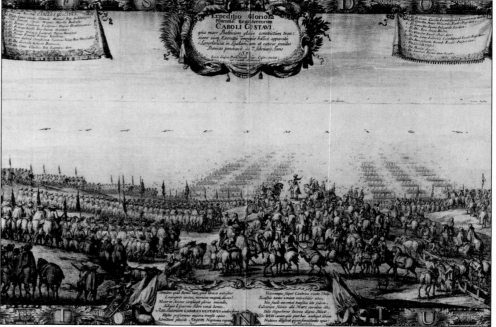

The Holy Roman Empire

See also
Reformation and Catholic Reformation, 1517–1648 p. 182
The ascendancy of France, 1648–1715 p. 192
The age of partition: eastern Europe, 1648–1795 p. 196
The rise of nationalism in Europe, 1800–1914 p. 214
Germany and Italy: the struggles for unification, 1815–71 p. 216

1500–12 *Division of Empire into ten 'Circles'*

1555 *Peace of Augsburg: temporary end to religious conflict*

1618 *Bohemian Revolt; start of the Thirty Years' War*

1629 *Edict of Restitution seeks to restore land secularized by Protestants since 1552*

1648 *Peace of Westphalia ends the Thirty Years' War*

1740–48 *War of the Austrian Succession*

1803 *Secularization of remaining ecclesiastical states*

1806 *Abdication of Emperor Francis II; end of Holy Roman Empire*

The Holy Roman Empire was a decentralized confederal system. While undoubtedly complex, it was effective enough to maintain a common currency and robust enough to survive religious division and the Thirty Years' War. After 1648, its institutions revived and it was regarded as the natural political framework for Germany until, undermined from outside, it collapsed in 1806.

> [IT] IS RIGHT TO CONSIDER THE EMPIRE AS A MODEL OF THE CHRISTIAN SOCIETY. IN THE EMPIRE, SUBJECTS CAN PLEAD AGAINST THEIR PRINCES, OR AGAINST THEIR MAGISTRATES ... JUDGES ARE NOT DEPENDENT UPON THE INSTRUCTIONS OF PRINCES, OR OF THE STATES WHICH HAVE APPOINTED THEM: THEY HAVE ONLY TO FOLLOW THE MOVEMENTS OF THEIR CONSCIENCE.
>
> **Leibniz**
> ***Observations on the Abbé de St Pierre's* Project for Perpetual Peace, *1715***

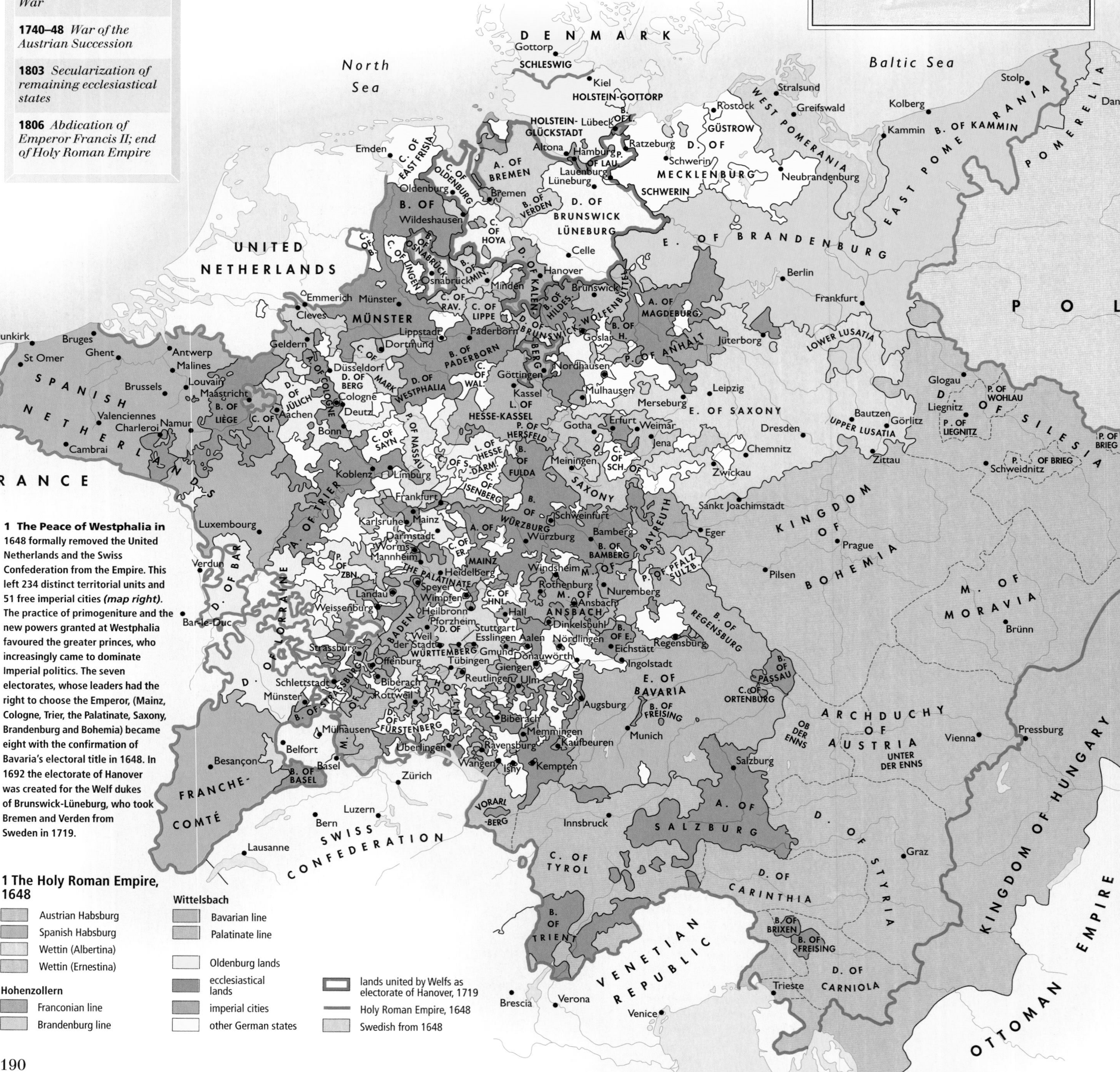

1 The Peace of Westphalia in 1648 formally removed the United Netherlands and the Swiss Confederation from the Empire. This left 234 distinct territorial units and 51 free imperial cities *(map right)*. The practice of primogeniture and the new powers granted at Westphalia favoured the greater princes, who increasingly came to dominate Imperial politics. The seven electorates, whose leaders had the right to choose the Emperor, (Mainz, Cologne, Trier, the Palatinate, Saxony, Brandenburg and Bohemia) became eight with the confirmation of Bavaria's electoral title in 1648. In 1692 the electorate of Hanover was created for the Welf dukes of Brunswick-Lüneburg, who took Bremen and Verden from Sweden in 1719.

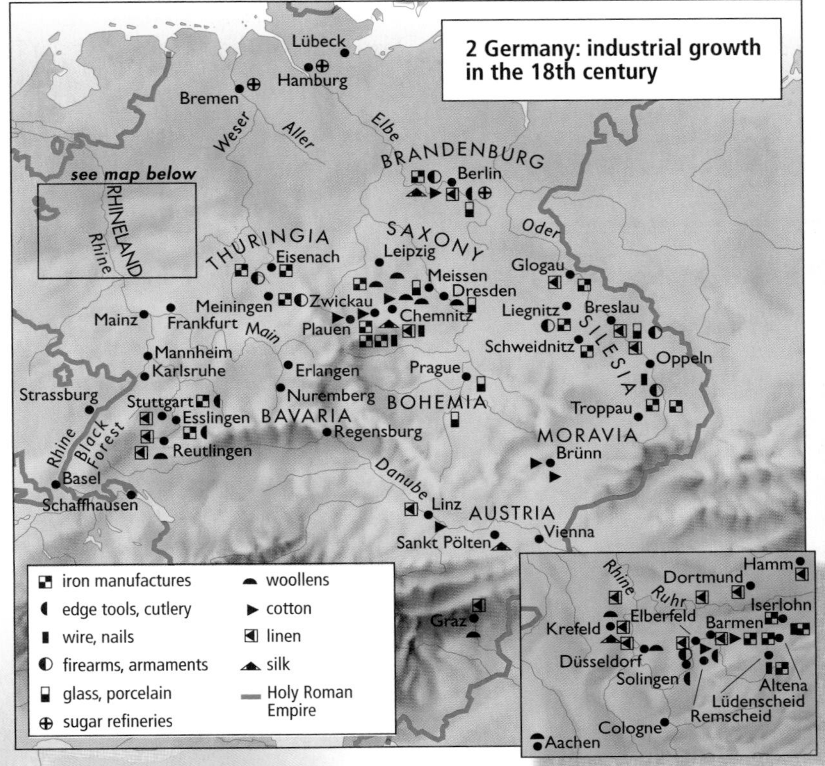

Abbreviations

- A. Archbishopric
- B. Bishopric
- C. County
- D. Duchy
- E. Electorate
- L. Landgraviate
- M. Margraviate
- P. Principality

B. of E.	Bishopric of Erchstätt
B. of H.	Bishopric of Halberstadt
B. of HILDES.	Bishopric of Hildesheim
B. of L.	Bishopric of Lübeck
B. of MIN.	Bishopric of Minden
C. of B.	County of Bentheim
C. of ER.	County of Erbach
C. of HNL.	County of Hohenlohe
C. of RAV.	County of Ravensberg
C. of SCH.	County of Schwarzburg
C. of S.	County of Solms
C. of WAL.	County of Waldeck
C. of L.	County of Limburg
D. of C.	Duchy of Cleves
L. of HESSE-DARM	Landgraviate of Hesse-Darmstadt
P. of LAU.	Principality of Lauenburg
P. of PFALZ-SULZB	Principality of Pfalz-Sulzbach
P. of ZBN.	Principality of Zweibrücken
HOZLN.	Hohenzollern

2 Although some formerly wealthy areas of Germany stagnated after 1648, new industries sprang up in rural districts where they could escape crippling guild restrictions. Mining, iron and textiles developed in Silesia *(maps left)* and Saxony, while water power provided the foundations of the new prosperity of the lower Rhineland.

Frederick II of Prussia (1740–88) inspects his troops *(above)*. When Emperor Charles VI died in 1740 leaving only a daughter, Maria Teresa, Frederick invaded Silesia, launching the War of the Austrian Succession. Although Frederick could not prevent the election of Maria Teresa's husband Franz as Emperor, he secured Silesia when peace was made in 1748.

At first sight, the Holy Roman Empire appears incoherent, with a high degree of political fragmentation and competing jurisdictions. In fact, considerable institutional consolidation took place after 1493 within what was a confederal system, with varying levels of authority which kept political control close to those affected by it. The Empire's division into ten 'Circles' improved its administration, with the Circles organizing taxation, regulating disputes and supervising the common currency, the Imperial thaler. The revival of the Imperial Cameral Tribunal and the Imperial Diet and the introduction of a common criminal code provided the empire with a complex but not unworkable constitution. From the election of Maximilian I (1493), the position of emperor became all but hereditary in the Habsburg dynasty, with a brief interlude in the reign of the Wittelsbach Charles VII (1742–5) during the War of the Austrian Succession.

The wars of religion

After 1517 two factors put the Empire under immense strain: the Reformation and the dramatic increase in Habsburg power following the election of Charles V (1519). Religion became a central issue, as princes sought to limit the Emperor's power while the secularization of church property in much of northern and western Germany sparked bitter disputes. Although the formation of the Protestant Schmalkaldic League in the 1530s brought a series of brief civil wars, all sides recoiled from all-out confrontation. At the peace of Augsburg (1555), a compromise was reached based on the principle that princes should determine the religion of their subjects.

Augsburg kept the peace for 60 years, but bitter disputes arose over its interpretation. Further instability was caused by conflict between the Habsburgs and their Austrian and Bohemian subjects, who by 1600 were largely Protestant. In 1618, the Bohemians rebelled, deposing Ferdinand II as their king in 1619. The rebels were defeated, but the war spread into the Empire after 1620. The Thirty Years' War devastated the empire, reducing a population in 1618 of between 20 and 25 million by a third.

3 In the first phase of The Thirty Years' War *(map right)* the Habsburgs extirpated Protestantism in their patrimonial lands and reclaimed church lands in Germany secularized by Protestants (the Edict of Restitution, 1629). This provoked a Swedish invasion supported by French subsidies and German Protestant princes (1630–2). Spanish intervention helped check the Protestant revival, but increasing involvement of foreigners brought the conciliatory Peace of Prague (1635) between the emperor and leading Protestant princes, although Calvinists were excluded. French intervention to shore up Sweden in 1635 ensured it was not until 1648 that peace was attained at Westphalia.

The Peace of Westphalia (1648), which ended it, brought religious compromise and established a new political framework. The power of the Emperor and the princes was better defined, and the Diet sat in permanent session at Regensburg from 1663; the way was opened for political and economic recovery. Nevertheless, Westphalia brought new problems. Princes gained the right to ally with foreign powers, while the creation of standing armies gave them an instrument to pursue ambitious foreign policies which increasingly they did. The electors of Brandenburg built a new power-base in Prussia, while in 1697 the elector of Saxony turned Catholic to secure election to the Polish throne as Augustus II. In 1714, the elector of Hanover became king of England as George I.

Economic growth

Despite its problems, most Germans still saw the empire as their natural political framework, and the 18th century saw economic expansion in many areas, particularly Silesia, where major landowners combined with government to invest in mining, iron and textiles, and the lower Rhineland and Saxony, which was probably the most advanced of all. But farming remained dominant, with three-quarters of Germany's population still rural in 1815, and towns and cities small compared with those of England and France: Berlin's 140,000 inhabitants in 1777 compared with 260,000 in Vienna, 670,000 in Paris and over 850,000 in London. Nevertheless, this reflected the empire's decentralized constitution, and in cities such as Weimar, Karlsruhe, Mannheim and Stuttgart attempts were made to implement Enlightenment ideas in ambitious reform programmes, often strikingly successful precisely because the principalities were so small. Germany experienced a literary revival in which Goethe and Schiller were figures of international significance. Yet with the import of French revolutionary ideas after 1789, the empire's institutions proved incapable of absorbing new ideas or adjusting to meet the challenge of Napoleon. In 1806, Francis II's abdication as Holy Roman Emperor ended a line which had begun 850 years earlier.

1648 to 1715
The ascendancy of France

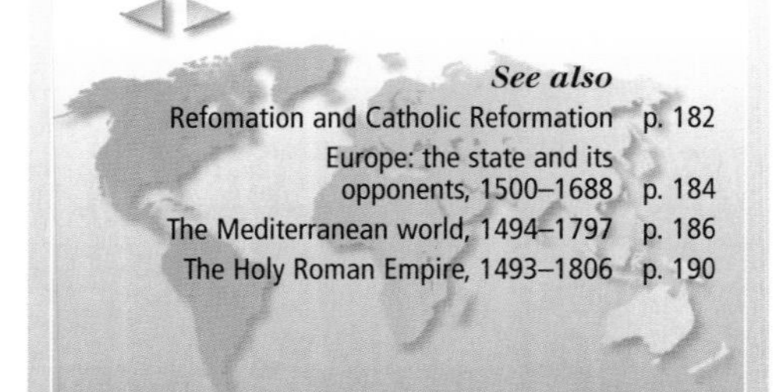
See also
Refomation and Catholic Reformation p. 182
Europe: the state and its opponents, 1500–1688 p. 184
The Mediterranean world, 1494–1797 p. 186
The Holy Roman Empire, 1493–1806 p. 190

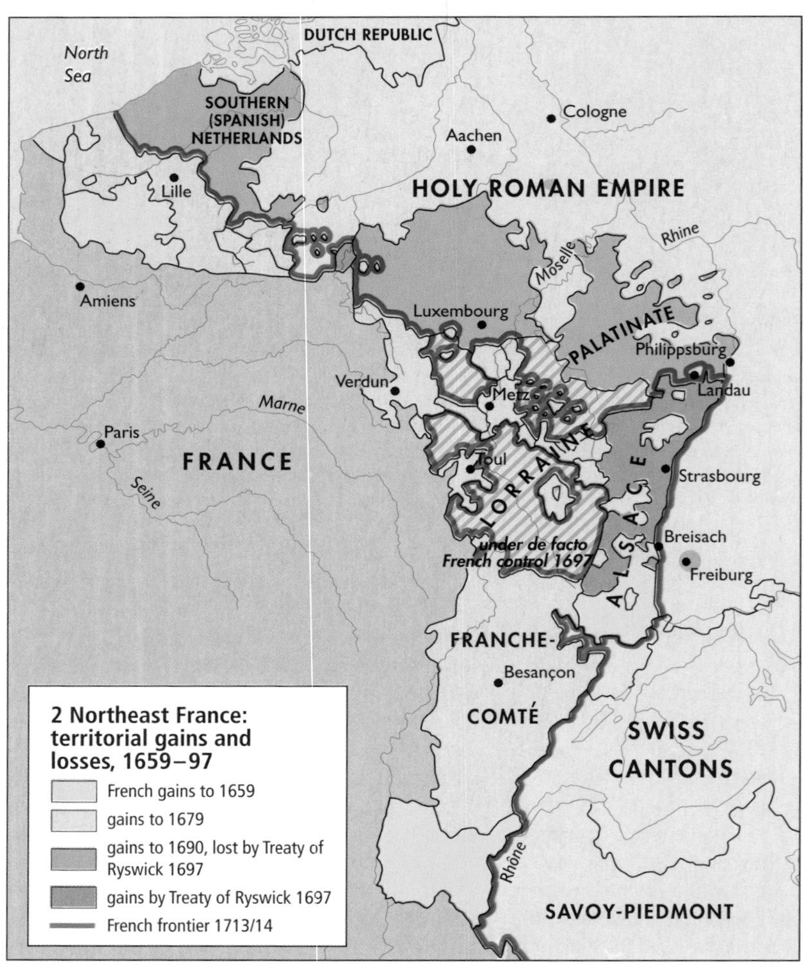

3 Carlos II, ruler of Spain, Spanish America, the south Netherlands and half of Italy, died childless in 1700, bequeathing his empire to Philip, grandson of Louis XIV. This concentration of territory in Bourbon hands overturned the balance of power in Europe, provoking war with Britain, the Dutch Republic, the Holy Roman Empire, Portugal and Savoy *(map below)*. Bourbon victories were followed by a string of defeats. By the peaces of Utrecht (1713) and Rastatt (1714), Philip kept Spain and Spanish America; Savoy and the Austrian Habsburgs partitioned the rest.

2 With Paris and later Versailles vulnerable to invasion from the northeast, Louis was anxious to expand into the Spanish Netherlands and to fortify the frontier defences *(map above)*. This can be partly explained by Louis's fear that at the death of Carlos II of Spain, Spanish possessions on Louis's northeast frontier would be left to the Austrian Habsburgs, raising the spectre of a resurrection of the empire of Charles V. For the same reason, he conquered Franche-Comté, widened his hold on Alsace, occupied Lorraine and in 1681 annexed Strasbourg.

Louis XIV's France was the most powerful state in Europe. By 1680 the king was acclaimed as 'Louis the Great' and military victories were matched by a flowering of the arts and economic and colonial expansion. Yet French success pushed the other great powers, England, the Dutch Republic and the Austrian Habsburgs into a coalition which, by 1709, had brought France close to invasion and defeat.

DURING THE REIGN OF Louis XIV France became so powerful that other states feared her ascendancy, regarding her as a danger to the balance of power on the Continent. Louis was suspected of plans to oust the Austrian Habsburgs from their traditional position as elected Holy Roman Emperor and of spearheading a second Catholic counter-reformation. He was generally held to be seeking French hegemony in Europe.

Such fears rested upon solid ground. After a century of foreign war and internal strife, Louis XIV and his able ministers took advantage of the peaceful years between 1659 and 1672 to make great progress in manufacturing, in trade, in overseas expansion and in ship-building. At the same time the French army was greatly expanded. The richness of French resources, including a population estimated at 20 million (Great Britain, in comparison, had a population of less than 8 million), played a significant part in these developments, but so did conscious effort and directives from the centre.

Territorial consolidation

Louis' objectives were at first limited and concerned the security of France's frontiers. Habsburg encirclement, forged by the family compacts of the Austrian and Spanish Habsburgs, was still felt to be pressing round France though the Peace of Westphalia (1648) brought sovereignty over Metz, Toul and Verdun and possession of the landgravates of Upper and Lower Alsace. The Peace of the Pyrenees (1659) plugged the gap in the southern frontier with Spain ceding Roussillon and northern Cerdagne. Yet France was still vulnerable from the Spanish Netherlands and Franche-Comté as well as through Lorraine and the Belfort Gap. This helps to explain the two aggressive wars of Louis' reign: the War of Devolution, fought to lay claim to part of the Spanish Netherlands in 1667–8; and the attack on the Dutch Republic in 1672. The latter, much to Louis' discomfiture, escalated into a European-wide war not settled until 1678–9.

Famine and war

Louis tried to avoid large-scale war after 1679 by resort to arbitration and treaties to settle European problems, but the memories of his early wars and the enormous power of France made the rest of Europe suspicious. He caused further unease by his 'reunion' policy to expand his control of German border areas and he lost the sympathy of all Protestant powers for his persecution of the Huguenots. The deleterious economic effects of the exodus of over 200,000 French Calvinists in the 1670s and 1680s have been greatly exaggerated, but the international consequences of Louis' revocation of the Edict of Nantes (1685) (*see* p. 182) were far-reaching, and contributed to the outbreak of the Nine Years' War (1688–97) and the War of the Spanish Succession (1701–14) (*see* map 3).

The defensive element in Louis' foreign policy is still disputed among historians, but can be demonstrated by the construction of a *barrière de fer* of fortresses around the whole of France (*see* map 1)

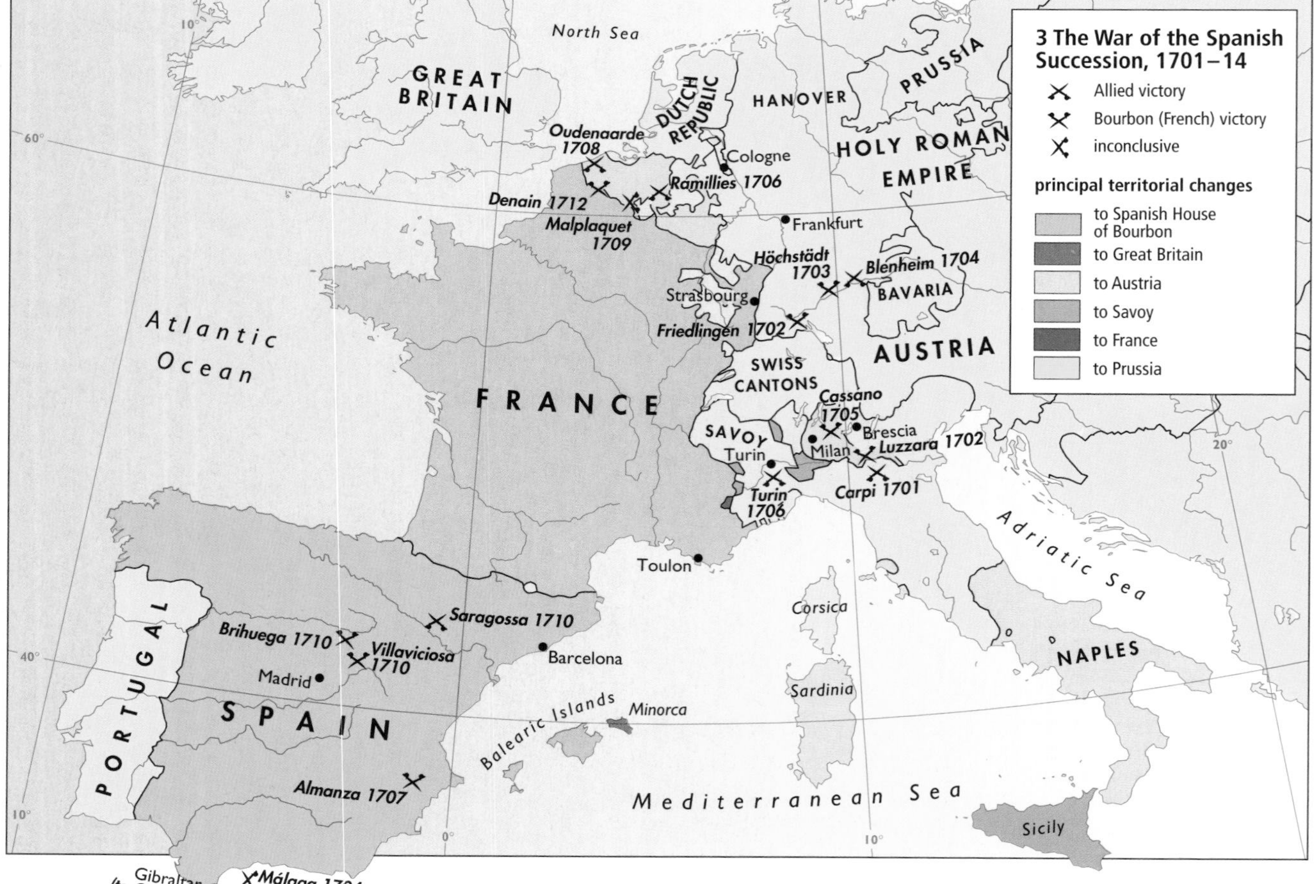

> HE UNITED IN HIS PERSON GREAT MAJESTY AND AFFABILITY. WHILE COMMANDING MEN HE REMEMBERED THAT HE WAS A MAN HIMSELF, AND HE HAD A TALENT FOR WINNING THE HEARTS OF ALL THOSE WHO HAD THE HONOUR OF APPROACHING HIM. IN HIM ALSO WERE GREAT PIETY AND JUSTICE ... IN THE MIDST OF THE DISORDERS OF WAR HE MADE GOOD GOVERNMENT FLOURISH AND SPREAD THE SCIENCES AND ARTS THROUGHOUT HIS KINGDOM ... ALL QUALITIES WORTHY OF FORMING THE PERFECT MODEL OF A GREAT KING ...
>
> **Papal Nuncio on the death of Louis XIV, 1715**

1643 *Accession of Louis XIV*

1661 *Start of Louis XIV's personal rule*

1667–8 *War of Devolution*

1672 *Louis launches the Dutch War (1672–9)*

1682 *Louis moves his court to Versailles*

1685 *Revocation of the Edict of Nantes*

1688 *Outbreak of Nine Years' War (1688–97); ends with Treaty of Ryswick*

1693–4 *Famine kills more than one million people in France*

1701–14 *The War of the Spanish Succession*

1715 *Death of Louis XIV*

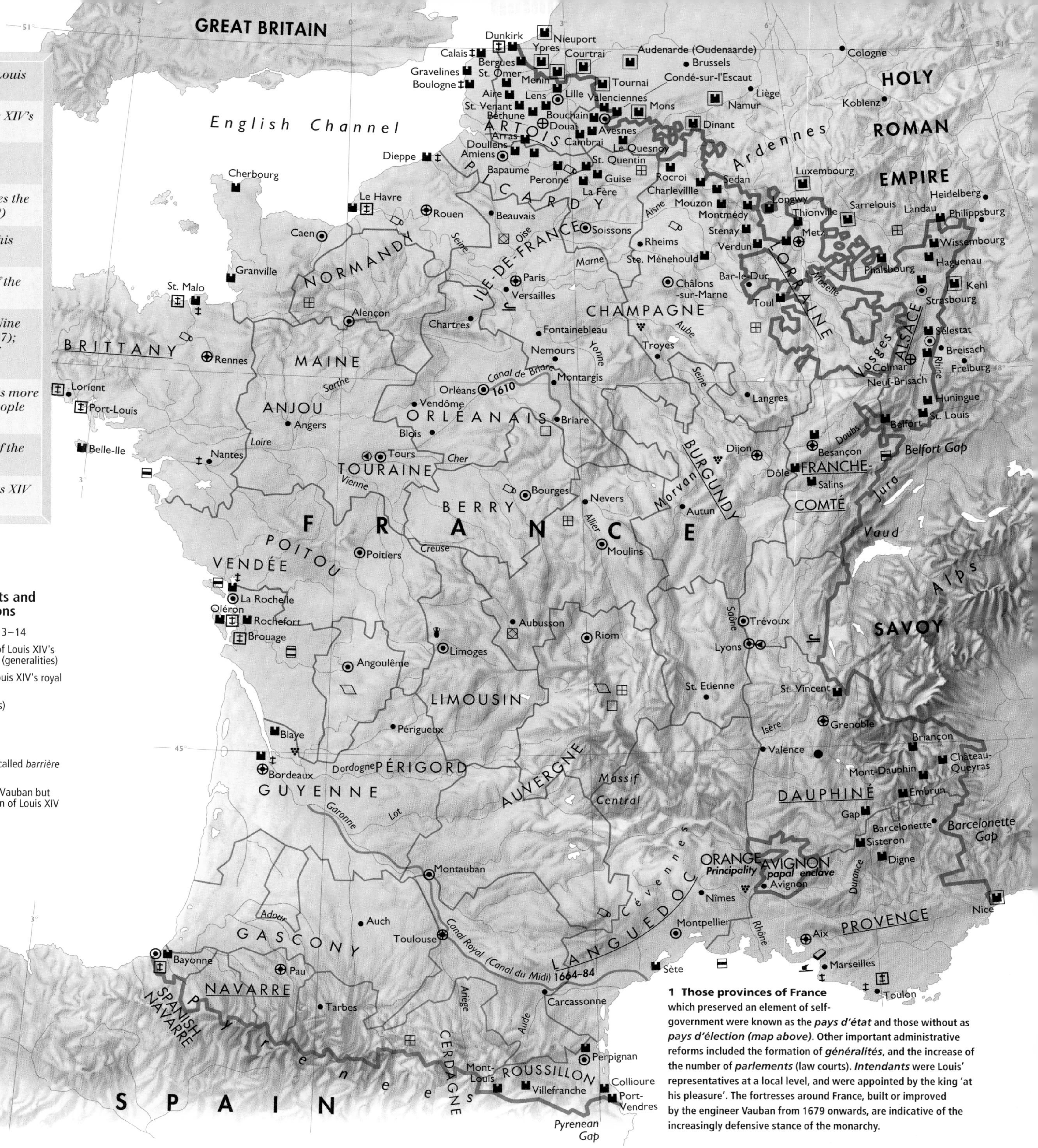

1 Administrative units and defensive fortifications

- frontier of France 1713–14
- administrative units of Louis XIV's reign, the *généralités* (generalities)
- seat of *intendants*, Louis XIV's royal commissioners
- *parlement* (law courts)
- ALSACE *pays d'état*

defence:

- fortifications (the so-called *barrière* or *frontière de fer*)
- fortifications built by Vauban but ceded during the reign of Louis XIV
- galley port
- naval port

economic:

- commercial harbours

major manufactures:

- brandy
- cloth
- glass
- iron
- madder dye
- paper
- pottery
- printing
- salt
- silk
- soap
- tapestry and carpets
- wine

1 Those provinces of France which preserved an element of self-government were known as the *pays d'état* and those without as *pays d'élection (map above)*. Other important administrative reforms included the formation of *généralités*, and the increase of the number of *parlements* (law courts). *Intendants* were Louis' representatives at a local level, and were appointed by the king 'at his pleasure'. The fortresses around France, built or improved by the engineer Vauban from 1679 onwards, are indicative of the increasingly defensive stance of the monarchy.

and by his willingness to promote a peaceful partition of the Spanish empire before the death of Carlos II. When that policy failed and the dying Spanish king offered the crown to his grandson, the future Philip V, Louis had no alternative but to accept. While understandable, it was a fateful decision for his subjects. Over a million had starved during the terrible famine of 1693–4 and nearly as many would perish as war combined with natural disaster to exact a terrible toll.

Cultural ascendancy

French ascendancy between 1648 and 1715 was not apparent only in the fields of politics, diplomacy and war. Louis' work for French architecture, learning, and for science and the arts in general, and his pensions paid to a great number of European poets, artists and scholars, whether they studied in France or not, may seem more important than his wars. His court at Versailles and his support for academies became models for other princes. French became the language of the educated classes all over Europe and helped to create the the country's cosmopolitan civilization of the late 17th and the early 18th centuries. France also made progress during his reign in the number of colleges and hospitals; in the codification of laws; in administrative practices and efficiencies; and in a range of practical improvements from street lighting and policing in Paris to the digging of the Canal Royal (completed by 1684), which provided cheap and efficient communication between the Atlantic and the Mediterranean. Taken as a whole, the reign fixed the French frontiers in Europe (though colonial cessions had to be made to Great Britain) and in the history of French civilization, the period is deservedly honoured with the title *Le Grand Siècle*.

In the vast palace of Versailles, seen *(right)* in the background behind Jean-Baptiste Tuby's bronze sculpture of Apollo rising from the waters, Louis XIV directed the fortunes of France. The court was household to the king, the centre of government and a source of inspiration – and envy – to monarchs throughout Europe.

1713 to 1815
The struggle for empire

See also
European expansion overseas p. 158
The Americas, 1500–1810 p. 162
Mughal India and the growth of British power p. 170
The ascendency of France, 1648–1715 p. 192
The emerging global economy p. 198
The age of revolt, 1773–1814 p. 202
Napoleon and the reshaping of Europe p. 204
European colonial empires, 1815–1914 p. 244

1754 *War breaks out between British and French colonists in North America*

1756 *Outbreak of Seven Years' War (1756–63)*

1757 *Clive's victory at Plassey gives Britain control of Bengal*

1759 *Britain takes Quebec*

1763 *Peace of Paris, France loses Canada*

1776 *American Declaration of Independence*

1778 *France enters American War of Independence*

1783 *Treaty of Versailles, Britain recognizes American independence*

1805 *Battle of Trafalgar*

From 1713 until 1815 Great Britain and France fought for global supremacy in India, North America and the Caribbean. Britain, with her great naval strength, was always at an advantage because France was first and foremost a continental power. Control of the seas allowed the British to defeat her enemy in North America and India.

EUROPEAN TERRITORIAL EXPANSION overseas continued throughout the 18th century and led to serious clashes between Portugal and Spain in the Banda Oriental (Uruguay), between Spain and Great Britain in Georgia and between Great Britain and France elsewhere in North America. Trading monopolies proved an even greater source of friction. Spanish attempts to suppress British and Dutch smugglers reduced the Caribbean to a state of undeclared war. Further north, British efforts to enforce similar restrictions upon its American colonists provoked resistance and finally, from 1775, open revolt.

The Anglo-French struggle

During 1739–40 the fragile peace brought about by the Treaty of Utrecht in 1713 (*see* p. 192) collapsed as Great Britain and Spain went to war in defence of their trading rights, while Frederick the Great's invasion of Silesia began the struggle for supremacy in eastern Europe (*see* p. 196). The outbreak of hostilities between Great Britain and France in 1744 brought the colonial conflict and the war for Silesia together into a single conflict that extended from North America to India and from the West Indies to Russia. This struggle, which lasted intermittently until 1815, rapidly became a duel between Great Britain and France for global supremacy. European states, American settlers, Native American chiefs and Indian princes all fought as subsidized and dependent allies of these two great powers.

Conflict in North America

The Treaty of Aix-la-Chapelle (1748) settled none of the outstanding questions, and fighting began again in North America in 1754. France quickly achieved local military superiority with its strategically sited forts preventing further British expansion. The outbreak of the Seven Years' War in Europe (1756–63) transformed the situation. France was handicapped by its continental commitments and Britain took control of the Atlantic, decisively defeating the French fleet at Quiberon Bay and Lagos in 1759. With French forces in Canada cut off from reinforcements Louisbourg fell in 1758, Quebec in 1759 and Montreal in 1760.

The British triumph was short-lived. Between 1763 and the American War of Independence (1776–83: *see* p. 202), France rebuilt both its navy and its alliances in pursuit of revenge. By 1781, confronted in home waters by a hostile coalition of France, Spain and the Dutch Republic and overstrained by the need to defend an empire stretching from Canada to India, Great Britain was forced to surrender control of North American waters. The French blockade of Yorktown forced a major British army to surrender, and in 1783 Great Britain was obliged to recognize American independence.

Rivalry in India

During these same years the British founded a new empire in India. The emergence of independent princes from the ruins of the Mughal empire in the early 18th century gave the English and the French East India companies opportunities to intervene in local politics. Here again sea power was decisive. Thus, after early French successes, Great Britain's ability to reinforce its position by sea enabled it to

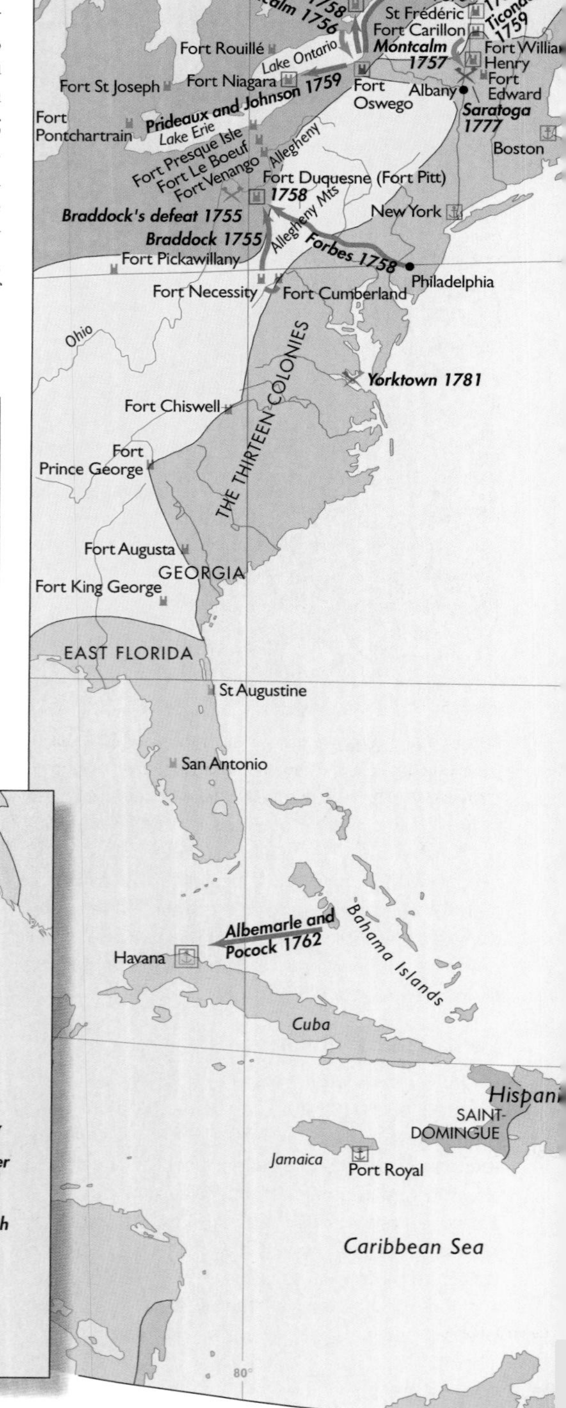

2 The capture of Madras by the French under Dupleix in 1746 began the struggle for India *(map below)*. As in America, British sea power proved decisive. Dupleix was checked at Trichinopoly in 1752, and after the capture of Bengal in 1757 the British could reinforce the Carnatic at will. The capture of Pondicherry in 1761 destroyed French power, and with control of the sea the British were able to hold off all subsequent challenges.

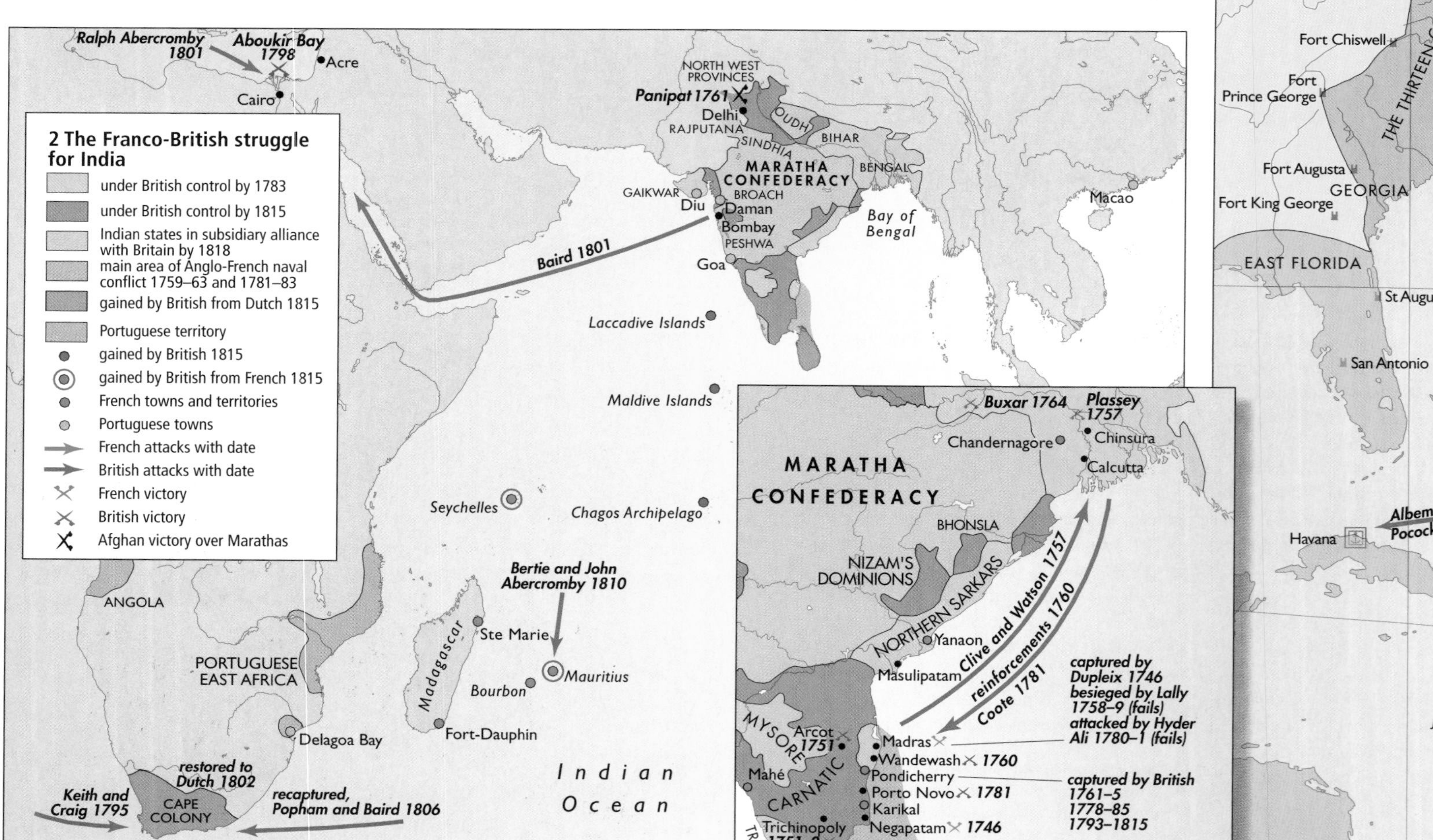

check France's ambitious designs in the Carnatic. But the real foundation of the British empire in India followed Clive's victory at Plassey (1757) which gave the British control of the rich province of Bengal (*see* p. 170). Reinforcements from Bengal enabled the British to eliminate French influence in the Carnatic and become the predominant European power in India.

The French revolution of 1789 shattered the French navy and left British naval power preeminent. This ruined Napoleon's plans for the invasion of Great Britain. By 1815, the French, Spanish, Dutch and Danish fleets were defeated, their colonies mostly in British hands. With the acquisition of the Cape, Ceylon and Mauritius, Great Britain secured the route to India, and laid the foundations for the second British empire.

3 In the final confrontation between Great Britain and France the decisive battles were fought in European waters ***(map right).*** Weakened by the revolution, the French fleet was no match for the British, and as successive invasion attempts foundered against British superiority at sea, Britain occupied its rival's possessions. By 1815, and the final defeat of Napoleon, British control of the key strategic colonies left it as the supreme imperial power.

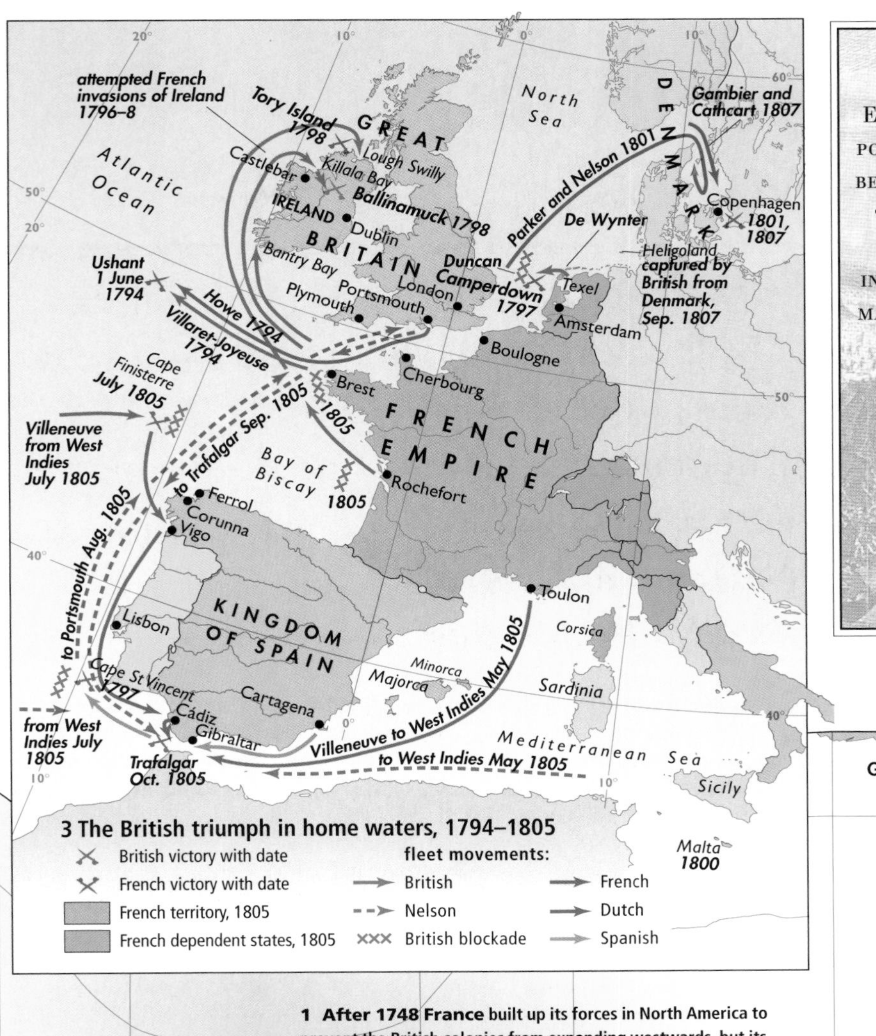

England is the declared enemy of your power and of your state; she always will be. Her avidity in commerce, the haughty tone she takes in the world's affairs, her jealousy of your power, the intrigues that she has made against you, make us foresee that centuries will pass before you can make a durable peace with that country which aims at supremacy in the four quarters of the globe.

Duke of Choiseul, French foreign minister, to Louis XV, 1765

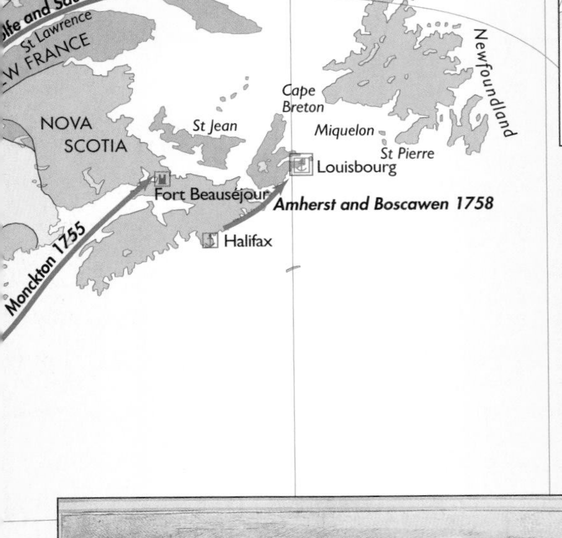

1 After 1748 France built up its forces in North America to prevent the British colonies from expanding westwards, but its position there and in the West Indies depended upon constant reinforcement from Europe ***(map below).*** Isolated by the British blockade of French ports, the position deteriorated rapidly after 1758 and the French overseas empire was lost. The sugar islands of the Caribbean were returned in 1763, but the fall of Montreal ended French power in North America. Twenty years later France gained revenge by aiding the American colonists in their successful fight for independence.

A View of the Taking of Quebeck by the English Forces Commanded by Genl. Wolfe Sep. 13 1759.

The fall of Quebec ***(above)*** in October 1759 signed the death warrant of the French empire in North America. The city was taken after a daring assault by British troops, commanded by General James Wolfe, who scaled the reputedly impregnable cliffs to surprise French forces led by General Montcalm. Both generals died in the battle. It was British control of the seas that made the triumph possible.

GREAT BRITAIN
London
Chatham
Portsmouth
Plymouth
Howe and Bligh 1758
Cherbourg
Brest
St Malo
Hawke
British blockade 1758, 1759
Confiens
Quiberon Bay 1759
Belle Isle
Keppel 1761
Hawke and Mordaunt 1757
Rochefort
FRANCE
Ferrol
Corunna
Toulon
La Galissonière
La Clue
Oporto
SPAIN
Madrid
PORTUGAL
Lisbon
Minorca
French 1756–63
Balearic Islands
Byng
Cartagena
Boscawen
Lagos 1759
Cádiz
Gibraltar 1782
Azores
Atlantic Ocean
Madeira Islands
Canary Islands
Cape Verde Islands

1 The struggle in the North Atlantic and North America, 1754–82

British operations and date
French operations and date
British victory
French victory
British fort
French fort
Spanish fort
British naval base
French naval base
Spanish naval base
British capture and date
French capture and date
British possessions
French possessions
Spanish possessions

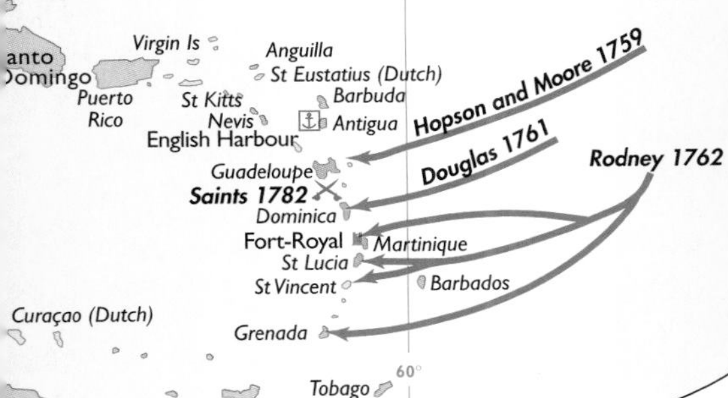

1648 to 1795

The age of partition: eastern Europe

See also
Russian expansion in Europe and Asia p. 160
The Early Modern Muslim empires, 1520–1700 p. 168
The struggle for the Baltic, 1523–1721 p. 188
The Holy Roman Empire, 1493–1806 p. 190
The rise of nationalism in Europe, 1800–1914 p. 214
The disintegration of the Ottoman empire, 1800–1923 p. 228

After 1648, a new balance of power in eastern Europe was brought about by the decline of both Poland-Lithuania and the Ottoman empire. Turkish resilience preserved the Ottoman empire from collapse, but Poland's internal weakness was cynically exploited by its neighbours to block reform and to destroy and partition the state.

> CATHERINE AND I ARE SIMPLY BRIGANDS, BUT I WONDER HOW THE QUEEN-EMPRESS MANAGED TO SQUARE HER CONFESSOR!...SHE WEPT AS SHE TOOK; THE MORE SHE WEPT, THE MORE SHE TOOK.
>
> **Frederick II of Prussia on Maria Theresa during the First Partition of Poland**

1652 *First use of the* liberum veto *in the Polish* Sejm

1669 *Ottoman conquest of Crete*

1672 *Peace of Buczacz: Ottomans take Podolia from Poland*

1683 *Siege of Vienna*

1699 *Peace of Carlowitz: Poland regains Podolia; Habsburgs gain all of Hungary*

1772 *First Partition of Poland-Lithuania*

1791 *Polish Constitution of 3rd May*

1793 *Second Partition of Poland-Lithuania*

1795 *Third Partition of Poland-Lithuania*

POLAND'S FAILURE TO CRUSH the revolt of the Zaporozhian Cossacks after 1648 (*see* p. 160) opened a new chapter in east European history. Poland-Lithuania was torn by foreign invasion in the Second Northern War (1655–60) and although it recovered it could not prevent the loss of Kiev and the left-bank Ukraine to Muscovy at the treaty of Andrusovo (1667) or rebuild its military system, with the result that the Ukraine remained a battleground for Poland, Russia and the Ottomans. The Cossacks divided into pro-Polish, pro-Russian and pro-Ottoman factions in the period known in Ukraine as 'the Ruin'.

Ottoman revival and decline

The renewed opportunities in Ukraine tempted the Ottoman empire, which pursued an expansionist policy under a succession of Grand Viziers from the Köprülü family. It reconquered Tenedos and Lemnos from Venice (1657) and seized Crete (1669). At the peace of Buczacz (1672) Podolia was then taken from Poland, before Grand Vizier Kara Mustafa led a huge army to besiege Vienna (1683). A combined Imperial and Polish army led by King John III Sobieski of Poland-Lithuania (1674–96) drove the Ottomans from the city wall. Thereafter the establishment in 1684 of the Holy League of Venice, Austria and Poland-Lithuania, supported by the Papacy, marked the start of a long campaign to push the Ottomans back. In 1686 Russia, too, joined the alliance.

The Ottomans could not combat the new military sophistication of European armies. At the peace of Carlowitz (1699), Podolia was returned to Poland, and Austrian possession of Hungary was confirmed. Yet division and distractions among the allies ensured that until 1739 the Ottoman empire, far from collapsing, was able to reverse some of its defeats. Azov, seized by Russia in 1696, was returned in 1711 after Peter I's army was surrounded on the river Prut, while Serbia and parts of Wallachia, ceded to Austria at Passarowitz in 1718, were regained in 1739 at the Peace of Belgrade. It was only after 1770 that Russian expansion to the Black Sea and the Caucasus was triumphantly resumed. Nonetheless Ottoman resilience was still enough to ensure that retreat was gradual. Only after 1815 did the balance tip decisively against the Ottomans and their final decline begin.

Sobieski's triumph at Vienna, however, marked the Commonwealth of Poland-Lithuania's last major victory as a significant European power, as the political problems which increasingly paralysed its institutions became clear to its neighbours. The Commonwealth's diet (the *Sejm*) was composed of delegates from provincial dietines (*sejmiki*). Decisions were consensual; in 1652, this saw the first acceptance of the *liberum veto*, by which a sole delegate had the right to block *Sejm* decisions. Henceforth, *Sejm* sessions regularly broke up without deciding anything, including the levying of taxes with which to pay the army.

The partitions of Poland

The first plans to partition Poland-Lithuania were drawn up in 1656–7, but after 1660 its neighbours recognized that there were advantages to be drawn from preserving it politically divided and weak. The *liberum veto* proved the perfect instrument: deputies could always be bribed to break the *Sejm*. Hopes of revival after the election of king Augustus II, elector of Saxony, (1697–1733) were dashed during the Great Northern War (1700–21), when Peter I's political acumen enabled him to establish a virtual Russian protectorate over the Commonwealth from 1717, when its army was limited to 24,000, tiny by 18th-century standards.

This situation suited Austria and Prussia, fighting for control of Silesia after the Prussian invasion of 1740. The War of Austrian Succession (1740–8) and the Seven Years' War (1756–63) left Prussia

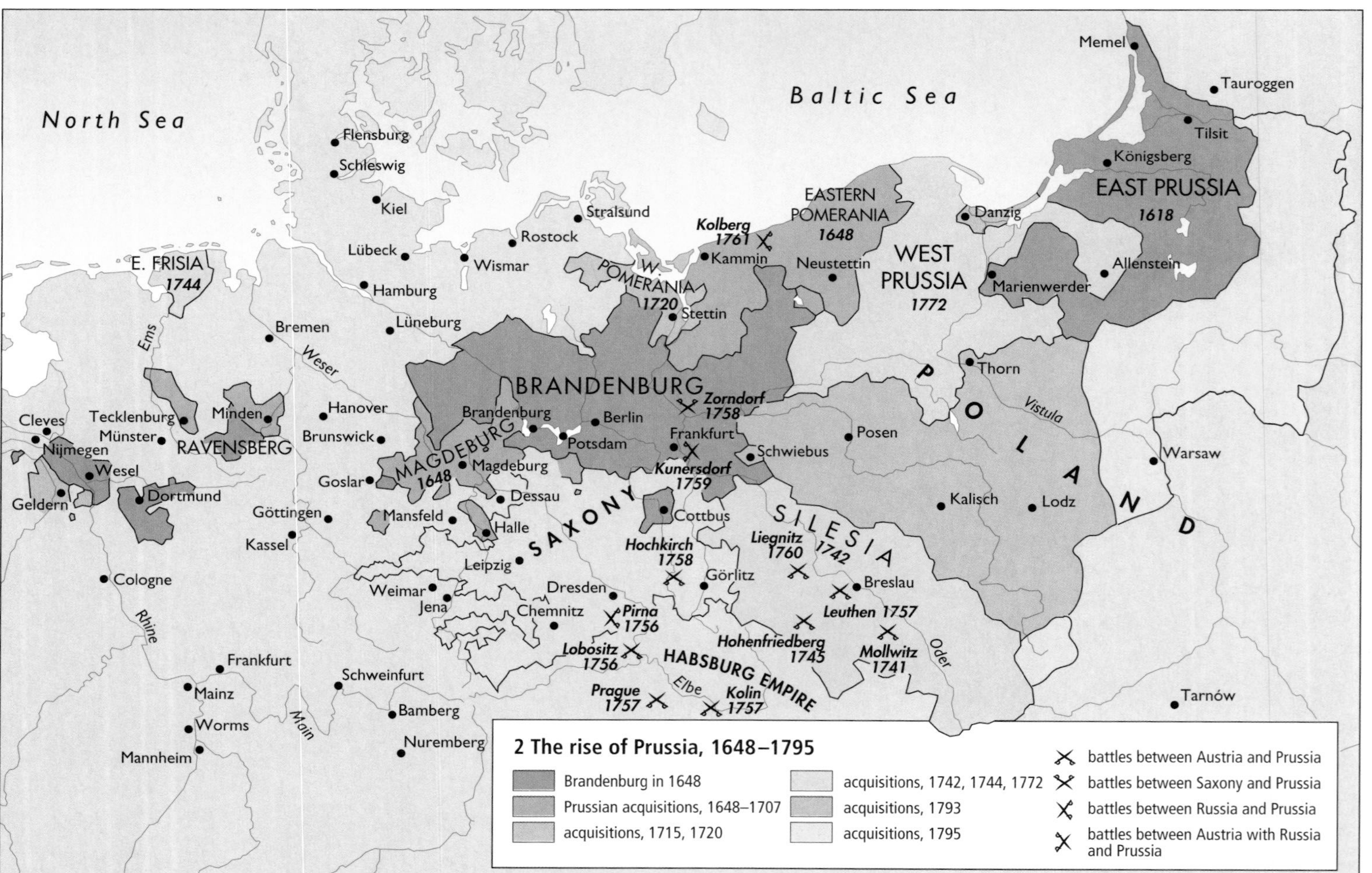

2 & 3 The electors of Brandenburg acquired a series of scattered territories in the 17th century ***(map left)***. Frederick William (the Great Elector) gained recognition of his full sovereignty from Poland in 1657; his son Frederick I was crowned king in Prussia in 1701. Frederick II (the Great) seized Silesia from the Habsburgs. Prussia's participation in the Partitions of Poland sealed its position as a Great Power. In three Partitions (1772, 1793, 1795), Russia, Austria and Prussia divided up the whole of Poland ***(map above)***. Austria gained 4,150,000 inhabitants, Russia 5,500,000 inhabitants and Prussia 2,600,000 inhabitants.

1 The Austrian branch of the Habsburg dynasty was founded by Charles V's brother Ferdinand, elected king of Bohemia and Hungary in 1526. For 200 years, the Habsburgs disputed possession of Hungarian territory with the Ottomans *(map left)*. After the Turkish defeat at the siege of Vienna (1683), the Habsburgs extended control rapidly down the Danube, consolidating their gains at the treaties of Carlowitz (1699) and Passarowitz (1718), though some territory was lost at the Peace of Belgrade (1739). Austria lost Silesia to Prussia in the War of the Austrian Succession (1740–8) and failed to recover it in the Seven Years' War (1756–63); compensation came in the shape of the land won in the First and Third Partitions of Poland, though Austrian possession of west Galicia was short-lived.

The Siege of Vienna in 1683 marked both the climax of the long Ottoman wars of expansion in the Balkans and the last great triumph of Polish arms *(picture below)*. The siege of Vienna by a massive Turkish army from July to September was lifted by a combined Imperial and Polish force, led by King John III Sobieski of Poland-Lithuania, which swept down the slopes of the Wienerwald on 12 September to win a dramatic victory

with Silesia; the two powers soon found common ground in the east where the election of Stanislaw Poniatowski as king of Poland in 1764 heralded the breakdown of the Russian protectorate over Poland as Poniatowski, inspired by Enlightenment teaching, sought to reform the unworkable Polish constitution. This provoked dangerous opposition: after the anti-Russian Confederation of Bar (1768–72) reduced the Commonwealth to political anarchy, Austria's seizure of the small territory of Zips (Spiz) stimulated Prussia and Russia to join in the First Partition.

Taking advantage of Russian distraction in the Turkish war of 1788–92 Poniatowski summoned the Four-Year *Sejm* (1788–92) which passed the Constitution of 3rd May 1791. This abolished the *liberum veto* and radically restructured the Commonwealth. The prospect of a revived Poland was too much for Russia and Prussia, who in 1793 agreed the Second Partition, in which Prussia secured Danzig. When the following year Tadeusz Kosciuszko led a rising in protest, Russia, Austria and Prussia combined to wipe Poland-Lithuania from the map in the Third Partition.

4 From the mid-17th century the western powers began to realize that the Ottoman empire was no longer an invincible force and had indeed become dangerously weak. As Austria and Russia sought advantage from Turkish disintegration, Prussia expanded, and France and Sweden tried to maintain the traditional balance *(map right)*. With France increasingly paralyzed and Britain preoccupied beyond Europe, the eastern powers were able to contrive the Partitions of Poland.

4 Territorial gains and losses in eastern Europe 1648–1795

Russian gains from Poland, 1667–1795
Russian gains from Sweden, 1700–43
Russian gains from Ottomans, 1768–92
Prussian gains from Austria, 1742
Prussian gains from Sweden, 1720
Prussian gains from Poland, 1772–95
Habsburg gains from Ottomans, 1683–1775
Habsburg gains from Poland, 1772–95
Ottoman gains from Venice, 1669–1718

The emerging global economy

See also
European voyages of discovery, 1487–1780 p. 156
The Americas, 1500–1810 p. 162
Trade and empire in Africa, 1500–1800 p. 164
Mughal India and the growth of British power p. 170
Southeast Asia and the European powers p. 176
The European economy: trade and industry, 1550–1775 p. 180
The struggle for empire, 1713–1815 p. 194

During the 18th century international trade made rapid strides, fuelled by the demand for luxury goods and foodstuffs from a Europe growing in wealth. The core of the trading system was the Atlantic triangle, dominated by Britain and France, which was based on the sale of slaves from Africa and the export of sugar and tobacco from the New World.

What was the sole cause of the revival of slavery by Christians, but the discovery of waste countries, and the disproportion which has ever since existed in those countries between the demand and supply of labour? And what is it that increases the number of slaves of Christian masters, but the increase of Christian capitalists wanting labourers, by the spreading of Christian people over regions heretofore waste?

Edward Gibbon Wakefield,
A Letter from Sydney, 1820

During the course of the 18th century, European and American merchants developed an extensive system of intercontinental trade routes which laid the foundation for the evolution of a sophisticated global economy in the next century. Trade on such a scale encouraged the development of large ocean-going merchant fleets, and the gradual development of modern commercial practices, particularly in the supply of insurance and trade credits. Nonetheless most trade in Europe and in the rest of the world remained local. In 1800 extra-European trade contributed an estimated 4 per cent to Europe's aggregate gross national product.

Mercantilism

For much of the century trade was still governed by mercantilist principles: trade should always be in surplus to provide a stream of bullion, and trade was always a war between states for a fixed quantity of commerce. In reality European merchants could see that trade was growing rapidly over the century, and bullion increasingly being replaced by bills of exchange. Nevertheless states still played an important part in inhibiting trade by pursuing mercantilist policies. British tariffs rose sharply over the 18th century, averaging 30 per cent, while British colonies were banned from producing industrial products that competed with domestic manufactures. Britain's Navigation Acts prevented any other power from engaging in trade in Britain's empire. Bullion was also essential for western European trade with the Baltic, Turkey and Asia, which supplied goods much in demand in Europe but had little market for European products.

There were other factors that made trade difficult. Piracy was widespread, and not until the defeat of the Mediterranean corsairs after 1815 and the elimination of Caribbean pirates by 1830 was trade in these seas secure. Piracy remained endemic in the Indian Ocean and the China Sea. War also interrupted trade development, for states permitted official piracy in time of war. Trade security could only be guaranteed by those states that possessed large navies, which meant that Britain, France and the Netherlands profited most from the growth of world commerce.

The slave economy

Trade growth owed a great deal to the emergence of the Atlantic economy, where most trans-oceanic trade was conducted. Much of this was based on the Spanish and Portuguese empires which still played an important part in the 18th century, chiefly through the mining of gold and silver and its shipment exclusively to the Iberian peninsula. But the growth of the American colonies, the Caribbean and Canada promoted a new trade. The most important commodity was slaves, and more than eight million Africans were shipped to the New World between the 17th and 19th centuries. Although outlawed by the United States and Britain in 1807, the slave trade continued until the 1860s.

The rise of the Atlantic slave economy was based on the growing demand in Europe for tobacco, sugar and cotton, all of which were produced in plantations in the New World. British trade in sugar grew six-fold over the 18th century, and the supply of tobacco, much of which was re-exported to Europe, grew from 32 million pounds to 50 million pounds. Europeans brought manufactured goods to the west African coast to trade for slaves which were then taken to the New World and sold. Plantation products were then exported to Europe. Half of the slaves died before shipping, perhaps a quarter more on board ship, another fifth in the first year of work. It was a brutal and inefficient trade, but it kept Europe supplied with cheap luxury products which it could not afford from Asia.

Trade with Asia

Trade with the rest of the world was small. Asian and African traders kept to inland routes, or engaged in coastal trade. Europeans bought silk, spices, coffee and china, but often paid with gold or silver. Trade was conducted through local chartered companies such as the East India Company, which enjoyed a monopoly of Britain's south Asia trade until 1813. The consolidation of British power in Bengal opened the way in the late century to the opening up of Asian trade. In 1700 Britain imported 70,000 pounds of teas; by 1800 the figure had risen to 15 million pounds. The development of Britain's cotton textile industry in the last third of the century produced a trading revolution. By then, the rapid pace of industrialization was poised to open the way for the domination of world markets by European traders in the 19th century and the development of a global system of communication, finance and production.

1696 *Britain begins official balance-of-trade statistics*

1697 *French found Saint-Domingue sugar colony*

1703 *Anglo-Portuguese trade treaty*

1731 *Sextant invented*

1750 *Britain bans iron- and steel-making in American colonies*

1783 *French slave trade act*

1813 *East India Company monopoly ended*

1830 *Last Caribbean pirate hanged*

1834 *Slavery abolished in British West Indies*

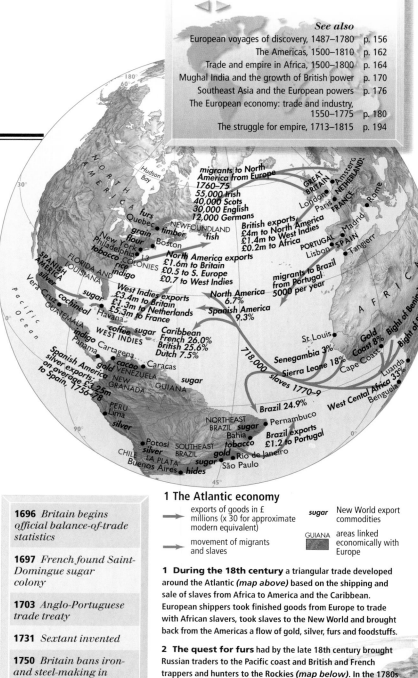

1 The Atlantic economy

exports of goods in £ millions (x 30 for approximate modern equivalent)
movement of migrants and slaves
sugar New World export commodities
GUIANA areas linked economically with Europe

1 During the 18th century a triangular trade developed around the Atlantic ***(map above)*** based on the shipping and sale of slaves from Africa to America and the Caribbean. European shippers took finished goods from Europe to trade with African slavers, took slaves to the New World and brought back from the Americas a flow of gold, silver, furs and foodstuffs.

2 The quest for furs had by the late 18th century brought Russian traders to the Pacific coast and British and French trappers and hunters to the Rockies ***(map below)***. In the 1780s sea trade linked up Kamchatka and Alaska, which became a Russian outpost until sold to the USA in 1867. Furs made up only 3 per cent of American-British trade in the 18th century, but the search for pelts opened up trade for other commodities.

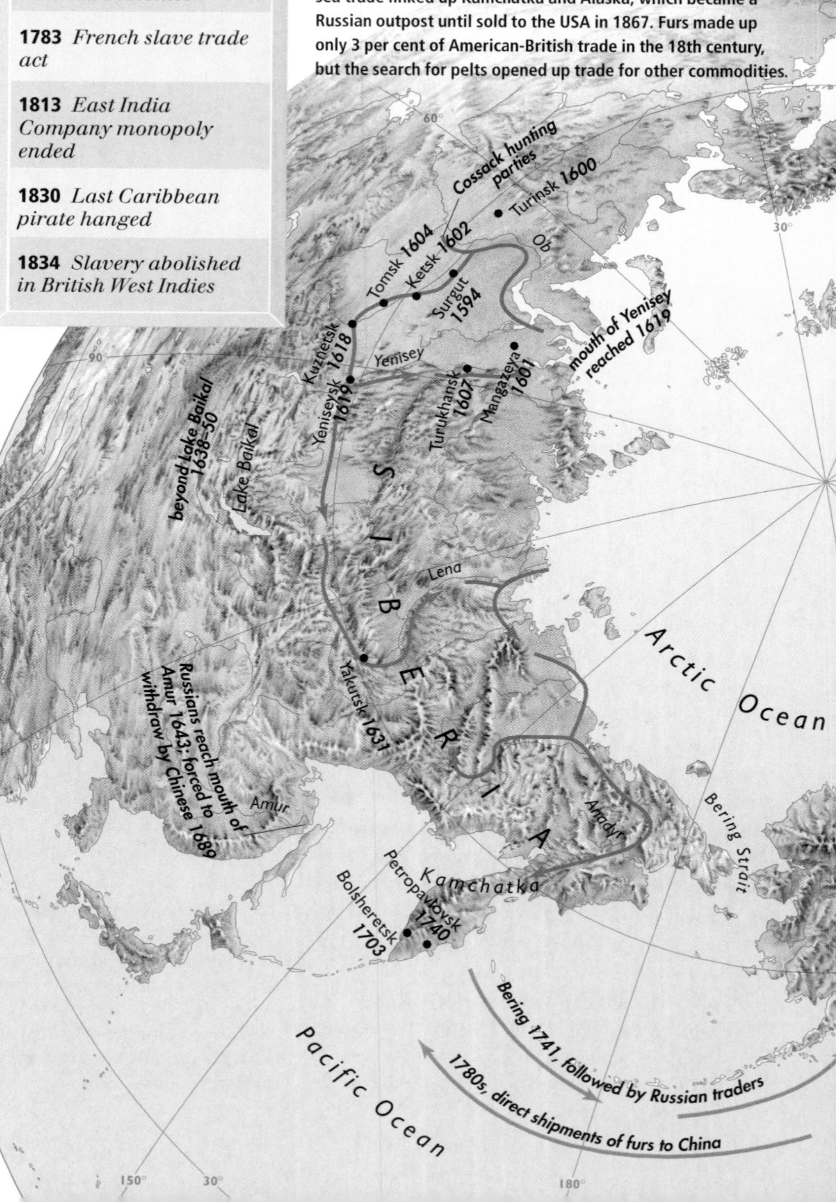

4 & 5 French trade grew remarkably over the course of the 18th century, at an average of 3 per cent a year ***(chart near right)***. By the 1780s 40 per cent of the Bordeaux trade was colonial, and the French merchant fleet plied the Atlantic routes in increasing numbers ***(chart far right)***: to Senegal for slaves; and from Saint-Domingue, Guadeloupe and Martinique laden with sugar. In 1792 the total tonnage of the French fleet was exceeded only by Britain's.

4 French exports and imports 1716–79

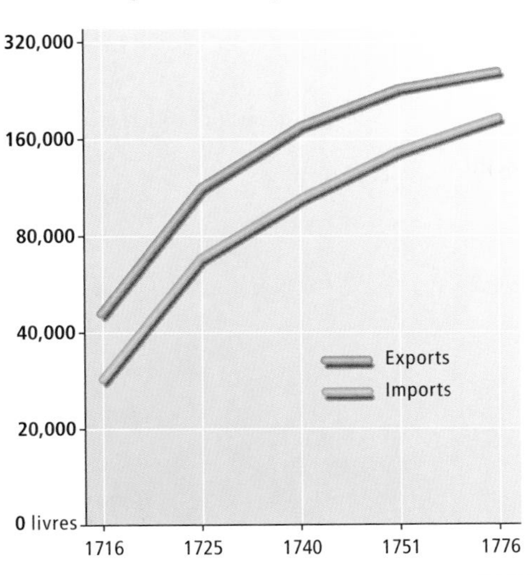

5 Foreign destination of the French merchant fleet, 1788

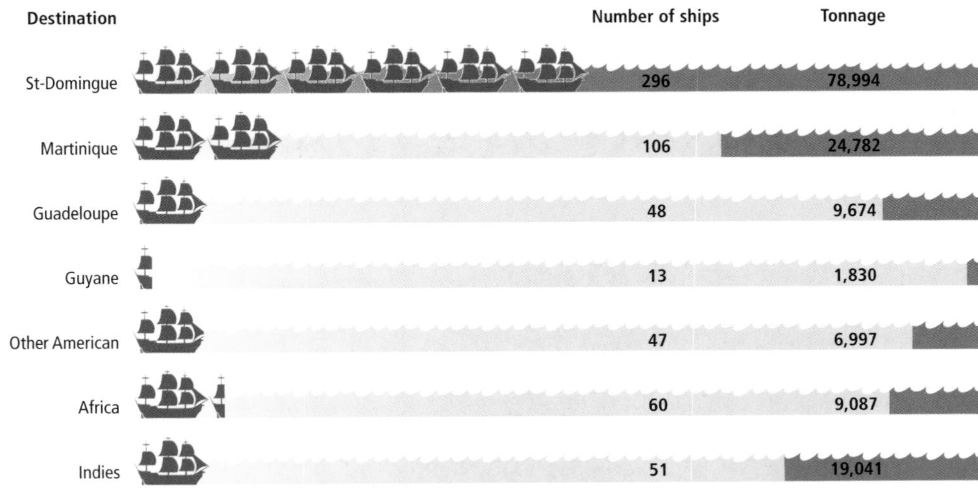

Destination	Number of ships	Tonnage
St-Domingue	296	78,994
Martinique	106	24,782
Guadeloupe	48	9,674
Guyane	13	1,830
Other American	47	6,997
Africa	60	9,087
Indies	51	19,041

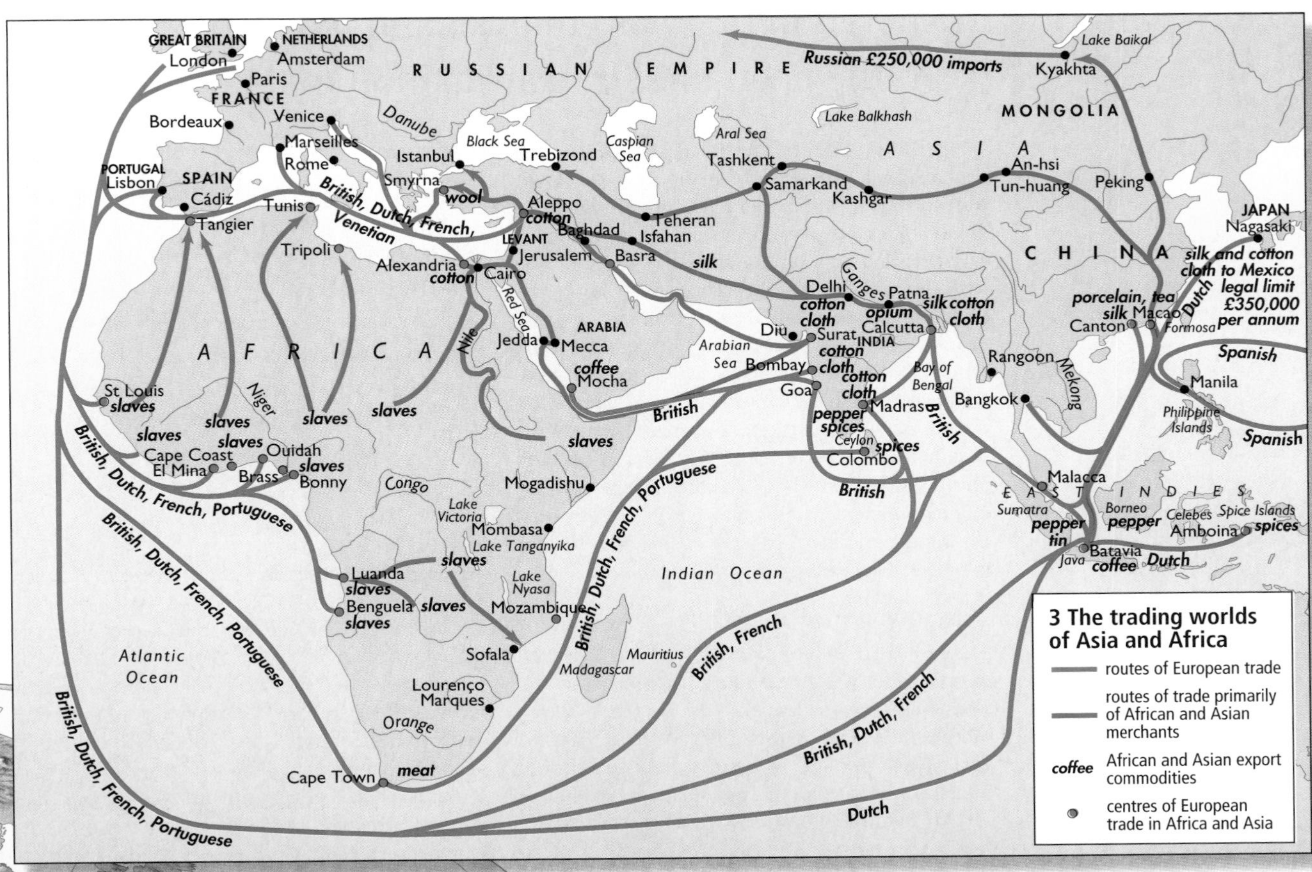

6 Slave prices in Africa, Brazil and the Caribbean

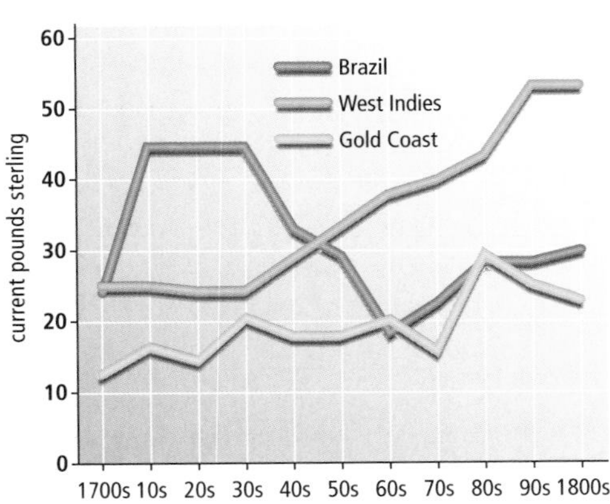

6 Slave prices ***(chart above)*** rose most sharply with increased demand from the Americas, particularly with the Brazilian gold rush of the early 18th century and the sugar boom in the Caribbean from the mid-century. In the 1770s prices paid for slaves in Africa expanded much faster than the selling price in the New World as African slavers exploited their monopoly.

3 European trade in Africa and Asia ***(map left)*** was restricted to high-value products bought mainly for silver since there was little demand for Europe's own products. In 1800 British trade with Africa and the Far East was only 10 per cent of her overseas trade. European trade was largely dominated by chartered companies which established forts and entrepôts around the rim of Africa and southern Asia.

Captain James Cook's ships at anchor at Nootka Sound ***(above)***. Cook reached the northwest coast of Canada in 1778 still searching for what might form part of the entrance to a Northwest Passage allowing seaborne trade to pass directly from the Atlantic to the Pacific. He did not locate the route he sought, but surveyed an area which was to become a point of severe conflict between the British, Spanish and Russians, all intent on expansion, the security of their existing territories and the dominance of trade in the north Pacific. The British were in the end to prevail.

1760 to 1860

The industrial revolution begins: Great Britain

See also
The European economy: agriculture and society, 1500–1815 p. 178
The European economy: trade and industry, 1550–1775 p. 180
The emerging global economy, c. 1775 p. 198
Population growth and movements p. 208
The industrial revolution in Europe, 1815–70 p. 210
The market revolution in the US, 1800–80 p. 220

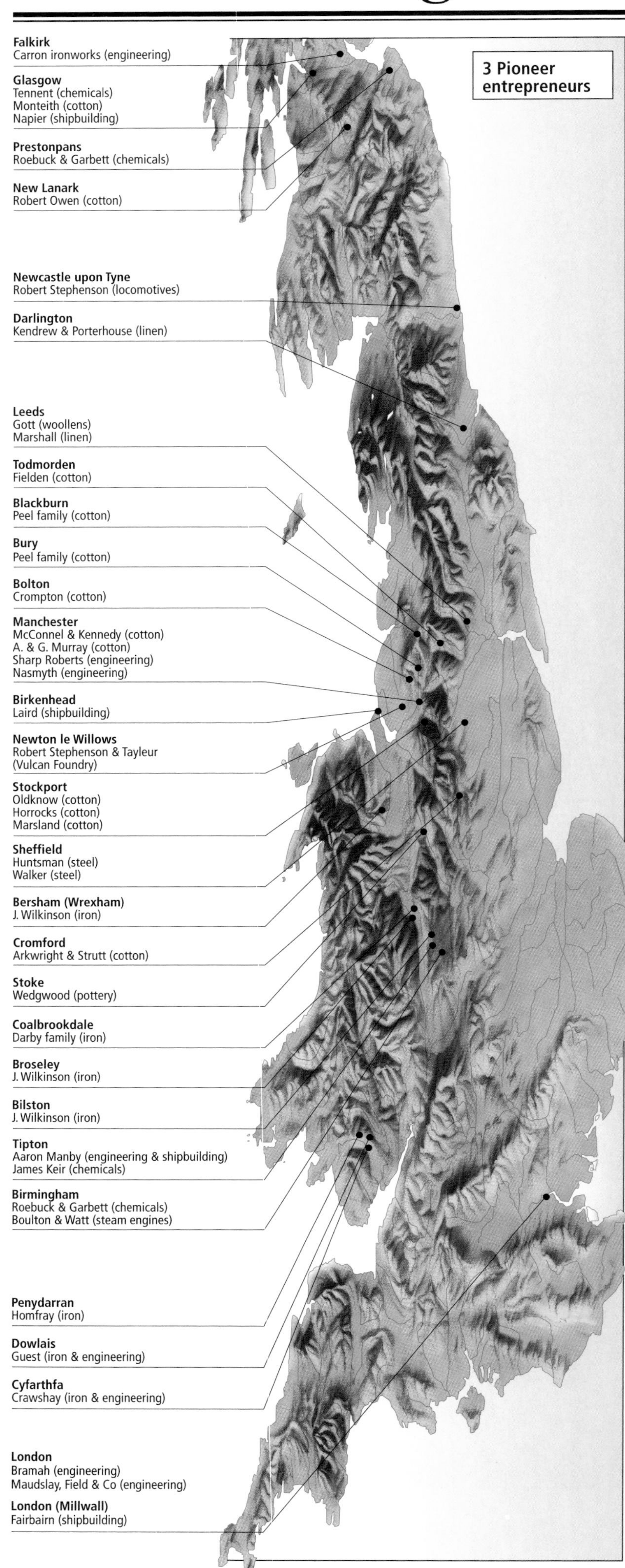

3 The expansion of manufacturing depended on the emergence of an entrepreneurial class *(map above)*. The pioneering enterprises shown here all played significant roles in the industrial revolution. Men from a variety of social backgrounds became inventors and businessmen. At the same time landowners and merchants also played their part by investing in new processes or developing the supply of raw materials and an improved transport system.

During the 18th century, Britain experienced the world's first industrial revolution as new technologies and overseas markets developed. British industry began to meet a growing demand for cheap consumer goods. It was a revolution that ushered in the mass market and paved the way for the economic transformation of the globe.

DURING THE SECOND HALF of the 18th century, the British economy was slowly transformed by the development of new industrial technologies that permitted cheaper production on a larger scale to meet the demands of a growing mass market. In fact the term 'industrial revolution' is misleading. The British economy had been growing steadily since the late 17th century, while much of the success of the new industries depended on changes in agriculture, transport and financial services and on the accelerated growth of the population. Nonetheless, at the heart of Britain's late 18th-century industrial transformation lay changes in the production of iron, textiles and machinery and a shift from wood to coal as the primary source of energy.

> THE WHOLE OF THE ISLAND ... SET AS THICK WITH CHIMNEYS AS THE MASTS STAND IN THE DOCKS OF LIVERPOOL; THAT THERE SHALL BE NO MEADOWS IN IT; NO TREES; NO GARDENS ... THAT, THE SMOKE HAVING RENDERED THE LIGHT OF THE SUN UNSERVICEABLE, YOU WORK ALWAYS BY THE LIGHT OF YOUR OWN GAS: THAT NO ACRE OF ENGLISH GROUND SHALL BE WITHOUT ITS SHAFT AND ITS ENGINE.
>
> **John Ruskin**
> ***The Two Paths, 1859***

The new technologies

The key lay in steam power. Steam engines had existed since the beginning of the century, but when the Scottish scientist James Watt developed a more reliable and powerful version in the 1760s it was rapidly applied in mining, then in the iron industry. The invention of a rotative motion engine in 1781 opened the way for steam power to drive machinery. By 1800 the cotton and brewing industries were regular users of steam power. When Watt's patents lapsed in 1800, steam power spread throughout the industrial economy and the transport system. In 1825 the first steam railway was opened, ushering in another new period of economic development.

Innovation was also important in manufacturing. In the cotton textile industry, production was slowly mechanized from the 1760s to the 1790s, though hand-loom weaving was not challenged by machines until the 1820s. Mechanization permitted the shift from small-scale craft output to factory production: by 1816, for example, Arkwright's mill at Cromford in northwest England employed over 700 people. In the iron industry the inventions of Henry Cort in 1784 permitted coal to be used as the main refining fuel for iron, while the steam engine was used to produce rolled and bar-iron for working. Large production units developed which both smelted the ore and produced the finished iron products. Better quality iron could be used in all forms of construction work. Innovation became a continuous process, producing a stream of cheaper and better products.

The conditions for growth

Britain was by no means the only country to produce industrial inventions, but it enjoyed a number of advantages which explain its rapid industrial development. In the first place agriculture experienced its own 'revolution', making it more prosperous and more productive. Improvements in patterns of land cultivation, greater use of fertilizers and improved stock breeding all contributed to raising farm incomes. The enclosure of common land accelerated after 1760 with Parliamentary Enclosure Acts, and had the effect of creating large integrated farms where modern practices could be introduced and yields and incomes raised. Farming generated growing demand for industrial goods and encouraged the creation of a wider market for farm products.

Agrarian change also encouraged the development of better transport and a more sophisticated capital market to meet the costs of farm improvement and canal-building. Both helped the emergence of early industry. Many businessmen came from humble social backgrounds with little access to finance. Landlord and merchant capital, derived largely from Britain's prosperous overseas and colonial trade, was mobilized for investment in expanding industries and in the building of canals, roads, ports and, from 1825, railways. The rapid growth of a largely unregulated capital market brought a serious bank crisis in 1825 which prompted bank reform in 1826 and, in 1844, the creation of a central bank and clearing-bank system. Without the emergence of this modern credit structure, the pace of industrial change might well have been much slower.

The social revolution

By 1820 Britain was in the throes of rapid social and economic transformation. Population growth produced a flow of cheap labour to the new cities and provided a large new market for mass-produced consumer goods. There were few social barriers to labour mobility or a business career, while governments favoured legislation that encouraged economic growth. It was between 1820 and 1851, when Britain hosted the Great Exhibition to trumpet its economic triumphs, that the industrialization of Britain finally overturned the agrarian social structure and traditional landlord rule. The new business class became an important political force, while the new urban workforce, toiling in appalling conditions with little security, laid the foundations for organized labour protest. 'Class' in its modern sense was the direct offspring of industrial change.

Falmouth
(mail port for New York)

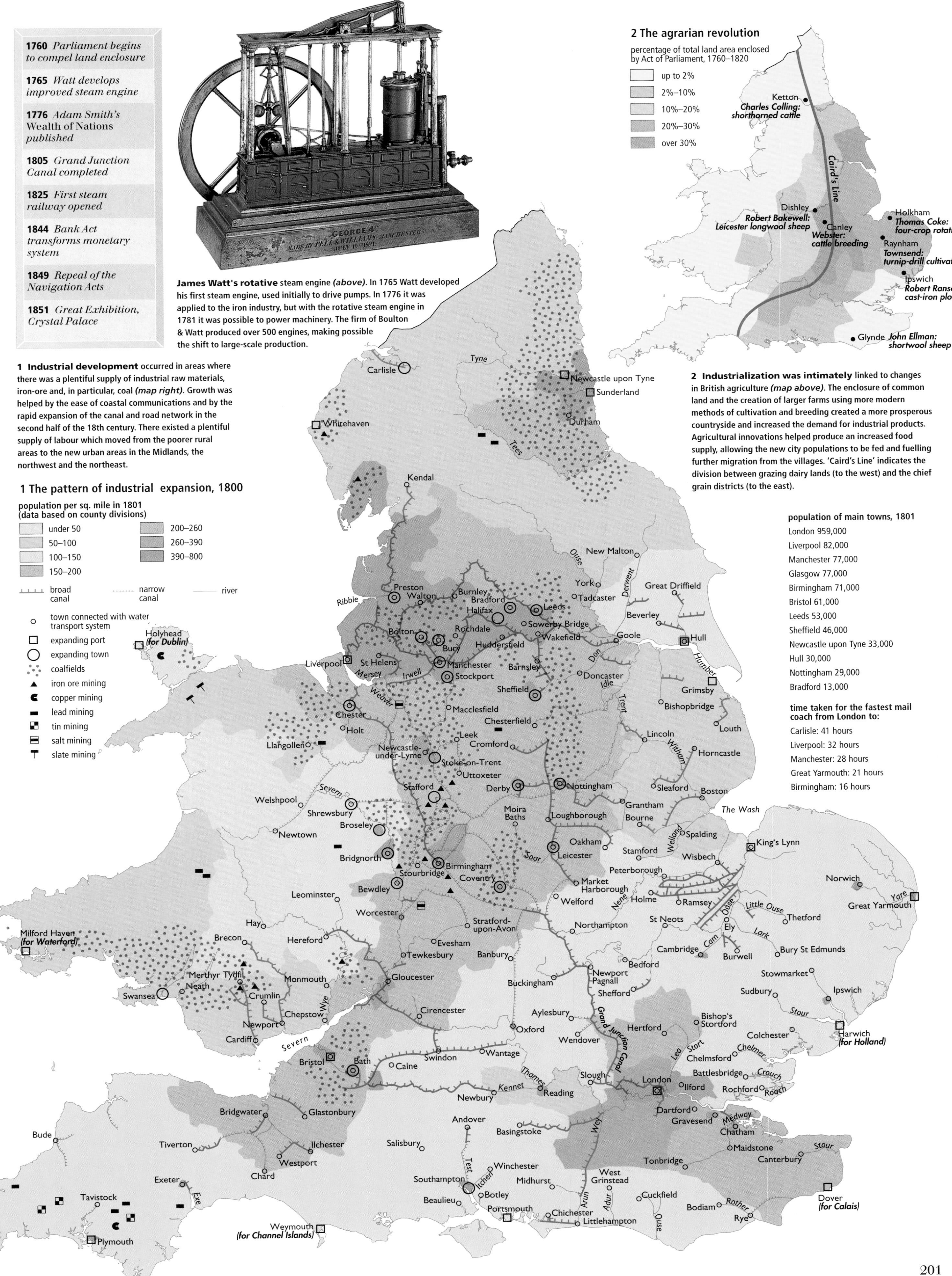

James Watt's rotative steam engine *(above)*. In 1765 Watt developed his first steam engine, used initially to drive pumps. In 1776 it was applied to the iron industry, but with the rotative steam engine in 1781 it was possible to power machinery. The firm of Boulton & Watt produced over 500 engines, making possible the shift to large-scale production.

1 Industrial development occurred in areas where there was a plentiful supply of industrial raw materials, iron-ore and, in particular, coal *(map right)*. Growth was helped by the ease of coastal communications and by the rapid expansion of the canal and road network in the second half of the 18th century. There existed a plentiful supply of labour which moved from the poorer rural areas to the new urban areas in the Midlands, the northwest and the northeast.

2 Industrialization was intimately linked to changes in British agriculture *(map above)*. The enclosure of common land and the creation of larger farms using more modern methods of cultivation and breeding created a more prosperous countryside and increased the demand for industrial products. Agricultural innovations helped produce an increased food supply, allowing the new city populations to be fed and fuelling further migration from the villages. 'Caird's Line' indicates the division between grazing dairy lands (to the west) and the chief grain districts (to the east).

See also
Napoleon and the reshaping of Europe, 1799–1815 p. 204
The rise of nationalism in Europe, 1800–1914 p. 214
The making of the United States: westward expansion, 1783–1890 p. 218
Latin America: independence and national growth, 1810–1930 p. 226

The age of revolt

> WHAT WERE FORMERLY CALLED REVOLUTIONS, WERE LITTLE MORE THAN A CHANGE OF PERSONS, OR AN ALTERATION OF LOCAL CIRCUMSTANCES. THEY HAD NOTHING … THAT COULD INFLUENCE BEYOND THE SPOT THAT PRODUCED THEM. BUT WHAT WE NOW SEE IN THE WORLD, FROM THE REVOLUTION OF AMERICA AND FRANCE, ARE A RENOVATION OF THE NATURAL ORDER OF THINGS, A SYSTEM OF PRINCIPLES AS UNIVERSAL AS TRUTH AND THE EXISTENCE OF MAN, AND COMBINING MORAL WITH POLITICAL HAPPINESS AND NATURAL PROSPERITY.
>
> Tom Paine
> *Rights of Man, 1791*

A wave of revolutions swept over Europe and the Americas in the late 18th century, inspired in part by ideas of freedom promoted in the Enlightenment. New social forces challenged the old royal regimes and traditional privileges. Revolutions in France and America symbolized the struggle against despotism and the triumph of a new ideal of citizenship.

1762 *Rousseau's* Social Contract *published*

1773–4 *Pugachev revolt in Russia*

1776 *American Declaration of Independence*

1789 *Fall of Bastille signals revolution in France*

1791 *Slave revolt in Haiti*

1793 *Execution of Louis XVI*

1798 *Irish rebellion under Wolfe Tone*

1815 *Congress of Vienna imposes 'legitimism' on Europe*

IN THE *SOCIAL CONTRACT*, published in 1762, the French philosopher Rousseau claimed that 'Man is born free, but everywhere he is in chains'. He was writing at the height of the European Enlightenment, an intellectual revolt against tradition and superstition. The spirit of the Enlightenment was the emancipation of the individual and the rational organization of society. Both ideas had profound political implications. Over the next 30 years much of the political order of Europe and America was overturned by revolutionaries who drew their inspiration from the concept of political liberty and civil rights embodied in Enlightenment political philosophy.

The pattern of revolt was unpredictable and diverse. It owed something to early stirrings of nationalism, evident in Corsica, Poland and Ireland. But the chief revolutions in the American colonies and in France were responses to royal authority which came to be regarded as arbitrary, inefficient and unjust. In 1775 Britain's American colonies rebelled against the existing tax regime and under George Washington fought a six-year war against British-led forces, finally winning independence in 1783. The 'founding fathers' of American liberty established a modern constitutional republic based on ideas on human rights culled from Enlightenment Europe.

The French revolution

The American revolution had a considerable impact in Europe. In 1787 the revolt in the Austrian Netherlands was modelled on America. It was here that the term 'democrat' first entered popular politics. Ideas of political emancipation spread widely throughout the Atlantic world and into eastern Europe. It was against this background that the crisis in France in 1788–9 must be understood. The French monarchy faced heavy financial demands, worsened by the costs of helping the American rebels. The attempt to centralize and strengthen royal authority was resented by vested interests and regional elites, and when the king convened the Estates General in 1789 in an effort to stave off political crisis, the assembly caught the mood of the country by declaring itself a national assembly, overturning royal authority and in 1791 drew up a

2 In 1789 revolution overthrew royal authority in France. Economic crisis and war provoked widespread popular violence culminating in the Great Terror of 1792–4 in which thousands of alleged counter-revolutionaries were murdered *(map below)*. Resistance to the revolution sprang up in the Vendée in western France and in major urban centres, and in 1794 a more moderate regime was installed in Paris, to be overturned by the revolutionary general Napoleon Bonaparte in 1799. By 1800 the revolution had been exported by force into the Low Countries, Italy and Switzerland.

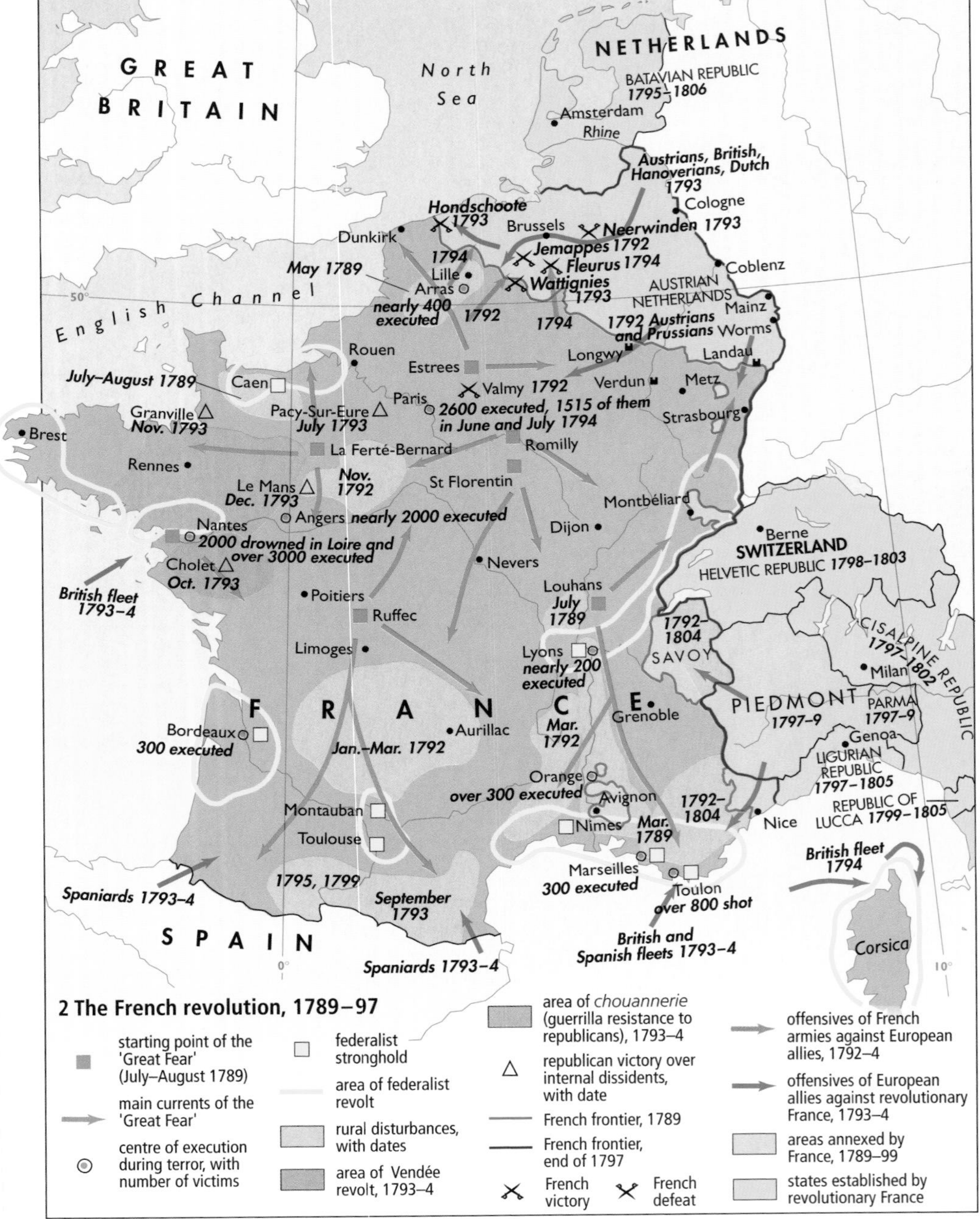

3 In 1775 the Thirteen Colonies on the eastern coast of North America revolted against British rule *(map below)*. Attempts by the British to reassert control over the colonists, such as the 1763 declaration of the 'Proclamation Line', forbidding settlement west of the Appalachians, had ended in failure. In 1774 the boundaries of the new Canadian province of Quebec had been enlarged to the Mississippi and Ohio rivers, a move bitterly resented in Virginia and Pennsylvania. When the situation escalated into warfare, the American army under George Washington suffered early defeats until Saratoga in 1777. With French assistance from 1778 a war of attrition set in which culminated in Franco-American victory at Yorktown in 1781. The Treaty of Versailles in 1783 granted independence to the colonies which organized themselves as the United States.

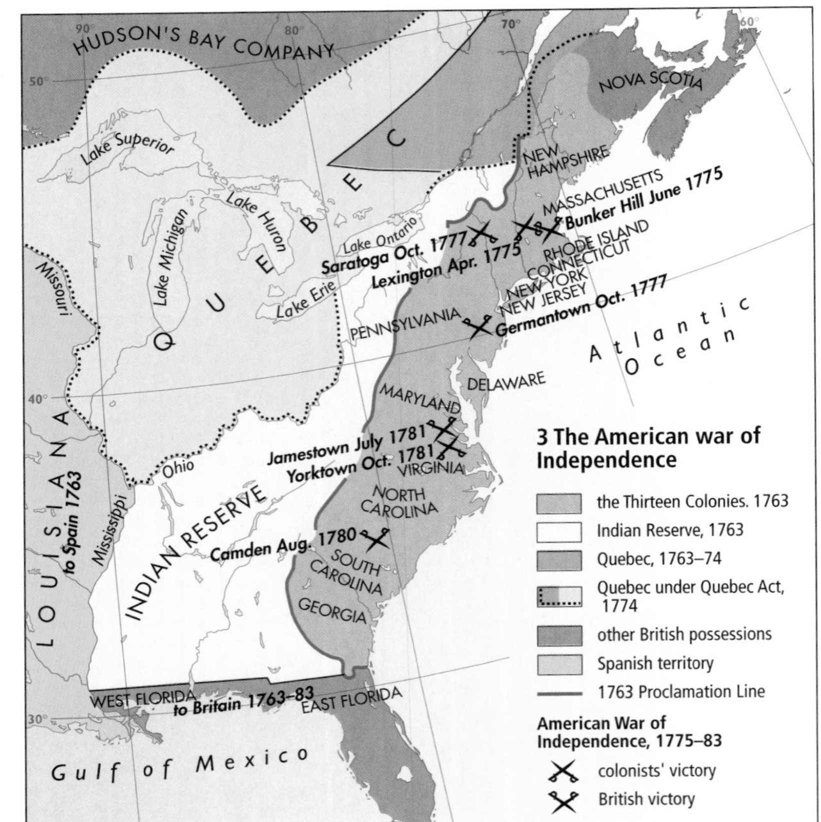

constitution with a limited parliamentary regime.

The attempt to introduce more representative government met with domestic resistance and the hostility of other powers. France was almost permanently at war from 1792, and in the process spread the revolution to Italy, Switzerland, the Rhineland and the Low Countries. The war produced a domestic radicalization with the triumph of the Jacobin faction in the assembly and the spread of the Terror which led to the death of thousands of alleged counter-revolutionaries and aristocrats. The Jacobins were themselves overthrown in 1794 and a more moderate Directory established. In 1799 Napoleon, who had made his name as a revolutionary general, was appointed First Consul to safeguard the moderate revolutionary achievement.

The French example inspired hope of liberty around the world. In India Tipu Sultan planted a symbolic 'Tree of Liberty' and declared himself an ally of revolutionary France against the British. In Haiti a slave revolt in 1791 freed the island from colonial rule. In Latin America the growing local hostility to Spanish rule was fuelled by news of the French revolution. Jacobin conspirators were discovered by the authorities in Quito and Buenos Aires. In Bogotá in 1793, 100 copies of the *Rights of Man* were printed, copied from the French declaration of 1789. In eastern Europe Jacobin activity was stamped out in Vienna and Budapest, while the 1794 Polish revolt, though led by the Polish nobility, used the French cry of 'liberty and equality' against its Russian and Prussian oppressors.

Counter-revolution

The wave of political revolt produced a strong counter-revolutionary reaction. Many of the revolutionaries in America and France were themselves conservative in outlook and worked to eliminate more radical or utopian revolutionary movements. Slave revolts in America were brutally suppressed in the 1790s. The revolutionary Directory unleashed a 'white terror' against the Jacobins in France, and Napoleon restored a strong centralist and authoritarian state after 1800. In eastern and central Europe reform from above introduced by so-called Enlightened despots was reversed or suspended and revolt in Poland, Hungary, Bohemia and the Ukraine violently quashed. Though Britain possessed the most liberal political system, the regime stamped hard on Irish nationalism and on any domestic threat of republicanism or domestic agitation.

In 1815 the Vienna Congress, summoned after the defeat of Napoleon, restored much of pre-1789 Europe by adopting the principle of 'legitimism'. But although monarchy was returned in France, the new ideas of liberty and nationhood were to find fertile ground throughout Europe and the Americas over the following century.

THE AGE OF REVOLT *(maps below)*

1755, 1793 Corsica Local clans led by Paoli rebelled against Genoese rule. France bought the island from Genoa in 1768 and crushed the revolt. A second attempt by Paoli to secure independence from (revolutionary) France in 1793, led to a brief British occupation; the rise of Bonaparte, himself a Corsican, put an end to the separatist movement.

1768 Geneva Middle-class citizens of the small city-state rebelled against domination by a few patrician families; with French support the latter reasserted predominance in 1782.

1773 Southeast Russia Cossacks, peasants and Asiatic tribes rebelled in the Volga and Ural regions under Pugachev, a Don Cossack. After fierce fighting, the Russian army put down the rebellion in autumn 1774.

1775 America Prolonged resistance by the Thirteen Colonies to Britain's financial policies resulted in open warfare and the Declaration of Independence, 1776. The defeat of Britain led to the formation of the United States in 1783. Numerous slave revolts from the 1790s.

1785, 1794–5 Dutch Netherlands Three-cornered struggle for power between the 'Stadholder', patrician families who controlled the Estates General, and the middle-class Patriot party which aimed to democratize the government. In 1787 Prussian troops defeated the Patriot army and restored the 'Stadholder' with greater powers. In 1794–5 the Patriot movement revived and with French help a republic was declared.

1787 Austrian Netherlands (Belgium) A revolt against the centralizing policy of Emperor Joseph II led to the proclamation of the Republic of the United Belgian Provinces in 1790. Austrian emperor re-took the area at the end of 1790.

1789 France In 1789 Louis XVI called the Estates General to try to solve the financial crisis, but the gathering turned into a national assembly and with army support royal authority was overturned. In 1791 a constitution was introduced loosely based on the 'rights of man', and in 1793 the king was executed and a republic declared. A moderate republic under the Directory ruled from 1795–9 until Napoleon assumed power in 1799.

1789 Liège Middle-class citizens, workers and peasants expelled the prince-bishop. The bishop was restored by Austrian troops in 1790.

1790 Hungary Magyar nobles rejected edicts of Austrian emperor and demanded greater independence for Hungary within Habsburg empire; later, frightened by peasant disturbances, they accepted a compromise with the monarchy.

1791 Poland The king, supported by patriotic nobles, adopted a constitution to modernize government. Catherine II of Russia organized a counter-revolution with the support of some of the greater nobles to restore the old regime, invaded Poland and divided large areas with Prussia. In 1794 a popular revolt led by patriotic nobles under Kosciuszko was brutally crushed by Russian armies and Poland was partitioned between Russia, Prussia and Austria.

1791 Haiti A slave rising in the western (French) part of the island (Saint-Domingue) resulted in the rise of a black leader, Toussaint l'Ouverture; by 1801 he had conquered the rest of the island from the Spaniards and secured virtual independence. The island was then seized by the French, the rising suppressed and independence not fully secured until 1825.

1793 Sardinia Islanders demanded autonomy within combined kingdom of Piedmont-Sardinia. The king reasserted his authority when the French threat subsided in 1796.

1798 Ireland The rebellion of United Irishmen seeking independence from England was put down by the British army. Leading conspirator, Wolfe Tone, committed suicide.

1804 Serbia Revolt against Ottoman atrocities led to demands for autonomy within the Ottoman empire and later for independence. Rebels under Kara George fought until the Ottoman reoccupation of Serbia in 1813.

1808 Spain A national rising against the French provided an opening for an expeditionary force under Wellington. A liberal constitution was proclaimed by Cortes of Cádiz in 1812, but did not survive the restoration of the Bourbon king in 1814.

1809 Tyrol Tyrol had been taken from Austria by Napoleon in 1805 and given to Bavaria. Peasants rebelled against the new rulers. In spite of a brave stand under Andreas Hofer, an innkeeper, the revolt was crushed by Bavarian and French troops.

1810 Spanish America Discontent increased after 1808 when the colonists were faced with the prospect of new imperialist policies from either Napoleon or Spanish liberals; beginning of the revolutionary movement which secured independence by 1826 (***see*** **p. 226**).

On 14th July 1789 a crowd of Parisians stormed the Bastille fort to release a handful of political prisoners housed there ***(above)***. The incident sparked off a more widespread revolt against the authority of Louis XVI, which led, four years later, to his imprisonment and execution. Bastille Day became the symbol for liberation struggles worldwide.

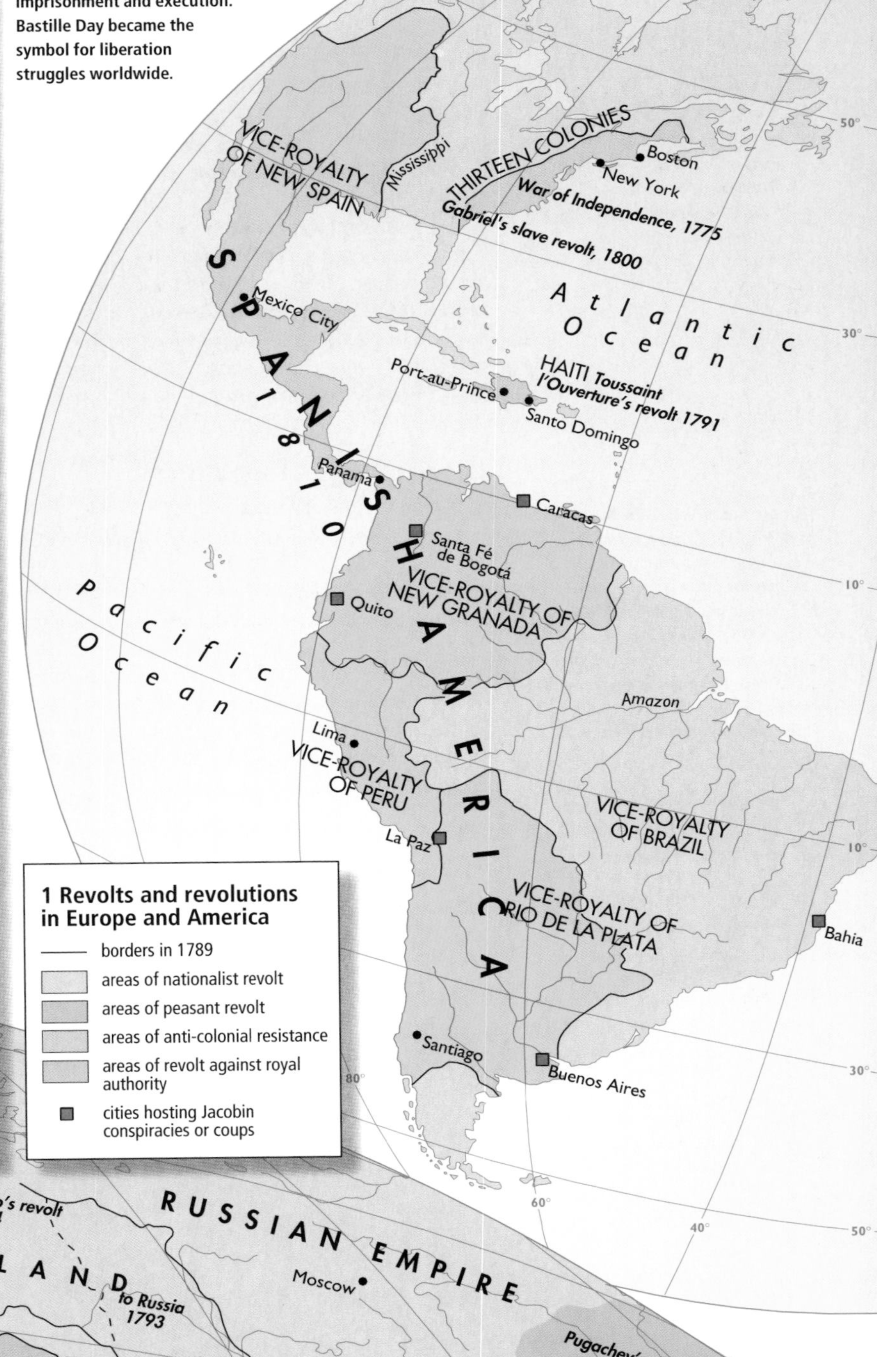

1 Revolts and revolutions in Europe and America

- borders in 1789
- areas of nationalist revolt
- areas of peasant revolt
- areas of anti-colonial resistance
- areas of revolt against royal authority
- cities hosting Jacobin conspiracies or coups

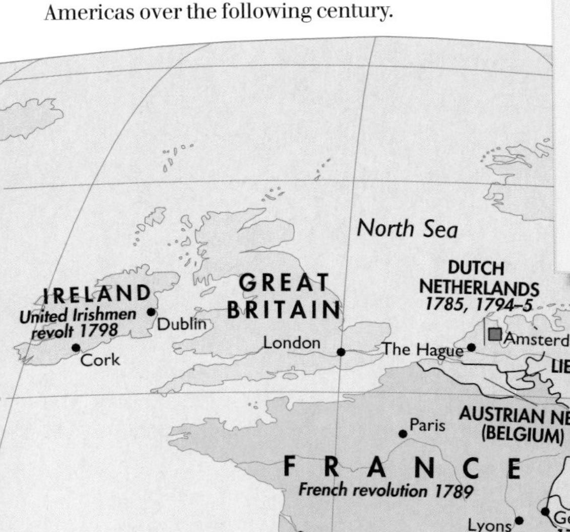

1799 to 1815

Napoleon and the reshaping of Europe

See also
The Mediterranean world, 1494–1797 p. 186
The struggle for empire, 1713–1815 p. 194
The age of revolt, 1773–1814 p. 202
The rise of nationalism in Europe, 1800–1914 p. 214

1799 *Napoleon appointed First Consul*

1804 Code Napoléon *published*

1805 *Battle of Trafalgar; Britain's naval supremacy uncontested*

1806 *Battle of Jena; Germany reshaped into French-dominated client states*

1809–14 *Spanish uprising against France drains French resources*

1812 *Russia invaded; Napoleon suffers catastrophic defeat*

1813 *Battle of the Nations, Leipzig; Napoleon defeated and exiled*

1815 *Battle of Waterloo; Napoleon's final defeat followed by exile to South Atlantic*

Between 1799 and 1815 Napoleon blazed across Europe, plunging the continent into near permanent war and ruthlessly imposing on it French Revolutionary institutions and his own tirelessly cultivated image as a latter-day Julius Caesar. Though he was ultimately defeated and exiled, the world of the *ancien régime* was swept aside for ever.

NAPOLEON, BORN IN 1769 to minor gentry in Corsica, was barely 30 years old when, in November 1799, he became First Consul and de facto ruler of the French First Republic. He had made his name as a Revolutionary general in northern Italy in 1796–7, where his defeat of Austria allowed him to create a new state, the Cisalpine Republic, run on French lines by pro-French Italian notables, a pattern reproduced throughout the areas later conquered by him.

Though Napoleon as First Consul inherited a system with an element of popular participation, within three years the Revolution's democratic aspirations had been smothered and France had been ruthlessly centralized. This concentration of power in his own hands reached its logical conclusion in 1804 with the creation of a French empire over which Napoleon presided as self-appointed emperor.

The primacy of the military

Napoleon's centralization of power took many forms – notably the *Code Napoléon* of 1804 which, in codifying and rationalizing French law, swept away *ancien régime* privilege and increased the power of the French state; the agreement with the Pope in 1802, which ended the dispute for primacy between state and church, again very much in the former's favour; and the creation of a paramilitary police force, the gendarmerie, which mercilessly suppressed opposition to the Revolution. But its overriding characteristic was the mobilization of France on an unprecedented scale in support of the army. With more than 1.5 million Frenchmen under arms, the French economy came to be dominated by the needs of the military.

This was not yet 'total war', but the demands of more than 20 years of conflict turned the Napoleonic empire into a militarized society. The military priorities explain the long string of military triumphs. In 1800 Italy was reconquered and French power extended in Germany. In 1805 Russia and Austria were defeated at Austerlitz and in 1806 Prussia humiliated at Jena. At Eylau in 1807 Russia was again defeated. Under the terms of the subsequent Treaty of Tilsit, French power was extended as far as Poland, where Napoleon established yet another puppet regime, the Grand Duchy of Warsaw.

Napoleon appointed kings, princes and dukes to enforce French rule throughout his empire. In the Kingdom of Westphalia he installed his youngest brother, Jerome. In Naples his brother Joseph was made king. When Joseph was transferred to Spain as its monarch in 1808, Naples was placed under the rule of Napoleon's brother-in-law, Joachim Murat. Holland was ruled by another brother, Louis, from 1806 to 1810. In all these areas, French officials introduced conscription and new taxes, helping finance the almost permanent state of war Napoleon faced.

By 1807 only Britain, at war with France almost

> BETWEEN OLD MONARCHIES AND A YOUNG REPUBLIC THE SPIRIT OF HOSTILITY MUST ALWAYS EXIST. IN THE EXISTING SITUATION EVERY TREATY OF PEACE MEANS TO ME NO MORE THAN A BRIEF ARMISTICE: AND I BELIEVE THAT, WHILE I FILL MY PRESENT OFFICE, MY DESTINY IS TO BE FIGHTING ALMOST CONTINUALLY.
>
> **Napoleon, 1802**
>
> I WISHED TO FOUND A EUROPEAN SYSTEM, A EUROPEAN CODE OF LAWS, A EUROPEAN JUDICIARY: THERE WOULD BE BUT ONE PEOPLE IN EUROPE.
>
> **Napoleon, writing in exile on St Helena**

2 Napoleonic institutions *(map below)*, including the system of departments and local prefects and the famous *Code Napoléon*, were introduced in many of the areas conquered by France. Though Napoleon won the support of local reformers, there was little real social change. In Spain the reforms lasted less than five years and were soon reversed.

1 By 1812 Napoleon dominated most of Europe west of Russia. In western Europe *(map right)* French administrators and local notables tried to modernize law and government. The persistent hostility of Britain undermined the empire. The British supported a series of shifting coalitions against Napoleon. Spain rebelled in 1809 and Russia refused to collaborate in 1812. The failure to conquer Russia weakened France and led to Napoleon's fall in 1814–5. The Congress of Vienna in 1815 tore up the Napoleonic empire.

1 Napoleon and the reshaping of Europe

- French territories ruled directly from Paris, c. 1812
- states ruled by members of Napoleon's family, c. 1812
- other dependent states, c. 1812
- British or British-occupied territory
- French victory / French defeat
- battles of the Italian campaign
- battles in the War of the Second Coalition
- battles of the War of the Third Coalition
- battles in the Austrian War of 1809
- battles in the Peninsular War
- battles of the Russian campaign
- battles of the War of Liberation from French rule
- battles in the defence of France
- battles in the War of the 100 Days

continuously since 1792, remained undefeated. Britain's chief weapon was its navy, largely unchallenged by Napoleon after its defeat of the combined French and Spanish fleets at Trafalgar in 1805. But unable to defeat Napoleon on land, Britain then blockaded French ports. Napoleon responded by forbidding trade with Britain in any of the territories of his empire. But though this, the Continental System, brought hardship to Britain, its effects on France were hardly less severe. The political crisis that followed was made all the more serious when in 1809 Spain revolted against French rule. The 'Spanish Ulcer' drained France of 70 million francs a year. In 1810, Tsar Alexander refused to exclude British trade. In June 1812 Napoleon invaded Russia.

Defeat and exile

It was a fatal miscalculation. With widespread unrest against French rule in much of northern Europe as well as in Spain, Napoleon had overreached himself. As his troops retreated from Moscow, ravaged by hunger, disease and cold, they were harried relentlessly by the Russians. 450,000 began the campaign; only 40,000 survived.

The cost broke the empire. Steep tax rises and conscription caused bitter popular protest. At the same time, Napoleon's enemies, realizing that he could after all be defeated, reformed the coalition against him. At Leipzig in October 1813, the French army was overwhelmed. The following year Napoleon was exiled and the Bourbon monarchy restored. Though Napoleon contrived a final throw, escaping from exile in 1815 and regrouping his army, this time his defeat, at Waterloo, was decisive and he was exiled to St Helena in the South Atlantic, where in 1821 he died.

The treaty drawn up by the Great Powers to decide the fate of Napoleon's empire – the Vienna Settlement of 1815 – aimed not just to overthrow his legacy but to make any further revolutionary upsurge impossible. In the longer term, it failed. Napoleon's reforms had shaken Europe's traditional structures to their foundations, creating the conditions for the emergence of recognizably modern states across Europe.

The remnants of Napoleon's army struggled across the Berezina river in November 1812 on the disastrous retreat from Moscow *(above)*. Thousands of wounded French soldiers had to be abandoned. Napoleon's catastrophic failure in Russia was decisive in his eventual defeat.

The Legion of Honour *(below)* was created in 1802 to reward soldiers and civilians for outstanding service to the state. By 1814 more than 32,000 had been awarded, almost all to soldiers. There were only 1,500 civilian awards, the bulk of them to judges, bishops and prefects.

6

The age of European dominance

BETWEEN 1815 and 1914 Europe thrust out into the world, impelled by the force of its own industrialization. Millions of Europeans poured overseas and into Asiatic Russia, seeking and finding new opportunities in the wider world. Between 1880 and 1900 Africa, a continent four times the size of Europe, was parcelled out among the European powers. And when in 1898 the United States of America, following Europe's lead, annexed Puerto Rico, the Philippines and other islands of the Pacific, and asserted a controlling voice in Latin American affairs, it seemed as though Western expansion had secured the domination of the white race over the non-white majority. But expansion carried with it the seeds of its own destruction. Even before European rivalries plunged the continent into the war of 1914–18, the beginnings of anti-European reaction were visible in Asia and Africa, and no sooner had the United States occupied the Philippines than they were met by a nationalist uprising.

Today, in retrospect, we can see that the age of expansive imperialism was a transient phase of history. Nevertheless, it left a lasting European imprint. The world in 1914 was utterly different from the world in 1815, the tempo of change during the preceding century greater than in entire millennia before it. Though industry in 1914 was only beginning to spread beyond Europe and North America, and life in Asia and Africa was still regulated by age-old traditions, the 19th century inaugurated the process of transformation which dethroned agricultural society as it had existed for thousands of years, replacing it with the urban, industrialized, technocratic society which is spreading – for good or for ill – like wildfire through the world today.

Head of Prince Albert, from the Albert Memorial, London, by John Foley, 1876

Population growth and movements

See also
The emerging global economy p. 198
The industrial revolution in Europe, 1815–70 p. 210
The industrial revolution in Europe, 1870–1914 p. 212
The making of the United States, 1783–1890 p. 218
The United States: a nation of immigrants p. 224
The Russian empire, 1815–1917 p. 230
European colonial empires, 1815–1914 p. 244
The formation of a world economy p. 254

1796 *Jenner introduces vaccination for smallpox*

1812–16 *Last major outbreak of bubonic plague in Europe*

1831–2 *Cholera reaches Europe from China*

1846–7 *Last major famine in Europe*

1870 *Large-scale Jewish emigration from Europe to America begins*

1871 *Austrian government terminates the quarantine frontier against bubonic plague entering Europe*

1877–8 *Famine in China and India*

1891 *USA establishes office to control immigration*

1907 *Peak year for immigration to the USA*

The 19th century witnessed the beginning of the remarkable population explosion which has continued ever since. Europe was at the centre of the surge, sending millions overseas to America, Africa and Australasia. Millions more left the land to work in the bustling cities whose populations grew faster than at any point in their history.

WHEN THOMAS MALTHUS wrote his *Essay on the Principle of Population* at the end of the 18th century the population of Europe, and of much of the rest of the world, had been stagnant for two centuries. Yet Malthus's belief that populations were always restricted – by famine, war and disease – was destroyed by the sudden explosion of world population in the century that followed.

The population explosion

It is estimated that the world's population grew in the 19th century from 900 million to 1,600 million. Much of the increase came from the expansion of the population of Europe, from 123 million to 267 million (excluding Russia). Europe also provided emigrants whose descendants populated the huge areas of the Americas, Australasia, southern Africa and Siberia. The population of these areas increased from 5.7 million to over 200 million between 1810 and 1910. The most heavily industrialized states grew fastest: the populations of the United States, Germany and Britain multiplied fivefold across the century.

Part of the explanation for this sudden burst of population growth lay in the decline of Malthusian checks. There were few major wars in the century after 1815; the spread of cultivation worldwide gradually overcame the regular incidence of famine or poor nutrition; above all, the effects of epidemic disease, particularly in Europe and America, declined significantly.

Smallpox, one of the major killers, was successfully combated by the introduction of Jenner's vaccination. Bubonic plague, still endemic in the Ottoman empire and in Asia, almost disappeared from Europe after 1816. The poor state of urban living produced a new cluster of epidemics – typhus and tuberculosis chiefly – but over the century better public-health measures and quarantine methods, and a general rise in living-standards in Europe and areas of European settlement reduced the general impact of disease. The crisis death-rates of the previous century receded. In France in 1801 only 5,800 out of every 10,000 lived to the age of 20; by 1901 7,300 reached that age.

The rapid growth of cities in Europe and America saw them overtake the greatest cities of India and China in size. In 1800 5.5 million Europeans lived in cities of more than 100,000; by 1900 the figure was 46 million. In cities people tended to marry younger and have more children. Legal controls over the age of marriage disappeared, while larger families provided a stream of young workers and a kinship group which could support the interests of the family as a whole. The rising birth-rate and the slowly falling death-rate produced a 'demographic gap', an excess of births over deaths that created a favourable cycle for further high growth.

> IN EXAMINING THE PRINCIPAL STATES OF MODERN EUROPE, WE SHALL FIND, THAT THOUGH THEY HAVE INCREASED VERY CONSIDERABLY IN POPULATION SINCE THEY WERE NATIONS OF SHEPHERDS, YET THAT, AT PRESENT, THEIR PROGRESS IS BUT SLOW. THE CAUSE OF THIS SLOW PROGRESS IN POPULATION CANNOT BE TRACED TO A DECAY OF THE PASSIONS BETWEEN THE SEXES ... WHY THEN DO NOT ITS EFFECTS APPEAR IN A RAPID INCREASE IN THE HUMAN SPECIES?
>
> **Thomas Malthus**
> ***An Essay on the Principle of Population*, *1798***

The movement of population

High population growth produced many pressures to migrate. In rural areas migration increased

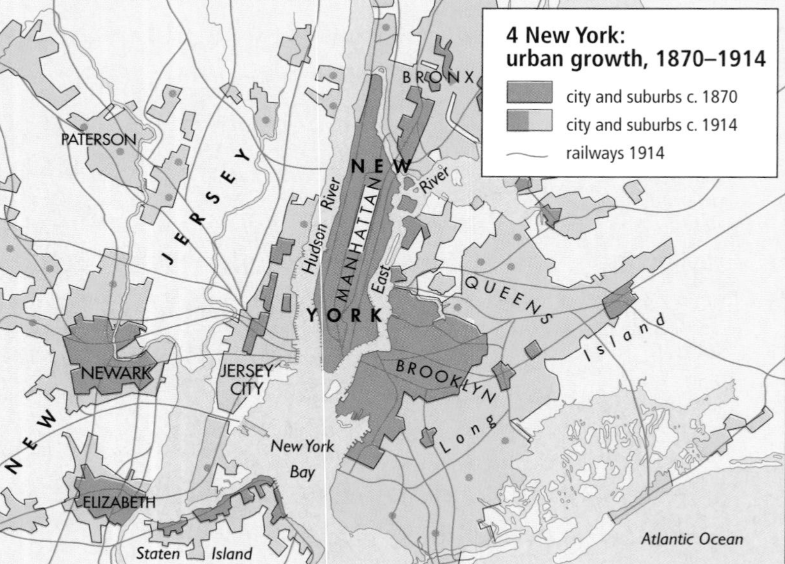

4 By 1810 New York *(map above)* **had outstripped its rivals to become the most dynamic urban centre in the New World. In 1810 its population was 100,000. By 1871 it had grown to more than a million, and by 1914 had reached over three million. More than two-thirds of all 19th-century immigrants to the United States passed through the city. The Statue of Liberty** *(below)* **symbolized to immigrants the promise of a new and better life held out to them by the New World.**

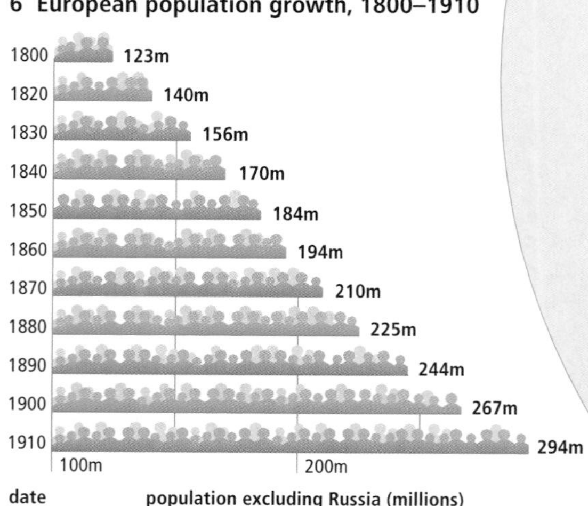

6 Population growth in Europe *(chart above)* **accelerated in the first four decades of the 19th century, slowed in the mid-century period of famine and revolution and revived strongly from the 1860s, when the peak of births over deaths was reached. From 1910 rates of growth slowed and have declined steadily since.**

rapidly as peasants left their villages to find city work. In Russia and Spain migrant workers were a traditional source of labour throughout the century. Elsewhere, workers flocked to where mines and factories were springing up. Polish workers moved to the Ruhr mines; Irish workers travelled to Scotland and Lancashire; Italians worked in France and Germany. By 1914 there were an estimated 3 million migrant workers in Europe.

The promise of economic opportunity also lured millions overseas. Between 1801 and 1840 only 1.5 million left Europe, mainly for the United States; between 1841 and 1880 the figure leapt to 13 million; and between 1880 and 1910 it leapt again to 25 million. Some migrants returned (estimates suggest as many as 25 per cent), but those who stayed in the vast expanses of America or Australia or southern Africa became buoyant population groups with high growth rates, better diets and more opportunities than Europe could provide. Some migrants were the victims of coercion – the threat of famine took millions from Ireland; political or racial persecution pushed out thousands more, particularly from eastern Europe – but most were lured by the promise of wealth, freedom or adventure. Between 1800 and 1930 the white proportion of the world's population expanded from 22 to 35 per cent.

Europeans were not the only ones on the move. Chinese and Indian emigrants reached the Caribbean and Africa in search of work and business openings. Japanese workers crossed the Pacific to west-coast America. Until the 1820s slaves were still shipped from Africa to the plantations of the New World, and continued to be shipped to the Middle East until the major slave markets of Zanzibar and Madagascar were closed in the 1870s. Gradually the movement of populations became regulated by governments as local labour forces, once migrants themselves, began to protest at the further flow of fresh recruits.

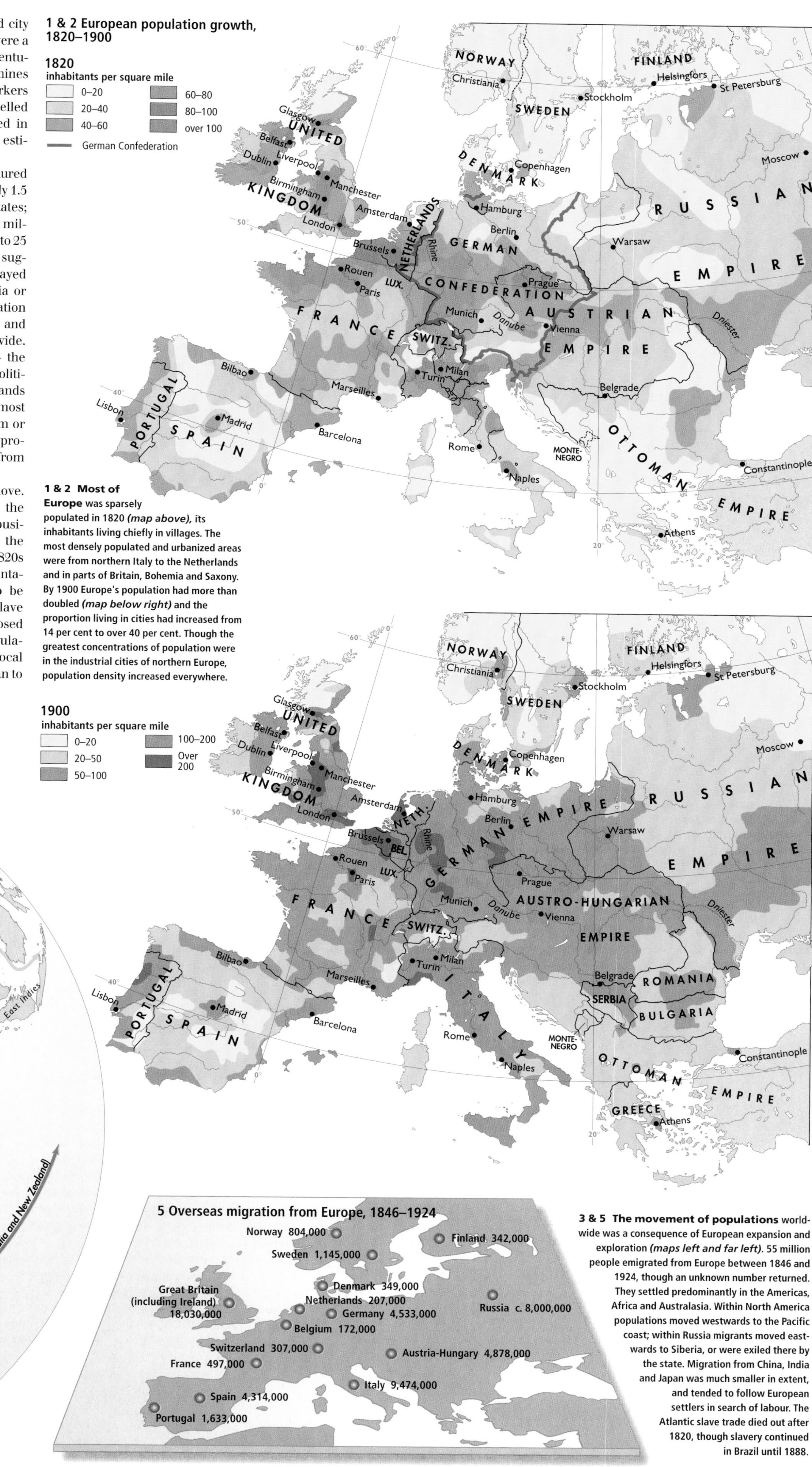

1 & 2 Most of Europe was sparsely populated in 1820 *(map above)*, its inhabitants living chiefly in villages. The most densely populated and urbanized areas were from northern Italy to the Netherlands and in parts of Britain, Bohemia and Saxony. By 1900 Europe's population had more than doubled *(map below right)* and the proportion living in cities had increased from 14 per cent to over 40 per cent. Though the greatest concentrations of population were in the industrial cities of northern Europe, population density increased everywhere.

3 & 5 The movement of populations worldwide was a consequence of European expansion and exploration *(maps left and far left)*. 55 million people emigrated from Europe between 1846 and 1924, though an unknown number returned. They settled predominantly in the Americas, Africa and Australasia. Within North America populations moved westwards to the Pacific coast; within Russia migrants moved eastwards to Siberia, or were exiled there by the state. Migration from China, India and Japan was much smaller in extent, and tended to follow European settlers in search of labour. The Atlantic slave trade died out after 1820, though slavery continued in Brazil until 1888.

The industrial revolution in Europe

See also
The industrial revolution begins: Great Britain, 1760–1860 p. 200
Population growth and movements p. 208
The industrial revolution in Europe, 1870–1914 p. 212
Germany and Italy: the struggles for unification, 1815–71 p. 216
European colonial empires, 1815–1914 p. 244
The formation of a world economy, 1870–1914 p. 254

1781 *Steam engine first used in Europe*

1828 *First modern blast furnace in Silesia*

1834 *Zollverein formed*

1837 *First French railway, Paris to St-Germain*

1846 *Central Bank established in Prussia*

1849 *Iron first produced from coke in the Ruhr*

1855 *Bessemer steel process developed by Krupp*

1857 *Danube and Danish Sound opened to free navigation*

1860 *Anglo-French Free Trade treaty*

Before 1870, industrialization spread only slowly across Europe. Industrial regions grew up around major ore- and coalfields, drawing in millions of workers from the villages to form a new class of labouring poor. Marx called them the proletariat, and defined the new era as the age of capitalism. Yet two-thirds of Europe still worked the land.

INDUSTRIALIZATION IN EUROPE was a slow and uneven process in the first half of the 19th century. Europe had a rich industrial heritage and was a far from undeveloped area in 1800, but most production was undertaken in villages or in small guild communities in the towns. Poor communications and shortages of capital ensured that these older forms of production survived long into the century until mechanized factory production and the railway finally forced the old trades to change.

Proto-industrialization

The early stage of industrial modernization has been described as 'proto-industrialization'. The term reflects the survival of traditional production methods alongside a small number of experimental firms using methods and technology borrowed, in many cases, from Britain. The textile industry in Europe was typical of this development. The mechanization of spinning developed very slowly. In Saxony, north Germany, British engineers introduced mechanical spinning in 1807, and the first steam driven machinery only in 1831. Hand-loom weaving survived in much of Europe until the late 19th century, and in France the proportion of Lyons silk produced in small rural workshops actually increased from 22 per cent in 1830 to 75 per cent in 1870.

The transformation of heavy industry was also slow. Coke-fired iron production had revolutionized British industry, but in Germany by the 1850s charcoal furnaces still provided 70 per cent of iron production. The first coke furnace in France was built in 1823, yet by 1850 only 41 per cent of iron was produced from coke. Belgium, thanks to its abundant supplies of easily mined coal, was the only country to emulate Britain. With the import of British technology and craftsmen, the Belgian coalfield became the first modern industrial region in continental Europe. As late as 1860 Belgium remained second to Britain in per capita output of coal and iron and in the density of its rail network.

> THE BOURGEOISIE HAS CREATED MORE MASSIVE AND MORE COLOSSAL PRODUCTIVE FORCES THAN HAVE ALL PRECEDING GENERATIONS TOGETHER. SUBJECTION OF NATURE'S FORCES TO MAN, MACHINERY, APPLICATION OF CHEMISTRY TO INDUSTRY AND AGRICULTURE, STEAM-NAVIGATION, RAILWAYS, ELECTRIC TELEGRAPHS ... CANALISATION OF RIVERS ... WHAT EARLIER CENTURY HAD EVER A PRESENTIMENT THAT SUCH PRODUCTIVE FORCES SLUMBERED IN THE LAP OF SOCIAL LABOUR?
>
> **Karl Marx**
> ***Manifesto of the Communist Party, 1848***

The mid-century boom

The European economy, like the British, depended for industrial development on changes in the wider economic framework. Between 1850 and 1870 Europe experienced a remarkable economic boom which helped to accelerate the drive to industrialize. There were a number of factors at work. The spread of the railway and steam navigation opened up markets, stimulated employment and permitted the supply of cheap foodstuffs. The reform of Europe's banking system in the 1850s saw the foundation of numerous investment and mortgage banks which channelled money towards business and helped to modernize agriculture. Under Napoleon III, France helped to set up modern systems of credit; note circulation there trebled between 1850 and 1870.

The role of the state was particularly important. After the severe credit and food crisis of the 1840s, which culminated in the failed 1848 revolutions (*see* p. 214), most regimes recognized the need to modernize the economy to strengthen the state. One way was to build railways. The main European networks outside Russia were laid between 1850 and 1870, usually with state regulation and financial assistance. There were 15,000 miles of track in 1850, most of it in Britain and Belgium; by 1870, another 50,000 miles had been added. Another way was to build up modern armed forces, which required high-quality weaponry and substantial investment in metalworking and machinery.

The state also played a key part in improving conditions for trade both within and between European states. Inspired by British ideas of Free Trade, many of the existing barriers to the movement and sale of goods were removed. In many cases guild regulations were suspended to allow free manufacture and trade. Usury laws were abolished (Britain 1854, Netherlands 1857, Prussia 1867) to allow a freer capital market. The major rivers of Europe were gradually opened up to international traffic and the hundreds of tolls and

4 Coal output, 1820–70*

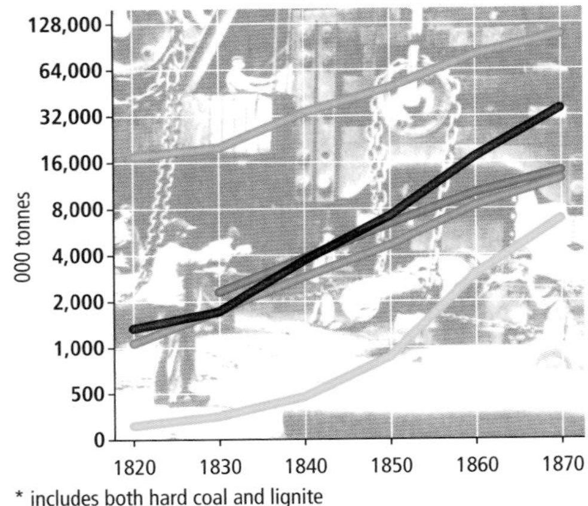

* includes both hard coal and lignite

5 Pig iron output, 1820–70

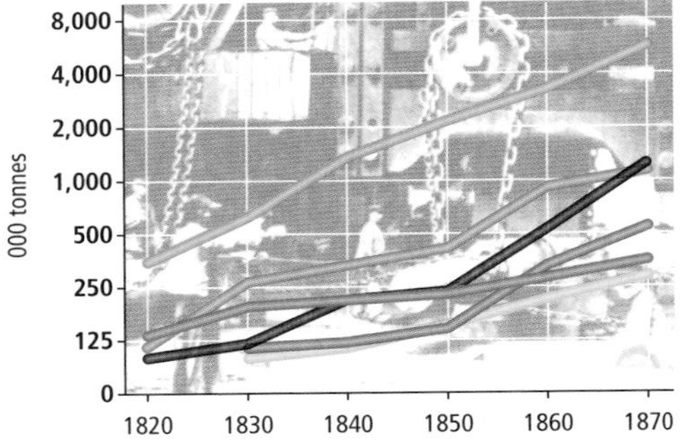

6 Length of railway line open, 1840–70

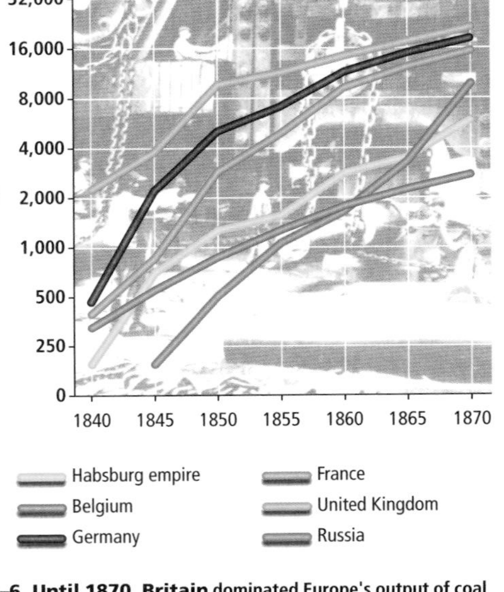

Habsburg empire
Belgium
Germany
France
United Kingdom
Russia

4–6 Until 1870, Britain dominated Europe's output of coal and iron and, despite its relative smallness, enjoyed a lead in railway development ***(charts above)***. In 1850 there were 2.1 miles of railway for every 60 square miles in Britain: the equivalent figures in France and Germany were 0.4 miles and 0.7 miles respectively. Railway-building in turn boosted iron and coal output, while the rail networks carried foodstuffs, fuel and raw material to hitherto inaccessible markets.

2 European trade was severely hampered in the pre-industrial age by thousands of local tariffs and tolls. Internal duties were scrapped in revolutionary France in 1791 and were progressively reduced in the German and Habsburg lands. In 1834 Prussia reached agreement with six other German states to establish a German free trade area or *Zollverein (map below)*. Trade between states, however, continued to be dominated by protective tariffs.

2 European customs unions from 1848

A French poster of 1842 celebrates the arrival of the railway in France *(right)*. The first railway was built between Paris and Saint-Germain in 1837 and its immediate success prompted railway mania. Within years there were 33 rail companies, many of which went bankrupt. In 1842 the 'Organic Railway Law' set up a national route system supervised by the state but operated by private companies. By 1850 France had over 2000 miles of track.

3 The Ruhr valley became the heart of the Prussian industrial revolution *(map below)*. The exploitation of the rich coalfield expanded steadily from the 1840s. In 1850 the Ruhr supplied 1.6 million tons of coal; by 1910 the figure was 88 million. Thanks to local supplies of 'blackband' ore, the iron industry expanded together with the coal. When the ore ran out supplies were imported from Spain and Sweden.

dues removed – the Danube in 1857, the Rhine in 1861, the Scheldt in Belgium in 1863. Finally, common commercial codes were drawn up to ensure respect for contracts and to remove the thousands of local regulations and privileges that had often made trade and production impossible.

A wave of entrepreneurial energy was released. In 1834 there were 15.4 million cotton spindles in Europe, 10 million of them in Britain. By 1877 there were 64 million, with 44 million in Britain. The output of iron increased sharply. In 1800 European iron output averaged approximately 9 kg per head; in 1870 the figure was 70 kg. Nonetheless, more than half of that iron was produced in Britain, which also produced 90 per cent of Europe's shipping and two-thirds of its textiles.

Though industry had made strides in Europe by 1870, most Europeans still lived and worked on the land and much production remained unmechanized and small in scale. Outside the major concentrations of industrial development traditional patterns of production still prevailed.

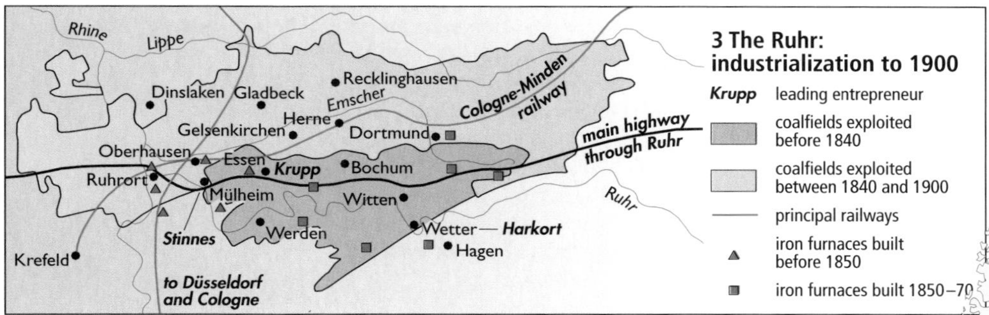

3 The Ruhr: industrialization to 1900

Krupp leading entrepreneur
coalfields exploited before 1840
coalfields exploited between 1840 and 1900
principal railways
iron furnaces built before 1850
iron furnaces built 1850–70

1 Europe: industrialization to 1870

percentage of total population living in cities of 100,000 or more (1850):
5% or less
6%–10%
20% or more
railway development by 1850
railway development, 1850–70
major coalfields
major lignite fields
major iron ore fields
centres of industrial development and concentration

1 Industrial development proceeded slowly in Europe until the coming of the railways in the 1840s and 1850s and the emergence of a more sophisticated banking system *(map right)*. The strong traditions of craft and luxury production survived, but on the coal- and ironfields close to navigable rivers or canals there grew up iron, steel and machinery production. Much manufacturing – textiles, metal goods, leatherwork – was still carried out in 'industrial villages.' Urbanization on any scale occurred only in Britain.

1870 to 1914

The industrial revolution in Europe

See also
The emerging global economy p. 198
Population growth and movements, 1815–1914 p. 208
The industrial revolution in Europe, 1815–1870 p. 210
The Russian empire: expansion and modernization, 1815–1917 p. 230
European colonial empires, 1815–1914 p. 244
The formation of a world economy, 1870–1914 p. 254

From 1870 to 1914 Europe experienced a 'Second Industrial Revolution' based on booming world trade and the establishment of a popular consumer market. Electricity, chemicals and motor vehicles replaced iron, coal and railways as the driving forces of economic change. Germany superseded Britain as the industrial heartland of Europe.

BETWEEN 1870 AND THE outbreak of the First World War in 1914, Europe moved into the so-called 'Second Industrial Revolution' based not on coal, iron and railways but on steel, chemicals, electricity and oil. Much of Europe remained underdeveloped even by 1914, but the new technologies and materials allowed economies less well-endowed than Britain's had been to move rapidly to the second stage of industrial expansion. Nonetheless, Britain still remained Europe's largest manufacturer and the world's leading trader. British capital and technology continued to play a part in the modernization of the continental economy, even though the new inventions which heralded the second stage of industrialization came mainly from Germany and the United States.

The new industries

After the boom of the 1850s and 1860s the European economy entered a long period of low growth popularly called the 'Great Depression' (1873–96). Rapid expansion of industrial output resulted in over-capacity leading to falling prices and profits, exacerbated by a shortage of gold in economies whose currencies were largely based upon the Gold Standard. Furthermore, there were limits to the exploitation of the technical breakthroughs that had made the first wave of industrialization possible.

Nonetheless, from the 1870s an exceptional period of scientific and technical invention set in, which in time opened the way to further industrial growth. Steelmaking was among the most important of the new sectors. The discovery of the Gilchrist-Thomas method for separating phosphorus from iron ore in 1879 allowed the exploitation of the ore deposits of the Ruhr, Lorraine, the English Midlands and Austria. Steel output in Europe expanded from 125,000 tons in 1861 to 38 million tons in 1913. The substitution of electric power for coal and gas was made possible with the development of modern generating equipment in the 1860s, particularly hydro-electricity, which was first used in the Alps and the Pyrenees. The electrical industry was dominated by the German firm of Siemens, which moved from electric cables to the production of telephones and electric railways in the 1870s. By 1914 half of the world's electrical trade originated in Germany.

The chemical industry, too, made great strides in Germany. Aniline dyestuffs developed in Britain and France in the 1850s were overtaken by alizarin dyes extracted from coal tar which were developed first in Germany. By 1913, 80 per cent of the world's dyestuffs were produced in Germany. It was thus no accident that in the 1880s Germany was home to the first true internal combustion engine and the first motor-car (developed separately by Daimler and Benz), and in the 1890s produced the Diesel engine and the carburettor.

The new industrial nations

Germany was the most successful of the new industrial powers that emerged in Europe after 1870, and by 1913 was second only to the United States. But the development of effective transport and finance networks, together with the growth of a wider world market and rising real incomes in Europe, encouraged the further spread of industry. The Austro-Hungarian empire, Italy, Spain and Russia all developed modern industrial regions within economies that remained primarily agrarian. Russia made the most progress. From a modest foundation in the 1880s, the Russian empire became the fifth largest industrial nation in 1913. Railways and foreign capital were the key to rapid expansion of the regions around Moscow, St Petersburg and the Donbass. Much of the technology had to be imported, along with the engineers and managers to run the large new factories. In the Caucasus there developed a remarkable oil rush which saw production increase from 2 million barrels in 1870 to 631 million in 1900, when Russia supplied one-third of the world's oil.

Russian modernization was helped by the remarkable boom in world trade which occurred from 1896 to 1913. Improved wage rates in the developed areas of Europe combined with falling food and commodity prices to release high levels of demand for consumer goods. The mass market became a reality after 1870, and businessmen catered for it with packaged and processed food, cheap household items and, from the 1890s, with bicycles, phonographs and box cameras. By 1914 European society demonstrated sharp contrasts – a modernized, prosperous urban core which embraced the new consumer age, and a large residue of poorer villagers and labourers whose way of life remained largely unchanged.

1873 *Onset of the 'Great Depression'*

1879 *Gilchrist-Thomas method for steel production*

1885 *Benz develops first petrol-driven car*

1888 *Hoechst develops first chemical painkiller*

1889 *Eiffel Tower built*

1890 *First electric tram, in Florence*

1891–1905 *Trans-Siberian railway built*

1896 *Marconi builds first radio transmitter*

1908 *First unassisted powered flight, in France*

One of the first motor-cars in Britain, a Daimler, pictured in Coventry in 1898 *(left)*. The invention of the internal combustion engine transformed the industrial face of Europe, amply living up to early prophecies that it would become 'the real power-machine of the masses'. Though the early breakthroughs were German, by 1900 France had become Europe's preeminent car manufacturer.

1 After 1870, industry began to spread out from Britain and northwest Europe into Italy, Spain, the Austro-Hungarian empire and Russia *(map below)*. By 1914 Britain had been replaced by Germany as the main industrial power and Russia was fast closing the gap. Yet even in Germany only 36 per cent of the workforce was employed in manufacturing; in the Austro-Hungarian empire it was 20 per cent and in Spain 13 per cent. Handicrafts and rural trades survived alongside the bustling industrial cities, which were transformed by electric light, tramcars and motor vehicles.

In the hundred years of the last century the organization of industry changed completely. The small producer was superseded by the captain of industry, and the small company gave way to the trust, sometimes so colossal as to stupefy the imagination ... A hundred years ago business was limited in area, now it is world-wide; the orders were given in person or by stage-coach post, now they are sent by letter, telephone, telegraph or wireless.

Frank McVey
Modern Industrialism, 1903

1 The industrialization of Europe, 1870–1914

areas of industrial concentration 1870–1914
centres of textile industry
centres of chemical industry
centres of shipbuilding
coalfields
centres of engineering, armaments and metal industries
iron ore fields
lignite fields
potash fields
centres of petroleum industry
European railway network, 1870
railway development, 1870–1914

2 Coal output, 1875–1913

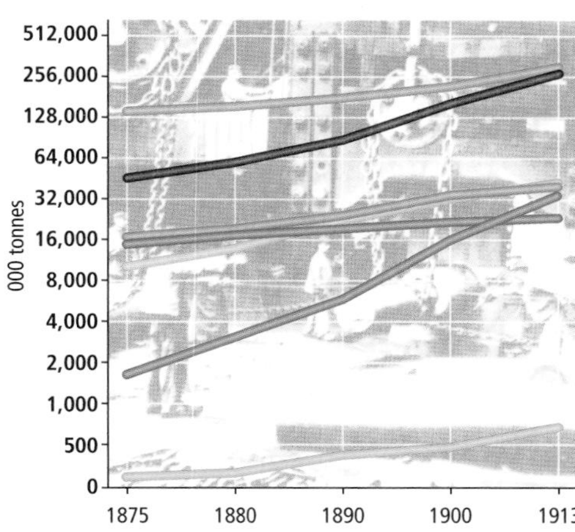

3 Pig iron output, 1875–1913

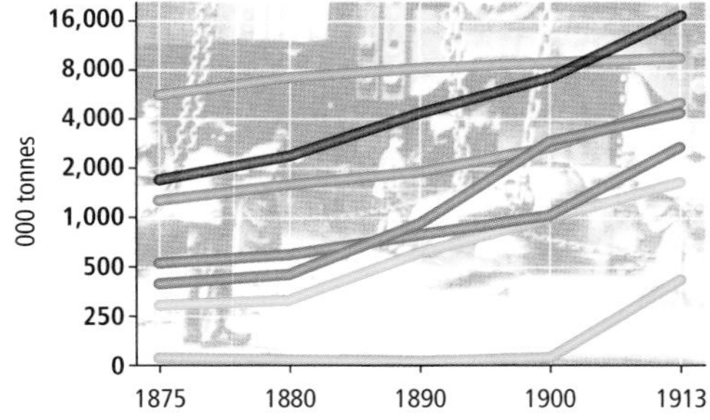

4 Length of railway line open, 1875–1913

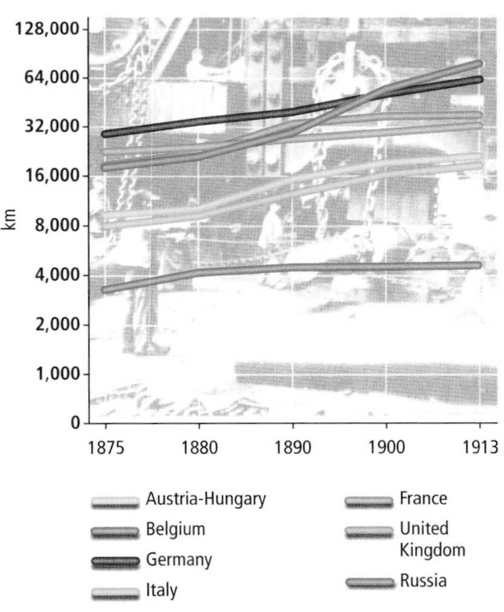

Austria-Hungary
Belgium
Germany
Italy
France
United Kingdom
Russia

2–4 The output of coal and iron (and of steel from the 1870s) expanded steadily after 1870 and rapidly in the decade before 1914 *(charts above)*. The exploitation of the Donbass region in Russia and the spread of Russian railways opened up the vast areas of eastern Europe to industrial development. The railways not only stimulated demand for the materials to build them, but also employed millions. By 1896 the largest economies produced more than 34 million horsepower from the application of steam, as much as 75 per cent of it on the railways. In 1860 the figure had been only 5.5 million.

The rise of nationalism in Europe

See also
The age of revolt, 1773–1814 p. 202
Napoleon and the reshaping of Europe p. 204
Germany and Italy: the struggles for unification p. 216
The disintegration of the Ottoman empire p. 228
European rivalries and alliances, 1878–1914 p. 248
The First World War, 1914–18 p. 250
Imperialism and nationalism, 1919–41 p. 258
European political problems, 1919–34 p. 262

NO PEOPLE EVER DIE, NOR STOP SHORT UPON THEIR PATH, BEFORE THEY HAVE ACHIEVED THE ULTIMATE AIM OF THEIR EXISTENCE, BEFORE HAVING COMPLETED AND FULFILLED THEIR MISSION. A PEOPLE DESTINED TO ACHIEVE GREAT THINGS FOR THE WELFARE OF HUMANITY MUST ONE DAY OR OTHER BE CONSTITUTED A NATION.

Giuseppe Mazzini, 1861

The French revolution paved the way for the modern nation-state. Across Europe radical intellectuals questioned the old monarchical order and encouraged the development of a popular nationalism committed to re-drawing the political map of the continent. By 1914 the days of the old multi-national empires were numbered.

1815 *The Congress of Vienna*

1822 *Greek declaration of national independence*

1848 *Nationalist revolts in Hungary, Italy and Germany*

1859–61 *Italy unified*

1863 *Polish national revolt*

1866–71 *Germany unified*

1867 *Hungary granted autonomy*

1878 *Congress of Berlin: Serbia, Romania, Montenegro granted independence*

1908 *Bulgaria becomes independent*

THE FRENCH REVOLUTION, by destroying the traditional structures of power in France and in the territories conquered by Napoleon, was the instrument for the political transformation of Europe. Revolutionary armies carried with them not only the slogan of 'liberty, equality and fraternity' but ideas of liberalism and national self-determinism. National awakening also grew out of an intellectual reaction to the Enlightenment that emphasized national identity and developed a romantic view of cultural self-expression through nationhood. The key exponent of the modern idea of the nation-state was the German philosopher Georg Hegel (1770–1831), who argued that a sense of nationality was the essential cement that held modern societies together in an age when dynastic and religious allegiance was in decline.

In 1815, at the end of the Napoleonic wars, the major powers of Europe tried to restore the old dynastic system as far as possible, ignoring the principle of nationality in favour of 'legitimism', the assertion of traditional claims to royal authority. With most of Europe's peoples still loyal to their local province or city, nationalism was confined to small groups of intellectuals and political radicals. Furthermore, political repression, symbolized by the Carlsbad Decrees published in Austria in 1819, pushed nationalist agitation underground.

The struggle for independence

Nevertheless there began to develop a strong resentment of what came to be regarded as foreign rule. In Ireland, Italy, Belgium, Greece, Poland, Hungary and Norway local hostility to alien dynastic authority started to take the form of nationalist agitation. Nationalism came to be seen as the most effective way to create the symbols of resistance and to unite in a common cause.

Success came first in Greece where an eight-year civil war (1822–30) against Ottoman rule led to the creation of an independent Greek state, while in 1831 Belgium obtained its independence from the Netherlands. Over the next two decades nationalism developed a more powerful voice, spurred by nationalist writers championing the cause of national self-determination. In 1848 revolutions broke out across Europe, sparked by a severe famine and economic crisis and mounting popular demands for political change. In Italy Giuseppe Mazzini used the opportunity to encourage a war for national unification; in Hungary Lajos Kossuth led a national revolt against Austrian rule; in the German Confederation a National Assembly was elected at Frankfurt, where it debated the creation of a German nation.

None of the nationalist revolts in 1848 was successful, any more than the two attempts to win

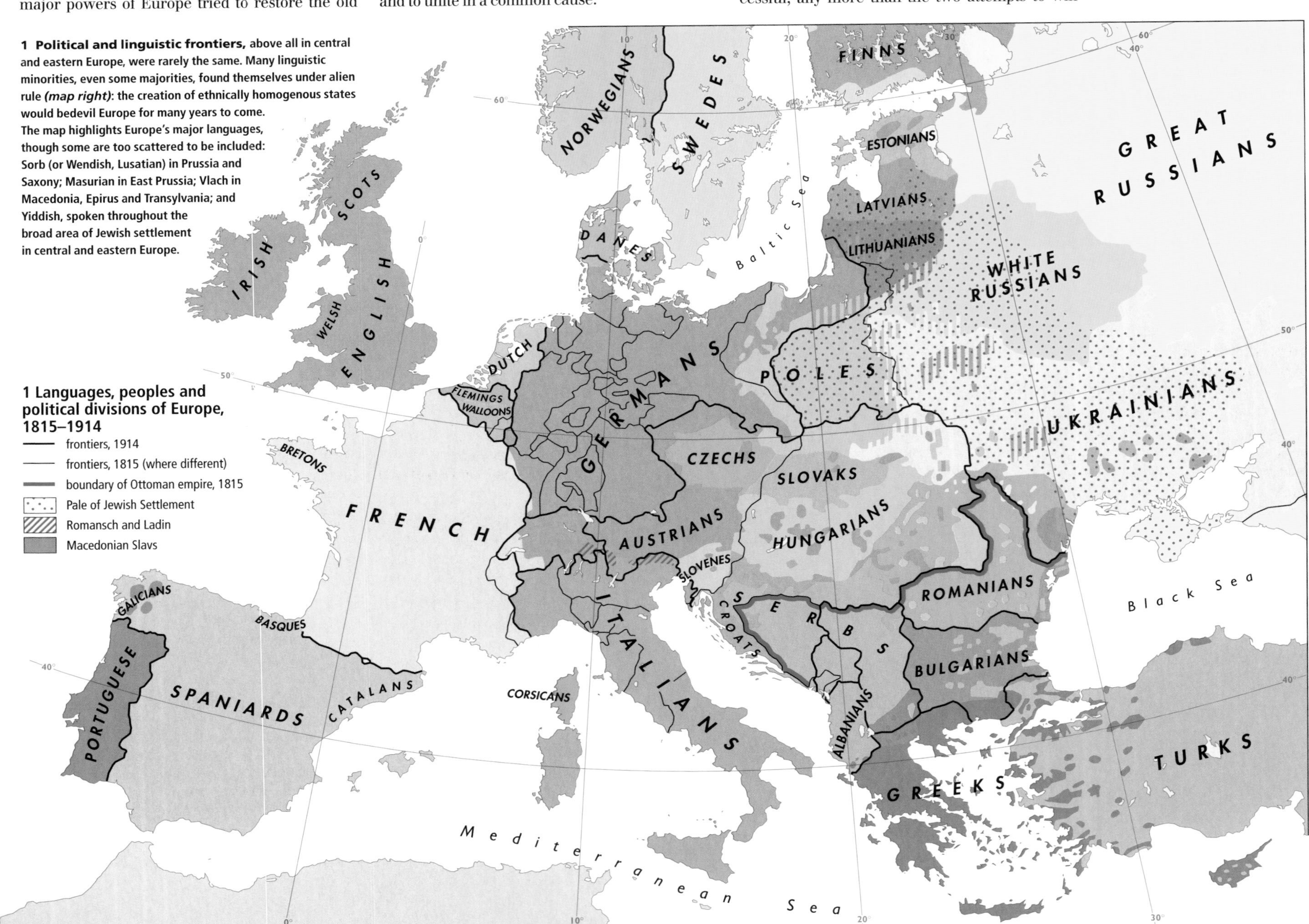

1 Political and linguistic frontiers, above all in central and eastern Europe, were rarely the same. Many linguistic minorities, even some majorities, found themselves under alien rule *(map right)*: the creation of ethnically homogenous states would bedevil Europe for many years to come. The map highlights Europe's major languages, though some are too scattered to be included: Sorb (or Wendish, Lusatian) in Prussia and Saxony; Masurian in East Prussia; Vlach in Macedonia, Epirus and Transylvania; and Yiddish, spoken throughout the broad area of Jewish settlement in central and eastern Europe.

2 The Balkans, 1830–1908

- frontier of Ottoman empire, 1800
- boundaries agreed by the Treaty of San Stefano, 1878

territories lost by Ottoman empire by Treaty of Berlin, 1878

- to Romania
- to Serbia
- to Montenegro
- frontier of Ottoman empire, 1908
- frontiers, 1908

Polish independence from Russian rule in 1831 and 1846 had been. Conservative forces proved too strong, while the majority of the populations little understood the meaning of national struggle. But the 1848 crisis had given nationalism its first full public airing, and in the 30 years that followed no fewer than seven new national states were created in Europe. This was partly the result of the recognition by conservative forces that the old order could not continue in its existing form. Conservative reformers such as Cavour and Bismarck (*see* pp. 216–7) made common cause with liberal political modernizers to create a consensus for the creation of conservative nation-states in Italy and Germany. In the Habsburg empire a compromise was reached with Hungarian nationalists in 1867 granting them a virtually independent state. In the Balkans (*see* map 2) the Greek example had inspired other national awakenings. Native history and culture were rediscovered and appropriated for the national struggle. Following a conflict between Russia and Turkey, the Great Powers met at Berlin in 1878 and granted independence to Romania, Serbia and Montenegro.

Nationalism exported

The invention of a symbolic national identity became the concern of racial or linguistic groups throughout Europe as they struggled to come to terms with the rise of mass politics, popular xenophobia and the decline of traditional social elites. Within the Habsburg empire the different races developed a more mass-based, violent and exclusive nationalism, even among the Germans and Magyars, who actually benefited from the power-structure of the empire. The Jewish population of eastern and central Europe began to develop radical demands for their own national state in Palestine. In 1897, inspired by the Hungarian-born nationalist Theodor Herzl (1860–1904), the First Zionist Congress was held in Basle. On the European periphery, especially in Ireland and Norway, campaigns for national independence became more strident. In 1905 Norway won independence from Sweden, but attempts to grant Ireland the kind of autonomy enjoyed by Hungary foundered on the national divisions in the island between the ethnic Irish and British migrants.

By this time the ideals of European nationalism had been exported worldwide and were now beginning to threaten the colonial empires still ruled by European nation-states.

2 In 1815 the Balkan peninsula *(above)* was still within the increasingly decrepit Ottoman empire. The combination of weakening Ottoman control, Russian and Austrian designs on the region and the rise of Balkan nationalism in territories far less ethnically homogenous than those in western Europe destabilized the region well into the 20th century. Only Greek independence proved relatively trouble free. Bulgaria's bitter fight for liberation, helped by Russia, was followed by the Russian-imposed Treaty of San Stefano. The huge Bulgarian state this created was unacceptable to the other Great Powers, who feared Russian influence in the region. The Treaty of Berlin, signed the same year, overturned it: Bulgarian resentment festered for years. The treaty also confirmed the independence of Serbia, Romania and Montenegro.

Seeing the Greeks as the modern heirs of the classical civilization of ancient Greece, the Great Powers put aside their instinctive desire to maintain the existing order and contributed decisively to their fight for independence. At the battle of Navarino *(right)*, fought in October 1827, a combined British, French and Russian force annihilated the Ottoman fleet, paving the way for Greek independence three years later.

1815 to 1871

Germany and Italy: the struggles for unification

See also
The Holy Roman Empire, 1493–1806 p. 190
Napoleon and the reshaping of Europe, 1799–1815 p. 204
The industrial revolution in Europe, 1815–70 p. 210
The rise of nationalism in Europe, 1800–1914 p. 214
European rivalries and alliances, 1878–1914 p. 248

The French revolution laid the foundation for a romantic nationalism in Italy and Germany that was harshly suppressed after 1815. The two regions were united in the end not by popular nationalism but by the ambitions of the major powers and the machinations of statesmen who preferred to unify from above rather than risk revolutionary demands.

THE ROOTS OF ITALIAN and German nationalism lay in the reaction to French domination under the Napoleonic empire. In both regions the experience of French revolutionary rule stimulated the emergence of a nationalist intelligentsia committed to the development of a native culture and language. National development was seen as the key to political freedom and economic success.

The struggle for nationhood

In 1815 the Vienna Settlement restored the conservative order in Germany and Italy. Secret societies kept nationalist aspirations alive – the *carbonari* in Italy, the student *Burschenschaften* in Germany – but the Habsburg empire, guided by Chancellor Metternich, smothered demands for national unification. What protest there was, for example in Italy in 1820–1 and 1830–1, was more anti-Austrian than actively nationalist in character. Most German and Italian liberals looked for constitutional reform, civil rights and economic freedoms rather than for unity.

The revolutionary upheavals of the 1840s gave impetus to the infant nationalist movements. Economic crisis combined with increasing resentment at the absence of political reform to produce growing demands for nationhood. In Italy Mazzini, who founded the Young Italy movement in 1831, inspired a generation of young nationalists. When revolt broke out in 1848, Mazzini was among the revolutionaries demanding a new national Italian state. Austrian forces crushed the revolutions and defeated the army of Charles Albert of Piedmont-Sardinia, who had briefly placed himself at the forefront of Italian revival, the *risorgimento*.

In Germany the 1848 crisis gave nationalist circles, drawn largely from the educated bourgeoisie, the opportunity to overturn the Habsburg-dominated German Confederation, which had been revived in 1815, and to replace it with a united German nation. Though a national assembly met at Frankfurt, it found itself split between those who wanted a Germany which included Austria (*Grossdeutschland*) and those who wanted a smaller Germany free of Habsburg interference (*Kleindeutschland*). The debate proved academic: in 1849 Prussian troops disbanded the parliament and reimposed the old order.

The failure of 1848 pushed nationalism to the margins again. Mazzini launched nationalist revolts in the 1850s, but with no success. It took ten years before a National Society was founded in Germany, and its numbers never exceeded 25,000. In the event the unification of Italy and Germany was made possible not through nationalist agitation but as a result of the changing character of the conservative order, both at home and abroad. In Germany and Italy conservative reformers emerged who were hostile to the continuation of Austrian dominance but fearful of mass politics and revolution. A programme of 'reform from above' was initiated, led by the major regional states, Prussia in Germany, Piedmont-Sardinia in Italy.

Unification from above

In Italy the lead was taken by Count Cavour, who became Piedmontese prime minister in 1852. He introduced economic, military and constitutional reforms that made Piedmont the most advanced state in the peninsula. When Austria found itself isolated internationally after the Crimean War (1853–5), Cavour opportunistically allied with

1831 *Mazzini founds Young Italy movement*

1848 *Italian states revolt against Austrian rule*

1848–9 *German national assembly tries to build united German state*

1852 *Cavour prime minister of Piedmont*

1858 *National Society established in Germany*

1859–60 *Piedmont leads drive to unify Italy*

1862 *Bismarck minister-president of Prussia*

1866 *War between Prussia and Austria*

1867 *North German Confederation founded*

1871 *William of Prussia crowned emperor of Germany*

The unification of Italy, and in particular the exploits of Garibaldi, excited artists all over Europe. This French painting *(above)*, entitled 'The Defenders of Italian Independence' shows from left to right, Garibaldi (holding his hat aloft), Victor Emmanuel II (on a white horse, wearing a green sash) and Napoleon III (on a black horse, wearing a red sash). Great efforts were made to portray the events leading to unification as heroic, rather than as the result of Great Power politics.

2 Italy was unified *(map above)* by war and revolution. In 1848 Charles Albert of Piedmont-Sardinia tried to expel Austria from northern Italy but was defeated at Custoza and Novara. Ten years later, with Napoleon III's France as an ally, Piedmontese forces together with nationalist volunteers defeated Austria at Magenta and Solferino. In return, Napoleon obtained Nice and Savoy, but Lombardy was joined to Piedmont, followed swiftly by the smaller central Italian duchies. When Sicily rose in revolt against the Kingdom of Naples in 1860, Garibaldi led a nationalist army southwards which defeated the Bourbon king. The northern states then joined with the liberated south to form a Kingdom of Italy ruled by the Piedmontese king, Victor Emmanuel.

Napoleon III of France to drive Austria out of northern Italy. Defeated at Magenta and Solferino, Austria signed the Treaty of Villafranca with France, giving up Lombardy but keeping Venetia. Lombardy then joined with Piedmont, and was followed by Tuscany, Parma, Romagna and Modena, where plebiscites overwhelmingly favoured a union with Piedmont. When Garibaldi, a flamboyant nationalist, lent his support to a peasant revolt against the Bourbon Kingdom of Naples, nationalists flocked to join him. Fearful that Garibaldi's success would result in popular uprisings throughout Italy, Cavour skilfully imposed Piedmontese control over Garibaldi, and in 1861 the Kingdom of Italy was declared with the Piedmont-Sardinian monarch, Victor Emmanuel II, its first king. Venetia was added in 1866, when Austria was defeated by Prussia, while in 1870 Rome was taken from the papacy to become the new capital.

> From day to day it is necessary that the governments and peoples of Germany be more convinced that national unity is the rock on which the edifice of their welfare, their honour, their power, their present security and existence, and their future greatness must be founded ... Nothing at this time so greatly impedes a closer union of the continent of Europe as the fact that its centre still has not taken the position for which it is naturally fitted.
>
> **Friedrich List, 1841**
> **German economist**

German unification

A similar process occurred in Germany, where Prussia embarked on a programme of conservative modernization, building up a strong industrial economy and reforming the army. With Bismarck as minister-president from 1862, Prussia began to dominate northern Germany. Following war with Denmark in 1864 over the duchies of Schleswig and Holstein, Prussian-Austrian relations deteriorated sharply. In 1866 Austria declared war on Prussia to prevent a repeat of her loss of influence in Italy. Defeated at Sadowa, Austria was effectively excluded from northern Germany and in 1867 Prussia established a North German Confederation. Napoleon III's ambition to revive French influence in the Rhineland then led to a crisis in Franco-Prussian relations which resulted in war in 1870 in which Germany decisively defeated the French, in the process occupying Paris. The southern German states, Bavaria, Baden and Württemberg, then allied with Prussia, and in 1871 agreed to join a larger federal structure, a German empire, rather than remain isolated and economically dependent on their much more powerful northern neighbour.

Nationalists in both Italy and Germany welcomed the new states, but in neither case had mass nationalism brought about unification. The old orders took the initiative to avoid popular revolution. When, later in the century, mass nationalism did develop in Italy and Germany it eventually led to fascism and the collapse of the conservative order that had ushered in the new nation states.

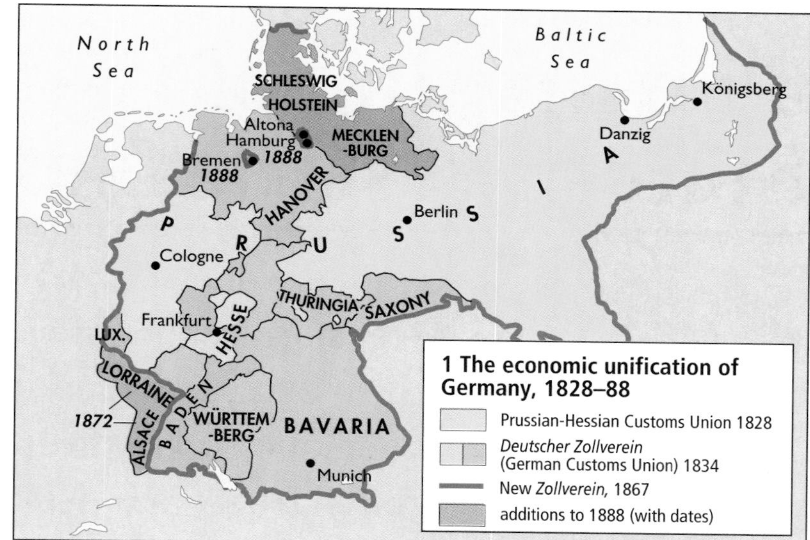

1 In 1834 Prussia established a customs union *(Zollverein)* between a number of the German states with the object of removing restrictions on trade *(map above)*. Austria was deliberately excluded, while northern Germany became the main area of trade and industrial expansion. Membership of the *Zollverein* did not stop most of Prussia's major economic partners, led by Saxony, from fighting on the side of Austria against Prussia in 1866.

3 In 1815 the German Confederation *(map below)* was a patchwork of city-states and principalities dominated by Prussia and Austria. From the 1850s relations between the two powers deteriorated, and after 1864 they squabbled over the administration of the annexed territory of Schleswig-Holstein. In 1866 Austria led the Confederation in a war against Prussia. After victory at Sadowa, Prussia absorbed Hanover, Hesse-Nassau and Frankfurt. In 1867 the North German Confederation was established, and following war with France in 1870, the southern states joined the Prussian-dominated federation in a new German empire.

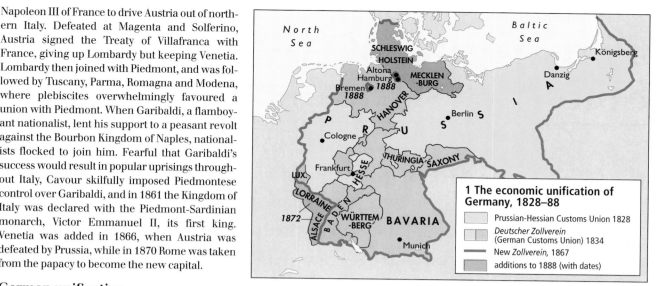

3 The unification of Germany, 1815–71

- Prussia in 1815
- acquired by Prussia 1815–66
- German Confederation, 1815
- North German Confederation, 1867
- Imperial territory of Alsace-Lorraine, 1871
- free city
- German Empire, 1871
- Austro-Prussian forces attack on Denmark, 1864
- Prussian armies in the war with Austria, 1866
- German armies in the Franco-Prussian war, 1870–71

The making of the United States: westward expansion

See also
The age of revolt, 1773–1814 p. 202
Population growth and movements, 1815–1914 p. 208
The market revolution in the US, 1800–80 p. 220
Slavery, civil war and Reconstruction p. 222
The United States: a nation of immigrants p. 224

1783 *American independence officially recognized*

1803 *Louisiana Purchase*

1838–9 *Final removal of the southern Cherokee tribes ('Trail of Tears')*

1845 *Annexation of Texas*

1849 *California Gold Rush*

1862 *The Homestead Act*

1869 *First trans-continental railroad completed*

1876 *Battle of The Little Big Horn*

1890 *US Bureau of Census declares the frontier closed*

At independence in 1783 most Americans lived on the eastern seaboard of the new country. Over the next 100 years there was a vast movement of population westwards into new lands acquired through treaty and exploration. It was a century of frontier towns, gold rushes and Indian wars. By 1890 railroads crossed the US and the 'frontier' was closed.

OUR MANIFEST DESTINY IS TO OVERSPREAD THE CONTINENT ALLOTED BY PROVIDENCE FOR THE FREE DEVELOPMENT OF OUR YEARLY MULTIPLYING MILLIONS.

John L. O' Sullivan, 1845

TELL YOUR PEOPLE THAT SINCE THE GREAT FATHER [THE PRESIDENT] PROMISED THAT WE WOULD NEVER BE REMOVED, WE HAVE BEEN MOVED FIVE TIMES … I THINK YOU HAD BETTER PUT THE INDIANS ON WHEELS AND YOU CAN RUN THEM ABOUT WHEREVER YOU WISH.

Chief Spotted Tail of the Sioux

GO WEST, YOUNG MAN, AND GROW UP WITH THE COUNTRY.

Horace Greeley's advice to the poor of New York City, 1850

WHEN IN 1783 THE INDEPENDENCE of the United States was at last recognized, most Americans – apart from a small settlement in Kentucky – lived between the eastern seaboard and the Appalachian mountains. Soon after independence, however, a vast westward movement of population began. This was assisted by the slow improvement in communications – first roads, later canals, and finally railroads. It was also encouraged by a series of political decisions through which, between the Louisiana Purchase of 1803 and the Gadsden Purchase of 1853 (*see* map 2), the new republic acquired vast new territories in the west and pushed its continental boundary as far as the Pacific Ocean.

After the political acquisition of new territory, 19th-century explorers – following in the footsteps of colonial predecessors such as Louis Joliet, James Marquette and Daniel Boone – visited and mapped the vast new lands. Many of these men, including William Clark, Meriwether Lewis, John C. Frémont and Zebulon Pike, were army officers. In their wake flowed pioneering settlers.

By 1820, the frontier of western settlement had reached the Mississippi River. It carried on shifting until by the 1840s it had reached the 100th meridian (bisecting present-day North Dakota and passing down through the middle of Texas). There, for a time, expansion faltered: the Great Plains to the west had too little rainfall to support mixed farming. It was only in the generation after the civil war and with the assistance of new technology – the railroads, barbed wire and steel ploughs – that this part of the west was finally settled and the region became the heart of American wheat production.

The move westwards

Beginning in the 1840s, sizeable wagon trains set out from Missouri and Midwestern states such as Illinois in order to cross the Rocky Mountains and settle near the Pacific coast. There were two basic routes: the Oregon Trail and, diverging away from it after the junction with the Snake River, the California Trail. It took most migrants about six months to complete the journey in ox-drawn, canvas-covered wagons. Often, they were under constant pressure from Indian attack or infectious disease. Some turned back. Others failed to reach the Far West – the notorious Donner party of 1846-7 experienced many fatalities when trapped by snow in the Rocky Mountains.

There were many different motives for western migration. The desire for cheap land was clearly a major one – especially in the wake of the Homestead Act of 1862 (which offered 160 acres of land free to anyone settling it). But not just farmers moved west. There were also professional folk interested in a new career in booming towns. Some of those booming towns went on to become great cities: Chicago, a small community on the shore of Lake Michigan when first incorporated as a city in 1837, had become a huge metropolis with a population of a million by 1890. Miners also moved west – especially during the California 'Gold Rush' of 1849. Some

1 There were several separate frontiers in American history ***(map below)***: the frontier of the explorer, the fur trader, the miner, the cattle-man and sheep-herder, and finally the farmers' frontier. Each of those westward movements had its own special rhythm, its own settlements and its own routes. By the 1850s settlers were crossing the Great Plains in vast numbers. In 1890 the Bureau of the Census deemed the frontier closed; by then San Francisco's population approached 300,000.

1 Westward expansion

explorers' routes
settlers' routes
cattle trails
cow town
fur traders' routes
fur station
pass
mining sites
Catholic mission
Protestant mission

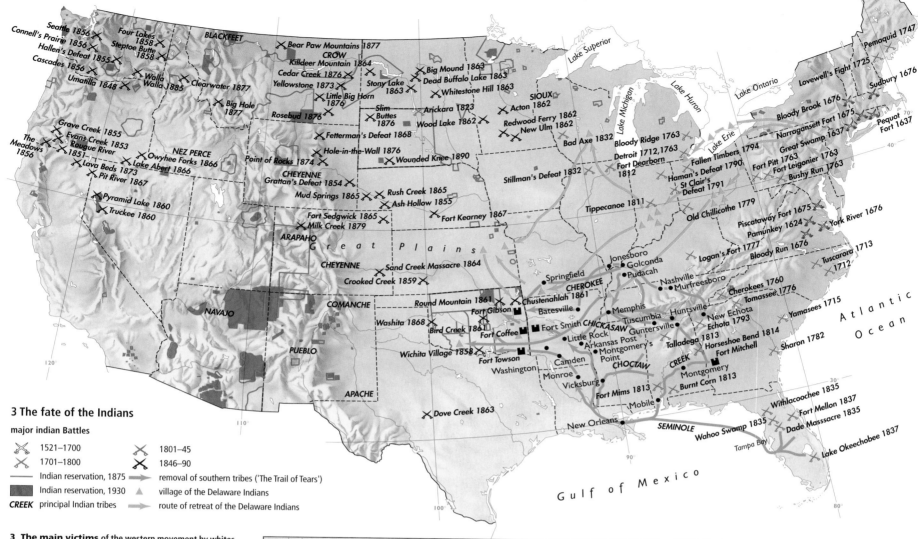

3 The fate of the Indians

major indian Battles

- 1521–1700
- 1701–1800
- 1801–45
- 1846–90
- Indian reservation, 1875
- Indian reservation, 1930
- CREEK principal Indian tribes
- removal of southern tribes ('The Trail of Tears')
- village of the Delaware Indians
- route of retreat of the Delaware Indians

3 The main victims of the western movement by whites were Indians *(map above)*. In the Great Plains and Far West, there were perhaps a quarter of a million Indians. As settlers moved into Indian areas there were a series of wars. The Indians had some temporary successes – for example – the defeat of General Custer's force at the Little Big Horn by Sioux and Cheyenne in 1876. But, by 1890 Indian resistance had effectively been brought to an end and the Indians themselves were largely confined to their reservations.

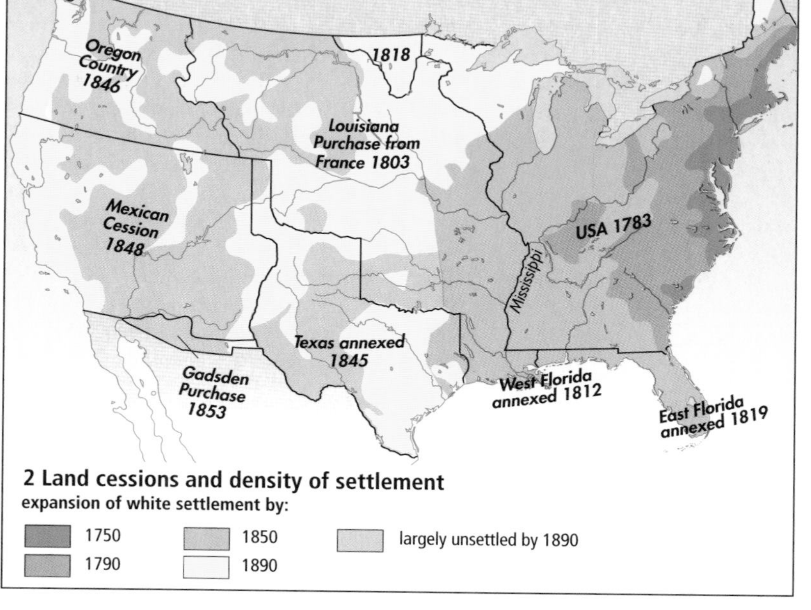

2 Land cessions and density of settlement

expansion of white settlement by:

- 1750
- 1790
- 1850
- 1890
- largely unsettled by 1890

2 In 1783 the new nation extended from the Atlantic coast to the Mississippi river. Its territory was enlarged in just two great spates of expansion *(map right)*. During the first (1803–19), three Virginian presidents acquired Louisiana and the Floridas. During the second, the heyday of 'manifest destiny' (1845–53), Texas, Oregon, California and the remainder of the southwest were added, thereby completing the area occupied by the 48 contiguous states of today.

4 The buffalo

Range of buffalo in:

- 1600
- 1800
- 1825
- 1850
- 1875
- railroads

4 On the Great Plains, the economic and spiritual base of Indian culture was destroyed when the buffalo herds *(map above right)* were cut in two by the first transcontinental railroad (1869) and then slaughtered in a deliberate campaign to starve out the Sioux. By the 1890s, the buffalo, like the Indians, survived only on reservations.

groups, such as the Mormons, who migrated to the Utah Territory in the 1840s, were in search of not simply economic opportunity but religious freedom as well. And others who moved west did so involuntarily, like the Cherokee Indians compelled to trek to Oklahoma in 1838. There were also large ethnic minorities, including blacks and Asians, in the west.

The development of communications

The story of the west was also one of faster communications. In 1851, a stagecoach service started between Independence, Missouri, and Salt Lake City. It was buttressed in 1857 by the Overland Mail between St Louis and San Francisco. In 1860, the Pony Express mail service was introduced – only to become immediately obsolete when the telegraph service between Kansas and California began just 18 months later. In 1869, the stagecoach suffered the same fate with the completion of the first transcontinental railroad. Abraham Lincoln thought that the settlement of the whole west would take 100 years. It was the railroads that proved him wrong. In 1890, only 21 years after the opening of the first transcontinental service, the US Census Bureau announced that it could no longer locate a continuous area of free land for settlement in the west. With the final disappearance of the frontier line, the western stage of American development effectively came to an end.

In the wake of the first settlers, railroads, stage coaches and covered wagons brought reinforcements. The lithograph *(right)*, from a painting of 1872 by John Gast, shows the figure of Progress (clasping a schoolbook under her arm and looping telegraph wires behind her) leading settlers westwards, where they drive darkness, buffaloes and Indians alike before them with peaceful but firm resolution.

1800 to 1880

The market revolution in the United States

See also
The Americas, 1500–1810 p. 162
Population growth and movements, 1815–1914 p. 208
The making of the United States: westward expansion, 1783–1890 p. 218
Slavery, civil war and Reconstruction, 1820–77 p. 222
The United States: a nation of immigrants, 1776–1924 p. 224

1811–18 *Building of Cumberland Road*

1813 *First cotton factory established in Waltham, Massachusetts*

1825 *Completion of Erie Canal*

1862 *Congress charters a Pacific Railroad*

1868 *Open-hearth process introduced in steel industry*

1882 *Organization of Standard Oil, first big business 'trust'*

1883 *Railroads introduce standard time zones across United States*

1886 *Railroads adopt standard track gauge*

The century between 1800 and 1900 witnessed a 'market revolution' in the United States. Small farms and workshops gave way to a national economy where manfacturers produced for a distant market place. Better transportation, vast resources and favourable government policies were all crucial in creating, by 1900, the world's most productive economy.

I CANNOT AVOID REFLECTING WITH PLEASURE ON THE PROBABLE INFLUENCE THAT COMMERCE MAY HEREAFTER HAVE ON HUMAN MANNERS AND SOCIETY IN GENERAL.

George Washington, 1785

WE HOLD IT BEST THAT THE LAWS SHOULD FAVOUR THE DIFFUSION OF PROPERTY AND ITS ACQUISITION, NOT THE CONCENTRATION OF IT IN THE HANDS OF THE FEW.

George Bancroft, historian, 1835

IN 1800, THE UNITED STATES had been internationally recognized as a nation for only 17 years. Most of its estimated population of 5,298,000 dwelt in small communities or on farms: there were only 73 towns and cities with a population of over 2,500, of which just one – New York – had over 50,000 inhabitants. By 1900, the nation had been transformed. The estimated population of the United States had grown to 76,094,000 (an increase of 1,337 per cent). There were now 827 settlements with a population between 2,500 and 50,000, and 75 cities of more than 50,000 people (including three of more than 1,000,000). The statistics of economic growth during the century show equally large increases: the net tonnage entering US ports grew by 3,400 per cent; total imports by 922 per cent; and exports by 2,011 per cent.

In 1800, not only was the United States primarily an agricultural nation, but most farm crops were grown for local consumption. Farming families produced either for themselves, or for their neighbours. There was little chance, because of the high cost of internal transportation, of moving towards a more national market-oriented type of economy. According to one estimate of 1816, shipping a ton of goods from Europe to America cost approximately $9; the same amount would enable it to be transported only nine miles by land.

Better transportation made possible a 'market revolution'. After 1800 , there were many improvements in communications. The building of the Cumberland Road (1811-18) between Cumberland, Maryland, and Vandalia on the Ohio river, symbolized the drive to build turnpike roads that, by the time the road construction boom collapsed in 1821, had seen 4,000 miles of such roads constructed. Return voyages by the *Clermond* between New York and Albany in 1807 and the *Washington* between Louisville and New Orleans in 1817 inaugurated an era of steamship navigation on rivers and inland lakes. The successful completion of the Erie Canal in 1825 also prompted a major boom in canal-building in subsequent years.

The arrival of the railroad

Most crucial of all was the arrival of the railroad. By 1840, the United States had 3,328 miles of railroad track (compared to 1,800 for the whole of Europe). A further 29,000 miles were built during the next 20 years. The last four decades of the 19th century saw a great expansion in railroad construction and the completion of five new transcontinental railroads. By 1900, the United States had 193,346 miles of rail track carrying about 142 billion ton-miles of freight (compared to 39 billion in 1866). The railroads, which had played so significant a part in creating a national market, both recognized it and regularized it with the introduction of standard time zones (1883) and a common track gauge.

Industrialization

During the 19th century, smaller-scale manufacturing gave place to industrial production in ever larger economic units. This process began during the war of 1812–14 between the United States and Britain, which saw considerable capital transferred from foreign trade into manufacturing. The organization of the first path-breaking cotton factory at Waltham, Massachusetts, was followed by the spread of the factory system throughout cotton manufacturing and then to other industries. The United States had a large pool of labour drawn from mass immigration, seemingly endless natural resources (for example, the huge iron ore fields around Lake Superior, the vast coal reserves of Appalachia, and the oil-fields of Pennsylvania), and great native inventiveness and ingenuity. It also had a class of entrepreneurs who,

3 Underpinning America's economic growth in the 19th century were the country's natural reserves ***(map right)***. Some of these – the vast Appalachian anthracite coal fields, the bituminous coal fields of the west and the iron ore reserves near Pittsburgh, in northern Michigan and in Minnesota – helped the enormous growth in iron and steel production in the 19th century. Others saw the beginnings of new industries, with a huge oil industry growing out of the discovery of petroleum by Edwin L. Drake in Pennsylvania in 1859. Many discoveries of precious metals were also made in the West, starting with the California 'Gold Rush' of 1849. In subsequent years, discoveries were also made in Colorado, Nevada (the location of the fabulous Comstock Lode), Idaho, Arizona and Montana.

3 Industrial growth and mineral wealth, 1799–1901

counties with 1,000 or more factory employees in 1899
principal coalfields
oil and mineral finds (with date)
gold
oil
copper
silver

1 The completion of the Erie Canal stimulated a great boom in canal construction *(map above)*. Although the boom itself collapsed after 1837, the canals already built – and later extensions to them – played a major role in spreading the market revolution to the west. Most canals and railroads were in New England and the Middle Atlantic States. By 1860, there were still comparatively few major railroads in the south

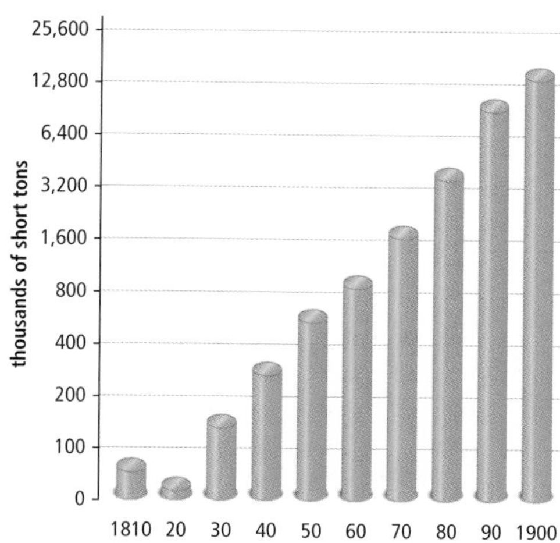

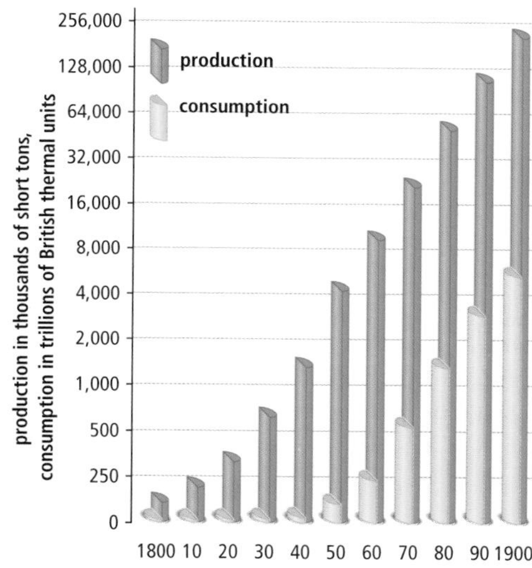

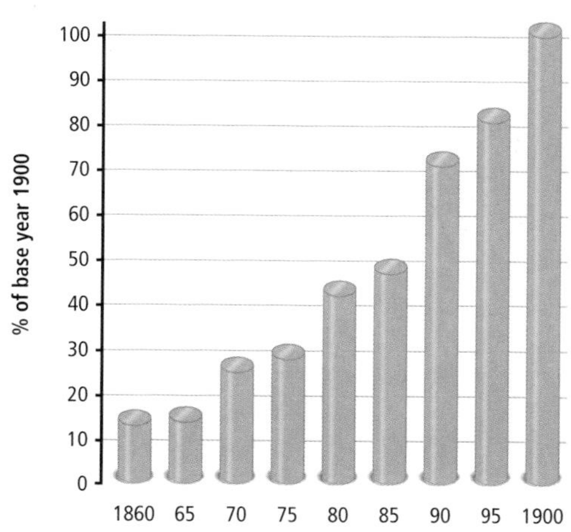

4, 5 & 6 The importance of iron to the 19th-century market revolution cannot be underestimated *(charts left)*. It literally provided the foundation for transportation (not for nothing was the railroad called the 'Iron Horse') and the construction industries. Industrialization also depended on the use of anthracite coal and, increasingly, on bituminous coal, which was considerably better for making the coke used to smelt iron.

2 When, in 1893, the Great Northern Railroad from Duluth and St. Paul finally reached Seattle, the United States had five transcontinental railroads, all built since 1862 *(map right)*. Beginning in 1866, enterprising Texas cattle ranchers drove their herds north to railheads, since beef would command a much higher price in northern markets. In subsequent years, as railroads and the farming frontier moved to the west, the cattle trails followed. Under the impact of the availability of cheap range cattle, the spread of railroads and the introduction of the refrigerator car, beef became an American staple.

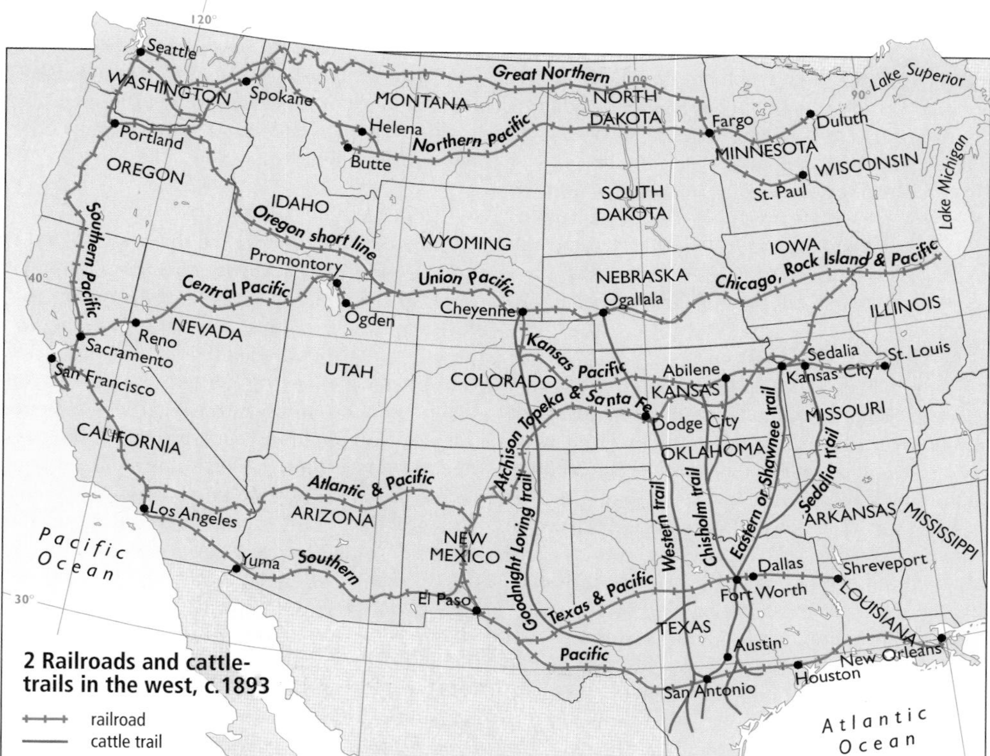

particularly towards the end of the century, organized themselves into larger and larger business corporations.

For most of the 19th century, Federal and state governments – while often paying lip service to laissez-faire principles – actively promoted the growth of industry and a market economy. The Erie Canal was built by the state of New York. The Federal government, which had financed the Cumberland Road, later took over the policy begun by the state of Illinois in the 1850s of promoting railroad construction through grants of land.

In 1800, the United States was a largely provincial and non-market economy. As the 19th century progressed, it not only developed a national marketplace, but also became part of the international economy. In terms of industrial production, by the end of the 19th century it was leading the world, with the most rapid developments coming in the last decades of the 19th century. In 1880, the US produced less steel than Britain. By 1900, it was producing more than the combined total of Britain and Germany, its nearest rivals. As the 20th century dawned, the United States was well on the way to developing into an economic colossus.

Pittsburgh, Pennsylvania *(left)*, surrounded by huge coal-fields and beds of iron and at the confluence of two important rivers, became the leading centre of iron and steel production in the United States. So vast and dramatic was the sight of its blast furnaces and coke ovens at work that early 20th-century artists and commentators began to refer to it as 'Hell with the lid off.'

1820 to 1877
Slavery, civil war and Reconstruction

See also
The Americas, 1500–1810 p. 162
The making of the United States: westward expansion, 1783–1890 p. 218
The market revolution in the United States, 1800–80 p. 220
The United States: a nation of immigrants, 1776–1924 p. 224

The civil war was the most dramatic event in American history. It caused the deaths of 620,000 men – more casualties than in all other American wars combined. The roots of the conflict lay in slavery. Where the North sought to abolish it, the South was determined on its preservation, as well as on protecting its rights in the Union as a whole.

> I STOLE THIS HEAD, THESE LIMBS, THIS BODY FROM MY MASTER, AND RAN OFF WITH THEM.
>
> **Frederick Douglass, escaped slave and abolitionist, 1842**

> A HOUSE DIVIDED AGAINST ITSELF CANNOT STAND. I BELIEVE THIS GOVERNMENT CANNOT ENDURE PERMANENTLY HALF SLAVE AND HALF FREE. I DO NOT EXPECT THE UNION TO BE DISSOLVED – I DO NOT EXPECT THE HOUSE TO FALL – BUT I DO EXPECT IT WILL CEASE TO BE DIVIDED.
>
> **Abraham Lincoln, 1858**

1820 *Missouri Compromise bans slavery north of 36 degrees 30'*

1846–8 *War with Mexico. US annexes California, Utah and New Mexico*

1854 *The Kansas-Nebraska Act*

1860 *Abraham Lincoln elected to the presidency. The South secedes*

1861 *Civil war begins*

1863 *Emancipation of the slaves*

14 April 1865 *Lincoln assassinated*

26 April 1865 *The South surrenders; Reconstruction begins*

1877 *Reconstruction formally comes to an end*

SLAVERY WAS AN EMBARRASSMENT to many of the early leaders of the American republic. Although they launched their new nation on the basis that everyone had a right to 'life, liberty, and the pursuit of happiness', many of them – including Thomas Jefferson – themselves owned slaves. In the northern states, slavery did begin to disappear at the start of the 19th century. In the South, however, the invention of the cotton gin by Eli Whitney in 1793 made cotton, grown principally by black slaves, a lucrative crop. Far from declining, slavery consolidated in the South.

The South and slavery

During the early 19th century, Southern slavery became intimately bound up with the issues raised by westward expansion. Southerners felt politically disadvantaged if new states were forbidden to enter the Union with slaves. In 1819 Missouri applied for admission to the Union as a slave state and the North refused. The problem was solved by the Compromise of 1820, which sought to balance the two interests by admitting Missouri as a slave state at the same time as Maine as a free one. It also drew a line at the latitude of 36 degrees 30 minutes across the Louisiana territory purchased in 1803 (*see* p. 218): future states entering the Union north of that line would be free, whereas south of it they could be slave states.

The Compromise of 1820 was finally brought down by a rising abolitionist clamour in the North and by the territories gained by the United States as a result of the war with Mexico (1846–8). California threatened to upset the sectional balance by applying to enter the Union in 1849 as a free state. This was opposed by the South, which feared Northern political dominance. Another compromise resulted: California was allowed into the Federal Union as a free state, but the territories of Utah and New Mexico were organized on a new principle: popular or squatter sovereignty. The decision on whether or not to have slavery was left to the settlers themselves. But this Compromise lasted less than four years: in 1854 an attempt was made to extend the same principle of popular sovereignty to the territories of Kansas and Nebraska. These lay north of the line of 36 degrees 30 minutes, so the possibility arose that they might decide to have slavery in an area from which it was banned by the Missouri Compromise of 1820.

The consequences of the Kansas-Nebraska Act were disastrous for the Union. Armed conflict broke out in Kansas between pro- and anti-slavery forces. A new political party, the Republicans, was born to resist any further expansion of slavery into the territories. Relations between the North and the South deteriorated rapidly. Finally, in 1860, when Abraham Lincoln, as the Republican candidate, was elected president solely on the basis of northern votes, the South began to secede from the Union. In spring 1861, war broke out between the 11 seceded Southern states, which formed a new collective government known as the Confederacy, and the Federal Union, which refused to accept the legality of secession. Eighteen months later, Lincoln added another war aim to the salvation of the Union when he issued his provisional proclamation emancipating the slaves, to become effective on 1 January 1863.

The civil war

During the first months of the war, volunteer armies on both sides were neither very disciplined nor very effective. Serious military operations really began in spring 1862. The North's strategy was based on denying the South vital resources by a naval blockade, controlling key river routes and capturing the Confederate capital of Richmond. Despite overwhelming superiority in manpower and resources, however, the Union took four years to win the war. There were two principal reasons: first, the South had superior generalship during the war's first two years; second, the North's goals demanded the occupation of the South and the destruction of its armies, while the South fought on home ground to defend its own territories. General Robert E. Lee thwarted two invasions of Virginia in 1862, and carried the war into the North, only to be stopped at Antietam, Maryland, in September 1862 and defeated at Gettysburg, Pennsylvania, in July 1863. By then, in the west, the Union had gained control of the Mississippi and Tennessee rivers and opened the way for an invasion of the lower South. In 1864, with the Union blockade increasingly effective, General Ulysses S. Grant began his invasion of Virginia which, combined with General Philip T. Sherman's march through Georgia and South Carolina, had destroyed the South's armies by the spring of 1865.

Reconstruction

With Lincoln's assassination and the end of the war, a political conflict arose between Congress and the new president, Andrew Johnson, over 'Reconstruction' – the process of re-admitting the South to the Union. Johnson wanted to be as lenient to the South as possible. Many Republicans, however, dismayed by the continuing intransigence of the Southern states, wished to follow a more radical policy centred around the enfranchisement of blacks in the South. In 1867, the Republicans imposed their version of Reconstruction on the South. But attempts to promote real equality for blacks were hampered by Southern resistance, through organizations such as the Ku Klux Klan, and the failure to provide land for the freed slaves. One by one, the Republican regimes supported by black voters in the South were overthrown. By 1876, only three states – South Carolina, Florida and Louisiana – were still undergoing Reconstruction. The withdrawal of Federal troops from these states, in the wake of the elections of 1876, caused the Republican regimes there to fall and Reconstruction finally came to an end.

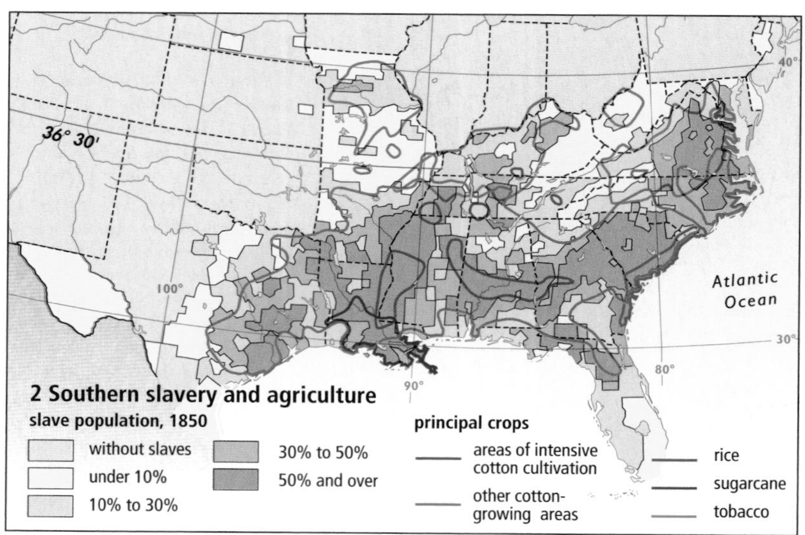

2 On the eve of the Civil War, cotton-producing areas stretched from eastern Texas to North Carolina *(map above)*. Sixty per cent of slaves worked in the fields producing cotton, which accounted for two-thirds of of US exports. Other Southern crops – often also cultivated by slaves – included sugarcane, rice and tobacco.

3 Some states, though they had slaves, declined to join the Confederacy *(map below)*. At the start of the Civil War, West Virginia split from Virginia in order to stay with the Union. Once the war was over, 'Reconstruction' governments were established in the South, backed by northern Republicans. The last of these survived until 1877.

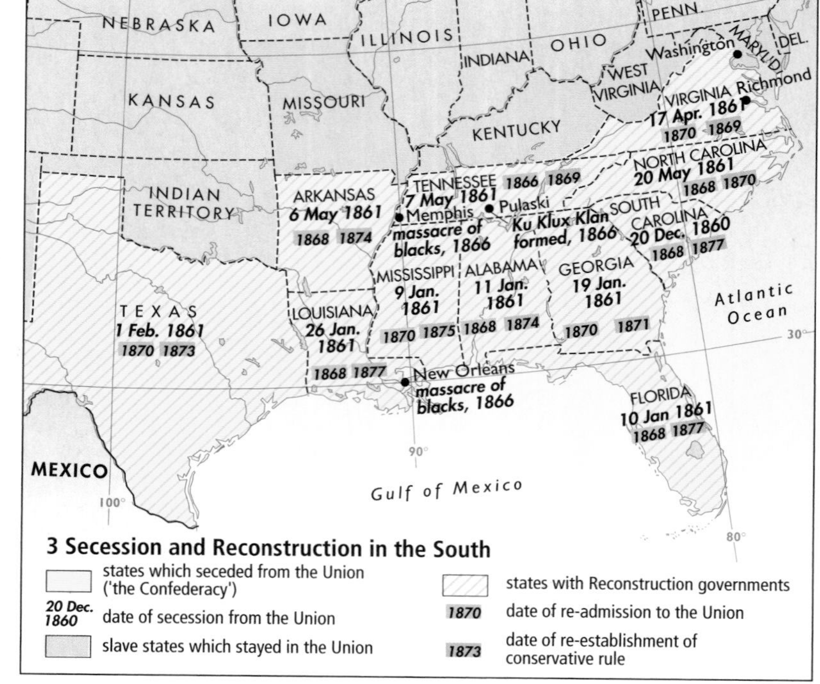

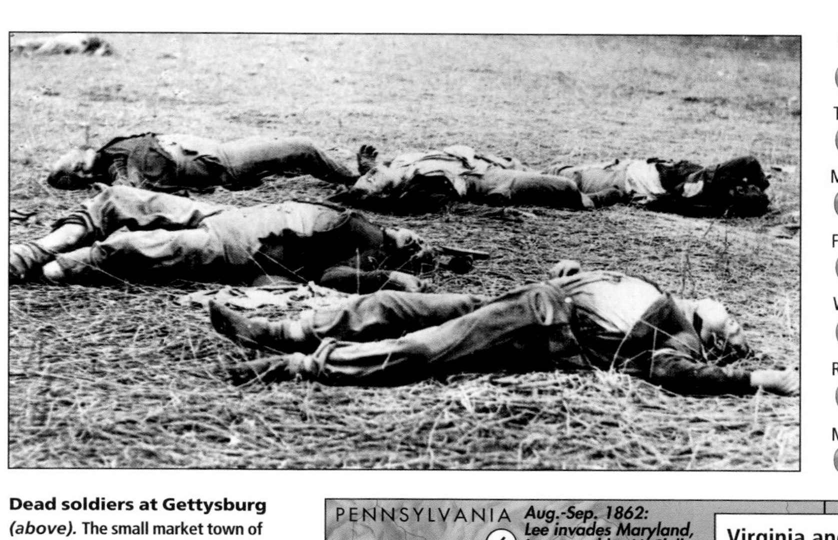

Dead soldiers at Gettysburg *(above).* The small market town of Gettysburg, Pennsylvania, was the scene of the greatest battle of the war. Lee, advancing into the North for a second time to force Lincoln to negotiate peace on the basis of Southern independence, attacked General Meade's Union army, but in the course of a three-day battle was comprehensively beaten. The Union lost 23,000 men, the Confederacy 28,000. Four months after the battle, at a ceremony dedicating a national cemetery on the Gettysburg site, Lincoln made perhaps his finest speech, declaring that the war would bring 'a new birth of freedom' and vowing that 'government of the people, by the people, for the people, shall not perish from the earth.'

4 Comparative resources: Union and Confederate states, 1861

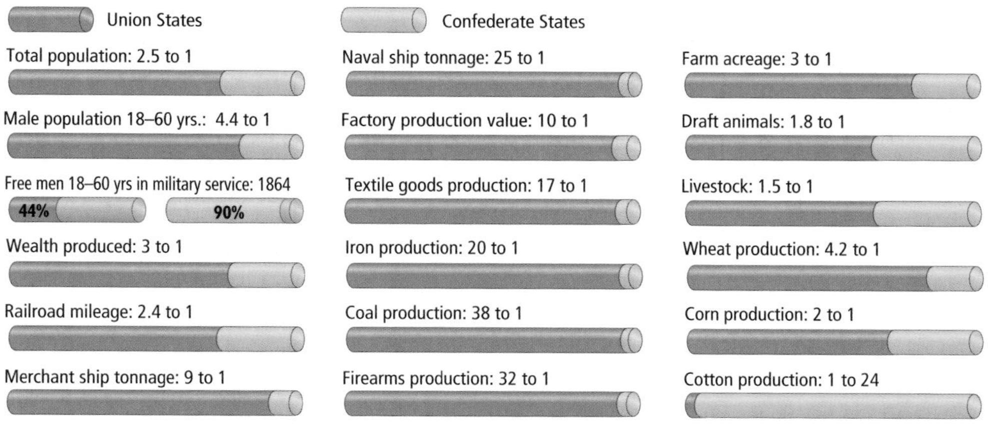

Union States
Confederate States
Total population: 2.5 to 1
Male population 18–60 yrs.: 4.4 to 1
Free men 18–60 yrs in military service: 1864
44%
90%
Wealth produced: 3 to 1
Railroad mileage: 2.4 to 1
Merchant ship tonnage: 9 to 1
Naval ship tonnage: 25 to 1
Factory production value: 10 to 1
Textile goods production: 17 to 1
Iron production: 20 to 1
Coal production: 38 to 1
Firearms production: 32 to 1
Farm acreage: 3 to 1
Draft animals: 1.8 to 1
Livestock: 1.5 to 1
Wheat production: 4.2 to 1
Corn production: 2 to 1
Cotton production: 1 to 24

4 Because the South lacked the North's industrial capacity *(chart above)*, the Confederacy was obliged to import or capture most of its arms. As the Union blockade tightened and the Confederate transport system broke down through inability to replace equipment, the agricultural South experienced difficulty even in feeding itself. The only area where the South had a decisive advantage was in the production of cotton.

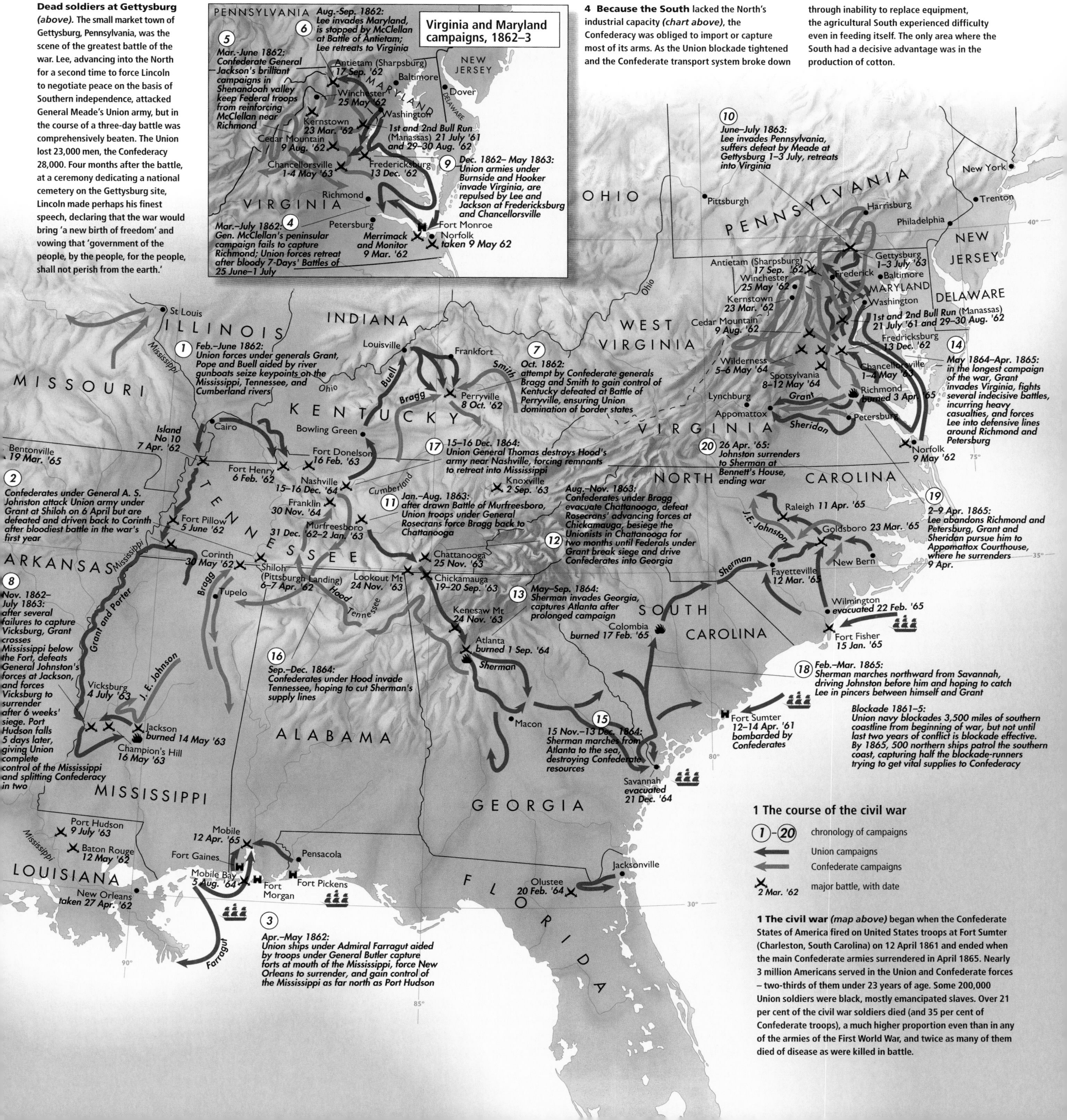

Virginia and Maryland campaigns, 1862–3
PENNSYLVANIA
NEW JERSEY
MARYLAND
DELAWARE
VIRGINIA
5 Mar.–June 1862: Confederate General Jackson's brilliant campaigns in Shenandoah valley keep Federal troops from reinforcing McClellan near Richmond
6 Aug.–Sep. 1862: Lee invades Maryland, is stopped by McClellan at Battle of Antietam; Lee retreats to Virginia
Antietam (Sharpsburg) 17 Sep. '62
Baltimore
Dover
Winchester 25 May '62
Washington
Kernstown 23 Mar. '62
1st and 2nd Bull Run (Manassas) 21 July '61 and 29–30 Aug. '62
Cedar Mountain 9 Aug. '62
Chancellorsville 1-4 May '63
Fredericksburg 13 Dec. '62
9 Dec. 1862– May 1863: Union armies under Burnside and Hooker invade Virginia, are repulsed by Lee and Jackson at Fredericksburg and Chancellorsville
Richmond
Petersburg
Fort Monroe
Norfolk taken 9 May 62
Merrimack and Monitor 9 Mar. '62
4 Mar.–July 1862: Gen. McClellan's peninsular campaign fails to capture Richmond; Union forces retreat after bloody 7-Days' Battles of 25 June–1 July
10 June–July 1863: Lee invades Pennsylvania, suffers defeat by Meade at Gettysburg 1–3 July, retreats into Virginia
OHIO
Pittsburgh
PENNSYLVANIA
Harrisburg
New York
Trenton
Philadelphia
NEW JERSEY
Gettysburg 1–3 July '63
Baltimore
Frederick
Antietam (Sharpsburg) 17 Sep. '62
Winchester 25 May '62
MARYLAND
DELAWARE
Kernstown 23 Mar. '62
Washington
Cedar Mountain 9 Aug. '62
1st and 2nd Bull Run (Manassas) 21 July '61 and 29–30 Aug. '62
Fredericksburg 13 Dec. '62
WEST VIRGINIA
Ohio
St Louis
ILLINOIS
INDIANA
Mississippi
MISSOURI
1 Feb.–June 1862: Union forces under generals Grant, Pope and Buell aided by river gunboats seize keypoints on the Mississippi, Tennessee, and Cumberland rivers
Louisville
Frankfort
7 Oct. 1862: attempt by Confederate generals Bragg and Smith to gain control of Kentucky defeated at Battle of Perryville, ensuring Union domination of border states
Buell
Bragg
Smith
Perryville 8 Oct. '62
KENTUCKY
Wilderness 5–6 May '64
Spotsylvania 8–12 May '64
Chancellorsville 1–4 May '63
14 May 1864–Apr. 1865: in the longest campaign of the war, Grant invades Virginia, fights several indecisive battles, incurring heavy casualties, and forces Lee into defensive lines around Richmond and Petersburg
Lynchburg
Grant
Richmond burned 3 Apr. '65
Appomattox
Petersburg
Sheridan
VIRGINIA
Norfolk 9 May '62
Island No 10 7 Apr. '62
Cairo
Bowling Green
Bentonville 19 Mar. '65
Fort Donelson 16 Feb. '63
Fort Henry 6 Feb. '62
17 15–16 Dec. 1864: Union General Thomas destroys Hood's army near Nashville, forcing remnants to retreat into Mississippi
20 26 Apr. '65: Johnston surrenders to Sherman at Bennett's House, ending war
NORTH CAROLINA
Nashville 15–16 Dec. '64
Cumberland
Knoxville 2 Sep. '63
2 Confederates under General A. S. Johnston attack Union army under Grant at Shiloh on 6 April but are defeated and driven back to Corinth after bloodiest battle in the war's first year
Franklin 30 Nov. '64
11 Jan.–Aug. 1863: after drawn Battle of Murfreesboro, Union troops under General Rosecrans force Bragg back to Chattanooga
Aug.–Nov. 1863: Confederates under Bragg evacuate Chattanooga, defeat Rosecrans' advancing forces at Chickamauga, besiege the Unionists in Chattanooga for two months until Federals under Grant break siege and drive Confederates into Georgia
12
Raleigh 11 Apr. '65
J. E. Johnston
Goldsboro 23 Mar. '65
19 2–9 Apr. 1865: Lee abandons Richmond and Petersburg, Grant and Sheridan pursue him to Appomattox Courthouse, where he surrenders 9 Apr.
Fort Pillow 5 June '62
Murfreesboro 31 Dec. '62–2 Jan. '63
TENNESSEE
Chattanooga 25 Nov. '63
Chickamauga 19–20 Sep. '63
New Bern
ARKANSAS
Mississippi
Corinth 30 May '62
Shiloh (Pittsburgh Landing) 6–7 Apr. '62
Lookout Mt 24 Nov. '63
Sherman
Fayetteville 12 Mar. '65
8 Nov. 1862–July 1863: after several failures to capture Vicksburg, Grant crosses Mississippi below the Fort, defeats General Johnston's forces at Jackson, and forces Vicksburg to surrender after 6 weeks' siege. Port Hudson falls 5 days later, giving Union complete control of the Mississippi and splitting Confederacy in two
Grant and Porter
Bragg
Tupelo
Hood
Tennessee
13 May–Sep. 1864: Sherman invades Georgia, captures Atlanta after prolonged campaign
Kenesaw Mt 24 Nov. '63
Atlanta burned 1 Sep. '64
Sherman
SOUTH CAROLINA
Colombia burned 17 Feb. '65
Wilmington evacuated 22 Feb. '65
Fort Fisher 15 Jan. '65
16 Sep.–Dec. 1864: Confederates under Hood invade Tennessee, hoping to cut Sherman's supply lines
18 Feb.–Mar. 1865: Sherman marches northward from Savannah, driving Johnston before him and hoping to catch Lee in pincers between himself and Grant
Vicksburg 4 July '63
J. E. Johnson
Jackson burned 14 May '63
Champion's Hill 16 May '63
ALABAMA
Macon
15 15 Nov.–13 Dec. 1864: Sherman marches from Atlanta to the sea, destroying Confederate resources
Fort Sumter 12–14 Apr. '61 bombarded by Confederates
Blockade 1861–5: Union navy blockades 3,500 miles of southern coastline from beginning of war, but not until last two years of conflict is blockade effective. By 1865, 500 northern ships patrol the southern coast, capturing half the blockade-runners trying to get vital supplies to Confederacy
MISSISSIPPI
Savannah evacuated 21 Dec. '64
GEORGIA
Port Hudson 9 July '63
Baton Rouge 12 May '62
Mobile 12 Apr. '65
Pensacola
Fort Gaines
Mobile Bay 5 Aug. '64
Fort Morgan
Fort Pickens
LOUISIANA
New Orleans taken 27 Apr. '62
Jacksonville
Olustee 20 Feb. '64
FLORIDA
Farragut
3 Apr.–May 1862: Union ships under Admiral Farragut aided by troops under General Butler capture forts at mouth of the Mississippi, force New Orleans to surrender, and gain control of the Mississippi as far north as Port Hudson
1 The course of the civil war
1–20 chronology of campaigns
Union campaigns
Confederate campaigns
major battle, with date
2 Mar. '62

1 The civil war *(map above)* began when the Confederate States of America fired on United States troops at Fort Sumter (Charleston, South Carolina) on 12 April 1861 and ended when the main Confederate armies surrendered in April 1865. Nearly 3 million Americans served in the Union and Confederate forces – two-thirds of them under 23 years of age. Some 200,000 Union soldiers were black, mostly emancipated slaves. Over 21 per cent of the civil war soldiers died (and 35 per cent of Confederate troops), a much higher proportion even than in any of the armies of the First World War, and twice as many of them died of disease as were killed in battle.

The United States: a nation of immigrants

See also
Population growth and movements, 1815–1914 p. 208
The making of the United States: westward expansion, 1783–1890 p. 218
The market revolution in the US, 1800–80 p. 220
Slavery, civil war and Reconstruction, 1820–1877 p. 222

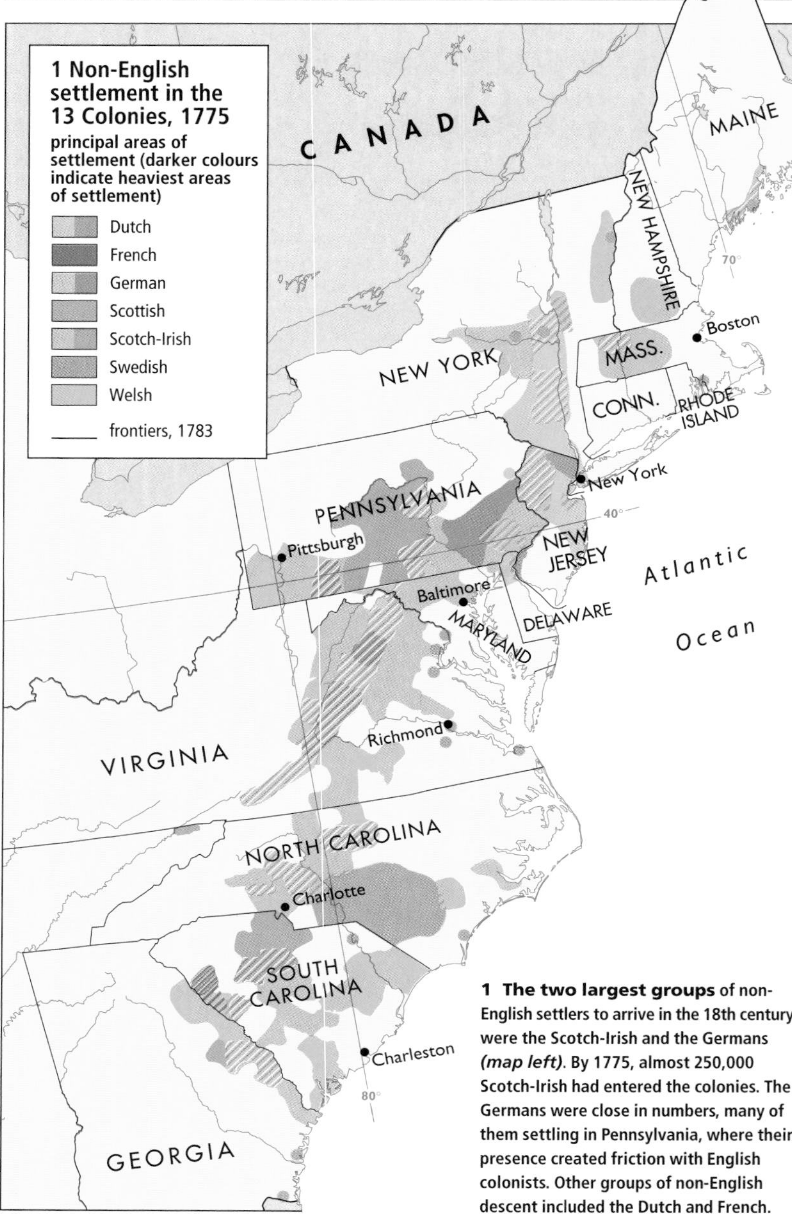

1 The two largest groups of non-English settlers to arrive in the 18th century were the Scotch-Irish and the Germans *(map left)*. By 1775, almost 250,000 Scotch-Irish had entered the colonies. The Germans were close in numbers, many of them settling in Pennsylvania, where their presence created friction with English colonists. Other groups of non-English descent included the Dutch and French.

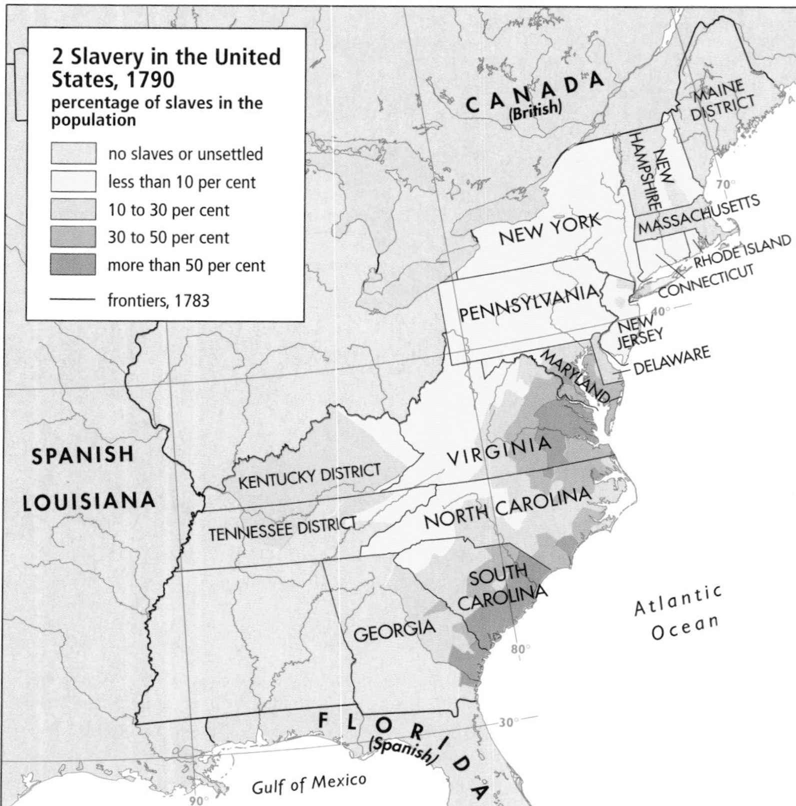

2 The numbers of black slaves rose sharply after 1700, partly as a result of the thriving slave trade *(map above)*. In 1700 there were perhaps 20,000 slaves; by 1763, there were over a third of a million. While slavery was to be found in the north, it never made up more than a small proportion of the population. In the South, on the eve of independence, two out of every five inhabitants were slaves.

Although the United States is not the only country to have been founded – and to have had much of its subsequent history shaped by – immigrants and their descendants, it is the most powerful, populous, and ethnically diverse of such countries. Between 1820 and 1920 the United States received a total of over 34 million immigrants.

UNTIL AROUND 1700, the great majority of immigrants to the British American colonies were English, Welsh or Scottish. Thereafter, as British governments discouraged voluntary emigration, the ethnic composition of the population changed, as growing numbers of German, Swiss, French, Dutch, Swedish and, above all, Ulster Scotch-Irish migrants arrived. Britain continued to transport involuntary emigrants to the American colonies, including around 200,000 slaves from Africa and 30,000 British convicted felons. As ethnic groups tended to settle in particular areas and (outside towns) there was comparatively little intermingling between them, the population of late colonial America very much resembled a mosaic.

> THERE SHE LIES, THE GREAT MELTING POT. LISTEN! CAN'T YOU HEAR THE ROARING AND THE BUBBLING? THERE GAPES HER MOUTH, THE HARBOUR WHERE A THOUSAND MAMMOTH FEEDERS COME FROM THE ENDS OF THE WORLD TO POUR IN THEIR HUMAN FREIGHT. AH, WHAT A STIRRING AND SEETHING! CELT AND LATIN, SLAV AND TEUTON, GREEK AND SYRIAN, BLACK AND YELLOW.
>
> ***The Melting Pot, 1909***

The early 19th century

In the early years following independence, immigration was on a comparatively small scale. But, after the Napoleonic Wars in 1815, more Europeans started to emigrate to the United States, thereby beginning a mass migration that would last for more than a century. Between 1820 and 1880, largely unaffected by the Civil War of 1861–65, over 10 million immigrants entered the US. Most came from northern and western Europe – mainly Germany, Ireland, Britain and Scandinavia. They sailed for America to better themselves economically, to escape (in the case of the Irish) the famine of the 1840s, or – more rarely – as political refugees (German 'Forty-Eighters', for example). Scandinavian immigrants often became farmers in Minnesota and Wisconsin, Germans in Illinois, Wisconsin, Iowa and Ohio. The Irish were the most urban of all immigrant groups: less than one in ten took up farming and New York, Philadelphia and Boston soon contained large Irish populations.

From the 1830s many native-born Americans were becoming increasingly disturbed by the extent of immigration. An anti-immigrant movement culminated in the 1850s in the emergence of a short-lived but, for a time, relatively successful 'nativist' party: the Know Nothings. But anti-immigrant feeling dissipated during the Civil War and in the years following it, when immigrants were welcomed as contributing to the American economy. It revived in the 1880s and '90s, in part in response to economic stresses and the huge increase in the numbers of immigrants (from 2.8 million in 1871–80 to 5.2 million in 1881–90), in part because of a perceived change in the origins of immigrants themselves.

The 'new' immigrants

The bulk of immigrants after 1880 came from southern and eastern Europe. These areas had suffered the collapse of the old agricultural order, huge population increases and anti-semitic pogroms. The immigrants, taking advantage of the easier and cheaper travel offered by steamships, arrived in a growing flood in the United States. Total immigration soared to 8.8 million in 1901–10 and 5.7 million in the subsequent decade. 'New' immigrants – to a far greater extent than the 'old' (other than the Irish) – tended to settle in cities. Cities like New York and Chicago developed a mosaic of ethnic neighbourhoods. Many Americans, between the 1880s and 1914, became increasingly uneasy over whether such groups could be assimilated and began to support demands for immigration restriction. The First World War, making Americans newly aware of their ethnic disunity, and the reaction against Europe that followed the war and the postwar recession, drove Congress, in 1921 and 1924, to impose ceilings on total immigrant numbers and introduce a 'quota' system that was heavily biased against the nations that had produced most of the 'new' immigration.

Controls and continuity

The legislation of the 1920s banned immigration from most Asian countries, but exempted the western hemisphere from its provisions since many southwestern employers regarded Mexican labour as essential. In 1943, the US government introduced the *braceros* system, allowing large numbers of Mexican agricultural labourers to enter the country. Meanwhile, immigration laws were relaxed to allow successive waves of refugees to enter: fugitives from communism in eastern Europe; Cubans after the revolution of 1959; and Vietnamese after the collapse of South Vietnam in 1975. The law was liberalized in 1965, allowing increased immigration from Asia. Indeed, throughout the 1970s, Asia (especially the Philippines and Korea) contributed more immigrants than Europe.

The poet Walt Whitman, writing in the 1850s, described America as 'not merely a nation but a teeming of nations.' Immigrants have made a massive contribution to American finance, society, politics and culture. American society today is recognisably and irreversibly multi-cultural. Yet anxieties persist on the part of some Americans towards immigration both legal and illegal (the so-called 'wetbacks') from Mexico that has transformed much of the South-West and Far West into predominantly Spanish-speaking areas.

3 Between 1840 and 1930, the United States accepted millions of immigrants from European countries *(map below)*. In the first decades of this tremendous migration, most immigrants came from northern and western Europe (Britain, with Ireland, Germany and Scandinavia). From about 1890, the main source of immigrants became southern and eastern Europe (especially Italy, Austria-Hungary and Russia). After the passage of the restrictive legislation of 1921 and 1924, total immigration into the United States fell sharply.

4 The total of immigrants from different nationalities over the period from 1820 to 1930 *(chart right)* demonstrates that, during this period, English-speaking immigrants from Ireland, Britain and Canada contributed a good proportion of total immigration. But to think of immigrants solely in terms of their 'national origins' is slightly misleading. There was comparatively little immigration from Russia or Poland before the 1880s, for example, and many of those who came from these countries thereafter were Jewish and identified themselves in this way rather than as Russian or Poles.

4 Total immigrants to the US, 1820–1930

6,400,000
3,200,000
1,600,000
800,000
400,000
200,000
100,000
50,000
25,000
0

Germany, Italy, Ireland, United Kingdom, Russia, Canada, Austria, Hungary, Sweden, Mexico, Norway, France, Caribbean, Poland, China, Japan, Portugal, Netherlands, South America, Aust/N. Zealand, Central America, Africa

3 Immigration to the United States, 1841–1930

numbers of immigrants in peak decades from selected countries:

- 1841–50
- 1881–90
- 1901–10
- 1921–30

USA, CANADA, MEXICO, CENTRAL AMERICA, CARIBBEAN, SOUTH AMERICA, AFRICA, RUSSIA, CHINA, JAPAN, AUSTRALIA, NEW ZEALAND, SWEDEN, NORWAY, POLAND, GERMANY, UK, IRELAND, NETHERLANDS, FRANCE, AUSTRIA, HUNGARY, PORTUGAL, ITALY

5 The population of the United States *(charts below)* increased steadily until the Civil War was over in 1865. It then began to rise much more sharply. Until around 1880, population grew fastest in towns. Stimulated by industrialization and mass immigration, some cities then expanded very fast: Chicago doubled in size between 1880 and 1890, to reach a population of a million for the first time. Because of the vast geographical size of the United States and its territorial expansion during the 19th century, the massive population increase since 1790 is only partly reflected in figures for population density.

5 Population of the United States, 1790–1995

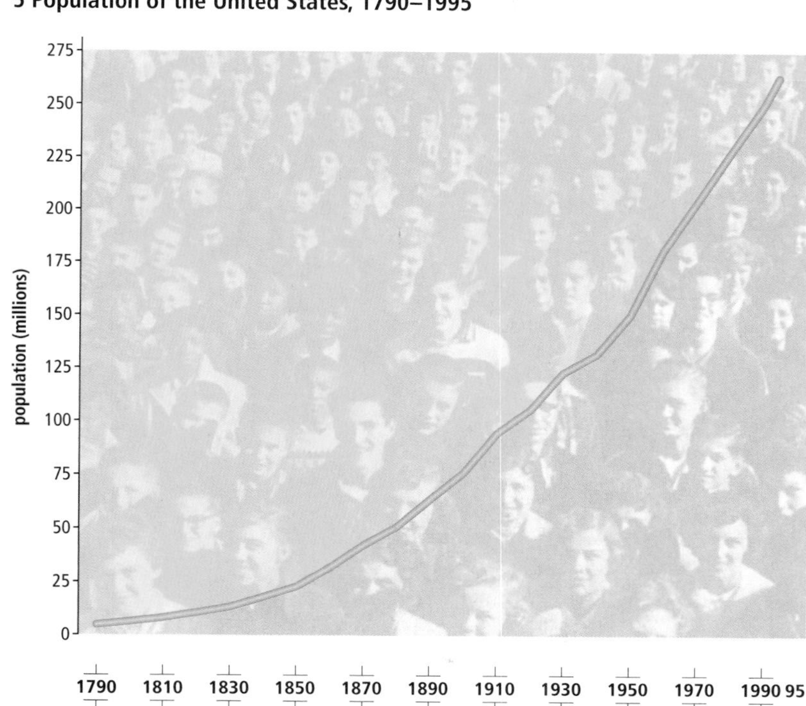

population per square mile
0
20
40
60
80
100

1619 *Arrival in Virginia of the first black slaves*
1840s *Irish potato famine*
1848 *Failed revolutions in Germany; 'liberals' leave for United States*
1882 *First Federal immigration law. First Chinese Exclusion Act*
1892 *Ellis Island becomes New York's immigrant reception depot*
1924 *Johnson-Reed Act introduces quota system based on national origins to limit immigration*
1943 *Introduction of* braceros *system*
1965 *Abolition of national origins system*

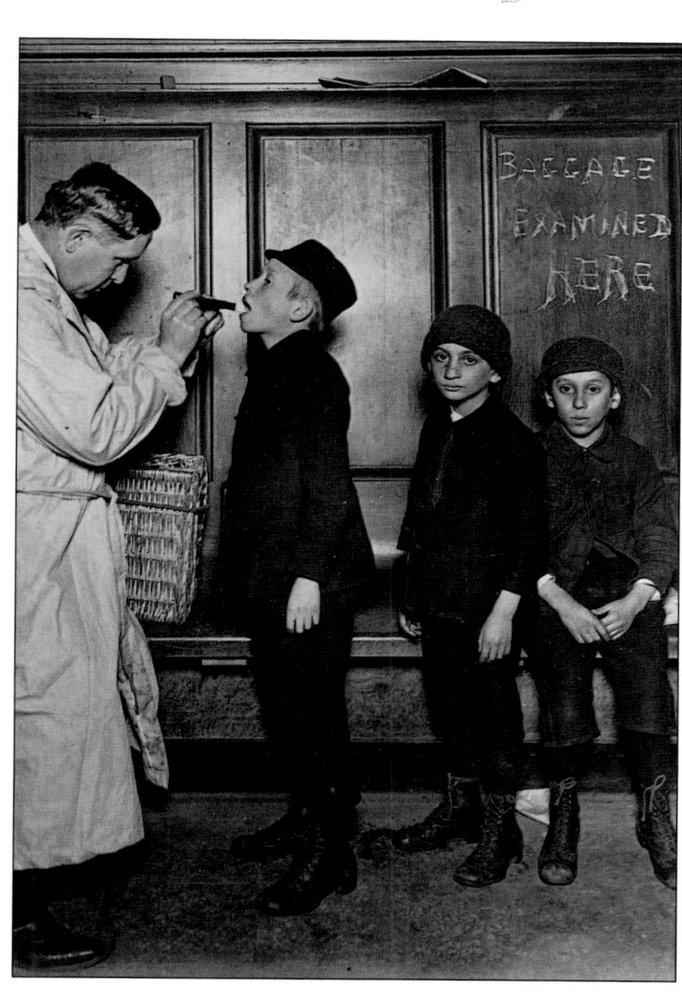

Children at Ellis island *(right).* In 1892 Ellis Island became New York's main reception depot for immigrants. Its immigration officers had the task of weeding out and excluding those regarded as undesirables. The first federal immigration law in 1882 began the task of defining exactly who was undesirable.

1810 to 1930

Latin America: independence and national growth

See also

European expansion overseas p. 158
The Americas, 1500–1810 p. 162
The emerging global economy, c. 1775 p. 198
The age of revolt, 1773–1814 p. 202
Napoleon and the reshaping of Europe, 1799–1815 p. 204
Latin America: revolution and reaction since 1930 p. 292

The early 19th century saw the Portuguese and Spanish colonies break away from their mother countries, in the latter case after a bitter military struggle. The new states which emerged were at first unstable; initial confederations soon broke up and military dictatorships flourished. By the early 20th century comparative stability had returned.

1808 *Napoleonic invasion of Portugal and Spain effectively begins the movement for independence*

1819 *Battle of Boyacá leads to independence of Colombia*

1821 *Battle near Carabobo finally secures Venezuelan independence*

1822 *Brazil declares independence*

1824 *Peru and Bolivia become independent*

1879 *War of the Pacific (Chile, Bolivia, Peru)*

1888 *Brazil becomes the last Latin American country to abolish slavery*

1910 *Start of Mexican revolution*

Simón Bolívar (1783–1830) ***(picture above right)*** **became known as 'The Liberator' for his role in the emancipation of South America from Spanish rule. After participating in several unsuccessful revolts, he and his army defeated the Spanish at Boyacá in 1819 and organized the republic of Gran Colombia. In 1821, he defeated the Spanish near Carabobo, ensuring Venezuelan independence. Between 1822 and 1824 he also helped free Ecuador and Peru. Southern Peru became a new republic, named Bolivia in his honour.**

BY THE LATE 18TH CENTURY, demands for political freedom, administrative autonomy and economic self-determination were growing throughout Latin America. Yet, while they were encouraged by the American and French revolutions, it was the Napoleonic invasion of Spain and Portugal in 1808 that enabled them to develop into successful movements for independence. Having fled from Lisbon to Rio de Janeiro, which then became the centre of their empire, the Portuguese royal family presided over the relatively peaceful transition of Brazil from colony to independent nation. After his father had returned to Portugal, Pedro I, renouncing his claims to the Portuguese throne and assuming the title emperor, declared the independence of Brazil. This, together with the fact that the planter elite were too fearful of slave revolts to split into factions, made for considerable political and institutional continuity.

> IT IS NOTORIOUS THAT THE MORE WE RELY ON FOREIGN INTERESTS TO SUPPLY OUR NEEDS, THE MORE WE DIMINISH OUR NATIONAL INDEPENDENCE; AND OUR RELIANCE NOW EVEN EXTENDS TO DAILY AND VITAL NEEDS.
>
> **Rafael Revenga, Venezuelan economist, 1829**
>
> MANY TYRANTS WILL ARISE ON MY TOMB.
>
> **Simón Bolívar, 1830**

The revolt against Spain

Spain, on the other hand, tried to crush revolts in her own Latin American colonies, and several years of conflict were necessary before her government acknowledged defeat. A southern revolution was carried by San Martín's Army of the Andes from Buenos Aires to Chile and beyond. A northern revolution, more vigorously opposed by Spain, was led by Bolívar from Venezuela to the battlefield of Boyacá in Colombia (then called New Granada). Both, by 1822, had converged on Peru, the fortress of Spain in South America. In the north, insurgency in Mexico followed a course of its own – frustrated social revolution, then prolonged counter-revolution and finally the seizure of power by Iturbide, an army officer, who proclaimed himself Emperor Agustín I.

The independence movement as a whole was essentially political. It involved a transfer of authority, but little social or economic change. Its leaders were mostly drawn from the Creole population, Iberians born in America. They were mainly politically inexperienced and, in many of the new Latin American republics, the decades between independence and mid-century were characterized by violent political conflicts. With the masses excluded from political decision-making, politics became a matter of rivalries amongst oligarchic families and military cliques. *Caudillos* – military leaders – fought with one another for political power without greatly affecting the mainly rural and traditional societies surrounding them.

Political stability

From the middle of the 19th century onwards, Latin American politics tended towards greater stability (even if still authoritarian), while economies began to orient themselves more towards overseas markets. Foreign capital helped rejuvenate the mining industry and build railways. Once Argentina became politically stable in the 1860s, British investors and southern European immigrants helped transform the agriculture of the pampas. Soon, Argentinian wheat and beef were major exports to Britain. Chilean nitrates, Brazilian rubber and Mexican copper also found European markets. Yet Latin American economies remained essentially 'colonial' – they provided raw materials rather than finished products. Apart from mills in Mexico and Brazil producing textiles primarily for domestic consumption, there was little industry. There was a brief, rapid surge of industrial development during the First World War, aimed at producing goods that were no longer available from Europe or the United States, but this was largely killed by a flood of cheap imports in the 1920s.

The early 20th century

At the beginning of the 20th century, urbanization occurred very rapidly, encouraged by European immigration and the displacement of peasants from the land as commercial agriculture expanded. Both the middle class and the working class were growing, altering the social profile of the population. Economic development, in the end, helped destroy many of the regimes that supported it. In Mexico, resentment at native *hacendados* and foreign investors led to the overthrow of the long Díaz regime (1876–1910) and a slow but successful social revolution that, over the next three decades, would nationalize foreign-owned oil companies and other corporations and expropriate most agricultural land in order to redistribute it to peasants. In Argentina (1916) and Chile (1920), electoral reform made it possible for radical parties supported by the middle class to win at the ballot box and elect their own candidate as president.

3 The new nations of Latin America **were classic export economies, exploiting cheap land and labour to produce raw materials for a world market** ***(map below)*****. After independence, they carried on exporting the same products to Europe as during the colonial period: silver, cacao, sugar, coffee, hides and tobacco. Economic development was discouraged for several decades by the survival of slavery, small domestic markets and foreign competition. But the last years of the 19th century saw an influx of foreign capital, above all from Britain and the US, that improved communications and encouraged the exploitation of new products.**

1 Latin American nationalists fought not only Spain and Portugal, but also each other. Uruguay split from Brazil in 1828, but otherwise Brazil preserved its territorial integrity. Elsewhere, fragmentation quickly followed emancipation from Spanish rule *(map below)*. In 1823, Central America seceded from Mexico and in 1839 itself split into five republics. In 1830, Venezuela and Ecuador seceded from Gran Colombia, the republic created by Bolívar. Subsequent boundary disputes led to several major wars, including the war between Mexico and the United States (1846–8) and the war of the Pacific (1879–83) between Chile, Peru and Bolivia.

2 In 1817, José de San Martín wrested Chile from Spanish forces *(map left)*. Simón Bolívar defeated the Spanish to free Colombia in 1819 and Venezuela in 1821. By 1824 their armies had liberated all of Spanish America.

population

	1825	1900	1930
Cuba	700,000	1.6m	3.8m
Mexico	6.8m	13.6m	16.6m
Guatemala	850,000*	1.4m	1.8m
El Salvador	370,000*	1.2m	1.8m
Honduras	350,000*	400,000	950,000
Nicaragua	300,000*	400,000	750,000
Costa Rica	100,000*	300,000	500,000
Brazil	4m	17m	33.6m
Colombia	1.3m	4.1m	7.4m
Peru	1.4m	3.8m	5.7m
Venezuela	800,000	2.3m	3m
Ecuador	550,000	1.4m	2.2m
Bolivia	1.1m	1.7m	2.2m
Argentina	630,000	4.7m	11.9m
Chile	1m	2.9m	4.4m
Uruguay	50,000	800,000	1.6m
Paraguay	180,000	690,000	900,000

* 1850

4 During the 19th century, most Latin American societies were composed of three main elements *(map above)*: a Creole elite of Iberians born in the Americas, many owning large landed estates or *haciendas*; a small, mostly urban middle class; and a huge mass of landless and largely illiterate Indians, mestizos (persons of mixed Indian and European ancestry), Blacks (predominantly slaves or the descendants of slaves) and mulattos (descendants of Blacks and another race).

1800 to 1923
The disintegration of the Ottoman empire

See also
The Early Modern Muslim empires, 1520–1700 p. 168
The rise of nationalism in Europe, 1800–1914 p. 214
The Russian empire: expansion and modernization, 1815–1917 p. 230
European rivalries and alliances, 1878–1914 p. 248
The First World War, 1914–18 p. 250
European political problems, 1919–34 p. 262

THE ORDER WENT OUT THAT NOT A SINGLE ARMENIAN WAS TO REMAIN IN THE TOWN. THE POLICEMEN AND GENDARMES RUSHED INTO THE ARMENIAN QUARTERS AND WITH BLOWS FROM STICKS AND RIFLE BUTTS FORCED ALL THE ARMENIANS TO FLEE ... SHORTLY, THE GENDARMES WITHDREW TO THE MOUNTAIN-SIDE AND BEGAN A HAIL OF RIFLE FIRE. AS SOON AS THE FIRST ARMENIANS FELL DEAD, THE THRONG WENT INTO TURMOIL ... ALL THE BEAUTIFUL ARMENIAN WOMEN JUMPED INTO THE RIVER. THE WHOLE SURFACE OF THE RIVER WAS COVERED WITH THEM.

Konstantinos Kaloyeridis, witness of the Armenian massacres

During the 19th century, the Ottoman empire – 'the sick man of Europe' – slowly disintegrated under the impact of foreign encroachment, popular anti-Turkish nationalism and a powerful reform movement. Defeat in the First World War brought complete collapse and the emergence of a modern Turkish national state under Kemal Atatürk.

1798 *Napoleon invades Egypt*

1830 *Greek independence*

1839 *Start of Tanzimat reform era*

1877 *Sultan Abdulhamid II suspends constitution*

1878 *Serbia, Romania, Montenegro and Bulgaria win independence*

1908 *Young Turk revolution*

1912–3 *Balkan Wars*

1915–6 *Armenian massacres*

1917–8 *Arab revolt: Ottoman territories in Middle East lost*

1920 *Atatürk abolishes sultanate*

1923 *Treaty of Lausanne creates new Turkish state*

BY THE END OF THE 18TH CENTURY, the Ottoman empire was no longer the military and cultural force it had once been. In 1798, the Ottoman province of Egypt was invaded and occupied by Napoleon. This was the first time since the Crusades that a European power had encroached directly on the Ottoman heartlands. Although Napoleon was ousted by the British, Egypt was seized by the Albanian general Muhammad Ali, who had been sent to attack the French by the Ottoman sultan, Selim III. From 1805, Egypt became independent of the empire, beginning a century-long process of territorial decline and persistent intervention by the European powers.

The Tanzimat reforms

Defeat at the hands of the Greeks and their European allies in 1827–9 (*see* p. 214) forced the Ottoman empire to modernize. The failure of the traditional janissary warriors during the war led to far-reaching military reforms based on European models. In 1839 a young generation of liberal officers and bureaucrats launched the Tanzimat reform movement, which culminated in 1876 with the granting of a parliamentary constitution.

Following Turkish defeat in war with Russia in 1877, which led a year later to the independence of Serbia, Montenegro and Romania, the new sultan, Abdulhamid II, suspended the constitution and ruled for 30 years as a modern authoritarian monarch.

Abdulhamid introduced further reforms and attempted to modernize the economy while suppressing popular politics. The chronic financial instability of the sultanate was brought under control by granting European powers tax-raising privileges within the empire in 1881. The growth of popular nationalism was brutally repressed. When Armenian nationalists, representative of the large Christian community living in Anatolia, developed their own national awakening, the Zartonk, it sparked the revival of popular Islam. In 1895–6 the state orchestrated a series of massacres in which 200,000 Armenians died at the hands of Muslim Turks.

The creation of modern Turkey

Abdulhamid was overthrown in 1908 by a revolution of 'Young Turks', who were drawn from among the new liberal intelligentsia and nationalist army officers organized through the Paris-based Committee of Union and Progress, founded in 1889. The sultanate was suspended and a modernizing regime installed. In 1913 the moderate liberals were overthrown by a military coup and hardline nationalists and Islamicists under Enver Pasha came to dominate Ottoman politics.

In October 1914 Enver Pasha brought Turkey in on Germany's side in the First World War and in November 1914 a *jihad*, or Holy War, was declared. On the grounds that Armenians in eastern Anatolia were a threat to the Turkish war effort, the regime unleashed a wave of savage violence against the Christian community. An estimated 1.5 million Armenians died, others were forced into slavery or made to convert to Islam. A fraction of the population arrived in deportation centres in Mesopotamia after enduring long 'death marches'.

Following Turkish defeat in 1918, the Young Turk regime was overthrown and the sultan briefly restored as an Allied puppet. But in 1920, Turkish nationalists led a war of liberation against the Allied occupying forces. Under the army officer Kemal Atatürk, and with the support of the emerging Turkish middle classes, the Turkish army reconquered Anatolia. The rest of the former empire was divided up between France and Britain by the League of Nations as mandated territories. In the Treaty of Lausanne in 1923, Turkish independence was recognized, and Atatürk began the process of building a modern nation state based on secular rule, mass education and economic reform.

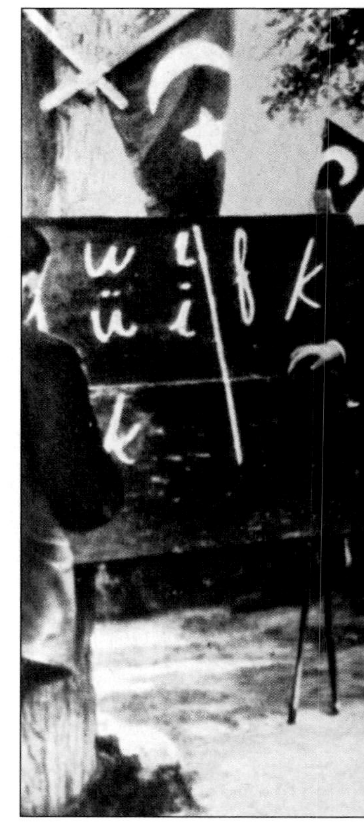

2 In the 19th century relations between Muslims and Armenian Christians in the empire slowly deteriorated. In the 1890s, a modest Armenian revolt was mercilessly crushed by the Ottomans. In 1915 under the impact of war and defeat a serious crisis erupted in eastern Anatolia which led to the deportation of the Christian population and the deaths of an estimated 1.5 million Armenians by 1923 *(map left)*. As Armenian populations were driven south towards Mesopotamia most were killed or died of hunger on the way. When the Turks regained eastern Anatolia in 1923, thousands of Armenians fled to join their co-religionists in the USSR.

4 Between 1750 and 1914 the territory of the Ottoman empire declined by almost 50 per cent as distant provinces were taken over by European colonial powers or lost to nationalist revolts *(chart below)*. By 1914 Turkey ruled only a fraction of its former European territory together with a swathe of territory from Anatolia to Arabia.

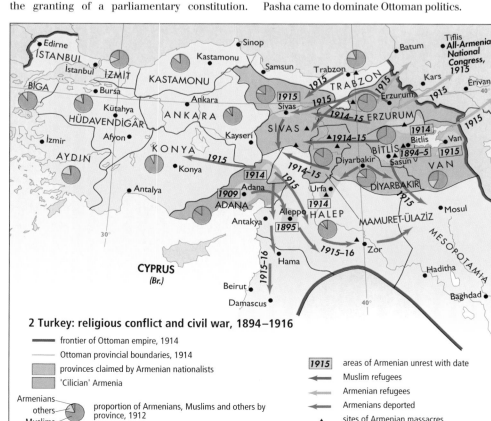

2 Turkey: religious conflict and civil war, 1894–1916

- frontier of Ottoman empire, 1914
- Ottoman provincial boundaries, 1914
- provinces claimed by Armenian nationalists
- 'Cilician' Armenia
- Armenians / others / Muslims: proportion of Armenians, Muslims and others by province, 1912
- 1915: areas of Armenian unrest with date
- Muslim refugees
- Armenian refugees
- Armenians deported
- sites of Armenian massacres

4 The contraction of the Ottoman empire

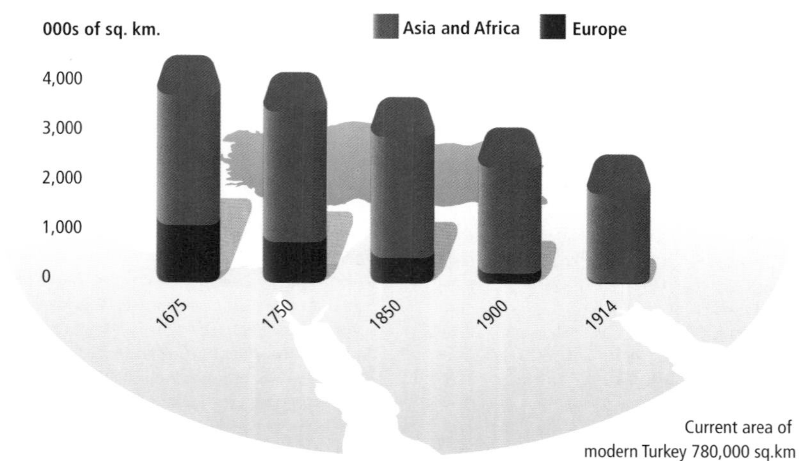

1 The Ottoman empire slowly disintegrated in the 19th and early 20th centuries *(map right)*. Egypt won its autonomy in 1805 while the Balkan nationalities broke away or had their independence confirmed one by one: Greece in 1830, Serbia, Romania and Montenegro in 1878, Bulgaria in 1908, Albania in 1912. Anatolia, the Ottoman heartland, became modern Turkey in 1923.

5 Ethnic composition of Ottoman empire, 1914

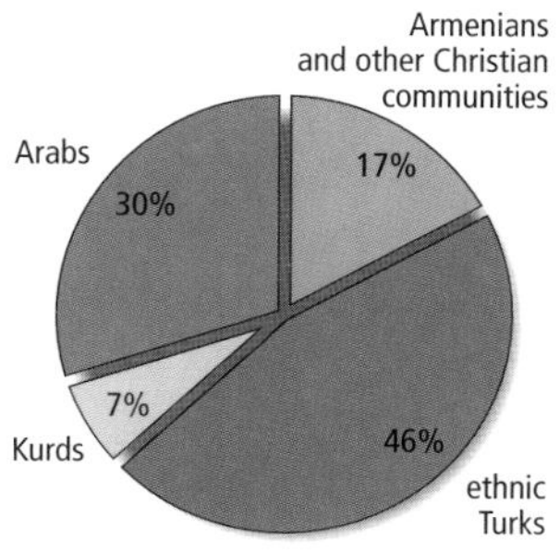

5 The Ottoman empire was a mix of ethnic groups in which Turks remained a minority *(chart above)*. Most of the empire's inhabitants were Muslim but there were almost three million Christians and Jews in Anatolia.

Kemal Mustapha, or Atatürk, – 'father of the Turks', as he styled himself *(below)* – was an Ottoman commander in the First World War. His effective leadership of Turkish forces in 1922 saw him become president of the new Turkish republic that year. He was determined to turn Turkey into a modern, industrialized, Western-style secular state.

3 Under the Allied-imposed Treaty of Sèvres, the remnants of the Ottoman empire were to be dismembered leaving a rump Turkish state *(map right)*. Parts of Anatolia were to be under Greek, French and British control and an independent Armenia and Kurdistan created. Greek occupation prompted a nationalist revival. The army overthrew the pro-Allied sultan and drove the Greeks out, recaptured parts of Armenia and defeated a Franco-Armenian force in Cilicia.

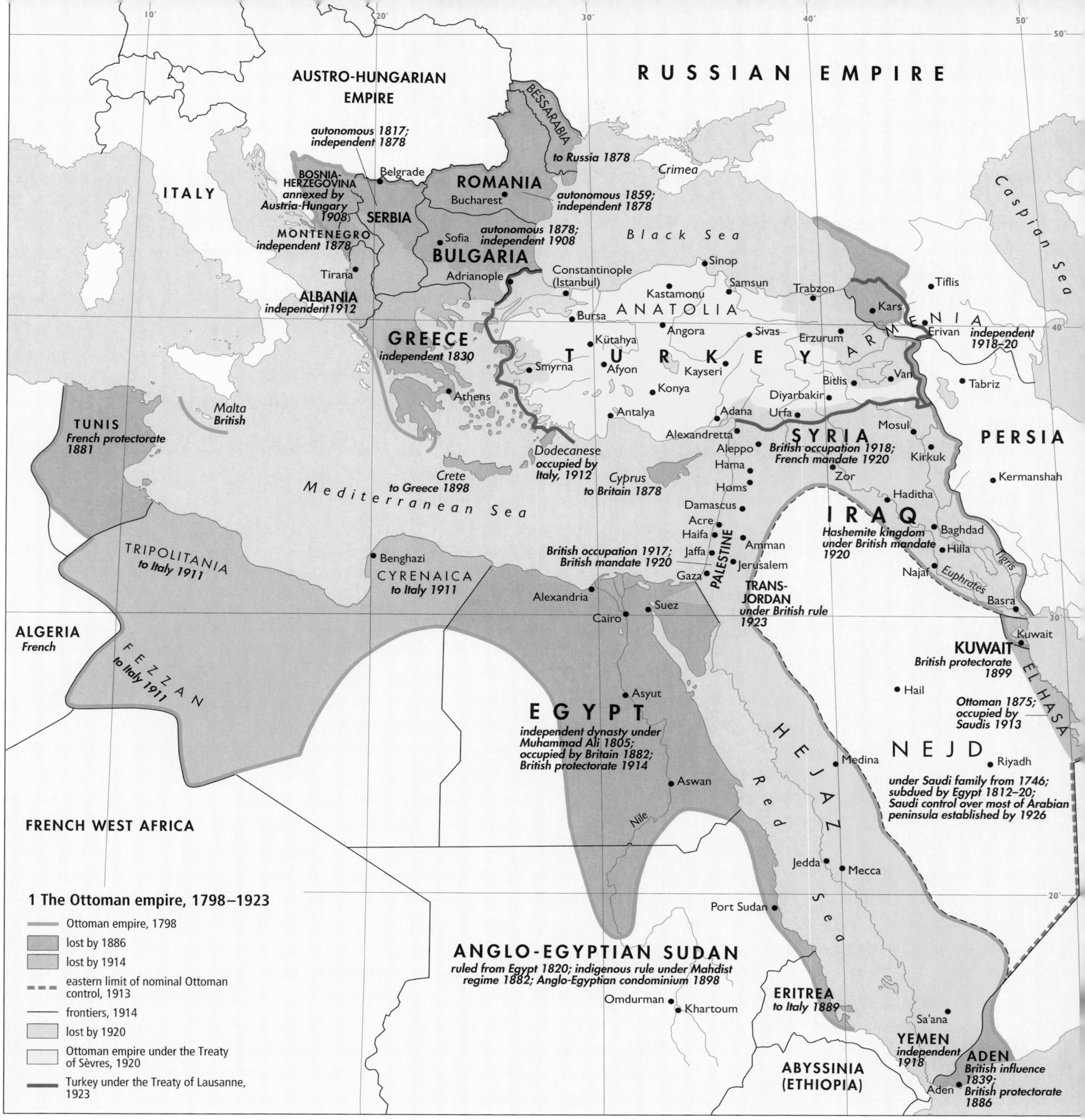

1 The Ottoman empire, 1798–1923

- Ottoman empire, 1798
- lost by 1886
- lost by 1914
- eastern limit of nominal Ottoman control, 1913
- frontiers, 1914
- lost by 1920
- Ottoman empire under the Treaty of Sèvres, 1920
- Turkey under the Treaty of Lausanne, 1923

RUSSIAN EMPIRE
AUSTRO-HUNGARIAN EMPIRE
BESSARABIA to Russia 1878
autonomous 1817; independent 1878
BOSNIA-HERZEGOVINA annexed by Austria-Hungary 1908
SERBIA
MONTENEGRO independent 1878
ROMANIA autonomous 1859; independent 1878
BULGARIA autonomous 1878; independent 1908
ALBANIA independent 1912
GREECE independent 1830
ITALY
Malta British
TUNIS French protectorate 1881
TRIPOLITANIA to Italy 1911
CYRENAICA to Italy 1911
FEZZAN to Italy 1911
ALGERIA French
FRENCH WEST AFRICA
Crete to Greece 1898
Dodecanese occupied by Italy, 1912
Cyprus to Britain 1878
TURKEY
ANATOLIA
ARMENIA independent 1918–20
SYRIA British occupation 1918; French mandate 1920
PALESTINE British occupation 1917; British mandate 1920
TRANS-JORDAN under British rule 1923
IRAQ Hashemite kingdom under British mandate 1920
PERSIA
KUWAIT British protectorate 1899
EL HASA Ottoman 1875; occupied by Saudis 1913
NEJD under Saudi family from 1746; subdued by Egypt 1812–20; Saudi control over most of Arabian peninsula established by 1926
HEJAZ
EGYPT independent dynasty under Muhammad Ali 1805; occupied by Britain 1882; British protectorate 1914
ANGLO-EGYPTIAN SUDAN ruled from Egypt 1820; indigenous rule under Mahdist regime 1882; Anglo-Egyptian condominium 1898
ERITREA to Italy 1889
ABYSSINIA (ETHIOPIA)
YEMEN independent 1918
ADEN British influence 1839; British protectorate 1886
Black Sea
Caspian Sea
Mediterranean Sea
Red Sea

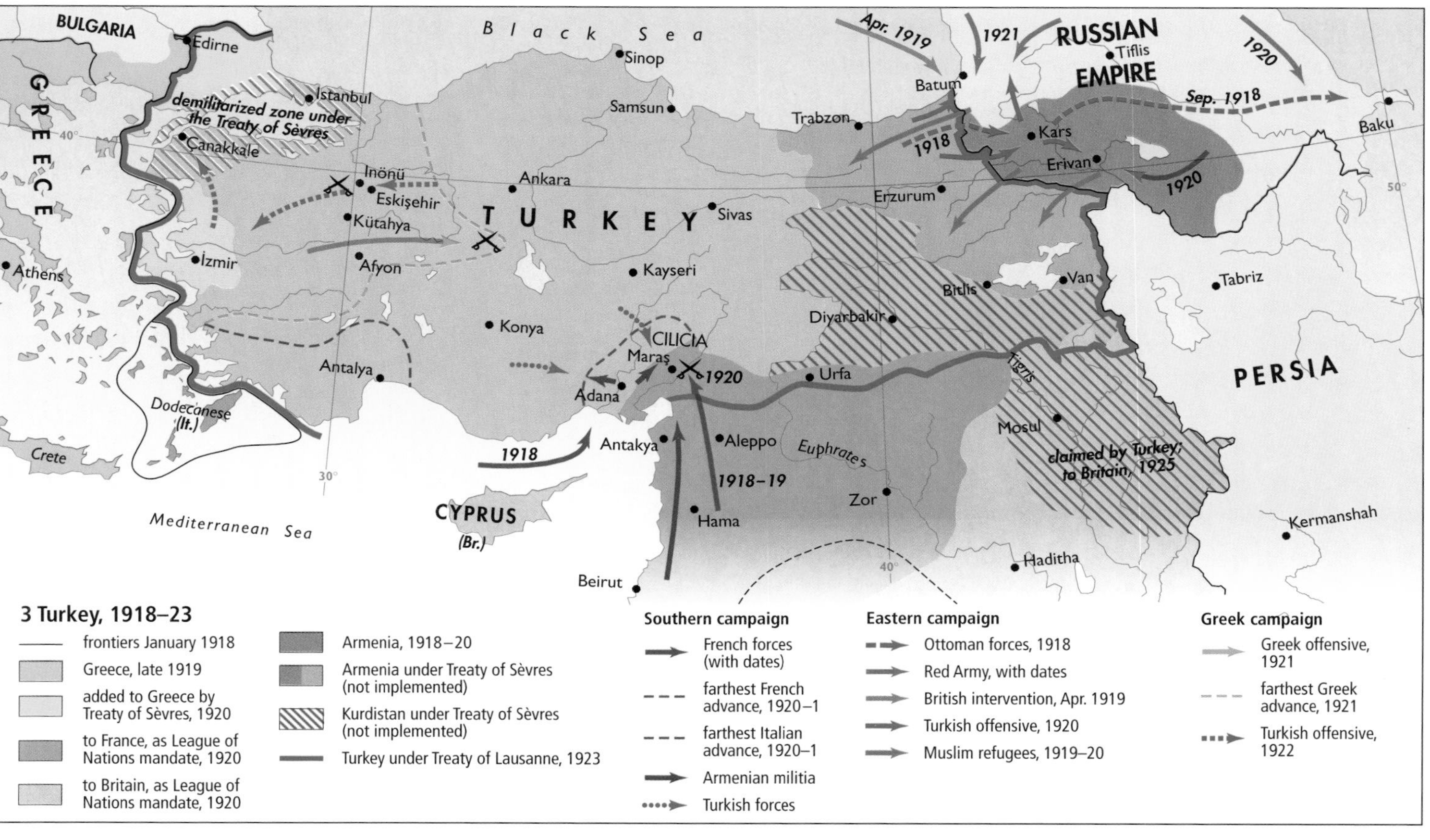

The Russian empire: expansion and modernization

See also
Russian expansion in Europe and Asia p. 160
The age of partition: eastern Europe, 1648–1795 p. 196
Napoleon and the reshaping of Europe p. 204
The disintegration of the Ottoman empire, 1800–1923 p. 228
The First World War, 1914–8 p. 250
The Russian revolution, 1917–29 p. 256

1825 *Nicholas I becomes tsar; 'Decembrist' uprising suppressed*

1853–5 *Defeat in Crimean War against France and Britain*

1861 *Emancipation of the serfs*

1881 *Alexander II, the 'reforming Tsar', assassinated*

1904–5 *Russia defeated in war with Japan*

1905 *Revolt forces constitutional reform*

1906–10 *Stolypin agrarian reforms*

Feb. 1917 *Tsar Nicholas II overthrown by popular revolution*

Though Russia emerged in the 19th century as one of the European Great Powers, her international status was compromised by economic backwardness and military failure. Efforts to modernize created demands for revolutionary change, and when Russia failed again on the battlefield in the First World War the monarchy collapsed in revolution.

IN 1815 RUSSIA WAS widely regarded as the foremost power in Europe. Its role in the defeat of revolutionary France had left it the largest military power on the continent and greatly reinforced the prestige of the ruling elite, which was able to reassert its own power while stifling liberal reform and modernization.

Under the tsars Alexander I (1801–25) and Nicholas I (1825–55) Russia remained a predominantly rural society, dominated by the crown, the nobility and corrupt bureaucrats and gendarmes. Attempts at political liberalization were ruthlessly suppressed. In December 1825, opponents of the autocracy, strongly influenced by Western models, tried to overthrow the tsar and install a modernizing regime. The 'Decembrists', drawn mainly from the army, were easily crushed, and Nicholas I, whose one-day-old reign they had tried to destroy, imposed a harsh regime of censorship and political oppression. The instrument of control, a forerunner of the secret police empires of the 20th century, was the notorious Third Department, set up in 1826 to suppress threats to the crown and any flirtation with Western ideas.

Abroad, Russia was seen as a force for conservatism in international affairs. Under Nicholas Russia tried to increase its influence in the Balkans and the Middle East, while opposing revolutionary and nationalist threats. In 1849 Russian troops put down revolution in Hungary, and in 1853 Russia seized the provinces of Moldavia and Wallachia from Ottoman Turkey and destroyed the Turkish Black Sea Fleet at Sinop. Alarmed by Russian ambitions in the Holy Land, France and Britain declared war and invaded the Crimean peninsula. In a campaign notable for military ineptitude on both sides, Russia was nonetheless defeated. Rebuffed in Europe, Russia thereafter turned her attentions more to expansion in Asia (*see* map 2). But the humiliation of defeat on her own soil had exposed Russian backwardness. The new tsar, Alexander II (1855–81), embarked on a widespread programme of reform.

> WITH EVERY DAY THE NEED AND MISERY OF THE PEASANTS GREW. THE SCENES OF STARVATION WERE DEEPLY DISTRESSING, AND IT WAS ALL THE MORE DISTURBING TO SEE THAT AMIDST ALL THIS SUFFERING AND DEATH THERE SPRAWLED HUGE ESTATES, BEAUTIFUL AND WELL-FURNISHED MANORS, AND THAT THE GRAND OLD LIFE OF THE SQUIRES, WITH ITS JOLLY HUNTS AND BALLS, ITS BANQUETS AND ITS CONCERTS, CARRIED ON AS USUAL.
>
> **Sergei Semenov, peasant leader, 1912**

The reforming tsars

Alexander's intention was not to liberalize Russia but to make it more efficient. Both he and his successor, Alexander III, were wedded to the idea of royal autocracy and saw reform as necessary to strengthen it rather than to alter its essential nature. Nonetheless, in 1861, following growing unrest, the serfs were emancipated while in 1864 new institutions of local government, the *zemstvos*, were introduced to stem the demand for liberal constitutional reform. In the same year Russia's legal system was overhauled on Western lines. Army reforms created a more effective fighting force. But Alexander set his face against political concessions or widespread industrialization. Radical groups turned to violent terrorism and in 1881, after three attempts, the 'People's Will' group succeeded in assassinating the tsar.

Regicide produced a backlash. Alexander III introduced industrialization schemes and encouraged modern banking and transport in order to build a strong Russia capable of resisting internal demands for change or pressure from the West. A conservative nationalism was whipped up against Westernizers and Jews, while reform groups were savagely repressed. In 1881 the *Okhrana* secret police was established. In 1889 Land Captains were instituted in the countryside to restore the influence of the gentry. In the new industrial centres trade unions were outlawed and socialist

3 In 1858 there were over 10 million serfs in Russia, 45 per cent of the adult male population *(map left)*. Many serfs paid dues (*obrok*) in kind or cash to their landlords; others were tied to the land through labour service (*barshchina*). By the 1850s there was widespread rural protest against serfdom and mass migrations from the major serf areas in western central Russia. In 1861 Tsar Alexander II granted emancipation to the serfs as part of a programme of modernization.

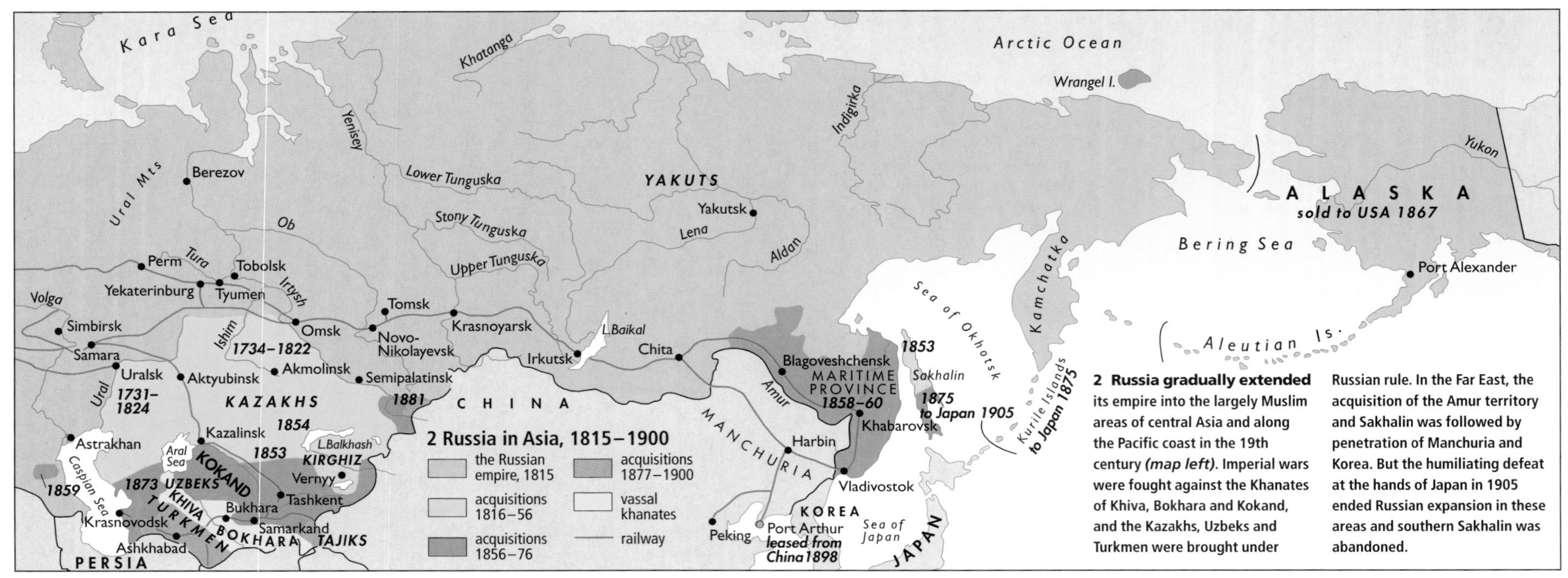

2 Russia gradually extended its empire into the largely Muslim areas of central Asia and along the Pacific coast in the 19th century *(map left)*. Imperial wars were fought against the Khanates of Khiva, Bokhara and Kokand, and the Kazakhs, Uzbeks and Turkmen were brought under Russian rule. In the Far East, the acquisition of the Amur territory and Sakhalin was followed by penetration of Manchuria and Korea. But the humiliating defeat at the hands of Japan in 1905 ended Russian expansion in these areas and southern Sakhalin was abandoned.

'It is better to abolish serfdom from above than wait for it to abolish itself from below,' declared Alexander II *(above)* in 1857. Four years later Alexander did indeed free the serfs. He soon found that it was one thing to emancipate them, another to feed, clothe and educate them. Radical though they were in Russian terms, Alexander's reforms failed to address the core problems facing his country.

movements persecuted. Russia in 1900 was more modern and militarily stronger, but its political system remained reactionary and unreformed.

Revolution and war

Under the last tsar, Nicholas II (1894–1917), the tension between the unreformed system and the new social forces thrown up by modernization reached a climax. Defeat in the Far East by Japan in 1905 saw protest reach a crisis-point. Revolt broke out across Russia. Sergei Witte, the leading architect of modernization, persuaded the tsar to grant a constitution. The October Manifesto of 1905 instituted a parliament, or Duma, a restricted franchise and the promise of civil rights.

Nicholas soon reverted to type. The Duma was prorogued twice until he got deputies he could work with; civil rights were never fully granted; the franchise became ever more narrow. The tsar still ruled by decree and through the vast police and bureaucratic apparatus. By 1914, when Russia entered the First World War, there was wide expectation of revolution. Defeat in battle, hunger in the cities and corrupt management of the home front produced irresistible pressure for a radical break. In February 1917 Nicholas abdicated, and the tsarist empire collapsed.

5 Foreign investment in Russia, 1861–1913

year	state bonds	private shares & bonds	total
1861	400*	8	408*
1881	2345*	115	2460*
1893	2713	238	2951
1900	3995	911	4910
1913	5461	1960	7585

in millions of roubles — * estimated

5 Russia was short of capital to begin the industrial modernization drive of the 1890s and relied on overseas loans *(chart above)*, much of them from France. By 1913 an estimated one-third of all capital in Russia was foreign-owned, concentrated in the oil, iron and steel and chemical sectors.

1 European Russia, 1815–1914

urban population increase, 1861–1914 the circle is proportionate to the size of growth
economic activity to 1861
economic activity 1861–1914
metallurgical and metalworking industry
coal mining
iron ore mining
textile industry
sugar refining
oil industry
railway
frontiers 1914

1 Despite her vast size Russia remained economically underdeveloped for most of the 19th century. Railway building and industrial development expanded from the 1880s with the help of foreign capital *(map above)*. Under the influence of the finance minister, Sergei Witte, Russia experienced high rates of industrial growth from the 1890s, particularly in the Donbass region of the Ukraine. But living-standards remained well below European levels and social tensions worsened as industry developed.

4 In 1853 Britain and France declared war on Russia following a dispute about who had custody of the Christian Holy Places in Ottoman-ruled Palestine *(maps below and right)*. Though the Anglo-French force was poorly equipped and undermined by disease and inter-allied squabbles, the Russian forces proved even more incompetent. Russian defeats at Balaklava and Inkerman in 1854 opened the way to the loss of the Black Sea base of Sevastopol in 1855. By highlighting Russian weaknesses, the war led to widespread reforms.

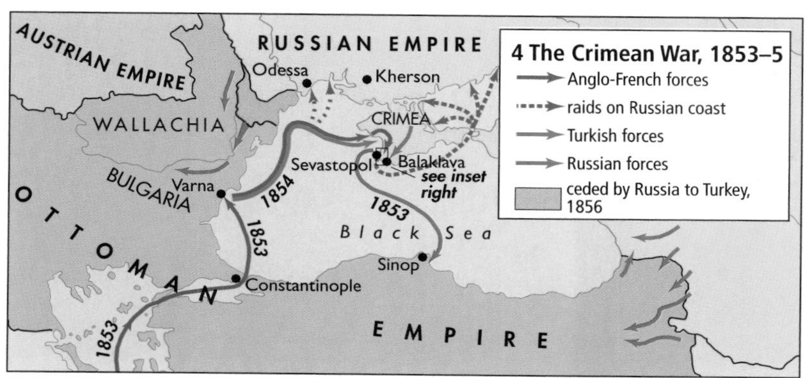

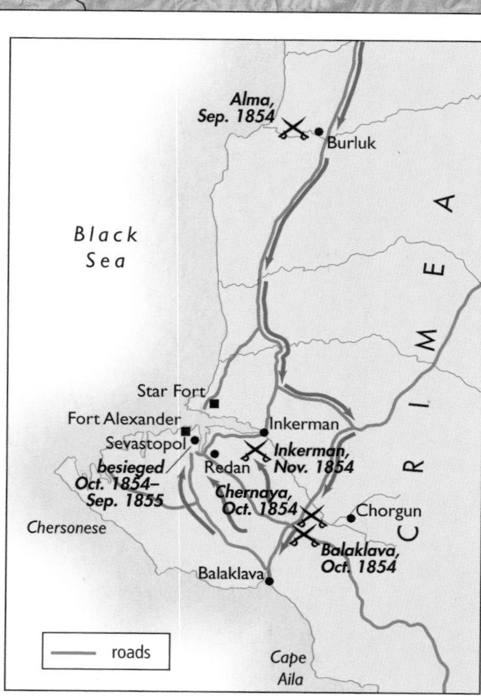

1839 to 1911

The collapse of the Chinese empire

See also

1839–42 *Opium War. China cedes Hong Kong to Britain and opens Treaty Ports*

1850–64 *T'ai-p'ing rebellion; immense loss of life*

1858 *Treaty of Tientsin; further Treaty Ports opened to foreign trade*

1860 *Treaty of Peking confirms Russian control of Maritime Province*

1894–5 *Sino-Japanese War: Japan occupies Taiwan*

1898 *Abortive 'Hundred Days' reform.*

1900 *Boxer uprising*

1911 *Revolution: Sun Yat-sen proclaimed provisional president of Chinese Republic*

During the 19th century China experienced a systemic crisis, with rebellions and humiliations by foreign powers. The Chinese leadership was slow to grasp how much internal change was needed. Realization came in the 1890s leading to sweeping reforms along Western lines and the overthrow of a dynastic system which had lasted over 2,000 years.

A survey of all states in the world will show that those states which undertook reforms became strong while those states which clung to the past perished. The consequences of clinging to the past and the effects of opening up new ways are thus obvious. If Your Majesty, with your discerning brilliance, observes the trends in other countries, you will see that if we can change, we can preserve ourselves, but if we cannot change, we shall perish.

K'ang Yu-wei, Confucian reformer
Memorial to the imperial throne, submitted 29 January 1898

For much of the 19th century the Chinese failed to understand the challenge presented by Western powers. Having reached a peak of prosperity under the Ch'ing in the 18th century, they regarded themselves as the centre of world civilization and were slow to realize that Western power, with its superior techonology, productivity and wealth, had overtaken them. Such attitudes informed their negative responses to British attempts to develop diplomatic relations from 1793. Matters came to a head when the Chinese tried to end the illicit trade in opium with its damaging economic effects. They were defeated by the British in the First Opium War and in 1842 forced to cede Hong Kong and five treaty ports in which foreigners were permitted to trade free from Chinese jurisdiction.

Defeat in the Opium War weakened imperial authority and exacerbated the systemic crisis which had been developing since the 18th century (*see* p. 172). Major rebellions broke out all over China, the most important of which was the T'ai-p'ing in which, together with the Nien rebellion, 25 million died (*see* map 1). Nevertheless, imperial support for traditional attitudes and institutions continued.

Foreign penetration

These serious disorders permitted further foreign penetration of China and her satellites (*see* map 2). From 1858 the Russians pressed forward their interests in northern China, and in 1860 Peking was occupied by the British and French. In 1884–5 the French defeated the Chinese over Indo-China. In 1894–5 the Japanese, having already intervened in Taiwan, the Ryukyu islands and Korea, overwhelmed China in a full-scale war.

Although this last defeat led in 1898 to an attempt at comprehensive reform headed by the Emperor, it was foiled by a reactionary coup. Meanwhile, the foreign powers, believing China on the point of collapse, scrambled for further concessions which in turn produced a wave of local xenophobia, leading to the Boxer uprising (*see* p. 246) and finally to the siege of foreign legations in Peking. The uprising was suppressed by foreign armies at the cost of further concessions and a huge indemnity.

After 1901 it was at last accepted that modernization was required throughout China's state and society. When the reformers, now including in their number many foreign-educated young Chinese, realised that the Manchu were still determined to cling on to power, they turned to revolution. A small army revolt at Wu-ch'ang in 1911 won support throughout China. The 2,000-year old imperial system came to an end, and the leader of the revolutionary alliance, Sun Yat-sen, was proclaimed provisional president on 1 January 1912.

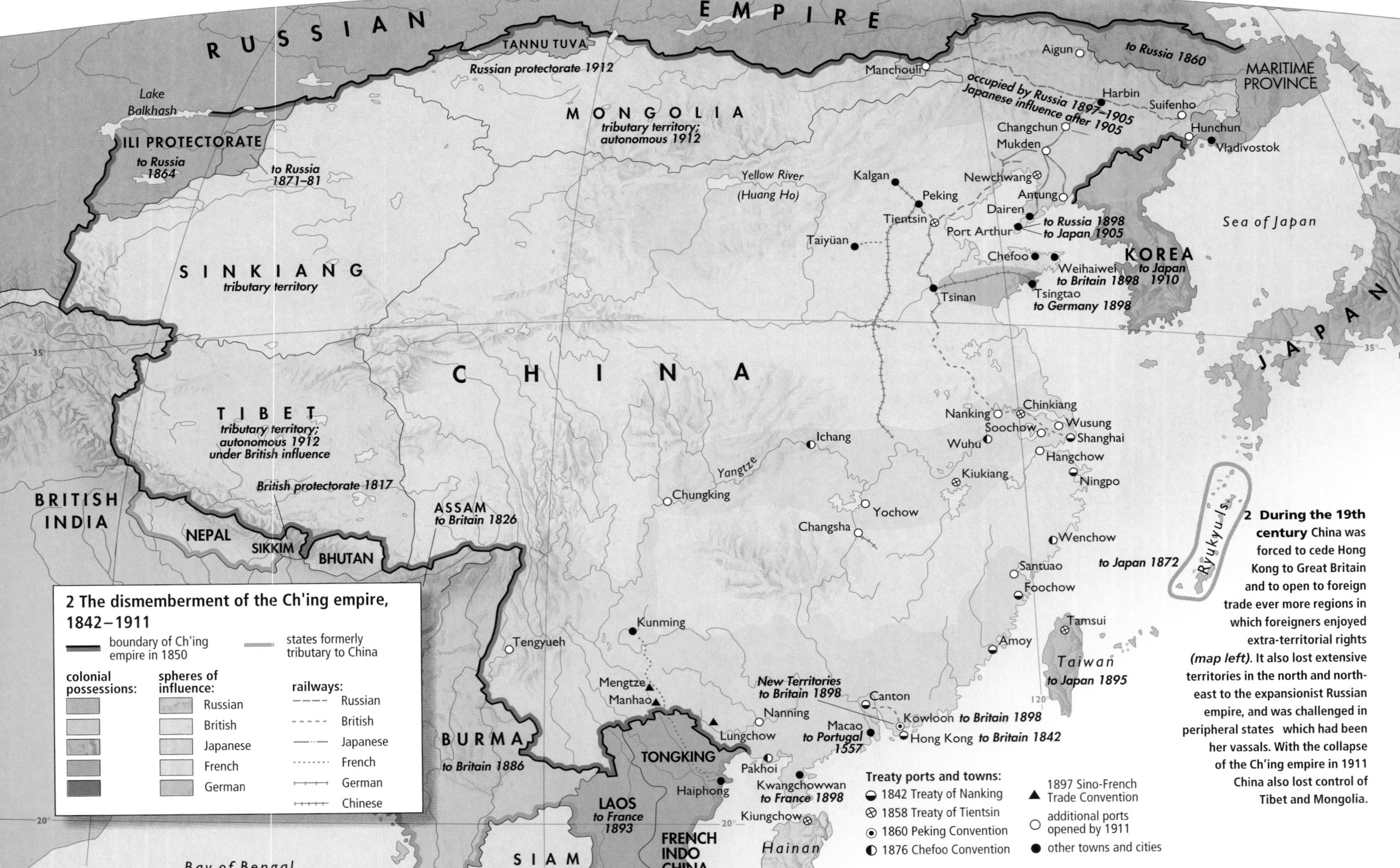

2 During the 19th century China was forced to cede Hong Kong to Great Britain and to open to foreign trade ever more regions in which foreigners enjoyed extra-territorial rights ***(map left).*** It also lost extensive territories in the north and north-east to the expansionist Russian empire, and was challenged in peripheral states which had been her vassals. With the collapse of the Ch'ing empire in 1911 China also lost control of Tibet and Mongolia.

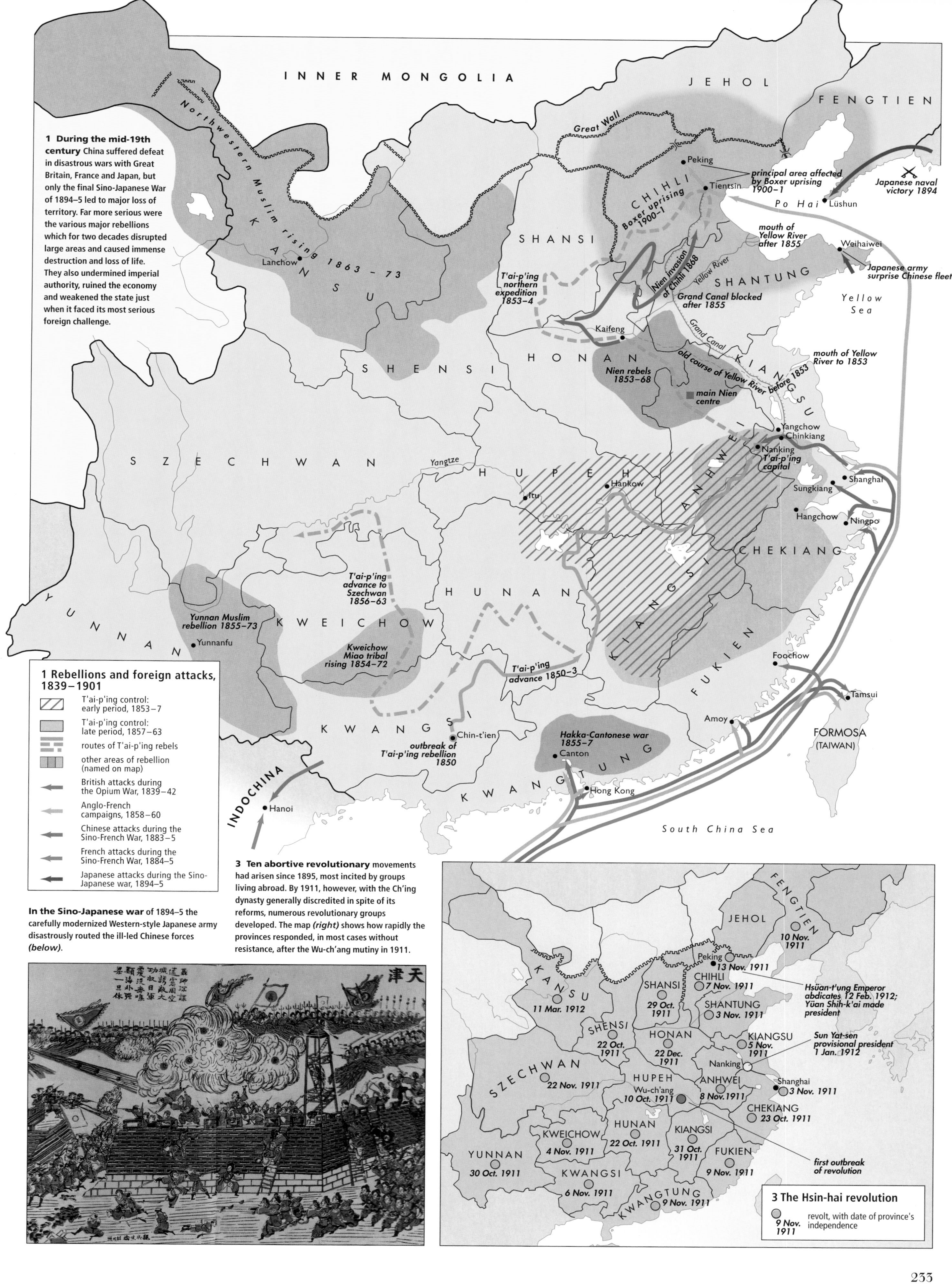

1 During the mid-19th century China suffered defeat in disastrous wars with Great Britain, France and Japan, but only the final Sino-Japanese War of 1894–5 led to major loss of territory. Far more serious were the various major rebellions which for two decades disrupted large areas and caused immense destruction and loss of life. They also undermined imperial authority, ruined the economy and weakened the state just when it faced its most serious foreign challenge.

In the Sino-Japanese war of 1894–5 the carefully modernized Western-style Japanese army disastrously routed the ill-led Chinese forces *(below)*.

3 Ten abortive revolutionary movements had arisen since 1895, most incited by groups living abroad. By 1911, however, with the Ch'ing dynasty generally discredited in spite of its reforms, numerous revolutionary groups developed. The map *(right)* shows how rapidly the provinces responded, in most cases without resistance, after the Wu-ch'ang mutiny in 1911.

1805 to 1935
India under British rule

See also
Mughal India and the growth of British power p. 170
Southeast Asia and the European powers p. 176
European colonial empires, 1815–1914 p. 244
The anti-colonial reaction, 1881–1917 p. 246
Imperialism and nationalism, 1919–1941 p. 258
Retreat from empire since 1939 p. 276
South Asia: independence and conflict p. 284

In the early 19th century, Britain consolidated its rule in south Asia, with India the focus of its imperial system. British rule encouraged the emergence of new national awareness within India, leading, in turn, to the foundation in 1885 of a national political organization, Congress. By 1935 the nationalists were close to their aim of independence.

1818 *British defeat the Marathas and become the effective rulers of India*

1824 *British begin conquest of Burma*

1833 *Death of Ram Mohan Roy (born 1772) father of modern Indian nationalism*

1843 *British conquer Sind*

1849 *British conquer the Punjab*

1853 *First railway and telegraph lines in India*

1857 *Outbreak of the Indian Mutiny*

1877 *Queen Victoria proclaimed Empress of India*

1885 *Foundation of Indian National Congress*

1920–2 *Non-Cooperation Movement against the British*

1935 *Government of India Act; Indians gain provincial autonomy*

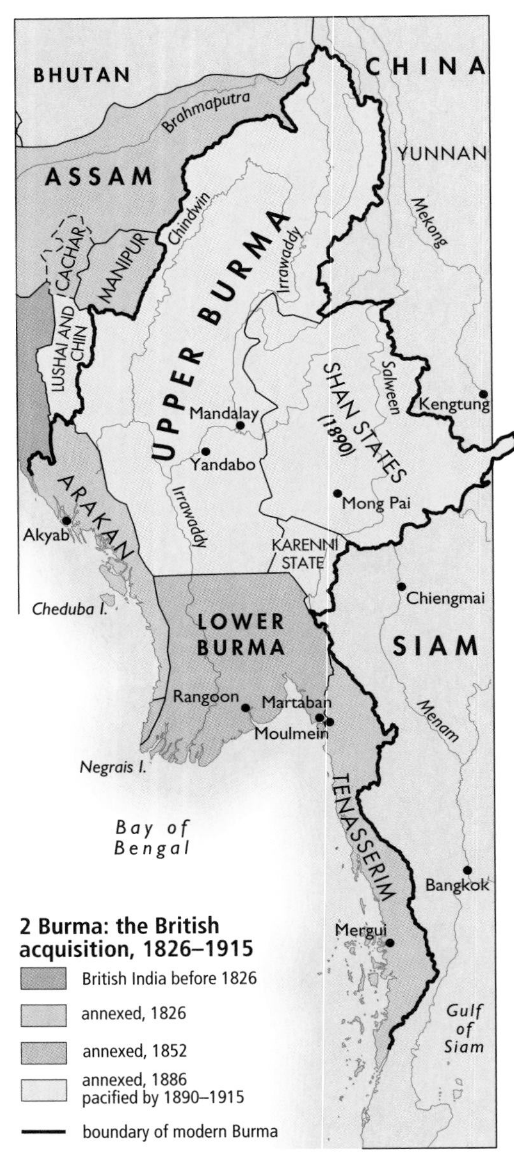

2 Burma: the British acquisition, 1826–1915

British India before 1826
annexed, 1826
annexed, 1852
annexed, 1886 pacified by 1890–1915
boundary of modern Burma

IN THE 50 YEARS after 1805 the supremacy of the English East India Company on the subcontinent was steadily consolidated. The third Anglo-Maratha War, which ended in 1818, eliminated the most serious threat to Company rule. The conquest of the Gurkhas (1816), the Sindhis (1843) and the Sikhs (1849) then saw the empire become coterminous with its natural frontiers in the north and west (*see* map 1). To the east the British clashed with the Burmese kingdom and from 1824 began the process of annexing all its territories (*see* map 2). In addition, within the subcontinent dependent states such as Oudh and some Maratha kingdoms were brought under direct rule.

However, increasing high-handedness towards Indian social customs fuelled a growing resentment which in 1857 exploded into a brutal rebellion. Beginning as a mutiny of the Company's army, it soon involved princes, landlords and peasants in north and central India; it was crushed only after 14 months of bitter fighting (*see* map 1). The direct administration of India was now taken over by the British Crown.

India then became the focus of the British imperial system, the source of rivalries with Russia in central Asia and France in southeast Asia, and a factor, too, in British involvement in the partition of Africa. From Abyssinia to China the Indian army protected British interests. Simultaneously India was absorbed into the world economy as a dependent of Britain. Indian communications, largely in the form of railways, were developed to facilitate the import of British manufactures and the export of raw materials.

Exploitation and dependency

As a result of this development and the opening of the Suez canal, India's foreign trade increased sevenfold between 1869 and 1929 and, despite severe British competition, some modern industries developed (*see* map 3). But by 1853 India had lost her worldwide market for textiles and was actually importing cloth from Britain. GNP per capita increased only slowly and, with sustained population growth (*see* maps 4 & 5), from 1921 even declined. India increasingly took on the typical characteristics of an underdeveloped economy while at the same time contributing substantially to Britain's balance of payments.

Administrative developments also contributed to India's absorption into a world order dominated by Europe. Britain's colonial administrators set out

1 The Indian Mutiny *(map below)* **began at Meerut on 10 May 1857 and spread swiftly to other parts of northern India. Hindus and Muslims alike rose against their British overlords. Sikh loyalty in the Punjab, coupled with passivity in the Deccan and the south, turned the tide in favour of the British after an orgy of bloodletting.**

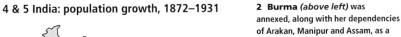

2 Burma ***(above left)*** **was annexed, along with her dependencies of Arakan, Manipur and Assam, as a result of three wars fought in 1826, 1852 and 1885. The Shan States were acquired in 1890.**

4 & 5 India: population growth, 1872–1931

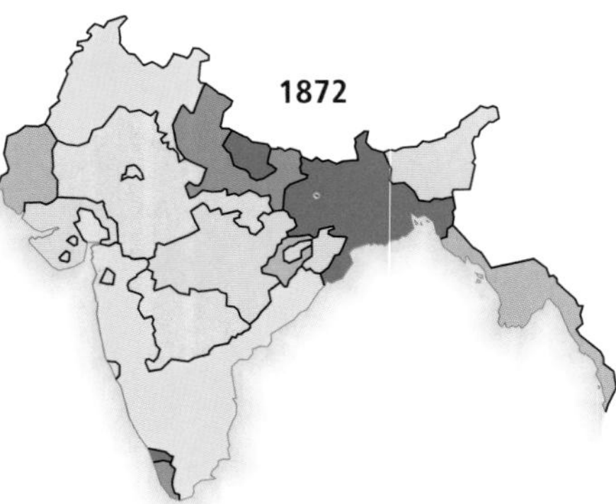

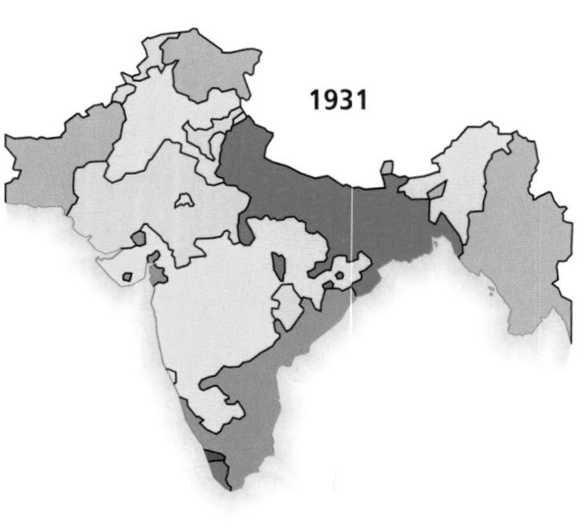

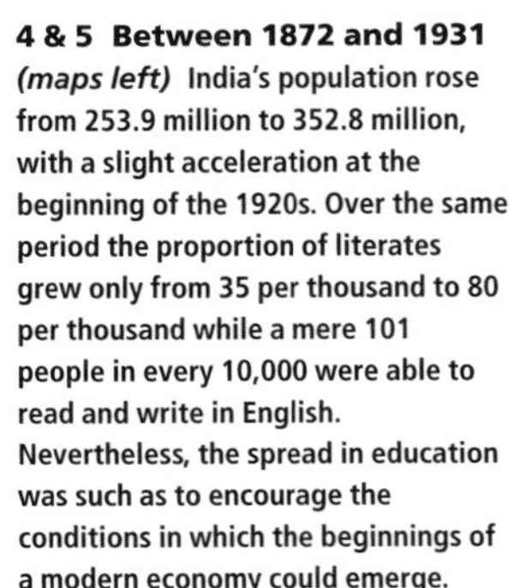

inhabitants per sq. km:
over 250
150 to 250
100 to 150
50 to 100
25 to 50
under 25

4 & 5 Between 1872 and 1931 ***(maps left)*** **India's population rose from 253.9 million to 352.8 million, with a slight acceleration at the beginning of the 1920s. Over the same period the proportion of literates grew only from 35 per thousand to 80 per thousand while a mere 101 people in every 10,000 were able to read and write in English. Nevertheless, the spread in education was such as to encourage the conditions in which the beginnings of a modern economy could emerge.**

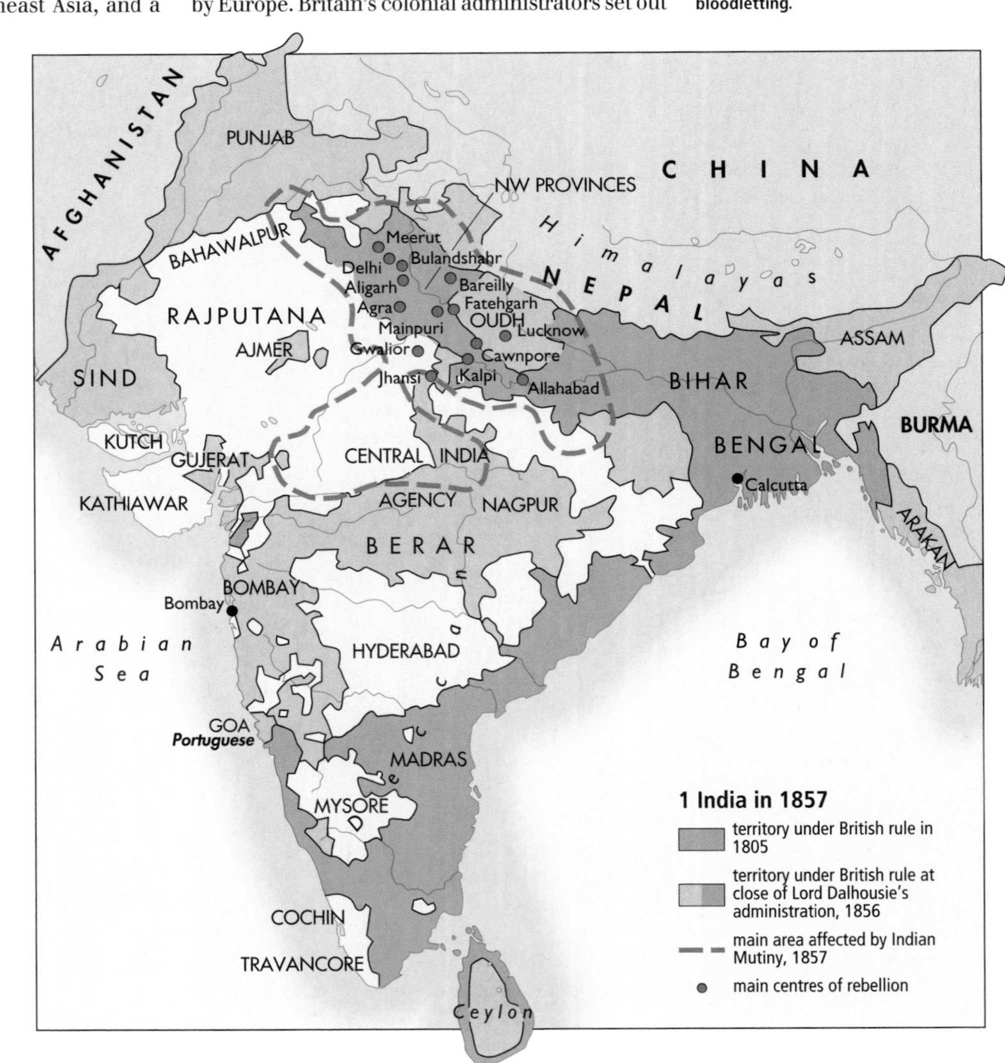

1 India in 1857

territory under British rule in 1805
territory under British rule at close of Lord Dalhousie's administration, 1856
main area affected by Indian Mutiny, 1857
main centres of rebellion

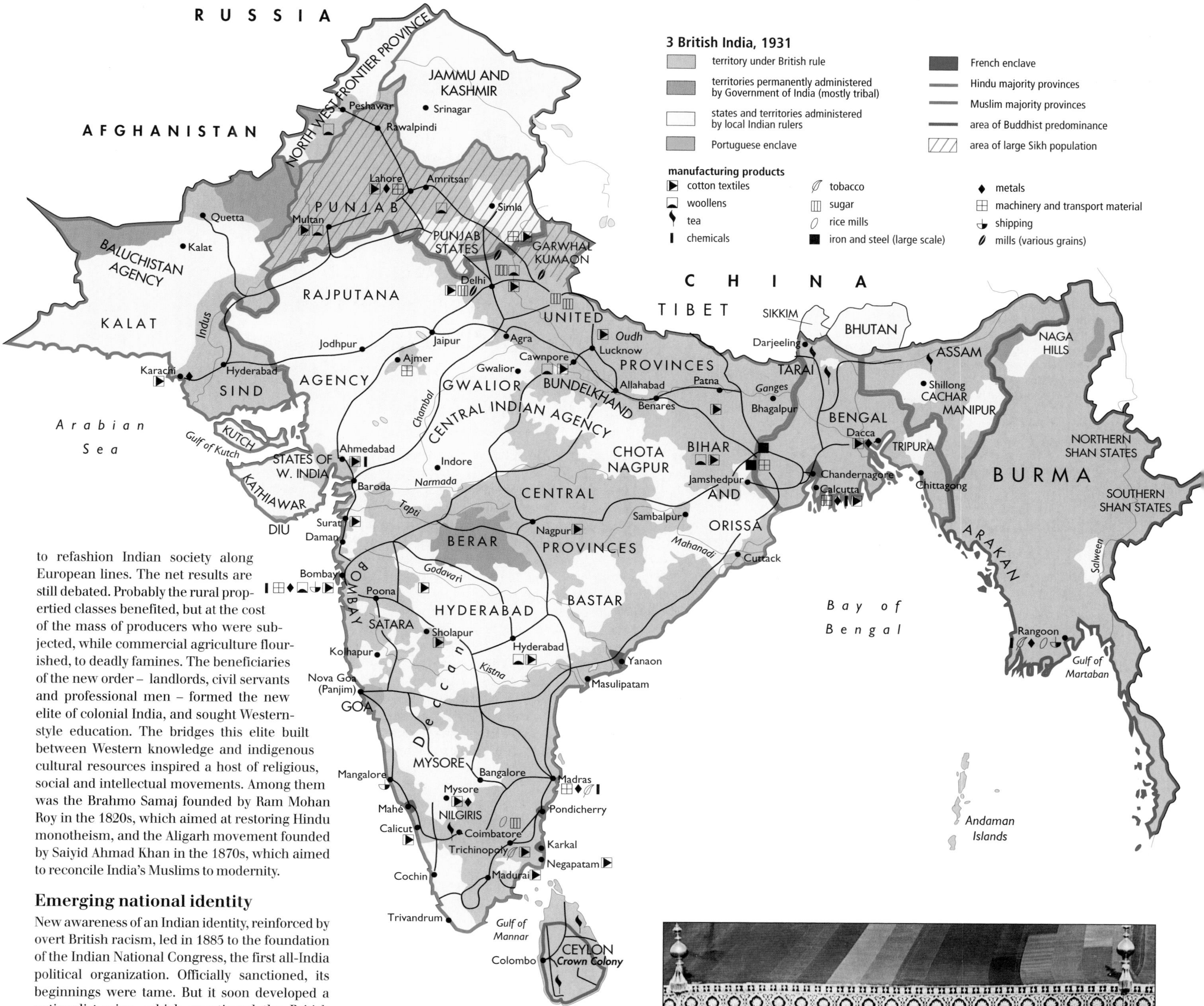

3 British India, 1931

- territory under British rule
- territories permanently administered by Government of India (mostly tribal)
- states and territories administered by local Indian rulers
- Portuguese enclave
- French enclave
- Hindu majority provinces
- Muslim majority provinces
- area of Buddhist predominance
- area of large Sikh population

manufacturing products

- cotton textiles
- woollens
- tea
- chemicals
- tobacco
- sugar
- rice mills
- iron and steel (large scale)
- metals
- machinery and transport material
- shipping
- mills (various grains)

to refashion Indian society along European lines. The net results are still debated. Probably the rural propertied classes benefited, but at the cost of the mass of producers who were subjected, while commercial agriculture flourished, to deadly famines. The beneficiaries of the new order – landlords, civil servants and professional men – formed the new elite of colonial India, and sought Western-style education. The bridges this elite built between Western knowledge and indigenous cultural resources inspired a host of religious, social and intellectual movements. Among them was the Brahmo Samaj founded by Ram Mohan Roy in the 1820s, which aimed at restoring Hindu monotheism, and the Aligarh movement founded by Saiyid Ahmad Khan in the 1870s, which aimed to reconcile India's Muslims to modernity.

Emerging national identity

New awareness of an Indian identity, reinforced by overt British racism, led in 1885 to the foundation of the Indian National Congress, the first all-India political organization. Officially sanctioned, its beginnings were tame. But it soon developed a nationalist wing, which questioned the British right to rule India. In 1905 it launched the first mass agitation, to resist the decision to partition the province of Bengal. By 1917, with the First World War quickening political expectations, the demand was for home rule. The British tried to counter these developments by slowly devolving power. As early as 1909 provincial councils had been established, while in 1917 Britain declared its aim to encourage responsible self-government. In 1919 the powers and electorates of the provincial councils were increased.

But after the First World War, increasingly repressive legislation seemed to question the sincerity of British intentions. Fuelled by Muslim fury at the destruction of the Ottoman sultan's power in the Middle East, the result was joint Hindu-Muslim action in the Non-Cooperation Movement (1920–2), in which Gandhi deployed his weapon of *satyagraha* or non-violent mass action. When this failed, Hindu-Muslim riots undermined the fragile national unity. In the late 1920s, however, a radical wing within Congress, led by Jawaharlal Nehru and Subhas Chandra Bose, pressed for renewed militant action against the British and from 1930–4 Gandhi led a civil disobedience movement. The Nationalists were rewarded with the 1935 Government of India Act, in which Indians gained full autonomy at the provincial level, a major step towards independence.

3 The racial and religious balance of the Indian empire – a crucial issue before and after independence – is shown *(above)* at the moment when the negotiations leading to the 1935 Government of India Act began. The almost equal weight of Muslims and Hindus in Bengal and the Punjab held the seeds of later violence (*see* pp. 284–5).

King George V was crowned King Emperor of India at a durbar, or assembly of notables, in Delhi in 1911 *(right)*. In an attempt to placate nationalist emotions, the decision to annul the unpopular partition of Bengal was announced at the durbar.

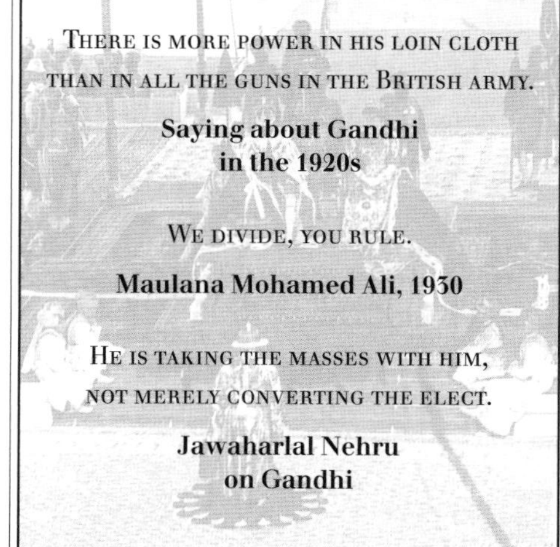

THERE IS MORE POWER IN HIS LOIN CLOTH THAN IN ALL THE GUNS IN THE BRITISH ARMY.

Saying about Gandhi in the 1920s

WE DIVIDE, YOU RULE.

Maulana Mohamed Ali, 1930

HE IS TAKING THE MASSES WITH HIM, NOT MERELY CONVERTING THE ELECT.

Jawaharlal Nehru on Gandhi

Since 1788

The development of Australia and New Zealand

See also
Australia and Oceania before European contact p. 48
European voyages of discovery, 1487–1780 p. 156
European expansion overseas p. 158
Population growth and movements, 1815–1914 p. 208
European colonial empires, 1815–1914 p. 244

European settlement of Australia and New Zealand began in the late 18th century. In both cases settlers pushed out existing indigenous peoples by force. By 1900 rich economies had emerged, still, however, dependent on British capital. It was only later in the 20th century that new policies on the economy and immigration signalled a new sense of independence.

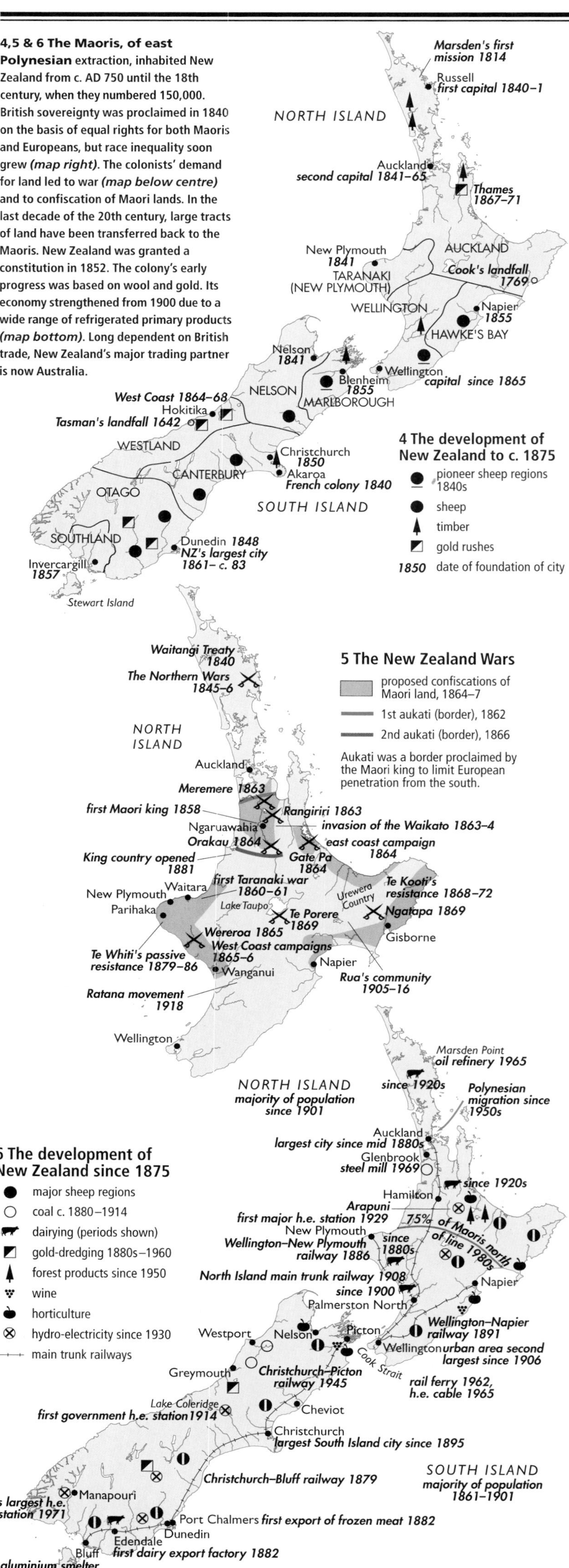

4,5 & 6 The Maoris, of east Polynesian extraction, inhabited New Zealand from c. AD 750 until the 18th century, when they numbered 150,000. British sovereignty was proclaimed in 1840 on the basis of equal rights for both Maoris and Europeans, but race inequality soon grew *(map right)*. The colonists' demand for land led to war *(map below centre)* and to confiscation of Maori lands. In the last decade of the 20th century, large tracts of land have been transferred back to the Maoris. New Zealand was granted a constitution in 1852. The colony's early progress was based on wool and gold. Its economy strengthened from 1900 due to a wide range of refrigerated primary products *(map bottom)*. Long dependent on British trade, New Zealand's major trading partner is now Australia.

Australia came into intermittent contact with Europeans from the 16th century and New Zealand had European visitors from the 17th, but neither the Portuguese nor the Dutch had any use for what they found there. The Englishman James Cook mapped both countries' coastlines extensively in 1769–70, though it was only in 1788, when Britain wanted to rid itself of the overflow from its prisons and establish a naval base on an alternative trade route to China, that European settlement in Australia began. New Zealand attracted itinerant whalers and sealers from soon afterwards, but European colonization did not start there in earnest until the 1840s.

New South Wales and Van Diemen's Land (Tasmania) were essentially convict colonies until the 1850s, though by then there were 'respectable' free settlements in Western Australia and South Australia. The search for staple products produced whaling and sealing, and later wool in great quantity. Graziers succeeded gaolers and traders as the elite in the eastern colonies. Wool also came to the fore in New Zealand and it continues today to be a major export of both countries.

The Aborigines and Maoris

There were about 750,000 Aborigines in Australia in 1788. Highly successful in the arts of survival off the land, they nevertheless retreated before the European invasion, decimated by disease, dispossession and the bullet. The Australian pastoral frontier witnessed much violence and bloodshed, most of it in guerrilla-type skirmishes, as it swept inland, not coming to a final halt until it reached the north of Western Australia and the Northern Territory in the 1930s. By then the Aboriginal population had been reduced to ten per cent of its original size. The pattern of settlement in New Zealand was rather different. Practising a more sophisticated way of warfare, and being more concentrated and relatively more numerous, the Maoris fought bloody campaigns against regular British forces in defence of their lands, notably in the 1860s in the Taranaki and Waikato wars. They were more successful in keeping title to some of their land and in making headway in European society.

Economic development

Gold rushes, in Australia in the 1850s and in New Zealand a decade later, led to huge population influxes and a vast expansion of wealth. On this basis, self-government was assured. Grain, frozen beef, sugar, dairy products and a range of minerals were also exported, as rail and steam 'tethered the mighty bush to the world', and by 1900 both societies were labelled 'workingmen's paradises', boasting the highest living standards in the world. Despite the wealth of agricultural produce, most Australians and New Zealanders, then, as now, were living in cities.

The separate Australian colonies federated into the Commonwealth of Australia in 1901 while New Zealand changed its name from colony to dominion in 1907. Each country, however, long depended on Britain for 'men, money and markets'. It was only after the Second World War and especially after Britain joined the European Community in 1973 that this cycle of dependence was broken. Now Australia and New Zealand trade much more with the Pacific Rim and the Middle East than with Europe. Significant mineral discoveries in Australia in the 1960s and '70s – notably oil, gas, iron, bauxite and uranium – gave the economy a boost; and New Zealand's government reforms in the 1980s again gave its economy a globally competitive edge.

Migration and national consciousness

Large-scale migration programmes after 1945 drew millions to Australia from Europe, more than half from countries other than Britain, notably Italy and Greece. Since the final dismantling of the White Australia policy in 1974, after over a century in place, several hundred thousand immigrants have arrived from Asia. New Zealand's prime source of recent immigrants has been the Pacific islands, making Auckland the world's largest Polynesian city. In both countries a new consciousness has emerged among the indigenous peoples and land rights and compensation are key political issues. These questions will almost certainly be resolved equitably in polities which still pride themselves in being advanced social democracies where citizens can count on a 'fair go'.

2 In 1788 there had been about 750,000 Aborigines and no Europeans, sheep or cattle. By the 1890s there were 106 million sheep, 12 million cattle, 3.5 million European Australians and some 100,000 Aborigines. As the frontier was pushed forward, the competition for land and water became fierce *(map right)*. Between 1788 and 1930 about 20,000 Aborigines and some 2,000 European Australians died directly in small frontier battles and skirmishes. Disease accounted for many more Aboriginal deaths. Since the 1970s considerable tracts of land have been returned to Aboriginal ownership. In 1997 the Aboriginal population was estimated at 327,000.

> We are approaching the 21st century and the centenary of our nationhood. As never before we are making our own way in the region ... Australia occupies a unique place in the world and makes a unique contribution to it. Our destiny is in no-one else's hands but our own: we alone bear responsibility for deciding what the nature of our government and society will be ... We share a continent. We share a past, a present and a future. And our Head of State should be one of us.
>
> **Paul Keating, Australian Prime Minister, addressing the Australian Parliament, 7 June 1995**

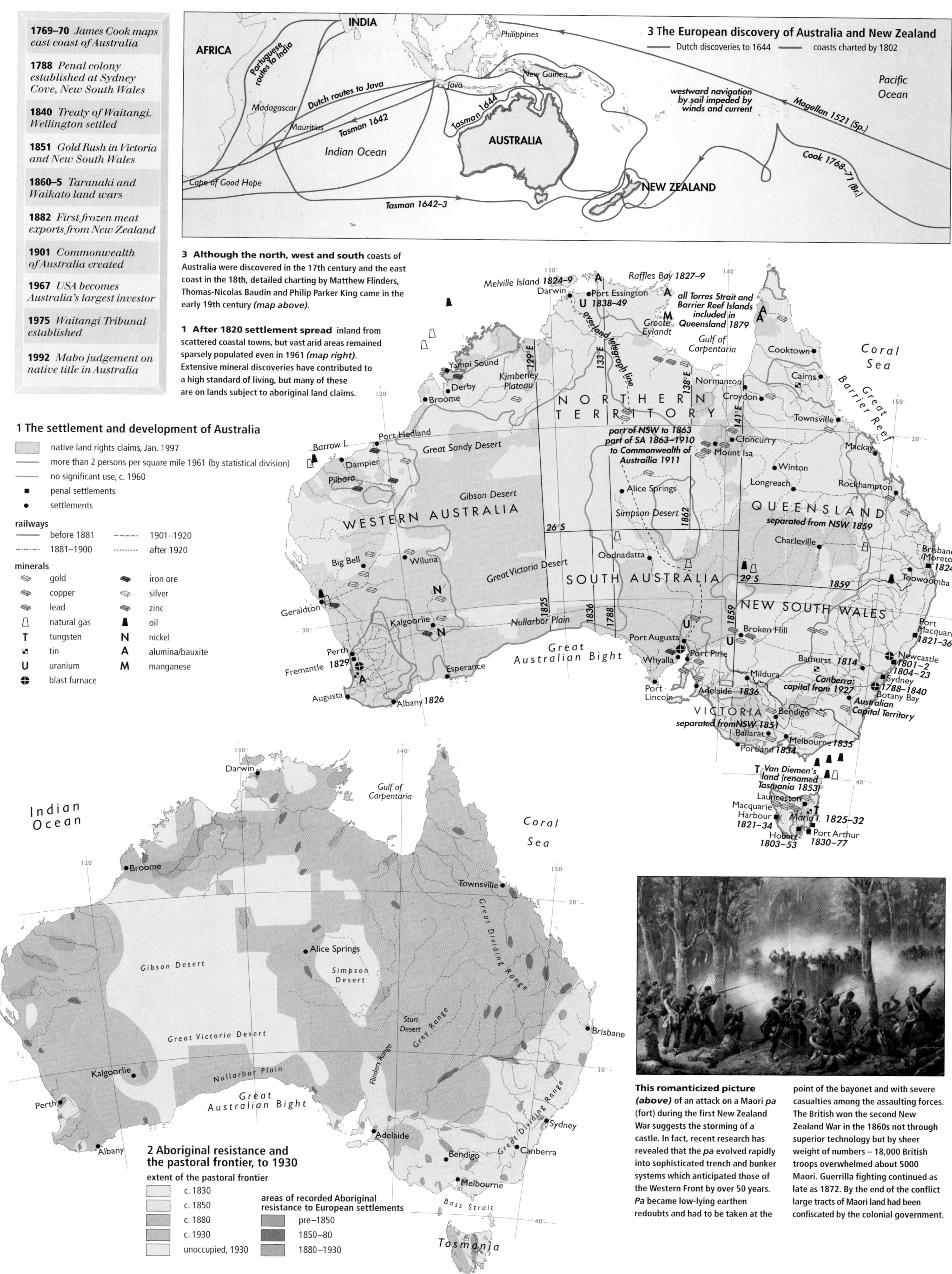

1769–70 *James Cook maps east coast of Australia*

1788 *Penal colony established at Sydney Cove, New South Wales*

1840 *Treaty of Waitangi. Wellington settled*

1851 *Gold Rush in Victoria and New South Wales*

1860–5 *Taranaki and Waikato land wars*

1882 *First frozen meat exports from New Zealand*

1901 *Commonwealth of Australia created*

1967 *USA becomes Australia's largest investor*

1975 *Waitangi Tribunal established*

1992 *Mabo judgement on native title in Australia*

3 Although the north, west and south coasts of Australia were discovered in the 17th century and the east coast in the 18th, detailed charting by Matthew Flinders, Thomas-Nicolas Baudin and Philip Parker King came in the early 19th century *(map above)*.

1 After 1820 settlement spread inland from scattered coastal towns, but vast arid areas remained sparsely populated even in 1961 *(map right)*. Extensive mineral discoveries have contributed to a high standard of living, but many of these are on lands subject to aboriginal land claims.

This romanticized picture *(above)* of an attack on a Maori *pa* (fort) during the first New Zealand War suggests the storming of a castle. In fact, recent research has revealed that the *pa* evolved rapidly into sophisticated trench and bunker systems which anticipated those of the Western Front by over 50 years. *Pa* became low-lying earthen redoubts and had to be taken at the point of the bayonet and with severe casualties among the assaulting forces. The British won the second New Zealand War in the 1860s not through superior technology but by sheer weight of numbers – 18,000 British troops overwhelmed about 5000 Maori. Guerrilla fighting continued as late as 1872. By the end of the conflict large tracts of Maori land had been confiscated by the colonial government.

1800 to 1880

Africa before the partition by the European powers

See also
Trade and empire in Africa, 1500–1800 p. 164
The partition of Africa, 1880–1913 p. 240
European colonial empires, 1815–1914 p. 244

Africa between 1800 and 1880 was shaped by indigenous societies and their rulers, intent as ever on pursuing their own ambitions. Europeans occupied little more than the tiniest of coastal footholds, and the commercial and political developments of the period represented more than the prelude to an inevitable European partition.

> THE AFRICANS ARE ALL DEEPLY IMBUED WITH THE SPIRIT OF TRADE. WE FOUND GREAT DIFFICULTY IN GETTING PAST MANY VILLAGES. EVERY ARTIFICE WAS EMPLOYED TO DETAIN US THAT WE MIGHT PURCHASE OUR SUPPERS FROM THEM ... THEY ARE ENTIRELY DEPENDANT ON ENGLISH CALICO FOR CLOTHING ... MANY OF THEIR VILLAGES WERE MODELS OF NEATNESS, AND SO WERE THEIR GARDENS & HUTS. MANY WERE INVETERATE MUSICIANS, AND MADE ONE REMEMBER HOW MUCH OF OUR ANGLO-SAXON ENERGY IS EXPENDED IN DRESS & IN THE HOWLING OF PIANOS.
>
> **David Livingstone to Arthur Tidman (Secretary, London Missionary Society), 12 October 1855**

1804 *Usuman dan Fodio begins to establish the Fulani empire*

1806 *Cape Colony recaptured by the British, and kept at the end of the Napoleonic wars in 1815*

1824 *British merchants establish post in Natal; first Anglo-Ashanti war*

1830 *French occupation of Algiers*

1852 *South African Republic (Transvaal) established by the Sand River Convention between Boers and British*

1853–6 *David Livingstone the first European to traverse the African continent*

1867 *Discovery of diamonds in Griqualand West near the Orange Free State*

1869 *Suez canal opens*

IN THE EARLY NINETEENTH CENTURY much of west Africa was profoundly affected by an Islamic religious revival manifested in Holy Wars (*jihads*) waged mainly against backsliding Muslim or partly-Islamicized communities. The great warriors of the *jihad* were the widely-scattered Fulani cattle-keepers of the Sudanic region. In the 18th century they had established theocracies in Futa Toro, Futa Jallon and in Masina on the upper Niger. Much larger, however, was the 19th-century Fulani state set up in Hausaland. In 1804 a Fulani religious leader, Usuman dan Fodio, was proclaimed Commander of the Faithful, and declared a *jihad* against the infidel. His formidable army of horsemen soon conquered the Hausa city states, and struck out into Adamawa, Nupe and Yorubaland. His son became the sultan of Sokoto, an empire still in existence in the 1890s.

An even fiercer *jihad* was conducted by al-Hajj Umar from Futa Jallon. Conquering the Bambara kingdoms and Masina, he was only kept from the Atlantic by the French on the Senegal river. In fact, Islam increasingly became a counterforce to European advance, especially in the case of the Mandingo leader Samory who carved out another empire south of the Niger; he was finally defeated by the French only in 1898.

New trade

In the forest states further south, the slave trade had long flourished but the British in particular began to try to replace it with 'legitimate trade'. Although a government-sponsored mission in 1841–2 to establish 'Christianity, commerce and civilization' inland failed, African responses to Europe's new commercial demands for palm oil and other products encouraged change.

Likewise in east and west central Africa new commercial patterns brought disruption. There the western world's almost insatiable appetite for ivory (for billiard balls and piano keys) caused the hunting and trading of elephant tusks to become a major economic activity, enriching many states and peoples – the Cokwe and King Msiri in central Africa, for instance, and Buganda and the Nyamwezi in east Africa. Foreign traders in central Africa were frequently Portuguese from Angola and Mozambique, and in east Africa Swahili-Arabs from Zanzibar, who often brought their Islamic religion with them. Some peoples, particularly around lakes Nyasa and Tanganyika, suffered severely from the Arab slave trade, which went hand-in-hand with that in ivory.

In northeast Africa, the expansion of Egypt, ruled by Khedives, nominally viceroys of the Ottoman sultan, brought a foretaste of the later European conquest. Muhammad Ali's armies conquered the northern Nilotic Sudan, founding the provincial capital at Khartoum in 1821, and his grandson, Ismail, consolidated Egyptian control over much of the Red Sea coast and Horn of Africa, as well as pushing south up the Nile towards the Great Lakes. Partly in response to this Egyptian activity, Ethiopian political power revived.

European colonization

Only two areas of Africa were colonized by European powers during this period. In 1830 France invaded Algeria and in a long and bitter struggle conquered and settled the territory. The British took the Cape from the Dutch during the Napoleonic wars and the south saw the presence of increasing numbers of Europeans, including the Boers – white farmers who left Cape Colony in the 'Great Trek' of 1836 to avoid British rule. In the 1850s Britain recognized the Transvaal and Orange Free State republics which the Boers founded, but by the 1870s were again in dispute with them.

2 Early European explorers *(map left)* generally travelled with African trading groups and proved remarkably receptive to the cultures they encountered. David Livingstone was the most able scientist among them and was also motivated by religious zeal and hatred of the slave trade. Later explorers, notably H. M. Stanley, were far more aggressive and exploitative, their expeditions resembling military campaigns.

The Battle of Isandhlwana *(below)* on 22 January 1879 was the first major engagement of the Zulu war. A British force of 1700 white and African troops under Lord Chelmsford was routed by 20,000 Zulu, the consequence rather of British arrogance and carelessness than of overwhelming numbers. It demonstrated the continuing possibility that African tactics and weaponry could triumph over well-armed European forces.

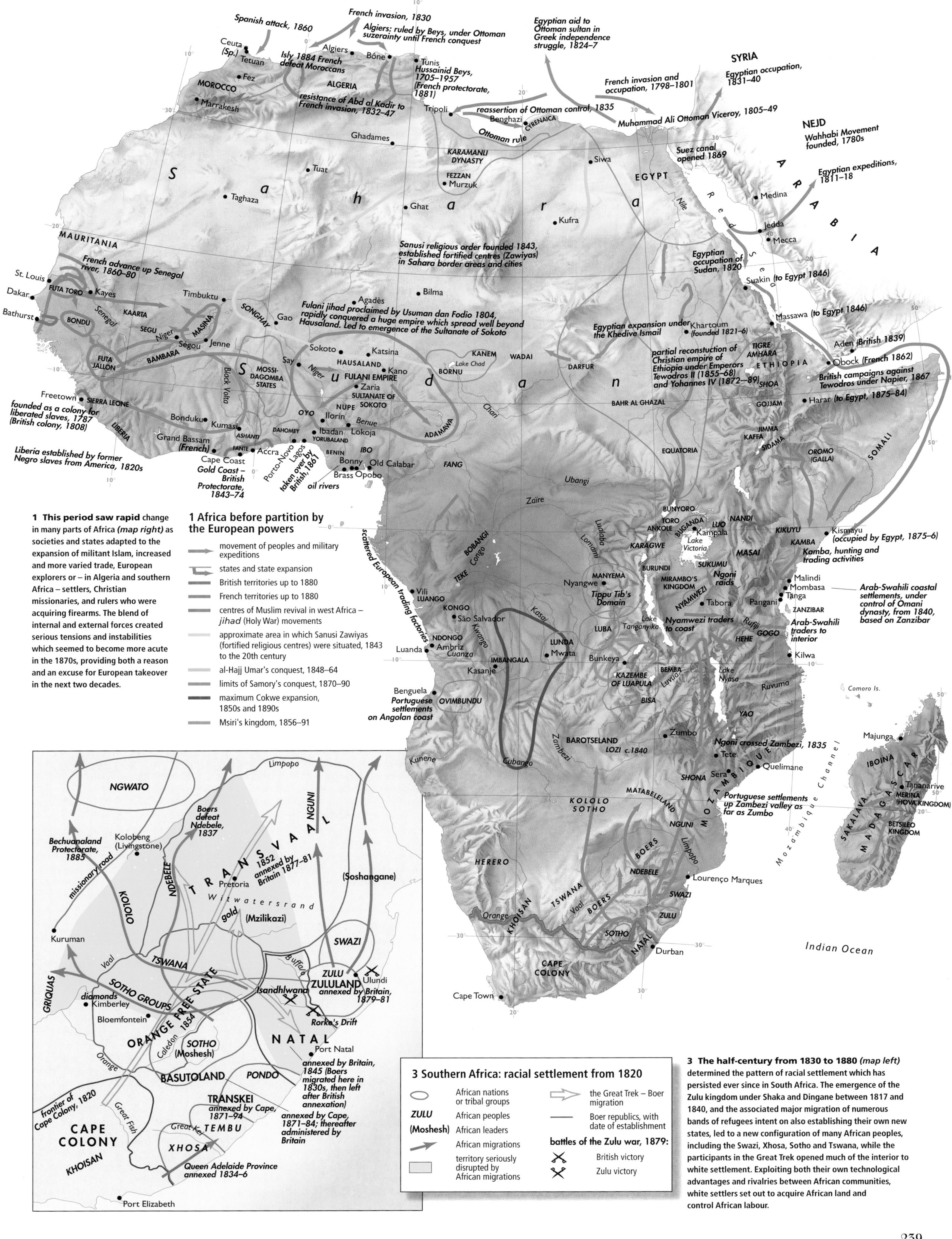

1 This period saw rapid change in many parts of Africa *(map right)* as societies and states adapted to the expansion of militant Islam, increased and more varied trade, European explorers or – in Algeria and southern Africa – settlers, Christian missionaries, and rulers who were acquiring firearms. The blend of internal and external forces created serious tensions and instabilities which seemed to become more acute in the 1870s, providing both a reason and an excuse for European takeover in the next two decades.

3 The half-century from 1830 to 1880 *(map left)* determined the pattern of racial settlement which has persisted ever since in South Africa. The emergence of the Zulu kingdom under Shaka and Dingane between 1817 and 1840, and the associated major migration of numerous bands of refugees intent on also establishing their own new states, led to a new configuration of many African peoples, including the Swazi, Xhosa, Sotho and Tswana, while the participants in the Great Trek opened much of the interior to white settlement. Exploiting both their own technological advantages and rivalries between African communities, white settlers set out to acquire African land and control African labour.

The partition of Africa

See also
Africa before the partition by the European powers, 1800–1880 p. 238
European colonial empires, 1815–1914 p. 244
The anti-colonial reaction, 1878–1917 p. 246
Imperialism and nationalism, 1919–41 p. 258
Retreat from empire since 1939 p. 276

Once Europe's partition of Africa began in the 1880s, the continent was carved up remarkably rapidly: 30 years later only Abyssinia and Liberia remained wholly independent. The scramble was completed with the redistribution of Germany's colonies after the First World War, when, for the first time, colonial administration began to be imposed effectively.

1881 *France establishes protectorate over Tunisia*

1882 *Britain occupies Egypt*

1884–5 *Berlin West Africa Conference: Berlin Act and recognition of the Congo Free State*

1883–6 *Discovery of gold in the Transvaal*

1896 *British reconquest of Sudan begins; Italy defeated at Adowa*

1898 *Fashoda Crisis: France confronts Britain on the Nile*

1899–1902 *South African War: Britain conquers Boer republics, Transvaal and Orange Free State*

1904–7 *Herero Revolt against German rule in South West Africa*

Little of Africa was directly ruled by Europeans in 1880: the French had been subjugating Algeria since 1830; there were small French and British colonies in west Africa; and there were moribund Portuguese settlements in Angola and Mozambique. Only in the south, where the British Cape colonists were in competition with the Afrikaners of the Transvaal and Orange Free State, did political control extend far inland. Yet within two decades the continent had been seized and partitioned. Of the 40 political units to which it was reduced by 1913, 36 were completely under European control. France was the largest beneficiary, ruling nearly one-third of Africa's 11.7 million square miles.

The scramble begins

Many ingredients contributed to this imperial explosion, among them the search for raw materials and new markets for Europe's rapidly expanding industries. At the same time, rivalries between European states were partly played out outside Europe, especially in Africa. As a result, often trivial incidents in Africa between competing European traders precipitated major international crises, accelerating the undignified scramble for the continent. Yet ironically, few European powers actively sought partition. At the Berlin West Africa Conference in 1884 the powers had agreed to avert partition and maintain access for all. Yet whatever their official hesitations, the process had acquired a momentum of its own.

In west Africa, French army officers, eager to recover their honour after their humiliating defeat by Germany in 1870 (*see* p. 216), sought glory advancing inland from Senegal in the late 1870s. This created conflict with the British in Gambia and Sierra Leone, and with African rulers such as Samory and al-Hajj Umar. Intense Anglo-French rivalry developed in the Gold Coast, Togo, Dahomey and Yorubaland and hardened after Britain's unilateral occupation of Egypt in 1882.

King Leopold of the Belgians' determination to become involved in Africa led him to recruit the explorer H. M. Stanley after his epic journey down the Congo River in 1877. In 1879 Stanley returned to the lower Congo to lay the foundations of the huge private domain the king eventually acquired in the Congo basin. His activities stimulated others in the region. The French naval officer de Brazza concluded vital protection treaties with African chiefs, which the government in Paris readily took up. Germany also entered the race, grabbing territory in Togoland, the Cameroons, southwest

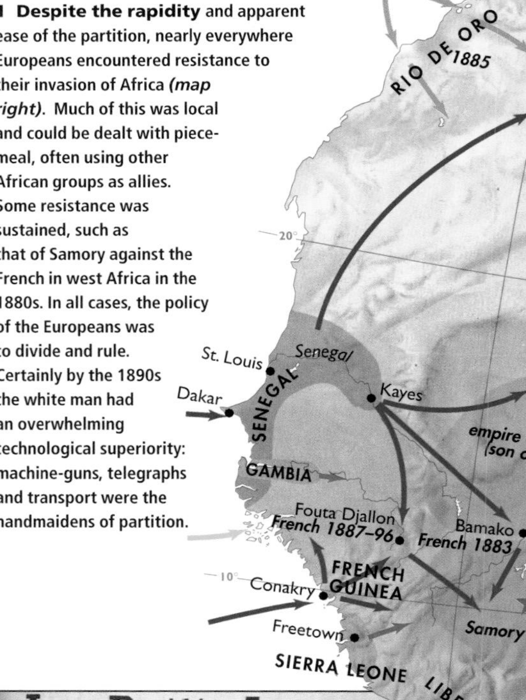

1 Despite the rapidity and apparent ease of the partition, nearly everywhere Europeans encountered resistance to their invasion of Africa *(map right)*. Much of this was local and could be dealt with piecemeal, often using other African groups as allies. Some resistance was sustained, such as that of Samory against the French in west Africa in the 1880s. In all cases, the policy of the Europeans was to divide and rule. Certainly by the 1890s the white man had an overwhelming technological superiority: machine-guns, telegraphs and transport were the handmaidens of partition.

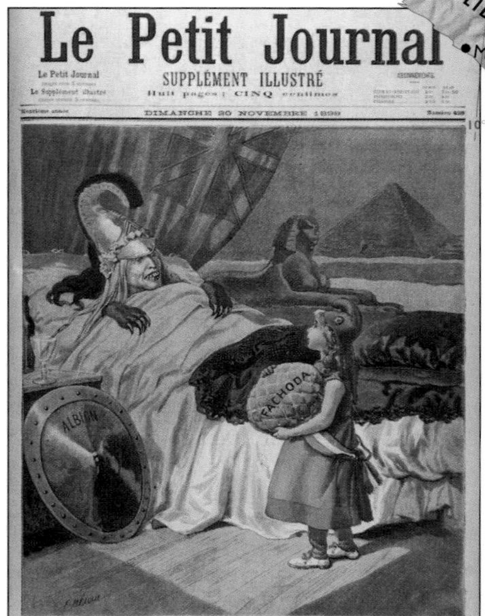

War between Britain and France in 1898 over their claims to Fashoda in the Sudan was only narrowly averted. The incident aroused nationalist fervour on both sides. Here *(right)* a French newspaper portrays an innocent France as Red Riding Hood confronted by Britannia as the wolf.

2 Colonial rule took many forms *(map below)*: the self-governing white territories of the Cape Colony and Natal; the manipulation of nominally independent local governments in the manner of the British in Egypt; and the incorporation of indigenous authorities into the autocratic administrations of French West Africa. Intended to be peaceful and cheap, colonial rule was often neglectful and oppressive.

3 The single-most effective resistance to the spread of white imperialism in Africa came not from native Africans but from existing European settlers, the Dutch farmers known as Boers. The discovery of gold in Boer-held territory saw Britain determined to bring the Boer republics under its control. Though eventually defeated, the Boer's brilliant guerilla tactics came close to inflicting a humiliating defeat. Britain was forced to field 300,000 troops against 75,000 Boers *(map below)*.

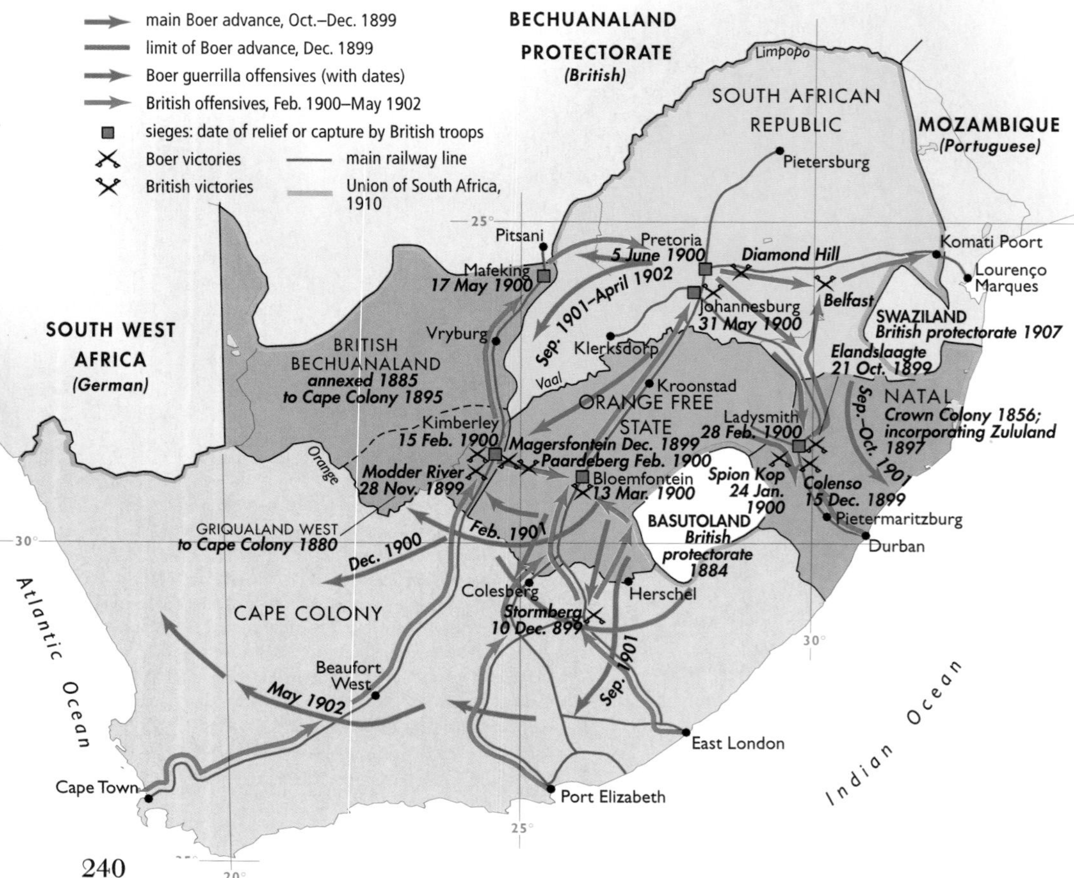

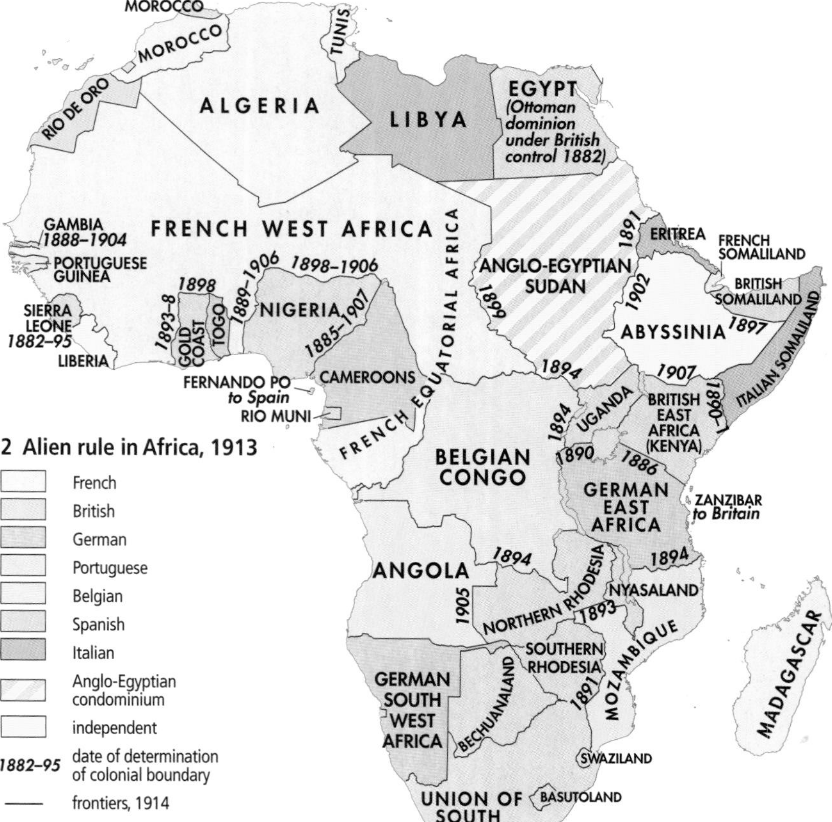

and east Africa. French and German initiatives in west Africa provoked British intervention, especially in securing the lands which became Nigeria. The far interior was left to the French, who by 1900 had swept right across the western Sudan.

Germany's presence in southern Africa revived Portuguese ambitions, and threats of Afrikaner expansion led to British thrusts into central Africa, aided decisively by the Cape politician Cecil Rhodes. Likewise, German colonization in Tanganyika prompted British claims to what became Uganda and Kenya. French conquest of Dahomey (1893) and her drive towards Lake Chad drew Britain and the Royal Niger Company into protecting its trading sphere, which in turn led to armed clashes with African states. Multiple tensions reached their height in 1898 at Fashoda on the White Nile where the two countries narrowly avoided war.

Conflict and war

Partition caused increasing bloodshed. Abyssinia routed the Italians at Adowa in 1896; some 120,000 Sudanese died in Britain's reconquest of the Mahdist state; and Rhodes' settlers fought bitterly with Ndebele and Shona as they moved north. Conflicts climaxed with the South African War (1899–1902) in which Britain with difficulty won the Transvaal gold fields and absorbed the Afrikaner republics (*see* map 3). Elsewhere black Africans, although bitterly opposing the European powers, could never offer concerted resistance and for the most part were easily overcome.

The expansion and modernization of Japan

See also
Japan under the shogunate, 1477–1868 p. 174
The Russian empire: expansion and modernization p. 230
The collapse of the Chinese empire p. 232
The Chinese revolution, 1912–1949 p. 260
The outbreak of the Second World War p. 266
Japan and east Asia since 1945 p. 278

1868 *Tokugawa shogunate ends and the Meiji emperor is restored*

1891 *Construction of the Trans-Siberian railway begins*

1894–5 *Sino-Japanese War; Japan occupies Formosa*

1904–5 *Russo-Japanese War; Japanese success stimulates Asian nationalism*

1910 *Japan annexes Korea*

1914 *Japan takes over German concessions in China*

1920 *Japan given permanent seat on the League of Nations*

Between the 1850s and the 1920s Japan emerged from isolation to become a major world power. Western pressure was the spur which led to the destruction of the feudal system and the unleashing of her great potential for rapid modernization. But by 1920 there were signs that her rapid growth was causing dangerous internal stresses.

THE ONE OBJECT OF MY LIFE IS TO EXTEND JAPAN'S NATIONAL POWER. COMPARED WITH CONSIDERATIONS OF THE COUNTRY'S STRENGTH, THE MATTER OF INTERNAL GOVERNMENT AND INTO WHOSE HANDS IT FALLS IS OF NO IMPORTANCE AT ALL. EVEN IF THE GOVERNMENT BE AUTOCRATIC IN NAME AND FORM, I SHALL BE SATISFIED WITH IT IF IT IS STRONG ENOUGH TO STRENGTHEN THE COUNTRY.

The leader of Japan's Liberal Party in the late 19th century

JAPAN AVOIDED EXCESSIVE interference by expansionist Western powers during the latter half of the 19th century by implementing successful policies for rapid modernization. The very countries that had threatened her independence became models for her own development and hence fuelled her own imperialist ambitions. The process began in the 1850s and by 1920 the Japanese empire was firmly established.

The spur to modernization was the demand from Western powers, led by the USA, for access to Japan's ports. The 'unequal treaties' concluded under threat in 1858 prompted the restoration of direct imperial rule in 1868 in the name of the Meiji emperor (*see* p. 174). Already the country had considerable strengths: an extensive network of commerce and credit; a labour intensive agriculture; reserves of copper, coal and iron; and scholars who, in spite of Japan's enforced isolation, had studied Western science and technology.

It was crucial to Japan's rapid modernization to bring these strengths into play. The abolition of feudalism, and the replacement in 1873 of feudal dues with cash payments based on the value of land, enabled wealth to be redirected to the purposes of central government. To encourage the transfer of technology and to stimulate investment, the government used this land tax to build model factories in strategic and import-saving industries, such as steel and textiles, and became directly involved in the development of transport and communications. There was also indirect encouragement in the form of subsidies and tax privileges.

The new leaders introduced complementary administrative reforms: feudal domains were replaced by modern bureaucracy (1871); the feudal army was replaced by a conscript one (1873); a bicameral legislature provided the basis for political unity and stability (1889); a national education system was instituted (1872); and legal codes based on those of France and Germany were introduced (1882).

Industrialization and trade

Within this framework capitalism made rapid headway: Japan quickly became the outstanding example of large-scale industrialization in the non-Western world. By 1918, when she had achieved major penetration of markets in China, the USA and elsewhere, she had become a major importer of raw materials and exporter of finished goods. Such developments meant considerable changes for Japanese society: by 1918 the population had risen to 55m (from 35m in 1873) and nearly one-third lived in towns of 10,000 or more.

National strength brought expansion overseas, motives being both strategic and economic. Japan began by claiming neighbouring islands such as the Ryukyus and Kuriles. The 'unequal treaties', were revoked in 1894. Then concerns that China was too weak to keep Russia out of Korea led to war (1894–5) in which Japan destroyed the Chinese forces and acquired Formosa (Taiwan). The Russian threat, however, was only resolved by Japan's overwhelming defeat of Russia on land and sea in 1904–5, which led to Japanese control over the Liaotung peninsula, extensive rights in southern Manchuria and the acquisition of southern Sakhalin (*see* map 2). There followed the annexation of Korea (1910), the acquisition of former German territories in China (1914), and the 'Twenty-one Demands' (1915), which made sweeping, though not wholly successful, claims over China. In 1919 the Paris Peace Conference confirmed most of these gains and granted Japan mandates to German colonies in the Pacific.

The cost of success

There was, however, another side to the story: the army was beginning to act independently of civil control, politicians were becoming too beholden to business, traditionalists objected to the sacrifice of Japanese values to the West, and the farmer and the labourer began to resent the subjection of their well-being to capital. The end of the war brought economic disruption, major disturbances in town and countryside, and the assassination in 1921 of the prime minister by a fanatic. These events presaged turbulent years ahead.

5 The three decades from 1888 to 1918 saw both a substantial growth in Japan's population ***(charts below right)*** from 39.5 to 55 million, and a significant shift from country to town. The proportion living in cities of over 100,000 people more than doubled in the period, and that in urban settlements of between 10,000 and 100,000 trebled. But the villages still remained preponderant.

5 Japanese population

- in towns of over 100,000
- in towns of 10,000–100,000
- in small towns and rural areas

1888 – 39.5 million

1918 – 55 million

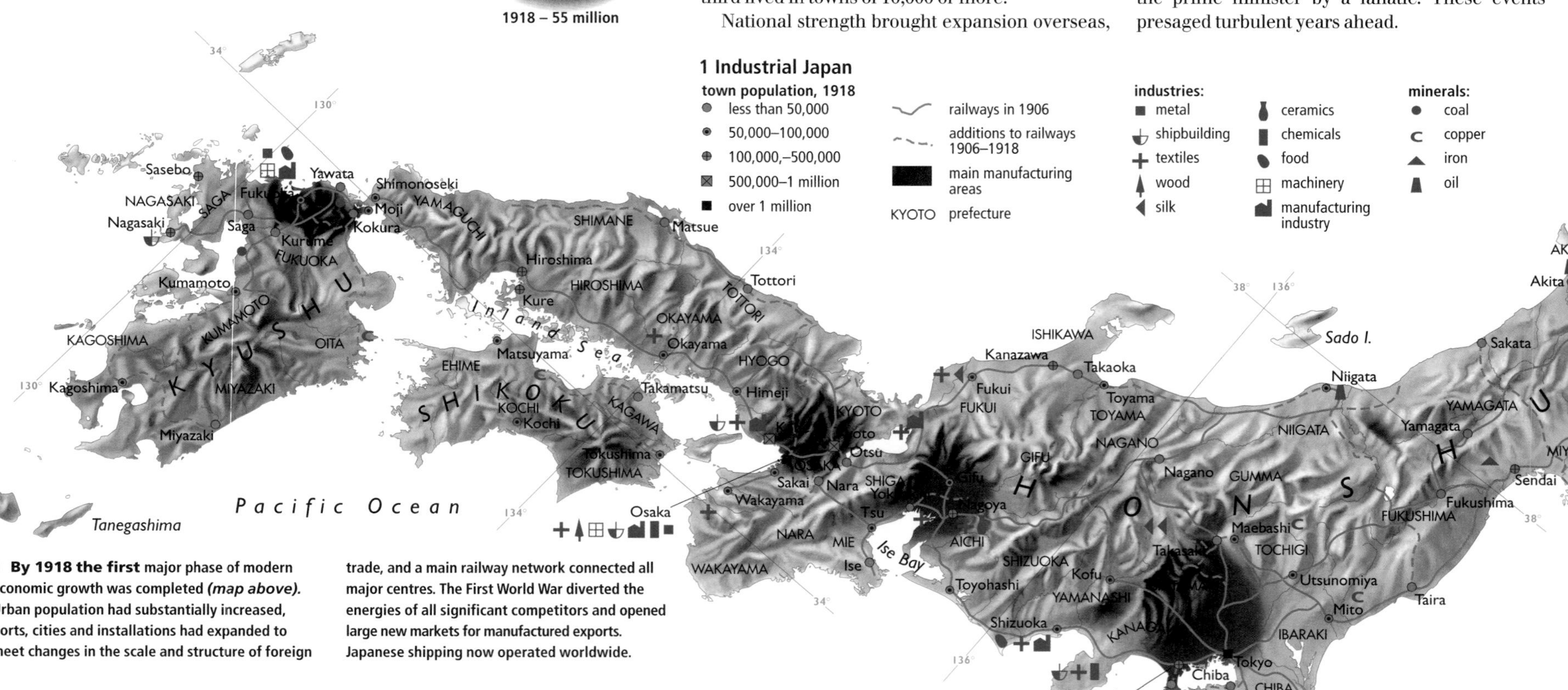

1 By 1918 the first major phase of modern economic growth was completed ***(map above).*** Urban population had substantially increased, ports, cities and installations had expanded to meet changes in the scale and structure of foreign trade, and a main railway network connected all major centres. The First World War diverted the energies of all significant competitors and opened large new markets for manufactured exports. Japanese shipping now operated worldwide.

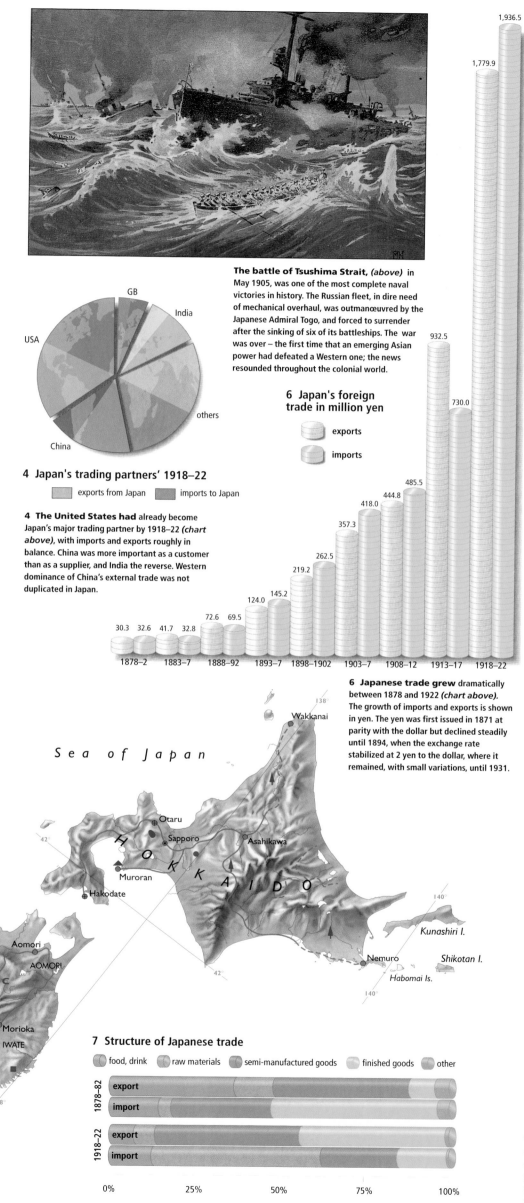

The battle of Tsushima Strait, ***(above)*** in May 1905, was one of the most complete naval victories in history. The Russian fleet, in dire need of mechanical overhaul, was outmanœuvred by the Japanese Admiral Togo, and forced to surrender after the sinking of six of its battleships. The war was over – the first time that an emerging Asian power had defeated a Western one; the news resounded throughout the colonial world.

GB
India
USA
others
China

4 Japan's trading partners' 1918–22

exports from Japan
imports to Japan

4 The United States had already become Japan's major trading partner by 1918–22 ***(chart above)***, with imports and exports roughly in balance. China was more important as a customer than as a supplier, and India the reverse. Western dominance of China's external trade was not duplicated in Japan.

6 Japan's foreign trade in million yen

exports
imports

30.3 32.6 41.7 32.8 72.6 69.5 124.0 145.2 219.2 262.5 357.3 418.0 444.8 485.5 932.5 730.0 1,779.9 1,936.5

1878–2 1883–7 1888–92 1893–7 1898–1902 1903–7 1908–12 1913–17 1918–22

6 Japanese trade grew dramatically between 1878 and 1922 ***(chart above).*** The growth of imports and exports is shown in yen. The yen was first issued in 1871 at parity with the dollar but declined steadily until 1894, when the exchange rate stabilized at 2 yen to the dollar, where it remained, with small variations, until 1931.

Sea of Japan
Wakkanai
Otaru
Sapporo
Asahikawa
HOKKAIDO
Muroran
Hakodate
Kunashiri I.
Shikotan I.
Nemuro
Habomai Is.
Aomori
AOMORI
Morioka
IWATE

7 Structure of Japanese trade

food, drink
raw materials
semi-manufactured goods
finished goods
other

1878–82: export, import
1918–22: export, import

0% 25% 50% 75% 100%

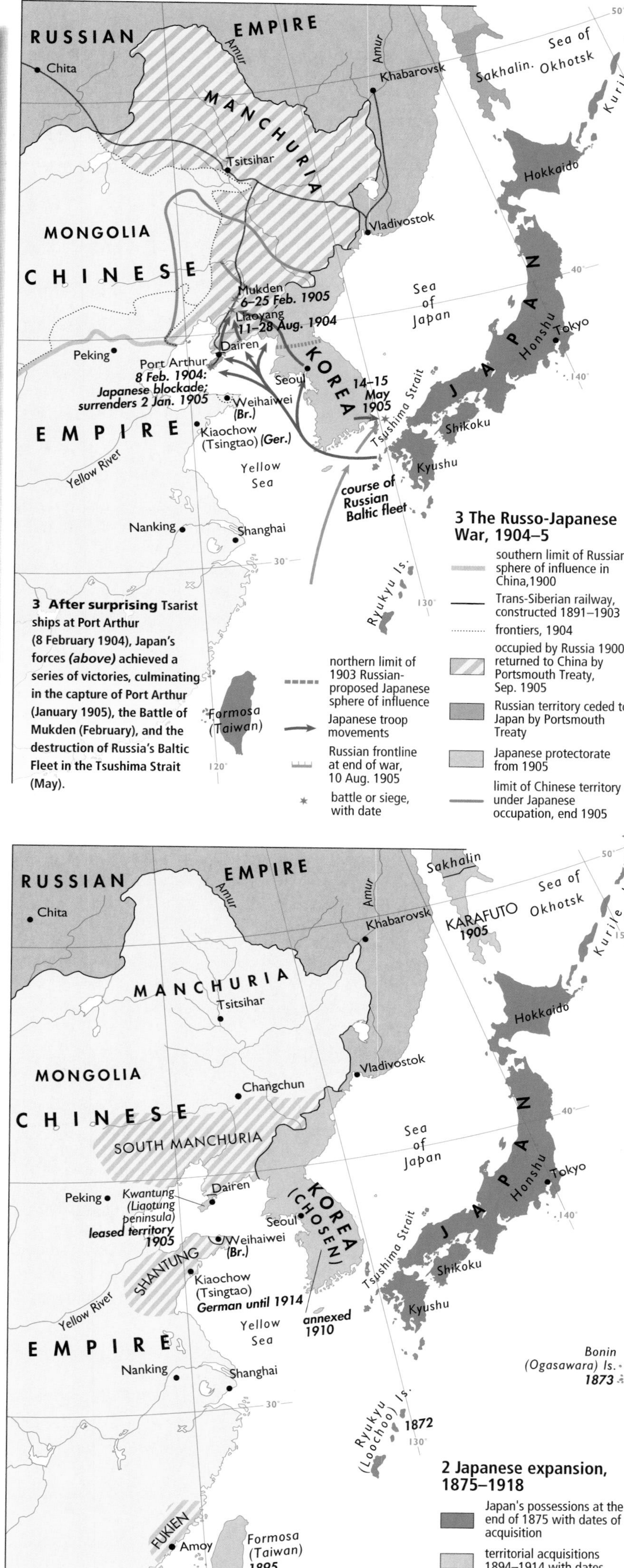

3 After surprising Tsarist ships at Port Arthur (8 February 1904), Japan's forces ***(above)*** achieved a series of victories, culminating in the capture of Port Arthur (January 1905), the Battle of Mukden (February), and the destruction of Russia's Baltic Fleet in the Tsushima Strait (May).

7 The structure of Japanese foreign trade ***(chart left)*** changed strikingly between 1878–82 and 1918–22. In the earlier period, manufactured goods represented half of all imports, but only 7.2 per cent of exports. Within 40 years the ratio had reversed: manufactures now accounted for over 40 per cent of sales and only 15 per cent of purchases.

2 The 1868 revolution was followed by an upsurge of Japanese interest in the West and in her neighbours ***(map above)***. By 1875, Japan had asserted her claims to a number of Pacific islands including the Kurile, Ryukyu and Bonin islands. By 1918 her holdings included Korea, Taiwan and half of the island of Sakhalin.

European colonial empires

See also
The Russian empire: expansion and modernization, 1815–1917 p. 230
The collapse of the Chinese empire p. 232
India under British rule, 1805–1935 p. 234
The partition of Africa, 1880–1913 p. 240
The anti-colonial reaction, 1881–1917 p. 246
Imperialism and nationalism, 1919–1941 p. 258
Retreat from empire since 1939 p. 276

In the first 50 years after 1815, there was a gradual extension of the European colonial empires as exploration opened up new regions to European traders and missionaries. But the later 19th century saw a heightening of imperial ambitions and rivalries that resulted in the partition of almost all of Africa, southeast Asia and the Pacific.

1823 *US Monroe Doctrine warns European powers against intervention in America*

1830 *French conquest of Algiers*

1833 *Slavery abolished in British empire*

1836 *Afrikaners begin 'Great Trek' in southern Africa*

1839–42 *First Opium War in China*

1856–60 *Second Opium War in China*

1857–8 *Indian mutiny sparks widespread rebellion*

1869 *Suez Canal opens*

1884–5 *Conference of Berlin on the partition of Africa*

1899–1902 *The South African ('Boer') War*

> I FEEL SURE THAT THE TIME FOR SMALL KINGDOMS HAS PASSED AWAY. THE FUTURE IS WITH THE GREAT EMPIRES AND IT RESTS WITH US TO SAY WHETHER OUR OWN SHALL BE COUNTED FOR MANY YEARS TO COME AS ONE OF THE GREATEST OR WE SHALL SPLIT UP INTO MINOR COMPARATIVELY UNIMPORTANT NATIONALITIES.
>
> **Joseph Chamberlain**
> ***letter to Sir George Reid***
> ***(prime minister of Australia 1904–5)***
> ***13 June 1902***

IN 1815 BRITAIN ALONE remained a great overseas power: France, Spain and the Netherlands had all lost colonial territories to the British. The decade after 1815 even saw a contraction of European colonial empires as in South and Central America Spanish and Portuguese colonies broke free. With Britain holding undisputed naval pre-eminence and discarding mercantilism (the theoretical underpinning of imperialism) in favour of free trade, the first half of the 19th century seemed unlikely to witness further British expansion.

Yet European colonial empires grew almost continuously between 1815 and 1914. The West Indies, with the decline of the Atlantic slave trade and failing economically, lost their 18th century importance, but in India further British conquests and, in Australia and New Zealand, emigration, pushed forward the boundaries of British imperialism. Britain also acquired Singapore (1819), Malacca (1824), Hong Kong (1842), Natal (1843), Lower Burma (1852) and Lagos (1861), and claimed sovereignty over Australia (1829) and New Zealand (1840). Many of these were to secure British commercial interests and to protect Britain's position in India; others were defensive reactions against France or necessitated by settler activity. Other European countries also steadily expanded. Russia sold Alaska to the United States in 1867, but continued its continental expansion: between 1801 and 1914 over 7 million Russians emigrated to Asiatic Russia. France, determined to replace the empire lost in 1815, conquered Algeria in the 1830s, annexed Tahiti and the Marquesas in the 1840s, expanded its colony in Senegal in the 1850s and began the conquest of Indo-China in 1858–9. Over and beyond the extension of formal empires, European technology and industrialization opened up other areas of the world – from Turkey and Egypt, to Persia and China, South America and even Japan – to European, particularly British, trade and finance. As Europe continued to disgorge missionaries, explorers and settlers overseas, relations with, and knowledge of the wider world was transformed.

The scramble for empire

After 1880, the pace of imperial expansion, fuelled by commercial competition, rivalries between imperial powers and changing conditions in Asia and Africa, quickened dramatically. By 1914, Europe had engrossed nine-tenths of Africa and a large part of Asia. Between 1871 and 1914 the French empire grew by nearly four million square miles and 47 million people. Defeat in Europe at the hands of Germany in 1870 redoubled French efforts – particularly by the army – to regain prestige through overseas conquests. Germany herself acquired an empire of one million square miles and 14 million subjects in southwest Africa, the Cameroons, east Africa and the Pacific islands. Italy, another power eager for reasons of prestige to enter the colonial race, obtained Tripoli and Libya, Eritrea and Italian Somaliland, though in 1896 failed to conquer Abyssinia. But the greatest gains of all were made by Britain, who, partly to secure areas for free trade, established control over Nigeria, Kenya, Uganda, Rhodesia, Egypt and the Sudan, Fiji and parts of Borneo and New Guinea. Nonetheless, India remained the keystone of the British empire and many of these acquisitions were made with a view to bolstering British control over and access to India.

Imperialism was not confined to Europe. The United States and Japan joined the race as well, the former acquiring the Philippines (from Spain) in 1898, the latter taking Formosa in 1895 and Korea in 1910. Of the great European trading nations, the Netherlands almost alone remained content with its existing rich possessions in the East Indies.

3 The Indian Ocean

British-controlled territory, 1900
British-controlled sea routes
British naval station, 1898
British army garrison, 1881

CYPRUS, Alexandria, Kuwait, Karachi, INDIA, Calcutta, Rangoon, Weihaiwei, Hong Kong, Bombay, Aden, Trincomalee, Colombo, CEYLON, Penang, Labuan, Singapore, Mombasa, Seychelles, Zanzibar, Cape York, Mauritius, Indian Ocean, Cape Town, Durban, Port Elizabeth, Perth, Adelaide, Sydney, Albany, Melbourne, Wellington

3 It was to Asia that Britain had increasingly looked for the expansion of its trade and territories since its defeat at the hands of the American colonists in 1783. The defence of India was to become a keystone of British imperial policy. By the late 19th century Britain controlled all the trade routes of the Indian Ocean *(map left)*; yet even so, Russia's advance towards India, French and German imperial expansion, and European, US and Japanese naval expansionism sparked new concerns about British paramountcy.

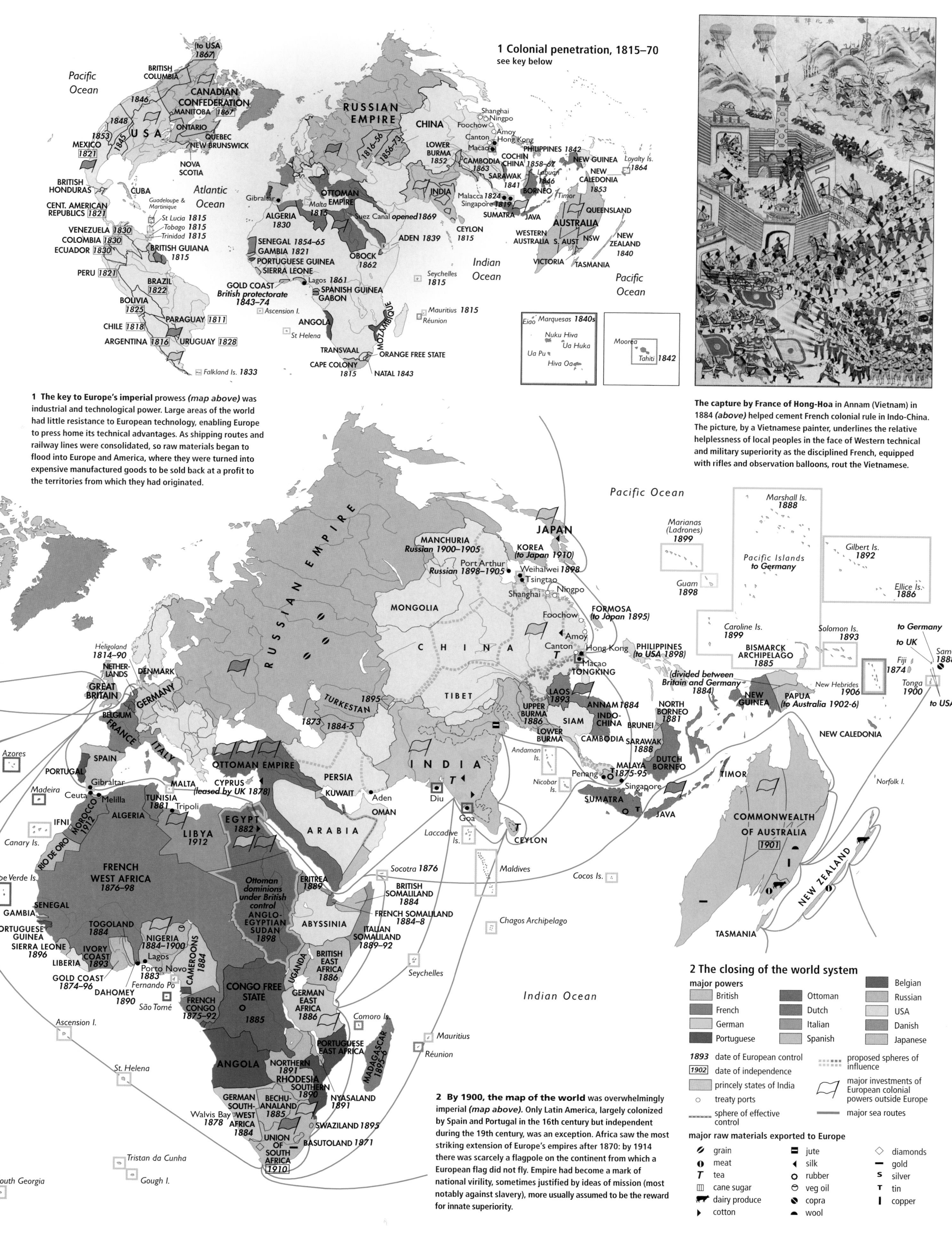

1 The key to Europe's imperial prowess *(map above)* was industrial and technological power. Large areas of the world had little resistance to European technology, enabling Europe to press home its technical advantages. As shipping routes and railway lines were consolidated, so raw materials began to flood into Europe and America, where they were turned into expensive manufactured goods to be sold back at a profit to the territories from which they had originated.

The capture by France of Hong-Hoa in Annam (Vietnam) in 1884 *(above)* helped cement French colonial rule in Indo-China. The picture, by a Vietnamese painter, underlines the relative helplessness of local peoples in the face of Western technical and military superiority as the disciplined French, equipped with rifles and observation balloons, rout the Vietnamese.

2 By 1900, the map of the world was overwhelmingly imperial *(map above)*. Only Latin America, largely colonized by Spain and Portugal in the 16th century but independent during the 19th century, was an exception. Africa saw the most striking extension of Europe's empires after 1870: by 1914 there was scarcely a flagpole on the continent from which a European flag did not fly. Empire had become a mark of national virility, sometimes justified by ideas of mission (most notably against slavery), more usually assumed to be the reward for innate superiority.

1881 to 1917
The anti-colonial reaction

See also

The disintegration of the Ottoman empire p. 228

The Russian empire: expansion and modernization, 1815–1917 p. 230

The collapse of the Chinese empire p. 232

India under British rule, 1805–1935 p. 234

The partition of Africa, 1880–1913 p. 240

European colonial empires, 1815–1914 p. 244

Imperialism and nationalism, 1919–41 p. 258

1884–5 *Berlin Conference on the partition of Africa*

1890 *Brussels Convention forbids export of European arms to Africa*

26 Jan. 1885 *Khartoum falls to the Mahdi; General Gordon killed*

1898 *Battle of Omdurman*

1899–1902 *South African ('Boer') War*

1900 *Boxer Rebellion in China*

1911 *Chinese revolution*

1914 *Outbreak of First World War*

From 1881 the European scramble for overseas territory provoked new and widespread resistance throughout Asia and Africa. Elsewhere, in China and the Ottoman empire, intense European commercial and political penetration was undermining the old order. By 1917 modern nationalist movements were emerging in many European colonies.

RESISTANCE TO EUROPEAN colonialism existed well before 1881. Furthermore, patterns of resistance were shaped just as much by struggles for economic advantage and by local and inter-state rivalries as by the imposition of European political control. Such resistance took many forms too, from mass migrations to, among African Christian converts, the establishment of indigenous Christian churches. Nevertheless, the unprecedented scale of the annexations of the 'new imperialism' after 1881 unleashed an anti-colonial wave that was bigger and more significant than anything that had preceded it. Nowhere was independence surrendered passively. Throughout Africa and Asia Europeans met prolonged and often bitter armed resistance.

In Annam the emperor, Ham Nghi, took to the mountains and resisted French occupation; Russia encountered Muslim resistance when it invaded central Asia; the United States became embroiled in a costly war with nationalist forces under Emilio Aguinaldo after it occupied the Philippines in 1898; and the Italians were defeated by the Abyssinians at Adowa in 1896. In Africa, Europeans faced resistance movements of varying strength. In many cases local groups alternated between diplomacy and armed opposition. Before and after mounting military resistance against the French, a west African leader, Samory, unsuccessfully sought British protection. Meanwhile oppressive German rule in South-West Africa and Tanganyika provoked the Herero and Maji-Maji revolts. In the Philippines resistance to the United States continued among the Islamic population of Mindanao while in

> IT SEEMS TO ME THAT THERE IS A CHANGE COMING OVER THE EAST ... IN CHINA THERE IS A MARKED MOVEMENT AGAINST THE FOREIGNERS ... IN EGYPT AND NORTH AFRICA IT IS SIGNALIZED BY A REMARKABLE INCREASE IN FANATICISM, COUPLED WITH THE SPREAD OF THE PAN-ISLAMIC MOVEMENT. PERHAPS THE EAST IS REALLY AWAKENING FROM ITS SECULAR SLUMBER, AND WE ARE ABOUT TO WITNESS THE RISING OF THESE PATIENT MILLIONS AGAINST THE EXPLOITATION OF AN UNSCRUPULOUS WEST.
>
> **E. G. Browne**
> ***The Persian Revolution of 1905–1909* (1910)**

2 Britain's occupation of Egypt led to intervention in the Sudan. When Khartoum was threatened by local Islamic forces under the 'Mahdi', General Gordon was sent there to evacuate the garrison. But he stayed and himself came under siege by the Mahdists. The failure of the relief attempt under Sir Garnet Wolseley *(map right)*, bedevilled by complacency and incompetence, caused outrage at home. In the second half of the 19th century Britain was almost continually involved with fighting small colonial wars. Sudan was not finally reconquered until 1898.

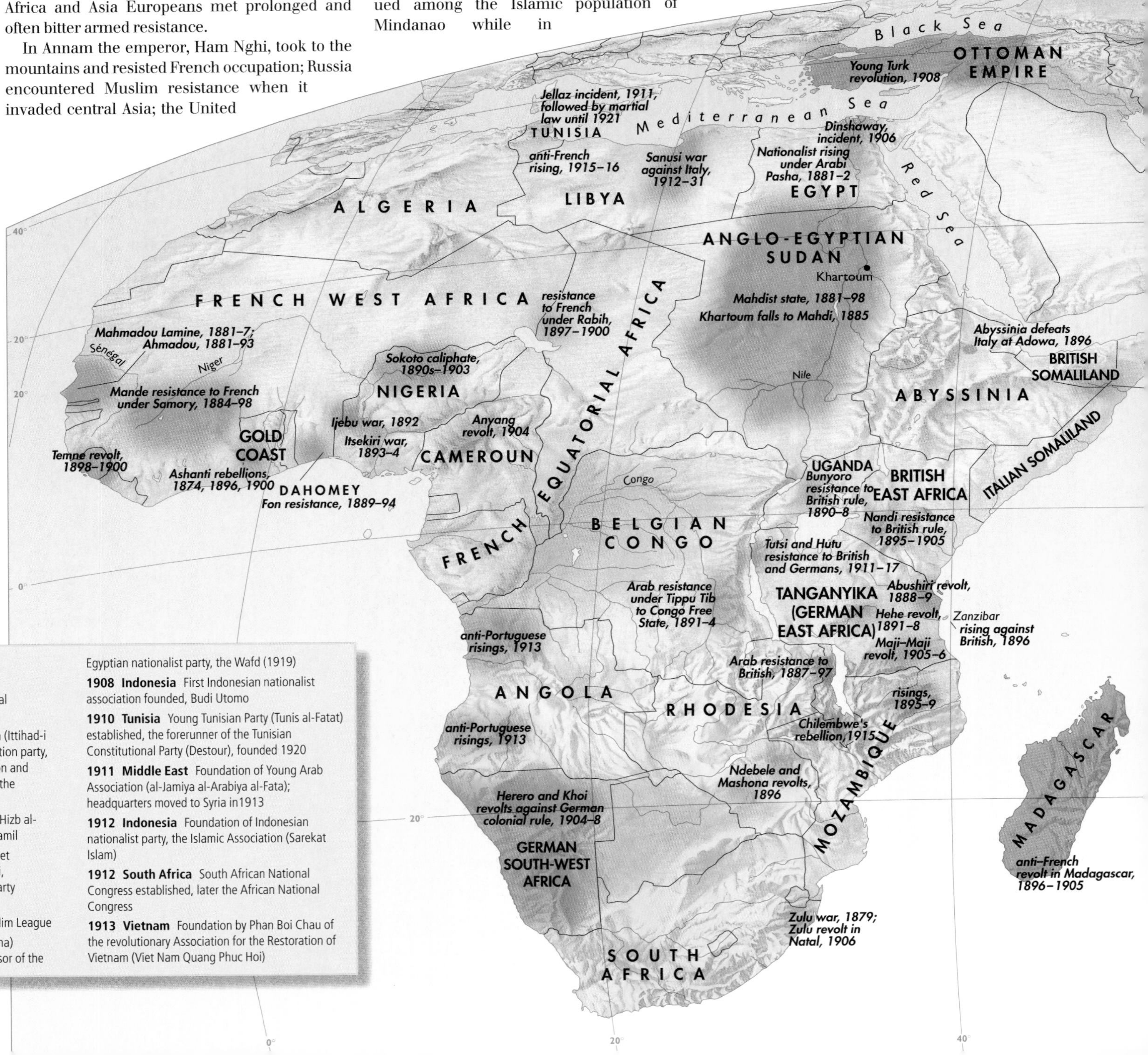

1 The reaction against European imperialism took many forms *(map right)*. In areas such as French Indo-China and the Dutch East Indies, native populations took up arms to fight for their independence. In the great Asian empires – the Ottoman empire and China – whose territorial integrity was threatened, the result of European intervention was revolt against the ruling dynasties and the beginnings of modernization so as to be able to confront the West on more nearly equal terms. In Africa, meanwhile, the partition of the continent by the European powers, a process inaugurated at the Berlin Conference of 1884, provoked resistance which was never quelled, despite harsh repression. Almost every one of the colonial powers was confronted by violent threats to its continued rule.

NATIONALIST PARTIES AND ASSOCIATIONS

1885 India Foundation of Indian National Congress

1889 Ottoman empire Ottoman Union (Ittihad-i Osmani), the first organized Turkish opposition party, established; name changed in1895 to Union and Progress (Ittihat ve Terakki), henceforward the organization of the Young Turk movement

1897 Egypt Egyptian National Party (al-Hizb al-Watani) established, headed by Mustafa Kamil

1905 China Sun Yat-sen founds the secret revolutionary organization T'ung Meng Hui, transformed in 1912 into the Nationalist Party (Kuomintang)

1906 India Foundation of All-India Muslim League

1907 Egypt People's Party (Hizb al-Umma) established, organ of Saad Zaghlul, precursor of the Egyptian nationalist party, the Wafd (1919)

1908 Indonesia First Indonesian nationalist association founded, Budi Utomo

1910 Tunisia Young Tunisian Party (Tunis al-Fatat) established, the forerunner of the Tunisian Constitutional Party (Destour), founded 1920

1911 Middle East Foundation of Young Arab Association (al-Jamiya al-Arabiya al-Fata); headquarters moved to Syria in1913

1912 Indonesia Foundation of Indonesian nationalist party, the Islamic Association (Sarekat Islam)

1912 South Africa South African National Congress established, later the African National Congress

1913 Vietnam Foundation by Phan Boi Chau of the revolutionary Association for the Restoration of Vietnam (Viet Nam Quang Phuc Hoi)

EGYPT
② Sep. 1884 Wolseley leaves Cairo (c. 600 miles to the north) for Khartoum relief expedition
2nd cataract
Wadi Halfa
Sarras
③ 6 Nov. Wolseley leaves Sarras
ANGLO-EGYPTIAN SUDAN
⑧ 24 Feb. river column ordered to return to Korti
3rd cataract
river column
Abu Hamed
Dongola
Kirbekan 11 Feb.
4th cataract
5th cataract
Korti
④ 28 Dec. at Korti, Wolseley sends small 'flying column' across desert to Metemmeh
Berber
Atbara
⑨ 2 May British forces ordered to leave Sudan
Abu Klea 17 Jan.
Abu Kru 19 Jan.
⑤ 24 Jan. small reconnaissance force proceeds to Khartoum
Gumbat
Metemmeh 21 Jan.
⑦ 28 Jan. flying column arrives; turns back under attack when it is clear the town has fallen
6th cataract
Khartoum
① 18 Mar. 1884 siege begins
Blue Nile
⑥ 26 Jan. 1885 Khartoum falls; death of Gordon
White Nile

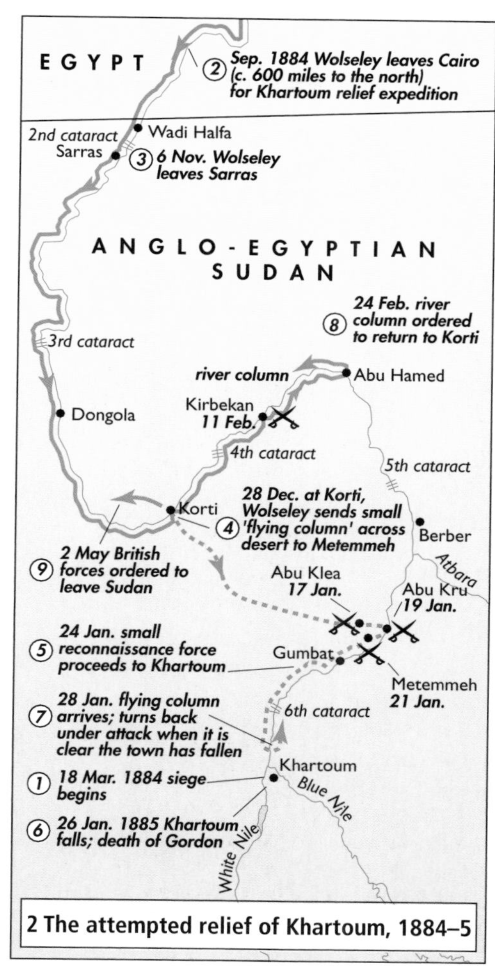

2 The attempted relief of Khartoum, 1884–5

Indo-China the 'Black Flags' and later De Tham took up the struggle after the emperor Ham Nghi was captured in 1888.

Even in areas not under colonial rule, European commercial and political penetration created local instability and provoked anti-western resistance. In China the disastrous wars with Japan in 1894–5, and the subsequent threat of partition, led to the abortive Hundred Days' Reform of 1898 and, after its failure, the anti-foreign Boxer Rebellion. In Turkey the Russian assault in 1877 and the dismemberment of the Ottoman empire's Balkan territories by the European powers at the Congress of Berlin fanned the patriotism of the Young Turks, who were to rise in revolution in 1908. In Egypt a revolt led by Arabi Pasha against the western-dominated khedive provoked British occupation in 1882.

Many of these movements were strongly religious in character. The Mahdiyya, which effectively controlled the Sudan from 1881 to 1898, was a Muslim revivalist movement, directed against Egyptians and Europeans alike. Hinduism played a similar role in fomenting resistance in India, as did Confucianism in China. Other movements were 'proto-nationalist' rather than nationalist in character: the disparate elements they brought together lacked unity and clearly defined objectives.

The consequences of resistance

But if African and Asian armed resistance was ultimately no match for European weaponry, technology and communications, its significance cannot be measured only in terms of its immediate military outcome. For the participants it often had important local political and economic consequences, and there were considerable continuities in rural resistance and in the ideologies of protest between the movements of this period and later anti-colonial opposition.

Even before 1914, 'modern' nationalist movements, characterized by the formation of nationalist associations and political parties, were emerging. Many of these were little more than small groups of disaffected intelligentsia whose impact was negligible, but a few, such as the Indonesian Sarekat Islam, quickly gained a mass following. In the First World War, with the European colonial powers simultaneously preoccupied with the war and forced to demand more from their colonies, new impetus was given to this incipient nationalism.

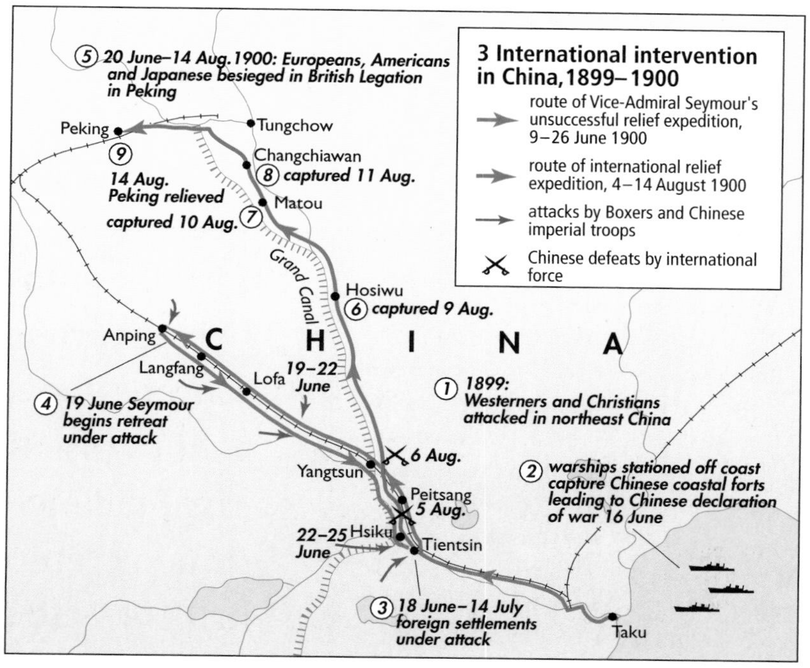

3 International intervention in China, 1899–1900
route of Vice-Admiral Seymour's unsuccessful relief expedition, 9–26 June 1900
route of international relief expedition, 4–14 August 1900
attacks by Boxers and Chinese imperial troops
Chinese defeats by international force
⑤ 20 June–14 Aug. 1900: Europeans, Americans and Japanese besieged in British Legation in Peking
Peking
Tungchow
⑨ 14 Aug. Peking relieved
Changchiawan
⑧ captured 11 Aug.
Matou
captured 10 Aug. ⑦
Grand Canal
Hosiwu
⑥ captured 9 Aug.
Anping
CHINA
Langfang
Lofa
19–22 June
① 1899: Westerners and Christians attacked in northeast China
④ 19 June Seymour begins retreat under attack
6 Aug.
Yangtsun
② warships stationed off coast capture Chinese coastal forts leading to Chinese declaration of war 16 June
Peitsang 5 Aug.
22–25 June
Hsiku
Tientsin
③ 18 June–14 July foreign settlements under attack
Taku

3 Western territorial encroachment provoked a violent uprising in northeast China. By early 1900 the 'Boxers' – practitioners of the martial arts who believed themselves to be invulnerable – had won the support of the Imperial court and Christians were attacked and representatives of 11 countries besieged in Peking *(map above)*. Peking was relieved in August at the second attempt as an international force brushed aside the imperial troops and the virtually unarmed Boxers. The uprising had revealed the extent of popular resistance to the foreign presence in China, but in 1901 further concessions had to be made to the Western powers. Such a striking display of impotence by the imperial government could not go unremarked by its subjects.

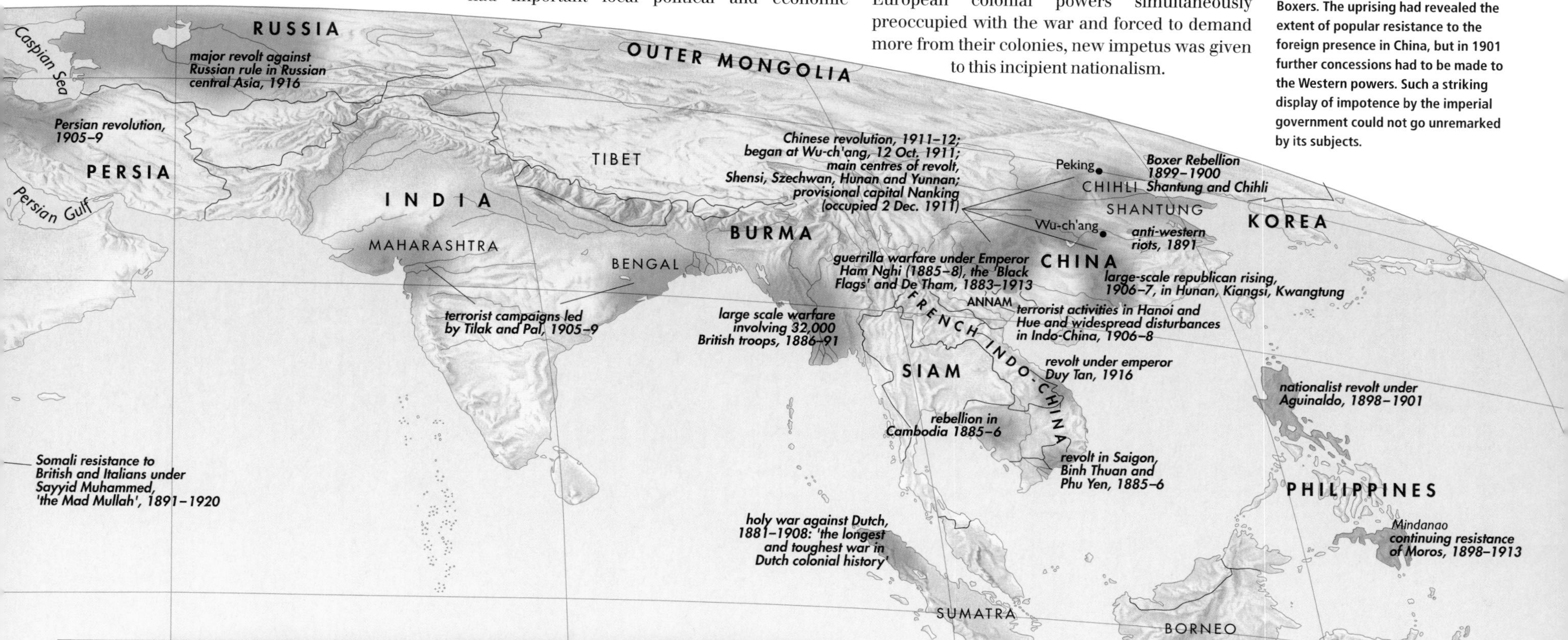

RUSSIA
Caspian Sea
major revolt against Russian rule in Russian central Asia, 1916
OUTER MONGOLIA
Persian revolution, 1905–9
PERSIA
Persian Gulf
TIBET
Chinese revolution, 1911–12; began at Wu-ch'ang, 12 Oct. 1911; main centres of revolt, Shensi, Szechwan, Hunan and Yunnan; provisional capital Nanking (occupied 2 Dec. 1911)
Peking
Boxer Rebellion 1899–1900 Shantung and Chihli
CHIHLI
SHANTUNG
KOREA
INDIA
Wu-ch'ang
anti-western riots, 1891
BURMA
MAHARASHTRA
BENGAL
guerrilla warfare under Emperor Ham Nghi (1885–8), the 'Black Flags' and De Tham, 1883–1913
CHINA
large-scale republican rising, 1906–7, in Hunan, Kiangsi, Kwangtung
ANNAM
terrorist activities in Hanoi and Hue and widespread disturbances in Indo-China, 1906–8
terrorist campaigns led by Tilak and Pal, 1905–9
large scale warfare involving 32,000 British troops, 1886–91
FRENCH INDO-CHINA
SIAM
revolt under emperor Duy Tan, 1916
nationalist revolt under Aguinaldo, 1898–1901
rebellion in Cambodia 1885–6
Somali resistance to British and Italians under Sayyid Muhammed, 'the Mad Mullah', 1891–1920
revolt in Saigon, Binh Thuan and Phu Yen, 1885–6
PHILIPPINES
holy war against Dutch, 1881–1908: 'the longest and toughest war in Dutch colonial history'
Mindanao continuing resistance of Moros, 1898–1913
SUMATRA
BORNEO
DUTCH EAST INDIES
Saminist peasant protest movement, beginning c. 1890, culminating in serious disturbances, 1914–17
JAVA
rebellion in Bali and Lombok, 1881–94
100°
60°
80°
120°
1 Reaction in Asia and Africa
rebellion against foreign or colonial power
rebellion against local rulers

After wars against Britain in 1874 and 1896, the final surrender of the Ashanti state came in 1900 *(left)*. This cleared the way for the British to extend its gold-mining in the region and also for the construction of railways into the interior. But the most lucrative activity – cocoa farming – remained in the hands of local farmers. On the back of this, by 1914 the Gold Coast was one of the most prosperous of the African colonies.

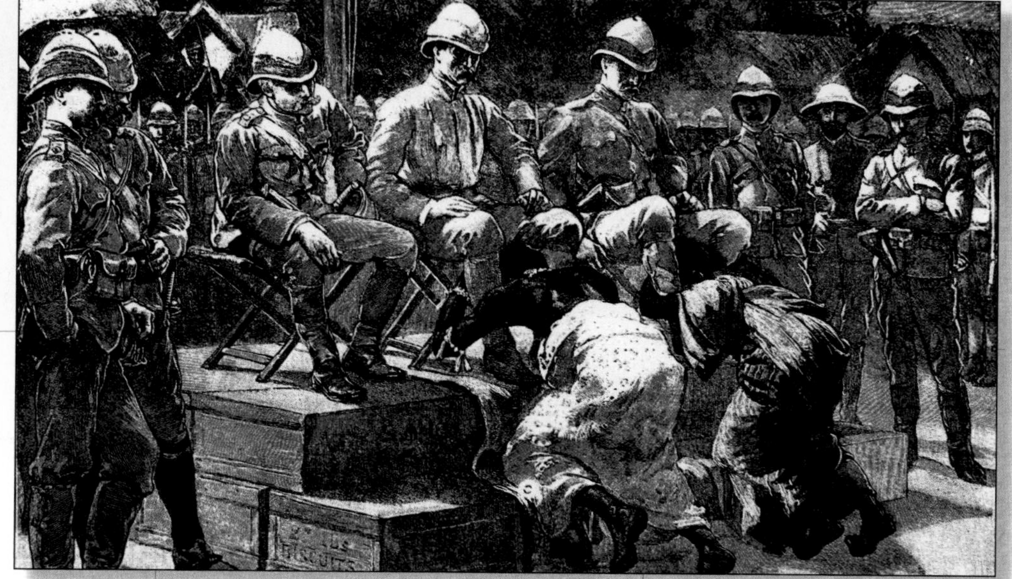

1878 to 1914

European rivalries and alliances

See also

The rise of nationalism in Europe, 1800–1914 p. 214

Germany and Italy: the struggles for unification, 1815–71 p. 216

The disintegration of the Ottoman empire p. 228

The First World War, 1914–18 p. 250

WHAT ARE THE FUNDAMENTAL MOTIVES THAT EXPLAIN THE PRESENT RIVALRY OF ARMAMENTS IN EUROPE? THEY ARE BASED ON THE UNIVERSAL ASSUMPTION THAT A NATION, IN ORDER TO FIND OUTLETS FOR EXPANDING POPULATION AND INCREASING INDUSTRY, IS NECESSARILY PUSHED TO TERRITORIAL EXPANSION AND THE EXERCISE OF POLITICAL FORCE AGAINST OTHERS; THAT NATIONS BEING COMPETING UNITS, ADVANTAGE, IN THE LAST RESORT, GOES TO THE POSSESSOR OF PREPONDERANT MILITARY FORCE, THE WEAKER GOING TO THE WALL, AS IN OTHER FORMS OF THE STRUGGLE FOR LIFE.

Norman Angell
The Great Illusion, 1909

Under the impact of mass nationalism and economic rivalry, relations between the Great Powers of Europe moved away from the balance-of-power politics practised since 1815 to a system based on rival alliance blocs. Rapid rearmament fuelled a growing tension in Europe which finally exploded in 1914 with the outbreak of the First World War.

1878 *The Congress of Berlin*

1879 *Austro-German alliance*

1884 *Berlin conference partitions Africa*

1894 *Franco-Russian alliance*

1904 *Anglo-French entente ends colonial rivalry*

1905 *First Moroccan crisis*

1907 *Anglo-Russian entente*

1908 *Bosnian crisis*

1912–13 *Balkan Wars: Turkey loses bulk of remaining European territory*

IN THE FORTY YEARS before 1914 the major European powers dominated the international order as never before. With military superiority assured, the search for security and economic expansion was expressed through a wave of imperialism and conquest. This sharpened rivalries between the powers and reduced the spirit of collaboration and collective settlement of disputes which had characterized the period since 1815.

Within Europe the traditions of 'concert diplomacy' were undermined by the sharp changes in the relative strength of the major players. The rise of Germany and Italy as major powers coincided with the decline of the Habsburg empire and the fatal weakening of the Ottomans. Under Bismarck Germany had played a cautious, even conservative role in Europe. After Bismarck's dismissal in 1890 German leaders began to pursue *Weltpolitik*, a global foreign policy, which brought them into conflict with the established colonial powers.

From the 1890s both Britain and France began a steady rearmament in response to the German threat. Russia, which since 1879 had been party to the League of the Three Emperors with Germany and Austria-Hungary, abandoned its traditional conservatism for an alliance with republican, democratic France, which was signed in 1894. By 1907 Britain had joined in agreements with them both to resolve colonial tensions.

The weakness of some countries was as much a source of instability as the growing strength of others. The Ottoman empire had been shored up by the Great Powers since 1815 in preference to their allowing any one of them to achieve a dominant position in the Middle East. But from the 1870s Ottoman influence declined sharply. Defeated by Russia in 1876–7 and then forced to grant independence to Romania, Serbia and Bulgaria, Ottoman Turkey found itself threatened all across the Middle East and north Africa.

The Balkan crisis

As Ottoman strength declined the Powers sought to reach agreement to prevent the 'Eastern Question' from precipitating a wider crisis. In 1887 Britain, Italy and Austria combined to limit French and Russian encroachments on Turkish territory. In 1897 Russia and Austria agreed to limit their ambitions in the Balkan region and this fragile collaboration lasted until 1908.

No other issue so divided the Powers in the years immediately before 1914 as the future of the Balkan peninsula. It was the one area of Europe where territorial and political advantage was still to be won as Ottoman imperialism waned. For Russia it had been an axis of advance since at least the 18th century; for Austria-Hungary it was the one region where Habsburg ascendancy could be maintained after defeat in Germany and Italy. When in 1908 Austria moved to annex Bosnia, an Ottoman territory under Austrian administration

2 In October 1912 the Balkan states (Bulgaria Greece, Serbia and Montenegro) drove Turkey from its remaining European territory ***(map right)***. The Balkan states divided up the spoils between them. In 1913 a second Balkan war broke out between Bulgaria and Serbia, Greece and Turkey, leading to a rapid Bulgarian defeat. Macedonia was divided between Greece and Serbia, leaving an enlarged and ambitious Serb state on the borders of the Habsburg empire.

HMS *Temeraire* *(below)*, depicted on a pre-war postcard. Britain responded to Germany's increased warship building after 1900 with a rival programme based on the most modern Dreadnought battleships. The Royal Navy was fully mobilized for exercises at the outbreak of war.

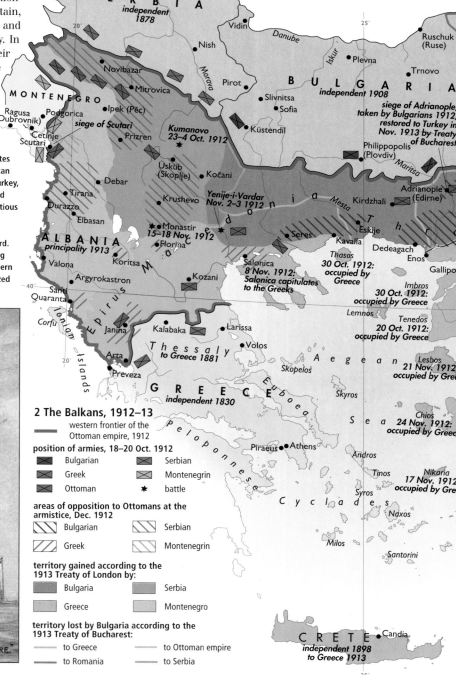

2 The Balkans, 1912–13

western frontier of the Ottoman empire, 1912

position of armies, 18–20 Oct. 1912: Bulgarian; Serbian; Greek; Montenegrin; Ottoman; ★ battle

areas of opposition to Ottomans at the armistice, Dec. 1912: Bulgarian; Serbian; Greek; Montenegrin

territory gained according to the 1913 Treaty of London by: Bulgaria; Serbia; Greece; Montenegro

territory lost by Bulgaria according to the 1913 Treaty of Bucharest: to Greece; to Ottoman empire; to Romania; to Serbia

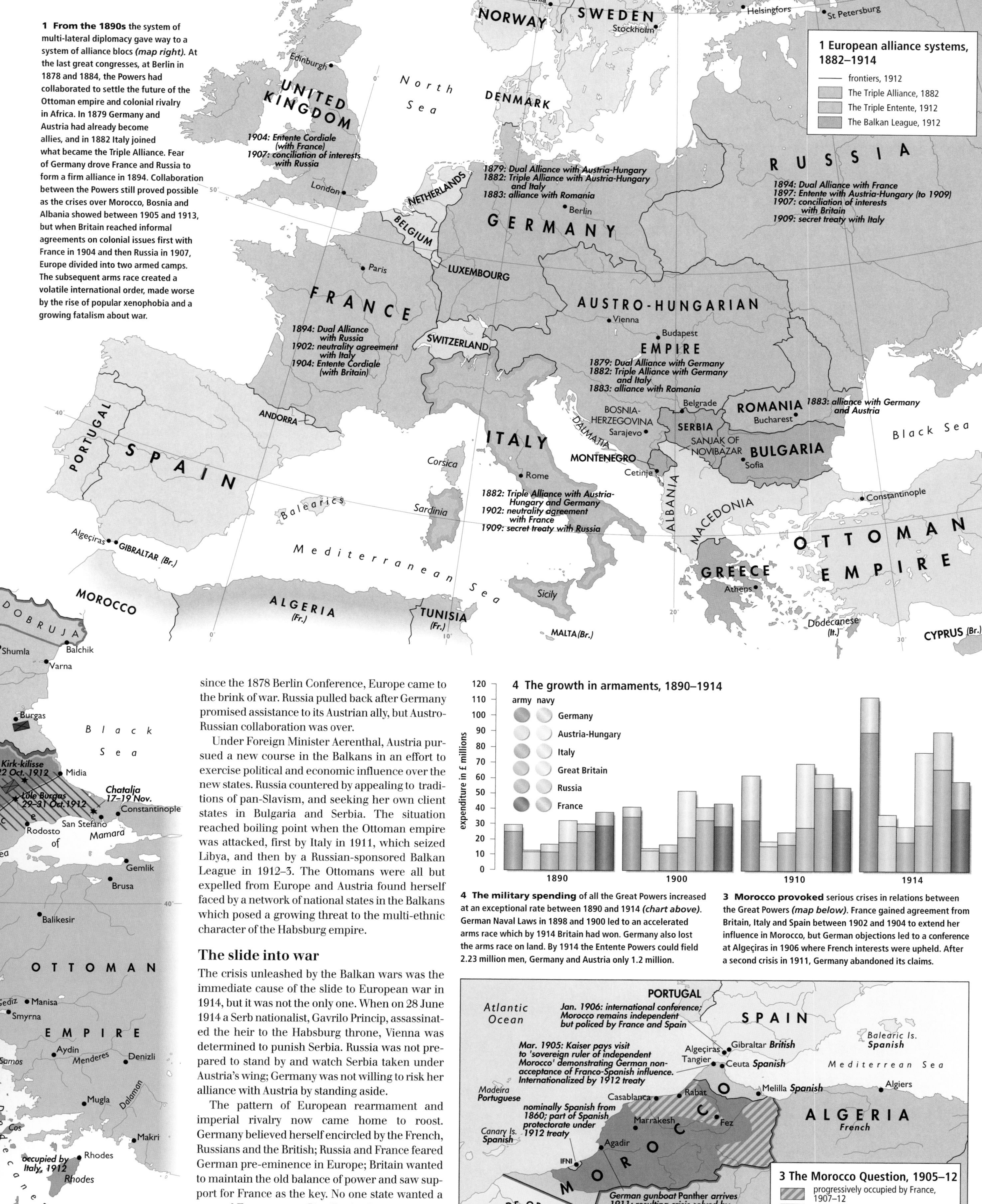

1 From the 1890s the system of multi-lateral diplomacy gave way to a system of alliance blocs *(map right)*. At the last great congresses, at Berlin in 1878 and 1884, the Powers had collaborated to settle the future of the Ottoman empire and colonial rivalry in Africa. In 1879 Germany and Austria had already become allies, and in 1882 Italy joined what became the Triple Alliance. Fear of Germany drove France and Russia to form a firm alliance in 1894. Collaboration between the Powers still proved possible as the crises over Morocco, Bosnia and Albania showed between 1905 and 1913, but when Britain reached informal agreements on colonial issues first with France in 1904 and then Russia in 1907, Europe divided into two armed camps. The subsequent arms race created a volatile international order, made worse by the rise of popular xenophobia and a growing fatalism about war.

4 The military spending of all the Great Powers increased at an exceptional rate between 1890 and 1914 *(chart above)*. German Naval Laws in 1898 and 1900 led to an accelerated arms race which by 1914 Britain had won. Germany also lost the arms race on land. By 1914 the Entente Powers could field 2.23 million men, Germany and Austria only 1.2 million.

3 Morocco provoked serious crises in relations between the Great Powers *(map below)*. France gained agreement from Britain, Italy and Spain between 1902 and 1904 to extend her influence in Morocco, but German objections led to a conference at Algeçiras in 1906 where French interests were upheld. After a second crisis in 1911, Germany abandoned its claims.

since the 1878 Berlin Conference, Europe came to the brink of war. Russia pulled back after Germany promised assistance to its Austrian ally, but Austro-Russian collaboration was over.

Under Foreign Minister Aerenthal, Austria pursued a new course in the Balkans in an effort to exercise political and economic influence over the new states. Russia countered by appealing to traditions of pan-Slavism, and seeking her own client states in Bulgaria and Serbia. The situation reached boiling point when the Ottoman empire was attacked, first by Italy in 1911, which seized Libya, and then by a Russian-sponsored Balkan League in 1912–3. The Ottomans were all but expelled from Europe and Austria found herself faced by a network of national states in the Balkans which posed a growing threat to the multi-ethnic character of the Habsburg empire.

The slide into war

The crisis unleashed by the Balkan wars was the immediate cause of the slide to European war in 1914, but it was not the only one. When on 28 June 1914 a Serb nationalist, Gavrilo Princip, assassinated the heir to the Habsburg throne, Vienna was determined to punish Serbia. Russia was not prepared to stand by and watch Serbia taken under Austria's wing; Germany was not willing to risk her alliance with Austria by standing aside.

The pattern of European rearmament and imperial rivalry now came home to roost. Germany believed herself encircled by the French, Russians and the British; Russia and France feared German pre-eminence in Europe; Britain wanted to maintain the old balance of power and saw support for France as the key. No one state wanted a general European conflict. Yet the Powers reacted with fear and uncertainty to the unexpected crisis in the Balkans, instead of displaying the collective crisis-management which they had brought to bear so often over the previous century.

The First World War

See also
The disintegration of the Ottoman empire, 1800–1923 p. 228
The Russian empire: expansion and modernization, 1815–1917 p. 230
European rivalries and alliances, 1878–1914 p. 248
The Russian revolution, 1917–1929 p. 256
European political problems, 1919–1934 p. 262
The outbreak of the Second World War p. 266

AS A TRIBUNAL FOR ASCERTAINING THE RIGHTS AND WRONGS OF A DISPUTE, WAR IS CRUDE, UNCERTAIN AND COSTLY ... LET ALL WHO TRUST JUSTICE TO THE ARBITRAMENT OF WAR BEAR IN MIND THAT THE ISSUE MAY DEPEND LESS ON THE RIGHTEOUSNESS OF THE CAUSE THAN ON THE CUNNING AND CRAFT OF THE CONTESTANTS. AND THE COST IS PROHIBITIVE. THE DEATH OF TEN MILLIONS AND THE MUTILATION OF ANOTHER TWENTY MILLIONS ... IS A TERRIBLE BILL OF COSTS TO PAY IN SUIT FOR DETERMINING THE RESPONSIBILITY AND PENALTY FOR THE MURDER OF TWO PERSONS.

David Lloyd George,
War Memoirs

In 1914, for the first time since the Napoleonic wars, most of Europe was convulsed by warfare. Expected to be short, the conflict became a long and bloody 'total war', mobilizing civilians as well as soldiers and killing millions. By 1918, the war had become a global conflict. Its legacy was economic dislocation, political violence and heightened nationalism.

Sep. 1914 *First Battle of the Marne*

1915 *Italy enters war on the side of the Allies*

1916 *Siege of Verdun leaves 600,000 dead*

June 1916 *Battle of the Somme fails to break German line*

1917 *German Navy begins unrestricted submarine warfare*

1917 *United States enters war on Allied side*

Mar. 1918 *Treaty of Brest-Litovsk ends war on Eastern Front*

May 1918 *German 'Spring Offensive' halted*

Sep. 1918 *Germans sue for armistice*

Nov. 1918 *Armistice on 11 Nov. ends the war*

WHEN ARCHDUKE FRANZ FERDINAND, heir to the Habsburg throne, and his wife were shot by Serb nationalists in Sarajevo on 28 June 1914, few Europeans expected the major powers to be locked in war within five weeks. Yet deeper fears for the balance of power and the preservation of national interest turned a minor incident into a diplomatic crisis. Once Austria-Hungary had decided to punish Serbia for the outrage it proved impossible to contain the conflict. German support for Austria and Russian support for Serbia created an explosive confrontation in which neither side would give way. When Austria invaded Serbia in late July, the two European blocs found themselves within a week fighting the first major European war since 1815.

Stalemate

Neither side thought the war would last more than six months. Both were ill-prepared for a brutal war of attrition. Germany expected to be able to deliver a swift knock-out blow against Belgium and France – the Schlieffen Plan – by sweeping round Paris and encircling French troops before swinging its forces east to confront the more slowly mobilizing Russian army. But the decision to hold forces in reserve in the industrial regions of Alsace-Lorraine and the Saar reduced the number of troops available and the weakened German offensive was blunted by Anglo-French forces on the Marne between 5 and 8 September. By November both sides had dug in along a 400-mile front from the English Channel to Switzerland. Behind a tangle of barbed wire, machine-guns and artillery each side confronted the other for almost four years of grim attritional warfare.

The war in the east

In the east the war was at first more mobile. The Russians pushed back German and Austro-Hungarian armies at Gumbinnen and Lemberg. Then, at the end of August, German forces defeated the Russians at Tannenberg and the Masurian Lakes. But trapped in a two-front war, Germany never had sufficient resources to consolidate its victories in the east. Elsewhere, the Central Powers found a decisive breakthrough similarly elusive. When Italy opened up a front against the Central Powers in 1915, Austro-Hungarian forces were stretched to the limit until German intervention helped crush the Italians at Caporetto in 1917. The conquest, with Bulgarian help, of Romania and Serbia by Austrian and German forces in 1916 was balanced by the Russian Brusilov offensive in June, limiting the threat of further territorial losses by Russia. The real breakthrough in the east for the Central Powers came with the overthrow of Russia's tsarist regime in February 1917, precipitating Russia's withdrawal from the war. In March 1918 the Treaty of Brest-Litovsk ended the war against Russia, allowing Germany to concentrate its efforts in the west.

Both sides had repeatedly tried to break the stalemate on the Western Front, launching offensives at terrible cost. In February 1916 German forces attempted to seize the French fortress of Verdun with no greater strategic object than to bleed the enemy white. More than 600,000 died. Verdun was saved in July 1916 by a British offensive on the Somme but at the cost of over 400,000 British casualties. By 1917, the constant blood-letting had produced protests. French units mutinied until concessions were granted; the German parliament passed a Peace Resolution to force the military to seek an honourable settlement. But by then Germany was under the virtual military dictatorship of Field Marshal Hindenburg and General Ludendorff, both determined on victory in what was now seen as a 'total war'. In February 1917 the German government authorized unrestricted submarine warfare to combat the Allied naval blockade. Outraged, in April the United States joined the war on the Allied side.

Victory in the west

The US decision to fight not only created a real world war, it tipped the balance against the Central Powers. America loaned over $10 billion to its allies and sent a stream of equipment and food. In March 1918 Ludendorff gambled on a last offensive. German forces broke through the Allied line towards Paris until, exhausted, poorly fed and short of weapons, they ground to a halt. With clear superiority in arms, the Allies pushed German and Austrian forces back in France and Italy. In September, Ludendorff sued for an armistice. When it was granted, on 11 November, Austria, Turkey and Bulgaria were already beaten. A prostrate Germany and revolution in Russia transformed Europe and ushered in an age of violent social confrontation.

1 The Great War in Europe, 1914–8

Allied Powers
Central Powers
major Allied Power offensive
major Central Power offensive
battles
battles costing over 250,000 killed
naval mutinies
army mutinies
naval bases
major naval battle
German raids on English coast
all battles, offensives, mutinies etc. coloured according to year
1914 1915 1916 1917 1918
farthest German advance in West, 1914
trench line, November 1914
farthest Russian advance in east, 1914–15
Russian front, November 1915
territory held by Central Powers, December 1917
front line at time of Brest-Litovsk armistice between Germany and Russia, December 1917
German penetration of Russia, March 1918
armistice line in West, November 1918

3 The war was fought between the Central Powers – Germany, Austria-Hungary, Bulgaria and the Ottomans – and the Allies – the British, Russian, French and Japanese empires *(map below)*. Italy joined the Allies in 1915; Romania, Greece and the USA also later joined them. Almost 70 million were mobilized, more than 9 million were killed, millions more were maimed or psychologically scarred.

3 Alliances and casualties

Central Powers
Allied Powers
states that later joined Central Powers, with date
states that later joined Allied Powers, with date
total mobilized forces:
Central Powers
Allied Powers
casualties
* estimated figures

On most fighting fronts soldiers' lives were dominated by the trench *(above)*. Conditions were at their worst on the Western Front. Prey to disease, living in damp, poorly ventilated bunkers, constantly shelled and occasionally gassed, the soldier's life was cheerless and brutal.

1 The war in Europe was fought on four fronts, but most resources were concentrated on the Western and Eastern fronts *(map above right)*. In the west the superiority of defensive systems led to a static war of attrition dominated by the machine-gun and the artillery barrage.

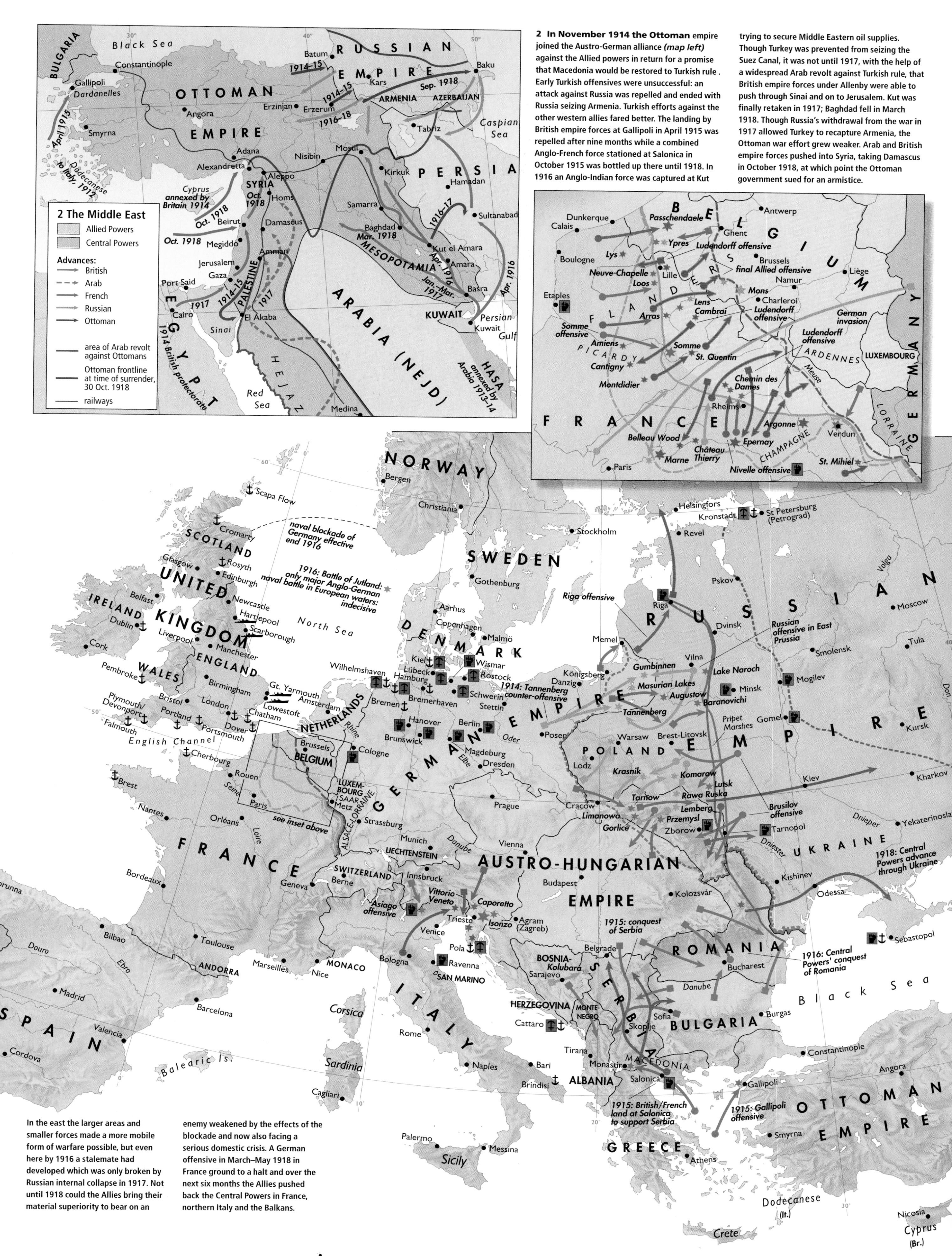

2 In November 1914 the Ottoman empire joined the Austro-German alliance *(map left)* against the Allied powers in return for a promise that Macedonia would be restored to Turkish rule . Early Turkish offensives were unsuccessful: an attack against Russia was repelled and ended with Russia seizing Armenia. Turkish efforts against the other western allies fared better. The landing by British empire forces at Gallipoli in April 1915 was repelled after nine months while a combined Anglo-French force stationed at Salonica in October 1915 was bottled up there until 1918. In 1916 an Anglo-Indian force was captured at Kut trying to secure Middle Eastern oil supplies. Though Turkey was prevented from seizing the Suez Canal, it was not until 1917, with the help of a widespread Arab revolt against Turkish rule, that British empire forces under Allenby were able to push through Sinai and on to Jerusalem. Kut was finally retaken in 1917; Baghdad fell in March 1918. Though Russia's withdrawal from the war in 1917 allowed Turkey to recapture Armenia, the Ottoman war effort grew weaker. Arab and British empire forces pushed into Syria, taking Damascus in October 1918, at which point the Ottoman government sued for an armistice.

In the east the larger areas and smaller forces made a more mobile form of warfare possible, but even here by 1916 a stalemate had developed which was only broken by Russian internal collapse in 1917. Not until 1918 could the Allies bring their material superiority to bear on an enemy weakened by the effects of the blockade and now also facing a serious domestic crisis. A German offensive in March–May 1918 in France ground to a halt and over the next six months the Allies pushed back the Central Powers in France, northern Italy and the Balkans.

7

The age of global civilization

THE DATE at which the European age gave way to the age of global civilization is a matter of debate. Some historians have picked out 1917 as a year of destiny. Others have seen 1947, the year of Indian independence, and 1949, the year of the Chinese revolution, as the decisive turning points. Certainly, America's declaration of war in 1917 turned a European conflict into a world war while the Bolshevik revolution in Russia split the world into two conflicting ideological camps. Similarly, the independence of India and the revolution in China symbolized the resurgence of Asia and the gathering revolt against the West.

Today it is obvious that we live in a post-European age. By making the world one, the European powers stirred up forces which spelled their own eclipse. The world wars between 1914 and 1945 whittled away the resources of the European powers, and only the healing of the wounds, in acts such as the formation of the European Economic Community in 1957, restored their fortunes. Europe's exhaustion after 1945 benefitted the Soviet Union and the United States, the two superpowers on the eastern and western flanks, whose rivalry produced an age of bipolarity. But bipolarity, too, proved to be a temporary phenomenon. The recovery of Europe, the emancipation of Asia and Africa, the rise of Japan and finally the collapse of the Soviet empire brought a new constellation into being, and with it the threat of confrontation between rich and poor nations and of the exhaustion of global resources through overpopulation. No one can foretell the shape of things to come. All this section can do is to show, in historical perspective, how the world of the 20th century changed and to chart the emergence of significant new factors.

The Statue of Liberty, New York

1870 to 1914
The formation of a world economy

See also
Population growth and movements, 1815–1914 p. 208
The industrial revolution in Europe, 1870–1914 p. 212
The market revolution in the US, 1800–80 p. 220
European colonial empires, 1815–1914 p. 244
The Great Depression, 1929–39 p. 264

1866 *First trans-Atlantic telegraph cable laid*

1869 *Suez canal opened*

1874 *Universal Postal Union founded*

1878 *Gold Standard established in Europe*

1880 *First refrigerated cargo ship (from Australia) reaches London*

1886 *Gold discovered on the Rand, South Africa*

1886 *Completion of Canadian Pacific railway*

1891 *Construction of Trans-Siberian railway begun*

1901 *First wireless message sent across the Atlantic*

1904 *Panama canal opened*

In the last third of the 19th century international trade, migration and capital flows expanded rapidly. Food and raw materials were now produced world-wide using European wealth. In return came a flow of industrial goods. This market operated informally, without state regulation. The 40 years before 1914 marked the zenith of economic liberalism

In those days when you left the shores of Europe you entered a kind of mercantile republic. Economic management on a world-wide basis actually existed. Europe devised it and Europe largely benefited by it. One could rely on a general stability in almost everything.

Andre Siegfried (1875–1959), French economist

The 40 years before the First World War witnessed a remarkable flowering of world-wide commerce, which in turn led to the establishment of an integrated and interdependent global economy. The creation of this world market derived from the economic expansion of Europe and North America, the wealthiest and most technically advanced areas of the world by 1870. Their search for markets and for new sources of raw materials and cheap food produced a restless economic imperialism at the expense of traditional native economies.

The transport revolution

To a large extent, this growth was governed by the spread of modern communications. The most significant development was the expansion of world shipping following the development of steamships. In 1850 most of the world's tonnage consisted of sailing ships; by 1914 only 8 per cent was still powered by sail. Between 1870 and 1910 European steam tonnage expanded from 1.5 million tons to over 19 million. Steam travel was faster, safer and allowed for much larger ships and cargoes. The average British steamship in 1914 was ten times the size of the average sailing ship in 1850.

There was also a remarkable expansion of the world rail network after 1870. While Europe possessed 60,400 miles of track in 1870 and the United States and Canada 56,300, the rest of the world had only 9100. By 1911 this had grown to 175,000. The American continent was first crossed by rail in 1869 and Canada in 1886, while the Russian empire completed the Trans-Siberian railway in 1904. Railways were essential in providing Europe with easy access to new sources of materials and food in the wider world.

The railway and the steamship also revolutionized commerce throughout the southern hemisphere. The development of effective means of refrigeration allowed meat, fruit and dairy produce to be sent across the equator to European customers. The first refrigerated cargo reached London from Australia in 1880. By the 1890s ships capable of carrying 150,000 frozen carcasses had been developed.

World commerce and banking

This revolution in transport produced an exceptional expansion of world trade. Between 1880 and 1913 the value of the world's imports and exports increased almost six-fold, from $7 billion to $40 billion. Europe dominated foreign trade, accounting for 57 per cent in 1913, of which Britain provided over one-quarter. But Europe's trade was overwhelmingly with other European states. The significant change since 1870 was the rising share of wider global trade, particularly inter-American trade and Japanese trade with Asia.

Trade expansion was closely linked with the development of foreign investment from Europe and America. The lead was taken by the world's wealthiest states, Britain and France. By 1914 they had invested the equivalent of 25 per cent and 15 per cent respectively of their national wealth abroad. Much of this money went to the United

1 Between 1870 and 1914 a genuinely global economy developed *(map right)*. A transport and communications revolution was fundamental to this new global economic boom. Shipping routes and telegraph lines linked continents; railways linked interiors to ports. Finance from Europe and the USA helped to fuel economic activity worldwide while world trade was helped, too, by the adoption of the Gold Standard and the development of an international banking network. Trade between European states and their overseas empires played a major role for Britain, France, Belgium and the Netherlands.

1 The development of the world economy

foreign investment, 1914 (in $ million)

535 United Kingdom
420 United States
3180 France
1050 Germany

busiest shipping routes
other major shipping routes, c. 1900
international telegragh cables

Colonial empires in 1900

Belgian
British
Danish
Dutch
French
German
Italian
Japanese
Ottoman
Portuguese
Russian
Spanish
USA
other countries

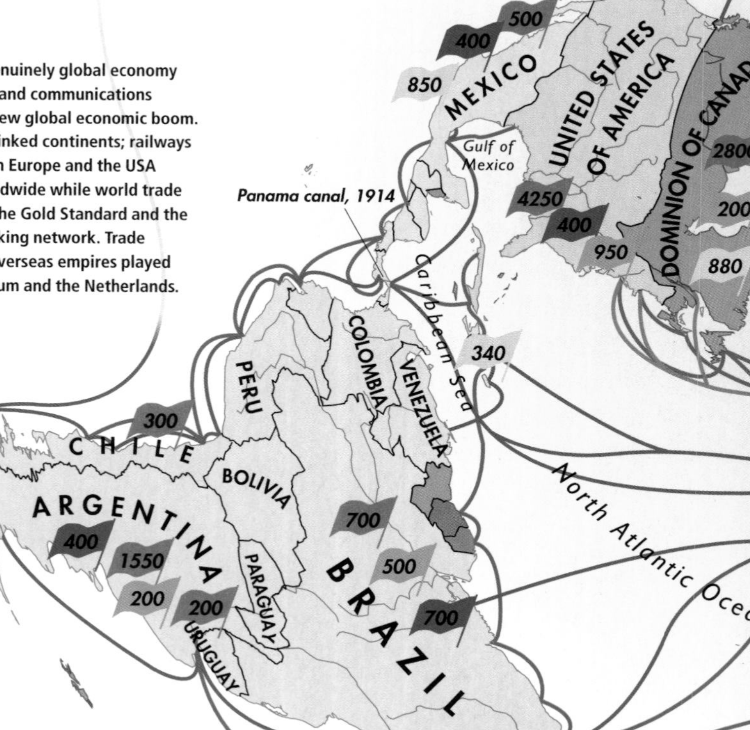

Miners at the Republic Gold Mining Company in the Transvaal, South Africa *(below)* fuelled the economic engine that drove the Gold Standard. This originated in Britain in 1821, but until Germany joined the system in 1871, most other countries had remained on a bi-metallic standard, gold and silver.

2 Average tariffs on industrial goods, 1914

United Kingdom 0%
Holland 4%
Switzerland 9%
Belgium 9%
Germany 13%
Denmark 14%
Austria-Hungary 18%
Italy 18%
France 20%
Sweden 20%
Russia 38%
Spain 41%

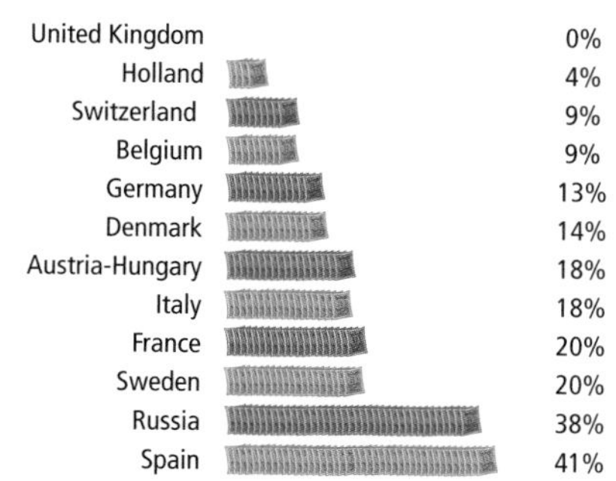

2 Though Britain encouraged freer trade in the 19th century, from the 1870s other states found that competition from Britain forced them to protect their trade by means of tariffs *(chart above).*

3 The opening of the Suez and Panama canals transformed world trade: journey times were dramatically cut and the dangerous routes around the Cape Horn and the Cape of Good Hope eliminated *(charts right).*

3 The Suez and Panama canals: journey times

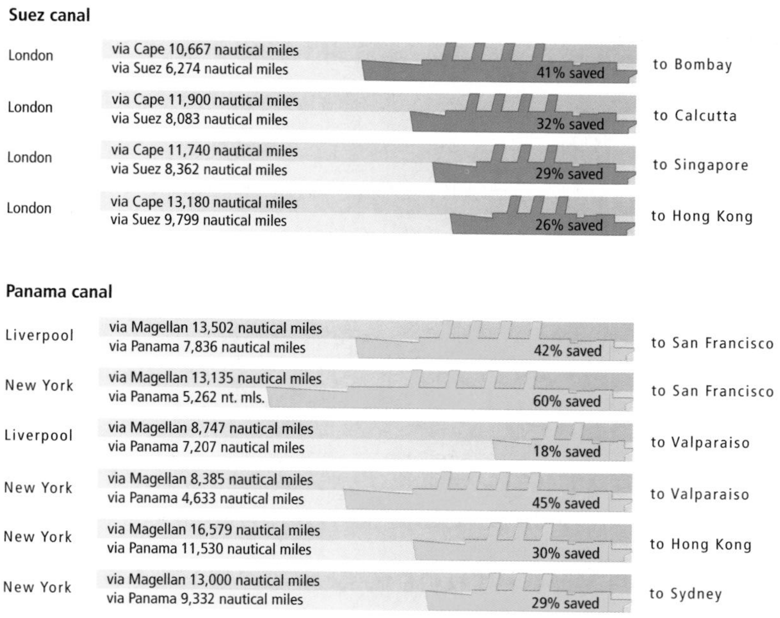

Suez canal
London
via Cape 10,667 nautical miles
via Suez 6,274 nautical miles
41% saved
to Bombay
London
via Cape 11,900 nautical miles
via Suez 8,083 nautical miles
32% saved
to Calcutta
London
via Cape 11,740 nautical miles
via Suez 8,362 nautical miles
29% saved
to Singapore
London
via Cape 13,180 nautical miles
via Suez 9,799 nautical miles
26% saved
to Hong Kong
Panama canal
Liverpool
via Magellan 13,502 nautical miles
via Panama 7,836 nautical miles
42% saved
to San Francisco
New York
via Magellan 13,135 nautical miles
via Panama 5,262 nt. mls.
60% saved
to San Francisco
Liverpool
via Magellan 8,747 nautical miles
via Panama 7,207 nautical miles
18% saved
to Valparaiso
New York
via Magellan 8,385 nautical miles
via Panama 4,633 nautical miles
45% saved
to Valparaiso
New York
via Magellan 16,579 nautical miles
via Panama 11,530 nautical miles
30% saved
to Hong Kong
New York
via Magellan 13,000 nautical miles
via Panama 9,332 nautical miles
29% saved
to Sydney

States and the settler colonies where it was used to promote railway building, farming and mining.

The rapid expansion of trade also raised issues of payment. From the 1860s, encouraged by the British example, most major states came to adopt the common Gold Standard against which their currencies could be valued. This was made possible by a great increase in gold production following discoveries in the United States in 1848, Australia in 1851 and South Africa in 1886. During the 1870s most European states adopted a Gold Standard. Japan followed in 1886, India in 1892, Russia in 1895–7 and the United States in 1900. The core measurement became the British pound, fixed at 113 grains of gold. The result was long-term stability in exchange rates and prices.

The regulation of commerce relied largely on the City of London, which became the world's financial and commercial centre in the half century before 1914, confidently exporting the virtues of free enterprise and economic liberalism. The growth of world trade and investment benefited the developed economies very substantially. Their share of world income in 1860 was 44 per cent; by 1913 it was 60.4 per cent. Though earnings in the developed world grew steadily, in the areas opened up by Europe and America they remained low, while native industries were often undermined by foreign imports. Only Japan succeeded in adopting modern technology and enterprise without becoming an economic satellite of the richer economies. Elsewhere local elites largely came to depend for their wealth and power on their links with the new world market, a relationship which in time provoked popular political resistance.

4 The rapid increase in the size and speed of Atlantic liners *(chart below)* was the result of the enormously improved efficiency of the new steam engines and of the greatly increased demand for travel. The fastest crossing times decreased from almost nine days in 1874 to just over four days in 1904.

4 The *Britannic* and *Mauretania*

	date	tonnage	length (feet)	indicated horse power	fuel consumption (tons per day)	speed (knots)	passengers	time to cross Atlantic
Britannic	1874	5,004	455	5,500	75	16	1,100	8 days 20 hours
Mauretania	1907	31,938	792	70,000	1,000	25	2,000	4 days 10 hours

Britannic
Mauretania

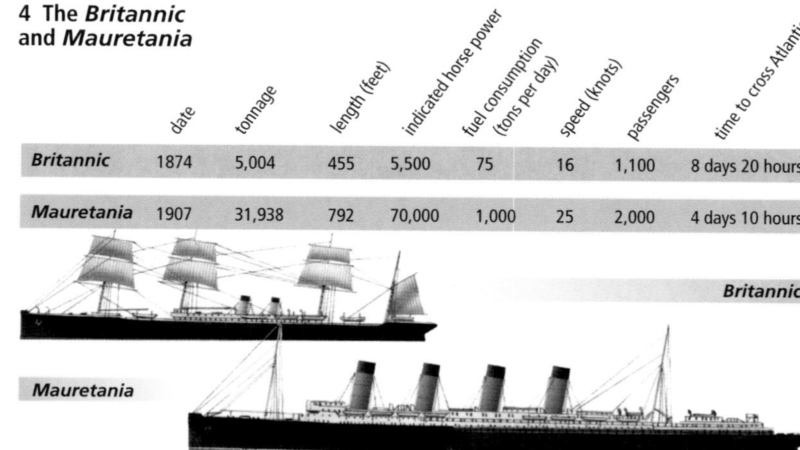

5 Foreign investment, 1914 (mill. of US dollars)

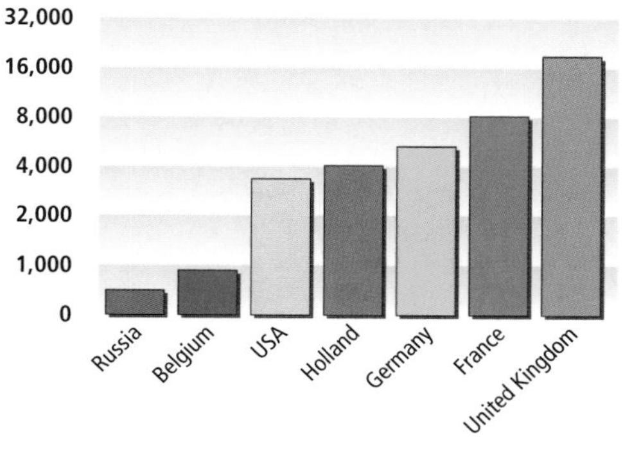

32,000
16,000
8,000
4,000
2,000
1,000
0
Russia
Belgium
USA
Holland
Germany
France
United Kingdom

5 Though its relative lead may have been declining, by 1914 British investment overseas was still twice as great as that of France, its nearest competitor and more than five times as great as that of the USA *(chart left).*

6 The period between 1860 and 1914 was one of remarkable price stability in which economies grew rapidly *(chart below).* The main beneficiaries were in Europe and the USA, which between them had two-thirds of the world's income in 1914.

6 Distribution of world income, 1860 and 1913

	1860 aggregate income ($ millions)	%	1913 aggregate income ($ millions)	%
North America	14,400	14.8	100,300	32.0
Oceania	500	0.5	4,100	1.4
Northwest Europe	28,500	20.4	84,000	27.5
Russia	7,000	7.0	22,500	7.4
Southeast Europe	9,500	9.7	26,000	8.5
Latin America	3,700	4.0	13,300	4.1
Japan	1,300	1.6	4,600	1.5
Near East	–	–	–	–
Far East	1,300	1.4	5,700	1.8
Central Africa	–	–	–	–
Southeast Asia	11,500	11.8	21,000	6.9
China	19,500	19.8	24,000	8.0
Total	**95,900**	**100.0**	**304,800**	**100.0**

300
NEW ZEALAND
COMMONWEALTH OF AUSTRALIA
1700
GERMAN NEW GUINEA
DUTCH NEW GUINEA
Pacific Ocean
JAPAN
500
DUTCH BORNEO
SARAWAK
200
INDO-CHINA
200
600
SIAM
BURMA
MONGOLIA
CHINA
RUSSIAN EMPIRE
550
400
2400
INDIA
1850
Indian Ocean
GREENLAND
investment in the rest of Europe
535
1050
420
3180
U K
NORWAY
SWEDEN
GERMANY
AUST.-HUNGARY
450
750
650
OTTOMAN EMPIRE
PERSIA
FRANCE
ITALY
Suez canal, 1869
ARABIA
SPAIN
Mediterranean Sea
200
500
200
LIBYA
EGYPT
ALGERIA
100
ANGLO EGYPTIAN SUDAN
ABYSSINIA
600
BRITISH EAST AFRICA
FRENCH WEST AFRICA
MADAGASCAR
all of Africa
500
NIGERIA
GERMAN E. AFRICA
CONGO FREE STATE
RHODESIA
ANGOLA
1550
GERMAN SOUTH WEST AFRICA
UNION OF SOUTH AFRICA
from 1910

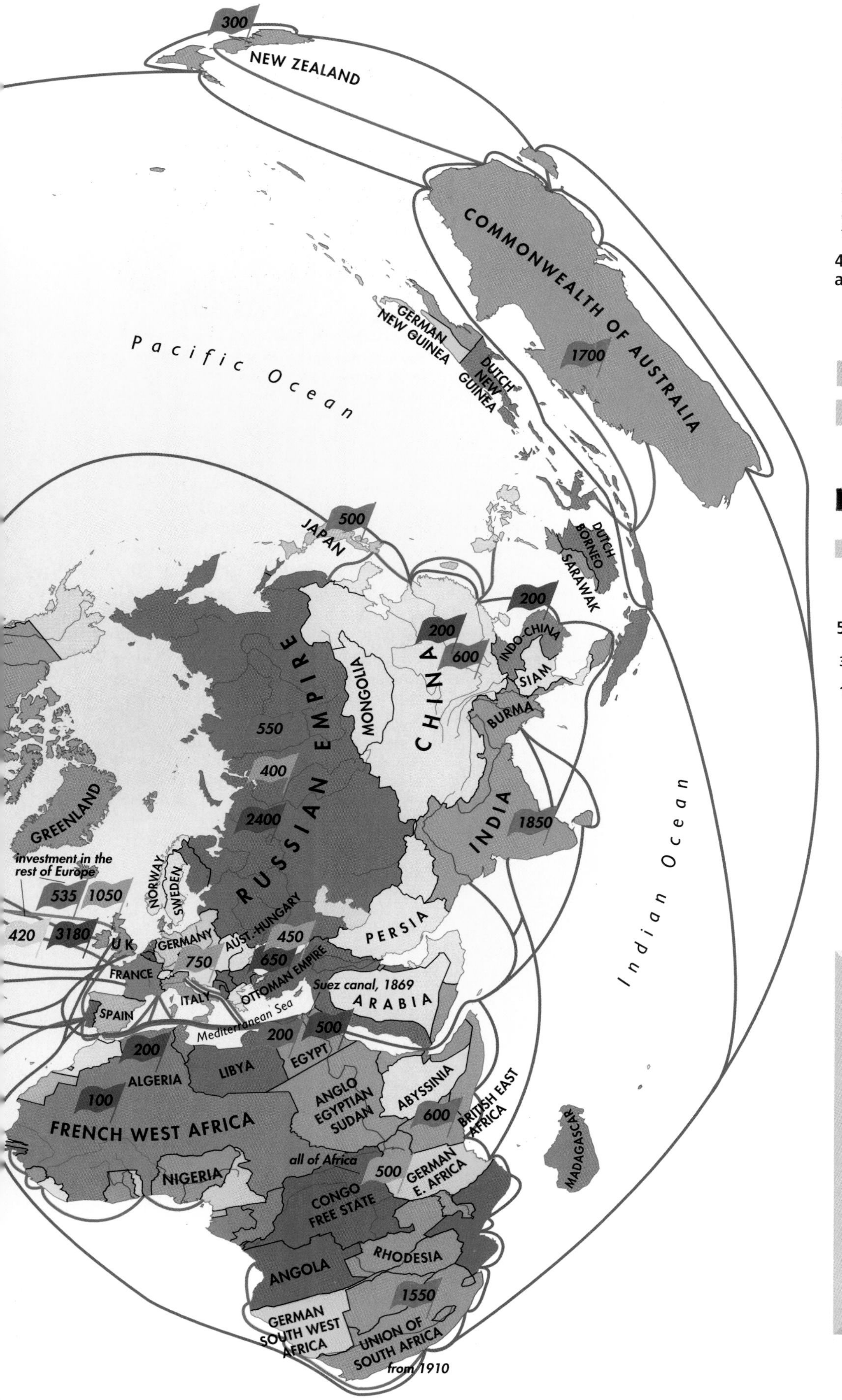

1917 to 1929

The Russian revolution

See also

The Russian empire: expansion and modernization, 1815–1917 p. 230

The First World War, 1914–18 p. 250

The development of the Soviet Union and Russia since 1929 p. 298

February 1917 *Tsar Nicholas II abdicates*

October 1917 *Lenin and the Bolsheviks seize power*

1918 *Treaty of Brest-Litovsk: Russia withdraws from First World War*

1918–20 *Russian civil war*

1921 *Lenin introduces NEP*

1922 *Stalin appointed General Secretary*

1924 *Death of Lenin*

1928 *Start of first Five-Year Plan*

In 1917 the Russian monarchy collapsed. For eight months liberals and moderate social democrats tried to set up a parliamentary regime, but in October radical communists under Lenin seized power and established a dictatorship which survived military intervention, civil war and economic crisis to forge the world's first communist state, the Soviet Union.

The tsarist system in Russia was faced with intolerable strains by the First World War. While Nicholas II did little to dispel hostility to his regime, the war effort went from bad to worse. Land was left untilled, the cities went hungry. The railway system threatened to collapse, towns were swamped with new workers who could not be adequately paid or housed. In February 1917 there were strikes and demonstrations in Petrograd. The army withdrew support from the tsar, and the Duma (parliament) called for a new order. In the face of the revolution, Nicholas abdicated. He was succeeded by a Provisional Government under the liberal Prince Lvov.

The second revolution

The first revolution in February solved none of Russia's problems. The Provisional Government had to work with a system of 'Dual Power' which it exercised with the Petrograd Soviet, a popularly-elected assembly representing workers and soldiers in the capital. A constitution was promised but constantly delayed and the economic situation deteriorated sharply. Soviets sprang up all over Russia, claiming to be the authentic voice of the people. When the war could not be continued effectively, the clamour for change pushed the population towards a more radical solution.

The main beneficiaries were the Social Revolutionaries and the Bolsheviks (Marxist Social-Democrats). In May a mainly socialist government was appointed under the leadership of a Social Revolutionary, Kerensky, but he was unable to stem the radical tide. By October land had been seized by the peasantry, the cities were in chaos, the authority of the government a hollow sham. The Bolshevik leader, Lenin, called for a second, communist revolution, and when Bolsheviks stormed the government building on 25 October 1917, resistance crumbled. The Bolsheviks seized power and established an emergency dictatorship.

Civil war

Bolshevik power extended only over the heartland of Russia; the rest of the empire broke into a series of smaller national states. On the fringes anti-Bolshevik forces gathered to destroy Russian socialism. After the new regime had agreed to end Russian participation in the First World War at Brest-Litovsk in March 1918, the Bolsheviks fought a three-year civil war against the 'White' counter-revolutionary armies, foreign forces sent to crush the revolution, and armed nationalist movements in the Ukraine, the Baltic states and the Caucasus.

A period of extraordinary confusion followed. By organizing a war effort on lines even more authoritarian than the tsar's, the Bolsheviks defeated one enemy after another. By 1920 the civil war was over, and by 1922, when the new state was established as the USSR, its power extended over the Ukraine, the far eastern territories and the Caucasus. In 1921 Lenin introduced the more liberal New Economic Policy, but the political system remained a tight Party dictatorship. During the 1920s an uneasy social peace reigned, but the issue of how to establish a modern industrial state in a peasant-based society had only been postponed. Under Stalin, General Secretary from 1922, the problem of modernizing Russia was addressed in 1928 in a savage 'revolution from above'.

> The working man must know that there really are no miracles, and that he will have to confront hunger, complete disorganization of industry, prolonged and bloody anarchy followed by reaction no less sanguinary and dark. That is where the proletariat is being led ... one must understand that Lenin is not an all-powerful magician, but a deliberate juggler, who has no feeling for the lives or the honour of the proletariat.
>
> **Maxim Gorky, November 1917**

The architect of the October Revolution was the lawyer-turned-revolutionary Lenin ***(above)***. Leader of the Bolsheviks in Russia since 1903, Lenin was a convinced Marxist who saw the collapse of the tsarist monarchy as the signal for worldwide communist revolution.

2 The Bolsheviks were convinced that their revolution would be the signal for a European revolt against the old imperialist order. At the end of the war communism surfaced in Hungary, Germany and other areas of eastern Europe, and social unrest was widespread in the west ***(map below)***. But the revolution was bloodily suppressed outside Russia, leaving the new revolutionary state dangerously isolated by 1921.

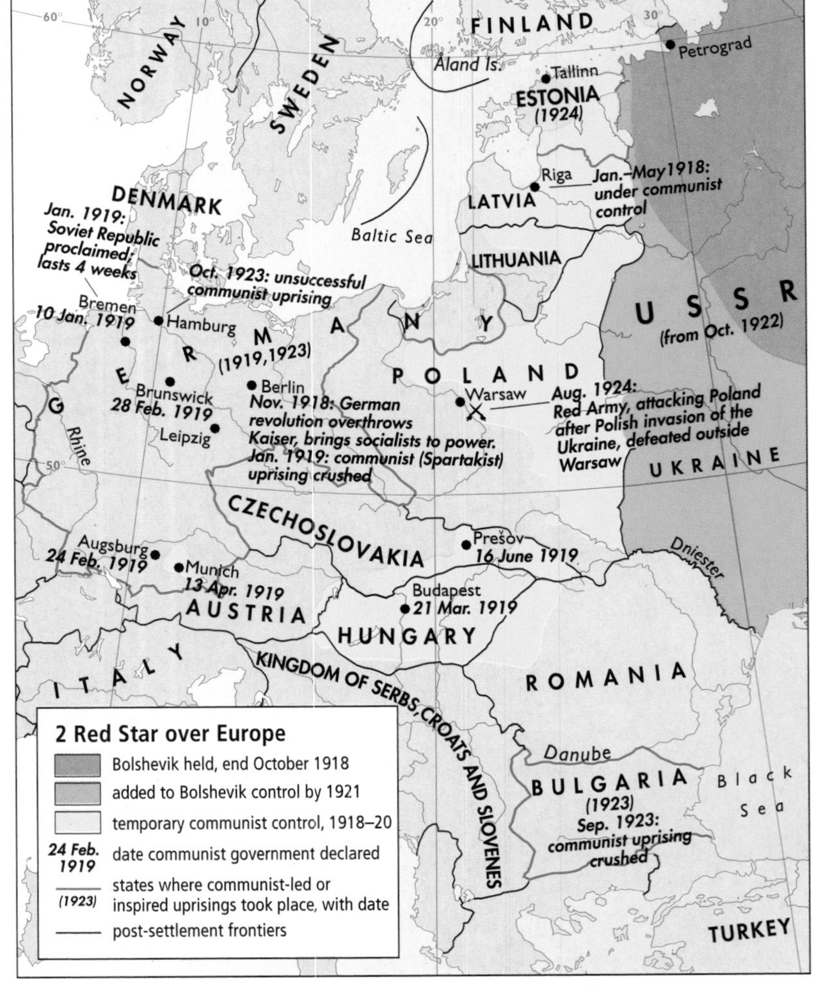

3 The Bolshevik message appealed much more to peasants than to workers, and the revolution spread rapidly across central Asia and into China, where a communist party was established in 1921 ***(map below)***. Autonomous communist states were set up in the east but, except for Mongolia, they were brought into the Soviet Union when it was established in 1922 as a federation of Bolshevik-dominated socialist republics.

1 Under the pressure of total war the Russian monarchy collapsed in February 1917 *(map below)*. The Provisional Government failed to halt either the Germans at the front or the tide of radical revolution at home. In October (by the old calendar), the Bolsheviks seized power and a bloody three-year civil war followed. Anti-Bolshevik 'White' forces, aided by foreign money and troops, almost destroyed the revolutionary state in 1919 until confronted with a reformed Red Army. By 1920 the war was over and the task of consolidating Communist rule in Russia began.

1919 to 1941
Imperialism and nationalism

See also
India under British rule, 1805–1935 p. 234
European colonial empires, 1815–1914 p. 244
The anti-colonial reaction, 1881–1917 p. 246
Retreat from empire since 1939 p. 276
South Asia: independence and conflict p. 284
Africa after emancipation since 1957 p. 286
Nationalism, secularism and Islam in the Middle East since 1945 p. 290

1919 *Former German colonies distributed as League of Nations mandates*

1920–2 *Gandhi leads Indian non-cooperation campaign*

1922 *Egypt independent*

1926 *British Dominions recognized as independent*

1930–1, 1932–4 *Civil disobedience campaigns in India*

1931 *Japan invades Manchuria*

1932 *Iraq independent*

1935–6 *Italy conquers Abyssinia*

1940–2 *Japan takes European colonies in Far East*

Though the First World War destroyed the German and Ottoman empires, the British and French empires reached their greatest territorial extent after 1919. Nevertheless, the war had eroded the foundations of imperialism in Asia and the Middle East while by the 1930s the stability of Europe's empires was being shaken by the Depression.

THE IMPERIAL CONTRIBUTION to the Allied cause during the First World War led Lloyd George to reflect that 'the British empire was not an abstraction but a living force to be reckoned with'. Britain, like France, then consolidated the strategic underpinning of its empire by the acquisition of new Middle East territories and expansion in Africa. This was possible because the new League of Nations distributed former Ottoman and German dependencies in the form of 'mandates' among the victorious powers. Britain gained trusteeships for Palestine, Iraq and Transjordan, as well as former German colonies in Tanganyika and, with France, Togoland and German Cameroon. France also gained Syria and Lebanon. Germany's Pacific islands and New Guinea (*see* p. 245) went to New Zealand and Australia respectively and German South West Africa went to South Africa.

Ironically, by 1919 the British faced significant challenges. National identities had been consolidated in the white self-governing colonies, and after the war these countries, termed 'dominions' since 1907, pressed for a definition of their status as independent countries within the British Commonwealth. At the same time, there was growing criticism of colonialism from the United States and the Soviet Union, while, despite the real economic rewards they brought with them, the empires were increasingly expensive to maintain.

Nationalist opposition

Above all the European empires faced growing opposition from within their territories, led by educated elites who sought a role in local administration or even national autonomy. The war lubricated the existing nationalist movements in India and Egypt, and intensified opposition in Ireland. Between 1920–2 and again in the early 1930s Mahatma Gandhi led the first nationalist Congress All-India campaigns for self rule. Confronted by mass opposition, in 1919 and 1935 Britain greatly extended Indian participation in government. Egypt, although Britain retained great influence and military rights, was given independence in

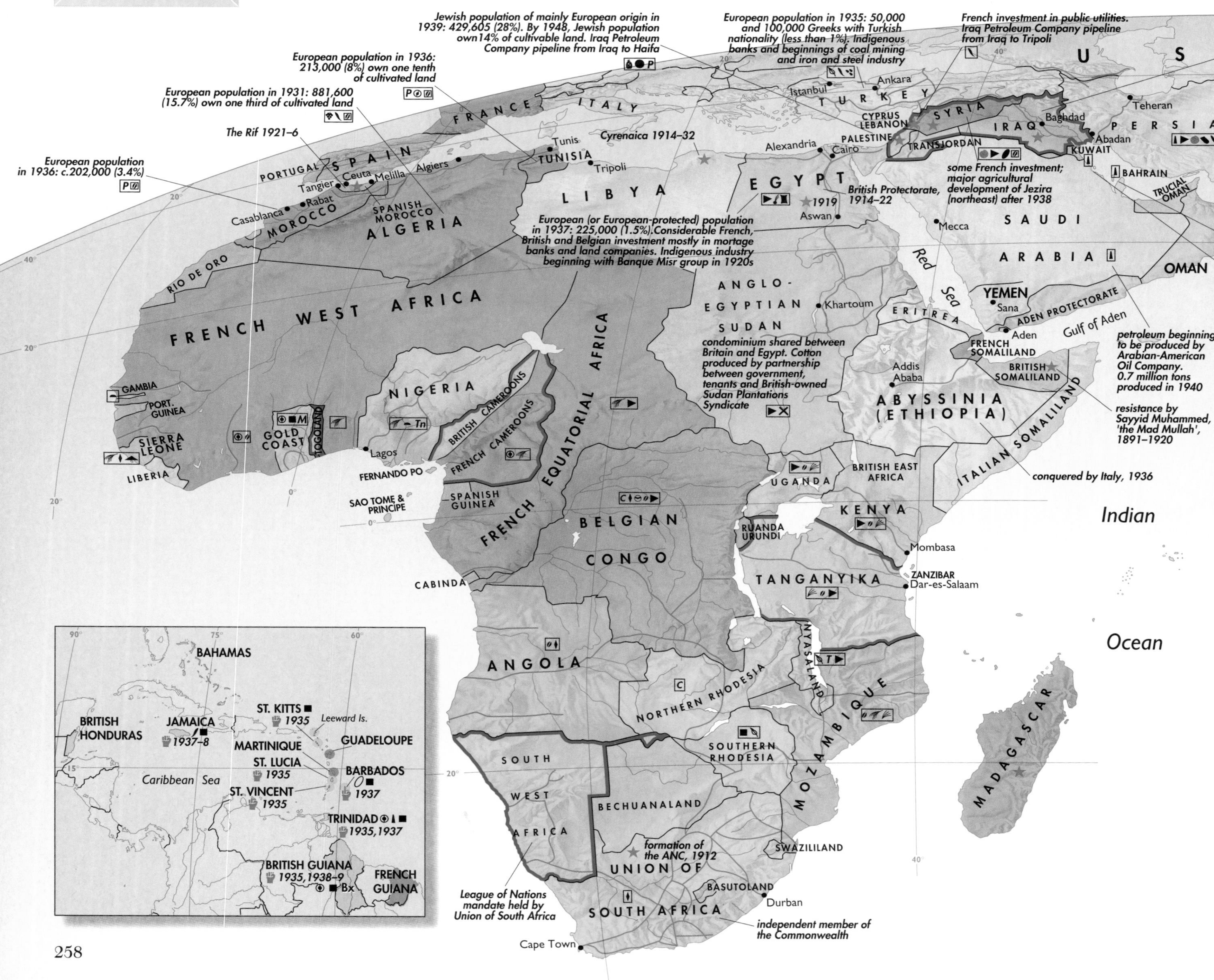

1922, while, after violently suppressing guerrilla warfare, Britain conceded 'dominion status' in 1921 to a new state created in southern Ireland. Meanwhile post-war uprisings in the newly acquired territories of the Middle East presaged problems to come. In Palestine, where Britain had committed itself to supporting the creation of a Jewish homeland, Jewish immigration after Hitler came to power in Germany led to a widespread Arab uprising after 1936. Iraq meanwhile had secured independence by 1932.

In other European colonies the 1920s were less troubled. In tropical Africa, a 'thin white line' of officials administered the colonies acquired in the late 19th century, and African chiefs were incorporated into colonial structures of local governance. Large settler communities developed in east and central Africa, especially in Kenya and southern Rhodesia.

Imperialism in the 1930s

The 1930s saw a last burst of imperialism as Japan invaded Manchuria in 1931 and Italy conquered Abyssinia in 1935–6. The League of Nations, however ineffective in practice at dealing with such aggression, had nonetheless, through its mandate system, introduced the idea of international accountability in colonial affairs. Together with the British idea of progress towards 'dominion status', it gave rise to a new conception of colonial rule as something temporary and limited. Other colonial powers also faced mounting opposition. In north Africa, Italy experienced continuous resistance while nationalist movements mushroomed in the French territories of Tunisia, Algeria and Morocco. In the Dutch East Indies, a phase of revolutionary movements, beginning with the communist revolt of 1926, was seen off with only limited changes in provincial government, but in Indo-China the preservation of firm French control led to unrest in the 1930s and the creation of a nationalist guerrilla organization, the Viet Minh, by Ho Chi Minh in 1941.

Differing political and social conditions meant that there were fewer challenges in sub-Saharan Africa; nonetheless discontent with colonial rule took a variety of forms, and the Depression in particular, hitting colonial economies vulnerable to changes in world trade, saw widespread unrest. Cocoa farmers in the Gold Coast were stirred to protest. In the West Indies, meanwhile, unemployment and falling export prices led to a series of strikes and riots between 1935 and 1938.

By 1939 the development of nationalism in Asia and north Africa and the rise of new, more radical nationalist leaders – Sukarno in Indonesia, Nehru in India, Bourguiba in Tunisia – was placing strains on the European colonial empires. It was the Second World War, however, which was to deliver the fatal blow to European colonialism.

1 The material advantages of the European overseas empires were offset by growing political and social conflict *(map below)*. Some of this was the result of impoverishment and trade decline but much came from nationalists hostile to colonial rule. Though concessions were made in the Middle East, India and the British Dominions, by 1939 the long-term prospects for the survival of colonial empires were bleak.

2 The Middle East saw numerous instances of opposition to British and French imperialism *(map above)* and attempts by rural or minority populations to resist the newly created central governments. Palestine experienced frequent anti-British disturbances and an Arab uprising (1936–9) in protest at Jewish immigration. Two national revolts in Syria-Lebanon (1925–7, 1943–5) sought to force the French to grant independence. In Egypt in 1919 the Wafd party organized a nationwide revolt in an attempt to overturn the British protectorate, which finally ended in 1922.

> THEY TALK TO ME ABOUT PROGRESS, ABOUT 'ACHIEVEMENTS', DISEASES CURED, IMPROVED STANDARDS OF LIVING. I AM TALKING ABOUT SOCIETIES DRAINED OF THEIR ESSENCE, CULTURES TRAMPLED UNDERFOOT, INSTITUTIONS UNDERMINED, LANDS CONFISCATED, RELIGIONS SMASHED, MAGNIFICENT ARTISTIC CREATIONS DESTROYED, EXTRAORDINARY POSSIBILITIES WIPED OUT.
>
> **Aimé Césaire**
> *Discourse on Colonialism, 1950*

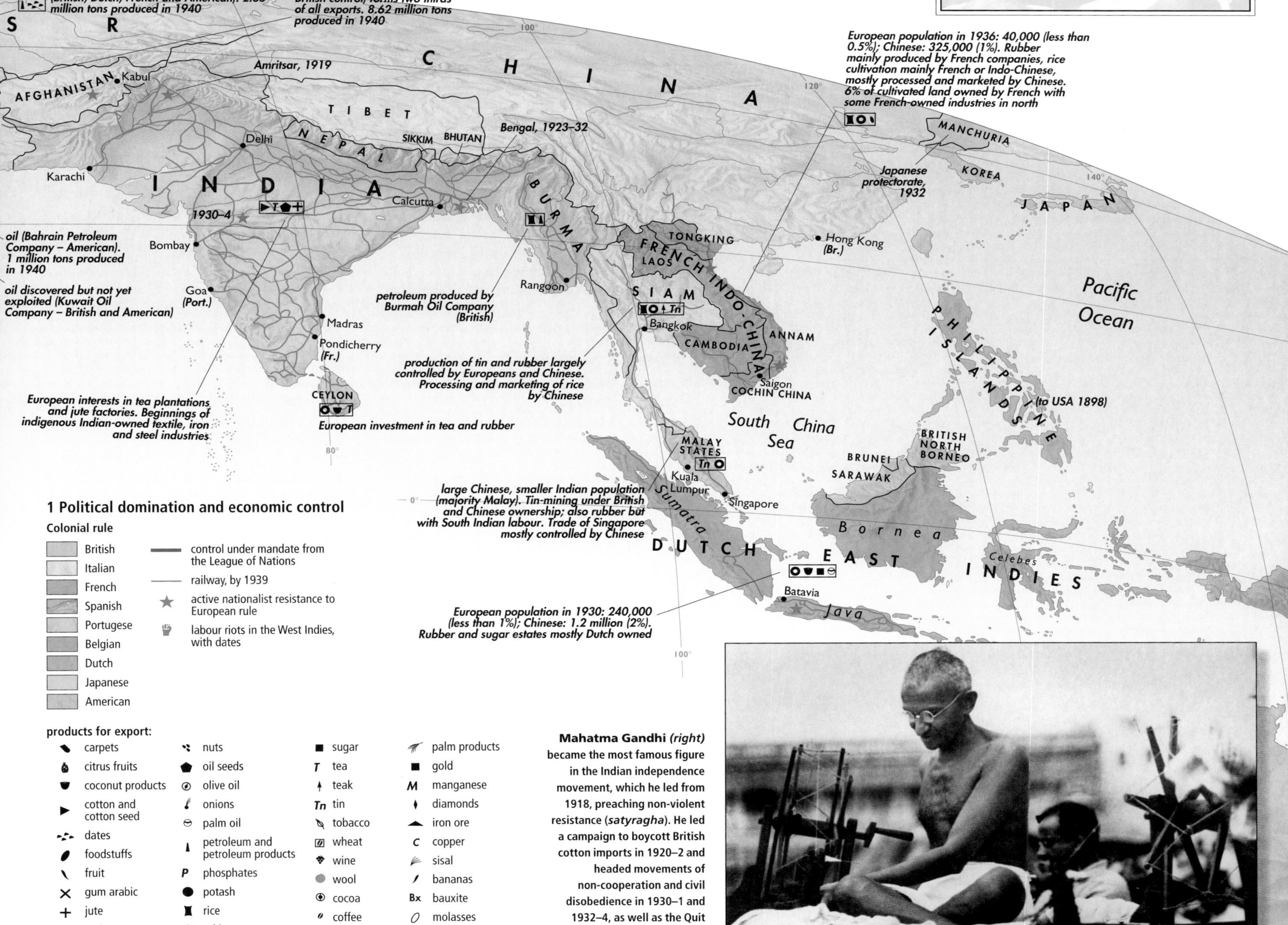

Mahatma Gandhi *(right)* became the most famous figure in the Indian independence movement, which he led from 1918, preaching non-violent resistance (*satyragha*). He led a campaign to boycott British cotton imports in 1920–2 and headed movements of non-cooperation and civil disobedience in 1930–1 and 1932–4, as well as the Quit India Movement of 1942.

1912 to 1949
The Chinese revolution

See also

The collapse of the Chinese empire, 1839–1911 p. 232
The anti-colonial reaction, 1881–1917 p. 246
The outbreak of the Second World War p. 266
The war in Asia and the Pacific, 1941–5 p. 268
Japan and east Asia since 1945 p. 278
China under communism since 1949 p. 280
Southeast Asia since 1945 p. 282

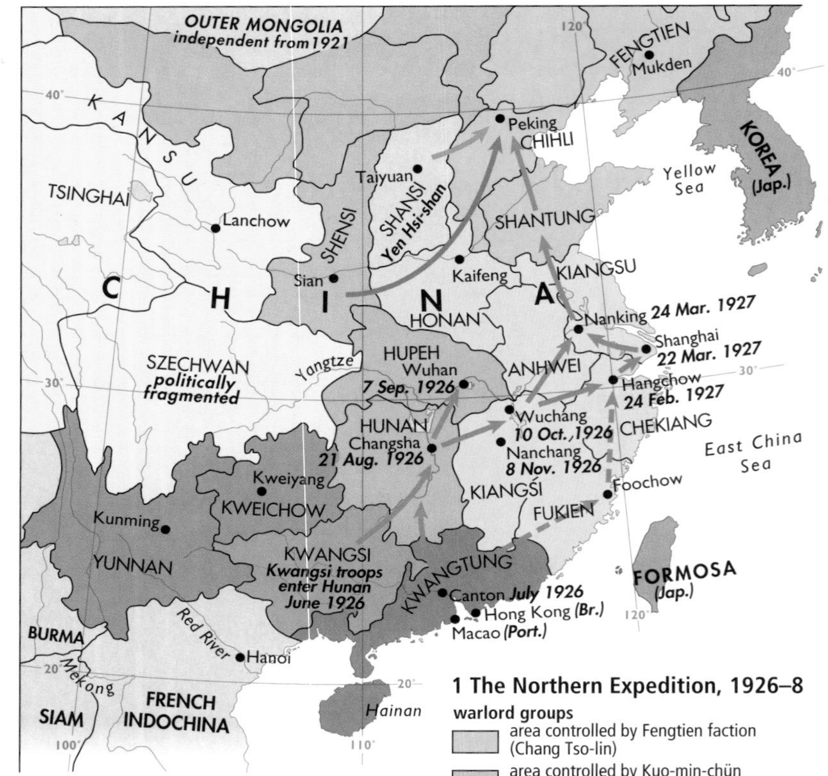

1 The Northern Expedition, 1926–8

warlord groups
- area controlled by Fengtien faction (Chang Tso-lin)
- area controlled by Kuo-min-chün (Feng Yü-hsiang)
- area controlled by Chihli faction (Sun Ch'uan-fang)
- area controlled by Chihli faction (Wu P'ei-fu)
- Kwangsi clique (group of warlords)
- T'ang Chi-yao, warlord of Yunnan and Kweichow
- area controlled by Kuomintang
- main Kuomintang forces
- minor Kuomintang forces
- Yen Hsi-shan (warlord of Shansi 1912 onwards)
- Kuo-min-chün

1 In 1926 the Kuomintang and their Communist allies launched a major drive to unify the country, the Northern Expedition *(map above)*. Their government was moved to Wuhan, which became the centre of the Left. In April 1927 Chiang Kai-shek carried out a purge of the Communists and transferred the capital to Nanking. Subsequent operations against the Fengtien faction in the north were joined by Yen Hsi-shan, warlord of Shansi, and Feng Yü-hsiang, leader of the Kuo-min-chün faction. Although the Kuomintang now claimed to rule all China, many areas remained outside their effective control.

2 The Nationalist (Kuomintang) regime, 1928–37

- occupied by Japan by 1933
- area in which Japan attempted to establish a puppet North China state, 1935

areas of effective control of Chiang Kai-shek's Nationalist government at Nanking
- 1928
- 1929–34
- 1935–7
- brought under Nanking influence 1935–7

2 The Kuomintang regime after 1928 controlled only part of China *(map above)*. The northeast was occupied by Japan from 1931, warlords ruled supreme in many provinces while other areas fell into anarchy. Large tracts of Kiangsi were under Communist control after 1931 while by 1936 the Communists possessed a new base in the northwest, at Yenan.

China from 1912 entered a phase of brutal internal anarchy. With no effective central government, warlords, Nationalists and Communists struggled for control while imperialist Japan occupied increasingly large areas of the north. Japan's defeat in 1945 saw a further civil war from which the Communists emerged victorious in 1949.

THE FOUNDATION OF THE REPUBLIC in 1912 (*see* p. 232) failed to produce a lasting solution to China's problems. Within weeks Sun Yat-sen, the revolutionary who had been elected China's provisional first president, was replaced by Yüan Shih-k'ai, the most powerful general of the imperial era. China's continuing weakness was clear: the government had to borrow huge sums abroad to offset the lack of a modern revenue system; the satellite states of Tibet and Mongolia fell under British and Russian dominance respectively; and Japan expanded her influence on Chinese territory. At the outbreak of the First World War Japan seized the German-leased territory in Shantung and presented 'Twenty-one Demands', which would have reduced China to a Japanese dependency. Though Yüan was able to resist most, he was forced to acknowledge Japanese dominance in Shantung, Manchuria and Inner Mongolia.

After Yüan died in 1916 power passed increasingly into the hands of provincial generals. For the next decade, although the Peking government claimed to rule China, it was the puppet of one group of generals or another. Some of these warlords established stable and reforming regimes, as in Shansi, Kwangsi and Manchuria, others, as in Szechwan, presided over anarchy. In the 1920s warlord coalitions fought devastating campaigns against each other. Only the Treaty Ports (*see* p. 232), under foreign protection, remained secure.

Nationalist reaction

After the First World War there was an upsurge of revolutionary activity driven by widespread popular reaction against foreign interference and economic exploitation, as well as disgust at the terms of the Paris Peace Conference, which reinforced Japan's position in Shantung. In 1919 the reaction erupted into the nationalist 'May 4th Movement' in which a new generation of Western-oriented students and intellectuals, joined by urban workers, became a force in politics for the first time. The Movement even succeeded in preventing the government from signing the Treaty of Versailles. There followed the transformation in 1923 of Sun Yat-sen's revolutionary party into the Nationalist (Kuomintang) Party.

With Sun's death in 1925, the Nationalists were headed by Chiang Kai-shek, who in 1926 led the 'Northern Expedition' from the Nationalist base in Canton to eliminate the warlords and unify the nation. By 1928 Chiang's armies had taken Peking. For much of this period the Nationalists operated in alliance with the Communist Party, which had been founded in 1920. The Communists showed themselves most effective at organizing support in the industrial cities until Chiang, in April 1927, decided he was strong enough to do without them, and they were ruthlessly purged.

Although the Nationalists now dominated China, serious competitors for power remained. With warlords still flourishing, Chiang's government had firm centralized control over only the rich provinces of the lower Yangtze (*see* map 2). There it modernized the administration and the army, built a road and railway system and established new industries.

> ... A REVOLUTION IS NOT A DINNER PARTY, OR WRITING AN ESSAY, OR PAINTING A PICTURE, OR DOING EMBROIDERY; IT CANNOT BE SO REFINED, SO LEISURELY AND GENTLE, SO TEMPERATE, KIND, COURTEOUS, RESTRAINED AND MAGNANIMOUS. A REVOLUTION IS AN INSURRECTION, AN ACT OF VIOLENCE BY WHICH ONE CLASS OVERTHROWS ANOTHER.
>
> **Mao Zedong**
> ***Report on an investigation of the peasant movement in Hunan, March 1927***

The Japanese, meanwhile, remained full of imperial ambition: in 1931 they occupied Manchuria, which they industrialized to great effect; in 1933 they occupied the neighbouring province of Jehol; and in 1935 they attempted, without success, to turn the whole of northern China into a puppet state. At the same time, the Communists were beginning to establish themselves effectively in the countryside. From 1929–34 they had made a great success of the Kiangsi Soviet at Jui-chin, where they pioneered a revolution in Marxist theory, developing reform programmes as a peasant-based party rather than as one of the urban proletariat. After the Nationalists forced them to leave the region in 1934, the Communists embarked on what they later saw as the achievement which established their national reputation, the 'Long March' to Yenan in northern China (*see* map 3). During the march, Mao Zedong, who had pioneered the peasant-based theory, came to dominate the Party.

Japanese advance

From 1936 a three-cornered struggle for power developed between the Nationalists, the Communists and the Japanese. In that year the Nationalists and Communists formed a united front against the Japanese, who responded by invading in force. By the end of 1938 the Japanese controlled most of north and central China, the main coastal ports and all the centres of modern industry. The Nationalist retreat to the far west of China provided the Communists with their opportunity. Using their reform policies they won support in the countryside of occupied China, and with this new peasant base they waged guerrilla warfare against the Japanese. By the end of the Second

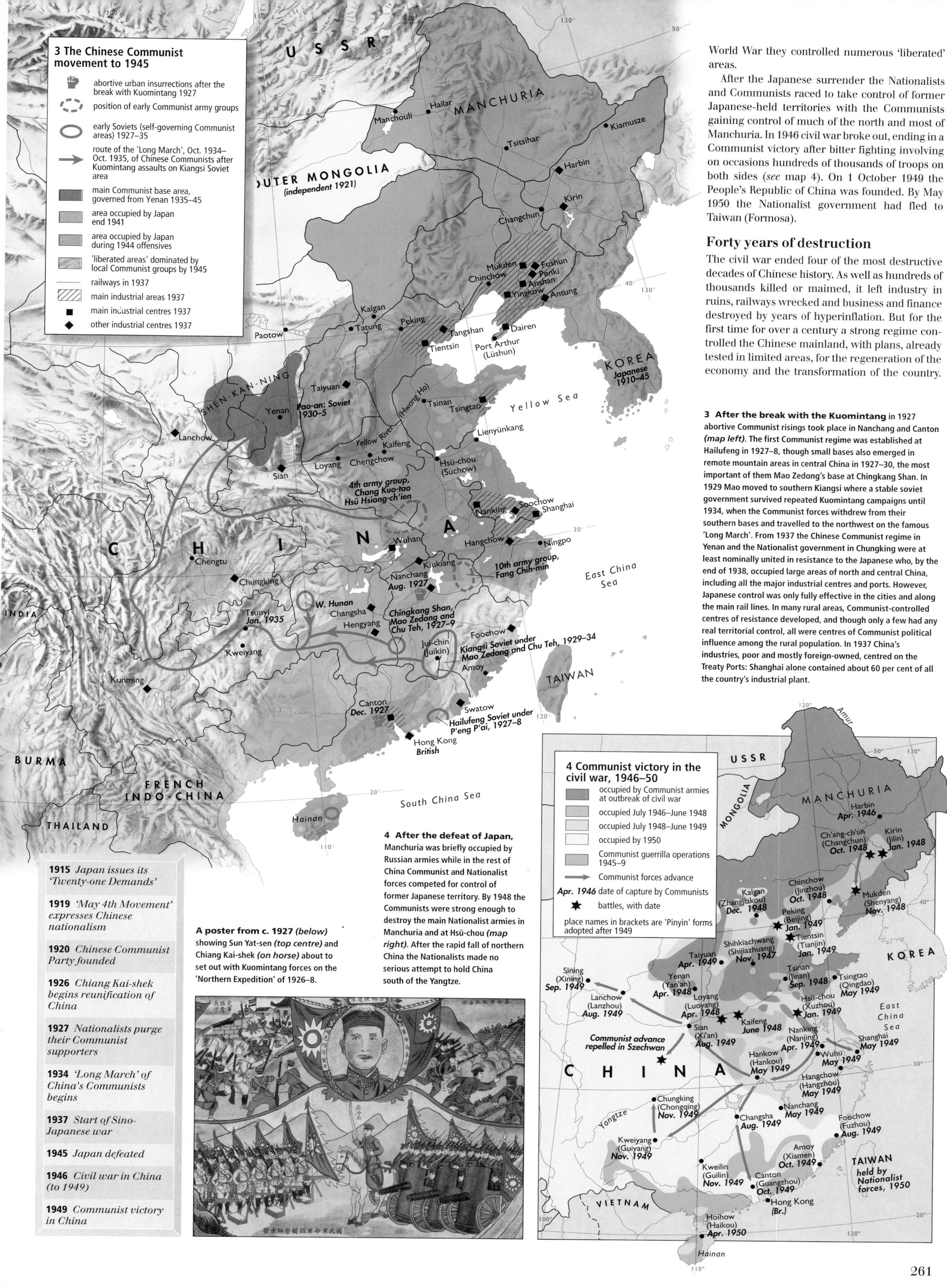

World War they controlled numerous 'liberated' areas.

After the Japanese surrender the Nationalists and Communists raced to take control of former Japanese-held territories with the Communists gaining control of much of the north and most of Manchuria. In 1946 civil war broke out, ending in a Communist victory after bitter fighting involving on occasions hundreds of thousands of troops on both sides (*see* map 4). On 1 October 1949 the People's Republic of China was founded. By May 1950 the Nationalist government had fled to Taiwan (Formosa).

Forty years of destruction

The civil war ended four of the most destructive decades of Chinese history. As well as hundreds of thousands killed or maimed, it left industry in ruins, railways wrecked and business and finance destroyed by years of hyperinflation. But for the first time for over a century a strong regime controlled the Chinese mainland, with plans, already tested in limited areas, for the regeneration of the economy and the transformation of the country.

3 After the break with the Kuomintang in 1927 abortive Communist risings took place in Nanchang and Canton *(map left)*. The first Communist regime was established at Hailufeng in 1927–8, though small bases also emerged in remote mountain areas in central China in 1927–30, the most important of them Mao Zedong's base at Chingkang Shan. In 1929 Mao moved to southern Kiangsi where a stable soviet government survived repeated Kuomintang campaigns until 1934, when the Communist forces withdrew from their southern bases and travelled to the northwest on the famous 'Long March'. From 1937 the Chinese Communist regime in Yenan and the Nationalist government in Chungking were at least nominally united in resistance to the Japanese who, by the end of 1938, occupied large areas of north and central China, including all the major industrial centres and ports. However, Japanese control was only fully effective in the cities and along the main rail lines. In many rural areas, Communist-controlled centres of resistance developed, and though only a few had any real territorial control, all were centres of Communist political influence among the rural population. In 1937 China's industries, poor and mostly foreign-owned, centred on the Treaty Ports: Shanghai alone contained about 60 per cent of all the country's industrial plant.

4 After the defeat of Japan, Manchuria was briefly occupied by Russian armies while in the rest of China Communist and Nationalist forces competed for control of former Japanese territory. By 1948 the Communists were strong enough to destroy the main Nationalist armies in Manchuria and at Hsü-chou *(map right)*. After the rapid fall of northern China the Nationalists made no serious attempt to hold China south of the Yangtze.

A poster from c. 1927 *(below)* showing Sun Yat-sen *(top centre)* and Chiang Kai-shek *(on horse)* about to set out with Kuomintang forces on the 'Northern Expedition' of 1926–8.

1915 *Japan issues its 'Twenty-one Demands'*

1919 *'May 4th Movement' expresses Chinese nationalism*

1920 *Chinese Communist Party founded*

1926 *Chiang Kai-shek begins reunification of China*

1927 *Nationalists purge their Communist supporters*

1934 *'Long March' of China's Communists begins*

1937 *Start of Sino-Japanese war*

1945 *Japan defeated*

1946 *Civil war in China (to 1949)*

1949 *Communist victory in China*

1919 to 1934
European political problems

See also
The First World War, 1914–18 p. 250
Imperialism and nationalism, 1919–41 p. 258
The Great Depression, 1929–39 p. 264
The outbreak of the Second World War, 1931–41 p. 266

The end of the Great War was supposed to usher in an age of peace and disarmament, but the conflict had undermined economic stability, opened up the threat of communist revolt and left a generation of veterans alienated from parliamentary politics. The slump of 1929 left European capitalism in deep crisis and opened the way to political extremism.

THE WHOLE OF EUROPE IS FILLED WITH THE SPIRIT OF REVOLUTION. THERE IS A DEEP SENSE NOT ONLY OF DISCONTENT BUT OF ANGER AND REVOLT. THE WHOLE EXISTING ORDER IN ITS POLITICAL, SOCIAL AND ECONOMIC ASPECTS IS QUESTIONED ... FROM ONE END OF EUROPE TO THE OTHER. THERE IS A DANGER THAT WE MAY THROW THE MASSES OF THE POPULATION THROUGHOUT EUROPE INTO THE ARMS OF THE EXTREMISTS.

David Lloyd George, Versailles, 1919

1919 *Germany signs the Treaty of Versailles*

1920 *Polish-Russian war ends with Treaty of Riga*

1922 *Mussolini appointed prime minister in Italy*

1923 *Treaty of Lausanne settles conflict between Turkey, Greece and the Allies*

1923 *Hyperinflation in Germany*

1925 *Treaty of Locarno brings France and Germany together*

1928 *Kellogg-Briand Pact outlaws war*

1932 *Lausanne Conference suspends German reparations*

1933 *Hitler appointed Chancellor*

1934 *February riots in Paris overthrow government*

IN 1919 THE POLITICAL map of Europe was transformed. The defeat of the German and Austro-Hungarian empires in 1918 (and the collapse of the Tsarist system in Russia the year before) brought to an end the long period of dynastic empires that had dominated central and eastern Europe. The victorious Allies met at Versailles in January 1919 to try to replace the imperial regimes with a system of independent states.

The Allies brought with them conflicting ambitions: the American president, Woodrow Wilson, hoped to broker a peace that would end war for ever and establish a liberal, democratic Europe of national states; the French wanted to punish Germany and prevent her revival; and Italy, Serbia, and Romania sought territorial concessions. The outcome was a messy compromise. Weak new democratic states were created, based only loosely on the principle of national self-determination, but the defeated countries were heavily penalized and their national territories dismembered. The political instability and violence of the post-war years can be traced back to the bitter legacy imposed by the peace settlement.

The settlement itself took four years to complete. New states were created (*see* map 1): Finland, Estonia, Latvia and Lithuania freed themselves from Russian rule; a Polish state was reconstituted after a bitter conflict with the new Soviet armies in the east and with German nationalist militia in the west; Czechoslovakia was carved out of the northern territories of the Habsburg empire, and Yugoslavia was created (*see* map 2).

The defeated powers were forced to relinquish territory, to pay substantial reparations and to disarm. The German army was reduced to a mere 100,000 men, the Austrian forces to 30,000 and the Hungarian to 35,000.

The League of Nations

Europe was now dominated by France, the most heavily armed state in the world in the 1920s. She played a key role with Britain in running the League of Nations, which was established in 1920 as a forum for the conduct of international politics on peaceful lines. The French aim was to find a system of 'collective security' which could protect her from any revival of German power. In 1926 Germany was admitted to the League and in 1928 the Kellogg-Briand Pact was signed in Paris by all the powers, committing them to the settlement of disputes without resort to war.

The collective system was a superficial one. The League had no agreed procedures for enforcing settlement and no military back-up. The Soviet Union did not join until 1934, and the United States refused to join at all. The expectation that Europe would embrace democracy as a foundation for collaboration soon evaporated. Economic crisis and bitter social conflict, engendered by the rise of socialism and the revolutionary activity of European communists, could not be contained within weak parliamentary systems by liberal politicians often quite out of touch with popular social and nationalist agitation. Between 1922 and 1926 democracy was torn up in Italy by Mussolini and the Fascist party; Spain had military rule imposed in 1923 by Primo de Rivera and, after a brief republican interlude between 1931 and 1936, the army imposed Franco's dictatorship. In Poland, Austria, the Baltic states, Yugoslavia, Hungary, Romania, Greece, and Bulgaria, democracy was eventually suspended and nationalist regimes installed based on royal dictatorship, military coup or single-party rule.

Even in the victor powers democracy was challenged. In Ireland a bloody civil war led to the creation of an independent Irish state and the break up of the Anglo-Irish Union. In 1926 a General

2 The formation of Yugoslavia, from 1918

- Serbia and Montenegro, 1913
- annexed by Serbia and Montenegro from Ottoman empire, 1913
- frontiers, 1914
- annexed from Bulgaria, 1919
- Austro-Hun. territory united with Serbia and Montenegro, 1920, to create the Kingdom of Serbs, Croats and Slovenes
- remained Austrian by plebiscite, 1920
- Kingdom of Serbs, Croats and Slovenes in 1929, when renamed Yugoslavia

2 The collapse of the Habsburg empire in 1918 created conditions for the establishment of a south Slav state *(map above)*. In December 1918 the Kingdom of the Serbs, Croats and Slovenes was set up in Belgrade, but arguments between the different national groups over the nature of the new state delayed until 1921 the full establishment of what was to be called Yugoslavia. The state was dominated by Serbs, who made up 43 per cent of the population.

The Versailles Conference *(below)* convened in Paris in January 1919. In all 32 states were invited to attend (but not the defeated powers or the infant Soviet Union). 70 plenipotentiaries were sent, but most decisions were taken by the three major powers, Britain, the USA and France, whose leaders can be seen at the centre of the picture.

1 National conflicts and frontier disputes, 1919–36

- German empire, 1914
- Austro-Hungarian empire, 1914
- Russian empire, 1914
- post-settlement frontiers
- plebiscites held
- new states
- areas of dispute
- areas temporarily autonomous or independent
- areas under armed occupation
- areas under League of Nations High Commissioners

PLEBISCITES AND TERRITORIAL DISPUTES

1. plebiscite Feb. 1920: divided between Denmark and Germany
2. occupied by France 1923–5
3. to Belgium 1919
4. to Belgium 1919
5. evacuated 1930, remilitarized 1936
6. League of Nations Mandate by plebiscite to Germany 1935
7. to France 1919
8. divided between Germany and Poland by plebiscite Mar. 1921
9. Allied occupation 1920–3, annexed by Lithuania 1923, autonomous 1924, to Germany 1939
10. to Germany July 1920
11. to Poland Dec. 1918
12. partitioned between Czechoslovakia and Poland 1920
13. to Hungary 1921
14. to Austria 1920
15. occupied by Poland 1920, annexed by Poland following elections 1922
16. to Greece from Bulgaria 1919
17. demilitarized 1924, remilitarized 1936
18. Greek-Bulgarian conflict, 1925

1 At the end of the war the victorious powers tried to redraw the political map of Europe *(map above)* by creating new states in the east at the expense of the defeated states: Germany, Austria-Hungary, Bulgaria and the Ottoman empire. Though not party to the peace settlement, the Soviet Union also lost extensive territories which had once formed part of the Tsarist empire. Millions of Europeans were expelled or fled from oppression, but there remained many areas where national aspirations were not satisfied, or where national minorities remained under the rule of another nationality. Irredentist conflict and national revolt created an unstable continent, marred by persistent violence and racial tension.

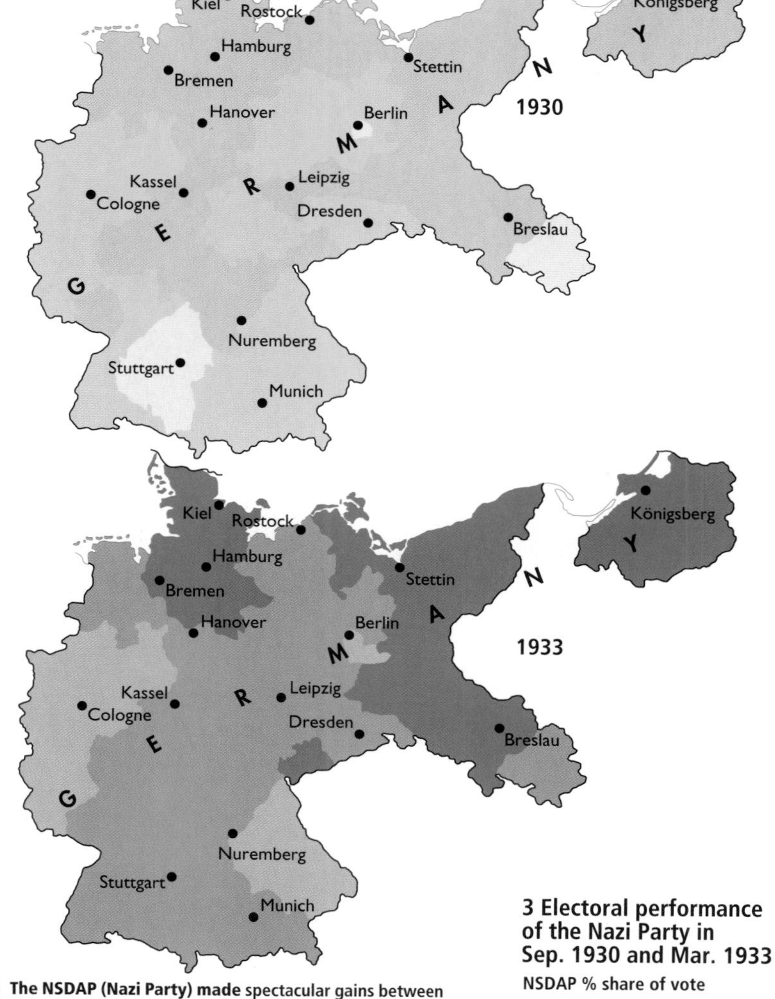

3 The NSDAP (Nazi Party) made spectacular gains between 1929 and 1933, when it won the largest vote any party had obtained in German history (44 per cent). Hitler's promise of national awakening, moral revival and social peace drew support from across German society, from workers to the aristocracy.

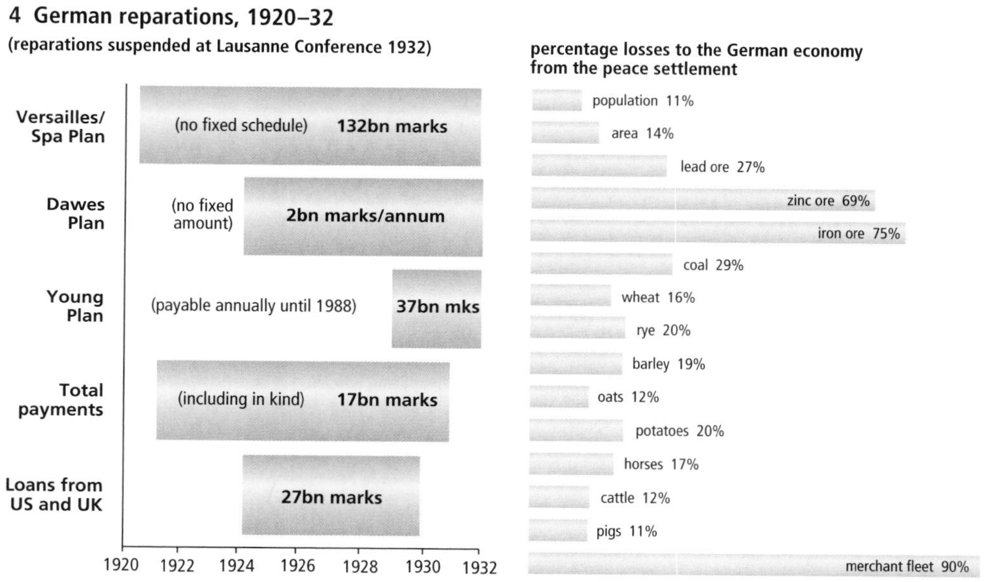

3 Electoral performance of the Nazi Party in Sep. 1930 and Mar. 1933

NSDAP % share of vote

- 50–59
- 40–49
- 30–39
- 20–29
- 10–19
- 0–9

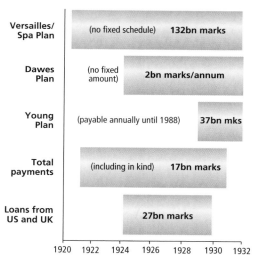

4 German reparations, 1920–32

(reparations suspended at Lausanne Conference 1932)

Versailles/ Spa Plan	(no fixed schedule)	132bn marks
Dawes Plan	(no fixed amount)	2bn marks/annum
Young Plan	(payable annually until 1988)	37bn mks
Total payments	(including in kind)	17bn marks
Loans from US and UK		27bn marks

1920 1922 1924 1926 1928 1930 1932

percentage losses to the German economy from the peace settlement

population	11%
area	14%
lead ore	27%
zinc ore	69%
iron ore	75%
coal	29%
wheat	16%
rye	20%
barley	19%
oats	12%
potatoes	20%
horses	17%
cattle	12%
pigs	11%
merchant fleet	90%

4 Reparations *(charts above)* were demanded from Germany by the victor powers in 1919. A final sum was agreed at Versailles in 1921 after much had been taken in kind. German economic problems led to the rescheduling of payments in 1924 (Dawes Plan) and in 1929 (Young Plan). They were finally suspended in 1932, though they were set to run to 1988.

Strike provoked sharp social conflict in Britain. In France conflicts between right and left led to growing violence, which culminated in the storming of the French parliament in 1934 and the overthrow of the government. Yet democracy survived in both states despite the noisy agitation of right and left.

The rise of Hitler

In Germany democracy was overcome by extremism. Despite efforts to make the new system work through coalition rule, the slump of 1929, which hit Germany harder than anywhere else, created an economic catastrophe that the government was powerless to ameliorate. German society was politically polarized. Communist support doubled, but millions of Germans turned to Adolf Hitler's Nazi Party (*see* map 3) with its promise of a New Order, neither socialist nor parliamentary. Hitler was committed to overturning Versailles, and his appointment as German chancellor in January 1933 challenged not only the German peace settlement but the whole system set up across Europe in 1919–20. Hitler emboldened radical nationalists and irredentists everywhere who rejected liberalism and collective security in favour of dictatorship and the violent revision of the peace treaties.

1929 to 1939

The Great Depression

See also

The formation of a world economy, 1870–1914 p. 254

European political problems, 1919–34 p. 262

The outbreak of the Second World War, 1931–41 p. 266

Latin America: revolution and reaction since 1930 p. 292

The United States: the age of abundance since 1939 p. 294

> THE DEFECTS OF THE CAPITALIST SYSTEM HAVE BEEN INCREASINGLY ROBBING IT OF ITS BENEFITS. THEY ARE NOW THREATENING ITS EXISTENCE. A PERIOD OF DEPRESSION AND CRISIS IS ONE IN WHICH ITS GREAT MERIT, THE EXPANSION OF PRODUCTIVE CAPACITY UNDER THE STIMULUS OF COMPETITIVE GAINS, SEEMS WASTED; AND ITS MAIN DEFECT, AN INCREASING INABILITY TO UTILISE PRODUCTIVE CAPACITY FULLY AND TO DISTRIBUTE WHAT IT PRODUCES TOLERABLY, IS SEEN AT ITS WORST.
>
> **Arthur Salter**
> ***Recovery*, *1932***

In 1929 the world was plunged into the worst slump in modern history. Trade and prices collapsed, millions were thrown out of work. As governments took responsibility for economic revival, the old economic order was replaced by state intervention. At the same time, the crisis provoked extreme nationalism, paving the way to dictatorship.

Oct. 1929 *New York stock market crashes*

1930 *Hawley-Smoot Tariff in USA*

1931 *Banks collapse in Germany and Austria*

1931 *National Government formed in Britain to combat slump*

1932 *Lausanne Conference suspends German reparations*

1933 *Roosevelt launches 'New Deal'*

1933 *World Economic Conference fails to find solution*

1934 *German 'New Plan' for controlling trade*

1936 *Large-scale rearmament begins in Germany, Britain and France*

THE GREAT INTER-WAR SLUMP is usually dated from 29 October 1929 when the New York stock market crashed. When in July 1933 the index at last stopped falling, shares stood at 15 per cent of their 1929 value. Thousands of Americans were bankrupt, millions unemployed and impoverished. In the developed world alone over 25 million were out of work by 1932. At its peak, unemployment affected one in four of the American workforce; in Germany almost nine million were thrown out of work in a workforce of 20 million.

The causes of the crisis

The crash of 1929 was a symptom as much as a cause of the worldwide slump that followed. The world economy had been weakened by the First World War and the massive debts it generated. It proved impossible to re-introduce the Gold Standard (*see* p. 254) system fully, or to revive an effective multilateral trading system. Over-production led to falling prices and declining profits. Despite the boom in America, business confidence elsewhere had been low and investment sluggish. When the US stock market crashed, it was against the background of an already declining and fragile world economy.

The effects of the slump

The effects unfolded slowly. Protective tariffs were set up worldwide to save domestic industry. Even laissez-faire Britain adopted Imperial Preference in 1932, a protected trading bloc within the empire. World trade in the 1930s never recovered its 1929 level, and bilateral trade agreements came to replace the liberal system of multilateral trade and exchange. Germany in 1934 adopted a 'New Plan' for state-regulated trade, and in 1936 a programme of 'autarky', or self-sufficiency.

Declining trade encouraged domestic sources of economic revival. In Britain, Sweden, Germany and the USA, experiments in state work-creation projects soaked up some of the millions of unemployed. In 1933 Roosevelt introduced a package of recovery policies known as the 'New Deal', which

SOCIAL AND POLITICAL CHANGE IN EUROPE, 1929–39

Protest movements of the left and right arose in almost every country in response to the slump, severely testing the social and political fabric. In countries where democratic traditions were weak – including most eastern and central European countries – some form of right-wing dictatorship resulted.

Albania Nov. 1927, virtual Italian protectorate established.

Austria Mar. 1933, Dollfuss dictatorship established; Feb. 1934, all parties banned, destruction of Austrian Socialists.

Belgium Mar. 1935, Government of National Union formed; June 1936, Social Improvement Programme stimulates reform.

Bulgaria May 1933, army coup; 1936, King Boris establishes royal dictatorship.

Estonia Mar. 1934, Päts dictatorship established.

France June 1936, Popular Front government installed; Mar. 1937, 'Breathing Spell' from reform proclaimed.

Germany Jan. 1933, Hitler chancellor; Mar., Enabling Act passed.

Greece 1935, George II restores monarchy; Aug. 1936, Metaxas establishes dictatorship.

Hungary 1931–5, Gömbös dictatorship.

Ireland 1932, De Valera president, oath of allegiance repudiated; 1932–3, tariff war with United Kingdom.

Latvia May 1934, Ulmanis coup establishes dictatorship.

Lithuania Dec. 1926, Smetona coup; Feb. 1936, all parties banned.

Netherlands 1933–9, Crisis Cabinet formed.

Norway 1935, Labour government institutes major reforms.

Poland 1926–35, Pilsudski dictatorship; 1935–9, Colonels' regime.

Portugal 1928, Salazar finance minister; 1930, National Union becomes only party; 1932, Salazar premier.

Romania 1930–40, King Carol II builds dictatorship; 1938, all parties banned, Front of National Rebirth founded.

Spain 1931, new constitution; Feb. 1936, Popular Front government elected; July 1936, civil war (to Mar. 1939).

Sweden 1932–6, socialists introduce public works programme; 1936–40, Socialist Agrarian Coalition.

Switzerland 1931, Labour largest party.

Turkey 1923–38, Kemal Atatürk modernizing programme; 1934, Five Year Plan adopted.

United Kingdom Aug. 1931, National Government formed to carry through economy measures.

Yugoslavia Jan. 1929, Alexander establishes royal dictatorship.

2 The slump radicalized European politics, pushing electorates towards the extreme right and left *(map below)*. Democracy was strong enough to survive in Britain and France, but in Spain, Germany and much of eastern Europe authoritarian anti-Marxist regimes appeared which violently repressed communism and abandoned the liberal parliamentary model.

2 Social and political change in Europe, 1929–39

political regimes

- democratic
- democratic, became fascist
- fascist or communist
- authoritarian
- democratic, became authoritarian
- percentage of industrial workers unemployed, 1932 (23.2)

major movements of protest and dissatisfaction, 1929–39

- ◆ strike wave
- ■ riot or demonstration
- ● right-wing activity
- frontiers, 1937

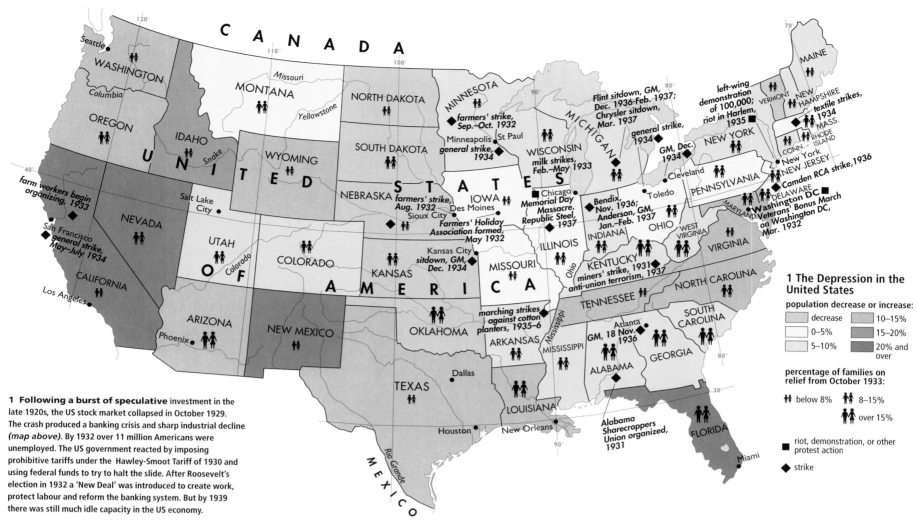

1 The Depression in the United States

population decrease or increase:

- decrease
- 0–5%
- 5–10%
- 10–15%
- 15–20%
- 20% and over

percentage of families on relief from October 1933:

- below 8%
- 8–15%
- over 15%

- ■ riot, demonstration, or other protest action
- ◆ strike

1 Following a burst of speculative investment in the late 1920s, the US stock market collapsed in October 1929. The crash produced a banking crisis and sharp industrial decline *(map above)*. By 1932 over 11 million Americans were unemployed. The US government reacted by imposing prohibitive tariffs under the Hawley-Smoot Tariff of 1930 and using federal funds to try to halt the slide. After Roosevelt's election in 1932 a 'New Deal' was introduced to create work, protect labour and reform the banking system. But by 1939 there was still much idle capacity in the US economy.

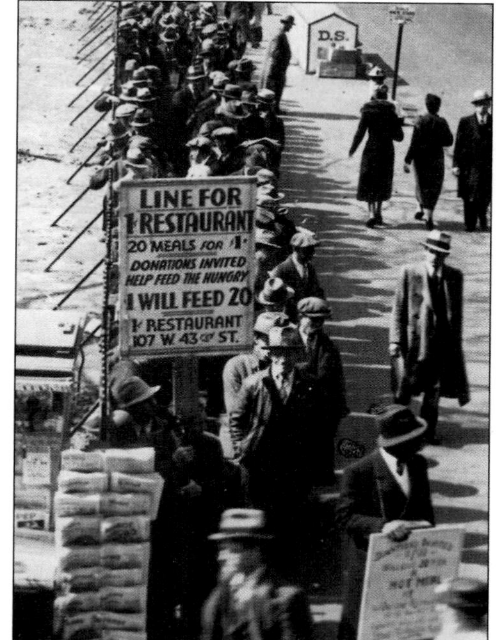

By 1932 17 million Americans were on public relief. For many the only source of food was to queue for meals and handouts organized by charities *(above)*. In May 1933 an Emergency Relief Act was passed to provide federal funds to tackle the desperate poverty and hunger.

4 The world economy during the slump

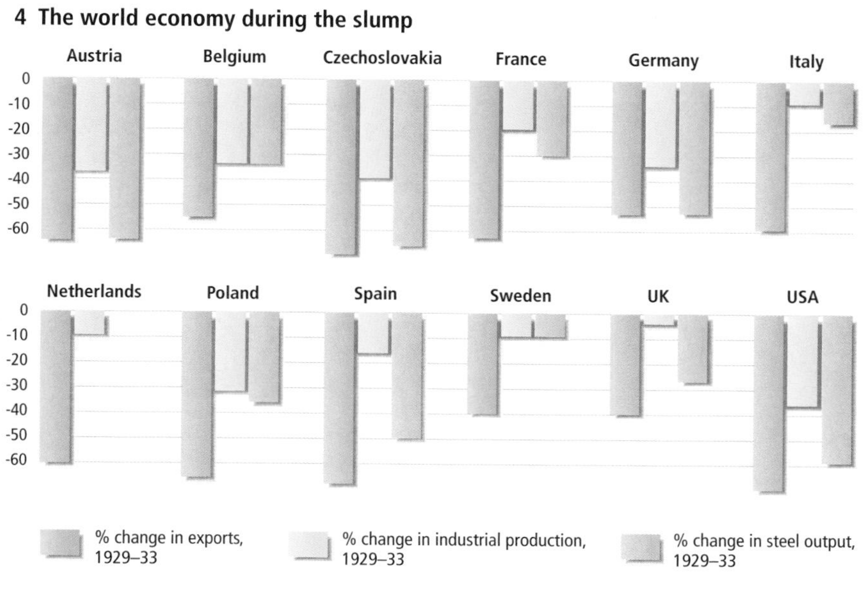

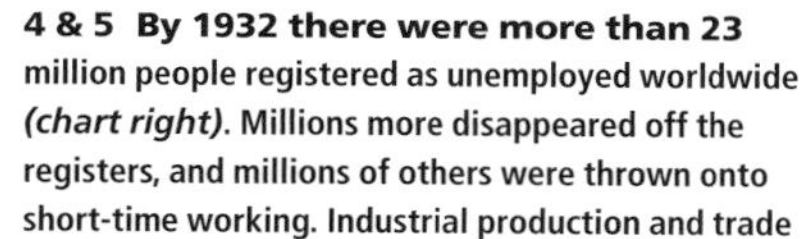

4 & 5 By 1932 there were more than 23 million people registered as unemployed worldwide *(chart right)*. Millions more disappeared off the registers, and millions of others were thrown onto short-time working. Industrial production and trade slumped *(chart above)*, causing severe price-falls and a further slump in output and profits. In Germany in 1932 some 40 per cent of the workforce was unemployed and production declined to the levels of the 1890s.

5 World unemployment, 1928–35

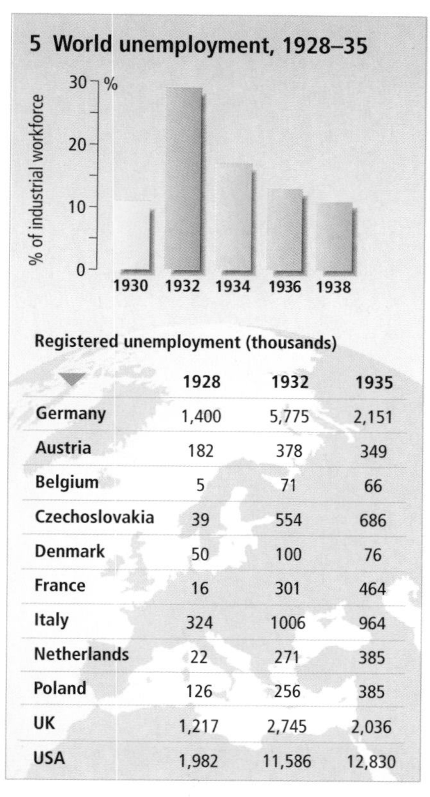

Registered unemployment (thousands)

	1928	1932	1935
Germany	1,400	5,775	2,151
Austria	182	378	349
Belgium	5	71	66
Czechoslovakia	39	554	686
Denmark	50	100	76
France	16	301	464
Italy	324	1006	964
Netherlands	22	271	385
Poland	126	256	385
UK	1,217	2,745	2,036
USA	1,982	11,586	12,830

extended state regulation of the economy in a country with little tradition of such government activity. In Britain and Germany state regulation by the late 1930s had produced what was called a 'managed economy', a forerunner of the mixed economies of the post-1945 era.

The political cost

The severity of the slump produced a political backlash. In more vulnerable economies such as Germany or Japan, radical nationalist groups argued for economic empire-building and an end to the old liberal capitalist order. In France and Spain economic crisis stimulated communism or anarchism, sparking prolonged social conflict. Only in Britain, with its large empire markets, did democracy survive and a modest prosperity set in during the 1930s. In much of Europe and Latin America various forms of dictatorship came to replace parliamentary systems now irrevocably associated with economic disaster.

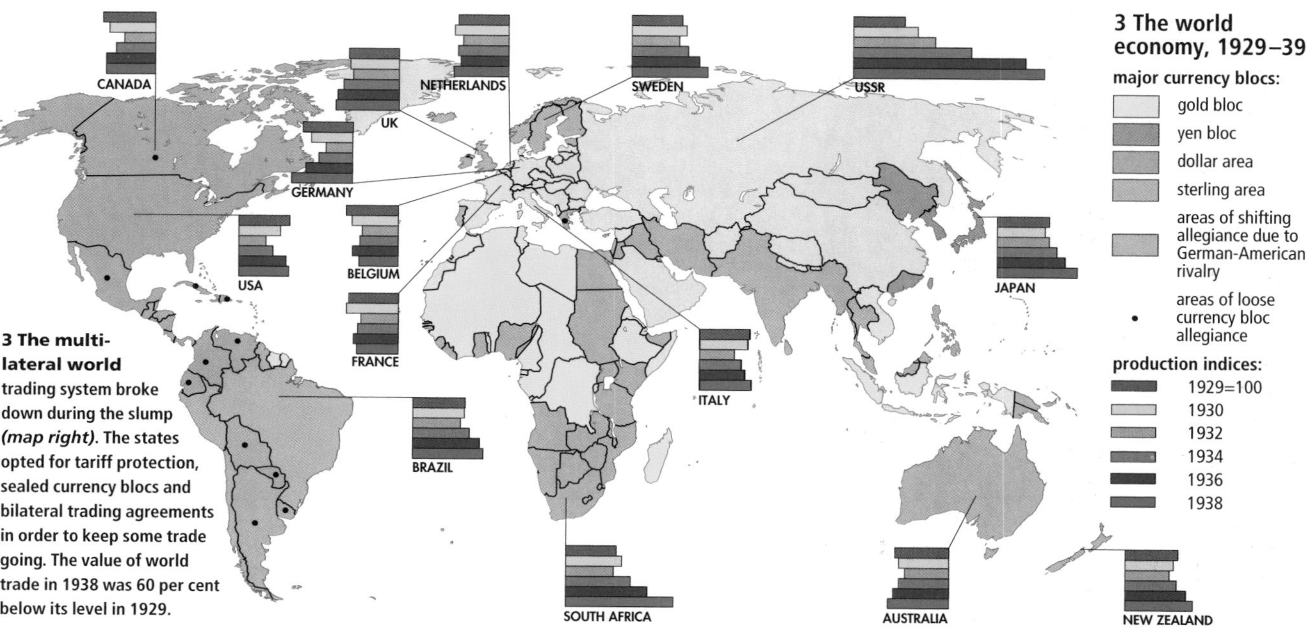

3 The multilateral world trading system broke down during the slump *(map right)*. The states opted for tariff protection, sealed currency blocs and bilateral trading agreements in order to keep some trade going. The value of world trade in 1938 was 60 per cent below its level in 1929.

3 The world economy, 1929–39

major currency blocs:

- gold bloc
- yen bloc
- dollar area
- sterling area
- areas of shifting allegiance due to German-American rivalry
- • areas of loose currency bloc allegiance

production indices:

- 1929=100
- 1930
- 1932
- 1934
- 1936
- 1938

The outbreak of the Second World War

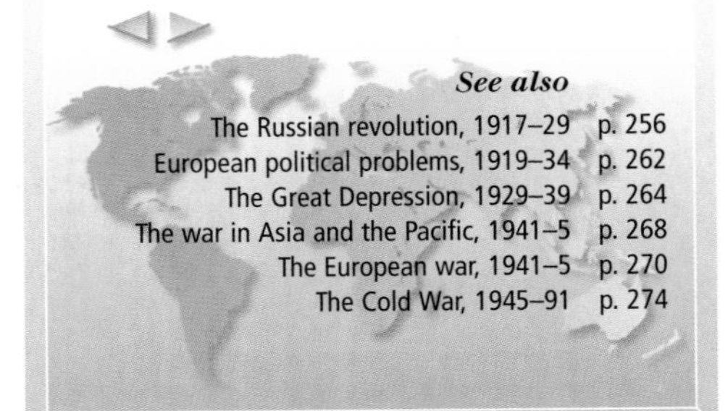

See also

The Russian revolution, 1917–29 p. 256
European political problems, 1919–34 p. 262
The Great Depression, 1929–39 p. 264
The war in Asia and the Pacific, 1941–5 p. 268
The European war, 1941–5 p. 270
The Cold War, 1945–91 p. 274

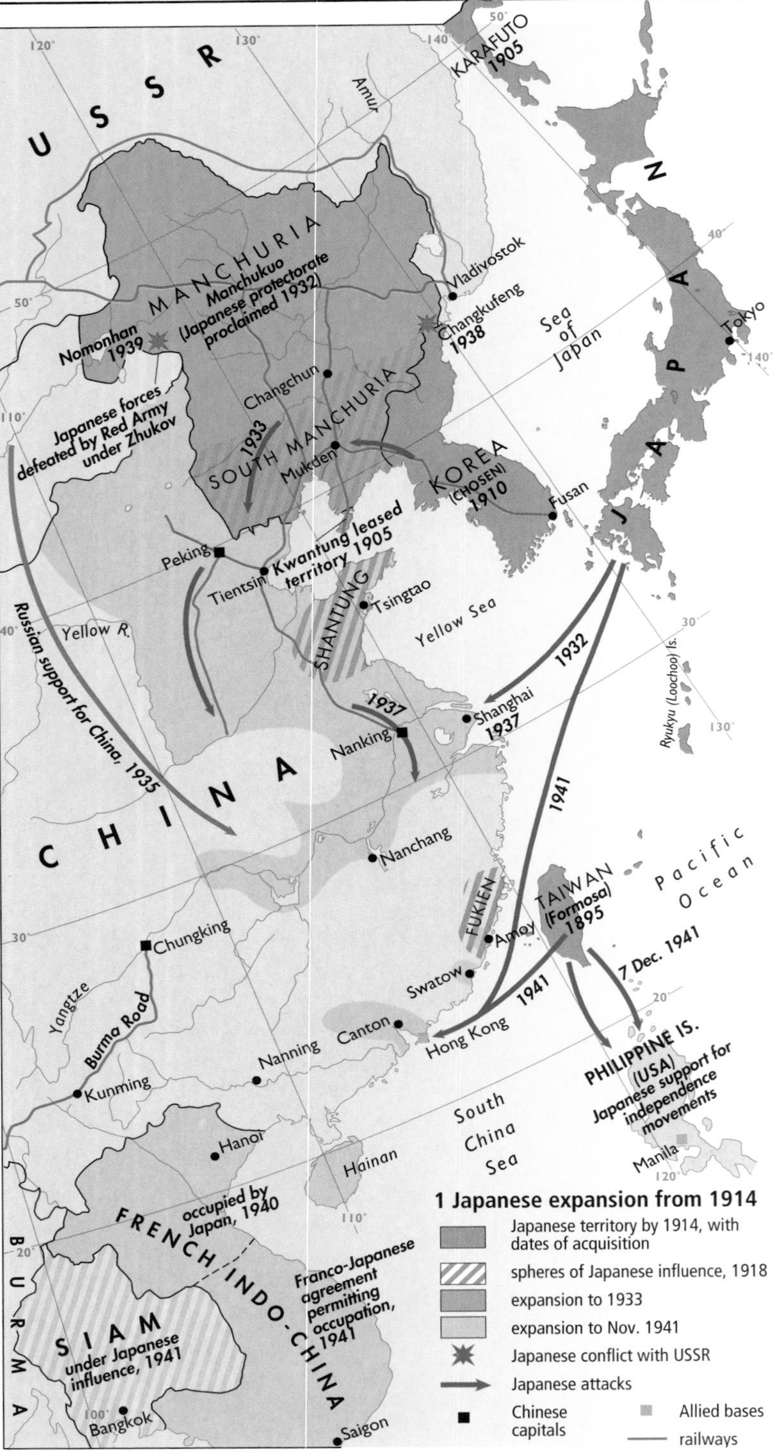

In the 1930s the world order was violently challenged by states committed to establishing a 'New Order' based on military conquest and brutal imperial rule. As the post-war system dissolved, bitter political conflicts between democrats, communists and fascists tore Europe apart and sent the world spiralling once again to war.

IN THE 1930s the international order constructed after the end of the First World War, based upon the League of Nations and 'collective security', collapsed under the violent impact of major revisionist powers bent on building a 'New Order' in their favour.

The crisis of the international system owed much to the effects of the worldwide slump, which encouraged strident nationalism and militarism in the weaker economies. In Japan the economic crisis provoked the military into seizing economic resources and markets by force to compensate for their declining trade. In 1931 the Chinese province of Manchuria was conquered and soon turned into a Japanese satellite state, Manchukuo, ruled by the last Manchu emperor, Pu Yi. Japan left the League and declared a 'New Order' in East Asia. With the League of Nations powerless in the face of this aggression, Japan continued to encroach on Chinese sovereignty until full-scale war broke out in 1937, bringing much of northern China under direct Japanese rule.

In Europe Mussolini's Italy also looked for a new economic empire. In 1935, expecting little reaction from the other major powers, Italy invaded Ethiopia. Though sanctions were half-heartedly applied by the League, by 1936 the conquest was complete. Italy, too, pulled out of the League.

1 Growing nationalist and militarist pressure at home pushed Japan into a policy of open imperialism in Asia *(map left)*. In 1931 Manchuria was occupied and over the next six years Japan encroached farther into China, exploiting its political disintegration. In 1932 Japan threatened the port of Shanghai with its large European population. After a restless peace, in 1937 Japan and China became embroiled in a brutal war. Japan then seized much of northern and eastern China.

German expansion

In 1935 Hitler began the process of overturning the Versailles settlement, declaring German rearmament in defiance of the Treaty. In March the following year, he ordered German troops back into the Rhineland. When the expected protest from Britain and France failed to materialize, his ambitions widened. In March 1938 Austria was occupied and united into a Greater Germany. In May Hitler's plans for the conquest of Czechoslovakia were frustrated only by belated protests from Britain and France. At the Munich conference in September that year, called to discuss the crisis, Britain and France nonetheless agreed to the incorporation of the Sudetenland, the German-speaking areas of Czechoslovakia, into Germany.

Far from marking an end to 'legitimate' German territorial aspirations, the Munich Pact encouraged Hitler further. In March 1939, in clear defiance of the Pact, Germany occupied Bohemia and Moravia. Slovakia, all that remained of Czechoslovakia, became a German puppet state. At the same time, Hitler forced Lithuania to agree the return of Memel on the Baltic coast to Germany. Hitler then formally demanded the return of Danzig, which had been made a Free City under League jurisdiction after the war.

The failure of Britain and France to respond to Hitler's aggression was largely the result of their horror of a further European conflict, a dilemma heightened by the events of the Spanish Civil War

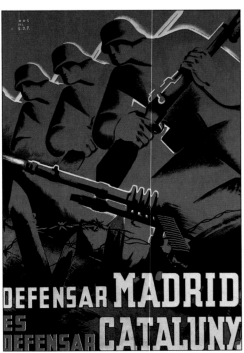

2 In 1936 the Spanish army under Franco rebelled against the Republic established in 1931 *(map right)*. The result was a bitter and sanguinary civil war between the nationalist right and the liberal and socialist left which came to symbolize the wider struggle between fascism and communism. Hitler and Mussolini sent help to the rebels; Stalin gave assistance to the left. Britain and France, in the face of widespread criticism, initiated an international non-intervention agreement to prevent the spread of the war. The fall of Madrid in spring 1939 brought Franco final victory in a conflict which left 600,000 dead.

A poster from the Spanish civil war *(left)* calls on republicans to defend Madrid and Catalonia. In 1933 the Catalans were granted partial autonomy from the capital but found themselves fighting on the same side in 1936. Catalonia and Madrid were the last areas to fall to Franco.

3 Between 1935 and 1939 Italy and Germany began programmes of imperial expansion *(map above)*. In 1936 Italy completed the conquest of Ethiopia and occupied Albania in 1939. Germany under Hitler overturned the Versailles settlement by taking back the Saar (1935), remilitarizing the Rhineland (1936), incorporating Austria (Mar. 1938), compelling Czechoslovakia to cede the Sudetenland (Oct. 1938) and occupying Bohemia and Moravia (Mar. 1939). Hitler's invasion of Poland finally provoked Britain and France to war.

and the crisis in eastern Europe. Nonetheless, despite political resistance at home they both in 1936 began a programme of large-scale rearmament, which they hoped would deter Hitler from further aggression. By the time Hitler threatened Poland in 1939 both western powers had reached the point where they could no longer postpone confronting the threat to the European balance of power. Hitler reacted to growing western firmness by concluding a non-aggression pact with the ideological enemy, the Soviet Union, in August 1939. Hitler was convinced that western resistance would crumble, but instead Britain signed a military alliance with Poland on 26 August, and when Germany invaded Poland on 1 September Britain and France declared war two days later.

War in Europe

Poland was defeated within two weeks and was divided between Germany and the Soviet Union on lines agreed in a secret protocol to the Pact. The western Allies sat behind the Maginot Line in eastern France waiting for a German attack. In April Germany occupied Norway to secure the northern flank, and on 10 May 1940 invaded the Netherlands, Luxembourg, Belgium and France. In six weeks all were defeated and British forces humiliatingly expelled from continental Europe. Emboldened by Hitler's success, Italy invaded France in June and Egypt in September 1940, and then attacked Greece in October.

Hitler wanted Britain to sue for peace. When Churchill, Britain's new prime minister, refused, German air forces tried to force a surrender. The ensuing Battle of Britain in the air was Hitler's first defeat. In the autumn he decided to attack the Soviet Union instead. Delayed by a campaign in the Balkans in April 1941 against Yugoslavia and Greece, the invasion began on 22 June 1941. After a series of spectacular victories German forces approached Leningrad and Moscow. The Axis seemed poised to remake the world order.

4 Thanks to the skills of her armed forces rather than numerical superiority, between 1939 and 1941 Germany conquered much of continental Europe *(map below)*. Poland was defeated in two weeks, Belgium, Luxembourg, Holland, France, Denmark and Norway in six weeks. The invasion of the USSR in 1941 seemed set to presage Hitler's greatest triumph as German forces swept aside a feeble Red Army.

THE GOVERNMENTS OF GERMANY, ITALY AND JAPAN CONSIDER THE PREREQUISITE OF A LASTING PEACE THAT EVERY NATION IN THE WORLD SHALL RECEIVE THE SPACE TO WHICH IT IS ENTITLED. THEY HAVE, THEREFORE, DECIDED TO STAND BY AND COOPERATE WITH ONE ANOTHER IN THEIR EFFORTS IN GREATER EAST ASIA AND THE REGIONS OF EUROPE RESPECTIVELY. IN DOING THIS IT IS THEIR PRIME PURPOSE TO ESTABLISH AND MAINTAIN A NEW ORDER OF THINGS.

Tripartite Pact, September 1940

1931 *Japan occupies Manchuria*

1935–6 *Italy attacks and seizes Ethiopia*

1937 *Sino-Japanese war*

March 1938 *Anschluss: union of Germany and Austria*

September 1938 *Munich Pact*

March 1939 *Germany occupies Bohemia and Moravia*

August 1939 *German-Soviet Pact partitions Poland*

September 1939 *Hitler invades Poland; Britain and France declare war*

May 1940 *Fall of France*

August–September 1940 *Battle of Britain*

June 1941 *Germany invades USSR*

4 The Axis advance, 1939–41

- Axis territory, 1 Sep. 1939
- Axis co-belligerents
- occupied by Axis after Sep. 1939
- Vichy France and territories
- Soviet annexed territory, 1939–41
- neutral powers
- frontiers, 1 Sep. 1939
- Axis advances, 1939
- Axis advances, 1940
- Axis advances, 1941
- Axis airborne landings
- Allied forces
- Soviet advances, 1939–40
- Allied retreat and withdrawal
- major cities severely damaged by bombing

1941 to 1945

The war in Asia and the Pacific

See also
The expansion and modernization of Japan p. 242
The Chinese revolution, 1912–49 p. 260
The outbreak of the Second World War p. 266
The European war, 1941–5 p. 270
Japan and east Asia since 1945 p. 278
Southeast Asia since 1945 p. 282
The United States: the age of abundance p. 294
The United States as a world power since 1945 p. 296

June 1941 *Japanese forces occupy Indo-China*

7 Dec. 1941 *Japanese air forces attack Pearl Harbor*

15 Feb. 1942 *Britain surrenders Singapore*

3–6 June 1942 *Battle of Midway: Japanese naval forces defeated*

March 1944 *Japanese Imphal offensive in Burma defeated*

April 1944 *Japanese launch Ichi-Go campaign in China*

Oct. 1944 *Japan defeated at Battle of Leyte Gulf*

Nov. 1944 *US bombing of mainland Japan begins*

6 and 9 Aug. 1945 *Atomic bombs dropped on Japan provoke unconditional surrender*

In 1941 Japan embarked on an ambitious programme of expansion in the Pacific and south-east Asia. War with US and Britain, together with the continuing war with China, proved more than Japanese resources could cope with. In 1945, after the US air force had reduced many of her cities to ruin, two by atomic weapons, Japan capitulated.

WHEN AIR RAIDS GOT SEVERE, AND THERE WAS NO OPPOSITION BY OUR PLANES, AND FACTORIES WERE DESTROYED, I FELT AS IF WE WERE FIGHTING MACHINERY WITH BAMBOO. WE COULD HARDLY STAND IT. THE GOVERNMENT KEPT TELLING US THAT THEY WOULD DEFEAT THE UNITED STATES FORCES AFTER THEY LANDED HERE, BUT AS MY HOUSE WAS BURNED DOWN AND I HAD NO FOOD, CLOTHING OR SHELTER, I DIDN'T KNOW HOW I COULD GO ON.

Japanese bombing victim, 1946

THE GERMAN VICTORIES in the Soviet Union in 1941 prompted Japanese leaders to establish a new order in southeast Asia and the Pacific while the colonial powers were weakened and before the United States began serious rearmament. The object was to create a southern zone which could be defended by the formidable Japanese navy while resources, particularly oil, were seized and shipped north to help the Japanese war economy and stiffen the Japanese army in its war with China.

The decision for war with the United States was taken in November 1941 and on 7 December Japanese aircraft attacked the Pearl Harbor naval base in the Hawaiian islands, crippling part of the US Pacific Fleet. Japan then occupied European colonial territories to the south – Burma, Malaya, Singapore, the East Indies – and captured a string of Pacific Islands stretching to the Solomons north of Australia. Though Japanese warships threatened Ceylon and Madagascar, there were no plans to occupy any larger region despite the rapid and comprehensive success of the original campaign.

The Japanese attack on Pearl Harbor brought the United States fully into the war. Within a year the US was turning out more vehicles, ships and aircraft than all the other combatant powers together. Japan could not hope to compete with American industrial might on this scale and planned instead to inflict a crippling defeat on what was left of the US Pacific Fleet, severing American communications across the Pacific and forcing a compromise peace. The naval battle sought by Admiral Yamamoto was fought off Midway Island between 3 and 6 June and resulted in a major Japanese defeat. In August 1942 US forces, commanded by General MacArthur, invaded Tulagi and Guadalcanal in the Solomons.

The Allied build-up

Though the Allies could not afford to allow the Pacific campaign to divert resources from the European theatre, sufficient supplies were made available to push the Japanese back island by island, using a combination of massive air power, fast carriers and submarines. The Japanese merchant fleet, on which the whole southern campaign relied, was reduced from over five million tons in 1942 to 670,000 tons in 1945. Communications were cut when US forces reoccupied the Philippines in 1944 and seized the Marianas. Japan threw its final air and naval reserves into these battles. Defeated in the Philippine Sea in June 1944 and at

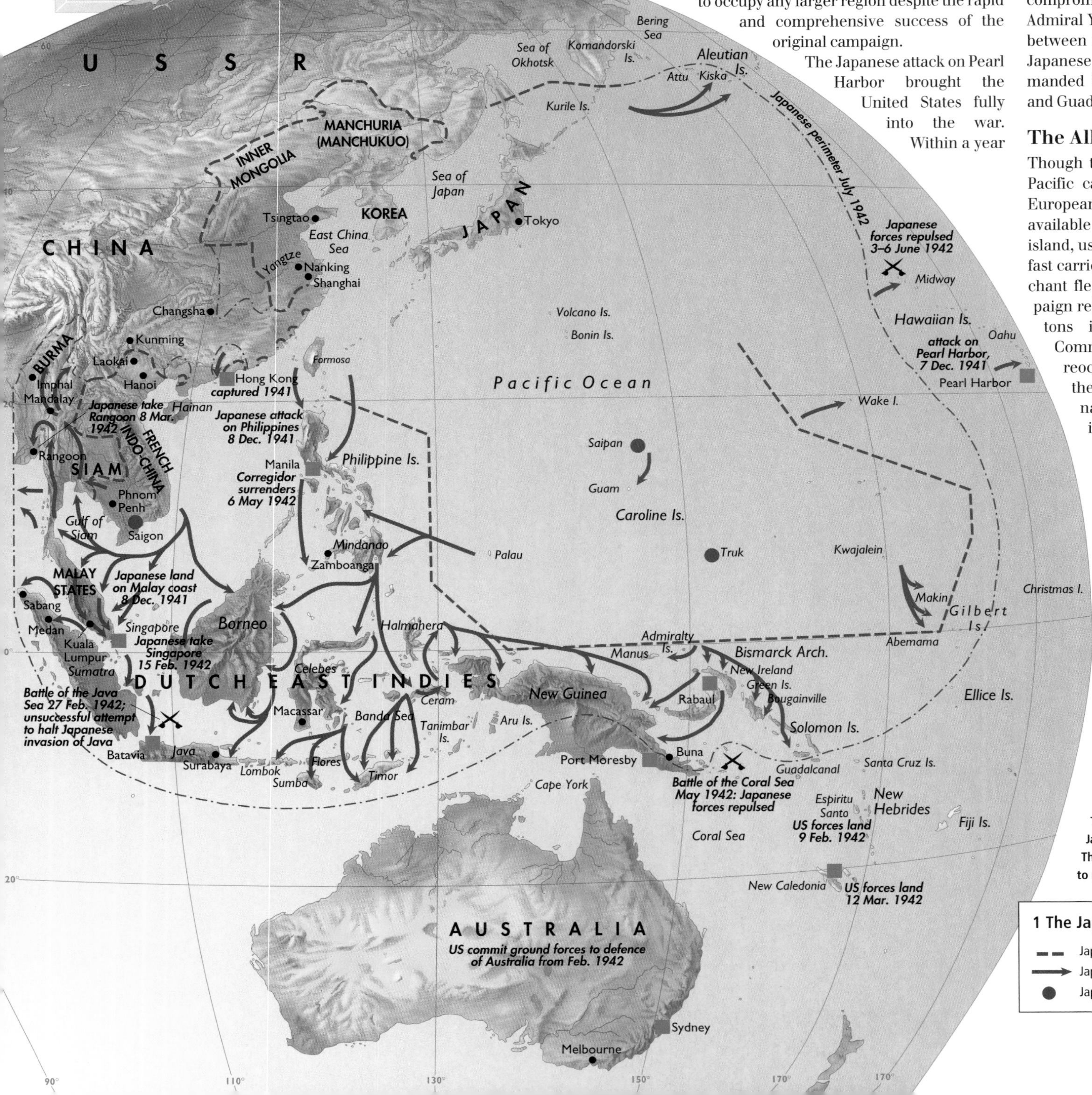

1 Japanese forces won startling victories in the first months of the Pacific War *(map left)*. By April 1942 they had captured Hong Kong, Malaya, Singapore, the East Indies, the Philippines, Burma and a string of Pacific islands and their armies threatened India and northern Australia. Japan planned to create a strong defensive perimeter around their new empire and compel the US and the colonial powers to reach an agreement respecting Japan's new conquests. Japan's successes were based on the use of small but highly trained forces protected by carrier-borne aircraft, which inflicted crippling losses on enemy warships. The whole of the southern campaign was conducted using only a handful of army divisions with almost no tanks and few advanced weapons. Japan's hopes of destroying what remained of America's naval power came to grief at Midway Island. The Japanese carrier force was destroyed and Japanese strategy was thrown into confusion. The disruption ensured that the Americans were able to recover their strength.

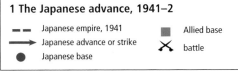

1 The Japanese advance, 1941–2

Japanese empire, 1941
Japanese advance or strike
Japanese base
Allied base
battle

Leyte Gulf in October, the remaining Japanese forces were stranded in what was left of the southern empire. Only fanatical resistance held up the Allied advance. By the spring of 1945, with the fall of Iwo Jima and Okinawa, America was in a position to attack mainland Japan.

The final defeat

The war in Asia made slower progress. In March 1944 Japan's forces in Burma attacked India, but were decisively defeated at Imphal with the loss of 53,000 men out of 85,000. In China, Japanese forces in the north fought both the Chinese Nationalists and the Communists under Mao Zedong. A million men were tied down in the Chinese war, which soaked up far more resources than the southern campaign. In 1944 Japan launched its last major offensive, Ichi-Go, which brought a large area of south-central China under Japanese rule, opened up a land-link with Indo-China and destroyed the Nationalist armies.

But victory in China came just as Allied forces in the Pacific could bring mainland Japan into their sights. Between March and June 1945, a series of devastating air raids were launched in which heavy B-29 bombers destroyed 58 Japanese cities, killing more than 393,000 Japanese civilians. Within the Japanese government arguments continued through the summer about surrendering, but the military refused to countenance such a dishonour. Suicide pilots (*kamikaze*) were sent out to attack Allied shipping, sinking or damaging 402 ships. America planned Operation Downfall for the invasion of the Japanese home islands, using 14,000 aircraft and 100 aircraft carriers, but the decision to drop atomic bombs on Hiroshima and Nagasaki in August 1945 ended Japanese resistance. On 15 August, with her cities in ruins and her economy devastated, Japan surrendered unconditionally to the Allies.

The devastation inflicted by the first atomic bomb *(above)*. It was dropped on the city of Hiroshima by the United States on 6 August 1945. Nagasaki suffered the same fate three days later. The combined death toll was 150,000. Japan immediately surrendered. The world had entered the atomic age.

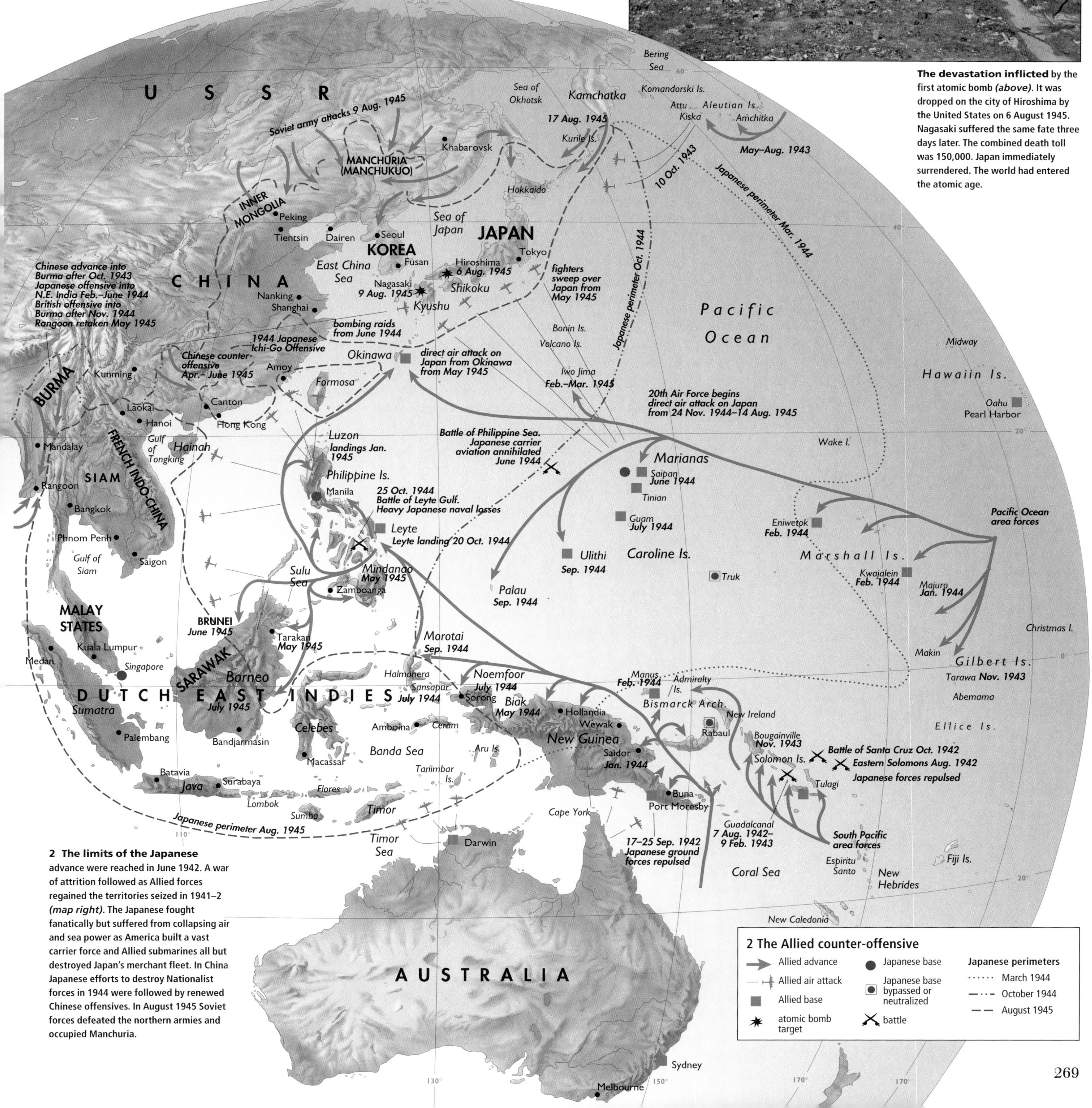

2 The limits of the Japanese advance were reached in June 1942. A war of attrition followed as Allied forces regained the territories seized in 1941–2 *(map right)*. The Japanese fought fanatically but suffered from collapsing air and sea power as America built a vast carrier force and Allied submarines all but destroyed Japan's merchant fleet. In China Japanese efforts to destroy Nationalist forces in 1944 were followed by renewed Chinese offensives. In August 1945 Soviet forces defeated the northern armies and occupied Manchuria.

2 The Allied counter-offensive

Allied advance
Allied air attack
Allied base
atomic bomb target
Japanese base
Japanese base bypassed or neutralized
battle

Japanese perimeters
March 1944
October 1944
August 1945

1941 to 1945
The European war

See also
European political problems, 1919–34 p. 262
The outbreak of the Second World War p. 266
The war in Asia and the Pacific, 1941–5 p. 268
Europe, 1945–73 p. 272
The Cold War, 1945–91 p. 274

> IT WAS THE BLOODIEST AND MOST FEROCIOUS DAY OF THE WHOLE BATTLE. ALONG A FRONT OF FOUR TO FIVE KILOMETRES, THEY THREW IN FIVE BRAND-NEW INFANTRY DIVISIONS AND TWO TANK DIVISIONS, SUPPORTED BY MASSES OF INFANTRY AND PLANES. THAT MORNING YOU COULD NOT HEAR THE SEPARATE SHOTS OR EXPLOSIONS; THE WHOLE THING MERGED INTO ONE CONTINUOUS DEAFENING ROAR.
>
> **General Chuikov on Stalingrad, 1942**

The Second World War was the largest and bloodiest conflict in human history, bringing the deaths of more than 55 million people and transforming the international order. In Europe, the main land battle was won in the east but the bombing offensive in the west destroyed German air power, paving the way for the invasion of German-held western Europe.

July 1941 *'Final solution' initiated*

Sep. 1942–Feb. 1943 *Battle of Stalingrad*

Nov. 1942 *Anglo-American landings in north Africa*

June 1943 *Combined Bomber Offensive launched*

July 1943 *Battle of Kursk: USSR defeats Germany*

Sep. 1943 *Italy surrenders to Allies*

6 June 1944 *D-Day: Allied invasion of France*

2 May 1945 *Fall of Berlin*

7 May 1945 *German surrender*

BY THE AUTUMN OF 1941 Hitler's empire in Europe had reached its zenith. German forces, buttressed by the industrial resources of a whole continent, seemed unconquerable. Yet within a year the balance began to tilt towards the Allies. Despite his failure to defeat the USSR in 1941, in December that year Hitler nonetheless declared war on the USA. Germany now faced not only a two-front war but enemies who were rapidly learning from their earlier mistakes and, above all in the shape of the USA, could claim immense and increasing military and industrial potential.

The turn of the tide

But in early 1942, the prospects for the Allies still looked bleak. The Soviet Union had suffered catastrophic losses, American rearmament was in its infancy and the U-Boat war in the Atlantic was strangling British trade. The Allied cause was saved by a remarkable resurgence of Soviet fighting power and morale in the face of the most barbarous conflict of the war and by the prodigious manufacturing record of American industry. In 1944 Allied aircraft production reached 168,000 against only 39,000 German.

Allied victory was also aided by German treatment of the conquered areas. Instead of winning the conquered peoples over to Hitler's European 'New Order' and to his crusade against communism, German rule was terroristic and exploitative. More than seven million Europeans, from France to Russia, were taken as forced labour to Germany. One-third of Germany's war costs was met by tribute extracted from occupied Europe. Thousands were executed or imprisoned for their ideological beliefs. Nazi racism was directed at the so-called lower races in the east, who were to be enslaved, and against Jews, Gypsies and the disabled. Around six million Jews were murdered in a state-sponsored campaign of genocide.

At the end of 1942 German forces suffered their first reverses, at El Alamein in north Africa and at Stalingrad. Anglo-American forces landed in Morocco and Algeria in November 1942, and in the same month the Red Army began an offensive on the Don river which initiated almost three years of continuous Soviet victories. The following spring the submarine offensive in the Atlantic was ended by the use of combined air and sea power, allowing American assistance to pour into Europe on a massive scale. In July 1943 the western Allies invaded Sicily, opening up a major southern front which drained German resources, while at Kursk on the Russian steppe the largest pitched battle in history was won by an increasingly well-organized Red Army.

The defeat of Germany

In June 1943 Anglo-American forces in Britain and the Mediterranean began the Combined Bombing Offensive, which by the spring of 1944 had imposed crippling destruction on the German urban population, undermined further expansion of German war production and almost destroyed the German air force. The campaign also paved the way for the massive Allied seaborne invasion of northern France in June 1944. France was liberated in four months, while Soviet forces continued their push into eastern Europe.

1 During the war German leaders planned a European 'New Order' *(map below)*. At its core was an enlarged 'Greater Germany', around it a ring of dependent and satellite states. In the east a vast colonial empire was to be established, economically exploited and ethnically cleansed. A continent-wide economy was to be centred on Berlin and Vienna.

Soviet victories raised the issue of the post-war order. As the likelihood of German defeat increased, the western powers found themselves facing a second authoritarian system in the form of their Soviet ally. Conferences at Teheran in 1943 and Yalta in 1945 exposed these growing divisions over the future of Europe. Yet this potential split, though it would come to dominate the post-war world, was never great enough to break up the alliance and in the last bitter months of fighting the Allies remained united in their determination to defeat Hitler. In 1945 a final assault on Germany brought western and Soviet forces face to face across central Germany. On 2 May Berlin fell, two days after Hitler had committed suicide. By 7 May German forces had surrendered.

The war was enormously costly. Worldwide, at least 55 million lost their lives, including an estimated 17 million Soviet citizens. Some 10 million Germans fled eastern Europe in 1944–5; millions of Soviet citizens were forced into internal exile or sent to Soviet labour camps (*see* p. 273). After four years of destruction, Europe lay in ruins, its economy shattered. The Second World War had exceeded by far the terrible cost of the First.

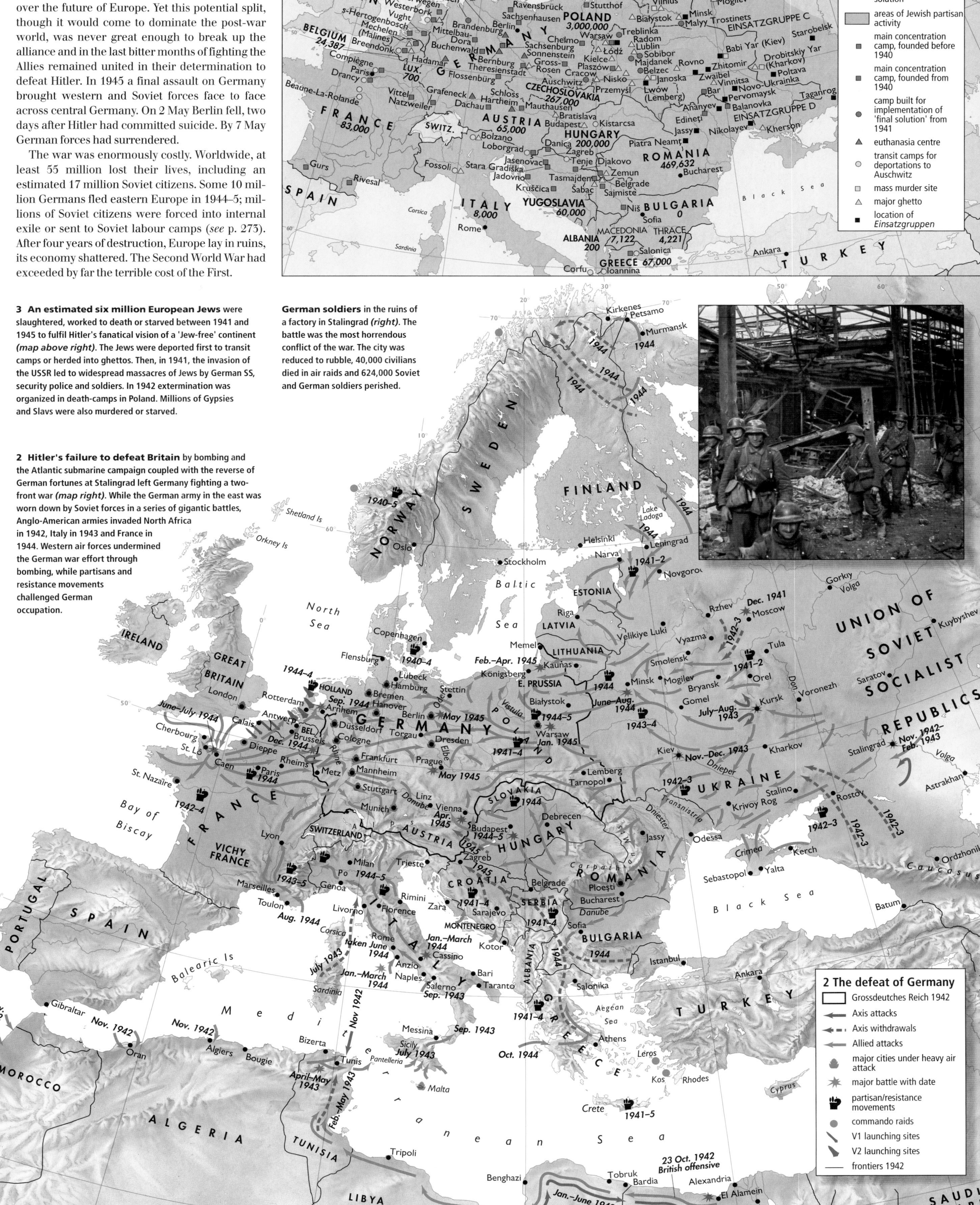

3 An estimated six million European Jews were slaughtered, worked to death or starved between 1941 and 1945 to fulfil Hitler's fanatical vision of a 'Jew-free' continent ***(map above right)***. The Jews were deported first to transit camps or herded into ghettos. Then, in 1941, the invasion of the USSR led to widespread massacres of Jews by German SS, security police and soldiers. In 1942 extermination was organized in death-camps in Poland. Millions of Gypsies and Slavs were also murdered or starved.

German soldiers in the ruins of a factory in Stalingrad ***(right)***. The battle was the most horrendous conflict of the war. The city was reduced to rubble, 40,000 civilians died in air raids and 624,000 Soviet and German soldiers perished.

2 Hitler's failure to defeat Britain by bombing and the Atlantic submarine campaign coupled with the reverse of German fortunes at Stalingrad left Germany fighting a two-front war ***(map right)***. While the German army in the east was worn down by Soviet forces in a series of gigantic battles, Anglo-American armies invaded North Africa in 1942, Italy in 1943 and France in 1944. Western air forces undermined the German war effort through bombing, while partisans and resistance movements challenged German occupation.

Europe

See also
The European war, 1941–5 p. 270
The Cold War, 1945–91 p. 274
The United States: the age of abundance p. 294
The United States as a world power since 1945 p. 296
The development of the Soviet Union and Russia since 1929 p. 298
Europe since 1973 p. 300

War-devastated Europe after 1945 was a continent on an ideological fault-line: capitalist and democratic in the west, communist and authoritarian in the east. The division was clear, too, in the west's superior economic performance. Despite the confrontation, the continent also experienced a growing stability and prosperity.

EUROPE WAS A REGION of extraordinary desolation in 1945. More than 30 million people had been killed and 16 million permanently displaced from their homes. Many of Europe's greatest cities lay in ruins. Industrial production had sunk to one-third of the pre-war level, agricultural production to half. The war also left a legacy of bitterness. Collaborators with fascism were ostracized, imprisoned or murdered while the revival of communism brought real fears of social collapse in the areas of Europe not under Soviet rule.

New frontiers

The first task was to dismantle Hitler's New Order in Europe (*see* p. 270). The new frontiers of Germany were agreed by the Allied powers at Yalta (February 1945) and Potsdam (July 1945). Germany lost its eastern territories to Poland and was separated from Austria. Czech and Yugoslav sovereignty was restored. In the east, however, the German New Order was replaced by a Soviet one. The USSR moved westward to absorb most of the territories of the former Tsarist empire – eastern Poland, the Baltic States, Bessarabia. Czech democracy, briefly restored in 1945, was overturned in 1948. Only Yugoslavia, under the rule of Tito's communists, retained real independence from Moscow. The other states of eastern Europe had traded one dictatorship for another.

Economic revival

The economic and social revival of Europe depended on the two super-powers: the USA and the Soviet Union. In western Europe revival was linked to American economic strength. Through

> A UNION BETWEEN FRANCE AND GERMANY WOULD GIVE NEW LIFE AND VIGOUR TO A EUROPE THAT IS SERIOUSLY ILL. IT WOULD HAVE AN IMMENSE PSYCHOLOGICAL AND MATERIAL INFLUENCE AND WOULD LIBERATE POWERS THAT ARE SURE TO SAVE EUROPE ... THE AMERICAN PEOPLE WOULD SEE SOME REAL RETURNS FOR THE BILLIONS OF DOLLARS THEY HAVE GIVEN TO EUROPE, BECAUSE THERE WOULD BE A GENUINE AND SIGNIFICANT CONTRIBUTION FROM WITHIN TO THE RECONSTRUCTION AND UNIFICATION OF EUROPE.
>
> **Konrad Adenauer, 1950**

3 As the Cold War confrontation hardened after 1945, Europe was divided into two armed camps *(map right)*. NATO was formed with the USA and Canada in 1949 as the centrepiece of Western security. In 1955 the Soviet Union created the Warsaw Pact, linking the states of the Communist bloc in a single defence pact. Economic union divided the continent along the same lines. In the west the EEC (1957) and EFTA (1960) created capitalist trading blocs matched by COMECON (1949) in the Soviet bloc.

3 European military and economic trading blocs, 1947–73

military partitions
- Nato 1949– (including United States and Canada)
- Warsaw Pact 1948–91

economic blocs
- Benelux customs union, 1947
- original European Economic Community (EEC) members, 1957
- joined EEC, 1973
- founder members of European Free Trade Association (EFTA), 1960
- subsequent EFTA members
- Council for Mutual Economic Assistance (COMECON) members, 1949
- subsequent COMECON members

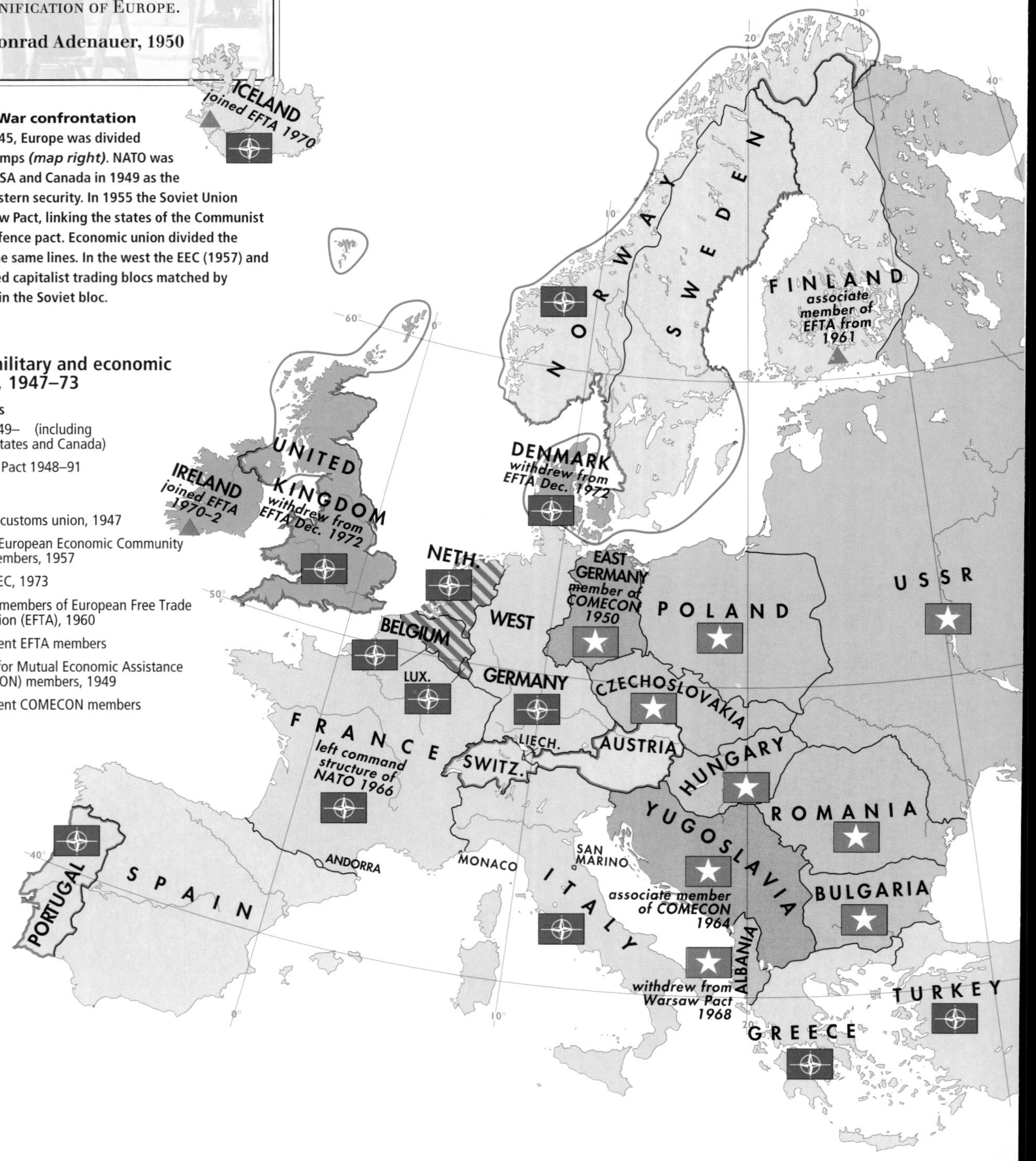

ICELAND joined EFTA 1970
IRELAND joined EFTA 1970–2
UNITED KINGDOM withdrew from EFTA Dec. 1972
DENMARK withdrew from EFTA Dec. 1972
FINLAND associate member of EFTA from 1961
EAST GERMANY member of COMECON 1950
FRANCE left command structure of NATO 1966
YUGOSLAVIA associate member of COMECON 1964
ALBANIA withdrew from Warsaw Pact 1968

2 The Marshall Plan
- applied for and received Marshall aid, with amounts (in US$)
- applied for Marshall aid but withdrew application
- did not apply
- 14.0% Net Marshall aid as percentage of national income 1948–9

Iceland $24 m 5%; Norway $236 m 5.8%; Sweden $118 m 0.3%; Denmark $257 m 3.3%; Ireland $116 m 7.8%; United Kingdom $2.825 bn 2.4%; Neth. $979 m 10.8%; Belgium $546 m 0.6%; West Germany $1.297 bn 2.9%; France $2.445 bn 6.5%; Austria $560 m 14.0%; Italy $1.314 bn 5.3%; Portugal $50 m; Greece $515 m; Turkey $152 m
Czechoslovakia applied for Marshall aid but received nothing
Spain denied Marshall aid because of Franco's pro-Axis sympathies

5 Rates of growth of selected European economies (average percentage per year)

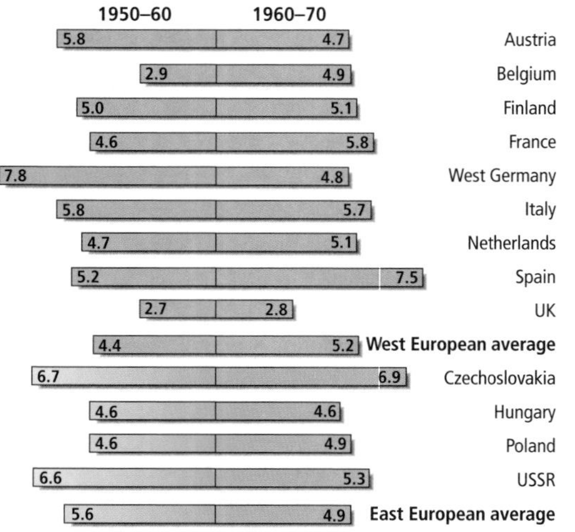

5 During the 1950s and 1960s all European states enjoyed exceptionally high rates of economic growth *(chart above)* thanks to expanding trade and a technological revolution that pushed chemicals, cars and electronics to a central role in the continent's industrial economies. West Germany above all emerged as Europe's economic powerhouse.

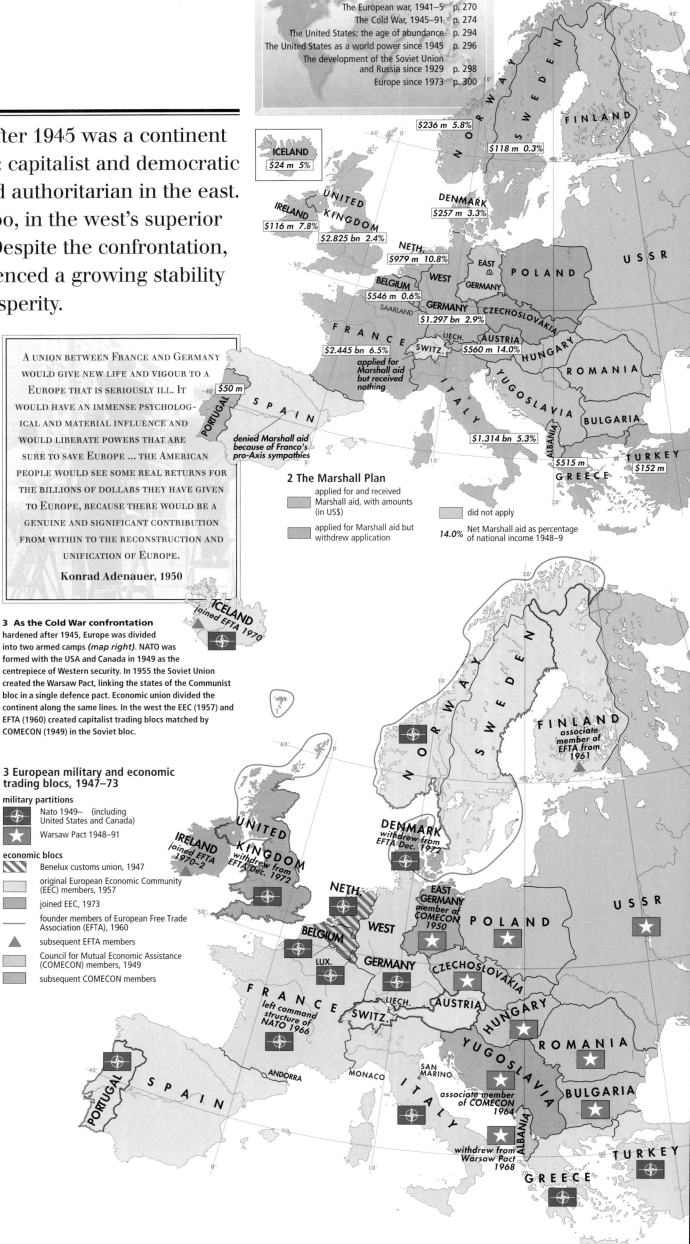

1947 *Marshall aid established*

1948/9 *Berlin airlift*

1949 *West and East Germany separate states; NATO and COMECON established*

1952 *European Coal and Steel Community founded*

1953 *Uprisings in East Germany and Poland*

1955 *Four-power occupation of Austria ended*

1956 *Hungarian uprising*

1957 *Treaty of Rome establishes EEC*

1961 *Berlin Wall built*

1968 *Soviet invasion of Czechoslovakia*

1973 *Britain, Denmark and Ireland join EEC*

2 In the spring of 1947 US Secretary of State George Marshall put his name to a European Recovery Programme backed by American finance. The Marshall Plan *(map left)* sought to get the European economy back on its feet by enabling Europe to purchase goods from the dollar area, and to promote a more stable political situation. The aid was intended for all European countries, capitalist and communist alike. However, Stalin refused to allow any countries of Soviet- dominated eastern Europe to accept it and the $11.8 billion went entirely to west and southern Europe.

6 Unemployment as a percentage of the labour force

	1950–60	1960–70
Austria	3.9	1.9
Belgium	4.0	2.2
France	1.3	1.4
West Germany	4.2	0.8
Italy	7.9	3.3
Netherlands	1.9	1.1
Norway	1.0	1.0
Sweden	1.7	1.7
Switzerland	0.2	0.0
UK	1.2	1.6
West European average	2.9	1.5

6 Unemployment was almost eliminated in the post-war boom *(chart above)*. Spending and tax policies boosted employment while training schemes produced a more employable workforce.

1 War and its aftermath drove millions of Europeans from their homelands *(map right)*. An estimated 30 million people became refugees, most of them permanently displaced. Territorially, the Soviet Union emerged as the major victor, its borders shifted dramatically to the west. Politically, it also dominated eastern Europe. Germany, greatly reduced, became two states in 1949, those areas occupied by the Western Allies becoming the Federal Republic, the Soviet zone becoming the German Democratic Republic, a division which endured until 1990.

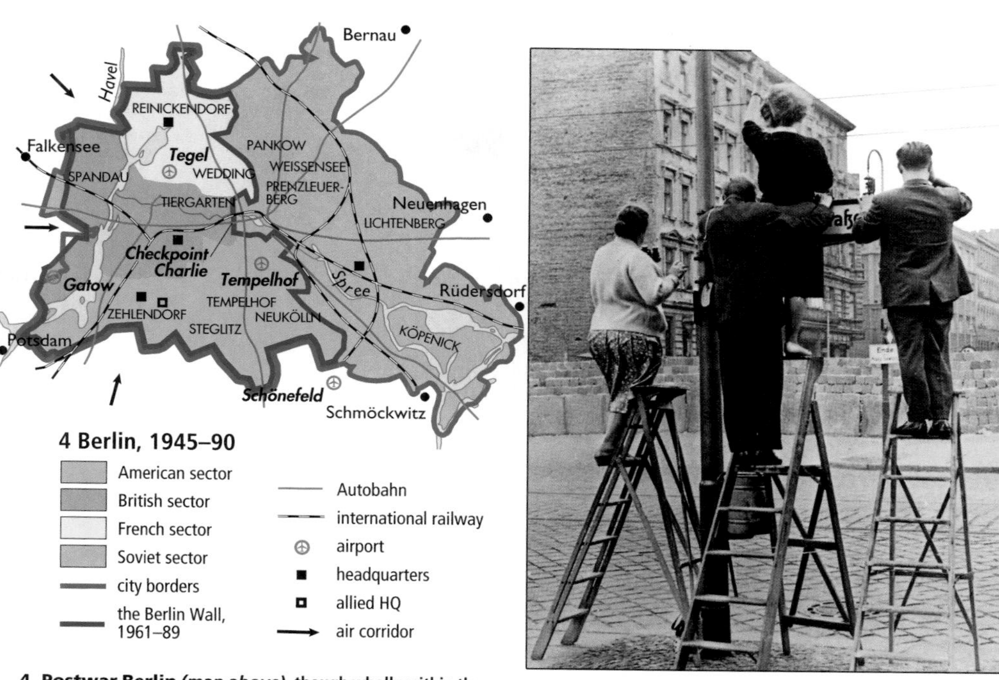

4 Postwar Berlin *(map above)*, though wholly within the Soviet sector of Germany, was divided into four zones administered separately by the victorious Allies. As the Cold War intensified, so the city became the focus of East-West tensions. Soviet attempts to drive the other Allies from the city in 1948 by blockading it were thwarted by a year-long airlift organized by the Western powers. A further Soviet attempt to isolate the city in 1958 also failed. In 1961, exasperated by the flood of refugees fleeing to the Western zones, the Soviets divided the city physically in two, erecting a wall across it overnight *(picture above right)*.

the UN and the International Bank for Reconstruction and Development the USA pumped $17 billion into Europe's economy. In 1947 a European Recovery Programme was set up which released another $11.8 billion. In 1948 the 16 nations qualifying for aid set up the Organization for European Economic Cooperation to coordinate the aid programme, the harbinger of much closer economic collaboration over the following decades. In 1952, France, Germany, Italy and the Benelux countries set up the European Coal and Steel Community to coordinate industry in their countries. In 1957 they moved to a full customs union, the European Economic Community.

Western Europe underwent the greatest economic boom in its history. By 1950 output of goods was 35 per cent higher than in 1938; by 1964 it was 250 per cent higher. Even in eastern Europe's command economy there was sustained economic growth though the price was high: low living standards, pollution and police oppression. The gap between the two economic systems widened greatly in the 1950s and 1960s, fuelling popular unrest in the East. There were strikes and political protests in East Germany and Poland in 1953, in Hungary in 1956 and Czechoslovakia in 1968, all violently suppressed by the USSR.

In the West, the EEC made another war between France and Germany virtually unthinkable and the two countries' relationship lay at the heart of the continent's new political alignment from the 1950s onwards. Economic growth encouraged political stability, too. Democracy was restored in Italy in 1946, in West Germany in 1949, in Austria in 1955. Authoritarianism survived in Portugal and Spain, and emerged briefly in Greece after 1967, but it remained the exception. Local independence movements in Northern Ireland, the Basque region of Spain and in Corsica produced sporadic violence, but the nationalist tensions that brought war twice since 1914 finally evaporated.

1 Post-war population movements and territorial change

Territorial change and population movements, 1945–9
cities divided into four occupation zones
frontiers, 1949
border of Germany, 1937
Allied control zones of Germany and Austria
annexed by Soviet Union 1940–5
states which became Communist 1945–8
Yugoslav gains from Italy, 1945
Federal Republic of Germany from 1949
German Democratic Republic from 1949

peoples resettled, evacuated or expelled (with numbers):
Germans
Finns driven from area bordering Russia
Baltic peoples
Russians
Russians forcibly repatriated
Poles
Czechs
peoples settled by International Refugee Organisation

1945 to 1991
The Cold War

See also
The European war, 1941–5 p. 270
Europe, 1945–73 p. 272
China under communism since 1949 p. 280
The United States as a world power since 1945 p. 296
The development of the Soviet Union and Russia since 1929 p. 298
Europe since 1973 p. 300

At the end of the Second World War, the world was dominated by the US and the USSR. Their ideological differences produced a complete polarisation between the capitalist west and the communist bloc. Both sides developed nuclear arsenals but the fear of nuclear destruction led to a 'Cold War', a confrontation short of armed conflict.

After 1945 the international order was dominated by the division between the capitalist west and communist east, each side grouped around the two new 'superpowers' that emerged from the defeat of Hitler: the United States in the west, the Soviet Union in the east. Yet though their hostility produced persistent confrontation, open conflict was avoided, a state described by the American journalist Walter Lippmann as 'Cold War'.

> Conscious of the special responsibility of the USSR and the US for maintaining peace, [they] have agreed that a nuclear war cannot be won and must never be fought. Recognizing that any conflict between the USSR and the US could have catastrophic consequences, they emphasize the importance of preventing any war between them, whether nuclear of conventional.
>
> **Reagan-Gorbachev Joint Statement, 1985**

The source of the conflict

The roots of the Cold War lay in the Russian revolution of 1917. Communism, with its belief in its own inevitable domination of the world, was seen as a profound threat to the world capitalist system, of which the USA was taking the leadership. The United States and the other Western allies had found themselves allied to the Soviet Union in the Second World War through force of circumstance: the imperatives of defeating Hitler overrode all other considerations, though this did not prevent persistently strained relations throughout the war. But with Hitler beaten, the underlying tensions resurfaced. The West saw in Soviet communism the spectre of a second expansionist authoritarian system, while for its part the USSR believed it had helped defeat one form of capitalist imperialism only to be confronted with an even more powerful one in the form of the USA.

The height of the Cold War

With both sides eager to avoid open conflict, the Cold War was fought out in a world of spies and secrets, political threat and subversion. In large measure it was a war fought by proxy. Both camps exploited or entered local conflicts in which they armed, equipped and trained the opposing sides, each seeking to extend their spheres of influence without coming to blows directly.

Tension was most acute in the period between 1947 and 1963, as the new political order in Europe and Asia was being fashioned, above all in central and eastern Europe where the USSR sought to impose itself on those territories it had liberated in the war. The consolidation of communist regimes in the region combined with the success of the communist revolution in China in 1949 under Mao Zedong created an apparently solid communist bloc from Europe to the Pacific, though by 1960 an open rift developed in Sino-Soviet relations.

America in 1947 committed itself to 'containing' communism (the Truman Doctrine) and lent support to countries fighting wars against the communist threat, in Greece (1947), in Korea (1950–3) and then in the long and draining conflict in Vietnam (1961–73). At the same time, the United States tried to bolster these efforts by creating security blocs – NATO in Europe in 1949, SEATO in southeast Asia in 1954 and CENTO in the Middle East in 1959. The Soviet Union and China retaliated by giving military aid and political support to anti-colonial or nationalist struggles against 'world imperialism' throughout Asia, Latin America and Africa. In 1955 the Soviet Union also sponsored a military alliance of its own, the Warsaw Pact.

The shadow of the bomb

The most important factor preventing the shift to 'hot war' was the existence of nuclear weapons. First used in 1945 against Japan, America's monopoly of the weapon was broken by the Soviet Union in 1949. In 1952 the USA developed thermonuclear weapons, with still more destructive power, and by 1953 the Soviet Union had them, too. By 1958 the American arsenal of warheads was estimated to be able to kill 200 million on a first strike. The development of intercontinental ballistic missiles and submarine-launched missiles

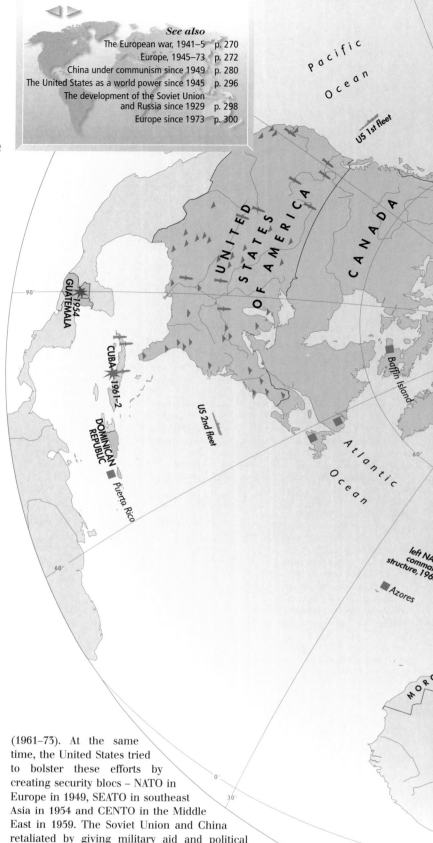

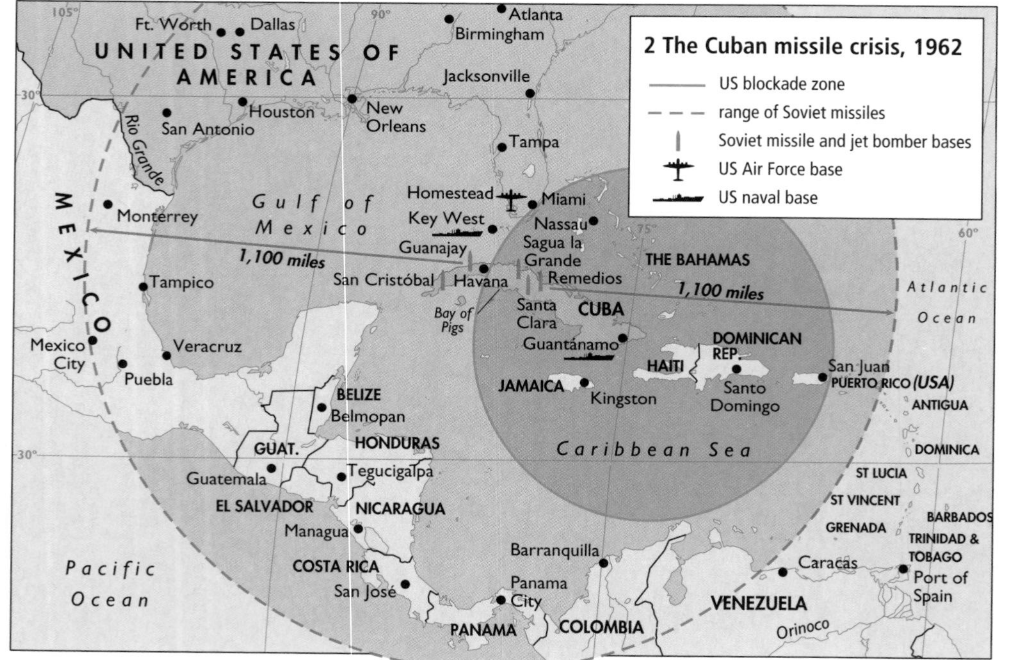

2 Following Castro's quasi-communist revolution in Cuba in 1959, the USA boycotted the new regime and in 1961 backed a failed counter-revolutionary invasion. Castro turned to the USSR for help, who in 1962 began to install nuclear missiles on the island. On 14 October the sites were spotted by a US reconnaissance plane, and President Kennedy ordered a quarantine of Cuba, to be enforced by the US Navy, while asking the USSR to withdraw the nuclear bases *(map left)*. On 26 October, following the most dangerous confrontation of the Cold War, Krushchev ordered the withdrawal.

1947 *Greek Civil War; Truman Doctrine announced*

1948–9 *Berlin airlift*

1949 *NATO formed*

1949 *Soviet Union detonates first nuclear bomb*

1950–3 *Korean War*

1955 *Warsaw Pact formed*

1962 *Cuban missile crisis*

1964–73 *US intervenes militarily in Vietnam*

1979 *Soviet Union invades Afghanistan*

1987 *INF treaty: phased elimination of inter-mediate range nuclear weapons*

1991 *Collapse of USSR; Cold War ends*

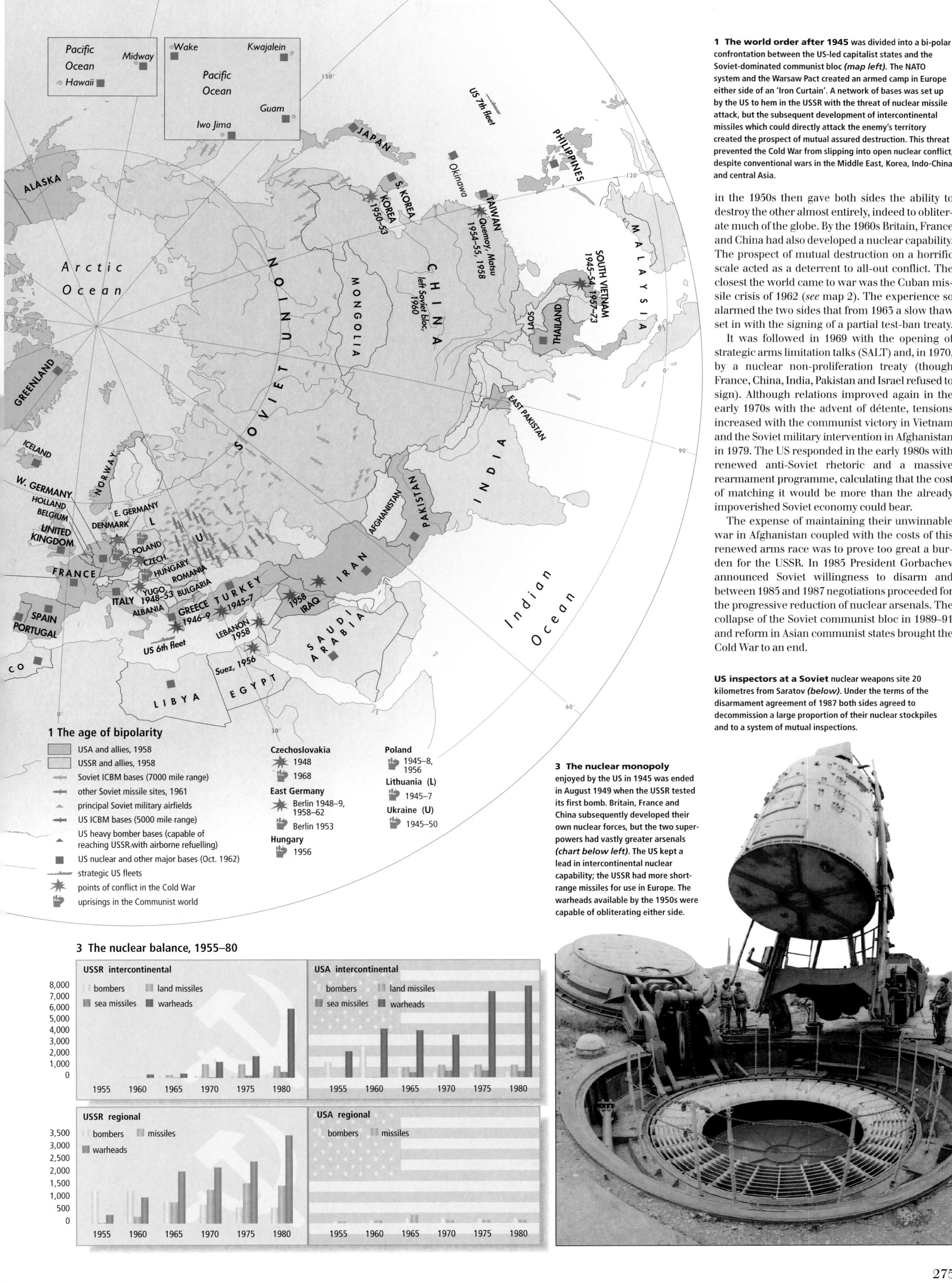

1 The world order after 1945 was divided into a bi-polar confrontation between the US-led capitalist states and the Soviet-dominated communist bloc *(map left)*. The NATO system and the Warsaw Pact created an armed camp in Europe either side of an 'Iron Curtain'. A network of bases was set up by the US to hem in the USSR with the threat of nuclear missile attack, but the subsequent development of intercontinental missiles which could directly attack the enemy's territory created the prospect of mutual assured destruction. This threat prevented the Cold War from slipping into open nuclear conflict, despite conventional wars in the Middle East, Korea, Indo-China and central Asia.

in the 1950s then gave both sides the ability to destroy the other almost entirely, indeed to obliterate much of the globe. By the 1960s Britain, France and China had also developed a nuclear capability. The prospect of mutual destruction on a horrific scale acted as a deterrent to all-out conflict. The closest the world came to war was the Cuban missile crisis of 1962 (*see* map 2). The experience so alarmed the two sides that from 1963 a slow thaw set in with the signing of a partial test-ban treaty.

It was followed in 1969 with the opening of strategic arms limitation talks (SALT) and, in 1970, by a nuclear non-proliferation treaty (though France, China, India, Pakistan and Israel refused to sign). Although relations improved again in the early 1970s with the advent of détente, tensions increased with the communist victory in Vietnam and the Soviet military intervention in Afghanistan in 1979. The US responded in the early 1980s with renewed anti-Soviet rhetoric and a massive rearmament programme, calculating that the cost of matching it would be more than the already impoverished Soviet economy could bear.

The expense of maintaining their unwinnable war in Afghanistan coupled with the costs of this renewed arms race was to prove too great a burden for the USSR. In 1985 President Gorbachev announced Soviet willingness to disarm and between 1985 and 1987 negotiations proceeded for the progressive reduction of nuclear arsenals. The collapse of the Soviet communist bloc in 1989–91 and reform in Asian communist states brought the Cold War to an end.

US inspectors at a Soviet nuclear weapons site 20 kilometres from Saratov *(below)*. Under the terms of the disarmament agreement of 1987 both sides agreed to decommission a large proportion of their nuclear stockpiles and to a system of mutual inspections.

3 The nuclear monopoly enjoyed by the US in 1945 was ended in August 1949 when the USSR tested its first bomb. Britain, France and China subsequently developed their own nuclear forces, but the two superpowers had vastly greater arsenals *(chart below left)*. The US kept a lead in intercontinental nuclear capability; the USSR had more short-range missiles for use in Europe. The warheads available by the 1950s were capable of obliterating either side.

Retreat from empire

See also
The disintegration of the Ottoman empire p. 228
European colonial empires, 1815–1914 p. 244
The anti-colonial reaction, 1881–1917 p. 246
Imperialism and nationalism, 1919–41 p. 258
Southeast Asia since 1945 p. 282
South Asia: independence and conflict p. 284
Africa after emancipation, since 1957 p. 286

1939–45 *Second World War: 1940, fall of France; 1942, Japan overruns Europe's Far Eastern colonies; 1943, Italy surrenders; 1945, Allied victory*

1947 *India partitioned; India and Pakistan independent*

1954 *Communist Vietnamese defeat French at Dien Bien Phu; start of the Algerian War*

1956 *Britain and France unsuccessfully invade Egypt after President Nasser seizes Suez Canal*

1957–68 *Independence for British African colonies*

1960 *Independence for all French sub-Saharan colonies and Belgian Congo.*

1962 *France withdraws from Algeria*

1965 *Rhodesian white settlers declare UDI (Unilateral Declaration of Independence), resulting in guerrilla war*

1975 *Portuguese rule in Africa ends*

1997 *Hong Kong returned to China*

In 1939 European colonial powers still controlled much of Asia, the Caribbean and the Pacific and almost all of Africa. The dissolution of their empires after 1945, frequently accompanied by violence, was one of the most remarkable transformations of the modern world. By the 1990s only a handful of European dependencies remained.

> THE WIND OF CHANGE IS BLOWING THROUGH THIS CONTINENT, AND, WHETHER WE LIKE IT OR NOT, THIS GROWTH OF NATIONAL CONSCIOUSNESS IS A POLITICAL FACT.
>
> **Harold Macmillan, 1960**
>
> NATIONAL LIBERATION, NATIONAL RENAISSANCE, THE RESTORATION OF NATIONHOOD TO THE PEOPLE, COMMONWEALTH: WHATEVER MAY BE THE HEADINGS USED OR THE NEW FORMULA INTRODUCED, DECOLONIZATION IS ALWAYS A VIOLENT PHENOMENON.
>
> **Franz Fanon**
> ***The Wretched of the Earth, 1961***

BY 1939 THERE WERE already significant nationalist movements in some European colonies. Britain, France and the Netherlands were also, to varying degrees, committed to the evolution of their colonial territories towards self-government, and this commitment was reinforced, in the case of Great Britain and France, by the terms under which they had been granted mandates by the League of Nations over territories formerly part of the German and Ottoman empires.

The Second World War accelerated these developments. The Italian empire was dismembered entirely, while after the war the remaining European colonial powers no longer had the economic muscle to enforce imperial rule. Furthermore, international politics were dominated by the two avowedly anti-colonial superpowers, the United States and the USSR. In addition, in east Asia, where the British, French and Dutch set about attempting to restore control of colonies overrun by the Japanese in the war, nationalists were unwilling to return to dependence. Similarly, in north Africa, Anglo-American occupation of French colonies during the war revitalized the independence movements there, while in British India independence had already been promised during the war in an unsuccessful attempt to secure the cooperation of the nationalist Congress.

Asia

It was in Asia that nationalists and, in some colonies, communists, presented the greatest challenges to European colonialism. The British, knowing they could not hold India on pre-war terms, advanced the sub-continent rapidly towards independence in 1947. Neither Britain nor Congress was able to resist the Muslim campaign for a separate state of Pakistan, and India was partitioned in circumstances of great violence. The following year Britain abandoned its mandate in Palestine, and withdrew from Ceylon and Burma. In Malaya a long struggle against communist insurgents culminated in Britain granting independence in 1957. The Dutch never regained control of the Dutch East Indies after the Japanese left and independence was finally achieved in 1949. In Vietnam communists and nationalists opposed the restored French administrations. After prolonged conflict and military defeat at Dien Bien Phu the French abandoned their Far Eastern empire.

The French were also engulfed in violent

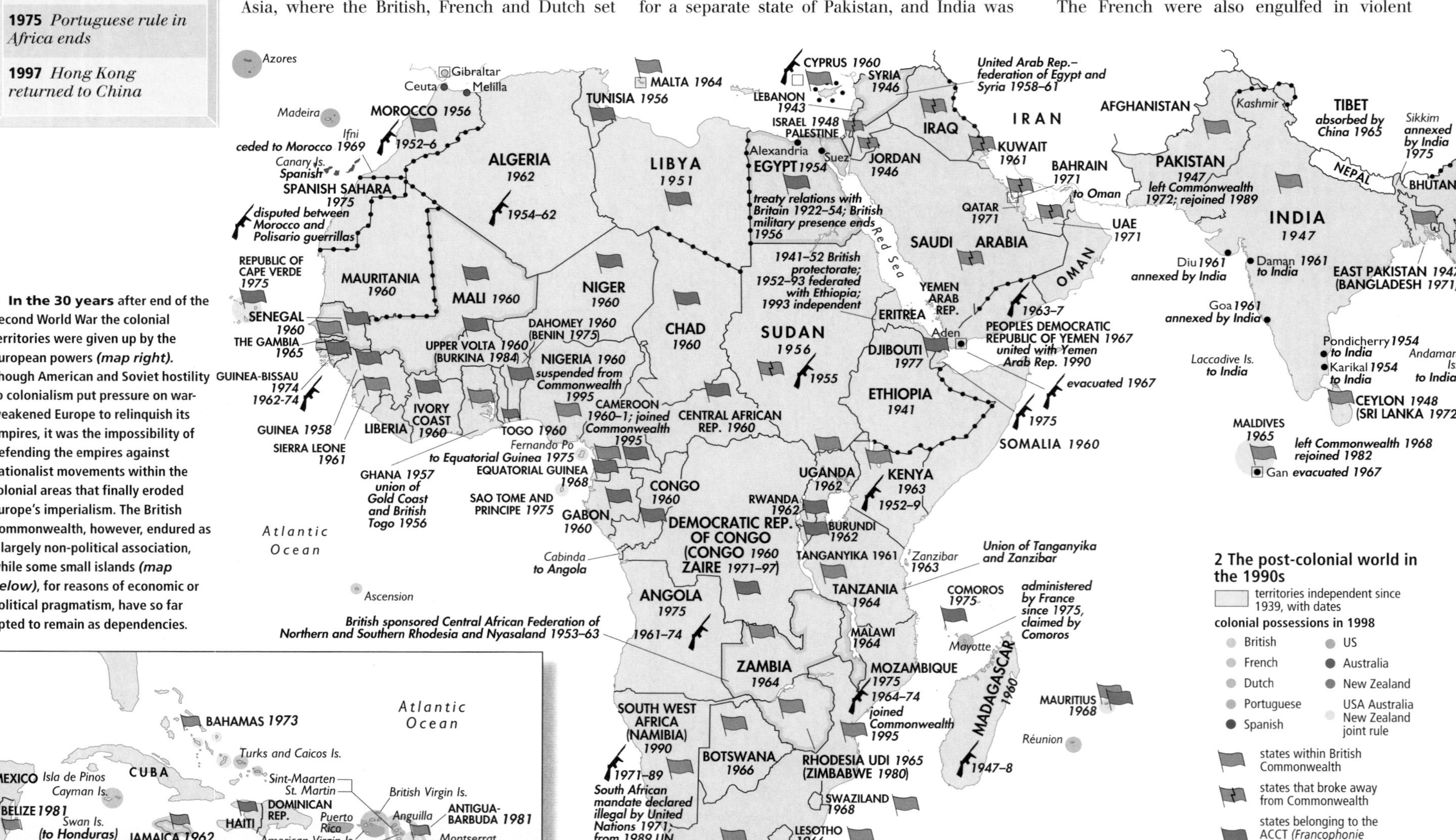

2 **In the 30 years** after end of the Second World War the colonial territories were given up by the European powers ***(map right).*** Though American and Soviet hostility to colonialism put pressure on war-weakened Europe to relinquish its empires, it was the impossibility of defending the empires against nationalist movements within the colonial areas that finally eroded Europe's imperialism. The British Commonwealth, however, endured as a largely non-political association, while some small islands ***(map below),*** for reasons of economic or political pragmatism, have so far opted to remain as dependencies.

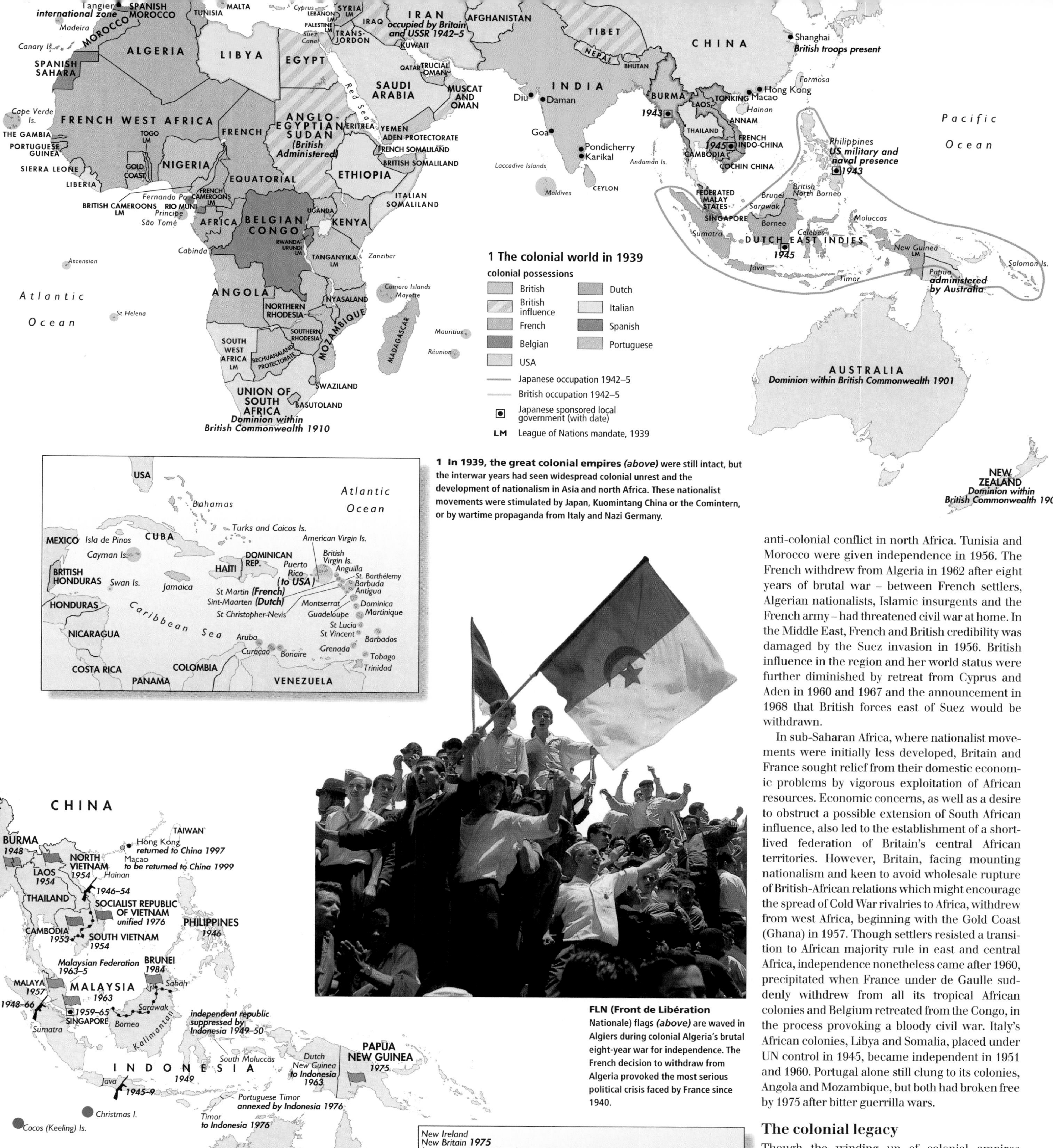

1 **In 1939, the great colonial empires *(above)* were still intact, but the interwar years had seen widespread colonial unrest and the development of nationalism in Asia and north Africa. These nationalist movements were stimulated by Japan, Kuomintang China or the Comintern, or by wartime propaganda from Italy and Nazi Germany.**

FLN (Front de Libération Nationale) flags *(above)* are waved in Algiers during colonial Algeria's brutal eight-year war for independence. The French decision to withdraw from Algeria provoked the most serious political crisis faced by France since 1940.

anti-colonial conflict in north Africa. Tunisia and Morocco were given independence in 1956. The French withdrew from Algeria in 1962 after eight years of brutal war – between French settlers, Algerian nationalists, Islamic insurgents and the French army – had threatened civil war at home. In the Middle East, French and British credibility was damaged by the Suez invasion in 1956. British influence in the region and her world status were further diminished by retreat from Cyprus and Aden in 1960 and 1967 and the announcement in 1968 that British forces east of Suez would be withdrawn.

In sub-Saharan Africa, where nationalist movements were initially less developed, Britain and France sought relief from their domestic economic problems by vigorous exploitation of African resources. Economic concerns, as well as a desire to obstruct a possible extension of South African influence, also led to the establishment of a short-lived federation of Britain's central African territories. However, Britain, facing mounting nationalism and keen to avoid wholesale rupture of British-African relations which might encourage the spread of Cold War rivalries to Africa, withdrew from west Africa, beginning with the Gold Coast (Ghana) in 1957. Though settlers resisted a transition to African majority rule in east and central Africa, independence nonetheless came after 1960, precipitated when France under de Gaulle suddenly withdrew from all its tropical African colonies and Belgium retreated from the Congo, in the process provoking a bloody civil war. Italy's African colonies, Libya and Somalia, placed under UN control in 1945, became independent in 1951 and 1960. Portugal alone still clung to its colonies, Angola and Mozambique, but both had broken free by 1975 after bitter guerrilla wars.

The colonial legacy

Though the winding up of colonial empires continued through the 1970s and 1980s in the Caribbean and the South Pacific and into the 1990s – Hong Kong was returned to China by the British in 1997 – by the beginning of the 1970s the age of European overseas empires was effectively past. In the process of decolonization, not only had many former dependencies faced rapid, sometimes violent, political change, a number then had to reconcile the demands of rival ethnic or religious divisions within their new borders. In varying degrees, most also confronted economic problems that for some would prove all but insuperable.

Since 1945

Japan and east Asia

See also
The expansion and modernization of Japan, 1868–1922 p. 242
The Chinese revolution, 1912–49 p. 260
The outbreak of the Second World War p. 266
The war in Asia and the Pacific, 1941–5 p. 268
China under communism since 1949 p. 280
Southeast Asia since 1945 p. 282
The world in the 1990s p. 302

1945 *Japan surrenders after two atom bombs dropped*

1950 *Korean War begins (to 1953)*

1951 *USA's occupation of Japan ends*

1964 *Olympic games in Tokyo*

1973 *Oil crisis; Japan recovers rapidly*

1975 *Death of Chiang Kai-shek*

1986 *Multi-party democracy introduced in Taiwan*

1988 *Olympic games in Seoul*

1994 *Death of Kim Il Sung*

1997–8 *Economic turmoil in east Asia*

In the years after 1945 east Asia struggled to throw off the legacy of the Second World War. After 1948, United States support for Japan, South Korea and Taiwan, perceived as its first line of defence in east Asia, transformed their economies. Until the late 1990s they seemed to form the core of one of the world's most dynamic economic regions.

For the new age, there is only one path open to Japan. Instead of arms, we must choose culture. Through our education and true morality, we must contribute to the world's progress.

Maeda Tamon, Japan's Minister of Education, 1945

As a result of defeat, the wall that secluded the Japanese mind from the outside world broke down. The Japanese people could see the world as it was for the first time.

Iyama Ikuo
Japan's Future Course, 1948

IN THE AUTUMN OF 1945 the future for Japan looked grim. The economy was in ruins; most of the towns and industrial plant had been destroyed; the navy had been sunk; nearly all foreign assets had been lost; domestic capital was run down; the victorious enemy demanded large reparations; all the necessities of life were short.

The reconstruction of Japan

The rebuilding of the country was led by the American occupation administration. Japan had to accept a new constitution which ended the divinity of the emperor and gave sovereignty to the people. An independent judiciary was established, free labour unions were permitted and war was renounced as a means of settling disputes. From 1948, with the advance of the Chinese communists, the United States increasingly came to see Japan not only as the key bulwark of Western power in east Asia but also as one whose effectiveness depended on the reconstruction of its economic power. In September 1951 the American occupation was ended.

For Korea Japan's defeat ended the harsh Japanese colonial regime imposed in 1910. But it also brought a division of the country between a communist state in the north backed by the Soviet Union and an anti-communist state in the south backed by the United States. In June 1950 war broke out and, when it came to an end in 1953, Korea was divided along the armistice line.

The Korean War provided the first boost to the Japanese recovery. There followed a period of exceptionally high economic growth – well over 10 per cent a year throughout the 1960s – which turned her into an economic superpower. In the years 1974–85 her economy grew at 4.3 per cent, faster than that of any other OECD country. A key feature of Japan's growth was her flexibility in pursuing economic objectives: in the 1950s she emphasized heavy industry, ship-building and iron and steel; in the 1960s she moved into high-technology consumer manufactures largely for export; from the 1970s she concentrated on technological innovation and higher value-added products while transferring the production of lower value-added goods overseas. There began an era of massive Japanese investment in Asia, Europe and North America (*see* map 4). In the early 1990s Japan had the world's strongest economy with the largest per capita GNP and the largest holding of foreign assets and debt. Amongst the causes of this remarkable success were: Japan's surplus labour in the 1950s-60s which kept prices down; the role of government intervention (and support); the high levels of domestic saving; and the distinctive character of employee-company relations which emphasized extensive consultation and group loyalty.

North and South Korea

Korea epitomized the relative success of the communist and capitalist projects. Until 1970 North Korea had the higher GNP per capita. By the 1990s GNP was declining at 5 per cent and the state, still communist, was close to economic and humanitarian disaster. From the mid-1960s South Korea embarked on rapid industrialization and emerged as one of the 'little tigers' amongst the Asian economies. By the 1990s it was the world's 13th largest economy with great strengths in car manufacture, shipbuilding and semi-conductors. For much of this period of rapid economic growth, however, its regime showed little tolerance of political dissent: open protest was forcefully crushed.

Taiwan, where the Chinese Nationalists established their government in 1949 after the Communist takeover on the mainland, experienced economic success similar to that of South

5 Japanese exports, 1960–96 (millions US $)

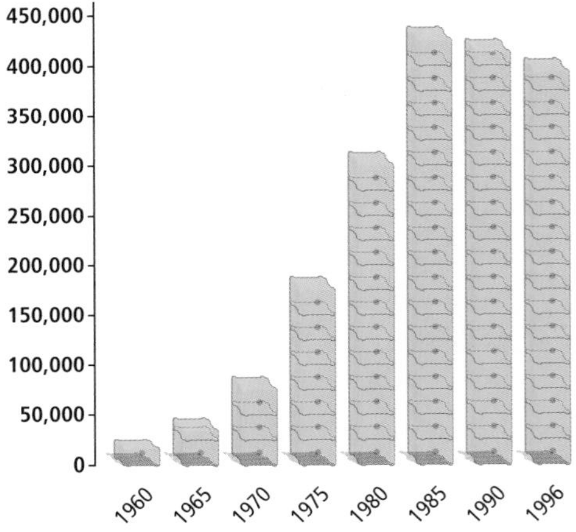

6 Japanese direct investment overseas, 1979–93 (billions US $)

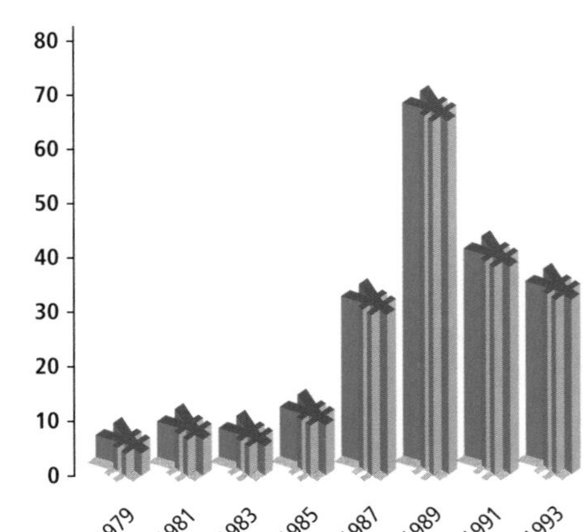

5 & 6 The economic progress of Japan has been startling since the 1960s *(charts right)*. As the level of Japanese exports grew after the war, so Japanese investment overseas increased. By the end of the 1980s the country was a long-established economic superpower. But however impressive Japan's economic performance since 1945, the country has had to contend with a sharp economic slowdown since the early 1990s. The end of the 'bubble economy' has brought depressed land prices, banking collapses and a series of less-than-successful attempts by successive Japanese governments to kick-start the economy. By the end of 1998, Japan was faced with negative growth, a serious overhang of debt in the financial sector and the threat of a deflationary spiral.

3 The Korean War *(map below)* carried the Cold War to the Far East. Occupied in 1945 by Soviet and American forces, the country was already divided de facto by 1948. In 1950, after the withdrawal of the occupying armies, the North Koreans attacked the South. The United States and United Nations immediately intervened. After initial North Korean successes, the Americans under General MacArthur counter-attacked and advanced to the Chinese frontier. This resulted in Chinese intervention and stalemate, ended only by the armistice of Panmunjom and the partition of the country along the 38th parallel.

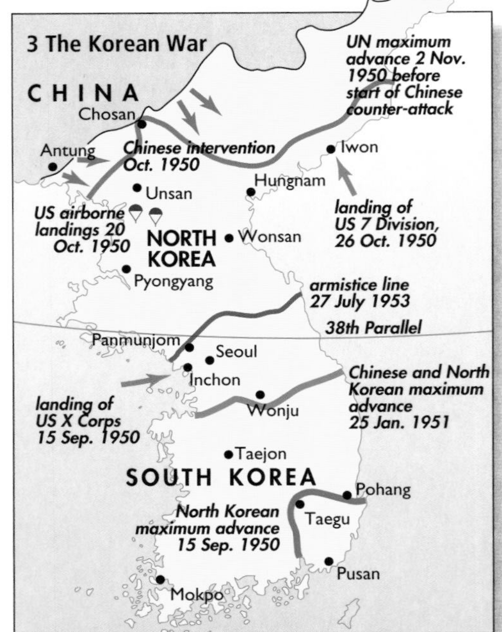

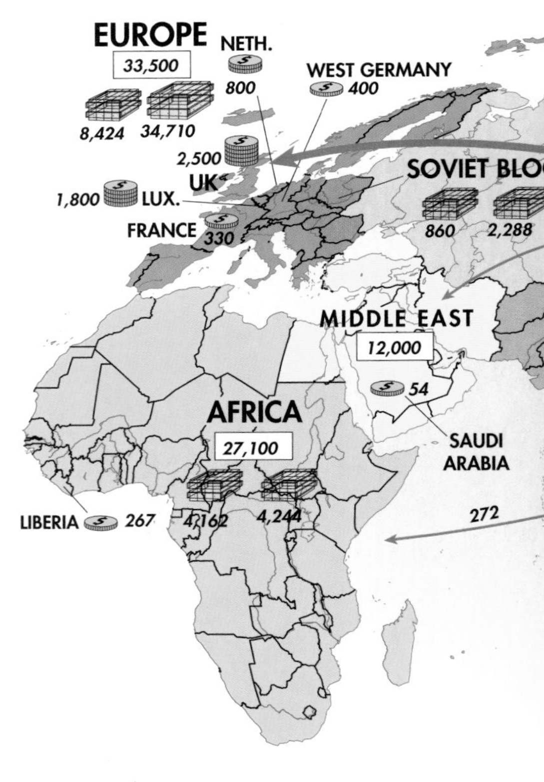

In 1948 the new state of North Korea was set up by the Korean Workers' Party led by Kim Il Sung ***(left).*** Kim imposed his own brand of communism on North Korea. Political dissidents were sent to concentration camps. The rest of the populace led strictly regimented lives. The economy was sealed off from the outside world and a personality cult of bizarre proportions arose. By his death in 1994 North Korea was impoverished and economically and politically isolated.

1 From the devastation at the end of the Second World War, Japan emerged as an economic powerhouse ***(map below)***, by the 1980s challenging even the United States. South Korea, though far from a model democratic state for much of the post-war period, has developed a thriving industrial base. Like Japan in the same period, it has specialized in high-tech industries. An economic crisis in 1997–8 showed that continued success would depend on financial reforms.

1 Japan and Korea

major industries

- major industrial areas
- research and development
- heavy engineering
- consumer goods
- vehicle manufacturing
- shipbuilding
- iron and steel
- electronics
- chemicals
- textiles
- telecommunications
- major roads
- airports
- bullet trains
- railways

Korea. A one-party state to 1986, it subsequently become a fully-functioning multi-party democracy. The growing diplomatic recognition from the 1970s of communist China, which saw Taiwan as a province, has left it isolated. Since 1990, however, Taiwan has been responsible for more than 60 per cent of inward investment into China.

The economic turmoil which hit the east Asian economies in 1997 exposed serious structural weaknesses, particularly in the inefficient and debt-laden finance and banking sectors. Yet the vast underlying strength of Japan suggests that the region, together with China and southeast Asia, will continue to play a critical role in the world economy in the early 21st century.

4 During the 1970s and 1980s Japan's economic presence abroad expanded dramatically ***(map below).*** By 1987 overseas investments were worth $139 billion. Foreign trade totalled only seven billion Yen in 1970 but was 40 billion by 1993. The US trade deficit with Japan reached $60 billion by 1987, over a third of the total trade deficit. The great bulk of Japanese exports was made up of machinery and equipment.

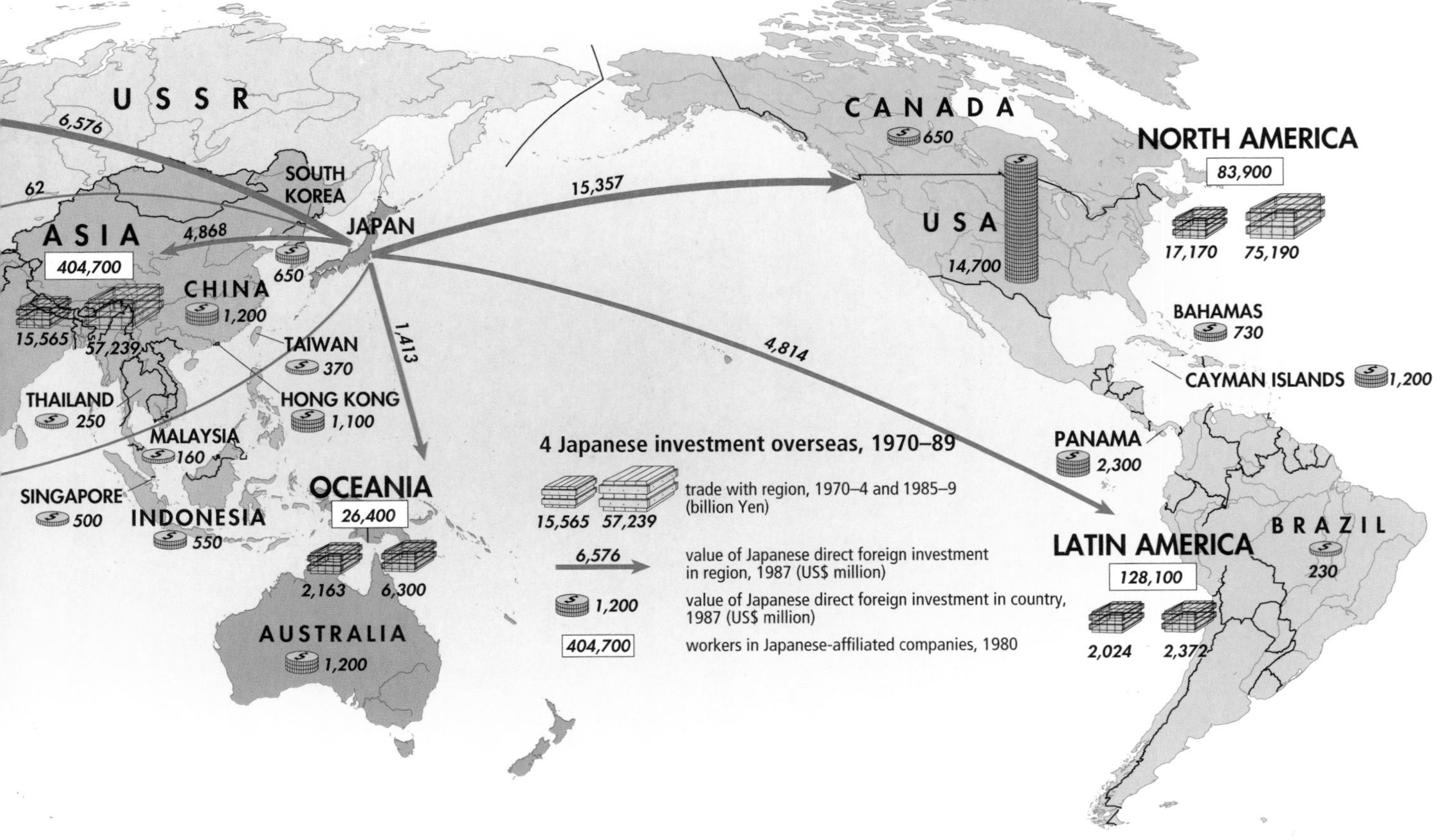

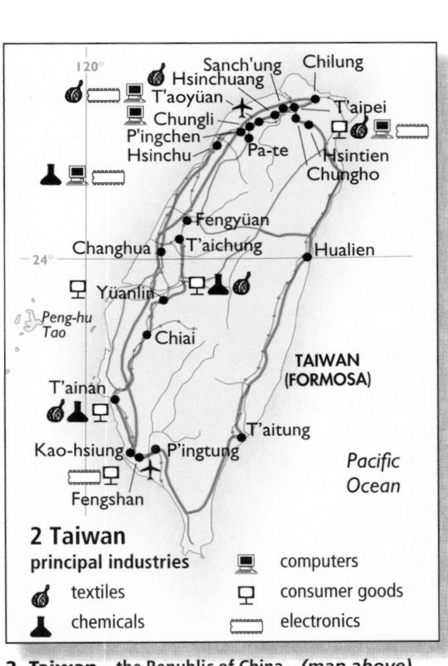

2 Taiwan – the Republic of China – ***(map above)*** was established in 1949 by Chiang Kai-Shek's Kuomintang, whose government in Beijing had been overthrown by Mao Zedong. The Kuomintang still claim to be the sole legitimate rulers of China, while communist China considers Taiwan to be one of its provinces. Taiwan has had one of the world's most successful economies since the 1950s, with growth rates over the period second only to those of Japan (and 6.6 per cent a year between 1985 and 1995).

Since 1949

China under communism

See also
The Chinese revolution, 1912–1949 p. 260
The Cold War, 1945–91 p. 274
Japan and east Asia since 1945 p. 278
The world in the 1990s p. 302

1949 *Communist victory in China*

1958 *Great Leap Forward (to 1961)*

1966 *Great Proletarian Cultural Revolution (to 1976)*

1972 *Nixon visits China; China begins to open up to the West*

1976 *Death of Mao; overthrow of 'Gang of Four'*

1986 *Pro-democracy agitation in China*

1989 *Student pro-democracy demonstration crushed in Beijing*

1997 *Death of Deng Xiaoping*

1997 *Hong Kong returned to China*

The establishment of the People's Republic of China launched China's economic modernization. Under Mao Zedong continuing revolutionary turmoil did as much to retard as to advance economic progress. From the late 1970s, however, China pursued economic liberalization with outstanding success. Its internal politics, however, remained repressive.

THE ESTABLISHMENT OF the People's Republic of China in 1949 marked a fundamental turning point in China's modern history. After a century of internal conflict and disintegration, exacerbated by external aggressors, China now experienced strong centralized government. Despite the excesses and failures since 1949, not least the systematic repression of much of the population, this is a fundamental achievement.

China under Mao

The central concern of the new regime was the economy, crucially the raising of agricultural production and the creation of a heavy industrial base. But by the late 1950s Mao Zedong was impatient with the slowness of progress. In February 1958 he launched the 'Great Leap Forward' which aimed to modernize China in three years. Rural China was divided into 26,000 communes which were required to abolish private property and to meet huge targets in agricultural and industrial production. 600,000 backyard furnaces sprang up across the countryside. The experiment was an unmitigated disaster: production declined sharply and 20-30 million died from starvation or malnutrition. In 1961 the project was abandoned. This failure strengthened the hands of moderates in the Chinese Communist Party (CCP) under Liu Shaoqi who preferred a more centrally-planned, Soviet-style development. Mao responded by forming an alliance with the People's Liberation Army (PLA) under Lin Biao and with Chinese youth who, as 'Red Guards', faithfully supported his policies.

In 1966 Mao launched the Great Proletarian Cultural Revolution. Red Guards were set loose to prevent the development of 'vested interests' and careerism in party and state by establishing permanent revolution. Chaos followed throughout China. Mao was forced to call on the PLA to restore order. On 9 September 1976 Mao died. His wife Jiang Qing with three conspirators, the 'Gang of Four', tried to seize power. By this time the PLA and the elite had had enough of revolution. The 'Gang of Four' were arrested, tried and expelled from the Communist Party.

From the late 1970s the dominant figure in China's politics was Deng Xiaoping. A beginning had been made in opening up China to the capitalist West with President Nixon's visit in 1972. Deng then launched a policy of economic liberalization.

OF ALL THE IMPORTANT THINGS, THE POSSESSION OF POWER IS THE MOST IMPORTANT. SUCH BEING THE CASE, THE REVOLUTIONARY MASSES, WITH A DEEP HATRED FOR THE CLASS ENEMY, MAKE UP THEIR MIND TO UNITE, FORM A GREAT ALLIANCE, [AND] SEIZE POWER! SEIZE POWER!! SEIZE POWER!!! ALL THE PARTY POWER, POLITICAL POWER, AND FINANCIAL POWER USURPED BY THE COUNTER-REVOLUTIONARY REVISIONISTS AND THOSE DIEHARDS WHO PERSISTENTLY CLING TO THE BOURGEOIS REACTIONARY LINE MUST BE RECAPTURED!

Editorial in pro-Cultural Revolution newspaper, 22 January 1967

He created special economic zones in areas bordering Hong Kong, Macao and Taiwan and in Shanghai with inducements to encourage foreign investment. By 1992 $36 billion had been invested. Other reforms followed: peasants were permitted to own land. By 1984, 98 per cent did so, the communes had vanished and agricultural output had increased 49 per cent in five years. Private businesses were also permitted. Their numbers grew from 100,000 in 1978 to 17 million in 1985. However, the success of liberalization brought its own problems: inflation, external deficits, migration to the cities and corruption.

Reform and protest

Economic reforms led to demands for political liberalization. In December 1986, students demonstrated for democracy in 15 cities. Deng responded with repression: 'troublemakers' were arrested;

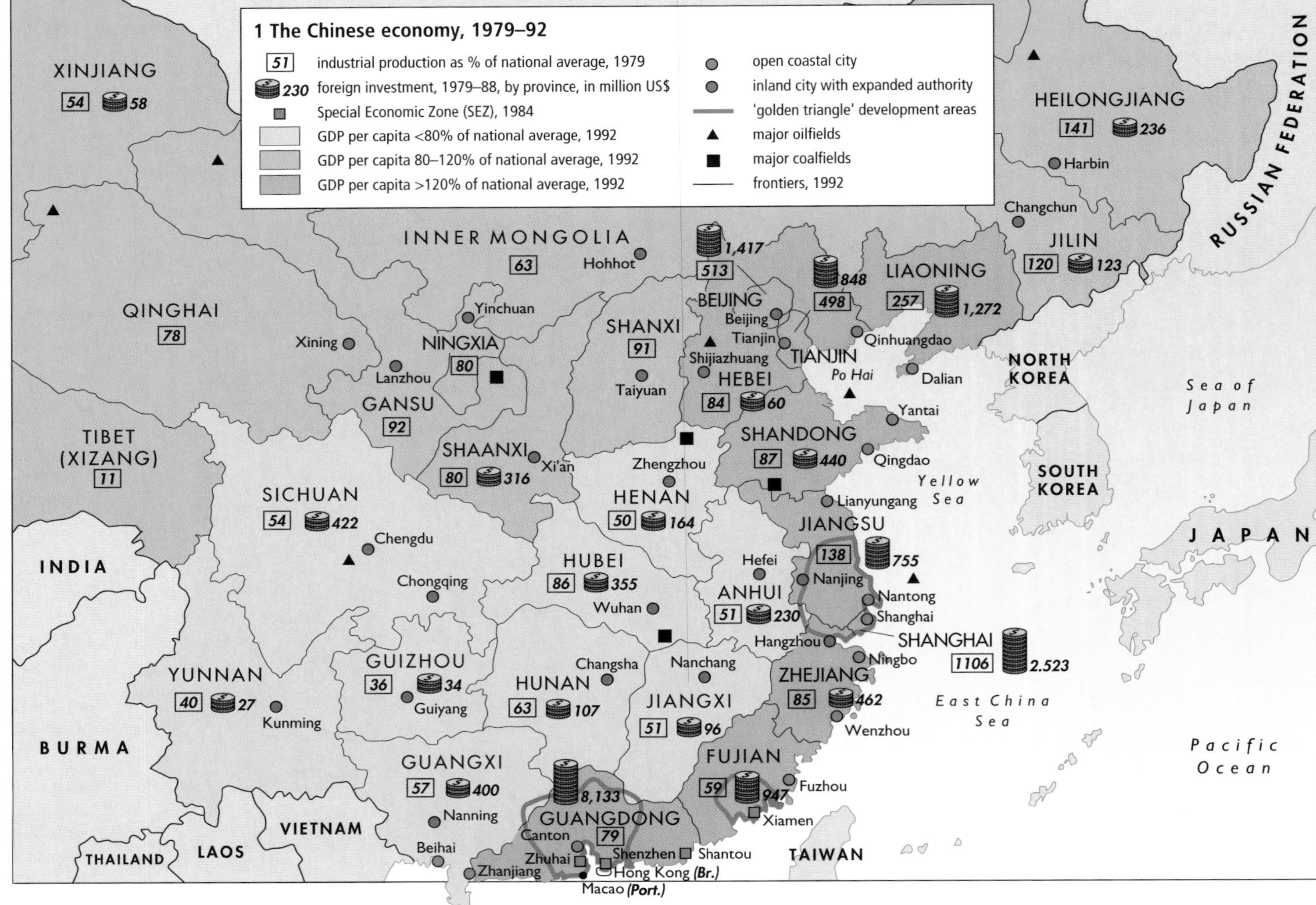

1 The world's most populous nation, China developed rapidly after the civil war and communist takeover in 1949 ***(map right)***. But the country's industrial and agricultural expansion was slowed by the Great Leap Forward of the late 1950s and the Cultural Revolution of the mid-1960s. From the late 1970s China experienced an economic revolution, following the decision to pursue the 'Four Modernizations' (agriculture, industry, national defence, science and technology). A massive programme of investment produced significant gains in output, but led to high inflation. In the mid-1980s a policy of retrenchment stabilized the economy, before the regime launched more thorough market reforms and a new expansionary wave from 1990. The fruits of this were seen in growth rates regularly in excess of 10 per cent, reaching 13 per cent in 1993 and an economy less affected than most in east and southeast Asia by the economic crisis of 1997–8.

2 From the 1970s communist China normalized relations with the outside world after years of isolation *(map above)*. Japan recognized China in 1972, and the United States switched allegiance from Taiwan to China in the spring of 1979. Frontier treaties were signed with neighbouring states, and Britain returned Hong Kong to Chinese sovereignty in 1997. Internally the period saw sporadic dissent movements. Massive student protests in 1989 *(right)* were ended by a massacre of pro-democracy demonstrators in Tiananmen Square on 4 June.

3 In 1966, threatened by growing opposition in the Party and the bureaucracy and impatient of their careerism and autocratic methods, Mao launched the Great Proletarian Cultural Revolution *(map above)*. In July 1966 he set his Red Guards loose. They rampaged through the cities attacking the 'Four Olds' (old ideas, culture, customs and habits) and took over many parts of the establishment. By mid-1968 there was chaos and the PLA was sent in to restore order.

4 Graphic demonstration of China's economic boom and its reintegration into the world economy is offered by the growth of its foreign trade since the late 1970s *(chart right)*. As far as possible China has been concerned to counteract the trade deficits consequent on a booming economy (with growth rates in excess of 10 per cent in the 1990s) by limiting foreign contracts and pursuing vigorous export policies.

Hu Yaobang, the liberal secretary-general of the CCP, was sacked. When Hu died in April 1989, students used the occasion to demand democracy. For six weeks they gathered in Tiananmen Square, at times numbering over a million. In June the PLA was sent in and the movement ruthlessly crushed.

After the Tiananmen massacre China moved quickly to reassure the world that it was a stable economic partner; the world largely ignored human rights concerns to assure itself of a share of China's economic boom. There was further economic liberalization: most of China now operated a 'socialist market economy'. Growth rates which averaged 10 per cent or more for the 1980s and 1990s were only slightly affected by the economic turmoil which hit east Asia in 1997–8. With growing freedom in many areas of life the issue of democracy remained the unfinished business of China's 20th-century achievement.

Southeast Asia

See also
Imperialism and nationalism, 1919–41 p. 258
The Chinese revolution, 1912–49 p. 260
The war in Asia and the Pacific, 1941–45 p. 268
Retreat from empire since 1939 p. 276
Japan and east Asia since 1945 p. 278
China under communism p. 280
The United States as a world power since 1945 p. 296

The early post-war history of southeast Asia was dominated by the struggles against European colonialism. While some European powers withdrew peacefully, others were driven out by force. By the 1990s, the states of the region were divided between those who had made great economic progress and those with weaker economies and uncertain politics.

SISTERS AND BROTHERS, HOW TERRIFICALLY DYNAMIC IS OUR TIME ... YES, THERE HAS INDEED BEEN A 'STURM ÜBER ASIEN' – AND OVER AFRICA TOO. THE LAST FEW YEARS HAVE SEEN ENORMOUS CHANGES. NATIONS, STATES HAVE AWOKEN FROM A SLEEP OF CENTURIES. ... HURRICANES OF NATIONAL AWAKENING AND RE-AWAKENING HAVE SWEPT OVER THE LAND...

Speech by President Sukarno to the Bandung Conference of non-aligned nations, April 1955

AFTER THE JAPANESE DEFEAT in 1945 the Western powers sought to return to their territories, but with differing ambitions. In July 1946 the United States left the Philippines. The British returned to Burma and Malaya committed to re-establishing colonial rule, but soon accepted that withdrawal was inevitable. In January 1948 they left Burma. The peninsular states of Malaya achieved independence in 1957, forming a wider union with Singapore, Sabah and Sarawak as the Federation of Malaysia in 1963. In 1965, Singapore became an independent republic.

The Dutch and French, who sought to re-impose their authority regardless of nationalist aspirations, both became enmeshed in bloody wars. The Dutch nearly defeated the infant republic of Indonesia. But world opinion turned against them and they withdrew in December 1949. The French struggle in Vietnam was bitter. After the Japanese defeat, Ho Chi Minh established a communist regime in the north while the French reimposed their rule in the south. For a year Ho Chi Minh tried to persuade the French to leave. In 1946 war broke out which ended in humiliating defeat for France at Dien Bien Phu in 1954. Vietnam was temporarily partitioned at the 17th parallel. The North Vietnamese assumed that elections scheduled for 1956 would lead to unification, but the South Vietnamese, guided by the United States, refused to sign an agreement or hold elections.

The Vietnam War

Vietnam became a major battlefield of the Cold War. The anti-communist South received massive American support, which from 1965 took active military form; the North received supplies from China and the Soviet Union. By the late 1960s it was clear that American intervention could not halt communist 'aggression' towards the South. By 1973 the United States had negotiated a withdrawal but continued to supply the South on a huge scale. But in 1975 Northern military victory

3 From 1957 communist guerrillas waged a war against the pro-Western government of South Vietnam. The government controlled the urban areas, the guerrillas most of the countryside *(map right)*. The Ho Chi Minh trail was the route by which supplies were funnelled from the north to the Viet Cong troops fighting in the south. In 1968 the guerrillas launched the 'Tet' offensive against the cities which prompted gradual US withdrawal. In 1973 the last US troops left the country. In 1975 the whole country was united under communist rule.

3 Indo-China, 1966–8
areas of control, early 1966:
- controlled by the Vietcong
- under Vietcong influence
- controlled by the Government
- under Government influence
- heavily contested area
- 'Tet' offensive, 1968

Vinh
Dong Hoi
NORTH VIETNAM
Vinh Linh
LAOS
Hue
Phu Bai
Da Nang
Ho Chi Minh trail
Chu Lai
Qui Nhon
CAMBODIA
SOUTH VIETNAM
Saigon
South China Sea
7th US fleet 1964
Mekong

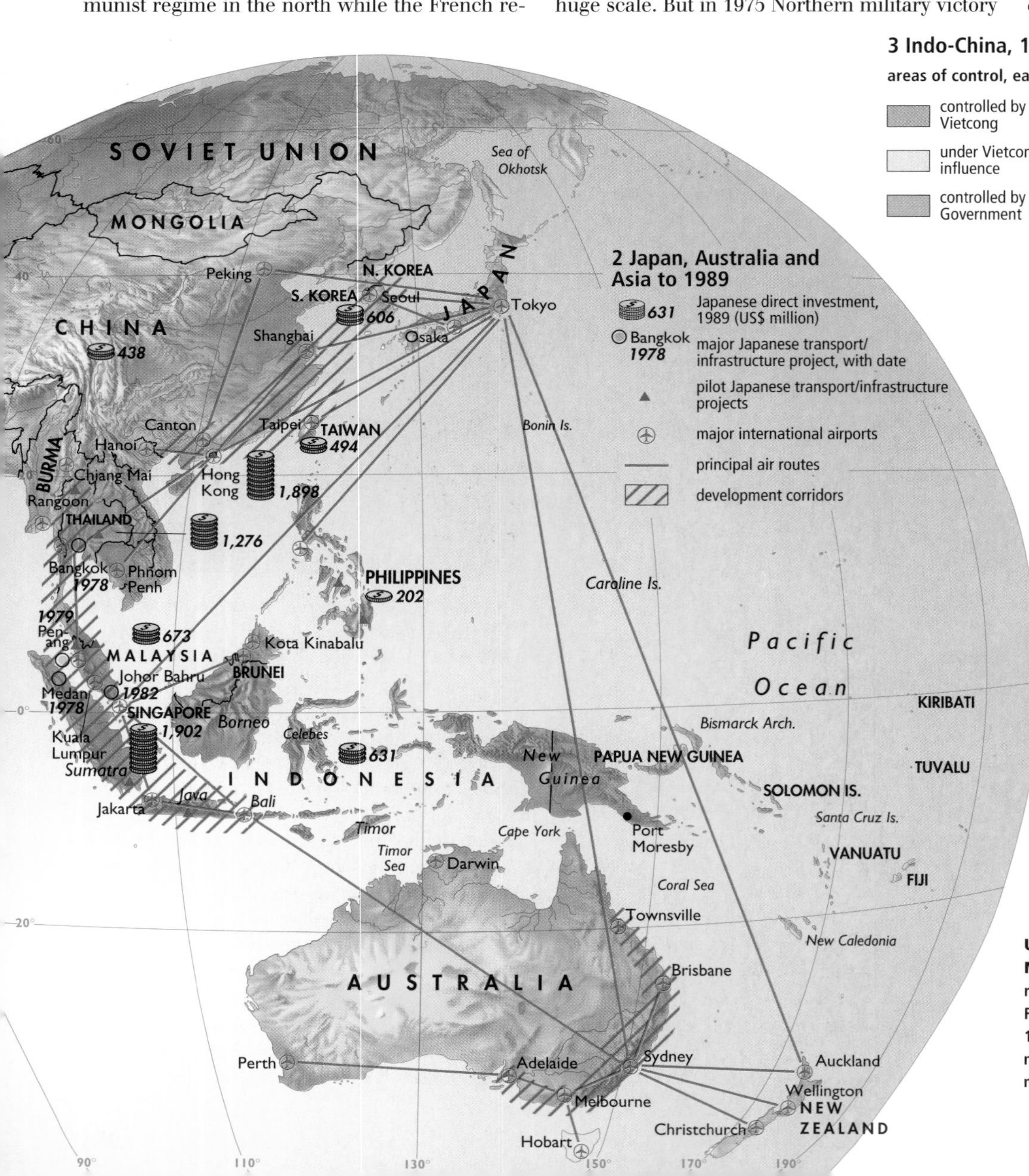

2 Much of southeast Asia's economic miracle was based on Japanese investment and help given to the industrializing countries of the Pacific. Japanese planners designated development corridors *(map left)* where investment was concentrated and communications developed.

US transport helicopters in the Mekong delta *(right)*. US forces reached a peak of 542,000 by February 1969, but by the end of 1972, shortly before the ceasefire negotiated by Henry Kissinger, their number had fallen to 25,000.

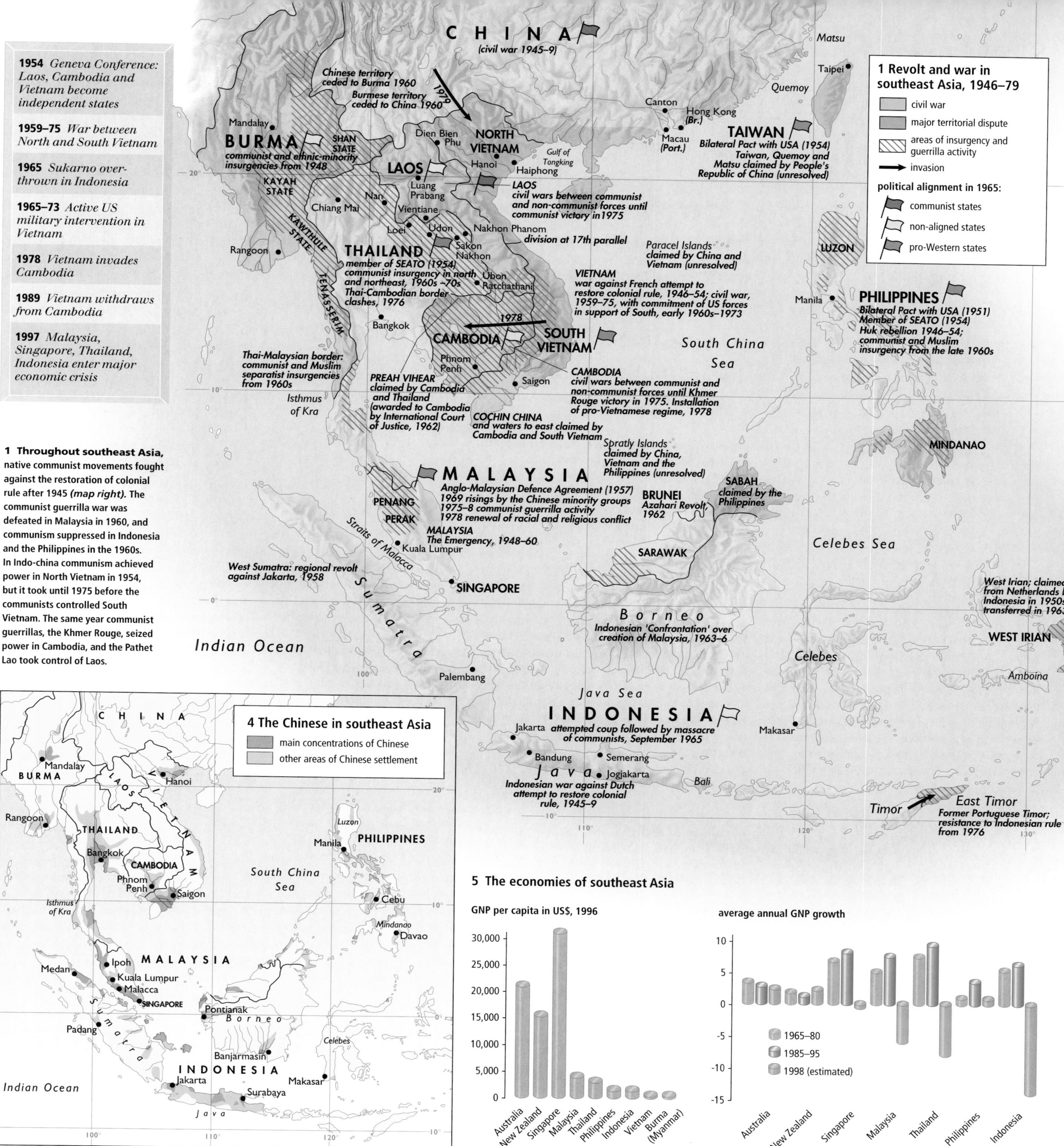

1954 *Geneva Conference: Laos, Cambodia and Vietnam become independent states*

1959–75 *War between North and South Vietnam*

1965 *Sukarno overthrown in Indonesia*

1965–73 *Active US military intervention in Vietnam*

1978 *Vietnam invades Cambodia*

1989 *Vietnam withdraws from Cambodia*

1997 *Malaysia, Singapore, Thailand, Indonesia enter major economic crisis*

1 Throughout southeast Asia, native communist movements fought against the restoration of colonial rule after 1945 *(map right)*. The communist guerrilla war was defeated in Malaysia in 1960, and communism suppressed in Indonesia and the Philippines in the 1960s. In Indo-china communism achieved power in North Vietnam in 1954, but it took until 1975 before the communists controlled South Vietnam. The same year communist guerrillas, the Khmer Rouge, seized power in Cambodia, and the Pathet Lao took control of Laos.

4 Many Chinese emigrated because of civil war or economic difficulties. The demand from European entrepreneurs for cheap labour also drew many Chinese abroad. By the 1980s there were over 20 million overseas Chinese, many of them in southeast Asia *(map above)*.The largest number was in Thailand, some 6 million, with over 4 million in Malaysia, and more than 3 million in Indonesia. Although contributing greatly to the dynamism of the economies where they settled, they often suffered political discrimination. At the time of the Sukarno's overthrow in 1965 in Indonesia, thousands were massacred. Anti-Chinese riots were also a feature of the disorder in 1998.

5 Economic growth in southeast Asia was exceptionally high from 1965–95 *(charts above)*. GNP per capita in Singapore exceeded many western countries. A financial crisis in 1997 began with a devaluation of the Thai baht, and led to a general economic crisis; Malaysian and Indonesia GDP had slumped by mid-1998. The economic turmoil spilled over into politics as the Suharto regime in Indonesia collapsed.

united the two Vietnams. Economic reconstruction after three decades of war was hampered by Vietnam's military intervention in Cambodia from 1978 and by its ostracism by the Western world. In 1989, however, the Vietnamese withdrew from Cambodia, the economy was liberalized and inward investment encouraged. By 1995 the economy was growing at over 8 per cent a year.

Political instability and ideological rigidity had damaging economic consequences in other parts of southeast Asia. In Burma, beset by one-party and military rule and strife between the Burmese and smaller ethnic groups, economic growth has been poor. In the Philippines, the economy was brought low by the 1980s by the corrupt Marcos regime, the opposition to it and the insecurity of the subsequent Aquino government. In Indonesia, Sukarno's politics of guided democracy, nationalization of Dutch businesses and campaigns for Indonesian sovereignty in West Irian and against the Malaysian Federation, led to economic chaos and his overthrow in 1965.

The 'tiger economies'

These histories of economic instability contrast with the rates of growth achieved by Malaysia, Singapore, Thailand and even Indonesia from the late 1960s. Each achieved an annual growth rate well in excess of 5 per cent, and created a substantial industrial base oriented towards exports. Many factors contributed to success: cheap labour; favourable labour legislation; tax incentives for investors; major infrastuctural development; and political stability. Growth was so rapid that the countries were dubbed the Asian 'tigers'.

All these economies suffered in the economic turmoil which hit east Asia in 1997, when a currency crisis was transformed into a general crisis of confidence in the Asian economic model. The Thai economy was seriously affected, while Indonesia was badly hit by a 75 per cent devaluation of the rupiah again exacerbated by a major political crisis, as the 33-year-old Suharto regime finally collapsed under the weight of nationwide protests.

Since 1947

South Asia: independence and conflict

See also

India under British rule, 1805–1935 p. 234
Imperialism and nationalism, 1919–1941 p. 258
The Cold War, 1945–91 p. 274
Retreat from empire since 1939 p. 276
Southeast Asia since 1945 p. 282
The world in the 1990s p. 302

> ALL OVER ASIA WE ARE PASSING THROUGH TRIALS AND TRIBULATIONS. IN INDIA ALSO YOU WILL SEE CONFLICT AND TROUBLE. LET US NOT BE DISHEARTENED BY THIS; THIS IS INEVITABLE IN AN AGE OF MIGHTY TRANSITION. THERE ARE A NEW VITALITY AND CREATIVE IMPULSES IN THE PEOPLES OF ASIA ... LET US HAVE FAITH IN THESE GREAT NEW FORCES AND THE DREAM WHICH IS TAKING SHAPE. LET US, ABOVE ALL, HAVE FAITH IN THE HUMAN SPIRIT WHICH ASIA HAS SYMBOLIZED FOR THESE LONG AGES PAST.
>
> **Jawaharlal Nehru, 1947**

After achieving independence from Britain in the late 1940s the states of south Asia found their politics cursed by religious, linguistic and ethnic conflicts. Their economic progress has been restricted by population growth, and the consolidation of parliamentary democracy – in Pakistan, Bangladesh and Burma – jeopardized by military intervention.

1947 *India and Pakistan independent*

1948 *Mohendas Gandhi assassinated*

1962 *China invades northern India*

1965 *War between India and Pakistan*

1971 *War between India and Pakistan leads to the creation of Bangladesh*

1977 *Military coup ends civilian rule in Pakistan (till 1988)*

1979 *USSR occupies Afghanistan (till 1989)*

1983 *Tamil revolt in Sri Lanka*

1984 *Sikhs assassinate Indira Gandhi*

1990 *Free elections in Burma; results annulled by military dictatorship*

1992 *Hindu zealots demolish Babur's mosque at Ayodhya*

1998 *India and Pakistan test nuclear devices*

INDEPENDENCE FROM BRITISH rule came to India and Pakistan in August 1947, to Burma in January 1948 and to Ceylon in February 1948.

The process was fraught with difficulty for India and Pakistan. The only basis on which the nationalists were able to agree to the transfer of power was to partition British India along religious lines. This included the break-up of the provinces of Punjab in the west and Bengal in the east (*see* maps 1 & 2). Also, massive numbers of Hindus and Muslims found themselves on the wrong sides of the new borders and, against a background of religious slaughter in which 500,000 were killed, as many as 15 million began the trek from one new state to the other. Resettlement of the refugees was a major burden and tensions between resident and immigrant communities still persist. In India, the new state also had to define the role of the 600 princely states, which had survived under British rule. Most joined either India or Pakistan but the Muslim-ruled state of Hyderabad had to be forcibly absorbed into India in 1948. In Kashmir, which was predominantly Muslim but ruled by Hindus, the two new states fought a war from October 1947 to January 1949, when the UN imposed a ceasefire and divided the area between India and Pakistan. The solution satisfied neither side and, following attempts by Pakistan to infiltrate troops into the Indian-held regions, war broke out again in 1965. Though a peace settlement was agreed, Kashmir remains part of the unfinished business of partition.

Ethnic conflict

All the states of South Asia have been troubled by demands from religious, ethnic and linguistic groups (*see* map 3). In India many early conflicts were over language (even after prime minister Jawaharlal Nehru agreed reluctantly in 1956 to reorganize state boundaries along linguistic lines) and ethnicity as, for instance, tribal groups in the northeast sought statehood or independence. By the 1970s serious religious conflicts began to emerge: there was the Sikh demand for a separate state, Khalistan, and their assassination of the prime minister, Indira Gandhi, in 1984; the rise of Hindu nationalism; the contestation of religious sites between Hindus and Muslims; and great insecurity among the Muslim minority in India.

In Pakistan this trend has been illustrated by ethnic strife between *muhajir* refugees from India and the local population in Sind and sectarian strife between Sunni Muslims and the Shia Muslim minority. Most important, however, was the political and economic subordination of East Pakistan by West Pakistan, which led to the emergence of Bengali nationalism and the creation, with Indian military assistance, of Bangladesh in 1971.

In Ceylon, there was little friction until 1972 when a new constitution named the country Sri Lanka and institutionalized the pursuit of a Buddhist- and Sinhala-only state. The Tamil minority who made up 15 per cent of the island's population, began to demand a separate state, Eelam. From 1983 to the 1990s the Tamils fought the Sri Lankan army for control of the northeast of the island (*see* map 4), a violent situation hardly helped by the intervention of an Indian peacekeeping force between 1987–90. In 1991 the Tamil Tigers assassinated the ex-prime minister of India, Rajiv Gandhi. Two years later, they also murdered Sri Lankan president Ranasinghe. In spite of extensive emigration among the Tamil population and the overrunning of the stronghold of Jaffna by government forces in early 1996, Tamil resistance to the Buddhist majority has continued and even pushed the Sinhalese government towards a version of federalism for the island.

Ethnic tension has also persisted in Burma where minority groups such as the Karens and Shans have struggled for self-determination against the Burmese majority. Here, as elsewhere in the region, ethnic and political conflict have become intertwined.

Military government

Though all the states of south Asia were launched into independence as democracies, Pakistan, Bangladesh and Burma have all endured periods of military intervention. Military rule has been most frequent in Burma where, despite a promise in 1990 of free multi-party elections to end 30 years of increasingly repressive communist rule, the military's grip on power continues unabated.

That said, despite widespread poverty and inequality, communism has otherwise generally been conspicuous by its absence in the region. But other notable political features have been: the death of many leaders by assassination; the Islamization of politics from the late 1970s in Pakistan and, to a lesser extent, Bangladesh; the decline of the Congress party in India and the rise of the Hindu nationalist BJP to challenge the secular basis of the Indian state; and simultaneously, and somewhat paradoxically, the rise of India's lower castes to positions of political leadership.

The rise of militant religious movements has not affected the trend in the 1990s in both India and Pakistan towards economic liberalization after decades in which nationalization and central planning have held sway. But throughout this period unrelenting population growth has held back economic development. Though the green revolution of the 1960s saw south Asia become self-sufficient in food grains, even able to export them, at the same time large proportions of the populations, except in Sri Lanka, live below the poverty line.

During the Cold War non-alignment was a feature of the external relations of south Asian states. The Chinese invasion of 1962 showed India the limitations of this policy. For most of the remainder of the Cold War India tilted towards the Soviet Union and Pakistan to the USA.

Soviet invasion

With the Soviet invasion of Afghanistan in 1979, the region reluctantly found itself in the frontline of the Cold War, with Pakistan a channel of assistance to the Afghan resistance. As US armaments poured into Pakistan to be transported to the Afghan rebels fighting the heavily armed, 100,000-strong Soviet forces, the region became awash with sophisticated weaponry. Huge numbers of refugees, combined with large-scale heroin-growing and processing, exacerbated the problems. Although south Asia was again freed from external occupation when the Soviet forces left Afghanistan in 1989, it was only to be replaced, once the rebels gained power in 1992, by bitter fighting between moderates and Islamic fundamentalists.

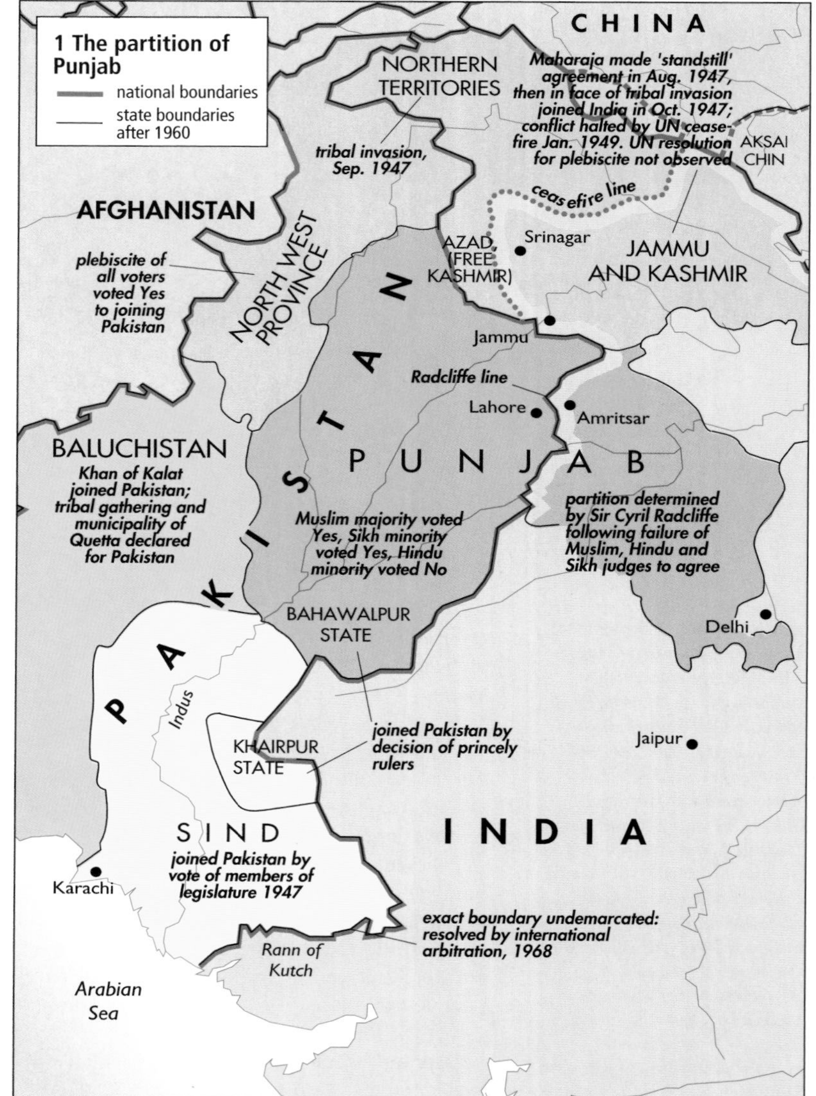

1 The partition of Punjab
national boundaries
state boundaries after 1960
CHINA
NORTHERN TERRITORIES
Maharaja made 'standstill' agreement in Aug. 1947, then in face of tribal invasion joined India in Oct. 1947; conflict halted by UN cease-fire Jan. 1949. UN resolution for plebiscite not observed
AKSAI CHIN
tribal invasion, Sep. 1947
ceasefire line
AFGHANISTAN
NORTH WEST PROVINCE
plebiscite of all voters voted Yes to joining Pakistan
AZAD (FREE KASHMIR)
Srinagar
JAMMU AND KASHMIR
Jammu
Radcliffe line
Lahore
Amritsar
BALUCHISTAN
Khan of Kalat joined Pakistan; tribal gathering and municipality of Quetta declared for Pakistan
PUNJAB
Muslim majority voted Yes, Sikh minority voted Yes, Hindu minority voted No
partition determined by Sir Cyril Radcliffe following failure of Muslim, Hindu and Sikh judges to agree
PAKISTAN
BAHAWALPUR STATE
Delhi
Indus
KHAIRPUR STATE
joined Pakistan by decision of princely rulers
Jaipur
SIND
joined Pakistan by vote of members of legislature 1947
INDIA
Karachi
exact boundary undemarcated: resolved by international arbitration, 1968
Rann of Kutch
Arabian Sea

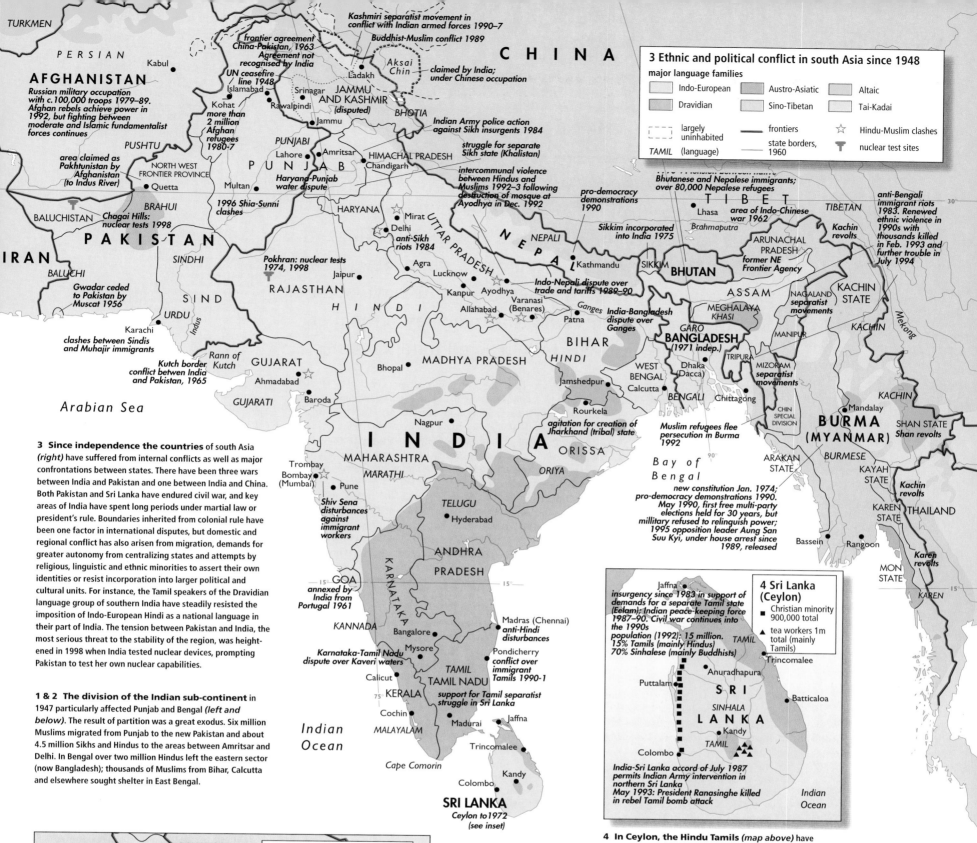

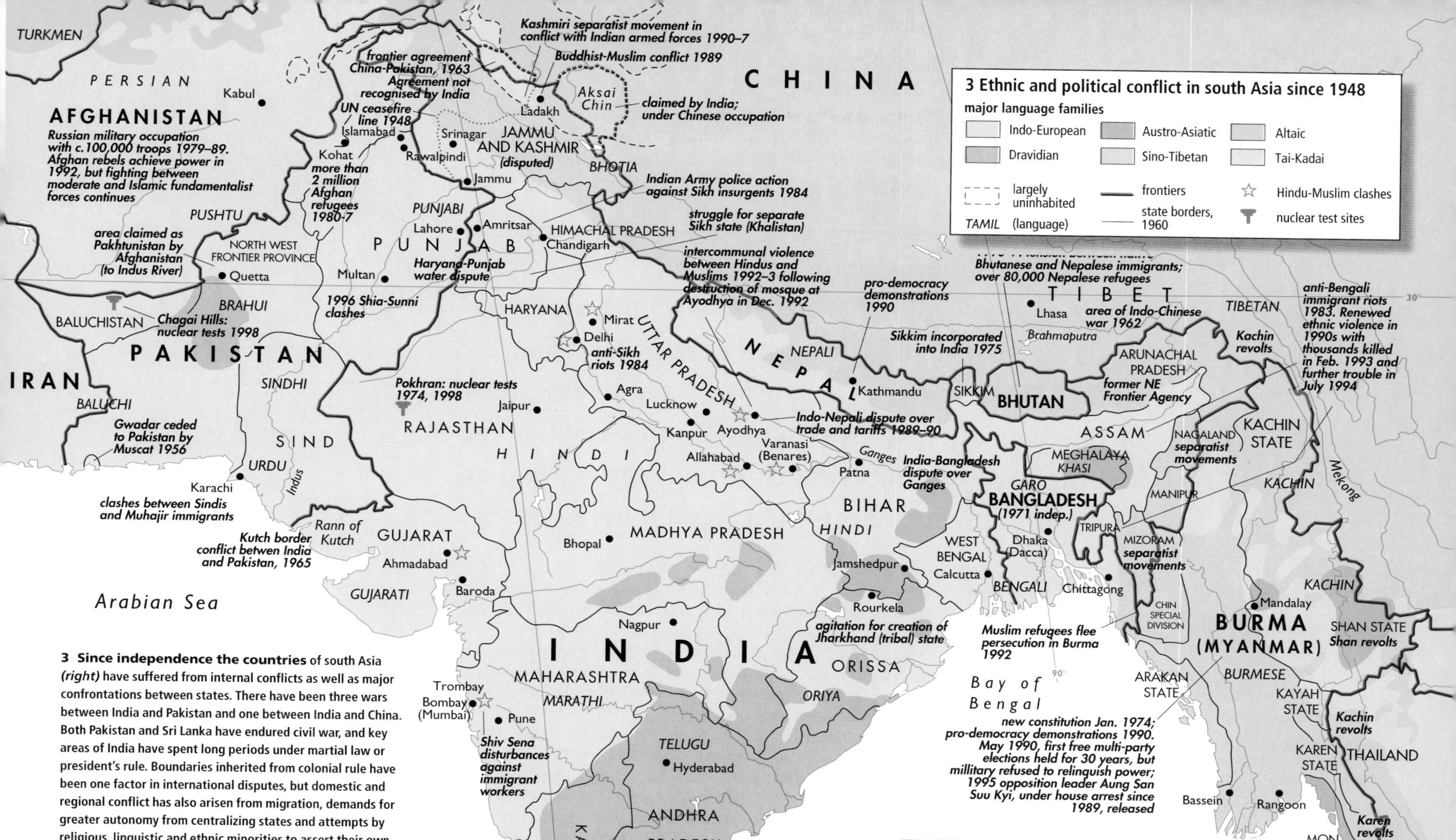

3 Ethnic and political conflict in south Asia since 1948
major language families
Indo-European
Austro-Asiatic
Altaic
Dravidian
Sino-Tibetan
Tai-Kadai
largely uninhabited
frontiers
Hindu-Muslim clashes
state borders, 1960
nuclear test sites
TAMIL (language)
TURKMEN
PERSIAN
Kabul
AFGHANISTAN
Russian military occupation with c.100,000 troops 1979–89. Afghan rebels achieve power in 1992, but fighting between moderate and Islamic fundamentalist forces continues
Kashmiri separatist movement in conflict with Indian armed forces 1990–7
Buddhist-Muslim conflict 1989
frontier agreement China-Pakistan, 1963
Agreement not recognised by India
UN ceasefire line 1948
Ladakh
Aksai Chin
claimed by India; under Chinese occupation
CHINA
Islamabad
Srinagar
JAMMU AND KASHMIR (disputed)
Rawalpindi
Kohat
more than 2 million Afghan refugees 1980–7
BHOTIA
Jammu
Indian Army police action against Sikh insurgents 1984
PUSHTU
PUNJABI
Amritsar
struggle for separate Sikh state (Khalistan)
area claimed as Pakhtunistan by Afghanistan (to Indus River)
NORTH WEST FRONTIER PROVINCE
Lahore
PUNJAB
HIMACHAL PRADESH
Chandigarh
Quetta
Multan
Haryana-Punjab water dispute
intercommunal violence between Hindus and Muslims 1992–3 following destruction of mosque at Ayodhya in Dec. 1992
Bhutanese and Nepalese immigrants; over 80,000 Nepalese refugees
BRAHUI
1996 Shia-Sunni clashes
HARYANA
pro-democracy demonstrations 1990
TIBET
Lhasa
area of Indo-Chinese war 1962
TIBETAN
anti-Bengali immigrant riots 1983. Renewed ethnic violence in 1990s with thousands killed in Feb. 1993 and further trouble in July 1994
BALUCHISTAN
Chagai Hills: nuclear tests 1998
Mirat
Delhi
anti-Sikh riots 1984
UTTAR PRADESH
NEPAL
NEPALI
Sikkim incorporated into India 1975
Brahmaputra
Kachin revolts
PAKISTAN
IRAN
SINDHI
Pokhran: nuclear tests 1974, 1998
Agra
Kathmandu
SIKKIM
BHUTAN
ARUNACHAL PRADESH
former NE Frontier Agency
BALUCHI
Jaipur
Lucknow
Indo-Nepali dispute over trade and tariffs 1989–90
Gwadar ceded to Pakistan by Muscat 1956
SIND
RAJASTHAN
Kanpur
Ayodhya
Varanasi (Benares)
ASSAM
NAGALAND separatist movements
KACHIN STATE
URDU
HINDI
Allahabad
Ganges
Patna
India-Bangladesh dispute over Ganges
MEGHALAYA
KHASI
GARO
KACHIN
Karachi
Indus
BIHAR
BANGLADESH (1971 indep.)
MANIPUR
Mekong
clashes between Sindis and Muhajir immigrants
Rann of Kutch
Kutch border conflict between India and Pakistan, 1965
GUJARAT
Ahmadabad
Bhopal
MADHYA PRADESH
HINDI
WEST BENGAL
Dhaka (Dacca)
TRIPURA
MIZORAM separatist movements
Jamshedpur
Calcutta
BENGALI
Chittagong
KACHIN
Baroda
GUJARATI
Arabian Sea
Rourkela
Mandalay
agitation for creation of Jharkhand (tribal) state
CHIN SPECIAL DIVISION
Muslim refugees flee persecution in Burma 1992
BURMA (MYANMAR)
SHAN STATE
Shan revolts
Nagpur
INDIA
ORISSA
Bay of Bengal
ARAKAN STATE
BURMESE
MAHARASHTRA
Trombay
Bombay (Mumbai)
MARATHI
ORIYA
KAYAH STATE
Pune
Kachin revolts
new constitution Jan. 1974; pro-democracy demonstrations 1990. May 1990, first free multi-party elections held for 30 years, but military refused to relinquish power; 1995 opposition leader Aung San Suu Kyi, under house arrest since 1989, released
Shiv Sena disturbances against immigrant workers
TELUGU
Hyderabad
KAREN STATE
THAILAND
Bassein
Rangoon
ANDHRA PRADESH
Karen revolts
MON STATE
GOA
annexed by India from Portugal 1961
KARNATAKA
KAREN
KANNADA
Madras (Chennai)
anti-Hindi disturbances
Bangalore
Mysore
Pondicherry
conflict over immigrant Tamils 1990-1
Karnataka-Tamil Nadu dispute over Kaveri waters
TAMIL
TAMIL NADU
Calicut
KERALA
support for Tamil separatist struggle in Sri Lanka
Cochin
Madurai
Jaffna
Indian Ocean
MALAYALAM
Trincomalee
Cape Comorin
Kandy
Colombo
SRI LANKA
Ceylon to 1972 (see inset)

3 Since independence the countries of south Asia *(right)* have suffered from internal conflicts as well as major confrontations between states. There have been three wars between India and Pakistan and one between India and China. Both Pakistan and Sri Lanka have endured civil war, and key areas of India have spent long periods under martial law or president's rule. Boundaries inherited from colonial rule have been one factor in international disputes, but domestic and regional conflict has also arisen from migration, demands for greater autonomy from centralizing states and attempts by religious, linguistic and ethnic minorities to assert their own identities or resist incorporation into larger political and cultural units. For instance, the Tamil speakers of the Dravidian language group of southern India have steadily resisted the imposition of Indo-European Hindi as a national language in their part of India. The tension between Pakistan and India, the most serious threat to the stability of the region, was heightened in 1998 when India tested nuclear devices, prompting Pakistan to test her own nuclear capabilities.

1 & 2 The division of the Indian sub-continent in 1947 particularly affected Punjab and Bengal *(left and below)*. The result of partition was a great exodus. Six million Muslims migrated from Punjab to the new Pakistan and about 4.5 million Sikhs and Hindus to the areas between Amritsar and Delhi. In Bengal over two million Hindus left the eastern sector (now Bangladesh); thousands of Muslims from Bihar, Calcutta and elsewhere sought shelter in East Bengal.

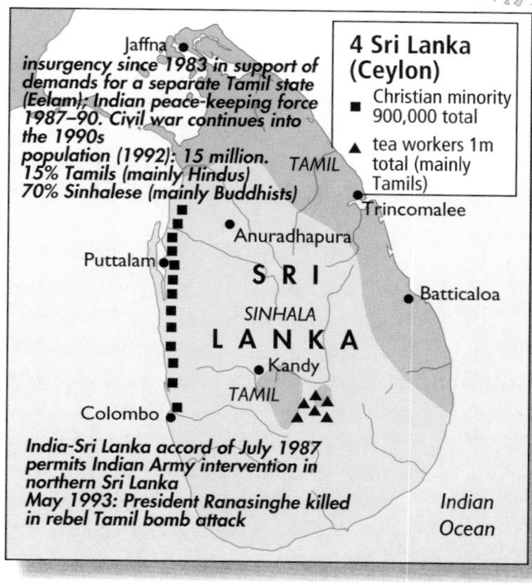

4 Sri Lanka (Ceylon)
Christian minority 900,000 total
tea workers 1m total (mainly Tamils)
Jaffna
insurgency since 1983 in support of demands for a separate Tamil state (Eelam); Indian peace-keeping force 1987–90. Civil war continues into the 1990s
population (1992): 15 million. 15% Tamils (mainly Hindus) 70% Sinhalese (mainly Buddhists)
TAMIL
Trincomalee
Anuradhapura
Puttalam
SRI LANKA
SINHALA
Batticaloa
Kandy
TAMIL
Colombo
India-Sri Lanka accord of July 1987 permits Indian Army intervention in northern Sri Lanka
May 1993: President Ranasinghe killed in rebel Tamil bomb attack
Indian Ocean

4 In Ceylon, the Hindu Tamils *(map above)* have resisted pressures, institutionalized in the new Sri Lankan Constitution of 1972, from the Sinhalese Buddhist majority. Tamil leaders demanded a separate state in a loose federation and after 1983 guerrilla activity by the Tamil Tigers and other militants precipitated a full-scale clash with the Sri Lankan army, with civilian massacres on both sides. Sinhala-Tamil tensions increased dramatically after 1985 and the Indian army intervened in 1987 to try to reimpose order.

2 The partition of Bengal
national boundaries
state boundaries after 1960
NEPAL
BHUTAN
COOCH BEHAR
BIHAR
Rangpur
Maharaja joined India. Separate state of Indian Union
ASSAM
to India subject to Sylhet plebiscite
Brahmaputra
Radcliffe line August 1947
Mymensingh
SYLHET
voted to join Pakistan by plebiscite
EAST PAKISTAN
Rajshahi
INDIA
East Bengal to Pakistan, Aug. 1947. Renamed East Pakistan, 1953. Independent as Bangladesh, 1971
TRIPURA
Maharaja joined India
WEST BENGAL
to India, Aug. 1947
Dacca
Comilla
BENGAL
Ganges
EAST BENGAL
Radcliffe line August 1947
Calcutta
Barisal
Chittagong
ORISSA
Mouths of the Ganges
BURMA
Bay of Bengal

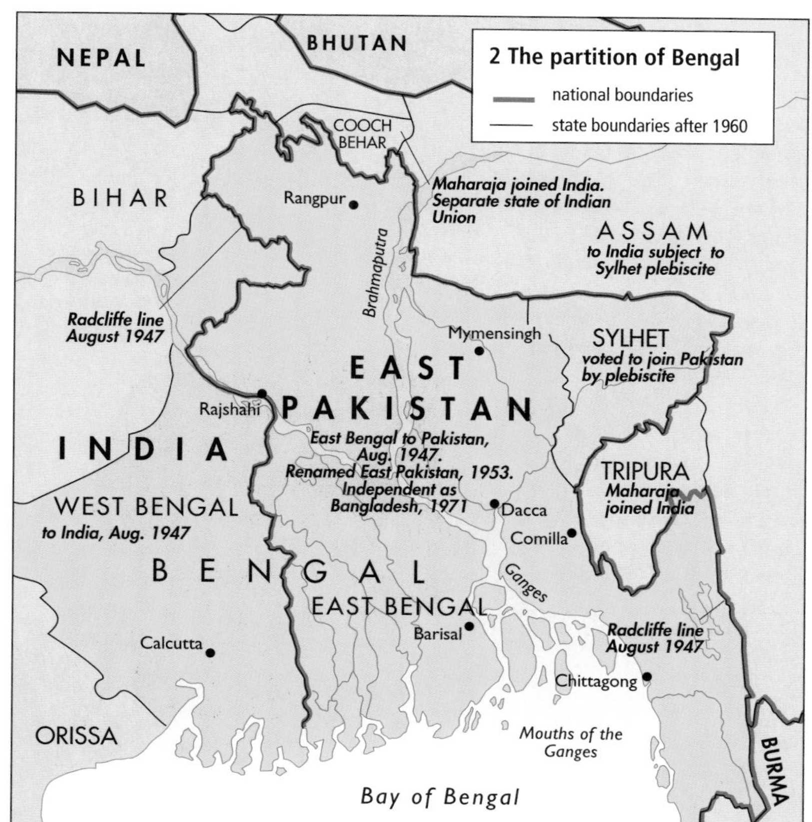

The Golden Temple, Amritsar *(right)*. The principal place of worship in the Sikh faith, the temple was begun by Arjan, the fifth Sikh guru, in 1589. It subsequently became a symbol of Sikh political as well as religious aspirations and in June 1984 was the scene of a five-day gun battle between the Indian Army and Sikh extremists. The severely damaged temple complex was later restored.

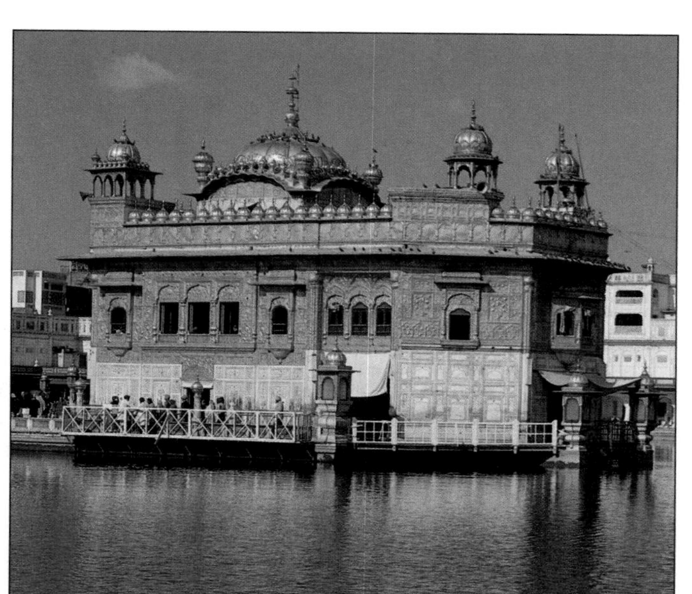

Since 1957

Africa after emancipation

See also

The partition of Africa, 1880–1913 p. 240
The anti-colonial reaction, 1881–1917 p. 246
Imperialism and nationalism, 1919–1941 p. 258
Retreat from empire since 1939 p. 276
Nationalism, secularism and Islam in the Middle East since 1945 p. 290
The world in the 1990s p. 302

1957 *Kwame Nkrumah leads the first black sub-Saharan African country, Ghana, to independence*

1960 *Sharpeville massacre and banning of African nationalist parties in South Africa*

1963 *Nationalist uprising against Portuguese rule in Angola*

1963 *Charter of Organization of African Unity signed, recognizing existing frontiers*

1965 *White settler regime in Rhodesia declares independence – UDI*

1967–70 *Civil war in Nigeria with secessionist Biafra*

1974 *Military coup in Lisbon ends Portuguese rule in Africa*

1986 *Soweto uprising by students in townships of South Africa*

1994 *South Africa's multi-racial elections won by ANC*

Africa's development since the ending of European colonial control has been anything but smooth. Poverty, corruption and ethnic rivalry have dogged parts of the continent, while wars, repressive one-party governments, disease and famine have meant that the lives of many Africans today are a mockery of the optimistic goals that greeted independence.

BY 1975 MOST AFRICAN STATES were independent of European colonial control. The process of transfer was mainly peaceful, although there were major wars in Algeria and in the Portuguese colonies (Angola and Mozambique).

At independence Africa inherited weak economies and fragile political systems. After 1957, population and urbanization grew rapidly. Increased pressure on land caused ecological problems which, at times of serious drought, as in the Sahelian region in 1972–3 and in the early 1980s, accelerated poverty. Epidemic disease was widespread including, since the 1980s, AIDS over much of east and central Africa. As poor economies, African states have low levels of capital accumulation, small markets, inadequate public utilities and limited welfare services. Corruption is often rampant. Many educated people have left the continent and within Africa the gulf between the rich and poor has widened.

Ethnic and political conflict

African states are politically fragile. Ethnic, religious and political rivalries have resulted in secessionist and civil wars; the most serious have occurred in the southern Sudan, between Nigeria and Biafra (1967–70) and in Ethiopia. Following a long war, Eritrea became effectively independent from Ethiopia in 1991. There are many other unresolved conflicts, for example that between Morocco and Western Sahara. In Rwanda, violence and massacres accompanied the long-standing ethnic rivalry between the Hutu majority and the Tutsi minority. In the genocidal war of 1994, 800,000 people, mainly Tutsi, were murdered, and two million fled the country. In civil wars in Somalia, Uganda, Liberia and Sierra Leone, alienated young men with guns continue to threaten social order. Africa has more refugees than any other continent, most the result of war and economic disorder.

At the same time sub-Saharan Africa has seen a rapid growth in Christianity and Islam. Large parts of east, cental and west Africa have become Protestant heartlands. Religious fervour has also led to tension, particularly in Nigeria where ethnic and political differences meet along the religious fault line dividing Christianity and Islam.

Economic failure

Early attempts at economic development were largely undertaken by the state, but with limited success. Governments' economic ambitions often exceeded their administrative capacities. Even plans which emphasized rural development, such as Tanzania's 'Ujamaa' policies, introduced in 1967, were largely failures. Several countries adopted political and economic policies patterned on those of communist countries, in particular the Marxist Ethiopian regimes from 1975–91.

African states remained heavily reliant on the export of primary products, but consumers rather than producers determined the world prices. African countries were weak players in a global economy largely dominated by Western capitalist powers, and on whom they were dependent for capital and markets. Foreign loans and global inflation led to increased indebtedness, so that the annual income of some countries amounted to less than the cost of servicing their debt.

Thus, since independence Africa has been vulnerable to foreign intervention. This happened during the Cold War, when West and East sought allies in strategic areas of Africa, particularly the extreme east of the continent. The collapse of the Soviet Union in 1991 made Africa less significant in global geopolitical terms. By the late 1980s, the World Bank and the International Monetary Fund, in pursuit of African debts, began to impose conditions upon African states through Structural Adjustment Programmes. African states were forced to adopt capitalist economic strategies, abandon single-party rule and embrace electoral politics. This new wave of 'democratization' brought many changes of government throughout the sub-Saharan continent.

2 South Africa's defensive 'total strategy' in the 1980s sought to destablize her northern neighbours by intervention in Angola and Mozambique's civil wars *(map below)*. Cuban troops aided the MPLA government in Angola and reached a stalemate with South African forces at Cuito Cuanavale. Unrest within South Africa, and increasing US financial pressure, helped bring about the end of the apartheid regime.

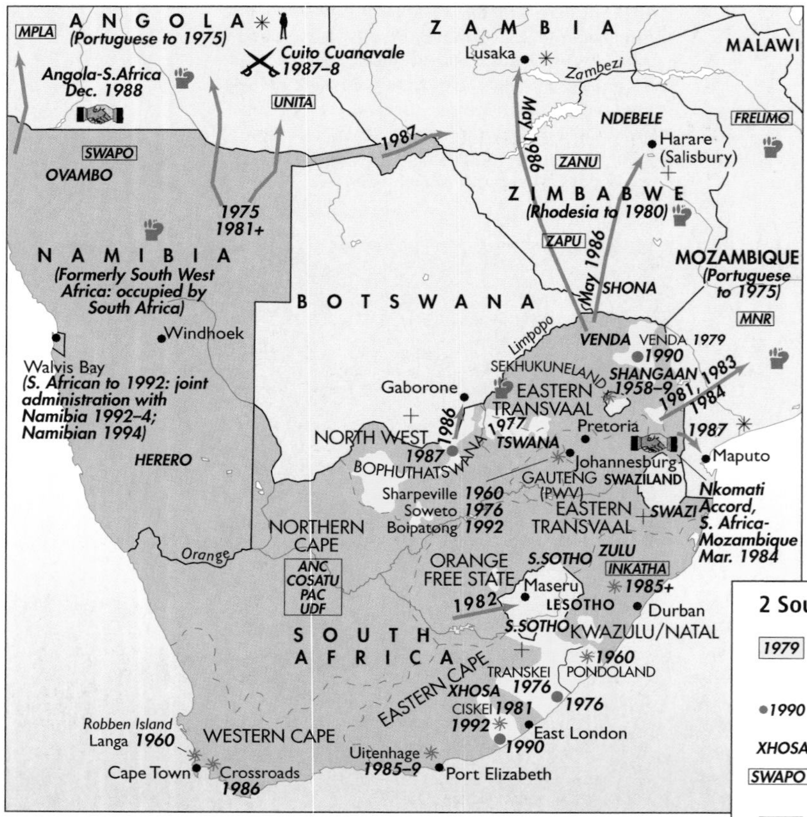

2 Southern Africa

1979	African homeland ('bantustan'), with date of 'independence'
•1990	army coups in bantustans, with date
XHOSA	major ethnic group
SWAPO	African nationalist parties
	Southern Africa Development Coordination Conference states
	ANC bases
	ANC offices
1986	South African Defence Force attacks, with date
	agreements
	guerrilla campaigns
	Cuban troops
	violent clashes, with dates
	South African provinces 1994

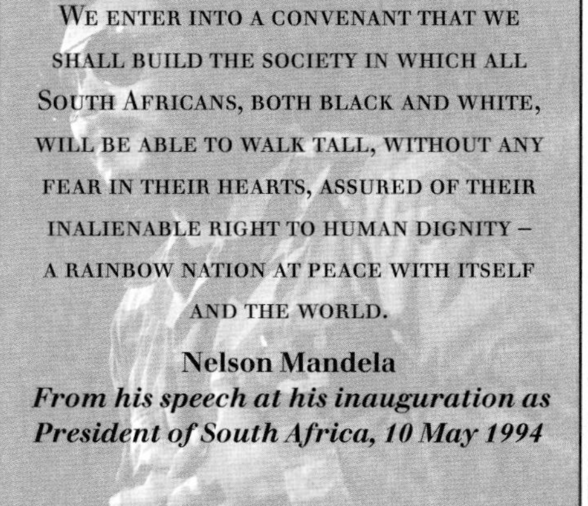

WE ENTER INTO A CONVENANT THAT WE SHALL BUILD THE SOCIETY IN WHICH ALL SOUTH AFRICANS, BOTH BLACK AND WHITE, WILL BE ABLE TO WALK TALL, WITHOUT ANY FEAR IN THEIR HEARTS, ASSURED OF THEIR INALIENABLE RIGHT TO HUMAN DIGNITY – A RAINBOW NATION AT PEACE WITH ITSELF AND THE WORLD.

Nelson Mandela
From his speech at his inauguration as President of South Africa, 10 May 1994

In two military coups, Fl. Lt. Jerry Rawlings *(below)* seized power in Ghana in 1979 but, in a pattern replicated across Africa, he later succeeded in being elected president. The initial radical policies of his PNDC regime were curtailed in the 1990s by pressure from the International Monetary Fund.

1 Independence and its aftermath

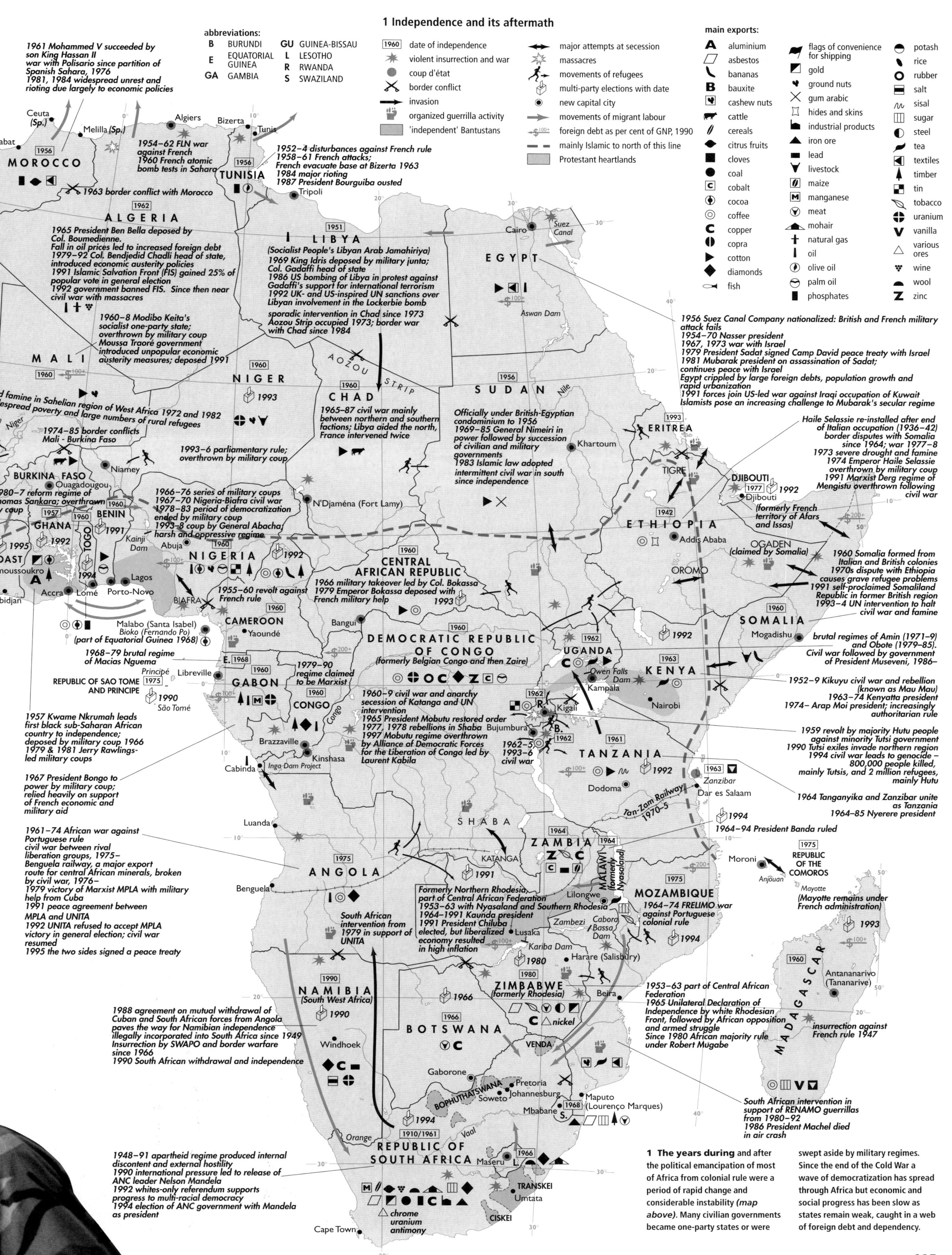

1 The years during and after the political emancipation of most of Africa from colonial rule were a period of rapid change and considerable instability *(map above)*. Many civilian governments became one-party states or were swept aside by military regimes. Since the end of the Cold War a wave of democratization has spread through Africa but economic and social progress has been slow as states remain weak, caught in a web of foreign debt and dependency.

Since 1947

Palestine, Zionism and the Arab-Israeli conflict

See also
The disintegration of the Ottoman empire, 1800–1923 p. 228
The First World War, 1914–18 p. 250
Imperialism and nationalism, 1919–41 p. 258
Retreat from empire since 1939 p. 276
Nationalism, secularism and Islam in the Middle East since 1945 p. 290
The world in the 1990s p. 302

The Arab-Israeli conflict has proved among the most intractable of the 20th century. Given tragic urgency by Hitler's mass extermination of the Jews, in 1948 the Zionist movement created a vibrant new state in the Middle East. While the Jews saw this as their rightful homeland, the Arabs of the region saw it as their land, taken from them and sustained by force.

THE RISE OF ZIONISM was part of the general movement of ethnic and linguistic nationalism in the 19th century. In the case of the Jews, the idea was particularly audacious: they were widely dispersed; they did not speak the same language; in conventional terms they were not even a people. But at the first Zionist Congress in 1896 it was nonetheless agreed that a Jewish homeland should be created. It was subsequently agreed that this should be in Palestine, or biblical Israel, then within the Ottoman empire (*see* p. 228).

With the collapse of Ottoman rule at the end of the First World War, Palestine became a British mandated territory under the League of Nations. The Arab population of Palestine, encouraged by British promises to further Arab aspirations, sought independence. At the same time, however, in the Balfour Declaration of 1917 Britain had committed itself to creating a Jewish homeland in Palestine. Throughout the 1920s and 1930s, Britain found itself caught between the conflicting, sometimes violent, demands of Arabs and Jews.

The State of Israel

Reviled by both sides, Britain turned the problem over to the United Nations. In November 1947, it divided Palestine into separate Jewish and Arab states. The following May Britain withdrew and the State of Israel was proclaimed. It was immediately invaded by Arab armies. After fierce fighting, a ceasefire was agreed early in 1949. It left an uneasy truce. Israel had beaten off the Arab forces, though had failed to take East Jerusalem. As important, up to 750,000 Palestinians had become refugees, crowded into the Gaza Strip and the West Bank, and the Arab state of Palestine had disappeared.

For over a hundred years, we have fought over the same strip of land: the country in which we, the sons of Abraham, have been fated to live together. Both peoples, Arabs and Israelis, have known suffering, pain and bereavement. Now the fanfares and festivals are over. Now the flags have been folded, the trumpets silenced, the stages dismantled – now the more difficult, more dangerous part has come. For a century of hatred does not dissolve suddenly with a handshake in Washington. All the bloodshed cannot be covered by the beating of drums. Peace will be built slowly, day by day, step by step, by people.

Yitzhak Rabin
Acceptance speech for the UNESCO Peace Prize, July 1994

The hostility which followed became a prime cause of instability within the Middle East as well as a major focus of Cold War rivalry. To Egypt, Syria and Iraq, buttressed by the Soviet Union, Israel represented not only an affront to Arab nationalism but, with its support from the United States, an extension of American imperialism in the region. Three further full-scale Arab-Israeli wars broke out after 1949: in 1956, over Suez, when Israel inflicted a humiliating defeat on Egypt; in 1967, when in the face of renewed Arab hostility Israel achieved a crushing pre-emptive strike against Egypt and then routed Jordanian, Syrian and Iraqi forces; and in 1973, when a combined Egyptian-Syrian attack was repulsed by Israel after days of desperate fighting. In all three cases, not only did Israel extend its territorial domination, occupying the West Bank, Sinai and the Golan Heights, but huge numbers of new Palestinian refugees were created in Jordan and Lebanon, increasing the Palestinian sense of injustice and giving rise to militant Arab movements dedicated to winning back the lost territories. In 1967, the Palestine Liberation

1948 *Establishment of State of Israel; first Arab-Israeli war*

1956 *Suez crisis; second Arab-Israeli war*

1964 *PLO established*

1967 *Third Arab-Israeli war (Six-Day War)*

1973 *Fourth Arab-Israeli war (Yom Kippur War)*

1978 *Egyptian-Israeli peace talks (Camp David)*

1982 *Israel invades Lebanon; withdraws from Sinai*

1985 *Israel withdraws from Lebanon*

1988 *PLO recognizes State of Israel*

1993 *Oslo Accords between Israel and PLO*

1994 *Limited Palestinian autonomy in Gaza Strip*

1995 *Israel and PLO sign agreement on West Bank autonomy*

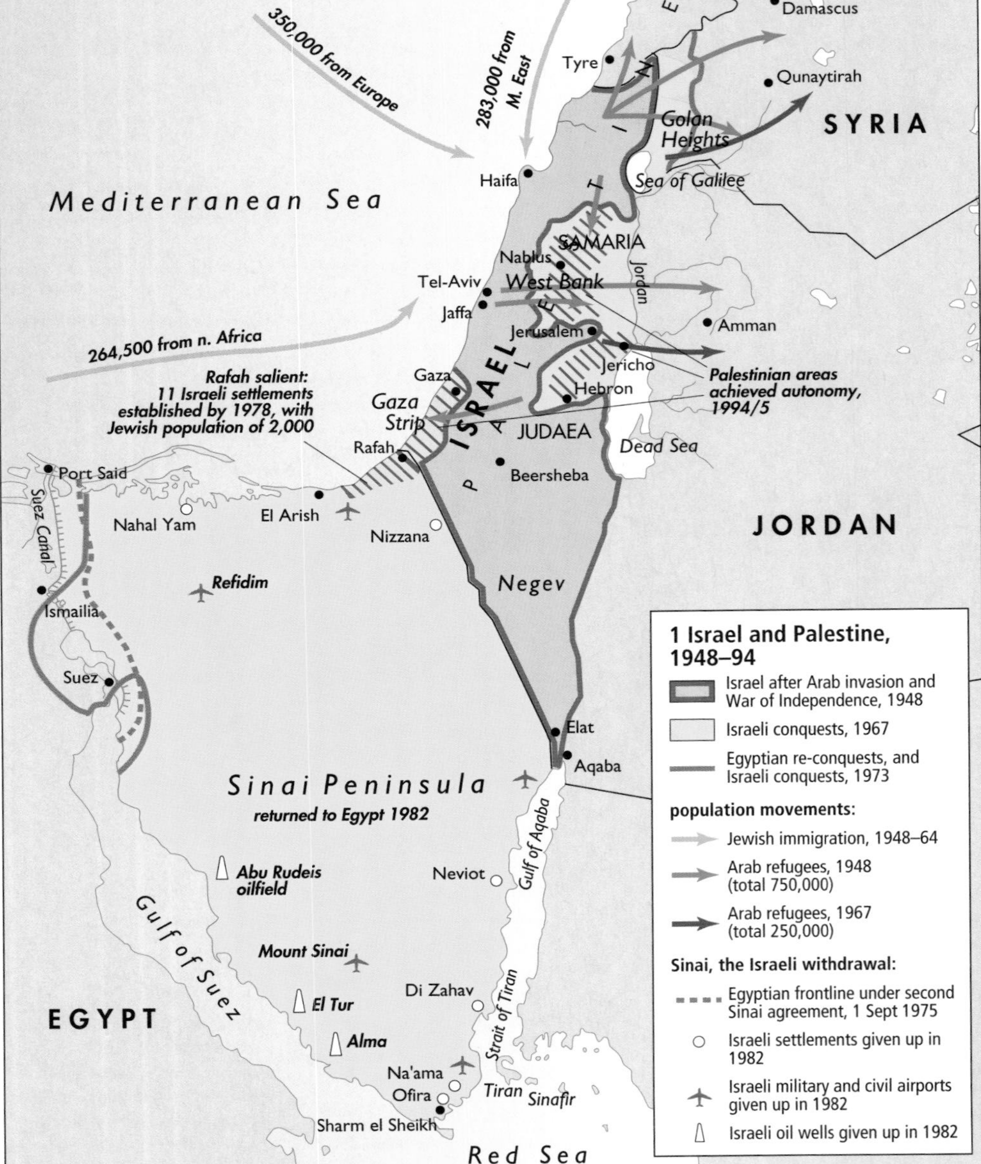

1 The years immediately before and after the establishment of the State of Israel in May 1947 saw massive movements of populations as Jews entered Palestine and Arabs fled ***(map left)***. Subsequent wars saw Israel annex the West Bank, Gaza Strip, Golan Heights and the Sinai Peninsula. The future of the West Bank, nominally now (with Gaza) under Palestinian self-rule, has proved the most intractable.

On 13 September 1993 the Israeli prime minister, Yitzhak Rabin, met President Clinton and PLO leader Yasser Arafat at the White House to sign the Oslo Accords ***(below)***. Yet however significant this breakthrough, differences between Israel and the Palestinians remain acute. Despite further progress in agreeing areas of Palestinian self-rule, the political will on both sides to arrive at a final and lasting settlement has generally been conspicuous by its absence.

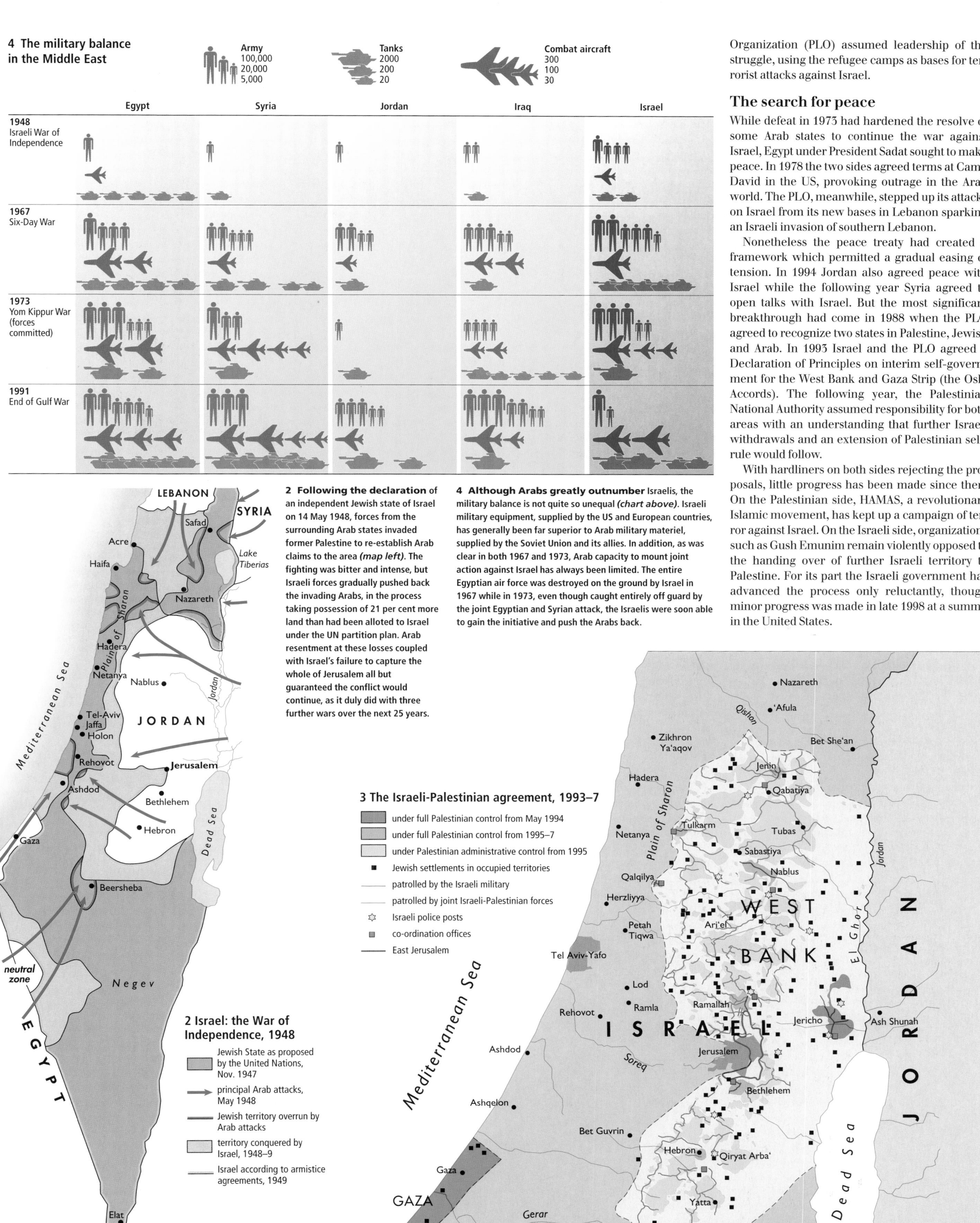

2 Following the declaration of an independent Jewish state of Israel on 14 May 1948, forces from the surrounding Arab states invaded former Palestine to re-establish Arab claims to the area *(map left)*. The fighting was bitter and intense, but Israeli forces gradually pushed back the invading Arabs, in the process taking possession of 21 per cent more land than had been alloted to Israel under the UN partition plan. Arab resentment at these losses coupled with Israel's failure to capture the whole of Jerusalem all but guaranteed the conflict would continue, as it duly did with three further wars over the next 25 years.

4 Although Arabs greatly outnumber Israelis, the military balance is not quite so unequal *(chart above)*. Israeli military equipment, supplied by the US and European countries, has generally been far superior to Arab military materiel, supplied by the Soviet Union and its allies. In addition, as was clear in both 1967 and 1973, Arab capacity to mount joint action against Israel has always been limited. The entire Egyptian air force was destroyed on the ground by Israel in 1967 while in 1973, even though caught entirely off guard by the joint Egyptian and Syrian attack, the Israelis were soon able to gain the initiative and push the Arabs back.

3 In 1993 the Israeli government and the PLO agreed, in secret, the Oslo Accords. These formed the foundation of the settlement negotiated in 1994 on the phased withdrawal of Israeli troops and limited Palestinian self-rule *(map right)*. The PLO was installed in the Gaza Strip and Jericho in summer 1994 while an interim agreement on the West Bank in autumn 1995 granted the PLO local authority over one-third of the area.

Organization (PLO) assumed leadership of the struggle, using the refugee camps as bases for terrorist attacks against Israel.

The search for peace

While defeat in 1973 had hardened the resolve of some Arab states to continue the war against Israel, Egypt under President Sadat sought to make peace. In 1978 the two sides agreed terms at Camp David in the US, provoking outrage in the Arab world. The PLO, meanwhile, stepped up its attacks on Israel from its new bases in Lebanon sparking an Israeli invasion of southern Lebanon.

Nonetheless the peace treaty had created a framework which permitted a gradual easing of tension. In 1994 Jordan also agreed peace with Israel while the following year Syria agreed to open talks with Israel. But the most significant breakthrough had come in 1988 when the PLO agreed to recognize two states in Palestine, Jewish and Arab. In 1993 Israel and the PLO agreed a Declaration of Principles on interim self-government for the West Bank and Gaza Strip (the Oslo Accords). The following year, the Palestinian National Authority assumed responsibility for both areas with an understanding that further Israeli withdrawals and an extension of Palestinian self-rule would follow.

With hardliners on both sides rejecting the proposals, little progress has been made since then. On the Palestinian side, HAMAS, a revolutionary Islamic movement, has kept up a campaign of terror against Israel. On the Israeli side, organizations such as Gush Emunim remain violently opposed to the handing over of further Israeli territory to Palestine. For its part the Israeli government has advanced the process only reluctantly, though minor progress was made in late 1998 at a summit in the United States.

Nationalism, secularism and Islam in the Middle East

◁ ▷
See also
Imperialism and nationalism, 1919–41 p. 258
The Cold War, 1945–91 p. 274
Retreat from empire since 1939 p. 276
Africa after emancipation since 1957 p. 286
Palestine, Zionism and the Arab-Israeli conflict p. 288
The world in the 1990s p. 302
The global economy p. 304

The Middle East has been among the world's most unstable and politically sensitive regions since the end of the Second World War. Independence struggles, the Cold War, Arab-Israeli conflict, military interventions, repression, regional rivalries, Islamic revival, oil riches and extremes of wealth and poverty have created near permanent turmoil.

Popular protest played a key role in the fall of the shah of Iran in 1979 and the assumption of power by Ayatollah Khomeini in February that year. The picture *(above)* was taken in 1987 on the eighth anniversary of the revolution. According to Khomeini, ultimate governmental authority should be vested in a supreme Islamic jurist. Subsequently, a rightly guided Iran should spread the message of true Islam to the rest of the Islamic world. But true Islam had first to be consolidated within Iran: an estimated 10,000 people had been executed by 1985 and 40,000 imprisoned.

IN THE IMMEDIATE POST-WAR period, war weariness, financial pressure and local opposition led Britain and France to abandon their colonial possessions in the Middle East. Despite efforts to keep a European military presence in an area of vital strategic importance to the West, by 1956 the Arab world was largely independent of European power.

But while the Europeans retreated, the United States and the Soviet Union advanced, both anxious to increase their influence in the region. In the process, the Middle East rapidly became a key theatre of the Cold War. Fearing Soviet expansion, the US underpinned Israel, Saudi Arabia and, until 1979, Iran, all of which became the principal surrogates of American interests. For its part, the Soviet Union, through its support for Egypt, Iraq and Syria, sought to portray itself as the champion of anti-imperialism, the Palestinian cause, revolutionary socialism and Arab nationalism.

Nationalism

It was nationalism that formed the keynote of Arab political goals in the period, with President Nasser of Egypt its principal standard bearer. Having led a military coup against the Egyptian monarchy in 1952, within two years he had become president of Egypt and the most charismatic Arab leader of the period even if his avowedly modernizing and secular policies alienated the more conservative Arab regimes and the cause of Arab unity, which he energetically pursued, was to prove no more than a chimera.

Nonetheless, with the active support of the Soviet Union, Nasser's influence was crucial to the development not just of Egypt but of Iraq, Sudan, Syria, South Yemen, Algeria and Libya, all of which owed much to eastern European economic and political models. In every case, the ruling regime was backed by the military while their economies were dominated by the state and all of them introduced ambitious and generally ineffectual land reforms and nationalized most of industry, banking and foreign trade. In common with most other Arab states, they all also maintained huge armies, supposedly to counter the threat posed by Israel, in reality to maintain the ruling regimes in power.

Rivalries and wars

Regional rivalries and tensions have also led to a series of Middle Eastern wars in addition to the persistent Arab-Israeli conflict (*see* p. 288). In Lebanon, divisions between Christians and Muslims, between Lebanese and Palestinians and between Sunni and Shi'a Muslims created a microcosm of the tensions in the wider Arab world. In 1975 full-scale civil war broke out in which both Israel and Syria became deeply involved. In 1980 Iraq's President Saddam Hussein launched a preemptive assault on Iran, then in the throes of revolutionary turmoil. The conflict turned into a lethal eight-year campaign of attrition reminiscent of the First World War. It cost an estimated 450,000 dead and 750,000 wounded. Undaunted, in 1990 Hussein invaded oil-rich Kuwait. Though Saddam Hussein survived Iraq's subsequent defeat at the hands of a US-led United Nations coalition force, the international isolation his country has since endured has only increased the brutality and misery endured by almost all Iraqis.

The rise of Islam

If the politics of the Arab world in the 1950s and 1960s were dominated by Cold War tension between conservative and radical Arab states, in the 1970s they gave way to a new development: the rise of revolutionary Islam. The Islamic movement dated back to the foundation of the Muslim Brotherhood in 1928 but was given new life partly by the military failures against Israel in 1967 and 1973 (*see* p. 288) and partly by the general sense of hopelessness and despair which pervaded the region. In such an atmosphere, militant Islamic activity seemed to give new hope, however illusory, for the future.

In 1978–9, a short-lived alliance of Islamic radicals overthrew the US-backed regime of the shah in Iran and an Islamic Republic was installed under the guidance of Ayatollah Khomeini. A wave of killings took place, both of members of the

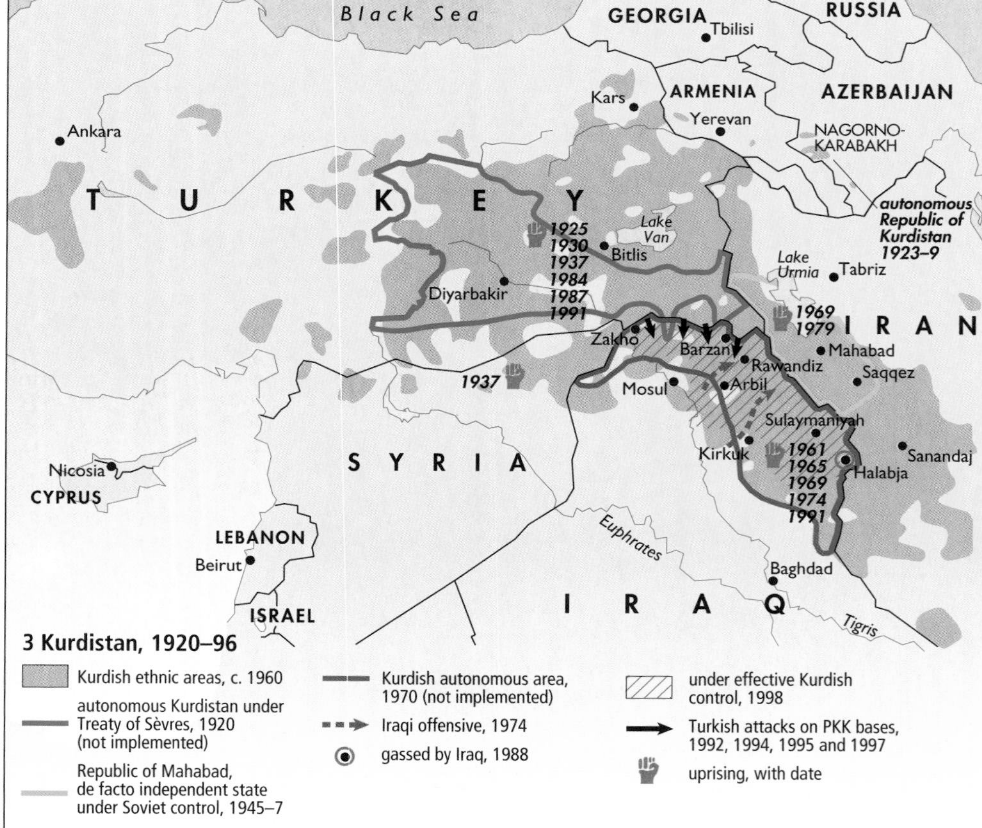

3 The Kurds, now divided between Turkey, Iran, Iraq and Syria, were promised an independent homeland under the Treaty of Sèvres in 1920. Largely confining their struggle to demands for autonomy within national frontiers *(map left)*, the Kurds of Turkey fought against their government in the 1920s and '30s, and have renewed their activities since the early 1970s. The Kurds of Iraq have waged an almost equally bitter struggle for most of this century. After the Gulf War, an autonomous Kurdish region was created in northern Iraq.

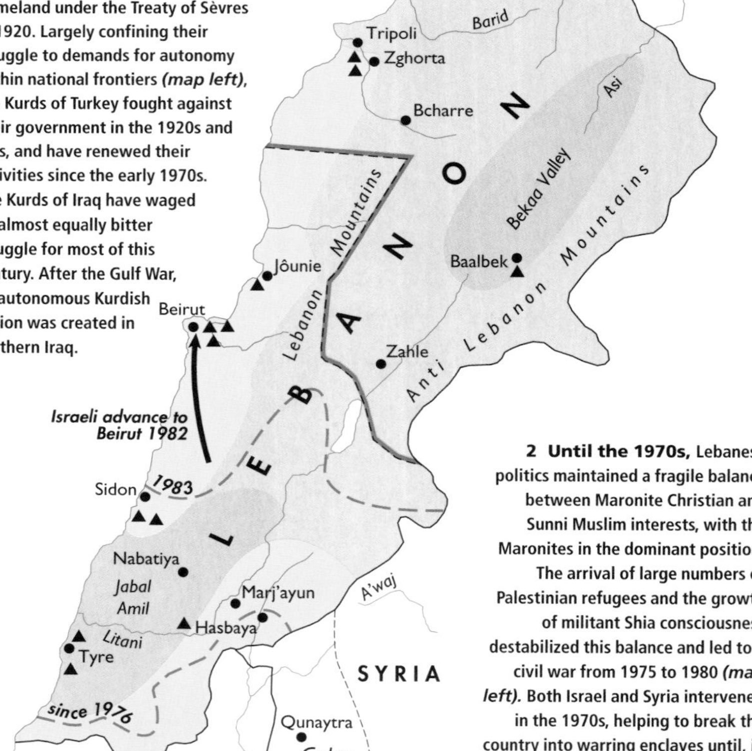

2 Until the 1970s, Lebanese politics maintained a fragile balance between Maronite Christian and Sunni Muslim interests, with the Maronites in the dominant position. The arrival of large numbers of Palestinian refugees and the growth of militant Shia consciousness destabilized this balance and led to a civil war from 1975 to 1980 *(map left)*. Both Israel and Syria intervened in the 1970s, helping to break the country into warring enclaves until, in 1992, an uneasy peace was restored.

1952 *Military coup in Egypt*

1953 *Military coup in Iran*

1956 *Nasser nationalizes Suez Canal; Israel, France, Britain invade*

1958 *United Arab Republic founded (Syria and Egypt)*

1973 *3rd Arab-Israeli war; oil crisis*

1975–92 *Lebanese civil war*

1979 *Islamic Republic established in Iran*

1980–88 *Iran-Iraq War*

1990 *Iraq invades Kuwait*

1991 *UN coalition forces defeat Iraq*

1992 *Algerian civil war*

4 Population and GNP, 1960–93

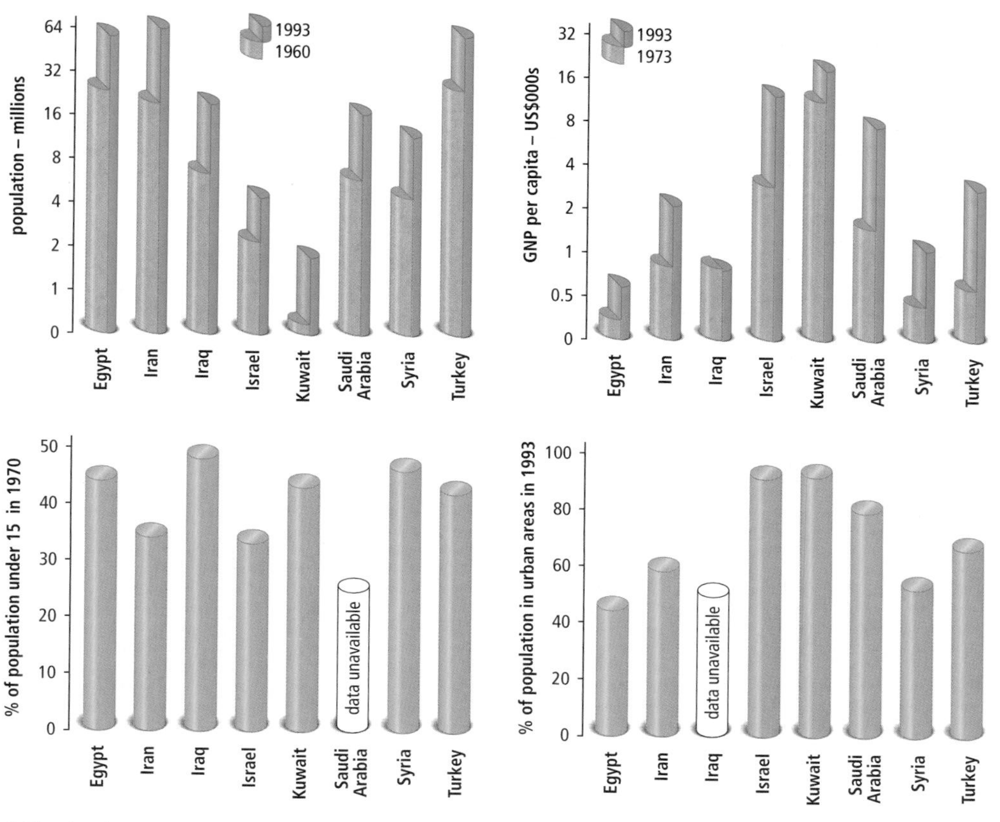

population – millions: 64, 32, 16, 8, 4, 2, 1, 0 — 1993, 1960

GNP per capita – US$000s: 32, 16, 8, 4, 2, 1, 0.5, 0 — 1993, 1973

% of population under 15 in 1970: 50, 40, 30, 20, 10, 0 — Saudi Arabia: data unavailable

% of population in urban areas in 1993: 100, 80, 60, 40, 20, 0 — Iraq: data unavailable

Egypt, Iran, Iraq, Israel, Kuwait, Saudi Arabia, Syria, Turkey

1 Between the 1930s and the 1960s. the states of the Middle East freed themselves from British and French rule and established themselves as independent nations. The region has been plagued by instability, partly because of the Arab-Israeli conflict, partly because of its role in the power struggle of the Cold War, and more recently because of the upheavals caused by the rise of militant Islam *(map below)*. In addition, it contains some 65 per cent of the world's oil reserves.

4 The tensions caused by political repression have been reinforced by differences in wealth between and within states *(graphs above)*. Iran, Iraq, Kuwait, Saudi Arabia and the UAE possess 50 per cent of the world's oil reserves. Though they have become enormously rich, their dependence on oil has left them vulnerable to stagnation or even decline in world oil prices. In countries with little or no oil reserves – Egypt, Sudan and Yemen – average per capita incomes are no higher than $800. Subsistence agriculture remains the occupation of most of the region's working populations.

former regime and of opponents of the new. In the 1980s, Iran then sought, unsuccessfully, to export its revolution. To date, however, Sudan is the only other country in the region with an avowedly Islamic government. Its long and bitter military campaign against its Christian citizens in the south has succeeded in making one of the world's poorest countries poorer still. Islamic militancy has also caused untold misery in Algeria, where a vicious civil war between the government and Islamic forces has waged since 1992, with devastating effects.

> Islamic government is a government of divine law. The difference between Islamic government and constitutional government ... lies in the fact that, in the latter system, it is the representatives of the people or those of the king who legislate and make laws. Whereas the actual authority belongs to God. No others, no matter who they may be, have the right to legislate, nor has any person the right to govern on any basis other than the authority that has been conferred by God ... It is the religious expert and no one else who should occupy himself with the affairs of government.
>
> **Ayatollah Khomeini (1900–89)**

1 The Middle East from 1945

invasion
major conflicts
guerrilla activity

TURKEY
1950 Democrat Party win elections
1960 military takeover
1961 restoration of civilian rule
1971 military takeover
1970s serious political instability and assassinations
1973 restoration of civilian rule
1974 invasion of Cyprus
1980 military takeover
1980 partial restoration of civilian rule under Özal
1990–1 support for US against Iraq
1997 (Jan.–Jun.) coalition led by (Islamist) Welfare Party
1997 Turkish application for EU membership rejected

SYRIA
1946 withdrawal of French troops
1958–61 union with Egypt (United Arab Republic)
1963 Ba'th Party seizes power
1967 Six Day War; Syria loses Golan Heights
1970 General Hafiz al-Assad seizes power
1973 October (Yom Kippur) War; Syria and Egypt attack Israel; Syrian forces expelled from Golan Heights and Israeli forces occupy Syrian territory
1976 Syrian forces intervene in Lebanese civil war
1980 Treaty of Friendship and Co-operation with USSR
1990–1 supports US-led coalition in Gulf War
1991 peace made with Lebanon

IRAQ
1955 anti-Soviet Baghdad Pact
1958 Hashemite dynasty overthrown in military coup; power seized by General Abdel-karim Kassem
1963 Kassem overthrown in military coup
1964–70 intermittent heavy fighting between government and Kurds
1968 Ba'th Party seizes power
1972–5 intermittent fighting between Kurds and government
1974–5 war against Iranian-supported Kurds; ends when Iran withdraws support
1979 Saddam Hussein becomes president
1980–8 Iraq-Iran War
1990 invasion of Kuwait by Iraq
1991 UN coalition expels Iraqi army from Kuwait; Shia and Kurdish rebels attempt overthrow of Saddam Hussein; massive reprisals ordered by Saddam Hussein; Western sanctions imposed; de facto independent Kurdish state established in north
1991–8 Western sanctions remain in place. UN weapons inspectors seek to locate and neutralize Iraqi weapons of mass destruction

USSR

CYPRUS
1963–74 intermittent intercommunal clashes
1974 Turkish invasion and occupation of northern part of island

LEBANON
1969 increase in Palestinian guerrilla activity
1975 Lebanese civil war breaks out
1976 Syrian invasion
1978 Israeli invasion
1982 attack on Beirut by Israel
1985 formal withdrawal of Israeli troops
1992 first elections for 20 years; Hrawi elected President

ISRAEL

Aleppo, Hama, Beirut, Damascus, Tel-Aviv, Jerusalem, Amman, Baghdad, Teheran, Cairo, Kuwait, Doha, Abu Dhabi, Riyadh, Medina, Mecca, Muscat, Khartoum, San'a, Aden

Euphrates, Tigris, Shatt al-Arab, Persian Gulf, Red Sea, Nile, Arabian Sea

IRAN
1941 forced abdication of Shah Reza Pahlavi following Anglo-Russian occupation of Iran; his son Mohammed Reza Pahlavi becomes Shah
1951 nationalization of oil industry; deterioration in relations with UK
1953–4 Prime Minister Mossadeq becomes de facto ruler; the Shah flees but is later reinstated by royalist military forces with covert US support; oil dispute settled
1961 Shah declares "White Revolution"
1975 Algiers agreement: Iran withdraws support from Iraqi Kurds; Shatt al-Arab waterway divided between Iran and Iraq
1978–9 revolution; the Shah is exiled; Ayatollah Khomeini returns from exile; Iran becomes an Islamic Republic
1980–8 Iran-Iraq War
1989 Khomeini dies, Rafsanjani president
1995 US imposes economic sanctions
1997 'moderate' Khatami elected president

AFGHANISTAN

PAKISTAN

JORDAN
1952 accession of King Hussein
1970 attempted destruction of PLO by Jordanian Army (Black September)
1990 King Hussein refuses to join coalition against Iraq
1994 peace accord and full diplomatic relations with Israel

EGYPT
1948 leads Arab coalition against Israel
1952 monarchy overthrown; military government led by Nasser after 1954
1956 nationalization of Suez Canal Company; tripartite invasion by Britain, France, Israel
1958–61 union with Syria (United Arab Republic)
1967,1973 wars with Israel
1970 Nasser dies; Sadat becomes president
1979 Egyptian-Israeli peace treaty
1981 Sadat assassination; Mubarak becomes president
1990–1 Egypt sends troops to anti-Iraq coalition
1990s attacks on Copts and foreign tourists by Muslim extremists

KUWAIT
1961 independent of Britain
1990 invaded by Iraq; Gulf Crisis
1991 iberated by UN coalition forces

BAHRAIN

QATAR

SAUDI ARABIA
1951 Mutual Defence Assistance Agreement with US
1960 Organization of Petroleum Exporting Countries formed
1981 Gulf Co-operation Council formed (with Bahrain, Kuwait, Oman, Qatar and UAE)
1973 Saudi Arabia embargos oil exports to USA; oil price soars
1990 base for UN Coalition attacks against Iraq
1992 tentative steps towards political openness
1996 King Fahd temporarily steps down

UAE
1971 created from former British-protected Trucial States after British evacuation

OMAN
1965–75 Marxist insurgency by People's Democratic Republic of Yemen defeated with British and Iranian help

SUDAN
1953 Anglo-Egyptian agreement on ending British condominium of 1899
1956 Sudan gains independence
1958 coup by General Ibrahim Abboud
1963–72 civil war between Arab Muslim rulers in north and Christian and animist Africans in south
1969 Abboud deposed; Colonel Gaafar Mohammed el-Nimeiri seizes power
1983 civil war re-erupts; food shortages increase
1985 military coup ousts Nimeiri
1989 military coup; National Islamic Front in effective control
1990–1 famine worsens; reports of military aid from Iraq
1994–5 ceasefire between feuding southern anti-government forces
1998 US attack on chemical weapons plant

YEMEN ARAB REPUBLIC
1962 death of Imam Ahmad; civil war 1962–70
1972–9 intermittent war with Aden

PEOPLE'S DEMOCRATIC REPUBLIC OF YEMEN
1967 coup by National Liberation Front; civil war; Britain withdraws troops from Aden
1986 Ali Nasar Muhammad overthrown as president by Haidar al Attas

YEMEN
1948 assassination of Imam Yahya; his son Ahmad takes power
1959 creation of the Arab Emirates of the South (later the Federation of South Arabia)
1962 civil war and revolution in San'a; Yemen Arab Republic (North Yemen) established
1967 withdrawal of British forces; declaration of People's Democratic Republic of Yemen (South Yemen)
1990 YAR and PDRY united

Since 1930

Latin America: revolution and reaction

See also

Latin America: independence and national growth, 1810–1930 p. 226

The Great Depression, 1929–1939 p. 264

The Cold War, 1945–91 p. 274

The United States as a world power since 1945 p. 296

The world in the 1990s p. 302

Latin America since the 1930s has experienced a cycle of economic crisis, radical politics and revolutionary movements, then right-wing reaction and a gradual return to democratic politics. Vulnerable to external economic shocks and political and military intervention from outside, the stability of the region has always been fragile.

THE ECONOMIC DEPRESSION of the 1930s hit Latin America exceptionally hard, cutting off foreign capital and reducing the price of its primary products. Many countries embraced industrialization programmes to provide substitutes for imports which could no longer be afforded. Poverty-stricken urban workers began looking to populist leaders who offered immediate relief, including Getúlio Vargas in Brazil and Juan Perón in Argentina. Backed by organized labour, these men accelerated the process of industrialization, offering in return higher wages and more jobs. Yet they were unable to overcome opposition from traditional politicians and the armed forces. In 1954 Vargas's support collapsed and he committed suicide. In 1955 Perón was overthrown by the military.

Land reform and revolution

In the 1940s and 1950s, attempts at radical land reform were frustrated. Even in Mexico, the homeland of social revolution, there was comparatively little land redistribution. In 1951, though President Árbenz of Guatemala did begin a programme of land reform, the project was short-lived and US-backed conservative forces ousted him in 1954. The episode highlighted the dilemma of creating a welfare state without the resources to sustain it.

In 1959, the Cuban revolution sought to create social change and economic growth simultaneously. Under Fidel Castro, businesses were nationalized, land collectivized and education and health care provided for all Cubans. Yet any gains remained theoretical. Political repression and economic collapse were the norm for most Cubans.

Despite its considerable failings, the Cuban revolution spawned many urban and rural social movements. In Bolivia, Che Guevara's rural guerilla movement posed a serious threat to security forces until his death in 1967. In Venezuela and Chile, however, left-wing movements sought to achieve social change by constitutional means. In 1970, Chile elected an avowed Marxist, Salvador Allende, as president. But he was overthrown (and assassinated) in a US-supported military coup in 1973. He was succeeded by the military dictatorship of General Pinochet, which lasted until 1989.

Both the Argentine and Brazilian military governments reacted to economic contraction and political opposition in the 1970s by employing repressive measures. Argentina invaded the Falklands (Malvinas) in 1982. Intended to rally support for the national cause, the Argentine invasion instead brought down the military government as Britain recaptured the islands. This raised important questions about the role of the military in domestic and international politics throughout the continent.

The 1980s saw the continuation of the long tradition of intervention by the US in Latin American affairs. In Nicaragua, the left-wing Sandinista government was compelled to fight a war against the US-backed right-wing 'contra' guerrillas before losing office in elections in 1989. In 1989, US troops invaded Panama and forcibly removed its head of state, Manuel Noriega, to be tried for drugs charges in an American court.

Latin America in the 1990s

By the 1990s most of the region's military dictatorships had given way to elected governments. Yet Latin America still faced massive problems. Fast-growing populations wiped out many of the gains of industrialization. Huge shanty towns grew up on the margins of major cities. Dependence upon imported technology and foreign capital (not to mention waste by corrupt regimes) led to the rapid rise of external debt in the 1980s. Latin American countries were obliged to produce more industrial goods and increase their share of world trade. Tariff-cutting agreements became increasingly fashionable in the 1990s: the North American Free Trade Agreement between Mexico, Canada and the US was inaugurated in 1994, and MERCOSUR (Argentina, Brazil, Paraguay, and Uruguay) and the Group of Three (Colombia, Mexico and Venezuela) in 1995. In the meantime, in December 1994, all the nations of the Americas (save Cuba) committed themselves to the introduction of a Free Trade Area throughout the western hemisphere by 2005.

AND NOW I HAVE GIVEN MY LAST LECTURE ... THE NEXT WILL BE GIVEN BY A COLONEL.

Bernardo Houssay, renowned Argentinian physiologist, 1943

[MILITARY RULE AIMED] TO MAKE CHILE NOT A NATION OF PROLETARIANS, BUT A NATION OF ENTREPRENEURS.

General Augusto Pinochet, dictator of Chile, 1973–89

3 Economic development ***(map below)*** Latin America's traditional primary-export economy was modified, though not transformed, by the Great Depression, which reduced demand and lowered prices, and the Second World War, which cut it off from foreign goods and capital. Industrialization met with a degree of success in some countries and impetus was given to import substitution. However, the area continued to depend upon the developed world for markets for its raw material exports, for imports of industrial capital goods, for technology and for finance.

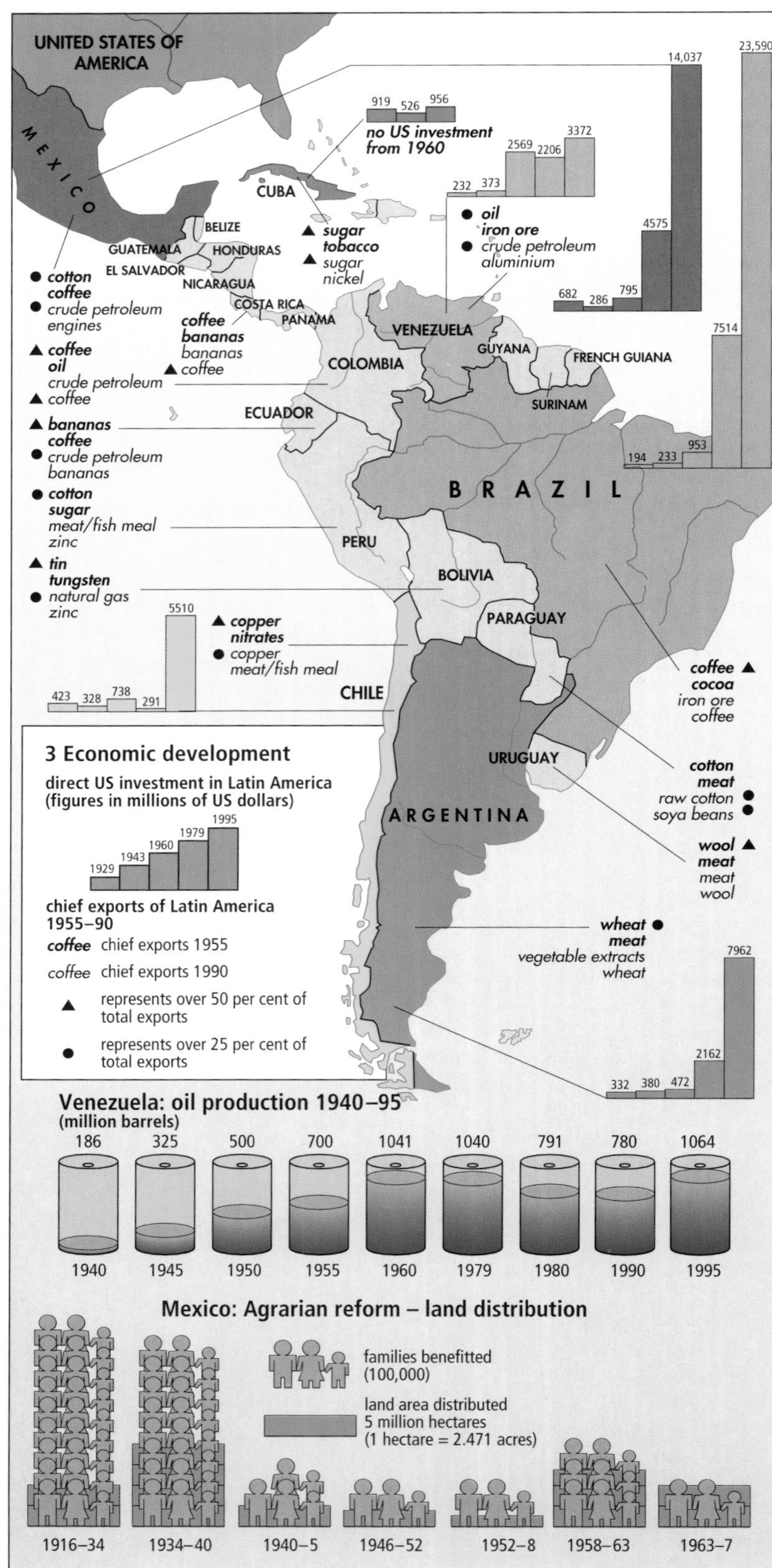

Juan Domingo Perón and his wife Eva (known as 'Evita') ***(right)*** at the height of their popularity in 1951. Perón became president of Argentina in 1946 through an alliance of workers and dissident soldiers. After Eva's death in 1952 and a prolonged economic downturn, he was overthrown in a military coup. In 1973 he returned from exile in Spain and became president once again.

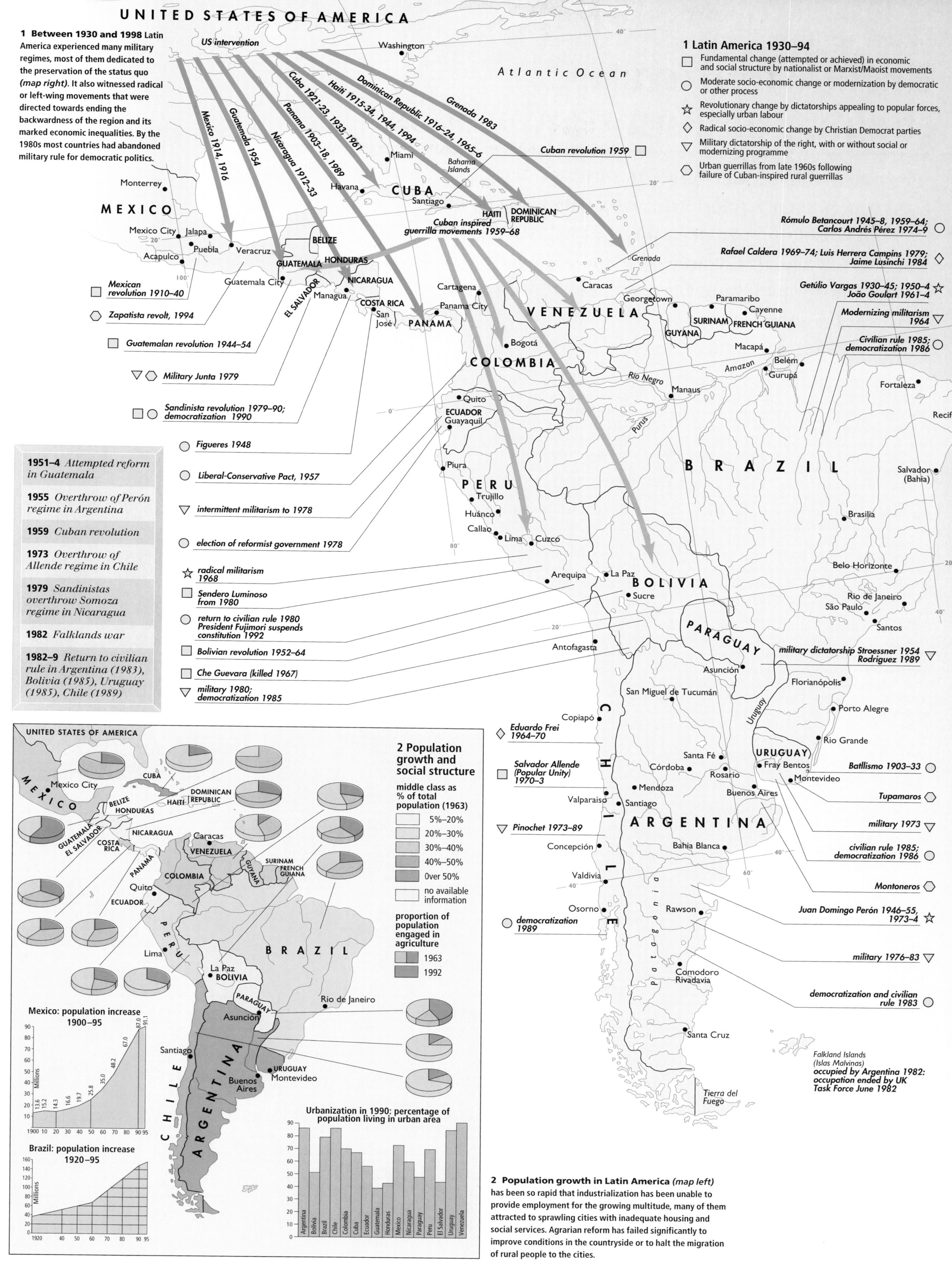

1 Between 1930 and 1998 Latin America experienced many military regimes, most of them dedicated to the preservation of the status quo *(map right)*. It also witnessed radical or left-wing movements that were directed towards ending the backwardness of the region and its marked economic inequalities. By the 1980s most countries had abandoned military rule for democratic politics.

2 Population growth in Latin America *(map left)* has been so rapid that industrialization has been unable to provide employment for the growing multitude, many of them attracted to sprawling cities with inadequate housing and social services. Agrarian reform has failed significantly to improve conditions in the countryside or to halt the migration of rural people to the cities.

Since 1939

The United States: the age of abundance

See also
The Great Depression, 1929–39 p. 264
The United States as world power since 1945 p. 296
The world in the 1990s p. 302
The global economy p. 304

For much of the 20th century the United States has seen exceptional economic growth, becoming by far the world's largest economy and enjoying a remarkable age of consumer-led abundance. Yet the fruits of this growth have been uneven with deprived rural communities and inner-city ghettoes remaining a serious problem.

THE 20TH CENTURY BEGAN with the United States poised to become the most powerful economy in the world. It had vast reserves of minerals and other natural resources. It had ample labour as a result of mass immigration and large-scale rural migration to the cities. Its business corporations were steadily becoming both bigger and more powerful. It had labour unions, in contrast, that were weak and small. It had well-developed – if largely unregulated – banks and financial services.

Before the First World War, the US was primarily a debtor nation. It emerged from the war as a creditor country, having advanced funds to the Allied nations to support their war effort. Despite a period of strikes and labour unrest attending the readjustment to a peacetime economy, the post-war years saw a 'New Era' of prosperity. Successive Republican governments adopted pro-business policies on corporate regulation, taxation and labour.

The Great Depression after 1929 affected the United States more deeply than any other nation. While President Franklin D. Roosevelt's 'New Deal' stabilized the economy and reformed financial and business regulation, unemployment remained high until the Second World War. The period after 1945, however, saw not a return to the economic difficulties of the 1930s but rather the start of a long economic boom. The American economy almost doubled in size between 1945 and 1960 and continued to grow sharply in the 1960s.

The post-war boom

A combination of consumer demand, military expenditure and technological innovation fuelled fast economic growth. The rate of personal income continued to grow and ownership of durable consumer goods increased markedly. While there were only around 7,000 television sets in the entire country in 1946, by 1960 there were over 50 million. Car ownership became much more widespread. By 1956, around 75 million cars and trucks were on American roads.

In 1955, the US, with just six per cent of the world's population, was producing and consuming half of all its goods. By 1970, with the same proportion of the total population, it accounted for two-thirds of the world's goods. Yet for all its vast wealth, there existed large pockets of poverty within

I HAVE A DREAM THAT ONE DAY THIS NATION WILL RISE UP AND LIVE OUT THE TRUE MEANING OF ITS CREED: 'WE HOLD THESE TRUTHS TO BE SELF-EVIDENT, THAT ALL MEN ARE CREATED EQUAL.'

Martin Luther King, 1963

WHAT I WANT TO SEE ABOVE ALL IS THAT THIS REMAINS A COUNTRY WHERE SOMEONE CAN ALWAYS GET RICH.

President Ronald Reagan, 1981

Perhaps against the odds, certainly to the dismay of liberal expectations, one-time Hollywood star Ronald Reagan, seen here on the campaign trail with his wife, Nancy, *(below)*, was elected US president in November 1980. Though a noted champion of economic individualism, Reagan proved nothing if not pragmatic in office and presided over a huge increase in government spending. The resulting economic boom, coupled with his genial personality and fierce anti-Soviet rhetoric, ensured him wide popularity and hugely reinforced American economic self-confidence after the uncertainty of the 1970s.

1952 *Eisenhower elected president*

1956 *Federal Highway Act*

1960 *Kennedy elected president*

1963 *President Kennedy assassinated*

1965 *Voting Rights Act becomes law*

1968 *Martin Luther King assassinated*

1973 *US withdrawal from Vietnam*

1974 *Nixon resigns after Watergate scandal*

1980 *Ronald Reagan elected president*

1987 *Stock market crash*

1994 *NAFTA established*

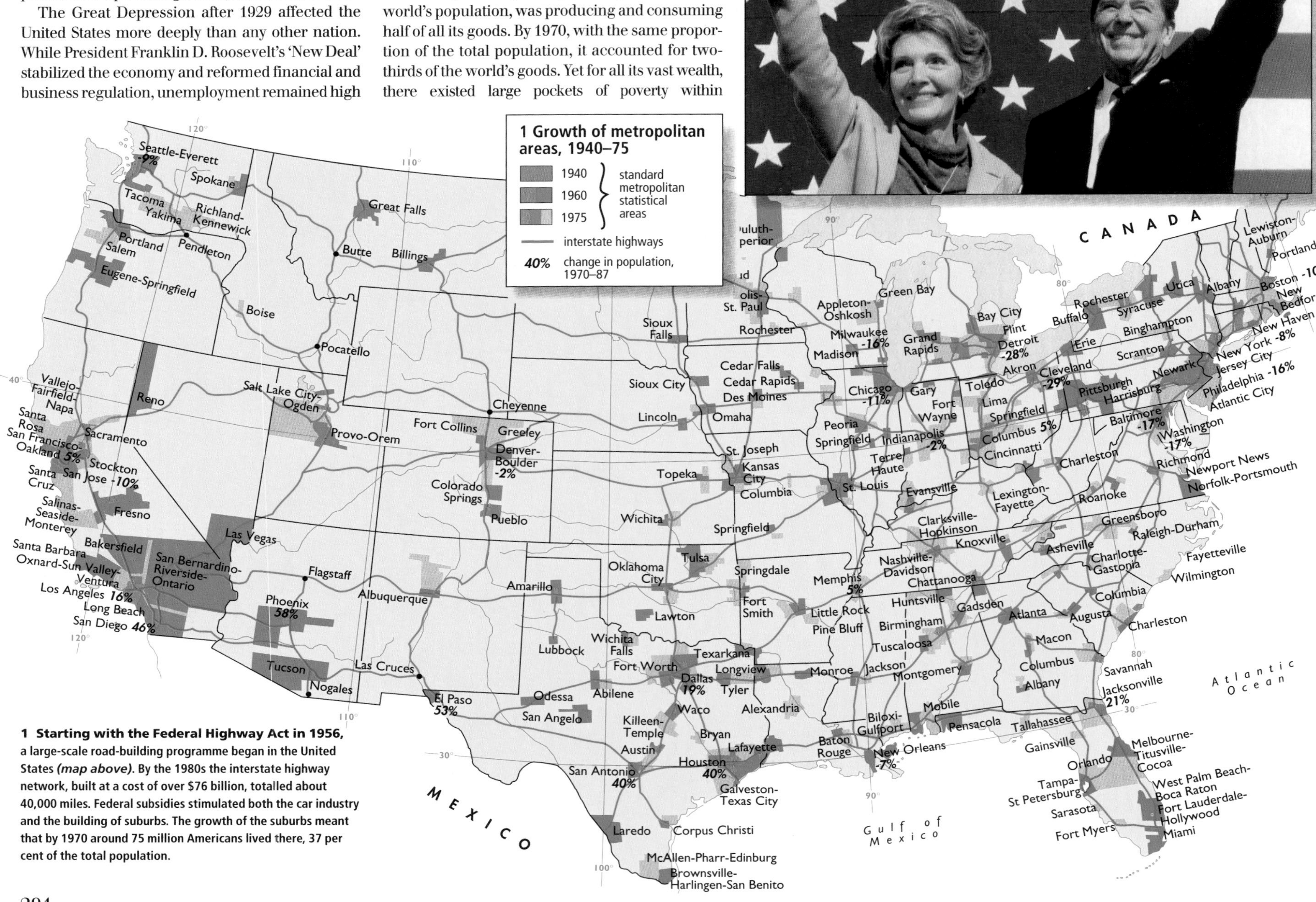

1 Starting with the Federal Highway Act in 1956, a large-scale road-building programme began in the United States *(map above)*. By the 1980s the interstate highway network, built at a cost of over $76 billion, totalled about 40,000 miles. Federal subsidies stimulated both the car industry and the building of suburbs. The growth of the suburbs meant that by 1970 around 75 million Americans lived there, 37 per cent of the total population.

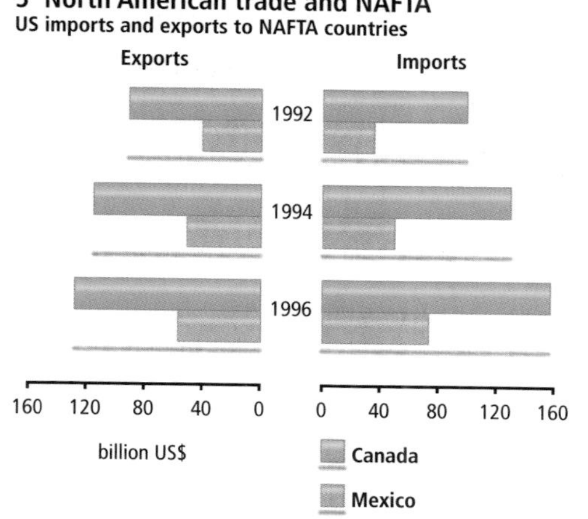

5 On 1 January 1994 Mexico joined the North American Free Trade Agreement (NAFTA), creating, with Canada and the US, the largest free-trade bloc in the world. NAFTA's total GNP was over $6 trillion, with a market of over 360 million people. Trade in the area has increased *(chart above)*, but initially this has led to a greater level of imports into the US.

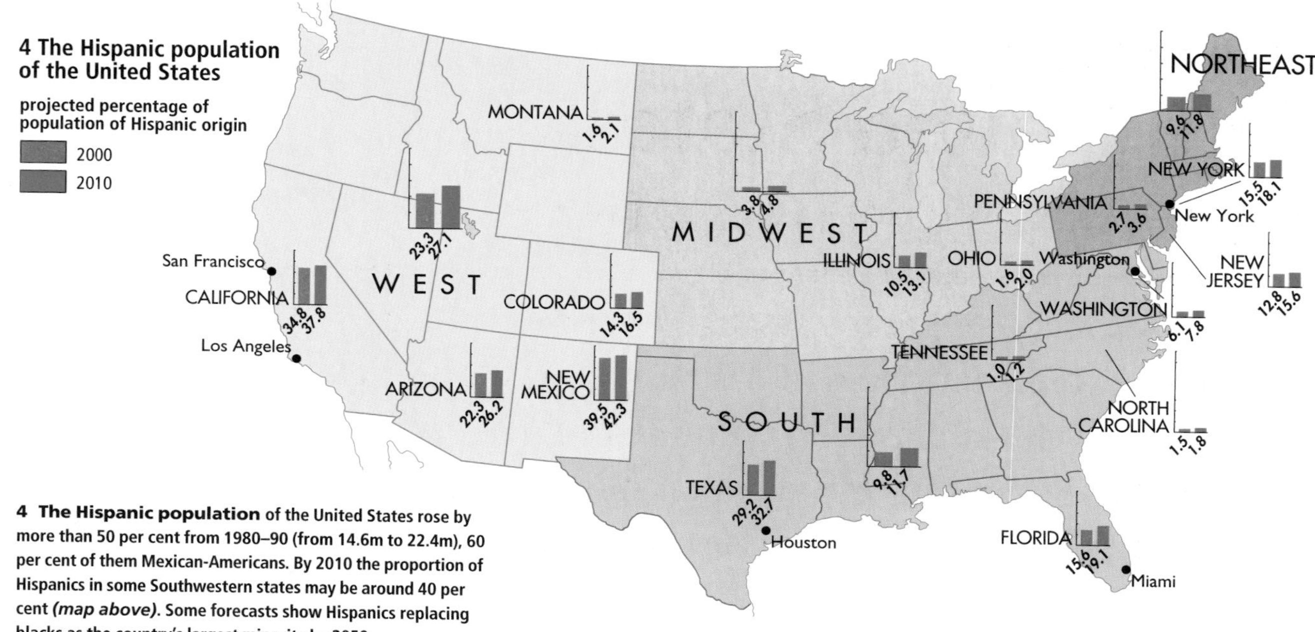

4 The Hispanic population of the United States rose by more than 50 per cent from 1980–90 (from 14.6m to 22.4m), 60 per cent of them Mexican-Americans. By 2010 the proportion of Hispanics in some Southwestern states may be around 40 per cent *(map above)*. Some forecasts show Hispanics replacing blacks as the country's largest minority by 2050.

American society itself. While much of this poverty was rural, particularly in the deep South, the increasing focus of attention of 1960s government programmes was in urban areas, where the issue of poverty became bound up with that of race.

Race and urban deprivation

Beginning in 1915–16, as a result of wartime demand for labour, African Americans began to move from the South to northern cities in search of jobs. This 'Great Migration' continued for several decades. The 1960 Census showed that for the first time a majority of blacks lived outside the deep South. As a result of social, economic, and discriminatory pressures, enclaves of many large cities came to contain black ghettoes, forming the home of a permanent black underclass. During the 1960s, beginning in the Watts district of Los Angeles in August 1965, many exploded into racial riots.

After the 1960s, as the political climate became less favourable to their aspirations, many blacks began to leave northern cities in search of jobs in the booming industries of the 'Sunbelt' – the South and Southwest states. The black middle and professional classes expanded in size. Yet many ghettoes remained, wracked by unemployment, drugs, crime, AIDS and violence.

Immigration, trade and NAFTA

By the 1990s, fresh flows of immigrants, above all from Latin America, had begun to transform American society anew. Between 1941 and 1970 approximately 800,000 legal immigrants from Mexico entered the United States, and many more did so illegally. By 1990 people of Hispanic origin made up 26 per cent of the population of California and 35 per cent of New Mexico, with the possibility of their becoming a majority in these states within a century. US relations with its Latin American neighbours had traditionally been uneasy, but by the early 1990s the need to institutionalize Mexican economic reform helped to promote the idea of a North American free-trade area. Canada had made such a pact with the US in 1985, and on 1 January 1994 Mexico joined in the North American Free Trade Agreement (NAFTA), the largest free-trade area in the world.

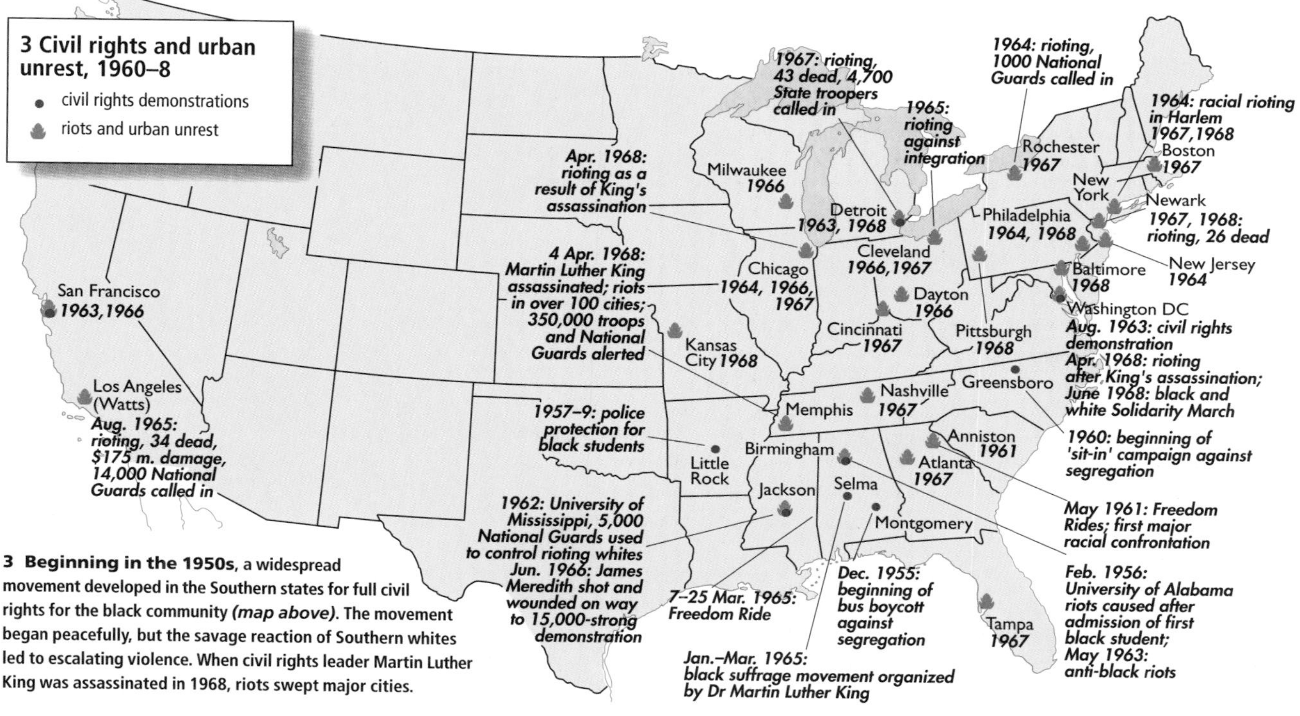

3 Beginning in the 1950s, a widespread movement developed in the Southern states for full civil rights for the black community *(map above)*. The movement began peacefully, but the savage reaction of Southern whites led to escalating violence. When civil rights leader Martin Luther King was assassinated in 1968, riots swept major cities.

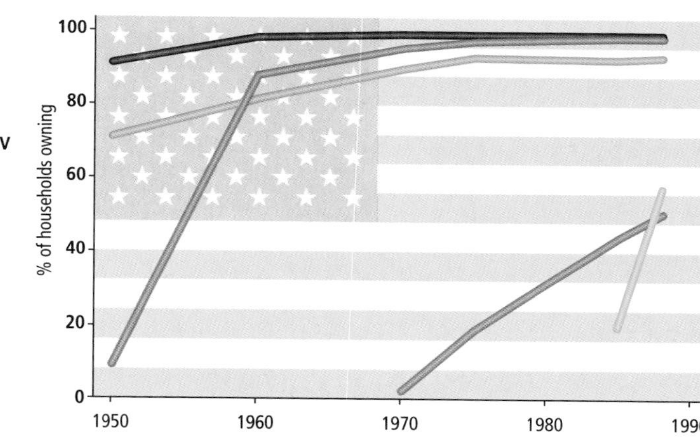

2 A striking migration since the Second World War has made California the most populous state. The states of the Northeast have the highest average income, while some Southern states have fared worse with regard to income and population *(map left)*. The black population, concentrated in the cities, has tended to grow faster than the white throughout the period. Migration from Latin America has boosted the Hispanic population, especially in the South and Southwest.

6 Consumerism boomed in the United States after 1945. Before the Second World War, only 25 per cent of the farming population even had electricity; by 1960 over 80 per cent had not just lighting but televisions and telephones as well *(chart above)*. By 1990 almost every household had these while an increasing number had cable television, video recorders and computers, too. Between 1945 and 1980 consumer expenditure in the US increased almost four-fold.

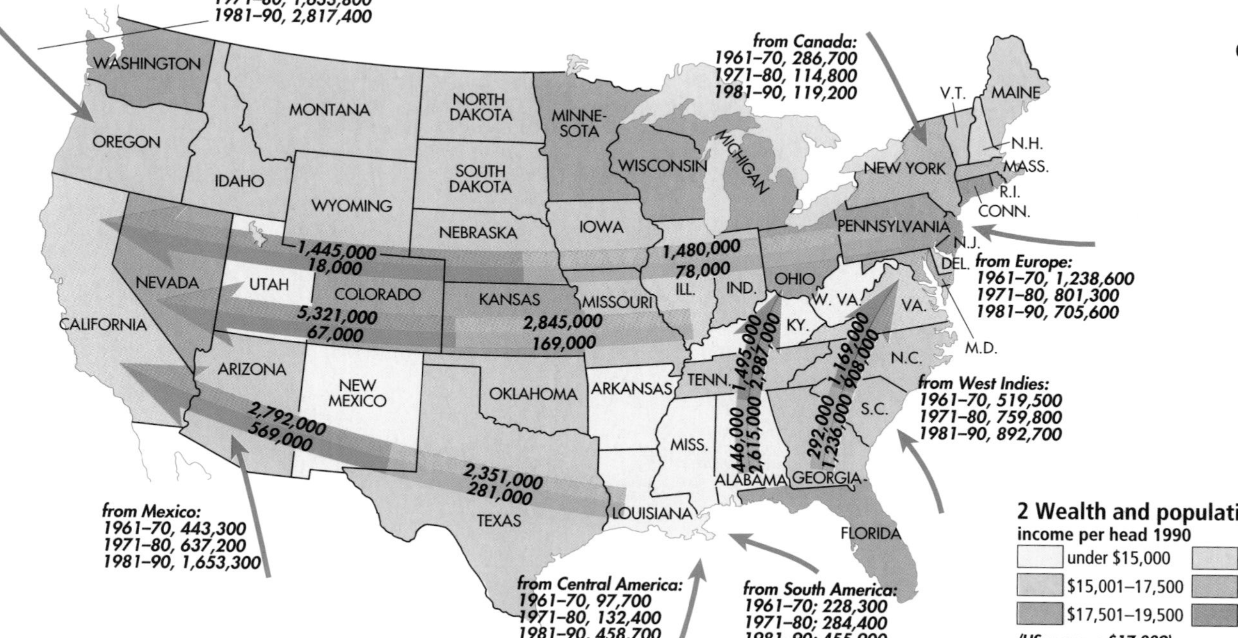

2 Wealth and population, 1930–90

income per head 1990

- under $15,000
- $15,001–17,500
- $17,501–19,500
- $19,501–21,500
- $21,501–23,500
- over $23,500

(US average $17,889)

- 1930–60 1965–79 movement of white population
- 1930–60 1965–79 movement of black population
- immigrants

The United States as a world power

See also
The war in Asia and the Pacific, 1941–45 p. 268
The European war, 1941–45 p. 270
The Cold War, 1945–91 p. 274
Southeast Asia since 1945 p. 282
Latin America: revolution and reaction p. 292
The United States: the age of abundance p. 294
The world in the 1990s p. 302

In the years following the Second World War, the United States found itself resisting the expansion of international communism. This led to American participation in two major wars – in Korea and Vietnam – and frequent military and diplomatic interventions in other areas. The break-up of the Soviet Union in 1991 left the US as the sole surviving superpower.

IN 1920, THE UNITED STATES declined to join the League of Nations and retreated into a period of isolationism, which was only brought to a close by the Japanese attack on the American fleet at Pearl Harbor in December 1941. When the war ended in 1945, the US and the Soviet Union were left as the two greatest military powers. The US found itself playing the leading role on the world scene in resisting the attempts of the Soviet Union to further the advance of international communism.

The policy of containment

In the spring of 1947, conscious of what appeared to be a Soviet threat in eastern Europe, Greece, and Turkey, the Truman administration adopted a policy of 'containing' communist expansionism. Containment remained the basis of American foreign policy until the 1980s. It had a number of successes in the late 1940s: Marshall Aid (introduced in 1948) which saved the economies of war-torn Europe; the Berlin airlift of 1948–9 which defeated a Soviet blockade of the city; and the creation of the North Atlantic Treaty Organisation (NATO) in 1949. Yet the policy also suffered reverses: the communist take-over of China in 1949 and, the same year, the Soviet Union's detonation of an atomic bomb. President Truman responded in 1950 by ordering the construction of the hydrogen bomb and accepting NSC-68, a document calling for the rearmament of America's conventional forces. In 1950, when communist North Korea invaded South Korea, Truman committed US forces against them and their Chinese allies in the Korean War (1950–3).

Under the Eisenhower administration from 1953, secretary of state John Foster Dulles talked not of containing communism but of the 'liberation' of eastern Europe. The hollowness of this rhetoric was demonstrated when the Russians suppressed East German workers' food riots in 1953 and by the Hungarian uprising of 1956. On both occasions the US proved powerless to help.

After an abortive US-backed attempt to overthrow the Castro regime in Cuba in 1961, Cuba became the scene (in October 1962) of the most dangerous moment of the Cold War. When the Soviet Union attempted to install Soviet nuclear missiles in Cuba, President Kennedy ordered a naval blockade of the island. Both sides seemed on the brink of nuclear war until the Russians agreed to withdraw their missiles in return for concessions over US missiles in Turkey. From 1962, relations between the two 'superpowers' – the US and the USSR – began slowly to improve, as symbolized by the 1963 treaty banning nuclear testing in the atmosphere and the first Strategic Arms Limitation Treaty (SALT) agreed in 1972. The Nixon Administration (1969–74) also began a process of rapprochement with Communist China.

The Vietnam War

Kennedy provided South Vietnam with military advisers, but not with troops, in an attempt to shore up a South Vietnamese government threatened by North Vietnamese-backed communist insurgents. In 1965, his successor, Lyndon Johnson, committed American ground forces to the preservation of South Vietnam. US involvement in the Vietnam War lasted eight years, cost 58,000 American dead, and had profound repercussions on domestic politics. It also failed: in April 1975, North Vietnam succeeded in unifying the country under communist rule.

The Vietnam War led to a period of 'neo-isolationism'. President Carter, elected in 1976, helped

3 US direct investment overseas, 1960 and 1984

1960 1984 percentage of total worldwide investment in area

3 & 4 The United States became the most important source of world investment funds between 1960 and 1984 *(map above)*. By 1984 US direct investment totalled US$223 billion with more than 75 per cent placed in the other developed economies of the world. The US used its foreign economic and military aid as a vital tool of foreign policy *(chart bottom left)*. In 1995 80 per cent of military aid went to the Middle East, principally to Egypt and Israel, while the bulk of the rest went to America's uneasy allies in the Aegean, Greece and Turkey. Economic aid was more widely dispersed, but Israel still received 10 per cent of the total, twice the figure for the whole of Asia, and not far short of American aid to all of Sub-Saharan Africa.

I BELIEVE THAT IT MUST BE THE POLICY OF THE UNITED STATES TO SUPPORT FREE PEOPLES WHO ARE RESISTING ATTEMPTED SUBJUGATION BY ARMED MINORITIES OR BY OUTSIDE PRESSURES.

President Harry S Truman, March 1947 (known as the 'Truman Doctrine')

IT IS CLEAR THAT THE MAIN ELEMENT OF ANY UNITED STATES POLICY TOWARD THE SOVIET UNION MUST BE THAT OF A LONG-TERM, PATIENT BUT FIRM AND VIGOROUS CONTAINMENT OF RUSSIAN EXPANSIVE TENDENCIES.

George F. Kennan, author of the containment policy, 1947

4 US economic and military aid, 1995

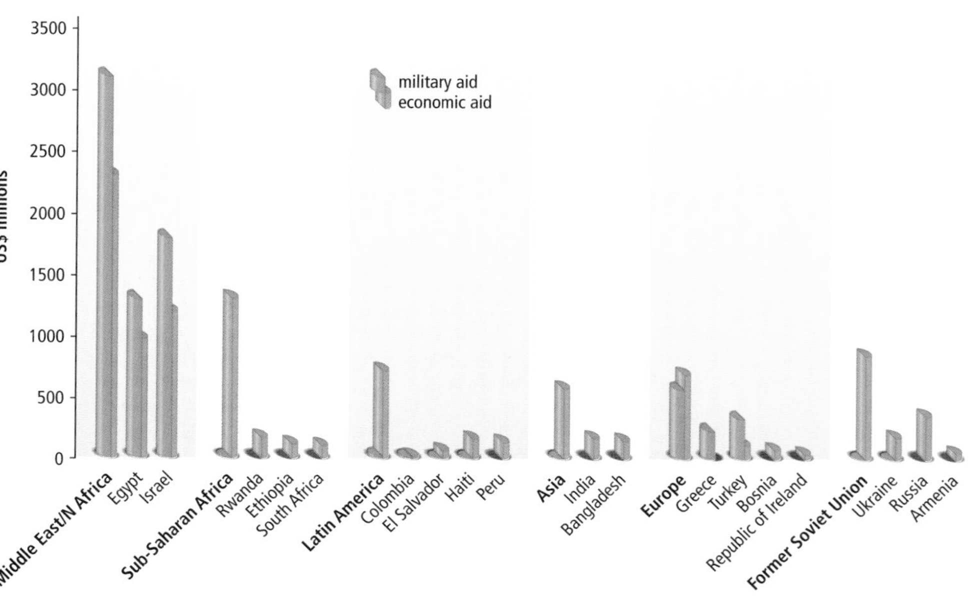

1 The United States and the world, 1945–85

anti-communist defensive line under Truman Doctrine, 1947
SEATO anti-communist defensive line, 1954
anti-communist defensive line under Formosa Resolution, 1955
anti-communist defensive line implied by Eisenhower Doctrine, 1958
returned to Japan, with date
S SEATO members, 1954–76
B Baghdad Pact members, 1955–8
C CENTO members, 1959–8
NATO and ANZUS members, 1985, including dependencies
Rio Pact (OAS) members, 1985
other US allies, 1985
former allies turned adversaries, with date
former adversaries turned allies, with date
US forces in action, with date
major overseas bases, 1965
870 American troops deployed in trouble spots, 1995, with number of troops

Israel and Egypt make peace (in the wake of the Yom Kippur War of 1973). But he had no answer to the Soviet invasion of Afghanistan in 1979 or the holding of American hostages by Iranian revolutionaries.

The collapse of communism

Ronald Reagan was elected president in 1980 promising a firmer line in foreign policy. He followed a two-prong strategy: large-scale rearmament, directed at the Soviet Union; and intervention, either open (as in Grenada in 1983) or covert (as in Nicaragua) to overthrow left-wing regimes.

The collapse of communism in eastern Europe in 1989 and the demise of the Soviet Union itself in 1991 left the US as the sole remaining superpower and replaced a bipolar with a multipolar world. With the ending of the Cold War, a whole series of ethnic, nationalist and separatist conflicts emerged. In many of these the United States played a crucial role – as in the 1995 bombing of Bosnian Serbs that persuaded them to join the Dayton peace negotiations (*see* p. 300). The US also led the coalition against Iraq in the Gulf War of 1991. Despite a strong post-Vietnam dislike of involving American forces in conflicts abroad, the 1990s saw American troops still deployed in many trouble-spots overseas.

1947 *Truman administration launches policy of containment*

1948 *Marshall Aid launched. Berlin airlift*

1949 *Communist takeover in China. USSR explodes an atomic bomb. Foundation of NATO*

1950–3 *The Korean War*

1962 *The Cuban Missile Crisis*

1965–73 *US forces engaged in Vietnam War*

1989 *Collapse of communism in eastern Europe*

1991 *The Gulf War. Demise of the Soviet Union*

1995 *Dayton Peace Agreement in former Yugoslavia*

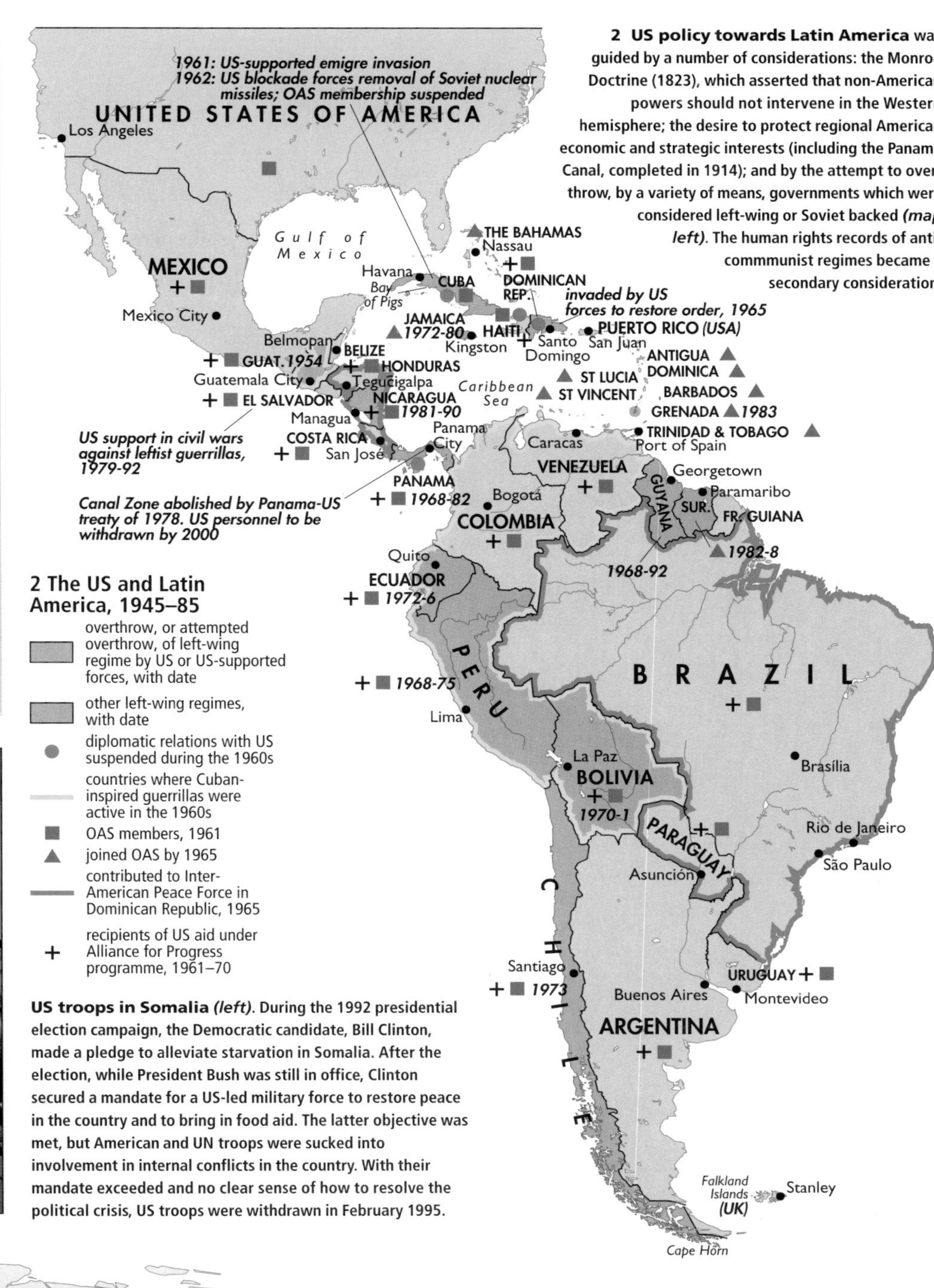

2 US policy towards Latin America was guided by a number of considerations: the Monroe Doctrine (1823), which asserted that non-American powers should not intervene in the Western hemisphere; the desire to protect regional American economic and strategic interests (including the Panama Canal, completed in 1914); and by the attempt to overthrow, by a variety of means, governments which were considered left-wing or Soviet backed *(map left)*. The human rights records of anti-commmunist regimes became a secondary consideration.

US troops in Somalia *(left)*. During the 1992 presidential election campaign, the Democratic candidate, Bill Clinton, made a pledge to alleviate starvation in Somalia. After the election, while President Bush was still in office, Clinton secured a mandate for a US-led military force to restore peace in the country and to bring in food aid. The latter objective was met, but American and UN troops were sucked into involvement in internal conflicts in the country. With their mandate exceeded and no clear sense of how to resolve the political crisis, US troops were withdrawn in February 1995.

1 The United States after 1945 maintained a world presence through a network of military bases and defence pacts in Europe, the Middle East and Asia *(map left)*. The desire to contain the threat of communism forced America into the role of the world's policeman, intervening militarily on numerous occasions. Many states saw America's role as a new imperialism, replacing the defunct colonial empires of Europe. In Iran and Libya rejection of American influence led to popular anti-imperialist revolutions.

The development of the Soviet Union and Russia

See also
The Russian revolution, 1917–29 p. 256
The European war, 1941–5 p. 270
Europe, 1945–73 p. 272
The Cold War, 1945–91 p. 274
Europe since 1973 p. 302
The world in the 1990s p. 304

1928 *First Five-Year Plan launched*

1929–33 *Soviet agriculture collectivized*

1941 *German invasion of Soviet Union*

1944–7 *Soviet control established in eastern Europe*

1953 *Death of Stalin*

1956 *Khrushchev launches 'de-Stalinization' campaign*

1964 *Brezhnev succeeds Khrushchev as Soviet leader*

1985 *Gorbachev begins programme of reforms*

1989 *Soviet influence in eastern Europe ended*

1991 *Soviet Union dissolved, Russian Federation established*

In 1929 Stalin led the drive to modernize the Soviet Union in a ten-year programme of forced industrialization and agrarian reform, generating a 'second revolution' and a wave of state terror. After the defeat of the German invasion, the Communist Party consolidated its grip on power, but demands for reform led in 1991 to the break up of the Union.

ONE FEATURE OF THE OLD RUSSIA WAS THE CONTINUAL BEATINGS SHE SUFFERED FOR FALLING BEHIND, FOR HER BACKWARDNESS ... WE ARE FIFTY OR A HUNDRED YEARS BEHIND THE ADVANCED COUNTRIES. WE MUST MAKE GOOD THIS DISTANCE IN TEN YEARS. EITHER WE DO IT, OR THEY CRUSH US.

Josef Stalin, 1931

A DECADE AFTER THE Russian revolution, the new Soviet Union had progressed little beyond the economic achievements of the pre-war Tsarist regime. Under Stalin's leadership the decision was taken to launch a 'second revolution' to modernize Soviet society and economic structure. The renewed modernization drive was necessary, Stalin believed, in order to reduce the size and economic preponderance of the peasantry – still 80 per cent of the population – and to strengthen the country against the threat of international conflict. It was also seen as the key to cementing the power of the Communist Party. The social upheaval that followed completed the social revolution only partially achieved in 1917.

The First Five Year Plan for economic development was launched in 1928, and was followed by two more, each one setting extravagant targets for the expansion of heavy industry. The whole enterprise rested on the ability to extract a grain surplus from the countryside to feed the cities. In the second half of 1929 the Party began a programme of collectivizing peasant landholdings (*see* map 1), and by 1935 90 per cent of land previously owned by the peasants had been taken, often by force, into large state-owned farms (*kolkhozy*). Peasant resistance resulted in the slaughter of millions of animals and the mass deportation of millions of farmers to work in the cities or to labour camps.

The consequences for the Soviet Union were mixed. Even allowing for Soviet exaggeration, industrial output expanded remarkably in the 1930s: the Soviet armed forces became the largest in the world, armed by 1941 with over 20,000 tanks and 10,000 aircraft. The social goal, too, was achieved, with the urban population expanding by 30 million between 1926 and 1939, and the peasantry falling to only 52 per cent of the population.

The cost of modernization

Yet the cost was high. To cope with modernization the state increased its policing of Soviet society. The regime whipped up popular hatred against spies and saboteurs which turned into a nationwide witch hunt every bit as brutal as the Terror of the French revolution. In 1937 and 1938 the terror reached a ghastly crescendo with the slaughter of more than 600,000 by the state security apparatus, including most of the senior officer corps (though only about one-fifth of all officers were purged, and most of these were dismissed rather than shot).

Modernization and terror also served to strengthen Stalin's personal grip on the Soviet Union. Victory over Germany in the Great Patriotic War of 1941–5 (*see* p. 270) showed how far Soviet society had come from the more feeble war effort of the Tsarist regime, and bolstered Stalin's domestic reputation even more. The war also saw Stalin order the shipment of millions from the country's smaller nationalities – including Germans, Poles, Chechens and Tatars – to the labour camps of the north and east.

After 1945 economic development continued with priority for heavy industry and armaments to compete in the Cold War arms race. The death of Stalin in 1953 was followed by a partial relaxation of the terror under Nikita Khrushchev. In the 1960s under Leonid Brezhnev greater efforts were made to help agriculture and the consumer industries. The Party, meanwhile, continued to dominate politics and dissent was relentlessly penalized. But by the 1980s the Soviet system was under pressure. Economic growth slowed (*see* chart 4 below), while the population became restless about the gap between the living standards of the West and those of the Communist bloc.

4 The Soviet economy, 1950–85

YEAR	steel (million tons)	coal (million tons)	exports (million roubles)	cars (thousands)	televisions (thousands)
1950	27.3	261	1.6	65	12
1960	65.3	509	5.0	139	1726
1970	116.0	624	11.5	344	6682
1980	148.0	716	49.6	1327	7528
1985	155.0	726	72.7	1332	9371

2 The Soviet Union was a patchwork of different nationalities *(map below)*. There were 22 with more than one million members by the 1980s and at least 80 other smaller ones. Russians made up just over half the population; Slavs as a whole (Russians, Ukrainians and Belorussians) about three-quarters. Slav dominance was reflected in the distribution of political power: in the 1970s, the leadership of the country was almost exclusively Slav; and while each major national area had its own political organization as one of the constituent republics of the USSR, none enjoyed political independence from the centre.

2 Principal ethnic groups of the Soviet Union, 1989

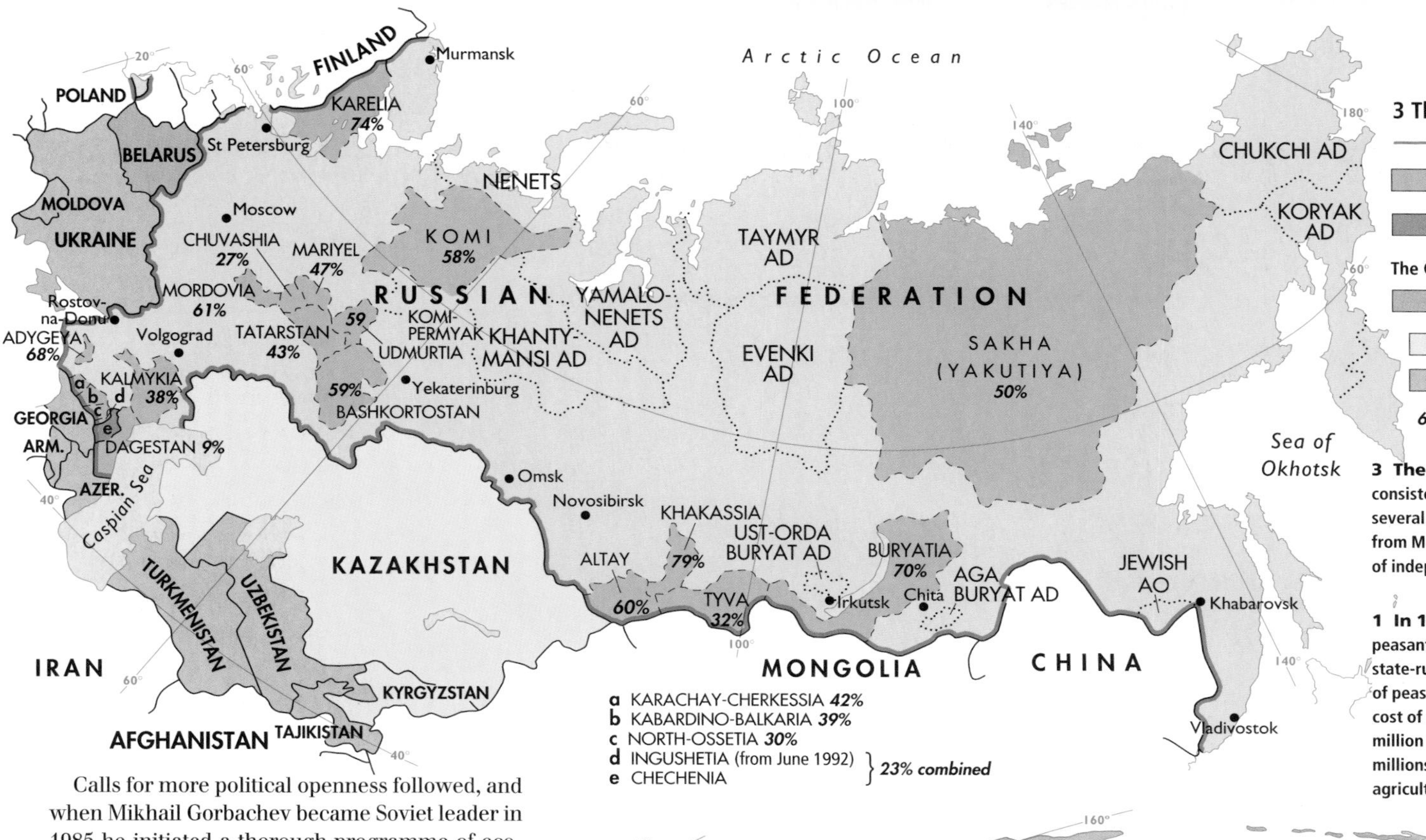

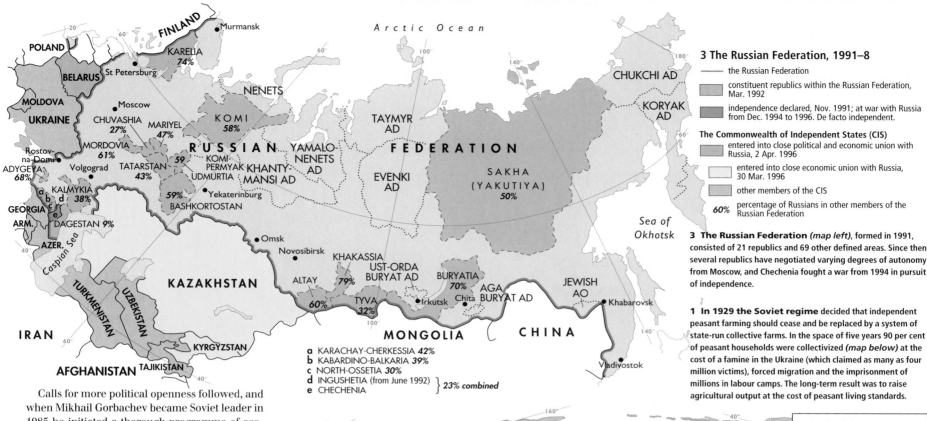

Arctic Ocean
FINLAND
Murmansk
POLAND
KARELIA 74%
BELARUS
St Petersburg
NENETS
MOLDOVA
Moscow
KOMI 58%
UKRAINE
CHUVASHIA 27%
MARIYEL 47%
TAYMYR AD
CHUKCHI AD
KORYAK AD
RUSSIAN FEDERATION
MORDOVIA 61%
YAMALO-NENETS AD
Rostov-na-Donu
TATARSTAN 43%
59
KOMI-PERMYAK
KHANTY-MANSI AD
ADYGEYA 68%
Volgograd
UDMURTIA
EVENKI AD
SAKHA (YAKUTIYA) 50%
KALMYKIA 38%
59%
Yekaterinburg
BASHKORTOSTAN
GEORGIA
ARM.
DAGESTAN 9%
AZER.
Caspian Sea
Omsk
Novosibirsk
Sea of Okhotsk
KHAKASSIA 79%
UST-ORDA BURYAT AD
BURYATIA 70%
KAZAKHSTAN
ALTAY 60%
TYVA 32%
Irkutsk
Chita
AGA BURYAT AD
JEWISH AO
Khabarovsk
TURKMENISTAN
UZBEKISTAN
IRAN
MONGOLIA
CHINA
KYRGYZSTAN
AFGHANISTAN
TAJIKISTAN
Vladivostok
a KARACHAY-CHERKESSIA 42%
b KABARDINO-BALKARIA 39%
c NORTH-OSSETIA 30%
d INGUSHETIA (from June 1992)
e CHECHENIA
23% combined

3 The Russian Federation, 1991–8

- the Russian Federation
- constituent republics within the Russian Federation, Mar. 1992
- independence declared, Nov. 1991; at war with Russia from Dec. 1994 to 1996. De facto independent.

The Commonwealth of Independent States (CIS)

- entered into close political and economic union with Russia, 2 Apr. 1996
- entered into close economic union with Russia, 30 Mar. 1996
- other members of the CIS
- *60%* percentage of Russians in other members of the Russian Federation

3 The Russian Federation ***(map left)***, **formed in 1991, consisted of 21 republics and 69 other defined areas. Since then several republics have negotiated varying degrees of autonomy from Moscow, and Chechenia fought a war from 1994 in pursuit of independence.**

1 In 1929 the Soviet regime decided that independent peasant farming should cease and be replaced by a system of state-run collective farms. In the space of five years 90 per cent of peasant households were collectivized ***(map below)*** **at the cost of a famine in the Ukraine (which claimed as many as four million victims), forced migration and the imprisonment of millions in labour camps. The long-term result was to raise agricultural output at the cost of peasant living standards.**

Calls for more political openness followed, and when Mikhail Gorbachev became Soviet leader in 1985 he initiated a thorough programme of economic and political reform (*perestroika*). In 1988 he launched a limited democratization, and was elected President in 1989.

Protest and reform

Popular demands for reform could not now be stemmed. A freer economic market and greater political and cultural freedoms (*glasnost*) opened the floodgates of popular protest. In August 1991 hard-line Communists staged a coup against Gorbachev, which was suppressed by Boris Yeltsin, head of the Russian Republic. By December the Soviet Union was fragmenting along nationalist and ethnic lines (*see* map 2), and Gorbachev bowed to reality. On 31 December 1991 the Soviet Union was wound up and replaced by a loose Commonwealth of Independent States. Russia itself (*see* map 3) became a presidential democracy with Yeltsin as its first head of state.

The 1990s were plagued by economic crisis as capitalist reforms were introduced. The state slowly disintegrated, the Red Army became corrupt and inefficient, and religious and ethnic conflict scarred the new democracy. Russia after communism became for many a much poorer and more violent society.

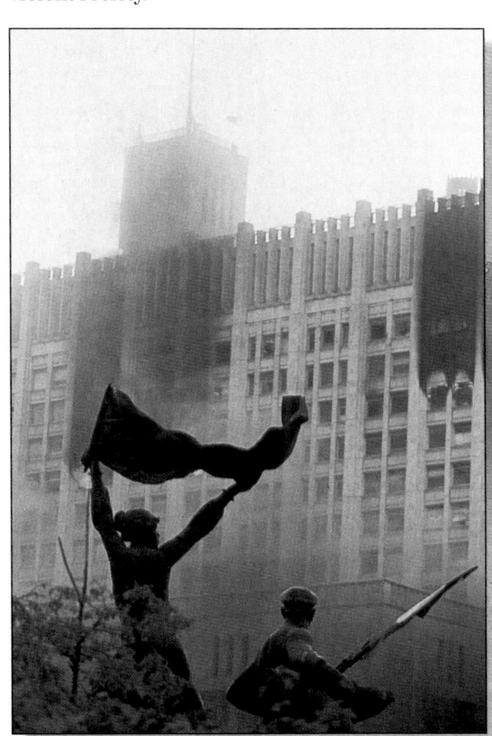

Russia established a fragile democracy in 1992. In October 1993 hard-line parliamentary delegates hostile to further reform tried to depose President Boris Yelstin. He ordered in tanks and special forces and bombarded the White House, the Russian parliament *(above)*. On 4 October, the rebels surrendered. There were 140 deaths in the fighting.

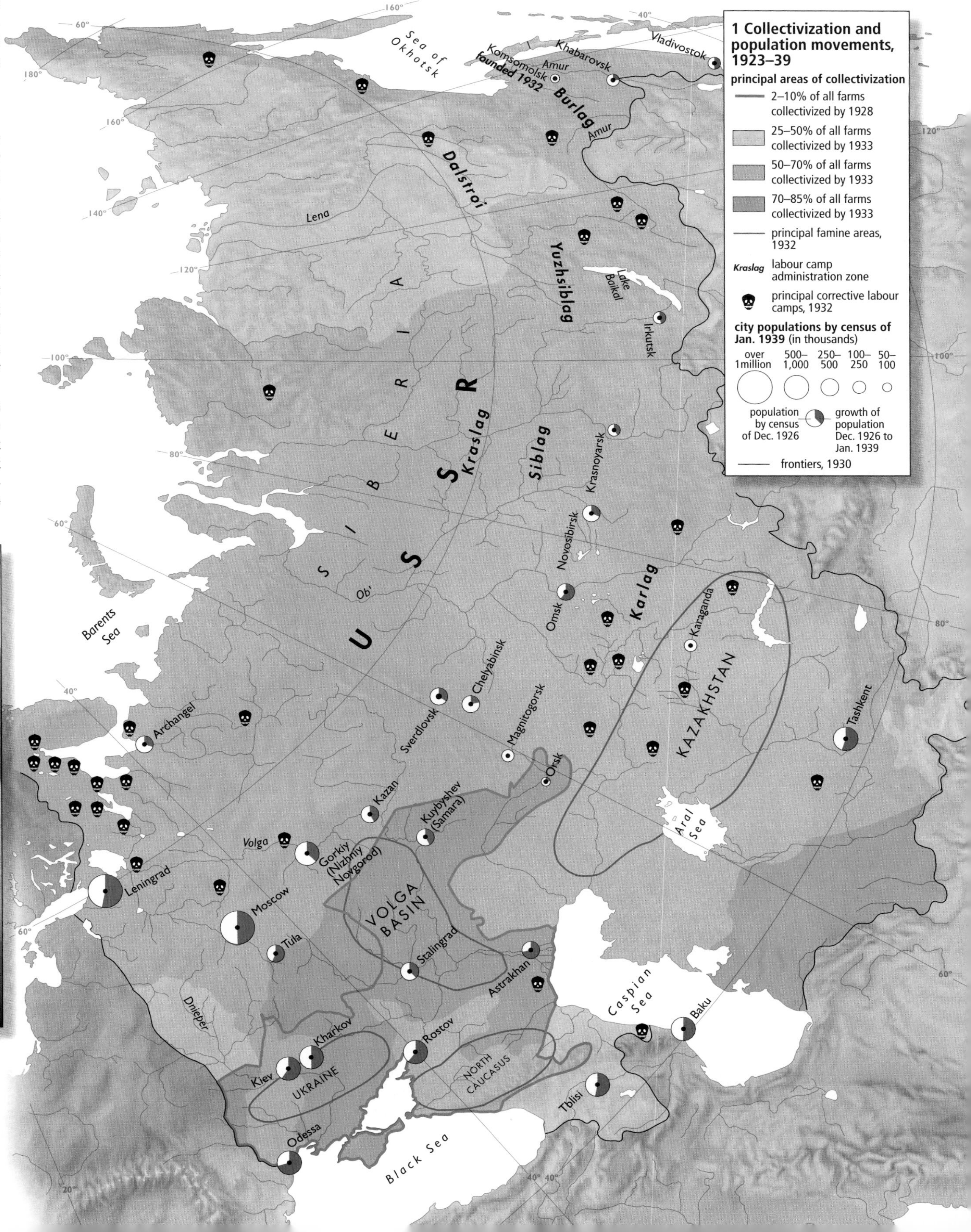

1 Collectivization and population movements, 1923–39
principal areas of collectivization
2–10% of all farms collectivized by 1928
25–50% of all farms collectivized by 1933
50–70% of all farms collectivized by 1933
70–85% of all farms collectivized by 1933
principal famine areas, 1932
Kraslag labour camp administration zone
principal corrective labour camps, 1932
city populations by census of Jan. 1939 (in thousands)
over 1million
500–1,000
250–500
100–250
50–100
population by census of Dec. 1926
growth of population Dec. 1926 to Jan. 1939
frontiers, 1930
Sea of Okhotsk
Komsomolsk founded 1932
Amur
Khabarovsk
Vladivostok
Burlag
Dalstroi
Lena
Yuzhsiblag
Lake Baikal
Irkutsk
SIBERIA
USSR
Kraslag
Siblag
Krasnoyarsk
Novosibirsk
Ob'
Omsk
Karlag
Karaganda
KAZAKHSTAN
Tashkent
Barents Sea
Chelyabinsk
Sverdlovsk
Magnitogorsk
Archangel
Orsk
Kazan
Kuybyshev (Samara)
Volga
Gorkiy (Nizhniy Novgorod)
Aral Sea
Leningrad
Moscow
VOLGA BASIN
Tula
Stalingrad
Astrakhan
Caspian Sea
Baku
Dnieper
Kharkov
Rostov
Kiev
UKRAINE
NORTH CAUCASUS
Tbilisi
Odessa
Black Sea

Europe

See also
Europe, 1945–73 p. 272
The Cold War, 1945–91 p. 274
The United States as a world power since 1945 p. 296
The development of the Soviet Union and Russia since 1929 p. 298
The world in the 1990s p. 302
The global economy p. 304

With the oil crisis of 1973, the post-war boom was replaced by slower, more uneven economic growth. In western Europe, plans for economic union were stepped up. Soviet-dominated eastern Europe disintegrated by the late 1980s, leaving a legacy of instability.

1973 *Oil crisis*

1974 *Salazar dies: democracy restored to Portugal*

1975 *Franco dies; democracy restored to Spain*

1980–1 *Solidarity campaign begins in Poland*

1985 *Gorbachev becomes Soviet leader; EEC agrees to create single market*

1989 *Communist bloc in eastern Europe disintegrates*

1990 *Germany reunified*

1991 *Maastricht Treaty signed*

1992–5 *Civil war in former Yugoslavia*

1995 *European Union formed*

Bosnian Muslim refugees in Han-Bila in July 1993 ***(below)*** at the height of the Serbian campaign against the Muslim population of the region. Thousands of Muslims were driven from their homes, tortured, imprisoned or starved to death in makeshift concentration camps. Later the most notorious perpetrators were put on trial for war crimes before the Court of Human Rights at the Hague.

IN 1973 THE OIL-PRODUCING states almost trebled the price of oil in a year, triggering worldwide price inflation. In Europe, the crisis coincided with a general slowdown in productivity and profit growth and mounting unemployment. The 1970s saw the onset of 'stagflation' – low rates of growth and soaring inflation. Unemployment, which had been almost eradicated in the 1960s, rose sharply, producing widespread labour unrest. Oil prices in the USSR affected the Soviet bloc as well. Economic performance stagnated behind the Iron Curtain, in some cases actually declined.

Economic integration

Across much of western Europe, the crisis was confronted by continuing the trend to greater economic integration. By the late 1960s, the original six members of the EEC (European Economic Community) had established themselves as the economic vanguard of the continent. Fearful that they were being left behind by their more dynamic neighbours, in 1973 Britain, Ireland and Denmark joined them. They were followed in 1981 by Greece, in 1986 by Spain and Portugal and in 1995 by Austria, Finland and Sweden.

Underpinning the EEC (renamed the EU, European Union, in 1995) was the belief, first proposed in the 1950s (*see* p. 272), that integrating the nations of western Europe was the only effective means of guaranteeing continued economic success. The massive economic bloc thereby created would allow Europe to compete effectively with the world's other leading economies, the USA and Japan. Such integration should in time evolve into full political union, with the aim of creating a single state. In 1985, the EEC agreed to create a single market under which it would became a free-trade zone. The Maastricht Treaty of 1991 then committed the EU to introduce a single currency, the Euro, by 1999. Despite misgivings – Britain and Denmark refused to join the Euro in the first wave – about the difficulties of coordinating so many disparate economies and the EU's lack of political accountability, the EU remained firmly committed to the project.

The coming of democracy

The combined effects of the economic slowdown after 1973 and the realization that by clinging to their pre-war authoritarian governments they were increasingly being pushed to the margins of Europe were sufficient to see the reintroduction of democracy to Portugal (1974) and Spain (1975). Greece also embraced democracy in 1974.

But these changes paled in comparison with events in eastern Europe in the late 1980s. These involved nothing less than the disintegration of the Soviet Union and the fall of communism in every one of its satellite states as well as in Yugoslavia and Albania. As remarkable as the collapse of this apparently permanent system was the creation in its wake of no less than 15 new countries. The reasons for this transformation were as much economic as political. Throughout the 1970s and 1980s, the economies

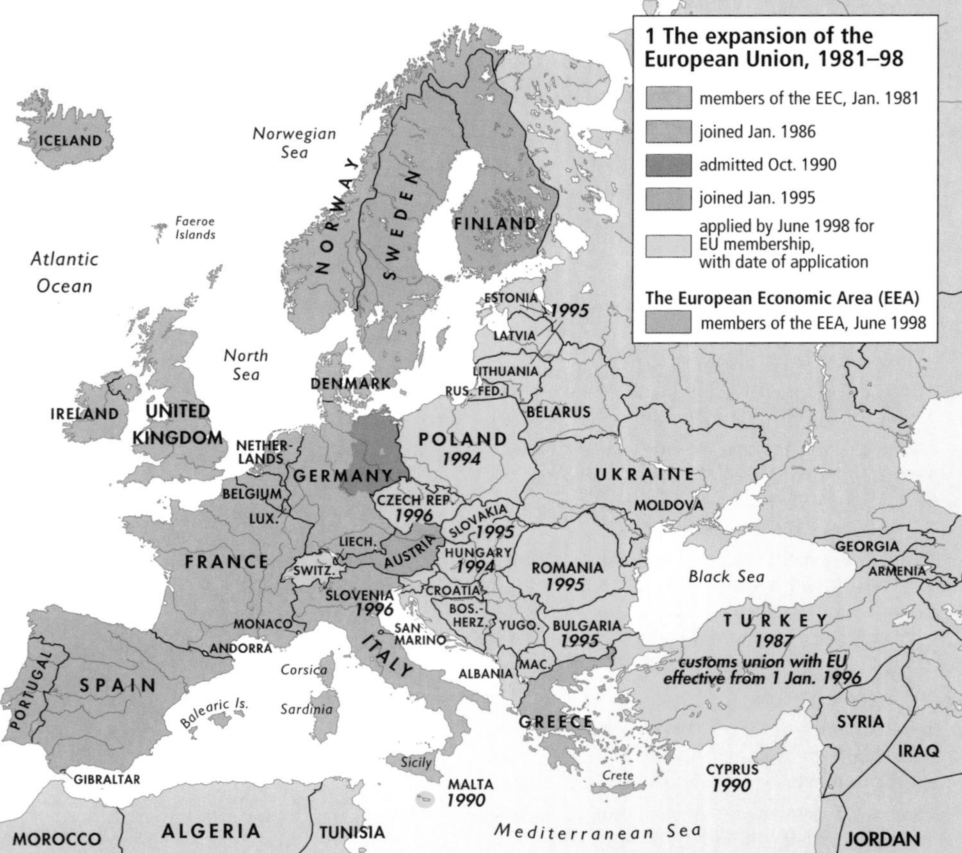

1 The EC in 1973 began a long-term programme of expansion ***(above)***. By 1995 it embraced most of western, southern and central Europe and, with reservations on the part of some member states, had agreed to create a single currency and to admit the former communist states of eastern Europe.

4 Referenda on European membership, 1972–98

Year	Country	Issue	Decision
1998			
	Denmark	whether to ratify Amsterdam Treaty	✓ yes
	Ireland	whether to ratify Amsterdam Treaty	✓ yes
1994			
	Norway	whether to join	✗ no
	Finland	whether to join	✓ yes
	Sweden	whether to join	✓ yes
	Austria	whether to join	✓ yes
1993			
	Denmark	Maastricht Treaty	✓ yes
	France	Maastricht Treaty	✓ yes
	Ireland	Maastricht Treaty	✓ yes
	Switzerland	whether to take part in European Economic Area	✗ no
1992			
	Denmark	Maastricht Treaty	✗ no
1987			
	Ireland	Single European Act	✓ yes
1986			
	Denmark	Single European Act	✓ yes
1982			
	Greenland	(1979 gained internal autonomy from Denmark) whether to withdraw	✓ yes
1975			
	UK	whether to remain in the EEC	✓ yes
1972			
	Denmark	whether to join	✓ yes
	Ireland	whether to join	✓ yes
	France	whether EEC should be enlarged	✓ yes
	Norway	whether to join	✗ no

4 The decision whether to join the European Community , or to accept its reform, aroused strong political feelings. Since 1971 referenda ***(right)*** have commonly been used to resolve important issues. Norway rejected membership in 1971, but re-applied in 1994 only to have its voters reject entry again. In Britain there was also widespread anxiety about commitment to Europe and in 1992 Prime Minister John Major refused a referendum on ratifying the Maastricht Treaty. In Denmark the Treaty was rejected in 1992 by the tiny margin of 40,000 votes, but a second referendum in May 1993 produced a vote of 58 per cent in favour. Britain and Denmark remain the only European Union states with large minorities opposed to the further development of an integrated Europe.

of the communist bloc had declined to the point where the region was effectively bankrupt. Unable to guarantee the survival of its client states, the Soviet Union under President Gorbachev abandoned them. By 1991 free elections had been held in every country of the region, including the Soviet Union, and the two Germanies had been reunited. Except for a short surge of violence in Romania, the transformation had been relatively peaceful.

The revival of nationalism

The euphoria which greeted the end of communism was followed swiftly by a fresh set of economic problems as the new regimes struggled to come to terms with democracy and economic liberalization. In the atmosphere of crisis old ethnic or religious conflicts revived. Slovakia won its independence from the Czechs in 1993. In 1991 Moldova declared independence and a brief civil war followed between the differing ethnic groups making up the new state.

But the most bloody and prolonged struggle took place in Yugoslavia, which in 1991 disintegrated under pressure from the long-suppressed rivalries of its ethnic groups, despite Serbian resistance. Between 1991 and 1995 Serbia fought first against Slovenian, then Croatian and finally Bosnian independence, declared in 1992 by its Muslim majority. Only the intervention of NATO in 1995 prevented further bloodshed in what had become the most barbarous European conflict since the Second World War. In 1998 civil war broke out in Serbia itself when ethnic Albanian separatists in Kosovo fought for independence.

Nationalist conflict continued in western Europe, too. Basque separatism in Spain and Irish nationalism in Ulster were both sustained by terrorism from the 1970s. In Ireland political agreement for closer cooperation between nationalists and Unionists was secured in 1998, though tensions survived. Although much of Europe became freer and more prosperous by the late 1990s, political stability and economic progress could not be guaranteed across the continent.

3 The Yugoslav civil war, 1991–5

3 After 1989 the Yugoslav Federation *(above)* began to break up into its constituent parts. In 1991 Croatia and Slovenia declared their independence. Though the Serb-dominated rump of Yugoslavia tried to force both states to remain in the federation, they became fully independent in 1992. When Bosnia tried to assert its independence a bitter civil war broke out between Serbs, Muslims and Croats which lasted until 1995, when NATO compelled Serbia to accept a ceasefire. The subsequent agreement divided Bosnia into two separate states, one Serb and one Croat/Muslim.

> In 1989 we experienced upheavals on our continent which have been unparalleled in peacetime since 1848, which was also a year of revolutions driven by a desire for political liberty and national self-expression. For the most part the revolutions of 1848 ended in violence and disappointment In 1989, as this astonishing pace of change continues, we have begun to hope that it might prove lasting. There may be halts and reverses, but it would be hard now to recreate the Iron Curtain.
>
> **Douglas Hurd, British Foreign Secretary, November 1989**

2 Between 1989 and 1991 communist eastern Europe was transformed *(map below)* from a Soviet-dominated bloc of authoritarian dictatorships to a patchwork of new regimes and states, most of them multi-party democracies. Growing popular dissatisfaction with the absence of civil rights and political freedom coupled with the region's poor economic performance produced widespread popular protest in 1989. Beginning in Hungary and Poland, the protests spread to East Germany. The fall of the East German government, precipitated by a mass emigration through Hungary, was a signal, like the Paris revolution in 1848, for the rest of eastern Europe to follow suit. By 1990 50 years of Soviet domination of eastern Europe had ended.

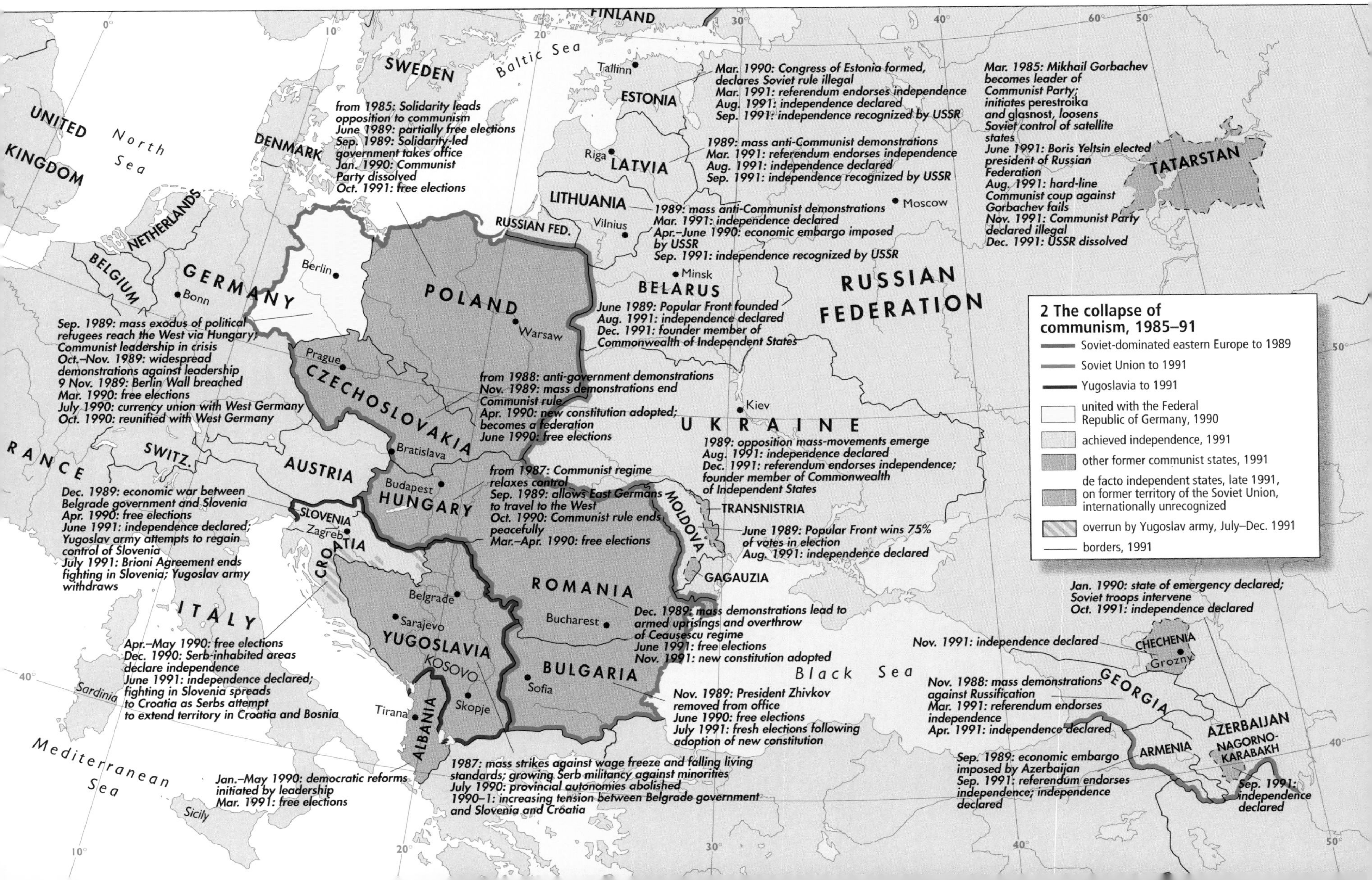

2 The collapse of communism, 1985–91

The world in the 1990s

See also
The Cold War, 1945–91 p. 274
Nationalism, secularism and Islam in the Middle East since 1945 p. 290
The United States as a world power since 1945 p. 296
Europe since 1973 p. 300
The global economy p. 304
Communications in the modern age p. 306
The global enviroment p. 308

The 1990s was a decade of progress in the spreading of democracy, in ending conflict, in superpower disarmament and in stabilizing economic development. Yet many critical issues remained for the 21st century. Ecological crisis, religious conflict and the threat of regional wars challenged the mood of optimism in the West as it prepared to celebrate the new millennium.

THROUGHOUT THE 1990s the world lived free of the shadow of the Cold War. The USA remained the world's largest military power, and on occasion exploited its muscle to enforce the peace, but the fragmented former Soviet bloc saw its formidable striking power dissipated. An uneasy peace arose between the two, reinforced by a commitment to nuclear disarmament. Yet the absence of global confrontation did not prevent regional disputes, many of which dragged in the major powers as arbiters.

A decade of conflict

The 1990s were punctuated by small wars and civil conflict. In 1990 the Iraqi leader Saddam Hussein invaded Kuwait, only to be expelled by the United Nations by force in 1991. Thereafter, tensions persisted as Iraq and the UN argued about the terms set for the inspection and destruction of Iraqi weapons of mass destruction. In Chechnya, Russian forces fought a grim civil war against Chechen nationalists which left the region desolate. Here, too, an uneasy peace was established in 1996. The largest war of all involved the states that emerged from the collapse of former Yugoslavia in 1991 (*see* p. 300). In 1995 NATO had imposed a settlement on the warring Serbs, Croats and Bosnians, but three years later fighting broke out again between Serbs and Albanian separatists in Kosovo.

The ability of small states to engage in warfare at all depended on a supply of arms from developed states. With the end of the Cold War both sides cut back military budgets and arms output. Weapons sales to the developing world became ever more vital. While military spending in the USA fell to 4.3 per cent of GDP by the mid-1990s, in the Middle East states spent up to 8 to 10 per cent. In east and south Asia, where countries were faced with the massive military weight of China, military spending rose steadily in the 1990s, reaching around 3 to 5 per cent of GDP. The trade in arms also led to an illicit trade in technology to support the development of weapons – chemical and biological warfare and nuclear devices – which the West tried to limit. In 1998 India and Pakistan both tested nuclear bombs, while other states (such as Israel) have nuclear know-how and, perhaps, weapons.

In 1994 Nelson Mandela ***(above)*** was elected the first president of a multi-racial South Africa. Active in the anti-Apartheid movement in the 1950s, he was imprisoned in 1962 by the white Nationalist regime. By the 1980s, he had become a symbol of the struggle for democracy. In 1990 Mandela (aged 72) was freed, and became leader of the African National Congress which in 1994 swept to power in South Africa's first multi-racial elections. He played a key part in re-integrating South Africa with the wider world after 30 years of isolation. His moral authority has helped hold together a society that faces serious problems of crime and poverty.

Many of the civil conflicts of the 1990s involved religious tensions. Throughout the Islamic world, including the large Islamic communities now living and working in the West, radical movements developed whose aim was to restore traditional Islamic law and drive out westernizing modernity. In Algeria, Egypt, Sudan, Lebanon and Israel the consequence was persistent terrorism; in Afghanistan it produced civil war throughout the 1990s, which threatened to spill over into the Islamic regions of southern Russia. In India the Hindu-Muslim conflict that divided the nation at independence in 1947 revived in a sharp form in the mid-1990s as both communities stressed a return to traditional religious values.

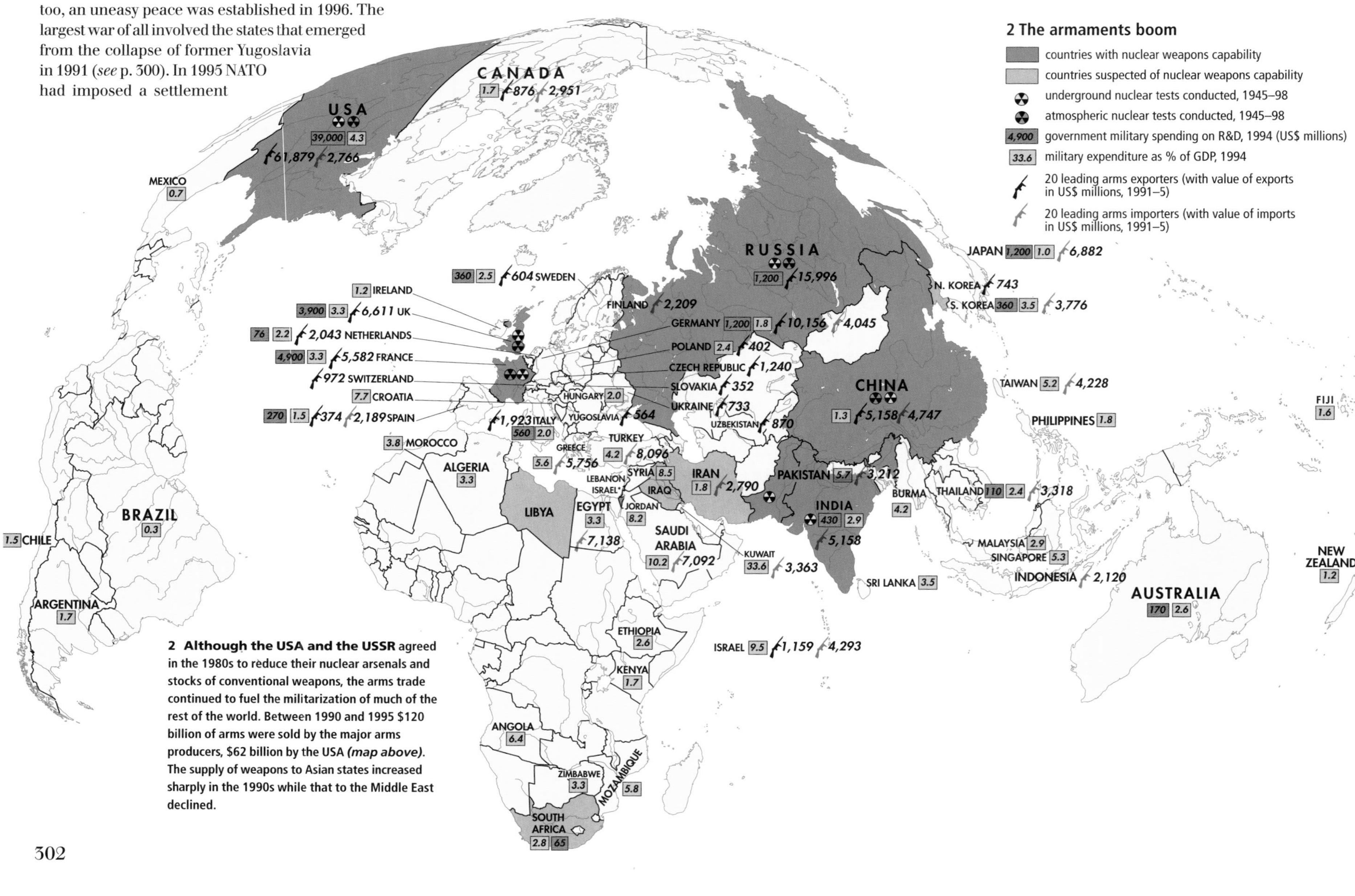

2 The armaments boom

- countries with nuclear weapons capability
- countries suspected of nuclear weapons capability
- underground nuclear tests conducted, 1945–98
- atmospheric nuclear tests conducted, 1945–98
- 4,900 government military spending on R&D, 1994 (US$ millions)
- 33.6 military expenditure as % of GDP, 1994
- 20 leading arms exporters (with value of exports in US$ millions, 1991–5)
- 20 leading arms importers (with value of imports in US$ millions, 1991–5)

2 Although the USA and the USSR agreed in the 1980s to reduce their nuclear arsenals and stocks of conventional weapons, the arms trade continued to fuel the militarization of much of the rest of the world. Between 1990 and 1995 $120 billion of arms were sold by the major arms producers, $62 billion by the USA ***(map above)***. The supply of weapons to Asian states increased sharply in the 1990s while that to the Middle East declined.

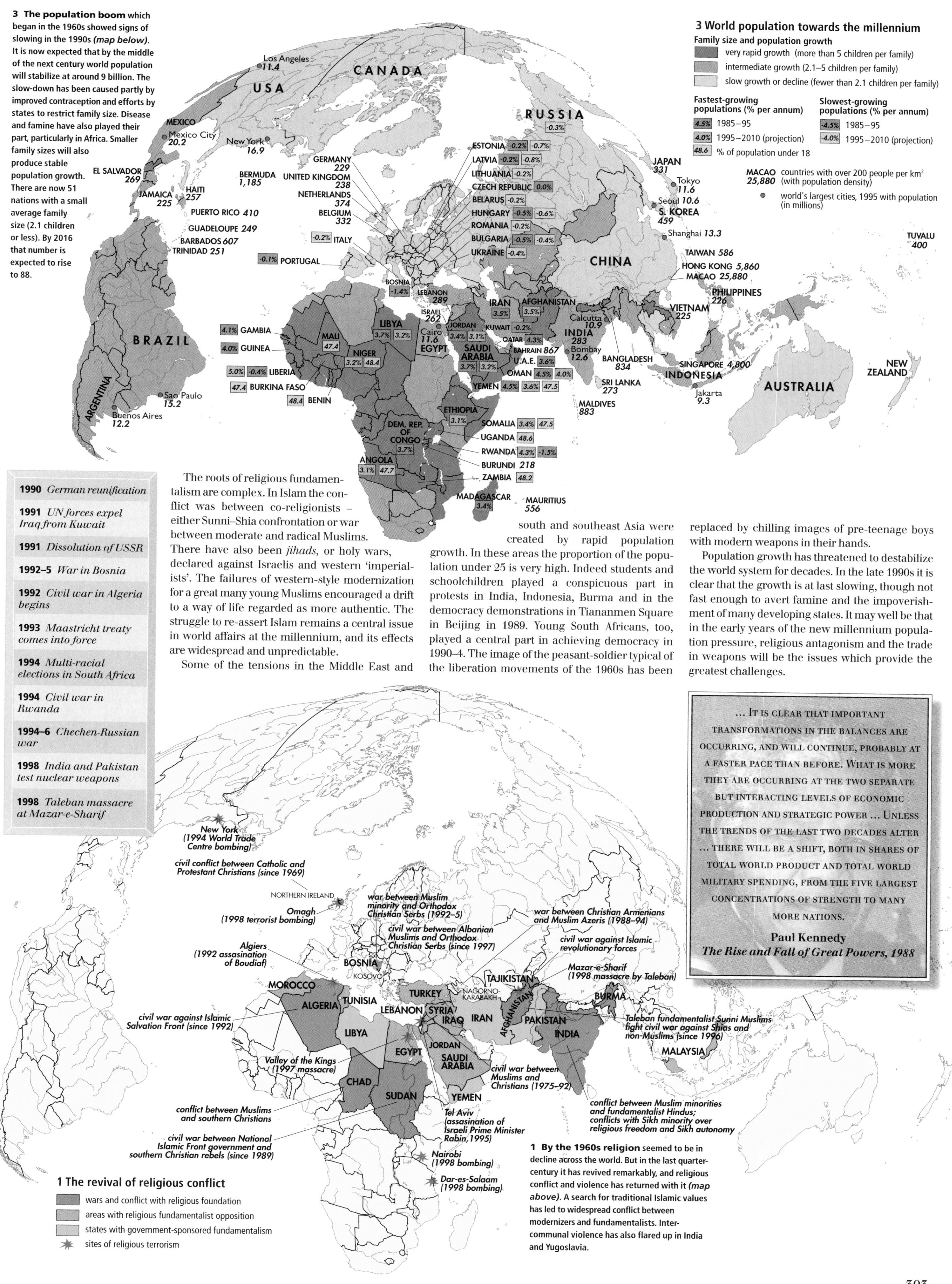

3 The population boom which began in the 1960s showed signs of slowing in the 1990s *(map below)*. It is now expected that by the middle of the next century world population will stabilize at around 9 billion. The slow-down has been caused partly by improved contraception and efforts by states to restrict family size. Disease and famine have also played their part, particularly in Africa. Smaller family sizes will also produce stable population growth. There are now 51 nations with a small average family size (2.1 children or less). By 2016 that number is expected to rise to 88.

1990 *German reunification*
1991 *UN forces expel Iraq from Kuwait*
1991 *Dissolution of USSR*
1992–5 *War in Bosnia*
1992 *Civil war in Algeria begins*
1993 *Maastricht treaty comes into force*
1994 *Multi-racial elections in South Africa*
1994 *Civil war in Rwanda*
1994–6 *Chechen-Russian war*
1998 *India and Pakistan test nuclear weapons*
1998 *Taleban massacre at Mazar-e-Sharif*

The roots of religious fundamentalism are complex. In Islam the conflict was between co-religionists – either Sunni–Shia confrontation or war between moderate and radical Muslims. There have also been *jihads*, or holy wars, declared against Israelis and western 'imperialists'. The failures of western-style modernization for a great many young Muslims encouraged a drift to a way of life regarded as more authentic. The struggle to re-assert Islam remains a central issue in world affairs at the millennium, and its effects are widespread and unpredictable.

Some of the tensions in the Middle East and south and southeast Asia were created by rapid population growth. In these areas the proportion of the population under 25 is very high. Indeed students and schoolchildren played a conspicuous part in protests in India, Indonesia, Burma and in the democracy demonstrations in Tiananmen Square in Beijing in 1989. Young South Africans, too, played a central part in achieving democracy in 1990–4. The image of the peasant-soldier typical of the liberation movements of the 1960s has been replaced by chilling images of pre-teenage boys with modern weapons in their hands.

Population growth has threatened to destabilize the world system for decades. In the late 1990s it is clear that the growth is at last slowing, though not fast enough to avert famine and the impoverishment of many developing states. It may well be that in the early years of the new millennium population pressure, religious antagonism and the trade in weapons will be the issues which provide the greatest challenges.

> ... It is clear that important transformations in the balances are occurring, and will continue, probably at a faster pace than before. What is more they are occurring at the two separate but interacting levels of economic production and strategic power ... Unless the trends of the last two decades alter ... there will be a shift, both in shares of total world product and total world military spending, from the five largest concentrations of strength to many more nations.
>
> **Paul Kennedy**
> ***The Rise and Fall of Great Powers, 1988***

1 By the 1960s religion seemed to be in decline across the world. But in the last quarter-century it has revived remarkably, and religious conflict and violence has returned with it *(map above)*. A search for traditional Islamic values has led to widespread conflict between modernizers and fundamentalists. Inter-communal violence has also flared up in India and Yugoslavia.

The global economy

See also
The Great Depression, 1929–39 p. 264
Japan and east Asia since 1945 p. 278
Southeast Asia since 1945 p. 282
The United States: the age of abundance p. 294
Europe since 1973 p. 300
The world in the 1990s p. 302
Communications in the modern world p. 306
The global environment p. 308

1978 *China declares 'Open Door' policy*

1987 *Single European Act for full economic union*

1991 *Russia begins programme of economic reform*

1992 *Maastricht Treaty*

1994 *Mexico joins North American Free Trade Area*

1995 *EEC becomes the European Union*

1997–8 *Financial crisis rocks east Asian economies*

1998 *Russian financial crisis*

1999 *European single currency (the 'euro') introduced*

By the 1990s electronic communication and world-wide investment and marketing had created a genuinely global economy. Giant transnational companies dominated finance and production. Yet the gulf between rich and poor nations remained, and the developing world relied on the developed world for aid, investment and export markets.

IN 1992 AN AMERICAN STATE Department official, Francis Fukuyama, published *The End of History*, in which he argued that the collapse of the Soviet bloc signalled the final worldwide triumph of modern free-market capitalism over all other systems. In the former Communist bloc capitalist free-market reforms had been introduced. Even in China, the remaining Communist superpower, the economy was liberalized and western capital and technology introduced. By the end of the decade an integrated global economy had emerged.

However, world economic development still depended in part on the central management of key economic factors by groups of states, and on collaboration between them. Representatives of the largest industrial economies met regularly as the Group of Seven to co-ordinate financial and trade policies. Additionally, regional agreements sought to expand trade between small groups of states.

Regional and global integration

The most successful of these groupings was the European Union, which grew from the original six members of the EEC in 1957 to embrace 15 states by 1996. Gradual economic integration culminated on 1 January 1999 in the introduction of a single currency, the euro. Economic groups elsewhere were looser associations aiming to enhance regional economic integration. In 1994, for example, the USA, Canada and Mexico joined together in the North American Free Trade Association (NAFTA).

Integration was also encouraged by the rapid growth of multinational (or transnational) enterprises and high levels of foreign direct investment. In the early 1990s it was estimated that the 37,000 multinationals employed 73 million people. The 100 largest companies controlled one-third of all foreign investment, most of it in the developed world. The existence of multinationals, many with assets larger than the GDP of smaller states, acted to stabilize the world economy, though at the cost of lack of supervision by sovereign states.

Global inequality

The fruits of the global economic success were spread very unevenly. Sustained expansion in Asia, Europe and the United States was accompanied by economic decline in Africa, Latin America and the former Soviet bloc. The Russian economy in particular faced serious crisis by 1998 as the rush for capitalism failed to generate the wealth to sustain employment and welfare at the level achieved under communism. Even in east Asia, which grew faster than anywhere else in the world from the 1960s to the mid-1990s, the boom turned sour in 1997. Burdened with debt, high population growth and excessive dependence on a cluster of manufacturing exports, the new Asian economies generated a financial crisis which threatened the health of the whole global economy.

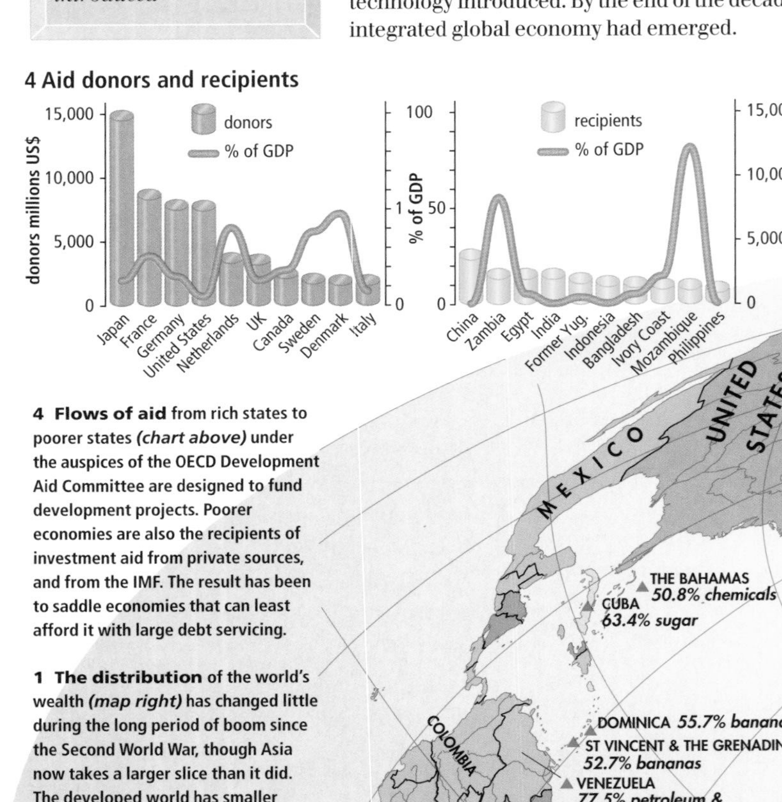

4 Flows of aid from rich states to poorer states *(chart above)* under the auspices of the OECD Development Aid Committee are designed to fund development projects. Poorer economies are also the recipients of investment aid from private sources, and from the IMF. The result has been to saddle economies that can least afford it with large debt servicing.

1 The distribution of the world's wealth *(map right)* has changed little during the long period of boom since the Second World War, though Asia now takes a larger slice than it did. The developed world has smaller populations and higher per capita incomes. Many states in the developing world, particularly in Africa and the Middle East, are heavily dependent on the sale of one commodity on world markets.

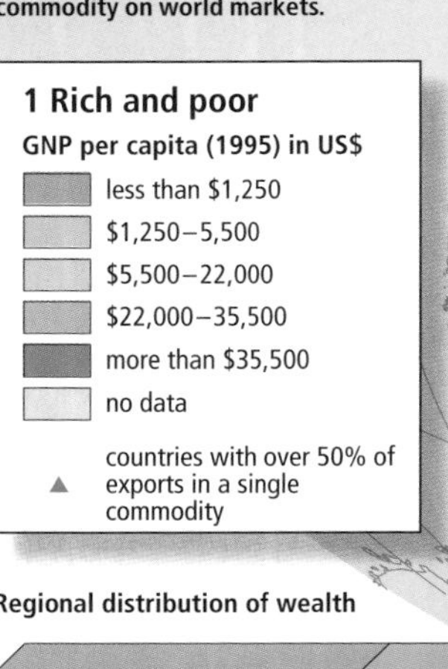

Regional distribution of wealth

total world GNP 1995: US$ 27,110,768 million

Europe 32.6%
Asia 30.4%
N. America 29.7%
S. America 4.3%
Africa 1.5%
Oceania 1.5%

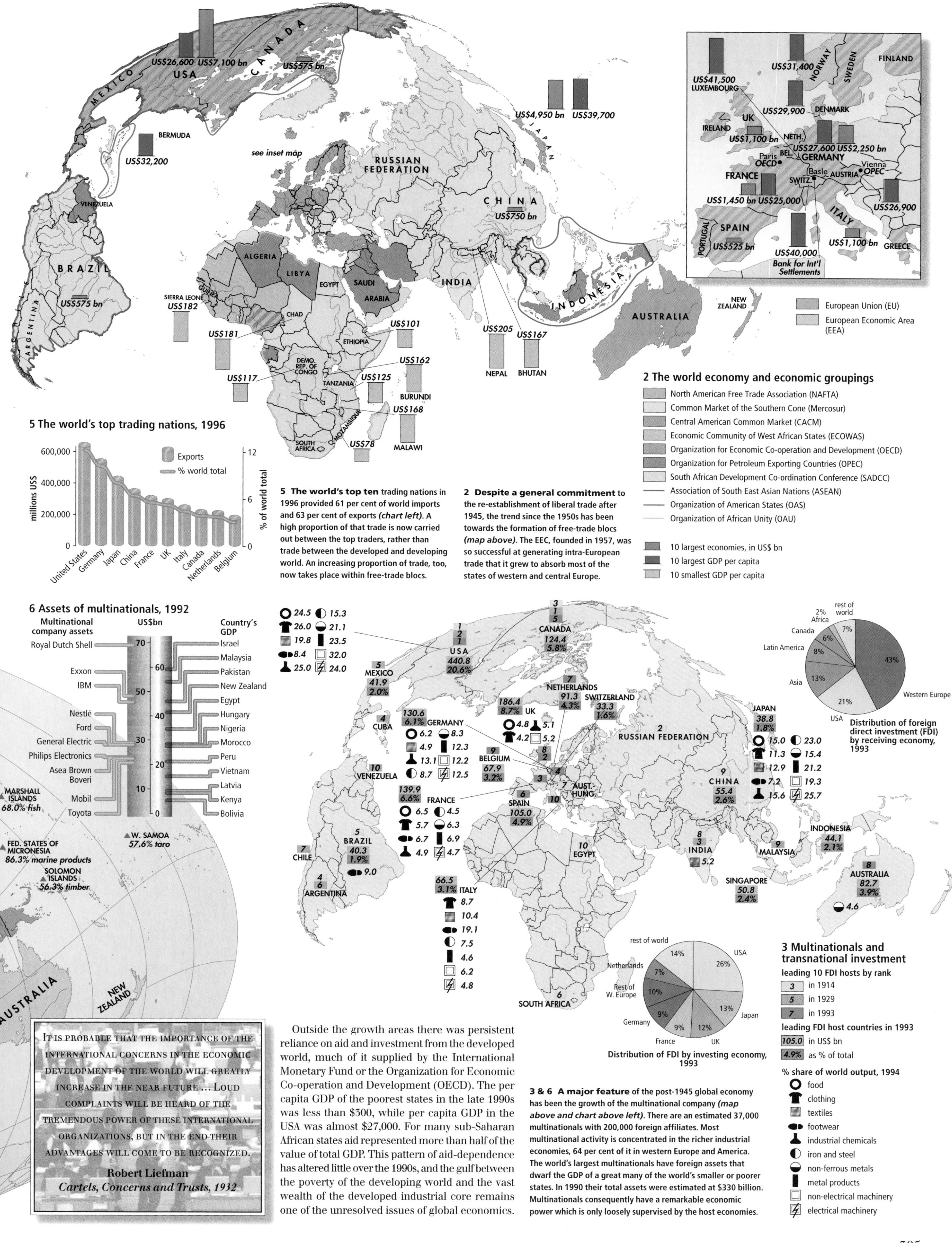

5 The world's top ten trading nations in 1996 provided 61 per cent of world imports and 63 per cent of exports *(chart left)*. A high proportion of that trade is now carried out between the top traders, rather than trade between the developed and developing world. An increasing proportion of trade, too, now takes place within free-trade blocs.

2 Despite a general commitment to the re-establishment of liberal trade after 1945, the trend since the 1950s has been towards the formation of free-trade blocs *(map above)*. The EEC, founded in 1957, was so successful at generating intra-European trade that it grew to absorb most of the states of western and central Europe.

> IT IS PROBABLE THAT THE IMPORTANCE OF THE INTERNATIONAL CONCERNS IN THE ECONOMIC DEVELOPMENT OF THE WORLD WILL GREATLY INCREASE IN THE NEAR FUTURE ... LOUD COMPLAINTS WILL BE HEARD OF THE TREMENDOUS POWER OF THESE INTERNATIONAL ORGANIZATIONS, BUT IN THE END THEIR ADVANTAGES WILL COME TO BE RECOGNIZED.
>
> **Robert Liefman**
> *Cartels, Concerns and Trusts, 1932*

Outside the growth areas there was persistent reliance on aid and investment from the developed world, much of it supplied by the International Monetary Fund or the Organization for Economic Co-operation and Development (OECD). The per capita GDP of the poorest states in the late 1990s was less than $300, while per capita GDP in the USA was almost $27,000. For many sub-Saharan African states aid represented more than half of the value of total GDP. This pattern of aid-dependence has altered little over the 1990s, and the gulf between the poverty of the developing world and the vast wealth of the developed industrial core remains one of the unresolved issues of global economics.

3 & 6 A major feature of the post-1945 global economy has been the growth of the multinational company *(map above and chart above left)*. There are an estimated 37,000 multinationals with 200,000 foreign affiliates. Most multinational activity is concentrated in the richer industrial economies, 64 per cent of it in western Europe and America. The world's largest multinationals have foreign assets that dwarf the GDP of a great many of the world's smaller or poorer states. In 1990 their total assets were estimated at $330 billion. Multinationals consequently have a remarkable economic power which is only loosely supervised by the host economies.

See also
The world in the 1990s p. 302
The global economy p. 304
The global environment p. 308

Communications in the modern age

The 20th century has witnessed a profound revolution in communication of every kind. Motor vehicles and aeroplanes have made the whole globe accessible, moulding the modern high-growth economy and transforming social life and leisure. The age of mass electronic communications has opened up possibilities undreamed of a century ago.

The world's airports have become increasingly congested *(above)* with the rapid growth of air travel. Chicago's O'Hare Airport handled 69 million passengers in 1996, London's Heathrow 56 million. Travel times have fallen dramatically. It took four perilous weeks to fly to Australia in 1919. Today, it takes less than a day.

THE 20TH CENTURY witnessed a revolution in communication that transformed practically every aspect of daily life. The changes were the fruit of a remarkable cluster of scientific breakthroughs in the 40 years before the First World War: the telephone, invented by Alexander Bell in 1876; the first automobiles powered by the internal combustion engine, pioneered by Karl Benz and Gottlieb Daimler in the 1880s ; the radio transmitter, developed by Guglielmo Marconi in 1896; the discovery of the electron in 1897 by Joseph Thomson; and the development of powered flight, begun by the Wright brothers in 1903. The development of the silicon microchip in the late 1950s completed this scientific foundation.

The internal combustion engine

The development of motorized transport on land and in the air was dependent on the development of a sufficiently powerful and efficient engine. The internal combustion engine, fuelled by refined oil, provided the key. Improvements in engine technology then made possible the evolution of mass-motoring and high-performance aircraft. Motor vehicles and aeroplanes gave transport a flexibility and speed unattainable by railways and horses.

Motorization began before the First World War in Europe and America. Henry Ford established his motor company in 1903, and within a decade had become the world's most successful mass producer of motor cars. The greater spread of wealth in the United States encouraged high levels of car ownership and by 1939 the majority of the world's motor vehicles were produced there. Rising incomes after 1945 fuelled growing demand worldwide. By 1959 there were 119 million vehicles in use; by 1974 the figure was 303 million. Motor transport transformed industry and commerce, produced a sharp change in social patterns and broke down the isolation of rural areas. Motorization also made possible mass leisure and mass tourism.

Air travel and telecommunications

In 1919 the first primitive airlines opened in Europe using the experience of the war years in producing larger and safer aircraft. The first modern multi-engined monoplane airliners were developed in the 1930s by the Boeing and Douglas companies in America, and in 1939 the first successful passenger services were opened across the Atlantic Ocean. Air travel expanded rapidly from the 1950s thanks to the development of a new generation of high-performance wide-bodied jet aircraft. The first jet airliner, the British Comet, flew in 1952, but world airliner markets were subsequently dominated by a succession of Boeing models.

Aircraft have made the world a smaller place. Journeys that took months in the 19th century now take less than a day. For the populations of the richer developed states global travel is taken for granted. Meanwhile, many poorer states now depend on tourism as their primary source of income. The shrinking of the globe has led to the emergence of a common global culture. The exotic may be within reach, but modern communication and

4 International tourist arrivals, 1950–94

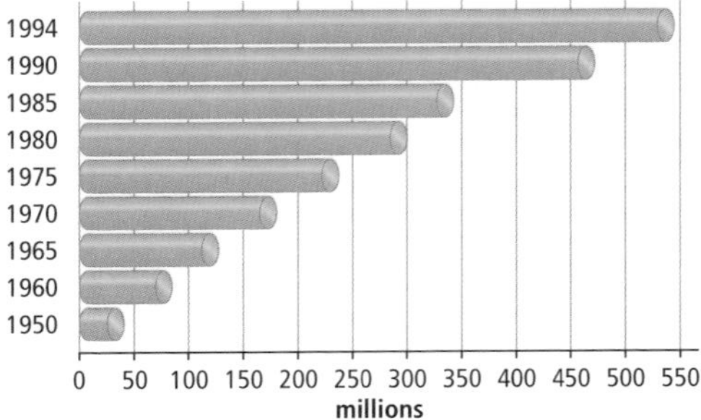

4 The introduction of cheap air travel combined with higher incomes and longer holidays in the developed world have generated mass tourism since the 1960s *(chart left)*. In 1994 almost 550 million tourist arrivals were recorded, the majority of them in Europe. Growing wealth in the West has led tourists to more exotic destinations in Africa, Asia and the Pacific.

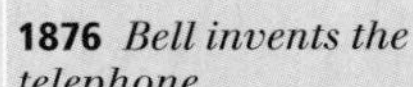

1876 *Bell invents the telephone*

1903 *Wright brothers make first powered flight*

1903 *Ford Motor Company founded*

1919 *First trans-Atlantic flight*

1928 *GEC develop first television images*

1948 *Transistor developed*

1948 *Britain develops first storage computer*

1952 *First jet airliner, the Comet*

1962 *Launch of first telecommunications satellite*

1969 *First Concorde flight*

1985 *Fax machines commercially available*

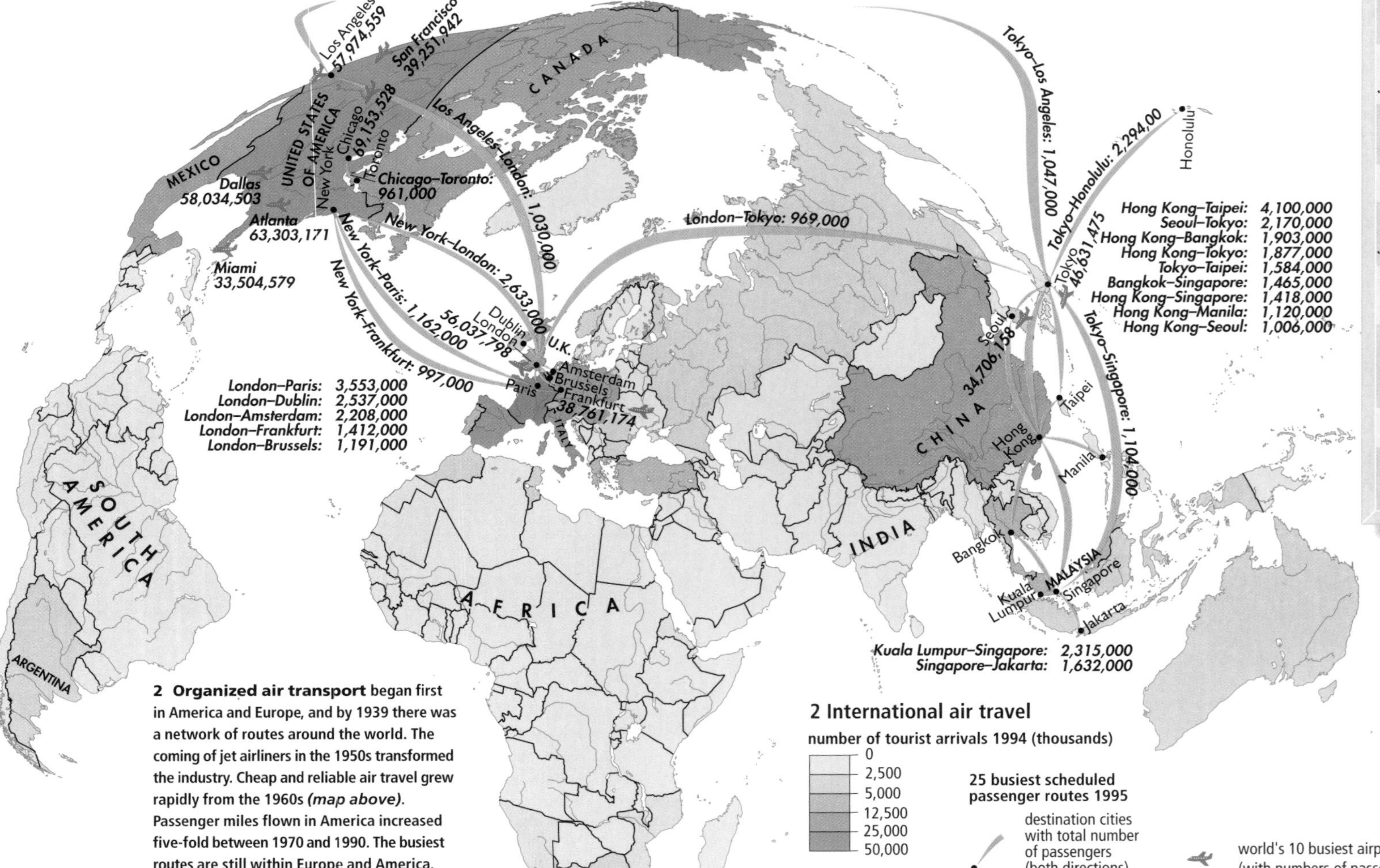

2 Organized air transport began first in America and Europe, and by 1939 there was a network of routes around the world. The coming of jet airliners in the 1950s transformed the industry. Cheap and reliable air travel grew rapidly from the 1960s *(map above)*. Passenger miles flown in America increased five-fold between 1970 and 1990. The busiest routes are still within Europe and America.

5 World communications equipment

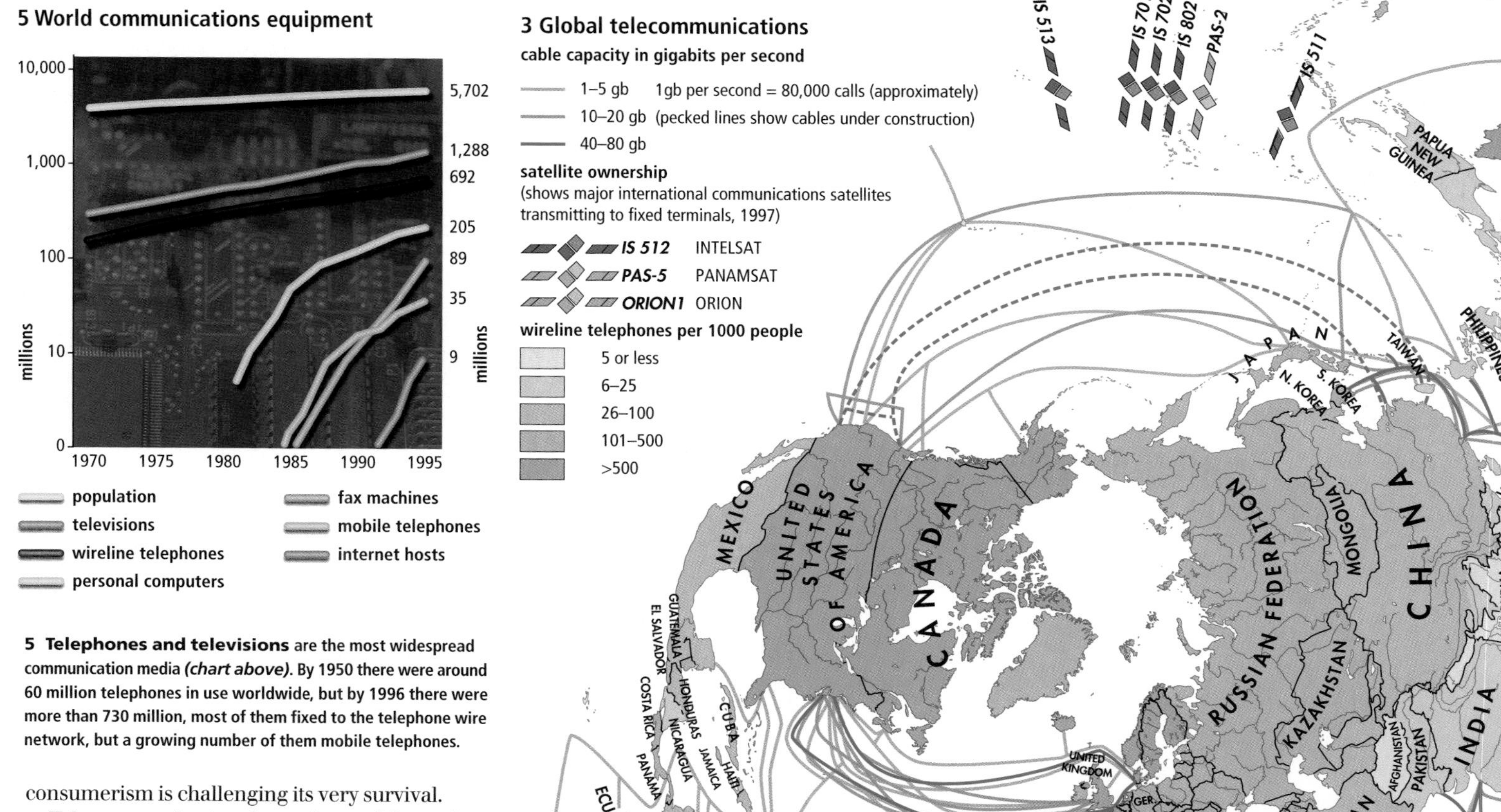

5 Telephones and televisions are the most widespread communication media *(chart above)*. By 1950 there were around 60 million telephones in use worldwide, but by 1996 there were more than 730 million, most of them fixed to the telephone wire network, but a growing number of them mobile telephones.

consumerism is challenging its very survival.

Telecommunications have changed faster than any other form of communication. The use of telephones expanded rapidly from the 1880s – there were just 50 million globally in 1930, but 350 million by 1975. Meanwhile in the 1920s television was developed, and the first public broadcasts followed in the 1930s. The development of the space programme after World War II encouraged the search for new forms of electronic communication. The development of the microchip opened up a new world of advanced communication. It allowed the development of small and increasingly efficient computer systems, and a modern global telephone network. In 1962 the first of many telecommunications satellites entered service. By the 1990s satellite communications were widely used for computer, television and telephone communication. In the early 1990s the growth of the Internet opened up a world of instant electronic information for its millions of users.

The electronic revolution has shrunk the worlds of finance, commerce and education. Billions of dollars or yen can be transferred at the press of a button. Information can be made instantly available. The pace of innovation shows no sign of slackening. The 21st century will see more changes in lifestyle and work as microchips perform work previously done by routine human labour.

3 The development of satellite communications since the 1960s and the revolution in microchip technology from the 1970s have created a global web of electronic communications by telephone, fax, television and computer *(map above)*. In the 1990s the growth of the Internet made possible instant communication world-wide via computer. The spread has been very uneven, however, with most electronic equipment concentrated in the world's most developed states.

> THE ADVANCE IN SCIENTIFIC KNOWLEDGE HAS PRODUCED OVER THE PAST 40 OR 50 YEARS CHANGES IN THE CONDITIONS OF LIFE WHICH HAVE RENDERED THE OLD WAYS OF LIVING AND OF CONDUCTING AFFAIRS UNWORKABLE ... IMPROVEMENT IN COMMUNICATIONS HAS LED TO A VIRTUAL NULLIFICATION OF DISTANCE ... A MAN CAN NOW CONVERSE OVER THE AIR WITH ANY OTHER MAN ANYWHERE ... AS WELL AS BEING ABLE TO TRAVEL ROUND THE WHOLE WORLD IN LESS TIME THAN IT TOOK TO GO FROM LONDON TO PARIS 150 YEARS AGO.
>
> ***Air Power and Civilization***
> **M.J. Davy, 1941**

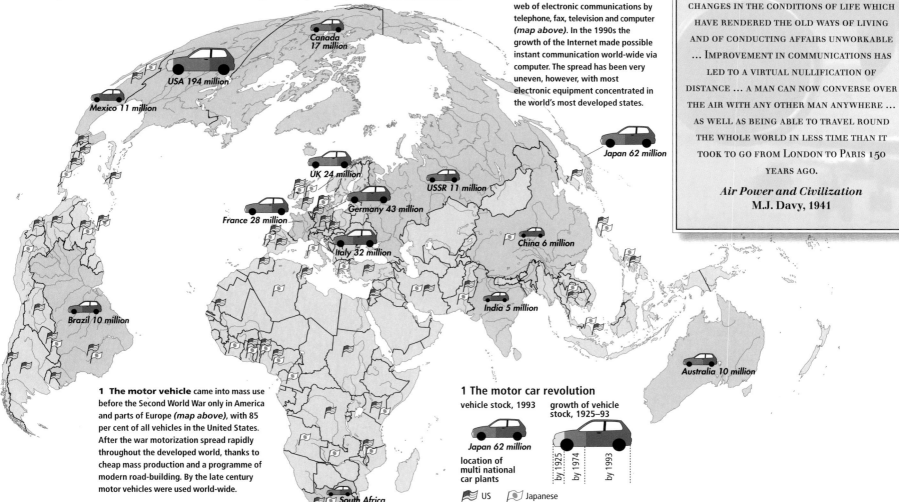

Canada 17 million
USA 194 million
Mexico 11 million
Japan 62 million
UK 24 million
USSR 11 million
Germany 43 million
France 28 million
Italy 32 million
China 6 million
India 5 million
Brazil 10 million
Australia 10 million
South Africa 5 million

1 The motor vehicle came into mass use before the Second World War only in America and parts of Europe *(map above)*, with 85 per cent of all vehicles in the United States. After the war motorization spread rapidly throughout the developed world, thanks to cheap mass production and a programme of modern road-building. By the late century motor vehicles were used world-wide.

1 The motor car revolution

vehicle stock, 1993
Japan 62 million
growth of vehicle stock, 1925–93
by 1925
by 1974
by 1993
location of multi national car plants
US
Japanese

The global environment

See also
The world in the 1990s p. 302
The global economy p. 304
Communications in the modern age p. 306

Until the 20th century, the environment was largely determined by natural changes. Industrialization, modern communications and mass consumption have combined to produce damaging man-made environmental change. Pollution now threatens the atmosphere itself. Ecological disasters have become among the most urgent of global problems.

> WE ESTIMATE THAT IF THE SEVEN BILLION PEOPLE OF THE YEAR 2000 HAVE A GNP PER CAPITA AS HIGH AS THAT OF PRESENT-DAY AMERICANS, THE TOTAL POLLUTION LOAD ON THE ENVIRONMENT WOULD BE AT LEAST TEN TIMES ITS PRESENT VALUE. CAN THE EARTH'S NATURAL SYSTEMS SUPPORT AN INTRUSION OF THAT MAGNITUDE? WE HAVE NO IDEA.
>
> Club of Rome, 1972
> *The Limits to Growth, 1972*

1970 *US Clean Air Act*

1972 *Publication of* The Limits to Growth

1973 *Oil price rise prompts worldwide crisis*

1986 *Chernobyl nuclear accident*

1987 *Montreal Protocol on CFC emissions*

1992 *Rio de Janeiro Earth Summit*

1997 *Smog from forest fires envelops Indonesia*

1997 *Kyoto Treaty on global warming*

1998 *Buenos Aires global warming conference*

EVER SINCE THE ONSET of large-scale population growth and industrialization in the 19th century (*see* p. 208), there has been a parallel rapid increase in man-made damage to the world's environment. Before 1945 this damage was largely localized, though very visible. However, the spread of industry worldwide after 1945 produced new threats to the environment which, if less visible, were nonetheless more deadly. Acid rain from waste in the atmosphere destroyed forests and eroded buildings. Pollutants in rivers and seas poisoned wildlife. High levels of carbon dioxide released from the burning of fossil fuels raised global temperatures, while other chemicals began to weaken the ozone layer in the earth's atmosphere.

Global warming

Between 1800 and 1900 the level of carbon dioxide in the atmosphere increased by only 4 per cent; in the 20th century it increased by 25 per cent, with most of the change occurring since the 1950s. The effect of this increase was to raise world temperatures artificially. The 1990s were the warmest decade of the millennium.

Global warming was due in part to a massive increase in energy consumption, most of which consisted of fossil fuels (oil, coal and natural gas). Between 1970 and 1990 energy consumption increased by 60 per cent, despite efforts to find more efficient ways of generating power and to reduce emissions. Fossil fuels released a range of chemicals into the atmosphere which blocked the natural loss of heat and created the so-called 'greenhouse effect', leading to a global rise in temperatures. Warming was also the result of extensive deforestation. The world's tropical rainforests absorb carbon dioxide and give out oxygen, but as the rise of population put pressure on the land in tropical regions it led to the spread of agriculture at the expense of forest.

From the 1960s, the developed world began to recognize the dangers. The Clean Air Act in the United States in 1970 helped reduce emissions. Motor vehicles, too, in most of the developed world have been adapted since the 1980s to reduce the release of harmful gases. At Kyoto in 1997 agreement was reached to reduce the emission of greenhouse gases by the year 2010. The main barrier in the fight against global warming, however, remains the developed world itself. The USA, Europe and Russia are still the chief sources of the gases that cause global warming.

By the 1990s, global warming threatened the delicate balance of the natural world. Climatic changes caused regular flooding and widespread droughts. The ice-caps have begun to melt, and the sea level will rise in the 21st century without effective control of the greenhouse effect. The changes also threaten the pattern of world agriculture and the distribution of animal and plant species.

Other damage to the natural world was even more avoidable. In the Soviet Union in the 1970s a decision to use the water of the Aral Sea to irrigate the surrounding area to grow cotton and rice produced an environmental disaster. By the late 1980s, two-thirds of the sea had disappeared, the fish stock had died out, the local climate had become hotter and drier and the water-table had contracted. The result was the collapse of local industries and rising levels of disease.

The ozone layer

The most notorious damage to the environment was the effect of the release of chlorofluorocarbons (CFCs) into the atmosphere. Discovered in the 1920s, CFCs were used in refrigeration, air-conditioning and in aerosol sprays. In the 1970s it was found that they were destroying the ozone layer in the atmosphere, which is responsible for reducing the harmful ultraviolet rays of the sun. International action on phasing out CFCs was agreed by the early 1990s, and the ozone layer may gradually regenerate itself in the 21st century.

Action on CFCs showed what the international community was capable of doing. Environmental issues were a central concern of the 1990s and state action did produce results. In Brazil deforestation fell from a rate of 21,000 square kilometres in 1988 to only 1000 square kilometres by 1993. At Rio de Janeiro in 1992 agreements were made to reduce harmful pollutants and emissions, a decision reinforced at Kyoto. The richer states subsidized industrial and agricultural projects in the developing world which respected environmental interests. In European states political movements developed based entirely on issues of the environment, and in 1998 the environmentalist Green Party won a share of power in Germany. Yet the future of the world eco-system depends on the willingness of the world's richest states to accept substantial changes in consumption patterns.

4 The Antarctic ozone hole, 1980–94

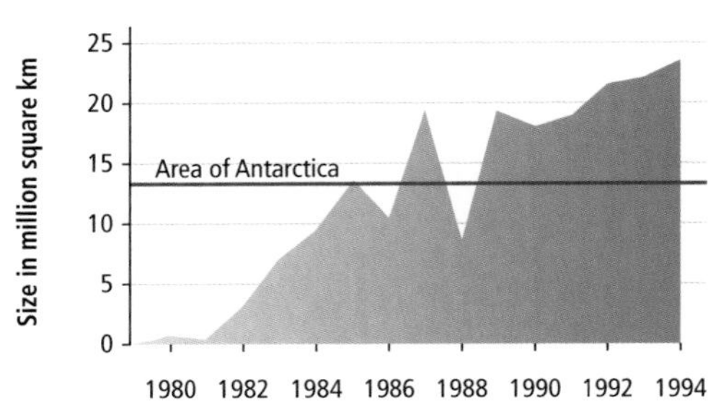

4 Since the 1970s the ozone layer in the atmosphere, which helps reduce the sun's ultraviolet radiation, has been thinning because of the emission of CFC chemicals from articles in everyday use, such as refrigerators and aerosols. One consequence is that a hole has opened in the ozone layer above the Antarctic and has been growing over the past two decades *(chart left)*. The Montreal Protocol, agreed in 1987, has reduced these emission levels, but it will be many years before the ozone layer is restored.

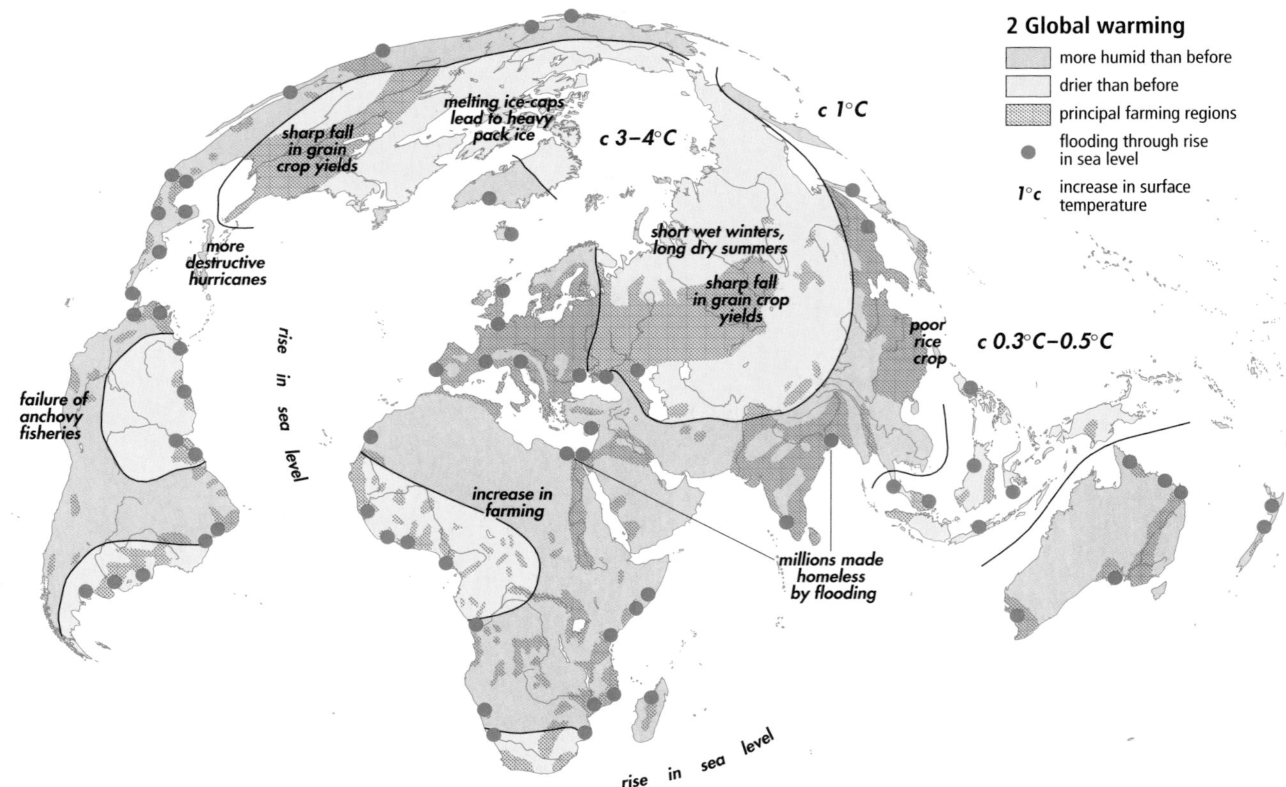

2 The emission of large quantities of carbon dioxide and other gases produced by industrial processes and by motor vehicles has raised world temperatures by creating a 'greenhouse effect' in the atmosphere *(map right)*. The consequence will be worldwide changes in the location of agricultural surplus areas and widespread flooding of coastal areas. Global temperatures have risen consistently since the 1930s. 1998 was the hottest year since formal records began.

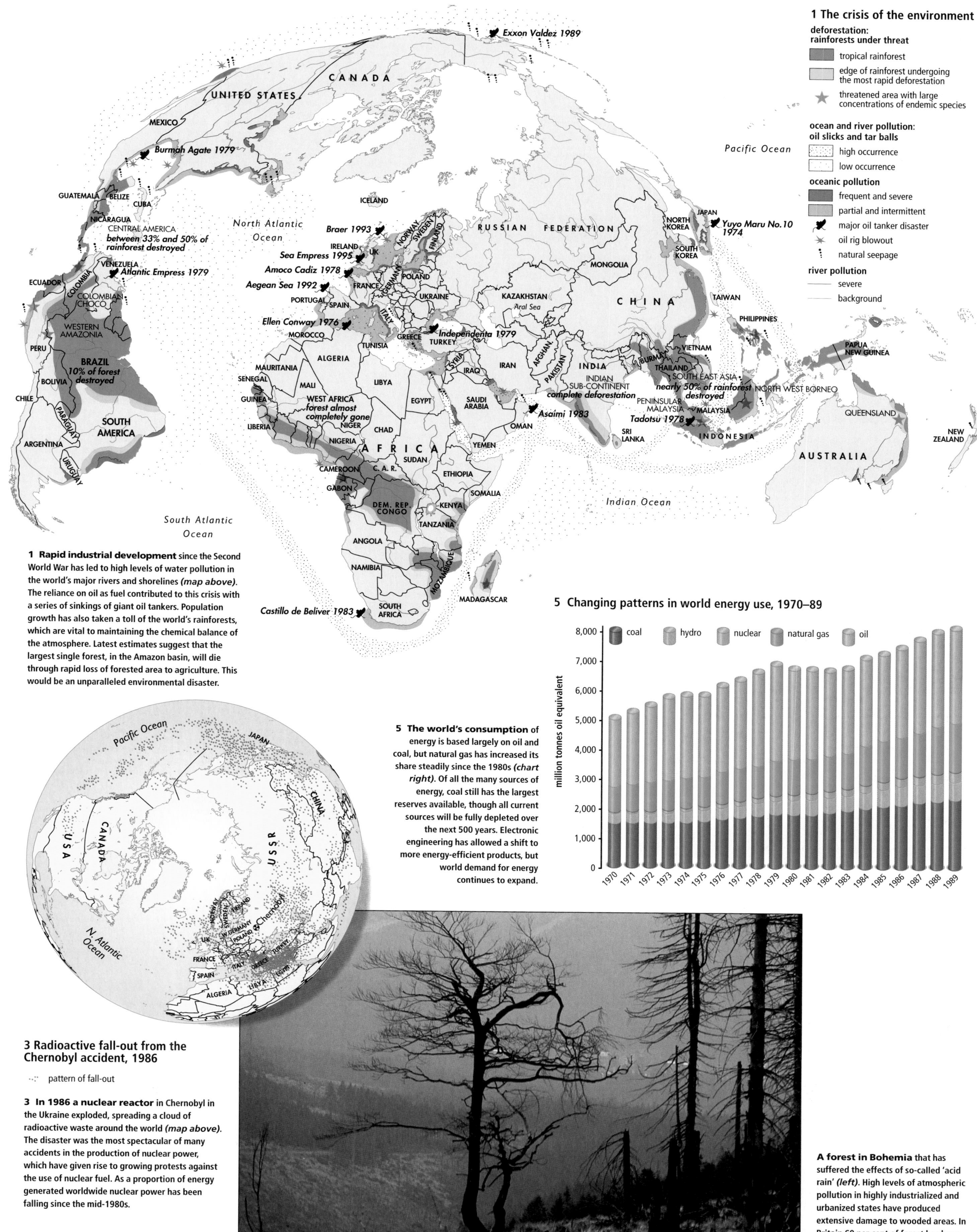

1 Rapid industrial development since the Second World War has led to high levels of water pollution in the world's major rivers and shorelines *(map above)*. The reliance on oil as fuel contributed to this crisis with a series of sinkings of giant oil tankers. Population growth has also taken a toll of the world's rainforests, which are vital to maintaining the chemical balance of the atmosphere. Latest estimates suggest that the largest single forest, in the Amazon basin, will die through rapid loss of forested area to agriculture. This would be an unparalleled environmental disaster.

5 The world's consumption of energy is based largely on oil and coal, but natural gas has increased its share steadily since the 1980s *(chart right)*. Of all the many sources of energy, coal still has the largest reserves available, though all current sources will be fully depleted over the next 500 years. Electronic engineering has allowed a shift to more energy-efficient products, but world demand for energy continues to expand.

3 In 1986 a nuclear reactor in Chernobyl in the Ukraine exploded, spreading a cloud of radioactive waste around the world *(map above)*. The disaster was the most spectacular of many accidents in the production of nuclear power, which have given rise to growing protests against the use of nuclear fuel. As a proportion of energy generated worldwide nuclear power has been falling since the mid-1980s.

A forest in Bohemia that has suffered the effects of so-called 'acid rain' *(left)*. High levels of atmospheric pollution in highly industrialized and urbanized states have produced extensive damage to wooded areas. In Britain 60 per cent of forest has been damaged, in Germany 52 per cent, and in the Czech Republic 27 per cent.

BIBLIOGRAPHY

HISTORY ATLASES

Atlas zur Geschichte 2 vols. Leipzig 1976
Bazilevsky, K V, Golubtsov, A, Zinoviev, M A *Atlas Istorii SSR*, Moscow 1952
Beckingham, C F *Atlas of the Arab World and the Middle East*, London 1960
Bertin, J (et al) *Atlas of Food Crops*, Paris 1971
Bjørklund, O, Holmboe, H, Røhr, *A Historical Atlas of the World*, Edinburgh 1970
Cappon, L (et al) *Atlas of Early American History*, Chicago 1976
Channon, J *The Penguin Historical Atlas of Russia*, London 1995
Darby, H C, Fullard, H (eds.) *The New Cambridge Modern History vol. XIV: Atlas*, Cambridge 1970
Davies, C C *An Historical Atlas of the Indian Peninsula*, London 1959
Engel, J (ed.) *Grosser Historischer Weltatlas*, 3 vols., Munich 1953-70
Fage, J D *An Atlas of African History*, London 1958
Fernández-Armesto, F (ed) *The Times Atlas of World Exploration*, London 1991
Gilbert, M *Russian History Atlas*, London 1972
Gilbert, M *Recent History Atlas 1860-1960*, London 1966
Gilbert, M *First World War Atlas*, London 1970
Gilbert, M *Jewish History Atlas*, London 1969
Haywood, J (ed) *The Cassell Atlas of World History*, London 1997
Hazard, H W *Atlas of Islamic History*, Princeton 1952
Herrmann, *A Historical and Commercial Atlas of China*, Harvard 1935
Herrmann, A *An Historical Atlas of China*, Edinburgh 1966
Jedin, H, Latourette, K S, Martin, J *Atlas zur Kirchengeschichte*, Freiburg 1970
Kinder, H, Hilgermann, W DTV *Atlas zur Weltgeschichte* 2 vols. Stuttgart 1964 (published in English as *The Penguin Atlas of World History*, London 1974 & 1978)
Magosci, P R *Historical Atlas of East Central Europe*, Toronto, revised ed. 1995
Matsui and Mori *Ajiarekishi chizu*, Tokyo 1965
May, H G (ed.) *Oxford Bible Atlas*, Oxford 1974
Mackay, A and Ditchburn, D (eds) *Atlas of Medieval Europe*, London 1997
McNeill, WH., Buske, M R, Roehm, A W *The World...its History in Maps*, Chicago 1969
Nelson's Atlas of the Early Christian World, London 1959
Nelson's Atlas of the Classical World, London 1959
Nelson's Atlas of World History, London 1965
Nihon rekishi jiten Atlas vol., Tokyo 1959
Palmer, R R (ed.) *Atlas of World History*, Chicago 1965
Paullin, C O *Atlas of the Historical Geography of the United States*, Washington 1932
Ragi al Faruqi, I (ed.) *Historical Atlas of the Religions of the World*, New York 1974
Roolvink, R *Historical Atlas of the Muslim Peoples*, London 1957
Scarre, C (ed) *Past Worlds: The Times Times Atlas of Arcaeology*, revised ed. London 1989
Schwartzberg, J E (ed.) *A Historical Atlas of South Asia*, Chicago 1978
The Times Atlas of European History (2nd ed), London 1997
Toynbee, A J, Mers, E D *A Study of History, Historical Atlas and Gazetteer*, Oxford 1959
Treharne, R F, Fullard, H (eds.) *Muir's Historical Atlas*, London 1966
Tubinger Atlas der Vorderen Orients, Wiesbaden (various vols) since 1972
Van der Heyden, A M, Scullard, H H *Atlas of the Classical World*, London 1959
Wesley, E B *Our United States...its History in Maps*, Chicago 1977
Westermann Grosser Atlas zur Weltgeschichte, Brunswick 1976
Whitehouse, D & R *Archaeological Atlas of the World*, London 1975
Wilgus, A C *Latin America in Maps*, New York 1943

GENERAL WORKS

Abu-Lughod, J L *Before European Hegemony: The World System AD 1250–1350*, Oxford 1991
Ajayi, J F A, Crowder, M *History of West Africa*, 2 vols., 3rd ed., 1985-
Allchin, B & R *The Birth of Indian Civilization*, London 1968
Australia, Commonwealth of, Department of National Development, *Atlas of Australian Resources*, 3rd series, 1980
Bakewell, Peter John *A History of Latin America: Empires and Sequels*, 1450–1930, Malden Mass, 1997
Bartlett, R *The Making of Europe: Conquest, Colonization and Cultural Change 950–1350*, London 1993
Basham, A L *The Wonder That Was India*, 2 vols., 3rd revised, London 1987
Bellwood, *P Prehistory of the Indo-Malay Archipelago*, Ryde NSW 1985
Bethel, Leslie (ed) *The Cambridge History of Latin America*, 11 vols., Cambridge 1984–95
Beresford, M *New Towns of the Middle Ages*, London 1967
Boardman, J (ed.) *The Oxford History of the Classical World*, Oxford 1989
Bolton, G (ed.) *Oxford History of Australia*, Oxford 1986
Bonney, R *The European Dynastic States 1494–1660*, Oxford 1991
Braudel, F *The Mediterranean and the Mediterranean World in the Age of Philip II*, 2 vols., London 1972-3
Brown, P *The Rise of Western Christendom: Triumph and Diversity 200–1000*, Oxford 1996
Bury, J B, Cook, S A, Adcock, F E (eds.) *The Cambridge Ancient History*, Cambridge 1923-; 2nd ed. 1982
Cameron, A M *The Mediterranean World in Late Antiquity AD 395–600*, London 1993
Campbell, P R *Louis XIV*, London 1994
Chang, K C *The Archaeology of Ancient China*, 4th ed., New Haven 1986
Chaudhuri, K N *Trade and Civilization in the Indian Ocean: An Economic History From the Rise of Islam to 1750*, Cambridge 1985
Chaudhuri, K N *Asia Before Europe: Economy and Civilization of the Indian Ocean from the Rise of Islam to 1750*, Cambridge 1991
Cook, M A (ed.) *A History of the Ottoman Empire to 1730*, Cambridge 1976
Coward, B *The Stuart Age*, London 2nd ed 1996
Crowder, M *West Africa Under Colonial Rule*, London 1968
Cunliffe, B (ed) *The Oxford Illustrated Prehistory of Europe*, Oxford 1994
Curtin, P D *The Atlantic Slave Trade*, Madison, 1972
Curtin, P D *Cross-cultural Trade in World History*, Cambridge 1984
Dalton, B J *War and Politics in New Zealand, 1855–1870*, Sydney 1967
Darby, H C (ed.) *An Historical Geography of England Before AD 1800*, Cambridge 1936 & 1960
Daniels, P and Lever, W *The Global Economy in Transition*, London 1996
Davis, R W *The Industrialization of Soviet Russia*, 3 vols., Cambridge 1989
Demand, N *A History of Ancient Greece*, New York 1996
East, W G *The Geography Behind History*, London 1965
East, W G *An Historical Geography of Europe*, 5th ed., London 1967
Edwardes, M *A History of India*, London 1961
Fage, J D and Oliver, R (eds.) *Cambridge History of Africa*, Cambridge 1975-
Ferguson, J *The Heritage of Hellenism*, London 1973
Fisher, C A *South-East Asia*, London 1964
Fletcher, A *Tudor Rebellions*, 3rd ed., London 1983
Geelan, P J M, Twitchett, D C (eds.) *The Times Atlas of China*, London 1974
Gernet, J *Le Monde Chinois*, Paris 1969; English translation 1982
Goodman, J and Honeyman, K *Gainful Pursuits: The Making of Industrial Europe 1600–1914*, London 1988
Graff, E, Hammond, H E *Southeast Asia: History, Culture, People*, 5th revised ed., Cambridge 1980
Grousset, R *The Empire of the Steppes: A History of Central Asia*, New Brunswick N J 1970
Guillermaz, J *Histoire du Parti Communiste Chinois*, Paris 1968; English translation 1972
Hall, D G E *A History of South-East Asia*, 4th ed., London 1981
Hallam, E *Capetian France 987–1328*, London 1980
Harlan, J R 'The Plants and Animals that Nourish Man', *Scientific American* 1976
Harlan, J R, Zohary, D 'The Distribution of Wild Wheats and Barleys, *Science* 1966
Harley, J B, Woodward, D *The History of Cartography*, 2 vols., Chicago 1987-
Hatton, R M *Europe in the Age of Louis XIV*, London 1969
Hawke, G R *The Making of New Zealand: An Economic History*, Cambridge 1985
Henderson, W O *Britain and Industrial Europe, 1750–1870*, Liverpool 1965
Higham, C F W *The Archaeology of Mainland Southeast Asia from 10000 BC to the Fall of Angkor*, Cambridge 1989
Higham, C F W and Thosarat, R *Prehistoric Thailand from Early Settlement to Sukhothai*, Bangkok 1999
Hopkins, A G *Economic History of West Africa*, London 1973
Hourani, A *A History of the Arab People*, Harvard 1991
Inalcik, H *The Ottoman Empire: The Classical Age, 1300–1600*, reprint, London 1989
Inikori, J E, Engerman, S L *The Atlantic Slave Trade: Effects on Economy, Society, and Population in Africa, America, and Europe*, Durham, NC 1992
Jeans, D N *An Historical Geography of New South Wales to 1901*, Sydney 1972
Jennings, J D *Prehistory of North America*, 3rd ed., Mountain View, Calif. 1989
Johnson, G (ed.) *New Cambridge History of India*, Cambridge 1989-
Jones, G *The Evolution of International Business*, London 1996
Josephy, Alvin M (ed) *America in 1492: the World of the Indian Peoples before the Arrival of Columbus*, New York 1992
Kahan, A *Russian Economic History*, Chicago 1991
Kennedy, J *A History of Malaya*, 1400-1959, London 1967
Koeningsberger, H G, Mosse, G L, Bowler, G Q *Europe in the 16th Century*, 2nd ed., London 1989
Kuhrt, A T L *The Ancient Near East c. 3000–330 BC*, London 1995
Laird, C E *Language in America*, New York 1970
Landes, D *The Wealth and Poverty of Nations*, London 1998
Langer, W L (ed.) *An Encyclopedia of World History*, revised ed., London 1987
Lapidus, I M *A History of Islamic Societies*, Cambridge 1988
Lattimore, O *Inner Asian Frontiers of China*, New York 1951
Lossky, A *Louis XIV and the French Monarchy*, London 1995
Lyashchenko, P I *History of the National Economy of Russia to the 1917 Revolution*, New York 1949
Majumdar, R C *The Vedic Age*, Bombay 1951
Majumdar, R C *History and Culture of the Indian People, Age of Imperial Unity*, Bombay 1954
Macmillan's *Atlas of South-East Asia*, London 1988
Mantran, R *Histoire de l'Empire Ottoman*, Paris 1989
McCarthy, J *The Ottoman Turks: an Introductory History to 1923*, London 1994
McKitterick, R *The Frankish Kingdoms under the Carolingians 751–987*, London 1983
McKitterick, R (et al) *The New Cambridge Medieval History*, Cambridge 1995
McNeill, W H *The Rise of the West: A History of the Human Community*, Chicago 1991
McNeill, W H *Plagues and Peoples*, New York 1992
McPherson, James M *Battle Cry of Freedom: the Civil War Era*, Oxford 1988
Meining, D W *On the Margins of the Good Earth*, New York 1962, London 1963
Mellaart, J *The Neolithic of the Near East*, London 1975
Milner, Clyde A (et al) *The Oxford History of the American West*, New York 1994
Morrell, W P, Hall, D O W *A History of New Zealand Life*, Christchurch 1962
Mulvaney, D J *The Prehistory of Australia*, London 1975
The National Atlas of the United States of America, Washington DC 1970
Neatby, H Quebec, *The Revolutionary Age 1760–1791*, London 1966
Ogot, B A (ed.) Zamani, *A Survey of West African History*, London 1974-1976
Oliver, R, Fagan, B *Africa in the Iron Age c. 500 BC–AD 1400*, Cambridge 1975
Oliver, R, Atmore, A *Africa Since 1800*, 3rd ed., Cambridge 1981
Oliver, W H, Williams, R R *Oxford History of New Zealand*, Oxford 1981
Osbourne, M E *Southeast Asia: An Introductory History*, 2nd ed., Sydney 1983
Ostrogorsky, G *History of the Byzantine State*, Oxford 1969
Overy, R *Why the Allies Won*, London 1995
Parker, W H *An Historical Geography of Russia*, London 1968
Phillips, J R S *The Medieval Expansion of Europe*, Oxford 1988
Piggott, S *Prehistoric India to 1000 BC*, London 1962
Pitcher, D E *An Historical Geography of the Ottoman Empire*, Leiden 1973
Postan, M M *Medieval Trade and Finance*, Cambridge 1973
Pounds, N J G *An Historical Geography of Europe 1800–1914*, Cambridge 1985
Powell, J M *An Historial Geography of Modern Australia: the Restive Fringe*, Cambridge 1988
Ragozin, Z *A History of Vedic India*, Delhi 1980
Reuter, T *Germany in the early Middle Ages, 800–1056*, London 1991
Rizvi, A A *The Wonder That Was India: 1200–1700*, 2 vols., London 1987
Roberts, J M *The Hutchinson History of the World*, revised ed., London 1987
Sanders, W T, Marino, J *New World Prehistory: Archaeology of the American Indian*, Englewood Cliffs, N J 1970
Saum, L O *The Fur Trader and the Indian*, London 1965
Sawyer, P (ed) *The Oxford Illustrated History of the Vikings*, Oxford 1997
Scammell, G V *The First Imperial Age: European Overseas Expansion, c. 1400–1715*, London 1992
Seltzer, L E (ed.) *The Columbia Lippincott Gazetteer of the World*, New York 1952
Shaw, I and Nicholson, P *British Museum Dictionary of Europe*, Oxford 1994
Shepherd, J and Franklin, S *The Emergence of the Rus*, London 1996
Simkin, C F *The Traditional Trade of Asia*, Oxford 1968
Smith, C D *Palestine and the Arab-Israeli Conflict*, Oxford 1994
Smith, C T *An Historical Geography of Western Europe before 1800*, revised ed. London & New York 1978
Smith, W S *The Art and Architecture of Ancient Egypt*, revised ed., London 1981
Snow, D *The American Indians: Their Archaeology and Prehistory*, London 1976
Sonyel, S R *The Ottoman Armenians*, London 1987
Stark, R *The Rise of Christianity: A Sociologist Reconsiders History*, Princeton 1996
Stravrianos, L S *The World Since 1500: A Global History*, 6th ed., Englewood Cliffs, N J 1991
Stavrianos, L S *The World to 1500: A Global History*, 5th ed., Englewood Cliffs, N J 1991
Stokes, M and Conway, S (eds) *The Market Revolution in America: Social, Political and Religious Expressions, 1800–1880*, Charlottesville, 1996
Stoye, J *The Siege of Vienna*, London 1964
Tate, D J M *The Making of South-East Asia*, Kuala Lumpur 1971
Thapar, R *A History of India*, London 1967
The Times Atlas of the World, 9th Comprehensive Edition, London 1992
Thompson, E A *The Huns*, 1996
Toynbee, A J *Cities of Destiny*, London 1967
Toynbee, A J *Mankind and Mother Earth*, Oxford 1976
Twitchett, D, Loewe, M (eds.) *The Cambridge History of China*, Cambridge 1979-
Van Alstyne, R W *The Rising American Empire*, reprint, Oxford 1974
Van Heekeren, H R *The Stone Age of Indonesia*, 2nd revised ed., The Hague 1972
Wadham, S, Wilson, R K, Wood, J *Land Utilization in Australia*, Melbourne 1964
Webster, L and Brown, M (eds) *The Transformation of the Roman World 400–900*, London 1997
Wheatley, P *The Golden Khersonese*, Kuala Lumpur 1966
Wheeler, M *Early India and Pakistan to Ashoka*, London 1968
White, Donald W *The American Century: the Rise and Decline of the United States as a World Power*, New Haven, 1996
Wickins, P L *An Economic History of Africa From Earliest Times to Partition*, New York 1981
Willey, G A *An Introduction to American Archaeology*, vols. 1 & 2, Englewood Cliffs, N J 1970
Williams, M *The Making of the South Australian Landscape*, London 1974
Williamson, Edwin *The Penguin History of Latin America*, London 1992
Wilson, M, Thompson, L *Oxford History of South Africa*, vols. 1 & 2, Oxford, 1969, 1971
Wood, I N *The Merovingian Kingdoms 450–751*, London 1994
Yarshater, E (ed) *The Cambridge History of Iran*, vol. 3, Cambridge 1983

PICTURE CREDITS

The Natural History Museum, London **31** (top); Science Photo Library **31** (bottom); Yoel Rak **33** (top); Science Photo Library **33** (bottom); AKG Photo London **34**; e.t. archive **35**; David Harris **37**; e.t. archive **39**; Janet & Colin Bord/Fortean Picture Library **40**; Werner Forman Archive, Tanzania National Museum, Dar es Salaam **42**; Werner Forman Archive, National Museum of Man, Ottawa **44** (top); Werner Forman Archive, Anthropology Museum, Veracruz University, Jalapa **44** (bottom); Ian Glover **47**; John Miles/Panos Pictures **48**; AKG Photo London **50/51**; Robert Harding Picture Library **53**; e.t. archive **54**; Robert Harding Picture Library **56** (left); Werner Forman Archive, Egyptian Museum, Cairo **56** (right); e.t. archive **58**; Werner Forman Archive, National Museum of Anthropology, Mexico **61**; Michael Holford **62**; e.t. archive **64**; Ancient Art & Architecture Collection **66**; AKG Photo London **68/69**; e.t. archive **70**; Spectrum Colour Library **73**; Sonia Halliday Photographs **75**; C.M Dixon **76**; Ancient Art & Architecture Collection **78**; Robert Harding Picture Library **80**; e.t. archive **82**; Skyscan Balloon Photography Ltd **84**; e.t. archive **87**; C.M. Dixon **88**; A.F. Kersting **90**; AKG Photo London **92** (top and bottom); Robert Harding Picture Library **94/95**; Scale **96**; C.M. Dixon **99**; Cive Hicks **100**; e.t. archive **101**; e.t. archive **103**; e.t. archive **104**; Werner Forman Archive, Viking Ship Museum, Bygdoy **107**; e.t. archive **108**; Philip Parker **111**; e.t. archive **113**; AKG Photo London **115**; AKG Photo London **117**; Skyscan Photo Library **119**; Anthony Kersting **120**; Boston Museum of Fine Arts **123**; Robert Harding Picture Library **124**; Werner Forman Archive, Christian Deydier, London **127**; National Museum of Ireland **129**; Daud Ali **131**; Hutchison Library **133**; Robert Harding Picture Library **134**; e.t. archive **136**; Christie's Images **138**; Robert Aberman **141**; Sonia Halliday Photographs **142**; Werner Forman Archive, University Library, Prague **145**; The British Library **147**; Werner Forman Archive, Schindler Collection, New York **149** (top); e.t. archive **149** (centre); The British Museum **151**; The Bridgeman Art Library **152/153**; e.t. archive **155**; e.t. archive **157**; The British Library **159**; Michael Holford **160**; Thomas Gilrease Institute of American History and Art, Tulsa **163**; Werner Forman Archive, British Museum, London **164**; National Palace Museum, Taiwan **167**; Sonia Halliday Photographs **168**; The Bridgeman Art Library **171**; e.t. archive **172** and **173**; Tokyo National Museum **175**; Werner Forman Archive, Jakarta Museum, Indonesia **177**; e.t. archive **179**; AKG Photo London **180**; AKG Photo London **183**; Beheer Collection, Gemeente Musea, Delft **185**; Sonia Halliday Photographs **187**; The Royal Library, National Linbray of Sweden **189**; AKG Photo London **191**; Robert Harding Picture Library **193**; e.t. archive **194**; e.t. archive **197**; National Maritime Museum, London **199**; Science and Society Picture Library **201**; e.t. archive **203**; e.t. archive **205** (top and bottom); English Heritage Photo Library **206/207**; Times Books **208**; AKG Photo London **211**; National Motor Museum **213**; e.t. archive **215**; e.t. archive **216/217**; National Library of Congress, Washington DC **219**; Corbis-Bettmann **221**; Corbis-Bettmann **223**; Corbis Bettmann **225**; e.t. archive **226**; AKG Photo London **228/229**; Novosti (London) **230**; e.t. archive **233**; Popperfoto **235**; e.t. archive **237**; e.t. archive **238**; Roger-Viollet, Paris **240**; e.t. archive **243**; Mary Evans Picture Library **245**; Mary Evans Picture Library **247**; Jane's Information Group **248**; Imperial War Museum **250**; Robert Harding Picture Library **252/253**; e.t. archive **254**; Popperfoto **256**; Hulton Getty **259**; e.t. archive **261**; e.t archive **262**; Aldus Archive **265**; David King Collection **266**; e.t. archive **269**; AKG Photo London **271**; AKG Photo London **273**; Popperfoto **275**; Keystone Press/Sygma **277**; Gamma **279**; J. Langevin/Sygma **281**; Magnum **282**; Anthony Kershing **284**; Magnum **286**; Gamma **288**; Sygma **290**; Popperfoto **292**; Corbis-Bettmann UPI **294**; Sygma **297**; Sygma **299**; Paul Popper **300**; Sygma **302**; Gamma **306**; Gamma **306**.

Map 2 on page 36 is based with permission on material published in *Last Hunters, First Farmers*, T. Douglas Price and Anne Birgitte Gebauer (eds), New Mexico 1995.

GLOSSARY

This glossary is intended to provide supplementary information about some of the individuals, peoples, events, treaties and processes which, through lack of space, receive only a brief mention on the maps and accompanying texts. It is not a general encyclopedia of world history. Names in **bold** *type within entries have their own main glossary entries.*

ABBAS I, THE GREAT (c. 1557–1629) Shah of Persia. Attaining the throne in 1587, he re-organized and centralized the **Safavid** state. His reign was marked by cultural efflorescence and territorial expansion. Having crushed the rebellious **Uzbeks** (1597) he drove the Ottomans from their possessions in western Iran, Iraq and the eastern Caucasus (1603–7), and extended **Safavid** territories (temporarily) from the Tigris to the Indus. He moved the capital to Isfahan.

ABBASIDS Second major dynasty in Islam, displacing the **Umayyads** in 750. It founded a new capital, Baghdad, in 762, but its political control over the Islamic world, almost complete in the 9th and early 10th centuries, gradually decayed. Its rulers frequently became figureheads for other regimes: the last true caliph was killed by Mongols in 1258 and later Abbasid caliphs, nominally restored in 1260, were merely court functionaries to Egypt's **Mamluk sultans.**

ABD AL KADIR (1808–83) Also known as Abd el-Kader and Abdal-Qadir. Algerian independence leader. He was elected in 1832 to succeed his father as leader of a religious sect; as emir, he took control of the Oran region, successfully fought the French, and in 1837 concluded the Treaty of Tafna; he extended his authority to the Moroccan frontier; renewed hostilities (1840–7) ended with his defeat and imprisonment, though he was freed in 1852.

ABD ALLAH (1846–99) Khalifa, or religious and political leader, in the Sudan after the death of the Mahdi in 1885. In 1880 he became a disciple of the **Mahdi, Mohammed Ahmed,** whom he succeeded. As leader of the Mahdist movement he launched attacks on Egypt and Ethiopia; he consolidated power within the Sudan, building up an effective centralized state, until invaded by Anglo-Egyptian forces under Kitchener. He lost the battle of Omdurman in 1898, and was killed the following year while resisting Anglo-Egyptian troops.

ABD EL-KRIM (1882–1963) Founded Republic of the Rif (1921–5), the north African precursor of many 20th-century independence movements. His forces defeated major French and Spanish armies until overwhelmed, in May 1926, by 250,000 Franco-Spanish troops. He was exiled to Réunion, but escaped to Egypt where he was given political asylum in 1947.

ABDULHAMID II (1842–1918) Last important Ottoman sultan, 1876–1909. He carried further some lines of modernization already begun, and used Islamic sentiment to resist European encroachments. The revolt by **Young Turks** in 1908 against his autocratic rule led to his deposition, 1909; he was imprisoned at Salonica, 1910, and died in Istanbul eight years later.

ABRAHAM First of three patriarchs of the **Jews** (Abraham, his son Isaac, Isaac's son Jacob). Born in Ur, he migrated via Harran in Syria to Canaan (Palestine), the land promised by God to his descendants. Abraham, Isaac and Jacob have been dated to the early or middle 2nd millennium BC. According to much later tradition, he was considered to be the progenitor of the Arabs through his other son, Ishmael.

ABREU, ANTONIO DE 16th-century Portuguese navigator, who in 1512 discovered the Banda Islands, Indonesia, during an exploratory voyage to the Moluccas.

ABU BAKR (c. 573–634) Close friend and advisor to **Mohammed,** and said to have been the first male convert to Islam. He became Mohammed's father-in-law, and accompanied him on the historic journey to Medina in 622. Accepted after Mohammed's death as caliph – 'successor of the Prophet of God'; under his two-year rule central Arabia accepted Islam and the Arab conquests began, with expansion into Iraq and Syria.

ABUSHIRI REVOLT An insurrection in 1888–9 by the Arab population of those areas of the East African coast which were granted by the sultan of Zanzibar to Germany in 1888. It was eventually suppressed by an Anglo-German blockade of the coast.

ACHAEMENIDS Ancient Persian dynasty of Fars province. **Cyrus II the Great,** a prince of the line, defeated the **Medes** and founded the Achaemenid empire, 550–330 BC. Descended traditionally from Achaemenes (7th century BC), the senior line of his successors included Cyrus I, Cambyses I, Cyrus II and **Cambyses II,** after whose death in 522 BC the junior line came to the throne with **Darius I.** The dynasty was extinguished with the death of Darius III in 330 BC after defeat by **Alexander the Great** (331 BC).

ACHESON, DEAN (1893–1971) US Secretary of State, 1949–53. He was responsible for many important policy initiatives under President **Truman,** including the implementation of the **Marshall Plan,** the **North Atlantic Treaty Organization,** non-recognition of Communist China and the re-arming of West Germany.

ADAMS, JOHN (1735–1826) Second President of the United States, 1797–1801. A leading advocate of resistance to British rule before the American War of Independence, in 1776 he seconded the Declaration of Independence. He was American envoy to Britain, 1785–8, and author of *Thoughts on Government* (1760).

ADAMS, JOHN QUINCY (1767–1848) Sixth President of the United States, 1825–9. The son of **John Adams** he was Secretary of State, 1817–25; in this post he contributed to the shaping of the **Monroe Doctrine.** In 1843 he led the opposition to the annexation of Texas.

ADENAUER, KONRAD (1876–1967) German statesman. He studied law and served in the Provincial Diet of the Rhineland (1920–33) until dismissed from office (1933). He suffered constant harassment by the **Nazis** until 1945 when he became active in the newly formed Christian Democratic Union. He became chancellor of the Federal Republic of Germany from 1949 until his retirement in 1963. Known affectionately as 'der Alte' (the Old Man), he remained deeply committed to close ties with the democratic Christian west.

AESCHYLUS (525/4–456 BC) Athenian dramatist, who also fought at the **Battle of Marathon,** 490 BC. He wrote at least 80 plays, mostly tragedies, of which seven survive in full: *The Persians, The Seven against Thebes, The Suppliants, The Oresteia* trilogy and *Prometheus Bound.* He was the creator of tragic drama.

ÆTHELRED II (d.1016) King of Wessex, England, from 898. His reign was marked by a steady increase in Danish influence; in 1013 he fled to Normandy and the English recognized the Danish king, **Sven Forkbeard,** as their ruler.

AFGHANI, JAMAL AD-DIN AL- (1838–97) Muslim agitator, reformer and journalist. Born in Persia, he was politically active in Afghanistan, Istanbul and Cairo. Exiled from Egypt in 1879 for political reasons, he published (1884) *The Firmest Bond,* a periodical attacking British imperialism and advocating Islamic reform. Exiled from Persia in 1892, he spent his remaining years in Istanbul; he instigated the assassination of the Shah in 1896.

AGLABIDS Muslim Arab dynasty, ruling much of North Africa from 800 to 909. They controlled Tunisia and eastern Algeria, conquered Sicily in 827 and invaded southern Italy. They were finally defeated and replaced by the **Fatimids.**

AGIS IV (c. 262–239 BC) King of Sparta who, in 243 BC, attempted to introduce a 'communist' programme of land redistribution and debt cancellation. Tricked by an unscrupulous uncle and unable to complete his reforms quickly enough, he was forced to leave the country for war with the Aetolians in 241; in his absence a counter-revolution put his enemies in power, and after a mock trial he was executed.

AGUINALDO, EMILIO (1869–1964) President of the short-lived Philippine Republic (1898–1901). Of mixed Chinese and Tagalog ancestry, he fought Spanish rule as leader of the revolutionary Katipunan Society. Exiled in 1897, he returned, first to cooperate with US forces, and then to lead a three-year insurrection. He was captured and deposed in 1901. In 1945 he was briefly imprisoned for supporting Japanese occupation. He became a member of the Philippine Council of State in 1950.

AGUNG, SULTAN Third ruler of Mataram, the Muslim kingdom which, in the 17th century, dominated central and much of eastern Java. He sought an alliance against Bantam and, when this was refused, attacked Batavia (now Jakarta), founded in 1619 by the **Dutch East India Company.** Defeated there in 1629, he undertook the Islamization of eastern Java by force; but failed in all attempts to conquer Bali, which remained loyal to traditional Hindu-Buddhist culture.

AGUSTIN I Emperor of Mexico *see* **Iturbide.**

AHMADU SEFU (1835–97) Son and successor of **al-Hajj Umar** (d.1864), a Tukolor chief whose kingdom was on the Upper Niger. He came to power some years after his father's death, but his kingdom was eventually destroyed by the French in the 1890s.

AHMED GRAN (c.1506–42) Muslim conqueror in 16th-century Ethiopia. He gained control of the Somali Muslim state, Adal, and declared a *jihad* (holy war) against Christian Ethiopia. By 1533, with help from Turkish troops and firearms, he had seized three-quarters of the country, and in 1541 defeated a Portuguese relief force. He was killed in battle against the new Ethiopian leader, Galawdewos.

AHMOSE *see* **Amosis I.**

AIDAN, ST (d.651) Born in Ireland, he trained as a monk at Iona, off the isle of Mull, west Scotland. He was consecrated bishop of the newly-converted Northumbrians in 635; he established his church and monastery on Lindisfarne, off the northeast coast of England, from where evangelists set out to convert large areas of northern England, under the protection of kings Oswald and Oswin of Northumbria.

AIUGUN, TREATY OF Agreement reached in 1858 by which China ceded the north bank of the Amur river to Russia. Together with further gains under the **Treaty of Peking** (1860), this gave Russia access to ice-free Pacific waters; the port of Vladivostok was founded in 1860.

AIX-LA-CHAPELLE, TREATY OF Agreement reached in 1748 which concluded the War of the Austrian Succession; Austria ceded Silesia to Prussia, Spain made gains in Italy, and **Maria Theresa** was confirmed in possession of the rest of the Austrian lands.

AKBAR (1542–1605) Greatest of India's **Mughal** emperors. Born in Umarkot, Sind, he succeeded his father, Humayun, in 1556. During his reign he consolidated Mughal rule throughout the sub-continent, winning the loyalty of both Muslims and Hindus; at his death he left superb administrative and artistic achievements, including the fortress-palace at Agra and the magnificent but now deserted city of Fatehpur Sikri.

AKHENATEN 18th Dynasty Egyptian pharaoh, reigned 1364–1347 BC; the son of Amenhotep III, he took the throne as Amenhotep IV. He promoted the monotheistic cult of Aten, the god in the sun disc; changed his name c.1373 BC and transferred the capital from Thebes to the new city of Akhetaten (el-Amarna). With his wife, Nefertiti, and six daughters, he devoted the rest of his reign largely to the cult of Aten, dangerously neglecting practical affairs.

AKKADIANS Name given to a wave of Semitic-speaking immigrants from the west, of increasing prominence in Mesopotamia from the first third of the 3rd millennium BC. **Sargon** of Agade was of Akkadian origin.

AK KOYUNLU Turcoman tribal federation, ruling eastern Anatolia, Azerbaijan and northern Iraq from c.1378 to 1508. The dynasty, whose name means 'white sheep', was founded by Kara Yüllük Osman (ruled 1378–1435), who was granted control over the Diyarbakir region of Iraq by **Tamerlane** in 1402. Under Uzun Jasan (1453–78) they expanded at the expense of the **Kara Koyunlu** ('black sheep') but were defeated by the Ottomans in 1473. They finally succumbed to internal strife and to pressure from the **Safavids.**

AKSUM Ancient city and kingdom of northern Ethiopia, an offshoot of one of the Semitic states of southern Arabia in the last millennium BC. By the start of the Christian era it was the greatest ivory market of northeast Africa. Converted to **Christianity** in the 4th century AD, it was gradually transformed, after the Muslim conquest of the Red Sea littoral in the 10th century, into the modern Amhara state of Ethiopia.

AL- For all Arabic names prefixed by al-, *see* under following element.

ALANS Ancient people, first noted in Roman writings of the 1st century AD as warlike, nomadic horse-breeders in the steppes north of the Caucasus Mountains. Overwhelmed by the **Huns** in 370, many Alans fled west, reaching Gaul with the **Vandals** and **Suebi** in 406 and crossing into Africa with the Vandals in 429.

ALARIC I (c. 370–410) Visigothic chief and leader of the army that captured Rome in AD 410. Born in Dacia, he migrated south with fellow-tribesmen to Moesia, and briefly commanded a Gothic troop in the Roman army. Elected chieftain in 395, he first ravaged the Balkans and then, in 401, invaded Italy; the 'sack' of Rome, following a decade of intermittent fighting, negotiation and siege, was in fact relatively humane and bloodless, as Alaric's main aim was to win land for the settlement of his people.

ALARIC II (d. 507) King of the **Visigoths.** From his accession in AD 484 he ruled Gaul south of the Loire and all Spain except Galicia. He issued a code of laws known as the Breviary of Alaric. He died after being defeated by **Clovis,** king of the Franks, at the Battle of Vouillé, near Poitiers.

ALAUDDIN KHALJI (d.1316) Sultan of Delhi who usurped the throne in 1296 from the sons of Jalaluddin. He unified much of northern India, thanks to heavy taxes and a standing army, and began the Muslim penetration of the south. He repelled a series of Mongol invasions between 1297 and 1306.

ALAUNGPAYA (d.1760) King of Burma and founder of the Konbaung dynasty which ruled until the British annexation of 1866. He rose from the position of village headman to lead resistance against invading Mons of Lower Burma; recaptured the Burmese capital, Ava, in 1753, finally seizing Pegu, the Mon capital, in 1757; and massacred staff of the **English East India Company**'s trading settlement on the island of Negrais, 1759. He was mortally wounded during the siege of the Siamese capital, Ayuttha.

ALBIGENSIANS (Albigenses) Members of a heretical Christian sect, following the **Manichaean** or **Cathar** teaching that all matter is evil. Strongly entrenched in southern France around the city of Albi in the 12th century, they were subjected to violent attack by northern French nobles in the Albigensian Crusade after 1208.

ALBUQUERQUE, AFONSO DE (1453–1515). Portuguese empire-builder. Appointed Governor-General of Portuguese India in 1509, he seized Goa and several Malabar ports, 1510; Malacca and the coast of Ceylon, 1511.

ALEMANNI Germanic tribe which in the 5th century AD occupied areas now known as Alsace and Baden; defeated in 496 by the Franks under **Clovis.**

ALEXANDER THE GREAT (356–323 BC) Most famous conqueror of the ancient world. The son of **Philip II of Macedon,** he was taught by **Aristotle.** Succeeding his father in 336, he reaffirmed Macedonian dominance in Greece and between 334 and 323 BC led his armies all but 'through to the ends of the earth'. He was only 32 when he died in Babylon. His victories, though never consolidated into a world empire, spread Greek thought and culture throughout Egypt, northern India, central Asia and the eastern Mediterranean. His body, sealed in a glass coffin and encased in gold, was preserved in Alexandria, the city he founded as his own memorial, but the tomb has never been located.

ALEXANDER I (1888–1934) King (1921–34) of the Serbo-Croat-Slovene state whose name he changed to Yugoslavia in 1929. Prince Regent of Serbia, 1914–21. Enthroned in 1921, he established a royal dictatorship in 1929. He was assassinated.

ALEXANDER II (1818–81) Tsar of Russia. The son of Nicholas I, he succeeded his father in 1855. He emancipated the serfs in 1861, and introduced legal, military, educational and local government reforms; he extended the Russian frontiers into the Caucasus (1859) and Central Asia (1865–8), and defeated Turkey in the last of the Russo-Turkish wars. (1877–8). He was assassinated.

ALEXANDER II (1198–1249) King of Scotland, son of William I the Lion. He succeeded to the throne in 1214, and sided with the rebel English barons against **King John** in the following year. He paid homage to Henry III in 1217, and in 1217 married his sister Joan. Under the Peace of York, which he concluded in 1237, Scotland abandoned English land claims and the border was fixed in more or less its present position.

ALEXANDER III (d.1181) Pope 1159–81. Distinguished canon lawyer, at one time professor at the University of Bologna. As pope, he opposed secular authority over the Church, allying successfully with the cities of Lombardy against Emperor **Frederick I Barbarossa,** and imposed a penance on **Henry II** of England for the murder of Thomas Becket, Archbishop of Canterbury.

ALEXIUS I COMNENUS (1048–1118) Byzantine emperor who seized the imperial throne in 1081. He was victorious over the Normans of Italy and the **Pecheneg** nomads; revived the Byzantine economy; founded the Comnene dynasty; and reluctantly accepted the arrival of the first **Crusade** in the East (1096–7).

ALFONSO X, THE WISE (1221–84) King of Castile and León, succeeding to the throne in 1252. He promulgated the *Siete Partidas*, Spain's great medieval code of laws; captured Cádiz and the Algarve from the Moors.

ALFRED THE GREAT (849–99) King of Wessex, England, succeeding his brother, Æthelred I, in 871. The early part of his reign was spent in hard struggle against Danish (Viking) invaders, in which he was gradually successful; Wessex itself was freed by 878, London retaken in 885, and the country divided on the line London–Chester. A notable lawgiver, he encouraged learning, vernacular translations of Latin classics and the compilation of an historic record, the *Anglo-Saxon Chronicle*; he also created many fortifications, a fast, mobile army and the beginnings of a fleet.

ALI (c. 600–61) Mohammed's cousin, second convert and son-in-law (married to the Prophet's daughter, **Fatima**), who became fourth caliph after the murder of Othman in 656. His accession led to civil war, he was murdered by a dissident supporter, Ibn Muljam. His descendants' claim to be imams, heirs of the Prophet as leaders of the community, still divides Islam (*see* **Shi'ism**).

ALLENBY, EDMUND HENRY HYNMAN (1861–1936) 1st Viscount; British field marshal. After service in France he commanded British forces in Palestine, 1917–18; he conducted a successful campaign against the Ottoman Turks culminating in the capture of Jerusalem (9 December 1917), victory at Megiddo (September 1918), and the capture of Damascus.

ALLENDE GOSSENS, SALVADOR (1908–73) Chilean statesman, elected president, 1970, becoming the world's first democratically chosen Marxist head of state. He instituted a major programme of political, economic and social change, but ran into increasing opposition both at home and abroad, and was killed during the successful right-wing military *coup d'etat* which brought to power General **Pinochet.**

ALMOHADS Berber dynasty ruling North Africa and Spain, 1130-1629, inspired by the religious teachings of Ibn Tumart. It defeated the **Almoravids**, 1147, and established its capital at Marrakesh; captured Seville, 1172. Its control over Islamic Spain was largely destroyed by the Christian victory of Las Navas de Tolosa in 1212.

ALMORAVIDS Saharan Berbers who built a religious and military empire in northwest Africa and Spain in the 11th and 12th centuries, after halting the advance of Castilian Christians near Badajoz, 1086; they ruled all Muslim Spain except El Cid's Christian Kingdom of Valencia. Their sober, puritanical style of art and architecture replaced the exuberant work of the **Umayyads** whose Córdoba government collapsed in 1031.

ALTAN KHAN (1507–82) Mongol chieftain who terrorized China during the 16th century. He became leader of the Eastern Mongols in 1543; in 1550 he crossed the Great Wall into northern China, and established his capital, Kuku-khoto (Blue City), just beyond the Wall; he concluded a peace treaty with China in 1570. In 1580 he converted the Mongols to the *Dge-bugs-pa* (Yellow Hat) sect of Lamaism, a mystical Buddhist doctrine originating in Tibet, and gave the head of the sect the title of Dalai ('all-embracing') Lama.

ALTMARK, ARMISTICE OF Truce concluded in May 1629 ending the war (since 1621) between Sweden and Poland. Sweden won the right to levy tolls along the Prussian coast, but renounced this when the agreement was renewed for 26 years in 1635.

AMBROSE, ST (c. 339–97) He served as governor of Aemilia-Liguria, in northern Italy, c. 370–4; appointed Bishop of Milan in 374, he was frequently in conflict with imperial authority. His writings laid the foundation for medieval thinking on the relationship between Church and state.

AMHARIC The most widely spoken language of Ethiopia, of Semitic origin, derived from Geez, a southern Arabian tongue related to Arabic and Hebrew, and still used in the liturgy of the Ethiopian Orthodox Church. It displaced and partially absorbed the indigenous Cushitic languages of the western highlands.

AMIN DADA, IDI (1925–) President of Uganda. He joined the British army in 1946, and was promoted to commander of the Ugandan army in 1965. He seized power in 1971 during the absence of President Milton Obote, and subsequently expelled all Asians (1972) and most Britons (1973). Having survived revolts against his repressive regime, he was overthrown in 1979 when Ugandan exiles seized power and (1980) restored Dr Obote.

AMORITES Immigrants from Syria into Mesopotamia, where they took over political supremacy from the **Sumerian** and **Akkadians** at the beginning of the 2nd millennium BC. Babylon's first dynasty was Amorite; to this belonged Hammurabi (1792–1750 BC). In the Bible, the term 'Amorite' is used to describe the pre-Israelite inhabitants of Palestine.

AMOSE I Founder of Egypt's 18th Dynasty. He completed the expulsion of **Hyksos** after the death of his brother, **Kamose**. Reigned c. 1550–1525 BC; with the aid of his mother, Queen Ahhotep, who may have acted as coregent early in his reign, he extended Egyptian control into Palestine and Nubia, and reopened trade with Syria. He died leaving the country prosperous and reunited.

AMSTERDAM EXCHANGE BANK Important early financial institution founded in 1609 with an official monopoly of foreign currency dealings in the city. It played a key part in the development of monetery instruments and commercial credit in western Europe.

ANAXAGORAS (c. 500–c. 428 BC) Greek philosopher. He taught a theory of cosmology based on the idea that the universe was formed by Mind; his particulate theory of matter opened the way to atomic theory. He was exiled as part of a political attack on his friend **Pericles**, perhaps c. 450 BC, after suggesting that the sun was an incandescent stone.

ANGEVINS Dynasty of English kings, often known as the Plantagenets, beginning with **Henry II** (reigned 1154–89). Descended from Geoffrey, Count of Anjou, and Matilda, daughter of Henry I; the direct line ended with **Richard II** (reigned 1377–99).

ANGLO-SAXONS Term originally coined to distinguish the Germanic tribes ruling England from 5th to 11th centuries AD, from the Saxons of continental Europe, the Angles and the Saxons being the most prominent of the invaders; later extended to mean 'the English' and their descendants all over the world.

AN LU-SHAN (703–57) Rebel Chinese general. Of Sogdian and Turkish descent, in 742 he became military governor of the northeast frontier districts. After the death of his patron, the emperor's chief minister Li Lin-fu, in 752, great rivalry developed between him and the courtier Yang Juo-chung; in 755 he turned his 160,000-strong army inwards and marched on the eastern capital, Lo-yang, proclaiming himself emperor of the Great Yen dynasty in 756 and capturing the western capital, Ch'angan. He was murdered the next year. The rebellion petered out by 763, but resulted in the serious weakening of the authority of the **T'ang** dynasty.

ANSKAR or Ansgar (801–65) Frankish saint, known as 'the Apostle of the North', who conducted missions to the Danes (826) and Swedes (829); first archbishop of Hamburg, 834.

ANTI-COMINTERN PACT Joint declaration by Germany and Japan, issued on 25 November 1936, that they would consult and collaborate in opposing the **Comintern** or Communist International. It was acceded to by Italy in 1937, and later became the instrument by which Germany secured the loyalty of its Romanian, Hungarian and Bulgarian satellites and attempted to bind Yugoslavia.

ANTIGONUS III DOSON (c. 263–221 BC) King of Macedonia from 227 BC, who created and led the Hellenic League (founded 224 BC) which defeated **Cleomenes III** of Sparta.

ANTIOCHUS III (242–187 BC) Seleucid king of Syria, who succeeded his brother, Seleucus III, in 223. After an inconclusive war with Egypt, he conquered Parthia, northern India, Pergamum and southern Syria, and invaded Greece (192), but was decisively driven back by the Romans at Thermopylae and defeated at Magnesia in Asia Minor (190). By his death the empire had been reduced to Syria, Mesopotamia and western Persia.

ANTONY (c. 82–31 BC) Marcus Antonius, best known as Mark Antony. A member of a prominent Roman family, he became joint consul with **Julius Caesar** in 44 BC; after Antony's defeat of Caesar's assassins, Brutus and Cassius, at Philippi, he controlled the armies of the Eastern empire; started liaison with **Cleopatra**; war broke out between him and Octavian, 32 BC. He committed suicide after naval defeat at Actium.

APACHE Indian hunters and farmers, located in the North American southwest. They probably originated in Canada, reaching their main hunting grounds, west of the Rio Grande, some time after the year 1000. The main groupings were the Western Apache, including the Mescalero and Kiowa tribes, and the Eastern Apache, including the Northern and Southern Tonto. In the colonial period they proved an effective barrier to Spanish settlement, and under such leaders as Cochise, Geronimo and Victorio in the 19th century, figured largely in the frontier battles fought in the American advance westward. After Geronimo's surrender in 1886, the remaining survivors became prisoners of war in Florida and Oklahoma; after 1913 they were allowed to move to reservations in Oklahoma and New Mexico.

APAMEA, PEACE OF Agreement ending the Syrian War between Rome and Seleucia; signed in 188 BC after the battle of Magnesia (190 BC). The Seleucid king, **Antiochus III**, paid an indemnity of 15,000 talents, surrendered his elephants and ships, and ceded all Asia Minor west of the Taurus Mountains.

APOLLONIUS (c. 295–c. 230 BC) Poet and director of the library at Alexandria in the 3rd century BC; known as 'Rhodius;' because he chose to retire to the island of Rhodes. His four-book epic, the *Argonautica*, tells the story of Jason's quest for the Golden Fleece.

ARABIAN AMERICAN OIL COMPANY (ARAMCO) Joint venture, set up in 1936 by **Standard Oil** of California and Texaco to exploit petroleum concessions in Saudi Arabia. It is now among the most powerful oil groups in the world, with additional partners Exxon and Mobil. In 1974 the Saudi Arabian government acquired a 60 per cent stake in the company and in 1979 took complete control. The services of the four US companies were retained to operate the production facilities on behalf of the government.

ARABI PASHA (1839–1911) Egyptian military leader. After service in the Egyptian-Ethiopian War, 1875–6, he was made a colonel; he joined the officers' mutiny, 1879, against **Ismail** Pasha, and in 1881 led the movement to oust Turks and Circassians from high army posts. Minister of War, 1882, he quickly became a national hero with his slogan *Misr lil Misriyin* ('Egypt for the Egyptians'); he was commander-in-chief, 1882, when the British navy bombarded Alexandria, and was defeated on 13 September at Tell-el-Kebir by British troops under Sir Garnet Wolseley. He was captured and sentenced to death, but instead was exiled to Ceylon.

ARAB LEAGUE Association of Arab states, with its headquarters in Cairo. Founded in 1945, by Iraq, Trans-Jordan, Lebanon, Saudi Arabia, Egypt, Syria and Yemen, it was later joined by other states as they became independent: Algeria, Bahrain, Djibouti, Kuwait, Libya, Mauritania, Morocco, Oman, Qatar, Somalia, Sudan, Tunisia, United Arab Emirates. The PLO has been a full member since 1976. Egypt was expelled between 1978 and 1989.

ARAUCANIANS (sometimes known as the Mapuche). A warlike Indian tribe in southern Chile which successfully resisted many Inca and Spanish incursions. The first native group to adopt the Spaniards' horses, they became brilliant cavalry fighters, and in 1598 three hundred mounted Araucanians wiped out a major Spanish punitive expedition. They retained effective independence, despite numerous Spanish and Chilean attempts to subdue them, until the late 19th century.

ARBENZ GUZMAN, JACOBO (1913–71) Guatemalan political leader of Swiss immigrant parentage. He rose to the rank of colonel in the Guatemalan army; played a leading role in the democratic revolution of 1945, and President of Guatemala, 1951; he inaugurated a radical leftwing land reform programme. He was overthrown in a United States-backed military coup in 1954.

ARCHILOCHUS Greek satirical poet, writing about 700 BC; many fragments of his work survive.

ARCHIMEDES (c. 287–212 BC) Greek mathematician and scientist. Born in Syracuse, he studied in Alexandria. He calculated the upper and lower limits for the value of π; devised a formula for calulating the volume of a sphere; invented, among many other things, Archimedes' Screw, for raising large quantities of water to a higher level, and also Archimedes' Principle, which enabled him to discover, with a cry of 'Eureka!', the impurity in King Hiero's crown by weighing it in and out of water in comparison with pure gold and pure silver. He returned to Sicily to design weapons and defence strategies for King Hiero, and was killed during the Roman siege of his native city.

ARDASHIR I (d.241) Founder of the Sasanid empire of Persia; born in the late 2nd century AD. Ardashir took the crown of Persis in 208. He rapidly extended his territory, defeating his Parthian overlords at Hormizdagan in 224, and occupying their capital, Ctesiphon. He made Zoroastrianism the state religion.

ARIANISM see Arius

ARISTOPHANES (c. 450–c. 380 BC) Athenian comic dramatist. Eleven of some 40 plays survive, including *The Frogs*, *The Birds*, and *Lysistrata*. They are highly political, brilliant in language and verse, dramatic situation, parody, satire, wit and farce, sparing neither men nor gods.

ARISTOTLE (384–322 BC) Greek philosopher and scienist. Born in Thrace, he studied in Athens under Plato. He taught the young **Alexander the Great**, then established his Lyceum in Athens, 335, and founded the Peripatetic school of philosophy. He was an outstanding biologist. His voluminous works, covering almost every aspect of knowledge, survive mainly in the form of lecture notes, edited in the 1st century AD.

ARIUS (c. AD 250–336) Originator of the Christian doctrine known as Arianism, later condemned as the Arian heresy. A pupil of Lucian of Antioch, he taught that the son of God was a creature, not consubstantial or coeternal with the Father. He was excommunicated for these views by the provincial synod of Alexandria in 321, unsuccessfully defended his belief in 325 before the **Council of Nicaea** and was banished. He died on the point of being reinstated by the Emperor **Constantine.** His controversial teachings divided the Church for many centuries.

ARKWRIGHT, SIR RICHARD (1732–92) English inventor and pioneer of the factory system, who invented the water-frame (1796) and other mechanized spinning processes.

ARMENIANS Indo-European people occupying in ancient times, the area now comprising north-east Turkey and modern Armenia. They were converted to Christianity in the late 3rd century. Armenians boast a highly distinctive culture, which flowered particularly during periods of independence and reached peaks in the 10th and 14th centuries. During the First World War the Ottoman government deported most Armenians in Asia Minor (about 1,750,000 people) to the Syrian and Mesopotamian provinces. Armenians claim that over 1 million deportees were systematically killed at this time in a policy of genocide.

ARMINIUS (c. 18 BC–AD 21) German tribal chief and early national hero, known also as Hermann. He became leader of the Cherusci after service and honour with Roman forces; in AD 9 he defeated and massacred three Roman legions at the Battle of Teutoburg Forest; held off Roman attacks, AD 16–17, but was murdered by his own people during a war with the Marcomanni, another German tribe. Described by Tacitus as *liberator haud dubie Germaniae* ('undoubtedly the liberator of Germany').

ARNOLD OF BRESCIA (c. 1100–55) Radical theologian and religious reformer who studied under Peter Abelard and was condemned with him at the Council of Sens in 1140. He later moved to Italy where, in alliance with the citizens of Rome, he strongly attacked Pope **Eugenius III** and forced him to leave the city. He was captured and executed at the pope's request by **Frederick Barbarossa.** His leading anti-clerical argument was that spiritual persons should not possess temporal goods.

ARPAD Magyar dynasty, ruling Hungary from late 9th century to 1301; named after Árpád, who was chosen in 889 to lead seven Magyar tribes westward from their homeland on the river Don. Under Béla III (1172–96), Hungary was established as a major central European power, but was later weakened by the Mongol invasion (1241–2); the dynasty died out with Andrew III (1290–1301), who left no heir.

ARTAXERXES II MNEMON (c. 435–358 BC) King of Persia, son of Darius II (reigned 423–404); he changed name from Arsaces on his accession in 404. He was challenged by his brother, Cyrus the Younger (c.430–401), but defeated and killed him at Cunaxa, near Babylon, 401.

ARTEVELDE, JACOB VAN (c. 1295–1345) Flemish leader during the early phases of the **Hundred Years' War.** In 1338 he emerged as one of five 'captains' governing the town of Ghent; formed an alliance with the English king, **Edward III**, against France and the Count of Flanders; ruled as chief captain until killed in a riot.

ARYAN Contentious term used at various times to describe a member of the Caucasian race from which the Indo-European peoples supposedly sprang; in **Hitler's** Germany, a member of the so-called 'master' or 'Nordic' race. Correctly applied to the Indo-Iranian branch of the eastern Indo-European group of languages, and at one time to the hypothetical parent language of that group.

ARYA SAMAJ Hindu reform movment; its followers reject all idolatrous and polytheistic worship and insist on the sole authority of the **Vedas**.

ASHANTI (Asante) One of several states of Akan-speaking peoples of southern Ghana, Togo and Ivory Coast. Also an independent kingdom in southern Ghana in the 18th and

19th centuries, taking an active part in the Atlantic slave trade. Ultimately failing to resist British penetration, it was annexed in 1901, and is now an administrative region of Ghana.

ASHANTI WARS Engagements fought in 1824–7, 1873–4, 1895–6 between the west African kingdom of Ashanti, which originated in the 17th century, and the British, at first to prevent Ashanti expansion into the British (coastal) colony of the Gold Coast and subsequently as resistance by the Ashanti to the attempted imposition of British rule over them. Final annexation of Ashanti came in 1901; it is now a province of independent Ghana.

ASHKENAZIM From the Hebrew word *Ashenaz*, meaning Germany. It refers to the Jews of the Germanic lands, many of whom emigrated eastward in the Middle Ages. Today it represents most of the Jews of Europe, the British Commonwealth, the United States, the USSR, South America and approximately half the Jewish population of Israel. The word is used in distinction to **Sephardim**, who have slightly different customs and rites.

ASHOKA (Asoka) (d.232 BC) Greatest of the Mauryan emperors of early India, succeeding his father, **Bindusara**, in 272 BC. In 260 BC he inflicted a crushing defeat on Kalinga (modern Orissa), the last major independent Indian state. He was converted to **Buddhism** and from then developed a policy of toleration and non-violence, renouncing conquest.

ASHURNASIRPAL II (d.859 BC) King of Assyria, 883–859 BC, who began the 1st millennium expansion of the Assyrian empire to the Mediterranean. Monuments and inscriptions describe with great frankness the harsh treatment of conquered peoples in ancient warfare. He created Calah (Nimrud) as his new capital.

ASIENTO Monopoly granted to an individual or company for the exclusive supply of Negro slaves to the Spanish colonies in America. The first asiento was signed by the Spanish court with Genoese entrepreneurs in 1517, later it passed mainly to the Portuguese until 1640, and then in succession to the French Royal Guinea Company and to the British South Sea Company (until 1750). It was finally extinguished in 1793, when all Spanish colonial trade was freed from central control.

ASKIA THE GREAT (d.1538) Founder of the Askia dynasty, rulers of the Songhay empire, centred round the capital of Gao in present day Mali, from 1492–1591. He rose to power in 1493, reigning as Mohammed I Akia; he promoted the spread of Islam in his domains and made a pilgrimage to Mecca in 1495–7. He was deposed in 1528 by his sons, led by Askia Musa.

ASSASSINS European name given to the Nizari branch of the Ismailis, organized by the leader of the 'new preaching', Hadan-i Sabbah (d.1124). They ruled parts of northern Persia and coastal Syria from strongholds of which Alamut in Persia was the most important, and played a part in the general history of Persia and Syria, partly because of their practise of killing opponents (hence 'assassination'). The leader of the Syrian group was known to Crusaders as the 'Old Man of the Mountains'. Their political power was ended by the Mongols in Persia, and by the **Mamluks** in Egypt.

ASSYRIANS Warlike people of northern Mesopotamia, remarkable for fighting prowess, administrative efficiency (after 745 BC) – which made possible the control of an empire of unprecedented size – and for the magnificent bas-reliefs in their palaces. They formed an independent state in the 14th century BC, and under the Neo-Assyrian empire dominated much of the Near East until destroyed by a Chaldaean-Mede coalition in 612 BC. In modern times the term is applied to an ancient Christian sect, found chiefly in Turkey, Iraq and Iran, whose members claim to be descended from the ancient Assyrians.

ASTURIAS, KINGDOM OF Founded in 718 in the extreme north of Spain by a group of Visigoths nobles after the Muslim invasions. Expanded and established on a firm basis under Alfonso I (739–57), it included northwest Spain and northern Portugal. For almost 200 years it remained the sole independent Christian bastion in Iberia; it survived many attacks and, particularly under Alfonso III (866–910), began to push its frontier further south. After 910 it continued as the kingdom of León.

ATAHUALLPA (c. 1502–33) Last independent ruler of the **Inca** empire in Peru. He was given the subsidiary kingdom of Quito on the death of his father, **Huayna Capac**; he fought a war with his brother **Huascar**, and deposed him in 1532, just before the Spaniards invaded the Inca realms. Taken prisoner by **Francisco Pizarro**, he was accused of complicity in his brother's murder and executed.

ATATÜRK (1881–1938) Founder and first president of the republic of Turkey. Originally named Mustafa Kemal, he was born in Salonica; he graduated from Istanbul Military Academy, in 1902. He resigned from the army in 1919 to support the Turkish independence movement, and in the same year was elected president of the National Congress. After British and Greek occupation (1920), he opened the first Grand National Assembly, was elected first president and prime minister, and directed operations in the Greco-Turkish War of 1920–2. After the peace treaty of 1923 he abolished the Ottoman caliphate and began a far-reaching reform and modernization programme. He took the name Atatürk, 'Father of the Turks', in 1934.

ATHANASIUS (c. 296–373) Theologian, statesman and saint, born in Alexandria (Egypt). He attended the **Council of Nicaea**, 325, and was appointed bishop of Alexandria in 328. He became both Egyptian national leader and the chief defender of orthodox Christianity against the heresy of Arianism. His major writings include a *Life of St Antony*, a short treatise *On the Incarnation of the Word* and *Four Orations against the Arians*.

ATTALUS III (d.133 BC) Last independent king of Pergamum, reigning 138–133 BC. On his deathbed he bequeathed his kingdom to Rome, which then (129) organized it into the province of Asia.

ATTILA (c. 406–453) Sole rule of the vast **Hun** empire after the murder of his brother Bleda c.445. He overran much of the Roman empire, reaching Orléans in Gaul, 451, and the river Mincio in Italy, 452; his empire collapsed after his death.

ATTLEE, CLEMENT (1883–1967) British prime minister. Educated at Oxford university, he briefly practised law, then spent 1907–22 (apart from war service) working among the poor in London's East End. He became Mayor of Stepney, 1919, and a Member of Parliament, 1922; a junior minister in the Labour governments of 1924 and 1929–31, leader 1935–55; and was a member of **Churchill**'s War Cabinet. As prime minister, 1945–51, he presided over the establishment of the Welfare State in Britain and the granting of independence to India, Pakistan, Burma and Ceylon; he relinquished British control of Egypt and Palestine. He was created Earl Atlee in 1955.

AUGUSTINE OF HIPPO, ST (354–430) Leading thinker of the early Christian Church. After a restless youth, recorded in his *Confessions* he was converted in 386, baptized by **St Ambrose** the following year, and in 396 appointed Bishop of Hippo, in North Africa. His greatest work, *The City of God*, was written between 413 and 426 as a philosophic meditation on the sack of Rome by the **Visigoths** in 410.

AUGUSTUS (63 BC–AD 14) First emperor of Rome, born Gaius Julius Caesar Octavianus; great-nephew, adopted son and heir of **Julius Caesar**. With **Antony** and Lepidus he emerged victorious in the civil war against Brutus and Cassius, after Caesar's murder. He broke with Antony and defeated him at Actium in 31 BC; offered sole command in Rome, he brought peace and prosperity to the empire, over which he effectively ruled from 27 BC until his death.

AURANGZEB (1618–1707) Last of India's great Mughal emperors. Son of the emperor **Shahjahan**; he succeeded in 1658 after a struggle with his brothers. Up to 1680 he successfully consolidated power over Hindu and Muslim subjects, but later his empire began to disintegrate through rebellions, wars with the **Rajputs** (erstwhile allies) and the **Marathas.**

AUSTRO-SERBIAN 'PIG WAR' Tariff conflict in 1906–11 between Austria-Hungary and Serbia, which also exacerbated anti-Habsburg agitation in Bosnia (occupied by Austria in 1878, annexed in 1908).

AVVOCATI (or Avogadro) Prominent family of medieval Vercelli, Italy. Supporters of the **Guelph** (anti-imperial) party, they engaged in a semi-permanent feud with their Ghibelline (pro-imperial) rivals until in 1335 the city came under the control of the **Visconti** of Milan.

AYLWIN, PATRICIO (1919–) Chilean lawyer and politician. He served as president of the Christian Democratic Party (PDC) in 1973 and 1987–91. He led the opposition coalition formed to reject General Pinochet in a national plebiscite in October 1988 and was President of Chile 1990–3.

AYYUBIDS Sunni Muslim dynasty, founded by **Saladin**. It ruled Egypt, Upper Iraq, most of Syria and Yemen from Saladin's death in 1193 until the **Mamluk** rise to power (1250).

BABUR (1483–1530) Founder of the **Mughal** dynasty of Indian emperors. Son of the ruler of Ferghana, central Asia, he lost this territory while seeking to conquer Samarkand (1501–4). He captured Kandahar, strategic point on the northern road to India, 1522; occupied Delhi, 1526, and established himself on the imperial throne. He wrote poetry and his memoirs.

BACSONIAN AND HOABINHIAN Stone Age cultures of southeast Asia, characterized by the fact that their typical implements and artefacts are worked on one side only. They were named after two provinces of northern Vietnam, Bac Son and Hoa Binh, where the largest concentration of examples have been found.

BAFFIN, WILLIAM (c. 1584–1622) English navigator; sailed (1612) with Captain James Hall's expedition in search of the Northwest Passage; in 1615 and 1616, with Captain **Robert Bylot**, he penetrated the waters between Canada and Baffin Island, and deep into Baffin Bay, both named after him. Working for the **English East India Company** he surveyed the Red Sea and the Persian Gulf.

BAGHDAD PACT *see* **Central Treaty Organization.**

BAIBARS (1223–77) Mamluk sultan, ruling Egypt and Syria, 1260–77. Born among the **Kipchak** Turks north of the Black Sea, he was sold as a slave to an Egyptian soldier. He fought and defeated both crusaders and Mongols before seizing the throne.

BAKEWELL, ROBERT (1725–95) English animal-breeder who revolutionized the development of meat-bearing strains in sheep and cattle. His successes included the Leicester Longhorn cow (now superseded by the Shorthorn) and the heavy, barrel-shaped, Leicester sheep. He was the first man to commercialize large-scale stud-farming.

BALAIADA Revolutionary uprising, 1838–41, in Maranhão province, Brazil; it was finally suppressed by the imperial general, Duque de Caxias.

BALBAN (1207–87) Sultan of Delhi, originally a junior member of the Forty, made up from personal slaves of Itutmish, who divided the kingdom after his death. He acted as deputy to Sultan Nasiruddin Mahmud (reigned 1246–66), whom he succeeded; he ably consolidated Muslim power, despite continual war with **Rajputs**, Mongols and Hindu states.

BALFOUR DECLARATION Letter from Britain's foreign secretary, Arthur Balfour, dated 2 November 1917, to Lord Rothschild, a leader of British Jewry, stating British support for the establishment in Palestine of a national home for the Jewish people, provided that the rights of the non-Jewish communities be respected. Approved at the San Remo Conference in 1920, it was incorporated into the mandate over Palestine granted to Britain by the **League of Nations** in 1922.

BALKAN LEAGUE The outcome of bilateral agreements made by Bulgaria with Serbia, Greece and Montenegro, leading to the Balkan Wars against Turkey, 1912–13. It collapsed completely in June 1913 when Bulgaria attacked Greece and Serbia in the hope of preventing them from acquiring the bulk of Macedonia.

BALKAN WAR, FIRST War that largely expelled the Ottomans from Europe. Montenegro, Bulgaria, Greece and Serbia attacked the Ottoman empire in October 1912; by December only the fortresses of Adrianople (Edirne), Scutari (Shkodër) and Yannin (Ioannina) remained in Turkish hands, and they too were lost to Turkey by the Treaty of London (May 1913) which also, at Austrian insistence, created the Albanian state to keep Serbia from the Adriatic.

BALKAN WAR, SECOND War among the victors of the First Balkan War over the division of Macedonia, June–Aug. 1913. Romania intervened on the side of Greece and Serbia against Bulgaria, which suffered a heavy defeat reflected in the Treaty of Bucharest (10 Aug. 1913); meanwhile, the Turks took the opportunity of regaining Adrianople (Edirne) from Bulgaria.

BALKE, HERMANN (d.1239) Provincial master of the **Teutonic Order**, who began the conquest of the pagan Prussians in 1231, at the head of a crusading army.

BAMBARA Also known as Banmana, west African people from the Upper Niger region of the Republic of Mali. Their spoken language is derived from the **Mande** group, but their method of writing is distinctive, as is its associated cosmological system. The Bambara states, Segu (founded c. 1600) between the Senegal River and the Niger, and Kaarta (c. 1753) on the Middle Niger, flourished until the mid-19th century.

BANDARANAIKE, SOLOMON (1899–1959) Prime minister of Ceylon, 1956–9. He resigned from the Western-orientated United National Party in 1951 to form the nationalist Sri Lanka Freedom Party; in 1956 his People's United Front, an alliance of four nationalist-socialist groups, won a sweeping electoral victory. As prime minister he replaced English with Sinhala as the official language, fostered **Buddhism**, and established diplomatic relations with Communist states. He was assassinated and succeeded by his widow.

BANK OF ENGLAND Central financial institution of Great Britain. It was founded in 1694 with the initial object of lending King William III £1,200,000 at 8 per cent. Originally a private, profit-making institution, its public responsibilities were extended and defined by Bank Charter Acts of 1833 and 1844; it was finally transferred to public ownership in 1946.

BANTU A large group of closely related languages, spoken by the majority of the black inhabitants in Africa south of the Equator. By association, the term is sometimes applied to the people themselves, especially in South Africa.

BAPTISTS Members of a Christian Protestant movement dating from the 16th century. They are now represented by many churches and groups of churches throughout the world, organized in independent congregations. Many follow the practise of baptism by total immersion, and insist that the rite should take place only when the initiate is old enough to appreciate its significance.

BARAKZAI Tribal group from which emerged Afghanistan's ruling dynasty, from 1837 to 1973. The brothers who founded the dynasty seized control of the country in 1826 and divided it between them; Dost Mohammed Khan consolidated and unified the family rule, c.1837, and his direct descendants held the throne until 1929 when, after the abdication of the reigning monarch, succession passed to a cousin's line; the military coup of 1973 overthrew the monarchy and a republic was declared.

BARBAROSSA Name of two Greek brothers, famous as Algerian Muslim pirates, Barbarossa I (c. 1473–1518) was killed by the Spaniards after a series of raids on the Spanish coast; Barbarossa II, also known as Khair ed-Din (c.1466–1546), took over command on his brother's death and in 1519 became a vassal of the Ottoman sultan, for whom he repulsed an invasion by the emperor **Charles V** in 1541.

BARDI Important Florentine family, established there in the 11th century, which flourished in trade and finance, especially from the mid-13th to the mid-14th century. It became the greatest merchant and banking company in Europe at that time, and exercised considerable political influence. Defaults on debt payment by **Edward III** of England and by Florence finally led to bankruptcy and collapse in 1345.

BARENTS, WILLEM (c. 1550–97) Dutch explorer of the Arctic, who in 1594 and 1595 rounded northern Europe to reach the Novaya Zemlya archipelago. He is remembered particularly for his charting of northern waters; the Barents Sea is named after him.

BARTH, HEINRICH (1821–65) German geographer and explorer. After travels in Tunisia and Libya (1845–7), he set off on a British-sponsored expedition across the Sahara. Returning after 10,000 miles, he wrote *Travels and Discoveries in North and Central Africa* (1857–8), still one of the richest sources of information on the area. He became Professor of Geography at Berlin in 1863.

BASIL I (d.886) Byzantine emperor. Of peasant stock, he was the founder of the Macedonian dynasty, so called from his place of origin. He rose to be co-emperor with Michael III in 866, but murdered Michael in 867. He began formulating the legal code (completed by his son **Leo VI**) known as the Basilica.

BASIL II (958–1025) Most powerful of Byzantium's Macedonian emperors. He was crowned co-emperor with his brother Constantine in 960; claimed sole authority, 985; extended Byzantine rule to the Balkans, Mesopotamia, Georgia and Armenia. His conquest of the Bulgarian empire earned him the nickname 'Bulgar Slayer'.

BASTIDAS, RODRIGO (1460–1526) Spanish explorer who discovered the mouths of the Magdalena river in modern Columbia, and founded the Columbian city of Santa Marta.

BATLLE Y ORDOÑEZ, JOSE (1856–1929) President of Uruguay. He founded a newspaper, *El Día*, 1866; elected president in 1903, by a narrow margin, he emerged victorious from the ensuing civil war (1904–5), and was re-elected, 1905–7, and again, after freely stepping down, 1911–15. He inaugurated a wide-ranging programme of social and economic reform. Defeated over constitutional reform in 1918, he went on to serve as president of the national executive council in 1920 and 1926.

BATU KHAN (d.1255) Leader of the **Golden Horde.** The grandson of **Genghis Khan**, in 1235 he was elected western commander-in-chief for the Mongol empire, and entrusted with the invasion of Europe. By 1240 he had conquered all Russia; by 1241, after defeating Henry II, Duke of Silesia, and the Hungarians, he was poised to advance further west. However, on hearing of the death of **Ogedei** (December 1241) he withdrew his forces to take part in the choice of successor. He later established the Kipchak khanate, or the Golden Horde, in southern Russia.

BAYEZID I, YILDIRIM (c. 1360–1403) Known as 'the Thunderbolt'. Ottoman ruler. Succeeding to the throne in 1389, he claimed the title of sultan and attempted to establish a strong centralized state based on Turkish and Muslim institutions. He conquered large areas of the Balkans and Anatolia; blockaded Constantinople, 1391–8; invaded Hungary, 1395, and crushed at Nicopolis in 1396 the crusaders sent to repel him. He was defeated by **Tamerlane**'s Mongol armies at Ankara in 1402, and died in captivity, with his empire partitioned between his sons and the restored Anatolian principalities.

BAYEZID II (c. 1447–1512) Ottoman sultan, succeeding to the throne in 1481. His reign marked a reaction from the policies of his father, **Mehmed II**. The conquest of Kilia and Akkerman (1484–5) gave the Ottomans control over the mouth of the Danube and the land route from Constantinople to the Crimea; the later years of Bayezid's reign were taken up by war with Venice (1496–1503), by growing social unrest in Anatolia connected with the rise of the **Safavids** under their leader Ismail, and by the struggle among the sons of Bayezid for the succession to the Ottoman throne.

BEAUMANOIR, PHILIPPE DE RÉMI, SIRE DE (c. 1246–96) French administrator and jurist; wrote *Coutumes de Beauvoisis* (c. 1280–3), one of the earliest codifications of French law.

BELGAE Ancient Germanic and Celtic people, inhabiting northern Gaul; some emigrated to southern Britain in the 1st century BC. Gallic Belgae were conquered by **Julius Caesar** in 57 BC and the British in 55–54 BC.

BELGRADE, TREATY OF Peace agreement of 1739 ending the Turkish–Austrian War of 1737–9. Austria surrendered most of its gains under the **Treaty of Passarowitz** (1718), and thus re-established the line of the rivers Danube and Save as the frontier between the two empires.

BELISARIUS (c. 494–565) Byzantine general. Under Emperor Justinian I he swept the **Vandals** out of North Africa and **Ostrogoths** out of Italy (533–40); repulsed Persian assaults (541–2).

BELL, JOHN (1797–1869) Nominee for president of the United States on the eve of the American Civil War. He entered Congress, 1827; became secretary for war, 1841, and a US senator, 1847–59. He opposed the extension of slave-holding, though a large owner himself; nominated on a Constitutional Union ticket, 1860, he at first opposed secession, then supported it.

BENEDICT OF NURSIA, ST (c. 480–c. 540) Founder of a Christian monastic order. He became a hermit, but c. 529 decided to form a monastic community, which he established at Monte Cassino in Italy, and for which, in the 530s, he composed the Benedictine Rule (a relatively short document of 73 chapters) which has served as the basis of Christian monastic organization.

BEN-GURION, DAVID (1886–1973) Israeli labour leader, politician and statesman; born in Poland. He became active in **Zionist** affairs, emigrated to Palestine in 1906 and became secretary-general of the labour movement in 1921. In the struggle to found an independent Jewish state, he cooperated with the British during the Second World War but led the political and military struggle against them, 1947–8. He was the first prime minister (and also minister of defence) of the new state of Israel, 1948–53, and again 1955–63. He continued to exert an influence as its founding father and elder statesman in retirement from the Negev Kibbutz of Sede Boker until his death.

BENTHAMITE Follower of the English utilitarian philosopher Jeremy Bentham (1748–1832). Benthamite thinking, summed up in the concept of the Pleasure Principle ('men seek pleasure and avoid pain') and the belief that institutions should be judged by their ability to promote 'the greatest happiness of the greatest number', influenced many later legal and political reforms.

BERBERS Original peoples of north Africa, who were colonized by Rome. Invaded by the Arabs in the 7th century AD, they were converted to Islam after some resistance. Those in or near cities were gradually absorbed into Arabic culture, but Berber languages continue to be spoken, particularly in mountain and pastoral regions of Morocco and Algeria.

BERING, VITUS JONASSEN (1681–1741) Danish navigator and discoverer of Alaska. After a voyage to the East Indies, he joined the Russian navy of **Peter the Great**; in 1724 he was appointed by the tsar to establish whether Asia was joined to North America, and in 1728 sailed through the strait which now bears his name, into the Arctic Ocean. He died when his ship was wrecked on Bering Island, east of the Kamchatka peninsula.

BERLIN, CONGRESS OF Meeting of European statesmen in June–July 1878 under the presidency of **Bismarck** to revise the Treaty of **San Stefano** (1878), concluded by Russia and Turkey. Bulgaria, greatly reduced in extent, became an autonomous principality. The independence of Romania, Serbia and Montenegro was confirmed. Austria-Hungary was given the right to occupy Bosnia and Herzegovina, and Russia was confirmed in its possession of Ardahan, Kars and Batum.

BERLIN WALL Heavily fortified barrier built in 1961 by the East German government around the Western zones of Berlin. The Berlin Wall was the single most potent symbol of the **Cold War**. As levels of emigration from East to West Berlin increased in the 1950s and early 1960s, the East German government determined to construct what it called the Anti-Fascist Exclusion Wall. Though its stated purpose was to keep West Berliners out of East Berlin, in reality the Wall was a crude but effective means of preventing East Germans from escaping to the West. The opening of the Wall in late 1989 after the collapse of the communist government of East Germany was a vivid symbol of the end of the Cold War.

BERNARD, ST (c. 1090–1153) He entered the Cistercian Order in 1113, only 15 years after the foundation of the monastery of Cîteaux, and soon became its leading light. Two years later, he founded the monastery of Clairvaux, also in southeast France, and remained its abbot for the rest of his life. Through personal influence, teaching and voluminous writings, he dominated the theological and to a large extent also the political life of his times, particularly by securing the recognition of Innocent II as Pope in 1130, by advice to his former pupil **Eugenius III** (Pope 1145–53), and by preaching the second **Crusade** in 1147.

BESANT, ANNIE (1847–1933) Theosophist, social reformer and Indian independence pioneer. She was a Fabian Socialist, with George Bernard Shaw, in the late 1880s, and was converted to the theosophic ideas of Helen Blavatsky, 1889–91. She spent much of her remaining life in India, jointly founding the Indian Home Rule League in 1916.

BESSEMER, SIR HENRY (1813–98) British inventor of the Bessemer steel-making process. He developed various mechanical devices, including a movable date stamp, and in the Crimean War the first rotary shell. In 1856 he announced a process for purifying molten iron with a blast of air; with contributions from other inventors, his work made possible the Bessemer converter and the mass production of cheap steel.

BETANCOURT, ROMULO (1908–81) Venezuelan political leader. Imprisoned while a student, and exiled to Colombia, he returned in 1936 to lead the anti-Communist left-wing underground movement; again exiled, 1939–41, in 1941 he organized Acción Democrática (AD), and became president of the revolutionary governing junta after the overthrow of President Medina Angarita, 1945. Forced yet again into exile by the Pérez Jiménez regime, 1948–58, he became president of Venezuela, 1959–64.

BHONSLAS Dynasty of **Maratha** rulers in western India, founded by the family of King **Sivaji**. They were leaders in the 18th-century Maratha confederacy formed to resist the British; later they became British clients (1816–53).

BINDUSARA (d.272 BC) Early Indian emperor, succeeding his father, **Chandragupta Maurya**, in 279 BC. He campaigned in the Deccan, as far south as Mysore, and brought most of the subcontinent under Mauryan control.

BISMARCK, PRINCE OTTO VON (1815–98) German statesman, known as 'the Iron Chancellor'. He was appointed minister-president of Prussia, 1862; after wars against Denmark (1864) and Austria (1866), he formed the North German Confederation (1867), and after the **Franco-Prussian War** (1870–1) inaugurated the German empire (1871–1918). As German chancellor (1871–90) he instituted important social, economic and imperial policies and played a leading role in the European alliance systems of the 1870s and 1880s.

BLACK FLAGS Chinese bandits and mercenary groups active in Annam and Tongking, 1873–5, led by Liu Yung-fu, a former T'ai-p'ing rebel. Called on by the mandarins of Hanoi to oppose the French (1873), they were responsible for the defeat and death of several French commanders during a decade of bitter guerrilla war.

BLACKFOOT INDIANS A group of Indian tribes of Algonquin stock. They were one of the strongest Indian confederations in the early 19th century but were gradually defeated and subdued by the US settlers. Their name derived from the colour of their moccasins.

BLAKE, ROBERT (1599–1657) English admiral; he commanded **Cromwell**'s navy in the English Interregnum, and defeated the Dutch, the Spaniards, and the Barbary corsairs.

BLIGH, WILLIAM (1754–1817) British vice-admiral. He served on Captain **James Cook**'s last voyage; he was commanding the *Bounty* when the crew mutinied in 1789 in the South Seas and set him adrift in an open boat. On his voyage of exploration of 1791 he made discoveries in Tasmania, Fiji and the Torres Straits. He fought at Gibraltar (1782), Camperdown (1797) and Copenhagen (1801). He was governor-general of New South Wales, 1805–8, from which post he was deposed by force and imprisoned until 1810.

BLITZ Second World War term for a sudden attack, particularly from the air; derived from the German word *Blitzkrieg*, or lightning war.

BOETHIUS (c. 480–524) Late classical scholar and statesman, born in Rome. He was appointed consul under **Theodoric** the Ostrogoth in 510. He translated **Aristotle**'s *Organon* and helped to preserve many classical texts; he wrote on music, mathematics and astronomy. His **Christianity**, clear from some short treatises, is not mentioned in his larger works. After falling from favour with Theodoric, he wrote his *De consolatione philosophiae* in prison. He was executed on charges of treason.

BOGOMILS Balkan religious sect, flourishing from the 10th to the 15th century. It inherited **Manichaean** doctrines from the **Paulicians**; believed the visible world was created by the devil; rejected baptism, the Eucharist, the cross, miracles, churches, priests and all orthodox Christianity. Its leader, Basil, was publicly burned in Constantinople c. 1100. Adopted by the ruling class in Bosnia, it also directly influenced the **Cathars** in Italy and **Albigensians** in France; it died out after the Ottoman conquest of southeast Europe because many of its adherents converted to Islam.

BOLESŁAW I CHROBRY, 'THE BRAVE' (966–1025) First fully accepted king of Poland, son of **Mieszko I**. He inherited the principality of Greater Poland, 992; reached the Baltic, 996, and seized control of Cracow and Little Poland. Crowned by Emperor **Otto III**, 1000, he was embroiled in wars, 1002–18, with Emperor Henry II over lands seized in Lusatia, Meissen and Bohemia. He defeated Grand Prince Iaroslav I of Kiev (1018), and placed his son-in-law on the Kievan throne.

BOLIVAR, SIMON (1783–1830) Venezuelan soldier-statesman who freed six South American countries from Spanish rule. He participated in Venezuela's declaration of independence in 1811, fleeing to Haiti after the Spanish counter-revolution; liberated New Granada (Colombia) in 1819; Venezuela, 1821; Ecuador, 1822; Peru, 1824; and Upper Peru, renamed Bolivia, in 1825. A liberal political thinker but an autocratic ruler, he failed in his real ambition to establish a union of Spanish-American peoples; most of the nations he had helped to create were in turmoil or conflict when he died.

BOLSHEVIKS Named from Bolsheviki Russian for 'those of the majority', the name adopted by **Lenin**'s supporters in the Russian Social-Democratic Workers' Party at the 1903 Congress when, advocating restriction of membership to professional revolutionaries, they won a temporary majority on the central committee. From 1912 they constituted a separate party. Seizing control of Russia in October 1917, in March 1918 they adopted the name 'Communists'.

BONAPARTE *see* **Napoleon I**

BONIFACE VIII (c. 1235–1303) Pope, 1294–1303. He reasserted papal claims to superiority over temporal powers; his Bull Clericis laicos (1296) led to conflict with **Edward I** of England, and particularly with **Philip IV** of France, over taxation of the clergy, but the dispute soon widened to cover the whole relationship of Church and state. He was briefly kidnapped at Anagni by the French, 1303, but soon released; to escape repetition of such treatment, the papacy took up residence at Avignon – the so-called 'Avignon Captivity'.

BONIFACE, ST (c. 675–754) Often called the Apostle of Germany; born in Nursling, Wessex. He was ordained priest c. 705 under his original name of Wynfrith. He left England in 716 to evangelize the Saxons. He was sent first into Hesse and Thuringia by Pope Gregory II (722–35), and then into Bavaria by Gregory III. He became Archbishop of Mainz, 751; organized German and reformed Frankish churches. He was martyred by pagan **Frisians**.

BOONE, DANIEL (1734–1820) American frontiersman, explorer and fighter in Kentucky and Missouri. He created the wilderness road, northwest of the Appalachians.

BOSE, SUBHAS CHANDRA (1897–1945) Indian nationalist leader; educated Calcutta and Cambridge, England. He was imprisoned (1924–7) for his part in **Gandhi**'s non-cooperation movement. On his release he was elected president of Bengal's provincial congress. He spent most of the next decade in prison or exile, until 1938 when he became president of the Indian National Congress; under house arrest (1940), he escaped to Germany. He formed an Indian volunteer force to attack the Western allies and in 1943, with Japanese support, invaded India from Rangoon. He died two years after his defeat, in an air crash in Taiwan.

BOURBONS European ruling family. Descended from Louis I, duke of Bourbon (1279–1341), grandson of King **Louis IX** of France (reigned 1226–70), the Bourbons held the thrones of France (1589–1791 and again 1814–48), Spain (more or less from 1700 to 1931), and Naples and Sicily (1735–1860). The Spanish line was restored after the death of **Franco** in 1975.

BOURGUIBA, HABIB (1903–) Tunisian politician. He became a journalist in 1930 on a paper which advocated self-government for Tunisia. He founded his own Neo-Déstour party in 1934 to achieve independence from France, but was imprisoned 1934–6, 1938–43 and 1952–4, and in exile 1945–9. He became first prime minister of independent Tunisia in 1956–7, its first president 1957–87, and 'President for Life' 1975–87.

BOXER REBELLION Chinese popular uprising in 1900, aiming to drive out all foreign traders, diplomats and particularly missionaries. The name is derived from a secret society, the I-ho-ch'üan (Right and Harmonious Fists), which had earlier violently opposed the ruling **Ch'ing** (Manchu) dynasty, but in 1899 began to attack westerners. On 18 June 1900, as hostilities grew, the Empress Dowager ordered the execution of all foreigners; hundreds were besieged in the Peking legation quarter until relieved on 14 August by an international expeditionary force, which then looted the capital. Peace and reparations were finally agreed in September 1901.

BRACTON, HENRY DE (d. c. 1268) Medieval English jurist, judge of King's Court under Henry III (1247–57). Author of *De legibus et consuetudinibus Angliae* ('On the laws and customs of England'), one of the oldest and most influential treatises on common law.

BRADDOCK, EDWARD (1695–1755) English general who in 1754 was appointed to command all British land forces in North America; he was ambushed (with his army) and killed by mixed French and Indian forces while leading an expedition against Fort Duquesne.

BRAHMA Hindu creator of the universe who, with **Vishnu** and **Shiva**, forms the leading trinity of Hindu gods.

BRAHMO SAMAJ Hindu theistic society, founded in 1828 by the religious reformer, **Rammohan Roy**. It split into two in 1865, when the philosopher Keshub Chunder Sen (author of *The Brahmo Samaj Vindicated*) founded a separate branch known as 'Brahmo Samaj of India'. It was the earliest modern reform movement in India.

BRASSEY, THOMAS (1805–70) English railway contractor, trained as a surveyor, in 1835 he built the Grand Junction line, and later helped to finish the London–Southampton link. Starting with the Paris–Rouen line (1841–3), he went on to build railway systems all over the world, including the 1100-mile Grand Trunk in Canada (1854–9).

BRAZZA, PIERRE SAVORGNAN DE (1852–1905) Piedmontese explorer and colonizer who made pioneering journeys through equatorial Africa, 1873–7. He negotiated treaties with African chiefs which were then taken up by the French, whose service Brazza subsequently entered, governing the region north of the Congo for France, 1887–97.

BRECKINRIDGE, JOHN CABELL (1821–75) Unsuccessful Southern Democrat candidate for the United States presidency on the eve of the American Civil War (1861–5). Born in Kentucky, he entered the US Congress in 1851; vice-president to James Buchanan, 1857–61; US Senator, 1861; expelled after joining the Confederate army. He served as brigadier, major-general and later secretary for war in the Confederacy; fleeing to England at the end of hostilities, he returned in 1868.

BREDA, TREATY OF Inconclusive agreement, signed 31 July 1667, ending the Second Anglo-Dutch War (1665–7). France, which had supported the Dutch, gave up Antigua, Montserrat and St Kitts, in the West Indies, to Britain, but recovered Acadia (now Canada's Maritime Provinces); England acquired New York and New Jersey from the Dutch; Holland won valuable sea-trading concessions.

BREST-LIVOTSK, TREATY OF Peace agreement, signed March 1918, between Russia and the Central Powers. Russia recognized the independence of Poland, Finland, Georgia, the Baltic States and the Ukraine, and agreed to pay a large indemnity. The treaty was declared void under the general armistice of 1918.

BREZHNEV, LEONID ILICH (1906–82) Soviet leader. He joined the Communist Party, 1931; became Red Army political commissar, major-general, 1943; a member of the Communist Party Central Committee, 1952. He succeeded **Khrushchev** as first secretary of the Party, 1964; enunciated the Brezhnev Doctrine to justify invasion of Czechoslovakia, 1968, by Warsaw Pact forces; replaced Podgorny as president of the USSR, 1977–82.

BRIAN BORU (c. 941–1041) High king of Ireland. He succeeded as ruler of a small Irish kingdom, Dal Cais, in 972, and also of Munster. Brian defeated Ivar, the Norse king, in Inis, Cathaig in 977; attacked Osraige (982); was recognized as ruler of southern Ireland (997) and by 1005 claimed his position as king of all Ireland. He was killed after the battle of Clontarf.

BRITAIN, BATTLE OF Series of aerial encounters between the German Luftwaffe and the British Royal Air Force, mainly over southern England, fought between July and October 1940. As a result of her failure to win air mastery, Germany abandoned plans for a seaborne invasion of Britain.

BRONZE AGE In the Old World, the first period of metal-use, based on copper and its alloys. Beginning in the Near East in the 3rd millennium BC, and in Europe after 2000 BC, and independently in southeast Asia at the same time, this technology spread among both peasant and urban societies – Bronze Age civilizations included Sumer, Egypt, the Indus and Shang China.

BROOKE, SIR JAMES (1803–68) Founder of a dynasty of 'white rajahs' in Sarawak, northwest Borneo. He served with the **English East India Company's** army in the Burma War 1824–6; assisted the Rajah of Brunei in suppressing various rebellions, and in 1843 was made Rajah of Sarawak.

BRUCE *see* **Robert I of Scotland**

BRUNHILDE (c. 545–613) Twice regent of Austrasia and for a period the most powerful ruler in **Merovingian** France. The daughter of Athanagild, Visigothic king in Spain, she married Sigebert, son of Lothar, king of the Franks. The murder of her sister, Galswintha, precipitated a 40-year feud in Gaul. The deaths of her husband and her son, **Childebert II**, placed her at the head of affairs until 599 when palace officials drove her out. In 613 she was executed by being tied to a wild horse.

BRÜNING, HEINRICH (1885–1970) German statesman. He became leader of the Catholic Centre Party, 1929, and formed a conservative government in 1930 without a Reichstag majority. After parliamentary rejection of his major economic plans, he began to rule by presidential emergency decree. He resigned the chancellorship in May 1932 after the failure of both his foreign and his domestic policies.

BRUSATI Prominent family of medieval Novara, Italy. Supporters of the **Guelph** (anti-imperial) party, they enjoyed a brief supremacy in the city 1305–15, but were overcome by their Ghibeline (pro-imperial) rivals, supported by the **Visconti** family in neighbouring Milan.

BRUSILOV, ALEKSEY ALEKSEYEVICH (1853–1926) Russian general who led the Russian offensive against Austria-Hungary in June–August 1916; he became the supreme Russian commander in 1917. Under the **Bolsheviks** he directed the war against Poland, 1920; he retired in 1924 as inspector of cavalry.

BRUSSELS PACT Defensive alliance of 1948 providing for military, economic and social cooperation, signed by France, Great Britain and the Benelux countries.

BUDDHA, GAUTAMA (c. 486–c. 400 BC) Founder of the world religion known as **Buddhism**. Born on the northern border between India and Nepal, the son of a nobleman of the Hindu Kshatiya caste, traditionally he was inspired to change his life at the age of 29 by the sight of an old man, a sick man, a corpse and an itinerant ascetic. In the Great Renunciation he gave up his privileges and for six years practised extreme asceticism, then abandoned it in favour of deep meditation, receiving enlightenment as he sat under a tree. The remainder of his life was spent teaching and serving the order of beggars which he founded.

BUDDHISM Religious and philosophic system based on the teaching of Gautama, the **Buddha**, who rejected important features of his native **Hinduism** in the 6th century BC. In his first sermon at Benares he preached the Four Noble Truths and the abandonment of desire and sorrow by systematic pursuit of the Noble Eightfold Path, the ultimate end of which is Nirvana, the elimination of all desire and anguish. This remains the basis for the Dharma or Teaching, carried out through the Samgha or monastic Order. Since the Buddha's death the religion has developed along two distinct and sometimes conflicting lines: Theravada (or Hinayana), in southeast Asia, stressing monasticism and avoiding any taint of theism or belief in a god; and Mahayana, in China, Japan, Tibet and Korea, which embraces more personal cults.

BUGANDA Former kingdom and later administrative region, occupying 17,311 square miles of present-day Uganda, inhabited largely by the Baganda tribe. It was an important independent power from the 17th to the 19th century, becoming a British protectorate in 1894; limited self-government, under British rule, was granted in 1900.

BUKHARIN, NIKOLAI IVANOVICH (1888–1938) Bolshevik economist and theoretician. He lived in exile in New York until the revolution, when he returned to Russia (May 1917) and became leader of the Communist Party's Right faction, which advocated cautionary progress to full socialism through the continuation of the New Economic Policy (NEP). A member of the Politburo, 1918–29, and head of the Third International, 1926–9, he was expelled from the Politburo in 1929 because of his association with Trotskyist opposition to **Stalin**. Restored in 1834, when he became editor of *Izvestia*, he was again expelled in 1938 and was executed after the last of the Great Purge Trials.

BUNYORO One of the earliest East African kingdoms, founded in the 16th century and occupying territory now part of Uganda. It prospered until the 19th century, when it lost ground and power to neighbouring **Buganda**. Its last ruler, Kabarega, was deposed by the British in 1894, and his kingdom absorbed into the British protectorate in 1896.

BUONSIGNORI Italian banking house, founded in Siena in 1209, which became the foremost company in Europe. It began to collapse in 1298 and finally closed its doors in 1309.

BURGUNDIANS Germanic people, originally from the Baltic island of Bornholm (Burgundaholm), 1st century AD. In the 5th century they established a powerful kingdom in the Saône and Rhône valleys, extending to the Rhine. They were defeated and absorbed by the Franks in 534.

BURKE, EDMUND (1729–97) British statesman, orator and political theorist. He entered Parliament in 1765, and made a reputation with eloquent speeches and writings on the American question and on the arbitrary government of George III. He sought abolition of the slave trade; in his *Thoughts on the revolution in France* (1790) he bitterly condemned the outbreak of revolution and predicted increasing violence.

BURTON, SIR RICHARD FRANCIS (1821–90) Explorer and English translator of *The Thousand and One Nights*. He visited Mecca in 1853 and was the first European to reach Harar, Ethiopia, in 1854; with **Speke** he discovered Lake Tanganyika in 1858.

BUSH, GEORGE HERBERT WALKER (1924–) US political leader and 41st president. From a wealthy Connecticut family and active in the navy during World War II, he graduated from Yale (1948). After two terms in the House of Representatives from Texas (1967–71), he was ambassador to the **United Nations**, chairman of the republican National Committee and Director of the Central Intelligence Agency during the 1970s. He served as **Ronald Reagan**'s vice president (1981–9) and as president (1989–93).

BUSHMEN *see* **San**

BUTTON, SIR THOMAS (d.1634) English navigator, and the first to reach the western shores of Hudson Bay (1612–13). He also discovered the Nelson River, which rises in Manitoba and runs into Hudson Bay.

BUWAYHIDS (Buyida) Dynasty originating in northern Persia. They occupied Baghdad, capital of the **Abbasid caliphate**, in 945; though **Shi'as**, they ruled the central lands of the caliphate in the name of the Abbasid caliph. Their power was ended by the occupation of Baghdad in 1055 by the **Seljuks**.

BYLOT, ROBERT English navigator and discoverer of Baffin Bay (1615); because he was suspected of disloyalty the bay was named after his lieutenant, **William Baffin**.

BYNG, JOHN (1704–57) English admiral, remembered mainly for an epigram by the French writer Voltaire who said that he was court-martialled and shot *'pour encourager les autres'* after failing to relieve Minorca.

C

CABANAGEM Revolutionary uprising, 1835–40, in the Paré region of Brazil. The term was coined from *cabana* or cabin, perhaps an allusion to the lowly origins of the insurgents.

CABOT, JOHN (c. 1450–c. 1499) Italian explorer (real name Giovanni Caboto). Precise details of his travels are much in dispute, but around 1484 he moved from Italy to London, and in 1496 was given authority by **Henry VII** to search for unknown lands; after one abortive attempt, he left Bristol in 1497 in a small vessel, the *Mathew*, and made landfall, probably in the region of Cape Breton, Nova Scotia. The fate of his second, larger expedition in 1498 remains unknown.

CABOT, SEBASTIAN (1476–1557) Explorer, cartographer and navigator. Before 1512 he worked for **Henry VIII** of England; seconded to assist Spain against the French, he was appointed in 1518 as pilot-major to the Spanish *Casa de la Contratación*; in 1526 he led an expedition intended for the Moluccas via the Magellan Straits, but diverted it to the Río de la Plata and spent three years exploring Paraná and Paraguay. He published a celebrated but unreliable world map 1544, and organized an expedition to seek the Northeast Passage.

CABRAL, PEDRO ALVARES (1467/8–1520) Reputed discoverer of Brazil, commissioned by the Portuguese king, Manuel I, to sail to India; he sighted and claimed Brazil for Portugal, 1500, before continuing the voyage in which he lost 9 out of his 13 ships in storms; he bombarded Calicut, established a Portuguese factory at Cochin and returned to Portugal with his four remaining ships loaded with pepper. He was not subsequently employed at sea.

CAINOZOIC Geological era, starting c. 65 million years ago, during which all surviving forms of mammal life (including Man) first evolved, and the earth's surface assumed its present form.

CALDERA RODRIGUEZ, DR RAFAEL (1916–) Venezuelan political leader. He was secretary of the Venezuelan Catholic youth organization 1932–4, and in 1936 founded the country's national union of students. In 1946 he founded the Committee of Independent Political Electoral Organizations (COPEI); an unsuccessful presidential candidate in 1947, 1958 and 1963, he finally became President, as the candidate of COPEI, in 1969, holding the post until 1974, in which year he was appointed senator for life.

CALIPHATE The office of caliph, regarded by **Sunnis** as successor to the Prophet **Mohammed** in his capacity as leader of the Islamic community. The first four caliphs ('patriarchal', 'rightguided' or 'orthodox' caliphs) ruled from Medina; they were succeeded first by **Umayyads** ruling from Damascus, 661–750; then by the **Abbasids** of Baghdad, whose dynasty continued until 1258, although effective power was held by various dynasties of sultans – **Buwayhids, Seljuks**. In the 10th century two other dynasties took the title of caliph; a branch of the Umayyads in Spain, and the **Fatimids** in Cairo. The last Abbasid caliph was killed by the Mongol conquerors of Baghdad in 1258, and the caliphate virtually came to an end. The title was revived by the Ottoman sultans in the 19th century, but abolished by the Turkish Republican government in 1924.

CALLIMACHUS (c. 305–c. 204 BC) Poet from Cyrene who worked in Alexandria, compiling a 120-volume critical catalogue of the great Library; only fragments of his 800 recorded works survive, but his Aetia (*'Origins'*) and his shorter poems had a profound influence on Roman authors, including Catallus and Propertius. He refused to write long epics, saying that 'a large book is a great evil'.

CALVIN, JOHN (1509–64) French theologian who established strict Presbyterian government in Geneva. He wrote *Institutes of the Christian Religion* (1536–59), setting out his teachings – that the state should support the Church, that biblical authority should override Church tradition, and that the sacraments, though valuable, are not essential to true religions. He strongly influenced the Huguenots in France, the Protestant churches in Scotland and the Netherlands, and the Puritan movement in England and North America.

CAMBYSES II (d.522 BC) Second Achaemenid Persian emperor, the eldest son of **Cyrus**, whom he represented in Babylon, 538–530 BC; he succeeded on Cyrus' death in 530. He invaded Egypt, taking Memphis in 525 and was returning home when he heard of the usurpation by his brother **Smerdis**, and died soon afterwards.

CAMINO, DA Medieval Italian family, prominent in the affairs of the city of Treviso. It first gained power through Gherado (c. 1240–1306), a noted soldier of fortune. His sons wavered between the rival **Guelph** and Ghibelline factions in Italian politics, resulting in the murder of one and the expulsion of the other from Treviso in 1312.

CANUTE *see* **Cnut the Great**

CAO, DIOGO 15th-century Portuguese navigator who explored much of the west coast of Africa. He was the first European to reach the mouth of the Congo (1482).

CAPETIANS Ruling dynasty of France, 987–1328. It was founded by Hugh Capet, elected king in 987 to replace the previous **Carolingian** line; gradually he and his successors extended their control, initially limited to the area around Paris, to cover the larger part of present-day France; they also began to develop many of the country's main political institutions, such as the *Parlements* (royal law courts) and the States General (representative assemblies). Notable Capetian kings included **Philip II Augustus** (reigned 1180–1223), (St) **Louis IX** (1226–70), and **Philip IV** the Fair (1285–1314).

CAPITALISM Economic system in which the principal means of production, distribution and exchange are in private hands, whether individual or corporate, and competitively operated for profit. A mixed economy combines the private enterprise of capitalism and a degree of state monopoly, as in nationalized industries.

CARACALLA (188–217) Roman emperor, born Marcus Aurelius Antoninus at Lugdunum (modern Lyons), son of Emperor Septimius Severus. He gained the imperial throne in 211 and in the following year extended Roman citizenship to virtually all inhabitants of the empire. He murdered his wife, Fulvia Plautilla, and younger brother, Geta. He was assassinated at Carrhae, Mesopotamia, while preparing his second campaign against Parthia.

CARDENAS, LAZARO (1895–1970) Mexican soldier and radical leader. Governor of home state of Michoacán, 1928–32; minister of the interior, 1931; president of Mexico, 1934–40. During his term of office he launched a Six-Year Plan, a land redistribution programme, the expropriation of foreign-owned oil companies (1938) and a renewed attack on the Catholic Church; he was minister of defence, 1942–5.

CARLOWITZ, TREATY OF A truce agreement, signed on 26 January 1699, ending hostilities (1683–99) between the Ottoman empire and the Holy League (Austria, Poland, Venice and Russia). Under its terms Transylvania and much of Hungary was transferred from Turkish control to Austrian, making Austria the dominant power in eastern Europe. In 1700 the armistice was confirmed by the Treaty of Constantinople.

CARNOT, LAZARE NICOLAS MARGUERITE (1753–1823) French military engineer and statesman who directed the early successes of the French revolutionary armies (1793–5); he was a member of the Directory, the five-man group ruling France, 1795–9. Although opposed to **Napoleon**'s rise to power Carnot later rallied to the emperor in resisting he invasion of France, 1814, and was minister of the interior during the **Hundred Days**, 1815; he died in exile.

CAROL II (1893–1953) King of Romania who supplanted his son Michael as legitimate ruler in 1930 and created a royal dictatorship. He was deposed in 1940.

CAROLINGIANS Royal dynasty descended from Pepin of Landen (d. AD 640), chief minister of the **Merovingian** king, Chlothar II. Pepin's illegitimate grandson was **Charles Martel**, after whom the dynasty was named. His great-great grandson was the emperor **Charlemagne**. The dynasty continued to rule in East Francia (Germany) until 911, and in West Francia (France) until 987.

CARRACK Large round sailing ship developed in the Middle Ages for both trade and naval warfare, particularly by the Genoese and Portuguese. Deep-keeled and high in the water, the vessel had two or three masts, castle fore and aft, and was usually well armed with cannon. Larger versions were used by the Portuguese in trade to the East Indies and Brazil in the 16th century.

CARRANZA, VENUSTIANO (1859–1920) President of Mexico. The son of a landowner, he was active in politics from 1877; as governor of Coahuila, in 1910, he supported **Madero**, and in 1913 led the opposition to Madero's successor, Victoriano Huerta. He set up a provisional government, defeated the armies of **Pancho Villa**, and was installed as first president of the Mexican Republic (1917). He fled during an armed uprising in 1920, and was betrayed and murdered in the mountains near Vera Cruz.

CARREIRA DA INDIA The round voyage between Portugal and India, inaugurated with **Vasco da Gama**'s pioneering expedition of 1497–8 and continuing until the age of steam. Under sail the journey averaged 18 months, including the stay at Goa.

CARRON Pioneer Scottish ironworks, established by John Roebuck. Founded with capital of £12,000 in 1760, it was first to use a cast-iron blowing-cylinder to increase airblast. Technicians trained there started iron-making in Russia and Silesia.

CARTIER, JACQUES (1492–1557) Explorer of Canada, commissioned by **Francis I** of France to sail in search of gold, spices and a new route to Asia; he entered the Gulf of St Lawrence in 1534, and on subsequent expeditions established a base at Quebec and reached Montreal.

CASIMIR I, THE RESTORER (1016–58) King of Poland. He ascended the throne in 1039. He recovered the former Polish province of Silesia, Masovia and Pomerania, lost by his father **Mieszko II**; he restored central government and revived the Catholic Church, but failed to throw off German suzerainty.

CASIMIR III, THE GREAT (1210–70) King of Poland. He succeeded to the throne in 1333. He concluded a favourable peace with the **Teutonic Order** in 1343, and annexed the province of Lwow from Lithuania during the 1340s. The last ruler of the **Piast** dynasty, he agreed in 1339 to the union of Poland and Hungary after his death. At home he unified the government, codified laws and founded new towns and the first university in eastern Europe at Cracow in 1364.

CASIMIR IV (1427–92) King of Poland. A member of the **Jagiellonian** dynasty, he succeeded to the Grand Duchy of Lithuania in 1440 and to the throne of Poland in 1447. He defeated the Teutonic Knights and recovered West Prussia for Poland by the Treaty of Thorn, 1466. Thereafter he sought to create a Polish empire stretching from the Baltic to the Black Sea but was checked by the Turks and, at the time of his death, by **Ivan III** of Russia.

CASTILLA, RAMON (1797–1867) President of Peru. Born in Chile, he fought for the Spaniards until captured by Chilean patriots; changing sides, he fought in Peru with **Bolívar** and **San Martín**. The first elected president, 1845–51 and again 1855–62, he built up Peru's economic strength by the exploitation of newly discovered guano and sodium nitrate deposits.

CASTRO, FIDEL (1926–) Prime minister of Cuba. Law graduate, 1950; after failure to win power by a coup, 1953, he led the guerrilla group '26th of July Movement'; invaded Cuba in 1956 but failed to raise a revolt and fled to the mountains; regrouped, and finally displaced the Batista regime in 1959. He was boycotted by the United States after his **Marxist** aims became apparent; survived the Bay of Pigs invasion of 1961, and the Cuban missile crisis, 1962; with Soviet aid (to 1990) he promoted a programme of land and economic reform. In 1976 he sent troops to Angola (withdrawn 1991), and embarked on an increasingly active African and Central American policy.

CATEAU-CAMBRÉSIS, TREATY OF Agreement signed in 1559 to end the war between France, Spain and England. Spain's claims in Italy were recognized by France, making the former the dominant power in southern Europe; France gained the bishoprics of Toul, Metz and Verdun; England finally surrendered Calais.

CATHARS (CATHARISM) A doctrinal heresy descended from the **Manichaeism** of the early Christian church but with some non-Christian roots, which from the mid-11th century spread rapidly in western Europe, throughout northern Italy and southern France (where the Cathars were known as **Albigensians**). Their chief tenet was the dualism of good and evil, which was contrary to Catholic belief although in some respects resembling it. They also devoted themselves to poverty and evangelism, in these respects resembling both the **Humiliati** and the monastic orders. **Innocent III** launched the Albigensian Crusade against them in 1208 and his successors combated them with the **Inquisition**.

CATHERINE II, THE GREAT (1729–96) Born a princess of the German principality of Anhalt-Zerbst, she married in 1744 Peter of Holstein-Gottorp who in 1762 became Tsar **Peter III**. Six months later she usurped his throne with the aid of her lover, G. Orlov. She advanced Russia's status as a great power, conquering the north shore of the Black Sea from Turkey, and with Prussia and Austria completed the partition of Poland in 1795. She carried out a number of domestic reforms, none of which improved the status of the serfs. She published her *Instruction for the drafting of a new code of laws* in 1767 and wrote many plays and historical works.

CATHOLIC LEAGUE Union of German Catholic princes, formed in 1609 in opposition to the Protestant Union of 1608, and headed by Maximilian I of Bavaria. Its armies, under Tilly (1559–1632), played an important part in the early stages of the Thirty Years' War (1618–48), in which they conquered Bohemia, 1619–22, and defeated Denmark, 1624–9.

CATHOLIC REFORMATION Movement initiated by the Catholic church at the Council of Trent (1545–63) to counter the spread of the **Reformation**. Extending into the 17th century, its dominant forces included the rise of the **Jesuits** as an educating and missionary group and the deployment of the Spanish **Inquisition** in other countries.

CAVALCABO Prominent family of medieval Cremona, Italy. Supporters of the **Guelph** (anti-imperial) party, they gained control of the city in the second half of the 13th century, retaining power until 1312 when they were driven out by Emperor Henry VII. In 1314 they returned, but were driven out permanently by the **Visconti** of Milan in 1344.

CAVOUR, COUNT CAMILLO BENSO (1810–61) Italian statesman. He abandoned court and an army career, visited England and then embarked on a career in finance, agriculture, industry and radical politics. In 1848 he founded the newspaper, *Il Risorgimento*, to champion monarchical and liberal aims, and promote democratic reforms. He entered the Piedmontese cabinet in 1850, and was given control of government, 1852, by the new king, **Victor Emmanuel II**. He was primarily responsible for creating the United Kingdom of Italy of 1861.

CEAUCESCU, NICOLAE (1918–89) Romanian political leader. Active in the illegal Communist party, he was imprisoned for eight years, before and during World War II. Minister of agriculture (1950–4); deputy armed forces minister (1950–4); Politburo member and president of Romania (1967–89). He enforced rigid domestic policies, suppressed political opposition ruthlessly, and concentrated on economic development along strict **Marxist**-Leninist lines. He was executed in 1989 after the overthrow of his government in a bloody revolution.

CELTS Ancient people of western Europe called by the Greek *Keltoi* and by the Romans *Celtae*. Now more generally used of speakers of languages descended from these, notably Breton in France, Welsh, Cornish, Gaelic (Scots and Irish), and Manx in the British Isles. Archaeologically often used as synonymous with **La Tène** style.

CENOZOIC *see* **Cainozoic**

CENTRAL TREATY ORGANISATION (CENTO) Defence alliance, originally known as the Baghdad Pact, between Iran, Iraq, Pakistan, Turkey and the United Kingdom, signed in 1955. The headquarters were moved from Baghdad to Ankara in 1958, and the name changed with the withdrawal of Iraq in 1959. The Pact was weakened from the first by the refusal of the United States, which had sponsored it, to become a full member. It aroused the hostility of **Nasser**, and an ill-judged attempt to recruit Jordan led to riots which nearly caused the fall of King Hussein. Dissolved in 1979.

CHALCEDON, COUNCIL OF Fourth ecumenical council of the Christian Church, called in 451 to pronounce on the nature of Christ; it condemned **Monophysitism** as a heresy.

CHALDEANS A group of Semitic tribes, related to the Aramaeans, who settled in the marsh areas of southern Babylonia c. 1000 BC. They eventually spread up the Euphrates, infiltrating into territories of many of the major cities of Babylonia, almost to Babylon. By the late 8th century BC, Chaldean chieftains, notably Ukinzer and Marduk-apal-iddina (Merodach-baladan of the Bible), sought the kingship of Babylonia, producing endemic disturbance. A Chaldean dynasty, whose best-known ruler was Nebuchadnezzar succeeded to the kingship from 625 to 539 BC. In the Hellenistic and Roman period the term 'Chaldeans' was used to describe Babylonian astrologers generally, without any ethnic basis.

CHAMBERLAIN, JOSEPH (1836–1914) British political leader. Mayor of Birmingham, 1873–6, and a pioneer of radical local government, he became a member of parliament in 1876. He was colonial secretary in the Conservative government, 1895–1903, during the last, and for Great Britain vital, stages of the partition of Africa; he was responsible for sending Kitchener to the Sudan, for declaring a protectorate over Uganda, and – most important – for the South African War of 1899–1902. He resigned to campaign for Imperial Preference (*see* **Ottawa Agreement**) and tariff protection for British industry.

CHAMORRO, VIOLETA BARRIOS DE (1939–) Nicaraguan politician and widow of the Nicaraguan journalist and writer Pedro Joaquin Chamorro, assassinated in 1978 because of his bitter opposition to the Somoza political regime. The National Opposition Union candidate for president in 1989–90, she was elected to the presidency in April 1990. She sought a balance between **Sandinista** and opposition forces in governmental programmes.

CHAMPA Ancient kingdom of Indo-China, originally occupying most of the central coastal region of modern Vietnam, and inhabited by the Chams, a people of Malay affinity. Founded c. AD 192, according to Chinese sources, it had close tributary relations with China down to the 16th century, but avoided a Chinese attempt at conquest in 1285. Frequent wars against the Vietnamese led to piecemeal loss of territory, and then to annexation of the main part of Champa by 1471; the kingdom disappeared completely c. 1700, apart from Cham communities surviving near Phan Thiet and Phan Rang. Its Hindu temples survive at various place, indicating Indian cultural influence.

CHANAK INCIDENT (1922) Landing of British troops at Çanakkale (Chanak) on the Dardanelles to oppose a Turkish takeover of the straits. **Lloyd George**, the British prime minister, was accused of recklessness and his government fell.

CHANCA Andean tribe occupying land in Andahuaylas, Peru. In 1440 they attacked but were heavily defeated by the neighbouring, previously insignificant, **Incas**.

CHANCELLOR, SIR RICHARD (d.1556) Navigator and pioneer of Anglo-Russian trade. In 1553 he was appointed pilot-general to Sir Humphrey Willoughby's expedition seeking a northeast passage to China. Separated from them by bad weather, he continued into the White Sea and overland to Moscow, where he was warmly received by Tsar **Ivan IV**. He returned to England in 1554 after negotiating the formation of the Muscovy Company.

CHANDELLAS Rajput warrior clan, ruling Bundelkhand, northern India, from the 9th to the 11th century. Defeated in 1001 by Muslim armies of **Mahmud of Ghazni** and expelled from their great fortress of Kalinjar (1023), they were reduced to vassalage by Prithviraja of Ajmer in 1082.

CHANDRAGUPTA II Indian king of the Gupta dynasty, reigning c. 375–415, son of Samadragupta. Traditionally renowned for his valour and chivalry, he fought a long campaign against the Shakas (388–409). He extended Gupta power, by war in northern India and by marriage in the Deccan, and took the title *Vikramaditya*, Sun of Prowess.

CHANDRAGUPTA MAURYA Founder of the first Indian empire, he usurped the throne of the Ganges Valley kingdom of Magadha, 321 BC. He exploited the power vacuum left by the retreat of **Alexander the Great** from northwest India, defeated the forces of **Seleucus I Nicator**, 305–303 BC and acquired Trans-Indus province (now part of Afghanistan). He is said to have been converted to **Jainism** at the end of his life, abdicating in 297 in favour of his son **Bindusara**, and dying, as a monk, by deliberate starvation.

CHANG CH'IEN (d. 114 BC) Chinese diplomat and explorer, sent in 138 BC by the Han emperor **Wu-ti** to establish contact with the **Yüeh-chih** tribes, and the first man to bring back to China reliable reports of central Asia. He was captured and held for 10 years by the **Hsiungnu** tribes but still completed his mission, returning after 13 years. He made many other journeys, his travels taking him as far as the Tarim Basin, Ferghana, Bactria, Sogdiana and the Hellenic outpost-states established by **Alexander the Great**. Besides information, his efforts gave China its first access to such valuable products as large, fast horses, grapes and alfalfa grass.

CHANG HSIEN-CHUNG (c.1605–47) Chinese rebel leader in the last days of the **Ming** dynasty. Trained as a soldier, he was dismissed from the imperial army and started bandit raids in northern Shensi, 1628. He moved into Honan and Hupeh in 1635. Forced to surrender in 1638, he was nevertheless allowed to retain his forces, and rebelled again in 1639. In 1643 he failed to set up administrations in Wuchang and Changsha. He retreated into Szechwan, but captured Cheng-tu in 1644 and took the title of King of the Great Western Kingdom. His government disintegrated in a reign of terror in 1646, and he was killed the following year.

CHANG KUO-T'AO (1897–1979) A founder of the Chinese Communist Party (CCP). After playing a minor role in the May 4 Movement, he represented Peking Marxists at the first CCP Congress at Shanghai in 1921. He helped to found the CCP-sponsored Labour movement and developed close ties with the **Comintern**. From 1929 he played a major role in Communist base areas on the borders of Honan, Anhwei and Hupeh, and led his forces through Szechwan on an important leg of the Long March. From 1935 he engaged in bitter debates with **Mao Zedong**; attempting to set up an independent base in the far northwest, his troops were disastrously defeated in Kansu. After 1938 he defected to the Nationalists and lived in semi-retirement, moving to Hong Kong in 1949, and writing his autobiography.

CHAN TSO-LIN (1873–1928) Chinese warlord known as 'the Old Marshal'. Originally an officer in a Manchurian army, he built up control of southern Manchuria and much of northern China until 1928. After 1921 he controlled Inner Mongolia. Attempts to control the Peking government led to war with **Wu P'ei-fu** in 1922, in which Chang was initially defeated. In 1924 he concluded a pact with the Soviet Union, which recognized his regime in Manchuria as independent. Later that year he invaded northern China, seriously defeating Wu P'ei-fu and driving south almost to Shanghai. His power was backed by the tacit support of the Japanese, who supported him in Manchuria as a buffer against Soviet influence, and to whom he granted major concessions in Manchuria. Unable to counter the growing power of the **Kuomintang** (Nationalist Party) armies under **Chiang Kai-shek**, which invaded his territories in 1927, he abandoned Peking to them. He was killed when Japanese extremists blew up his private train.

CHARLEMAGNE (742–814) Emperor of the **Franks**, son of **Pippin III**. Succeeded as joint king, 768; sole ruler from 771. He conquered most of the Christian territory in western Europe, defeating the Lombards and converting the pagan Saxons, and he allied with the papacy to counter the dominance of Byzantium. On Christmas Day 800 in St Peter's, Rome, he was crowned and anointed by the Pope and became the first emperor of non-Roman origins and the first of the German emperors of the Middle Ages.

CHARLES I, OF ANJOU (1226–85) Angevin king of Naples and Sicily, younger brother of **Louis IX** of France. He acquired the country of Provence, 1246; defeated the last **Hohenstaufen** in 1266 and 1268 to conquer Naples and Sicily, and in 1277 became heir to the kingdom of Jerusalem. Transferring his capital from Palermo to Naples, he set off the revolt of the Sicilian Vespers, 1282, and was defeated by the alliance of the Sicilians and Peter III of Aragon in the Bay of Naples, 1284.

CHARLES I (1600–49) King of England, Scotland and Ireland, son of **James VI (and I)**. Succeeding in 1625, he came increasingly into conflict with his English parliament over religion, foreign policy and taxation. After being forced to sign the Petition of Right (1628), he ruled without Parliament until 1640; rebellion broke out in Scotland in 1638, in Ireland in 1641 and in England in 1642. Defeated in the civil wars that followed, he was captured in 1647 by the English army under **Cromwell**, tried and beheaded.

CHARLES IV (1316–78) King of Bohemia, 1346–78, and ruler of the German empire from 1355, son of John of Luxembourg and Elizabeth, sister of the last native Bohemian king. He reformed the finances and legal system, and built up the power of the monarchy in Bohemia, but left Germany largely to the princes; in 1356 he issued the **Golden Bull**, laying down a permanent constitution for the empire.

CHARLES V (1500–58) Holy Roman Emperor. He was the son of Philip I (died 1506), heir to the Burgundian states, and of Joanna (declared insane in 1506), heiress to Castile and Aragon, to which he succeeded in 1516. Elected Emperor in 1519, he annexed Lombardy (1535), and several Netherlands provinces, but was eventually defeated (1551–5) by an alliance of Turks, French and German Lutherans. He abdicated in 1556, leaving his German possessions to his brother Ferdinand (elected Emperor in 1558), and the rest to his son **Philip II**. He retired to a monastery in 1557.

CHARLES IX (1550–1611) Effective ruler of Sweden from 1599, and king 1604–11. The third son of **Gustavus I Vasa**; in 1568 he helped his brother, then crowned as **John III**, to depose their half-brother **Eric XIV**. A strong Lutheran, he first broke with John over religion and then, after the accession of John's Catholic son, **Sigismund III**, called the Convention of Uppsala, 1593, to demand the acceptance of **Lutheranism** as the state religion. Appointed regent in Sigismund's absence, he precipitated a civil war and deposed the king, 1599. He died after strengthening Sweden's metal-based economy and provoking the Kalmar War with Denmark, 1611–13.

CHARLES X GUSTAV (1622–60) King of Sweden, son of John Casimir, Count Palatine of Zweibrücken, and Catherine, eldest daughter of **Charles IX**. He fought with the Swedish armies in Germany, 1642–5. His cousin, Queen Christina of Sweden, appointed him commander of the Swedish forces in Germany and also her official successor. He was crowned in 1654, invaded Poland in 1655 and Denmark in 1657–8, and won an advantageous peace.

CHARLES XI (1655–97) King of Sweden, succeeding his father, **Charles X Gustav**, in 1660. He was kept in tutelage by aristocratic regents until Sweden's defeat by Brandenburg at Fehrbellin in 1675; he then established absolute rule, expanding the royal estates to cover 30 per cent of Sweden and Finland and rebuilding the armed forces to match those of Denmark. In 1693, the Swedish Diet granted him unrestricted powers to ensure his reforms.

CHARLES XII (1682–1718) Warrior king of Sweden, eldest son of **Charles XI**, succeeding to the throne in 1697. Brilliantly defeated the anti-Swedish coalition (formed in 1699 to crush Sweden's Baltic hegemony) of Denmark, Russia, Poland and Saxony, invading each in turn (1700–6). He invaded Russia again with Cossack help in 1708 but was routed at Poltava, 1709, taking refuge in Turkey which he succeeded in turning against Russia. Forced to leave Turkey in 1714, he was killed while fighting in Norway.

CHARLES ALBERT (1798–1849) King of Sardinia-Piedmont. Son of the Prince of Carignano, he was exiled from Italy and brought up in revolutionary Paris and Geneva, succeeding his father in 1800. He was involved in an abortive plot to displace his cousin as king of Piedmont in 1821. He ascended the throne on his cousin's death in 1831. He sought to lead the unification of Italy, granting representative government and declaring war on Austria in 1848. Defeats at Custoza, 1848, and Novara, 1849, forced his abdication. He died in Portugal.

CHARLES THE BOLD (1433–77) Duke of Burgundy, son of **Philip the Good**, inheriting the title in 1467. He attempted to conquer the lands dividing his territories of Luxembourg, Burgundy, the Low Countries and Franche-Comté; but was defeated and killed in battle. Soon after this, in the year 1483, Burgundy passed to the French crown, and Charles' other domains became part of the **Habsburg dominions**.

CHARLES MARTEL (c. 688–741) Reunifier of the **Franks**. The illegitimate son of Pippin of Herstal, Mayor of the Palace of Austrasia, he emerged, after a five-year struggle, as his father's successor and as effective ruler of all the Franks, 719. He defeated the Muslims, advancing north from Spain, near Tours, 733/4; subdued Burgundy, 733, the **Frisians**, 734, and the Aquitainians 735. He retired in 741, and died the same year.

CHEOPS (Khufu) Second king of Egypt's 4th Dynasty (early 26th century BC), succeeding his father, Snefru. He built the Great Pyramid of Giza and three subsidiary pyramids for his principal wives.

CHEPHREN (Khafre) Fourth king of Egypt's 4th Dynasty (late 26th century BC). The son of **Cheops**, he succeeded his brother, Djedefre. He built the second of the three pyramids of Giza and the granite valley temple linked to it by a causeway.

CH'I Large and powerful Chinese state in the period 771–221 BC, located on the eastern edge of the North China Plain (modern Shantung and Hopeh). In the 7th and 6th centuries BC Ch'i began to expand, absorbing its smaller neighbours; during this period it was also the most technologically advanced state in China. Under the semi-legendary Duke Huan it gained short-lived hegemony over all Chinese territories in 651. In the 3rd century BC a new ruling house again attempted to impose sole dominance on China, but it failed, and in 221 Ch'i was absorbed by Western **Ch'in**.

CHIANG KAI-SHEK (1887–1975) Chinese general and political leader. He took control of the **Kuomintang** in 1926 and established a stable republican government in Nanking, 1928–37. He fought warlords, Japanese invaders and the Chinese Communist Party (with occasional periods of alliance) until finally defeated in 1949. He withdrew to Taiwan (Formosa) to form the Chinese Nationalist government, of which he remained president until his death.

CHICHIMECS Barbarian and semi-civilized Indian groups who invaded central Mexico from the north in the 12th and 13th centuries and ended the rule of the **Toltecs**; the Aztecs originated as one of the Chichimec tribes.

CHILDEBERT II (570–95) King of Austrasia, son of Sigebert and **Brunhilde**. After the murder of his father he became the pawn of various aristocratic factions in Austrasia, which favoured alliance with one or other of his two uncles, Chilperic or Guntram. He led an expedition to Italy in 584; ousted the supporters of Chilperic in 585 and allied with Guntram; and after Guntram's death in 593 controlled almost all of Gaul.

CHILDERIC (d.481) Chieftain of the Salian Franks, occupying territory between the rivers Meuse and Somme. He helped the Romans to defeat the **Visigoths**, near Orléans in 463, and again in 469; and cleared the Saxon pirates from the area of Angers. He died in Tournai, where his richly equipped tomb was discovered in 1653, and was succeeded by his son **Clovis**.

CHILEMBWE, JOHN (1860–1915) Nyasaland missionary and rebel leader, now regarded as one of the spiritual forebears of modern Malawi. He worked closely with the European fundamentalist Joseph Booth, 1892–5. In 1897 he received a degree from the United States Negro theological college. On his return to Nyasaland in 1900 he founded the Providence Industrial Mission with Negro Baptist finance. He protested in 1914 against economic oppression and the use of Nyasa troops in the First World War. He was shot after leading a suicidal revolt against British rule.

CHIMU South American Indians, famous for their goldware and pottery, whose rule immediately preceded that of the **Inca** in Peru. Their comparable, though small-scale, civilization, centred at Chanchán in the Moche Valley about 300 miles north of Lima, was conquered by **Pachacuti** in 1465–70.

CH'IN First great Chinese imperial dynasty: founded by **Shih Huang-ti**; *see* pp. 80–81.

CH'IN-CH'UAN RISINGS Series of risings of the aboriginal peoples of western and northwest Szechwan in 1745–9, flaring up intermittently again until 1776. The risings tied down large Manchu armies in difficult mountain terrain, and their suppression was extremely costly.

CHIN FU (1633–92) Chinese official responsible for major water improvements under the early **Ch'ing** dynasty. From 1677 he dredged and banked up the frequently flooding Yellow River, and made large-scale repairs to the Grand Canal.

CH'ING Last imperial dynasty in China. *See* pp. 172–3, 232–3.

CHOU Chinese dynasty, c. 1122–221 BC. The Western Chou (c. 1122–771 BC) were originally semi-nomadic barbarians from west of the North China Plain. They conquered the lands ruled by the previous Shang dynasty and extended them. Their territory was organized in a 'feudal' system of virtually independent fiefs; in 771 central authority finally broke down. During the Eastern Chou (771–221 BC), China became one of the world's most advanced regions; its greatest philosophers, **Confucius** and **Lao-tzu**, lived at this time, and from this period date many of it most characteristic innovations.

CHREMONIDES' WAR The last flicker of Athenian aggression. In 267 BC a citizen called Chremonides called for a Greek league of liberation with the support of Egypt against the Macedonian king, Antigonus Gonatus; few others joined, and after an intermittent siege Gonatus captured the city in 262. Athens never again sought political leadership in classical times.

CHRISTIANITY Religion of those who have faith in **Jesus**. In the central traditions of Christianity the single God is nonetheless a trinity – the Father, the Son (incarnate in the human life of Jesus of Nazareth) and the Holy Spirit. Christianity spread despite persecution, and in the 4th century was adopted by the Roman ruling class. Despite divisions it has remained one of the great world religions, sending its missionaries all over the world.

CH'U One of the Chinese states which, with **Ch'i**, **Ch'in** and later, Chin, contended between 771–221 BC for the domination of China. Based on present-day Hupeh, in the fertile Yangtze valley of southern China, Ch'u had a completely distinctive culture of its own. It expanded very rapidly into Anhwei and Hunan, and eventually controlled all central China. In 223 BC it was finally absorbed by Ch'in, but 15 years later, when Ch'in collapsed, a Ch'u aristocrat, Hsiang Yü, briefly became emperor of China; but his reign only lasted a few months before the advent of the **Han** dynasty.

CHURCHILL, SIR WINSTON LEONARD SPENCER (1874–1965) British statesman and author. The son of Lord Randolph Churchill, he served as a soldier and journalist in Cuba, India, the Sudan and South Africa before becoming a Conservative member of parliament in 1900. He was a minister in both the Tory and Liberal governments between 1908 and 1929, serving as first lord of the admiralty, 1911 to 1915. During the 1930s he warned of the growing threat from **Nazi** Germany, and later directed Britain's war effort as first lord of the admiralty in 1939–40, then as prime minister and minister of defence, 1940–5. He was prime minister again in 1951–5. His works, written while out of office, include *The World Crisis, 1916–18* (1923–9), *The Second World War* (1948–53) and *A History of the English-speaking Peoples* (1956–8). He won the Nobel Prize for literature in 1953.

CHU TE (1886–1976) 'Father' of the Chinese Red Army. Originally a military officer in Yunnan and Szechwan, he went to Shanghai in 1921 and joined the Chinese Communist Party in 1922. After studying in Germany (1922–6) he took part in the abortive rising in Nanch'ang in 1927. With **Mao Zedong** he built a famous fighting unit in the Kiangsi Soviet, took part in the Long March, commanded Communist forces in the Sino-Japanese War and became commander-in-chief during the civil war with the Nationalists. During the 1930s and 1940s he played a major role in developing Communist policies in rural areas, and in strategic planning. In 1949 he became vice-chairman of the central people's government and by 1958 was looked on as natural successor to Mao as head of state. However, in 1959 he was passed over in favour of Liu Shao-ch'i, and had little real power after that time.

CHU YÜAN-CHANG (1328–98) Chinese emperor, founder of the **Ming** dynasty. Born in Anhwei province, he joined a monastery, but between 1356 and 1364 led insurgent forces, gradually gaining control of the region north of the Yangtze, being proclaimed Prince of Wu in 1364. Driving out the Mongols in 1368, he established the Ming dynasty with its capital at Nanking and reigned for 30 years under the title Hung Wu.

CIMMERIANS Indo-European people driven from their homelands in southern Russia, north of the Caucasus and the Sea of Azov, by the closely-related **Scythians** in the 8th century BC. They were turned aside into Anatolia when they conquered Phrygia, 696–95. After their rout by Alyattes of Lydia, c. 626, they were absorbed by surrounding groups.

CISTERCIAN Religious order founded at Cîteaux, in southeast France, in 1098. It rose to great prominence under the influence of **St Bernard**; and by the end of the 12th century it had more than 500 monasteries all over Europe. The motive of the foundation was the re-establishment of the primitive rigour of the Rule of St Benedict, which had lately been neglected.

CLAPPERTON, HUGH (1788–1827) Scottish explorer of West Africa. He joined an expedition journeying south from Tripoli across the Sahara; in 1823 he reached Lake Chad, and travelled in what is now northern Nigeria. He made a second expedition to southern Nigeria; he died near Sokoto after crossing the Niger.

CLARK, WILLIAM (1770–1838) American explorer. With Meriwether Lewis he led a momentous expedition (1804–8) up the Missouri River and over the Rocky Mountains to the Pacific, opening vast territories to westward expansion.

CLAUDIUS I (10 BC–AD 54) Fourth Roman emperor, born Tiberius Claudius Drusus Nero Germanicus, nephew of the emperor **Tiberius**. He achieved power unexpectedly in AD 41, after the murder of his elder brother's son, **Caligula**; annexed Mauretania, north Africa, 41–2; invaded Britain, 43, and extended the empire in the east. He had his third wife, Messalina, killed on suspicion of conspiracy, and was almost certainly poisoned by his fourth, his niece Agrippina.

CLAUSEWITZ, CARL von (1780–1831) Prussian general and philosopher of war. He played a prominent part in the military reform movement after the disastrous defeat by **Napoleon** at Jena in 1806. He served as a staff officer with the Russian army, 1812–13, but returned to Prussian service in 1814–15. After the defeat of Napoleon he was appointed director of the War Academy, a purely administrative post which gave him ample time for historical and theoretical writings. His most famous and still influential book, *On War*, was published posthumously.

CLEMENT OF ALEXANDRIA (c. AD 150–c. 213) Saint, and principal reconciler of early Christian beliefs with the mainstream of Graeco-Roman cultural tradition. Born in Athens, he settled in Egypt, and became head of the Catechetical School, Alexandria. He taught many future theologians (e.g. Origen) and church leaders (Alexander, Bishop of Jerusalem), and wrote important ethical and theological works.

CLEMENT OF ROME Saint, first Apostolic Father of the Christian Church and Bishop of Rome at the end of the 1st century AD. Author of the *Letter to the Church of Corinth*, an important source for the Church history of the period.

CLEMENT IV (d.1268) Pope 1265–8. A Frenchman who had been in the service of **Louis IX**, his pontificate signified the growth of French influence in the Church which predominated during the next 100 years. He allied with **Charles of Anjou** to drive the **Hohenstaufen** out of Italy.

CLEOMENES III (d.219 BC) King of Sparta, succeeding his father, Leonidas, in 235 BC. He successfully fought the Achaean League, 228–26; usurped the constitutionally jointly-held Spartan throne to establish virtual autocracy, 227; reintroduced many of the 'communist' ideas of **Agis IV**. His predominance in the Peloponnese was challenged by the Macedonian, **Antigonus Doson**; defeated by Doson at Sellasia in 222, he escaped to Egypt and was interned by Ptolemy IV. He committed suicide after an abortive attempt at revolution in Alexandria.

CLEOPATRA (c. 70–31 BC) Last Ptolemaic ruler of Egypt, the daughter of King Ptolemy Auletes. Joint heir with her brother, she was made queen by **Julius Caesar** in 48 BC. She went to Rome as his mistress, but transferred her affections to **Antony**, who then left for four years, but returned after breaking with Octavian. She committed suicide after the Egyptian fleet was defeated at Actium and the troops of her ally, Antony, refused to fight.

CLINTON, BILL (1946–) US politician and 42nd president. He studied international affairs at Georgetown (1968) and as a Rhodes Scholar at Oxford (1968–70), then received his law degree from Yale (1973). He served as attorney general of Arkansas (1977–9); governor of Arkansas (1979–81; 1983–92) and, as the national Democratic candidate, in 1993 defeated George Bush to become US president. He was re-elected president in 1997 but his presidency was dogged by growing scandals .

CLIVE, ROBERT (1725–74) Conqueror of Bengal and founder of British power in India. He arrived in India in 1743 as a clerk in the **English East India Company**. He fought French, and later (1757) Indian, forces to establish British control in Bengal, where he was twice governor (1757–60) and 1765–7). His rule was marred by corruption scandals; despite successful Parliamentary defence in 1773, he committed suicide the following year.

CLOVIS I (c. 466–511) Founder of the kingdom of the **Franks**, succeeding his father, **Childeric**, as ruler of the Salian Franks in 481, and gradually uniting all other Frankish groups under his rule. He defeated the last Roman authority in northern Gaul in 486, defeated the **Burgundians** and the Aleman, and drove the **Visigoths** from Aquitaine in 507. Sometime before 508 he converted to Catholic Christianity, and was baptized at Rheims; he issued the Salic law for his people, and established his capital at Paris. His descendants, the **Merovingians**, ruled the Frankish kingdom until 751.

CLUNIAC The monastery of Cluny (near Mâcon, Burgundy) was founded in 910 by the Duke of Aquitaine, and wielded a tremendous influence on the life of the Church for the next two centuries. The respect in which the Cluniacs were held through their many foundations all over western Europe, the statesmanlike activity of their leaders and the hierarchical organization of the Order under the abbot of Cluny, combined to make it one of the foundation stones of the general reform of the Church led by Pope **Gregory VII**.

CNUT THE GREAT (c. 995–1035) King of England (where he is remembered as Canute), Denmark and Norway. The son of **Sven Forkbeard**, he went to England with his father in 1013; he divided the country with Edmund II in 1016, assuming rule over all the country on Edmund's death in the same year. He succeeded to the Danish throne in 1019 and invaded Scotland in 1027.

COELHO, DUARTE (c. 1485–1554) Portuguese soldier. He was granted the captaincy of Pernambuco in 1534, and developed it into the most flourishing colony in Brazil.

COKWE (Bajokwe) People occupying the southern region of Zaire, northeast Angola and northwest Zambia, formed by a mixture of aboriginal groups and **Lunda** invaders; they were famous ivory-hunters in the 19th century.

COLBERT, JEAN BAPTISTE (1619–83) Minister of Finance to **Louis XIV** of France. Personal assistant to Cardinal **Mazarin**, he became a dominant member of Louis' Council of Finance, and in 1665 was made Controller-General. He reformed taxes, founded state manufactures, created the French merchant fleet and laid the basis for France's economic dominance in late 17th-century Europe.

COLD WAR Global tension caused by super-power rivalry after the end of the Second World War. *See* pp. 274–5.

COLIJN, HENDRIKUS (1869–1944) Dutch statesman. Fought in Sumatra where he was later colonial administrator. He entered the Dutch parliament in 1909; became war minister, 1911–13; finance minister, 1923–5; prime minister, 1925–6 and 1933–9. In his second term as premier he instituted successful anti-Depression policies. He was forced to resign in 1939. Arrested by the Germans in 1941, he died three years later in a concentration camp.

COLLA People of the high Andes who in pre-Columbian times occupied the area south of Lake Titicaca. They were conquered by the **Incas** in the early 15th century.

COLLING BROTHERS English 18th-century stockbreeders, farming near Darlington, who developed the shorthorn cow, c. 1780, into an animal equally good for milk and meat.

COLTER, JOHN (c.1775–1813) United States trapper and explorer, who in 1807 discovered the area now known as Yellowstone National Park. He was also a member of the Lewis and **Clark** expedition.

COLUMBA (521–579) Irish saint, famous as the missionary who carried Christianity to **Picts** in Caledonia (Scotland). He founded the monastery at Iona, 563, the mother house of numerous monasteries on the Scottish mainland.

COLUMBUS, CHRISTOPHER (1451–1506) Genoese navigator, discoverer of America and founder of the Spanish empire in the Americas.

In 1492 he obtained finance from the Spanish court to seek the east by sailing west. His three ships, the *Pinta*, *Niña* and *Santa María*, sighted San Salvador on 12 October 1492. During his second voyage, in 1493, he founded Isabela, the first European city (now deserted) in the New World, in the Dominican Republic. His third journey, 1498–1500, revealed the mainland of South America. He was embittered when administrative disasters and lack of political sense made the king of Spain reluctant to trust his governorship. His last voyage, 1502–4, coasted Honduras, Nicaragua and the isthmus of Panama, and ended with his ships beached off Jamaica.

COMINTERN The Third Socialist International, set up in 1919 to replace the **Second International** by those who condemned it for its failure to prevent the First World War. Captured immediately by the leadership of Bolshevik Russia, it split the world socialist movement between evolutionary and revolutionary parties, fomenting a number of uprisings in Europe and in European colonies in southeast Asia in the 1920s. Extensively purged by **Stalin**'s secret police in the 1930s, it was formally dissolved in 1943.

COMMUNISM Revolutionary socialism based on the theories of the political philosophers Karl **Marx** and Friedrich Engels, emphasizing common ownership of means of production and a planned economy. The principle held is that each should work according to their needs. Politically, it seeks the overthrow of **capitalism** through a proletarian revolution. The first communist state was the USSR after the revolution of 1917. Revolutionary socialist parties and groups united to form communist parties in other countries. After the Second World War, communism was enforced in those countries that came under Soviet occupation. China emerged after 1961 as a rival to the USSR in world communist leadership and other countries attempted to adopt communism to their own needs. With the collapse of the USSR in 1990, communism disappeared from Europe. It survives in China and a small number of unreconstructed hardline states.

COMNENES Byzantine dynasty holding the imperial throne, 1081–1185. Isaac I, son of Manuel Comnenus, a Paphlagonian general, became emperor briefly from 1057 to 1059, but his nephew, **Alexius I** (reigned 1081–1118), consolidated the family's power. The elder line died out in 1185, but after the sack of Constantinople by crusaders (1204) relatives founded the empire of Trebizond, lasting until 1461, when David Comnenus was deposed.

CONFEDERATION OF THE RHINE Created by **Napoleon I** in 1806 after the dissolution of the **Holy Roman Empire**, to gather his client states into a federation of which he was 'protector'. Excluding Austria and Prussia, it formalized French domination over German territory, and lasted until Napoleon's defeat.

CONFLANS, TREATY OF Agreement concluded in 1465 between **Louis XI** of France and the League of the Public Weal, under which Louis agreed to return land captured on the Somme to the League's leader, **Charles the Bold**, duke of Burgundy, and promised him the hand of his daughter, Anne of France, with the territory of Champagne as dowry.

CONFUCIUS Chinese philosopher. He served as a public administrator, c. 552–c. 517 BC, then spent the rest of his life teaching and editing the ancient Chinese classics. His sayings, collected after his death as *The Analects*, formed the basis for Chinese education and social organization until the 20th century. His philosophy was conservative: he advocated submission to one's parents and of wives to husbands, loyalty of subject to ruler, and conformity to established social forms. He advocated the supremacy of ethical standards and rule by 'humanity' and moral persuasion rather than brute force, and laid great stress on ritual observance. Confucianism has been deeply influential in Japan, Korea and Vietnam as well as in China.

CONGREGATIONALIST Member of one of the independent Protestant churches established in the 16th and 17th centuries in the belief that each congregation should decide its own affairs. Among its famous followers were John Winthrop, founder of the Massachusetts Bay Colony in 1629, and **Oliver Cromwell**, Lord Protector of England, 1649–60. Congregationalism became the established religion in 17th-century New England; many such churches still survive in North America and in Great Britain.

CONSTANTINE I (c. 287–337) Roman emperor, known as 'the Great'. Born in Naissus, now Nis, Serbia, he was brought up at the court of **Diocletian**, and became Western emperor in 312 and sole emperor in 324. Committed to Christianity, he issued the **Edict of Milan**, 313, extending toleration to all faiths; addressed the **Council of Nicaea**, 325, called to resolve some of its crucial theological disputes; founded many churches and was baptized shortly before his death. He built Constantinople as a new Rome on the site of Byzantium, 324, as his permanent capital, and was largely responsible for the evolution of the empire into a Christian state.

CONSTANTINOPLE, COUNCILS OF The first council, an ecumenical gathering of the Christian Church held in AD 381, reaffirmed the teaching of the **Council of Nicaea** and defined the doctrine of the Holy Trinity. The second, in 553, rejected the Nestorian version of Christianity and defined the unity of the person of Christ in his two natures, human and divine. This was reasserted in the third council in 680–1. The fourth, summoned in 869–70, excommunicated Photius, Patriarch of Constantinople (he was reinstated ten years later) and forbade lay interference in the election of bishops.

CONTRAS A counter-revolutionary insurgent force formed by the **Reagan** administration (1981–9) to fight against the **Sandanista** government in Nicaragua (1979–89). They included former supporters of the Somoza regime, members of the National Guard and disaffected opposition leaders. With substantial US military training and aid, they carried out military operations from Honduras, but proved unable to topple the Sandinistas and were demobilized in exchange for free elections in 1989.

COOK, JAMES (1728–79) Explorer of the Pacific Ocean. Appointed 1768 to take members of the British Royal Society to Tahiti and locate *Terra Australis Incognita*, or Unknown Southern Continent, he instead charted the coasts of New Zealand and established its insular character, explored the east coast of Australia, navigated the Great Barrier Reef (1770); on his second voyage of circumnavigation, 1772–5, he finally disposed of the notion of an inhabited southern continent; on the third voyage, 1776–80, he discovered the Sandwich (Hawaiian) Islands and proved that no navigable passage connected the north Pacific and north Atlantic. He was famous for his radical dietary methods, which protected all his men from the previously unavoidable scourge of scurvy. He was killed in Hawaii.

COPT Member of the Coptic Church, an ancient **Monophysite** branch of **Christianity**, founded in Egypt in the 5th century. Persecuted by Byzantines for theological reasons, but relatively secure after the Muslim conquest of Egypt, the Church, with its strong monastic tradition, survived. Its 3 to 4 million followers today still use the Coptic language, derived from ancient Egyptian, for their version of the Greek liturgy.

CORNISH REBELLION English uprising in 1497 against the heavy taxes levied by **Henry VII** to pay for his Scottish wars. The rebels killed a tax collector at Taunton (Somerset) and marched on London, but they were attacked and defeated in their camp at Blackheath by government troops; 2000 rebels died and the leaders were hanged.

CORREGIO, DA Italian family, prominent in the affairs of the Emilian city of Corregio from the 11th century until 1634, and of Parma in the 14th century. Its territories were sold to the house of **Este** in 1634. The dynasty finally died out in 1711.

CORSAIRS Pirates, particularly on the Maghreb ('Barbary') Coast of north Africa.

CORTE-REAL, GASPAR and MIGUEL Portuguese explorer brothers who made a series of voyages in the late 15th and early 16th centuries under royal commission to discover lands in the northwest Atlantic within the Portuguese domain. Gaspar travelled along the coast of southeast Greenland and crossed the Davis Strait to Labrador; Miguel visited Newfoundland and possibly the Gulf of St Lawrence in 1502. Both were lost at sea.

CORTÉS, HERNAN (1485–1547) Conqueror of Mexico. At the age of 19 he settle in Hispaniola and in 1511 sailed with Diego de Velásquez to conquer Cuba; from there, in 1518, he headed an expedition to colonize the Mexican mainland, and achieved a complete and remarkable victory over the Aztec empire. In 1542 he led an arduous and profitless expedition to Honduras. The rest of his life was spent fighting political enemies and intriguers both in New Spain and at home in Spain.

COSA, JUAN DE LA (c. 1460–1510) Spanish geographer and traveller. He owned **Columbus**' flagship, the *Santa Maria*, and served as his pilot. He compiled a celebrated map, dated 1500, showing Columbus' discoveries, **Cabral**'s landfall in Brazil, **Cabot**'s voyage to Canada, and **da Gama**'s journey to India. Sailed with **Bastidas** in 1500; explored Darien, 1504. He died during an expedition to central America and Columbia.

COSSACKS Bands of warlike adventurers recruited mainly from Ukrainian, Polish, Russian and Tatar fugitives and runaway serfs. Renowned for their horsemanship, courage and ruthlessness, they were active on the borders of the Ottoman empire with Poland and Russia from the 15th century. One of their bands in the service of the Stroganov family, under Yermak, conquered the Siberian Khanate for **Ivan IV**. The Cossacks' principal settlement was at Zaporzhye on the Dnieper, and from here they rebelled against Poland in 1648. The settlement was destroyed after the Peace of Kücük Kaynarca in 1774, but other Cossack hosts entered Russian service as cavalry regiments (e.g. Don Cossacks). They survived as semi-autonomous societies into the Soviet period, when they set up short-lived anti-Bolshevik governments.

COUGHLIN, FATHER CHARLES EDWARD (1891–1979) Populist and anti-semitic Catholic priest; born in Canada. From 1930 he broadcast weekly to large audiences in the United States, at first supporting President **F.D. Roosevelt**, but then dropping him in 1936. He edited an increasingly right-wing journal, *Social Justice*, until publication ceased in 1942 after the magazine was banned from the mails for infringing the Espionage Act.

COVENANTERS Those who signed the Scottish National Covenant in 1638, pledging to defend Presbyterianism against all comers. Covenanting armies entered England in 1640, 1644 and 1651; they were defeated by **Cromwell** at Dunbar (1650) and Worcester (1651). The Westminster Confession (1643), drawn up after agreeing the Solemn League and Covenant with the English Parliamentarians, defined the worship, doctrines and organization of the Church of Scotland. The movement faded away after 1690, when the official Scottish religion became Episcopalianism.

COVILHA, PERO DE 15th-century Portuguese explorer sent by the crown in 1487 to see whether the Indian Ocean connected with the Atlantic. His reports from Ethiopia, which he reached after travels in India and Arabia, were important in the Portuguese decision to send the fleet of **Vasco da Gama** to India in 1497–8. Covilha reached the court of the emperor of Ethiopia, whom he thought was a descendant of **Prester John**.

CRASSUS, MARCUS LICINIUS (c. 112–53 BC) Wealthy Roman, third member of the First Triumvirate with **Julius Caesar** and **Pompey**. He sought power and prestige to equal his political colleagues; invaded Mesopotamia. He was ignominiously defeated and killed by Parthian at the battle of Carrhae.

CRIPPS, SIR STAFFORD (1889–1952) British lawyer and politician. He became a member of the Labour Party in 1929, and served in the Cabinet 1930–1. A leading left-wing MP during the 1930s, he was ambassador to Moscow, 1940–2, and headed missions sent to India with plans for self-government in 1942–3 and 1946 (both plans were rejected by the Indian leaders). He held Cabinet office 1942–50, including the post of chancellor of the exchequer, 1947–50.

CROATS East European people who migrated in the 6th century from White Croatia, now in the Ukraine, to the Balkans. Their conversion to Roman Catholicism in the 7th century has continued to divide them from their Orthodox neighbours, the **Serbs**. The first Croatian kingdom, formed in the 10th century, was united by marriage with the crown of Hungary in 1091. In 1918 an independent Croatia was proclaimed, but it immediately entered the union of Slav states known as Yugoslavia; a Fascist-led independent state of Croatia, under Ante Pavelic, lasted from 1941 to 1945 before reunification with Yugoslavia under the Communist partisans. Independent again from 1991.

CROMPTON, SAMUEL (1753–1827) British inventor who pioneered the automatic spinning mule, 1779, so called because it combined the principles of the jenny and the water frame.

CROMWELL, OLIVER (1599–1658) Head of republican Britain. Elected to the English Parliament in 1640; he led the 'New Model' army to victory in the Civil War, and supported the execution of **Charles I** in 1649. He crushed uprisings by the **Levellers**, 1649, and by opponents in Ireland and Scotland, 1649–51, unifying the British Isles for the first time in a single state. He was appointed Lord Protector (effectively dictator) by army council in 1653. He declined the offer of the monarchy in 1657.

CROQUANTS Peasants who rose in large-scale and well-organized revolts in the Saintonge, Angoumois and Périgord regions of France in 1593–5, 1636–7 and 1643–5. The colloquial meaning of the name is 'clodhopper' or 'nonentity'.

CRUSADES The First Crusade, a holy war waged from 1096 until 1099 by Christian armies from western Europe against Islam in Palestine and Asia Minor, was inspired by a sermon of Pope **Urban II** in 1095. Its leaders included Robert of Normandy, Godfrey of Bouillon, Baldwin and Robert II of Flanders. Nicaea and Antioch were successfully besieged, Jerusalem stormed in 1099, and the Christian kingdom of Jerusalem established by Godfrey of Bouillon.

The Second Crusade, 1147–9, was inspired by **St Bernard**. It was led by the emperor, Conrad III, and by **Louis VII** of France, but foundered on quarrels between its leaders and the barons of the kingdom of Jerusalem, who were in alliance with Muslim Damascus, which the newly-arrived crusaders wished to attack. The Crusade petered out fruitlessly, and the Latin kingdom was soon weaker then ever.

The Third Crusade, 1189–92, was led by Emperor **Frederick I Barbarossa** (who died before reaching Palestine), King Richard I of England and King **Philip II Augustus** of France. It aimed to regain Jerusalem, which had been captured by the Muslim leader **Saladin** in 1187. It failed to do so, but the coast between Tyre and Jaffa was ceded to Christians and pilgrimage to Jerusalem was allowed.

The Fourth Crusade (1202–4) was originally intended to attack Egypt, centre of Muslim power in the late 12th century. The crusading armies, heirs to a long hostility towards Byzantium, were diverted by Venice, which provided the transport first to Zara on the Adriatic, and then to Constantinople, which fell on 13 April 1204 and was subjected to three days of massacre and pillage. A horrified Pope **Innocent III**, who had called the crusade, was unable to re-establish control, and his legate absolved the crusaders from the vow to proceed to the Holy Land.

CULTURE SYSTEM A system of land cultivation introduced in the 19th century by the governor-general of the Dutch East Indies, van den Bosch. Under the system each cultivator set aside an agreed portion of his land for the cultivation of certain cash crops – primarily coffee, tea, sugar, indigo and cinnamon – to be delivered at fixed prices to the government in lieu of land rent. It was such a success that all the safeguards against exploitation of labour gradually broke down; Javanese agriculture benefited in various ways, but at the price of oppression and, in places, famine. The system was strongly attacked by the Dutch Liberals, who came to power in 1848, and abolition began in the 1860s. Coffee, the most profitable item in the system, was removed from it only in 1917.

CURZON LINE Ethnically defined frontier between the former USSR and Poland, proposed in 1919 by the British foreign secretary Lord Curzon (1859–1925). At the time it was not accepted by either party; after victory in the Russo-Polish war of 1919–20, Poland, as a result of the **Treaty of Riga**, 1921, retained over 50,000 square miles each of the line. The Russo-Polish frontier as settled in 1945 in some respects conforms to the Curzon recommendations.

CUSHITIC Group of languages, related to Egyptian and Berber, spoken originally in the western highlands of Ethiopia; many elements are now partially absorbed into **Amharic**, the official national language. The most widely used Cushitic dialects today include Galla, Somali and the much-divided Sidamo group.

CYNICS Followers of the way of life of Diogenes of Sinope (c. 400–325 BC), nicknamed the Dog (hence Cynic, i.e. doglike), who pursed non-attachment or self-sufficiency by a drastic attack on convention, and by renouncing possessions, nation and social obligations, and choosing self-discipline and a simple life. Cynicism returned to prominence in the early Roman empire.

CYNOSCEPHALAE, BATTLE OF First decisive Roman victory over a major Greek army, fought in Thessaly in 197 BC against **Philip V of Macedon**, who commanded 25,000 troops.

CYPRIAN, ST (c. 200–58) Early Christian theologian. He practised law in Carthage, and was converted to **Christianity** c. 246. Elected Bishop of Carthage, c. 248, in 250 he fled from Roman persecution, but regained his authority on his return the following year. He was exiled in 257 in a new persecution under Emperor **Valerian**. After attempting to return, he was tried and executed.

CYRIL (826–69) and METHODIUS (816–85) Brother saints, known as 'the apostles of the Slavs'. They worked to convert the **Khazars**, northeast of the Black Sea; sent by Byzantine Emperor Michael III into Greater Moravia, 863. They translated the scriptures into the language later known as Old Church Slavonic, or Old Bulgarian. The 'Cyrillic' alphabet, used today in most Slavonic countries, is named after St Cyril.

CYRUS II, THE GREAT (d.529 BC) Known as 'the Elder' or 'Cyrus the King' in the Old Testament. Founder of the Persian **Achaemenid** empire. Originally a vassal king to the **Medes** in Anshan (Fars province), 559 BC, he rebelled. After capturing the Median capital Ecbatana in 550, he conquered and in most cases liberated Babylonia, Assyria, Lydia, Syria and Palestine. He ordered the rebuilding of the Temple in Jerusalem.

D

DALHOUSIE, JAMES ANDREW BROUN-RAMSEY, 1st Marquis (1812–60) British colonial administrator. He was appointed the youngest-ever Governor-General of India in 1847; during his nine-year term he annexed vast territories, including the Punjab and Lower Burma, built railways, roads and bridges, installed a telegraph and postal system, opened the Ganges canal, acted against thuggee (murder and robbery), dacoity (armed robbery) and the slave trade, and opened the Indian Civil Service to native Indians.

DANEGELD Tax levied in Anglo-Saxon England by King Æthelred II (978–1016) to finance the buying-off of Danish invaders; it was preserved as a revenue-raising device by the Anglo-Norman kings who last made use of it in 1162. The name itself is Norman, replacing the earlier, Old English *gafol* (tribute).

DANELAW Region of eastern England, north and east of a line from the Dee to the Tees rivers, governed in the 9th and 10th centuries under the Danish legal code. Some of its legal and social elements survived the **Norman Conquest**, gradually dying out in the course of the 12th century.

DANTE ALIGHIERI (1265–1321) Italian poet, born in Florence. He was sentenced to death in 1301 on political charges, but escaped; the remainder of his life was spent in exile. His greatest work, the *Commedia* (written c. 1308–20, known since the 16th century as the *Divina Commedia*), is the earliest masterpiece written in Italian. It traces an imaginary journey through Hell, Purgatory and Heaven, and symbolically describes the progress of the soul from sin to purification.

DANTON, GEORGE-JACQUES (1759–94) French revolutionary who helped to found the Cordeliers Club, 1790; as Minister of Justice, 1792, he organized the defence of France against the Prussians. He was a member of the Committee of Public Safety 1793, but was overthrown by his rival, **Robespierre**, and guillotined.

DAOISM Ancient cult of China, tracing back philosophically to the legendary **Lao-tzu**, who held that there is a Way (*dao*), a sort of natural order of the universe, and that it is the duty of individuals to ensure that their life conforms to it. It developed as a mass religious movement in the 2nd century AD, with its own church and hierarchy; it emphasizes salvation, aided by magical practices based on the interaction of *yin* and *yang*, the powers of darkness (female) and light(male).

DARBY Family of English iron-masters whose enterprise helped to create the industrial revolution. Abraham Darby (c.1678–1717) was the first man to smelt iron ore successfully with coke instead of charcoal. His son, Abraham II, built over 100 cylinders for the **Newcomen** steam engine. His grandson Abraham III built the world's first iron bridge, over the Severn at Coalbrookedale, 1779, and the first railway locomotive with a high-pressure boiler (for Richard Trevithick, 1802). The new smelting process had a slow start, but in the second half of the 18th century developed rapidly, leading to a great increase in the output of pig-iron and of cast-iron goods.

DARIUS I (c. 550–486 BC) King of ancient Persia (reigned 522–486 BC). Son of Hystaspes, satrap of Parthia and Hyrcania; he extended Persian control in Egypt and western India; invaded Scythia across the Bosporus, 513. His attack on Greece was defeated at **Marathon**, 490; he died while preparing a second Greek expedition.

DAVID (d. c. 972 BC) King of the Israelites, son of Jesse. Reared as a shepherd boy, he slew the giant Goliath, champion of the Philistines. He was disaffected from Saul, king of Israel, but was accepted as king after Saul's death; he established his capital at Jerusalem. Traditionally believed to have composed many of the Biblical Psalms. Christian tradition claims that **Jesus** was among his descendants, as a member of the House of David, from which, according to Jewish belief, the Messiah must spring.

DAVIS, JOHN (c. 1550–1605) English explorer, who in 1585 made the first of three unsuccessful attempts to find a Northwest Passage through the Canadian Arctic; detailed in his later treatise, *The World's Hydrographical Description*, 1595. He fought against Spanish Armada, 1588; discovered the Falkland Islands, 1592; sailed with Walter Raleigh to Cádiz and the Azores, 1596–7. He was killed by Japanese pirates on the last of three voyages to the East Indies.

DELIAN LEAGUE Confederation of ancient Greek states, with its headquarters on the sacred island of Delos, originally created under the leadership of Athens in 478 BC to oppose **Achaemenid** Persia. Initially successful; however, freedom to secede was not permitted. In 454 BC the treasury was transferred to Athens, and the League became effectively an Athenian empire.

DEMOCRACY From the Greek *demos*, the community, and *kratos*, sovereign power. Government by the people, usually through elected representatives. In the modern world, democracy has developed from the American and French revolutions.

DEMOSTHENES (384–322 BC) Ancient Greek statesman and orator. He led the democratic faction in Athens; engaged in bitter political rivalry with his fellow-orator Aeschines; roused the Athenians to oppose both **Philip of Macedon** and **Alexander the Great**. He died by self-administered poison.

DENG XIAOPING (1904–97) Chinese statesman. In 1924 he joined the Chinese Communist Party. Following the split between nationalists and communists (1927) he worked for the central committee in Shanghai. He participated in the 'long march' led by **Mao Zedong** (1934–5), served in the Red Army against the Japanese and nationalists and was elected to the central committee after the establishment of the People's Republic of China (1949). Falling from power during the Cultural Revolution (1966–9), he was reinstated as vice-premier (1973), only to be removed again in 1976. In 1977 he returned as the dominant political figure, introducing free market policies in agricultural and industrial sectors and promoting cultural and scientific exchanges with Western powers.

DENIKIN, ANTON IVANOVICH (1872–1947) Russian general. After the revolution in 1917 he joined the anti-Bolshevik armies in south Russia. Promoted to commander in 1918, he led an unsuccessful advance on Moscow in 1919 and in 1920 resigned and went into exile.

DE THAM (c. 1860–1913) Vietnamese freedom fighter. He joined a local pirate band and started organizing formidable attacks on the French colonists. As 'the tiger of Yen Tri' he built up a large guerrilla army; the great-uncle of Ho Chi Minh was a member. He attacked the French railway, 1894, and temporarily ran Yen Tri district as an autonomous empire. In 1906–7 he linked with the other main anti-French group under **Phan Boi Chau**. Implicated in the abortive 'Hanoi Poison Plot' in 1908, he was later assassinated.

DIARMAT, MAC MAEL (1010–71) King of Leinster, Ireland, between 1040 and 1071. He extended his authority over much of the Scandinavian kingdom of Dublin (1071) and planned to make himself High King, but death intervened and Ireland disintegrated into warring sub-kingdoms until the Norman invasion of 1170.

DIAZ, PORFIRO (1830–1915) Dictatorial President of Mexico. He joined the army fighting against the United States (1846–8), in the War of the Reform (1857–60), and in opposition to the French (1862–7). Involved in unsuccessful revolts in 1871 and 1876, he returned later in 1876 from the US and defeated the government at the battle of Tecoac. Elected president in 1877, he gradually consolidated power; he was re-elected in 1884 and effectively ruled the country until 1910, modernizing its economy at great social cost. The military supporters of **Madero** forced him to resign in 1911. He died in exile in Paris.

DIESEL, RUDOLF (1858–1913) Inventor of the heavy oil internal combustion engine bearing his name. Trained at Technische Hochschule, Munich; worked two years at the Swiss Sulzer Machine Works, and then in Paris at Linde Refrigeration Enterprises. He started work on his engine in 1885, making his first working model in 1893.

DENSHAWAI INCIDENT Anti-British incident in Egypt in 1906. British officers shooting pigeons near a village in the Delta became involved in a fight with peasants who owned the pigeons; one officer died of sunstroke. Savage punishment of villagers provoked strong demonstrations against the British.

DIOCLETIAN (245–316) Roman emperor, born Aurelius Valerius Diocletianus, in Dalmatia. Acclaimed by his soldiers as emperor in 284, at a time of deep economic, political and military trouble, he took sole control of affairs in 285 and forced through an immense programme of legal, fiscal and administrative reform, restoring much of Rome's former strength. He abdicated in 305.

DIODOTUS I Founder of the ancient Greek kingdom of Bactria, originally subject to the **Seleucid** kings, Antiochus I and II. He rebelled and made himself king (250–230); he was succeeded by his son, Diodutus II Soter.

DISRAELI, BENJAMIN (1804–81) 1st Earl of Beaconsfield, statesman, novelist and twice British prime minister; born of a Jewish family but baptized as a Christian. He first stood for Parliament as a radical, but was elected as Conservative MP in 1837. Quarrelled with Sir Robert **Peel** over the repeal of the Corn Laws, 1846, and emerged as a leader of the rump of the Conservative Party. He succeeded Lord Derby as prime minister for a few months in 1868 and became prime minister again, 1874–80. He incorporated concern for the empire into the Conservative programme in his Crystal Palace speech of 1872 and saw a link between imperialism and social reform at home; his real concern was for India and the route to India. Represented Britain at the **Congress of Berlin** in 1878; his ministry was associated with a forward policy in Afghanistan and South Africa.

DOENITZ, KARL (1891–1981) German naval commander and briefly head of state. In the First World War he served as a submarine officer. After the succession of **Hitler** he supervized the clandestine construction of a new U-boat fleet; he was appointed commander of submarine forces in 1936, head of the Germany navy in 1943 and head of the northern military and civil command in 1945. Named in Hitler's political testament as the next president of the Reich, he assumed control of the government for a few days after Hitler's suicide on 2 May 1945. Sentenced to ten years' imprisonment as a Nazi war criminal in 1946, he was released in 1956.

DOLLFUSS, ENGELBERT (1892–1934) Chancellor of Austria, 1932–4, who effectively made himself dictator until he was assassinated by Austrian Nazis.

DOMINICANS *see* **Friars**

DOMITIAN (AD 51–96) Roman emperor, born Titus Flavius Domitianus, son of Emperor **Vespasian**; succeeded his brother **Titus**, in AD 81. He is remembered for his financial rapacity and the reign of terror (particularly 93–6) waged against his critics in the Senate; he was murdered by conspirators, including his wife, Domitia Longina.

DONATUS (d. c. 355) Leader of the Donatists, a north African Christian group named after him, which broke with the Catholic Church in 312 after a controversy over the election of Caecilian as Bishop of Carthage; Donatus, appealing against the appointment, was overruled by a council of bishops, 313, by another at Arles, 314, and finally by Emperor **Constantine**, 316. The dissidents were persecuted, 317–21, then reluctantly tolerated; they continued to gain strength (perhaps through African nationalist feeling). In 347 Donatus was exiled to Gaul, where he died. The movement continued but, thanks to the teaching of St Augustine, and to state persecution, it had disappeared by c. 700.

DORIANS Last of the Hellenic invaders to press into Greece from the north, c. 1100 BC, perhaps from Epirus and southwest Macedonia, traditionally via Doria in central Greece. They recognized three 'tribes', the Hylleis, perhaps coming down the east, the Dymanes down the west, and the Pamphyloi covering minor groupings. They spread through the Peloponnese and to the islands of Cythera, Melos, Thera, Crete, Rhodes, Cos and into southern Anatolia. Many unresolved questions about them continue to challenge archaeologists.

DOUGLAS, STEPHEN ARNOLD (1813–61) United States Senator. He was elected to Congress in 1843 and to the Senate in 1846. He strongly supported 'popular sovereignty' (local option) on the question of slavery. In 1858 he engaged in a series of highly publicized debates with **Abraham Lincoln**, to whom he lost in the presidential election. He condemned secession on the outbreak of the Civil War.

DRAKE, SIR FRANCIS (c. 1540–96) English seaman who led buccaneering expeditions to west Africa and the Spanish West Indies, 1566–73, 1585–6 and 1595–6. He circumnavigated the globe in his ship the *Golden Hind*, 1577–80; raided the Spanish fleet in Cádiz, 1587, and fought against the Spanish Armada, 1588.

DRAVIDIAN Group of seven major and many minor languages, including Tamil, Telugu, Kanarese, Malayalam, Gondi and Tulu, spoken mainly by some 110 million people in southern India (also known collectively as Dravidians); characteristically these are darker, stockier, longer-headed and flatter-faced than the Indic or Aryan races of northern India.

DRUID Member of a pre-Christian religious order in Celtic areas of Britain, Ireland and Gaul. It has been retained as a name for officers in the modern Welsh Gorsedd.

DUAL MONARCHY OF AUSTRIA-HUNGARY Political system, 1867–1918, established by the Compromise of 1867 which granted a large measure of autonomy to the Hungarian lands of the former Austrian empire.

DULLES, JOHN FOSTER (1888–1959) US lawyer and statesman. He began legal practice in 1911; became counsel to the US commission to negotiate peace after the First World War, 1918–19, and to other government bodies. He was special adviser to the secretary of state, 1945–51, and filled that post himself, 1953–9. He was associated with a vigorously anti-communist US foreign policy.

DUMA Lower house of the Russian parliament, established by Tsar **Nicholas II** in 1905; on the collapse of tsarism in February 1917 leading Duma politicians formed the Provisional Government.

DUPLEIX, JOSEPH FRANÇOIS (1697–1763) French administrator, Governor-general of Chandernagore 1731–41, and of Pondichery 1741–54. His expansionist ambitions in southern India were checked by **Robert Clive**, 1751–2; he was recalled in 1754.

DUTCH EAST INDIA COMPANY (Vereenigde Oostindische Compagnie, VOC). Powerful trading concern set up in 1602 to protect Dutch merchants in the Indian Ocean and to help finance the war of independence with Spain. Under able governors-general, such as Jan Pieterszoon Coen, 1618–23, and Anthony van Diemen, 1636–45, the company effectively drove both British and Portuguese out of the East Indies, and established Batavia (now Jakarta) as its base for conquering the islands. Growing corruption and debt led to the company's dissolution in 1799.

DUY TAN (1888–1945) Emperor of Annam, the son of Emperor Thanh Thai, whom he succeeded in 1907. His reign was a period of revolt against the French colonial power; after one revolt, which sought to make him a real emperor, he was deposed and exiled to Réunion in 1916. Later he served with the Free French forces in the Second World War; he died in an air crash.

E

EADGAR (c. 943–75) English king; younger son of Edmund I. He became king of Mercia and **Danelaw**, 957, on the deposition of his brother Eadwig, and in 959 succeeded to the throne of West Saxons and effectively all England. He reformed the Church in England.

EAM (Initials in Greek for National Liberation Front). One of the Greek resistance movements, formed in 1941 to fight the German and Italian armies of occupation. By 1944, when the Germans evacuated, it controlled two-thirds of the country. It rejected Allied orders to disarm in December 1944, but accepted the Varkiza Peace Agreement, 1945; it participated in large-scale civil war, 1946–9.

EAST INDIA COMPANY *see* **English East India Company** and **Dutch East India Company**

EC Founded in 1957 with the Treaty of Rome, which was signed by six nations and called originally the European Economic Community, the European Community was formed to promote economic and political cooperation as part of the process of post-war reconstruction. From 1986 it had 12 member nations. Despite undoubted benefits (between 1958 and 1962 trade between member states increased by 130 per cent) economic cooperation brought many problems – for example, the Common Agricultural Policy, developed to ensure a fair standard for farmers, led to massive over-production and higher prices. In 1992 Europe became in theory a single market, and the removal of physical, technical and financial barriers began. The **Maastricht Treaty** (1991) called for closer political union among EC member states and committed the EC to introduce a single currency, the Euro, by 1999. Though Britain and Denmark refused to join, the remaining states of the EC introduced the Euro in Jaanuary 1999. In 1995 the EC became the EU, or European Union

EDEN, Anthony, 1st Earl of Avon (1897–1977) British statesman and foreign secretary, 1935–8, 1940–5 and 1951–5. He supported the **League of Nations** in the 1930s and was **Churchill**'s deputy for a decade before succeeding him as prime minister (1955–7). Eden's determination to confront President **Nasser** of Egypt resulted in the **Suez** Crisis of 1956 which, added to poor health, led to his resignation.

EDEN TREATY Trade agreement between Britain and France, negotiated in 1786–7 by William Eden, 1st Baron Auckland (1744–1814), which gave the British free access to French markets. By encouraging the export of French corn to Britain, the treaty contributed to popular tension during the food crisis preceding the French revolution.

EDWARD THE CONFESSOR (c. 1003–65) King of England, son of **Æthelred II** the Unready. Exiled after Æthelred's death (1016) when the Danes again seized power in England, he returned from Normandy, 1041, and succeeded to the throne of his half-brother, Harthacnut, 1042; however, the main power in the kingdom remained first with Godwin, Earl of the West Saxons, then with his son, Harold, named as king on Edward's death. Claims that Edward had previously promised the throne to Duke William of Normandy led to the **Norman Conquest** (1066)

EDWARD I (1239–1307) King of England; the son of Henry III. He led the royal troops to victory in the Barons' War (1264–6); succeeded to the throne, 1272; conquered Wales (1277–83); established suzerainty over Scotland and defeated the Scottish revolt under **William Wallace**, 1298. His consistent utilization of Parliament in wide-ranging legislation consolidated its institutional position. He died on an expedition to suppress the revolt of **Robert Bruce** of Scotland.

EDWARD II (1284–1327) King of England, son of **Edward I**, whom he succeeded in 1307. He ruled, weakly and incompetently, through favourites such as Piers Gaveston (murdered 1312) and the Despensers (executed 1326). He was heavily defeated by the Scots at Bannockburn, 1314, and strongly opposed by the English barons, who in 1311 tried to subject him to control by a committee of 'lords ordainers'. He was deposed and put to death when his queen, Isabella, invaded from France with her ally, Roger Mortimer.

EDWARD III (1312–77) King of England, son of **Edward II**, succeeding in 1327. By 1330 he had freed himself from subjection to his mother, Isabella, and her ally, Roger Mortimer. Defeated the Scots, 1333 and 1346; at the start of the **Hundred Years' War** he defeated the French fleet at Sluys, 1340, and invaded France. His notable victories at Crécy, 1346, and Calais, 1347, with that of his son at Poitiers, 1356, were consolidated by the Peace of Brétigny in 1360. He resumed war in 1369, and by 1375 had lost all his previous gains except Calais, Bordeaux, Bayonne and Brest.

EIGHT TRIGRAMS Secret north Chinese sect, part-religious, part-political. It flourished, particularly in Chihli, Shantung and Honan, in the 19th century, and was involved in the palace revolution in Peking in 1814.

EISENHOWER, DWIGHT DAVID (1890–1969) 34th president of the United States, 1953–61. He was commander of the American forces in Europe, and of the Allies in north Africa, 1942; directed the invasions of Sicily and Italy, 1943; became Supreme Allied Commander, 1943–5, and Commander, NATO land forces, 1950–2. Under his presidency, the Korean War was ended (1953), **SEATO** formed, and federal troops were ordered (1957) to enforce racial desegregation of US schools at Little Rock, Arkansas.

EISNER, KURT (1867–1919) German socialist leader. In 1914 he opposed German aid to Austria-Hungary, and became leader of the pacifist Independent Social Democratic Party in 1917; he was arrested as a strike-leader the following year. After his release he organized the overthrow of the Bavarian monarchy and proclaimed an independent Bavarian republic. He was assassinated by a right-wing student.

ELCANO, JUAN SEBASTIAN DE (d.1526) First captain to make a complete circumnavigation of the earth. A Basque navigator, he sailed in 1519 as master of the *Concepción* under **Magellan**; after Magellan's death he took command of the three remaining ships and returned to Spain, 1522, with one ship, the *Victoria*. henceforth his family coat-of-arms carried a globe and the motto *Primus circumdedisti me* ('You were the first to circle me').

ELECTOR Historically, one of the small group of princes who, by right of heredity or office, were qualified to elect the Holy Roman Emperor. Originally, in the 13th century, there were six; from 1356 to 1623 there were seven – the archbishops of Mainz, Trier and Cologne, the king of Bohemia, the count palatine of the Rhine, the dukes of Saxony and the Margrave of Brandenburg. By 1806, when the Empire ended, there were ten.

ELIZABETH I (1533–1603) Queen of England. The daughter of **Henry VIII** and Anne Boleyn, she succeeded to the throne in 1558. Her re-establishment of a Church of England independent of Rome, 1559, led to her excommunication by Pope Pius V in 1571. She survived a Spanish attempt to put the sentence into effect (Spanish Armada, 1588). She made English authority effective in Ireland (1601).

ELLMAN, JOHN English 18th-century sheep-breeder, farming at Glynde, Surrey, who in about 1780 began developing short wool varieties, a process which eventually transformed the Southdown sheep from a light, long-legged animal into one solid, compact and equally good for mutton and for wool.

ENCYCLOPEDISTS Group of French writers, scientists and philosophers connected with the influential *Encyclopédie ou dictionnaire raisonné des sciences, des arts et des métiers*, edited 1751–72 by Denis Diderot (1713–84) assisted by d'Alembert (1717–83); the work and its contributors powerfully expressed the new spirit of 18th-century rationalism.

ENGLISH EAST INDIA COMPANY Founded in 1600 to trade with the East Indies, but excluded by the Dutch after the Amboina Massacre in 1623. The company negotiated concessions in Mughal India and won control of Bengal in 1757, but its political activities were curtailed by the Regulating Act of 1773 and the India Act of 1784. Its commercial monopoly with India was broken in 1813, and that with China in 1833. It ceased to be the British government's Indian agency after the Rebellion in 1857; its legal existence ended in 1873.

ENTREPOT Commercial centre, specializing in the handling, storage, transfer and dispatch of goods.

EON OF STEILA (d.1148) Christian heretic. He preached opposition to the wealth and organization of the Roman Catholic Church, gaining followers in Brittany and Gascony before being imprisoned by Pope **Eugenius III** at the Synod of Rheims. He died in prison; his followers, such as the **Henricians** and **Petrobrusians**, faded away.

EPICUREANS Followers of the Greek philosopher Epicurus (341–271 BC). To Epicurus happiness ('pleasure') was all; it consisted in freedom from disturbance. So the wise men free themselves from fear, through scientific understanding, and from desire by 'doing without'. The structure of the universe is atomic; death is annihilation; gods exist but do not intervene in human affairs. The Epicureans fostered friendship and discouraged ambition. The system was expounded by the Roman poet Lucretius (c. 94–55 BC).

EPIRUS, DESPOTATE OF Byzantine principality in southern Albania and northwest Greece, organized as a rival principality during the Western occupation of Constantinople after the Fourth Crusade. Founded in 1204 by Michael Angelus Ducas, it was continually attacked by Nicaea, Bulgaria and later, after the restoration of Michael VIII Palaeologus, by Byzantium itself. In the 13th century it was a pre-Renaissance centre for classical studies; it was re-annexed to Byzantium in 1337.

EPISCOPALIAN Member of the Protestant Episcopal Church of Scotland and the United States, a believer in the principle that supreme authority in the Church lies with the bishops assembled in council, rather than with a single head.

ERATOSTHENES (c. 276–c. 194 BC) The first systematic geographer. He directed the library at Alexandra, c.255 BC; wrote on astronomy, ethics and the theatre; compiled a calendar, showing leap years, and a chronology of events since the siege of Troy; calculated the earth's circumference with remarkable accuracy. He was known as Beta, because he was good without being supreme in so many fields. He is said to have starved himself to death after going blind.

ERIC XIV (1533–77) King of Sweden, 1560–8, the son of **Gustavus I Vasa**. He seized strategic territory in Estonia, prompting Denmark and Norway to initiate the Nordic Seven Years' War. He was accused of insanity and deposed by his half-brothers, 1568, after failing to win the war and after defying the Swedish nobility in order to make his commoner mistress, Karin Mansdotter, queen. He died in prison.

ERIK BLOODAXE (d. 954) King of Norway and of York in the 10th century, named to commemorate his murder of seven of his eight brothers. The son of **Harald Finehair**, he was expelled from Norway, 934; by 948 he was king of York and ruled there until expelled in 954. He was killed at Stainmore.

ESSENE Member of an ancient Jewish sect founded between the 2nd century BC and 2nd century AD. It was characterized by stern asceticism, withdrawal, communistic life, ceremonial purity, a rigorous novitiate lasting three years, identification of Yahweh with the Sun, and a mystic belief in immortality. The Dead Sea Scrolls, found in the Qumran (1947–1956), probably belonged to an Essene community; attempts to link **Jesus** to them are implausible.

ESTE Italian family which presided over an unusually brilliant court, ruling as princes in Ferrara from the 13th century until 1598, and as dukes in Reggio and Modena from 1288 until the mid-19th century. The dynasty was founded by the margrave Albert Azzo II (c. 1097); their connection with Ferrara ended when Clement VIII imposed direct papal rule.

ETRUSCANS A people in Italy inhabiting Etruria, the land between the rivers Tiber and Arno, west and south of the Apennine hills. Their origins are unknown, but they possibly came from Asia Minor. From 800 BC to their decline in the 5th century BC, they developed an elaborate urban civilization, particularly notable for its tombs; they were ultimately absorbed by Rome. The Etruscan language is still largely undeciphered.

EUGENIUS III (d.1153) The first Cistercian Pope (1145–53), a pupil of **St Bernard**, whose *De Consideratione* presented his views on how the pope should lead the Church. Forced to leave Rome because of conflict with the city and with **Arnold of Brescia**, he was finally re-established by the Treaty of Constance (1153) with **Frederick Barbarossa**.

EURIPIDES (480–406 BC) Last of the three great Athenian tragic dramatists; 19 of his 92 plays survive, distinguished by their concentration on real human problems expressed in contemporary language. He left Athens in 408, moved to Thessaly and then Macedon, where he wrote *The Bacchae*; he died at the court of King Archelaus.

EUROPEAN COMMUNITY *see* EC

EUSEBIUS (c. 265–340) Bishop of Caesarea. His *History of the Church* is the first scholarly work on the early institutions of Christianity.

EXARCHATE Under the Byzantine and the Holy Roman Empires, it referred to the governorship of a distant province; in the eastern Catholic Church, to the area of responsibility of certain high-ranking ecclesiastics known as exarchs (approximate equivalents of patriarchs or archbishops).

FAIRBARN, SIR WILLIAM (1789–1874) Victorian authority on factory design who wrote the classic treatise, *Mills and Millwork*. A builder of ships and bridges, he constructed many iron ships at Millwall, London, between 1835 and 1849, and also invented the rectangular tube used on **Robert Stephenson**'s Menai Bridge.

FANG CHIH-MIN (1900–35) Early leader of the Chinese Communist Party. He became prominent in Communist and **Kuomintang** affairs in Kiangsi during the 1920s; helped to found the Communist base in northeast Kiangsi, which developed into the Fukien-Chekiang-Kiangsi Soviet in the early 1930s. He led the 10th Army Corps when encircled by the Nationalist Army in mid-1934, and the following year was captured and executed by the Nationalists.

FAROUK I (1920–65) King of Egypt. The son of Fuad 1, he succeeded to the throne in 1936. He was involved in the long struggle for power with the nationalist party, the **Wafd**; during the Second World War Britain, then in occupation of Egypt, forced him to appoint a Wafdist government. He was deposed and exiled after the military *coup d'état* organized by **Neguib** and **Nasser**.

FARROUPILHA REVOLUTION Provincial uprising in Rio Grande do Sul, southern Brazil; it flared intermittently, 1834–45, until finally suppressed by the armies of Pedro II under the Duque de Caxias. The name means 'rags', alluding to the rebels' lack of uniforms.

FASCISM Originally the anti-democratic and anti-parliamentarian ideology adopted by the Italian counter-revolutionary movement led by **Mussolini**; characterized by advocacy of the corporate, one-party state, to which all aspects of life are subordinated. It was later extended to describe any extreme right-wing political creed that combines absolute obedience to the leader with a willingness to use force to gain power and suppress opposition.

FATIMA (c. 616–33) Mohammed's daughter, and first wife of **Ali**. The imams recognized by the **Shi'as** are her descendants, and Shi'as have a special reverence for her; her descendants led a moderate wing of the Shi'as, the second major division of Islam, and some of those claiming descent from her founded the **Fatimid** dynasty.

FATIMIDS North African dynasty claiming descent from **Fatima**, **Mohammed**'s daughter, founded in 908 in Tunisia by the imam, Ubaidallah. Muizz, the fourth Fatimid caliph, conquered Egypt and founded Cairo, 969. In the 11th century, they supplanted the **Abbasids** as the most powerful rulers in Islam, but were finally abolished by **Saladin** (1171).

FEDERALISTS Name, first used in 1787, to denote the supporters of the newly written United States' Constitution; and later for a conservative party which was hostile to the revolution in France, favourable to an alliance with Great Britain and generally supportive of central authority in America. From 1791 to 1801 Federalists controlled the national government, organized the new nation's administrative and tax machinery, and formulated a policy of neutrality in foreign affairs. In 1801 they were displaced by an opposition group led by **Thomas Jefferson**, and never again held national office.

FEITORIA Fortified factory or trading post, established by the Portuguese during their period of maritime dominance.

FENG YÜ-HSIANG (1882–1948) Chinese warlord, nicknamed 'the Christian general'. At first an officer in the Hwai army under **Yüan Shih-k'ai**, he served in the Peiyang army after the 1911 revolution. From 1918 he created a private army, controlling a large part of northwest China, 1912–20; he was involved in a series of *coups d'état* and civil wars, 1920–8, but never acquired a permanent territorial base. To relieve chronic financial pressures he sought the help of Russia, but in 1929 was forced to relinquish control of his troops to **Chiang Kai-shek**. His army, joined by **Yen Hsi-shan**, attempted to form a northern coalition against Chiang, and in 1929–30 they fought a bitter war. When it ended he joined the Nationalist government, but never again had any real power.

FENLAND REVOLT Prolonged local opposition, 1632–8, to government-sponsored measures to drain and enrich the fens of eastern England, thus depriving the local population of common rights. **Oliver Cromwell** was one of the leaders of the revolt.

FERDINAND III (c. 1199–1252) Saint and king of Castile (1217–52) and León (1230–52). He united the crowns of Castile and León, and completed the conquest of all Moorish dominions in Spain except **Granada**.

FERDINAND OF ARAGON (1452–1516) The son of John II of Aragon. His marriage in 1469 to Isabella of Castile united the two principal kingdoms in the Iberian peninsula. The kingdom of Granada was annexed by Castile in 1492, while in 1504 Ferdinand conquered Naples which remained under Spanish control until 1713. In 1512 he acquired Navarre. It was during the joint rule of Ferdinand and Isabella that the **Inquisition** was established in Castile in 1478, **Columbus**'s first voyage to the new world was supported, and the **Jews** were expelled from Castile in 1492.

FEUDALISM Political system of medieval Europe, based on the mutual obligations of vassal and superiors, linked by the granting of land (the feud, or fee) in return for certain services. The feudal lord normally had rights of jurisdiction over his tenants, and held a feudal court. Similar systems (sometimes also termed 'feudal' by analogy) are found in other parts of the world (e.g. early China and Japan) at a similar stage of development.

FIANNA FÁIL Irish political party; founded in 1926 by **de Valera** to espouse republican nationalism and erase all English influence from Irish public life.

FIELDEN, JOSHUA (d.1811) Cotton industry pioneer. In 1780 he was still a peasant farmer, operating two or three weaving looms; by 1800 he owned a five-storey cotton mill in Todmorden, Yorkshire. After his death his sons developed the business – Fielden Brothers, Waterside Mills – into one of the largest cotton mills in Britain.

FIGUERES FERRIER, JOSÉ (1906–90) Costa Rican political leader. He worked as a coffee planter and rope-maker; exiled to Mexico 1942–4, he became Junta president of the Republic, 1948, but resigned in 1949; he was president of Costa Rica 1953–8 and 1970–4.

FISSIRAGA Prominent family of medieval Lodi, Italy. Supporters of the **Guelph** (anti-imperial) party, they rose to prominence in the 1280s; in 1311 their leader, Antonio Fissiraga, was captured by the **Visconti** of Milan and died in prison (1327).

FIUME INCIDENT Unsuccessful attempt to seize the Adriatic sea port in September 1919, by a private Italian army, led by the poet Gabriele d'Annunzio, to forestall its award to Yugoslavia at the Paris Peace Conference.

FIXED EXCHANGE RATES Regime under which the value of one currency bears a constant relationship to that of another: e.g. the pound sterling in the period 1949–67, when it was always worth US$ 2.80. Such relations linked most major currencies in the period 1947–71, under the so-called Bretton Woods System, but that then gave place to a period of mainly 'floating' rates.

FLAMININUS (c. 227–174 BC) Principal Roman general and statesman during the period when Greece became a Roman protectorate. He defeated **Philip V of Macedon** at **Cynoscephalae** in 197 BC; declared that all Greeks should be free and governed by their own laws in 196; and supported Greek autonomy in Asia Minor during Rome's wars with the **Seleucids**.

FLAVIANS Dynasty ruling the Roman empire from AD 69 to 96. It was founded by **Vespasian** (69–79) and continued by his sons, **Titus** (79–81) and **Domitian** (81–96).

FLINDERS, MATTHEW (1774–1814) Maritime explorer of Australia, born in Lincolnshire, England. He entered the Royal Navy in 1789, from 1795 to 1799 he charted much of Australia's east coast between Fraser Island and Bass Strait, and circumnavigated Tasmania; in 1801–2, as commander of the

Investigator, he surveyed the whole southern coast, and in 1802–3 circled the entire continent. He was interned by the French in Mauritius, 1802–10; his *Voyage to Terra Australis* was finally published about the time of his death.

FOCH, FERDINAND (1851–1929) French soldier, marshal of France, a teacher of military history and author of many standard works. Appointed a general in 1907, he won distinction during the First World War in the first battle of the Marne, 1914, the first battle of Ypres, 1915, and the battle of the Somme, 1916. He was appointed as commander-in-chief of the French armies in 1917, and after the onset of the German offensive in spring 1918 was appointed to command all French, British and American forces.

FORREST, JOHN (1847–1818) 1st Baron Forrest, Australian explorer and statesman. He led several expeditions across Western Australia from 1869; became surveyor-general of Western Australia, 1883–90 and its first premier, 1890–1901. He held cabinet office in several ministries in the federal government of the new Commonwealth of Australia between 1901 and 1918.

FOURTEEN POINTS Programme put forward by United States President **Woodrow Wilson** in 1918 for a peace settlement following the First World War. Several of the Points related to the right of self-determination of peoples; although statesmen at the Peace Conference were thinking of the rights of the successor states of the Austro-Hungarian and Ottoman empires, the principle was noted by colonial peoples in Asia and Africa. The final proposal for a 'general association' to guarantee integrity of 'great and small states alike' led to the setting up of the **League of Nations**.

FRANCIS I (1494–1547) King of France; he succeeded his cousin, **Louis XII**, in 1515. In 1520 he attempted unsuccessfully to win the support of the English king, **Henry VIII**, for his struggles with the **Habsburgs**; he pursued his rivalry alone in a series of Italian wars (1521–5, 1527–9, 1536–7, 1542–4), but finally abandoned Italian claims in 1544. He was a noted patron of Renaissance art.

FRANCIS II (1768–1835) The last Holy Roman Emperor. The son of Leopold II, he succeeded to the imperial title in 1792 and held it until dissolution of the empire by **Napoleon** in 1806. He continued to reign as the first emperor of Austria, under the title Francis I; through his chancellor, **Metternich**, he confirmed Austria's position as a leading European power.

FRANCISCANS *see* **Friars**

FRANCO, FRANCISCO (1892–1975) Spanish dictator. A general in the Spanish army, he organized the revolt in Morocco in 1936 which precipitated the Spanish Civil War of 1936–9, from which he emerged as head of state ('El Caudillo'). He was named regent for life in 1947. In 1969 he proposed that Prince Juan Carlos of Bourbon should ultimately take the throne, as indeed he did at Franco's death.

FRANCO-PRUSSIAN WAR Struggle provoked by rivalry between France and the growing power of Prussia, reaching a head over the candidacy of Leopold of Hohenzollern for the throne of Spain. Prussian armies under von Moltke invaded France and quickly won victories at Wörth, Gravelotte, Strasbourg, Sedan and Metz between August and October 1870. **Napoleon III** abdicated, and the Third French Republic was declared on 4 September 1870; Paris, under siege for four months, surrendered on 28 January 1871. Under the Treaty of Frankfurt (May 1871) France ceded Alsace and East Lorraine to the newly established German empire, and agreed to pay an indemnity of 5 billion francs.

FRANKS Germanic peoples who dominated the area of present-day France and western Germany after the collapse of the West Roman empire. Under **Clovis** (481–511) and his **Merovingian** and **Carolingian** successors they established the most powerful Christian kingdom in western Europe. Since the disintegration of their empire in the 9th century the name has survived in France and Franconia, In the Middle East, the crusaders were generally referred to as Franks, and the word came into several oriental languages to mean 'European'.

FRANZ FERDINAND (1863–1914) Archduke of Austria, nephew of, and from 1896 heir to, the Emperor Franz Joseph I (1830–1916). He was assassinated on 28 June 1914 at Sarajevo, an incident which provoked the Austrian ultimatum to Serbia that led directly to the outbreak of the First World War.

FREDERICK THE GREAT (1712–86) King of Prussia, son of **Frederick William I**, whom he succeeded in 1740. He entered the War of the Austrian Succession, won the battle of Mollwitz, 1741, and acquired the economically valuable province of Silesia, which he retained through the **Seven Years' War** (1756–63). He annexed West Prussia in the First Partition of Poland, 1772; formed the Fürstenbund (League of German Princes), 1785. He patronized writers and artists, including Voltaire; wrote *L'Antimachiavel*, 1740, and *History of the House of Brandenburg*, 1751.

FREDERICK I BARBAROSSA (c. 1123–90) King of Germany, 1152, emperor 1155; second of the **Hohenstaufen** dynasty. In 1154 he launched a campaign to restore royal rights in Italy; captured Milan, 1162, and Rome, 1166; s upported the anti-pope against the powerful Pope **Alexander III**, but was defeated by the **Lombard League** (Legnano 1176); reached a *modus vivendi* with the papacy and Italian cities at the Peace of Venice (1177) and Peace of Constance (1183). He was drowned in Syria while leading the Third **Crusade**.

FREDERICK II (1194–1250) Last great **Hohenstaufen** ruler. He was elected German king in 1212, after civil war and disorder in Germany, Italy and Sicily following the early death of his father, **Henry VI**, in 1197. He left Germany for Italy in 1220 to concentrate his energies on restoring royal authority in Sicily (Constitution of Malfi, 1231); he was crowned emperor by Pope Honorius III in 1220, and led the Fifth Crusade, 1228–9, but his Italian ambitions brought him into conflict with Honorius' successors, Gregory IX and **Innocent IV**. He was excommunicated and deposed at the Council of Lyon (1245), and forced to make lasting concessions to German princes to win their support against the papacy and the Lombard cities. The conflict was continuing at the time of his death, and was only resolved when **Charles of Anjou** defeated Frederick's son and grandson at Benevento (1266) and Tagliacozzo (1286).

FREDERICK II OF PRUSSIA *see* **Frederick the Great.**

FREDERICK AUGUSTUS I (1670–1733) Elector of Saxony (1694–1733) and, as Augustus II, king of Poland, 1697–1733. He succeeded as Elector of Lutheran Saxony in 1694, then became a Catholic in order to be elected king of Poland in 1697; elected by a minority of Polish nobles, he used his Saxon army to secure his coronation. He entered the **Great Northern War** and was defeated by **Charles XII** of Sweden (1702). Deposed in 1706 and his kingdom occupied until 1709 by Stanislaw Leszczynski, a rival Polish king, he was restored at the treaty of Stockholm, 1719. He was succeeded by **Frederick Augustus II**, his son (Augustus III of Poland).

FREDERICK AUGUSTUS II (1696–1763) Elector of Saxony (1733–63) and, as Augustus III, king of Poland (1733–63). The only legitimate son of **Frederick Augustus I** of Saxony. He married Maria Josepha, daughter of the Emperor Joseph I, in 1719. In 1733 he succeeded as elector of Saxony, and in the same year drove his rival Stanislaw I Leszczynski into exile and was elected King of Poland (as Augustus III) by a minority vote. He supported Austria against Prussia in the War of the Austrian Succession (1740–8) in 1742, and again in 1756 in the **Seven Years' War**. He failed to counter the growing influence of the Czartoryski and Poniatowski families.

FREDERICK WILLIAM (1620–88) Elector of Brandenburg, known as the Great Elector. He succeeded in 1640 and successfully reconstructed his domain after the ravages of the Thirty Years' War; created a standing army after agreement with the Estates; fought France and Sweden, 1674; defeated the Swedes at Fehrbellin, 1675, and concluded the **Peace of Nijmegen**.

FREDERICK WILLIAM I (1688–1740) King of Prussia, son of Frederick I, and father of **Frederick the Great**. After succeeding to the throne in 1713, he reorganized the administration and economy to sustain an army of 83,000 men, and won most of western Pomerania from Sweden under the Treaty of Stockholm, 1720.

FREI, EDUARDO (1911–82) Chilean political leader, and a founder member, in 1935, of the National Falange, later renamed the Christian Democrat Party. He edited a daily newspaper, *El Tarapacá*, 1935–7. He held office as minister of public works, and was president of Chile from 1964 until 1970, when the Christian Democrats were defeated by **Allende** in the presidential election.

FRÉMONT, JOHN CHARLES (1813–90) United States' explorer and mapmaker who headed expeditions to survey the Des Moines River (1841), the route west to Wyoming (1842), the mouth of the Columbia River (1843), and California (1845). He was the Republican Party's nominee for president of the United States, 1856; he was governor of Arizona, 1878–83.

FRIARS During the first decade of the 13th century St Francis (1181–1226) and St Dominic (1170–1221) were independently moved to raise the standard of religious life in Europe by instructing the populace (particularly in the towns) through preaching and example, in order to counteract the growing menace of heresy. The Franciscans (Order of Friars Minor, or Grey Friars) were informally recognized by Pope **Innocent III** in 1209 and formally established in 1223; the Dominicans (Order of Preachers, or Black Friars) were formally established in 1216. The Franciscan St Bonaventura (1221–74) and the Dominican St Thomas Aquinas (1226–74) were among their most prominent early members. Friars took the monastic vows of poverty, chastity and obedience, but differed from monks in two main respects; their convents were bases for preaching tours, not places of permanent residence like monasteries, and they sought education at the newly founded universities. Other 13th-century Orders of friars were the Austin Friars and the Carmelites.

FRISIANS Germanic people. They first entered the coastal provinces of western Germany and the Netherlands in prehistoric times, ousting the resident Celts; after the collapse of Rome, the territory was infiltrated by Angles and **Jutes** on their way to England. The Frisians were conquered and converted to Christianity by **Charlemagne**.

FROBISHER, SIR MARTIN (c.1535–94) Explorer of Canada's northeast coasts, who sailed in 1567 with three ships in search of a Northwest Passage to Asia; he reached Labrador and Baffin Island, but failed to find gold or establish a colony. He became vice-admiral to **Drake** in the West Indies, 1585, was prominent in fighting the Spanish Armada, and was mortally wounded fighting Spanish ships off the coast of France.

FRONDE Complex series of uprisings against the French government under **Mazarin** during the minority of **Louis XIV**. Leaders of the Paris *parlement* were imprisoned in 1648 after violent protests against taxation. They were freed by popular revolt in Paris, supported by a separate rebellion of the nobility in alliance with Spain, which escalated into open warfare. The Fronde disintegrated soon after the victory of the royal armies at Faubourg-St Antoine in 1652.

G

GADSDEN PURCHASE Sale to the United States of some 30,000 square miles of land along the Mexico-Arizona border, required by the US to provide a low pass through mountains for railway construction. The purchase was negotiated by US minister James Gadsden in 1853 at a cost of $10 million.

GAIKWARS Powerful **Maratha** family which made its headquarters in the Baroda district of Gujarat, west-central India, from 1734 to 1947. In 1802 the British established a residency on Baroda to conduct relations between the **East India Company** and the Gaikwar princes.

GAISERIC (428–77) King of the **Vandals**, also known as Genseric. He transported his whole people, said to number 80,000, from Spain to north Africa in 429; sacked Carthage, 439, after defeating the joint armies of Rome's Eastern and Western Empires, and declared independence. By sea he attacked, captured and looted Rome, 455; and fought off two major Roman expeditions (460 and 468).

GALLA Large ethnic group in Ethiopia. Cushitic-speaking camel nomads, in a series of invasions from their homelands in the southeast of the country they migrated north and east, and by the end of the 16th century had reached almost to Eritrea. Since then they have largely been assimilated into, and dominated by, the rival Amharic and Tigrean cultures.

GALLEON Powerful sailing ship developed in the 15th and 16th centuries for Mediterranean and ocean navigation. Larger than the galley, with a ratio of beam to length of 1 to 4 or 5, usually with two decks and four masts (two square-rigged and two lateen), it was heavily armed and used in particular by Spain in fleets across the Atlantic and in the annual voyage from Acapulco to Manila.

GALLIC WARS The military campaigns in which the Roman general **Julius Caesar**, won control of Gaul. As described in his account, *De Bello Gallico*, the conquest took eight years, from 58 to 50 BC; in the first phase, 57–54 BC, Roman authority was fairly easily established, but suppression of a large-scale revolt in 53 BC, led by the Gallic chieftain, Vercingetorix, required all Caesar's skills.

GAMA, VASCO DA (1462–1524) First discoverer of a continuous sea route from Europe to India via the Cape of Good Hope. In 1497–9 he led a Portuguese expedition round Africa to India; a second voyage in 1502 established Portugal as controller of the Indian Ocean and a world power. He died shortly after his arrival to take up an appointment as the Portuguese viceroy in India.

GANDHI, INDIRA (1917–86) Indian prime minister and head of state, 1966–77 and 1980–6. The daughter of **Nehru**, she was elected to the premiership in 1966, and won national elections in 1967 and 1971; she led India in war against Pakistan, 1971. She declared a national emergency in 1975, after an adverse legal decision on her own election. Defeated in the elections of 1977, she was returned to office in 1980 as leader of the Congress I party. She was assassinated in 1986 by Sikh extremists.

GANDHI, MOHENDAS K (1869–1948) Indian independence leader. Born in a strict Hindu community, he studied law in England 1889–92, then worked in South Africa as a lawyer and subsequently as a leader of the civil rights movement of Indian settlers, 1893–1914. Entering politics in India in 1919, he turned the previously ineffectual Indian National Congress into a potent mass organization. He perfected the disruptive techniques of mass disobedience and non-violent non-cooperation; during protest against the Salt Tax (1930) 60,000 followers were imprisoned. Three major campaigns, in 1920–2, 1930–4 and 1940–2, played a major part in accelerating India's progress to Dominion status in 1947. He bitterly opposed partition, and worked incessantly to end the Hindu-Muslim riots and massacres accompanying the emergence of independent India and Pakistan. He was assassinated by a Hindu fanatic.

GARCIA MORENO, GABRIEL (1821–75) Theocratic president of Ecuador, 1860–75. He based his regime on ruthless personal rule and forcible encouragement of the Roman Catholic Church. All education, welfare and much state policy were turned over to clerics; political opposition and alternative religions were suppressed. He encouraged agricultural and economic reform, and Ecuadorian nationalism. He was assassinated.

GARIBALDI, GIUSEPPE (1807–82) Italian patriot and member of **Mazzini**'s Young Italy movement. He was a guerrilla leader in South America, and a founder of an independent Uruguay in her war against Argentina. He established himself as a national hero in 1849 as the defender of the Roman Republic against the French. In 1860 he led the expedition of 'The Thousand' in Sicily, and occupied Naples, thus ensuring the unification of Italy. He had led a victorious force against the Austrians in 1859, and repeated the operation in 1866, but was defeated by the French in his attack on Rome in 1867.

GAUGAMELA Battlefield near the river Tigris, scene of **Alexander the Great**'s most notable victory, in 331 BC, when, greatly outnumbered, his Macedonian cavalry and Thracian javelin-throwers routed the Persian armies of Darius III by brilliant tactics, and opened the way to Babylon and Susa for him.

GAULLE, CHARLES DE (1890–1970) French soldier and statesman. He escaped to London after the French surrender to Germany, 1940; organized the Free French forces and led the French government-in-exile from Algiers, 1943–4. He was first head of the post-war provisional government, 1944–6. In 1953 he withdrew from public life, but returned in 1958 to resolve the political crisis created by the civil war in Algeria; hostilities ceased in 1962. He established the Fifth Republic, becoming its first President, 1959 and presided over France's spectacular economic and political recovery. Resigned in 1969 after an adverse referendum vote on constitutional reform.

GEDYMIN (c.1275–1341) (or Giedymin) Grand Duke of Lithuania, ancestor of the **Jagiello** dynasty. Came to power in 1316, ruling a vast pagan principality based on Vilna. He built the strongest army in eastern Europe to hold his empire in the east and south, while repelling the advances of the Knights of the **Teutonic Order** against the Prussians, who were one of his Lithuanian tribes.

GENERAL MOTORS America's largest industrial manufacturing corporation; in 1988 General Motors' worldwide sales of cars and trucks totalled 8.1 million units.

GENERAL PRIVILEGE Legal document, compiled in 1293, setting out limits of royal power in Aragon and Valencia. Approved, under protest, by King **Peter III** of Aragon, it was a source of acrimony between king and subjects until abolished in 1348 by Peter IV, the Ceremonious, after defeating his nobles at the battle of Epila.

GENGHIS KHAN (c. 1162–1227) Mongol conqueror. According to the anonymous *Secret History of the Mongols* Temujin (his personal name) first became leader of an impoverished central Asian clan. He overcame all rivals, gathering a fighting force of 20,000 men, and by 1206 was acknowledged as Genghis Khan by all the people of the Mongol and Tatar steppes. He invaded northern China, capturing Peking in 1215, and destroyed the Muslim empire of **Khwarizm**, which covered part of central Asia and Persia, between 1216 and 1223.

GEORGE II (1890–1947) King of Greece, 1922–3, but exiled on the formation of the republic in 1923. Restored in 1935, he was again exiled during the Second World War. He returned to Greece in 1947.

GERMAN CONFEDERATION A grouping of 38 independent German states under the presidency of Austria, set up at the **Congress of Vienna** (1815). Superseded by the Frankfurt Parliament in 1848, it was re-established in 1851, and then dissolved by Prussia after the Seven Weeks' War of 1866.

GHAZNAVIDS Afghan dynasty, founded by Sebuktigin, father of **Mahmud of Ghazni**, in 977. At its greatest extent the empire stretched from the Oxus river in central Asia to the Indus river and the Indian Ocean. Under Mahmud's son, Masud (reigned 1037–41), much northern territory was lost to the **Seljuks**; the last Indian possessions were conquered by **Muizzudin Muhammad** in 1186.

GHURIDS Dynasty ruling northwest Afghanistan from the mid-12th to the early 13th century. Under **Muizzudin Muhammad** the empire was extended into northern India, helping the establishment of Muslim rule in the sub-continent.

GIRONDINS Members of a moderate republican party during the French revolution, so named because the leaders came from the Gironde area. Many were guillotined, 31 October 1793, after the group had been overthrown by the rival Jacobins the previous June.

GLADSTONE, WILLIAM EWART (1809–98) British prime minister. Entered Parliament in 1832 as a Tory; president of the Board of Trade, 1843–5, and colonial secretary, 1845–6. He resigned after the repeal of the Corn Laws; later became chancellor of the exchequer, 1853–5 and 1859–66. He led the newly-formed Liberal Party to victory, 1868, and was four times prime minister, 1868–74, 1880–5, 1886 and 1892–4. He was responsible for many military, educational and civil service reforms, and for the Reform Act of 1884; he was repeatedly defeated over attempts to bring abut Irish home rule.

GODUNOV, BORIS FYODOROVICH (c.1551–1605) Tsar of Muscovy. He rose in power and favour at the court of **Ivan IV**, the Terrible, and was appointed guardian of Fyodor, the Tsar's retarded son, when Fyodor succeeded in 1584. Godunov banished his enemies and became effective ruler, and was himself elected tsar when Fyodor died without heirs in 1598. Plagued by war, pestilence, famine and constant opposition from the boyars (the old Russian nobility), he was unable to fulfil his desired programme of social, legal, diplomatic and military reforms. His sudden death during civil war with a pretender known as 'the false Dmitri' precipitated Russia into a devastating 'time of troubles'.

GOEBBELS, PAUL JOSEPH (1897–1945) **Hitler**'s Minister of Propaganda. He entered journalism in 1921, and in 1926 was appointed by Hitler as district administrator of the National Socialist German Workers' Party (NSDAP), becoming its head of propaganda in 1928. On Hitler's accession to power (1933) he was appointed minister for public enlightenment and propaganda, controlling the press, radio, films, publishing, theatre, music and the visual arts. He committed suicide, with his wife and six children, in Hitler's besieged Berlin bunker.

GOETHE, JOHANN WOLFGANG VON (1749–1832) Most famous of all German poets, novelists and playwrights, Minister of State to the Duke of Saxe-Weimar, 1775, and one of the outstanding figures of European literature. His early novel, *The Sorrows of Young Werther*, 1774, expressed the reaction against the Enlightenment, the sensation of 'emotion running riot' and the conflict between the artist and society. He returned to classicism after a visit to Italy, 1786–8, which affected his whole life and work; from this period onwards his work (*Faust*, part I and part II, 1808, 1832, *Wilhelm Meister*, 1791–1817, *Tasso*, 1789) has a philosophical content which lifts it out of time and place and gives it a universal quality.

GOKHALE, GOPAL KRISHNA (1866–1915) Indian independence leader. He resigned in 1902 from a professorship of history and political economy at Ferguson College, Poona, to enter politics; advocated moderate protest and constitutional reform. He was President of the Indian National Congress, 1905, and founder of the Servants of India Society, dedicated to the alleviation of poverty and service to the underprivileged.

GOLDEN BULL OF 1356 Constitution of the Holy Roman Empire, promulgated by the Emperor **Charles IV**; confirmed, *inter alia*, that succession to the German throne would continue to be determined by seven electors, convened by the Archbishop of Mainz, but that henceforth the electoral lands and powers would be indivisible, and inheritable only by the elder son, thus removing confusion over the right to vote; it sanctioned the primacy of the territorial princes under loose imperial suzerainty. It also rejected traditional papal claims to rule during periods when the throne was vacant.

GOLDEN HORDE Western portion of the Mongol empire, also known as the Kipchak khanate. Founded by **Batu** c. 1242, it dominated southern Russia to the end of the 14th century. It was finally broken up by **Tamerlane** to form three **Tatar** khanates: Kazan, Astrakhan and the Crimea.

GOLD STANDARD Monetary system in which the value of currency in issue is legally tied to a certain quantity of gold. During the last quarter of the 19th century virtually all major trading nations adopted this policy and most attempted to return to it after the break caused by the First World War; this attempt was abandoned in the slump of the 1930s. The US dollar finally came off gold in 1971.

GÖMBÖS, GYULA (1886–1936) Hungarian prime minister. In 1919 he set up a proto-fascist movement and helped organize the overthrow of the Communist government. At first he opposed the conservative premier, István Bethlen (1921–31), but joined his administration in 1929 and in 1932 was swept to power by the 'radical right' movement. He advocated a reactionary, anti-Semitic programme and alliance with Germany and Italy, but was restrained by the head of state, Admiral Horthy.

GOMES, FERNÃO 15th-century Portuguese merchant who in 1469 was granted a monopoly to explore the West African coast and keep all trading profits. Gomes and his captains explored as far as the Congo River, and prepared the way for the voyages of **Vasco da Gama** to Indian in 1497–9.

GOMULKA, WLADYSLAW (1905–82) Polish Communist leader. A youth organizer for the banned Communist Party, 1926, and a wartime underground fighter, he was stripped of Party membership in 1949 after incurring the displeasure of Stalin, but re-admitted in 1956 to become First Secretary of the Central Committee. Resistance to his regime erupted in riots in 1968; he was deposed and retired in 1970.

GORBACHEV MIKHAIL (1931–) Soviet statesman. After studying law at Moscow university (1953) he headed the Young Communist League in his native Stavropol. He became agriculture secretary of the central committee of the Soviet Communist Party (1978); a full member of the Politburo (1980); general secretary of the Soviet Communist Party (1985–91) and president of the Soviet Union (1988–91). He promoted economic and social reforms programs known as *glasnost* (openness) and *perestroika* (restructuring), and negotiated two arms limitation treaties (1987, 1990), effectively ending the Cold War. Opposed to the breakup of the Soviet Union, he met with growing opposition which brought about his resignation in 1991.

GORDON, CHARLES GEORGE (1833–85) British general, first distinguished for bravery in the Crimean War (1854–6). He volunteered for service in China, where his exploits in the 'Arrow' war, the T'ai-p'ing Rebellion and the burning of the emperors Summer Palace earned him the nickname 'Chinese Gordon'. In 1884 he was sent to the Sudan (where he had earlier been Governor-General) to evacuate British troops from Khartoum; he was besieged and killed by Sudanese followers of **Mohammed Ahmed al-Mahdi.**

GORGIAS OF LEONTINI (c. 483–c. 376 BC) Ancient Greek rhetorician, noted for his poetic language and carefully balanced clauses. In his treatise *On Nature* he argued the essential non-existence, unknowability and incommunicability of Being. He was portrayed with respect by **Plato** in *Gorgias*.

GORM King of Denmark, father of **Harald Bluetooth**; died after 935.

GOTHIC Relating to the art and language of the **Ostrogoths** and **Visigoths**. During the Renaissance, the word was used to typify the barbarism of the Middle Ages; it still refers to the style of church architecture, with characteristic pointed arches, predominant from the 12th to the 15th century, and to the painting and sculpture associated with it.

GOTT, BENJAMIN (1762–1840) English manufacturer of woollen cloth and philanthropist. In 1793 he established a woollen mill in Leeds, introducing an improved mechanical cloth-cutting device in spite of much hostility.

GOTTFRIED VON STRASSBURG German medieval poet, author of *Tristan*, the classic version of the story of Tristan and Isolde. He lived and worked in the late 12th and early 13th centuries.

GOULART, DR JOAO (1918–76) Brazilian political leader. He joined the Brazilian labour party, Partido Trabalhista, in 1945 and became national party director in 1951, minister of labour and commerce, 1953–4, vice-president of Brazil, 1956, was re-elected in 1061 and became president that year. He was deposed in a military *coup d'état*, 1964.

GOVERNMENT OF INDIA ACT British Act of Parliament of 1935 embodying a number of constitutional reforms, including 'provincial autonomy' and a federal structure at the centre. Only the provisions relating to the provinces were implemented, the proposals for federation being rejected by the Indian political parties.

GRANADA, KINGDOM OF Last foothold of the Muslims in Spain. Ruled by the **Nasrid** dynasty, 1238–1492, it prospered by welcoming Moorish refugees from Seville, Valencia and Murcia; it built one of Islam's most famous architectural achievements, the Alhambra (Red Fortress). The kingdom was finally conquered by Christian forces in 1492.

GRANT, ULYSSES SIMPSON (1822–85) 18th president of the United States, 1869–77. He was commander-in-chief of the Union armies during the American Civil War. His administration (Republican) was marked by corruption and bitter partisanship between the political parties.

GREAT ELECTOR *see* **Frederick William, Elector of Brandenburg**

GREAT FEAR Series of rural panics, spreading through the French countryside between 20 July and 6 August 1789, at the onset of the French revolution. Following a series of peasant disorders, during which stores of grain were looted and châteaux burned, rumours of invasion by armed brigands spread in five main currents covering the greater part of the country, which stimulated further disorders that petered out as suddenly as they had begun.

GREAT NORTHERN WAR Struggle between Sweden and Russia, 1700–21, mainly for control of the Baltic. **Charles XII** of Sweden at first defeated an alliance of Russia, Denmark, Poland and Saxony (1700–6), but was heavily defeated at Poltava by **Peter the Great** of Russia in 1709. This advantage was lost when Turkey declared war on Russia in 1710, and fighting continued in Poland and Scandinavia until Charles' death in 1718. In the final settlement Sweden lost Livonia and Karelia to Russia (which gained permanent access to the Baltic Sea), and abandoned its claims to be a great power.

GREAT SCHISM A political split in the Catholic Church, lasting from 1378 to 1417, during which rival popes – one in Rome, the other in Avignon – attempted to exert authority. The result of a serious split among cardinals and high churchmen on ecclesiastical reform, and the political influence of the French monarchy, the Schism was resolved by the Council of Constance, 1414–17.

GREGORY I 'THE GREAT' (c. 540–604) Pope, saint and one of the Fathers of the Christian Church. During his papacy (590–604), he strengthened and reorganized the Church administration, reformed the liturgy, promoted monasticism, asserted the temporal power of the papacy, extended Rome's influence in the West and sent St Augustine of Canterbury on his mission to convert the English.

GREGORY VII (c. 1020–85) Pope and saint, born in north Italy and given the name Hildebrand. He served under Pope Gregory VI during the Pope's exile in Germany after deposition by the Emperor **Henry III**. He was recalled to Rome by Pope **Leo IX**, and thereafter was often the power behind the papal throne. He was made a cardinal by **Alexander II** (1061–73) and elected by acclaim as his successor. From 1075 he was engaged in the contest over **lay investiture** with Emperor **Henry IV** , whom he excommunicated in 1076; after absolving him at Canossa in 1077, he re-excommunicated him after fresh attacks. Gregory was driven from Rome in 1084. He was canonized in 1606.

GRIJALVA, JUAN DE (c. 1489–1527) Spanish explorer. Sailing along the coast of Mexico, where he discovered the River Grijalva (named after him) in 1518, he was probably the first of the *conquistadores* to hear of the rich Aztec civilization of the interior.

GRUFFYDD AP LLEWELYN (d.1063) Briefly king of all Wales. He challenged the authority of existing dynasties holding power over Welsh kingdoms; seized control in Gwynedd in the northwest, Deheubarth in the southwest, and for a short period the whole country; he devastated the borderland with England.

GUELPH and GHIBELLINE The two great rival political factions of medieval Italy, reflecting the rivalry of Guelph dukes of Saxony and Bavaria and the **Hohenstaufen**. The names Guelph and Ghibelline came to designate support for the papal (Guelph) side against the imperial (Ghibelline) side in the struggle between the **Papacy** and the **Holy Roman Empire**.

GUEST, SIR JOSIAH (1785–1852) British industrialist. He created an improved smelting process at the family ironworks at Dowlais (near Merthyr Tydfil, Wales) and raised its annual iron production to 65,000 tons, mostly in the form of rails for the new railways.

GUEVARA, ERNESTO 'CHE' (1928–67) South American revolutionary leader, born in Argentina. He qualified as a doctor of medicine, 1953; became chief aide to **Fidel Castro** in his successful Cuban revolution, 1959; wrote *Guerrilla Warfare*, 1960 and *Episodes of the Revolutionary War*, 1963. He was killed in Bolivia, trying to establish a guerrilla base there.

GUGGENHEIM, MEYER (1826–1905) Founder of modern American metal-mining industry; born in Switzerland, he emigrated to the United States in 1847. In the early 1880s he bought control of two Colorado copper mines, and quickly built up a worldwide network of mines, exploration companies, smelters and refineries. With his son Daniel (1856–1930) he merged all the family interests in 1901 into the American Smelting & Refining Company.

GUPTA Imperial dynasty, ruling in northern India from the 4th to the 6th centuries AD. It first rose to prominence under Chandragupta I, ruling over Magadha and parts of Uttar Pradesh, (c. 319–35). Its power was extended and reinforced under **Samudragupta** (reigned c. 335–75), **Chandragupta II** (c. 375–45) and Kumaragupta (c. 415–54). The dynasty was later weakened by domestic unrest and **Hun** invasion, and effectively eliminated as a major political force by 510.

GURJARAS Central Asian tribe, reaching India with the **Hun** invasions of the 4th and 5th centuries AD. They settled in Rajasthan, in western India, and were reputed ancestors of the **Pratiharas**.

GUSTAVUS I VASA (c. 1496–1560) King of Sweden (1523–60), founder of the Vasa dynasty. He fought in Sweden's 1517–18 rebellion against Denmark, was interned but returned in 1520 to lead another rebellion against Denmark. He was elected king of Sweden in 1523, thus breaking up the **Union of Kalmar**. He introduced the **Lutheran** Reformation; and in 1 544 persuaded the Diet to make the monarchy hereditary in his Vasa family line.

GUSTAVUS II ADOLPHUS (1594–1632) King of Sweden, grandson of **Gustavus I Vasa**. He succeeded to the throne in 1611 and made Sweden a major political and military power. He entered the Thirty Years' War on the side of the Protestants, 1630, and conquered most of Germany. He was killed at the battle of Lützen.

GUTIANS (Guti) Ancient mountain people from the Zagros range, east of Mesopotamia. They destroyed the empire of Akkad, c. 2230 BC, and exercised sporadic sovereignty over much of Babylonia for the next century. Traditionally they were eclipsed as a history force after the defeat of the last king, Tirigan, by Utu-Khegal of Uruk, c. 2130 BC. The Gutians were primarily remembered in later tradition as barbarians.

GUZMÁN BLANCO, ANTONIO (1829–99) President of Venezuela. He was appointed special finance commissioner to negotiate loans from Great Britain, seized control of the government in 1870; as head of the Regeneration party was elected constitutional president, 1873; ruled as absolute dictator until 1877, and again 1879–84 and 1886–8, laying the main foundations of modern Venezuela, and accumulating a vast personal fortune. Ousted by a *coup d'état* during one of his visits to Europe, he died in Paris.

HABSBURGS Major European royal and imperial dynasty from the 15th to the 20th century. The ascendancy of the family began in 13th century Austria. Frederick V Habsburg was crowned Holy Roman Emperor in 1452, as Frederick III; the title remained a family possession until the Empire was dissolved in 1806. At their peak, under Charles V (Charles I of Spain), Habsburg realms stretched from eastern Europe to the New World; after Charles' death, the house split into the Spanish line, which died out in 1700, and the Austrian line, which remained in power – after 1740 as the House of Habsburg-Lorraine – until 1918.

HADRIAN IV (c. 1100–59) Pope 1154–9. Born Nicholas Breakspear, and the only English Pope, he renewed the initiative of the papacy in the spirit of **Gregory VII**, notably in the incident of Besançon, when he claimed that the imperial crown was held from the Pope. He expelled the heretic **Arnold of Brescia** from Rome.

HADRIAN, PUBLIUS AELIUS (AD 76–138) Roman emperor. Adopted by **Trajan** as his son, whom he succeeded in 117. He abandoned the policy of eastern expansion in order to consolidate frontiers and initiated far-reaching military, legal and administrative reforms; his fortifications in Britain and Syria still stand. He travelled widely in the empire, encouraging the spread of Greco-Roman civilization and culture.

HAFSIDS Dynasty of **Berber** origin, ruling Tunisia and eastern Algeria c. 1229–1574. The most famous ruler, Mustansir (1249–77), used the title of caliph; his diplomacy averted danger from the Crusade of **Louis IX** and extended his influence into Morocco and Spain.

HAIDAR ALI (1722–82) Muslim ruler of Mysore, southern India. He created the first Indian army equipped with European firearms and artillery. He deposed the local rajah and seized the throne, c. 1761. He defeated the British several times between 1766 and 1780, but finally lost in the three battles of Porto Novo, Pollilu and Sholinghar. Before his death he implored his son **Tipu** to make peace with the invaders.

HAIG, DOUGLAS (1861–1928) 1st Earl Haig. British field marshal, commander-in-chief of the British forces in Flanders and France 1915–18, during the First World War. His strategy of attrition on the Somme (1916) and in Flanders (1917), especially at the third battle of Ypres (or Passchendaele), resulted in enormous British casualties.

HAILE SELASSIE I (1892–1975) Emperor of Ethiopia. A close relative of Emperor **Menelik II** (1889–1913), he was appointed to provincial governorships from 1908, became regent and heir apparent to Menelik's daughter Zauditu in 1916. He took Ethiopia into the **League of Nations** in 1923, and became emperor in 1930, introducing bicameral Parliament the following year. He was driven out by the Italian occupation of 1936–41 but he led the reconquest, with British aid, and began to modernize the country. He survived a coup threat in 1960, but in 1974 news of the famine in the Wollo district and an armed mutiny provoked a revolution which deposed him. He died under house arrest.

HAJJ UMAR, AL- (1794–1864) West African Tukolor warrior-mystic, founder of the Muslim empire based on Masina in the western Sudan (now in the republic of Mali). He became a member of the newly-founded militant religious order, the Tijaniyya. He made a pilgrimage to Mecca in 1826 and returned inspired to propagate Islam in the western Sudan. In 1852 he embarked upon a great and bloody *jihad* (holy war) which resulted in the conquest of much of the western Sudan. The campaign brought him into violent conflict with the French, who were expanding up the Senegal river. He was killed in battle. By the end of the 19th century his empire was finally conquered by the French.

HAKKA North Chinese people who migrated south under the Sung dynasty (1126–1279) to Kwangtung and Fukien where they remained a distinct social group, living in separate communities, usually in poor uplands. They were involved in many bitter communal feuds in the 18th and 19th centuries, culminating in the Hakka-Punti war in the 1850s. Many emigrated after the T'ai-p'ing rebellion, and they are now widely spread throughout East Asia.

HALLSTATT Early Celtic Iron Age culture, flourishing in central Europe c. 750–450 BC, named after an Austrian village in the Salzkammergut, where an archaeologically important cemetery was found in the 19th century. The culture was notable for elaborate burials, in which the dead person was placed in a four-wheeled chariot, of which examples have been found from the Upper Danube region to Vix in Burgundy.

HAMAGUCHI, OSACHI (1870–1931) Japanese statesman. Official of the finance ministry, 1895–1924, and finance minister 1924–6. In 1927 he was elected leader of the new Rikken Minseito (Constitutional Democratic) Party, and became Japanese prime minister in 1929. He decreed drastic deflationary policies, but was assassinated before they could take effect. The army forced his colleagues to resign, thus bringing democratic government to an end.

HAMDANIDS Bedouin dynasty controlling Mosul and Aleppo, 905–1004; renowned warriors and patrons of Arab art and learning.

HAMMADIDS North African Berber dynasty, a branch of the **Zirids**. In the reign of the Zirid leader Badis Ibn al-Mansur (995–1016) they gained control of part of Algeria; in 1067, under attack from the **Fatimids** and their Bedouin allies, they established themselves in the port of Bejaia (Bougia), and developed a successful trading empire until conquered by the **Almohads** in 1152.

HAMMARSKJÖLD, DAG (1905–61) Swedish and international statesman. Son of a Swedish prime minister, he entered politics in 1930 and became deputy foreign minister in 1951. Elected as secretary-general of the **United Nations** in 1953, he greatly extended the influence both of the UN and of its secretary-general striving to reduce the tensions caused by decolonization in Africa, particularly in the Congo (1960–1), where he was killed in an air crash.

HAMMURABI King of Babylon, reigning 1728–1686 BC. He succeeded his father, Sin-Mabullit, and extended his small kingdom (originally only 80 miles long and 20 miles wide) to unify all Mesopotamia under Babylonian rule. He published a collection of laws on a basalt stele, 8 feet high, now in the Louvre museum.

HAM NGHI (1870–c. 1940) Emperor of Vietnam. He reached the throne in 1884 after intense intrigue following the death of his uncle, the emperor Tu Duc; at the instigation of his regents, Nguyen Van Tuong and Thou That Thuyet, he led a revolt against the French, 1885; he fled after its failure, was deposed in 1886, captured and exiled to Algeria.

HAN Chinese imperial dynasty, ruling from 206 BC to AD 9 (Former Han), and AD 25–220 (Later Han); see pp. 80–1.

HAN FU-CHÜ (1890–1938) Military officer who served under **Feng Yü-hsiang**, 1912–28. He was appointed governor of Honan in 1928; defecting from Feng in his confrontation with **Chiang Kai-shek**, in 1929, he controlled Shantung from 1930 to 1938 and brought it under the control of Nanking. In 1937 the Japanese invaded Shantung; he put up only token resistance and was executed for dereliction of duty the following year.

HANNIBAL (247–183 BC) Most famous Carthaginian general, son of another great soldier, Hamilcar Barca. He was commander-in-chief in Spain aged 26; after the outbreak of the Second **Punic war** against Rome (218–201) he led 40,000 troops, with elephants, over the Alps to smash the Roman armies at Lake Trasimene, 217, and Cannae, 216. Forced to abandon Italy in 203 as Rome had attacked Carthage itself, he was finally defeated at Zama in 202 and later driven into exile. He committed suicide.

HANSEATIC LEAGUE Association of medieval German cities and merchant groups which became a powerful economic and political force in northern Europe. With a centre for meetings in the city of Lübeck, the members established an important network of Baltic trade, and a string of commercial bases stretching from Novgorod to London and from Bergen to Bruges. In its heyday during the 14th century the Hansa included well over 100 towns; its influence gradually faded with the emergence of powerful competitor states, and the last meeting of the Diet was held in Lübeck in 1669.

HARALD BLUETOOTH (d.c. 985) King of Denmark from c. 940. He accepted the introduction of Christianity into his kingdom, and strengthened its central organization; he successfully defeated German and Norwegian attacks on Denmark, unifying its disparate elements.

HARALD I FINEHAIR (c. 860–c. 940) First king claiming sovereignty over all Norway, in the second half of the 9th century, the son of Halfdan the Black, ruler of a part of southeast Norway and a member of the ancient Swedish Yngling dynasty, whom he succeeded when very young. His conquests culminated in the battle of Hafrsfjord, c. 900; many defeated chiefs fled to Britain and possibly Iceland. The best account of his exploits is given in Snorri Sturlson's 13th century saga, the *Heimskringla*.

HARALD II GREYCLOAK (d.c. 970) Norwegian king, son of **Erik Bloodaxe**. He overthrew his half-brother, Haakon the Good, c. 961, ruling oppressively, with his brothers, until c. 970. He is credited with establishing the first Christian missions in Norway. He was killed in battle against an alliance of local nobles and his former supporter, **Harald Bluetooth**.

HARA TAKASHI (1856–1921) First 'commoner' (i.e. untitled) prime minister of modern Japan. Graduated from Tokyo university into journalism and then entered foreign service in 1882. He became ambassador to Korea in 1897, chief editor of the Osaka *Mainichi* newspaper in 1899. He helped to found the Rikken-Seiyukai (Friends of Constitutional Government) Party, 1900, and built it into an American-style party machine, meanwhile rising to ministerial and finally prime ministerial rank in 1918. He was assassinated by a right-wing fanatic after opposing the use of Japanese troops in Siberia.

HARKORT, FRIEDRICH (FRITZ) (1793–1880) Pioneer entrepreneur in the German engineering industry. In 1918 Harkort and Kamp, in partnership with Thomas (an English engineer), established works producing textile machinery and steam engines at Wetter in the Ruhr district. The plant was later expanded to include the puddling process. Harkort twice visited England to recruit skilled mechanics. He was a pioneer in the construction of steamships on the Weser and the Rhine, and was also a leading advocate of railway building in Germany.

HARSHA (c. 590–c. 647) Indian ruler, second son of a king in Punjab. He ultimately exercised loose imperial power over most of northern India. Converted from **Hinduism** to **Buddhism**, he was the first to open diplomatic relations between India and China (c. 641); his court, at Kanauj, his early years and his model administration are described in Bana's poem *The Deeds of Harsha*, and the writings of the Chinese pilgrim Hsüan Tsang.

HARUN AL-RASHID (c. 763–806) Fifth caliph of the **Abbasid** dynasty, immortalized in *The Thousand and One Nights*. He inherited the throne in 786, ruling territories from northwest India to the western Mediterranean; his reign saw the beginning of the disintegration of the **caliphate**.

HASHEMITES Direct or collateral descendants of the prophet **Mohammed**, who was himself a member of the house of Hashem, a division of the Quraysh tribe. In the 20th century, Hussein ibn Ali, descendant of a long line of Hashemite *sharifs* or local rulers of Mecca, and King of Hejaz, 1916–24, founded the modern Hashemite dynasty, carried on by his sons, King Feisal of Iraq and King Abdullah of Jordan.

HASSAN II (1929–) King of Morocco, 17th monarch of the Alaouite dynasty. The son of **Mohammed V**, he became commander-in-chief of the Royal Moroccan Army in 1957. Succeeding to the throne in 1961, he held the posts of prime minister, 1961–3 and 1965–7, minister of defence, 1972–3, and commander-in-chief of the army from 1972. He established strong monarchical government, and was the main force behind the abortive attempt to partition the former Spanish Sahara between Morocco and Mauritania.

HASTINGS, FRANCIS RAWDON-HASTINGS (1754–1826) 1st Marquis. Early governor-general of Bengal. He landed in India, 1813; defeated the Gurkhas, 1816; conquered the Maratha states and cemented British control east of the Sutlej river. He purchased Singapore, 1819, but resigned under a financial cloud, 1823; he was Governor of Malta 1824.

HASTINGS, WARREN (1732–1818) First governor-general of British India, 1774–85. He carried out important administrative and legal reforms, but was impeached on corruption charges, 1788; he was finally acquitted, after a long and famous trial, in 1795.

HAUSA West African people, organized from about the 11th century into a loose groupings of states centred to the west of Lake Chad. In the 16th century Kano became the greatest of the Hausa cities, but the Hausaland region only came under unified control after conquest by the Fulani in the early 19th century. They are now one of the largest ethnic groups in Nigeria.

HAVEL, VACLAV (1936–) Czech playwright and politician. Widely regarded as the leading Czech playwright of his generation, he commented on the struggles of contemporary intellectuals in his plays. His works were banned after the Soviet invasion (1968), but remained available abroad. In the 1970s he became spokesman for human rights groups and was imprisoned. After the resignation of the entire politburo, he formally entered politics to become the first president of an independent Czechoslovakia (1989) in the 'Velvet Revolution'. In January 1993 he was elected president of the new Czech Republic.

HAWLEY-SMOOT TARIFF United States tariff, passed in 1930, which set the highest import duties in American history, attracted immediate retaliation from European governments, and is considered to be one of the factors responsible for deepening the Great Depression.

HAY, JOHN (1838–1905) US secretary of state (1898–1905). A skilful diplomat, he is best known for his Open Door Policy in China (1900). He also helped negotiate the end of the Spanish-American war (1898), was active in the decision to retain the Philippines, thus marking the US as a major imperialist power, and completed the second **Hay-Pauncefote Treaty** (1901), granting the US exclusive rights to build a canal across the Isthmus of Panama. He assisted in diplomatic efforts to assure Panamanian independence and the beginning of canal construction (1903).

HAY-PAUNCEFOTE TREATY Composite name for two Anglo-American agreements, signed in 1900 and 1901, freeing the US from a previous commitment to international control of any projected Central American canal. It freed US hands for the building of the Panama canal, which was completed in 1914.

HAYES, RUTHERFORD B. (1822–93) 19th president of the United States, and the first chief executive to say openly that an isthmian canal must be American-owned. This pronouncement correlates with the beginning of a programme of naval expansion.

HEAVENLY PRINCIPLE SECT (T'ien-li chiao) Secret sectarian movement connected with the **White Lotus** society, with a large following during the last 18th century in northern China (Hopei, Honan, Shantung), led by Lin Ch'ing and Le wen-ch'eng, who began a rebellion in Honan in 1813. A small group infiltrated Peking and entered the palace.

HEGIRA (hijra) Arabic word for 'emigration', and the starting date of Muslim era. By order of **Omar I**, the second caliph, in AD 639, Islamic letters, treaties, proclamations and events were to be dated by reference to the day, 16 July 622, on which the Prophet **Mohammed** migrated from Mecca to Medina.

HELLENISM Culture, philosophy and spirit of ancient Greece, spread across Asia and across Europe through the Roman adoption of Greek models; through thought and art, it touched Buddhism, Christianity, Hinduism and Islam. It was revived in the western world in the Renaissance and other renaissances. It is often associated with humanism, rationality and beauty of form.

HELLENISTIC The era from 323 to 30 BC when the eastern Mediterranean and the Near East were dominated by dynasties and state governments founded by the successors of **Alexander the Great**.

HENRICIANS Followers of Henry of Lausanne, an itinerant preacher of southern France in the 12th century, whose criticisms of the Church followed those of the **Petrobrusians** and were transmitted to the more numerous and better organized **Waldensians**.

HENRY II (1133–89) King of England. Grandson of Henry I, he became Duke of Normandy in 1150 and Count of Anjou in 1151. He married Eleanor of Aquitaine in 1152 after her repudiation by Louis VII of France. He succeeded to the English throne in 1154; in his own right and that of his wife, he ruled over domains extending from Ireland to the Pyrenees and Mediterranean. He was noted for his expansion of the judicial and administrative authority of the English crown; his generally successful reign was marred by quarrels with Thomas Becket, Archbishop of Canterbury, and with his own family.

HENRY II (1333–79) King of Castile, 1369–79. The natural son of Alfonso XI, Henry drove his brother Pedro (1356–69) from the throne with French aid and founded the Trastámara dynasty, which continued until 1504.

HENRY III (1027–56) German king 1039–56, and emperor 1046–56. He brought Church reform to Rome at the Synod of Sutri, 1046, and appointed a succession of Germans – notably **Leo IX** – to the papacy.

HENRY IV (1050–1106) German emperor, son of **Henry III** and Agnes of Poitou. He succeeded in 1056 under his mother's regency. He broke with Pope **Gregory VII** over the investiture issue in 1075, was excommunicated and declared deposed by him, but restored after performing penance to the Pope at Canossa in 1077; he was excommunicated again in 1080. He appointed Clement III as anti-Pope in 1084, but was outmanoeuvred by Pope **Urban II** and his position was weakened by the revolts of his sons Conrad and the future emperor, **Henry V**. He died after defeating Henry at Visé, near Liège.

HENRY IV (1533–1601) King of France, 1589–1610, son of Antoine, King of Navarre. He married Marguerite of Valois, daughter of the French king, **Henry II**, in 1572. He emerged as Protestant leader in the French wars of religion, and was excommunicated, 1585. Reconciled with King Henry III in 1589, he abjured the Protestant faith in 1593 and was crowned king in 1594. In 1598 he signed the **Edict of Nantes**, granting toleration to French Protestants. He married Marie de' Medici, 1600; authorized **Jesuits** to reopen colleges in Paris, 1603. He was assassinated.

HENRY V (1387–1442) King of England, son of **Henry IV**, whom he succeeded in 1413. In 1415 he reopened the **Hundred Years' War** in support of his claims to the French throne; won the battle of Agincourt, 1415, and conquered Normandy, 1419. Under the Treaty of Troyes he married Catherine of Valois and became heir to the French king, Charles VI. Renewed war, 1421, the year before his death.

HENRY VI (1165–97) Son of **Frederick I Barbarossa**, he was chosen as German king in 1169; married Constance, daughter of **Roger II** of Sicily in 1186, and inherited Roger's kingdom in 1189; crowned emperor in 1911, after Frederick's death on the Third **Crusade**. The ransom of Richard I, whom he held prisoner, 1193–4, enabled him to overcome internal opposition in the Lower Rhineland and Saxony led by **Duke Henry**, and then to finance his conquest of Sicily after the death of the rival claimant, King Tancred, in 1194. He died of malaria while preparing a crusade. Because his son **Frederick II** was then aged only two years, his death caused a succession dispute in the Empire.

HENRY VII (1457–1509) King of England. He became head of the royal House of Lancaster which challenged their cousins, the House of York, for the crown of England; exiled until 1485, when he defeated and killed the Yorkist, Richard III, he then became king and ended the civil war (**Wars of the Roses**). He founded the **Tudor** dynasty, which lasted until 1603, creating a strong central government in England after almost a century of disruption.

HENRY VIII (1491–1547) King of England, son of **Henry VII**, succeeding in 1509. His desire for a male heir caused his search for a means to declare his first marriage, to Catherine of Aragon, invalid; after papal refusal, and non-recognition of his second marriage in 1533 to Anne Boleyn, Parliament passed the Act of Supremacy, 1534, declaring Henry head of the English Church; monasteries were suppressed (1536, 1539). Wales was brought into legal union with England, 1534–6.

HENRY, DUKE OF SAXONY (c. 1130–95) Known as 'the Lion'. He spent his early years fighting for his father's duchies. He was granted Saxony in 1142 but had to wait until 1156 for Bavaria; founded Munich in 1157 and Lübeck in 1159. Stripped of his lands after breaking with **Frederick I Barbarossa**, 1179–80, he was twice exiled, 1181–5 and 1189–90, but was reconciled with Emperor **Henry VI** in 1194.

HENRY THE NAVIGATOR (1394–1460) Portuguese prince, third son of John I and Philippa of Lancaster. He helped in the capture of Ceuta, Morocco, in 1415, and at the age of 26, was made Grand Master of Portugal's crusading Order of Christ. Thereafter, he devoted much of his life to the encouragement of maritime trade and discovery, to the organization of voyages to west Africa and to occasional crusading operations in Morocco.

HERACLIAN DYNASTY Byzantine dynasty, ruling from AD 610 to 711, founded by emperor Heraclius (610–41 – and ending with Justinian II (685–95, and again 705–11).

HERACLIUS (c. 575–641) Eastern Roman emperor. The son of a governor of Africa, in 610 he seized the crown from emperor Phocas; fought and defeated the Persians, 622–8; restored the True Cross to Jerusalem, 630; persecuted the **Jews**, 632. His armies were beaten by Muslim Arabs in 636, and Syria and Palestine (640) and Egypt (642) lost to Islam. In the meantime he restored the administration of the remaining provinces and laid the foundations for the medieval Byzantine state.

HERDER, JOHANN GOTTFRIED VON (1744–1803) German critic, linguist and philosopher who wrote on the origins of language, poetry and aesthetics. he was a leading figure in the literary movement known as *Sturm und Drang*. He made a famous collection of German songs (*Volkslieder*, 1778–9), wrote the *Essay on the Origin of Language* (1722), and at Weimar, where he became superintendent of schools in 1776, *Reflections on the Philosophy of the History of Mankind* (1178–91).

HEREDIA, PEDRO DE (c. 1500–54) Spanish soldier who founded Cartagena in modern Colombia in 1533, and several other New World cities. He amassed a vast fortune through his many expeditions to the interior.

HERERO Bantu-speaking peoples of southwest Africa, mostly in central Namibia and Botswana.

HERERO REVOLT A protest which broke out in 1904 against German colonial oppression of the Herero and other peoples of southwest Africa. In 1907, when the risings ended, over 65,000 Hereros out of an original 80,000 had been killed, starved in concentration camps or driven into the Kalahari Desert to die.

HERNANDEZ DE CORDOBA, FRANCISCO Name of two Spanish soldier-explorers active in the New World at the beginning of the 16th century. The first, born c. 1475, went in 1514 to the Isthmus of Panama with Pedro Arias de Avila, and in 1524 was sent to seize Nicaragua from its rightful discoverer, Gil González de Avila; after finding the towns of Granada and León and exploring Lake Nicaragua he defected to **Cortés**, and was executed by a rival in 1526. His namesake went to Cuba with Velázquez in 1511 and later commanded the expedition that coasted Yucatán and made the first recorded European contact with **Mayan** civilization; he died in 1517.

HEROD ANTIPAS (21 BC–AD 39) Tetrarch of Galilee during the lifetime of **Jesus**.The son of Herod the Great, he inherited part of his father's kingdom under the Roman suzerainty, c. 4 BC. He was goaded into beheading John the Baptist, but later refused to pass judgement on Jesus himself.

HERODOTUS (c. 484–c. 420 BC) Greek writer, known as 'the father of history'. He travelled widely in Asia, Egypt and eastern Europe; his *Histories*, a history of the Greco-Persian wars and the events preceding them, is one of the world's first major prose works, incorporating many vivid and, to contemporaries, almost incredible travellers' tales; modern research has sometimes shown even the wildest of them to contain an element of truth.

HIDEYOSHI *see* **Toyotomi**

HINDENBURG, PAUL VON (1847–1934) German soldier, president of Germany 1925–34. Recalled from retirement in 1914 to take command in east Prussia after the Russian invasion, he won the victory of Tannenberg, and the first and second battles of the Masurian Lakes (1914–15). Appointed a field-marshal and supreme commander of all German armies, 1916, he became virtual dictator of German domestic policy, too, until the armistice. As President he was persuaded to appoint **Hitler** as Chancellor in 1933.

HINDENBURG LINE Fortified line on the Western Front in the First World War, taken up by German armies following the battle of the Somme in 1916. A formidable defence system, it was eventually pierced in September 1918 by the British and French forces.

HINDUISM Predominant religion of India; all-embracing in its forms, capable of including eternal observances and their rejfection, animal sacrifice and refusal to take any form of life, extreme polytheism and high monotheism.

HIPPOCRATES (c. 460–c. 377 BC) Ancient Greek physician, traditionally regarded in the West as the father of medicine. He believed in the wholeness of the body as an organism, in the close observation and recording of case-histories, and in the importance of diet and climate. The works making up the Hippocratic Collection, forming the library of the medical school at Cos, where he taught, reflect the continuing effects of his work. The Hippocratic Oath is still used as a guide to conduct by the medical profession.

HIPPODAMUS OF MILETUS Ancient Greek architect who flourished in the 5th century BC. He is best known for the grid system of street planning, developed for the Athenian port of Piraeus, the pan-Hellenic settlement of Thurii and perhaps the new city of Rhodes.

HIROHITO (1901–89) Emperor of Japan, supposedly the 124th direct descendant of Jimmu, Japan's legendary first ruler. An authority on marine biology, and the first Japanese crown prince to travel abroad (1921), he succeeded his father in 1926. He tried, ineffectually, to avert war with the United States, and broke political deadlock in 1945 to sue for peace. He ended centuries of public imperial silence to broadcast Japan's announcement of surrender on 15 August 1945. He became a constitutional monarch, with greatly restricted powers and was succeeded, in 1989, by his son, Akihito.

HITLER, ADOLF (1889–1945) German dictator. Born in Austria, he moved to Munich in 1913, served in the German army, joined the National Socialist German Workers' Party and re-organized it as a quasi-military force. He tried unsuccessfully to seize power in Bavaria, 1923; wrote *Mein Kampf (My Struggle)* in prison, elaborating his theories of Jewish conspiracy and **Aryan** superiority. Appointed chancellor, 1933; in 1936 he remilitarized the Rhineland, in 1939 invaded Austria and Czechoslovakia and in 1939 Poland. His sweeping initial successes in the Second World War were followed by defeats in Russia and north Africa, 1942–3. He survived an assassination plot in 1944, but committed suicide in 1945 as the Russians entered Berlin.

HITTITES A people speaking an Indo-European language who occupied central Anatolia by the beginning of the 2nd millennium BC, quickly absorbing the older population. The Old Hittite kingdom, c. 1750–1500 BC, later expanded into the Hittite empire, c. 1500–1190, which at its greatest extent controlled all Syria and briefly much of northern Mesopotamia. After the collapse of the empire, various neo-Hittite kingdoms survived in the region for a further 500 years.

HOABINHIAN *see* **Bacsonian**

HOCHE, LOUIS-LAZARE (1768–97) French revolutionary general. He enlisted in the French Guards, 1748, was appointed corporal, 1789, as commander of the army of the Moselle (1793) he drove Austro-Prussian forces from Alsace. He suppressed the **Vendée** counter-revolution, 1794–6. He commanded an expedition to Ireland to help rebels against England which failed due to storms at sea.

HO CHIEN (1887–1956) Warlord who controlled Hunan province, 1923–37. He played a major role in the campaigns against the Communists, 1930–5, supported by Kwangsi and Kwangtung. On the outbreak of the Japanese war he became a minister in the National government. He resigned in 1945.

HO CHI MINH (1890–1969) President of the Democratic Republic of Vietnam (North Vietnam), 1945–69. He was a founding member of the French Communist Party, 1920, and founded the Indo-Chinese Communist Party, 1930. He escaped to Moscow, 1932, but returned to Vietnam, 1940. Imprisoned in China, 1942–3, he emerged as leader of the **Viet Minh** guerrillas; he declared Vietnam independent, 1945, and played a dominant role in both the first and the second Indo-China wars, 1946–52, and from 1959 until his death.

HOHENSTAUFEN German royal dynasty, ruling Germany and the **Holy Roman Empire**, 1138–1254, and Sicily, 1194–1268. It restored German power and prestige after the setbacks during the Investiture Contest (*see* **Lay Investiture**); it became increasingly embroiled with the papacy for control of Italy following the marriage of **Henry VI** to the Sicilian heiress in 1186. The extirpation of the dynasty by the French allies (**Charles of Anjou**) of Pope **Clement IV** in 1268 continued a period of disunity and territorial fragmentation in Germany and Italy. The Hohenstaufen period marked the high point of German courtly culture, exemplified by the works of Wolfram von Eschenbach, **Gottfried von Strassburg** and Walther von der Vogelweide.

HOHENZOLLERN German dynastic family, ruling in Brandenburg-Prussia, 1415–1918, and as German emperors 1871–1918. They were originally descended from Burchard I, Count of Zollern, in Swabia (d.1061); a subsidiary branch, the Hohenzollern-Sigmaringens, held the throne of Romania from 1866 to 1947.

HOLKARS Ruling dynasty of Indore, southern India, founded by Malhar Rao Holkar, a Maratha soldier who, at his death in 1766, had become virtual king in the region of Malwa. Power crystallized during the long reign of his son's widow, Ahalyabai (1767–95); family forces were defeated by the British in 1804, and princely power ended with Indian independence in 1947.

HOLY ROMAN EMPIRE Name first bestowed in 1254 to denote the European lands ruled by successive dynasties of German kings. It was used retrospectively to include the empire of **Charlemagne**, on whom Pope Leo III conferred the title of Roman Emperor in 800; and also applied to the domains held by **Otto II** (d.983) and his successors. At its fullest extent the empire included modern Germany, Austria, Bohemia, Moravia, Switzerland, eastern France, the Netherlands and much of Italy. The title lapsed with the renunciation of imperial dignity by Francis II in 1806.

HOMER Putative author of the two great Greek national epic poems, *The Iliad* (or *The Wrath of Achilles*) and *The Odyssey*. The poems stand in a bardic tradition, using verse formulas, but each suggests composition by a single mind. Homer may have composed *The Iliad* in the 8th century BC in the eastern Aegean; the date of *The Odyssey* is less certain.

HOMFRAY family British industrialists. They built an ironworks at Penydarren, near Merthyr Tydfil, Wales, and built the first true railway from there to the sea; in 1804 Richard Trevithick made the first journey in a locomotive engine there, pulling truckloads of iron.

HOMININE Man, considered from the point of view of zoology; a member of the mammalian family **Hominidae**, which includes only one living species, **Homo sapiens**.

HOMINOID Animal resembling man, or with the form of a man.

HOMO SAPIENS Biological genus and species incorporating all modern human beings. It is characterized by a two-legged stance, high forehead, small teeth and jaw, and large cranial capacity; it dates back some 350,000 years.

HONECKER, ERICH (1912–94) German communist politician, in power 1973–89, elected chair of the council of state (head of state) 1976. He governed in an outwardly austere and efficient manner and, while favouring East-West detente, was a loyal ally of the USSR. He was replaced as head of state with the breaching of the Berlin Wall in 1989. He died in Moscow.

HONORIUS (384–423) Roman emperor, son of **Theodosius I**. He succeeded to the western half of the empire when it was divided after his father's death in 395.

HOOVER, HERBERT CLARK (1874–1964) 31st president of the United States. He organized American relief to Europe after the First World War; he was elected Republican president, 1929–33, but bitterly criticized for his failure to combat the depression. He opposed **Roosevelt's New Deal**; he sat as Chairman of the Hoover Commission, 1947–9 and 1953–5, on simplification of government administration.

HORROCKS, JOHN (1768–1804) Cotton manufacturer. In 1786 he erected a cotton mill at Preston, Lancashire. He was appointed by the **English East India Company** to be the sole supplier of cotton goods to India.

HOTTENTOTS *see* **Khoi**

HOUPHOUET-BOIGNY, FÉLIX (1905–93) President of the Ivory Coast. A planter and doctor, in 1945 he formed his own political party and was elected to represent the Ivory Coast in the French National Assembly, 1945–58. He entered the French Cabinet, 1956–9, working closely after 1958 with **General de Gaulle** to achieve peaceful decolonization. He became the first prime minister of the Ivory Coast in 1959, was elected its first president after independence in 1960, and was re-elected president in October 1990.

HOWE, WILLIAM (1729–1814) 5th Viscount Howe. British general who, after a distinguished career in the **Seven Years' War** (1756–63), commanded British forces during the American War of Independence (1175–8).

HOYSALAS Central Indian dynasty, ruling lterritory centred on Dorasamudra, near modern Mysore. It was founded by Vishnuvardhana in the first half of the 12th century, consolidated under his grandson, Ballala II, who won control of the southern Deccan, but overthrown in the 14th century by the Turkish sultans of Delhi.

HSIENPEI Group of tribes, probably of Turkic origin but according to some scholars of mixed Tungusic and Mongolian race. They first emerged as one of the Eastern Hue people in southern Manchuria, becoming vassals of the **Hsiungnu** after 206 BC. From the late 1st century AD they developed into a powerful tribal federation which dominated south Manchuria and Inner Mongolia. The final collapse of Chinese power in the early 4th century enabled them to invade north China repeatedly. Individual Hsienpei tribes established several short-lived dynasties during the 4th century, and from that time Hsienpei royal families ruled the dynasties Northern (Toba) Wei, Western Wei, Northern Chou, Eastern Wei and Northern Ch'i, which unified and controlled all of north China.

HSIUNGNU Chinese name for the vast alliance of nomad tribes that dominated much of central Asia from the late 3rd century BC to the 4th century AD. They were first identified in the 5th century BC, when their constant raids prompted construction of the fortifications which later became the Great Wall of China. Their power was largely broken by the emperor **Wu-ti**; around 51 BC the tribes split into two great groups; the eastern horde, more or less submitting to Chinese control, and the western, which migrated to the steppes. Later, after the collapse of the **Han** dynasty, Hsiungnu generals, hired as mercenaries, founded the short-lived Earlier Chao and Later Chao dynasties in northern China, c. AD 316–30. No reference to them after the 5th century is extant; the theories linking then with the European **Huns** or the early Turkish empire of central Asia remain unsubstantiated.

HSÜAN-T'UNG (1906–67) Last emperor of China, succeeding at the age of three on the death of his uncle. He reigned under a regency for three years before being forced to abdicate in 1912 in response to the success of the 1911 revolution. He continued to live in the palace at Peking under the name of Henry Pu-yi until 1924, when he left secretly for a Japanese concession in Tientsin. He ruled as puppet emperor of Manchukuo, 1936–45, was tried as a war criminal in 1950 and pardoned in 1959, when he went to work as a gardener.

HSÜ HSIANG-CH'IEN (1902–91) Commander in Chinese Communist Army, a subordinate of **Chang Kuo-t'ao**, during the Long March, and commander of the Eighth Route Army troops in the early part of the Sino-Japanese War. He was a leading general in Shansi in the late 1940s during the civil war with the Nationalists, and a member of the Communist Party Central Committee in 1945. He re-emerged as a leading figure in the Cultural Revolution of 1966, and became a member of the CCP Politburo the following year.

HUARI Early Andean civilization (c. AD 600–1000), named after its most characteristic archaeological site, in the highlands of present-day Peru. Its distinctive motif, the 'doorway god' with its rectangular face and rayed headdress, is also found among the vast ruins of Tiahuanaco, on the southern shore of Lake Titicaca, with which it appears to have been linked in its period of imperial expansion.

HUASCAR (d.1533) Son of **Huayna Capac**, on whose death (probably in 1525) he succeeded to the southern half of the Inca empire, based on Cuzco. He was soon involved in a succession war with his half-brother **Atahuallpa**, who had inherited the northern half of the empire and ruled from Quito. Huascar fled from Cuzco after a series of defeats, but he was captured and forced to watch his family and supporters being murdered. He was himself assassinated by Atahuallpa on the arrival of the

Spanish invaders under **Pizarro**, for fear they would restore him to power.

HUAYNA CAPAC (d. c.1525) Inca emperor, young son of the principal wife (and sister) of the Inca **Topa**, whom he succeeded in 1493. He reigned most peacefully after an initial succession struggle. He conquered Chachapoyas, in northwest Peru, and later northern Ecuador, returning home on hearing that an epidemic (probably measles or smallpox, brought by Spanish settlers at La Plata) was sweeping his capital, Cuzco; he died after contracting the disease. (Scholars now suggest that his death may have occurred as late as 1530, but that the early date was given by the Cuzco Incas as an effort to 'legitimize' **Huascar**'s rule.)

HUDSON, HENRY (c. 1550–1611) English seaman, after whom Hudson River, Hudson Strait and Hudson Bay are all named. He explored the islands north of Norway, 1607–8, in search of a Northeast Passage to Asia; in 1609, commissioned by the **Dutch East India Company** to find a Northwest Passage, he sailed up the Hudson river. In 1610, working again for the English, he passed through Hudson Strait and Hudson Bay, but died the following year after being abandoned by his mutinous crew.

HUDSON'S BAY COMPANY Incorporated in England, 1670, to seek a Northwest Passage to the Pacific, to occupy land around Hudson Bay and to engage in profitable activities. The company concentrated on fur-trading for two centuries; armed clashes with competitors led to a new charter, 1821. It lost its monopoly, 1869, as territories were transferred to the Canadian government but is still one of the world's major fur-dealing and general retailing organizations.

HUGUENOTS French followers of the Swiss religious reformer, **John Calvin**. Huguenot rivalry with the Catholics erupted in the French wars of religion, 1562–98; under the **Edict of Nantes**, 1598, the two creeds were able to co-exist, despite another religious war 1621–9, but when this edict was revoked by **Louis XIV** in 1685 many Huguenots preferred to flee the country; they settled, to the great benefit of the host states, in Great Britain, the United Provinces, north Germany and in those colonies overseas in which Protestants were tolerated.

HÜLEGÜ (c. 1217–65) Mongol leader, grandson of **Genghis Khan** and younger brother of **Möngke**, who led the epic campaign from east Asia to capture Baghdad in 1258; on the disruption of the Mongol empire after the death of Möngke, he remained to found the Il-Khan state, dominating Persia and the Middle East.

HUMILIATI A society of penitents in 12th century Europe who followed a life of poverty and evangelism. This brought them into conflict with the hierarchy of the Church, and they were condemned as heretics by Pope Lucius III in 1184. They were in some respects similar to the **Cathars**, but unlike the latter did not originally hold doctrines at variance with the Catholic faith. They were finally suppressed in the late 16th century.

HUNDRED DAYS, WAR OF Napoleon's attempt, after being defeated and exiled in 1814, to re-establish his rule in France. It began with his return to Paris from Elba in 1815 and ended with his defeat by Great Britain and Prussia at the battle of Waterloo.

HUNDRED YEARS' WAR Prolonged struggle of England and France, beginning in 1337 and ending in 1453. English forces twice came close to gaining control of France: once under **Edward III** (victories at Crécy, 1346, and Poitiers, 1356; treaty of Brétigny, 1360), and again under **Henry V** (victory at Agincourt, 1415; Henry was recognized as heir to the French throne, 1420). England's resources were insufficient to consolidate these gains, however, and by 1453 the only remaining English possession in France was Calais, which was lost in 1558.

HUNS Mounted nomad archers who invaded southeast Europe across the Volga c. 370, and dominated lands north of the Roman frontier until the defeat of their most famous, leader, **Attila**, in Gaul at the battle of the Catalaunian Fields in 451. Their empire broke up and disappeared from history, c. 455. The Huna who attacked Iran and India in the 5th and 6th centuries, and the **Hsiungnu** of central Asia, may have been related to the Huns, but this is unproven.

HUNTSMAN, BENJAMIN (1704–50) English steelmaker who invented the crucible process for making high-quality cast steel, c. 1750.

HURRIANS Near Eastern people, possibly from the region of Armenia, who briefly controlled most of northern Syria and northern Iraq in the 15th century BC. The principle Hurrian political unit was the kingdom called Mitanni, centred on the Khabur.

HUS, JAN (1372/3–1415) Czech religious reformer, born in Husinec, Bohemia. In 1409 he was appointed rector of the University of Prague; he was fatally involved in the struggles of the **Great Schism**; tricked by a promise of safe conduct into attending the Council of Constance, he was tried and burned for heresy. His death sparked off a Czech national revolt against the Catholic Church and its German supporters, particularly the Emperor Sigismund. *See also* **Hussites**.

HUSSEIN (d.1931) Hashemite sharif of the Hejaz, western Arabia. In 1915 he agreed to join the war of Great Britain against his Ottoman overlords. He proclaimed himself king of the Arabs in 1916 and began the war, aided by T.E. Lawrence, a British agent (Lawrence of Arabia), but his title was challenged by **Ibn Saud**, sultan of Nejd, after 1919. Hussein was forced to abdicate in 1924 and by 1926 Ibn Saud had conquered all of Arabia, although Hussein's sons ruled in Iraq and Transjordan.

HUSSEIN-McMAHON CORRESPONDENCE Letters exchanged in 1915 between Sir Henry McMahon, British High Commissioner in Cairo, and Hussein, sharif of Mecca and later king of Hejaz, setting out the area and terms in which Great Britain would recognize Arab independence after the First World War. Unpublished for decades, they remained a potent source of controversy and tension in the Middle East, especially in their ambiguous references to the future of Palestine.

HUSSEIN, SADDAM (1937–) Iraqi political leader. Active in the Ba'ath Socialist party since 1957, he brought his party to power through a bloodless coup (1968). He served as deputy chairman of the Revolutionary Command Council (1969–79) and as President of Iraq (1979–). He declared war on Iran (1980) but the war ended in stalemate in 1988. After invading Kuwait in 1990, he faced war with the US-led forces in 1991. Despite overwhelming defeat, he maintained himself in power. Continuing economic sanctions have done little to prise loose his tenacious grip on Iraq or to halt a massive re-armament programme.

HUSSITES Followers of **Jan Hus**. They broke with the papacy, used the Czech liturgy, and made many converts in Bohemia. From 1420 they repelled numerous attacks by Catholic neighbours, retaining freedom of worship until the battle of the White Mountain in 1620 restored Roman Catholicism and forced the Hussites (and others) into exile.

HYKSOS Asiatic invaders, sometimes known as the Shepherd Kings, who overran northern Egypt c. 1648 BC, and established the 15th Dynasty. Their capital, Avaris, was located in the eastern delta of the Nile. They were said to have introduced the horse and chariot into Egypt. Their rule collapsed c. 1540 BC.

HYWEL DDA (d.950) Also known as Hywel the Good, and to chroniclers as 'King of all Wales'. On the death of his father, Cadell, c. 910, he succeeded as joint ruler of Seisyllwg (roughly, modern Cardiganshire and the Towy valley) and from 920 ruled alone following the death of his brother Clydog; he acquired Dyfed (southwest Wales) and Gwynedd (northwest Wales) by marriage and inheritance. His reign was noted for its peacefulness – internally and with England. Hywel's name is associated with the earliest written Welsh law-code.

I

IBALPIEL II An Amorite dynast, King of Eshnunna (modern Tell Asmar) in the Diyala region of ancient Iraq. He reigned from 1725 to 1696 BC, when he was overthrown by **Hammurabi** of Babylon.

IBO (now Igbo) People (and language) of southeast Nigeria; they were associated with the attempt to secede from Nigeria and set up the state of Biafra in the 1960s.

IBN BATTUTA (1304–c. 1368) A Moroccan and possibly the greatest of all travellers. On a pilgrimage to Mecca in 1325 he conceived an ambition to travel 'through the Earth'. Though he rarely ventured beyond the Muslim world he nonetheless reached the Niger in west Africa and Kilwa in east Africa. His Asian travels took him across Transoxiana, Afghanistan, India, the Maldives, Ceylon and Sumatra to China. He left a reputation as the most-travelled man on earth. Though received with stupefaction in Fez, his accounts of his journeys are almost entirely convincing.

IBN SAUD (c. 1880–1953) Founder of Saudi Arabia; born at Riyadh, now the Saudi Arabian capital. A member of an exiled ruling family, he recaptured Riyadh in 1902 and began the conquest of central Arabia. He established close relations with Britain in the First World War, occupied Hejaz in 1926 and formally established the kingdom of Saudi Arabia in 1932. He signed the first oil-exploration treaty in 1933.

ICONOCLASM The policy of banning, and often destroying, religious images, officially imposed in 8th- and 9th-century Byzantium. Veneration of icons, previously encouraged, was first prohibited by **Leo III** in 730; the resulting persecutions reached their peak in 741–75. The policy was reversed, 787–814, but then reimposed until the death of Emperor Theophilus, 842; the final restoration of icon veneration, promulgated in 843, is still celebrated as the Feast of Orthodoxy in the Eastern Church.

ICTINUS Ancient Greek architect working in the 5th century BC. He was largely responsible for the Parthenon at Athens, the Temple of the Mysteries at Eleusis and the Temple of Apollo Epicurius at Bassae; he was joint author of a lost treatise.

IDRIS (1890–1893) Former king of Libya. Leader of the Sanusi Order, 1916; he was proclaimed king of Libya at independence in 1950. He was deposed in a coup by the army in 1969, fled the county for exile in Egypt and in 1971 was sentenced to death *in absentia*.

IDRISI, ABU ABD ALLAH MUHAMMAD AL- (1100–c. 1166) Medieval geographer. After travel in Spain and north Africa, he entered the service of **Roger II** of Sicily in about 1145; he became a leading mapmaker and scientific consultant to the court of Palermo. He constructed a silver planisphere showing the world, a 70-part world map and a great descriptive work completed in 1154, *The Pleasure Excursion of One who is Eager to Traverse the Regions of the World*.

IDRISIDS Islamic dynasty, ruling a kingdom occupying the northern part of what is now Morocco from 789 to 926. It was founded by Idris I, a descendant of the Prophet **Mohammed**'s son-in-law, **Ali**; after his death in 791 his son, Idris II, reigned until 828, when the kingdom split into a number of principalities. The Idrisids founded the important city of Fez.

IEYASU *see* **Tokugawa**

IGNATIUS OF LOYALA, ST (1491–1556) Founder of the order of Jesuits. A page and soldier of **Ferdinand of Aragon**, he made a barefoot pilgrimage to Jerusalem, 1523–4; studied at Alcalá, Salamanca and Paris, where in 1534 he planned a new religious order, the Society (or Company) of Jesus, devoted to converting the infidel and counteracting the Protestant Reformation. His Society was approved by the Pope in 1540, and he was appointed its first Superior, or general, in 1541. He was canonized in 1622.

IGOR SVYATOSLAVICH (1151–1202) Russian warrior who succeeded to the title of Prince of Novgorod-Seversk in 1178, and that of Prince of Chernigov in 1198. He led an ambitious but unsuccessful campaign against the Kuman or **Polovtsy** nomads, ending in total defeat in 1185; escaping from captivity in 1186, he returned to resume his role.

ILIAD Ancient Greek epic poem in 24 books, better called *The Wrath of Achilles*, describing an episode in the Trojan War; attributed to **Homer**.

ILKHANIDS Mongol rulers of Iran, 1256–1353. The dynasty was founded by **Hülegü** after he seized Persia with an army of 13,000 men; captured Baghdad by 1258. They lost contact with the Chinese Mongols after the conversion of **Mahmud of Ghazni** (1255–1304) to Sunni Islam; the dynasty was later weakened by divisions between **Sunni** and **Shi'as**.

ILTUTMISH Founder of the Delhi sultanate, son-in-law successor of **Qutbuddin Aibak** as ruler of the Muslim conquests in India. During his reign, 1211–36, Delhi established itself as the largest, strongest state in northern India.

IMHOTEP Chief minister of **Zoser**, second king of Egypt's 3rd Dynasty (27th century BC); later worshipped as the god of medicine in Egypt. He was architect of the world's oldest hewn-stone monument, the step pyramid at Saqqara, the necropolis of Memphis.

IMPERIALISM The policy of extending the power and rule of a government beyond its own borders. A country may attempt to dominate others by direct rule or by less obvious means such as control of markets for goods or raw materials. Imperialism has been a constant feature of human history.

INCA Name for the Indian group which dominated the central Andes region in the 15th and 16th centuries; also for their emperor and any member of the royal dynasty. From the capital, Cuzco in Peru, they controlled in the 16th century a region extending from Ecuador to north Chile; although lacking either knowledge of the wheel or any form of writing, their society reached a high level of civilization before being destroyed by the Spaniards in 1533. Occasional Inca uprisings occurred until the 19th century.

INDULF King of Alba (Scotland), 954–62. He captured Edinburgh from the Angles of Northumbria before being killed in battle by the Danes.

INNOCENT III (1160–1216) Pope, 1198–1216. In conflicts with the empire, France and England he asserted superiority of spiritual over temporal power as **Gregory VII**, **Urban II** and **Alexander III** had done, but more widely and more successfully. With him the medieval papacy reached its highest points of influence over European life. He claimed to dispose of the imperial crown, and excommunicated **King John** of England. His methods were mainly but not entirely political; he reconciled some heretics as well as launching the Albigensian Crusade against them, showed favour to St Francis at the beginning of his mission, and in the Fourth **Lateran Council** (1215) imposed spiritual regulations on the whole Church. The Fourth **Crusade** was the major blemish on his career as Pope.

INNOCENT IV (c. 1190–1254) Pope, 1243–54. Continued the struggle of previous popes to establish the superiority of spiritual over temporal power in bitter conflicts with the Emperor **Frederick II**.

INÖNÜ, ISMET (1884–1973) Turkish soldier and statesman, succeeding **Atatürk** as president of the Turkish Republic (1938–50). He commanded the Fourth Army in Syria, 1916, became under-secretary for war in 1918, joined the independence movement and in 1921 led the Turks to victory in the two battles of Inönü (1921), from which he took his name. He successfully negotiated the **Treaty of Lausanne** and was the first Republican prime minister, 1923–38. He advocated one-party rule, 1939–46, but later, in opposition, ardently advocated democratic reform.

INQUISITION Established by Pope Gregory IX in 1233 as a supreme Church court to repress heresy following the Albigensian Crusade, it brought about a considerable reduction in the number of heretics. Torture was permitted in 1252, though used less in the 13th century than later. The Inquisition was reorganized as the 'Sacred Congregation of the Roman and Universal Inquisition or Holy Office' in 1542, again as the 'Congregation of the Holy Office' in 1908, and as the 'Sacred Congregation for the Doctrine of the Faith', 1965. The Spanish Inquisition was established in 1478, abolished in 1820, and played an important part in imposing religious and civil obedience.

INUIT People of the western Arctic region, thinly spread in small settlements across the northern coasts of North America, from Alaska to Greenland. Of closely related physical type, language and culture, these groups, totalling some 50,000 people, share a common adaptation to the harsh living and hunting conditions of the Arctic tundra.

INVESTITURE CONTEST *see* **Lay Investiture**

IRAQ PETROLEUM COMPANY International consortium, set up to exploit oil concessions in Iraq under an agreement signed in 1925. In 1952 a 50-50 share agreement was reached with the government; in 1961, 99 per cent of the group's undeveloped concessions were nationalized, including the rich North Rumaila field. Under the arrangement finally agreed in 1975, IPC paid £141 million in a tax settlement, receiving 15 million tons of crude oil and the right to continue operating in South Rumaila.

IRON AGE The final period among archaeological periods of the prehistoric and early historic Old World, it takes in the barbarian tribes which were contemporaries of the classical civilizations of the Mediterranean, and much of Africa down to colonial times. Iron began increasingly to replace bronze after 100 BC, and can still be considered one of the world's most important materials.

IROQUOIS American Indians living round the lower Great Lakes. The Iroquois League, founded between 1570 and 1600, united five tribes – the Mohawk, Oneida, Onondaga, Cayuga and Seneca – as 'the People of the Long House', playing a key part in early American history. After defeating their native enemies, they turned on the French; when joined by the Tuscarora in 1722, they became the 'Six Nations'; split during the American revolution, the League disbanded under the Second Treaty of Fort Stanwix, 1784.

ISAIAH Old Testament prophet, son of Amoz, who stood alongside the kings of Judah in the last part of the 8th century BC. The book that bears his name falls into two parts; there is glorious poetry and profound insight in all, and many passages are taken by Christians to presage the coming of Christ.

ISAURIAN emperors Dynasty of Byzantine (East Roman) emperors, 717–802.

ISMAIL (1830–95) Khedive, or viceroy, of Egypt under Ottoman sovereignty, grandson of **Mohammed Ali**. He studied in Paris, and became viceroy in 1863; in 1867 he persuaded the Ottoman sultan to grant him the title of khedive. He opened the Suez canal in 1869 and expanded Egyptian rule in the Sudan. He carried further the process of economic and educational change begun by Mohammed Ali, but in doing so incurred a large foreign debt (£100 million by 1876) which ultimately led to British occupation in 1882. He was deposed in 1879 by the Ottoman sultan, in favour of his son.

ISMAIL I (c. 1487–1524) Shah of Persia (1501–24) and founder of the **Safavid** dynasty. In 1501 he established what some historians have regarded as the first truly Iranian dynasty since the Arab conquests, although the dynasty was Turkish-speaking and religious affiliation to **Shi'a** Islam provided the prime focus of loyalty to it. The strength of the state, resting on the Kizilbash (Turcoman tribes owing allegiance to the shah) enabled it to hold off serious threats from the Ottomans and the **Uzbeks** in 1510, and to stabilize its power on the Iranian plateau.

ISMAILIS Branch of the **Shi'a** division of Islam, which split from other branches over the question of succession to the sixth imam, and gradually developed theological doctrines of its own. Some Ismaili groups were politically active from the 9th to the 13th centuries establishing local rule in Bahrain and eastern Arabia then, on a larger scale, in Tunisia and Egypt (**Fatimid** caliphate); from there a further group, the 'new preaching' led by Hasan-i Sabbah, established itself in northern Persia (*see* **Assassins**). Ismailis of different groups still exist in Syria, Iran, Yemen, Pakistan and India, where the Aga Khan is head of the most important group.

ISMET *see* **Inönü**

ISOCRATES (436–338 BC) Athenian orator and pamphleteer, Too nervous to speak, he nevertheless composed eloquently for others. He preached in favour of enlightened monarchy and Greek unity in face of the threat from Persia.

ITURBIDE, AUGUSTIN (1783–1824) First emperor of independent Mexico. An officer in the Spanish colonial army, 1797; in 1810 he rejected an invitation to join anti-Spanish revolutionaries, and successfully defended Valladolid for the royalists. After 1820, he led a conservative independence movement. He crowned himself Emperor Agustín I in 1822, but in 1823 abdicated in the face of mounting opposition. Returning from Europe, unaware of the death sentence passed in his absence, he was captured and shot.

IVAN III (1440–1505) Grand Duke of Moscow, succeeding his father, Vasily II, in 1462. By conquering Novgorod in 1478 he made Moscow supreme among the principalities of west Russia, known henceforth as Muscovy. He declared Muscovite independence of the Mongols and stopped tribute payments to the **Golden Horde**.

IVAN IV VASILIEVICH 'THE TERRIBLE' (1530–84) Grand Duke of Moscow, 1533–84, and from 1547 Tsar of Russia. he conquered Kazan in 1552, Astrakhan in 1554, destroyed the free city of Novgorod in 1570, and annexed much of Siberia, to create a unified Russian state. Notoriously cruel, he killed his elder son in anger in 1581. His reign of terror was renowned for the establishment of the **oprichnina**, the forerunner of the political police.

JACKSON, ANDREW (1767–1845) Seventh president of the United States, 1829–37. A lawyer, planter and general, he defeated the British attack at New Orleans in 1815. He was elected as the champion of individual freedom and the common man in 1828. In 1832 he vetoed a bill for establishing a national bank, but otherwise supported strong federal government. He is credited – unjustly – with the introduction of the 'spoils system', the dispensing of official jobs as rewards for political support, into American public life.

JACKSON, THOMAS JONATHAN 'STONEWALL' (1824–63) Confederate general in the American Civil War, best known for his mobile tactics in the Virginia theatre, 1861–3.

JACOBINS Members of a French revolutionary club, founded in May 1789 among the deputies at Versailles. It was named from the former Dominican monastery where early meetings were held. Under the leadership of **Robespierre** the group became increasingly extreme, overthrowing the moderate **Girondins** in 1793 and instituting the Terror. The movement was eliminated after the *coup d'état* of July 1974.

JACQUARD, JOSEPH-MARIE (1752–1834) French textile-machinery inventor. He started work on the Jacquard loom in 1790, broke off to fight in the French revolution, and completed his designs in 1801. The machine, working on a punch-card system, was capable of duplicating all traditional weaving motions: it replaced all previous methods of figured silk-weaving. In 1806 his invention was declared public property, winning him a pension and a royalty on all sales. At first his looms were burned and he himself attacked by the handweavers of Lyons, fearing loss of employment, but by 1811, 11,000 looms were installed in France.

JACQUERIE Popular uprising in northeast France in 1358, named from the contemporary nobles' habit of referring to all members of the lower classes as 'Jacques'. Unrest began near Compiègne and quickly spread; peasant armies destroyed numerous castles and killed their inmates. Under their leader, Guillaume Cale (or Carle) the peasants joined forced with the Parisian rebels under **Étienne Marcel**, Cale's forces were crushingly defeated at Clermont-en-Beauvaisis on 10 June, and a general massacre followed.

JADWIGA (1371–99) Queen of Poland in her own right. Her marriage to **Władysław II Jagiełło** linked the thrones of Poland and Lithuania (1386).

JAGIEŁŁO, GRAND DUKE OF LITHUANIA *see* **Władysław II Jagiełło**

JAGIELLONIAN dynasty East European ruling family, prominent from the 14th to the 16th century. Founded by Jagiełło, Grand Duke of Lithuania, grandson of **Gedymin**, who married Queen **Jadwiga** of Poland in 1386, thus uniting the two crowns. It later also ruled Bohemia and Hungary.

JAINISM Early Indian religion, emphasizing non-violence, frugality, and the purification of the soul; it regards the existence of God as irrelevant. Shaped and organized in the 6th century BC by the prophet Mahavira, its basic doctrines, at first transmitted orally, were finally codified in the 5th century AD. Much practised among merchants, traders and money lenders, it is followed today by several million people in western and northern India and around Mysore.

JAMES I OF ARAGON (1208–76) Known as 'the Conqueror'. Born in France, he was acknowledged as king of Aragon and Catalonia in 1214, taking full power in 1227. He conquered the Balearic Islands, and in 1233 began a successful campaign to recover Valencia from the Moors. He renounced his French territories in 1258. He formulated an important code of maritime law, and established the Cortes as a parliamentary assembly.

JAMES VI and I (1566–1265) King of Scotland, Ireland and England. The son of Mary Queen of Scots, he succeeded to the throne of Scotland, as James VI, on his mother's enforced abdication in 1567, and to that of England and Ireland, as James I, in 1603 on the death of **Elizabeth I**. In Scotland he created a strong government for the first time, but in England his absolutist policies, extravagant court spending and High Church and pro-Spanish attitudes made him unpopular.

JAMESON RAID Abortive attack launched from Bechuanaland into the South African Republic (Transvaal) in 1895–6, led by Dr (later Sir) Leander Starr Jameson, a colleague of **Cecil Rhodes**. It was intended to overthrow the Afrikaner government of Paul Kruger (1825–1904), but it resulted in the resignation of Rhodes, the worsening of Anglo-Boer relations and Jameson's imprisonment. Jameson, however, returned to public life as Prime Minister of Cape Colony 1904–8.

JARUZELSKI, WOJCIECH (1923–) Polish military and political leader. Working his way up the ranks of the military and the Communist Party he became chief of the general staff (1965–8), defence minister (1968–83), and party Politburo member (1970–90). As prime minister (1981–5) he proved unable either to reach a compromise agreement with the powerful independent union, Solidarity, or solve the country's economic problems. He became president in 1985 but resigned in 1990.

JASSY, TREATY OF Pact signed on 9 January 1792 to end the Russo-Ottoman war of 1787–92. It confirmed the **Treaty of Küçük Kaynarca** (or Kuchuk Kainarji), advanced the Russian frontier to the Dniester river, and reinforced Russian naval power in the Black Sea.

JATAKA A popular tale, relating one of the former lives of **Buddha**. The largest collection, the Sinhalese *Jatakatthavannana*, contains 547 stories; other versions are preserved in all branches of Buddhism, and some reappear in non-Buddhist literature, such as *Aesop's Fables*.

JEFFERSON, THOMAS (1743–1826) Third president of the United States, 1801–9. He trained as a lawyer; opposed British colonial rule; became a member of the committee which drafted the Declaration of Independence. He was minister to France, 1785–9; secretary of state in Washington's administration, 1790–3; vice-president, 1797–1801. As president he defended the rights of states and completed the **Louisiana Purchase**. In his old age he founded the University of Virginia.

JEM (d.1495) Claimant to the Ottoman sultanate, the younger son of **Mehmed II**. On his father's death in 1481 he attempted to seize the succession, but was pre-empted by his elder brother **Bayezid II**. He declared himself sultan but was defeated at Yenishehir (1481); after a further vain assault on Konya in 1482 he fled, first to Rhodes, then to France. In 1489 he came under the control of Pope Innocent VIII, who received a pension from Bayezid for keeping him safe. For 14 years he was the centre of European intrigues and schemes to invade the Ottoman realms. Charles VIII of France was making plans to use him in a **crusade** when he died.

JEROME, ST (c. 342–419/20) Born at Stridon, now in Yugoslavia, and educated at Tome, he was baptized c. 366. He retired for two years as a desert hermit in 375, was ordained priest in Syria in 378 and in 382 returned to Rome as secretary to Pope Damasus. In 385 he left for Palestine, and established a monastery at Bethlehem. He wrote voluminously, including his influential Latin translation of the Bible and numerous controversial polemics.

JESUIT Member of the Society of Jesus, a Roman Catholic order founded in 1534 by **St Ignatius of Loyola**. Organized to support the papacy, to fight heresy and to conduct overseas missionary activity, it quickly established a dominant influence in the Church. Though suppressed, 1773, by Pope Clement XIV and expelled by many European countries in the 18th century, it was restored by Pope Pius VII in 1814, and is now widely entrenched, particularly in education, with schools and universities all over the world.

JESUS OF NAZARETH (8/4 BC–c. AD 29) Jewish teacher whose preaching, personal example and sacrificial death provide the foundations for the religion of Christianity. The name is the Greek form of Joshua, Hebrew for 'Jehovah is salvation'; to this is often added Christ, from the Greek *Christos*, the Hebrew *Messiah*, or 'anointed one'. Born near the end of the reign of Herod the Great, his ministry and Passion are recounted in the four Gospels of the New Testament. He was crucified, but is believed by his followers to have risen from the dead and ascended to heaven as the son of God.

JEW Originally a member of the tribe of Judah, the fourth son of Jacob, one of the 12 tribes of Israel which took possession of the Biblical Promised Land of Palestine; later a member of the kingdom of Judah, as opposed to the more northerly kingdom of Israel. After the Assyrian conquest in 721 BC, it applied to all surviving adherents of **Judaism**. In modern times it refers to an adherent of the Jewish religion whether by birth or by conversion, or to the child of a Jewish mother.

JEWISH UPRISING First of two major revolts, AD 66–73, against Roman rule in Judaea. The Romans were expelled from Jerusalem, 66, and the country rose in revolt; a revolutionary government was set up. Jewish forces finally succumbed to the Roman armies of **Vespasian** and **Titus**; Jerusalem was stormed, the temple burned and Jewish statehood ended in 70, and the Jews' last outpost, Masada, fell in 73. A second revolt, in 132–5, in the days of Emperor **Hadrian**, was suppressed with difficulty by the Romans after three years.

JINNAH, MOHAMMED ALI (1876–1948) Hailed as *Qaid-i-Azam*, 'Great Leader', by Indian Muslims, he was founder and first Governor-General of Pakistan. Born in Karachi, he became a highly successful barrister, and in 1906 entered the Indian National Congress. He supported Hindu-Muslim unity until the rise of **Gandhi**. As president of the Muslim League, which he transformed into a mass movement, he adopted the demand for separate Muslim states in 1940, and headed the Muslims in their independence negotiations, 1946–7, securing the partition of India.

JOHANNES IV (d.1889) Christian emperor of Ethiopia. Originally a *ras*, or prince, of Tigre in northern Ethiopia, his strong, militaristic policies were largely thwarted by external threats – from Egypt, Italy and the Mahdist Sudan – and by the internal rivalry of Menelik, ruler of Shoa. Successful against Egypt, 1856–7, and Italy, 1887, Johannes was finally killed at the battle of Matama in a retaliatory invasion against the khalifa **Abd Allah** of the Sudan.

JOHN (1167–1216) King of England, youngest son of **Henry II**. He tried to seize the throne in 1193 while his brother Richard I was away on **crusade**. He succeeded in 1199 on Richard's death; lost Normandy and other English possessions to the French; was excommunicated, 1209, in a quarrel with Pope **Innocent III**. In 1215, after six years of strife with his barons, he was forced to accept **Magna Carta**, a charter confirming feudal rights and limited abuses of royal power. He died during renewed civil war.

JOHN II (1455–95) King of Portugal, nicknamed 'the Perfect Prince'; succeeded his father, Alfonso V, in 1481. He broke the power of the richest family in Portugal, the Braganzas; organized expeditions to explore west and central Africa.

JOHN II CASIMIR VASA (1609–72) King of Poland, son of **Sigismund III**. He fought with the **Habsburgs** in the Thirty Years' War and was imprisoned by the French 1638–40. Created a cardinal in 1647, he was elected King of Poland in 1648 on the death of his brother Władysław IV; he fled in the face of the Swedish invasion of 1655. He lost large areas of Polish territory to Sweden at the Peace of Oliva (1660) and to Russia at the Treaty of Andrusovo (1667). He abdicated in 1668, retiring to France as titular abbot of St-Germain-des-Prés.

JOHN II COMNENUS (1088–1143) Byzantine emperor, 1118–43. He fought unsuccessfully to end Venetian trading privileges, 1122; defeated **Pecheneg**, Hungarian, Serbian and Norman threats to the empire; attempted to confirm Byzantine suzerainty over the Norman kingdom of Antioch.

JOHN III (1537–92) King of Sweden, 1568–92. The elder son, by his second marriage, of **Gustavus I Vasa**, he overthrew his half-brother, **Eric XIV** in 1568 to seize the throne. A learned theologian, he hoped to reconcile the beliefs of **Lutheranism** and Roman Catholicism, and fought hard but unsuccessfully to impose his own liturgy, known as *The Red Book*, on the Protestant Swedes. He died bitter and frustrated, leaving an impoverished and divided kingdom to his son **Sigismund III**.

JOHN III SOBIESKI (1642–96) King of Poland and Grand Duke of Lithuania. In 1655–60 he fought in the Swedish war. He became commander-in-chief of the Polish army in 1668 and won victories over **Tatars**, Turks and **Cossacks**. He was elected king in 1674. In 1683 he led the army which drove the Turks back from the gates of Vienna, but failed in a long campaign (1684–91) to extend Poland's influence to the Black Sea.

JOHN XXII (1249–1334) Second Avignon Pope, elected 1316. A lawyer and administrator, he was accused of financial extortion and involvement in politics and lowering the reputation of the papacy as a religious force. He contested the election of Louis of Bavaria as German emperor (1324); declared a heretic by Louis and by the Spiritual Franciscans, whom he had criticized, in return he excommunicated and imprisoned Louis's candidate, the anti-Pope, Nicholas V (1328).

JOHN OF AUSTRIA (1545–78) Spanish military commander, often known as Don John, the illegitimate son of Emperor **Charles V**. He commanded a Christian fleet against the Turks in the Mediterranean, 1570–6, winning the battle of Lepanto in 1571. He was commander of the Spanish army against the Dutch Revolt until his death.

JOHN CHRYSOSTOM, ST (c. 347–407) Father of the Christian Church. He became a hermit-monk, and was ordained priest in 386. A renowned preacher, he was appointed Archbishop of Constantinople in 398. In 403 he was indicted on 29 theological and political charges, was deposed and banished.

JOHNSON, LYNDON BAINES (1908–73) 36th president of the United States, 1963–9. Elected to Congress, 1937; senator for Texas, 1949; majority Senate leader, 1955–61. He was largely instrumental in passing civil rights bills of 1957 and 1960. He was elected vice-president in 1960, and succeeded after **John F. Kennedy's** assassination in 1963. He inaugurated the Great Society programme, but came under increasing criticism over the US involvement in the Vietnam War; he refused renomination in 1968.

JOHNSTON, ALBERT SYDNEY (1803–62) Confederate general in the American Civil War. He was appointed a second-ranking Confederate commander in 1861, and in the following year was mortally wounded leading a surprise attack at the battle of Shiloh.

JOINT-STOCK System of business finance in which the capital is contributed jointly by a number of individuals, who then become shareholders in the enterprise in proportion to their stake. It is usually, but not necessarily, combined with the principle of limited liability, under which the shareholders cannot be legally held responsible for any debts in excess of their share-capital.

JOLLIET, LOUIS (1645–1700) French Canadian explorer and cartographer. He led French parties of exploration from Lake Huron to Lake Erie, 1669, and down the Mississippi, 1672. This latter expedition reached the junction of the Mississippi and Arkansas rivers, but all Jolliet's maps and journals were lost when his canoe overturned; only the diary of the expedition's chaplain, **Jacques Marquette**, survived. He explored the coast of Labrador, 1694, and in 1697 was appointed Royal Hydrographer for New France.

JOSEPH II (1741–90) Holy Roman Emperor. Son of **Maria Theresa** and the Emperor Francis I, he succeeded to the empire in 1765, and to **Habsburg** lands in 1780. He continued his mother's attempts to reform and modernize the Habsburg dominions; introduced a new code of criminal law, 1787; suppressed the Catholic contemplative orders; agreed to the first partition of Poland. He was harassed by disaffection in Hungary and the Austrian Netherlands which compelled him to revoke some reforms.

JUAN-JUAN (also called Avars). Central Asian nomad people, controlling the northwest border areas of China from the early 5th to the mid-6th century and spreading to Europe, where they were finally destroyed by **Charlemagne** at the end of the 8th century.

JUÁREZ, BENITO (1806–72) National hero of Mexico. Of Indian parentage, he studied law and entered politics in 1831. Exiled to the United States in 1853, he returned in 1858 and fought in the civil war. After his election as Mexico's first Indian president in 1861, he instituted large-scale reforms, led opposition to the French-imposed **Emperor Maximilian** and defeated him in 1867. He was re-elected president in 1867 and again in 1871.

JUDAH Hebrew patriarch, fourth son of Jacob; also the Israelite tribe to which he was ancestor, and the kingdom established by this tribe in southern Palestine, c.932–586 BC.

JUDAH HA-NASI (c. 135–c. 220) Jewish sage, known as 'the rabbi' or 'our saintly teacher', son of Simeon ben Gamaliel II. He succeeded his father as patriarch (head) of the Jewish community in Palestine. He codified the Jewish Oral Law (supplementing the Written Law, found in the Pentateuch of Moses), and set down his findings in the **Mishnah** (Teaching), which included regulations for all aspects of Jewish life.

JUDAH MACCABEE (d.160 BC) Third son of the priest Mattathias the Hasmonean, who initiated the revolt against the **Seleucid** king, Antiochus IV, and his decrees against **Judaism**. He succeeded his father and recaptured most of Jerusalem, re-dedicating the temple in 164 BC; he was killed in battle. Eventually, under his brother Simon, an independent Judaea emerged in 140 BC.

JUDAISM Religion of the Jewish people, distinguished by its pure monotheism, its ethical system and its ritual practices, based on the Pentateuch as interpreted by the rabbis of the Talmudic period (first five centuries AD) and their successors up to the present.

JULIAN (c. 331–63) Roman emperor, known as 'the Apostate'. He was educated as a Christian but reverted to paganism and tried to make the empire pagan again after his election as emperor in 360.

JULIUS CAESAR (c. 100–44 BC) Dictator of Rome. He was a patrician, general, statesman, orator, historian – one of the greatest leaders produced by the Roman republic. He wrote vivid accounts of his conquest of Gaul and his civil war with **Pompey**. He was murdered by Brutus and other conspirators.

JUPITER *see* **Zeus**

JUSTINIAN I (483–565) Byzantine emperor, born at Tauresium in the Balkans, Flavius Anicius Justinianus. He went to Constantinople, where his uncle was the Emperor Justin I, becoming co-emperor and then emperor in 527. He was most successful as a legal reformer (Codex Justinianus, 534) and a great builder (the Santa Sophia). His foreign policy, directed at defending and re-extending the imperial frontiers, achieved the reconquest of north Africa, Italy, southern Spain and western Yugoslavia, but the victories proved fragile.

JUTES Germanic people inhabiting Jutland; with the Angles and Saxons they invaded Britain in the 5th century AD, settling mainly in Kent, Hampshire and the Isle of Wight.

K

KABIR (1440–1518) Indian mystic, who attempted to combine what he regarded as the best elements in **Hinduism** and Islam, a project completed by his disciple **Nanak**. Kabir's thinking, much of it incorporated into the **Adi Granth**, the sacred book of the **Sikhs**, also contributed to the development of several Hindu cults, notably the Kabirpanth, with its total rejection of caste.

KACHINS Rice-farming tribesmen in northern Burma. They total some 500,000 people, with their own Kachin state, capital Myitkyina.

KADAR, JANOS (1912–89) Hungarian statesman. He became a member of the then illegal Communist Party in 1932, was elected to the Central Committee in 1942 and to the Politburo in 1945. Post-war minister of the interior; he was expelled in 1950. Rehabilitated in 1954 he joined Imre Nagy's government, forming a new administration after the suppression of the Hungarian revolution in 1956. Premier 1956–8 and 1961–5, and later first secretary of the Hungarian Socialist Workers Party.

KALMAR, UNION OF An agreement, concluded in 1397, under which Norway, Sweden and Denmark shared a single monarch. It broke down in 1523 with the rebellion of Sweden led by **Gustavus I Vasa.**

KALMYKS Buddhist Mongolian nomads, now mainly occupying the Kalmyk Autonomous Soviet Socialist Republic which is located in the steppes around the delta of the Volga.

KAMOSE Last king of Egypt's 17th Dynasty (c. 1648–1552 BC). He ruled the southern part of the country after the death of his father, Seqenenre II; he began the expulsion of the **Hyksos** from the northern part. He was succeeded by his brother, **Amose I**, founder of the 18th Dynasty.

KARA KHANIDS Turkic dynasty ruling the central Asian territory of Transoxania from 992 to 1211. In 992 they occupied Bukhara, capital of the then disintegrating Samanid dynasty. Split by internal rivalries, the land fell under the domination of the **Seljuks** in the latest 11th century and then under the Kara Khitai. After a brief resurgence under Uthman (ruled 1204–11) the dynasty was extinguished in battle with the **Khwarizm**-shah.

KARA KOYUNLU (Black Sheep) Turcoman tribal confederation, ruling Azerbaijan and Iraq c. 1375–1467. They seized independent power in Tabriz under Kara Yusuf (ruled 1390–1400 and 1406–20); were routed by **Tamerlane** in 1400; captured Baghdad, 1410; annexed much of eastern Arabia and western Persia under Jihan Shah (ruled 1437–66). They were finally defeated in 1466 and absorbed by the rival **Ak Koyunlu** (ruler Uzun Hasan).

KARENS Agricultural tribesmen occupying a mountainous area in southeast Burma.

KASAVUBU, JOSEPH (c.1910–69) First president of independent Congo. He entered the Belgian Congo civil service, 1942; he became an early leader of the Congo independence movement, and in 1955 president of Abako (Alliance des Ba-Kongo). Joined with **Lumumba** in an uneasy alliance to share government power in 1960. He dismissed Lumumba in Ssepteniber 1960; he was deposed by **Mobutu** in 1965.

KAUNDA, KENNETH (1924–97) First president of independent Zambia. A school headmaster from 1944–7, he became in 1953 secretary-general of the North Rhodesia branch of the African National Congress, and in 1958 broke away to form the Zambia African National Congress. He became prime minister of Northern Rhodesia, and president of Zambia in 1964, but was defeated in the presidential election in October 1991.

KAZAKHS Traditionally pastoral nomads occupying a semi-arid stepped region in former Soviet central Asia to the east of the Ural river and extending into China. Their territory was incorporated into the Russian empire between 1830 and 1854. Russian colonization encroached on their best grazing lands before the revolution, and during the 1930s they were settled on collective farms. There are now over 5 million Kazakhs in the former USSR, most of whom live in Kazakhstan.

KEIR, JAMES (1735–1820) Scottish chemist. A retired army officer, he opened a glass factory in Stourbridge in 1775. Three years later he was placed in charge of the Boulton & Watt engineering works at Soho (Birmingham). In 1779 he patented an alloy capable of being forged or wrought when red hot or cold. In partnership with Alexander Blair he set up a chemical plant to make alkali products and soap.

KEMAL, MUSTAPHA *see* **Atatürk**

KENG, CHING-CHUNG (d.1682) Chinese general, son of Keng Chi-mao (d.1671) who became provincial governor of Fukien after 1660. On Chi-mao's death he succeeded him and in 1674 joined in the rebellion of the **Three Feudatories** to prevent losing control over the province. After initial success in southern Chekiang, he was attacked by superior forces and surrendered in 1676. For a time restored to his province, he was later taken to Peking and was executed.

KENNEDY, JOHN FITZGERALD (1917–63) 35th president of the United States, 1961–3. Member of the House of Representatives 1947–53, senator for Massachusetts 1953–61. He was the youngest candidate and the first Roman Catholic to be elected to the White House. He confronted the USSR in 1962 and successfully insisted that Russian missiles be withdrawn from Cuba. During his administration, the US launched its first manned space flights. He was assassinated on 22 November 1963 in Dallas, Texas.

KENYATTA, JOMO (1891–1978) First president of independent Kenya. He returned from studying in London, 1946, and became president of the Kenya African Union the following year. Convicted and imprisoned for allegedly running the Mau Mau revolt in 1953, he was released in 1959 under restriction. He was leader of the Kenyan delegation to the London constitutional conference of 1962. He became prime minister, 1963–4, and president 1964.

KEPPEL, AUGUSTUS (1725–86) British admiral and politician. He served in the British navy from the age of ten. During the **Seven Years' War** (1756–63) he captured Belle Isle in 1761; he participated with **Pocock** and his brother Albemarle in the capture of Havana; he commanded the Channel fleet in 1776. He was court martialled after an indecisive battle with the French off Ushant, 1778, during the American War of Independence. A member of parliament from 1761, he became first lord of the Admiralty, 1782–3.

KETT'S REBELLION English uprising in protest against the enclosure of common land. It was named after Robert Kett, a Norfolk smallholder who led the revolt and stormed Norwich in 1549. He was soon defeated by government forces and executed.

KHALIFA *see* **Abd Allah**

KHANATE State, region or district governed by a khan; the title 'khan' or 'kaghan' was first assumed by the chiefs of a tribe – perhaps of Mongol speech and origin – inhabiting the pastures north of the Gobi desert in the 5th century AD, and known to the Chinese as **Juan-Juan.** The title was destined later to adorn half the thrones of Asia.

KHAZARS Turkic and Iranian tribes from the Caucasus, who founded a major trading empire in southern Russia in the 6th century AD. In 737 they moved the capital north to Itil, near the mouth of the Volga, adopted the Jewish religion, and started massive westward expansion. At their peak in the late 8th century they ruled a huge area, from Hungary and beyond Kiev almost to Moscow. Two Byzantine emperors, Justinian II (in 704) and Constantine V (in 732) took Khazar wives. The Khazars were crushed by **Svyatoslav** in 965.

KHITAN Nomadic tribes who, under the Liao dynasty (974–1125), controlled most of present-day Manchuria, Mongolia and part of northeast China. During the Five dynasties, when China was weak and divided, they destroyed the Po-hai state in Manchuria and invaded northeast China before establishing a Chinese-style dynasty in 947 and adopting many Chinese administrative techniques. They carried on a border war with the Sung dynasty for control of northern China until 1004 when the Sung agreed to pay an annual tribute. The dynasty was destroyed in 1125 by one of its subsidiary peoples, the Jurchen (*see* **Ch'in**).

KHMER The predominant people of Cambodia; there are also communities of them in eastern Thailand and the Mekong Delta region of Vietnam. Their ancient civilization is exemplified by the remarkable, mainly Hindu temple complex of the Angkor area, dating from the 9th to the 13th century. After the 14th century most lowland Khmers became Theravada Buddhists; the conflicts with the neighbouring Thai and Vietnamese led to wars in the 17th and 19th centuries, and have re-emerged during and since the Cambodian war of 1970–5 (*see also* **Khmer Rouge**).

KHMER ROUGE Communist regime in Cambodia between 1975 and 1979. Originally organized to oppose the right-wing government of **Lon Nol**, President 1970–5. After defeating him and depopulating the capital, Phnom Penh, it subjected the country to a continuing reign of terror until its overthrow in 1979 by the Vietnamese. In 1991 the movement gained two of the twelve seats on the Cambodian Supreme National Council (composed of representatives of the country's warring factions).

KHOI (HOTTENTOTS) A nomadic pastoral people from Namibia, Botswana and the Northern Cape. Probably related to the **San**.

KHOISAN Relating to the Stone Age Bushmen (**San**) and Hottentot (**Khoi**) inhabitants of southern Africa.

KHOSRAU I ANOHSHIRVAN (d.579) Known as 'the just', shahinshah of **Sasanid** Persia 531–79. He succeeded his father Kavadh, whom he helped to suppress the Mazdakite heretics. He also reorganized the bureaucracy and religious establishment, fought back against Byzantium, and restored the dynasty's flagging fortunes. He patronized both Greek and Sanskrit learning, and is reputed to have brought the game of chess to the West from India.

KHOSRAU II 'THE VICTORIOUS' (d.628) (also known as Chosroes). The last great **Sasanid** king of Persia. He made a bid for power on the assassination of his father, Hormizd IV, in 590, but was expelled. He fled to Byzantine territory, and after being provided with forces by the Emperor Maurice (586–602) gained the Persian throne in the following year. When Maurice was murdered by the usurper Phocas in 601, Khosrau pledged vengeance against the whole Byzantine people, and invaded the empire with vast forces. Eventually he captured Antioch, Jerusalem and Alexandria, camping repeatedly along the Bosporus opposite Constantinople, but for lack of ships was never able to cross. **Heraclius**, a capable general, overthrew Phocas and, after numerous brilliant campaigns in Asia Minor, finally threatened the Sasanid capital at Ctesiphon. By this time both empires were exhausted, and social unrest at Ctesiphon forced Khosrau's son Shiruya (Siroes) to acquiesce in the killing of his father, and the ending of the war, in 628.

KHRUSHCHEV, NIKITA (1894–1971) Soviet statesman, first secretary of the Soviet Communist Party (1953–64) and prime minister (1958–64). A close associate of **Stalin**, he emerged as leader after his death. He promoted a policy of 'peaceful coexistence' with other foreign powers, but the Cuban missile crisis with the US (1962) and a dispute with China over borders and economic aid brought about his downfall in 1964.

KHWARIZM Ancient central Asian territory along the Amu Darya (River Oxus) in Turkestan; part of **Achaemenid** Persia, 6th to 4th centuries BC. Conquered for Islam in the 7th century AD; it was ruled by an independent dynasty, the Khwarizm-shahs, from the late 11th to the early 13th century; successively conquered by Mongols, Timurids and **Shaybanids**, in the early 16th century it became centre of the khanate of Khiva, under the **Uzbecks**. After repelling many invasions, it was absorbed as a Russian protectorate in 1873. As a result of the 1917 revolution it became the short-lived Khorezm Peoples' Soviet Rrepublic (1920–4). From 1924–91 the region was split into the Turkmen and Uzbeck SSRs, which became the independent states of Turkmenistan and Uzbeckistan respectively in 1991, following the collapse of the Soviet Union.

KIKUYU Bantu-speaking people of Kenya and their language; they were associated with the Mau Mau revolt against the British in the 1950s.

KILLIAN, ST (d.697) Irish bishop, known as the Apostle of Franconia; he was martyred at Würzburg.

KIM IL-SUNG (1912–94) North Korean leader. Involved in guerrilla resistance to Japanese occupation (1930s), he fought in World War II in the Soviet Red Army, returning to Korea in 1945. Head of the Democratic People's Republic of Korea (1948-94), he also became the nation's premier (1948–72) and president from 1972. His lengthy rule was characterized by rigid adherence to communist orthodoxy, economic backwardness and suppression of political opposition. He was succeeded by his son, Kim Jong Il.

KING, PHILIP PARKER (1791–1856) British naval officer, explorer of Australia and South America. He conducted surveys of Australia's tropical and western coasts from 1818 to 1822, and of the coasts of Peru, Chile and Patagonia from 1826 to 1830.

KING PHILIP'S WAR Savage conflict between Indians and English settlers in New England, 1675–6. King Philip (Indian name, Metacom) was chief of the Wampanoag tribe; during the fighting 600 white men died and entire Indian villages were destroyed.

KING WILLIAM'S WAR North American extension of the War of the Grand Alliance (1689–97) between William III of England, supported by the **League of Augsburg**, and **Louis XIV**'s France. The British captured parts of eastern Canada but failed to take Quebec; France penetrated into present-day New England but failed to seize Boston. the **status quo** was restored under the **Treaty of Ryswyck**. *See also* **Nine Years' War**.

KIPCHAKS *see* **Polovtsy**

KIPCHAK KHANATE *see* **Golden Horde**

KIRGHIZ Turkic-speaking people of central Asia. They were widely dispossessed of their traditional nomad grazing lands during Russia's 19th century expansion. Their protest revolt in 1916 was bloodily suppressed, with more than a third of the Kirghiz survivors fleeing to China. The remainder now live mostly in Kirghizia.

KLONDIKE Tributary of the Yukon river, Canada. It became world-famous in 1896, when gold was found in Bonanza Creek; 30,000 prospectors swarmed in from all over the world. By 1911 the main deposits had been worked out and the population reduced to 1000; all mining ceased in 1966.

KNÄRED, PEACE OF Treaty concluding the Kalmar war of 1611–13, fought between Denmark and Sweden over the control of north Norway. It was provoked by Sweden's king,

Charles IX, claiming sovereignty over the region. The Danes took the Swedish ports of Kalmar (1611) and Älvsborg's vital western harbour (1612). The ignominious peace, including the payment of a massive ransom for the return of Älvsborg was signed by Charles' son and successor, **Gustavus II Adolphus**.

KNIGHTS HOSPITALLERS OF ST JOHN Members of a military and religious order, the Hospital of St John of Jerusalem, founded in the 11th century to help poor and sick pilgrims to the Holy Land. The Order was recognized by the papacy in 1113; it became active in the **Crusades** but was driven from Palestine in 1291. It conquered Rhodes in 1310, and as the Knights of Rhodes grew in wealth and power until expelled by the Turks in 1522. The Order was moved by **Charles V** to Tripoli (to 1551), and thereafter to Malta until it was deposed by **Napoleon** in 1798, after which it took refuge in Russia. Reformed in 1879 as the charitable order of St John, its English branch is now widely known for its ambulance and first aid work.

KOHL, HELMUT (1930–) German statesman. He joined the Christian Democratic Union in his youth, becoming the party's deputy chairman in 1969. He was the party's candidate for the chancellorship in 1976 but was defeated. The collapse of Schmidt's centre-left coalition in 1982 enabled Kohl to recover and he led the CDU to victory in the elections which followed. As chancellor, Kohl adopted a cautious economic policy and reduced government spending. His foreign policy involved support for closer European integration. The CDU's disappointing showing in the 1987 elections forced him to rely increasingly on coalition partners. After the collapse of the **Berlin Wall** in November 1989, Kohl was able to bring about German re-unification during 1990. This success led to victory in 'all-German' elections soon afterwards. Re-unification caused serious economic difficulties, however, and Kohl's austerity measures created discontent. He was defeated in the elctions for chancellor in 1998.

KOLCHAK, ALEXANDER VASILYEVICH (1874–1920) Russian counter-revolutionary admiral. He led a *coup d'état* within the **White** (Provisional) government in Siberia in 1918, and was recognized as ruler of Russia by the Western allies; but he was betrayed to the **Bolsheviks** and shot.

KONIEV, IVAN STEPANOVICH (1897–1973) Marshal of the Soviet Union. He was a front commander, 1941–3; senior commander in the liberation of the Ukraine, the Soviet drive into Poland (1944), and the attack on Berlin and liberation of Prague, 1945. Between 1956 and 1960 he was commander-in-chief of the **Warsaw Pact** forces.

KÖPRÜLÜ (also spelled Kuprili) Family of Pashas and generals of Albanian origin, who held high office in the Ottoman state in the second half of the 17th century. The founder of the family's fortunes, Köprülü Mehmed Pasha, was called to the grand vizierate in 1656 by **Mehmed IV** at the age of 80, being succeeded as grand vizier by his son Fazil Ahmed Pasha in 1661 and by his son-in-law Kara Mustafa Pasha (1676–83). The last significant member of the family was Köprülüzade Mustafa Pasha, grand vizier 1689–91. Their military and administrative reforms did much to arrest the decline of the Ottoman house (final reduction of Crete, 1669; conquest of Podolia, 1672), but the over-confident policies of Kara Mustafa Pasha, culminating in his failure before Vienna in 1683, severely damaged the fabric of the state and sowed the seeds of future defeat.

KORAN Holy book of Islam, believed by Muslims to be the word of God communicated to the Prophet, **Mohammed**. The text is said to have been definitely fixed by order of the third caliph, **Othman**; containing 114 chapters of different lengths and content, it serves as a basis of law and social morality as well as of doctrine and devotion.

KORNILOV, LAVR GEORGIYEVICH (1870–1918) Russian general. An intelligence officer during the Russo-Japanese war of 1904–5, and military attaché in Peking 1907–11, he was captured by the Austrians in 1915, escaping the following year. He was placed in charge of Petrograd military district after the February Revolution, 1917; he was appointed commander-in-chief by Kerensky. Accused of attempting a military *coup d'état* he was imprisoned, but escaped and took command of the anti-Bolshevik (White') army in the Don region. He was killed at the battle for Yekaterinodar.

KOŚCIUSZKO, TADEUSZ (1746–1817) Polish general and patriot. After military training in Warsaw, he went to America to join the 'struggle for liberty' there (1777–80). He fought Russia and then Prussia in 1792–3 in an unsuccessful attempt to save Poland from a second partition. He led a national uprising against Russia and Prussia in 1794 which failed, and precipitated the final partition of Poland the following year. He spent much of the rest of his life in exile, attempting to enlist foreign support for the recreation of a Polish state.

KRUM (d.814) Khan of the Bulgars, 802–14. After **Charlemagne**'s defeat of the Avars in 796, he greatly extended the power and territory of the Pannonian Bulgars. His early forays against Byzantium were repulsed, but he decisively defeated Emperor Nicephorus I in 811, and besieged Constantinople in 813, though he died during a second siege the following year.

KRUPP, ALFRED (1812–87) German industrialist and arms manufacturer. He was the son of Friedrich Krupp (1787–1826), founder of the family's cast-steel factory at Essen in 1811. Alfred perfected techniques to produce first railway track and locomotive wheels, then armaments. The **Franco-Prussian War** (1870–1) was won largely with Krupp field-guns, and the firm became the largest weapon manufacturer in the world, at one time supplying the armies of 46 nations.

KUBLAI KHAN (1215–94) Mongol emperor of China, founder of the Yüan dynasty. Grandson of **Genghis Khan**, he was proclaimed Great Khan in 1260 in succession to his brother **Möngke**. He reunited China, divided since the eclipse of the **T'ang** dynasty. His court was first described to the west by the Venetian, **Marco Polo**.

KÜÇÜK KAYNARCA, TREATY OF (also known as Kuchuk Kainarji) A pact signed on 21 July 1774 to end the Russo-Ottoman war of 1768–74. Under its terms the Ottomans renounced their previously undisputed control of the Black Sea and allowed Russia the privilege of representing the interests of the Orthodox Christians in Moldavia, Wallachia and the Aegean Islands; this provided the basis much later for Russian interference in the affairs of the Ottoman empire.

KU KLUX KLAN American anti-Negro secret society, founded in 1866 to assert white supremacy and oppose the rule of the 'carpet-baggers' in the southern states. It was declared illegal in 1871, but was relaunched in 1915, and broadened to attack not only Negroes but also Jews, Roman Catholics and foreigners. Violently active during the early 1920s in the mid-West and South, and again in the South in the 1960s, it came under increasing attack as a result of Federal enforcement of the Civil Rights Acts of 1964 and 1965.

KUMANS *see* **Polovtsy**

KUN, BELA (1886–?1937) Hungarian revolutionary leader. He led the Communist insurgents who overthrew the Karolyi regime in 1918. On becoming premier in 1919, he attempted to reorganize the country on Soviet principles but was forced into exile four months later.

KUO-MIN CHÜN (People's Army) Group of warlord armies led by **Feng Yü-hsiang, 1924–8.**

KUOMINTANG (also known as Chinese Nationalist Party) Political Party, ruling mainland China from 1928 to 1949, and since then (from Taiwan) claiming to be the only legitimate Chinese government. It evolved from a revolutionary group formed after the Chinese Republican Revolution of 1911 and was outlawed in 1913. Three short-lived governments were established under **Sun Yat-sen**, between 1917 and 1923 when the party allied with the Chinese Communists. Jointly they conquered most of the country, but split, 1927–8; cooperation was renegotiated in face of a Japanese invasion, 1937. Civil war was resumed in 1946, ending with Communist victory in 1949.

KURDS A Muslim people, speaking an Indo-European language, numbering up to 19 million, mostly in the mountains where Iran, Iraq and Turkey meet. Hopes of an autonomous Kurdistan emerging from a defeated **Ottoman** empire, raised by the 1920 **Treaty of Sèvres**, were still-born: Atatürk suppressed the Kurds. The Soviet Union, whose forces occupied part of Iran in the Second World War, encouraged the proclamation of a Kurdish republic but this collapsed after the Russians withdrew. In Iraq, fighting broke out with government troops in 1961. Nine years later, Baghdad offered the Kurds limited autonomy but the war restarted in 1974. Iranian support for the Kurds was withdrawn following an Iraqi-Iranian agreement in 1975. The Iraqis gassed Kurds at Halabja in 1988. The US-led coalition, which drove Iraq from Kuwait in 1991, encouraged an unsuccessful rising against Baghdad and created a safe haven for Kurds inside northern Iraq.

KUSHANAS Imperial dynasty, ruling in central Asia and northern India from the late 1st to the mid-3rd century AD, and traditionally founded by Kanishka, who succeeded to the throne of a kingdom extending from Benares in the east to Sanchi in the south, some time between AD 78 and 144. The Kushana empire lasted abut 150 years, until its kings in Taxila and Peshawar were reduced to vassals of the Persian **Sasanids**.

KYANZITTHA (1084–1112) One of the first great kings of Burma, responsible for the expansion of **Buddhism**.

L

LA For all personal names prefixed by la, le, etc, see under following element.

LAIRD, MACGREGOR (1808–61) Scottish explorer, shipbuilder and trader. He designed the first ocean-going iron ship, the 55-ton paddle-steamer *Alburkah*, and in it in 1832 accompanied an expedition to the Niger delta. He ascended the river's principal tributary, the Benue, developed west African commerce in an attempt to undermine the slave trade and pioneered trans-Atlantic shipping routes. He promoted a second major expedition, penetrating 150 miles further up the Niger than any previous European, in 1854.

LAMAISM Form of **Buddhism**, established in Tibet c. 750. It is derived from Mahayana beliefs, combined with elements of erotic Tantrism and animistic Shamanism. In 1641 the Mongols inaugurated the appointment of the Dalai Lama, to rule Tibet from Lhasa, while the Panchen Lama from the Tashi Lhunpo monastery near Shigatse became spiritual head of the religion. The last Dalai Lama, fourteenth in a line claiming descent from Bodhisattva Avalokiteshvara, ancestor of the Tibetans, accepted exile in India in 1959. Lamaism temporarily lost its hold in Tibet, but again now has widespread support.

LANGOSCO Prominent family of medieval Pavia, Italy. Supporters of the **Guelph** (anti-imperial) party, they gained control of Pavia in 1300–15 and 1357–9, but lost it to their rivals, the **Visconti** of Milan.

LAO-TZU Originator of the Chinese Daoist philosophy. Little definite is known of his life, though he is traditionally said to have met Confucius during the 6th century BC. His authorship of the *Dao-te Ching*, one of the central Daoist texts, is unproven, and it certainly dates from a later period (probably 3rd century BC). Since his death he has been venerated as a philosopher by Confucians, as a saint or god by many Chinese, and as an imperial ancestor during the **T'ang** dynasty (AD 618–907).

LAPPS Inhabitants of northern Scandinavia and the Kola peninsula of Russia. The origin of these people is obscure, but their history goes back at least 2,000 years. The best known, but smallest, group are nomadic reindeer herders; their forest and coastal cousins rely on a semi-nomadic hunting and fishing economy.

LA TÈNE Celtic Iron Age culture, flourishing in central Europe from c. 500 BC until the arrival of the Romans, and in remote areas such as Ireland and northern Britain until the 1st century AD. It was named after an archaeological site excavated near Lake Neuchâtel, Switzerland. Most surviving near Celtic art – weapons, jewellery, tableware, horse and chariot decoration – is characteristically La Tène in motif and design.

LATERAN COUNCILS Four Church Councils were held at the Lateran Palace in Rome during the Middle Ages. The first (1123) confirmed the **Concordat of Worms** which ended the Investiture Contest; the second (1139) reformed the Church after the schism at Innocent II's election; the third (1179) marked the end of the conflict with **Frederick I Barbarossa** and introduced a two-thirds majority rule for papal elections; the fourth (1215), the high water mark of **Innocent III**'s pontificate, inaugurated large-scale reform to deal with the recent widespread dissatisfaction with the Church, and proclaimed a **Crusade**.

LATIN EMPIRE OF CONSTANTINOPLE From 1204 to 1261 the Byzantine capital, Constantinople, was ruled by a succession of western European crusaders after its capture by the Venetian-backed armies of the Fourth **Crusade**; its wealth was systematically pillaged before it was captured by Michael VIII Palaeologus, the Greek Emperor of Nicaea, in 1261.

LAUSANNE, TREATY OF Agreement signed on 24 July 1923 by First World War Allies with Turkish nationalists. It recognized the territory and independence of the New Turkish Republic which had replaced the Ottoman empire. Turkey abandoned claims to its former Arab provinces, recognized British and Italian right in Cyprus and the Dodecanese Islands, and opened the Turkish straits (Dardanelles) linking the Aegean and the Black Sea to all shipping.

LAY INVESTITURE The right claimed by many medieval rulers to appoint and install their own bishops. The denial of this right by the papacy gave rise to the Investiture Contest (1075–1122); a form of settlement was reached at the **Concordat of Worms**.

LEAGUE OF NATIONS Organization set up by the Allies for international cooperation at the Paris Peace Conference in 1919 following the end of the First World War. Weakened by the non-membership of the United States, it failed to halt German, Japanese and Italian aggression in the 1930s. Moribund by 1939, it was replaced in 1946 by the **United Nations**.

LEE, KWAN YEW (1923–) Political leader of the Republic of Singapore. An outstanding law student at Cambridge, he worked for labour unions before entering politics (1954). He founded the People's Action Party in 1955. When Singapore became a self-governing state he was elected prime minister, holding office for over 25 years (1965–90). He promoted economic development, regional cooperation and a policy of non-alignment. A conservative politician of authoritarian temperament, he was also a major spokesman of the Association of Southeast Asian Nations (ASEAN).

LEE, ROBERT E (1807–70) Commander-in-Chief of the Confederate (Southern) army in the American Civil War, 1861–5. He graduated top cadet from West Point military academy, 1829; fought in the Mexican War of 1846–8. In 1861 he resigned his commission to lead the Virginian forces; he was military adviser to Jefferson Davis, commander of the Army of Northern Virginia, and General-in-Chief of the Confederate Armies. He surrendered at Appomattox Court House on 9 April 1865. After the war he served as president of Washington College (later Washington and Lee University), Virginia.

LEGALISM Ancient school of Chinese thought, advocating institutional rather than ethical solutions in politics, and teaching that governments should rule by rigid and harshly enforced laws, irrespective of the views of their subjects. It was first adopted as a state ideology by the **Ch'in** dynasty (221–206 BC) and regularly revived since, particularly during periods of national crisis.

LENIN (1870–1924) Architect of the Russian revolution; born Vladimir Ilych Ulyanov. Converted to Marxism while training to be a lawyer, he was exiled to Siberia, 1897–1900. He led the Bolshevik wing of the Social Democratic Party from 1903. He returned from Switzerland in 1917 at the outbreak of revolution and in October overthrew Kerensky's government to become first head of the Soviet government, 1917–24. His influential writings include *What Is To Be Done?*, *Imperialism, the Highest Stage of Capitalism*, *The State and Revolution* and *The Development of Communism*.

LEO I, THE GREAT (d. 461) He succeeded to the papacy in 440, and was the founder of papal primacy. As a theologian he defined Catholic doctrine, and secured the condemnation of the **Monophysites** at the **Council of Chalcedon** (451). He asserted the primacy of the Roman see against Constantinople. In 452 he saved Rome from the **Huns**.

LEO III (675–741) Byzantine emperor, founder of the Isaurian, or Syrian, dynasty. He seized the throne in 717, defeated the Arab attack on Constantinople, and went on to drive them from Anatolia. He launched the policy of **iconoclasm**, which opened deep religious conflict in the empire.

LEO VI (866–912) Byzantine emperor, known as 'the Wise' or 'the Philosopher'. Son of Basil I the Macedonian, he became co-emperor in 870, and attained full power in 886. He issued a set of imperial laws, the **Basilica**, which became the accepted legal code of Byzantium.

LEO IX (Bruno of Egisheim) (1002–54) Pope and saint. He became Bishop of Toul in 1026, and in 1048 was appointed Pope by **Henry III** of Germany, a relation. He showed his reforming spirit by demanding also to be elected by the clergy of Rome; and also by condemning simony and clerical marriage, and by travelling widely in order to spread reforming ideas. He was defeated and briefly held captive by the Normans of southern Italy. His assertion of papal supremacy led to the great schism of 1054 between the Eastern and Western churches.

LEOPOLD II (1835–1909) King of the Belgians. The son of Leopold I, he succeeded in 1865. He was instrumental in founding the Congo Free State, 1879, over which he secured personal control in 1885. Under his guidance, Belgium became a significant industrial and colonial power. He handed over sovereignty in the Congo to his country in 1908.

LETTOW-VORBECK, PAUL VON (1870–1964) German general. He served in the Southwest Colonial Forces, helping to suppress the Herero and Hottentot rebellions; as commander of the (German) East African Colonial forces, he repelled a British landing in Tanganyika, in 1914, and with less than 17,000 troops pinned down British, Portuguese and Belgian forces of over 300,000 in East Africa, 1914–18. He led the right-wing occupation of Hamburg, 1919. He became a member of the

Reichstag, 1929–30 and tried without success to organize conservative opposition to **Hitler**.

LEVELLERS Members of a radical movement both in the Parliamentary army and in London during the English Civil War. It advocated total religious and social equality among 'freeborn Englishmen', and sought an extreme form of republican government based on the pamphlet *The Agreement of the People* (1648) written by its leader, John Lilburne (c. 1614–57). It was suppressed by **Oliver Cromwell** at Burford, Oxfordshire in 1649.

LEWIS, JOHN LLEWELLYN (1880–1969) United States labour leader. In 1905 he became legal representative to the United Mine Workers of America, and its president from 1920 to 1960. With the American Federation of Labour (AFofL), he encouraged the organization of mass production workers into industrial unions. Expelled from the AFofL, these unions then set themselves up in 1935 as the Congress of Industrial Organizations (CIO), with Lewis as president. He himself resigned from CIO in 1940, and withdrew the mineworkers in 1942.

LEWIS, MERIWETHER (1774–1809) American explorer, *see under* **Clark, William**

LIBERATION FROM FRENCH RULE, WAR OF Penultimate struggle of the Napoleonic Wars, when the French armies, after their retreat from Russia in 1812, suffered a series of setbacks against a new coalition of Britain, Prussia, Sweden and Austria, culminating in defeat at the battle of the Nations (1813). The allies then advanced to Paris, Napoleon abdicated, peace was made with France and the **Congress of Vienna** was called (1814) to make a settlement for the rest of Europe.

LIGUE *see* **Catholic League**

LILUOKALANI (1838–1917) Queen of Hawaii, 1891–5; born in Honolulu. She opposed the renewal of the Reciprocity Treaty, 1887, under which her brother, King Kalakaua, granted the US commercial rights and Pearl Harbor; she supported Oni Pa's party, whose motto was 'Hawaii for the Hawaiians'. Deposed by the US-inspired provisional government in 1893, she abdicated in 1895 after a loyalist revolt. In 1893 she composed the famous Hawaiian song *Aloha Oe*.

LINCOLN, ABRAHAM (1809–65) Sixteenth president of the United States, 1861–5. Raised in the backwoods of Indiana, he was a self-taught lawyer. He entered Congress in 1847, eventually being elected president, on an anti-slavery platform. He fought the Civil War (1861–5) to preserve national unity; proclaimed the emancipation of slaves in 1863, and was assassinated in 1865 by John Wilkes Booth, a fanatical southerner.

LI TZU-CH'ENG (c. 1605–45) Chinese rebel leader, born in Shensi. He was a bandit chieftain, 1631–45, during the final disturbed years of the **Ming** dynasty. After first operating in Shensi, he overran parts of Honan and Hupeh in 1639, and captured Kaifeng (1642) and all of Shensi (1642–4). In 1644 he also invaded Shansi, and in April seized Peking and proclaimed himself emperor. He was defeated by the combined tribes of General **Wu San-kuei** and the **Manchus**, and was driven from Peking, retreating first to Sian and then into Hupeh.

LIVINGSTONE, DAVID (1813–73) Scottish missionary and explorer. He started his mission career in the Botswana region in 1841. He crossed the Kalahari Desert; reached the Zambezi, 1851; and Luanda, 1853; discovered the Victoria Falls, 1855; and explored the basin of Lake Nyasa and the Upper Congo. He was feared lost in early 1870, but was found by **Stanley** near Lake Tanganyika in 1871.

LIVONIAN ORDER Society of German crusading knights, also known as Brothers of the Sword, or Knights of the Sword. They conquered and Christianized Livonia (covering most of modern Latvia and Estonia) between 1202 and 1237, but were reprimanded by both pope and emperor for their brutal approach to conversion. They were destroyed by pagan armies at the battle of Saule in 1236, and the following year were disbanded and reorganized as a branch of the **Teutonic Order**. After secularization (1525) the last Grand Master of the Order became Grand Duke of Courland, a fief of the Polish crown.

LLOYD GEORGE, DAVID (1863–1945) British statesman. Born into a poor Welsh family, he was elected a Liberal Member of Parliament in 1890, and entered the Cabinet as president of the Board of Trade (1905–08) and chancellor of the exchequer (1908–15), introducing an ambitious welfare and pension programme. When a coalition Cabinet was formed during the First World War, he became minister of munitions (1915–16), and minister of war (1916), replacing the Liberal Party leader, H.H. Asquith, as prime minister later the same year. In 1918 the coalition won a general election and Lloyd George represented Great Britain at the **Paris Peace Conference**, where he exercised a moderating influence on his allies. In 1922 the Conservative party withdrew its support from the coalition and the Liberals, divided between Asquith and Lloyd George, were heavily defeated in a new general election. Although Lloyd George became party leader, 1926–31, and remained in Parliament almost until his death, he became an increasingly isolated political figure, and the Liberal Party steadily declined as a political force.

LOCARNO PACT A treaty, signed 1 December 1925, between Great Britain, France, Germany, Italy and Belgium. Under its terms Britain and Italy agreed to guarantee the frontiers of Germany with Belgium and France and the continued demilitarization of the Rhineland. **Hitler** repudiated it on 7 March 1936, stationing troops on both sides of the Rhine and re-fortifying it.

LOCKE, JOHN (1632–1704) English philosopher. His most important political work, the second *Treatise of Civil Government* (1690) provided the theoretical justification for government with only limited and revocable powers; his main philosophical work, *An Essay concerning Human Understanding* (1690) was the basis for most 18th century European thought on the function of reason and the importance of environment in life.

LOESS Fine, yellowish, often very fertile soil, carried by the wind; large deposits are found in Europe, Asia and North America.

LOLLARDS Members of a reforming religious movement, influential in the 14th and 15th centuries in Europe, especially in England under **John Wyclif**. It was widely popular for its attacks on Church corruption and its emphasis on individual interpretation of the Bible as the basis for a holy life, but was repressed under the English King Henry IV.

LOMBARDS German people ruling northern Italy, 568–774. Originally one of the tribes forming the **Suebi**, they migrated south from north-west Germany in the 4th century. By the end of the 5th century they occupied approximately the area of modern Austria north of the Danube, and in 568 crossed the Alps into Italy. The Lombard kingdom of Italy was conquered by the **Franks** in 774.

LOMBARD LEAGUE Association of north Italian cities, established in the 12th and 13th centuries to resist the authority of the **Holy Roman Empire**. The League was originally founded in 1167, with 16 members and the blessing of Pope **Alexander III** to defy **Frederick I Barbarossa**, hostilities ending in 1177 with the Peace of Venice and in 1183 with the Peace of Constance. In 1226 the League was revived and strengthened to avert new imperial ambitions by **Frederick II** but was dissolved after Frederick's death in 1250.

LONDON RIOT Popular demonstrations in 1641 by Londoners outside the House of Parliament and **Charles I**'s palace at Whitehall, demanding that the king's chief minister, Strafford, should be sentenced to death.

LONG, HUEY PIERCE (1893–1935) United States senator and governor of Louisiana. He was elected governor in 1928 after a noisy demagogic campaign for the redistribution of wealth and became a senator in 1932. He was assassinated.

LON NOL (1914–85) President of Cambodia, 1970–5. He became a general in the army, then prime minister, 1966–7, and again in 1969. He seized power from Prince **Sihanouk** in a right-wing coup in 1970 but was ousted and fled to Bali in 1975 when the communist **Khmer Rouge** overran the country.

LOUIS I, THE GREAT (1326–82) King of Hungary, 1342–82. He succeeded his father, Charles Robert, a member of the Neapolitan dynasty of Anjou, who was invested with the kingdom after the extinction of the Arpád dynasty in 1301. Louis fought wars against Naples and Venice; in 1370 he acquired the Polish crown, but with little power, and won most of Dalmatia in 1381. One of his daughters, Maria, became Queen of Hungary; the other, **Jadwiga**, Queen of Poland.

LOUIS THE PIOUS (778–840) Emperor of the Franks, son of **Charlemagne**. He was crowned co-emperor in 813, was twice deposed by his four sons and twice restored (830 and 834); his death preceded the break-up of the empire.

LOUIS VI (1081–1137) King of France, also known as Louis the Fat. Son of Philip I, he was designated his successor in 1098, and crowned in 1108. He made substantial progress in extending French royal power and fought major wars against Henry I of England (1104–13 and 1106–20). He arranged an important dynastic marriage between his son. **Louis VII**, and Eleanor, heiress of Aquitaine.

LOUIS VII (c. 1120–80) Known as **Le Jeune** (the Young). King of France, succeeding his father, **Louis VI**, in 1137, after marrying Eleanor, heiress to the dukedom of Aquitaine, and thus effectively extending his lands to the Pyrenees. He repudiated Eleanor for misconduct in 1152, upon which she married his great rival, **Henry II** of England, who took over the claim to Aquitaine. The later years of his reign were marked by continual conflict with the English.

LOUIS IX (1214–70) Capetian king of France, canonized as St Louis. He was crowned at the age of 13. In 1228 he founded the Abbey of Royaumont, and in 1248 led the Sixth **Crusade** to the Holy Land. He sought peace with England by recognizing Henry III as Duke of Aquitaine. He died on a second Crusade, to Tunisia.

LOUIS XI (1423–83) King of France, son of Charles VIII. He succeeded in 1461; in 1477 he defeated a rebellion of nobles, led by **Charles the Bold**, Duke of Burgundy. By 1483 he had united most of France with the exception of Brittany.

LOUIS XII (1426–1515) King of France. Son of Charles, Duke of Orléans, he succeeded his cousin, Charles VIII, in 1498. He embarked on fruitless Italian wars (1499–1504, 1508–13), and was finally driven out by the Holy League – an alliance of England, Spain, the Pope and the Holy Roman Empire – in 1513.

LOUIS XIV (1638–1715) The Sun King (*Le Roi Soleil*), ruler of France without a First Minister, 1661–1715, hence looked upon as the archetype of an absolute monarch. The son of Louis XIII and Anne of Austria, he succeeded in 1643 but remained under **Mazarin**'s tutelage until the cardinal's death. He extended and strengthened France's frontiers, built the palace of Versailles and set a European-wide pattern for courtly life. He founded or refashioned academies, supported artists and craftsmen, writers, musicians, playwrights and scholars, French and non-French. He was hated by Protestants for his revocation of the **Edict of Nantes**; and opposed by the maritime powers and the Austrian Habsburgs who feared that he aimed at European hegemony.

LOUIS XVI (1754–93) King of France, grandson of Louis XV. He married the Austrian Archduchess Marie-Antoinette in 1770, and succeeded to the throne, 1774. The early years of his reign saw France in a state of progressive financial and political collapse; with the outbreak of the French revolution in 1789 the royal family became virtual prisoners of the Paris mob. Their attempted flight in 1791 led to deposition, trial for treason and execution by guillotine in 1793.

LOUIS-PHILIPPE (1773–1850) King of France, son of Louis-Philippe Joseph, Duke of Orléans. Exiled, 1793–1815, during the French revolution and the Napoleonic period, he succeeded to the throne in 1830 after the reactionary regime of Charles X had been ended by the July revolution. His reign was characterized by financial speculation, the ostentatious affluence of the emerging middle class, and growing failure in foreign policy. He abdicated in 1848 after renewed revolutionary outbreaks, and fled to England.

LOUISIANA PURCHASE The western half of the Mississippi Basin, bought from Napoleon in 1803 by President **Thomas Jefferson** for under 3 cents an acre. It added 828,000 square miles to the United States, at the time doubling its area, and opened up the West.

LUBA Also known as Baluba. Bantu-speaking peoples, widespread in southeast Zaire. The main present-day groups all trace their history back to the Luba empires which flourished, but finally broke down, in the 16th and 17th centuries. With the **Lunda** they established a series of satellite states, trading with and buying firearms from the Portuguese in Angola until colonized by the Belgians in the late 19th century.

LUDDITE Machine-smasher, originally a member of one of the bands of workers who systematically broke looms, textile plant and machine tools in Lancashire, Yorkshire and the east Midlands of England during the early industrial revolution (1811–16). Traditionally named after Ned Ludd, a possibly mythical leader of the rioters.

LUDENDORFF, ERICH VON (1865–1938) German soldier. Chief of staff to **Hindenburg** throughout the First World War, he was increasingly influential in German military and (after 1916) domestic policies. After the failure of the offensives on the Western Front of March 1918 he insisted upon an immediate armistice. He fled to Sweden at the end of the war, but returned in 1919 to take part in the Kapp Putsch (1920) and Munich Beer-Hall Putsch (1923). An early supporter of **Hitler**, he sat as a Nazi deputy in the Reichstag, 1924–8.

LUMUMBA, PATRICE (1925–61) First prime minister of Congo (later Zaire). He was educated at a Protestant mission school; became local president of the Congolese trade union, 1955; founded the Mouvement National Congolais, 1958, to work for independence from Belgium. Imprisoned in 1959, he was asked to form the first independent government in 1960. He was removed from office after opposing the Belgian-backed secession of Katanga province. He was murdered.

LUNDA Bantu people, originating in the Katanga-Shaba district of Congo (the central Lunda kingdom) and now spread widely over southeast Congo, eastern Angola, northwest Zambia and the Luapula valley. The Lunda of Kazembe were famous throughout central Africa as ivory and slave traders, especially with the Portuguese.

LUNG YÜN (1888–1962) Chinese warlord. A member of the Lolo minority peoples, he trained as a military officer and joined the staff of **T'ang Chih-yao** in Yunnan. In 1915 he joined the rebellion of Yunnan against **Yüan Shih-k'ai**, which left T'ang in control of the province. In 1927 Lung Yün ousted T'ang , and ruled the Yunnan region as an independent satrapy until 1945. He fostered the cultivation of the opium poppy and inflicted savage taxes on the population. He collaborated unwillingly with **Chiang Kai-shek** during the Japanese War 1937–45, but in 1944 joined a group opposed to the Nationalist government. In 1945 Chiang organized a coup which deposed him, but Lung was given a government post and Yunnan placed under his close relative Lu Han. In 1950 Lung went to Peking as a member of the Communist government, and served until he was purged in 1957.

LUPACA Andean people in the Lake Titicaca region of South America. In alliance with the Incas in the early 15th century they defeated their neighbouring rivals, the **Colla**, but were in turn overthrown and absorbed by the Incas in the 1470s.

LUTHER, MARTIN (1483–1546) German theologian and initiator of the Protestant Reformation. He was ordained priest in 1507, and taught at the University of Wittenberg, 1508–46. His attack on papal abuses provoked excommunication in 1520, but Luther advanced an alternative theology which was adopted by many states of northern Europe (the Lutheran Reformation).

LUTHERANISM A system of theology, originated by **Martin Luther** (1483–1546) and expressed in *The Book of Concord* (1580), which incorporated the three traditional Creeds, the Augsburg Confession, Luther's two Catechisms and the Formula of Concord (1577). The main tenets of Lutheranism are that justification is by faith alone and that the scriptures are the sole rule of faith. The Lutherans have traditionally made a sharp distinction between the kingdom of God and the kingdom of the world, so that the state has sometimes seemed autonomous in its own field.

LUVIANS (LUWIANS) A people established in southern Anatolia by the beginning of the 2nd millennium BC, speaking a language closely related to that of the **Hittites**. Many inscriptions are extant in the Luvian language, written in hieroglyphs commonly called 'hieroglyphic Luvian'.

LUXEMBOURGS European ruling dynasty. Initial line, founded by Count Conrad (d.1086) held the lordship of Luxembourg but became extinct in 1136; a collateral descendant, Henry II, Count of Luxembourg, founded a second line including four emperors of the **Holy Roman Empire**: Henry VIII, **Charles IV**, Wenceslas and Sigismund; on the death of Sigismund in 1438 the family was replaced on the imperial throne by Albert II of Habsburg and his descendants.

LYNN RIOTS Popular revolt at King's Lynn, Norfolk, England in 1597 against the high price of food and the high taxes imposed by the government of **Elizabeth I** to pay for the war against Spain and for the conquest of Ireland.

M

MAASTRICHT, TREATY OF (1991) The agreement between the 12 European Community leaders to promote monetary and political union, thereby expanding the European Community's powers over matters previously controlled by national governments. The treaty also called for the introduction of a single currency for the **EC** by 1999 and laid the groundwork for a common defence policy.

MACARTHUR, DOUGLAS (1880–1964) American general who commanded the defence of the Philippines, 1941–2. From 1942–5 he was Commander, United States Forces in the Pacific. He headed United Nations forces in the Korean War (1950–1) until dismissed by President **Truman** after a policy disagreement.

McCLELLAN, GEORGE BRINTON (1826–85) American general, commander-in-chief of the Union forces in 1861–2 during the American Civil War.

McCONNEL & KENNEDY Machinery manufacturers for the rapidly expanding

English cotton industry in the late 18th and 19th centuries. For many years the firm was virtually the sole supplier of spinning mules to the industry. John Kennedy (1769–1855) made several improvements in the machines used to spin fine yarns.

McKINLEY, WILLIAM (1843–1901) 25th president of the United States. He served in the Civil War under Colonel (later president) **Rutherford Hayes**. He was a member of Congress, 1877–91, and governor of Ohio in 1891–5. He defeated the Populist candidate, **William Jennings Bryan**, in the presidential election in 1896 without ever leaving his front porch. He led the country into the Spanish-America war, 1896, and in the suppression of the subsequent Filipino revolt (1899–1902). Re-elected in 1900 with a huge majority, he was shot the following year by an anarchist at the Pan-American Exhibition in Buffalo.

MACEDONIAN DYNASTY Family of Byzantine emperors, founded by Basil I (867–86) and ruling, with some interruptions, until the death of Theodora (1056). Originally peasant marauders, murdering their way to power, they presided over almost two centuries of Byzantium's highest military, artistic and political achievements.

MACHIAVELLI, NICCOLO (1469–1527) Florentine statesman, historian and political theorist. In response to foreign invasions and the anarchic state of Italy in his time, he wrote his most famous work, *Il Principe (The Prince)* in 1513, advocating the establishment and maintenance of authority by any effective means.

MACMILLAN, HAROLD (1894–1986) British statesman. A Conservative MP 1924–9 and 1931–64, he was noted for progressive social views and for opposition to the policy of appeasement of the dictators, voting against his party on abandonment of sanctions against Italy in 1936. He was British minister resident at Allied headquarters in northwest Africa, 1942–5. He entered the Cabinet in 1951 and held various offices before becoming prime minister, 1957–63, and presiding over the peaceful decolonization of British Africa.

MADERO, FRANCISCO (1873–1913) President of Mexico 1910–13. He inspired, organized and eventually led the movement to displace the dictator **Porfirio Díaz**. His arrest in 1909 was soon followed by release and escape to Texas. In 1910 he declared himself the legitimate resident, and was elected in 1911 after the military successes of his supporters, Pascual Orozco and **Pancho Villa**. He failed to implement **democracy** or stem corruption. He was arrested and assassinated in 1913 after betrayal by an army commander, Victoriano Huerta, in the course of a military revolt.

MADISON, JAMES (1751–1836) Fourth president of the United States, 1809–17. A member of the Continental Congress, 1780–3 and 1787–8, he played a leading role in framing the US Constitution (1787). He broke with the **Federalists** and helped to found the Democratic-Republican party; served **Thomas Jefferson** as secretary of state, 1801–9. During his presidency war broke out between America and Great Britain (1812–14).

MADRID, TREATY OF Agreement, also known as 'Godolphin's Treaty', between England and Spain in 1670 to end piracy in American waters; Spain also confirmed the English possession of Jamaica, captured in 1655.

MAGELLAN, FERDINAND (c. 1480–1521) (Portuguese name, Fernão de Magalhães) First European to navigate in the Pacific Ocean. He was prominent in Portuguese naval and military expeditions to Africa, India and the East, 1505–16. In 1518 he was commissioned by Spain to find a southwest route to the Spice Islands; after sailing through the strait later named after him between South America and Tierra del Fuego, he crossed the Pacific and reached Guam in 1521, with three of his five original ships, but their crews in a state of near-starvation. The round-the-world voyage (the first) was completed by **Elcano** with one ship and 18 survivors, of an original 270 men, after Magellan had been killed by local people near Mactan in the Philippines.

MAGGI Prominent family of Brescia, Italy, which gained control of the city in the later 13th century until the siege by Emperor Henry VII in 1311, after which other families replaced them.

MAGNA CARTA The Great Charter issued under duress by King **John** of England in 1215. Though its provisions, promptly repudiated by John, concerned primarily the relationships of a feudal ruler with vassals, subjects and the Church, revisions and reconfirmations in 1216, 1217, 1225 and most notably by **Edward I** in 1297 asserted the supremacy of the laws of England over the king. Thus it came to be regarded as a keystone of British liberties.

MAGNUS OLAFSSON 'THE GOOD' (1024–47) King of Norway and Denmark, illegitimate son of Olaf Haraldsson (St Olaf). He was exiled to Russia, with his father, at the age of four by **Cnut the Great**. Elected as king in 1039 by Norwegian chieftains, he gained sovereignty over Denmark by 1042. He was unsuccessfully challenged by Cnut's nephew, Sweyn. He agreed to share thrones with his uncle, Harald Hardrada, in 1045. He was killed in a Danish battle while planning to claim the English crown.

MAHABHARATA 'The Great Epic of the Baharata Dynasty'. This vast work of early Indian literature, running to 100,000 couplets (seven times as long as *The Odyssey* and *The Iliad* combined) related the struggle between two families, the Kauravas and the Pandavas, as well as incorporating a mass of other romantic, legendary, philosophic and religious material from the heroic days of early **Hinduism**. Traditionally ascribed to the sage Vyasa, it was more probably the result of 2000 years of constant accretion and reshaping before reaching its present form c. AD 400. Included in it is the *Bhagavadgita (The Lord's Song)*, probably Hinduism's most important text.

MAHAVIRA Indian religious teacher of the 6th century BC, principal founder of **Jainism**. At the age of 30 he renounced his family and became an ascetic, wandering for 12 years in the Ganges valley seeking enlightenment. He shaped and organized the Jaina sect, named from his honorific title of *Jina*, the Conqueror.

MAHDI Islamic concept of the messianic deliverer, who will one day fill the earth with justice, faith and prosperity. The title has been frequently adopted by social revolutionaries since Islam's upheavals in the 7th and 8th centuries – notably by Ubaidallah, founder of the **Fatimid** dynasty in 908, Mohammed ibn Tumart, leader of the 12th century **Almohad** movement, and in 1881 by **Mohammed Ahmed al-Mahdi** on declaring rebellion against the Egyptian administration in the Sudan.

MAHDI, MOHAMMED AHMED AL- (d.1885) Mystic founder of a vast Muslim state in the Sudan. He gathered a growing band of supporters through his preaching and interpretation of Islam; in 1881 he proclaimed a divine mission to purify Islam under the title of al-Mahdi, the Right-Guided One. He swiftly mastered virtually all territory once occupied by Egypt; captured Khartoum in 1885, and created the theocratic state of the Sudan. He died in that year at his new capital, Omdurman; the theocratic state fell to forces under the British general Kitchener in 1898.

MAHMUD OF GHAZNI (971–1030) Muslim warrior and patron of the arts. He was the son of Sebuktigin, a Turkish slave who became ruler of Ghazni (compromising most of modern Afghanistan and northeast Iran). He succeeded to the throne in 998, and from 1001 to 1026 led 17 invading expeditions to India, amassing an empire including the Punjab and most of Persia. His capital, Ghazni, became an Islamic cultural centre rivalling Baghdad.

MAHMUD II (1785–1839) Reforming Ottoman sultan, nephew of Sultan Selim III. He was brought to the throne in 1808 in a coup led by Bayrakdar Mustafa Pasha, later his grand vizier. He was heavily defeated in wars with Russia, Greece, France and Britain, and by **Mohammed Ali**'s insurgents in Syria. He destroyed the moribund janissary corps in 1826, establishing a modern, European-style army in 1831 and a military academy in 1834. He introduced cabinet government, postal service, compulsory education and European dress.

MAIRE, JAKOB LE (1585–1616) Dutch navigator and South Sea explorer. With **Willem Schouten**, in 1615–16 he sailed through Le Maire Strait, rounded Cape Horn for the first time, and discovered some of the Tuamotus, the northern-most islands of the Tonga group, and the Hoorn islands.

MAJAPAHIT Last of the Javanese Hindu-Buddhist empires, founded after the defeat of the Mongol seaborne expedition against Java in 1292. It rose to greatness under Gaja Mada (d.1364), chief minister of King Hayam Wuruk, with whose death in 1389 its decline began. Its size is a matter for dispute; its effective sway was probably limited to east and central Java, Madura, Bali and Lombok, while its powerful fleets ensured the allegiance and tribute of the Spice Islands and the chief commercial ports of southern Sumatra and southern Borneo.

MAJI-MAJI East African revolt against German colonialism which broke out in 1905 and was suppressed in 1907.

MALAN, DANIEL FRANÇOIS (1874–1959) South African politician. Before entering politics, he studied for the Dutch Reformed Church, receiving a doctorate in divinity at the University of Utrecht, Holland (1905). In 1948 he led a 'purified' National party faction to victory, serving as prime minister (1948–54) of the Republic of South Africa's first exclusively Afrikaner government. A right-wing nationalist, Malan is best known for introducing apartheid into South Africa. He retired from public office in 1954.

MALATESTA Italian family, ruling Rimini from the late 13th century until 1500. They first became lords of the city in 1295, when the **Guelph** leader, Malatesta di Verruchio (d.1312) expelled his Ghibelline rivals. Sigismondo Malatesta (1417–68) is often represented as the ideal Renaissance prince – a soldier who also cultivated the arts. In 1461 he was the subject of a **Crusade** launched by Pope Pius II which deprived the family of most of its powers. Sigismondo's son, Roberto il Magnifico (d.1482), recovered Rimini in 1469, but the dynasty was finally driven out by Cesara Borgia in 1500.

MALFANTE, ANTONIO 15th-century Genoese merchant, sometimes known, exaggeratedly, as 'the first explorer of the Sahara'.

MALINKE People of the ancient west African empire of Mali. As the Dyula, or travelling merchants, their traders have remained a potent factor in the economy of the region since the 13th century.

MAMLUKS Generically, military slaves or freedmen, mainly from the Caucasus or central Asia, and employed by many medieval Muslim states. A group of them established a sultanate which ruled Egypt and Syria 1250–1517, until defeated by the **Ottomans**.

MANBY, AARON (1776–1850) English engineer. In 1821 he patented his design for an oscillating steam engine, widely used for marine propulsion, and in 1822 launched the first practical iron ship, the **Aaron Manby**, sailing from London to Paris. He also founded an iron works at Charenton (1810) which made France largely independent of English engine-builders, and in 1822 formed the first company to supply gas to Paris. He returned to England in 1840.

MANCHESTER SCHOOL Group of 19th-century British political economists advocating free trade and *laissez-faire*, led by Richard Cobden (1804–65) and John Bright (1811–89).

MANCHUS People of Manchuria (northeast China) who in 1644 founded the imperial dynasty known as the **Ch'ing**.

MANDATE Former colonial territory, assigned by the **League of Nations** to a victorious Allied power after the First World War under supervision of the League, and in some cases with the duty of preparing it for independence. Great Britain thus assumed responsibility for Iraq, Palestine (from the Ottoman empire) and Tanganyika (from Germany); France for Syria and Lebanon and Belgium for Ruanda-Urundi. The arrangement was replaced by the **United Nations**' Trusteeship System in 1946, except for southwest Africa (Namibia), where South Africa retained its mandate until 1990.

MANDE A west African language group, the Mande-speaking people, found primarily in the savannah plateaux of the western Sudan, where they developed such complex civilizations as the Solinke state of Ghana, around 900 to 1100, and the empire of Mali which flourished in 14th and early 15th centuries. Today the most typical Mande groups are the Bambara, the Malinke and the Solinke, speaking characteristic Mande versions of the Niger-Congo group of languages.

MANDELA, NELSON (1918–) Born in Umtata in the Transkei, Mandela moved to Johannesburg and qualified as a lawyer. In 1944 he joined the African National Congress, becoming its deputy national president in 1952. In 1956 he was arrested and charged with treason but was discharged after a five-year trial. After the Sharpeville massacre and the banning of the ANC in 1960, Mandela went underground but was captured and condemned to life imprisonment in 1964. He was released in February 1990, an event marking the real beginning of political change in South Africa, and resumed leadership of the ANC in the search for a negotiated political settlement. In 1994 he was elected the first president of a multi-racial South Africa.

MANDINGO West African people, related to the larger **Mande** language group, occupying parts of Guinea, Guinea-Bissau, Ivory Coast, Mali, Gambia and Senegal. The many independent tribes are dominated by a hereditary nobility which in one case, the Kangaba, has ruled uninterruptedly for 13 centuries: starting as a small state in the 7th century, Kangaba (on the Mali-Senegal boundary) became the focus for the great Malinke empire of Mali, reaching its peak around 1450.

MANICHAEISM Dualist religion founded in Persia in the 3rd century AD by Mani, 'the Apostle of Light', who tried to integrate the messages of **Zoroaster, Buddha** and **Jesus** into one universal creed. It is often regarded, wrongly, as a Christian heresy: properly it is a religion in its own right, and has influenced many other sects, Christian and otherwise, in both East and West. It became extinct in the Middle Ages, but some scriptures have been recovered in this century in Egypt and Chinese Turkestan.

MANSA MUSA Most famous of the emperors of ancient Mali, he reigned 1312–37. He pushed the frontiers of the empire out to the edges of the Sahara, the tropical rain forest, the Atlantic and the borders of modern Nigeria. He made a lavish pilgrimage to Mecca and actively promoted Islam among his subjects; he also developed Saharan trade, introduced brick buildings and founded Timbuktu and Jenne as world centres of Muslim learning.

MANSUR, ABU AMIR AL- (c. 938–1002) ('Almanzor' in medieval Spanish and Latin texts) Chief minister and effective ruler of the **Umayyad** caliphate in Córdoba, 978–1002. He overthrew and succeeded his vizier in 978, and fought 50 campaigns against the Christians of northern Spain, including an expedition against the great shrine of Santiago de Compostela in 997.

MANSUR, ABU JAFAR AL- (c. 710–75) Second caliph of the **Abbasid** dynasty, great-grandson of **Abbas**, **Mohammed**'s uncle; he succeeded to the caliphate in 754 on the death of his brother as-Saffah. He completed the elimination of the deposed **Umayyad** dynasty, and founded the city of Baghdad, begun in 762.

MANUEL I COMNENUS (1122–80) Emperor of Byzantium, son of **John II Commenus**, he succeeded in 1143. He tried but ultimately failed to build alliances in the West; was defeated in 1156 at Brindisi and expelled from Italy. He forced Jerusalem to recognize Byzantine sovereignty in 1159. In 1167 he added Dalmatia, Bosnia and Croatia to his empire. He broke ties with Venice in 1171. His armies were destroyed by the **Seljuk** Turks at Myriokephalon in 1176.

MANZIKERT, BATTLE OF Fought near the town in Turkish-held Armenia (today Malazgirt, Turkey) in 1071; the **Seljuks**, under Sultan Alp-Arslan (1063–72) decisively defeated the Byzantine armies under Emperor Romanus IV Diogenes (1068–71). The victory led to Seljuk conquest of almost all Anatolia, and fatal weakening of Byzantine power.

MAORI Member of the aboriginal Polynesian people inhabiting New Zealand at the time of its European discovery.

MAO ZEDONG (1893–1976) First chairman of the People's Republic of China (1949–77). He helped to found the Chinese Communist Party in 1921, and until 1926 organized peasant and industrial unions. After the Communist split with the **Kuomintang** in 1927 he set up Communist bases in Hunan, and later in Kiangsi. In 1934–5 he led the Long March of the Red Army from Kiangsi to Yenan. He became the dominant figure in the Party after 1935, establishing it as a peasant-based party. During the second Sino-Japanese War (1937–45) he worked for national unity, and after a bitter civil war in 1949 expelled Nationalist forces from mainland China. In 1966 he launched the Cultural Revolution.

MARATHAS Hindu people of western India, famous in the 17th and 18th centuries for their warlike resistance to the **Mughal** emperors. Now the term covers the 10 million or so members of the Maratha and Kunbi castes in the region bounded by Bombay, Goa and Nagpur, or more loosely the 40 million speakers of the Marathi language.

MARATHON, BATTLE OF A famous victory in 490 BC won on the coastal plain northeast of Athens by the Greeks, under the Athenian general Miltiades, over an invading army of Persians. It is remembered *inter alia* for the feat of the runner Philippides, who raced 150 miles in two days to warn the Spartans and to return with the news that their forces would be delayed by a religious festival.

MARCEL, ÉTIENNE (c. 1316–58) Provost of merchants of Paris, deputy to the Estates General (the French national assembly). He proposed in 1355–6 that the Estates should control royal revenues and purge crown officials. He led Paris in a revolt against the crown in 1357–8, and supported the **Jacquerie**. He was assassinated in 1358 after the revolt collapsed.

MARCHAND, JEAN-BAPTISTE (1863–1934) French explorer and general who in 1897 led a remarkable 18-month march from Libreville, in Gabon, to the Upper Nile, occupying Fashoda in 1898. He withdrew after a prolonged confrontation with Kitchener which provoked an international diplomatic crisis.

MARCION (c. 100–160) Originator of a religious sect challenging Christianity throughout Europe, north Africa and western Asia from the 2nd to the 5th century. Possibly the son of a bishop of Sinope, he went to Rome c. 140, formed separate communities and was excommunicated in 144. He preached the existence of two gods: the Old Testament Creator or Demiurge, i.e. the God of Law, and the God of Love revealed by Jesus, who would overthrow the first. He compiled his own version of the New Testament (the *Instrumentum*), largely based on St Luke and St Paul's Epistles. After his death the Marcionite sect survived many persecutions and remained significant, particularly in Syria, until the 10th century.

MARGARET (1353–1412) Queen of Norway. The daughter of Valdemer III of Denmark, she married Haakon VI of Norway (1343–80), and became effective ruler of Norway and Denmark, c. 1387, and of Sweden, 1389. She was regent on behalf of her great-nephew, Eric of Pomerania, who was crowned ruler of Sweden, Denmark and Norway at the **Union of Kalmar** in 1397.

MARI (Cheremiss) Finno-Ugrian speaking peoples now living mainly in the Autonomous Republics of Mari, on the middle Volga, and Bashkir.

MARIA THERESA (1717–80) Elder daughter of the Emperor Charles VI, and one of the most capable **Habsburg** rulers. She was Archduchess of Austria and Queen of Hungary and Bohemia in her own right, and always overshadowed her husband, the elected Emperor Francis I (1745–65). She died after 15 years of widowhood and a troublesome co-regency with her son, **Joseph II**.

MARINIDS Berber dynasty, ruling in Morocco and elsewhere in north Africa from the 13th to the 15th centuries, replacing the **Almohads** on the capture of Fez (1248) and Marrakesh (1269). They launched a holy war in Spain which lasted until the mid-14th century. Despite many attempts, they failed to re-establish the old Almohad empire; after a period of internal anarchy, the related Wattasids assumed control of Morocco in 1465, but were finally expelled, by the **Saadi** sharifs, in 1549.

MARQUETTE, JACQUES (1637–75) French Jesuit missionary and explorer, the first Frenchman to sail on the Mississippi (1673); he explored much of its length with **Jolliet**.

MARRANO Insulting Spanish term for a **Jew** who converted to **Christianity** in Spain or Portugal to avoid persecution but secretly continued to practise **Judaism**; also used to designate the descendants of such a person.

MARSHALL PLAN Popular name given to the European recovery programme, proposed in 1947 by US Secretary of State General George C. Marshall (1880–1959), to supply US financial and material aid to war-devastated Europe. Rejected by Eastern European countries under Soviet pressure, it came into force in Western Europe in 1948 and was completed in 1952.

MARSHALL, WILLIAM (1745–1818) Agriculturalist and leading improver, famous for his 12-volume *General Survey, from personal experience, observation and enquiry, of the Rural Economy of England* (1787–93). He proposed setting up a governmental Board of Agriculture, put into effect by Parliament in 1793.

MARTIN IV (c. 1210–85) Pope from 1281 to 1285. He supported **Charles I** of Naples and Sicily, and opposed the Aragonese claims after the **War of the Sicilian Vespers**.

MARX, KARL HEINRICH (1818–1883) German philosopher, economist and social theorist whose account of change through conflict is known as historical, or dialectical, materialism. His *Das Kapital* is the fundamental text of **Marxist** economics and his systematic theses on class struggle, history and the importance of economic factors in politics have exercised an enormous influence on later thinkers and political activists.

MARXIST Follower of the social, political and economic theories developed by Karl **Marx**. Characteristic beliefs include dialectical materialism, the collapse of **capitalism** through its internal contradictions, the dictatorship of the proletariat and a withering away of the state after the achievement of a classless society.

MASON-DIXON LINE Originally a boundary line between the American states of Pennsylvania and Maryland named after the English surveyors, Charles Mason and Jeremiah Dixon, who first delineated it, 1763–7. It later became a symbolic frontier between slave and free states in the American Union.

MATABELE (also known as Ndebele) Southern African people, who broke away from the **Nguni** of Natal in the early 19th century. Under **Mzilikazi** they migrated to the High Veld area of modern Transvaal, and later the Marico valley. In 1837, after confrontation with Dutch settlers in the Transvaal, they crossed the river Limpopo into `Matabeleland (southern Rhodesia). The resulting state grew powerful under the leadership of Mzilikazi's successor, Lobengula. They were finally defeated by settlers of the British South Africa Company in 1893.

MATACOS South American Indians, forming the largest and most important group of the Chaco Indians in the Gran Chaco region of northwest Argentine. They were first encountered by Europeans in 1628, and resisted Christianity and colonization, suffering large-scale massacre, before being placed on reservations and in Spanish government colonies. They are now gradually being incorporated into the *mestizo* (mixed blood) population of the Chaco.

MATILDA (1046–1115) Countess of Tuscany. She was a strong supporter of Pope Gregory VII. Having acknowledged (c. 1080) papal overlordship of her lands, strategically placed across the route of German invasions of Italy, she eventually made Emperor Henry V her heir, thus giving rise to much conflict between the Empire and the Papacy.

MATTHIAS CORVINUS (1440–90) Elected King of Hungary (1458) and claimant to the throne of Bohemia from 1469. He acquired Moravia, Silesia and Lusatia in 1478, Vienna in 1485, and built up the most powerful kingdom in central Europe. He was also a patron of science and of literature.

MAURYAS First Indian dynasty to establish rule over the whole sub-continent. The dynasty was founded in 321 BC by **Chandragupta Maurya**, and steadily extended under his son Bindusara and Grandson **Ashoka**. Power was gradually eroded under **Ashoka**'s successors, finally dying out c. 180 BC.

MAXIMILIAN I (1459–1519) Holy Roman Emperor, son of Frederick III. He married Mary of Burgundy in 1477; was crowned king of Germany in 1486 and emperor in 1493. He achieved a partial reform of the imperial administration, but failed in 1499 to subjugate the Swiss cantons. He was succeeded by his grandson **Charles V**.

MAXIMILIAN (1832–67) Emperor of Mexico. Younger brother of the Austrian emperor, Francis Joseph I, in 1863 he accepted the offer of the Mexican throne as an unwitting pawn in the plot by Mexican opponents of **Juárez** and the French emperor, **Napoleon III**. He was installed by French troops and crowned, 1864. His attempts at liberal reform were nullified by local opposition and lack of funds. He was deserted by the French in 1867, surrounded, starved and tricked into surrender by the armies of Juárez and shot in June that year.

MAYA Indian people of the Yucatán peninsula and the adjoining areas of southern Mexico, Guatemala and Honduras. The Classic period of Maya civilization (marked by fine buildings, magnificent art and an advanced knowledge of mathematics and astronomy) falls between the 3rd and 9th centuries AD. Archaeologically it is best represented at the southern cities of Tikal, Copán, Uaxactún, Quiriguá and Piedras Negras. In the 9th century, for reasons still poorly understood, Classic Maya civilization declined. Mexican (*see* **Toltec**) influence became important, and the main centres of power shifted to Chichén Itzá and Mayapán in northern Yucatán. Although the Spanish conquest destroyed much of the political and religious life, the Maya still exist as a linguistic and cultural unit in their original homelands.

MAYFLOWER Famous ship that carried the 102 pilgrims of the later United States from England to found the first permanent New England colony at Plymouth, Massachusetts, in 1620. Her precise size is not recorded, but she was probably about 180 tons and some 90 ft (27m) long. Originally she set out for Virginia, but was blown north first to Cape Cod and then to Plymouth.

MAZARIN, JULES (1602–61) Italian-born French statesman. He pursued a career in papal service, 1625–36, was brought into the service of Louis XIII by **Richelieu** in 1639 and, on French nomination, was made a cardinal in 1641. He inherited Richelieu's position as Louis XIII's first minister. The king made him godfather to the future **Louis XIV**, over whose training for kingship he had a good deal of influence. He showed skill both in handling the civil wars of the **Fronde** and in negotiating gains for France under the treaties of **Westphalia** (1648) and the Pyrenees (1659).

MAZZINI, GIUSEPPE (1805–72) Italian revolutionary and patriot. He founded the highly influential Young Italy movement and a journal of that name in 1831. Following the failure of the invasion of Savoy in 1834, and banished from Switzerland, he arrived in London in 1837. In 1849 he was First Triumvir, in effect executive ruler, of the Roman Republic, an office filled with tolerance and enlightenment. As a republican, he refused to acknowledge the Italian Kingdom of 1861.

MEADE, GEORGE GORDON (1815–72) Union general in the American Civil War, best remembered for his victory in the battle of Gettysburg (1863).

MEDES The branch of the Iranian invaders settled in the northwest of present-day Iran. Under Cyaxares (c. 625 BC) the Medes became a major military power which, once it had settled accounts with the Scythian invaders of northern Iran, made an alliance with Babylon to destroy the hated Assyrian empire. Under the last king, Astyages, the Medes were defeated by the Persian **Cyrus II the Great** in 550 BC, in whose empire the 'Medes and Persians' were held in equal honour. Thereafter, especially under the Sasanids, the Medes became effectively merged with the other groupings which came to constitute the Iranian nation-state.

MEDICI Most important of the great families of Florence. Their origins are obscure, but they were established in the 13th century in the cloth trade and in finance, and soon exercised considerable political influence. The family developed three lines: that of Chiarissimo II, who failed to gain power in Florence in the 14th century; that of Cosimo the Elder (1389–1464) who became the hereditary, although uncrowned, monarch of Florence; and that of Cosimo, who became Grand Duke of Tuscany in 1569. Tthe line ended with the death of Gian Gastone, 1737. The family provided many rulers and patrons, and three Popes.

MEGALITH (meaning 'great stone') Monument constructed of large undressed stones or boulders, usually as a ritual centre (e.g. a stone circle) or burial monument (e.g. chambered cairn). Of many different kinds, megaliths were erected by simple agricultural communities in many parts of the world, most notably in **Neolithic** Europe during the 3rd millennium BC.

MEHMED I, ÇELIBI (d.1421) Younger son of **Bayezid I** and reunifier of the Ottoman state after the defeat of Ankara (1402), the death of his father and the civil war (1403–13) with his brothers. Mehmed, from a territorial base at Amasya, moved to defeat successively Isa in Brusa, Süleyman in Edirne (1403–11), and Musa in Rumeli (1411–13), while maintaining nominal allegiance to the Timurids, and later overcoming both dangerous social revolts and Byzantine-inspired attempts to place his brother Mustafa on the throne (1415–16). By his death the prestige, if not the full authority, of the sultanate was restored, enabling it to survive the further shocks of the first years of **Murad II**'s reign.

MEHMED II, FATIH ('the Conqueror') (1432–81) Ottoman Sultan succeeding in 1451. By the conquest of Constantinople in 1453 Mehmed II obtained for the Ottoman state a fit site for the capital of a would-be universal world empire. His reign is a record of unceasing warfare: against Hungary, Venice, the **Ak Koyunlu** and the Knights of St John. The last vestiges of Greek rule disappeared (in the Morea 1460, in Trebizond 1461); Serbia (1459), Bosnia (1463) and Karaman (1466) were annexed; Moldavia (1455) and the khanate of the Crimea (1475–8) rendered tributary.

MEHMED IV AVCI ('the Hunter') (1642–93) Ottoman sultan, succeeding in 1648. His reign was most notable for the emergence in 1656 of the grand vizierate as the dominating institution of the state under the ministerial family of **Köprülü**. He fought incessant and not altogether unsuccessful wars in the Mediterranean (reduction of Crete, 1644–69, ended by the 13-year siege of Candia); and on the northern frontiers of the empire (invasion of Translyvania 1654, conquest of Podolia 1672). Against the **Habsburgs** he was less successful (St Gotthard campaign 1663, second unsuccessful siege of Vienna 1683). The subsequent loss of Hungary (1684–7) fuelling popular resentment, and exacerbated by the Sultan's withdrawal from matters of state and notorious obsession with hunting, precipitated his deposition in 1687 and detention until his death.

MEIJI Name meaning 'enlightened rule' by which the Japanese emperor, Mutsuhito, was known during his long reign. Mutsuhito (1852–1912) came to the throne in 1867; within a year the 'Meiji Restoration' ended two and a half centuries of semi-isolation in Japan under the **Tokugawa** shogunate. Under his rule, industrialization and modernization began, and a Western democratic constitution was adopted (1889). By the time of his death, Japan was widely accepted as a world power; his role was largely symbolic, new political leaders being more directly responsible for the reshaping of the nation.

MELGAREJO, MARIANO (1818–71) Bolivian dictator. A general in the Bolivian army, he deposed José Maria Achá in 1864 to become president. He conceded to Chile some of Bolivia's claim to the rich nitrate deposits of the Atacama Desert. He was deposed and assassinated in the same year.

MENELIK II (1844–1913) Emperor of Ethiopia. He was enthroned in 1889, and in 1896 defeated an Italian invasion at Adowa to ensure his country's independence and consolidate its power. He greatly expanded the boundaries of Ethiopia by conquering Galla lands in the southwest and Ogaden in the east.

MENES Traditionally, the first king to unite Upper and Lower Egypt, c. 3100 BC; he may also have founded the royal capital of Memphis. He is said by the historian Manetho to have ruled for 62 years and to have been killed by a hippopotamus.

MENSHEVIKS Named from **Mensheviki**, Russian for 'the minority'. Moderate faction in the Russian Social Democratic Party, which generally supported the **Bolshevik** regime during the civil war, after which most Mensheviks were either liquidated or absorbed into the Russian Communist Party, or emigrated.

MENTUHOTEP I Governor of the Theban province who, according to tradition, in c. 2120 became the first king of the 11th Dynasty and 'ancestor' of the Middle Kingdom, c. 2040 BC.

MENTUHOTEP II (d.c. 2010 BC) King of Egypt's 11th Dynasty. He acceded c. 2060 to the throne of Upper Egypt. In 2046 he launched a campaign against the Herakleopolitan kingdom of Lower and Middle Egypt and by c. 2040 had reunited the country.

MERCANTILISM Economic theory much favoured in the 16th and 17th centuries, under which a country's prosperity was held to depend on its success in accumulating gold and silver reserves. It favoured a strict limitation of imports and the aggressive promotion of export trade.

MEROVINGIANS Frankish dynasty, ruling much of Gaul from the time of **Clovis** to their replacement by the **Carolingians** in 751.

MESOLITHIC The middle part of the **Stone Age** in Europe, representing hunting and collecting groups in the period of present-day climatic conditions after the end of the last glaciation, 10,000 years ago. It succeeded the reindeer-hunting groups of the **Palaeolithic**, and was gradually displaced by the incoming farmers of the **Neolithic**.

METAXAS, IOANNIS (1871–1941) Greek military leader. After reaching the rank of general he emerged as dictator of Greece in 1936; he defeated the Italians when they invaded the country in 1940.

METHODIST Member of one of the several Protestant denominations which developed after 1730 from the Church of England revival movement led by John and Charles Wesley. it emerged as a separate church in 1791 with supporters in both North America and Great Britain.

METHODIUS, ST *see* **Cyril**

METHUEN TREATY Commercial agreement signed in 1703 between England and Portugal. It was named after John Methuen (c. 1650–1706), at that time British ambassador to Lisbon. The treaty gave a preferential tariff on Portuguese wine in exchange for freer import of English woollens, and helped to promote the drinking of port in England.

METTERNICH, PRINCE KLEMENS WENZEL LOTHAR VON (1773–1859) Austrian statesman. he was ambassador to various nations, and minister of foreign affairs, 1809; following a period of collaboration with France, he then joined the victorious alliance against **Napoleon**. He was a leading figure at the **Congress of Vienna**, 1814–15, during which he restored the Habsburg empire to a leading place in Europe. He continued to be dominant in the Austrian government until the revolution of 1848.

MEWAR Independent state in northern India, first prominent in the 8th century under the Rajput clan of the Guhilas. Under Hamir in the 14th century it defied the Muslim armies of **Alauddin**; enriched by the discovery of silver and lead, it continued to battle with the Delhi sultanate and their **Mughal** successors. The state was in decline after Rana Sanga's defeat by Babur in 1527; **Akbar**'s long war against Rana Pratap was inconclusive, but Pratap's son accepted Mughal suzerainty.

MEZZOGIORNO Name for the region of Italy south of Rome, covering roughly the area of the former kingdom of Naples. Its longstanding backwardness, unemployment and low standard of living (half the per capital income of the north) have made it a perpetual preoccupation of Italian governments and planners.

MIAO Mountain-dwelling people of China, Vietnam, Laos and Thailand. Divided into more than a hundred groups distinguished by dress, dialect and customs, its members all share a heritage of Sino-Ttibetan languages. In China they are concentrated in the provinces of Kweichow, Hunan, Szechwan, Kwangsi and Yunnan and Hainan island.

MIDLAND RISING Peasant rebellion in 1607 in several shires of the English east Midlands, caused mainly by the enclosure of common land by landlords which deprived the local population of grazing rights.

MIESZKO I (d.992) First ruler of united Poland, a member of the **Piast** dynasty. He succeeded as Duke of Poland c. 963; he expanded his territories into Galicia and Pomerania. In 966 he accepted (Roman) **Christianity** from Bohemia, and placed his country under the protection of the Holy See (mainly in the hope of securing papal protection against the 'crusade' of the Germans against the Slavs).

MIESZKO II (930–1034) King of Poland, succeeding to the throne in 1025. He lost much territory to Bohemia and the **Holy Roman Empire**.

MILAN, EDICT OF Proclamation issued in AD 313, granting permanent religious toleration for people of all faiths throughout the Roman empire. It was jointly promulgated by the emperors Licinius in the Eastern and **Constantine I** in the Western empire.

MILNER, ALFRED (1854–1925) 1st Viscount Milner, British statesman and imperialist. As High Commissioner for South Africa, 1897–1905, he was responsible for the reconstruction of the Transvaal and Orange River Colony after the South African War. He was a member of the War Cabinet, 1916–18, War Secretary, 1918, and Colonial Secretary, 1919–21.

MILITARY FRONTIER The Habsburg frontier (*Militärgrenze*) consisted at the end of the 16th century of a long strip of southern Croatia in which immigrants, holding land in return for military service, manned a line of forts. The system was later extended to Slavonia and subsequently to the Banat of Temesvár and Transylvania, thus covering the whole frontier with the Ottoman empire. Highly unpopular among the Croats and Hungarians, it was finally abolished in 1872.

MING Chinese imperial dynasty ruling 1368 to 1644; *see* pp. 166–7

MINISTERIALES Originally of servile status, from the 11th century onwards they served as stewards, chamberlains and butlers to kings and other lords in Germany. Gradually, as they assumed military, administrative and political functions, their social status improved until, in the 14th century, their estates and offices became hereditary, and they were accepted as members of the nobility.

MINOS Early king of Crete, referred to by **Homer** and Thucydides. According to legend he was the son of Zeus and Europa, and husband of Pasiphae. Knossos was said to have been his capital and the focus of his vast seapower. The 'Minoan' civilization of Crete (c. 3000–1500 BC) was named after him by Sir Arthur Evans, excavator of Knossos.

MISHNAH Compilation of the oral interpretations of legal portions of the Bible by the **Pharisees** and Rabbis; codified by **Judah ha-Nasi**, in Palestine around AD 200, it served as the basis for the **Talmud**.

MITCHELL, SIR THOMAS LIVINGSTONE (1792–1855) Australian explorer. Born in Scotland, he joined the British Army in 1811 and served in the Peninsular War. As surveyor-general of New South Wales (from 1828) he surveyed the province, constructed roads and (1831–47) led four major expeditions to explore and chart the Australian interior. He produced *Australian Geography* (1850) for use in schools – the first work to place Australia at the centre of the world – and published his expedition journals.

MITHRAISM Worship of Mithra or Mithras, ancient Indian and Persian god of justice and law; in pre-Zoroastrian Persia a supporter of Ahura Mazda, the great god of order and light. In the Roman empire Mithraism spread as a mystery-cult with Mithras as a divine saviour, underground chapels, initiation rites, a common meal, and the promise of a blessed immortality. The adherents were men only, mostly soldiers, traders and civil servants. In the 4th century it was ousted by **Christianity**.

MITHRIDATES (120–63 BC) King of Pontus, in Asia Minor. He assumed the throne as Mithridates VI, known as 'the Great'. He fought three wars with Rome, finally being defeated by **Pompey**.

MITTERAND, FRANÇOIS (1916–96) French president. He was active in the resistance in the Second World War and became a deputy in 1946, holding various offices in the Fourth Republic. He was critical of **de Gaulle**'s Fifth Republic, set up in 1958, and unsuccessfully challenged the general in the 1965 presidential elections. He tried to unify the French left, achieving success with the setting-up of the Parti Socialiste in 1971. He displaced Giscard d'Estaing as president in 1981 and introduced a policy of nationalization. Economic problems soon forced him to adopt austerity measures and abandon many socialist principles. He was obliged to cooperate with a Gaulist prime minister, Jacques Chirac, after 1986. Mitterand defeated Chirac in the 1988 presidential elections, restoring socialist pre-eminence. Despite ill-health and troubles with his party, he managed to remain in office until 1995, when he retired and was replaced by Chirac.

MOBUTU SESE SEKO (1930–97) President of Zaire (formerly Congo). He enrolled as a clerk in the Belgian Congolese army in 1949. In the mid-1950s he edited a weekly newspaper *Actualités Africaines*. He joined **Lumumba** in 1958 as a member of *Mouvement National Congolais*; and became chief of staff of the Force Publique after Congo gained independence in 1960. He supported **Kasavabu** and then ousted him in a coup in 1965, put down a white mercenary uprising in 1967 and nationalized the Katanga copper mines. In 1977 he defeated an invasion of Shaba province (Katanga) from Angola. By 1992 he found himself challenged by a growing pro-**democracy** movement, which criticised the harshness of his rule and laid accusations of human rights abuses. In May 1997 Mobutu was forced to give up the presidency. His successor, Laurent Kabila, renamed the country the Democratic Republic of Congo.

MOHAMMED (Muhammad) (c. 570–632) Prophet and founder of Islam, born in Mecca in western Arabia (now part of Saudi Arabia). When aged about 25 he married Khadija, widow of a wealthy merchant (later he made several other marriages, some for political reasons). In about 610 he received a religious call, regarded by himself and his followers as revelations from God, later written down in the **Koran**. He was forced by opposition in Mecca to emigrate to Medina in 622 at the invitation of some Arab groups there; this emigration, or **Hegira**, is the starting point of the Muslim calendar. In Medina he became first arbitrator, then ruler of a new kind of religious and political community, the Umma. He conquered Mecca in 630 and then unified much of Arabia under his leadership. After his death he was succeeded as leader of the Umma, but not as prophet, by **Abu Bakr**, first of the line of caliphs.

MOHAMMED ABDUH (1849–1905) Islamic religious reformer, born in Egypt. In 1882 he was exiled for his political activity after the British occupation of Egypt. Returning, he was appointed appellate judge in 1891. He suggested many modernizing liberal reforms in Islamic law, education, ritual and social thought.

MOHAMMED ALI (1769–1849) Founder of modern Egypt; born in Macedonia. He was appointed Ottoman viceroy in Egypt, 1805. He took Syria from the Turks in 1831 but was forced to give it up in 1840 after European intervention. In the following year he was compensated by recognition as hereditary ruler of Egypt and the Sudan.

MOHAMMED V (1906–61) King of Morocco. He succeeded his father as sultan of Morocco in 1927, then under French tutelage which he worked to remove. Deposed and exiled by the French, 1953–5, he was first reinstated as sultan and then recognized as sovereign (1956) and first king of Morocco (1957).

MÖNGKE (d.1259) Mongol leader, grandson of Genghis Khan. He played a prominent part in the great Mongol drive into western Asia and Europe. Elected Great Khan in 1251, he planned a world conquest, from China to Egypt.

MONISM Philosophic doctrine that asserts the single nature of phenomena and denies duality or pluralism (i.e. the separateness of mind and matter). Religiously, it is also the doctrine that there is only one Being, not an opposition of good and evil, or a distinction of God from the world.

MONOPHYSITES Those who followed Eutyches and Dioscorus, Patriarch of Alexandria (d.454), who taught that there was only one nature, not two, in the person of **Jesus** Christ. This doctrine was condemned by the **Council of Chalcedon** (451). Modern churches which grew out of Monophysitism are orthodox in belief though they retain some Monophysite terminology, notably the Coptic, Syrian and Armenian variations.

MONROE, JAMES (1758–1831) Fifth president of the United States. He negotiated the **Louisiana Purchase** (1803). During his presidency, 1817–25, he drew up with his secretary of state, **John Quincy Adams**, the Monroe Doctrine, which has aimed at excluding foreign influence from the Western Hemisphere ever since.

MONTAGNARDS Hill-dwellers in Indo-China. In Vietnam they cultivate rice on burned-out forest land, live in longhouses or huts raised on piles, trace their descent through the female line, and speak a variety of Mon-Khmer and Malayo-Polynesian languages.

MONTANIST Follower of the heretical Christian sect founded in Phrygia by Montanus and by two women, Prisca and Maximilla, in the 2nd century AD. The group was ecstatic and prophetic, restoring belief in the present power of the spirit; there was mystical identification with the divine and ascetic practice. **Tertullian** was a notable convert, but by the 3rd century the sect was under condemnation; it persisted in Phrygia until the 5th century.

MONTCALM, LOUIS, MARQUIS DE (1712–59) French general who as commander-in-chief of the French Canadian forces defended Canada against the British in the French and Indian War (1756–60). He was killed during the battle for Quebec on the Heights of Abraham.

MONTESQUIEU, BARON DE (1689–1755) French political philosopher. His main works included *Lettres Persanes* (1721), satirizing French life and politics, and *L'Esprit des Lois* (1748), his masterpiece, which first set out many of the key ideas in modern democratic and constitutional thought, characteristic of the Enlightenment and of rationalism.

MONTFORT, SIMON DE (c. 1160–1218) Baron of Montfort (near Paris). He became a leader of the Albigensian Crusade and Count of Toulouse after the battle of Muret; 1213, he extended north French and Catholic influence in the south of France. He was the father of Simon de Montfort, Earl of Leicester, the opponent of Henry III of England.

MORDAUNT, SIR JOHN (1698–1780) British general. In 1756 he commanded the army assembled in Dorset to repel an expected French invasion; in 1757 he led an unsuccessful expedition (with Admiral Hawke) to attack the French naval base at Rochefort, and was court-martialled for his failure.

MORELOS, JOSÉ MARIA (1765–1815) Mexican priest and revolutionary. He joined Hidalgo's insurrection against the Spanish colonial government, 1811, and took command in southern Mexico after Hidalgo's death, leading a successful guerrilla army but with too few men to consolidate his victories. In 1813 he called the Congress of Chilpancingo, which declared Mexican independence, but two years later was captured, defrocked and shot as a traitor after directing a heroic rearguard action against the Spaniards.

MORENO, MARIANO GARCIA (1778–1811) Argentine independence leader. He practised as a lawyer in Buenos Aires; in 1809 published his 'Landowners' petition' (*Representación de los hacendados*) attacking restrictive Spanish trade laws, and in 1810 joined the revolutionary junta which replaced the Spanish administration. He became secretary for military and political affairs; founded Argentina's national library and official newspaper, *La Gaceta de Buenos Aires*. He was forced to resign after prematurely advocating complete separation on a diplomatic mission to London.

MORGAN, JOHN PIERPONT (1837–1913) United States financier. In 1871 he joined the New York firm of Drexel, Morgan & Co. (renamed J.P. Morgan & Co. in 1895); under his guidance this became one of the world's greatest financial institutions, deeply involved in US government borrowing, reorganization of the US railways and the formation of such massive industrial groups as US Steel, International Harvester and the General Electric Company. By the time of his death his name was accepted everywhere as a symbol of 'money power'; he had also formed a great art collection.

MOSES Israelite leader, prophet and lawgiver who flourished some time between the 15th and 13th centuries BC. According to the Old Testament, he was born in Egypt; he led the Israelites out of slavery, and travelled forty years in the Sinai desert seeking Canaan, the land promised to the descendants of **Abraham**. He received the Ten Commandments, the basis of Jewish law; he died within sight of the promised land.

MOSLEY, SIR OSWALD (1896–1980) Leader of the British Union of Fascists. He served as a member of parliament, successively as a Conservative, Independent and Labour representative. He left the Labour Party in 1930 to found the right-wing 'New Party' and, later, the BUF or Blackshirts. He was imprisoned by the British government during the Second World War, and subsequently lived in France.

MOSSADEQ, MOHAMMED (?1880–1967) Iranian politician. As prime minister, 1951–3, he nationalized the Anglo-Iranian oil company. After a struggle for power with the Shah and his supporters, and with Western oil interests, he was overturned by a *coup d'état* in 1953 and imprisoned until 1956.

MOUNTBATTEN, LOUIS, EARL (1900–79) British military commander. A grandson of Queen Victoria, he entered the Royal Navy in 1913. He was allied chief of combined operations, 1942–3; supreme commander Southeast Asia, 1943–6; last viceroy (1947) and first governor-general (1947–8) of India; commanded the Mediterranean fleet (1948–9 and 1952–4); became first sea lord (1955–9), chief of UK defence staff and chairman of chiefs of staff committee (1959–65); and personal aide-de-camp to the British sovereign from 1936. He was killed by Irish terrorists in 1979.

MSIRI (d.1891) African king, also known as Ngetengwa and Mwendo. Born near Tabora, now in Tanzania, in 1856 he settled in southern Katanga (Shaba); with a handful of Nyamwezi supporters, he seized large parts of this valuable copper-producing region, and by 1870 had largely displaced the previous Lunda rulers. His rejection of overtures from the British South Africa Company in the 1880s resulted in the Copper Belt being divided between Great Britain (Zambia) and Belgium (Zaire). He was shot while negotiating with emissaries from **Leopold II** of Belgium's Congo Free State.

MUGABE, ROBERT (1924–) Zimbabwean political leader. He worked as a schoolteacher before joining the nationalist movement in 1960. A Marxist, he co-founded the Zimbabwe African National Union (ZANU) in 1963, but was subsequently imprisoned for 11 years. After his release, he joined the Patriotic Front in 1976 and waged a guerrilla war against the white supremacist government of **Ian Smith**. After the ceasefire (1980) he was elected the first prime minister of independent Zimbabwe.

MUGHALS Dynasty of Muslim emperors in India; *see page* 168

MUHAMMAD IBN TUGHLUQ (c. 1290–1351) Indian empire-builder, who succeeded his father in 1325 as ruler of the Delhi sultanate. He extended the frontiers far into southern India, fighting many campaigns to consolidate his gains; he failed, however, to impose coherent control, and saw his domains begin to crumble before he died.

MUIZZUDIN MUHAMMAD (d.1206) Greatest of the **Ghurids**. He helped his brother to seize power in Ghur, northwest Afghanistan, c. 1162, expelled Turkish nomads from Ghazni, 1173; invaded northern India, 1175; annexed the **Ghaznavid** principality of Lahore, 1186. He was defeated by a **Rajput** coalition at Tara, 1191, but returned to rout them in 1192. He was assassinated in 1206.

MUJIBUR RAHMAN (1920–75) East Pakistan (now Bangladesh) political leader. He worked for Bengali rights until independence from British rule (1947), founded the Awami League (1949) opposed to the domination of West Pakistan, of which he became general secretary (1953) and president (1966). Tensions resulting from his party's majority victory and demand for autonomy from West Pakistan (1970) resulted in an India-Pakistan war, and an independent Bangladesh (1971). In 1975 he became president with dictatorial powers, but was killed in a coup the same year.

MUKDEN, BATTLE OF Main land engagement of the Russo-Japanese War (1904–05). Mukden (Shen-yang), the industrial centre of Manchuria, became a tsarist stronghold after Russia obtained extensive railway building rights in the region (1896). The battle lasted over two weeks, starting in late February 1905 and ending with Japanese occupation of the city on 10 March.

MULVANY, WILLIAM THOMAS (1806–85) Irish industrialist. An engineer and civil servant 1833–49, he went to the German Ruhr district in 1854 and directed the opening of coalmines and ironworks there. In 1858 he organized an association of Ruhr industrialists (the *Bergbauverein*) which transformed the Ruhr into the largest coalfield and industrial complex on the European continent.

MÜNSTER, TREATY OF An agreement signed in January 1648 as part of the arrangements known collectively as the Peace of Westphalia, which ended the Thirty Years' War. It brought Spanish recognition of the independence of the Dutch Republic and brought to an end the Dutch Revolt.

MURAD I (c. 1326–89) Third ruler of the Ottoman state, succeeding **Orkhan** in 1362. He controlled (or profited from) the continuing Turkish expansion in the Balkans which brought Thrace and later Thessaly, the south Serbian principalities and much of Bulgaria under Ottoman control. Byzantium, Bulgaria and Serbia were successively reduced to vassalage after the defeat of hostile coalition forces at Chirmen (Chermanon) in 1371 and Kossovo in 1389; Murad was killed during the latter battle. Ottoman territory was also expanded in Anatolia (acquisition of Ankara, 1354; hostilities with the Karaman in the 1380s).

MURAD II (1404–51) Ottoman sultan, son of **Mehmed I**. Succeeding to the throne in 1421, he spent the early years of his reign overcoming rival claimants backed by Byzantium or Karaman. After a seven-year war with Venice, Murad took Salonika in 1430. The later years of his reign were dominated by the struggle with Hungary for the lands of the lower Danube, Serbia and Wallachia. Murad gained control over Serbia in 1439 but in 1440 failed to take Belgrade; by 1443 the Ottomans were forced on to the defensive at Izladi, and in the following year, having made an unfavourable peace with Hungary and Karaman, Murad abdicated in favour of his 12-year-old son **Mehmed II**. Following the penetration of the Balkans by a Christian army, Murad led the Ottoman forces to a crushing victory at Varna in 1444. Two years later he reassumed the throne; in 1448 he defeated the Hungarians once more at Kossovo.

MUSSOLINI, BENITO (1883–1945) Italian dictator. He practised as a schoolteacher and journalist; having been expelled in 1914 from the Socialist party for advocating support of the Allied powers, in 1919 he organized the Fascist party, advocating nationalism, syndicalism and violent anti-**communism**, backed up by a para-military organization, the Blackshirts. He organized a march on Rome in 1922. He was appointed prime minister and then, as Il Duce (the Leader), established himself as totalitarian dictator. He invaded Ethiopia in 1935, formed the Rome-Berlin Axis with **Hitler** the following year, and in 1940 declared war on the Allies. He was defeated in 1943, installed by Hitler as head of a puppet state (Republic of Salo) in northern Italy and shot by Italian partisans in 1945.

MWENEMUTAPA (later Mashonaland) Kingdom of southeast Africa between the 14th and 18th centuries, with its capital probably at Zimbabwe; famous for its gold deposits, which attracted Portuguese traders, based in Mozambique, from 1505 onwards.

MYCENAEAN Ancient Greek civilization flourishing c. 1600–1100 BC, culturally influenced by **Minoan** Crete. It was centred on the city of Mycenae, in Argolis, where the most famous surviving monuments include the citadel walls with the Lion gate, and the treasury of Atreus.

MZILIKAZI (d.1870) Matabele (Ndebele) chief. He fled from Zululand to set up a new kingdom north of the Vaal river, but was defeated by the Boers, 1836; he withdrew across the Limpopo river and established the Matabele kingdom.

N

NABOPOLASSAR (d. 605 BC) King of Babylon and destroyer of Assyria, a notable of one of the Kaldu (Chaldaean) tribes of southern Babylonia. While governor of the Sea-land province, he assumed leadership of an insurrection against the Assyrians in 627 BC. He founded the last native Babylonian dynasty, the Chaldaean, in 626, quickly gaining control of much of Babylonia. He unsuccessfully besieged Ashur, 616, formed an alliance with the **Medes**, 614, and made a joint assault on Nineveh which was completed in 612. He was succeeded by his son, Nebuchadnezzar.

NANAK (1469–1539) Founding guru of the Sikh faith, combing Hindu and Muslim beliefs into a single doctrine. The son of a merchant, he made an extended pilgrimage to Muslim and Hindu shrines throughout India, returning to the Punjab in 1520 and settling in Kartarpur. His teaching, spread by a large following of disciples, advocated intensive meditation on the divine name; many of his hymns still survive.

NANKING TREATY *see* **Opium War**

NANTES, EDICT OF Order, issued in 1598 by **Henry IV** of France, guaranteeing freedom of worship to French Protestants. Its revocation in 1685 by **Louis XIV** forced many non-Catholics to flee the country, weakening the French economy and creating much international friction.

NAPIER, SIR CHARLES JAMES (1782–1853) British general and prolific author. He served under **Wellington** in the Peninsular War; and led the British conquest of Sind, 1841–3.

NAPOLEON I (NAPOLEON BONAPARTE) (1769–1821) Emperor of the French; *see* pp. 202–3, 204–5

NAPOLEON III (CHARLES LOUIS NAPOLEON BONAPARTE) (1808–73) Emperor of the French, son of Louis Bonaparte and nephew of **Napoleon I**. He was exiled, like his uncle, after 1815. He wrote *Les Idées Napoléoniennes* in 1839, was involved in two unsuccessful insurrections, in 1836 and 1840, and returned to France after the 1848 revolution, to be elected president by a huge majority, and to become emperor in 1852. During his highly prosperous reign, central Paris was rebuilt, Cochin China was acquired and the Suez canal opened. He was defeated by **Bismarck** in the **Franco-Prussian War** (1870–1), and after the collapse of his regime in 1871 went into exile in England.

NARAI (d.1688) (also Narayana) King of Siam from 1657 until his death. In his struggle to free his country's foreign trade from Dutch control he sought the help of the **English East Indian Company**'s factors at Ayutthaya. Their inability to help caused him to turn to the French, whose cause was espoused by his Greek adviser, **Constant Phaulkoni**, a convert to Catholicism. After an exchange of missions between Versailles and Lopburi, Narai's up-country residence, **Louis XIV** sent a naval expedition which seized the then village of Bangkok and the port of Mergui (now in Burma) with the declared aim of converting Siam to **Christianity**. The resulting national uprising, led by Pra Phetraja, forced the French to withdraw; Pra Phetraja became regent, and on Narai's death a few months later his successor.

NARAM-SIN The last great ruler of Sumer and Akkad, in ancient Mesopotamia, and grandson of **Sargon**. He reigned c. 2213–2176 BC, and was a famous warrior whose victories are commemorated in several extant carvings and monuments, including the impressive stele found at Susa, now in the Louvre museum.

NASRIDS The last Muslim dynasty in Spain, which rose to power under Muhammad I al-Ghalib (died 1272) and ruled Granada from 1238 until its conquest by the Christians in 1492.

NASSER, GAMAL ABDEL- (1918–70) Egyptian politician. As an army officer he became the leading member of the group which overthrew King **Farouk** in 1952, under the nominal leadership of General **Neguib**. In 1954, after a power struggle with Neguib, he became prime minister, and in 1956 president until his death. His regime was marked by socio-economic changes – reform of land-tenure, building of the Aswan High dam – and initially by a foreign policy of neutralism between the great powers and leadership of the Arab nationalist movement, which led to the short-lived union with Syria in the United Arab Republic (1958–61), two wars (with Israel, Great Britain and France, 1956, with Israel, 1967), and increasing dependence on the USSR.

NATIONALISM A movement that consciously aims to unify a nation, create a state or liberate it from foreign or imperialist rule. Nationalist movements became a potent factor in European politics in the 19th century. Since 1900, nationalism has been a strong force in anti-imperialist movements in Asia and Africa.

NATO *see* **North Atlantic Treaty Organization**

NAVAJO North American Indian tribe which probably emigrated from Canada to the region of the southwest United States between 900 and 1200. After a long history of raids against white settlers in New Mexico, 8000 Navajo were captured by a force under Colonel Kit Carson (1863–4) and interned for four years in New Mexico; in 1868 they were released and sent to a reservation. Today some 100,000 Navajo survive, many still occupying the 24,000 square mile reservation in New Mexico, Arizona and Utah. They form the largest Indian tribe in the United States.

NAZISM Term formed from the abbreviation for the National Socialist Germany Workers' Party – leader **Adolf Hitler**. Its creed covered many of the features of **Fascism**. Its special characteristics were a belief in the racial superiority of the '**Aryan** race' and of the German people who, as the purest carriers of Aryan blood, constituted a master race destined to dominate the sub-human Slav peoples of eastern Europe and Russia; virulent anti-semitism expressed in the systematic extermination of the Jewish population throughout Europe, the Jews being accused of an insatiable desire to corrupt and destroy Aryan purity and culture; anti-urbanism and anti-intellectualism, the peasant being held to be purified by his contact with the land; the personality and ruthless political leadership of Hitler, who believed himself destined to risk all to lead the German people to the empire which would last for 1000 years.

NAZI-SOVIET PACT (also known as Molotov-Ribbentrop Pact) Mutual non-aggression pact signed on 23 August 1939 between Germany and Soviet Russia, containing secret protocols which divided eastern Europe between the signatories: eastern Poland, Latvia, Estonia, Finland and Bessarabia to Russia; western Poland and Lithuania (later transferred to the Russian sphere) to Germany. The Russians invaded Poland 17 days after the Germans, on 17 September 1939.

NDEBELE *see* **Matabele**

NEGUIB, MOHAMMED (1901–84) Egyptian soldier and president. He was second in command of Egyptian troops in Palestine in the first Arab-Israeli war in 1948. Adopted as their titular head by the Egyptian officers who made the revolution of 1952, after the revolution he became prime minister and president of the republic, 1953–4. He was deprived of office after a struggle for power with the real leader of the officers, **Nasser**.

NEHRU, JAWAHARLAL (1889–1964) The first prime minister of independent India, 1947–64. Educated in England, in 1920 he joined the nationalist movement led by **Gandhi**, and was imprisoned eight times between 1920 and 1927. He was four times president of the Indian National Congress Party: 1929–30, 1936–7, 1946 and 1951–4.

NELSON, HORATIO (1758–1805) 1st Viscount Nelson. British naval hero, who rose to the rank of admiral in 1797 during the French Revolutionary Wars, winning decisive victories at the Nile (1798) and at Copenhagen (1801). He was killed in 1805 during his most famous battle, Trafalgar, which effectively ended the threat of a French invasion of England.

NEOLITHIC The last part of the **Stone Age**, originally defined by the occurrence of polished stone tools, but now seen as more importantly characterized by the practice of agriculture, for which sharp stone axes were essential forest-clearing equipment. Such cultures emerged in the Near East by 8000 BC, and appeared in Europe from 6000 to 3000 BC.

NERCHINSK, TREATY OF Peace agreement signed in 1689 between Russia and China, as a result of which Russia withdrew from lands east of the Stanovoy mountains and north of the Amur river. The settlement lasted until the treaties of **Aigun** (1858) and **Peking** (1860) brought Russia to its present boundary with China in the Far East.

NERO (AD 37–68) Roman emperor, succeeding to the imperial title in AD 54. He murdered his mother, Agrippina, in 59. After the fire of Rome in 64 he began a systematic persecution of Christians, and in the following year executed many opponents after the discovery of a plot to depose him. He committed suicide when the governors of Gaul, Spain and Africa united in revolt.

NESTORIANS Followers of Nestorius whose Christian teachings, condemned by the councils of Ephesus (431) and Chalcedon (451), stressed the independence of the divine and human natures of Christ. They are represented in modern times by the Syrian Orthodox Church (approximately 100,000 members in Iran, Syria and Iraq) which first accepted this version of **Christianity** in 486.

NEVSKY, ALEXANDER (c. 1220–63) Prince of Novgorod. He defeated the Swedes on the river Neva (hence his name) in 1240; and the Teutonic Knights on frozen Lake Peipus, 1242. He thought resistance to the Mongols hopeless and cooperated with them; in return the Khan made him Grand Prince of Vladimir (i.e. ruler of Russia) in 1252.

NEWCOMEN, THOMAS (1663–1729) English inventor of the atmospheric engine. As an ironmonger, he saw the high cost and inefficiency of using horses to drain the Cornish tin mines, and after ten years of experiment produced a steam machine for this purpose. The first known engine was erected near Dudley Castle, Staffordshire, in 1712. He also invented an internal-condensing jet to produced a vacuum in the engine cylinder, and an automatic valve gear.

NEW DEAL Social and economic programme, instituted 1933–9 by President **F.D. Roosevelt** to combat the effects of world depression in the United States. He used the Federal government to promote agricultural and industrial recovery, to provide relief to the unemployed, and to institute moderate economic and social reform.

NE WIN (1911–) Military dictator of Burma. He joined the nationalistic 'We-Burmans Association' in 1936, and in 1941 went to Taiwan (Formosa) for military training with the Japanese. He was chief of staff, Burma National Army, 1943–5, commander-in-chief of the Burmese army after independence in 1948, and served as prime minister in the 1958 'caretaker' government. He stepped down in 1960 on the restoration of parliamentary administration, but in 1962 led a *coup d'état*, establishing a Revolutionary Council of the Union of Burma and declaring the Burmese Road to Socialism. He broke Chinese and Indian control of the economy and expelled 300,000 foreigners. He resigned in 1988 under pressure from pro-**democracy**, communist and nationalist forces.

NGO DINH DIEM (1901–63) President of the Republic of Vietnam. Born into one of Vietnam's royal families, he was interior minister of the emperor Bao Dai's government in the 1930s. In 1945 he was captured by **Ho Chi Minh**'s communists, and fled after refusing Ho's invitation to join his independence movement. Returned in 1954 to head the US-backed government in South Vietnam, but took dictatorial powers, and as a Roman Catholic imprisoned and killed hundreds of Buddhists. He was abandoned by the US, and was assassinated during a military *coup d'état*.

NGUNI One of the two main Bantu-speaking groups of southern African peoples, including the Swazi, Pondo, Thembu, **Xhosa**, **Zulu** and **Matabele** (Ndebele) nations, mainly occupying land east of the Drakensburg mountains, from Natal to Cape Province.

NICAEA, COUNCILS OF The first council, which was also the first ecumenical gathering of the Christian Church, was called in 325 by the Emperor **Constantine**; it condemned the heresy of Arianism and promulgated the Nicene Creed, which affirms the consubstantiality of Christ the Son and God the Father. The second Nicaean (or seventh ecumenical) council took place in 787 as an attempt to resolve the controversy over **iconoclasm**; it agreed that icons deserved reverence and veneration but not adoration, which was reserved for God.

NICAEA, EMPIRE OF Founded in 1204 by the Byzantine leader Theodore I Lascaris after the Western occupation of Constantinople during the fourth **Crusade**. Crowned emperor in 1208, Theodore gradually extended his territory to include most of western Anatolia. His successors, while fighting off the despots of Epirus and the Mongols, also attempted to retake Constantinople; success came in 1261 when the Nicaean general, Michael Palaeologus, was able to establish himself as Michael VIII and found the last dynasty of Byzantine emperors.

NICEPHORUS II PHOCAS (c. 913–69) Byzantine emperor, who fought as a general under Constantine VII and Romanus II and usurped the throne in 963. He defeated Arab, Bulgarian, Italian and Western imperial enemies. He was murdered in 969 by his own general John Tzimisces, who in turn usurped the throne as John I.

NICHOLAS II (1869–1918) Last tsar of Russia, son of Alexander III. He succeeded in 1894; granted, but then largely withdrew liberal reforms after the revolution of 1905. He was forced to abdicate in March 1917, and was shot at Yekaterinburg (Sverdlovsk, now again Yekaterinburg) by the **Bolsheviks** in July 1918.

NIEN REBELLION Insurrection led by peasant bandit confederations in Anhwei, Honan and Shantung, areas which had suffered from the disastrous flooding of the Yellow River in the 1850s.

NIJMEGEN, TREATIES OF Agreements signed 1678–9 to end the Dutch War (1672–8) between France, Spain and the Dutch Republic. France returned Maastricht to the United Provinces and suspended her anti-Dutch tariff of 1667; Spain gave up Franche-Compté, Artois and 16 Flemish garrison towns to France, thus losing its 'corridor' from Milan to the Spanish Netherlands (the Spanish Road). In 1679 the German emperor, Leopold I, accepted the terms, slightly strengthening French rights in Alsace, Lorraine and on the Rhine.

NIMITZ, CHESTER WILLIAM (1885–1965) American admiral, commander-in-chief of the Pacific Ocean Area, 1942–5.

NINE YEARS' WAR Conflict between **Louis XIV** of France and his neighbours, 1689–97, led by William II of England and the Netherlands, allied in the **League of Augsburg**. Their aim was to restrain French territorial expansion, mainly at the expense of the Spanish empire, and in this they eventually succeeded. *See also* **King William's War**.

NIVELLE, ROBERT-GEORGES (1856–1924) French general. After two brilliant victories at Verdun, he was appointed commander-in-chief of the French armies on the Western Front in 1916, but was replaced by Pétain in 1917 after the disastrous failure of the spring offensive and widespread mutiny.

NIXON, RICHARD MILHOUS (1913–94) 37th president of the United States. Trained as a lawyer he was elected to the House of Representatives in 1946 and 1948; elected Republican senator for California, 1950. He was vice-president to **Dwight D. Eisenhower** (1953–61); defeated for the presidency by **John F. Kennedy**, 1960, and in the contest for California governorship, 1962. He re-entered politics to defeat Humphrey in the presidential election, 1968, and was re-elected in a landslide victory, 1972. He resigned office in 1974 at the climax of the investigation into the Watergate scandal arising out of an attempt to burgle the Democratic election headquarters during the 1972 campaign.

NIZAM Hereditary title of the rulers of the Indian state of Hyderabad; members of the dynasty founded by Asaf Jah, Subadhar of the Deccan, 1713–48.

NKRUMAH, KWAME (1902–72) The first prime minister of independent Ghana (formerly the Gold Coast colony). He graduated from Achimota College in 1930. He wrote *Towards Colonial Freedom* in 1947 in opposition to British rule, and in 1949 formed the Convention People's Party, instituting a programme of non-cooperation. After independence (1957) he became first president of the Ghana republic, 1960; in 1964 he declared a one-party state, but was deposed two years later by the army while on a visit to China.

NOBEL, ALFRED BERNHARD (1833–96) Swedish industrialist, chemist and inventor of dynamite. He began the manufacture of nitro-glycerine in Sweden in 1860; his first factory blew up, killing his younger brother Emil. He perfected a much safer dynamite, and patented it in 1867–8. He made an immense fortune from this and from his share of the Russian Baku oilfield. When he died he left the bulk of his money in trust to establish the Nobel prizes for peace, literature, physics, chemistry, medicine and, more recently, economics.

NOK One of the Iron Age cultures in west Africa, flourishing on the Benue plateau of Nigeria between 500 BC and AD 200. It is characterized by its distinctive clay figurines depicting both animals and men.

NORIEGA, MANUAL ANTONIO (1938–) Panamanian military and political leader. Educated at the Military Academy in Peru before becoming a lieutenant in the Panamanian National Guard in 1962. In 1970 he became head of Intelligence Services and in 1983 dictator and president of the republic of Panama. Courted by the CIA during the 1960s, he was eventually charged with drug trafficking and forcibly deposed and removed by US troops in 1989 to be indicted.

NORMANS Name derived from Nordmanni, or Northmen, to describe the Viking invaders who in the late 9th century established themselves on the lower Seine, in France. In 911, under their leader Hrolfr (Rollo), they obtained from the French king, Charles the Simple, rights to territory in northern Normandy; in 924 and 933 their control was extended, particularly westward, to include the whole area now known as Normandy. In the 11th century, under Robert and Roger Guiscard, and Duke William (**William I, the Conqueror**) respectively, their descendants conquered both Sicily and England.

NORMAN CONQUEST Name given to the successful invasion of England in 1066 by Duke William of Normandy, crowned king as **William I, the Conqueror**. English resistance was broken and the whole country overrun by 1071. Stabilization was achieved by expelling the **Anglo-Saxon** landowners and parcelling out the conquered territory among Williams' followers, as tenants-in-chief and vassals of the king.

NORTH ATLANTIC TREATY ORGANIZATION (NATO) Defensive alliance signed in 1949 between Belgium, Canada, Denmark, France, Iceland, Italy, Luxembourg, Netherlands, Norway, Portugal, United Kingdom and United States. Greece and Turkey joined in 1951; West Germany in 1954. France ceased to participate fully in 1966. NATO's headquarters are in Brussels; it deployed some 800,000 land troops in Europe.

NORTHERN RISING Attempted rebellion in northern England against **Elizabeth I** in 1569–70. Led by the Catholic earls of Northumberland and Westmorland, its object was to restore Catholicism by placing the imprisoned (Catholic) Mary Queen of Scots on the English throne. Faced by royal armies, the rebels melted away, although 800 of them died in the only direct clash; the leaders fled abroad.

NORTH GERMAN CONFEDERATION Political union of north German states set up under Prussian leadership after the Seven Weeks' War in 1866. It was enlarged in 1871 after the Franco-Prussian War to become the new German empire.

NOVATIAN (c. 200–c. 258) Roman theologian, author of *De Trinitate (On the Trinity)*. He at first supported those Christians whose faith lapsed under persecution, but later strongly condemned all apostasy, After 251, when Cornelius became Pope, this led him to break with the Church and set himself up as a rigorist anti-Pope, at the head of the Novatianist Schism. He was excommunicated in 251, and probably martyred c. 258 under the Emperor **Valerian**, but the sect continued to spread in East and West and lasted until the 6th century.

NU-PIEDS Peasants who rebelled in protest against high taxes in Normandy, France, in 1639; named after the salt-gathers of Avranches, who walked barefoot on the sands. They feared that the introduction of a salt tax (*gabelle*) would reduce sales of their product, and took a leading part in the uprising, which was crushed after four months in a pitched battle with government forces outside Rouen.

NURI ES-SAID (1888–1958) Iraqi statesman. An officer in the Ottoman army, in 1916 he joined the revolt of Sharif **Hussein** against the Ottomans, and in 1921 joined Hussein's son Faysal when he became king of Iraq. He held various ministerial posts, including that of prime minister. In 1941 he fled Iraq with the regent, Abdullah, during the period of rule by **Rashid Ali**, returned after the British military re-occupation, and dominated Iraqi politics, with intervals, until he was killed during an army coup. He was associated with the strongly pro-Western policy which led to the formation of the Baghdad Pact (**Central Treaty Organization**) in 1955.

NYAMWEZI A Bantu-speaking people of east Africa, occupying a large area between Lake Victoria and Lake Rukwa. In the 19th century they played a major part in the opening up of the east African interior to European trade from the coast.

NYERERE, JULIUS (1922–) President of Tanzania. Founder president of the Tanganyika African National Union in 1954, he was elected to the Tanganyika legislative council in 1958, and became chief minister, 1960–1, and prime minister, 1961–2. He was president, first of Tanganyika, 1962–4, and then of Tanzania from 1964–85. He remained in power after 1985 as leader of the only legal party, but in 1992 promised to end the one-party system. The author of *Freedom and Unity* (1967) and Swahili translations of Shakespeare, he developed theories of African socialism, and put these and other economic self-sufficiency policies into practice. He resigned in October 1995.

NYSTAD, TREATY OF Agreement in 1721 between Russia and Sweden to end the **Great Northern War**. Russia gained Sweden's Baltic provinces (Estonia and Livonia) and thus a 'window on the west', but restored Finland to Sweden.

OCTAVIAN *see* **Augustus**

OFFA (d.796) King of Mercia, central England, in the 8th century. He constructed an earthwork which still survives (Offa's Dyke) between his kingdom and Wales. He claimed the title 'King of the English' after establishing control over most of the country south of the river Humber.

OGEDEI (d.1241) Mongol ruler, third son of **Genghis Khan**. He was given chief command, in preference to his brothers, Jochi and Chagatai, during the latter part of the Khwarizian campaign, 1220–2; elected Great Khan in 1229, in 1235 he completed the conquest of the **Ch'in** in northern China and declared war on China's Sung dynasty, and in 1236 conquered Korea. He planned the western campaign that finally carried the Mongols from Siberia to the Adriatic.

O'HIGGINS, BERNARDO (1778–1842) Liberator of Chile, and its first head of state. The son of a Spanish officer of Irish origin; he became a member of the Chilean national congress in 1811; and then led Chilean forces in **San Martín**'s Army of the Andes, triumphing over the royalists at the battle of Chacabuco in February 1817. In 1823 he was exiled to Peru, where he died.

OJEDA, ALONSO DE (1465–1515) Spanish adventurer, who sailed under, and later quarrelled with, **Columbus**. In 1499, with **Vespucci**, he explored the coasts of Venezuela and Guiana, landing in the area later claimed by Spain (1595) under the name Surinam. He commanded the first mainland settlement in South America, on the Gulf of Urabá, 1509 – a disastrous failure.

OLDENBURGS Danish royal family, of German origin. Christian, Count of Oldenburg, was elected king of Denmark and Norway in 1448; his direct descendants ruled until 1863, when the succession passed to the present Glücksburg branch.

OLGIERD (d.1377) Grand Duke of Lithuania, reigning 1345–77, son of **Gedymin**, father of **Wladyslaw II Jagiello**. He invaded Mongol-dominated Russia in 1362–3, seizing the principality of Kiev, but failed to take Moscow in 1368–72. He died fighting the **Tatars**.

OLOF SKÖTKONUNG (d.1022) 'The Tax King'. Christian king of the Swedes and the Gantat; son of Erik the Victorious. He joined the Danish king, **Sven Forkbeard**, to defeat Norway in 1000; though he became a Christian he failed to impose the new religion on his subjects.

OMAR IBN AL-KHATTAB (c. 591–644) Second Muslim caliph, and the first to assume the title 'Commander of the Faithful'. At first he opposed Islam, but was converted c. 617; his daughter Hafsa became **Mohammed**'s third wife. He aided the first caliph, **Abu Bakr**, in his campaigns, succeeding him without opposition in 634, and carried further the conquests he had begun in Palestine, Syria, Iraq, Persia and Egypt. He was assassinated by a slave of Persian origin.

OPEC *see* **Organization of Petroleum Exporting Countries**

OPIUM WAR Fought between Britain and China, 1839–42, over Chinese attempts to prevent the import of opium from British India in payment for British imports of Chinese tea and silk which had previously been paid in silver, the only exchange acceptable to the Chinese. After a series of defeats, under the terms of the Nanking Treaty China ceded Hong Kong Island to Britain, opened five Treaty Ports to British trade, and relaxed many economic restrictions on foreign merchants.

ORGANIZATION OF PETROLEUM EXPORTING COUNTRIES (OPEC) Multinational organization established by Iran, Iraq, Kuwait, Saudi Arabia and Venezuela (1961) to coordinate petroleum policies and provide members with technical and economic aid. In 1973, in support of the Arab war against Israel, OPEC first halted oil production and then increased prices by 250%, triggering a major worldwide economic recession, but increasing both the revenues and the political influence of the member states. By 1982, however, many nations had reduced their consumption of OPEC oil, forcing a decrease in production and a fall in prices.

ORIGEN (c. 185–254) Scholar and theologian, deeply influential in the emergence of the early Greek Christian Church. He wrote many important commentaries, treatises and polemics, culminating c. 232 in his *Hexapla* which reconciles six different versions of the Old Testament.

ORKHAN (1274/88–1362) Second ruler (*beg*) of the Muslim principality founded by his father, **Osman I**, whom he succeeded in c. 1324. He captured Bursa in 1326, Nicaea (Iznik) in 1331 and Nicomedia (Izmit) in 1337 from Byzantium; by annexing the neighbouring emirate of Karasi in 1345 he was able to involve the Ottomans in the civil wars in Byzantium, and secured a bridgehead in Europe (Rumeli). Orkhan's sons seized Tzympe in 1352, Gallipoli in 1354 and Adrianpole (Edirne) in 1361, thus opening the Balkans to Turkish conquest and Ottoman expansion.

ORMEE REVOLT Part of the **Fronde** rebellion against **Louis XIV** of France, 1648–53. Bordeaux defied authority until reduced by siege; the rebellion took its name from the *ormes* (elm trees) under which the rebels met to discuss policy.

ORTELIUS, ABRAHAM (1527–1606) Publisher of the first modern atlas, *Theatrum orbis terrarum* (Antwerp, 1570). He worked as a cartographer, antiquary and book dealer.

OSMAN (c. 1258–c. 1324) Founder of the Ottoman dynasty, a leader active among the Turks settled in the northwest Anatolian borderlands with Byzantium in the latter part of the 13th century. He emerges into history c.1301; after a constant struggle he had by his death conquered most of Bithynia from Byzantium.

OSTROGOTHS Germanic people who occupied the Ukraine in the 4th century AD. During the reign of their great hero King Ermanaric (d.372), they extended their empire from the Black Sea to the Baltic, but were dispossessed c. 370 by the advancing Huns. The tribe then wandered and fought in eastern and central Europe until the end of Hunnish domination, c. 455. Under their king, **Theodoric** (ruled 493–526), they moved into Italy and established themselves as rulers, with their capital at Verona, until finally dispersed by the armies of **Justinian I** in the mid-6th century.

OTHMAN (d.656) Third Muslim caliph after the death of **Mohammed**. Born into the rich and powerful **Umayyad** clan of Mecca, c. 615 he became Mohammed's first influential convert, and was elected caliph in 644 after the death of **Omar**. He promulgated the first official version of the **Koran**, and continued the policy of conquest.

OTTAWA AGREEMENTS A series of arrangements, concluded at the Imperial Economics Conference in 1932, under which Great Britain, having reversed its traditional Free Trade policies and imposed tariffs on most foreign food and raw material imports, allowed free or preferential entry to goods from the British empire. In return, the colonies and dominions agreed to use tariffs against British goods only to protect their own domestic industries. The underlying doctrine, known as Imperial Preference, was substantially modified by the General Agreement on Tariffs and Trade (GATT) in 1947, and finally evaporated on Britain's entry to the European Economic Community (EC) in 1973.

OTTO I, THE GREAT (912–73) German emperor. As king of East Francia he crushed rebellions involving his brothers Thankmar and Henry (938–9) and his son Liudolf (953–4). He defeated the Magyars at the battle of the Lechfeld (955). He received the imperial crown in 962 by marrying his son **Otto II** to the Byzantine Princess Theophano, 972, he achieved recognition of his Western Empire in Constantinople.

OTTO II (955–83) Son of **Otto I**, and German king from 961, he held the imperial throne jointly with his father from 967 and alone from 973. He tried without success to drive the Greeks and Arabs from southern Italy, 982.

OTTO III (980–1002) German emperor, son of **Otto II**. He was German king from 983 under the regency of his mother (until 991) and grandmother (until 994), being crowned emperor in 996.

OTTO OF FREISING (c. 1111–58) German bishop, historian and philosopher, half-brother to King Conrad III. He entered the Cistercian monastery at Morimond, Champagne, c.1132, and became bishop of Freising in 1138. He wrote a world history from the beginning to 1146, and also the *Gesta Friderici*, celebrating the deeds of the **Hohenstaufen** dynasty, particularly of his nephew, **Frederick I Barbarossa**.

OTTOCAR II (1230–1278) King of Bohemia, son of Wenceslaus I, reigning 1253–78. He made his kingdom briefly the strongest state in the **Holy Roman Empire**. He led crusades against the heathen Prussians and Lithuanians, and annexed lands from Styria to the Adriatic. Eclipsed after the election of Rudolf of Habsburg as emperor in 1273, he was forced to renounce all territory save Bohemia, and Moravia. He was killed at the battle of Dürnkrut, attempting to reconquer Austria.

OTTOMANS Turkish Muslims; *see* pp. 142–3, 186–7, 214–5, 228–9.

OWEN THE BALD (d.1015) Last king of the Britons of Strathclyde, a state between Scotland and England, centred on Glasgow, which was annexed by Scotland after Owen's death.

OWEN, ROBERT (1771–1858) Early British socialist and social reformer. He was manager of a model cotton mill at New Lanark, 1799, and pioneered shorter working hours, employee housing, education and co-operative stores. He was partly responsible for the Factory Act of 1819; he formed the Grand National Consolidated Trades Union in 1843.

OXFORDSHIRE RISING Popular revolt in 1596 in the English Midlands against the enclosure of common land by landlords, depriving the local population of grazing rights.

PACHACUTI (d.1471) The ninth **Inca** emperor, reigning from 1438 until his death. He led his people's victorious expansion out of the Cuzco valley towards Lake Titicaca; with his son, **Topa** Inca, he conquered the **Chimú**; he founded the great fortress of Sacsahuaman. His mummified body was found by Juan Polo de Ondegardo, Spanish *Corregidor* of Cuzco, in 1559.

PÁEZ, JOSÉ ANTONIO (1790–1873) First President of Venezuela. Part-Indian, he joined the revolution against Spain in 1810 and became one of the chief Venezuelan commanders to **Simon Bolívar**. He participated in the defeat of the Spaniards at Carabobo, 1821, and Puerto Cabello, 1823; in 1829 he led the movement to separate Venezuela from the larger state of Gran Colombia, and effectively controlled the country from his election as president in 1831 until 1846, when he was forced into exile, returning as dictator in 1861. Driven out again in 1863, he retired to New York.

PAHLEVIS Dynasty in Iran, founded by **Reza Shah Pahlevi**in 1925. Overthrown 1979.

PAL, BIPIN CHANDRA (1851–1932) Indian schoolmaster, journalist and propagandist. After a brief visit to the United States in 1900, he became involved in the movement for Indian self-government (*swaraj*) editing newspapers and giving lectures which advocated non-cooperation with the British. In 1908 he was arrested; he lost his influence to **Tilak** and later to **Gandhi**.

PALAEOLITHIC The first part of the **Stone Age**, from the first recognizable stone tools in Africa over 2 million years ago, to the advanced reindeer-hunters who decorated their caves with wall-paintings in France and Spain around 20,000 years ago. It is divided into the Lower Palaeolithic, associated with early types of man, and the Middle and Upper Palaeolithic, associated with anatomically modern man.

PALAS Warrior dynasty of northern India, controlling most of Bengal and Bihar from the 8th to the 10th century. Founded by Gopala, under his son, Dharmapala, it became a dominant power in east India, with alliances from Tibet to Sumatra. It reached Benares in the 10th century but was blocked by the **Chola** king, Rajendra, and was forced back to defend Bengal, under King Mahipala, after whose death the dynasty declined, giving way to the Sena line.

PAN CH'AO Chinese general, explorer and administrator. Born into a famous scholarly family, he preferred a military life, and was dispatched with a small expedition in 73 to repacify the **Hsiungnu** tribes. He quickly established a highly effective technique for fomenting inter-tribal tensions. Appointed Protector-General of the Western Regions in 91, during the next ten years he briefly conquered virtually the whole area from the Tarim basin and the Pamirs almost to the shores of the Caspian – the greatest westward expansion China has ever known.

PANTAENUS (d.c. 190) Christian teacher, convert from Stoicism. He made a missionary journey to India. The first head of the Christian Catechetical School in Alexandria, he influenced his associate and successor, **Clement of Alexandria**.

PAOLI, PASQUALE (1725–1807) Corsican patriot, elected president by the islanders during the struggle against Genoese rule. He was forced to submit after Genoa sold the island to France in 1768 and went into exile in Britain 1769–90. He returned in 1793 to lead the revolt against the French revolutionary government. He persuaded the British to take control of Corsica, 1794–6.

PAPACY The office or position of the Pope, as head of the Roman Catholic church. Also the papal system of government, both ecclesiastical and political, particularly during the centuries in which the papacy counted among the major states of Europe.

PAPANDREOU, ANDREAS (1919–1996) Greek socialist politican, founder of the Pan-Hellenic Socialist Movement (PASOK), prime minister 1981–89 and 1993–96. In 1989 he became implicated in the alleged embezzlement and diversionm of funds to the Greek government of $200 million from the Bank of Crete. The subsequent scandal lead to his loss of the Greek prime ministership. In 1992 Papandreou was cleared of all corruption charges. He was re-elected prime minister the following year.

PAPEN, FRANZ VON (1879–1969) German politician, elected chancellor in 1932. He played a substantial part in **Hitler**'s rise to power, and helped to prepare the German annexation of Austria in 1938. He was found not guilty of war crimes at the Nuremberg Trials in 1945, but was sentenced to eight years' imprisonment; he was released in 1949.

PARAMARAS Rajput clan, prominent in northern India from the 9th to the 12th century. Mainly based in Malwa, with their capital at Dhar, near Indore, they were defeated by Turks from Afghanistan in 1192.

PARIS COMMUNE Name assumed on 26 March 1871, in emulation of the Jacobin Assembly of 1793, by a Central Committee established by rioters who had refused on 18 March to recognize the Assembly of Bordeaux which had accepted Prussian peace terms; the revolutionary socialist movement was crushed, with thousands of casualties, by government troops between 21 and 28 May.

PARIS, FIRST PEACE OF Signed on 30 May 1814, it consisted of seven separate treaties negotiated between the restored Louis XVIII of France and the principal European allies. The limits of France were fixed at approximately those of 1 January 1792; Britain restored certain colonies to France and acquired Malta. (*See also* **Congress of Vienna**.)

PARIS PEACE CONFERENCE *see* **Versailles, Treaty of**

PARIS, SECOND PEACE OF Signed on 20 November 1815, following the **'Hundred Days'**. It deprived **Napoleon** of Elba, reduced France to the limits of 1790, provided for an army of occupation and imposed an indemnity of 700 million francs. (*See also* **Congress of Vienna**.)

PARIS, TREATY OF (1763) Treaty which ended the **Seven Years' War** (known in North America as the French and Indian War). France ceded to Great Britain all her territory east of the Mississippi, including Canada; Spain similarly gave up Florida to Great Britain, but received the Louisiana Territory and New Orleans from France.

PARK, MUNGO (1771–1806) Scottish explorer of Africa, who sought the true course of the river Niger; his account *Travels in the Interior of Africa* (1797) made him famous. He returned in 1805 to head a second expedition, but was drowned during a skirmish.

PARSEES Modern followers of the Iranian prophet **Zoroaster**. The majority of the sect is descended from the Persian Zoroastrians who fled to India in the 7th century to escape Muslim persecution.

PARSONS, SIR CHARLES ALGERNON (1854–1931) Inventor of the steam turbine. He entered Armstrong engineering works, Newcastle upon Tyne, in 1877 and in 1884 patented the steam turbine, at the same time thus producing the first turbo-generator. In 1897 his powered experimental ship, the *Turbinia*, attained the then record speed of 34 knots.

PARTHIAN EMPIRE Founded in 247 BC when Arsaces, a governor under **Diodotus**, king of the Bactrian Greeks, rebelled and fled west to found his own kingdom south of the Caspian Sea. Under **Mithridates** (171–138 BC) Parthia extended its control over the whole Iranian plateau and into the Tigris-Euphrates region. After the famous Parthian victory over the Romans at Carrhae (53 BC) Parthia was almost continuously at war with Rome, and prevented any permanent Roman expansion beyond the Euphrates. The empire was finally eclipsed in AD 224 by the rise of the **Sasanids**.

PASSAROWITZ, TREATY OF Signed on 21 July 1718, it ended the Austro-Turkish and Venetian-Turkish wars of 1716–18, and marked the end of Ottoman expansion into Europe. Under its terms, the Ottoman empire lost substantial Balkan territories to Austria.

PATHET LAO Left-wing nationalist movement in Laos, founded in 1950. It joined with the **Viet Minh** to oppose French colonial rule in Indo-China. The first Congress of Neo Lao Hak Sat (Lao Patriotic Front) was held in 1956; throughout the 1960s and early 1970s it fought a civil war against the US-supported government in Vientiane. Its control of the northeast provinces of Sam Neua and Phong Saly was recognized in 1954, when Laos gained independence; it won control of the entire country in 1975.

PATRICK, ST (5th century) British cleric who brought Christianity to Ireland in the mid-5th century. Patron saint of Ireland; associated particularly with Armagh. He wrote *Letter to the Soldiers of Coroticus* and *Confessions*, an account of his work.

PÄTS, KONSTANTIN (1874–1956) President of independent Estonia. He founded the nationalist newspaper, *Teataja (The Announcer)* in 1901, and entered politics in 1904. He was sentenced to death by the Russian authorities in 1905 after an abortive rising. Returning from exile in 1910, in 1918 he became head of the provisional government despite his arrest by German occupation forces. He was prime minister 1921–2, 1923–4, 1931–2, 1932–3 and 1933–4, and became dictator after an attempted Fascist coup in 1934. He was deported to the USSR after the Soviet invasion in 1940 and was believed to have died some 16 years later.

PAUL, ST Jewish convert to **Christianity**, who became the leading missionary and theologian of the early Church. He was born a Roman citizen in Tarsus, now in Turkey. Brought up a **Pharisee**, he persecuted the followers of **Jesus** until his conversion by a vision on the road to Damascus. He became the Apostle to the Gentiles, undertaking three great journeys to the cities of Asia Minor and Greece. His letters, maintaining contact with the communities established there, remain fundamental documents of the Christian faith. Paul was arrested in Jerusalem, c. 57, taken to Rome in 60, and probably martyred during the reign of the Emperor **Nero**, between 62 and 68.

PAULICIANS Sect of militant Armenian Christians, founded in the mid-7th century. Influenced by earlier dualist thought, notably **Manichaeism**, its members believed that there were two gods: an evil one, who created the world, and a good one responsible for the world to come. It was suppressed by Byzantine military expeditions in the late 7th and early 9th centuries; many followers then moved to Thrace as frontier soldiers, where they helped to form the ideas of the **Bogomils**.

PEASANTS' REVOLT 14th century uprising in the English countryside and towns of villeins, free labourers, small farmers and artisans. Initially in protest against the Poll Tax of 1381 and stringent labour regulations imposed after the Black Death, it was concentrated mainly in East Anglia and the southeast. Under the leadership of Wat Tyler, a vast mob invaded London, executing royal ministers and destroying the property of supposed enemies of the common people, extracting promises of redress from the young king, Richard II. However, the insurgents were dispersed, Tyler slain, and insurgent action in other areas vigorously suppressed; the reforms and royal pardons were then revoked.

PEASANTS' WAR A series of rural uprisings in 1524–5 in Austria and central Germany, mainly directed against heavy manorial duties and exactions. Despite the accusations of Catholics that the rebellion was provoked by Lutheran theology, there is little evidence for this. **Luther** himself condemned the peasants, and the rebels were cut down, in several bloody battles, by the combined forces of Lutheran and Catholic landlords.

PECHENEGS Turkic nomads, ruling the steppes north of the Black Sea from the 6th to the 12th century. In the 10th century they controlled the land between the rivers Don and Danube; held back with difficulty by Russians and Hungarians, they then attacked Thrace and increasingly threatened the Byzantine empire until they were finally annihilated, at the gates of Constantinople, by Emperor **Alexius I Comnenus** in 1091.

PEEL family. The first Robert Peel introduced the calico printing industry to Lancashire, England, when he took the initiative in founding the firm of Haworth, Peel & Yates in Blackburn in 1764. His son Robert (1750–1830) greatly expanded the business and by the end of the 18th century employed some 15,000 workers in various mills. He was an enlightened employer, and when he became a member of parliament introduced the first Factory Act (1802). He had been created a baronet in 1800. His son Sir Robert Peel (1788–1850) was prime minister from 1841 to 1846.

PEKING CONVENTION Series of agreements made in 1860, reaffirming and extending the Tientsin treaties of 1858. Tientsin was opened as a Treaty Port; Britain obtained control of Kowloon, the city on the mainland opposite Hong Kong island; French missionaries were given a free hand to buy and develop land; war vessels and merchant ships were allowed to navigate in the interior; and Russia obtained the Maritime Provinces east of the Ussuri river.

PELAGIUS Christian teacher and monk, whose belief in man's responsibility for his own good and evil deeds led him into bitter controversy with the 4th-century Church fathers. In Rome c. 380 he attacked the lax morality he attributed to the doctrines of Augustine., Cleared of heresy charges at Jerusalem in 415, he responded to further attacks from **Augustine** and **Jerome** by writing *De libero arbitrio (On Free Will)*. He was excommunicated by Pope Innocent I in 417, and condemned at Carthage in 418; the date of his death is unknown.

PENINSULAR WAR Struggle, fought in the Iberian peninsula, 1808–14, between France and an alliance of Britain, Spain and Portugal, in the course of the Napoleonic Wars. Initially forced to evacuate from Corunna (1809), the British, under the future **Duke of Wellington**, returned to fight first a defensive engagement at Torres Vedras, then a successful offensive (1812–14) which drove all French troops from the region.

PEQUOT WAR Massacre of the Pequot tribe of North American Indians by British colonists in 1636–8, precipitated by the murder of a Boston trader. By the early 20th century hardly any of the tribe remained in their ancestral lands in Connecticut.

PERICLES (c. 495–429 BC) Athenian statesman. As a radical democrat he dominated the city-state from c. 460 BC until his death. He converted the League of Delos from an equal alliance into an Athenian empire, and led Athens in the Peloponnesian War against Sparta. His famous *Funeral Speech*, setting out his vision of an ideal Athens, is reported by **Thucydides**.

PERKIN, SIR WILLIAM HENRY (1838–1907) Discoverer of aniline dyes. In 1853 he entered the Royal College of Chemistry, London, and while working as a laboratory assistant attempted the synthesis of quinine, but instead obtained a substance later named aniline purple, or mauve. In 1856 he produced tyrian purple, the first dyestuff to be produced from coal tar. He was knighted in 1896.

PERMIANS Finno-Ugrian-speaking peoples, including the Votyaks and the **Zyrians**, living in the northwest region of Russia.

PERON, JUAN DOMINGO (1895–1974) Argentine head of state. He entered the army, 1911, became minister of war and secretary for labour, 1944; vice-president, 1944–5, and president, with strong backing from the trade union movement, 1946. Removed from office during the 1955 revolution and exiled to Spain, he returned and was elected to the presidency, 1973.

PERRY, MATTHEW (1794–1858) US naval commander who headed the expedition to Japan of 1853–4 which forced that country to end its 200-year old isolation and open trade and diplomatic relations with the world. Perry had earlier captained the first US steamship, the *Fulton* (1837–40); his Japanese exploit, taking four warships into the fortified harbour of Uraga, made him world-famous. Later he strongly urged US expansion in the Pacific.

PERSEUS (c. 212–165 BC) Last king of classical Macedonia, son of **Philip V**. He succeeded to the throne in 179 after plotting his brother's execution. He tried to dominate Greece, but by his success precipitated the Third Macedonian War (171–168) with Rome; he was finally defeated at Pydna, southern Macedonia, by the armies of Lucius Aemilius Paullus, and died after three years in captivity.

PERUZZI Important family of Florence, prominent in trade and finance in Europe in the late 13th century, and second only to the **Bardi**. During the **Hundred years' War** the firm made large loans to **Edward III** of England; these were cancelled in 1342. The king of Naples also defaulted and the king of France exiled them and confiscated their goods; bankruptcy and collapse, both financial and political, followed.

PETER, ST (d.c. AD 64) Foremost of **Jesus**' disciples and recognized by the Roman Catholic Church as its first pope. Originally a fisherman called Simon, or Simeon, from Bethsaida, he was named by Jesus 'Cephas', meaning rock (in Greek, *petros*). After Jesus' death he emerged as the first leader of the early Church, preaching and healing. His later career is obscure, but his residence, martyrdom and burial in Rome can be taken as certain.

PETER I, THE GREAT (1672–1725) Tsar of Russia. He succeeded to the throne in 1682, and took full control in 1689. War with the Ottoman empire, 1695–6, gave Russia access to the Sea of Azov. He made an extensive tour of western Europe, 1697–8, introduced western technology to Russia, and drastically reformed the system of government. With the **Great Northern War** (1700–21) he won through to the Baltic, and founded the city of St Petersburg which he made his capital.

PETER III (1728–62) Tsar of Russia. He succeeded his aunt, the Empress Elizabeth, in 1762, and immediately ordered Russia's withdrawal from the **Seven Years' War**, thereby causing discontent among his army officers, who deposed and killed him after a reign of only six months. He was succeeded by his wife, **Catherine the Great**.

PETROBRUSIANS Followers of Peter de Bruys, leader (1104–25) of a radical opposition in France to the doctrine and organization of the Roman Church. He rejected infant baptism, transubstantiation, the sacrifice of the Mass, and the organization of worship. He claimed scriptural authority for all his teachings, but he was burned in 1125 as a heretic. His ideas were also taken up by the **Henricians**.

PHAN BOI CHAU (1867–1940) First 20th century Vietnamese resistance leader. He trained for the mandarin examinations; in 1903 he wrote *Cau huyet thu le than (Letters Written in Blood)* urging expulsion of the French colonial rulers. He directed, from Japan, the Duy Tan Hoi (Reformation Society) aiming to put Prince Cuong De on the throne; after exile from Japan in 1908 he reorganized in China and planned the assassination of the French governor, Albert Sarraut, in 1912. He was imprisoned until 1917; converted to Marxism; seized in 1925 and taken to Hanoi, but released after immense public protest.

PHARISEES (and Sadducees) Leading, and antagonistic, Jewish religious sects during the second temple period (to AD 70). Emphasizing the interpretation of the Bible, the development of the oral law and adaptation to new conditions, the Pharisees evolved eventually into the Rabbis of the **Mishnah** and the **Talmud**. The Sadducees believed in the literal truth of the Bible and excluded all subsequent interpretations as well as beliefs in immortality, or devils and angels. The Pharisees, with their dislike of violence, survived the destruction of the temple by the Romans (AD 70); the Sadducees did not.

PHAULKON, CONSTANT (1647–88) An innkeeper's son from Cephalonia who ran away to serve as cabin boy on an English trading vessel and was later taken to Siam by a merchant of the **English East Indian Company**. Entering the service of King **Narai**, he was promoted to superintend foreign trade. After a quarrel with the chief of the English factory at the capital, Ayutthaya, he supported the French cause at court, but his support for **Louis XIV**'s intervention in Siam in 1687 brought about his downfall in the following year when his patron died. Narai's successor had him publicly executed.

PHIDIAS (c. 490–?) Ancient Athenian sculptor. Appointed by **Pericles** to oversee all the city's artistic undertakings, he was responsible for the design and composition of the marble sculptures of the Parthenon. None of his most famous works – three monuments to Athena on the Acropolis and a colossal seated Zeus at Olympia – survive in the original. Exiled on political charges some time after 432 BC he went to Elis; his date of death is unknown.

PHILIP 'THE BOLD' (1342–1404) Duke of Burgundy, son of the French king John II. As a boy he distinguished himself at the battle of Poitiers in 1356; succeeding to his title in 1363, he was co-regent (1382–8) to Charles VI and effective ruler of France during much of the rest of his life.

PHILIP 'THE GOOD' (1396–1467) Duke of Burgundy, son of John the Fearless, he succeeded in 1419. He supported the claims of the English king **Henry V** to the French throne but made peace with the rival monarch, Charles VII, in 1435. He also acquired extensive territories in the Netherlands, and founded the Order of the Golden Fleece in 1429.

PHILIP II AUGUSTUS (1165–1223) First great Capetian king of France, son of Louis VII. He succeeded to the throne in 1179; fought a long, mainly successful campaign to win control of English possessions in France; took part in the Third **Crusade**, 1190–1; acquired major territories in the west and north of France, and began the Capetian conquest of the territory of Languedoc.

PHILIP IV (1268–1314) Known as 'the Fair'. Capetian king of France, the second son of Philip III, he became heir on the death of his brother Louis in 1276, and succeeded in 1285. He fought major wars against England, 1294–1303, and Flanders, 1302–5. Continually in conflict with the papacy from 1296, he transferred the papal Curia to Avignon during the Pontificate of Pope Clement V (1305–14).

PHILIP II OF MACEDON (c. 380–336 BC) Ruler of Macedon from 359 to 336 BC; father of **Alexander the Great**. He made Macedon a major power. He penetrated Greece by war and diplomacy, defeating Athens and Thebes at the battle of Chaeronea, 338, and bringing the warring city-states of Greece into a forced unity through a federal constitution with himself as leader. He was assassinated while planning an invasion of Persia.

PHILIP V (238–179 BC) King of Macedon, succeeding his cousin, **Antigonus Doson**, in 221. He allied with Carthage against Rome in the Second **Punic War**, and ended the resulting First Macedonian War (215–205) on favourable terms, but suffered a decisive defeat in the Second War at **Cynoscephalae** in 197. The resulting peace treaty confined him to Macedonia and imposed severe indemnities. Seven years of cooperation with Rome relaxed these conditions and his last decade was spent in trying to re-establish control in the Balkans.

PHILIP II (1527–98) King of Spain, Spanish America and the Two Sicilies (1556–98), also ruler of the Netherlands and Lombardy (1555–98) and, as Philip I, King of Portugal (1580–98). Son of Emperor **Charles V**, he became King of England, 1554–8, through his marriage to Mary Tudor. Sought unsuccessfully to suppress the revolt of the Netherlands from 1566 onwards; conquered Portugal in 1580; failed to invade England with his Armada in 1588.

PHRYGIANS Ancient Anatolian people, dominating central Asia Minor from the 13th to the 7th centuries BC. Traditionally of Thracian origin, they settled in northwest Anatolia in the 2nd millennium BC, and after the collapse of the **Hittites** founded a new capital, Gordium, in the central highlands. In about 730 BC the eastern territories fell to Assyria; c. 700 BC the legendary king Midas was defeated by the Cimmerians, who burned Gordium and transferred the land to the Lydians.

PIAST First ruling dynasty in Poland, traditionally named after the wheelwright whose son, Ziemowit, inherited the estates of the Prince of Gniezno in the late 9th century. The dynastic territories were consolidated under **Mieszko I**; his son **Bolesław I** was the first king of Poland, and established the Polish frontiers in east and west. Tthe last Piast in the main line, **Casimir III the Great**, died in 1370.

PICTS A group of tribes occupying Scotland north of the river Forth in early Christian times. The name, signifying 'painted people', was first mentioned in Latin texts in AD 297. Known for their fierce raiding and their characteristic towers ('brochs') and symbol stones, they successfully blocked Anglian attempts to control them at the battle of Nechtansmere in 685. The connections between the kings of the Picts and the Scots (Irish immigrants in southwest Scotland) grew closer in the 9th century, leading to the creation of the medieval kingdom of Scotland.

PIKE, ZEBULON MONTGOMERY (1779–1813) American explorer. Commissioned in the US army in 1799, he led parties to the headwaters of the Mississippi, 1805–6, and Arkansas and Red rivers, 1806–7. He was promoted to the rank of brigadier-general in 1813, but was killed in the same year in the assault on York (now Toronto, Canada).

PILGRIMAGE OF GRACE Popular uprising in 1536 in the English counties of Yorkshire and Lincolnshire. The participants were mainly protesting against the religious policies of **Henry VIII**, especially the closure of the monasteries. Its leaders were executed in 1537.

PILGRIM FATHERS Group of English puritan refugees, mostly of the Brownist sect, who sailed in the **Mayflower** in 1620 to found Plymouth Colony, New England.

PILSUDSZKI, JOSEF (1867–1935) Polish general and statesman who struggled to liberate Poland from Russian control from 1887. He was imprisoned in Siberia, 1887–92. After the outbreak of the First World War, he commanded Polish legions under Austro-Hungarian sponsorship, 1914–16. After the Russian revolution he assumed command of all Polish armies and proclaimed himself head of a new independent Polish state. He defeated the Soviet Union in the war of 1919–21 (*see* **Treaty of Riga**). He resigned in 1922, but a right-wing military *coup d'état* in 1926 brought him back to supreme power until his death.

PINEDA, ALVAREZ 16th-century Spanish explorer. In 1519 he led an expedition which followed the Caribbean coast from Florida to the Pánuco river, already reached from the south by **Grijalva** in 1517. Pineda's voyage ended all hope of finding a direct sea contact between the Caribbean and the Pacific.

PINOCHET UGARTE, GENERAL AUGUSTO (1915–) Former Chilean head of state. He rose to prominence when appointed commander of the Santiago zone by Chile's Marxist President **Allende** in 1972. He succeeded General Carlo Prats as commander of the army, and emerged after a violent coup as head of the ruling military junta, 1973; he assumed sole leadership in 1974, but stood down as head of state in 1989 following a plebiscite in favour of democratic elections. He remained army commander. During his rule, Chile's economy was transformed and the country emerged as one of the most stable and successful in Latin America.

PINZÓN, MARTÍN ALONSO (c.1411–93) Part-owner of **Columbus**'s two ships, the *Pinta* and the *Niña*, which took part in the discovery of the Americas. Pinzón commanded the *Pinta* under **Columbus**, but left the expedition after reaching the Bahamas to search independently for gold. After rejoining the main body he broke away again on the homeward voyage, hoping – but failing – to be first with the news.

PINZÓN, VICENTE YAÑEZ (c. 1460–1523) Spanish explorer, younger brother of **Martin Alonso Pinzón**. Commanded the caravel *Niña* in **Columbus**'s fleet throughout the 1492–3 voyage to the Americas. Later he probably sighted the Amazon estuary and sailed with **Juan Díaz de Solís** along the coast of central America.

PIPPIN III ('the Short') (d.768) First **Carolingian** king, son of **Charles Martel** and father of **Charlemagne**. He became effective ruler of the **Franks** in 747. In 751 he deposed the last Merovingian king and was crowned king himself.

PITT, WILLIAM (1759–1806) Known as 'the Younger'. English statesman, second son of the 1st earl of Chatham (the elder Pitt). He entered Parliament in 1781, became chancellor of the exchequer 1782–3, and prime minister 1783–1801 and again 1804–6. He played a leading part in organizing coalitions against France on the outbreak of the Revolutionary Wars (1793–1802); passed the Act of Union with Ireland, 1800; resigned after George III refused to grant Catholic emancipation in 1801 but was recalled to organize new opposition to the French.

PIZARRO, FRANCISCO (c. 1478–1541) Conqueror of Peru, illegitimate son of a Spanish soldier. He went to the Caribbean in 1502, and in 1513 was deputy to Vasco Balboa when he discovered the Pacific Ocean. He led a small force of Spanish adventurers to conquer (and, in fact, to destroy) the **Inca** empire in Peru, 1531–3, and founded the city of Lima in 1535.

PIZARRO, HERNANDO (c. 1501–78) Spanish conquistador, the younger half-brother of **Francisco Pizarro**. He accompanied Francisco to Peru in 1531, and in 1534 returned to Spain with the royal share of the Inca **Atahuallpa**'s ransom. He returned to Peru, and in 1537 was seized at Cuzco by the Pizarros' rival, Diego de Almagro. After his release he led an army to defeat and execute his captor, 1538. He was imprisoned in Spain, 1540–60.

PLANTAGENETS *see* **Angevins**

PLATO (c. 427–347 BC) Athenian philosopher, an associate of **Socrates** and the teacher of **Aristotle**. He is best known through his 25 surviving Dialogues, his letters, and his *Apology*, in defence of Socrates. The ten books of *The Republic*, later modified by *The Laws*, outline a complete system for the ideal society. His Academy, outside Athens, was founded to train statesmen; it lasted nearly 900 years after his death, being closed finally by Emperor **Justinian** in 529.

PLEISTOCENE Geological era, characterized by a series of major ice advances, starting approximately 2.5 million years ago and ending in about 8000 BC. During this period Man evolved from pre-human origins to his present appearance and bodily form.

PLINY, THE ELDER (AD 23–79) Roman encyclopedist, accepted as the foremost Western authority on scientific matters until medieval times. After a short army career he settled down to accumulate knowledge and to write. His only surviving work (out of seven known titles) is the vast *Historia Naturalis*; its information, though fascinating and far-ranging, varies considerably in accuracy when checked with other sources.

PLO (Palestine Liberation Organization) Formed in 1964 as an umbrella organization to represent the world's estimated 4.5 million Palestinians, dedicated to the creation of a 'democratic and secular' Palestinian state. Its charter also called for the elimination of Israel. In 1969, Yasir Arafat, moderate leader of the major faction al-Fatah, became chairman. The PLO formed the effective government over the Palestinian enclaves in Gaza and the West Bank after the 1993 peace agreement.

POCOCK, SIR GEORGE (1706–92) British admiral. He commanded a squadron in the Indian Ocean, 1757–9, and in 1762–3 commanded the fleet which carried an expeditionary force under the Earl of Albemarle to Cuba.

POLENTA, DA Italian family dominating the city state of Ravenna from the end of the 13th to the middle of the 15th century. It first rose to power under Guidoe da Polenta, a leader of the **Guelph**, or pro-papal faction in the city; from 1322 it was rent by violent intra-family rivalries, and in 1441 the city fell under Venetian control.

POLO, MARCO (1254–1324) Medieval traveller from Venice. He went to Asia in 1271 as a merchant and jeweller with his father and uncle, who had already visited the court of the Mongol khan at Karakorum. He stayed for almost 17 years in China and neighbouring territories in the service of **Kublai Khan**. He escorted a Chinese princess to Persia in 1292 and returned to Venice in 1295. Captured at sea by the Genoese, while in prison he began to dictate an account of his travels: the book has been a bestseller ever since, and subsequent investigation has confirmed almost all its observations, although at the time Polo was thought to have invented most of them.

POLOVTSY Russian name for the Kipchak (Turkish) or (Kuman) Byzantine tribes who dominated the Eurasian steppes in the mid-11th century. They controlled a vast area between the Aral and Black Seas; fought Russians, **Pechénegs**, Byzantines and Hungarians. Dispersed in 1237, when the Mongols killed Bachman, the eastern Kipchak leader, some were absorbed into the **Golden Horde**, others (the Kumans) fled to Hungary.

POLYGNOTUS Ancient Greek painter from Thasos, at work in Athens and elsewhere, 475–447 BC, and famous for works such as the Fall of Troy in the Stoa Poikile at Athens and the vast murals in the Hall of the Cnidians at Delphi, now known only from contemporary descriptions. He was noted for his realism (e.g. transparent drapery) and for moralism.

POMPEY THE GREAT (103–48 BC) Roman statesman and general. He campaigned in Spain and Italy against pirates in the Mediterranean, and against **Mithridates** of Pontus. Consul in 70 BC, in 61 he formed the First Triumvirate with **Crassus** and **Julius Caesar**. He raised an army to defend the state when civil war broke out in 49, but was defeated by Caesar at Pharsalus (Greece) in 48 and fled to Egypt, where he was murdered.

PONCE DE LÉON, JUAN (1460–1521) Discoverer of Florida, in search of the mythical Fountain of Youth. He sailed with **Columbus** in 1493; in 1508–9, as deputy to the governor of Hispaniola, he helped to settle Puerto Rico. In 1513 he reached Florida, without realizing it was part of the North American mainland; he probably sighted the north coast of Yucatán on his return passage to Puerto Rico. He was mortally wounded in 1521 by **Seminole** Indians when on a second expedition to explore his discovery.

PORTSMOUTH, TREATY OF Agreement signed in New Hampshire, USA, to end the Russo-Japanese War of 1904–5. Russia recognized Japan as the dominant power in Korea, and ceded the lease of Port Arthur, railway concessions in the south Manchurian peninsula, and the southern half of Sakhalin Island. Both powers agreed to recognize Chinese sovereignty in Manchuria.

POTASSIUM-ARGON METHOD Technique for dating the original formation of rocks of igneous origin. It involves measuring the ratio of radioactive argon to radioactive potassium in the sample, and depends for its validity on several crucial assumptions about initial purity, steadiness of decay rates, absence of other factors affecting the radioactive decay process, etc; but in modern, improved forms it has been used to establish geological age as remote as 4500 million years and as recent as 20,000 years.

POTSDAM CONFERENCE Last inter-Allied conference of the Second World War, held from 17 July to 2 August 1945. The main participants were **Truman**, **Churchill** (with **Clement Attlee**, who became prime minister during the conference) and **Stalin**; they discussed the continuation of war with Japan and the form of the forthcoming European peace settlement.

POWELL, JOHN W. (1834–1902) United States Professor of Geology who led four expeditions to explore 900 miles of the Green and Colorado rivers, 1869–75; director of the geological survey of the Rocky Mountains, 1875–80, and of the US Geological Survey, 1880–94.

PRAIEIRA Last significant revolutionary uprising in imperial Brazil. The anti-conservative, anti-Portuguese rebellion broke out in Pernambuco in 1848 and was suppressed by 1850. 'Praieira' was the nickname given to liberals whose newspaper was printed in the Rua da Praia in Recife.

PRATIHARAS Warlike people of northern India, reputedly descended from the **Gurjaras**. By the end of the 8th century they ruled a large part of Rajasthan and Ujjain, and controlled the strategic city of Kanauj. Under King Bhoja they successfully held back the Arab advance into northern India, but were eclipsed by various enemies when a Turkish army sacked Kanauj in 1018.

PRAXITELES Ancient Athenian sculptor, working between 370 and 330 BC. Only one of his works survives in the original, the marble *Hermes carrying the infant Dionysus*, but by transforming the aloof, majestic style of his archaic and classical predecessors into more graceful and sensuous forms he changed the whole culture of Greek art. A few Roman copies of his works exist, including two of the masterpiece *The Aphrodite of Cnidus*, now in the Vatican and the Louvre.

PREMYSLIDS First Czech ruling family, founded by Premysl, a ploughman, who married the Pricess Libuse. They held the throne of Bohemia from c. 800 to 1306. In 1198 Premysl Ottocar I raised the country from a principality to a hereditary kingdom within the **Holy Roman Empire**.

PRESTER JOHN Legendary Christian king, variously believed to rule in central Asia and east Africa. His fabled kingdom, and its riches, captured the medieval imagination between the first **Crusades** and the early 16th century. His story, probably based on garbled reports of the Negus of Abyssinia, played a part in the motivation of many well-financed expeditions, including the final successful efforts of Portugal to reach Asia by sea.

PRODICUS Greek Sophist from the island of Ceos (Kea), active in the 5th century BC and renowned for his precise distinctions between words.

PROTAGORAS (c. 485–c. 412 BC) Most famous of the Greek Sophists, author of the constitution for the pan-hellenic settlement of Thurii, and best known for his assertion that 'man is the measure of all things'. He taught in Athens and other cities for 40 years. He expressed agnosticism in his text *Concerning the Gods*, but the story of his trial for impiety may be a later invention.

PROTESTANTISM One of the three main branches of **Christianity** since the Reformation of the 16th century. It was originally characterized by belief in justification by grace through faith, the priesthood of all believers and the over-riding authority of the Bible. The main early groups were **Lutherans**, **Calvinists**, and **Zwinglians**, with the Church of England including both Catholic and Protestant elements. Other groups from the Anabaptist and Independent traditions, as well as those emerging later such as the Society of Friends (**Quakers**) and the **Methodists**, are also included within the term.

PRUTH, TREATY OF THE A pact signed on 23 July 1711, after the Ottomans had defeated the armies of **Peter I the Great** of Russia on the river Pruth (now the frontier between Romania and Moldavia). Russia agreed to relinquish the fortress of Azov, to demilitarize Taganrog and the Dnieper forts, cease interfering in Poland and the affairs of the Crimean Tatars, and allow safe conduct to **Charles XII** of Sweden. His delay in complying with these terms led to a renewed declaration of war in 1712 and the conclusion of a new, though similar, peace agreement at Adrianople (Edirne) in 1713.

PTOLEMAIC DYNASTY Line of Macedonian kings, founded by **Ptolemy I Soter**. They ruled Egypt from 323 to 30 BC, the last of the line being **Cleopatra**.

PTOLEMY Greek astronomer and geographer of the 2nd century AD. He worked in Alexandria, and wrote a *Geography*, with maps, which became the standard medieval work on this subject; an *Optics*, and a mathematical and astronomical treatise, popularly known as *Great Collection or Almagest*, which pronounced that the Earth was the centre of the Universe. He worked out a close approximation to the value of π in sexagesimal fractions; he divided the degree of angle into minutes and seconds.

PTOLEMY I SOTER (c. 367–c. 282 BC) Founder of the Ptolemaic dynasty, rulers of Egypt from 323 to 30 BC. He was born in Macedonia, rose to become a general of **Alexander the Great**, and after Alexander's death became satrap of Egypt, Libya and Arabia. He fought off Macedonian attacks (322–1 and 305–4) and in 304 assumed the titles of King and Soter (Saviour). An outstanding administrator, he was also author of a history of Alexander (since lost), and founder of a library and museum.

PUGACHEV, YEMELYAN IVANOVICH (1726–75) Pretending to be Peter III, the murdered husband of **Catherine II**, he led a revolt, in September 1773, among a group of *Cossacks* in the Urals, and was joined by factory serfs, Bashkirs, state peasants and serfs. In August 1774 he sacked the city of Kazan, but then turned south down the Volga, where he was defeated by Russian troops in August 1774. He was executed the following year.

PUNIC WARS Three wars in which Rome and Carthage, hitherto friendly, contested supremacy in the western Mediterranean in the 3rd and 2nd centuries BC.

First Punic War (264–41 BC): the clash came when Carthage threatened to gain control of the Straits of Messina. Carthage was a sea-power, Rome a land-power: to defeat their enemy the Romans had to build a large fleet, which gained a series of brilliant victories. The war, which was also fought by land in Sicily, resulted in the ejection of the Carthaginians from Sicily; Rome made the island its first overseas province.

The Second Punic War (218–201 BC) was caused by **Hannibal**'s advance from Spain into Italy, where after a series of great victories (especially Cannae in 216) he was gradually forced on to the defensive. In 204 Publius Scipio led an expeditionary force to Africa, thus compelling the return of Hannibal, and defeated him at Zama. Scipio had also driven the Carthaginians from Spain, which became a Roman province. Carthage survived but was no longer a great Mediterranean power.

Third Punic War (149–146 BC): Roman suspicions led to the outbreak of a final war. The Romans invaded north Africa; after a desperate siege the city of Carthage was totally destroyed and its territory made into the Roman province of Africa.

PUTTING-OUT SYSTEMS Method of industrial production, widely practised in 17th-century Europe. Raw materials were supplied by manufacturers to workers in their own homes or small workshops, and the finished output was then collected and sold, after payment on a piecework or wage basis; it was gradually superseded by the development of the factory system.

PYRRHUS (319–272 BC) King of Epirus, northwest Greece. He fought Macedon, and was then called to help Greek cities in Sicily and southern Italy against the expanding power of Rome. He defeated the Romans, but with crippling losses, at Asculum in 279 BC (hence a 'Pyrrhic victory'), and was forced out of Italy in 275 BC. He died in a street fight in Argos three years later.

PYTHAGORAS (c. 580–497 BC) Greek philosopher and mathematician. He emigrated from Samos to southern Italy; founded a school based on the belief that the soul could be purified by study and self-examination; taught transmigration of souls; discovered the numerical basis of the musical scale; taught that numbers form the basis of the universe. Pythagoras' Theorem, which states that the square on the hypotenuse of a right-angled triangle is equal to the sum of the squares on the other two sides, is probably attributable to his school.

QADISIYYA, AL- Battle, 637, in which the armies of Islam defeated the **Sasanid** Persians, and completed the conquest of Iraq.

QAJARS Iranian dynasty, ruling a unified Persia, 1779–1925. The reign of Fath Ali Shah (1797–1834) saw the beginning of intense European rivalry for control of the country; Nasir ud-Din Shah (1848–96) exploited Anglo-Russian suspicions to preserve its independence, but the Anglo-Russian division of Persia into spheres of influence in 1907, followed by Russian and British occupation of parts of the country in the First World War, led to a *coup d'état* (1921) and the emergence of the **Pahlevi**. Ahmed Shah, the last Qajar, was formally deposed in 1925.

QUAKERS (also known as the Society of Friends). Radical religious movement without clergy or creed, originating in mid-17th century England and rapidly developing in North America from the colony of Pennsylvania, founded by Quaker William Penn under royal charter in 1681. Today Quakers in the world number around 200,000.

QUEBEC ACT One of the Intolerable Acts or Coercive Acts which led up to the American War of Independence. This measure (1774) established a new administration for the Northwest Territory, ceded to Great Britain by France after the **Seven Years' War** (1756–63), and extended its frontiers to the Ohio and Mississippi rivers; the trans-Appalachian claims of the other (largely Protestant) American colonies were thus jeopardized in favour of French Catholics.

QUTBUDDIN AIBAK (d.1210) Muslim ruler in India. Born in Turkestan and sold as a child slave, he entered the service of **Muizzudin Muhammad** where he rose from the position of stableman to that of general. He led many mounted campaigns between 1193 and 1203, and was freed after Muhammad's death in 1206. He laid the foundations for the emergence of the Delhi sultanate under **Iltutmish**.

RABIH ZOBEIR (d.1900) Leader of native opposition to the French in Equatorial Africa from 1878 until his death at the battle of Lakhta.

RADCLIFFE, WILLIAM (1760–1841) An improver of cotton machinery in England. With the aid of Thomas Johnson he invented a cotton dressing machine which enabled the fabric to be starched before the warp was put on to the loom; he went bankrupt in 1807. He started another mill, but this was destroyed by **Luddite** rioters in 1812. He was the author of *Origin of the New System of Manufacture, commonly called Power Loom Weaving* (1828).

RAFFLES, SIR THOMAS STAMFORD (1781–1826) Founder of Singapore. He was appointed assistant secretary to the newly formed government of Penang in 1804, and lieutenant-governor of Java in 1811. He was recalled to England in 1816, but returned to the East as lieutenant-governor of Benkulen, 1818-24, and in 1819 established a British port at Singapore, henceforth the centre of British colonial activity in southeast Asia.

RAHMAN, MAJIBUR (1920–75) Usually known as Sheikh Majib, First president of Bangladesh. He founded the East Pakistan Students' League, and during the 1950s was secretary and organizer of the Awami League, seeking autonomy for East Pakistan. He was imprisoned in 1958, and the resulting mob violence led to the breakaway of the province in 1971 as the new state of Bangladesh. Rahman was elected as its first head of state in January 1972. He was assassinated in 1975.

RAJARAJA (d.1014) King of the **Cholas** in southern India, reigning 985–1014. He attacked the alliance between Kerala, Ceylon and the Pandyas, seized the Arab trading centre of Malabar, launched a naval attack on the Arab-held Maldive Islands, devastated Ceylon and its capital Anuradhapura. He was succeeded by his son Rajendra after two years of joint rule.

RAJPUTS Literally 'Sons of Kings'; members of landowning and military castes, according to one view descendants of central Asian invaders, who dominated large parts of north and western India, especially Rajasthan, from about the 8th to the 18th century.

RAMAYANA Shorter of India's two great epic poems, composed by the poet Valmiki. Its surviving text runs to 24,000 couplets celebrating the birth, education and adventures of Rama, the ideal man and king, and his ideal wife, Sita.

RAMSES II, THE GREAT (d. 1224 BC) Third king of Egypt's 19th Dynasty; son of **Seti I**. He succeeded c. 1304 BC; fought the Hittites in an indecisive battle at Qadesh on the Orontes in the fifth year of his reign; 16 years later he signed a lasting peace treaty with the Hittite king, Khattushilish. He is remembered for his military prowess and vast building activities; he constructed the famous rock-temples of Abu Simbel.

RAMSES III The last great pharaoh of Egypt, reigning 1184–1152 BC as the second pharaoh of the 20th Dynasty. He fought two major wars against the Libyans and one against a confederation of northerners, who included Philistines, and two minor campaigns in Palestine and Syria. His greatest monument was his funerary temple at Medinet Habu (western Thebes), in which his wars are represented; he also built a small temple at Karnak, which he dedicated to Amun. Late in his reign he survived a palace conspiracy to murder him.

RAMMOHAN ROY (1774–1833) Hindu religious reformer. He published a tract against idolatry in 1790; in 1816 he founded the Spiritual Society in Calcutta, which in 1828 developed into the **Brahmo Samaj** movement. He was active in the campaign to abolish suttee, the ritual burning of Hindu widows; he was granted the title of rajah by the Delhi emperor.

RANJIT SINGH (1780–1893) Known as the Lion of the Punjab, he was the son of a **Sikh** chieftain. In 1799 he seized Lahore, capital of the Punjab, and proclaimed himself maharajah in 1801. His aim to unite all Sikh territories in India was thwarted by the British in 1809. With a modernized army, he inflicted many defeats on Afghans and Pathans in the 1820s and 1830s, and jointly with the British planned to invade Afghanistan in 1838.

RAPALLO, TREATY OF Agreement signed in 1922 between Germany and Soviet Russia, which established trade relations and cancelled pre-1914 debts and war claims.

RASHID ALI AL-GAILANI (1892–1965) Iraqi prime minister. He supported German war aims in 1939; resigned his post, January 1941, and then seized power in April; he refused the British permission to move troops through Iraq (agreed under a 1930 treaty), but lost out in a sharp, 30-day war when promised German help failed to arrive, and went into exile in Iran as a pro-British government was formed.

RASHTRAKUTAS South Indian dynasty, founded in the 8th century AD by Dantidurga, a feudatory of the Chalukyas. From their central territory in the north Deccan, they fought wars and formed alliances throughout India. The best-known king, Amoghavarsha (reigned 814–80), patronized **Jainism**. They were eclipsed in the late 10th century by the later Chalukyas.

RASULIDS Muslim dynasty, ruling Yemen and the Hadhramaut from 1229 to 1454, named after Rasul, a Turkish officer of the **Abbasid** caliph. His grandson Umar I ibn Ali controlled Yemen and Mecca 1229–50; later Rasulid rule was confined to the Yemeni highlands.

RATANA, T W (1870–1939) Maori religious and political leader in New Zealand. In 1920 he founded the Ratana Church, which had widespread popular appeal among Maoris and helped create for them a stronger supra-tribal identity in society and politics, notably through the Ratana-Labour Party Alliance.

RATHENAU, EMIL (1838–1915) German industrialist and electrical pioneer. In 1883 he founded Deutsche Edison-Gesellschaft to exploit German rights in the patents of Thomas Edison; the company was renamed Allgemeine-Elektrizitäts-Gesellschaft (AEG) in 1887. With **Werner von Siemens** he founded the Telefunken company in 1903.

RATHENAU, WALTHER (1867–1922) German statesman. He succeeded his father, Emil, as head of the vast electrical engineering firm, AEG. In 1914 he set up the War Raw Materials Department to organize the conservation and distribution of raw materials essential to Germany's war economy. He founded the Deutsche Demokratische Partei (DDP) and advocated industrial **democracy** and state intervention in industry. He was minister of reconstruction, 1921, and as foreign minister in 1922 he negotiated the **Treaty of Rapallo** which normalized relations with the Soviet Union. He was assassinated after accusations that he favoured 'creeping **communism**'.

RAZIYYA Briefly sultana of Delhi, she succeeded to the throne during the period of anarchy following the death of her father, Iltutmish, in 1236. She provided both political stability and military leadership, but her sex and her unwillingness to share power created growing resentment, and ultimately she was murdered.

REAGAN RONALD (1911–) US actor, Republican politician and 40th president (1981–9). After acting in over 50 Hollywood films and becoming leader of the actors' union he joined the Republican Party in 1962 and secured the governorship of California for two terms (1967–75). He defeated Democratic incumbent Jimmy Carter in the presidential election of 1980 and served two consecutive terms. As president he supported deflationary policies aimed at reducing taxes and government spending, popularly called 'Reaganomics'. In foreign policy he increased military spending, maintained a tough anti-Soviet posture, authorized US intervention in Grenada (1983), CIA operations in Nicaragua and the bombing of Libya (1986).

REFORMATION Religious and political movement in 16th-century Europe to reform the Roman Catholic church which led to the establishment of Prostestant churches. Anticipated from the 12th century by the Waldenses, Lollards and Hussites, it was set off by the German priest Martin **Luther** in 1517 and became effective when the absolute monarchies gave it support by challenging the political power of the papacy and confiscating church wealth.

RENÉ OF ANJOU (1409–80) Duke of Lorraine, 1431–52, of Anjou, 1434–80, and Count of Provence, 1434–80. He made an unsuccessful bid to become king of Naples, 1435–42; in 1442 he retired to Anjou and later (1473) to Provence, where he patronized poets and artists. In 1481 his lands (except for Lorraine) passed to the French crown.

RESTITUTION, EDICT OF (1629) Decree of the Holy Roman Emperor Ferdinand II (1619–37) that all imperial Church lands taken by secular princes since 1552 should be restored. The measure was brutally enforced by a large imperial army and provoked an alliance of German Protestant rulers against the Emperor. With Swedish aid provided by **Gustavus Adolphus**, the alliance defeated the imperial forces at the battle of Breitenfeld, 1631.

REULEAU, FRANZ (1829–1905) French engineer, best known for his geometric studies on the underlying principles of machine design, set out in his *Theoretische Kinematic*, published in Germany in 1875 and translated into English as *The Kinematics of Machinery* in 1876.

REZA SHAH PAHLEVI (1878–1944) Ruler of Iran, 1925–41. An army officer, he organized a successful revolution in 1921 and deposed the **Qajar** dynasty to become shah in 1925. He instituted a reform and modernization programme; he abdicated in 1941, when British and Russian armies occupied Iran.

RHEE, SYNGMAN (1875–1965) South Korean political leader. Jailed and tortured in his early twenties for his nationalist views, he then studied for six years at American universities until 1910 and lived in exile, working for the Korean Methodist Church in the US (1912–45). A leader of the independence movement, he returned to the newly established Republic of Korea to become its president (1948–60). Known for his dictatorial and militant anti-communist stance, he was forced to resign amid accusations of election fraud and corruption.

RHODES, CECIL JOHN (1853–1902) Financier and imperialist. He emigrated from Great Britain to South Africa in 1870, and made a fortune from Kimberley diamond mines and Transvaal gold. In 1881 he entered the Cape Colony parliament and strongly advocated British expansion in Africa: he negotiated the annexation of Bechuanaland in 1884, and having sent white settlers into Mashonaland 'founded' Rhodesia. He became prime minister of Cape Colony, 1890–6, but resigned after the **Jameson Raid** into the Transvaal.

RICHARD II (1367–1400) King of England, 1377–99. Son of Edward the Black Prince, he succeeded his grandfather, **Edward III**; he was in conflict with a baronial group, the Lords Appellant, to 1397, and was deposed in 1399 by a cousin, Henry of Lancaster, later crowned **Henry IV**; he died in prison, possibly murdered.

RICHELIEU, ARMAND-JEAN DU PLESSIS, DUC DE (1585–1642) French cardinal and statesman. As secretary of state (1616–17) and chief minister (1624–42) to Louis XIII, he destroyed French Protestant power (the siege of La Rochelle, 1628), undermined Spanish power in Italy (war of Mantua, 1627–31), declared war on Spain and intervened in the Thirty Years' War against the **Habsburgs** from 1635, although he died before much success had been gained (*see also* **Mazarin**)

RIENZO, COLA DI (c. 1313–54) Popular leader in medieval Rome. In 1343 he was sent to Avignon to plead the cause of Rome's new popular party before Pope Clement VI. In 1347 he assumed dictatorial powers with popular acclaim and reformed taxes, courts and political structure, attempting to re-establish Rome as the capital of a 'Sacred Italy'. He successfully suppressed an uprising by the nobles, but was forced to resign before the end of the year; reinstated in 1354 (but for only two months) he was seized and killed trying to quell a riot.

RIGA, TREATY OF (1920) Agreement by which Soviet Russia recognized the independence of Latvia (formerly a Russian province).

RIGA, TREATY OF (1921) Agreement between Poland and Soviet Russia following a war (1919–21) provoked largely by the claim of the new Polish state (created in 1918) that its eastern frontier of 1772 (prior to the first partition) should be restored. The treaty gave Poland large parts of Belorussia and the Ukraine. It lasted until the **Nazi-Soviet Pact** of 1939.

RIM-SIN Last ruler of Larsa, in ancient Mesopotamia, who reigned c. 1747–1688 BC. Son of Kudur-Mabuk, probably an **Amorite** chieftain from the borders of Elam, in 1719 he overthrew Isin, the old rival of Larsa, for control of southern Babylonia. He fought frequently with **Hammurabi** of Babylon, who finally defeated him in 1688.

RIPON, GEORGE FREDERICK SAMUEL ROBINSON (1827–1909) 1st marquis and 2nd earl of Ripon, viceroy of India. He was appointed viceroy in 1880, and attempted many reforms but generated much opposition, resigning in 1884 after the forced withdrawal of his proposal to give Indian judges power over European defendants. He became secretary for the colonies, 1892–5, and Lord Privy Seal, 1905–8.

RIZAL, JOSÉ (1861–96) Filipino novelist, poet and patriot, born in Manila. At the University of Madrid he led a movement for reform of Spanish rule in the colony; he returned to the Philippines in 1892, and founded the non-violent Reform society, *Liga Filipina*. Exiled to

Mindanao, he was arrested after an insurrection by a secret nationalist group, the Katipunan; although he had no connection with it, he was shot. His martyrdom and his masterly verse-farewell, *Ultimo Adiós*, inspired the fight for Filipino independence.

ROBERT I 'THE BRUCE' (1274–1329) King of Scotland, crowned in 1306 in defiance of the English king, **Edward I**. He consolidated his power during the weak reign of **Edward II**, and inflicted a heavy defeat on the English at Bannockburn in 1314. The title and Scotland's independence were recognized by the English in 1328, the year before his death.

ROBERT OF ANJOU (1278–1343) King of Naples 1309–43; he was the grandson of Charles I, conqueror of Sicily from the **Hohenstaufen** (1286). He unsuccessfully attempted to secure a dominant position in Italy, in alliance with France and the papacy. The kingdom rapidly declined after his death.

ROBESPIERRE, MAXIMILIEN FRANÇOIS MARIE-ISIDORE DE (1758–94) French revolutionary leader. He practised as a provincial lawyer; led the radical **Jacobin** faction, and played a leading part in the 1793 overthrow of the **Girondins** by the extremist Mountain group. As a member of the Committee of Public Safety, 1793–4, he became virtual dictator, establishing the Terror and eliminating his rivals Hébert and **Danton**; he introduced the cult of the Supreme Being. He was overthrown and executed after the *coup d'état* of July 1794.

RODNEY, GEORGE BRYDGES (1718–92) British admiral who commanded in the West Indies in the **Seven Years' War** and again in the American War of Independence. He captured Martinique (from the French) and the neutral islands of St Lucia, Grenada and St Vincent in 1762; and defeated the Spanish fleet to relieve Gibraltar in 1780. His subsequent failures were redeemed by his victory over the French fleet at the battle of the Saints (Dominica) in 1782, for which he was created Baron Rodney.

ROGER II (1095–1154) Founder of the Norman kingdom of Sicily. He succeeded his brother as Count of Sicily in 1105; made Palermo his capital, 1130; acquired Calabria, 1112, and Apulia, 1127; was crowned King of Sicily, 1130. He made Sicily a major meeting place for Christian and Arab scholars.

ROGGEVEEN, JACOB (1659–1729) Dutch explorer. After retirement from law practice in Batavia, he fitted out a private fleet to search for the reputed southern continent in the South Pacific, 1721–2. Though he circumnavigated the globe, his only significant discovery was Easter Island.

ROMANCE The group of languages derived from the spoken Latin of the Roman empire. Influenced by local languages in the successor states of Rome, the romance group comprised French, Spanish, Italian, Portuguese, Romanian, Catalan and Romansch.

ROMANOVS Ruling dynasty in Russia from 1613 until the Revolution of 1917. The family came to prominence when Anastasia Romanova married **Ivan IV the Terrible**. In 1613 the grandson of Anastasia's brother, **Michael Romanov**, was elected tsar; the succession thereafter, though remaining within the family, was frequently disorderly. In 1917 **Nicholas II** abdicated in favour of his brother Michael, who refused the throne, thus ending the royal line.

ROMANOV, MICHAEL (1596–1645) First of the Romanov tsars in Russia, reigning 1613–45. Distantly related to Fyodor I (reigned 1584–98), last tsar of the previous Rurik dynasty, he reluctantly accepted popular election to the throne at the end of Russia's 15-year 'Time of Troubles'. The 16-year-old tsar at first shared power with relatives of his mother, who had been forced to become a nun by **Boris Godunov**, and later with his father, who had been forced to become a monk, the Patriarch Filaret.

ROOSEVELT, FRANKLIN DELANO (1882–1945) 32nd president of the United States, first elected 1932. He formulated the **New Deal** policy to combat world depression; inaugurated the Good Neighbour Policy in Latin America; in 1933 he recognized the USSR. He was re-elected in 1936 and again in 1940, when he provided lend-lease support for Great Britain. With **Churchill**, he issued the Atlantic Charter; after the Japanese attack at Pearl Harbor he led the US into the Second World War, and with **Chiang Kai-shek** at Cairo in November 1943 resolved to continue the war until Japan's unconditional surrender. Re-elected for a fourth term, he died after the 1945 **Yalta** conference of Allied leaders.

ROOSEVELT, THEODORE (1858–1919) 26th president of the United States. He worked as a writer, explorer and soldier before entering politics in 1881. He became assistant navy secretary, then led the US **Rough Riders** in Cuba during the Spanish-American War (1898). He was governor of New York, becoming vice-president in 1900 and succeeding to the presidency in 1901 after the assassination of **McKinley**. He acquired the Panama Canal Zone in 1903. He left office in 1909, and failed to win back the presidency in 1912.

ROSAS, JUAN MANUEL DE (1793–1877) Dictatorial governor of Beunos Aires, 1829–52. Born into a landowning and military family, he acquired large ranches and controlled a force of *gauchos* (cowboys); in 1827 he was appointed head of the provincial militia, and distinguished himself fighting insurgents (1828–9) and Indians (1833). He accepted the governorship, 1829–32 and from 1835, and ran a ruthless police state. He was overthrown in 1852 by a coalition of Brazilians, Uruguayans and Argentine opponents at the battle of Caseros. He fled to England and died in exile.

ROSES, WARS OF THE Civil war between rival claimants to the English throne: the dynasty of York (whose emblem was a white rose) and that of Lancaster (a red rose). The Yorkists rose against the Lancastrian king, Henry VI, in 1455, and deposed him in 1461. After a series of struggles involving Edward IV, Edward V and Richard III, the conflict was finally resolved in 1485, when Richard was defeated at Bosworth Field by the Lancastrian claimant, Henry Tudor, who was enthroned as **Henry VII** and married the Yorkist princess, Elizabeth, daughter of Edward IV, thus uniting the warring factions.

ROSKILDE, PEACE OF Treaty ending the war between Sweden and Denmark (1655–8) for control of the Baltic; it gave Sweden permanent possession of the strategically important region of Scania, Blekinge and Bohuslän.

ROUGH RIDERS Popular name for the First Volunteer Cavalry, recruited by **Theodore Roosevelt** from cowboys, police, miners and athletes to fight in the Spanish-American War, 1898.

ROUSSEAU, JEAN-JACQUES (1712–78) Swiss-French writer, born in Geneva. He quarrelled with most of the accepted conventions and established authorities of his time, and explored many of the themes later to form the basis of 19th century Romanticism and modern **democracy**. His main works include *Du Contrat Social* (1762), setting out a new theory of the relationship between the individual and the state; his autobiographical *Confessions* (published posthumously); and his novels *La Nouvelle Héloïse* (1761) and *Emile, ou l'éducation* (1762).

ROYAL NIGER COMPANY British trading company in west Africa. In 1886 Sir George Goldie's National African Company received a royal charter, changed its name, and was authorized to administer the delta and territories adjoining the course of the rivers Niger and Benue. It engaged in complex struggles with the French, the Germans and local rulers, conquering several emirates; in 1899, after many complaints and disputes, the charter was transferred to the British government.

RUDOLF IV (d.1365) Habsburg Duke of Austria, reigning 1358–65. He forged a charter, the *privilegium majus*, claiming vast lands, privileges and the hereditary title of archduke from his brother-in-law, Emperor **Charles IV**. The document was declared fraudulent by Italian scholar-poet Petrarch; the resulting war ended with the granting of Austria's claim to the Tyrol. He founded the University of Vienna (1365).

RYSWYCK, TREATY OF Agreement, signed September–October 1697, ending the War of the Grand Alliance (1689–97). **Louis XIV** (for France) accepted William III's right to the English throne, restoration of the *status quo* in the French and British colonies, the return of Catalonia, Luxembourg and parts of the Spanish Netherlands to Spain, and a favourable trade treaty with the Dutch. The German emperor recovered many French-fortified places along the Rhine, while Lorraine was restored to Duke Leopold.

S

SAAD ZAGHUL *see* **Zaghul, Saad**

SAADIS Muslim dynasty, claiming to be descendants of the Prophet ('sharifs') and ruling Morocco from the mid-16th to the mid-17th century.

SAAVEDRA, BALTAZAR DE LA CUEVA HENRRÍQUEZ ARIAS DE (1626–86) Spanish colonial administrator. In 1674 he was appointed Viceroy of Peru, Chile and Tierra Firme (a territory which included the Isthmus of Panama); his prosperous rule ended in outcry in 1678, when he tried to relax commercial monopolies. He was held captive for two years while charges were heard, and was exonerated in 1680. He returned to Spain, and held a seat on the Council of the Indies.

SABINES Ancient Apennine people of central Italy, northeast of Rome. According to legend the Sabine women were abducted by the Romans under Romulus; by the 3rd century the Sabines had become fully Romanized.

SADAT, MOHAMMED ANWAR EL- (1918–1981) Egyptian President. Commissioned in the Egyptian army in 1938, he was one of the group of officers, headed by **Nasser**, who planned the 1952 revolution. He was vice-president, 1964–6 and 1969–70, and became president after Nasser's death in 1970. In alliance with Syria he launched war against Israel in October 1973. In 1977 he opened a new round of discussions on peace between Israel and Egypt with his visit to Jerusalem; assassinated in 1981 by Muslim fundamentalists.

SAFFARIDS Muslim dynasty ruling much of eastern Persia in the 9th century. By 873 the empire stretched from northeast India to Khurasan; after failing to annex Transoxania in 900 its wider empire collapsed, but Saffarids retained local power in eastern Persia until the 15th century.

SAID, AL BU Muslim dynasty ruling in Oman, c. 1749 to the present, and Zanzibar, c. 1749–1964. It was founded by Ahmed ibn Said, who displaced the Yarubid imams of Oman to seize power there and in east Africa. In the 18th century they held Bahrain and parts of Persia; at the peak of their power under Said ibn Sultan (1806–56) they established commercial relations with the United States, France and Great Britain. The dominions were divided by Great Britain on the death of Said. The Zanzibar line was overthrown in 1964 when the island became part of Tanzania.

ST BARTHOLOMEW'S DAY MASSACRE Massacre of **Huguenots** (French Protestants) by French Catholics, which began on St Bartholomew's Day, 24 August 1572, and quickly spread from Paris to other French towns.

SALADIN (c. 1137–93) Western name of the founder of the **Ayyubid** dynasty, and the crusaders' most successful foe. He became sole ruler of Egypt and Islamic Syria, 1186; destroyed the crusaders' army at Hattin, northern Palestine and re-entered Jerusalem, 1187. He also neutralized the gains of the Third **Crusade**.

SALAZAR, ANTONIO DE OLIVEIRA (1889–1970) Dictator of Portugal. He was finance minister during the Depression, 1928–32, and became prime minister in 1932 after restoring economic order. He established authoritarian rule on Fascist lines in 1933 and maintained personal control until his death.

SALIANS One of many Frankish tribes which moved from central Europe (3rd century AD) and settled in the area north of the Rhine, near the modern Ijsselmeer. Thence, in the 5th century, they expanded south approximately to the river Loire. From them sprang the **Merovingian** dynasty, later superseded by the **Carolingians**, which conquered Aquitaine and Burgundy and reunited most of Gaul. The term is also used of the dynasty which came to power in Germany with Conrad II in 1024; the line died out with his great-grandson in 1125.

SALISBURY, ROBERT CECIL, 3rd MARQUESS OF (1830–1903) British statesman. He entered politics as a Conservative, and became foreign secretary 1878–80, a post which he also held through most of his three periods as prime minister, 1885–6, 1886–92, 1895–1902. On the whole he inclined towards cooperation with the **Triple Alliance** against Great Britain's imperial rivals, France and Russia, but was reluctant to conclude 'binding alliances' in Europe and was therefore often associated with the co-called policy of splendid isolation.

SALLE, ROBERT CAVELIER SIEUR DE LA (1643–87) French explorer. He emigrated to Montreal in 1666; traded and surveyed along the Illinois and Mississippi rivers from the Great Lakes region to the gulf of Mexico. He founded Louisiana in 1682.

SAMANIDS Iran's first native dynasty after the Muslim conquests, ruling 819–999. It developed Samarkand and Bukhara as centres of art and culture and assumed the economic leadership of northern Persia, but weakened after the mid-10th century.

SAMNITES Ancient Italian peoples occupying the territory of Samnium, in the southern Apennines in Italy, who were subjugated by Rome in the 4th to the 3rd century BC.

SAMORY (c. 1830–1904) Islamic hero and defender of the western Sudan against French colonial expansion in the late 19th century. Between 1865 and 1870 he built up a powerful chiefdom, and by early 1880 ruled an empire stretching from the Upper Volta and Upper Niger to Futa Jallon. In 1890 he set up his own firearms industry. He was finally defeated in 1898 on the Cavalla River, and died in exile.

SAMOYEDS People of the northern coasts of the former Soviet Union, from the White Sea to the Taymyr peninsula. Speaking a Uralic language, they are noted reindeer herders, fishermen and hunters.

SAMUDRAGUPTA (d.c. 375) Indian king, succeeding his father Chandragupta I, founder of the **Gupta** dynasty, c.335. From his capital, Pataliputra, in the Ganges valley, he extended control or exacted tribute throughout the greater part of the sub-continent.

SAMURAI Japanese warrior caste. Originally restricted to landed military houses, it became more open to able warriors of all kinds, especially during periods of civil war, such as that which lasted from c. 1450 to 1600. After 1603, when the rule of the **Tokugawa** ***shoguns*** initiated 250 years of peace, the Samurai became a closed hereditary class, often turning from military to administrative and artistic pursuits. Its feudal privileges were quickly abolished after the **Meiji** restoration of 1868.

SAN (Bushmen) Nomadic people, speaking a distinctive click language, living in the Kalahari Desert area of Namibia and Botswana.

SANDINISTAS Members of Sandinist National Liberation Front, (Frente Sandinista de Liberación Nacional: FSLN), named for César Augusto Sandio (1893–1934), assassinated guerrilla leader of the Nicaraguan resistance against US military occupation (1927–33). The FSLN, founded in 1962, began as a guerrilla campaign and ended in a full scale civil war, resulting in the overthrow of the Somoza regime (1979). They pursued a course of social **democracy**, with Daniel Ortega as president of the National Assembly (1985–90), in spite of pressure from the US-supplied counter-revolutionary forces through the 1980s. In free elections (1989), **Violeta Chamorro**, the opposition candidate was elected president.

SAN-FAN REBELLION *see* **Wu San-kuei**

SAN MARTÍN, JOSÉ DE (1778–1850) Argentine liberator; with **Simon Bolívar**, he led an army of liberation in the epic crossing of the Andes; with **Bernardo O'Higgins** he freed Chile in 1818, and in 1821 invaded Peru from the sea and took the Spanish stronghold of Lima. After a quarrel with Bolívar, he retired to France.

SANSKRIT Classical language of ancient India, in use mainly from c. 500 BC to c. AD 1000, but kept alive to the present day as the sacred language of the Hindu scriptures as well as of much secular literature. Also used in early inscriptions in south and southeast Asia, notably in ancient Cambodia. It is an Indo-European language, and hence ultimately related to Greek and Latin.

SAN STEFANO, TREATY OF Agreement ending the Russo-Turkish War, 1877–8. It created a large tributary state of Bulgaria, stretching from the Danube to the Aegean and covering all Macedonia except Salonika, granted independence to and enlarged Serbia, Montenegro and Romania, and gave Russia acquisitions in the Caucasus and a large indemnity. Fiercely opposed by Britain and Austria, the treaty was largely overturned at the **Congress of Berlin** in 1878.

SANTA ANNA, ANTONIO LÓPEZ DE (1794–1876) Mexican *caudillo*. He fought off the Spanish reconquest attempt in 1829, and became president of Mexico in 1834. He quelled Texan resistance at the Alamo, 1836, but was later defeated and captured; seizing power again in 1839 he ruled until 1845, but was routed by US troops in the Mexican War of 1864–8. His services were refused by both Emperor **Maximilian** and his enemies, and Santa Anna died poor and blind.

SANUSI WAR Resistance between 1912 and 1931 to Italian attempts to annex Libya, led by a brotherhood formed among the desert tribes (the 'Sanusis', founded in 1837). While the European powers were involved in the First World War, the Sanusis drove the Italians back to the coast and directed opposition to the French in Tunisia. In the 1920s they were defeated, but after the Second World War their leader became King of Libya.

SAPPHO (born c. 612 BC) Greek poetess, who lived at Mytilene in Lesbos. Her affection for a group of young women and girls associated with her in celebrating the cult of Aphrodite is ecstatically described among the surviving fragments from her seven books of poems in the Aeolic dialect. She looks at her emotions honestly and expresses them with a rare gift of verbal music.

SARGON Semitic king of Akkad, reigning c. 2296–2240 BC. One of the world's earliest empire-builders, he defeated the Sumerian ruler Lugalzagges of Uruk, seized all southern Mesopotamia, and achieved conquests as far afield as northern Syria, southern Anatolia and Elam in western Persia.

SASANIDS Iranian dynasty, named after Sasan, an ancestor of **Ardashir I**, who founded the family fortunes in AD 224. Under his leadership, Persis defeated the **Parthians** and created a major but frequently fluctuating empire extending from the Roman and Byzantine frontier in the west to central Asia where it absorbed most of the territories of the **Kushanas**. They were finally eclipsed by the Islamic invasions of 637–51.

SATAVAHANAS Indian dynasty, controlling the Andhra region in the delta of the Krishna and Godavari rivers. First mentioned in the 1st century AD, when King Satakarni made many conquests, it revived under Gautamiputra and his son Vasishthiputra in the early 2nd century, under whom lands were acquired from Kathiawar on the west coast to northern Madras on the east. They were displaced by the **Vakataka** dynasty.

SATNAMIS Members of one of a group of Hindu sects in India. The oldest, founded by Birbham in the 16th century, was part of an attempt to bring together **Hinduism** and Islam. Another was launched at the end of the 17th century by the Rajput religious leader, Jagjivan Das. Modern Satnamis are found mainly among the Chamars, northern India's hereditary caste of leather-tanners; they follow the teachings of the 19th century Chamar saint, Rai Das.

SAUDI (as-Saud) dynasty Founders and rulers of Saudi Arabia. Originally small rulers in central Arabia, they created their first – but short-lived – large state in the 18th century. The present state was created by Ibn Saud, who was followed after his death (1953) by four sons in succession: Saud (deposed 1964), Faisal (assassinated 1975), Khaled (d.1982) and Fahd.

SAUNDERS, SIR CHARLES (1713–75) British admiral. He commanded the fleet which carried General **James Wolfe**'s army to conquer French Canada in 1759. He was appointed First Lord of the Admiralty in 1766.

SAXONS German people originating in Schleswig-Holstein and along the Baltic. They responded to the decline of the Roman empire with a policy of active piracy in the North Sea, developing in the 5th century AD into substantial settlements along the coasts of Britain and Gaul. The Saxon wars, initiated by **Charlemagne**, lasted 32 years and ended with the absorption of the continental Saxons into the Frankish empire.

SAYYID MUHAMMAD BEN ABDULLAH (d.1920) Known as the 'Mad Mullah', a Somali chief who proclaimed himself **Mahdi** (religious leader) in the 1890s and began systematic raids against British and Italian positions around the Red Sea. He won territorial recognition in 1905 but resumed raids after 1908, keeping the Europeans confined to the coast until his death.

SCALA, della Italian dynastic family, also known as Scaligeri, hereditary rulers of Verona, founded by Mastino I (d.1277). Power was built up by his descendants, notably Cangrande I (1291–1329), the patron of **Dante**, but then frittered away in family quarrels. Their power was terminated by the **Visconti** of Milan, who conquered Verona in 1387.

SCANIAN WAR Fought between Sweden and Denmark, 1674–9, over the rich and strategically important province of Scania, or Skåne (at the southern tip of modern Sweden), which had been captured from the Danes in 1658. The Danish army reconquered Scania, but **Louis XIV** vetoed the return of the territory.

SCHLEICHER, KURT VON (1882–1934) Last chancellor of Germany's Weimar Republic, nicknamed 'the Hunger Chancellor'. He joined the German army in 1900, and in 1919 entered the newly-formed Reichswehr, becoming a major-general in the ministry of war in 1929. He helped bring down **Brüning**, and succeeded **Papen** as chancellor in 1932. He offered to aid **Hitler** if he could retain control of the Reichswehr, but was dismissed by **Hindenburg** in January 1933 after Hitler's refusal, and was murdered by the SS during the 'night of the long knives' the following year.

SCHLIEFFEN, ALFRED GRAF VON (1833–1913) German field-marshal, and chief of the German general staff, 1891–1906. In 1905 he devised the Schlieffen Plan, which, in the event of war, would involve the defeat of France by a vast outflanking movement through the Low Countries; in a revised form this provided the basis of German strategy at the outbreak of the First World War.

SCHOUTEN, WILLEM (1567–1625) Flemish navigator, discoverer of Le Maire Strait, between Tierra del Fuego and Staten island, and of Cape Horn. He was the first captain to traverse the Drake passage, linking the Atlantic and Pacific south of Tierra del Fuego; Drake himself followed the Magellan passage, further north.

SCOTTSBORO BOYS Nine Negro youths of Alabama, USA, charged in 1931 with the rape of two white girls in a railway freight car. The death sentences pronounced by the Alabama courts provoked accusations of racial prejudice from Northern liberals and radicals, and the US Supreme Court twice reversed the Alabama court decisions. In 1937 four were finally sentenced to life imprisonment, and the others released.

SCYTHIANS Nomadic Indo-European people, settling in Scythia, north of the Black Sea, on the lower Don and Dnieper rivers, before the 7th century BC. They were famous for the skill of their mounted archers and their rich gold jewellery; they were displaced by the closely-related Sarmatians in the 3rd century BC.

SEATO *see* **Southeast Asia Treaty Organization**

SECOND COALITION, WAR OF THE Struggle between France and a combination of Austria, Britain and Russia in support of Turkey, 1799–1802. After initial success in Italy and Switzerland, the alliance was crippled by France's victories over Austria at Marengo and Hohenlinden in 1800. Peace was signed with Austria at Lunéville (1801) and with Britain at Amiens (1802).

SECOND INTERNATIONAL Socialist organization founded in 1889 after the collapse of the First International. One of its main objects was to reconcile the working classes of Germany and France and to prevent war, possibly by means of a general strike, but it broke up when the main socialist parties of Europe decided to support their governments on the outbreak of war in 1914.

SÉGUIN, MARC (1786–1875) Distinguished French engineer who constructed railways, locomotives and suspension bridges. In 1828 he invented a multi-tubular locomotive boiler at almost exactly the same time as – but independently of – a similar invention in England by **Robert Stephenson** and Henry Booth. In 1831 a Séguin locomotive ran on the St Étienne-Lyons line, the first railway in France.

SELEUCIDS Near Eastern dynasty dominating Syria and Asia Minor from 312 to 63 BC. It was founded by **Seleucus I Nicator** (reigned 312–280 BC), a close associate of **Alexander the Great**. Its capital established at Antioch-on-the-Orontes, the dynasty sought to Hellenize Asia through Greek settlements; it was constantly at war with the Ptolemies. Power in the east was lost in the 3rd century, in Asia Minor in 198; after 129 it became a local dynasty in northern Syria, and it was finally eclipsed during the Roman invasion of Syria and Cilicia, 65–63.

SELEUCUS I NICATOR (c. 358–280 BC) Founder of the Seleucid dynasty, rulers of Asia Minor until the reign was largely absorbed into the Roman empire. He fought alongside **Alexander the Great** in Persia and married a Bactrian princess, 324. After Alexander's death he became governor of Babylon, and allied with **Ptolemy I** to prevent Antigonus Monophthalmus of Macedonia from inheriting Alexander's imperial throne; he helped to defeat Antigonus at Ipsus, 301; moved his capital to Antioch-on-the-Orontes. A ruler of high integrity, he was murdered by Ptolemy Ceraunus, son of Ptolemy I.

SELIM I YAVUZ (the Inexorable) (1470–1520) Ottoman sultan, 1512–20. The youngest son of **Bayezid II**, he rebelled against his father in 1511, engineering his deposition and overcoming his own brothers Ahmed and Korkut, 1512–13. He proscribed and massacred the Anatolian Turcoman adherents of the **Safavid** shah, **Ismail**, defeating him at Chaldiran and occupying Tabriz, his capital. This radical shift in the Middle Eastern balance of power brought **Selim** into conflict with the **Mamluks** of Egypt: in 1516–17 he successively conquered Syria and Egypt, abolished the Mamluk sultanate and annexed its territories to the Ottoman state. By the time of his death the Ottomans ruled in Jerusalem, in Cairo and in Mecca and Medina: a vast increase in the size, prestige and wealth of the empire.

SELJUKS Ruling family of the Oghuz branch of the Turkish peoples who began settling in lands of the **Abbasid** caliphate, becoming Muslims, in the 10th century. They established a local power, quickly expanded it and occupied Baghdad, capital of the caliphate, in 1055. They ruled most of the lands of the caliphate, under Abbasid suzerainty, with the title of sultan. The empire split after the death of Nizam al-Mulk, but a branch remained as rulers of part of Anatolia (incorporated in the Muslim world by Seljuk conquest from the Byzantines) from the early 12th century until the Mongol conquest in the 13th century.

SEMINOLE North American Indian tribe. In the early 18th century they separated from the Creek Indians ('seminole' means separate) and moved from Georgia into northern Florida. They fought two wars against the United States to avoid deportation and repel white encroachment (1817–18, while still under Spanish rule, and 1835–42); after the final surrender most of the tribe settled in Indian territory, which in 1907 became the state of Oklahoma.

SEMITES Speakers of the Semitic group of languages, of which Arabic, Hebrew and **Amharic** are the main languages still current. Akkadian, the language of Babylon and Assyria, was superseded by Aramaic during the 1st millennium BC, though still written for certain purposes down to the first century AD; Aramaic, once widespread, survives in small enclaves and in the liturgy of the **Jews** and some Eastern churches.

SENDERO LUMINOSO *see* **Shining Path**

SENGHOR, LEOPOLD SEDAR (1906–) President of Senegal 1960–90. He studied in France (the first black African to obtain his *agrégation*), served in the French army (1939–40) and in the Resistance. He helped to draft the constitution of the Fourth French Republic in 1946 and sat in its Assembly between 1946 and 1958. He formed his own political party in Senegal in 1948, which won power in 1951, and worked in both Paris and Dakar for a federation of independent French west African states; when this failed he ran for office as resident of Senegal, and was elected (1960). He resigned in 1980 and became the first African to be accepted by the French Academy (1984).

SENNACHERIB King of Assyria, 704–681 BC. He gained experience as a senior commander during the reign of his father, Sargon II, and on his accession devoted himself energetically to the defence of the empire. The rising strength of **Chaldean** and Aramaean tribes in Babylonia, backed by Elam, produced a dangerous instability, which Sennacherib made repeated attempts to resolve by both political and military means, finally sacking the capital, Babylon, in 689 BC. A rebellion in the west, politically linked to the disaffection in Babylonia, led to a campaign in 701 BC, which included the attack on Jerusalem mentioned in the Bible. Sennacherib had a keen interest in technological innovation; his most enduring work was the replanning of Nineveh as the Assyrian capital. He was murdered by a son or sons.

SEPHARDIM From the Hebrew word *Sepharad* for Spain, it refers to the **Jews** of Spain, and after the expulsion of 1492–7 their descendants down to the present day. It is used in distinction to **Ashkenazim** who have slightly different customs and rites.

SERBS Slav people. Serbia, the largest and most populous republic of Yugoslavia, emerged as a separate principality in the 9th century and an independent kingdom in 1217. It was conquered by the Turks (1389) and incorporated into the **Ottoman** empire (1459); it regained its independence in 1829. Blamed for the assassination of Archduke **Franz Ferdinand**, which precipitated the First World War, it became part of Yugoslavia in 1918. Serbia backed Croatian and Bosnian Serb separatists in civil war from 1991, after Croatia, Slovenia and Bosnia-Herzegovina declared independence. Formed new Yugoslav state in 1992 comprising Serbia and Montenegro.

SESTERCE A small silver coin, originally worth one-quarter of a Roman denarius. It was the most common unit of Roman currency.

SETI I King of Egypt's 19th Dynasty, he reigned 1318–1304 BC. He campaigned in Syria, continued work on the Temple of Amun at Karnak, and built his own splendid temple at Abydus.

SEVEN YEARS' WAR Complex struggle, fought 1756–63, between Prussia, supported by Britain, and a coalition of Austria, Russia and France. It arose from Austrian attempts to regain Silesia, lost to Prussia in 1748 (War of the Austrian Succession) and extended by colonial rivalries between Britain and France. The untimely death of Elizabeth of Russia saved Prussia from annihilation while, overseas, Britain destroyed French power in North America, the Caribbean and India.

SÈVRES, TREATY OF Agreement between First World War allies and the Ottoman empire providing for dismemberment of the empire and Greek occupation of part of its Turkish heartland (Izmir and its surrounding region). It was signed reluctantly by the sultan's government on 10 August 1920, but was totally rejected by Turkish nationalists under Mustafa Kemal (**Atatürk**); it was replaced in 1923 by the **Treaty of Lausanne**.

SEWARD, WILLIAM (1801–72) US secretary of state, 1861–9, best remembered for negotiating the purchase of Alaska in 1867 from Russia, called at the time 'Seward's Folly'. He was a leading anti-slavery agitator; he became governor of New York, 1839–43, and helped to found the Republican Party, 1855. A close adviser to **Lincoln**, he was stabbed by a co-conspirator of Lincoln's assassin, John Wilkes Booth, but survived.

SHAHJAHAN (1592–1658) Mughal emperor of India and builder of the Taj Mahal. Third son of the emperor Jehangir, and grandson of **Akbar**, he rebelled in 1622 in an ineffectual bid to win the succession, was reconciled with his father in 1625, and in 1628 proclaimed himself ruler after his father's death. He created the city of Shahjahanabad, and the Taj Mahal (1623–49), in memory of his favourite wife, Mumtaz Mahal. He was imprisoned in 1657 during a power struggle between his four sons, and died in captivity.

SHAILENDRA DYNASTY Rulers from c. 700 to 1293 of the Sri Vijaya kingdom. Their ardent support of **Buddhism** is reflected in such architectural masterpieces as the great Borobudur complex in Java.

SHAKA (c.1787–1828) Zulu king. He was appointed in 1810 by the **Nguni** leader, Dingiswayo, to train and command the fighting men of northeast Natal; he pioneered the highly disciplined use of the short, stabbing assegai. He established himself as ruler on Dingiswayo's death in 1818 and crushed all rivals in Natal-Zululand before being assassinated by his half-brothers.

SHALMANESER III King of Assyria, 858–824 BC. He was the son and successor of Ashurnasirpal II, whose imperialist policies he continued, although stability and not expansion was his primary objective, as shown in Babylonia where he provided massive military aid to support the ruling dynasty without seeking personal kingship. In a long series of campaigns he broke the power of the Aramaean and neo-Hittite state of Syria and Cilicia, consolidating control of the routes from the Mediterranean and Asia Minor. In the north he acted to defend Assyria against the growing power of Urartu (Armenia). He defended the eastern borders by sorties into the Zagros mountains to secure recognition of Assyrian suzerainty.

SHAMIL (c. 1830–71) Caucasian resistance leader. In 1830 he joined the Muridis, a Sufi sect engaged in a holy war against the Russians who had seized the former Persian province of Daghestan. He succeeded as imam in 1834, establishing Daghestan as an independent state; surviving the capture of his main stronghold, Ahulgo, in 1838, he was finally defeated by massive Russian forces in 1859, and was exiled to the Moscow district. He died on a pilgrimage to Mecca.

SHAMSHI-ADAD I A major king in northern Mesopotamia, 1749–1717 BC, and older contemporary and possibly former suzerain of **Hammurabi**. The son of a minor ruler of nomad **Amorite** stock, he first gained control of Assyria, and from that base annexed the kingdom of Mari on the middle Euphrates. This gave him an empire controlling important trade routes, stretching from the Zagros mountains to the Euphrates and at times beyond, and northwards to the borders of the Anatolian plateau. Much of his correspondence, and that of his two sons appointed as sub-kings, has been found on clay tablets which haves been excavated at Mari, and shows his skill and attention to detail in diplomatic, military and administrative matters.

SHANS A Thai people now forming the Shan state of the Union of Burma. The word is a variant of 'Siam', but the Siamese came to call themselves **Thai**, 'free', and their country Thailand. The Shans infiltrated Upper Burma in the 13th century, and when Pagan fell, c. 1300, strove for nearly three centuries with the Burmans for dominance; they sacked Ava, the capital, in 1527. In the 1550s the rulers of the Sittang state of Toungoo finally forced the Shan states to accept Burman overlordship. After the British annexation of Upper Burma in 1886, their *sawbwas* (chieftains) accepted British overlordship; later they were joined into the Shan States Federation. After independence in 1948 the Union government abolished the powers of the *sawbwas*.

SHANG CHIH-HSIN (1636–80) Son of Shang K'o-hsi (d.1676), governor of Kwangtung 1650–71, who succeeded his father. In 1673 his father's retirement provoked the rebellion of **Wu San-kuei**; in 1676 he joined the rebels, but the following year submitted to the **Manchus**. In 1680 he was accused of plotting a fresh rebellion, was arrested and ordered to commit suicide.

SHANKARACHARYA (c. 788–820) Brahmin philosopher. He was a famous interpreter of *Vedanta* and originator of the Monist (*Advaita*) system of Hindu thought. He established influential religious centres (*mathas*) at Badrinath in the Himalayas, Puri in Orissa, Dwarka on the west Indian coast, and Sringeri in the south; he argued that the visible world is an illusion (*maya*) and that reality lies beyond the senses.

SHARIFIAN DYNASTY Saadi rulers of south Morocco from 1511. They secured Ottoman aid and managed to extend their control over the rest of Morocco in the 1550s and to expel the

Portuguese in 1578. In 1591 they sent an expedition of Ottoman-trained troops across the Sahara and destroyed the Songhay empire. Disputed successions after 1610 weakened their authority, and the last Saadi was assassinated in 1660.

SHAYBANIDS Central Asian dynasty, controlling Transoxania in the late 15th and early 16th centuries after defeating the descendants of **Tamerlane**; it was replaced at Bukhara by the Astrakhanids in 1599.

SHENG SHI-TS'AI (1895–1970) Warlord from Manchuria, sent to Sinkiang in 1929. He established control there, 1933–43, with strong support from the USSR, giving extensive concessions to the Soviet Union in return. In 1942 he went over to the Nationalists and demanded Soviet withdrawal, which was completed in 1943. In 1944 he tried to renew Russian links; he was removed from the province.

SHERIDAN, PHILIP HENRY (1831–88) Union general in the American Civil War. He cut off the Confederate retreat at Appomattox in 1865, forcing the surrender of the Southern commander, General **Robert E. Lee** to General **Ulysses S. Grant**. He was army commander-in-chief from 1883 until his death.

SHERMAN, WILLIAM TECUMSEH (1820–91) Union general in the American Civil War. He entered the army but resigned his commission in 1853; reappointed a colonel in 1861, he was promoted to general after the first Battle of Bull Run. He destroyed the Confederate forces on his famous march through Georgia, 1864; he was appointed commanding general of the army in 1869.

SHER SHAH (c. 1486–1545) Afghan emperor of northern India. A soldier under the **Mughal** king of Bihar, he became ruler of Bihar, and conquered Bengal in 1539. He defeated the Mughal emperor, Humayan, in 1539 and again in 1540, and took the royal title of Fariduddin Sher Shah. He effected notable fiscal, social and administrative reforms.

SHIH HUANG TI (c. 259–210 BC) Creator of the first unified Chinese empire. He attained the throne of Ch'in, northwest China, in 246 BC. By 221 he had annexed the territories of his six major rivals and proclaimed empire over them. He expanded Chinese control into southern China, establishing centralized administration and a network of roads, extending and consolidating the Great Wall, and unified the Chinese writing system. He entered into bitter controversy with Confucian scholars at his court, culminating in the Burning of the Books in 213.

SHI'ISM One of two main divisions of Islam, which split from the other, the **Sunni**, over the question of succession to the Prophet **Mohammed**, which Shi'as believe to have gone to his son-in-law **Ali** and then to a line of imams (hence their name, *Shi'at Ali*, party of Ali). They later split into a number of groups recognizing different lines of imams: Zaidis in Yemen, **Ismailis**, and the main or Twelver group recognizing a line of twelve imams, the last of whom is believed to have gone into hiding. This kind of Shi'ism is widespread today in Lebanon, Iraq, India, Pakistan and Iran, where it is the state religion.

SHIMONOSEKI Treaty of agreement ending the first Sino-Japanese war (1894–5). China recognized the independence of Korea, ceded Taiwan, the Pescadores Islands and the Liaotung peninsula (including Port Arthur) to Japan, paid a large indemnity, and opened four new ports to foreign trade. Later in 1895 Russia, France and Germany forced Japan to return south Liaotung to China in return for a larger indemnity.

SHINING PATH (Sendero Luminoso) Peruvian revolutionary movement employing guerrilla tactics and extreme violence in the name of Maoism, founded as the Communist Party of Peru in Ayacucho (1970) as an offshoot of other parties. The leader, philosophy professor Abimael Guzmán, and his followers envision revolution as a long-term military offensive aimed at the destruction of all traces of 'bourgeois' influence, including political and military figures, and municipal targets. Expanding their activities from the highlands to the capital city of Lima, they remained a formidable force in Peru despite the capture of Guzmán in September 1992.

SHINTO Ancient religion of Japan. It lacks both an acknowledged founder and an organized body of teaching. It is characterized by worship of ancestors and heroes, a wide variety of local cults, and belief in the divinity of the emperor. It was largely superseded in the 6th century by **Buddhism**, but revived in the 17th century and was the official state religion from 1867 to 1946.

SHIVA Hindu god, combining within himself many apparently contradictory qualities: destruction and restoration, asceticism and sensuality, benevolence and revenge. In Sanskrit the name means 'suspicious one'; he is worshipped as the supreme deity by various Shiva sects in India.

SICILIAN VESPERS Revolt against the French conqueror of Sicily, **Charles I of Anjou**, during the hour of vespers on Easter Monday, 30 March 1282. Encouraged by Peter III of Aragon, the Sicilians massacred 2000 French officials; after long wars between France and Aragon, Peter III's son, Frederick III, won recognition as king under the Peace of Caltabellotta, 1302.

SIEMENS, ERNST WERNER VON (1816–92) German engineer and inventor who discovered a process for galvanic gilding and plating, 1841. He supervised the construction of the first long telegraph line in Europe (Berlin to Frankfurt-am-Main, 1848–9). With Halske he set up a telegraph factory which constructed many telegraph lines in Russia; his brother Carl ran a subsidiary company in Russia while another brother, William, was in charge of the London branch. A new company (Siemens Brothers) manufactured and laid underwater cables. He invented the electric dynamo in 1866 and was actively concerned with the application of electric power to locomotives, trams, lifts and street lighting.

SIENIAWSKI, MIKOLAJ HIERONIM (1645–83) Polish general *Voivode* (Army leader) of Volhynia (1680) and *Hetman* of the crown (1682), he fought successfully against **Tatars** and **Cossacks**. In 1683 he led the advance guard of the army led by King **John III Sobieski** to relieve Vienna.

SIGISMUND III (1655–1632) King of both Sweden and Poland, son of John III of Sweden and Catherine of Poland. Sigismund thus belonged to both the Vasa and the **Jagiełło** dynasties, but his efforts to unite the two lines and the two countries ended in disaster. Elected to the throne of Poland, 1587, he also inherited the Swedish crown in 1592, and tried to restore Catholicism to Sweden. When he left Sweden for Poland, the regent, his uncle (later **Charles IX**), rebelled, defeating him at Stängebrö, 1598, and deposing him, 1599. The two countries remained intermittently at war until 1660.

SIHANOUK, PRINCE NORODOM (1922–) Cambodian statesman, King of Cambodia from 1941–55, he then became its prime minister 1955–60, and head of state, 1960–70. In 1970 he was deposed by the National Assembly and Council of the Kingdom, and in Peking set up a Government of National Union. He returned as nominal head of state after the Communist (**Khmer Rouge**) victory in 1975, but was removed from office the following year. He became Cambodian head of state again in 1991.

SIKHS Members of an Indian religious community founded by the 16th-century teacher **Nanak**. Outwardly distinguished by carrying the five K Symbols: Kesha (uncut hair), Kanga (a small comb), Kara (an iron bangle), Kirpan (a small dagger) and Kacha (a type of underwear), in the 18th and early 19th centuries they emerged as a militant warrior brotherhood, particularly under the leadership of **Ranjit Singh**.

SIMON THE HASMONEAN (d.135 BC) Younger brother of **Judah Maccabee** who in 142 established a new Jewish state independent of the **Seleucid** rulers of the Near East; the state survived until quarrels among the descendants of Simon led to the establishment of Roman control in 63 BC.

SINCLAIR, UPTON (1875–1963) American novelist. His first major success, *The Jungle* (1906), embodied his personal, bitterly controversial investigation into working conditions in the Chicago stockyards; a series of similar works established him as a leading Socialist critic of US **capitalism**. He ran for governor of California as the Democratic candidate in 1934.

SINDHIAS Ruling dynasty of Gwalior, western India, founded by Ranoji, a **Maratha** official, in the 18th century. Under Sindhia Mahaduji (reigned 1761–94) the family established a virtually independent empire in northwest India, holding off the troops of the **English East India Company**, 1775–82, defeating the **Rajputs** and the **Marathas**, 1793, and taking the **Mughal** emperors, Shah Alam, under their protection. Later Sindhias, however, accepted British pre-eminence (from 1818); their kingdom survived as a native princedom under the British, and was later absorbed into the Indian union.

SIOUX (also called Dakota). North American Indian tribes once occupying vast areas of Minnesota, Montana, the Dakotas and the Western plains. From 1851 to 1876 they organized a resolute and often successful resistance to the advance of white settlers; discovery of gold in the Black Hill of Dakota brought a vast new influx of white fortune-hunters. Despite victory at the Little Big Horn (1876), the Sioux were finally crushed in the Tongue River valley.

SIVAJI (c. 1627–80) Founder of the 17th-century **Maratha** kingdom in west India. He carved out his kingdom from **Mughal** and Bijapur territory and carried on a protracted war against the former. He was enthroned as an independent sovereign in 1674 and devoted his later life to social reform and the advancement of religious toleration.

SLOVENES South Slav people inhabiting the former Yugoslav province of Slovenia; they number about two million. Gained independence in 1991, after brief opposition from the Yugoslav army.

SMERDIS Short-lived Persian emperor in 522 BC, son of **Cyrus II the Great** and younger brother of **Cambyses II**, on whose order he was secretly put to death by the king's officer Prexaspes. Subsequently imperial powers were usurped by Gaumata, the majordomo, who put his brother in the place of the vanished prince ('Pseudo-Smerdis') while Cambyses was campaigning in Egypt. After Cambyses' death, 'Smerdis' was recognized as king for eight months before being killed by **Darius I**.

SMETONA, ANTANAS (1874–1944) Lithuanian statesman who signed the Lithuanian declaration of independence, 1918; he became first president, 1919–20, and again after a *coup d'état* from 1926–40. After the Soviet invasion, he fled to western Europe in 1940, and then to the United States.

SMITH, ADAM (1723–90) Scottish economist and philosopher. Professor of Logic, Glasgow University, 1751, and of Moral Philosophy, 1752–64. His *Inquiry into the Nature and Causes of the Wealth of Nations*, 1776, laid the foundations for the new science of political economy.

SMITH, IAN DOUGLAS (1919–) Rhodesian political leader. Served in the British Royal Air Force, 1941–6. He became a member of the South Rhodesia legislative assembly, 1948–53; of the parliament of the federation of Rhodesia and Nyasaland, 1953–61, and of the right-wing Rhodesia Front Party. As prime minister of Rhodesia (1964–79) he declared unilateral independence (UDI) in 1965. In 1979 a peaceful trasnfer to black majority rule was engineered. Smith remained a member of parliament in the renamed Zimbabwe until 1987, when he was suspended. He susequently resigned as leader of the opposition party.

SOCIALISM Belief in communal or collective ownership of the means of economic production and distribution, and the right of all to share equally in the benefits and opportunities created by society. In Europe it reached back to the Middle Ages ('when Adam delft and Eva span, who was then the gentilman?') and was influential in the 16th and 17th centuries (e.g. the **Levellers** in England); in the 19th century it broke up into various sub-divisions – Utopian (or Saint-Simonian) socialism, Marxian socialism, Christian socialism, democratic socialism – each differing in the emphasis placed on particular parts of the programme, and the political methods considered acceptable to achieve them.

SOCRATES (469–399 BC) Athenian thinker. None of his own work survives; he is best known through **Xenophon**'s memoirs and the early *Dialogues* of his pupil **Plato**. He was independent but critical of **democracy**, and was condemned to death by a popular jury. Plato's *Apology* and *Phaedo* purport to be accounts of his defence and last days.

SOLIDUS Byzantine gold coin, first issued by the Emperor **Constantine** in the 4th century AD. One of the most stable units of currency in economic history, it remained important in international trade for over 700 years.

SOLÍS, JUAN DÍAZ DE (c.1470–1516) Spanish explorer. He first visited central America in 1508 with **Vicente Yáñez Pinzón**. In 1515 he left Spain with three vessels and a commission to explore the lands 1700 leagues (5000 miles/8000 km) south of Panama. He reached the Plate River in 1516, sailed up the Uruguay River and was killed and eaten by Charrua Indians in sight of his crew; the survivors gave valuable information to **Sebastian Cabot**.

SOLOMONIDS Ruling dynasty in Ethiopia from 1770 to 1975. It was founded by Yekuno Amlak, prince of the inland province of Shoa, who claimed direct descent from the biblical King Solomon. Under Amda Sion (1314–44) and Zara Yaqob (1434–68) it consolidated power at home and repelled the Muslims to the north. It was finally eclipsed with the deposition of **Haile Selassie**.

SOPHIST Name applied to itinerant purveyors of higher education for fees in 5th and 4th century Greece. Their leading figures, such as **Protagoras**, were spoken of with much respect, but conservative opinion found their influence disturbing.

SOPHOCLES (c. 496–406 BC) Athenian dramatist. Also a statesman, general and priest. He won first prize at Athenian festivals with 24 tetralogies, i.e. 96 of his 123 plays. Seven plays survive: *Ajax, The Women of Trachis, Antigone, King Oedipus, Electra, Philoctetes, Oedipus at Colonus*, and a fragment of *The Trackers*. He said that he created men as they ought to be, whereas **Euripides** wrote about men as they are.

SOTHO/TSWANA One of two main Bantu-speaking groups of southern African peoples, occupying the areas of Botswana, Lesotho, Orange Free State, and the north and east Transvaal since c. 1000.

SOTO, HERNANDO DE (c. 1500–42) Spanish explorer. He first sailed to Central America, c. 1519, and in 1532 took part in the conquest of Peru. He was appointed governor of Cuba in 1537 by **Charles V**, and given a contract to conquer Florida: landing near Charlotte Bay in 1539, he fought his way through today's southern United States as far west as Oklahoma, discovering the Mississippi river in 1541. He died on the return journey.

SOUTHEAST ASIA TREATY ORGANIZATION (SEATO) Set up in 1954 between Australia, France, New Zealand, Pakistan, the Philippines, Thailand, the United Kingdom and the United States to resist possible aggression by Communist China after the Korean War. Pakistan withdrew in 1972; at the 1975 Council meeting it was agreed that the organization should be phased out.

SOVIETS Originally revolutionary councils elected by workers during the Russian revolution of 1905. They were revived in 1917 to include bodies elected by workers, peasants and soldiers; it signified the primary units of government in the former USSR.

SPARTAKISTS Members of the *Spartakusbund*, a German revolutionary socialist group in the First World War, led by Rosa Luxembourg and Karl Liebknecht, and named after the Roman slave-rebel, Spartacus. It later became the nucleus of the German Communist Party.

SPEER, ALBERT (1905–81) German architect and **Nazi** leader. A member from 1931 of the German Nazi party; as minister of armaments between 1942 and 1945 he made widespread use of slave labour from concentration camps for which, at the end of the Second World War, he was sentenced to 20 years' imprisonment. His brilliant and efficient organization of industry contributed greatly to German strength. His memoirs, *Inside the Third Reich*, present an intimate picture of life in the entourage of **Adolf Hitler**.

SPEKE, JOHN HANNING (1827–64) British explorer who with Richard **Burton** reached Lake Tanganyika in 1858, and then journeyed alone, becoming the first European to see Lake Victoria and identify it as a source of the Nile.

SPUTNIK First artificial space satellite put into orbit, in 1957, by the USSR. Meaning 'companion', 'fellow traveller', it signalled the Soviet Union's growing technical capability and helped to precipitate a new phase in the US-USSR arms race.

SRI VIJAYA Maritime empire, controlling the Strait of Malacca and much of the Malay Archipelago from the 7th to the 11th century.

STALIN (1879–1953) Born Joseph Vissarionovich Dzhugashvili. Son of a Georgian shoemaker, he trained for the priesthood but was expelled in 1899 after becoming a **Marxist**. In 1917 he became Peoples' Commissar for Nationalities in the Soviet government, and general secretary of the Communist Party of the Soviet Union from 1922 until his death. He eliminated all rivals after the death of **Lenin** in 1924; promoted an intensive industrialization, the forced collectivization of agriculture, and the development of a police state. He signed a non-aggression pact with Nazi Germany in 1939, resulting in the Russian occupation of eastern Poland and Finland; and led resistance to German invasion, 1941–5. Three years after his death his regime was denounced by **Khruschev** and a 'destalinization' programme instituted.

STANDARD OIL US company formed in 1870 by John D. Rockefeller to refine and distribute petroleum. By 1879 it controlled almost 95 per cent of all oil refined in the United States and became the first industrial 'trust', provoking the Sherman Anti-Trust Law of 1890. It was dissolved by the Supreme Court in 1911 and forced to operate as separate corporations charters in different states. Its principal component, the Exxon Corporation, became the company with the highest turnover in the world in 1975, with annual sales of nearly $50,000 million.

STANISŁAW II PONIATOWSKI (1732–98) Last king of independent Poland, being elected king with the support of **Catherine the Great** after the death of Augustus III in 1763. He failed to counter successive partitions of Poland by Russia, Austria and Prussia, despite the short-lived revival of 1788–94, and abdicated in 1795 as the three countries finally absorbed all Polish territory.

STANLEY, SIR HENRY MORTON (1847–1904) British explorer. As a young war-correspondent, he was sent by a New York newspaper to find the Scottish missionary traveller **David Livingstone**; he met him near Lake Tanganyika in 1871, to secure the 'scoop of the century'. He crossed Africa from Zanzibar to the mouth of the Congo, 1874–7, and founded the Congo Free State in 1879 on behalf of **Leopold II** of the Belgians, after Great Britain had turned down his offer to acquire the territory. He was a member of parliament, 1859–1900.

STAUFEN *see* **Hohenstaufen**

STAVISKY, SERGE ALEXANDRE (1886–1934) French financier who founded a credit organization in Bayonne and issued bonds later found to be fraudulent. The scandal that followed his death – said by police to be suicide but widely believed to be murder – precipitated a major political crisis, culminating in the resignation of two prime minsters and a riot outside the Chamber of Deputies in which 15 died.

STEFAN DUSHAN (1308–55) Most famous king of medieval Serbia. He deposed his father and seized the throne in 1331; annexed Macedonia, Albania and large areas of Greece from Byzantium; took the title 'Tsar of the Serbs and Greeks'; granted a major new code of laws.

STEIN, BARON HEINRICH VON (1757–1831) Prussian statesman. As chief minister, 1807, he instituted a programme of reform including the emancipation of serfs and municipal self-government; exiled by **Napoleon**, 1808, he became counsellor to Tsar Alexander I, 1812–13, and played a leading part in forming the anti-Napoleonic alliance between Russia and Prussia.

STEPHEN (c.1097–1154) King of England, third son of Stephen, Count of Blois and Chartres, and Adela, daughter of **William I**. Raised by Henry I and given large estates in England and Normandy, he pledged his support to Henry's daughter Matilda, but instead usurped the crown in 1135. Most of his reign was spent in civil war with Matilda (finally defeated 1148); after the death of his son, Eustace, he reluctantly designated Matilda's son, later **Henry II**, as his successor.

STEPHEN I (977–1038) First king of Hungary, a member of the Arpád dynasty, and son of the leading Magyar chief, Geisa (Geza). He decisively defeated a pagan uprising after the death of his father in 997, and was anointed king in 1000. He founded bishoprics, abbeys and encouraged church-building; and fought off an invasion by Emperor Conrad I in 1030. He was canonized in 1083.

STEPHEN OF PERM, ST (1335–96) Russian Orthodox bishop who led a mission to the **Zyrians**.

STEPHENSON, GEORGE (1781–1848) English railway pioneer. He built the first successful steam locomotive, 1814; constructed the Stockton and Darlington line, 1825; his *Rocket* won the first open speed contest for railway engines, 1829. With his son, Robert, he built many early track systems both in Great Britain and overseas.

STEPHENSON, ROBERT (1803–59) Civil engineer. He was a partner with his father, George Stephenson, and others in the firm of Robert Stephenson & Co. which built locomotives for British and many Continental railways.

STIMSON, HENRY LEWIS (1867–1950) American statesman. He was secretary for war, 1911–13, in the Cabinet of William Howard Taft, and went on to serve in the administration of five presidents, of both parties, up to 1945. He was secretary for war to **F.D. Roosevelt**, 1940–5, and chief advisor to both Roosevelt and **Truman** on atomic policy: he justified the bombing of Hiroshima and Nagasaki on the grounds that it saved more lives than it cost.

STINNES, HUGO (1870–1924) German industrialist, grandson of **Matthias Stinnes**. He trained as a mining engineer, and founded the Stinnes Combine. Head of German industrial production in the First World War, he took advantages of the post-war hyper-inflation to extend interests in coal, iron, power and transport into timber, insurance, paper manufacture and newspapers. At his death he was probably the most powerful financier in Europe; the company is known now as Stinneskonzern.

STINNES, MATTHIAS (1790–1845) German industrialist who built up large coal mining and river transport interests in the Ruhr; the sinking of a deep shaft in his colliery Graf Beust (near Essen) in 1839–41 began the northward expansion of mining in the Ruhr.

STOICS School of philosophers, founded by Zeno (c. 332–264 BC), who taught in Athens at the Stoa. To the Stoics, 'God is all and in all. Call him Zeus, Nature, Universe, Reason – all is in his hands. Virtue is the only good, moral weakness the only evil; to all else – health, wealth, position, pain – man should be indifferent.' Notable Stoics were Zeno's successors, Cleanthes and Chrysippus; Panaetius and Posidonius, who transplanted the philosophy to Rome; and, under the Roman empire, the statesman Seneca, the ex-slave Epictetus, and the half-agnostic Emperor Marcus Aurelius.

STOLBOVO, PEACE OF Settlement ending the Russo-Swedish war, 1610–17. The Swedes invaded northern Russia and captured Novgorod in 1611; expelled from there, they besieged Pskov. Anglo-Dutch mediation produced an agreement that Sweden would withdraw its troops, but retain Karelia and Ingria, between Finland and Estonia, thus effectively denying Russia any 'window to the Baltic' for the next century.

STOLYPIN, PIOTR ARKADEVICH (1863–1911) Russian statesman. Minister of the interior and prime Minister, 1906–11, he tried to save imperial Russia by agrarian reform and the forcible suppression of the revolutionary movement. He was assassinated.

STONE AGE The earliest stage in the development of human culture, characterized by the use of stone, as opposed to metal tools. It is normally sub-divided into an Old Stone Age (**Palaeolithic**), Middle Stone Age (**Mesolithic**) and New Stone Age (**Neolithic**). The Old Stone Age covers the whole of human development during the **Pleistocene** Ice Age; the other two occupy the earlier part of the post-glacial period from 8000 BC onwards.

STROESSNER, ALFREDO (1912–) President of Paraguay; son of a Bavarian immigrant father and Paraguayan mother. He fought in the Chaco War (1832–35); rose to be general in the Paraguayan army in 1951, associated with the Colorado party and became president in 1954 after a palace revolution. He steadily accumulated dictatorial powers, and was voted resident for life in 1977. He was deposed by Andrés Rodríguez in a military takeover in 1989.

STRUTT, JEDEDIAH (1726–97) A pioneer in the development of the early English cotton industry. In 1758–59, he patented an improved stocking frame and set up a mill in Derby, England, to manufacture the 'Derby Patent Rib'. In 1768 he entered into partnership with **Arkwright** to exploit Arkwright's new spinning frame.

STUART, JOHN McDOUALL (1815–66) Explorer of south Australia. Born in Scotland, he served as draughtsman in **Sturt**'s expeditions of 1844–46 before making six expeditions (1856–62) to the Australian interior, reaching Van Dieman Gulf.

STURT, CHARLES (1795–1869) Explorer of Australia. Born in Bengal, he was educated in England. Military secretary to the governor of New South Wales in 1827, in 1828–9 he traced the Macquarie, Bogan and Castlereagh rivers, then traversed the Murrumbidgee and Murray rivers, 1829–30, and in 1844–6 penetrated north from Adelaide to the Simpson Desert.

SUCRE, ANTONIO JOSÉ DE (1795–1830) Liberator of Ecuador. Born in Venezuela, at the age of 26 he was appointed by **Bolívar** to free the southern part of Gran Colombia, now Ecuador, from Spanish control. He defeated the royalists at Quito, May 1822, and routed 9,000 Spaniards at Ayacucho, forcing withdrawal. He dislodged the last Spanish survivors from Upper Peru, now Bolivia, whose legal capital carries his name.

SUEBI (SUEVES) Germanic peoples, including the Marcomanni, Quadi, Hermunduri, Semnones and Langobardi (**Lombards**). In the 1st century AD they mostly lived along the river Elbe, apart from the Lombards, who established long-lasting control in northern Italy, their best-known group, dislodged by the **Huns**, entered Spain in 409 and consolidated a quasi-independent kingdom in the northwest (Galicia, Lusitania, Baetica). Their Christian king, Rechiar, was defeated by the **Visigoths** in 456, but the Visigoths finally absorbed the last Suebian territory in 585.

SUEZ WAR Joint military intervention by Great Britain, France and Israel after Egypt nationalized the Suez Canal Company in 1956. After some early success, the action was condemned and halted by the intervention of the **United Nations**, and especially the United States. The Canal, blocked by Egypt during the fighting, was reopened in 1957.

SUHARTO, RADEN (1921–) Indonesian political leader. During World War II he served with the Japanese defence forces and then fought in the anti-Dutch guerrilla movement. After independence (1949) he led the army which in 1965 slaughtered more than 300,000 communists and leftists after an attempted coup. Suharto took control of the government in 1967 and was elected president five consecutive times. He maintained close ties with Japan and the west and was chair of the Non-Aligned movement. He resigned from the presidency in 1998 amid accusations of nepotism and corruption and against a background of nationwide protest sparked by economic collapse.

SUI Short-lived but important Chinese dynasty, ruling from AD 581. It reunited China in 589, after three centuries of disorder following the collapse of the Han dynasty. The Sui built a great network of canals linking Lo-yang with Yangchow, Hangchow and the northern territories near Peking. It fell in 618, to be replaced by the T'ang dynasty the following year.

SUKARNO (1901–70) Indonesian statesman; he helped to found the Indonesian Nationalist party in 1928. Imprisoned by the Dutch colonial authorities, 1933–42, he was released by, and cooperated with, the Japanese, 1942–5. At the end of the Second World War he proclaimed himself president of an independent Indonesia, and spent the next four years trying to force the Dutch to relinquish their hold on the country. In 1959, after ten years of democratic rule, he assumed dictatorial powers (he declared himself president for life in 1963), and increased contacts with the Chinese Communists. Following a military coup in 1965 Sukarno was deposed (1967) and kept under house arrest until his death.

SULEIMAN I (c. 1496–1566) Ottoman Sultan known as 'the Lawgiver', and to the West as 'the Magnificent'. He succeeded his father **Selim I** in 1520; expanded and reinforced the Ottoman empire and encouraged the development of art, architecture, literature and law. He conquered Belgrade (1521) and Rhodes (1522); defeated the Hungarians at Mohács (1526); seized large parts of Persia and Iraq. He developed a formidable navy to dominate the Mediterranean, and brought the Ottoman empire to the practical limits of its power and expansion (unsuccessful siege of Vienna 1529, and of Malta 1565).

SULLA (138–78 BC) Roman general, led the aristocratic party in civil war with the popular leader Marius, and made himself dictator after Marius' defeat. He initiated sweeping constitutional and legal reforms, giving more power to the Senate, but was notorious for cruelty to political and military opponents.

SUMERIANS The predominant people in southern Mesopotamia from the beginning of the 3rd millennium. Immigration of Semites (*see* **Akkadians, Amorites**) changed the balance by the end of the millennium, the last Sumerian dynasty collapsing in 1940 BC. Their cultural achievements included the invention of writing and the creation of the first cities. Their language, of agglutinative type, has not been positively related to any other.

SUN CH'UAN-FANG (1884–1935) Warlord who controlled Kiangsu, Chekiang, Anhwei, Fukien and Kiangsi in 1925–7 at the time of the Northern Expedition. He lost control of his provinces in 1927, allowing the Nationalists to capture the lower Yangtze valley. With the aid of **Chang Tso-lin** he attempted to recapture Nanking in August of that year but was routed; he retired from public life. He was assassinated.

SUNNI One of the main two division of Islam, and the majority in most Muslim countries. It split from the other main group, the **Shi'as**, over the question of succession to the Prophet **Mohammed**, which Sunnis believe to have passed to the caliphs. The name is derived from *Sunna*, or words and deeds of the Prophet as recorded in the Hadith or Traditions; Sunnis thus claim to be following the example of the Prophet.

SUNNI ALI Emperor of Songhay in west Africa, who reigned c. 1464–92. From his home territories on the Middle Niger he reduced many former Mali provinces to Songhay dependencies; he created a professional army and river-navy; seized Timbuktu, controlled the commerce of the western Sudan, and introduced many advanced administrative reforms.

SUN YAT-SEN (1866–1925) First (provisional) president of the Republic of China (1912). He studied medicine in Hong Kong and Canton; entered politics with the formation of the Revive China Society, 1884, and was exiled in 1896 after instigating an abortive uprising, but attempted to organize a series of further uprisings in south China. He returned from the US in 1911 during the anti-**Ch'ing** (Manchu) revolution, and was elected provisional head of state but resigned after a few months. In 1923 he gained control of the country, with Russian support; reorganized the **Kuomintang** to resemble the Soviet Communist Party. His Three Principles of the People inspired both Nationalists and Communists.

SUN YEN-LING (d.1677) Chinese general. His wife was the daughter of a commander in Kwangsi, and in 1660 she was given command of his former army. In 1666 Sun was sent to Kwangsi as its military governor; in 1673 he joined **Wu San-kuei**'s rebellion; wavering in his allegiance after 1676, he was killed on Wu San-kuei's orders.

SUPPILULIUMA (d.c. 1322 BC) King of the **Hittites**, who won the throne c. 1344 BC. He successfully invaded northern Syria, driving back Egyptians and Mitannians to add territory as far as Damascus to his empire.

SUTRI, SYNOD OF Council of the Roman Church held in 1046, convoked at a diocesan seat north of Rome by Pope Gregory VI at the insistence of Henry III, king of Germany. The synod deposed Gregory, who had purchased his post, and two other rival pontiffs; it elected a German as Pope Clement II (1046–7), who inaugurated a thorough reform of the Church culminating in the pontificate of **Gregory VII**.

SVEN ESTRIDSSON (c. 1020–74) King of Denmark, nephew of the English and Danish king, **Cnut the Great**. He was chosen as ruler by the Danish nobles in 1047 after the death of **Magnus**; his title was vigorously disputed by Harald Hardrada, but the struggle ended early in 1066, when Harald was killed during an invasion of England (battle of Stamford Bridge). Sven himself sponsored a serious Danish attack on England in 1069, withdrawing after an agreement with **William I** in 1070. His dynasty ruled Denmark for 300 years.

SVEN FORKBEARD (d.1014) King of Denmark, son of the Danish king, **Harald Bluetooth**. After a rebellion against his father, he seized the throne c. 986. He unsuccessfully invaded Norway, and in 994 attacked England, being expensively bought off by **Æthelred II**. He was virtual ruler of Norway after 1000. He led a series of expeditions against England, and became king in 1013 after forcing Æthelred into exile.

SVYATOSLAV (d.972) Early Russian hero, grand Prince of Kiev. He attempted to establish a Russian commercial empire over the steppes from Bulgaria to the Volga, 962–972; crushed the **Khazars, Volga Bulgars** and Danubian Bulgars, but was defeated by Byzantine Emperor John Tzimisces in 871. He was ambushed and killed by the **Pecheneg**.

SWAZI Bantu-speaking herdsmen and cultivators, living mainly in the independent African kingdom of Swaziland and in the adjacent South African territory of the eastern Transvaal.

SYAGRIUS Last Roman ruler of Gaul, overthrown by **Clovis** near Soissons in 486.

SYKES-PICOT AGREEMENT Secret pact between the First World War allies for the dismemberment of the Ottoman empire. it was signed on 7 May 1916, with the assent of imperial Russia, by Sir Mark Sykes for Great Britain and François Georges-Picot for France.

TACITUS, CORNELIUS (c. AD 55–c. 120) Roman historian. His works include *Dialogue on Orators* (c. 79–81), *Agricola* (c. 98), *Germania* (c. 98) and fragments of two longer works, the *Histories*, covering the period 68–70 (the original probably went down to 96), and the *Annals*, covering 14–68.

TAJIKS (Tadzhiks) Ancient Iranian people within Tajikistan, a mountainous country adjoining Afghanistan, Pakistan and India. They are mainly livestock keepers by occupation and Muslims by religion.

TALAS, BATTLE OF (751) The prince of Tashkent called upon the Muslims to oust the Chinese after their invasion (747). In this battle the Arabs decisively defeated general Kao Hsien-chih, transferring control of the area west of the Pamirs and Tien Shan mountains (Transoxania) from China to Islam and establishing the boundary between the two civilisations.

TALLEYRAND, CHARLES-MAURICE DE (1754–1883) French statesman and diplomat. Destined for the army but crippled by an accident in childhood, he entered the Church in 1775; became Bishop of Autun in 1788, but was excommunicated for his radical Church reorganization during the French revolution. Foreign minister under the Directory, 1979–9, and to **Napoleon I** until resigning in 1807. He intrigued with Tsar Alexander I for Napoleon's defeat, and in 1814 became foreign minister to Louis XVIII. At the **Congress of Vienna** (1814–51) he secured favourable terms for France. He was made Duc de Talleyrand-Périgord in 1817, and French ambassador to England, 1830–4.

TALMUD Principal repository of Jewish law and lore. It consists of the **Mishnah** and the Gemarra, an explanation of the Mishnah and a general presentation of the traditions taught and transmitted in the Rabbinical academies and preserved in two versions: the Palestinian, edited around AD 400, and the Babylonian, around 500.

TAMERLANE (1336–1405) Known as Timur Lang, from his lame leg, hence Tamerlane. Born near Samarkand, later his capital, he concluded the Mongol age of conquest, although his background was Turkish rather than Mongol, and he was no nomad but a product of the sophisticated Islamic society of Transoxania. He conquered, with legendary barbarity, a vast Asian empire stretching from southern Russia to Mongolia and southwards into northern India, Persia and Mesopotamia. He adorned his capital with splendid buildings, many of which still stand today. He died on an expedition against **Ming** China; after his death the empire soon fell apart.

TAMIL Dravidian language spoken by some 30 million southern Indians, one-third of the population of Sri Lanka (Ceylon), and scattered communities in South and east Africa, Mauritius, Malaysia and Fiji. Tamil literature dates back to the 3rd century BC; it remains the official languages in the Indian state of Tamil Nadu (Madras).

TANCHELM (d.1115) Religious radical who criticized the Roman Church, especially its hierarchical organization. He preached to large congregations in the Low Countries (mainly Utrecht and Antwerp) but was eventually murdered by a priest.

T'ANG Imperial Chinese dynasty ruling AD 618 to 907; *see* pp. 126–7.

T'ANG CHI-YAO (1881–1927) Chinese military leader. Appointed military governor of Kweichow, 1912, and of Yunnan Province, 1915 until his death, he gave crucial support to rebels opposing **Yüan Shih-k'ai** in his bid to re-establish the empire. After the death of **Sun Yat-sen** in 1925, he made an abortive bid to lead a new national government.

TANGUTS Tibetan-speaking peoples of northwest China, who established the 11th-century kingdom of Hsi-hsia in the area of present-day Kansu and northern Shensi. The Tangut tribes, straddling the main trade route from China to the West, remained tributaries to the Sung dynasty from 960 to 1038; from 1038 to 1044 they attempted, under their emperor, Li Yüan-hao, to conquer the whole of China, but withdrew on payment of an annual tribute. The kingdom then survived until 1227, when it was overrun by the Mongols.

TANTRIC BUDDHISM This form of belief, evolved chiefly between the 6th and the 11th centuries AD, aimed at recreating in the individual the original spiritual experience of Guatama the **Buddha**, and emphasized sexo-yogic practices. Tantric art and sculpture made much use of male and female images to symbolize the process of spiritual growth and fulfilment; *Vajra-Yana* or the 'adamantine path' was its largest school.

TASMAN, ABEL JANSZOON (c. 1603–c.1659) Dutch explorer, discoverer of New Zealand, Tasmania, Tonga and the Fiji Islands. He served with the **Dutch East India Company**, 1633–53, carrying out two major voyages in the Indian Ocean and the South Pacific, reaching Tasmania (named after him) in 1642; he circumnavigated Australia without seeing it.

TATAR (also spelled Tartar) First found in an inscription of 731, the name came to be applied to the forces of **Genghis Khan** and his successors, and in Europe was confused with Tartarus, the classical hell, which seemed an appropriate place of origin for these dreadful hordes. The name was later loosely and in accurately applied to some of the Turkic peoples of the Russian empire for example, Volga Tatars, Crimean Tatars. At the present time there is a Tatar Autonomous Republic within the Russian Federation with its capital at Kazan on the Volga.

TEHERAN CONFERENCE Meeting held from 18 November 1943 to 12 January 1944 at which the Allied leaders – **Churchill**, **Roosevelt** and **Stalin** – concerted plans for an Anglo-American invasion of France and a Russian offensive against eastern Germany.

TE KOOTI (c. 1830–93) New Zealand Maori resistance leader. While imprisoned, he founded the Ringatu cult, which is still extant. After escaping, he conducted skilful guerrilla campaigns (1868–72).

TENNANT, CHARLES (1768–1858) Scottish pioneer industrial chemist. He set up a bleachworks and in 1798 patented a new liquid for bleaching textile fabrics, which was soon widely used by Lancashire bleachers. In 1780 with three partners he set up a chemical plant near Glasgow to manufacture bleaching powder and other alkali products. When he died the firm was operating one of the largest chemical plants in the world.

TENNESSEE VALLEY AUTHORITY (TVA) United States federal agency, formed in 1933 to develop natural resources (particularly hydro-electric power) in the states drained by the Tennessee River system – Tennessee itself, Kentucky, Mississippi, Alabama, North Carolina, Georgia and Virginia.

TEN YEARS' WAR (1868–78) Cuba's first war for independence from Spain. It ended inconclusively with promises of political and economic reform, set out in the Convention of Zanjon, 1878. The nationalist leader, Antonio Maceo, refused to accept the accompanying conditions and fled the island to prepare for renewed struggle.

TERTULLIAN (c. 170–c. 220) Early Christian theologian. Born in Carthage and trained as a lawyer, he was converted to **Christianity** c. 195. Writing in Latin rather than Greek, he provided the Western Church with much of its basic terminology; his *De Praescriptions Haereticorum* (197–8) championed orthodoxy; in *De Testimonio Animae* he claimed that the soul is naturally Christian; in his great *Apology* he praised the martyrs: 'the blood of Christians is seed'.

TEUTONIC ORDER (also called Knights of the Cross). Organization of German crusaders, founded in 1190 at Acre, Palestine. It moved to central Europe in 1211, and in 1226, at the invitation of the Polish duke, Conrad of Masovia, began the conquest of pagan Prussia. Under its Grand Masters, with its headquarters at Marienburg, it controlled the eastern Baltic, conquering Pomerania and other areas of Poland. It absorbed the **Livonian Order** (Knights of the Sword) in 1237. It was defeated by the alliance of Poland and Lithuania at Tannenberg (Grünwald) in 1410, and broken by the Treaty of Thorn (Torun) in 1466. It was secularized as the duchy of Prussia (1525) becoming a fief of Polish kings.

TEWFIK PASHA (1852–92) First khedive of Egypt under the British occupation. He was appointed Khedive in 1879 by the Ottoman sultan in succession to **Ismail** Pasha. The growth of tension between England and France, representing the interests of foreign creditors of Egypt, and nationalist sentiment with **Arabi Pasha** as its chief spokesman, led to the weakening of Tewfik's power in favour of Arabi, but British military intervention and occupation in 1882 restored him as a figurehead under British control.

TE WHITI, ORONGOMAI (1831–1907) New Zealand Maori leader. He claimed to be a prophet and refused to take part in the Maori rebellions of the 1860s, preaching instead passive resistance and complete segregation from the Europeans. Imprisoned by the British 1881–3 and 1886, he still exercised great influence on the Maoris.

THATCHER, MARGARET (1925–) British Conservative politician and first woman prime minister (1979–90). With degrees in chemistry from Oxford (1947) and law, she entered parliament in 1959 and served as secretary of state for education and science (1970–4), establishing a reputation for toughness. Following Conservative election defeat (1974), she won the party leadership (1975), and became prime minister in 1979. Her programme, which beame know as 'Thatcherism', combined a restraint on public spending, privatization of major industries, and fiscal caution. In 1990 she was succeeded as prime minister by her chancellor of the exchequer, John Major.

THEOCRITUS (c. 300–250 BC) Pastoral poet from Syracuse, who worked in Cos and Alexandria. His *Idylls* and his lyrical descriptions of country life seem a form of escape from urban Alexandria; he strongly influenced Virgil and, through him, all pastoral poetry.

THEODORET (c. 393–c. 455 BC) Christian theologian. Born in Antioch, he was appointed Bishop of Cyrrhus in Mesopotamia, and played a prominent part in the **Nestorian** controversy (for long defending Nestorians against **Cyril**), culminating with his appearance at the **Council of Chalcedon** in 451, where he finally agreed to condemn Nestorian beliefs. His works include a *Church History* and a brilliant defence of **Christianity** against paganism.

THEODORIC THE GREAT (c. 454–526) Ostrogothic king of Italy, son of a chieftain. He succeeded his father in 471, led migrations of his people into the Balkans and (in 489, on orders of the Emperor Zeno) Italy. He murdered Odoacer, the previous Italian ruler, in 493, to gain control of the country, though acknowledging imperial supremacy; he issued an edict imposing Roman law on his followers, tolerated Catholicism and sought friendship between Goths and Romans.

THEODORUS Known as Theodorus the Lector, an early Greek Church historian of the 6th century. Though only fragments of his work have survived, it is an essential source for events between the time of **Constantine I** (313) and Justin I (518).

THEODOSIUS I, THE GREAT (c. 346–95) Roman emperor, 379–95. Appointed by Gratian to rule the Eastern empire after the death of **Valens**, he also administered the Western empire after the death of Maximus in 388. He established Catholicism as the official Roman religion, 380; condemned Arianism and paganism; after the massacre of Thessalonica he submitted in penance to **Ambrose**. After his death the empire was finally divided into two halves.

THEOPHRASTUS (c. 372–c. 287 BC) Ancient Greek philosopher taught by **Aristotle** whom he succeeded as head of the Lyceum. Theophrastus was a great teacher, with classes attended by as many as 2000; he influenced the foundation of the Museum at Alexandria. Of his works, the *Enquiry into Plants* and the *Etiology of Plants* survive intact, and his *Doctrines of Natural Philosophers*, reconstructed by 19th century scholars, provide the main foundation for the history of early thought. His entertaining *Characters* has been much enjoyed and imitated.

THIRD COALITION, WAR OF THE Struggle between Napoleonic France and an alliance of Britain, Austria, Russia and Sweden, formed in April 1805. Britain's naval victory at Trafalgar established Allied supremacy at sea, but on land there were only defeats: Austria at Ulm (1805), Austria and Russia at Austerlitz (1805), and Prussia, joining late, at Jena (1806). Further Russian defeats, at Eylau and Friedland (1807) and the elimination of Sweden brought hostilities to an end with the treaty of Tilsit (1807).

THIRTY TYRANTS Vituperative name given to the men who ruled Athens on behalf of Sparta for eight months after its defeat (404 BC) in the Peloponnesian War. The group included **Socrates's** former associate, Critias, who died in May 403 when a democratic army under Thrasybulus defeated the tyrants at Piraeus; the survivors were massacred two years later in Eleusis, where they had taken refuge.

THOMAS, ST One of the twelve Apostles. He doubted the Resurrection until he saw and touched the wounds of **Jesus**; he is traditionally believed to have gone to India as a missionary.

THOMAS, SIDNEY GILCHRIST (1850–85) English metallurgist and inventor, who discovered a new process for making steel which eliminated phosphorus from pig iron. It was applied both to the Bessemer converter (1875) and to the Siemens open-hearth process, perfected by Percy Carlyle Gilchrist.

THREE FEUDATORIES REBELLION *see* **Wu San-kuei**

THUCYDIDES (c. 460–c. 400 BC) Athenian historian. He served as a general in the Peloponnesian War but was exiled after failing to defend an important strongpoint in Thrace. He had already begun his classic history of the war and completed eight books, breaking off at 411, seven years before the end of hostilities.

THURINGIANS Germanic people, first documented c. AD 350. They were conquered by the **Huns** in the mid-5th century; by 500 their revived kingdom stretched from the Harz Mountains to the Danube, but they were defeated by the **Franks** in 531 and were subsequently ruled by them.

TIBERIUS (42 BC–AD 37) (Tiberius Claudius Nero Caesar Augustus). Second Roman emperor, stepson of the Emperor **Augustus**, he succeeded in AD 14 at the age of 56. In his first years he greatly strengthened Rome's finances and institutions; after his son's death in 23 he gradually withdrew from affairs, retiring to Capri in 27 where he gained the reputation of an arbitrary, cruel and merciless tyrant. In 31 he arranged the execution of Sejanus, to whom he had delegated his authority and who plotted against him.

TIENTSIN TREATIES Agreements forced on the Chinese government in 1858 by Britain and France to allow free access, the posting of resident officials in Peking, and the opening of the new trade ports. Similar agreements were then made by Russia and the United States.

TILAK, BAL GANGADHAR (1856–1920) Militant Indian nationalist. He taught mathematics, owned and edited two weekly newspapers, was twice imprisoned by the British; in 1914 he founded the Indian Home Rule League; he signed the Lucknow Pact in 1916 as the basis for a Hindu-Muslim political alliance. His books include *Secret of the Bhagavad-gita*, written in prison between 1908 and 1914.

TIMES, THE London newspaper, founded in 1785 by John Walter under the title *Daily Universal Register*, its present name was adopted in 1788. Known as 'The Thunderer' under the editorship of Delane (1840–79) for its incorruptibility and independence of government.

TIMUR *see* **Tamerlane**

TIPU (c. 1749–99) Indian sultan, known as 'the Tiger of Mysore'; son of **Hader Ali**. He fought frequently against the **Marathas**, 1769–79, despite being publicly caned by his father for cowardice in 1771. He defeated the British on the Coleroon river in 1782 and succeeded to the Mysore throne in the same year. He signed the Treaty of Bangalore with the British in 1784, though he fought several further aggressive and partially successful campaigns against them. He was killed during the final British assault on his capital, Seringapatam; he is remembered in the Mysore saying: 'Haidar was born to create an empire, Tipu to lose one'.

TITO, MARSHAL (1892–1980) (Born Josip Broz). Yugoslav head of state. He led Communist resistance to German occupation of Yugoslavia, 1941–5 and in 1945 became head of the Federal People's Republic with Soviet support; he broke with the USSR in 1948 to pursue a neutralist foreign policy and an independent version of **communism**. He served as president from 1953 until his death.

TITUS (AD 39–81) Roman emperor, son of Vespasian. He served in Britain, Germany and under his father in Judaea; on Vespasian's accession as emperor he took charge of the Jewish War, killed many (reputedly one million) Jews and sacked Jerusalem in 70; he was made commander of the Praetorian Guard in 71. He was much criticized for taking Berenice, sister of the Jewish king, Herod Agrippa II, as his mistress. He succeeded his father as emperor in 79, helped to rebuild Rome after the fire of 80, and completed the Colosseum.

TLAXCALANS Indians of the central Mexican plateau. Relations between the Tlaxcalans and the Aztec confederation were always uneasy, and at the time of the Spanish conquest they joined **Hernán Cortés** as his principal local ally; continued loyalty to Spain brought many privileges.

TOCHARIANS Central Asian peoples, occupying the basin of the upper Oxus river in the 2nd century BC. They were joint founders, with the **Kushanas**, of the Kushana empire. They are not necessarily identical to the speakers of the 'Tocharian' language, one of the Indo-European group, whose main surviving manuscripts, found in Chinese Turkestan (Tarim Basin) date from the period AD 500–1000.

TOJO, HIDEKI (1884–1984) Japanese general and statesman, he was prime minister at the time of the Japanese attack on Pearl Harbor. After a military career he became vice-minister (1938–9), then minister (1940–4) of war, and also prime minister, 1941–4. He resigned after the fall of Saipan; tried, after the war, by the Tokyo War Crimes Court, he was found guilty and hanged.

TOKUGAWA Dynasty of hereditary *shoguns* or military dictators, effectively ruling Japan from 1603–1868. It was founded by Ieyasu (1542–1616), who mastered the country after the death of **Toyotomi Hideyoshi** and established his capital at the fishing village of Edo (now Tokyo). He organized a new pattern of fiefs and administration which lasted unchallenged until the 19th century. Under his son, Hidetada (1579–1632), and grandson, Iemitsu (1603–51), Japan eliminated Christianity and virtually closed itself to foreign trade and influence. These three rulers consolidated the family's control, which lasted until the 19th century. When Tokugawa Keika accepted the near-peaceful handing over of power to the emperor, **Meiji**.

TOKUGAWA IEYASU (1542–1616) Founder of the **Tokugawa** shogunate.

TOLTECS Ruling people in Mexico from the 10th to the 12th century. The name is associated with their capital, Tula, or 'place of the reeds', located 50 miles (80 km) north of Tenochtitlán, present-day Mexico City. They captured and sacked the great city of Teotihuacán c. 900; under their leader Quetzalcoatl and his successors they established a wide-ranging empire, introducing to it metal-work and ambitious architectural and sculptural techniques. They were overwhelmed by nomad **Chichimec** invaders, including the **Aztecs**, who destroyed Tula in the mid-12th century.

TOPA (d.1493) Inca emperor, who succeeded to the title in 1471 after the abdication of his father, **Pachacuti**. After an early setback, invading the rain forests near the Tono River, he established a reputation as a great conqueror: he defeated the revolt led by the **Colla** and **Lupaca**, extended the boundaries of his empire to highland Bolivia, northern Chile and most of northwest Argentina; and finally succeeded in incorporating the previously unconquered southern coast of Peru.He devoted the rest of his reign to administration.

TORAH Hebrew name for the Law of Moses, or Pentateuch, the first five books of the Old Testament of the Bible: *Genesis, Exodus, Leviticus, Numbers* and *Deuteronomy*; also the scroll containing these books, used ceremonially in the synagogue.

TORDESILLAS, TREATY OF Treaty between Spain and Portugal, 1494, to determine ownership of lands discovered or to be discovered in the west. It granted Spain exclusive rights west of a north-south line 370 leagues west of the Cape Verde islands – a 1493 Bull of the Spanish Pope Alexander VI had put the line 270 leagues further east – with Portugal taking lands east of the line. Portugal thus established claim to the so far undiscovered Brazil; but the treaty was never accepted by the other Atlantic powers.

TOTONAC Central American Indians, farming both the highlands and the hot coastal lowlands of eastern Mexico, mainly in the states of Vera Cruz, Puebla and Hidalgo. The two Totonac languages, Totonac and Tepehuan, are believed to be related to ancient **Mayan**.

TOURÉ, AHMED SEJOU (1922–84) President of the Republic of Guinea. A trade union organizer, in 1952 he started a political party, the Guinea Democratic Party; he became vice-president of the government council in 1957, and first president of Guinea on independence in 1958.

TOUSSAINT-L'OUVERTURE (1743–1803) Haitian independence leader, born into a family of African slaves in the part of Haiti which formed the French colony of St Domingue. He joined the slave rebellion and declared in favour of the French Revolutionary government; recognized by the French Directory as lieutenant-governor in 1797, he expelled British and Spanish forces and gained control of the whole island in 1801. The French government, now under Napoleon, sent invasion forces in 1802, and he was defeated and taken to France where he died in prison. The French restored slavery to Haiti.

TOWNSEND, FRANCIS (1867–1960) US doctor who helped lay the foundations for the modern American social security programme. He devised the Old Age Revolving Pension Plan which mobilized support for federal action in this area.

TOYOTOMI HIDEYOSHI (1536–98) Unifier of 16th-century Japan. He served as a chief lieutenant to the feudal general, Oda Nobunaga (1534–82), and after his death became the emperor's chief minister (1585). In 1590 he conquered the islands of Shikoku and Kyushu to unify the country; he energetically promoted internal peace, economic development and overseas expansion. He died after an unsuccessful invasion of Korea.

TRAJAN (AD 53–117) (Marcus Ulpius Trajanus). First Roman emperor to be born in the provinces – in Italica, near Santiponce, Seville. He served in the army in Syria, Spain and Germany, was named consul in 91 and chosen as emperor in 98. He is famous as a builder, social reformer and extender of the empire in the East and in Dacia, modern Romania (celebrated by Trajan's Column, still standing in Rome). He died in Cilicia after invading Mesopotamia and taking Ctesiphon, the Parthian capital.

TRASTÁMARA *see* **Henry II, King of Castile**

TRIPARTITE PACT Agreement signed on 27 September 1940 between Germany, Italy and Japan, setting up a full military and political alliance (the Rome-Berlin-Tokyo Axis) to support one another in the event of a spread of the Second World War to the Far East.

TRIPLE ALLIANCE (1882–1915) Defensive treaty signed on 20 May 1882 pledging Germany and Italy to mutual support in the event of a French attack, and obliging Austria-Hungary to support Italy in such an event in return for a promise of Italian neutrality in the event of a Russian attack on Austria-Hungary. It was extended between 1887 and 1909 by supplementary agreements providing for diplomatic support in the Near East and north Africa.

TROTSKY, LEON (1879–1940) Russian revolutionary leader and theorist. Born Lev Davidovich Bronstein, he spent long periods in prison and in exile before returning to Russia in 1917 to play a major part in bringing the **Bolsheviks** to power. He was commissar for foreign affairs, 1917–18, and commissar for war, 1918–25. The most prominent revolutionary after **Lenin**, he was an effective organizer of the Red Army during the civil war. After Lenin's death in 1924 he was increasingly in conflict with **Stalin**, and was exiled in 1929. He founded the Fourth International in 1938, and published the *History of the Russian Revolution*. He was murdered by a Soviet agent in Mexico.

TRUMAN, HARRY S (1884–1972) 33rd president of the United States, 1945–53. The son of a Missouri mule trader, he entered politics as country judge, 1922–4; US senator, 1935 and re-elected 1940; vice-president in 1944, succeeding as president in 1945 on the death of **F.D. Roosevelt**. He ordered the atomic bombing of Hiroshima and Nagasaki in 1945; in 1947 enunciated the Truman Doctrine on the 'containment' of the Soviet Union, and established the Central Intelligence Agency (CIA). He inaugurated the **Marshall Plan** and was re-elected, 1948, and supported in 1949 theformation of the **North Atlantic Treaty Organization** (NATO); he ordered the US engagement in Korea in 1950.

TSHOMBE, MOÏSE (1919–69) Congo (Zaire) political leader. He became a member of the Katanga Provincial Council, 1951–3, and president of Conakat (*Confédération des Associations Tribales du Katanga*) in 1959. His plans for a federated Congo after independence were rejected in favour of a central state. He declared Katangan independence in 1960, but was defeated by UN forces in 1963. Appointed by **Kasavubu** as premier of the Congo in 1964, he was dismissed in 1965 and was sentenced to death *in absentia* in 1967. Hijacked to Algeria in 1967, he died in captivity.

TUAREG Berber nomads from the central and western Sahara; Hamitic-speaking Muslims.

TUDORS English ruling dynasty from 1485 until 1603, founded by **Henry VII** and continued through his descendants **Henry VIII**, Edward VI, Mary I and **Elizabeth I**.

TULUNIDS Muslim dynasty ruling in Egypt and Syria from 868 to 905. It was founded by Ahmed ibn Tulun, a Turk who arrived in Egypt as vice-governor under the **Abbasids**.

TUNG-MENG-HUI Chinese political party, originally founded as a secret society by **Sun Yat-sen** in 1905.

TUNGUSY People of the sub-arctic forest in eastern Siberia. Originally nomadic hunters, fishers and reindeer breeders, they moved from the Ob and Yenisey river basins east to the Pacific, and north from the Amur basin to the Arctic Ocean. Since the Russian revolution (1917) most were settled on collective farms.

TUPAMAROS Members of a Uruguayan urban guerrilla movement. It first came to prominence in 1968, preaching socialist revolution on the Cuban pattern. Its violent campaign of bombing, assassination, robbery, kidnapping – and a spectacular prison break in 1971 when 106 leading Tupamaros escaped from the Uruguayan national penitentiary – brought increasingly severe retaliation; by 1974 over 2000 members were held in a new maximum-security prison and the movement had apparently been crushed.

TUTANKHAMUN King of Egypt's 18th Dynasty. Of uncertain parentage, as a child he succeeded his brother Smenkhkare, who had been co-regent and successor to **Akhenaten**. During his reign (1345–1335 BC) the worship of the old gods, suppressed by Akhenaten, was restored. In 1922 his long-lost tomb was discovered almost intact by the British archaeologist Howard Carter.

TUTHMOSIS III (d.1436 BC) Greatest of Egypt's warrior kings of the 18th Dynasty. Son of Tuthmosis II and a minor wife named Isis, he ascended the throne as a young boy but was overshadowed for nearly 20 years by his stepmother, Queen Hatshepsut, until her death in 1482 BC. He conducted 17 campaigns in Palestine and Syria, extending Egypt's empire to the banks of the Euphrates; his campaigns in Nubia gave Egypt control over all the gold mines and territory as far as the Fourth Cataract of the Nile.

TWENTY-ONE DEMANDS Claims pressed by Japan on China during the First World War, asking for privileges similar to, but more extensive than, those enjoyed by the Western powers, including railway and mining concessions, coastal access and power to intervene in financial, political and police affairs. An ultimatum, presented on 5 May 1915, forced capitulation on most points by the Chinese president on 25 May and greatly increased anti-Japanese feeling in China.

U

UIGHURS Nomadic Turkic-speaking peoples of central Asia, who ruled a substantial area north and northwest of China in the 8th and 9th centuries and later settled in Kansu and the Tarim Basin, establishing a distinct way of life and a literary language. The modern Uighars live mainly in Sinkiang and the former Soviet central Asia.

ULFILAS (c. 311–c. 382) Converter of the Goths to Christianity. In 341 he was consecrated Bishop of the Gothic Christians by Eusebius, the Arian patriarch of Constantinople. After initial persecution, the **Visigothic** leaders accepted the **Arianist** doctrine, while Ulfilas created a Gothic alphabet and made the first Germanic translation of the Bible, some of which still survives.

ULMANIS, KARLIS (1877 – post 1942) Latvian independence leader. Trained in agronomy, he worked to free Latvia from the century-old Russian control during the 1905 revolution. He fled to the US, was amnestied in 1913 and founded the Latvian Farmers' Union, 1917. Appointed head of the provisional government by the national independence council, 1918, he held power from 1918–21 and then in 1925-6, 1931-2 and 1934-40. He resigned in 1940 in the face of a Russian military ultimatum; was arrested in July by the Soviet authorities and deported. His fate is unknown.

UMAYYADS Dynasty of caliphs, founded by Muawiya in 661, in opposition to **Ali, Mohammed**'s son-in-law and fourth caliph. They were deposed by the **Abbasids** in 750 although a branch continued to rule Muslim Spain from 756 to 1031.

UNION, ACT OF Treaty signed in 1707 under which Scotland and England (which had shared the same rulers since 1603) became jointly the Kingdom of Great Britain. The agreement stipulated a single government, but separate churches and legal systems; Scotland recognized the Hanoverian succession.

UNITARIANS Members of a Protestant Christian denomination, characterized by belief in one God, as opposed to the more orthodox doctrine of the Trinity. It first emerged as a distinct church in Poland and Transylvania in the late 16th and 17th centuries, and was widely followed in England and North America in the 18th and 19th centuries.

UNITED FRUIT COMPANY United States-based multinational company, specializing in the shipment of tropical produce. Founded in 1899 in a merger of Central American shipping, railroad and banana-planting interests, it was merged into the United Brands Company in 1968.

UNITED NATIONS International organization, founded in 1945 as a successor to the **League of Nations**. Its aims are to maintain world peace and security, and to promote economic, social and cultural cooperation among nations. The original membership of 50 had risen to 183 by May 1993. Its main divisions are the Security Council and the General Assembly; special agencies include the World Health Organization (WHO), Food and Agriculture Organization (FAO), United Nations Educational, Scientific and Cultural Organization (UNESCO), etc.

U NU (1907–) Burmese independence leader. He was expelled from Rangoon university in 1936, and in 1940 was imprisoned by the British for sedition. He became foreign minister in 1943 in the pro-Japanese government, and was first prime minister of independent Burma in 1948–58 and 1960–2, when he was ousted by General **Ne Win** in a *coup d'état*. Released from prison in 1969, he began to organize a resistance movement from abroad.

UPANISHADS Prose and verse reflections on the **Vedas** and forming with them the central corpus of Hindu sacred literature. Numbering 108 in their surviving form, the oldest were composed probably c. 900 BC; teaching based on their mystical and philosophic speculations is known as the *Vedanta* – the conclusion of the *Vedas*.

URBAN II (c. 1042–99) Pope, 1088–99. He inherited many of **Gregory VII**'s ideas about the freedom of the Church from state interference, and in addition established at Rome the administrative organizations to operate it. He preached the First **Crusade** in 1095.

URNFIELD Late Bronze Age culture in central Europe, flourishing from the late 2nd to the early 1st millennium BC. It is characterized by the practice of burying the cremated ashes of the dead in ceramic urns. It was a direct predecessor of the Celtic **Hallstatt** period.

USUMAN DAN FODIO (1754–1817) Muslim Fulani mystic and revolutionary reformer, and founder of a militant Islamic state in what later became northern Nigeria. He began teaching Sufi doctrines in 1775, and was hailed as deliverer by oppressed Hausa and fellow Fulani peoples. He launched a *jihad* (holy war) from Gabir in 1804, conquering most of northern Nigeria and beyond, establishing the Fulani-ruled Sokoto caliphate before retiring in 1815, disillusioned by the corruption of his supporters.

UTRECHT, PEACE OF Treaties concluded in 1713 which, with those of Rastadt and Baden (1714), ended the War of the Spanish Succession. **Louis XIV**'s grandson Philip was recognized as king of Spain on condition that the kingdoms of France and Spain would never be united and with the cession of the Spanish Netherlands and Spain's Italian territories to Austria and Savoy. Gibraltar and Minorca were ceded to Great Britain, with a 30-year monopoly on supplying slaves to the Spanish colonies. Portugal obtained frontier rectifications in South America at Spain's expense. Louis XIV recognized the Protestant succession in Great Britain (thus abandoning the Stuart cause) and the title of king for the ruler of Brandenburg-Prussia. He also ceded Nova Scotia, Hudson's Bay, Newfoundland and St Kitts to the British, against incorporation of the principality of Orange and the Barcelonette valley into France. The Dutch Republic secured the right to garrison, at Austrian expense, fortresses in the southern Netherlands. At the 1714 treaties between the Emperor Charles VI and Louis XIV, Landau was ceded to France and the electorros of Bavaria and Cologne, Louis XIV's allies, were restored to their lands and dignities. Formal peace between Austria and Spain was not made until 1720.

UZBEKS A people of Turkish origin who arrived in the area around Samarkand and Tashkent in the 6th century AD. In the 14th century they became the core of the empire of **Tamerlane**, and in the 16th century the basis for the conquests of **Babur**. Later the area disintegrated into small city-states. Russia annexed the region in the 1860s, although incorporation was not complete until the 1920s; now mostly concentrated in Uzbekistan.

UZKOKS Balkan Christians who fled from the Ottoman conquest in the late 15th century and settled around the Adriatic port of Fiume, whence they attacked both Turkish and Christian (especially Venetian) shipping.

V

VACA, ALVARO NUÑEZ CABEZA DE (c. 1490–1560) One of two Spanish survivors of a voyage of exploration from Florida to New Mexico, 1528–36, who wrote a description of the fabulous riches he claimed to have seen. Many others were thereby encouraged to go to their deaths prospecting there.

VAKATAKAS South Indian dynasty, dominating the western Deccan from the mid-3rd to the later 4th century AD. It achieved its greatest power under King Pravaresena I in the early 4th century; Rudrasena II married the daughter of **Chandragupta II**, and after his death, c.390, the Vakataka territory was absorbed into the **Gupta** empire.

VALENS (c. 328–378) Eastern Roman emperor, who on the death of the Emperor Jovian was appointed co-emperor by his brother, Valentinian I, in 364. He twice devastated the Visigothic lands north of the Danube (in 367 and 369); fought an inconclusive war with Persia 376; was defeated and killed by the **Visigoths** at the battle of Adrianople.

VALERA, EAMON DE (1882–1975) Irish statesman. He was elected president of the Irish Nationalist Party, Sinn Fein, in 1917, and president of the Irish Parliament, the Dáil, while imprisoned in England in 1918–19. He refused to accept the Irish independence treaty in 1921; in 1926 he formed a republican opposition party, Fianna Fáil. He was prime minister of the Irish Free State, 1937–48, and again – following full independence – in 1951–4 and 1957–9; and president of the Irish Republic 1959–73.

VALERIAN (c. 190–c. 260) (Publius Licinius Valerianus) Roman emperor. He gained the throne in 253, but left government to his son Gallienus while he led campaigns against the Goths and the Persians. He was captured by the Persians in 260 and died in captivity.

VANDALS Germanic people, displaced from central Europe by the 4th-century incursion of the Huns. They reached north Africa, via Spain, and established their kingdom there in AD 429. At first federated with Rome, they seized their independence in 439 and captured Rome itself briefly in 455. Attacked in 533 by the Byzantine armies under **Belisarius**; they were obliterated in 534.

VARGAS, GETULIO DORNELLES (1883–1954) President and dictator of Brazil. He became state president of Rio Grande do Sul in 1928, and Liberal candidate for national president in 1929, seizing the presidency by force in 1930 after his defeat. Under a new constitution he was re-elected in 1934, and in 1937 he introduced the corporate-style dictatorship of Estado Nôvo (New State). He laid the foundations for the modern nation, and linked Brazil to the Western alliance in the Second World War. He was ousted in 1945, re-elected constitutional president in 1951, and committed suicide during the 1954 political crisis.

VARUS, PUBLIUS QUINTILIUS (d.AD 9) Roman general. He became consul in 13 BC, governor of Syria, 6–4 BC, and commander in Germany, AD 6–9. He committed suicide after the destruction of his army by the Germans in the Teutoburg forest.

VASVAR, TREATY OF Agreement signed on 10 August 1664, ending an Austro-Turkish war (1663–4) after Austria had been called in to help the then independent principality of Transylvania repel a Turkish invasion. Under its terms Hungary, which had not been consulted, lost numerous fortresses to the Turks, and the resulting fury generated several later anti-Habsburg rebellions.

VAUBAN, SEBASTIEN LE PRESTRE DE (1633–1707) French engineer, military architect and town planner. He revolutionized defensive fortification, building a ring of fortresses on France's frontiers; he planned port fortifications and also towns connected with the many forts. He was made a marshal of France in 1703.

VEDANTA Most influential among the Six Systems of Hindu philosophy. Decisive in refuting non-Brahminical schools of Hindu thought, it argues the existence of Absolute Soul in all things, and the union of the individual and his Absolute Soul as salvation. It was forcefully promoted by the Brahmin **Shankaracharya**.

VEDAS Collection of ancient Sanskrit hymns, sacred verses and devotional formulae (*mantras*), preserved by Hindu tradition – first oral, then written – since the first appearance of Aryan-speaking peoples in north India, c. mid-2nd millennium BC. The three major compilations – *Rig, Yajur* and *Sama* – form the *Trayividya* or 'threefold knowledge'; a fourth, the *Artharvaveda*, is made up of more homely chants, spells and incantations, of lesser religious significance.

VENDÉE UPRISING Largest and most successful royalist counter attack against the first French Republic. In 1793 peasant troops, under their own and various aristocratic leaders, scored a number of victories, but were unable to hold the region's coastal ports and establish contact with Britain. Defeat came in October 1793, but the trouble continued sporadically until finally put down by **Napoleon**.

VERONA, LEAGUE OF Alliance of Italian city states (1164), including Vicenza, Verona and Padua, formed to oppose the Emperor **Frederick I Barbarossa**; it was absorbed into the larger **Lombard League** in 1167. Verona was ruled by the da Romano and **della Scala** families from the mid-13th century until conquered by the **Visconti** family of Milan in 1387; it was then subject to Venice from 1404 until 1797.

VERRAZZANO, GIOVANNI DA (c. 1485–c. 1528) Florentine who in 1524 explored the North American coast from Cape Fear, North Carolina, probably as far north as Cape Breton, Nova Scotia. During his voyage he became the first European to sight New York Bay and Narragansett Bay, and he proved North America to be a continuous landmass. His name is commemorated in New York's Verrazzano-Narrows Bridge, linking Brooklyn and Staten island.

VERSAILLES, TREATY OF (1783) Also known as the Treaty of Paris. Treaty which ended the American War of Independence. Great Britain recognized US sovereignty to the Mississippi River and ceded Florida to Spain. The agreement also called for payment of debts, US access to Newfoundland fishing-grounds and fair treatment for Americans who had stayed loyal to Great Britain.

VERSAILLES, TREATY OF (1919) Agreement signed on 28 June 1919 between Germany and the Allies after the First World War. Germany was made to accept responsibility for paying heavy war reparations, to give up Alsace-Lorraine to France, yield much territory to Poland, Belgium, Denmark and Japan, and to lose all its overseas colonies. Danzig became a Free City under a **League of Nations** High Commission; the Saar was also placed under League control until 1935, when by plebiscite its citizens voted to be reunited with Germany. The Rhineland was to be permanently demilitarized and occupied by the Allies for 15 years. The Treaty embodied the Covenant of the League of Nations; failing to secure a two-thirds majority in the United States Senate, it was not ratified by the US. The Versailles Treaty with Germany was paralleled by the treaties of Trianon with Hungary, of Neuilly with Bulgaria, of St Germain with Austria and of Sèvres with the Ottoman empire.

VESPASIAN (AD 9–79) Roman emperor. Of humble parentage, he became proconsul in Africa, 63–66, led victorious armies in Palestine, 67–68; was proclaimed emperor by troops during the civil wars following the death of Nero, and was recognized by the senate in 69. He reorganized provinces in the Eastern empire; secured the pacification of Wales and much of north Britain; and used tax reform, tolerance and a vast building programme to restore political stability.

VESPUCCI, AMERIGO (1454–1512) Explorer, cosmographer and propagandist. Born in Florence, he moved in 1492 to Seville as the **Medici** representative. He participated in several voyages of exploration, including one along the north coast of Brazil and Venezuela in 1499, and down the east coast of Brazil, possibly as far as Rio de la Plata, in 1501–02. He is credited, on slender evidence, with the first suggestion that America was a continent separate from Asia; even, by some contemporaries, with being its discoverer – hence the name 'America', first used on the world map of Martin Waldseemüller in 1507. From 1508 to 1512 Vespucci was pilot-major of the House of Trade of the Indies.

VICTOR EMMANUEL II (1820–78) First king of united Italy, son of **Charles Albert**, king of Sardinia-Piedmont, whom he succeeded on his father's abdication in 1849. He entrusted government in 1852 to Count **Cavour**, and led Italian troops in the Franco-Piedmontese victories over the Austrians at Magenta and Solferino, 1859. Rather against the wishes of his ministers, he secretly encouraged **Garibaldi** to conquer Sicily and Naples. Proclaimed king of Italy in 1861, he acquired Venetia in 1866 and Rome in 1870.

VICTORIA (1819–1901) Queen of Great Britain and Ireland, 1837–1901, and Empress of India, 1876–1901. She succeeded her uncle, William IV; married in 1840 Prince Albert of Saxe-Coburg-Gotha (1819–61) later styled the Prince Consort. She attached particular significance to her right to be consulted about foreign affairs and, in the latter part of her reign, identified herself with her people's imperial aspirations. She went through a period of intense unpopularity when she shut herself away from the public after the Prince Consort's death, but re-emerged as the symbol of both national and imperial unity. Her diamond jubilee in 1897 was an ostentatious celebration of the apogee of Great Britain's world power.

VIENNA, CONGRESS OF Convened in fulfilment of Article XXXII of the **First Peace of Paris** and formally opened at the end of October 1814. The principal powers reconstructed Europe following the many territorial changes of the previous two decades, their decisions being embodied in the final Act of Vienna of 9 June 1815. Legitimate dynasties were restored in Spain, Naples, Piedmont, Tuscany and Modena; the Marches, Legations and other territories were restored to the Holy See; the Swiss Confederation was restored and guaranteed; 39 German states were formed into a confederation; Belgium, Holland and part of Luxembourg were united under the kingdom of the Netherlands; the kingdom of Lombardy-Venetia was placed under the Emperor of Austria; the Congress Kingdom of Poland was created and placed under the Tsar of Russia, the rest of Poland gong to Austria and Prussia; Prussia in addition acquired nearly half of Saxony, Swedish Pomerania and certain territories on both banks of the Rhine; Dalmatia, Carniola and Salzburg went to Austria.

VIET MINH League for the independence of Vietnam, founded in 1941 by **Ho Chi Minh**. It emerged as a coalition of nationalist and Communist groups, and between 1946 and 1954 successfully fought to expel the French colonial administration. The dominant element of the party in North Vietnam, and since the military victory of 1975 throughout the country, is Lao Dong (Workers Party or Communist Party).

VIJAYANAGAR Powerful Hindu kingdom of southern India, founded in 1336 by a local prince, Harihara, who in 1343 built his new capital of Vijayanagara (City of Victory) to give the state its name. In 1485 a change of dynasty brought the Saluva family to the throne. Its greatest influence was achieved under Krishna Deva Raya (1509–30); the continued struggles with the Muslim Deccan culminated in a crushing defeat at the battle of Talikota in 1565 from which the kingdom never recovered.

VILLA, PANCHO (1877–1923) Mexican revolutionary leader, son of a farm worker. He joined **Madero** in 1909 and led a north Mexican troop in his successful revolution. Imprisoned in 1912, Villa escaped to the United States, returning in 1913 to form his famous División del Norte. He was joint leader of the successful revolt against Madero's successor, the dictator Victoriano Huerta, in 1914, but broke with his co-revolutionary **Carranza**, and fled to the mountains. He was pursued by a United States expedition in 1916 after executing 16 Americans and attacking New Mexico, but was pardoned in 1920. He was assassinated three years later.

VILLAFRANCA, PEACE OF (1859) Preliminary peace between **Napoleon III**, **Victor Emmanuel II** and Francis Joseph I of Austria which brought to an end the Franco-Piedmontese hostilities against Austria. A definitive peace, which provided for the cession of Lombardy to Sardinia-Piedmont, was signed at **Zürich** on 10 November 1859.

VILLARET-JOYEUSE, LOUIS THOMAS (1750–1812) French vice-admiral. He led the French fleet during the Revolutionary Wars; ordered to protect a grain convoy by the Committee of Public Safety in 1794, he suffered severe losses at the hands of the British at the battle of the 'Glorious' First of June, but succeeded in getting the convoy safely home to Brest; recalled by **Napoleon I** to lead the abortive expedition to recover St Domingue. In 1802 he was made governor of Martinique, which he was forced to yield to the British in 1809. In 1811 he became governor of Venice, where he died.

VILLENEUVE, PIERRE-CHARLES-JEAN-BAPTISE-SILVESTRE DE (1763–1806) French vice-admiral. He commanded the French fleet at the battle of Trafalgar in 1805; disgraced in the eyes of **Napoleon I** by his failure, he committed suicide.

VIRACOCHA (d.c. 1438) Inca emperor who took his name from the ancient Inca god of creation. He began in the early 15th century to substitute permanent conquest for his predecessors' pattern of intermittent raiding, successfully extending Inca influence into the Titicaca basin. He became embroiled in a civil war with his son, later **Pachacuti** Inca.

VISCONTI Milanese family dominating northern Italy in the 14th and 15th centuries. The family probably became hereditary viscounts of Milan in the 11th century, adopting the title as their surname; by war, diplomacy and marriage they extended their control over large territories between 1300 and 1447. The name died out with Filippo Maria (1392–1447) when he was succeeded by his son-in-law, the *condottiere* Francesco Sforza, who founded his own dynasty, ruling the Visconti domains until the 16th century. Through the female line, Visconti blood was transmitted to almost all the great European ruling houses: Valois in France, Habsburg in Austria and Spain, and Tudor in England.

VISCONTI, GIANGALEAZZO (1351–1402) Lombard ruler. He succeeded his father in 1378 as joint ruler of Pavia and Lombardy with his uncle, Bernabo, whom he put to death in 1385. Recognized as Duke of Milan in 1395, he became master of northern Italy, including Verona, Bologna and Perugia; in 1399 he bought Pisa and seized Siena; he founded Milan cathedral. He died of plague, with the conquest of Florence and his project for a great unified state in northern Italy incomplete.

VISHNU Hindu deity: God the Preserver in the Hindu trinity; the object of special or exclusive worship to Vaishnavas, a major sect of Hindu belief. Traditionally, Vishnu manifested himself in nine incarnations (most recently as the **Buddha**) to save men from evil; his tenth and final incarnations is still to come.

VISIGOTHS Germanic people, closely linked with the **Ostrogoths**, who occupied the former Roman province of Dacia (modern Romania) in the 3rd century AD. Forced by the **Huns** to take refuge in the Roman empire in 376, they revolted and defeated the Romans at Adrianople in 378 and began the wars and wanderings that included the Sack of Rome in 410 and the establishment of the Visigothic kingdom which, from 418 to 507, covered most of Spain and Gaul. They were defeated by the **Franks** at Vouillé in 511 and retreated to Spain, where their Christian state (first Arian, but Catholic from 589) was finally destroyed in 711 by Muslims invading from north Africa.

VLADIMIR (c. 956–1015) Grand prince of Kiev, saint and first Christian ruler of Russia. Son of **Svyatoslav** of Kiev, he became Prince of Novgorod in 970, and by 980 had linked Kiev and Novgorod, and consolidated Russia from the Ukraine to the Baltic. He signed a pact c. 987 with the Byzantine emperor **Basil II** to give military aid and accept Christianity. He agreed to the appointment of a Greek Metropolitan, or archbishop, in Kiev, thus checking Roman influence on Russian religion. During his reign he expanded education, legal institutions and poor relief.

V.O.C. *see* **Dutch East India Company**

VOLGA BULGARS A Turanian people, emigrating northwards from the Black Sea in the 9th century to the junction of the Volga and Kama rivers. They adopted Islam, founded an independent state, and built up a rich fur trade based on the cities of Bulgar and Suvar (early 11th century). They were conquered by the Mongols, 1237; their territory was won by Muscovy after the capture of Kazan (1552) but they themselves seem to have vanished long before.

VOLSCI Ancient Italian People, mainly known for their opposition to Roman expansion in the 5th century BC. Originally related to the Osco-Sabellian tribes of the upper Liris valley, they later moved into the fertile area of southern Latium where for 200 years they fought against Rome and the Latins. Defeated during the Latin revolt in 338 BC, they finally submitted in 304, and were quickly Romanized.

W

WAFD Egyptian nationalist party during the generation after the First World War. The name refers to the delegation, led by **Saad Zaghlul** which asked the British High Commissioner in Cairo for permission to put the Egyptian case for independence to the British government. Exile of leaders by the British in 1919 led to violence, martial law, and a long crisis which ended in the British declaration of limited Egyptian independence in 1922, the grant of a constitution, 1923, and the assumption of power by the Wafd, now organized as a party, in 1924. It soon lost office, but its leaders, Zaghlul and then Nahas, played an important part in later activities and negotiations which led ultimately to the Anglo-Egyptian treaty of 1936. Subsequently Nahas was prime minister on several occasions, including during much of the Second World War, and the Wafd continued to play the leading role as spokesmen of Egyptian aspirations for complete independence until dissolved after the military revolution of 1925. Reformed in 1978, the party soon dissolved itself. The New Wafd party boycotted the elections in 1990.

WAHHABI Member of the Muslim puritan movement founded by Mohammed ibn Abd al-Wahab in the 18th century. Originating in the Nejd district of central Arabia, it was adopted by a local dynasty, the **Saudis**, who created the first Wahhabi empire, crushed by **Muhammad Ali** of Egypt acting on behalf of the Ottomans in 1818; revived in the mid-19th century, it was again destroyed, this time by the Rashidis of northern Arabia. The state was reformed, and expanded by Ibn Saud to become the modern kingdom of Saudi Arabia in 1932, with the Wahabi version of Islam as its official faith.

WALDENSIANS (Waldenses) Christian movement founded around 1170 by Peter Waldo (or Valdez) (c. 1140–1217), characterized by its poverty, simplicity and evangelism. The Waldensians (also known as the Poor Men of Lyons) exalted personal conduct and the setting of a good example above priestly ordination. Waldo preached no doctrinal heterodoxy (which distinguished his movement from that of the **Cathars** with their dualistic **Manichaeism**), but he was nevertheless critical of the manners of the clerical hierarchy of his time. He was condemned at the Council of Verona (1184) for preaching without licence. As they operated in much the same areas as the Cathars, the Waldensians were also attacked in the Albigensian Crusade of 1208. Although the victim of continual persecution, the Waldensian church still survives in some districts of northern Italy.

WALESA, LECH (1943–) President of Poland. The son of a carpenter, he became an electrician at the **Lenin** Shipyard in Gdansk (1967–76), the scene of violent anti-government protest in 1970. Although dismissed for unauthorized labour agitation, he remained active in the underground labour movement, founding Solidarity, a free trade union in 1979. Solidarity was crushed in 1981, by the Communist government, but survived under Walesa's leadership to win recognition again in 1989, in the wake of mass strikes and demonstrations. In 1990, Walesa was elected president of the Polish Republic.

WALLACE, SIR WILLIAM (c. 1270–1305) Scottish national hero, son of Sir Matthew Wallace, a landowner near Renfrew. He organized resistance to the claims of the English king, **Edward I**, to rule Scotland, and annihilated a large English army near Stirling in 1297. He ravaged Northumberland and Durham, was badly defeated and discredited at Falkirk in the following year, and was arrested in Glasgow and executed in London in 1305.

WALLIS, SAMUEL (1728–95) Circumnavigator, discoverer of Tahiti, the Wallis Islands and some of the Tuamotu and Society Islands; in 1767 the British Admiralty sent him to survey the extent of Oceania.

WANG FU-CH'EN (d.1681) Chinese general. He was a subordinate of Wu San-kuei in the campaigns against the remnants of Ming forces in southwest China in the 1650s. In 1670 he became governor of Shensi. Wu San-kuei asked him to rebel in 1673 – he refused, and offered to lead his army against Wu. In 1674 he quarrelled with the Manchu commander sent against Wu and murdered him, joining the rebellion. In 1675–6 he controlled much of Shensi and Kansu, but surrendered to the Manchus in 1676 and committed suicide after the final failure of the rebellion.

WANG MANG (d.AD 23) Chinese emperor, known as 'the Usurper', founder of the short-lived Hsin dynasty, AD 9–23, which separated the two halves of the long Han period. He became regent to the imperial throne in 8 BC, at a time when the Han succession was confused; dismissed in 5 BC and reinstated four years later, he finally manoeuvred his way to supreme power in AD 9. By the time of his death a series of natural disasters and widespread rebellion, known as the Revolt of the Red Eyebrows, had precipitated his overthrow. This brought about the restoration of the Han line in AD 25. He instituted many reforms of administration and the economy, for which he claimed Confucian scriptural precedents. These sweeping reforms raised much discontent: for example, he attempted to nationalize land and free all slaves.

WARSAW PACT (Treaty of Friendship, Co-operation and Mutual Aid) Agreement signed in 1955 which formed the basis for mutual defence cooperation within the former Soviet bloc. The original participants were Albania, Bulgaria, Czechoslovakia, East Germany, Hungary, Poland, Romania and the Soviet Union, but Albania withdrew after the

Soviet-led invasion of Czechoslovakia in 1968. East Germany withdrew after unification (1990). The Pact was formally wound up in March 1992.

WASHINGTON, GEORGE (1732–99) American soldier and statesman. A farmer and country gentleman of Virginia, as a lieutenant-colonel in the Virginia militia he fought against the French, 1754–8; married 'the prettiest and richest widow in Virginia' in 1759, and became one of the largest landowners in t he state. He was a member of the Virginia House of Burgesses, 1759–74, and delegate to the first Continental Congress. Appointed commander of the colonial armies in 1775 on the suggestion of **John Adams**, despite several military defeats in 1777–8 he retained the confidence of Congress, and forced the British surrender at Yorktown in 1781. After the peace of 1783 he resigned his command and returned to farming. He was elected chairman of the Constitutional Convention, 1787, and first president of the United States, 1788 (inaugurated 30 April 1789); he was re-elected in 1792. Declining to serve a third term, he gave his 'Farewell Address' in September 1796.

WATERLOO, BATTLE OF Final defeat in 1815 of **Napoleon I**, emperor of the French, by the armies of his enemies: Dutch and British forces led by the **Duke of Wellington**, Prussian led by Marshal von Blücher.

WATT, JAMES (1736–1819) Scottish inventor. At the age of 17 he started making mathematical instruments. In 1764, while repairing a model Newcomen pump, he started a series of improvements which transformed the steam engine into the major power unit of the industrial revolution: separate condenser (1765), sun-and-planet gear (1781), double-acting engine (1782), centrifugal governor (1788), pressure gauge (1790). He was elected a Fellow of the Royal Society in 1786.

WEDGWOOD, JOSIAH (1730–95) Leading English potter in the 18th century. He introduced great improvements in the manufacturing process, and in 1769 he opened his new Etruria factory, and in 1774 he made two dinner services for **Catherine II** of Russia. Wedgwood played an active part in securing the construction of the Trent and Mersey Canal in 1777, which greatly improved the transport facilities of the pottery industry.

WEICHSEL GLACIAL STAGE *see* **Würm Glacial Stage**

WELLESLEY, RICHARD COLLEY (1760–1842) Marquis of Norragh, Anglo-Irish statesman and administrator, brother of the Duke of Wellington. Governor-general of Madras and of Bengal, 1797–1805, he defeated **Tipu**, Sultan of Mysore, but was recalled and threatened with impeachment over the cost and scale of his military annexations. As lord lieutenant of Ireland, 1821–8, and 1833–4, he tried to reconcile Protestants and Catholics.

WELLINGTON, DUKE OF (1769–1852) Victor of Waterloo and later prime minister of Great Britain. Born Arthur Wellesley, he gained an early military reputation in India, and was raised to the peerage after victories in the Peninsular War (1808–14). With the Prussian Marshal von Blücher he defeated **Napoleon I** in 1815 at Waterloo. A member of various Conservative Cabinets between 1818 and 1827, he became prime minister 1828–30, and opposition leader after the passing of the 1832 Reform Act.

WENCESLAS (1361–1419) King of Germany and Bohemia; son of Emperor Charles IV. His drunken and ineffective rule reduced Germany to anarchy between 1378 and 1389; deposed there in 1400, he clung on in Bohemia as a pawn of the aristocracy. He supported **Jan Hus** but failed to protect him from execution.

WESTERN RISINGS A popular English rebellion in 1549 in Cornwall and Devon against the introduction of a Protestant liturgy by Edward VI, which was defeated by government troops; also, in 1628–31, riots in southwest England against the efforts of **Charles I**'s government to enclose and cut down royal forests and thus deprive the local population of common rights.

WESTMINSTER, STATUE OF (1931) Act of the Parliament of the United Kingdom declaring that the self-governing dominions of Canada, Australia, New Zealand, South Africa, Ireland and Newfoundland were to be regarded equally as 'autonomous communities' within the British empire, though united by a common allegiance to the Crown. It recognized their sovereign right to control domestic and foreign affairs and to establish their own diplomatic corps.

WESTPHALIA, PEACE OF Name given to 11 separate treaties signed in 1648, after five years of negotiation, to end the Thirty Years' War. The **Habsburg** emperors lost most of their authority over the German princes, promised full toleration for Calvinist princes, promised full toleration for Calvinist states, accepted the secularization of all Church land (carried out 1555–1624), and formally recognized the independence of the Swiss Confederation. Sweden and Brandenburg made substantial territorial gains in north Germany; France gained extensive rights and territories in Alsace and Lorraine.

WETTIN Ancient Germany ruling dynasty, named after the castle of Wettin on Saale below Halle, which played a major role in German eastern expansion. Conrad (d.1156) received the March of Meissen. The dynasty split into two branches in 1485: the Ernestines in Thuringia, the Albertines in Saxony. The latter was a leading territorial state in Germany from 1555 to 1815.

WHITE LOTUS REBELLION The White Lotus was a Buddhist millenarian sect founded before the 13th century. Under the Manchu (**Ch'ing**) dynasty (1644–1911) it became an anti-dynastic movement, aiming to restore the **Ming**. Between 1796 and 1805 White Lotus leaders led a series of large-scale risings in the mountainous regions of central China, using guerrilla tactics; however, there was no coordination of the rebels, who were eventually contained and put down by the organization of local militias at vast expense.

WHITE RUSSIANS Traditional name for the people of Belarus (White Russia).

WHITES, THE Name used during the Russian Civil War (1918–20) to describe the anti-Bolshevik forces which fought against the Communist Red Army, and after that to describe Russian emigrés.

WILFRID, ST (c. 634–c.709) Born in Northumbria, he entered the monastery of Lindisfarne and, after the Synod of Whitby, became bishop of York. He fought to establish Roman customs; helped to convert the **Frisians** and the South Saxons; established monasteries at Ripon and Hexham; and encouraged **Willibrord** and Suidbert to evangelize the Saxons of Germany. His forceful personality and strong principles led to him twice being deposed from his see.

WILKINSON, JOHN (1728–1803) A pioneer English ironmaster who developed a greatly improved method of boring cylinders. The new technique was first used to bore cannon, and was then adapted to the production of boilers for steam engines. In 1779 Wilkinson cast the components for the first iron bridge, over the Severn at Coalbrookedale, and in 1787 built a small iron ship on the Severn.

WILLIAM I, THE CONQUEROR (c. 1028–87) First Norman king of England, son of Robert I of Normandy whose dukedom he inherited in 1035, becoming effective ruler in 1042. In 1063 he annexed Maine, and in 1066 successfully invaded England, where he introduced major legal and religious reforms. From 1072 he spent most of his time in Normandy; in 1085 he ordered the compilation of the Domesday Book, a unique survey of England's landholdings.

WIILIBALD, ST (c. 700–86) Anglo-Saxon missionary in the eastern Mediterranean and Germany, a nephew and associate of **St Boniface**. He was made bishop of Eichstätt in 741.

WILLIBRORD, ST (658–739) Anglo-Saxon bishop and missionary, disciple of St Egbert in Ireland, 678–90. He was sent to convert the **Frisians**, and became their archbishop in 695. He worked with the **Merovingian** kings, Pippin II and **Charles Martel**, to extend Christianity in northern Europe. He died at his monastery of Echternach, and was adopted as the patron saint of Holland.

WILLOUGHBY, FRANCIS (c. 1613–66) Founder of the British colony of Surinam. He first supported Parliament in the English Civil War, then joined the Royalists. As Lord Willoughby of Parham he was appointed governor of Barbados in 1650, and the following year successfully implanted settlers in Surinam.

WILSON, WOODROW (1856–1924) 28th president of the United States, an outstanding chief executive whose two terms in office (1913–21) covered the First World War and the Paris Peace conference. A controversial figure during the first years, Wilson won temporary fame as the world's greatest leader after the war, but his power and influence later declined. The US Senate repudiated the **League of Nations**, which he had ardently advocated, and ill-health sapped his capacity to govern.

WISCONSIN GLACIAL STAGE *see* Würm

WITOLD (1350–1430) Grandson of **Gedymin**, Lithuanian grand duke and national leader, also known in Lithuania as Vytautas the Great. He fought a long struggle with his cousin **Władysław II Jagiełło**, king of Poland, which ended in 1401 when Władysław recognized him as Grand Duke of Lithuania, while remaining his suzerain. In alliance,the cousins broke the power of the **Teutonic Order** at the battle of Tannenberg (Grünwald) in 1410.

WITTELSBACH Bavarian dynasty enfeoffed with the duchy of Bavaria after the fall of **Henry, Duke of Saxony** in 1180. A collateral line held the Palatinate from 1214 to 1777. The Bavarian Wittelsbachs, imperial supporters in the **Thirty Years' War**, were rewarded with the Upper Palatinate in 1684. Raised to the rank of king by Napoleon in 1806, they continued to rule until 1918.

WITTE, SERGEI YULYEVISH (1849–1915) Russian politician. Promoted the building of the Trans-Siberian railroad (begun 1891), known as the 'Witte system', linking European and Asiatic Russia. Rrussian minister of communication (1892) and finance (1892–1903) and first constitutional prime minister of the Russian empire (1905–6). He sought to combine authoritarian rule with modernization along Western lines and persuaded Tsar Nicholas II to issue the 'October Manifesto' (1905) supporting a measure of representative government but fell from favour in 1906. He opposed Russia's entry into World War I and died dispirited, foreseeing disaster for the tsarist empire.

WŁADYSŁAW II JAGIEŁŁO (1351–1434) Grandson of Gedymin, son of **Olgierd**, grand duke of Lithuania (from 1377). On his marriage to Queen **Jadwiga** of Poland in 1386, he united the two crowns and styled himself Władysław II, King of Poland. At the head of Polish and Lithuanians armies he defeated the knights of the **Teutonic Order** at the battle of Tannenberg (Grünwald) in 1410. He gave his name to the **Jagiełłonian** dynasty.

WOLFE, JAMES (1727–59) British general. He served in the Low Countries, Scotland and Cape Breton Islands before commanding the British army at the capture of Quebec in 1759; after defeat at Beauport, he climbed the heights of Abraham to surprise and rout the French army. He thus gained Canada for Britain, but died of wounds during the battle.

WORMS, CONCORDAT OF Agreement concluded in 1122 between Pope Calixtus II and Emperor Henry V, which ended the Investiture Contest in compromise. The Emperor conceded full freedom of election to episcopal office, surrendering the claim to bestow spiritual authority by investiture; but bishops were to be elected in his presence so that he might nevertheless influence the elector's choice. Thus neither side gained all that **Gregory VII** and **Henry IV** had demanded, but each secured valuable concessions from the other; papal headship of the Church was recognized, but the emperor retained some control over its leaders in Germany.

WRIGHT BROTHERS American aviation pioneers. Together Orville Wright (1871–1948) and his brother Wilbur (1867–1912) built the first stable, controllable, heavier-than-air flying machine, which made its first successful flights (the longest of 852 feet) at Kitty Hawk, North Carolina, in 1903.

WU P'EI-FU (1874–1939) Chinese warlord. He served with the Pei-yang armies under **Yüan Shih-k'ai**, and with the Japanese army during the Russo-Japanese War of 1904–5. After Yüan's death in 1916, Wu became the most powerful general of the Pei-yang armies, and in 1922 drove back the Manchurian armies of **Chang Tso-lin**. This made him China's most powerful military figure, and he dominated the shaky Peking government from 1922–4. His ruthless suppression of a workers' strike on the Hankow-Peking railway in 1923 cost him much of his popularity and the support of his main ally **Feng Yu-hsiang**. Decisively defeated by Chang near Tientsin in 1924, he retreated to Hupeh; in 1925–6 allied himself with Chang in a war against Feng Yu-hsiang and invaded Honan. In 1926–7 he was defeated by **Chiang Kai-shek**'s Northern Expedition and took refuge in Szechwan; he took no further major part in affairs.

WÜRM GLACIAL STAGE The latest phase of major ice advance in Alpine Europe, starting c. 70,000 years ago and ending around 10,000 years ago; it is equivalent to the Wisconsin period in North American and Weichsel in Scandinavia.

WU SAN-KUEI (1612–78) Chinese general. He served in the **Ming** armies, defending the northeast frontier against the **Manchus**, but he appealed to the Manchus for aid when Peking was attacked in 1644 by the rebel **Li Tzu-ch'eng** (c. 1605–45), and with their aid drove Li from Peking, where the Manchus set up the **Ch'ing** dynasty. He refused appeals to aid a restoration of the **Ming** emperors, and commanded the southwest province of Yunnan on behalf of the Manchus, growing increasingly powerful and eventually controlling much of southwest and west China. In 1673 he led the Rebellion of the Three Feudatories and attempted to set up his own Chou dynasty, invading central China in 1674. He died of dysentery three years before the rebellion was finally crushed in 1681.

WU-TI (156–87 BC) Powerful Chinese emperor of the former **Han** period, eleventh son of Emperor Ching Ti. He succeeded to the throne in 140 BC; aggressively extended China's frontiers to include much of south and southwest China; north Vietnam, northern Korea and much of central Asia, and established effective defences against the **Hsiungnu** in the north. He finally established the supremacy of the emperor, created a tightly knit bureaucracy, levied unprecedented taxes and made Confucianism the state religion.

WYATT'S REBELLION English uprising in 1554 against the marriage of Mary Tudor (reigned 1553–8) to Philip II of Spain. Three thousand men from Kent marched on London and reached Fleet Street before surrendering; their leader, Sir Thomas Wyatt (son of the poet of the same name), was executed, and Princess Elizabeth, later Queen **Elizabeth I** (whom Wyatt had wished to place on the throne) was imprisoned in the Tower of London.

WYCLIF, JOHN (c. 1330–84) Religious reformer and translator of the Bible into English. As a vigorous anti-clerical he was patronized by John of Gaunt, who continued to support him, but not his views, when he denied the miracle of transubstantiation in the Mass; he was condemned as a heretic in 1381. His followers are known as **Lollards**.

WYNFRITH *see* **Boniface, St**

WYNTER, JAN WILLEM DE (1761–1812) Dutch admiral and politician. In 1785 he led the 'patriot party' which deposed the Stadholder William V, but fled to France when William was restored in 1787. In 1795 he accompanied the French army which conquered the Netherlands, and the French placed him in charge of the Dutch navy; in 1797 he led it to its defeat by the British at the battle of Camperdown.

XENOPHON (c. 430–c. 355 BC) Greek soldier and author. He studied with Socrates, about whom he wrote the *Memorabilia*, *Symposium* and *Apology*. His *Anabasis* describes the epic retreat of 10,000 mercenaries from Persia after the failure of Cyrus the Younger's expedition against Artaxerxes II. In exile he wrote the *Hellenica*, a history of Greece, and other works on sport and politics.

XERXES I (c. 520–465 BC) King of Persia (reigned 486–465 BC). Son of **Darius I** by his second marriage; chosen to succeed over his elder brother. He reconquered Egypt, which had rebelled at the end of Darius's reign; invaded Greece in 480 after digging a canal through the Mount Athos peninsula, forced the pass at Thermopylae and occupied Athens before meeting a crushing defeat at Salamis (480) by sea and at Plataea (479) by land. He was responsible for the finest work at the Persian capital of Persepolis. He was assassinated by conspirators headed by his chief guard, Artabanus.

XHOSA A people, and their Bantu language, in Cape Province, South Africa; now the inhabitants of the Transkei, the first so-called 'independent homeland' inside South Africa.

YAHYA KHAN, AGHA MOHAMMED (1917–82) Pakistan soldier and politician. Commander in East Pakistan (now Bangladesh), 1962–4; commander-in-chief of the Pakistan army, 1966–9, and president of Pakistan and chief administrator of martial law, 1969–71. He was forced to resign after his failure to suppress the revolt in East Pakistan which led to the setting up of the state of Bangladesh.

YALTA CONFERENCE Meeting of Allied war leaders (led by **Roosevelt, Churchill** and **Stalin**) at Yalta in the Crimea, 4–11 February, 1945. It reaffirmed the decision to demand unconditional Axis surrender, planned a four-power occupation of Germany, and agreed a further meeting to finalize plans for the **United Nations**. It was also agreed that the British and Americans would repatriate all Russians in Allied hands. Stalin, for his part, was prompted to declare war on Japan.

YAO Mountain-dwelling people of south and southwest China and of Southeast Asia, related to the Miao who share a similar heritageof Sino-Tibetan languages. in Kwangtung some have turned to wet-rice cultivation, but most remain in the highlands practising primitive slash-and-burn agriculture.

YELTSIN, BORIS (1931–) Russian president. He joined the Soviet Communist Party in 1961 and its central committee in 1981. After **Gorbachev**'s takeover in 1985, he became party leader in Moscow, where he introduced a programme of rapid reform. However, his outspoken attacks on communist hardliners led to his demotion. In May 1990 he became president of the Russian Republic and his criticism of Gorbachev became more open. In August 1991 he played a key role in defeating the hardline coup mounted against Gorbachev. The prominence he gained led swiftly to his elevation to the leadership of the new Russian Federation after the collapse of the USSR at the end of 1991. He survived another coup attempt in 1994, but growing lawlessness and economic hardship weakened his leadership. Though re-elected in 1996, by 1998 the rapid decline of the Russian economy and of his health had left him an isolated figure.

YEN HSI-SHAN (1883–1960) Chinese general and military governor. A Japanese-trained army officer, he emerged as a warlord in Shansi after the overthrow of the **Ch'ing** (Manchu) dynasty in 1911, and ruled as absolute dictator of the whole region from 1917 until the end of the Second World War. In 1930 he joined **Feng Yu-hsiang** in an abortive northern alliance against **Chiang Kai-shek**, but was afterwards confirmed in command of Shansi, where he instituted a sweeping programme of provincial reforms in 1934. In 1937 he lost most of Shansi to the Japanese, and from 1939 was in constant conflict with the Chinese communists. He was driven from the province in early 1949; he went to Taiwan and became premier until 1950.

YEZHOV, NIKOLAI IVANOVICH (1894–1939?) Soviet political leader who joined the Communist party in 1917 and served as a political commissar in the Red Army. He was a member of the central Committee of the Soviet Communist party from 1934 and headed the people's commissariat of internal affairs (NKVD) (1936–8), which under his direction carried out **Stalin**'s purges. As a result, his name became inextricably linked with the great Terror (Yezhovshchina). He was probably assassinated in 1939, but the circumstances surrounding his death remain unknown.

YORKSHIRE RISING Major revolt in 1489 against the attempts of the English King **Henry VII** to collect a parliamentary grant of £75,000. The king's lieutenant, the earl of Northumberland, was killed before the rebels were suppressed.

YOUNG TURKS Popular name for the committee of Union and Progress, an association of army officers and others who compelled sultan **Abdül Hamid II** to restore the 1876 constitution in 1908 and deposed him in 1909. Subsequently it became the Ottoman empire's dominant political party, in 1814 bringing Turkey into the First World War. It was disbanded after the Central Powers' defeat in 1918.

YÜAN SHIH-K'AI (1859–1916) First President of the Republic of China. He was sent to Korea with the Anhwei army, 1882, and became Chinese commissioner in Seoul, 1885–94; he helped to create a new model army after defeat by Japan in 1895. In 1901 he became viceroy of China's metropolitan province, Chihli, and commander of China's most powerful army, the Pei-yang chün. He was removed from his post in 1907 but exercised power through his former military subordinates, and was recalled by the **Ch'ing** (Manchus) after the outbreak of the 1911 revolution as supreme commander. In 1912 he was recommended by the emperor to be president, replaced the provisional president, **Sun Yat-sen**; increasingly dictatorial, he precipitated civil war in 1913 by murdering the revolutionary party chairman, and in 1916 tried to create a new imperial dynasty.

YUDENICH, NIKOLAI NIKOLAYEVICH (1862–1933) Russian general. After service in the Russo-Japanese war and the First World War, he took command of the anti-Bolshevik forces in the Baltic after the Russian revolution. In 1919, with some British support he led an unsuccessful advance on Leningrad (then called Petrograd, now reverted to St Petersburg), and went into exile.

YÜEH-CHIH Central Asian peoples, first identified in Chinese sources in the 2nd century BC, living as nomads in Kansu, northwest China. Under attack by the **Hsiungnu**, they moved west into Sogdiana and Bactria, displacing the Greek rulers there, c.150 BC. Their descendants, with the **Tocharians**, founded the Kushana empire, ruling northern India and central Asia until about AD 300. Yüeh-chih and Kushana missionaries helped spread **Buddhism** and Indian culture in China.

YUNG-LO (CHU TI) (1360–1424) Chinese emperor, the third of the **Ming** dynasty, and fourth son of Hung-we. He rebelled against his nephew in 1399, and seized the throne in 1402 after two years of destructive civil war. He invaded Annam, 1406–7, and began a series of major maritime expeditions into the Indian Ocean. He personally conducted campaigns to crush the Mongols in 1410, 1414 and 1422–4, and expanded Chinese power in Manchuria and the Amur valley. He rebuilt the Grand Canal, and transferred the capital from Nanking to Peking in 1421.

ZAGHLUL, SAAD (1857–1927) Leader of Egyptian **nationalism** during that period when it first became a mass movement. He became prominent as a minister and politician before 1914; from 1918 he was leader of the **Wafd**, and in 1924 was appointed prime minister shortly after the British declaration of limited independence for Egypt; he was, however, forced to resign soon afterwards.

ZAGWE Ethiopian dynasty of Semitic origin which displaced the Aksumite kings in the 12th and 13th centuries. It did much to expand and centralize the Christian empire of Ethiopia.

ZAIBATSU Large-scale Japanese business groups, normally organized around the commercial, industrial and financial interests of a single family. The biggest and best known were the Mitsui, Mitsubishi, Yasuda and Sumitomo empires, all of which grew up and flourished in the period from 1868 to 1945. In 1946, after Japan's defeat, the Zaibatsu were ordered to dissolve into their component companies, but most are now, for practical purposes, reassembled.

ZAIDI Dynasty of rulers in Yemen, southern Arabia. Founded by imam al-Hadi in northern Yemen in the 9th century, they expanded their power in the 12th century, and again after 1635, when they expelled the Ottoman Turks. Driven back to northern Yemen in the 1710s, they were forced to recognize Ottoman suzerainty in 1849. After the Ottoman collapse in 1918 they became rulers of all Yemen until a military coup in 1962 deposed the last Zaidi imam.

ZANGI (1084–1146) Iraqi warrior who inflicted the first serious defeat on Christian crusaders, recapturing Edessa in 1144. He founded the Zangid dynasty, which ruled northern Iraq and Syria, 1127–1222.

ZANGIDS Muslim Turkish dynasty, ruling northern Iraq and part of Syria from 1127 to 1222. It was founded by Zangi (1127–46), who mounted the first Islamic counterattack against the Christian **Crusades. Saladin**, founder of the **Ayyubid** dynasty in Egypt, was a Zangid general, and ultimately brought the family territories under his rule.

ZAPATA, EMILIANO (1879–1919) Mexican revolutionary leader. He supported **Madero** in the 1911 overthrow of **Díaz**; forbidden to redistribute land to the peasants, he issued the Plan of Ayala and renewed revolution under the slogan 'Land Liberty'. He fought constantly, first against the dictator Huerta in 1913, and then with **Pancho Villa** against the moderate government of **Carranza**. He was ambushed and assassinated.

ZARATHUSTRA *see* **Zoroaster**

ZEALOTS Extreme Jewish resistance party against the Roman domination of Judaea. It played a major part in the **Jewish uprising** of AD 66–73.

ZENO OF CITIUM (c. 334–c. 262 BC) Ancient Greek philosopher, best known for his paradoxes demonstrating the unreality of motion.

ZEUS Supreme god of Greek mythology, also identified with the Roman Jupiter; born in Crete (Mount Ida), son of Rhea and Cronus, whom he overthrew.

ZHIVKOV, TODOR (1911–) Bulgarian political leader. He worked as a printer in Bulgarian communist circles in the 1920s. Some claim he led the coup overthrowing the pro-German regime in 1944. He served as secretary of the Bulgarian communist party in 1954, premier in 1962 and president in 1971 but resigned in November 1989 when communist power in eastern Europe collapsed.

ZHUKOV, GEORGIY KONSTANTINOVICH (1896–1976) Marshal of the Soviet Union and leading Russian hero of the Second World War. He served in the Imperial Russian Army, 1915–17, joining the Red Army in 1918; he was cavalry commander in the Civil War. In command of the Mongolian-Manchurian frontier in 1939, he became general officer commanding the Kiev Military district in 1940, and in 1941 chief of the general staff. He directed the defence of Leningrad and then Moscow after the German invasion; was appointed marshal in 1943; and led the final assault on Berlin in 1945. He was briefly commander-in-chief of the Soviet forces in Germany, GOC of Odessa military district 1948–52; minister of defence 1955, after supporting **Khrushchev** against Malenkov. He was dismissed in 1957 and retired into private life.

ZIONISM Jewish national movement. it emerged in the latter part of the 19th century, and was placed on a firm and permanent organizational basis by Theodor Herzl, author of *The Jewish State*, who convened the first Zionist Congress at Basle in 1897. It sought the creation of a Jewish national homeland in Palestine which most Jews regarded as their ancestral land; this aim was achieved in 1948 when the United Nations voted to create the state of Israel.

ZIRID Muslim Berber dynasty ruling, under various branches, Tunisia, eastern Algeria and Granada from 972 to 1152. They were given a free hand in northwest Africa when their suzerain, the **Fatimid** caliph al-Muizz, moved his capital to Cairo. They were finally conquered by the **Almohads**.

ZOLLVEREIN German customs union established in 1834 when 18 states, some of which had formerly belonged to the Prussian, central German and southern German customs unions, formed, under Prussian auspices, a free trade area. By 1841 most German states had joined; Hanover and Oldenburg joined in 1854; Austria remained outside; Schleswig-Holstein, Lauenburg, Lübeck and the Mecklenburgs joined after the defeat of Austria in 1866 by Prussia, whose power in Germany had been much enhanced by the Zollverein. Hamburg and Bremen joined in 1888.

ZOROASTER (Zarathustra) Prophet and religious reformer of ancient Iran, the founder of Zoroastrianism. His personal writings were the Old Iranian texts known as the *Gathas*, in which he emphasized the ethical aspects of religion against mere conformity with ritual requirements. Theologically, these ideas were expressed in the cult of Ahura Mazda, 'the Wise Lord', as the highest god, in opposition to beliefs never defined but which some have thought included forms of Mithraism. Thus arose the 'dualistic' theology of later Zoroastrianism, which depicts creation not as the immediate rule of an omnipotent just god, but as a long contest between the divine forces of good and evil. This theology provides a simple solution for the problem of suffering, and may have influenced theories concerning the role of Satan in developing Christianity.

ZOSER (Djoser) Second king of Egypt's 3rd Dynasty; he is traditionally said to have reigned for 19 years during the 27th century BC. With his chief minister and architect, **Imhotep**, he built the first of the great stone pyramids at Saqqara, near his capital, Memphis.

ZULU Nguni-speaking group in Natal, southern Africa. In the early 19th century they joined with related peoples under Shaka, their leader, to form the Zulu empire. They engaged in sporadic warfare with other African peoples and with the advancing European settlers, and were finally defeated in 1879 at Ulundi.

ZÜRICH, PEACE OF Agreement in 1859 between **Napoleon III** of France and Franz Joseph of Austria to settle the Italian problem after a general rebellion against Austrian rule. Lombardy was ceded to Piedmont, Venetia remained Austrian (to 1866); the central states of Italy voted to join Piedmont, and Nice and Savoy voted to become French (1860).

ZWINGLI, HULDREICH (1484–1531) Swiss religious reformer. He was pastor in Glarus, 1506, and rector and teacher of religion at the Great Minster, Zürich, 1519. He established the Protestant **Reformation** in Zürich, 1520–3, although failing to agree about doctrine with **Luther** and other German reformers, 1529. He was killed at the battle of Kappel while serving as chaplain in Zürich's army during its campaign against the Swiss Catholics.

ZYRIANS Finno-Ugrian speaking Arctic people, mostly inhabiting the Komikomi area of northwest Russia.

INDEX

1 HISTORICAL PLACE NAMES

Geographical names vary with time and with language, and there is some difficulty in treating them consistently in an historicalwork which covers the whole world from the beginning of human pre-history, especially for individual maps within whose time span the same place has been known by many different names. We have aimed at the simplest possible approach to the names on the maps, using the index to weld together the variations.

On the maps forms of names will be found in the following hierarchy of preference:-

a English conventional names or spellings, in the widest sense, for all principal places and features, e.g., Moscow, Vienna, Munich, Danube (including those that today might be considered obsolete when these are appropriate to the context, e.g., Leghorn).

b Names that are contemporary in terms of the maps concerned. There are here three broad categories:-
i names in the ancient world, where the forms used are classical, e.g., Latin or latinized Greek, but extending also to Persian, Sanskrit, etc.
ii names in the post-medieval modern world, which are given in the form (though not necessarily the spelling current at the time of the map (e.g., St. Petersburg before 1914, not Leningrad); whose language reflects the sovereignty then existing, e.g., Usküb (Turkish) rather than Skoplje (Serbian) or Skopje (Macedonian) in maps showing Ottoman rule.
iii names in the present-day world, where the spelling generally follows that of *The Times Atlas of the World*, though in the interests of simplicity there has been a general omission of diacritics in spellings derived by transliteration from non-roman scripts, e.g., Sana rather than Ṣan'ā'.

On the spelling of Chinese names, readers will be increasingly aware of the Pinyin romanizations that have come into use over the last ten years (eg., Beijing, Qin dynasty) but this book continues to spell Chinese names in the conventional forms and Wade-Giles romanizations that are still more generally found in historical contexts (e.g. Peking, Ch'in dynasty). However, all Chinese names that occur as main entries in the index give the Pinyin spelling in brackets, and there are cross-references from all Pinyin forms to the traditional spellings used in the book.

Alternative names and spellings have occasionally been shown in brackets on the maps to aid in identification.

2 THE INDEX

The index does not include every name shown on the maps. In general only those names are indexed which are of places, features, regions or countries where 'something happens', i.e., which carry a date or symbol or colour explained in the key, or which are mentioned in the text.

Where a place is referred to by two or more different names in the course of the book, there will be a corresponding number of main entries in the index. The variant names in each case are given in brackets at the beginning of the entry, their different forms and origins being distinguished by such words as *now*, *later*, *formerly* and others included in the list of abbreviations *(right)*.

'Istanbul (*form.* Constantinople, *anc.* Byzantium)' means that the page references to that city on maps dealing with periods when it was known as Istanbul follow that entry, but the page references pertaining to it when it had other names will be found under those other names.

Places are located generally by reference to the country in which they lie (exceptionally by reference to island groups or sea areas), this being narrowed down by where necessary by location as E(ast), N(orth), C(entral), etc. The reference will normally be to the modern state in which the place now falls unless (a) there is a conventional or historical name which conveniently avoids the inevitably anachronistic ring of some modern names, e.g., Anatolia rather than Turkey, Mesopotamia rather than Iraq, or (b) the modern state is little known or not delineated on the map concerned, e.g., many places on the Africa plates can only be located as W., E., Africa, etc.

All variant names and spellings are cross-referenced in the form 'Bourgogne (Burgundy)', except those which would immediately precede or follow the main entries to which they refer. The bracketed form has been chosen so that such entries may also serve as quick visual indications of equivalence. The Bourgogne (Burgundy) means not only 'see under Burgundy' but also that Burgundy is another name for Bourgogne.

Reference is generally to page number/map number (e.g., pages 114/2) unless the subject is dealt with over the plate as a whole, when the reference occurs as 114-5 (i.e., pages 114 and 115). All entries with two or more references have been given sub-headings where possible, e.g., Civil War 268/3. Battles are indicated by the symbol ✕.

3 ABBREVIATIONS

a/c also called
AD Autonomous District (Okrug)
Alb. Albanian
anc. ancient
AO Autonomous Oblast
Ar. Arabic
a/s also spelled
ASSR Autonomous Soviet Socialist Republic
Bibl. Biblical
Bulg. Bulgarian
C Century (when preceded by 17, 18 etc.)
C Central
Cat. Catalan
Chin. Chinese
Cz. Czech
Dan. Danish
Dut. Dutch
E. East(ern)
Eng English
Est. Estonian
f/c formerly called
Finn Finnish
form. former(ly)
Fr. French
f/s formerly spelled
Ger. German
Gr. Greek
Heb. Hebrew
Hung. Hungarian
Indon. Indonesian
Ir. Irish
Is. Island
It. Italian
Jap. Japanese
Kor. Korean
Lat. Latin
Latv. Latvian
Lith. Lithuanian
Maced. Macedonian
Mal. Malay
med. Medieval
mod. modern
Mong. Mongolian
N. North(ern)
n/c now called
Nor. Norwegian
n/s now spelled
NT New Testament
obs. obsolete
O.E. Old English
OT Old Testament
Pers. Persian
Pol. Polish
Port. Portuguese
Prak. Prakoit
Rom. Romanian
Russ. Russian
S. South(ern)
s/c sometimes called
Skr. Sanskrit
Slk. Slovak
Som. Somali
Sp. Spanish
S. Cr. Serbo-Croat
SSR Soviet Socialist Republic
Sw. Swedish
Turk. Turkish
Ukr. Ukrainian
US(A) United States (of America)
var. variant
W. West(ern)
Wel. Welsh
W/G Wade-Giles
WW1 The First World War
WW2 The Second World War

Aachen (*Fr.* Aix-la-Chapelle *anc.* Aquisgranum) W Germany Frankish royal residence 105/2; imperial city 190/1,2; industrial development 212/1; WW1 251/2
Aargau Switzerland Reformation 183/1
Aarhus (*n/s* Aårhus) Denmark bishopric 101/2; archbishopric 109/2
Abada C Mesopotamia Chalcolithic site 39/1
Abaj Takalik Mexico Maya site 44/2
Abasgia region of Caucasus 113/1
Abbas I the Great shah of Persia 168
Abbasids Muslim dynasty 98; Islam; 137/1; challenged 136
Abbeville N France 17C revolt 185/1
Abdera NE Greece Greek colony 77/1
Abdera (*mod.* Adra) S Spain Phoenician city 79/1
Abdulhamid II Ottoman sultan 228
Abellinum (*mod.* Avellino) C Italy 87/1
Abemama Gilbert Is WW2 266-7
Abenaki NE Canada Indian tribe 149/1
Abd ar-Rahman III caliph of Córdoba 102
Abhisara NW India kingdom 79/1; 83/2
Abilene C USA cow town 218/1
Abipon Argentina Indian tribe 149/1
Abo (Turku)
Abodrites Germany tribe 116/2
Aborigines way of life 48; and European invasion 236
Aboukir Bay Egypt ✕ 194/2
Abrotonum (Sabrata)
Abu Aweigila Sinai captured by Israel 282/2
Abu Bakr 1st caliph 98
Abu Dhabi United Arab Emirates 291/1
Abu Hammu 139
Abu Hureyra N Mesopotamia Neolithic site 38/1
Abu Khamis NE Arabia Chalcolithic site 39/1
Abu Klea C Sudan ✕ 247/2
Abu Kru C Sudan ✕ 247/2
Abu Roash N Egypt site 58/1
Abu Rudeis Sinai Israeli capture 288/1
Abu Salabikh S Mesopotamia early city 55/3
Abu Simbel Upper Egypt temple 59/3
Abusina S Germany Roman fort 88/2
Abusir N Egypt site 58/1
Abydus W Turkey Persian War 77/2; Dorian colony 77/1; Byzantine Empire 113/1
Abydus Upper Egypt site 52/1, 58/1
Abyssinia (*now* Ethiopia) 214/1, 245/2
Acadia (Nova Scotia)
Acalan Mexico Maya state 148/2
Acancéh E Mexico Maya site 60/2
Acanthus NE Greece Greek colony 79/1
Acapulco Mexico early trade 154/1
Acarnania country of ancient Greece 76/4
Accho (Acre)
Accra Ghana early European settlement 165/1; British settlement 239/1
Aceh (Achin)
Achaea (*a/s* Achaia) Greek parent community 77/2, 77/1; Roman province 89/1; Venetian principality 139/1, 147/1
Achaemenid Empire 74; 79/1
Achaia (Achaea)
Acheh (Achin)
Achin (*mod.* Aceh *var.* Acheh, Atjeh) N Sumatra early trade 158/2
Açores (Azores)
Acquebouille C France medieval *villeneuve* 121/6
Acragas (*Lat.* Agrigentum *mod.* Agrigento) Sicily Dorian colony 77/1
Acre (*OT* Accho *NT* Ptolemais *Fr.* St Jean-d'Acre *Heb.* `Akko) Palestine Crusades 111/1
Actium W Greece battle of, and Roman annexation of Egypt 79; ✕ 86/3; 89/1; Octavian victorious 87,88
Acton SE USA ✕ 219/3
Adab Mesopotamia 55/3
Adad-nirari I king of Assyria 58
Adal E Africa early state 141/1, 165/1, 239/1
Adamawa W Africa 239/1
Adamgarh C India site 65/1
Adan (Aden)
Adana W Turkey Neo-Hittite city-state 59/3; Jewish community 103/4; Byzantine Empire 113/1; Ottoman Empire 225/1
Ad Decimum Tunisia ✕ 98/1
Addis Ababa Ethiopia Italian penetration 241/1
Adelaide S Australia founded 237/1; British naval base 244/2
Aden (*Chin.* Adan *W/G* A-tan) S Arabia early trade 41/1; Muslim trade 137/1; early town 159/1; Ottoman Empire 169/1, 229/1; taken by British 239/1; British base 276/2; 291/1
Aden Protectorate (*successively renamed* Protectorate of South Arabia, Federation of South Arabia, People's Republic of South Yemen, People's Democratic Republic of Yemen) British protectorate 245/2, 258/1, 277/1
Adiabene region of Assyria 103/4
Adichanallur S India site 65/1
Adium battle of 79, 88
administration Carolingian 105; China 167, 172, 260; France under Louis XIV 193; British India 234-5; Japan 242; European colonial 259
Admiralty Islands S Pacific Japanese attack 267/1
Adowa N Ethiopia ✕ 241/1; battle of 246
Adra (Abdera)
Adramyttium (*mod.* Edremit) W Turkey 110/3
Adrar region of W Africa rock painting 43/1
Adrar Bous N Africa cattle domestication 43/1
Adrar Tiouiyne N Africa cattle domestication 43/1
Adrianople (*anc.* Adrianopolis *mod.* Edirne) W Turkey battle of 90; ✕ 98/1; Goths 97; Byzantine Empire 113/1, 133/2; Ottoman centre 168/1; 16C urban development 180/1;taken by Bulgaria 248/2; 18C urban development 181/2; occupied by Greece 263/1
Adrianopolis (Edirne, Adrianople)
Adriatic early trade routes 52/1
Adulis Red Sea Iron Age site 43/1; port 41/1, 82/4, 141/1
Adyge AD (*n/c* Adygeya) Caucasus 300/2, 299/3
Aeclanum C Italy early town 87/1
Aegean early movements of people 67/1; Balkan Wars 248/2
Aegospotamus (*Turk.* Karaova Suyu) NW Turkey ✕ 76/3
Aegyptus (*mod.* Egypt) Roman province 89/1,
Aelana (*a/c* Aela *mod.* Aqaba) N Arabia port 41/1, 82/4; Roman Empire 88/2
Aelia Capitolina (*mod.* Jerusalem) Judaea Roman city 88/2
Aenus (*mod.* Enez) W Turkey Aeolian colony 77/1
Aerenthal, Count Aloys Lexa von 249
Aeschylus 77
Aesernia (*mod.* Isernia) C Italy Latin colony 87/1
Aesis (*mod.* Lesi) N Italy 87/1
Aethelred II 'the Unready' king of the English 108
Aetolia ancient country of C Greece 77/2
Afars and Issas, French Territory of (*form.* French Somaliland *now* Rep. of Djibouti) NE Africa 295/1
Afghanistan under Abbasid sovereignty 137/1; under Mughal rule 171/1; Anglo-Afghan war 259/1; territorial claim against Pakistan 285/3; establishment of republic 291/1; Soviet occupation 285/3, 291/1; religious conflict 303/1
Africa early man 31/1, 31/1, 35/1; agricultural origins 37/1; early cultures 42-3; spread of epidemics 71/2; expansion of Christianity 100/1; early trade 139/1, 140/2; early states 145/1; early European voyages of discovery 156/1, 155/8; early Chinese exploration 154/1; early Indian exploration 154/4; early Muslim exploration 155/7; Portuguese exploration 164/2; early empires 165/1; Ottoman expansion 165/1; Chinese expedition to east coast 167/4; slave trade 194/3; 18C trade 195/1; colonial strategy 236/3; European exploration 238/2; before partition 239/1; partition 240-1; colonial empires 245/2, 258/1; anti-colonial resistance 246/1; decolonization 276/2; Japanese investment 278/4; modern political developments 280-3; US military involvement 297/1; armaments 302/2; population 303/3; economy 304-5; communications 307/3; environment 308-9
Africa (*mod.* Tunisia and Libya) Roman province 86/3, conversion to Christianity 72/1; Byzantine province 112/1
Africa Nova (*mod.* Tunisia) Roman province 86/3
Aga Buryat AD E Russia 300/2, 299/3
Agade empire and city of S Mesopotamia 54/1, 55/3; empire 55
Agadès (*var.* Agadez) W Africa 63/2, 140/2, 141/1, 165/1, 241/1
Agadir S Morocco Portuguese enclave 168/1; German involvement 249/3
Agathe (*mod.* Agde) SW France Ionian colony 77/1
Agathopolis Bulgaria Byzantine Empire 112/4
Agau tribe of NE Africa 141/1
Agde (Agathe)
Aggersborg N Denmark circular fortification 109/2
Aghlabids Muslim dynasty of N Africa 137/1
Agincourt (*mod.* Azincourt) N France ✕ 145/4
Aglar (Aquileia)
Agnadello N Italy ✕ 186/2
Agra N India region 171/1; centre of Mutiny 234/1
Agram (Zagreb)
agrarianismmedieval Indian empires 130; effect of agrarian change 200
agriculture in decline of Ice Age 34; origins of 36; earliest agricultural communities 40; prehistoric African 42; prehistoric Americas 44; rice 46, 130; ancient Eurasia 52; China 62, 80, 124, 126, 167, 172, 280; India 64, 65, 82, 170, 235; Crete 66; economy of Greek city-states 77; and Hellenistic economy 78; 15C North America 148-9; plough cultivation 154; hand cultivation in non-European civilizations 154; cash crops 155; revolution 178; Holy Roman Empire 191; agricultural revolution in Britain 200; Great Plains 242; Japan 242; Latin America 226; World War II and European production 272; Soviet Union 298; global warming 308
Agri Decumates region of NE Gaul abandoned by Rome 90/2
Agrigentum (*Gr.* Acragas *mod.* Agrigento) Sicily Roman Empire 86/2,3, 89/1, 88/2
Agropoli S Italy Saracen occupation 107/1
Aguascalientes state of C Mexico 227/1
Aguinaldo, Emilio 246
Ahar NW India site 65/1,3
Ahicchatra N India 65/1,3, 83/1, 133/1
Ahmadabad (Ahmedabad)
Ahmad ibn Tulun 126
Ahmadnagar W India sultanate 132/4; state 171/1
Ahmad Gran of Adel 164
Ahmad Shahis early state of N India 133/3
Ahmedabad (*n/s* Ahmadabad) W India industry 214/1, 231/3; Hindu-Muslim clashes 285/3
Ahmed Khan, Sir Saiyid 235
Ahvenanmaa (Åland islands)
Ahwaz (*a/s* Ahvaz) W Persia 82/3
Aichi prefecture of C Japan; industry 242/1
Aigun (*n/c* Heihe *a/c* Aigui) NE China treaty port 232/2
Ain Gev Jordan early site 38/1
Ain Ghazal Jordan Neolithic site 38/1
Ain Jalut Palestine ✕ 128/1, 137/1; battle of 129
Ain Qannas NE Arabia Chalcolithic site 39/1
Ain Mallah (*a/c* Eynan) Palestine early site 38/1
Ain Salah NW Africa Saharan trade 140/2, 164/2, 165/1
Air early state of W Africa 141/1, 165/1
Aire NW France fort 193/1
Airikina C India ✕Hun defeat of Guptas 83/4
air power World War II 270; Soviet Union 298
Aisne *river* NE France WW1 250-1
Aithaia S Greece Mycenaean site 67/1
Aix (*or* Aix-en-Provence *anc.* Aquae Sextiae) S France archbishopric 106/3; university founded 144/2; St Bartholomew Massacre 191/3; 17C revolts 185/1; parlement 193/1
Aix-la-Chapelle (*Ger.* Aachen) W Germany Carolingian capital 109/6; Treaty of 194
Aja early kingdoms of Nigeria 145/1
Ajanta C India Buddhist site 73/1
Ajayameru (*mod.* Ajmer) C India 83/1
Ajmer (*form.* Ajayameru) N India Mughal province 171/1; British rule 234/1; industry 235/3
Ajnadain Palestine ✕ 98/1
Akamagaseki (*n/c* Shimonoseki) W Japan 174/1
Akaroa S island, New Zealand French colony 236/4
Akbar Mughal emperor 170
Akhetaten (El Almarna]
Akhisar (Thyatira)
Akhmin S Egypt site 58/1
Akhtiar (Sevastopol)
Aki W Japan feudal province 123/2
Akita town and prefecture of N Japan; industry 242/1
Akkerman (*from 1946* Belgorod-Dnestrovskiy *anc.* Tyras

B

Bakhchesaray (*Turk.* Bahçesaray) Crimea Ottoman Empire 143/1
Bakhtrish (Bactria)
Baku Azerbaijan conquered by Ottomans 169/1; urban growth 231/1, 303/1; Russian Revolution 257/1; British occupation 257/1; WW2 271/2; industry 213/1, 231/1
Balaclava S Russia Crimean War 231/4
Balagansk SC Siberia founded 160/2
Bala-Kot NW India Harappan site 65/2
Balambangan district of Java Dutch control 176/3
Balanovka W Ukraine concentration camp 272/3
Balanovo C Russia early settlement 52/1
Balboa Panama 242/2
Bâle (Basle)
Baleares Insulae (*mod.* Baleares *Eng.* Balearic Islands) W Mediterranean Roman province 86/3; Byzantine Empire 112/1
Balearic Islands W Mediterranean taken by Vandals 97/2; attacked by Saracens 107/1; conquest by Pisa 121/2; reconquered by Aragon 111/2
Balfour Declaration 288
Bali early state of E Africa 145/1
Balita S India early port 21/1
Balkan League 249
Balkans rise of nationalism 211/2;alliances 248-9
Balkan Wars 249
Balkh (*anc.* Bactra *a/c* Zariaspa) Afghanistan Sasanid Empire 79/3; early church 101/1; Muslim conquest 99/1; Empire of Ghazni 128/2
Ballarat SE Australia goldfield 237/1
Ballinamuck Ireland ⚔ 195/3
Ballynagilly Ireland site 41/1
Baltic Viking trade 110/3; Swedish settlement 107/1; 188-9
Baltic Empire 189
Baltic States (Estonia, Latvia, Lithuania)
Baltimore E USA industry 287/1
Baluchistan region of NW India tribal agency 235/3; joins Pakistan after Partition 284/1, 285/3
Bamako W Africa reached by Mungo Park 234/2; occupied by French 241/1
Bamangwato tribe of S Africa 239/3
Bambara tribe of W Africa 239/1
Bamberg S Germany bishopric 101/2, 117/1, 190/1; massacre of Jews 103/3; medieval trade 120/1
Bamburgh NE England ⚔ 97/4
Bamiyan region of NW India 133/1
Bamongo tribe of W Belgian Congo 280/2
Banas dynasty of S India 130/2
Banat region of Hungary/Romania/Yugoslavia conquered by Habsburgs 197/4, 197/1; WW1 251/2
Banbury C England Industrial Revolution 201/1
Ban Chiang N Siam early site 47/1
Ban Chieng Hian N Thailand early site 47/1
Banda early state of E Africa 145/1
Bandar Abbas (*form.* Gombroon) SW Persia early trade 158/2; Ottoman siege 169/1
Bandjarmasin (*n/s* Banjarmasin) S Borneo Islamic town 134/2; early trading centre 177/1; WW2 269/2
Ban Don Ta Phet W Thailand early site 47/1
Bandung W Java early Japanese settlement 174/1
Bangalore S India industry 214/1
Bangarh E India site 64/3
Banghazi (Benghazi)
Bangka island E Sumatra Dutch settlement 177/1
Bangkok (*Thai.* Krung Thep) S Thailand early trade centre 174/1, 177/1; captured by Japanese 266/2
Bangladesh (*form.* East Pakistan *or* East Bengal) part of Pakistan 285/2; independence 276/2; 285/3; industry 304/1
Bangor N Ireland monastery 101/3
Bangor Wales monastery 101/3
Banja Luka N Bosnia civil war 301/3
Baniyas (Paneas)
Banjarmasin (Bandjarmasin)
Banjul (Bathurst)
banking Black Death and economic crisis 144; growth of 181; creation of modern credit structure 200; reform of European banking system 210; Middle East nationalization 290
Ban Llum Khao W Thailand early site 47/1
Ban Na Di N Thailand early site 47/1
Bannockburn C Scotland battle of 118; ⚔ 119/1, 118/2
Bannu (*form.* Edwardesabad) NW Pakistan industry 214/1
Banpo (Pan-p'o)
Ban Prasat C Thailand early site 47/1
Bantam (*form.* Banten) Java Islamic town 134/2; early trade 158/2, 177/1; sultanate under Dutch control 176/3
Banten (Bantam)
Ban Tha Kae S Thailand early site 47/1
Banyu (Pan-yü)
Banzart (Bizerta)
Bao'an (Pao-an)
Baoji (Pao-chi)
Baotou (Pao-t'ou)
Bapaume NW France fort 193/1
Bar W Ukraine concentration camp 272/3
Bar region of NE France/W Germany Burgundian possession 151/3; independent fief 151/2,3; duchy 190/1
Bara-Bahau SW France cave art 34/2
Barake S India early port 21/1
Baranovichi (*Pol.* Baranowicze) W Russia WW1 251/2
Barbados island of West Indies settled by English 158/3; British colony 227/1; 245/2; labour riots 258/1 (inset); independence 276/2 (inset); population growth 294/2
Barbalissus Syria ⚔ 78/3
Barbaricum port of NW India 41/1, 82/4
Barbuda island of West Indies settled by English 158/3; dependency of Antigua 276/2 (inset); population growth 294/2
Barca Libya ⚔ 78/1
Barcelona (*anc.* Barcino) NE Spain Jewish settlement 102/1, 103/3; Mediterranean trade 121/2, 145/1; urban revolt 145/1; 16C financial centre 180/1; 18C urban development 181/2; ⚔ 204/1; industrial development 211/1; Civil War 266/2
Barcelonette SE France fort 193/1
Barcino (Barcelona)
Bardaa NW Persia early archbishopric 101/1
Bardia (*n/s* Bardiyah) Libya WW2 271/2
Barduli (Barletta)
Bareilly N India Mutiny 234/1
Barguzinsk (*now* Barguzin) SC Siberia founded 160/2
Bari (*anc.* Barium) S Italy Saracen occupation 107/1; captured by Normans 121/2; university founded 144/1; 14C trade 145/1; WW2 271/2
Barium (*mod.* Bari) S Italy Roman Empire 87/1; Jewish community 103/4
Bar-le-Duc E France 190/1
Barletta (*anc.* Barduli) S Italy medieval city 117/1
Barmen-Elberfeld (*since 1930* Wuppertal) W Germany industrial development 211/1, 212/1
Barnard Castle N England ⚔ 185/1
Barnaul C Asia founded 160/2; industry 288/3, 289/1
Barnsley C England Industrial Revolution 201/1
Baroda C India industry 214/1
Barotseland SC Africa early state 239/1
Bar-sur-Aube C France medieval fair 120/1
Barygaza (*Skt.* Bhrigukaccha *mod.* Broach *n/s* Bharuch) NW India trading centre 71/1, 82/4, 83/1
Basel (*Fr.* Bâle *Eng.* Basle) Switzerland bishopric 190/1
Bashkir ASSR (*n/c* Bashkortostan) C Russia 300/2
Bashkirs Turkic people of C Russia 161/1, 300/2
Bashkortostan (*form.* Bashkir ASSR) C Russia 299/3
Basil II Bulgaroctonus Byzantine emperor 112
Basingstoke S England Industrial Revolution 201/1
Basle (*Fr.* Bâle *Ger.* Basel) Switzerland medieval trade 120/1; Reformation 183/1; bishopric 190/1; industrial development 211/1, 212/1
Basque Provinces N Spain reconquest by Castile 111/2; Spanish civil war 266/2; revolt of Vizcaya 184/2
Basque Republic N Spain autonomy 260/1
Basques people of N Spain and SW France 91/4, 97/3, 210/1
Basra (*Ar.* Al Basrah) Mesopotamia ⚔ 99/1; early archbishopric 101/1; Ottoman conquest 169/1; 18C trade 195/1; British control 224/2, 225/1; WW1 251/3
Bassano N Italy ⚔ 205/1
Bassein Burma early trade centre 177/1
Bassein (*Port.* Baçaim) W India Portuguese settlement 158/2, 171/1
Basse-Yutz E France Celtic site 85/1
Bastar princely state of C India 235/3
Basti district of N India ceded to Britain 170/3
Basutoland (*now* Lesotho) S Africa state 239/3; British colony 240/2, 245/2, 258/1, 277/1
Batanaea district of Judaea 103/3
Batavi tribe of the Netherlands 89/1
Batavia (*form.* Sunda Kalapa, *since 1949* Jakarta *f/s* Djakarta) Java early trade 158/2, 177/1, 195/1; Dutch control 176/3; port 195/1; WW2 268-9
Batavian Republic (*mod.* Netherlands) state established by French Revolution 202/2
Bath W England Industrial Revolution 201/1
Bathurst SE Australia founded 237/1
Bathurst (*now* Banjul) Gambia, W Africa British settlement 234/1; 287/1
Bato Cave E Philippines early site 47/1
Baton Rouge S USA ⚔ 218/1
beaurocracy Japan 242
battles *see individual entries*
Batu Khan invasion of Russia 114; invasion of Europe 128
Batumi (*f/s* Batum) Caucasus British occupation 257/1
Baturong N Borneo Neolithic cave 47/1
Batungan C Philippines early site 47/1
Bau Tro C Vietnam neolithic cave 47/1
Bautzen E Germany ⚔ 205/1
Bavaria (*Ger.* Bayern) conversion to Christianity 101/3; part of Frankish Empire 107/3; Magyar invasions 107/1; Wittelsbach territory 150/1; at 1382 147/1; Electorate 190/1; German Empire 217/3; customs union 217/1; short-lived soviet republic 256/2
Baxter Spring C USA cow town 218/1
Bayern (Bavaria)
Bayeux N France Scandinavian settlement 106/2
Bayezid II Ottoman sultan 142
Bayonne (*anc.* Lapurdum) SW France 18C financial centre 181/2; 17C revolt 185/1; 193/1
Bayreuth S Germany margraviate 190/1
Bayrut (Beirut)
Beans Store C USA cow town 218/1
Bear Island Spitsbergen discovered 156/1
Béarn region of SW France under English rule 119/1; acquired by France 147/4
Bear Paw Mountains C USA ⚔ 219/3
Bear Valley W USA mining site 218/1
Beas Valley NW India site 65/1
Beaulieu S England Industrial Revolution 201/1
Beaumanoir, Philippe de Remi sire de 118
beaurocracy Japan 242
Beauvais N France 17C revolt 185/1
Beaver NW Canada sub-arctic Indian tribe 149/1
Beç (Vienna)
Bechuanaland (*now* Botswana) country of S Africa, British protectorate 239/3, 240/2, 245/2, 258/1, 277/1
Bedcanford S England ⚔ 97/4
Bédeilhac S France cave art 34/2
Bedford S England Viking fort 106/2; Industrial Revolution 201/1
Bedsa (Karli)
Beersheba (*Heb.* Beer Sheva) S Israel WW1 251/3
Begho W Africa early trade 140/2
Begram (*anc.* Kapisa, *mod.* Begram) W Afghanistan Alexander's route 79/1
Beidha S Palestine early village 38/1
Beihai (Pakhoi)
Beijing (*Eng.*Peking, *W/G* Pei-ching) city-province of N China 280/)
Beiqu (Pei-ch'ü)
Beira SE Africa Portuguese occupation 241/1
Beirut (*anc.* Berytus *Fr.* Beyrouth *Ar.* Bayrut) Lebanon Mediterranean trade 137/1, 143/1; French control 225/1; disturbances under French mandate 259/2; civil war 283/4
Beisamoun S Syria early village 41/1
Beiyu (Pei-yü)
Beizhou (Pei-chou)
Bejaia (Saldae, Bougie, Bugia)
Bekaa Valley Lebanon occupied by Syria 290/2
Belarus (*a/c* Belorussia) economic union with Russia 299/3; independence from USSR 301/2
Belchete NE Spain Civil War 266/2
Belfast N Ireland industrial development 212/1
Belfast S Africa ⚔240/3
Belfort E France fort 193/1
Belgian Congo (*form.* Congo Free State *then* Zaire *now* Democratic Republic of Congo) colony 240/2, 245/2, 258/1, 277/1; uprising 246/1; independence 277/1,2
Belgica Roman province of NE France 89/1
Belgium (*form.* Spanish Netherlands *or* Southern Netherlands) industrial revolution 211/1, 212/1; colonial empire 245/2; WW1 250-1; overseas trade 254-5; acquisition of Eupen and Malmédy 263/1; economic and social development 1929-39 265/3-5, 264/2; WW2 267/4, 270-1; Marshall aid 276/2; EEC and NATO 273/1; economy 295/1; EU 300/1
Belgorod S Russia founded 161/1; WW2 269/5
Belgorod-Dnestrovskiy (Akkerman)
Belgrade (*anc.* Singidunum *S. Cr.* Beograd) C Yugoslavia ⚔ 129/1; Ottoman conquest 168/1; 18C urban development 180/1; peace of 196; WW1 251/2; WW2 267/4, 270-1
Belisarius Roman general takes Africa 91; Justinian's general 97
Belize city of C America founded by British 158/3, 163/1
Belize (*form.* British Honduras) independence 276/2 (inset); economy 295/1
Bell, Alexander 306
Bellary district of S India ceded to Britain 170/3
Belleau Wood NE France WW1 251/2 (inset)
Belorussia (Byelorussia, Belarus) SSR 300/2
Belostok (*now* Białystok) Poland in Russian Empire 231/1
Belsen (*correctly* Bergen-Belsen) N Germany concentration camp 272/3
Belzec S Poland concentration camp 272/3
Bemba tribe of Rhodesia 165/1, 239/1
Benares (*anc.* Kasi *now* Varanasi) N India 82/1, 130-1, 170/3; Hindu-Muslim clashes 285/3
Bender (*mod.* Bendery *Rom.* Tighina) S Russia Ottoman conquest 168/1
Bendigo SE Australia goldfield 237/1
Benevento (*anc.* Beneventum) C Italy 107/1; dukedom under Byzantine Empire 113/1; ⚔ 146/3 principality 209/5
Beneventum (*mod.* Benevento) C Italy Roman Empire 87/1, 89/1
Bengal country of E India 132/4; under Mughal Empire 169/1, 171/1; under British rule 170/3, 194/2, 235/3; anti-colonial revolt 247/1, 259/1; partition between India and Pakistan 285/2, 285/3
Benghazi (*anc.* Berenice *Ar.* Banghazi) Libya Ottoman rule 225/1, 239/1; Italian occupation 241/1; WW2 267/4, 271/2
Benguela Angola Portuguese settlement 165/1, 239/1, 241/1; 18C trade 195/1
Beni Hasan N Egypt site 58/1
Benin early state of Nigeria 141/1, 165/1, 239/1
Benin (*form.* Dahomey) country of W Africa independence 276/2
Benkulen Sumatra trading post 177/1
Benqi (Penki)
Bentheim W Germany country 190/1
Bentonville E USA ⚔ 223/1
Bent's Fort C USA fur station 218/1
Benz, Karl 306
Beograd (Belgrade)
Beothuk Newfoundland Indian tribe 149/1
Berar C India sultanate 132/4, 171/1; tribal territory 235/3
Berbati S Greece Mycenaean site 67/1
Berbera Somalia Muslim Colony 141/1; British occupation 241/1
Berbers people of NW Africa 91/4; attack Roman Africa 94/1; incursions into Morocco 136/1
Berenice Red Sea early trading port 41/1, 82/4; Roman Empire 88/2
Berenice (*mod.* Benghazi) Libya city of Roman Empire 89/1, 88/2
Berezina river of W Russia ⚔ 205/1
Berezov (*now* Berezovo) W Siberia founded 161/1
Berg W Germany Reformation 191/3; duchy 190/1, 204/2
Berg S Norway concentration camp 272/3
Bergama (Pergamum)
Bergamo (*anc. Bergomum*) N Italy medieval city 117/1
Bergen Norway bishopric 101/2; 14C trade 145/1; WW2 267/4
Bergen (Mons)
Bergen Belsen (Belsen)
Bergomum (*mod.* Bergamo) N Italy invaded by Huns 98/1
Bering Strait N Pacific European discovery 157/3,199/2
Berlin Germany 18C urban development 181/2; urban development 191/2; industrial development 211/1, 212/1; Congress of 247; WW1 251/2; Communist uprising 256/2, 260/2; WW2 270-1; divided 273/4; Cold War 292/2; airlift 296
Bermuda British colony in W Atlantic, 245/2
Bern (*Fr.* Berne) Switzerland Zähringen town 121/6; Reformation 183/1; industrial development 212/1
Bernburg C Germany concentration camp 272/3
Bernicia region of NE England Anglo-Saxon invasion 97/4
Bernifal S France cave art 34/2
Beroea (*mod.* Veroia) N Greece Christian community 93/1; Jewish community 103/4
Beroea (Aleppo) Syria rebuilt 78/1
Berry region of C France Frankish Royal domain 119/1, 151/3; province 193/1
Bersham N England Industrial Revolution 201/1
Berytus (*mod.* Beirut) Lebanon Roman Empire 89/1, 88/2
Besançon (*anc.* Vesontio) E France archbishopric 104/2; gained by France 192/2; French Revolution 202/2
Beshbalik W Mongolia 129/1,3
Besigheim W Germany Mithraic site 72/1
Bessarabia region of Romania/Russia acquired by Russia 161/1; Ottoman province 229/1; lost to Romania 257/1; regained by Russia 263/1, 267/4; regained by Romania 273/1
Beta king of Aragon 110
Beth Katraye SE Arabia early church 101/1
Bethlehem Palestine Christian centre 93/1, 2
Béthune N France fort 193/1
Betsileo Kingdom Madagascar 239/1
Beverley NE England Industrial Revolution 201/1
Bewdley W England Industrial Revolution 201/1
Beyrouth (Beirut)
Bhabra (Bairat)
Bhagatrav NW India Harappan site 65/2
Bhagavad-gita 130
Bhaja (Karli)
Bhakra-Nangal N India dam 285/3
Bharuch (Broach)
Bhilai C India steel plant 285/3
Bhonsla state of C India 170/3; alliance with Britain 194/2 (inset)
Bhopal C India chemical plant 285/3
Bhubaneshwar E India attacked by Cholas 131/1
Bhutan Himalayan kingdom 235/3, 285/3; end of Chinese tributary status 232/2; British influence 277/1
Biafra E Nigeria civil war 287/1
Białystok (*Russ.* Belostok) W Poland to Germany 1941 273/1
Biak NW New Guinea captured by US 269/2
Bianzhou (Pien-chou)
Bibracte C France Roman Empire 86/3
Bicocca N Italy ⚔ 186/2
Bidar sultanate of S India, 132/4
Big Bell W Australia gold town 237/1
Big Hole NW USA ⚔ 219/3
Big Mound N USA ⚔ 219/3
Bigorre region of SW France under English rule 119/1; independent fief 151/3
Bihac N Bosnia civil war 303/4
Bihar state of E India Muslim expansion 99/2; Sultanate of Delhi 133/1; Mughal Empire 171/1; under British control 170/3, 194/2; 235/3, 285/3
Bijapur sultanate of SW India, 132/4, 171/1
Bilá Hora (White Mountain)
Bilbao N Spain 18C financial centre 181/2; industrial development 211/1, 212/1; Civil War 266/2
Bilma W Africa early trade 140/2, 165/1; occupied by French 241/1
Biloxi S USA fur station 218/1
Bilston C England Industrial Revolution 200/3
Bilzingsleben Germany site of early man 32/2
Bimlipatan NE India Dutch settlement 171/1
Bindon SW England ⚔ 97/4
Bingcheng (Ping-ch'eng)
Bingen W Germany Mithraic site 72/1
Bingham Canyon W USA mines 220/3
Binh Chau C Vietnam early site 47/1
Binh Dinh (Vijaya)
Bioko (Fernando Po)
Bird Creek C USA ⚔ 219/3
Birkenhead N England Industrial Revolution 200/3
Birmingham C England 18C urban development 181/2; Industrial Revolution 200/3, 201/1; industrial development 211/1, 212/1; bombed in WW2 267/4
Bisa tribe of C Africa, 239/1
Bisbee SW USA mine 220/3
Bishapur S Persia town of Parthian Empire 79/3
Bishopbridge E England Industrial Revolution 201/1
Bishop's Stortford S England Industrial Revolution 201/1
Bismarck, Otto Furst von German unification 215; minister-president 217; German role in Europe 248
Bithynia ancient country of NW Anatolia 77/1, 78/1; Roman province 86/3; Byzantine Empire 113/1
Bithynia and Pontus Anatolia Roman province 89/1
Bitlis E Anatolia Byzantine Empire 113/1
Bitolj (*n/s* Bitola *Turk.* Manastir *a/s* Monastir) S Yugoslavia Ottoman control 143/1
Biysk Russ. C Asia founded 160/2
Bizerta (*anc.* Hippo Zarytus *Fr.* Bizerte *Ar.* Banzart) Tunisia Spanish occupation 187/1; WW2 271/2
Bjerre N Denmark Megalithic site 40/2
Blackburn NE England Industrial Revolution 200/3
Blackburn S Africa Iron Age site 43/1
Blackfoot W Canada Plains Indian tribe 149/1
Black Forest SW Germany colonization 121/3; 18C industrial growth 191/2
Blackheath S England ⚔ 185/1
Black Patch S England Megalithic site 40/2
Black Sea early trade 52/1
Blagoveshchensk Russ. Far East 227/2
Blekinge region of S Sweden under Danish rule 109/2; acquired by Sweden 188/3
Blemmyes early people of NE Africa 99/2
Blenheim (*Ger.* Blindheim) W Germany ⚔ (called Höchstädt by French and Germans) 192/3
Blenheim S Island, New Zealand founded 236/4
Blinkklipkop S Africa early site 43/1
Bloemfontein S Africa Boer War siege 240/3
Blois region of N France 151/3
Bloody Brook NE USA ⚔ 219/3
Bloody Ridge NE USA ⚔ 219/3
Bloody Run NE USA ⚔ 219/3
Blue Fish Caves Alaska site of early man 31/1
Blue Turks tribe of Mongolia 95/1
Bluff S Island, New Zealand aluminium 236/6
Bobangi early state of C Africa 239/1
Bobo Dioulasso W Africa early trade 140/2
Bobriki (Novomoskovsk)
Bodhgaya NE India Buddhist site 73/1, 82/1
Bodiam SE England Industrial Revolution 201/1
Bodrum (Halicarnassus)
Boeotia ancient country of C Greece, Persian influence 77/2
Boer Republic S Africa 239/3
Boers 238
Boğazköy (*anc.* Hattushash *Gr.* Pteria) C Anatolia site 66/1
Boğdan (*Eng. Moldavia*) vassal state of Ottoman Empire 143/1
Bohai (Po-hai)
Bohemia (*Ger.* Böhmen) W part of mod. Czechoslovakia occupied by Poland 108/3; medieval German Empire 117/1; Black Death 145/1; acquired by Habsburgs 150/1,2, 187/1, 197/1; Thirty Years' War 191/3; Reformation 183/1; 18C industrial growth 191/2; kingdom within Holy Roman Empire 190-1; conquest by Prussia 196/2; Austro-Hungarian Empire 197/1, 263/1
Bohuslän province of S Sweden acquired from Denmark 188/1
Boker Tachtit E Egypt site of early man 31/1
Boleslaw I Chrobry 1st king of Poland 109
Boleslaw I prince of Bohemia 109
Bolgar (*a/c* Bulgar) C Russia city of the Volga Bulgars 114/4, 115/1, 128/1
Bolivar, Simón 226
Bolivia country of S America independence 226-7, 245/2; exports and foreign investments 226/3; population 222/4; 20C revolutions 292-3; economy 294/1
Bologna (*anc.* Felsina *later* Bononia) N Italy Mithraic site

72/1; medieval city 117/1, 146/3; university founded 144/2; 18C urban development 181/2
Bolsheretsk Russ. Far East founded 160/2,199/2
Bolsheviks 256
Bolton N England Industrial Revolution 200/3, 201/1
Bombay W India early church 100/1; early trade 158/2, 170/2, 195/1; British settlement 171/1; British rule 234/1; industry 235/3; British naval base 244/2; Shiv Sena disturbances and Hindu-Muslim clashes 285/3
Bombo Kaburi E Africa Iron Age site 43/1
Bona (*mod.* Annaba *Fr.* Bône) N Algeria acquired by Habsburgs 150/1,2; Spanish occupation 187/1
Bonaire island of Dutch West Indies 227/1, 245/2, 276/2 (inset)
Bonampak E Mexico Maya site 60/2
Bonaparte, Jerome 204
Bonaparte, Joseph 204
Bonaparte, Louis 204
Bondu early state of W Africa 234/1
Bône (*mod.* Annaba *Sp.* Bona *anc.* Hippo Regius) N Algeria Pisan raids 121/2; French invasion 239/1
Boniface VIII, Pope 'two sword' theory 100, kidnapped 117; Sardinia 146
Bonin Islands (*a/c* Ogasawara Islands) N Pacific annexed by Japan 243/2; WW2 268-9
Bonna (*mod.* Bonn) W Germany Roman Empire 88/2
Bonny W Africa 18C trade 195/1
Bono early state of W Africa 145/1
Bono Manso W Africa early trade 140/2
Bononia (*earlier* Felsina *mod.* Bologna) N Italy Roman Empire 87/1, 89/1
Boomplaas S Africa cave art 35/1
Boone, Daniel 218
Bophuthatswana S Africa independent Bantustan 286/2, 287/1
Bordeaux (*anc.* Burdigala) SW France Christian centre 92/1; early archbishopric 104/2; occupied by English 140/4; university founded 144/2; 14C trade 145/1; 16C urban development 180/1; 18C financial centre 181/2; Ormée revolt 185/1; St Bartholomew Massacre 191/3; industry 193/1; French Revolution 202/2
Border Cave S Africa site of early man 31/1
Borger Holland site 40/2
Borgu States W Africa 145/1, 165/1
Borneo (*Indon.* Kalimantan) island of East Indies Muslim expansion 98/3, 134/2; Dutch trade 177/1; Dutch and British colonization 245/2; WW2 268-9; confrontation with Malaysia 283/1
Bornholm Danish island of S Baltic Swedish Rule 189/1
Bornhöved N Germany ⚔ 117/1
Borno Nigeria early state 165/1, 239/1
Borobudur C Java Buddhist site 73/1; political centre 135/1
Borodino W Russia ⚔ 205/1
Bororo forest Indian tribe of S Brazil 149/1
Bosanska Krupa N Bosnia civil war 301/3
Bose, Subhas Chandra 235
Bosiljgrad (*n/s* Bosilegrad) E Serbia annexed from Bulgaria 1919 262/2
Bosna Saray (*n/c* Sarajevo) C Yugoslavia captured by Ottomans 143/1
Bosnia country of C Yugoslavia vassal state of Ottoman Empire 143/1; Black Death 145/1; at 1380 147/1
Bosnia-Herzegovina (*S. Cr.* Bosna i Hercegovina) region of S Yugoslavia part of Austria-Hungary 211/2; under Ottoman rule 229/1; Balkan Wars 248/2; after WW1 263/1; civil war 301/2
Bosnians people of C Yugoslavia 261/3; 302
Bosporan Kingdom S Russia 86/3, 89/1
Boston E England Industrial Revolution 201/1
Boston NE USA founded 162/2; British naval base 194/1; trade 194/3
Boston Post Road NE USA 218/1
Bostra S Syria Roman fort 88/2
Botany Bay SE Australia penal settlement 237/1
Botocudo Indian tribe of S Brazil 149/1
Botsu S Japan early port 174/1
Botswana (*form.* Bechuanaland) S Africa independence 276/2; political development 287/1; economy 304/1
Bouchain N France fort 193/1
Bouga S Greece Mycenaean site 67/1
Bougainville one of Solomon Islands, W Pacific WW2 268-9
Bougie (*anc.* Saldae *Sp.* Bugia *mod.* Bejaia) N Algeria Genoese raids 121/2; captures by Almohads 136/2; 14C trade 145/1
Bougon N France Megalithic site 40/2
Boulogne (*anc.* Gesoriacum) N France fort 193/1
Boulonnais region of NE France Burgundian possession 151/2
Bouqras SE Syria early village 39/1
Bourbon (*now.* Réunion) island of Indian Ocean French possession 194/2
Bourbon (Bourbonnais)
Bourbons 205
Bourbonnais (*a/c* Bourbon) region of C France Royal domain 119/1; annexed to France 150/1, 151/3
Boure early state of W Africa 134/1
Bourges (*anc.* Avaricum) C France massacre of Jews 103/3; 17C revolt 185/1; St Bartholomew Massacre 191/3;193/1
Bourg-la-Reine C France medieval *villeneuve* 121/6
Bourgogne (Burgundy)
Bourg-St Andéol S France Mithraic site 72/1
Bourguiba, Habib 259
Bourne E England Industrial Revolution 201/1
Boussargues S France early settlement 41/3
Bouvines NE France ⚔ 119/1, 119/1
Boxer Rebellion matters leading to 232; Sino-Japanese war and 247
Boxgrove S England site of early man 31/1
Boyacá Colombia ⚔ 227/2
Bozeman Trail and Pass NW USA 218/1
Brabant region of Belgium/Holland medieval German Empire 117/1, 119/1; at 1380 147/1; Burgundian possession 151/2
Bracara (*mod.* Braga) Portugal archbishopric
Bracton, Henry de 118
Bradford N England Industrial Revolution 201/1
Braga (*anc.* Bracara) N Portugal Christian centre 92/1
Brahmagiri S India site 64/3
brain evolution of human 30, 31; Neanderthal 33
Branč Czechoslovakia burial site 41/3
Branco, Cape W Africa Portuguese exploration 164/2
Brandenburg region of E Germany Black Death 145/1; Hohenzollern territory 150/1; at 1380 147/1; Electorate 190-1; 18C industrial growth 191/2; Thirty Years' War 191/3; Reformation 191/3, 183/1; part of Prussia 217/3
Brassempouy S France cave art 34/2
Brass Nigeria 18C trade 195/1; early European settlement 239/1
Bratislava (*Ger.* Pressburg *Hung.* Pozsony) Slovakia WW1 251/2
Bratsk SC Siberia founded 160/2
Braunschweig (Brunswick)
Brazil early sites 45/1, 61/1; Portuguese colony 154/1, 163/1; discovered 156/1; Atlantic trade 194/3; immigration from Europe 209/3; population 222/4; exports and foreign investment 226/3; independent Empire 227/1, 245/2; industrialization and economy 265/3-5, 284-5, 294/1, 302-7; Japanese investment 279/4; environment 309/1
Brazza, Pierre Savorgnan de 240
Brcko E Bosnia civil war 301/3
Brecon W Wales Industrial Revolution 201/1
Breedonk Belgium concentration camp 272/3
Bredveit S Norway concentration camp 272/3
Breisach W Germany gained by France 192/2
Breitenfeld E Germany ⚔ 191/3; battle of 267
Bremen N Germany bishopric 101/3; archbishopric 190/1; 14C trade 145/1; Reformation 191/3, 183/1; urban development 191/2; industrial development 211/1; German customs union 217/1; WW1 251/2; short-lived Soviet Republic 256/2; WW2 271/2
Bremen and Verden region of N Germany Swedish rule 188/1
Bremerhaven N Germany WW1 251/2
Brenta, River N Italy ⚔ 107/1
Brescia (*anc.* Brixia) N Italy medieval city 117/1, 146/3
Breslau (*n/c* Wrocław) W Poland Jewish settlement 102/1; 18C financial centre 181/2; Reformation 183/1; urban and industrial development 191/2, 211/1, 213/1; WW1 251/2
Brest NW France fort 193/1; naval base 195/1; French Revolution 202/2
Brest (*a/c* Brest-Litovsk *Pol.* Brześć nad Bugiem) W Russia Jewish settlement 102/1; 231/1, 257/1; WW1 251/2
Bretagne (Brittany)
Bretons Celtic people of NW France, 91/4, 105/1, 210/1
Bretteville-le-Rabet N France Megalithic site 40/2
Brezhnev, Leonid agriculture and industry 298
Brian Boru king of Ireland 108
Briançon SE France fort 193/1
Bridgnorth W England Industrial Revolution 201/1
Bridgwater W England Industrial Revolution 201/1
Brieg (*Pol.* Brzeg) W Poland Reformation 191/3
Brigantes Britain early tribe 88/1
Brigetio Hungary Mithraic site 72/1; Roman Empire 88/2
Brihuega C Spain ⚔ 192/3
Brindisi (*anc.* Brundisium) S Italy captured by Normans 121/2; WW1 251/2
Brisbane E Australia founded 237/1
Bristol W England 18C urban development 181/2; industrial development 201/1, 212/1; bombed in WW2 267/4
Britain Celtic sites 45/1, 61/1; conversion to Christianity 72/1; invasion by Germanic tribes 96/1, 97/4; 18C trade 194; battle of 267. See also England, Kingdom
Britanniae Roman prefecture of Britain 88/2
Britannia Inferior Roman province of N England, 88/1
Britannia Superior Roman province of S England 88/1
British Bechuanaland S Africa 241/1, 240/3
British Cameroons (*now part of* Cameroon) W Africa protectorate 258/1, 277/1
British Columbia province of W Canada border dispute with Alaska 242/3; joins Confederation 245/2;
British East Africa (*now* Kenya) colony 240/2, 241/1, 245/2, 246/1, 258/1
British Empire 195; 245/2
British Guiana (*now* Guyana) S America colony 227/1, 245/2; labour riots 258/1 (inset)
British Honduras (*now* Belize) C America colony 227/1, 245/2, 243/4
British North Borneo (*now* Sabah) protectorate 259/1, 277/1
British Somaliland (*now part of* Somalia) E Africa protectorate 240/2, 245/2, 258/1, 276/2
British, the voyages of exploration 157; and Southeast Asia 176; American immigrants 224
Britons tribe of SW England, movement to Brittany 98/1
Brittany (*Fr.* Bretagne) NW France on borders of Frankish Empire 104/2; Angevin Empire 118/3; conquered by Normans 119/1; Black Death 145/1; annexed to France 151/3
Brivas C France monastery 93/3
Brixia (*mod.* Brescia) N Italy attacked by Goths 98/1
Brno (*Ger.* Brünn) Moravia WW1 251/2
Broach (*anc.* Barygaza *mod.* Bharuch) NW India ceded to Britain 170/2
Brody SE Poland WW1 251/2
Broederstroom S Africa early site 43/1
Brogne S Belgium monastic reform 116/3
Broken Hill SE Australia mining 237/1
Bronze Age southeast Asia 46; collapse of empires 58; China 62; Mycenaean power 67; Europe 84
bronze North Africa 42; ancient Eurasia 52, 53; bronze-working under Hyksos 56
Broome W Australia early settlement 237/1
Broseley C England Industrial Revolution 200/3, 201/1
Brouage W France port 193/1
Bucer, Martin 182
Buddha, Gautama (personal name Siddhārtha Gautama) background 65; teaching of 73
Buddhism basis for development of 64; reaction to tensions of the age 73; formulation 82; Ashoka 82; Kanishka 82; spread of 82; Japan 122; under Western Chin 124; Mongols and 128, 129; early India 130; university 130; in southeast Asia 134; Sri Lanka 284
Bruges (*Dut.* Brugge) Belgium medieval city 117/1, 120/1; urban revolt 145/1; Hanseatic city 142/1; 16C urban development 180/1; town of Spanish Netherlands 185/1; WW1 250-1
Brundisium (*mod.* Brindisi) S Italy Latin colony 87/1; Roman Empire 89/1, 88/2; Byzantine Empire 113/1
Brunei sultanate of N Borneo spread of Islam 98/3, early Japanese settlement 174/1; early trade 177/1; recaptured from Japanese 269/2; independence 276/2; British troops 278/3; Azahari revolt 283/1; oil 304/1
Brunete C Spain Civil War 266/2
Bruniquel S France cave art 34/2
Brünn (*Cz.* Brno) Czechoslovakia urban and industrial development 191/2, 213/1
Brunswick (*Ger.* Braunschweig) N Germany early city and duchy 117/1; urban revolt 145/1; German state 217/3; WW1 251/2
Brunswick-Lüneburg duchy of N Germany Reformation 183/1; 190/1
Brunswick-Wolfenbüttel duchy of N Germany 190/1
Brusa (Bursa)
Brussels (*Fr.* Bruxelles *Dut.* Brussel) Belgium 16C urban development 180/1; 18C urban development 181/2; city of Spanish Netherlands 185/1, 190/1; industrial development 211/1, 212/1; WW1 251/2; WW2 267/4, 271/2
Bruttii ancient tribe of S Italy 86/2
Bruxelles (Brussels)
Bryansk W Russia town of Novgorod-Seversk 115/1; WW2 271/2,5
Brycheiniog early principality of S Wales 109/1
Brzeg (Brieg)
Bubastis (mod. Tell Basta) Lower Egypt 58/1; Jewish community 103/4
Bucellarian Theme Byzantine province of C Anatolia, 113/3
Bucephala NW India on Alexander's route 79/1, 82/3
Bucharest (*Rom.* București *Turk.* Bükreş) Romania in Ottoman Empire 225/1; WW1 251/2; railway strike 264/2; WW2 270-1
Buchenwald W Germany concentration camp 272/3
Buckingham S England Industrial Revolution 201/1
București (Bucharest)
Buczacz, peace of 196
Buda Hungary Ottoman conquest 168/1
Budapest Hungary Jewish settlement 102/1; 18C urban development 181/2; industrial development 211/1, 213/1; WW1 251/2; WW2 270-1
Budaun region of N India 133/1
Buddha (*personal name* Siddhartha Guatama) teaching of 73
Buddhism reaction to tensions of the age 73
Buddhists Tamils and 284
Buenos Aires Argentina colonized 154/1, 163/1; trade 194/3
Buganda state of E Africa 165/1
Bugia (anc. Saldae *Fr.* Bougie *mod.* Bejaia) Algeria acquired by Habsburgs 187/1
Bugojno C Bosnia civil war 301/3
Buhen S Egypt 12th Dynasty fort 57/3
Bui Ceri Uato E Timor Neolithic cave 47/1
buildings Neolithic temples 39; prehistoric mudbrick 40; Mesoamerican pyramids 44; Egyptian pyramids 56; Karnak temples 56; Nimrud palace 58; Minoan 'Old Palaces' and 'New Palace Period' 66; Greek temples 76; cathedral of St Sophia 91; Rhineland cathedral-building 120; Kalaisanatha temple at Ellora 130; Hindu temples 133, 134; Aztec monumental stone 148; Taj Mahal 168, 170
Bujak vassal state of Ottoman Empire in SW Russia 143/1
Bukavu E Belgian Congo Congo crisis 280/2
Bukhara city and province of C Asia limit of Alexander's route 79/1, 822; early church 101/1; Muslim conquest 99/1; under Abbasids 109/1; in Timur's empire 128/4; khanate 169/1, 225/1, 230/2
Bukit Tengku Lembu N Malaya Neolithic cave 47/1
Bukit Tinggi (Fort de Kock)
Bukovina region of Romania gained by Habsburgs 197/1; WW1 251/2
Bükreş (*Eng.* Bucharest *Rom.* București) Romania Ottoman control 143/1
Bulandshar N India Indian Mutiny 234/1
Bulgar (Bolgar)
Bulgaria conversion to Christianity 101/2; Muslim control 107/1; Slav settlement 112/2; Empire 112/4; Mongol invasion 129/2; Christian state 142/2; under Ottoman rule 143/1, 229/1; Black Death 145/1; at 1382 147/1; population growth 209/2; independence 211/2, 231/4; Balkan Wars 248/2; Balkan League 249/1; WW1 250-1; Communist uprising 256/2; conflict with Greece 263/1; socio-political change 1929-39 264/2; WW2 267/4, 270-1; 273/1; communism overthrown 301/2,
Bulgarians emigration from Greece and Turkey 261/3
Bulgars tribe of Europe 98/1; Christianity 110; settle in Balkans 112; middle Volga 114
Bull Run (*a/c* Manassas) SE USA ⚔ 223/1
Buna SE New Guinea recaptured by Allies 269/2
Bunce Island Sierra Leone British settlement 158/2, 164/1
Bundelkhand district of C India 235/3
Buni W Java early site 47/1
Bunker Hill NE USA ⚔ 202/3
Buntoto early state of E Africa 239/1
Bunyoro early state of E Africa 165/1
Büraburg W Germany bishopric 101/3
Burdigala (*mod.* Bordeaux) SW France Roman Empire 88/1, 88/2
Buret Siberia cave art 35/1
Burgdorf E Switzerland Zähringen town 121/6
Burgos N Spain massacre of Jews 103/3; Santa Junta 184/2; Civil War 266/2
Burgundiones (*Eng.* Burgundians) early tribe of Germany 89/1; invade France 98/1,2
Burgundy (*Fr.* Bourgogne) region of E France kingdom 91/4, 97/3; kingdom conquered by Franks 105/1,3; 107/1; province of medieval German Empire 116-7; French Royal domain 119/1; acquisitions 14C and 15C 140/4; Black Death 145/1; annexed to France 150/1, 151/3; possessions in Low Countries 151/2; 16C revolts 185/1; province of France 193/1
Burgundians 97
Burkina Fasso (*f/c* Upper Volta) country of W Africa political development 287/1
Burlag Siberia labour camp zone 299/1
Burma (*a/c* Myanmar) spread of Buddhism 73/1; early state 135/1; tributary state of Chinese Empire 173/1, 232/2; conquests 177/1; annexed by Britain 234/2; under British rule 235/3, 245/2, 259/1; anti-colonial resistance 247/1; Japanese support for independence movements 266/1; Japanese occupation 268/1; British recapture 269/2; independence 276/2; boundary agreements with China 283/1; economic development 278/3, 285/3; Chinese settlement 283/4; armaments 302/2; environment 309/1
Burma Road SW China 266/1, 266/2
Burmese empire 176
Burnley N England Industrial Revolution 201/1
Burnt Corn SE USA ⚔ 219/3
Bursa (*anc.* Prusa *later* Brusa) W Anatolia Jewish settlement 102/1; Byzantine Empire 133/2; centre of Ottoman state 143/1
Burundi (*form.* Urundi) country of C Africa native state 165/1, 239/1; independence 276/2; political development 287/1; economy 304/1. See also Ruanda-Urundi
Burwell E England Industrial Revolution 201/1
Bury N England Industrial Revolution 200/3, 201/1
Buryatia (*form.* Buryat Mongol ASSR) E Russia 299/3
Buryat-Mongol ASSR (*n/c* Buryatia) E USSR 300/2
Buryats Mongolian tribe 129/1
Bury St Edmunds E England Industrial Revolution 201/1
Bushehr Bushire)
Bushire (*Pers.* Bushehr) Persian Gulf 128/2
Bushmen tribe of S Africa 239/3
Bushy Run NE USA ⚔ 219/3
Busiris Lower Egypt ancient city 58/1
Bussa W Africa reached by Mungo Park 234/2
Buto (*mod.* Tell el Fara'in) Lower Egypt capital 58/1
Butte NW USA mine 220/3
Buwayhids (Buyids)
Buxar NE India ⚔ 194/2 (inset)
Buxentum S Italy Roman colony 87/1
Buyids (*a/c* Buwayhids) Muslim dynasty of Persia 137/1
Byblos (*mod.* Jubail) Syria early trade 54/1, 58/1, 66/3; Phoenician city 59/3, 77/1; Alexander's route 78/1
Byelorussia (Belorussia)
Bylany Czechoslovakia site 41/1, 85/1
Byneskranskop S Africa early site 43/1
Byzantine Empire (*a/c* East Roman Empire) 98/1, 112-3, 121/2; dismembered 111; loss of territory 112; Crusades and 112; last centuries 113; conflict with Seljuks 137/1; decline 142/2; at 1382 147/1; overthrow of 182
Byzantines ousted 97; Asia Minor 98; Orthodox church 100; missionaries 110; Fatimids, Umayyads and 136
Byzantion W India early port 71/1
Byzantium (*Eng.* Constantinople *Norse* Mikligard *mod.* Istanbul) E Thrace Roman Empire 41/1, 89/1, 88/2; Achaemenid Empire 74/1; Dorian colony 76-7

Cabeço da Arruda C Portugal Megalithic site 40/2
Cabinda coastal district of SW Africa occupied by Portuguese 241/1; part of Angola 277/1
Cacas dynasty of NW India 130/1
Cacaxtla Mexico Classic site 60/2
Cáceres W Spain Civil War 266/2
Cachar district of E India 234/2
Cacheu W Africa Portuguese settlement 164/1
Caddo S USA Indian tribe 149/1
Cádiz (*anc.* Gades) SW Spain reconquered from Muslims 111/2; 18C urban development 181/2; imperial trade 194/3; naval base 195/1; Civil War 266/2
Caen N France university founded 144/1; 185/1, 193/1; French Revolution 202/2; WW2 271/2,6
Caere (*mod.* Cerveteri) C Italy Etruscan city 77/1; Roman Empire 87/1
Caerleon (Iscal)
Caernarvon (*Wel.* Caernarfon *anc.* Segontium) N Wales ancient principality 119/1
Caesaraugusta (*mod.* Zaragoza *Eng.* Saragossa) N Spain Roman Empire 89/1, 88/2
Caesarea C Israel Roman Empire 89/1, 88/2, 92/2; Christian centre 93/1; town of Judaea 103/3; Byzantine Empire 112/2
Caesarea (*mod.* Cherchell) N Algeria Roman Empire 89/1; Christian centre 92/1
Caesarea (*mod.* Kayseri) C Anatolia Roman Empire 89/1, 92/2; Jewish community 103/4; Byzantine Empire 113/1,5
Caesarea Cappadociae (*mod.* Kayseri) C Anatolia Christian centre 93/1
Caesarea Philippi (Paneas)
Caesar, Julius 88
Caesarodunum (Tours)
Caesaromagus (Chelmsford)
Cagayan N Philippines early site 47/1
Cafer Höyük E Anatolia Neolithic site 38/1
Caffa (*a/s* Kaffa) Crimea 14C trade 145/1
Cagliari (*anc.* Carales)Sardinia Christian centre 92/1; 14C trade 145/1
Cahokia C USA early site 61/1, 3; French post 162/2; fur station 218/1
Cahors S France university founded 144/2; 17C revolt 185/1
Cahuachi C Andes site 61/1
Cai (Ts'ai)
Caiguá forest Indian tribe of S Brazil 149/1
Cairns E Australia early settlement 237/1
Cairo (*Fr.* Le Caire *Ar.* Al Qahirah and Al Fustat - Old Cairo) Egypt Muslim conquest 99/1; early trade 141/1; captured by Ottomans 143/1; Ottoman Empire 168/1, 225/1; WW1 251/3
Cajamarca C Andes site 60/4, 5; 149/3; Pizarro captures Atahuallpa 161/4
Cajamarqilla C Andes site 60/5
Cajon Pass SW USA 218/1
Calabria region of S Italy part of Kingdom of Naples 146/3
Calagurris (*mod.* Calahorra) N Spain Roman Empire 88/1
Calah (*OT* Kalhu *mod.* Nimrud) Mesopotamia capital of Assyria 58/1
Calahorra (Calgurris)
Calais N France WW1 251/2; WW2 271/2
Calakmul E Mexico early site 60/2
Calcutta E India trade 158/2, 195/1; British settlement 171/1; 18C trade 195/1; industry 214/1, 235/3; British naval base 244/2
Çaldiran (*a/s* Chaldiran) E Turkey battle of 142; ⚔ 143/1
Caldy Island S Wales monastery 101/3
Caledonia (*mod.* Scotland) Roman Empire 91/2, 96/1
Cales C Italy Latin colony 87/1
Calicut (*a/c* Kozhikode) SW India trade 151/1, 159/1;

attacked by Mongols 129/1; invaded by Japan 166/1; invaded by Manchus 173/1; end of Chinese tributary status 232/2; Russo-Japanese war 243/3; acquired by Japan 243/2, 245/2, 258/3; 268-9; 278-9; 1950-3 war 278/3; development after 1941 279/1
Korea, North economy 295/1; armaments 302/2
Korea, South US bases 275/1;Japanese investment 279/4, 282/2; armaments 302/2; population 303/3
Korean War and Japanese economic recovery 278; US involvement 296
Korsun (Khersones)
Korti C Sudan Relief of Khartoum 247/2
Kortrijk (Courtrai)
Koryak AD Russ. Far East 300/2, 299/3
Koryaks tribe of Russ. Far East 160/2
Koryo (Korea)
Kos S Aegean WW2 271/2
Kosala early kingdom of N India 82/1, 83/2
Kosciuszko, Tadeusz 197
Koselsk C Russia town of Chernigov 115/1
Koshu-kaido early highway of C Japan 175/2
Košice (*Hung.* Kassa) Czechoslovakia industrial development 213/1
Kosogorsk SE Siberia founded 160/2
Kosovo (*properly* Kosovo Polje *a/s* Kossovo *Ger.* Amselfeld) S Yugoslavia battle of 142; ⚔ 143/1, 139/1
Kossuth, Lajos 214
Koster C USA early site 45/1
Kostenki W USSR site of early man 31/1, 35/1
Kostroma W Russia Russian Revolution 257/1
Köszeg (Güns)
Kota Tampan W Malaya early site 47/1
Kot Diji N India Harappan site 65/2
Kotor (Cattaro)
Kotosh C Peru early site 45/3
Kottayam S India early church 100/1
Koufonisi E Crete Minoan site 67/2
Koukounara S Greece Mycenaean site 67/1
Koumasa C Crete Minoan site 67/2
Kouphia Rachi N Greece Mycenaean site 67/1
Kovno (*Pol.* Kowno *now* Kaunas) W USSR industry 231/1; WW1 251/2
Kowloon S China acquired by Britain 232/2
Kowno (Kovno)
Kow Swamp Australia site of early man 31/1
Kozhikode (Calicut)
Krain (Carniola)
Krak des Chevaliers Syria 111/1, 132/3
Kraków (Cracow)
Krapina N Yugoslavia site of early man 32/2
Kraslag Siberia labour camp zone 299/1
Krasnik C Poland WW1 251/2
Krasnodar (*until 1920* Yekaterinodar) Caucasus WW2 268/1
Krasnoi W Russia ⚔ 205/1
Krasnopol'ye S Russia early trade 41/1
Krasnovodsk (*n/c* Turkmenbashi) Russ. C Asia on railway 230/2; Revolution 257/1; industry 289/1
Krasnoyarsk S Siberia founded 160/2; railway 230/2; urban growth 299/1
Kremlin 160
Kremsmünster Austria monastery 107/3
Krisa C Greece Mycenaean site 67/1
Kristiania (Oslo)
Krivichi E Slav tribe of C Russia 115/1
Krivoy Rog S Ukraine WW2 271/2
Kromdraai S Africa site of early man 31/1
Kronstadt (*Russ.* Kronshtadt) NW Russia 231/1, 257/1; WW1 251/2
Krukath (Cyropolis)
Krung Thep (Bangkok)
Kruscica W Bosnia concentration camp 272/3
Krym (Crimea)
Ku (*n/s* Gu) C China Western Chou domain 63/3
Kua-chou (*n/s* Guazhou) NW China Ming military post 166/1
Kuala Lumpur Malaya occupied by Japanese 268/1
Kuala Selinsing Malaya early site 47/1
Kuan (*n/s* Guan) C China Western Chou domain 63/3
Kuang-chou (*n/s* Guangzhou *Eng.* Canton) S China early church 100/1Sung provincial capital 127/5; Ming provincial capital 166/1
Kuang-chou-wan (*n/s* Guangzhouwan) S China acquired by France 232/2
Kuang-han (*n/s* Guanghan) W China Han commanderie 80/2
Kuang-hsi (Kwangsi)
Kuang-ling (*n/s* Guangling) E China early trade 80/2
Kuang-nan Hsi (*n/s* Guangnan Xi) SW China Sung province 127/5
Kuang-nan Tung (*n/s* Guangnan Dong) S China Sung province 127/5
Kuang-nei (*n/s* Guangnei) N China T'ang province 126/1
Kuang-tung (Kwangtung)
Kuang-wu (*n/s* Guangwu) N China Han prefecture 80/2
Kuba early state of C Africa 165/1
Kublai Khan 1st emperor of Mongol dynasty 167
Kucha (*Chin.* K'u-ch'e) NW China early trade 82/4; Han prefecture 81/3; early church 100/1
K'uei (*n/s* Kui) W China Western Chou domain 63/3
Kuei-chou (Kweichow)
Kuei-lin (*n/s* Guilin) C China Ming provincial capital 166/1
Kuei-tzu (*n/s* Guizi) N China Han prefecture 80/2
Kuei-yang (*n/s* Guiyang) W China Ming provincial capital 166/1
Kui (K'uei)
Kukawa WC Africa Barth's journey 234/2
Ku Klux Klan 222
Kulasekharas dynasty of S India 131/1
Kuldja (*n/s* Gulja *Chin.* I-ning) Sinkiang on silk route 71/1
Kullania NW Syria Neo-Hittite city-state 59/3
Kullyspell House NW USA fur station 218/1
Kulm (*Pol.* Chelmno) N Poland university founded 144/2
Kulmerland region of E Germany occupied by Teutonic Knights 146/2
Kültepe (Kanesh)
Kumamoto city and prefecture of W Japan 242/1
Kumanovo S Serbvia ⚔ 248/2
Kumasi Gold Coast, W Africa 239/1, 241/1
Kumbi Saleh W Africa possible site of capital of Ghana Empire 141/1
Kumma S Egypt 12th Dynasty fort 57/3
Ku-mu (*n/s* Gumu) NE China Han prefecture 80/2
Kumul (*W/G* Ha-mi) Sinkiang early church 101/1
Kunduz (Drapsaca)
Kunersdorf (*now* Kunowice) W Poland ⚔ 196/2
K'un-ming (*n/s* Kunming *form.* Yün-nan-fu) W China French sphere of influence 232/2; industry 261/3, 278/3; WW2 268/1, 269/2
Kunowice (Kunersdorf)
Kurdistan region of Iran/Iraq/Turkey issue of independence 1920-1996 290/3
Kurds people of N Iraq, uprisings 259/2, 291/1
Kurile Islands (*Russ.* Kurilskiye Ostrova *Jap.* Chishima-retto) acquired by Japan 243/2; reoccupied by Russia 279/1
Kurland (Courland)
Kurnool district of SE India ceded to Britain 170/3
Kurs early people of Baltic 115/1
Kursk W Russia 115/1, 161/1; battle of 270; WW2 271/2
Kuru early kingdom of N India 82/1
Kuruman S Africa 239/3
Kurume W Japan 170/4
Kushana Empire S Asia 41/1, 75/2, 79/1, 82/3, 83/5
Kushans tribe of S Asia, migration into Persia 79/1
Kushanas 70
Kusinagara (*Prak.* Kusinara) N India Buddhist site 73/1, 82/1
Kutch (*f/s* Cutch) region of W India border dispute with Pakistan 285/3
Kutchin sub-arctic Indian tribe of NW Canada 149/1
Kut el Amara (*a/c* Kut) C Mesopotamia WW1 251/3
Kutikina SE Australia cave art 35/1
Kutno C Poland WW2 267/4
Kuwait country of Persian Gulf Ottoman sovereignty 229/1; British protectorate 245/2, 258/1; WW1 251/3; independence 276/2, 291/1; Gulf War 291/1; oil 304/1
Ku-yüan (*n/s* Guyuan) NW China Ming frontier defence area 166/1
Kuybyshev (*n/c* 5 Samara) E Russia urban growth 299/1
Kuznetsk S Siberia founded 160/2; fur trade 199/2
Kwajalein Marshall Islands, C Pacific occupied by US 269/2; US base 275/1 (inset)
Kwakiutl coast Indian tribe of W Canada 149/1
Kwale E Africa Iron Age site 43/1
Kwangchowwan S China French treaty port 232/2
Kwangju S Korea industrial centre 279/1
Kwangsi (*n/s* Guangxi *W/G* Kuang-hsi) province of SW China Mesolithic sites 63/1; under Ming 167/2, 166/1; rebellion against Ch'ing 173/2; Manchu expansion 173/1; T'ai-p'ing rebellion 233/1; Hsin-hai revolution 233/3; shifting control 265/1,2
Kwangtung (*n/s* Guangdong *W/G* Kuang-tung) province of S China Mesolithic sites 63/1; under Ming 167/2, 166/1; rebellion against Ch'ing 173/2; Manchu expansion 173/1; Hakka-Cantonese war 233/1; Hsin-hai revolution 233/3; shifting control 265/1, 2
Kwantung Leased Territory NE China 243/2, 268/1
Kwararafa early state of W Africa 141/1, 165/1
Kwazulu/Natal province of South Africa 268/2
Kweichow (*n/s* Guizhou *W/G* Kuei-chou) province of SW China under Ming 167/2, 166/1; rebellion against Ch'ing 173/2; Manchu expansion 173/1; Miao tribal rising 233/1; Hsin-hai revolution 233/3; warlord control 265/1; independent 262/2
Kweilin (*n/s* Guilin)S China captured by Communists 263/4
Kweiyang (*n/s* Guiyang) S China captured by Communists 263/4
Kwidzyn (Marienwerder)
Kyakhta S Siberia Russian trade with China 173/1, 195/1
Kydonia W Crete Minoan site 67/2
Kyongju S Korea Buddhist site 73/1
Kyoto C Japan Buddhist site 73/1; early imperial capital 123/2; city and prefecture 171/4; industry 175/1, 242/1
Kypros (Cyprus)
Kyrgyzstan (*form.* Kirghiz SSR, *a/c* Kirshizia) economic union with Russia 299/3
Kyushu W Island of Japan 214/2, 242/1

L

Laang Spean Cambodia early site 47/1
Labastide SW France cave art 34/2
La Baume-Latrone SE France cave art 34/2
Labici C Italy Latin colony 87/1
labour Black Death and scarcity of 144; urban workforce and organized protest 200; migrant workers 209; US 220, 294, 295; unemployment 294, 295, 300
labour camps Soviet 271, 298
Labrador region of NE Canada rediscovered 156/1
Labuan N Borneo British colony 245/2 (inset); British naval base 244/2
Labuhanmeringgai S Sumatra early Japanese settlement 174/1
Laccadive Islands (*n/c* Lakshadweep) SW India conversion to Islam 99/2; gained by British 194/2
Lacedaemon (*a/c* Sparta) S Greece Byzantine Empire 113/1
La Chapelle-aux-Saints C France site of early man 32/2
La Chaussée-Tirancourt N France Megalithic site 40/2
La Clape S France Megalithic site 40/2
Laconia ancient country of S Greece, 77/2, 76/4
La Coruña (*Eng.* Corunna) NW Spain Civil War 266/2
Ladhiqiyah (Latakia)
Ladoga, Lake (*Russ.* Ladozhskoye Ozero) NW Russia waterway trade route 115/1
Ladrones (Marianas)
Lae SE New Guinea retaken by Allies 269/2
Laetolil E Africa site of early man 31/1
La Fère Champenoise NE France ⚔ 205/1
La Ferrassie S France site of early man 32/2
La Ferté-Bernard N France French Revolution 202/2
La Florida S Peru early site 45/1, 3
La Forêt-le-Roi C France medieval *villeneuve* 121/6
La Forêt-Sainte-Croix C France medieval *villeneuve* 125/1
La Frebouchère NW France Megalithic site 40/2
La Galgada N Peru early site 45/3
Lagash (*a/c* Shipurla) ancient city of Mesopotamia, trade 55/3
Lagny C France medieval fair 120/1
Lagoa Santa SE Brazil early site 45/1
Lagos S Portugal battle of 194; ⚔ 195/1
Lagos Nigeria Slave Coast 165/1; taken by British 239/1; British colony 245/2; British base 244/2
La Graufesengue (Condatomagus)
Laguna de los Cerros C Mexico Olmec site 44/2
La Habana (Havana)
La Halliade SW France Megalithic site 40/2
Laharia-Dih NE India cave art 35/1
La Hogue English Channel Megalithic site 40/2
Lahore NW India in Delhi Sultanate 133/1; trade 170/3; 171/1; industry in British India 235/3; capital of Pakistan Punjab 285/3
Lake Albert W USA ⚔ 219/3
Lake Coleridge S Island, New Zealand hydroelectric station 236/6
Lake Kerinci S Sumatra early site 47/1
Lake Mungo Australia cave art 35/1
Lake of the Woods (Fort Charles)
Lake Okeechobee SE USA ⚔ 219/3
Lake Trasimene battle of 86
Lakhmids 75
Lakhnauti N India district of Delhi Sultanate 133/1
L'Aldène C France cave art 34/2
Lalibela Ethiopia monastery 100/1
Lallo N Philippines early site 47/1
La Madeleine C France site of early man 22/2, 34/2
La Magdaleine S France cave art 34/2
Lamanai E Mexico Maya site 60/2, 148/2
La Marche NW France cave art 34/2
La Mata N Venezuela early site 61/1
Lambaesis (*mod.* Tazoult) Algeria Mithraic site 72/1; Roman Empire 89/1
Lambakannas dynasty of Ceylon 82/3, 131/1
Lamongan E Java early site 47/1
La Mouthe SW France cave art 34/2
Lampsacus (*mod.* Lâpseki) NW Anatolia Greek colony 77/1; Byzantine Empire 113/3
Lamu Kenya Muslim colony 141/1
Lamuts Siberian tribe 160/2
Lanchow (*n/s* Lanzhou *W/G* Lan-chou) NW China early trade 71/1; T'ang prefecture 126/1; Sung provincial capital 127/5; captured by Communists 263/4; industry 261/3
land clearance in Megalithic Age 40; held of the king 118; reclamation 120, 178; *shiki* 122; land-holding rights under Western Chin 124; enclosure 178, 184; Maoris defend their lands 236; Middle East land reform 290; Latin American land reform 292
Landau W Germany gained by France 192/2; French Revolution 202/2
Landriano N Italy ⚔ 186/2**Lang Co** N Vietnam early site 47/1
Langobardi early tribe of NW Germany 89/1. See also Lombards
languages of Neanderthals 33; Indo-European 40; Bantu 42, 140, 164; Na-Dene 44; Sumerian 54, 55; Addadian 55; of ancient India 64; Mycenaean Greek 67; Greek 78; Prakrit 82; Sanskrit 82, 134; Latin 91; Arabic 98; Persian 133; of indigenous Americans 148; disparity between subjects' and government 184; French 193; Spanish 224; Jews' 288
Languedoc region of S France French Royal domain 119/1, 151/3; 17C revolts 185/1; province of France 193/1
Lang Vac N Vietnam early site 47/1
Lanka (Ceylon)
L'Anse aux Meadows Newfoundland Norse colony 61/1, 107/3
Lan-t'ien (*n/s* Lantian) C China prehistoric site 31/1; Late Chou site 63/3; Han prefecture 80/2
Lanzhou (Lanchow)
Laodicea (*a/c* Laodicea ad Lycum) *mod.* Denizli) W Anatolia founded 78/1; Roman Empire 89/1; early Christian community 93/1; Jewish community 103/4; Byzantine Empire 113/3
Laodicea (*a/c* Laodicea ad Mare, *mod.* Latakia *Fr.* Lattaquié) Syria founded 78/1; early Christain centre 93/1; Byzantine Empire 113/3, 113/1
Laodicea in Media (*mod.* Nehavend) W Persia founded by Alexander 79/1
Laon N France ⚔ 205/1
Laos country of SE Asia 135/1; kingdom of Luang Prabang 177/1; end of Chinese tributary status 232/2; French protectorate 259/1; independence 276/2; civil wars 283/1; Pathet Lao 277/3
Laozi 73
Lâpseki (Lampsacus)
Lapurdum (Bayonne)
Lardavif Wales bishopric 92/1
Larisa (*a/s* Larissa *Turk.* Yenişehir) C Greece Jewish community 103/4; Byzantine Empire 113/1,5
La Rochelle W France 16-17C revolts 185/1; commercial harbour 193/1
Larsa (*Bibl.* Ellasar) Mesopotamia Amorite kingdom 55/2; early city 55/3
Las Bela NW India Alexander's Empire 82/3
Lascaux C France cave art 34/2
Las Conchas N Chile early site 45/1, 3
Las Haldas N Peru early site 45/1, 3
Lashio E Burma WW2 266/2
Las Navas de Tolosa S Spain ⚔ 111/2, 136/1
La Starza S Italy early settlement 41/3
Latakia (*anc.* Laodicea *Fr.* Lattaquié *Ar.* Ladhiqiyah) Syria 139/1
La Tène E France Celtic site 85/1
Later Liang dynasty of N China 127/3
Latin America (America, South)
Latini early tribe of Italy, 86/2
Latin Way (Via Latina)
Lato E Crete Minoan site 67/2
Lattaquié (Latakia)
Latvia country of the Baltic corn shipments 177/4; independence from Russia 257/1, 263/1; socio-political change 264/2; WW2 270-1; annexed by Russia 267/4, 273/1; Soviet Socialist Republic 300/2; independence 1991 290/3; EU 300/1, 301/2
Latvians emigration from Russia 261/3; in USSR 300/2
Lauenburg principality of N Germany 190/1
Laugerie Basse C France cave art 34/2
Laugerie Haute C France cave art 34/2
Launceston W England 16C riots 185/1
Launceston Tasmania gold 237/1
Laupen W Switzerland Zähringen town 121/6
Laurentide ice-sheet N America 34/3
Lauricocha N Peru early site 45/3
Lausanne Switzerland 1924 Conference 263/1
Lausitz (Lusatia)
Laussel C France cave art 34/2
Lava Beds W USA ⚔ 219/3
Laval NW France 17C revolts 185/1
Lavenham E England rebellion against Henry VIII, 185/1
La Venta C Mexico Olmec site 44/2
Lavinium C Italy Roman Empire 87/1
Lavriya Nandangarh N India Buddhist site 83/2
law Jewish 102; under Carolingian regime 105; instrument of royal authority 118; France under Louis XIV 193; Russia 230; Japan 242
Lazaret S France site of early man 32/2
Lazica early country of the Caucasus 113/1
Leang Buidane NE Indonesia early site 47/1
Leang Burung E Indonesia early site 47/1
Leang Tuwo Mane'e NE Indonesia early site 47/1
League of Nations and former Ottoman empire 228/2; mandates 258, 276; and colonial rule 259; purpose of 262; Japan 266; Italy 266; Palestine 288; US 296
League of the Three Emperors 248
learning support from royal women of German empire 16; medieval European civilization 98; Louis XIV's patronage 193
Lebanon French mandate 258/1; political disturbances 259/2; independence 276/2, 291/1; US landing 292/5; Middle East conflict 290/2, 275/1; civil war 303/1
Lebda (Leptis Magna)
Lechfeld S Germany battle of 106; ⚔ 107/1, 116/2
Le Creusot C France industrial development 211/1, 212/1
Ledosus (*mod.* Lezoux) C France Roman Empire 88/2
Leeds N England industrial development 200/3, 201/1, 211/1
Leek C England Industrial Revolution 201/1
Lee, Robert E 222
Leeward Islands West Indies British and French settlement 158/3
Le Gabillou W France cave art 34/2
Leghorn (Livorno)
legislation Rome 86; king's authority 118; British India 235
legislature Japan 242
Legnica (Liegnitz) battle of 128
Le Havre N France trading port 176/3; fortified naval port 193/1; French Revolution 202/2; industrial development 211/1, 212/1; WW2 269/6
Leicester (*anc.* Ratae) C England Scandinavian settlement 106/2, 107/1; Industrial Revolution 201/1
Leiden (Leyden)
Leinster province of SE Ireland early kingdom 117/1; conquered by Normans 119/1
Leipen N Germany Megalithic site 40/2
Leipzig E Germany massacre of Jews 103/3; university founded 144/2; 18C financial centre 181/2; industrial development 211/1, 212/1; WW1 251/2; Communist insurrection 256/2
Leipzig (Battle of the Nations) E Germany ⚔ 205/1
Le Kef (Sicca Veneria)
Leling (Lo-ling)
Le Mans NW France Viking raid 107/1; bishopric 117/1; French Revolution 202/2; industrial development 211/1
Le Mas-d'Azil S France cave art 34/2
Lemberg (*Pol.* Lwów *now* Lvov) N Austria-Hungary WW1 251/2; E Germany WW2 271/2
Lemnos island of the Aegean Byzantine naval victory 121/2
Lenca Indian tribe of central America 149/1
Lenin *pseud.* of Vladimir Ilich Ulyanov 256
Leninakan (*until 1924* Aleksandropol) Armenian SSR industry 289/1
Leningrad (St Petersburg *Russ.* Sankt-Peterburg, *between 1914 and 1923* Petrograd) NW Russia WW2 265/1, 271/2; population growth 299/1
Lens NE France WW1 251/2 (inset)
Lenzen N Germany ⚔ 116/2
León early kingdom of C Spain 111/2; 16-17C revolts 184/2; city of N Spain, Civil War 266/2
Leontini E Sicily Greek colony 79/1
Leontopolis (*mod.* Tell el-Yahudiya) N Egypt site 58/1 early Jewish community 103/4
Leopold II king of the Belgians 240
Léopoldville (Kinshasa)
Lepanto (*mod. Gr.* Navapaktos) C Greece battle of, Habsburg victory 168, 186; ⚔ 168/1
Le Placard N France cave art 34/2
Le Poisson SW France cave art 34/2
Leptis N Libya Iron Age site 43/1
Leptis Magna (*a/s* Lepcis Magna *mod.* Lebda) N Libya Mithraic site 72/1; Carthaginian city 86/3; Roman Empire 89/1, 88/2; early Christian centre 93/1
Le Puiset C France medieval *villeneuve* 121/6
Lera, cave of (Akrotiri)
Lérida (*anc.* Ilerda) NE Spain university founded 144/2
Leros S Aegean WW2 271/2
Les Bolards C France Mithraic site 72/1
Lesbos (*mod. Gr.* Lesvos *a/c* Mytilene) island of E Aegean acquired by Turks 151/1; ceded to Greece 211/2, 248/2
Lesotho (*form.* Basutoland) S Africa independence 276/2; South African attack 286/2; political development 287/1; economy 304/1
Lespugue S France cave art 34/2
Les Trois Frères S France cave art 34/2
Letts people of Latvia, NW Russia 257/1
Le Tuc d'Audoubert S France cave art 34/2
Leucas (*mod. Gr.* Levkas *It.* Santa Maura) W Greece Greek colony 77/1
Leucecome early port of W Arabia 41/1
Leucos Limen Red Sea early trade 71/1; Roman Empire 88/2
Leuthen (*Pol.* Lutynia) SW Poland ⚔ 196/2
Leuven (*Fr.* Louvain) Belgium Viking raid 107/1; town of Sp. Netherlands university founded 144/2; 185/1
Leuwiliang W Java early site 47/1
Levant Company 107
Levkas (Leucas)
Lewes S England ⚔ 119/1
Lewis, Meriwether 218
Lexington NE USA ⚔ 202/3
Leyden (*n/s* Leiden) Netherlands 16C urban development 180/1; 18C urban development 181/2
Leyte SE Philippines US landing 269/2
Leyte Gulf SE Philippines ⚔ 271/2

Phalaborwa SE Africa early site 43/1; 141/1
Phanagoria S Russia Greek colony 77/1
pharaohs of Egypt 58
Pharsalus (*Gr.* Pharsalos) C Greece Roman Empire 86/3
Phaselis SW Anatolia Greek colony 77/1; Alexander's route 78/1
Phasis Caucasus Greek colony 77/1; Roman Empire 89/1
Phazania (*mod.* Fezzan) region of S Libya 89/1
Philadelphia (*mod.* Alaşehir) W Anatolia founded 78/1; early church 93/1
Philadelphia N Egypt Jewish community 103/4
Philadelphia E USA founded 162/2; industry 287/1
Philip II Augustus king of France 118
Philip IV king of France kingship 118; battle of Courtrai 118
Philip II king of Macedon 77
Philip II king of Spain Portuguese nobles rise against 184; retains Italian territories 186
Philip IV king of Spain 193
Philip V king of Spain offered crown 193; secures throne 187
Philiphaugh S Scotland ✕ 185/1
Philippi N Greece Roman Empire 86/3; 89/1; early Christian community 93/1; Jewish community 103/4
Philippines spread of Islam 98/3, 134/2; early sites 130/1; early trade 159/1, 158/2; Spanish conquest 176/2, 177/1; imperial trade 195/1; acquired by US 245/2; anti-colonial revolts 247/1; occupied by Japanese 266/1, 268/1; retaken by US 269/2; insurgency 283/1; Chinese settlement 283/4; US bases 277/1, 275/1; industry and economy 278/3, 304/1; Japanese investment 282/2; environment 309/1
Philippine Sea ✕ 269/2
Philippopolis (*mod.* Plovdiv *Turk* Filibe) Bulgaria founded 78/1; Roman Empire 89/1; attacked by Goths 90/2; Byzantine Empire 113/1; Ottoman Empire 168/1
Philistines 59/2; displaced 67/3
Philomelium (*mod.* Akş ehir) C Anatolia Byzantine Empire 110/3
philosophy 87
Phimai C Thailand early town135/1
Phnom Penh Cambodia early town 135/1; Khmer capital 177/1; Vietnam war 292/4
Phocaea W Anatolia Greek parent community 79/1
Phoenicia at time of Greeks 77/1, 78/1; Roman province 89/1; 102/2
Phoenicians move into Africa 43/1; 76
Phylakopi SE Greece early settlement 41/1
Phrygia ancient country of W Anatolia 77/1, 78/1, 92/2; spread of Christianity 72/1; Byzantine Empire 113/1
Phrygians early people of Anatolia 59/2, 67/3
Phu Lan N Thailand early site 47/1
Phung Nguyen N Vietnam early site 47/1
Phylakopi Aegean Mycenaean palace site 41/3, 67/1
Piacenza (*anc.* Placentia) N Italy Lombard League 117/1; Signorial domination 146/3; medieval fair 142/1; university founded 144/2
Piast dynasty 109
Piauí state of NE Brazil 277/1
Picardy (*Fr.* Picardie) region of N France annexed from Burgundy 151/3; 193/1; WW1 251/2 (inset)
Picentes early tribe of N Italy 86/2
Pichincha Colombia ✕ 227/2
Picton S Island, New Zealand railway 236/6
Picts early tribe of Scotland 88/2, 96/1; 108
Piedmont (*It.* Piemonte) region of N Italy occupied by France 199/3; 216/2
Pien-chou (*n/s* Bianzhou) N China T'ang prefecture 126/1
Pietrasanta N Italy Tuscan principality 183/3
Pigs, Bay of Cuba CIA invasion 293/6
Pike, Zebulon 218
Pikimachay S Peru early site 45/3
Pilbara W Australia early settlement 237/1
pilgrimage to Mecca 98; to Holy Land 110
Pilgrimage of Grace 184
Pilos (Pylos)
Pilsen (*Cz.* Plzeň) Czechoslovakia industrial development 211/1
Pima Indian tribe of N Mexico 149/1
Pinega N Russia town of Novgorod Empire 115/1
Ping-ch'eng (*n/s* Bingcheng) N China Northern Wei capital 124/3
P'ing-yin (*n/s* Pingyin) C China Han prefecture 80/2
P'ing-yüan (*n/s* Pingyuan) NE China Han prefecture 80/2
Pinochet, Augusto 292
Pinsk W Russia town of Turov-Pinsk 115/1; WW1 251/2
Pintu N Philippines early site 47/1
Piombino N Italy Mediterranean trade 142/1; duchy 186/2; French rule 205/1
Pippin II mayor of the palace 104
Pippin III the Short Frankish king 105
Piqillacta C Andes early site 60/5
piracy in western Mediterranean 106; Japanese pirates 123, 224; Barbary pirates 138, 187; attacks on Chinese coast 167; danger to international trade 198; Indian Ocean and China Sea 198
Piramesse (Qantir)
Pirna E Germany ✕ 196/2
Piro forest Indian tribe of S America 149/1
Pisa (*anc.* Pisae) N Italy medieval city 117/1; Mediterranean trade 120/1, 145/1; raids and conquests 121/2; Republican commune 146/3; 150/1; university founded 144/2; republic 186/2
Pisae (*mod.* Pisa) N Italy Roman Empire 87/1, 89/1
Pisaurum (*mod.* Pesaro) N Italy Roman colony 87/1
Piscataway Fort NE USA ✕ 219/3
Pisidia ancient country of C Anatolia 78/1, 86/3, 113/1
Pistoia (*anc.* Pistoriae) N Italy Roman Empire 87/1; medieval city 117/1
Pitcairn Island C Pacific British colony 276/2 (inset)
Pithecusae S Italy Greek colony 79/1
Pit River W USA ✕ 219/3
Pittsburgh E USA industry 215/1
Pittsburg Landing (Shiloh)
Pityus Caucasus
Placentia (*mod.* Piacenza) N Italy Latin colony 87/1
Plain of Jars N Laos early site 47/1
PLA (People's Liberation Army) Mao forms alliance with 280; Tiananmen massacre 281
Plassey E India ✕ 170/3, 19/2 (inset); battle of 195
Plaszow (*mod.* Pamplona) N Spain Roman Empire 88/1
Plataea C Greece ✕ 77/2
Platanos C Crete Minoan site 67/2
Plate River (*Sp.* Rio de la Plata) Argentina explored 156/1
Plati E Crete Minoan site 67/2
Plawangan C Java early site 47/1
Pleistocene Age Australasia 48
Plenty, Bay of N Island, New Zealand Maori settlement 49/4
Plevna (*now* Pleven) Bulgaria WW1 251/2
Pliny the Elder 70
Pliska Bulgaria early city 108/1
Pločnik S Yugoslavia early settlement 41/1
Ploeşti (*n/s* Ploieşti) Romania WW2 271/2
PLO (Palestine Liberation Organization) 288-9
Plovdiv (Philippopolis)
Plussulien NW France Megalithic site 40/2
Plymouth SW England naval base 195/1; Industrial Revolution 201/1; WW1 251/2; WW2 267/4
Plymouth NE USA founded 162/2
Plzeň (Pilsen)
Poço da Gateira S Portugal Megalithic site 40/2
Poduca S India early port 71/1
Poetovio (*mod.* Ptuj *Ger.* Pettau) N Yugoslavia Mithraic site 72/1; Roman Empire 89/1; early bishopric 93/1
poetry ancient Greece 76; Córdoba centre of 136
Po-hai (*n/s* Bohai *Kor.* Parhae *mod.* Manchuria) NE China early state 122/1, 127/2
Pohang S Korea 1950-3 war 278/3; industry 279/1
Point of Rocks C USA ✕ 219/3
Poitiers (*anc.* Limonum) C France early Christian centre 92/1; ✕ 98/1, 119/1;Viking raid 107/1; ✕ 140/4; monastery 104/2; university founded 144/2; 17C revolts 185/1; seat of intendant 193/1; centre of French Revolution 202/2
Poitou region of W France English possession 119/1; French Royal domain 151/3; province of France 193/1
Pola (*mod.* Pula) N Yugoslavia Roman Empire 89/1; WW1 251/2
Polabii Slavic tribe of N Germany 116/2
Poland conversion to Christianity 101/2; under Boleslaw Chrobry 108/3; Mongol invasion 129/2; Black Death 145/1; at 1382 147/1; Empire of Casimir IV 151/1; acquired by Russia 161/1; agriculture and peasant emancipation 178/1; Reformation 183/1; Great Northern War 189/2; Partitions 197/3; revolt against Russia 203/1; industry under Russian rule 231/1; independence after WW1 257/1, 263/1; socio-political development 265/3-5, 264/2; WW2 267/4; Warsaw Pact and Comecon 270/3; communism overthrown 300/1,2
Poles post-WW2 migration to West 273/1; to Soviet labour camps 298; in USSR 300/2
police Paris under Louis XIV 193; Russia 231; policing of Soviet society 298
Polish Corridor 263/1
politics Muslim 98; Anglo-Saxon England 108; Poland-Lithuania 196; papacy and 116; 19C Latin American 226; of Arab world 290
Polochanye NW Russia E Slav tribe 115/1
Polo, Marco 128
Polotsk W Russia bishopric 101/2; 114; early city and principality 115/1
Polovtsy (*a/c* Cumans) tribe of C Russia 114-5
Poltava Ukraine town of Pereyaslav 115/1; Great Northern War; battle of 160; ✕ 189/2; defeat of Charles XI of Sweden 189; industry and urban growth 231/1; Bolshevik seizure 257/1
Polyane Slav tribe of the Ukraine, 115/1
Polynesia island group of C Pacific early settlement 49/1; Polynesians 49
Pomerania (*Ger.* Pommern *Pol.* Pomorze) region of N Europe acquired by Poland 108/3; medieval German Empire 117/1; Black Death 145/1; Reformation 183/1; unification of Germany 217/3
Pomerania, East part of Germany 190/1
Pomerania, Swedish 189/1,2; 196/2
Pomerania, West to Sweden 188-9, 190/1,4
Pomerelia (*Ger.* Pommerellen) region of N Europe occupied by Teutonic Knights 146/2
Pomo Indian tribe of NW USA 149/1
Pompaelo (*mod.* Pamplona) N Spain Roman Empire 88/1
Pompeii S Italy early Christian community 92/1; Jewish community 103/4
Pompeiopolis S Anatolia Roman Empire 89/1
Pondicherry (*Fr.* Pondichéry) SE India French settlement 158/2, 171/1; ✕ 172/3; captured by British 194/2 (inset); imperial trade 195/1; French enclave 235/3; returned to India 276/2
Pondo (*a/c* Pondoland) region of SE Africa British administration 239/3; civil unrest 286/2
Pons Saravi E France Mithraic site 72/1
Pontecorvo principality of N Italy 209/5
Ponthieu region of NE France Frankish royal residence 104/2; under English rule 119/1; Burgundian possession 151/2
Pontia (Ponza)
Pontiae (*a/c* Pontine Islands *mod.* Isole Ponziane) C Italy Roman Empire 87/1
Pontianak W Borneo Dutch settlement 177/1
Pontine Islands (Pontiae)
Pontnewydd N Wales early man 32/2
Pontus district of N Anatolia 79/3; Roman province 86/3, 89/4, 88/2; Byzantine Empire 113/1
Ponza (Pontia) *island* C Italy Mithraic site 72/1
Ponziane, Isole (Pontiae)
Poona W India industry 214/1, 235/3
population Ice Age 34; prehistoric evolution 36; prehistoric Africa 42; Maoris 49; ancient Eurasia 52, 53; Teotihuacán 60; Mayan 60; China 80, 81, 126, 127, 154, 167, 172; of western Europe by AD 1000 120; Incas re-locate 148; 15C native Americans 148; food supplies and growth of 155; Russia 160; Thirty Years' War reduces 191; France 192; and industrial revolution 200; 19C explosion 208, 209; movement 208-9, 218-19; US 220; British India 234; Aborigines 236; gold rushes lead to influx 236; Japan 242; French and German empires 244; south Asia 284; growth in Africa 286; Latin America 292; Soviet Union 298; pressure 303; and environmental damage 308
Populonia N Italy Etruscan city 77/1, 86/2
Porolissensis Roman province of E Europe 89/1
Porolissum Romania Roman Empire 89/1
Portage la Prairie (Fort La Reine)
Port Arthur (*Chin.* Lüshun *Jap.* Ryojun) Manchuria ceded to Russia and Japan 230/2, 232/2, Russo-Japanese war 243/3; 261/3
Port Arthur Tasmania penal settlement 237/1
Port Augusta S Australia settlement 237/1
Port-aux-Choix E Canada early site 45/1
Port Chalmers S Island, New Zealand 236/6
Port Elizabeth SE Africa British settlement 239/3
Port Essington N Australia founded 237/1
Port Hedland W Australia early settlement 237/1
Port Hudson S USA ✕ 218/1
Porti C Crete Minoan site 67/2
Port Jackson (Sydney)
Portland S England WW1 251/2
Portland SE Australia founded 237/1
Port Lincoln S Australia settlement 237/1
Port Macquarie SE Australia penal settlement 237/1
Port Moresby SE New Guinea Allied base in WW2 267/1
Porto Novo SE India ✕ 194/2
Porto-Novo W Africa French settlement 239/1
Port Pirie S Australia settlement 237/1
Port Royal Jamaica British naval base 194/1
Port Said N Egypt Egyptian-Israeli war 288/1
Portsmouth S England naval base 195/1; Industrial Revolution 201/1; WW1 251/2
Portsmouth NE USA settlement 162/2
Portugal (*anc.* Lusitania) early settlement 40-1; Jewish migration 102/1; Muslim conquest 98/1; reconquest 111/2; expansion overseas 156-9; expansion in Morocco 168/1; annexed to Spain 182/1; agriculture 175/1; revolt against Spain 184/2; trade and industry 180-1, 198-9; population growth 209/1,4; railway development 212/1; colonial empire 245/2; WW1 248/1; inter-war alliances 260/2; general strike 264/2; Marshall aid 276/2; NATO and EEC 273/1; US bases 275/1; EU 302/1; economy 304/2; ; environment 309/1
Portuguese East Africa (*now* Mozambique) 245/2
Portuguese Empire 198
Portuguese Guinea (*now* Guinea-Bissau) W Africa Portuguese colony 240/2, 245/2, 258/1, 277/1; independence 276/2
Portuguese Timor E Indies annexed by Indonesia 276/2, 283/1
Portuguese, the Ceuta falls to 136, 147; voyages of exploration 157; Indian Ocean trade 158; and Ottoman navies 168
Portus Herculis Monoeci (Monaco)
Portus Namnetum NE France Roman Empire 88/1, 91/4
Porus early kingdom of NW India 79/1
Poseidonia (*later* Paestum *mod.* Pesto) S Italy Greek colony 77/1
Posideium (*mod.* Al Mina) W Syria Greek colony 79/1
Posen (*Pol.* Poznań) W Poland industrial development 211/1; North German Confederation 217/3; WW1 251/2; ceded by Germany 263/1
Potaissa Romania Roman Empire 88/2
Potawatomi Indian tribe of C USA 149/1
Potchevash N Russia site 71/1
Potentia (*mod.* Potenza) N Italy Roman colony 87/1
Potidaea N Greece Dorian colony 77/1
Potosí Peru Spanish silver mine 154/1
Potsdam Conference 272
pottery Neolithic 39; of prehistoric agricultural communities 40; prehistoric South and Central America 44; prehistoric southeast Asia 46; Lapita 48-9; coast of Central Andes 61
Pouey-Mayon SW France Megalithic site 40/2
poverty 286; Latin America 292; US 294-5; of developing world 305
Poverty Point N America site 45/1
Powhatan Indian tribe of E USA 149/1
Powys early principality of N Wales 109/1
Pozsony (Bratislava)
Poznań (*Ger.* Posen) W Poland bishopric 108/3; 139/1
Pozzuoli (Puteoli)
Praeneste (*mod.* Palestrina) C Italy Roman Empire, 87/1
Pragjyotisa region of NE India 83/2
Prague (*Cz.* Praha) Czechoslovakia bishopric 101/2, 108/3; medieval trade 120/1; university founded 144/2; 16C urban development 180/1; ✕ 196/2; industrial development 211/1, 213/1; communist coup 292/2
Praia das Maçãs C Portugal burial site 41/3
Praisos E Crete Minoan village 67/2
Prambanan C Java Hindu-Buddhist temple 135/1
Pratiharas early dynasty of N India 131/1, 2; 130
Pravdinsk (Friedland)
Prayaga N India sacked by Huns 83/4
Preah Khan C Cambodia early town 135/1
Preah Vihear district of Cambodia claimed by Thailand 279/1
Preanger district of Java Dutch control 176/3
Prekmurje region of E Slovenia to Yugoslavia 1920 262/2; to Hungary 1941 273/1
Premadasa, Ranasinghe 284
Premyslid dynasty 109
Preslav Bulgaria early city 108/1
Presov Slovakia Communist republic 256/2
Pressburg (*mod.* Bratislava) 107/1
Prester John 129
Preston N England ✕ 180/1; Industrial Revolution 201/1
Prestonpans S Scotland Industrial Revolution 200/3
Pretoria S Africa on Boer trek 239/3; Boer War 240/2
Preussen (Prussia)
Preussisch-Eylau (Eylau)
Preveza C Greece ✕ 168/1
Primo de Rivera, Miguel marquas de Estalla 262
Primorskiy Kray (Maritime Province)
Prince Edward Island (Ile St Jean)
Prince's Town Ghana early French settlement 164/1 (inset)
Princip, Gavrilo 249
Principe *island* W Africa Portuguese settlement 165/1, 241/1; colony 258/1
Prinias E Crete Minoan site 67/2
Priniatiko Pyrgos E Crete Minoan site 67/2
printing Jews engaged in 103; increased exploitation of 150; invention of 182
Princip, Gavrilo assassin 249
Prizren Serbia WW1 251/2
Procolitia (*mod.* Carrawburgh) N Britain Mithraic site 72/1
Prome C Burma Buddhist site 73/1
Protestants and Reformation 182-3; Habsburgs' subjects 191; and persecution of Huguenots 192; Africa 286
Prosymna S Greece Mycenaean site 67/1
Provence region of S France temporarily held by Visigoths 97/2; Frankish Empire 105/1,3; medieval German Empire 117/1, 119/1; Arabs expelled 121/2; annexed to France 151/3; 16-17C revolts 185/1; province of France 193/1
Providence NE USA founded 162/2
Provins C France medieval fair 120/1
Prusa (*mod.* Bursa) W Anatolia Byzantine Empire 113/1
Prussia (*Ger.* Preussen) region of E Germany conquest by Teutonic Knights 146/2; Polish fief 202/3; Reformation 183/1; Great Northern War 189/2; Duchy 190/1; conquests in Europe 197/4,4; 193/1; opposition to Napoleon 204-5; unification of Germany 216-7
Przemyśl Austria-Hungary WW1 251/2
Psammetichus I king of Egypt 56
Pseira E Crete Minoan site 67/2
Pskov W Russia town of Novgorod Empire 115/1, 161/1; acquired by Muscovy 151/1; Russian Revolution 257/1
Pteria (*mod.* Boğazköy) C Anatolia ✕ 74/1
Ptolemais Egypt Roman Empire 89/1
Ptolemais (*mod.* Tulmaythah *It.* Tolmeta) Libya Roman Empire 89/1, 88/2; early Christian centre 93/1
Ptolemais (Acre, `Akko)
Ptolemais Theron NE Africa early port 71/1
Ptolemies, the (dynasty of Macedonian kings of Egypt) re-establish Ancient Egyptian power 56; warfare 78
Ptuj (Poetovio)
Puebla C Mexico early Spanish city 154/1; province 227/1
Pueblo Indian tribe of SW USA 45/1, 61/1; 149/1; 46/3; villages 60; way of life 149
Pueblo Bonito N America site 61/1
Puerto Hormiga N Colombia early site 45/1
Puerto Marquez S Mexico early site 44/2
Puelche Indian tribe of Argentina 149/1
Puerto Rico W Indies Spanish settlement 158/3; conquered by US 227/1
Puig Roig NE Spain Megalithic site 40/2
Pukow (*n/s* Pukou *W/G* P'u-k'ou) E China British influence 232/2
Pula (Pola)
Pulakesin II Indian king 130
Pulicat SE India Dutch settlement 171/1
Pultusk N Poland Great Northern War ✕ 189/2
Pundravardhana region of E India 82/3
Punjab region of NW India Muslim expansion 99/1; limit of Abbasid sovereignty 137/1; state of British India 235/3; partition between India and Pakistan 279/1, 280/3; water dispute with Haryana 285/3
Punic Wars 86-7
Punta de Jauari C Brazil early site 45/1
Pupitz W Poland Great Northern War ✕ 189/2
Puri district of NE India cession to Britain 170/3
Puritjarra C Australia cave art 35/1
Purusapura Afghanistan trade 82/3, 83/5
Purushkhaddum early town of C Anatolia 54/1
Pusan (*Jap.* Fusan) S Korea 1950-3 war 278/3; industry 279/1
P'u-shan (*n/s* Pushan) Sinkiang Han expansion 81/3
Pushkari W USSR cave art 35/1
Puskalavati NW India Ashokan site 83/2
Pusybhutis dynasty of N India 130/1; 130
Puteoli (*mod.* Pozzuoli) C Italy Roman colony 87/1; Roman Empire 88/2
P'u-t'o Shan (*n/s* Putuo Shan) *mountain* E China Buddhist site 73/1
Pu Yi last Manchu emperor 266
Pyatigorsk Caucasus 161/1
Pydna C Greece battle of 79; ✕ 79/3; Roman Empire 86/3
Pylos (*a/s* Pilos *It.* Navarino) SW Greece Mycenaean palace site 67/1
Pyongyang (*Jap.* Heijo) N Korea 1950-3 war 278/3; industry 279/1
Pyramid Lake W USA ✕ 219/3
Pyrenees, Peace of 192
Pyrgi C Italy Roman colony 87/1
Pyrgos C Crete Minoan palace 67/2
Pyrgos C Greece Mycenaean site 67/1
Pyrgos E Crete Minoan palace 67/2
Pyu S Burma Buddhist kingdom 127/2, 135/1

Qadi Burhaneddi Turcoman principality of C Anatolia 142/2
Qadisiyya battle of 75
Qandahar (Kandahar)
Qantir (*anc.* Piramesse) N Egypt site 58/1
Qarabagh region of the Caucasus conquered by Ottomans 169/1
Qarakhanids (*a/s* Karakhanids) Muslim dynasty of Central Asia 137/1
Qarqan (Ch'ieh-mo)
Qatar sheikdom of Persian Gulf oil 304/1
Qatna Syria Amorite kingdom 55/2
Qermez Dere N Mesopotamia early site 39/1
Qi (Ch'i)
Qiancheng (Ch'ien-ch'eng)
Qiang (Ch'iang)
Qiankang (Ch'ien-K'ang)
Qiantong (Ch'ien-t'ang)
Qianxian (Ch'ien-hsien)
Qianzhong (Ch'ien-chung)
Qichun (Ch'i-ch'un)
Qiemo (Ch'ieh-mo)
Qift (*anc.* Koptos) S Egypt site 58/1
Qin (Ch'in)
Qinfeng (Ch'in-feng)
Qingdao (Tsingtao)
Qinghai (*W/G* Ch'ing-hai, *a/s* Tsinghai) province of NW China economy under communism 280/1; minority unrest 287/1
Qingjiang (Ch'ing-chiang)
Qingzhou (Ch'ing-chou)
Qiongzhou (Ch'iung-chou)
Qiqihar (Tsitsihar)
Quadi Germanic tribe 89/1
Quanterness N Scotland Megalithic site 40/2
Quanzhou (Ch'üan-chou)
Quban S Egypt 12th Dynasty fort 57/3
Quebec city, E Canada capital of New France 162/2; captured by British 194/1

Teotenango S Mexico early site 60/2
Teotitlán Mexico site 148/2
Teopantecuanitlan C Mexico early site 44/2
Tepe Gawra N Mesopotamia early settlement 39/1
Tepe Guran W Persia Neolithic site 39/1
Tepe Hisar N Persia 55/1
Tepehuan Indian tribe of N Mexico 149/1
Tepexpan Mexico site of early man 32/1
Tepic state of N Mexico 227/1
Te Porere N Island, New Zealand ✕ 236/5
Teramo (Interamna)
Terebovl W Russia town of Galich 115/1
Teremembé forest Indian tribe of NE Brazil 149/1
Terezin (Theresienstadt)
Tergeste (*mod.* Trieste) N Italy Roman Empire 89/1
Terhazz (Taghaza)
Ternate Moluccas, East Indies early village 47/1; Islamic town 134/2; sultanate 135/1; Portuguese settlement 176/2
Ternifine Algeria site of early man 31/1
Ternopol (Tarnopol)
Terracina (Anxur, Tarracina)
Terranova di Sicilia (Gela)
Terror, the 203
terrorism 302
Tertry battle of 105
Teruel E Spain Civil War 266/2
Teschen (*Cz.* Těšin *or* Český Těšín *Pol.* Cieszyn) city and district divided between Poland and Czechoslovakia 263/1; Czech part retaken by Poland 267/3
Teshik-Tash C Asia site of early man 31/1
Těšín (Teschen)
Tete Mozambique Portuguese settlement 165/1; Stanley's travels 234/2
Tetuán Morocco Spanish control 224/1
Teurnia Austria Roman Empire 89/1
Teutonic Order Crusades 111/1; Baltic 115/1; conquest of Prussia 146/2, 139/1; at 1380 147/1; territory lost to Poland 151/1; 188
Teverya (Tiberias)
Te Waiponamu (South Island, New Zealand)
Tewkesbury W England Industrial Revolution 201/1
Texas state of S USA independent 227/1; Civil War and Reconstruction 226/3; Depression 265/1; income and population 295/2
Texel I and II N Netherlands English/Dutch naval battles 185/1, 195/3
textiles 50,000 years ago 32; Chavan 44; Black Death and 144; Italian cloth industry 178; Holy Roman Empire 191; industrial revolution 200, 210-1; Mexico and Brazil 226; British India 234; Japan 242
Teyjat NW France cave art 34/2
Thagaste Tunisia early Christian centre 92/1
Thailand (*f/c* Siam) early Iron and Bronze Age sites 130/1; occupied by Japanese 268/1, 267/1; militarization and insurgency 283/1; Chinese settlement 283/4; US bases 275/1; Japanese investment 279/4; armaments 302/2. See also Siam
Thais people of SE Asia, expansion 135/1
Thames N Island, New Zealand gold rush 236/4
Thames Valley N Island, New Zealand Maori settlement 48/3
Thamugadi (*a/c* Timgad) Algeria ancient city 89/1
Thapsacus (*Bibl.* Tiphsah *mod.* Dibse) Syria Alexander's route 78/1; Achaemenid Empire 79/1; Alexander's Empire 82/3
Thapsus Tunisia Punic city 74/1; Roman Empire 86/3, 89/1
Thara N Persia Alexander's route 79/1
Tharro NW India Harappan site 65/2
Tharros Sardinia Punic town 79/1
Thasos *island* N Greece ancient city 77/1; occupied by Greece 248/2
Thaton S Burma early town 135/1
Thebes (*mod. Gr.* Thivai) C Greece Mycenaean palace 67/1; Jewish community 102/1, 103/4
Thebes (*Lat.* Thebae *earlier* Diospolis Magna) Upper Egypt Iron Age site 43/1; 58/1; Achaemenid Empire 74/1; Roman Empire 89/1, 88/2
Theodoric the Great Ostrogothic king of Italy 97
Theodosia (*mod.* Feodosiya) Crimea Greek colony 77/1; Roman Empire 89/1
Theodosiopolis E Anatolia under Seljuks of Rum 110/3
Theodosius I the Great Roman emperor 92
Thera (*mod.* Thira *a/c* Santorini) island of S Aegean 67/1; Greek parent community 79/1
Theresienstadt (*now Cz.* Terezin) C Germany concentration camp 272/3
Thermopylae C Greece ✕ 77/2, 78/1
Thessalonica (*a/c* Salonika *Gr.* Thessaloniki) N Greece Roman Empire 86/3, 89/1, 88/2; early Christian centre 93/1; Jewish community 103/4; Byzantine Empire 113/1; WW2 267/4
Thessaly (*Gr.* Thessalia) region of C Greece Slav settlement 112/4; district of Byzantine Empire 113/1; ceded to Greece 211/2, 248/2
Thetford E England Scandinavian settlement 106/2, 107/1; Industrial Revolution 201/1
Theveste (*mod.* Tebessa) Algeria Roman Empire 89/1, 88/2
Thiel (Tiel)
Thionville (Diedenhofen)
Thira (Thera)
Thirsk N England rebellion against Elizabeth I 185/1
Thirteen Colonies N America 194/1, 203/1
Thirteen Years' War 160
Thirty Years' War Germany importance of northern Italy to Spain during 187; Sweden 188; devastates Holy Roman Empire 191; 191/3
Thivai (Thebes)
Thmuis N Egypt early Christian centre 93/1
Thompson, Joseph 306
Thonburi Thailand early trade centre 177/1
Thorikos E Greece Mycenaean site 67/1
Thorn (*Pol.* Toruń) N Poland founded by Teutonic Knights 146/2, 139/1; Peace of 188
Thrace (*anc.* Thracia) region of SE Europe 77/1, 78/1; divided between Bulgaria and Turkey 211/2; East occupied by Greece 263/1
Thracesian Theme W Anatolia district of Byzantine Empire 113/3
Thracia (*Eng.* Thrace) SE Europe Roman province 89/1; Byzantine Empire 113/1
Thraciae Roman prefecture of SE Europe 88/2
Thracian Theme Byzantine province of SE Europe 113/3
Thracians early people of SE Europe 67/3, 74/1
Three Days Battle S England English naval victory 185/1
Three Forks NW USA fur station 218/1
Three Feudatories rebellion 172
Thrimbokambos W Crete Minoan early village 67/2
Thucydides 77
Thule culture 60
Thun C Switzerland Zähringen town 121/6
Thurgau Switzerland Reformation 183/1
Thurii Copia S Italy Latin colony 87/1
Thuringia (Thüringen) region of E Germany Frankish Empire 107/3; Magyar invasions 107/1; medieval German Empire 117/1; 18C industrial growth 191/2; German unification 217/3
Thuringians E Germany Germanic tribe 97/3
Thyatira (*mod.* Akhisar) W Anatolia early Christian centre 93/1
Ti early people of C China 125/2
Tiahuanaco Empire C Andes site 60/4, 5; 149/3
Tiananmen massacre student demonstrations 281, 303
Tianjin (*W/G* T'ien-chin, *a/s* Tientsin) city-province of NE China 212/1
Tianshui (T'ien-shui)
Tiantai Shan (T'ien-t'ai Shan)
Tiberias (*Heb.* Teverya) Israel town of Judaea 103/3
Tiberius Roman emperor 88
Tibesti Massif N Africa rock painting 43/1
Tibet (*Chin.* Hsi-tsang *n/s* Xizang *form.* T'u-fan) C Asia spread of Buddhism 73/1; unified kingdom 127/2; part of Mongol Empire 129/1; Chinese protectorate 173/1; British sphere of influence 232/2, 245/2; absorbed by China 276/2; economy under communism 280/1; minority unrest 281/2
Tibur (*mod.* Tivoli) C Italy Roman Empire 87/1
Tiburon Hills W USA early site 61/3
Tichitt W Africa early site 43/1; early trade 140/2
Ticinum (Pavia)
Ticonderoga (*Fr.* Fort Carillon) NE USA British capture of French fort 194/1
Tidore *island* Moluccas, E Indies early village 47/1; Islamic town 134/2; sultanate 135/1; Portuguese settlement 176/2; Dutch settlement 177/1
Tiel (*f/s* Thiel) Netherlands early market 110/3; 117/1
Tien (*n/s* Dian) early state of W China 81/1
T'ien-chin (Tientsin)
T'ien-fang (Mecca)
T'ien-shui (*n/s* Tianshui) NW China Han commanderie 80/2
T'ien-t'ai Shan (*n/s* Tiantai Shan) *mountain* E China Buddhist site 73/1
Tientsin (*n/s* Tianjin *W/G* T'ien-chin) NE China industry 214/1, 259/1; treaty port 232/2; Boxer uprising 233/1, 247/3; Civil War battle 263/4; Japanese occupation 266/1
Tievebulliagh N Ireland Megalithic site 40/2
Tiflis (*n/c* Tbilisi) Caucasus Muslim conquest 99/1, 137/1; Mongol conquest 128/4; Safavid Empire 143/1; Ottoman conquest 169/1; urban growth 231/1, 288/3
Tighina (Bender)
Tiglath-pileser III king of Assyria 58
Tigranocerta (*mod.* Siirt) E Anatolia Roman Empire 86/3, 89/1
Ti-hua (Urumchi)
Tikal E Mexico Maya site 60/2
Tikulti-ninurta I king of Assyria 58
Tilantongo S Mexico early site 60/2
Tilmun (Dilmun)
Tilsit treaty of 204
Tilya-tepe C Asia treasure 79/1
Timbira forest Indian tribe of N Brazil 149/1
Timbuktu (*Fr.* Tombouctou) W Africa captured by Almoravids 136/2; trans-Saharan trade 140/2, 141/1, 164/2; conquered by Al Hajj Umar 239/1; occupied by French 241/1
Timgad (Thamugadi)
Timor island of E Indies early Portuguese colony 159/1, 158/2, 177/1; Dutch/Portuguese control 245/2; WW2 268-9; resistance to Indonesian occupation of E Timor 279/1
Timucua Indian tribe of SE USA 149/1
Timurids Muslim dynasty of C Asia 137/1
Tingis (*mod.* Tangier) Morocco Roman Empire 88/1, 88/2
Tingitana NW Africa region of Roman Empire 88/1
Ting Kayu N Borneo early site 47/1
Tinian *island* Marianas, C Pacific occupied by US in WW2 269/2
Tinmallal N Morocco captured by Almohads 136/2
Tinnevelly district of S India ceded to Britain 170/3
Tiphsah (Thapsacus)
Tippecanoe NE USA ✕ 219/3
Tippemuir C Scotland ✕ 185/1
Tippu Tib's Domain E Africa 239/1, 241/1
Tipton C England Industrial Revolution 200/3
Tipu E Mexico Maya centre 148/2
Tipu sultan of Mysore power of Mysore increased under 170; allies with France 203
Tiran *island and strait* Red Sea Egyptian-Israeli war 288/1
Tirana Albania Ottoman Empire 225/1
Tîrguşor Romania Mithraic site 72/1
Tirol, Tirolo (Tyrol)
Tiryns S Greece Mycenaean palace 67/1
Tiszapolgár N Hungary burial site 41/3
Tito (b. Josip Broz) 272
Titus Roman emperor 88
Titusville NE USA oil well 220/3
Tiverton SW England Industrial Revolution 201/1
Tivertsy Slav tribe of W Russia 115/1
Tivoli (Tibur)
Tiz SE Persia Abbasid Caliphate 137/1
Tjeribon (Cheribon)
Tlapacoya C Mexico early site 44/2
Tlatilco C Mexico early site 44/2
Tlaxcala region of C Mexico early kingdom 148/2; defence against Cortés 162/3; modern state 227/1
Tlemcen NW Africa Jewish settlement 102/1; early trade, 140/2, 141/1
Tlngit coast Indian tribe of NW Canada 149/1
Tmutarakan S Russia 115/1
tobacco American Indians 155; and slave trade 158
Tobago island of W Indies French rule 158/3; dependency of Trinidad 276/2 (inset)
Tobolsk W Siberia founded 160/2; on railway to east 230/2
Tobruk (*Ar.* Tubruq) N Libya WW2 267/4, 271/2
Tocharians early tribe of C Asia 75
Tochigi prefecture of C Japan industry 242/1
Tod S Egypt site 58/1
Todi (Tuder)
Todmorden N England Industrial Revolution 200/3
Togo (*form.* Togoland) country of W Africa French mandate 268/1; independence 276/2; political development 287/1
Togoland W Africa German colony 240/2, 241/1, 245/2; League of Nations mandate 258/1; Trans-Volta area transferred to British protection 277/1, to Ghana 276/2. For French mandate see Togo
Tokaido early highway of C Japan 171/4
Tok-do (Takeshima)
Tokugawa shogunate 174-5
Tokushima city and prefecture of W Japan 242/1
Tokyo (*form.* Edo) C Japan industrialization 175/1, 242/1; WW2 266/1, 268-9
Toledo (*anc.* Toletum) C Spain bishopric 101/2; Muslim conquest 98/1, 136/2; urban revolt 144/1; Santa Junta 184/2; Civil War 266/2
Toletum (*mod.* Toledo) C Spain Roman Empire 89/1, 88/2; Jewish community 102/1, 103/4
Tolmeta (Ptolemais)
Tolosa (*mod.* Toulouse) S France Roman Empire 86/3, 88/1, 88/2
Toltecs 60
Tolyatti (*until 1964* Stavropol) C Russia foundation and industry 288/3
Tomara S Thailand trading port 83/5
Tomassee SE USA ✕ 219/3
Tombouctou (Timbuktu)
tombs Neanderthal burial of the dead 33; megalithic 40; prehistoric North American 44; pyramids 56; Moche 61; southern Indian megalithic 65; Mycenaean 'shaft-graves' and tholos tombs 66
Tomi (*now* Constanţa) Romania Greek colony 77/1; Roman Empire 89/1, 88/2
Tomsk C Siberia founded 160/2; fur trade 199/2; on railway to east 230/2
Tonbridge SE England Industrial Revolution 201/1
Tong (T'ung)
Tonga island kingdom of S Pacific early settlement 49/1; British protectorate 245/2; independence 276/2 (inset); population growth 294/2
Tongking (*a/s* Tonking *Fr.* Tonkin) region of N Indo-China Hindu-Buddhist state 134/2; tributary state of China 173/1; French control 259/1
Tongking, Gulf of Vietnamese war 292/4
Tonglian C China cave art 35/1
Tonina E Mexico Mayan site 60/2
tools stone 30; handaxe 31, Neanderthal use of 33; plough 40; axe 40; prehistoric southeast Asian 46; Pleistocene Australasia 48; New Zealand 49; metal-working 84
Toowoomba E Australia early settlement 237/1
Toprakkale NW Persia early trade 41/1
Tordesillas N Spain Spanish and Portuguese claim under Treaty of 157; Treaty of 162; Spanish and Portuguese in New World 162; Santa Junta 184/2
Torfou C France medieval *villeneuve* 121/6
Torhout Belgium medieval fair 120/1
Torino (Turin)
Torki people of S Russia 115/1
Torksey C England Viking trading centre 106/2
Toro early state of E Africa 239/1
Toro N Spain Santa Junta 184/2
Torone N Greece Ionian colony 77/1
Toropets W Russia early town of Smolensk 115/1
Torres Strait Australia/New Guinea European discovery 157/3
Tortoise Cave S Africa early site 43/1
Tortona N Italy Lombard League 117/1
Toruń (Thorn)
Tory Island N Ireland ✕ 195/3
Torzhok W Russia early town of Novgorod Empire 115/1
Tosali E India Ashokan site 83/2
Toscana (Tuscany)
Tosu S Japan industrial centre 279/1
Totonac Indian tribe of C Mexico 60/2, 149/1
Tottori city and prefecture of W Japan 242/1
Touat (Tuat)
Toul NE France annexed 151/2,3; WW1 251/2
Toulon (*anc.* Telo Martius) S France naval base 193/1, 195/1; executions during French Revolution 202/2
Toulouse (*anc.* Tolosa) S France Kingdom regained from Visigoths 97/2; Muslim conquest 98/1; university founded 144/2; massacre of Jews 103/3; 16C urban development 180/1; St Bartholomew Massacre 191/3; parlement 193/1; French Revolution 202/2
Toumba N Greece Mycenaean site 67/1
Toungoo C Burma 135/1,3
Touraine region of C France English possession 119/1; French Royal domain 151/3; 193/1
Tourane (*mod.* Da Nang) C Vietnam early trade 177/1
Tournai region of Belgium Burgundian possession 151/2
Tours (*anc.* Caesarodunum *later* Turones) C France early Christian centre 92/1; early bishopric 101/2; 17C revolt 185/1; seat of intendant 193/1; industrial development 211/1
Townsville E Australia early settlement 237/1
Toyama city and prefecture of C Japan 242/1
Toyotomi Hideyoshi 174
Trabzon (*Eng.* Trebizond *anc.* Trapezus) NE Anatolia 143/1
Trachonitis ancient district of N Palestine 103/3
trade in early Eurasian civilizations 52, 53; China 62, 127, 167, 172; ancient India 64; ancient Eurasia 70; Hellenistic economy 78; Chinese silk 81, 84; early India and the West 82; in Celtic world 84; early Middle Ages 120; eastern India and southeast Asia 130; spice 136, 139, 158, 176; gold 139, 140, 164; trans-Saharan 140; Black Death and 144; Hansa 144; 'triangular' 155; Indian Ocean 158-9; European involvement in Africa 164; ivory 164, 238; slaves 164, 198, 238; silk 168; Mughal India 170; opium 172; southeast Asia 176; maritime powers 180; Baltic 188; 17C France 192; Napoleonic wars 205; Free Trade 210, 244;Australia and New Zealand 236, 295; Japan 242; and imperialism 244; late 19C global 254-5; effect of inter-war slump on 264; Latin America 292; NAFTA 295; arms 302, 303
trade unions 230
Traelleborg C Denmark circular fortifications 109/2
Trafalgar S Spain battle of 205; ✕ 195/3, 204/1
Trajan Roman emperor 88
Trajectum (Utrecht)
Tra Kieu C Indo-China early town 135/1
Trang Kenh N Vietnam early site 47/1
Tranquebar S India Danish settlement 171/1
Transeuphrates Syria/Iraq satrapy of Achaemenid Empire 74/1
Transjordan country of N Arabia Ottoman province 229/1; British mandate 258/1, 259/2, 276/2
Transkei region of SE Africa annexed by Cape Province 239/3; independent Bantustan 286/2, 287/1
Transnistria SW Russia WW2 270-271; secession from Moldova 301/2
Transoxiana (*or* Transoxania) ancient region of C Asia, Muslim conquest 99/1, 127/2; under Abbasid sovereignty 137/1
transport sea transport and trade 155; agrarian change and 200; and US 'market revolution' 220; development in Japan 242; revolution in 254; motor vehicles and airplanes 306
Transvaal S Africa Boer republic 281/3, 24/1
Transylvania region of Hungary/Romania 143/1; Empire of Mathias Corvinus 151/1; Ottoman vassal state 168/1, 187/1; WW1 251/2 part of Austro-Hungarian Empire 197/1, 263/1; north to Hungary 1941 273/1
Trans-Siberian Railway 266/1
Traostalos E Crete Minoan site 67/2
Trapezus (*mod.* Trabzon *Eng.* Trebizond) NE Anatolia Greek colony 77/1; march of Cyrus the Younger 74/1; Roman Empire 86/3; 89/1, 88/2; attacked by Heruli 90/2; spread of Judaism 72/1
Trasimene, Lake N Italy ✕ 86/3
Travancore former state of S India 170/3, 194/2 (inset), 234/1
Traverse des Sioux N USA fur station 218/1
Trebizond (*Turk.* Trabzon *anc.* Trapezus) NE Anatolia Byzantine Empire 113/1; Ottoman Empire 168/1; 18C trade 195/1
Trebizond, Empire of NE Anatolia 143/1
Treblinka Poland concentration camp 272/3
Trelleborg S Sweden circular fortification 109/2
Trengganu state of Malaya tributary to Siam 177/4
Trent (*It.* Trento, *or (district)* Trentino *Ger.* Trient *anc.* Tridentum) N Italy bishopric 190/1; district in Austrian Tyrol 216/2,3; to Italy 263/1
Trent, Council of 182
Tres Zapotes C Mexico early site 44/2
Treves (Trier, Augusta Treverorum)
Treviso (*anc.* Tarvisium) N Italy Lombard League 117/1; Signorial domination 146/3
Trevoux E France seat of intendant 193/1
tribute Novgorod 114; Aztec tribute-extraction 148
Trichinopoly S India ceded to Britain 170/3 ✕ 194/2; industry 235/3
Trient (Trent)
Trier (*Eng.* Treves *Fr.* Trèves *anc* Augusta Treverorum) W Germany archbishopric 190/1
Trieste (*anc.* Tergeste *S. Cr.* Trst) WW1 251/2; WW2 271/2
Trimontium Bulgaria Roman Empire 89/1
Trincomalee Ceylon captured by France 194/2; British naval base 244/2; Tamil majority 285/4
Trinidad island of W Indies discovery 157/2; Spanish settlement 158/3; British colony 227/1; 245/2; labour riots 258/1 (inset); independence 276/2 (inset)
Trinil Java site of early man 31/1, 47/1
Trio Indian tribe of S America 149/1
Tripoli (*Ar.* Tarabulus al Gharb *anc.* Oea) N Libya Muslim conquest 98/1; occupied by Normans 136/2; trans-Saharan trade 140/2, 195/1; Jewish settlement 102/1; Mediterranean trade 136/1; Ottoman rule 168/1, 239/1; Italian occupation 241/1
Tripoli (*Ar.* Tarabulus ash Sham *anc.* Tripolis) Syria Roman Empire 89/1; Jewish community 103/4; Crusades and Kingdom of 111/1; Byzantine Empire 113/3, 113/1; Venetian trade 121/2; WW2 267/4; 287/1
Tripolitania N Africa district of Byzantine Empire 113/1; under Almohads 136/1; vassalized by Turks 187/1; Ottoman rule 229/1; Italian occupation 241/1
Tripura district of NE India 237/3; Partition 284/1; anti-Bengali riots 285/3
Tristan da Cunha S Atlantic British colony 245/2
Trizay W France burial site 41/3
Trnovo Bulgaria early Slav settlement 112/4
Troas (*Eng.* Troy) W Anatolia early Christian centre 93/1
Troesmis Romania Roman Empire 89/1
Trois Rivières Quebec French post 162/2
Trombay W India atomic energy plant 285/3
Trondheim (*f/c* Nidaros *Sw.* Trondhjem) C Norway bishopric 101/2; Swedish Empire 188/3; WW2 267/4
Tropaeum Traiani Romania Roman Empire 89/1
Trowulan E Java early town 135/1
Troy (*Lat.* Ilium *Gr.* Troas) NW Anatolia early city 52/1, 59/2, 66/3
Troyes NE France Jewish settlement 102/1; medieval fair 120/1; St Bartholomew Massacre 191/3; French Revolution 202/2
Trst (Trieste)
Trucial Coast (*later* Trucial Oman, Trucial States *now* United Arab Emirates) E Arabia British control 225/1, 258/1, 227/1; WW1 251/3
Truckee W USA ✕ 219/3
Truk Caroline Islands, C Pacific Japanese base in WW2 268-9
Truman Doctrine 274
Truman, Harry S 296
Ts'ai (*n/s* Cai) N China Chou domain 63/3, 63/4
Ts'ang-chou (*n/s* Cangzhou) NE China T'ang prefecture 126/1
Tsang-k'o (*n/s* Zangku) SW China Han commanderie 80/2
Ts'ang-wu (*n/s* Cangwu) S China Han commanderie 80/2
Ts'an-luan (*n/s* Canluan) NW China Han prefecture 80/2
Ts'ao (*n/s* Cao) N China Late Chou domain 63/4
Tsaritsyn (*1925-61* Stalingrad *now* Volgograd) S Russia founded 161/1; urban growth 231/1; industry 231/1; Bolshevik seizure 257/1
Tsimshian Indian tribe of NW Canada 149/1
Tsinan (*n/s* Jinan *W/G* Chi-nan) N China railway 261/3; captured by Communists 263/4
Tsinghai (*n/s* Qinghai *W/G* Ch'ing-hai) province of NW China incorporated into Manchu (Ch'ing) Empire 173/1
Tsingtao (*n/s* Qingdao *W/G* Ch'ing-tao) E China German treaty port 232/2; industry 259/1; Japanese occupation 268/1; captured by Communists 263/4